Encyclopedia of Small Business

THIRD EDITION

Encyclopedia of Small Business

THIRD EDITION

VOLUME I

A–I

Arsen J. Darnay
Monique D. Magee

EDITORS

Detroit • New York • San Francisco • New Haven, Conn. • Waterville, Maine • London

Encyclopedia of Small Business, Third Edition

Arsen J. Darnay and Monique D. Magee, Editors

Project Editor
Virgil L. Burton III

Editorial
Julie Gough
Sonya D. Hill
Kristen Peltonen

Composition and Electronic Prepress
Evi Seoud

Manufacturing
Rita Wimberley

©2007 Thomson Gale, a part of The Thomson Corporation.

Thomson and Star Logo are trademarks and Gale is a registered trademark used herein under license.

For more information, contact
Thomson Gale
27500 Drake Rd.
Farmington Hills, MI 48331-3535
Or you can visit our internet site at
http://www.gale.com

ALL RIGHTS RESERVED
No part of this work covered by the copyright hereon may be reproduced or used in any form or by any means—graphic, electronic, or mechanical, including photocopying, recording, taping, Web distribution, or information storage retrieval systems—without the written permission of the publisher.

For permission to use material from this product, submit your request via Web at http://www.gale-edit.com/permissions, or you may download our Permissions Request form and submit your request by fax or mail to:

Permissions Department
Thomson Gale
27500 Drake Rd.
Farmington Hills, MI 48331-3535

Permissions Hotline:
248-699-8006 or 800-877-4253, ext. 8006
Fax: 248-699-8074 or 800-762-4058

Since this page cannot legibly accommodate all copyright notices, the acknowledgments constitute and extension of the copyright notice.

While every effort has been made to ensure the reliability of the information presented in this publication, Thomson Gale does not guarantee the accuracy of the data contained herein. Thomson Gale accepts no payment for listing; and inclusion in the publication of any organization, agency, institution, publication, service, or individual does not imply endorsement of the editors or publisher. Errors brought to the attention of the publisher and verified to the satisfaction of the publisher will be corrected in future editions.

LIBRARY OF CONGRESS CATALOGING-IN-PUBLICATION DATA

Encyclopedia of small business / Arsen J. Darnay, Monique D. Magee, editors. -- 3rd ed.
    p. cm.
    Rev. ed. of: Encyclopedia of small business / Kevin Hillstrom, Laurie Collier Hillstrom. 2nd ed. © 2002
    Includes bibliographical references and index.
    ISBN-13: 978-0-7876-9112-7 (set hardcover : alk. paper) --
    ISBN-10: 0-7876-9112-7 (set hardcover : alk. paper) --
    ISBN-13: 978-0-7876-9113-4 (vol. 1 hardcover : alk. paper) --
    ISBN-10: 0-7876-9113-5 (vol. 1 hardcover : alk. paper) --
[etc.]
    1. Small business--Management--Encyclopedias. 2. Small business--Finance--Encyclopedias.
I. Darnay, Arsen. II. Magee, Monique D. III. Hillstrom, Kevin, 1963– .

    HD62.7.H553 2007
    658.02'2--dc22

                                                                                    2006022623

ISBN-13:
978-0-7876-9112-7 (set)
978-0-7876-9113-4 (vol. 1)
978-0-7876-9114-1 (vol. 2)

ISBN-10:
0-7876-9112-7 (set)
0-7876-9113-5 (vol. 1)
0-7876-9114-3 (vol. 2)

This title is also available as an e-book
ISBN-13: 978-1-4144-1040-1, ISBN-10: 1-4144-1040-9
Contact your Thomson Gale sales representative for ordering information.
Printed in the United States of America

10 9 8 7 6 5 4 3 2

Contents

CONTENTS

Introduction and User's Guide

INTRODUCTION

Amidst the triumphs, turmoils, mergers, acquisitions, and lately the dramatic scandals and collapses of Big Business in America during the early years of the 21st century, small business just keeps on going and going. Thus, the third edition of *Encyclopedia of Small Business* has been prepared for and is dedicated to the largely silent majority of companies that, together, weave the extremely varied multi-colored fabric of American commercial life. Of the nation's roughly 5.8 million firms with employees, well over 95 percent are classified as small, whether using the official measures published by the U.S. Small Business Administration (SBA) or a simpler metric under which all firms employing fewer than 100 people qualify. To these small companies with employees must be added America's "micros," nearly 19 million businesses that do not have hired help and represent countless individuals and couples in business for themselves—a rapidly growing segment of the business population. Small business is small, but it is everywhere. It is innovative, adaptive, quick on its feet—and, according to the SBA—it creates three out of every four new jobs. Given the vast extent, productivity, ubiquitous presence, and deep integration of this element of commerce in American life, it is appropriate to adapt a phrase from Hollywood and say: "There is no business like small business."

Encyclopedia of Small Business is itself a relative newcomer, no longer a start-up, to be sure, but still energetically changing and growing. The third edition, like the second, features new entries and reflects the rapidly changing environment by intensive updating of its contents. Since the second edition the U.S. has experienced the traumatic events of 9/11, descended into a brief recession in the wake of the terrorist attacks, has seen budget surpluses turn into budget deficits, has seen gas prices spike, has witnessed the bursting of the dot-com boom but has also seen the resilient recovery of electronic commerce—has, indeed, seen many changes in public perception, government policy, securities legislation, economic structures, and in technology. EOSB-3 reflects all these changes. Virtually every entry has had to be revised, many rather extensively, to mirror accurately a dynamically changing economic environment.

EOSB-3, like earlier editions, is intended as a resource for the small business owner, for the would-be entrepreneur, and for students of business generally. It deals extensively with most aspects of business activity, from human resources on up to organizational issues; production and productivity; financial activities from accounting details on up to stock trading; purchasing, sales and marketing; accounting and measurement issues including various forms of valuation and assessment; and also with legal forms and regulatory requirements. It deals with starting, buying, and selling businesses—as well as taking them public or buying them back from the public. *EOSB* also attempts to cover major issues that shape the business environment, like globalization, or shape the company, like business ethics. Not least, *EOSB* also covers emerging and fading management fads and attempts to highlight the lasting virtues as well as the more ephemeral aspects of these attempts at improving sales, profits, quality, services, etc. In most cases, however, the point of view reflected is that of the small business owner. All events in all companies have the same fundamental character. But the same issue confronting a small business will very often play out differently than it will in huge organizations where often choirs upon choirs of committees must have their say.

EOSB-3 has 605 entries of which eight are new. These are Business to Business, Business to Consumer (both reflecting trends in electronic commerce), Board of Directors, Code of Ethics, Entrepreneurial Networks, Global Businesses, Sarbanes-Oxley (radical new securities legislation), and Small Business. Yes, somewhat surprisingly, perhaps, *EOSB* has delayed until its third edition to tackle the subject of actual definition: What exactly *is* small business? The reader who wonders why it took so long needs only to read the entry to realize that it took real courage to tackle the subject!

Many of the other existing entries have also been rewritten from the ground up on the basis of new research that has suggested—or new events that have necessitated—a fresh look. Users of *EOSB* who like to follow a subject closely might wish to look up and read again entries that have helped them in the past. All other entries have been carefully reviewed and updated in light of regulatory, market, legislative, technological, or global changes.

USER'S GUIDE

The essays in *EOSB-3* are presented alphabetically by topic in two volumes, with Volume 1 covering essays beginning with A-I and Volume 2 containing essays J-Z. In the very nature of things, some topics are covered in more than one entry depending on context. An example is the broad subject of Internet-based commercial activities. Some cross-referencing is provided at the bottom of entries under the **See Also** heading. A look at the index will provide references to other essays in which the topic may be covered in part or touched upon. Each entry is also followed by a **Further Reading** section in which the reader can identify books, periodicals, and government or other Web sites from or on which additional information may be obtained.

EOSB-3 features a Master Index at the back of Volume 2. The index contains alphabetical references to important terms in accounting, finance, human resources, marketing, operations management, organizational development, and other areas of interest to small business owners; names of institutions, organizations, associations, government agencies, and relevant legislation; and "see also" references. Each index term is followed by volume and page numbers, which easily direct the user to main topics as well as to all secondary reference terms as mentioned above.

EOSB-3 works equally well as a reference work—to look up some category on which more information is needed, e.g., Discounted Cash Flow—or as a book used for browsing and as a source of general information on trends or practices, the reader sampling an essay and being moved, perhaps, to read another that comes up in the context of the first. However used, it is the editors' hope that *EOSB* will have served the reader well in presenting the subjects and in provoking thought and—best of all—profitable action.

COMMENTS AND SUGGESTIONS

We welcome any questions, comments, or suggestions regarding the *Encyclopedia of Small Business.* To reach us, please contact:

Editor
Encyclopedia of Small Business
Thomson Gale
27500 Drake road
Farmington Hills, MI 48331-3535
Toll-free Phone: 800-347-GALE

A

ABSENTEEISM

Absenteeism is the term generally used to refer to unscheduled employee absences from the workplace. Many causes of absenteeism are legitimate—personal illness or family issues, for example—but absenteeism can also be traced to factors such as a poor work environment or workers who lack commitment to their jobs. If such absences become excessive, they can adversely impact the operations and, ultimately, the profitability of a business.

COSTS OF ABSENTEEISM

Unscheduled absences are costly to business. According to the U.S. Department of Labor, companies lose approximately 2.8 million workdays a year because of employee injuries and illnesses. The inability to plan for these unexpected absences means that companies hire last minute temporary workers, or pay overtime to their regular workers, to cover labor shortfalls; they may also maintain a higher staffing level regularly in anticipation of absences. According to Matt Lewis, in an article entitled "Sickened by the Cost of Absenteeism," which appeared in *Workforce* in the fall of 2003, "Three to 6 percent of any given workforce is absent every day due to unscheduled issues or disability claims ... To compensate, most companies continually overstaff by 10 to 20 percent to mask lost productivity. That's a colossal cost."

Small businesses are, of course, not immune to such "expenses." There are obvious costs associated with an absent employee, including consequences difficult to measure. The most obvious cost is in the area of sick leave benefits—provided that the business offers such benefits—but there are significant hidden costs as well.

The *SOHO Guidebook* cites the following as notable hidden cost factors associated with absenteeism:

- Lost productivity of the absent employee
- Overtime for other employees to fill in
- Decreased overall productivity of those employees
- Costs incurred to secure temporary help
- Possible loss of business or dissatisfied customers
- Problems with employee morale

The costs associated with absenteeism can be controlled. While scheduled time off for vacations and illnesses is an inevitable cost of doing business, managing things in such a way as to discourage excessive absenteeism is well worth the effort.

DEVELOPING AN ABSENCE POLICY

Many small business owners do not establish absenteeism policies for their companies. Some owners have only a few employees, and do not feel that it is worth the trouble. Others operate businesses in which "sick pay" is not provided to employees. Workers in such firms thus have a significant incentive to show up for work; if they do not, their paycheck suffers. And others simply feel that absenteeism is not a significant problem; they see no need to institute new policies or make any changes to the few existing rules that might already be in place.

But many small business consultants counsel entrepreneurs and business owners to consider establishing formal written policies that mesh with state and federal laws. Written policies can give employers added legal protection from employees who have been fired or disciplined for excessive absenteeism provided that those policies explicitly state the allowable number of absences, the consequences of excessive absenteeism, and other relevant aspects of the policy. Moreover, noted *The SOHO Guidebook,* "a formal, detailed policy that addresses absences, tardiness, failure to call in, and leaving early can serve to prevent misconceptions about acceptable behavior, inconsistent discipline, complaints of favoritism, morale problems, and charges of illegal discrimination. General statements that excessive absenteeism will be a cause for discipline may be insufficient and may lead to problems."

Changes in company culture and policy have been cited as effective in reducing absenteeism. The use of flexible schedules, whenever possible, is one way to offer employees a means of managing their own personal time needs and thus reducing unscheduled absences. Many small businesses that have introduced flextime, compressed work weeks, job sharing, and telecommuting options to their workforce have seen absenteeism fall significantly; these policies provide employees with much greater leeway to strike a balance between office and home that works for them (and the employer).

ABSENTEEISM POLICIES

Most employees are conscientious workers with good attendance records (or even if they are forced to miss significant amounts of work, the reasons are legitimate). However, it is estimated that as many as three of hundred workers are likely to exploit the system by taking more than the allotted sick time or more days than actually necessary.

To address absenteeism, then, many small businesses that employ workers have established one of two absenteeism policies. The first is a traditional absenteeism policy that distinguishes between excused and unexcused absences. Under such policies, employees are provided with a set number of sick days (also sometimes called "personal" days in recognition that employees occasionally need to take time off to attend to personal/family matters) and a set number of vacation days. Workers who are absent from work after exhausting their sick days are required to use vacation days under this system. Absences that take place after both sick and vacation days have been exhausted are subject to disciplinary action. The second policy alternative, commonly known as a "no-fault" system, permits each employee a specified number of absences annually (either days or "occurrences," in which multiple days of continuous absence are counted as a single occurrence); this policy does not consider the reason for the employee's absence. As with traditional absence policies, once the employee's days have been used up, he or she is subject to disciplinary action.

"Use It or Lose It" Some companies do not allow employees to carry sick days over from year to year. The benefits and disadvantages of this policy continue to be debated in businesses across the country. Some analysts contend that most employees do not require large numbers of sick days and that systems that allow carryovers are more likely to be abused by poor employees than appropriately utilized by good employees, who, if struck down by a long-term illness, often have disability alternatives.

A friendly feature that can be added onto a "use it or lose it" sick day policy is the option of donating unused earned days to a leave bank for colleagues suffering from catastrophic illnesses. Although this may not be an incentive to all employees to conserve sick days, it does offer dedicated employees a means of putting what they may consider legitimately earned hours to a positive use.

ESTABLISHING A SYSTEM FOR TRACKING ABSENCES

Absenteeism policies are useless if the business does not also implement and maintain an effective system for tracking employee attendance. Some companies are able to track absenteeism through existing payroll systems, but for those who do not have this option, they need to make certain that they put together a system that can: 1) keep an accurate count of individual employee absences; 2) tabulate company wide absenteeism totals; 3) calculate the financial impact that these absences have on the business; 4) detect periods when absences are particularly high; and 5) differentiate between various types of absences.

SEE ALSO *Employee Motivation; Sick Leave and Personal Days*

BIBLIOGRAPHY
Allerton, Haidee E. "How To." *Training and Development,* August 2000.

Anderson, Tom "Employers Lax on Absence Management." *Employee Benefit News,* June 15, 2005.

Ceniceros, Roberto. "Written Policies Reduce Risk in Firing Workers Comp Abusers." *Business Insurance.* April 21, 1997.

"Don't Let Unscheduled Absences Wipe You Out." *Workforce,* June 2000.

Gale, Sarah Fister. "Sickened by the Cost of Absenteeism." *Workforce,* September 2003.

Hunt, David. "'There's a Bit of Flu Doing the Rounds, Boss,'" *Employee Benefits,* April 2000.

"Link Absenteeism and Benefits—And Help Cut Costs," *HR Focus,* April 2000.

The SOHO Guidebook. CCH Incorporated, 1997.

Hillstrom, Northern Lights
updated by Magee, ECDI

ACCELERATED COST RECOVERY SYSTEM (ACRS)

The Accelerated Cost Recovery System (ACRS) is a method of depreciating property for tax purposes; it allows individuals and businesses to write off capitalized assets in an accelerated manner. Adopted by the U.S. Congress in 1981 as part of the Economic Recovery Tax Act, ACRS assigns assets to one of eight recovery classes—ranging from 3 to 19 years—depending on the assets' useful lives. These recovery classes are used as the basis for depreciation of the assets.

The idea behind ACRS was to increase the tax deduction for depreciation of property and thus increase the cash flow available to individuals and businesses for investment. It was put in place during an economic recession and "unleashed a torrential flow of corporate cash," according to Elizabeth Kaplan in *Dun's Business Month*. In fact, at the time it was enacted, ACRS was expected to add between $50 and $100 billion to the incomes of individuals and businesses over a 10-year period.

Proponents of ACRS claimed that this depreciation method and related changes in tax law led to a huge increase in investment that helped the U.S. economy recover. But other people criticized ACRS for making reported business earnings look better than they actually were. "The dangers of treating depreciation as merely an accounting convention—and not a real economic cost that provides for the eventual replacement of plant and equipment—were exacerbated by ACRS, which allowed companies to take ultra rapid depreciation on capital-intensive assets," Kaplan explained. "By reducing corporate tax bills, ACRS also exaggerated the disparity between cash flow and reported earnings. The cash generated by a company's operations is being hailed as a far more reliable barometer of financial health than the more traditional earnings yardstick, which can be skewed by accounting conventions."

Perhaps the most dangerous trend to grow out of the favorable tax treatment of capitalized assets was a large number of hostile takeovers. "ACRS inadvertently unleashed a potent weapon for corporate raiders who specialize in leveraging the assets of the target company to finance their attacks," Kaplan noted.

Responding to criticism, the U.S. Congress revised the ACRS as part of the 1986 Tax Reform Act. The new depreciation method for tangible property put in use after 1986 is called the Modified Accelerated Cost Recovery System (MACRS). The main difference between ACRS and MACRS is that the latter method uses longer recovery periods and thus reduces the annual

depreciation deductions granted for residential and non-residential real estate.

Some people expressed concern that the change would spur consumption at the expense of investment and thus end the period of economic recovery and growth. Others worried that the frequency of changes would unnecessarily complicate the tax code. After all, taxpayers were required to use the "useful life" method to depreciate property put in service prior to 1981, the ACRS method for property put in use between 1981 and 1986, and the MACRS method for property put in use after 1986.

MACRS actually encompasses two different depreciation methods, called the General Depreciation System (GDS) and the Alternative Depreciation System (ADS). GDS is used for most types of property. ADS applies only to certain types of property—that which is used for business purposes 50 percent of the time or less, is used predominantly outside the United States, or is used for tax-exempt purposes, for example—but can also be used if the taxpayer so chooses.

In March 2004, temporary and proposed changes to MACRS were published by the IRS. The changes concern how depreciation is handled for property acquired in one of two very specific ways. Property acquired in a like-kind exchange and/or as a result of an involuntary conversion are to be handled differently if both the relinquished and the replacement property are subject to MARCS in the acquiring taxpayer's hands. The property in question must also have changed hands prior to February 27, 2004. According to Lynn Afeman, in an article discussing these changes in *The Tax Adviser* "The temporary regulations, fortunately, provide an election out of these rules. However, some taxpayers may make the election simply to avoid complexity, rather than to gain the most advantageous depreciation regime."

SEE ALSO *Depreciation*

BIBLIOGRAPHY

Afeman, Lynn, and Sarah Staudenraus. "Practical Application of the New MACRS Depreciation Regs." *The Tax Adviser.* June 2004.

Blumenfrucht, Israel. "Depreciation of Personal Property." *Management Accounting.* April 1987.

Duncan, William A., and Robert W. Wyndelts. "The Accelerated Cost Recovery System after the Tax Reform Act of 1986." *Review of Taxation of Individuals.* Summer 1987.

Flynn, Maura P. "Property Located Outside United States Subject to Different Depreciation Rules." *The Tax Adviser.* August 1992.

"The Future of Depreciation Rules." *Nation's Business.* February 1986.

Internal Revenue Service. *IRS Publication 946: How to Depreciate Property.* 2000.

Kaplan, Elizabeth. "Wall Street Zeroes in on Cash Flow." *Dun's Business Month.* July 1985.

Tandet, Steven N. "Modified Accelerated Cost Recovery System." *The Tax Adviser.* April 1989.

Hillstrom, Northern Lights
updated by Magee, ECDI

ACCOUNTING

Accounting has been defined as "the language of business" because it is the basic tool keeping score of a business's activity. It is with accounting that an organization records, reports, and evaluates economic events and transactions that affect the enterprise. As far back as 1494 the importance of accounting to the success of a business was known. In a book on mathematics published that year and written by the Franciscan monk, Luca Paciolo, the author cites three things any successful merchant must have. The three things are sufficient cash or credit, an accounting system to track how he is doing, and a good bookkeeper to operate the system.

Accounting processes document all aspects of a business's financial performance, from payroll costs, capital expenditures, and other obligations to sales revenue and owners' equity. An understanding of the financial data contained in accounting documents is regarded as essential to reaching an accurate picture of a business's true financial well-being. Armed with such knowledge, businesses can make appropriate financial and strategic decisions about their future; conversely, incomplete or inaccurate accounting data can cripple a company, no matter its size or orientation. The importance of accounting as a barometer of business health—past, present, and future—and tool of business navigation is reflected in the words of the American Institute of Certified Public Accountants (AICPA), which defined accounting as a "service activity." Accounting, said the AICPA, is intended "to provide quantitative information, primarily financial in nature, about economic activities that is intended to be useful in making economic decisions—making reasoned choices among alternative courses of action."

A business's accounting system contains information relevant to a wide range of people. In addition to business owners, who rely on accounting data to gauge the financial progress of their enterprise, accounting data can communicate relevant information to investors, creditors, managers, and others who interact with the business in question. As a result, accounting is sometimes divided into two distinct subsets—financial accounting and management accounting—that reflect the different information needs of the end users.

Financial accounting is a branch of accounting that provides people outside the business—such as investors or loan officers—with qualitative information regarding an enterprise's economic resources, obligations, financial performance, and cash flow. Management accounting, on the other hand, refers to accounting data used by business owners, supervisors, and other employees of a business to gauge the enterprise's health and operating trends.

GENERALLY ACCEPTED ACCOUNTING PRINCIPLES

Generally accepted accounting principles (GAAP) are the guidelines, rules, and procedures used in recording and reporting accounting information in audited financial statements. In order to have a vibrant and active economic marketplace, participants in the market must have confidence in the system. They must be confident that the reports and financial statements produced by companies are trustworthy and based on some standard set of accounting principles. The stock market crash of 1929 and its aftermath showed just how damaging uncertainty can be to the market. The results of U.S. Senate Banking and Currency Committee hearings into the 1929 crash caused public outrage and lead to federal regulation of the securities market as well as a push for the development of professional organizations designed to establish standardized accounting principles and to oversee their adoption.

Various organizations have influenced the development of modern-day accounting principles. Among these are the American Institute of Certified Public Accountants (AICPA), the Financial Accounting Standards Board (FASB), and the Securities and Exchange Commission (SEC). The first two are private sector organizations; the SEC is a federal government agency.

The AICPA played a major role in the development of accounting standards. In 1937 the AICPA created the Committee on Accounting Procedures (CAP), which issued a series of Accounting Research Bulletins (ARB) with the purpose of standardizing accounting practices. This committee was replaced by the Accounting Principles Board (APB) in 1959. The APB maintained the ARB series, but it also began to publish a new set of pronouncements, referred to as Opinions of the Accounting Principles Board. In mid-1973, an independent private board called the Financial Accounting Standards Board (FASB) replaced the APB and assumed responsibility for the issuance of financial accounting standards. The FASB remains the primary determiner of financial accounting standards in the United States.

Comprised of seven members who serve full-time and receive compensation for their service, the FASB identifies financial accounting issues, conducts research related to these issues, and is charged with resolving the issues. A super-majority vote (i.e., at least five to two) is required before an addition or change to the Statements of Financial Accounting Standards is issued.

The Financial Accounting Foundation is the parent organization to FASB. The foundation is governed by a 16-member Board of Trustees appointed from the memberships of eight organizations: AICPA, Financial Executives Institute, Institute of Management Accountants, Financial Analysts Federation, American Accounting Association, Securities Industry Association, Government Finance Officers Association, and National Association of State Auditors. A Financial Accounting Standards Advisory Council (approximately 30 members) advises the FASB. In addition, an Emerging Issues Task Force (EITF) was established in 1984 to provide timely guidance to the FASB on new accounting issues.

The Securities and Exchange Commission, an agency of the federal government, has the legal authority to prescribe accounting principles and reporting practices for all companies issuing publicly traded securities. The SEC has seldom used this authority, however, although it has intervened or expressed its views on accounting issues from time to time. U.S. law requires that companies subject to the jurisdiction of the SEC make reports to the SEC giving detailed information about their operations. The SEC has broad powers to require public disclosure in a fair and accurate manner in financial statements and to protect investors. The SEC establishes accounting principles with respect to the information contained within reports it requires of registered companies. These reports include: Form S-X, a registration statement; Form 10-K, an annual report; Form 10-Q, a quarterly report of operations; Form 8-K, a report used to describe significant events that may affect the company; and Proxy Statements, which are used when management requests the right to vote through proxies for shareholders.

On December 20, 2002, the SEC proposed a series of amendments to the rules and forms that it imposes on companies within its jurisdiction. These changes were mandated as part of the passage of the Sarbanes-Oxley Act of 2002. This law was motivated, in part, by accounting scandals that came to light involving firms as well known as Enron, WorldCom, Tyco, Global Crossing, Kmart, and Arthur Andersen to name a few.

ACCOUNTING SYSTEM

An accounting system is a management information system responsible for the collection and processing of data useful to decision-makers in planning and controlling the activities of a business organization. The data processing cycle of an accounting system encompasses the total structure of five activities associated with tracking financial information: collection or recording of data; classification of data; processing (including calculating and summarizing) of data; maintenance or storage of results; and reporting of results. The primary—but not sole—means by which these final results are disseminated to both internal and external users (such as creditors and investors) is the financial statement.

The elements of accounting are the building blocks from which financial statements are constructed. According to the Financial Accounting Standards Board (FASB), the primary financial elements directly related to measuring performance and the financial position of a business enterprise are as follows:

- Assets—probable future economic benefits obtained or controlled by a particular entity as a result of past transactions or events.

- Comprehensive Income—the change in equity (net assets) of an entity during a given period as a result of transactions and other events and circumstances from non-owner sources. Comprehensive income includes all changes in equity during a period except those resulting from investments by owners and distributions to owners.

- Distributions to Owners—decreases in equity (net assets) of a particular enterprise as a result of transferring assets, rendering services, or incurring liabilities to owners.

- Equity—the residual interest in the assets of an entity that remain after deducting liabilities. In a business entity, equity is the ownership interest.

- Expenses—events that expend assets or incur liabilities during a period from delivering or providing goods or services and carrying out other activities that constitute the entity's ongoing major or central operation.

- Gains—increases in equity (net assets) from peripheral or incidental transactions. Gains also come from other transactions, events, and circumstances affecting the entity during a period except those that result from revenues or investments by owners. Investments by owners are increases in net assets resulting from transfers of valuables from other entities to obtain or increase ownership interests (or equity) in it.

- Liabilities—probable future sacrifices of economic benefits arising from present obligations to transfer assets or provide services to other entities in the future as a result of past transactions or events.

- Losses—decreases in equity (net assets) from peripheral or incidental transactions of an entity and from all other transactions, events, and circumstances affecting the entity during a period. Losses do not include equity drops that result from expenses or distributions to owners.

- Revenues—inflows or other enhancements of assets, settlements of liabilities, or a combination of both during a period from delivering or producing goods, rendering services, or conducting other activities that constitute the entity's ongoing major or central operations.

FINANCIAL STATEMENTS

Financial statements are the most comprehensive way of communicating financial information about a business enterprise. A wide array of users—from investors and creditors to budget directors—use the data it contains to guide their actions and business decisions. Financial statements generally include the following information:

- Balance sheet (or statement of financial position)—summarizes the financial position of an accounting entity at a particular point in time as represented by its economic resources (assets), economic obligations (liabilities), and equity.

- Income statement—summarizes the results of operations for a given period of time.

- Statement of cash flows—summarizes the impact of an enterprise's cash flows on its operating, financing, and investing activities over a given period of time.

- Statement of retained earnings—shows the increases and decreases in earnings retained by the company over a given period of time.

- Statement of changes in stockholders' equity—discloses the changes in the separate stockholders' equity account of an entity, including investments by distributions to owners during the period.

Notes to financial statements are considered an integral part of a complete set of financial statements. Notes typically provide additional information at the end of the statement and concern such matters as depreciation and inventory methods used in the statements, details of long-term debt, pensions, leases, income taxes, contingent liabilities, methods of consolidation, and other matters. Significant accounting policies are usually disclosed as the initial note or as a summary preceding the notes to the financial statements.

ACCOUNTING PROFESSION

There are two primary kinds of accountants: private accountants, who are employed by a business enterprise to perform accounting services exclusively for that business, and public accountants, who function as independent experts and perform accounting services for a wide variety of clients. Some public accountants operate their own businesses, while others are employed by accounting firms to attend to the accounting needs of the firm's clients.

A certified public accountant (CPA) is an accountant who has 1) fulfilled certain educational and experience requirements established by state law for the practice of public accounting and 2) garnered an acceptable score on a rigorous three-day national examination. Such people become licensed to practice public accounting in a particular state. These licensing requirements are widely credited with maintaining the integrity of the accounting service industry, but in recent years this licensing process has drawn criticism from legislators and others who favor deregulation of the profession. Some segments of the business community have expressed concern that the quality of accounting would suffer if such changes were implemented, and analysts indicate that small businesses without major in-house accounting departments would be particularly impacted.

The American Institute of Certified Public Accountants (AICPA) is the national professional organization of CPAs, but numerous organizations within the accounting profession exist to address the specific needs of various subgroups of accounting professionals. These groups range from the American Accounting Association, an organization composed primarily of accounting educators, to the American Women's Society of Certified Public Accountants.

ACCOUNTING AND THE SMALL BUSINESS OWNER

"A good accountant is the most important outside advisor the small business owner has," according to the *Entrepreneur Magazine Small Business Advisor*. "The services of a lawyer and consultant are vital during specific periods in the development of a small business or in times of trouble, but it is the accountant who, on a continuing basis, has the greatest impact on the ultimate success or failure of a small business."

When starting a business, many entrepreneurs consult an accounting professional to learn about the various tax laws that affect them and to familiarize themselves with the variety of financial records that they will need to maintain. Such consultations are especially recommended for would-be business owners who anticipate buying a business or franchise, plan to invest a substantial amount of money in the business, anticipate holding money or property for clients, or plan to incorporate.

If a business owner decides to enlist the services of an accountant to incorporate, he/she should make certain that the accountant has experience dealing with small corporations, for incorporation brings with it a flurry of new financial forms and requirements. A knowledgeable accountant can provide valuable information on various aspects of the start-up phase.

Similarly, when investigating the possible purchase or licensing of a business, a would-be buyer should enlist the assistance of an accountant to look over the financial statements of the licensor-seller. Examination of financial statements and other financial data should enable the accountant to determine whether the business is a viable investment. If a prospective buyer decides not to use an accountant to review the licensor-seller's financial statements, he/she should at least make sure that the financial statements that have been offered have been properly audited (a CPA will not stamp or sign a financial statement that has not been properly audited and certified).

Once in business, the business owner will have to weigh revenue, rate of expansion, capital expenditures, and myriad other factors in deciding whether to secure an in-house accountant, an accounting service, or a year-end accounting and tax preparation service. Sole proprietorships and partnerships are less likely to have need of an accountant; in some cases, they will be able to address their business's modest accounting needs without utilizing outside help. If a business owner declines to seek professional help from an accountant on financial matters, pertinent accounting information can be found in books, seminars, government agencies such as the Small Business Administration, and other sources.

Even if a small business owner decides against securing an accountant he or she will find it much easier to attend to the business's accounting requirements if a few basic bookkeeping principles are followed. These include maintaining a strict division between personal and business records; maintaining separate accounting systems for all business transactions; establishing separate checking accounts for personal and business; and keeping all business records, such as invoices and receipts.

CHOOSING AN ACCOUNTANT

While some small businesses are able to manage their accounting needs without benefit of in-house accounting personnel or a professional accounting outfit, the majority choose to enlist the help of accounting professionals. There are many factors for the small business owner to consider when seeking an accountant, including personality, services rendered, reputation in the business community, and expense.

The nature of the business in question is also a consideration in choosing an accountant. Owners of small businesses who do not anticipate expanding rapidly have little need of a national accounting firm, but business ventures that require investors or call for a public stock offering can benefit from association with an established accounting firm. Many owners of growing companies select an accountant by interviewing several prospective accounting firms and requesting proposals which will, ideally, detail the firm's public offering experience within the industry, describe the accountants who will be handling the account, and estimate fees for auditing and other proposed services.

Finally, a business that utilizes a professional accountant to attend to accounting matters is often better equipped to devote time to other aspects of the enterprise. Time is a precious resource for small businesses and their owners, and according to the *Entrepreneur Magazine Small Business Advisor*, "Accountants help business owners comply with a number of laws and regulations affecting their record-keeping practices. If you spend your time trying to find answers to the many questions that accountants can answer more efficiently, you will not have the time to manage your business properly. Spend your time doing what you do best, and let accountants do what they do best."

The small business owner can, of course, make matters much easier both for his/her company and for the accountant by maintaining proper accounting records throughout the year. Well-maintained and complete records of assets, depreciation, income and expense, inventory, and capital gains and losses are all necessary for the accountant to conclude her work; gaps in a business's financial record only add to the accountant's time and, therefore, her fee for services rendered.

The potential management insights that can be gained from a study of properly prepared financial statements should not be overlooked. Many small businesses see accounting primarily as a paperwork burden and something whose value is primarily in helping to comply with government reporting requirements and tax preparations. Most experts in the field contend that small firms should recognize that accounting information can be a valuable component of a company's management and decision-making systems, for financial data provide the ultimate indicator of the failure or success of a business's strategic and philosophical direction.

SEE ALSO *Certified Public Accountants*

BIBLIOGRAPHY
Anthony, Robert N., and Leslie K. Pearlman. *Essentials of Accounting.* Prentice Hall, 1999.

Bragg, Steven M. *Accounting Best Practices.* John Wiley, 1999.

Fuller, Charles. *The Entrepreneur Magazine Small Business Advisor.* Wiley, 1995.

Lunt, Henry. "The Fab Four's Solo Careers." *Accountancy.* March 2000.

Pinson, Linda. *Keeping the Books: Basic Record Keeping and Accounting for Successful Small Business.* Business & Economics, 2004.

Strassmann, Paul A. "GAAP Helps Whom?" *Computerworld.* December 6, 1999.

Taylor, Peter. *Book-Keeping & Accounting for Small Business.* Business & Economics, 2003.

Hillstrom, Northern Lights
updated by Magee, ECDI

ACCOUNTING METHODS

Accounting methods refer to the basic rules and guidelines under which businesses keep their financial records and prepare their financial reports. There are two main accounting methods used for record-keeping: the cash basis and the accrual basis. Small business owners must decide which method to use depending on the legal form of the business, its sales volume, whether it extends credit to customers, whether it maintains an inventory, and the tax requirements set forth by the Internal Revenue Service (IRS). Some form of record-keeping is required by law and for tax purposes, but the resulting information can also be useful to managers in assessing the company's financial situation and making decisions. It is possible to change accounting methods later, but the process can be complicated. Therefore it is important for small business owners to decide which method to use up front based on what will be most suitable for their particular business.

CASH BASIS Accounting records prepared using the cash basis recognize income and expenses according to real-time cash flow. Income is recorded upon receipt of funds, rather than based upon when it is actually earned; expenses are recorded as they are paid, rather than as they are actually incurred. Under this accounting method, therefore, it is possible to defer taxable income by delaying billing so that payment is not received in the current year. Likewise, it is possible to accelerate expenses by paying them as soon as the bills are received, in advance of the due date.

ACCRUAL BASIS A company using an accrual basis for accounting recognizes both income and expenses at the time they are earned or incurred, regardless of when cash associated with those transactions changes hands. Under this system, revenue is recorded when it is earned rather than when payment is received; expenses are recorded when they are incurred rather than when payment is made.

CASH VS. ACCRUAL BASIS

As we've seen, the key difference between the two methods of accounting has to do with how each method records cash coming into and going out of the company. At any one point in time, a company's accounts will look very different depending on which accounting method was used to prepare those accounts. Over time, these differences diminish since all expenses and revenues are eventually recorded.

If a company called, say, Cash Method Company, pays its annual rent of $12,000 in January, rather than paying $1,000 per month all year, it will show a rent expense of $12,000 in January and no rent expense for the rest of the year. If another organization, Accrual Method Company, made the same rental payment in January, its records would show a $1,000 rent expense in January as well as in each month of the year. At the end of the year, the expense records of the two companies will look very similar. At any point earlier in the year, however, the two company records will look very different.

The cash method offers several advantages: it is simpler than the accrual method; it provides a more accurate picture of cash flow; and income is not subject to taxation until the money is actually received. A disadvantage of the cash method is that expenses and revenues are not matched in time. For example, if a company provides landscaping services to a client in early April, it will likely send that client an invoice in May and may not receive payment for the services provided until June. Meanwhile, employees will be paid for the time they spent on the project in April and May. Accordingly, the accounting records will show high expenses in April and May with no corresponding income.

In contrast, the accrual method is designed to recognize income and expenses in the period to which they apply, regardless of whether or not money has changed hands. Under the accrual basis of accounting, the income associated with the landscaping services described above would be recorded in April, the month in which the services were provided, even though the payment for those services may not arrive until June. Consequently, the company using an accrual method of accounting will have records that show expenses and revenues for the landscaping job in the same month. The main advantage of the accrual method is that it provides a more accurate picture of how a business is performing over the long-term than the cash method. The main disadvantages are that it is more complex than the cash basis and that income taxes may be owed on revenue before payment is actually received.

Under generally accepted accounting principles (GAAP), the accrual basis of accounting is required for all businesses that handle inventory, from small retailers to large manufacturers. It is also required for corporations and partnerships that have gross sales over $5 million per year, although there are exceptions for farming businesses and qualified personal service corporations—such as doctors, lawyers, accountants, and consultants. A business that chooses to use the accrual basis must use it consistently for all financial reporting and for credit purposes. For anyone who runs two or more businesses, however, it is permissible to use different accounting methods for each.

CHANGING ACCOUNTING METHODS

In some cases, businesses find it desirable to change from one accounting method to another. Changing accounting methods requires formal approval of the IRS, but new guidelines adopted in 1997 make the procedure much easier for businesses. A company wanting to make a change must file Form 3115 in duplicate and pay a fee. A copy should be attached to the taxpayer's income tax return and the other copy must be sent to the IRS.

Any company that is not currently under examination by the IRS is permitted to file for approval to make a change. Applications can be made at any time during the tax year, but the IRS recommends filing as early as possible. Taxpayers are granted automatic six-month extensions provided they file income taxes on time for the year in which the change is requested. The amended tax returns using the new accounting method must also be filed within the six-month extension period. In considering whether to approve a request for a change in accounting methods, the IRS looks at whether the new method will accurately reflect income and whether it will create or shift profits and losses between businesses.

Changes in accounting methods generally result in adjustments to taxable income, either positive or negative. For example, say a business wants to change from the cash basis to the accrual basis. It has accounts receivable (income earned but not yet received, so not recognized under the cash basis) of $15,000, and accounts payable (expenses incurred but not paid, so not recognized under the cash basis) of $20,000. Thus the change in accounting method would require a negative adjustment to income of $5,000. It is important to note that changing accounting methods does not permanently change the business's long-term taxable income, but only changes the way that income is recognized over time.

If the total amount of the change is less than $25,000, the business can elect to make the entire adjustment during the year of change. Otherwise, the IRS permits the adjustment to be spread out over four tax years. Obviously, most businesses would find it preferable for tax purposes to make a negative adjustment in the current year and spread a positive adjustment over subsequent years. If the accounting change is required by the IRS because the method originally chosen did not clearly reflect income, however, the business must make the resulting adjustment during the current tax year. This provides businesses with an incentive to change accounting methods on their own if they realize that there is a problem.

BIBLIOGRAPHY

Cornwall, Dr. Jeffrey R., David Vang, and Jean Hartman. *Entrepreneurial Financial Management.* Prentice Hall, May 13, 2003.

Epstein, Lita. *Reading Financial Reports for Dummies.* December 2004.

Pinson, Linda. *Keeping the Books: Basic Record Keeping and Accounting for the Successful Small Business.* Business & Economics, 2004.

Sherman, W. Richard. "Requests for Changes in Accounting Methods Made Easier." *The Tax Adviser.* October 1997.

Walsh, Joseph G. "More Accounting Method Changes Granted Automatic Consent." *Practical Tax Strategies.* July 1999.

Hillstrom, Northern Lights
updated by Magee, ECDI

ACCOUNTS PAYABLE

Accounts payable is the term used to describe the unpaid bills of a business; the money owed to suppliers and other creditors. The sum of the amounts owed to suppliers is listed as a current liability on the balance sheet. The accounts payable category is, along with accounts receivable, a major component of a business's cash flow. Aside from materials and supplies from outside vendors, accounts payable might include such expenses as taxes, insurance, rent (or mortgage) payments, utilities, and loan payments and interest.

For many small businesses, limited access to capital leaves little room for error in managing cash flow and accounts payable. Mismanaging of accounts payable can lead to significant problems with overdue payments. For this reason, it is absolutely essential for entrepreneurs and small business owners to deal with the accounts payable side of the business ledger in an effective manner. Bills left unpaid or addressed in a less than timely manner can snowball into major credit problems; these can easily cripple a business's ability to function.

By making informed projections and sensible provisions in advance, the small business can head off many credit problems before they get too big. Obligations to creditors should be paid off concurrently with the collection of accounts receivable whenever possible. Payment checks should not, however, be dated any earlier than the bills' actual due date. In addition, many small companies will find that their business fortunes will take on a cyclical character; they will need to plan for accounts payable obligations accordingly.

For instance, a small grocery store located near a major factory or mill may experience surges in customer traffic in the day or two immediately following the days on which the neighboring facility pays its workers. Conversely, the store may see a measurable drop in customer traffic during weeks in which the factory or mill is not distributing paychecks to employees. The observant shop owner will learn to recognize these patterns and address the accounts payable portion of his or her business accordingly.

Generally, not all bills will need to be paid at once. Expenses such as payroll, federal, and local taxes, loan installment payments, and obligations to vendors will, in all likelihood, be due at various times of the month. Some—such as taxes—may only be due on a quarterly or annual basis (tax payments should always be made on schedule, even if it means delaying payment to vendors; it is far better to dispute a tax bill after it's been paid than to run the risk of being charged with costly fines). It is important, then, for small business owners to prioritize their accounts payable obligations.

PRIORITIZING AND MONITORING

Every business must work to keep a reasonable balance between the money coming into and flowing out of its coffers. This task is especially important for small business owners who often have limited flexibility in dealing with shortfalls of cash. Entrepreneurs who find themselves struggling to meet their accounts payable obligations have a couple of different options of varying levels of attractiveness. One option is to "rest" bills for a short period in order to satisfy short-term cash flow problems. This basically amounts to waiting to pay off debts until the business's financial situation has improved. There are obvious perils associated with such a stance: delays can strain relations with vendors and other institutions that are owed money, and over-reliance on future good business fortunes can easily launch entrepreneurs down the slippery slope to bankruptcy.

Another option that is perhaps more palatable is to make partial payments to vendors and other creditors.

This good-faith approach shows that an effort is being made to meet financial obligations; it can help keep interest penalties from raging out of control. Partial payments should be set up and agreed to as soon as payment problems are foreseen or as early as possible. It is also a good idea to try to pay off debts to smaller vendors in full whenever possible unless there is some clear benefit to be had in making installment payments to them.

Usually, signs of cash flow problems will start to show up well before the company's financial fortunes become truly desperate. One clean sign of cash flow problems is an increase in aged payables. Aged payables are those for which the due date has passed. Bills should never be allowed to "ripen" more than 45 to 60 days beyond the due date unless a special payment arrangement has been made with the vendor in advance. At 60 days, a company's credit rating could be jeopardized; this could make it harder to deal with other vendors and/or loaning institutions in the future.

Outstanding balances can drive interest penalties way up, and this trend is obviously compounded if many bills are overdue at the same time. Such excessive interest payments can seriously damage a business's bottom line. Explaining to vendors and creditors one's current problems and their planned solutions can deflect ill feelings and buy more time. It is often in the best interest of the vendor or other creditor to keep a fledgling business solvent so that continued business may be done with this client. Some—though by no means all—creditors may be willing to waive, or at least reduce, growing interest charges, or make other changes to the payment schedule.

It is crucial to the success of a small business that accounts payable be monitored closely. Ideally, this aspect of the firm's operations would be supervised by a financial expert (either inside or outside the company) who is not only able to see the company's financial "big picture" but is able to analyze and act upon fluctuations in the company's cash flow. This also requires detailed record keeping of outstanding payables. Reports ought to be checked on a weekly basis, and when payments are made, copies should be filed along with the original invoices and other relevant paperwork. Any hidden costs, such as interest charges, should also be noted in the report. Over a period of time, these reports will start to paint an accurate cash flow picture.

Effective monitoring practices not only ensure that payments are made to vendors in a complete and timely fashion, but also serve to protect businesses against accidental overpayment. These overpayments, which often take the form of overpaying sales and use taxes, can be caused by any number of factors: internal miscommunication, encoding errors, sloppy or inadequate record keeping practices, or ignorance of current tax codes.

Internal audits of accounts payable practices can be an effective method of addressing this issue, especially for expanding companies. "As companies grow, owners tend to become less involved in day-to-day operations and relinquish control of some functions to staff," stated Cindy McFerrin in *Colorado Business Magazine*. "Set up systems and procedures in your company that encourage communication, provide for staying current with tax codes, and lessen the risk of multiple payments and other mistakes. Laying the groundwork for accuracy today can keep you profitable and in control tomorrow."

SEE ALSO *Cash Management*

BIBLIOGRAPHY

Anthony, Robert N., and Leslie K. Pearlman. *Essentials of Accounting*. Prentice Hall, 1999.

Bannister, Anthony. *Bookkeeping and Accounts for Small Business*. Straightforward Company Ltd, April 1, 2004.

Longenecker, Justin G., Carlos W. Moore, J. William Petty, and Leslie E. Palich. *Small Business Management*. Thomson South-Western, January 1, 2005.

Ludwig, Mary S. *Accounts Payable: A Guide to Running an Efficient Department*. John Wiley, 1998.

McFerrin, Cindy. "Understanding Overpaying." *Colorado Business Magazine*. December 1997.

Hillstrom, Northern Lights
updated by Magee, ECDI

ACCOUNTS RECEIVABLE

Accounts receivable is a term used to describe the quantity of cash, goods, or services owed to a business by its clients and customers. The manner in which the collection of outstanding bills is handled, especially in a small business, can be a pivotal factor in determining a company's profitability. Getting the sale is the first step of the cash flow process, but all the sales in the world are of little use if monetary compensation is not forthcoming. Moreover, when a business has trouble collecting what it is owed, it also often has trouble paying off the bills (accounts payable) it owes to others.

Making Collections By extending credit to a client—selling on payment terms other than cash up front—you are, in essence, lending them money. Collecting this money is of critical importance to the health of a company. Nonetheless, many small business owners depend primarily on the good will of their clients as a collection policy. They simply send out an invoice and them wait,

and wait. A collection policy designed to minimize payment delays is a good idea for companies of any size.

In an ideal world, a company's accounts receivable collections would coincide with the firm's accounts payable schedule. In the real world, there are many outside factors working against timely payments some of which are well beyond the control of even the most vigilant manager. Seasonal demands, vendor shortages, stock market fluctuations, and other economic factors can all contribute to a client's inability to pay bills in a timely fashion. Recognizing those factors and incorporating them into the cash flow contingency plan can make a big difference in establishing a solid accounts receivable system for your business.

By looking at receipts from past billing cycles, it is often possible to detect recurring cash flow problems with some clients, and to plan accordingly. Small business owners need to examine clients on a case-by-case basis, of course. In some instances, the debtor company may simply have an inattentive sales force or accounts payable department that needs repeated prodding to make its payment obligations. But in other cases, the debtor company may simply need a little more time to make good on its financial obligations. In many instances, it is in the best interests of the creditor company to cut such establishments a little slack. After all, a business that is owed money by a company that files for bankruptcy protection is likely to see very little of what it is owed. However, a business that has determined that its late paying customer is well managed may decide by giving that customer a little more time and by doing so, perhaps a chance to grow and prosper becoming a valued long-term client.

Methods of Collecting A good way to improve cash flow is to make the entire company aware of the importance of accounts receivable, and to make collections a top priority. Invoice statements for each outstanding account should be reviewed on a regular basis, and a weekly schedule of collection goals should be established. Other tips in the realm of accounts receivable collection include:

- Get credit references for new clients, and check them out thoroughly before agreeing to extend the client credit

- Do not delay in making follow-up calls, especially with clients who have a history of paying late

- Curb late payment excuses by including a prepaid payment envelope with each invoice

- Know when to let go of a bad account; if a debt has been on the books for so long that the cost of pursuing payment is proving exorbitant, it may be time to consider giving up and moving on (the wisdom of this depends a lot on the amount owed, of course)

- Collection agencies should only be used as a last resort

The longer it takes to collect on an invoice, the less likely collection of the money becomes. As a rule of thumb, according to Dr. Cornwall, Director of the Belmont University, Center for Entrepreneurship, "never let any one customer represent a larger percentage of your total sales than your average profit margin. That way if you need to fire a customer, you can still pay your bills."

ACCOUNTS RECEIVABLE FINANCING

Accounts receivable financing provides cash funding on the strength of a company's outstanding invoices. Instead of buying accounts, lenders use invoices as collateral against which they extend short-term loans. Besides benefiting a business in debt, accounts receivable financiers can assume greater risks than traditional lenders, and will also lend to new and vibrant businesses that demonstrate real potential. An accounts receivable lender will also handle other aspects of the account, including collections and deposits, freeing the company to focus on other areas of productivity. However, risks are involved in this sort of undertaking and agreements are typically lengthy and steeped in legal lingo. Before considering this type of financing it is recommended that an expert assessment of the specific collection situation be sought.

SEE ALSO *Cash Management*

BIBLIOGRAPHY
Bannister, Anthony *Bookkeeping and Accounts for Small Business.* Straightforward Company Ltd, April 1, 2004.

Bragg, Steven M. *Accounting Best Practices.* John Wiley, 1999.

"Collecting Yourself." *Inc.* March 2000.

Cornwall, Dr. Jeffrey R., David Vang, and Jean Hartman. *Entrepreneurial Financial Management.* Prentice Hall, May 13, 2003.

Flecker, Cody. *Collect Your Money: A Guide to Collecting Outstanding Accounts Receivable.* Cobra, 1998.

Longenecker, Justin G., Carlos W. Moore, J. William Petty, and Leslie E. Palich. *Small Business Management.* Thomson South-Western, January 1, 2005.

Schechter, Karen S. "Compare Costs, Benefits of Billing Service Vs. In-house." *American Medical News.* July 24, 2000.

Schmidt, David. "Agents of Change." *Business Credit.* October 2000.

Hillstrom, Northern Lights
updated by Magee, ECDI

ACTIVITY-BASED COSTING

Activity-based costing (ABC) is an accounting method that allows businesses to gather data about their operating costs. Costs are assigned to specific activities—planning, engineering, or manufacturing—and then the activities are associated with different products or services. In this way, the ABC method enables a business to decide which products, services, and resources are increasing their profitability, and which are contributing to losses. Managers are then able to generate data to create a better budget and gain a greater overall understanding of the expenses that are required to keep the company running smoothly. Generally, activity-based costing is most effective when used over a long period of time.

Activity-based costing emerged in the 1980s as a way to more accurately measure all of a business's costs and associate them to the goods and services produced. Traditional cost accounting methods were designed for the companies operating in the early days of the 20th Century, a time when direct labor and materials were the two largest costs associated with producing goods and services. There was little automation at the time and overhead costs were very small as a percentage of total costs. Furthermore, most companies offered a narrow range of products and/or services. All this was changing by the middle of the century. Automation was being incorporated into all businesses and overhead costs rose as the support services needed to design and manage this automation were removed from the production floor. Yet traditional cost accounting methods stayed in place. Owners continued to measure primarily the costs of direct labor and materials; they allocated overhead costs somewhat arbitrarily. As overhead costs grew as a share of total costs, the distortions that this method introduced also grew.

Harvard Business School Professor Robert S. Kaplan was among the first to articulate a need for a more sophisticated system with which to more accurately allocate costs directly to the goods and services produced by that business. ABC is based on the principle that the majority of business activities support the production and delivery of goods and services. Therefore, in order to get a true picture of the cost of producing a good or service, one must allocate the costs of all business activity to specific products and services. The ABC method does this by assigning factory and corporate overhead, as well as other indirect resource costs, to activity categories. Then, an assessment is made as to how much overhead each product, product line, or service consumes. In this way, according to Professor Kaplan, in an article he wrote for *The CPA Journal* in 1990, "ABC offers management accurate information by delineating support costs and tracing them to individual products and product lines."

HOW ACTIVITY-BASED COSTING PROGRAMS WORK

Implementing an activity-based costing program requires planning by and a commitment from upper management. If possible, it is best to do a trial study or test run on a department whose profit-making performance is not up to snuff. These types of situations have a greater chance of succeeding and demonstrating that an ABC program is worth the effort. If the pilot study yields no savings in cost, the activity-based costing system has either been improperly implemented or, it may not be right for the company.

The first thing a business must do when using ABC is set up a team charged with determining which activities are necessary for the product or service in question. This team needs to include experts from different areas of the company (including finance, technology, and human resources); an outside consultant may also be helpful.

After the team has assembled data on such topics as utilities and materials, it is time to determine the elements of each activity that cost money. Attention to detail is very important: many of these costs may be hidden and not entirely obvious. As Joyce Chutchian-Ferranti wrote in an article for *Computerworld*: "The key is to determine what makes up fixed costs, such as the cost of a telephone, and variable costs, such as the cost of each phone call." Chutchian-Ferranti goes on to note that even though in many instances technology has replaced human labor costs (such as in voice-mail systems), a business manager must still examine the hidden costs associated with maintaining the service. Nonactivity costs like direct materials and services provided from outside the company usually do not have to be factored in because this has previously been done.

Once all of these costs are determined and noted, the information must be input into a computer application. Chutchian-Ferranti explains that the software can be a simple database, off-the-shelf ABC software, or a customized software program written for the specific job. Over time, this accumulation of data will eventually give the company a detailed picture of exactly where in the process they are spending most and in which areas they are most efficient.

After a business has had enough time to analyze the data obtained through activity-based costing and to determine which activities are cost effective, it can decide what steps can be taken to increase profits. Activities deemed cost prohibitive can then be outsourced, cut back, or eliminated altogether. The implementation of these changes is known as activity-based management (ABM).

ACTIVITY-BASED COSTING AND SMALL BUSINESSES

It used to be that large corporations were the only businesses involved in activity-based costing. Not so today. Service industries such as banks, hospitals, insurance companies, and real estate agencies have all had success with ABC. But since its inception, activity-based costing has seemed to have been more successful when implemented by larger companies rather than by smaller ones. As Henrick noted, "Companies with only a few products and markets aren't likely to get as much benefit from basing costs on activities as companies operating with diverse products, service lines, channels and customers." But since setting up activity-based costing for a business usually takes less time for a smaller project, a small business that is unsure about the effectiveness of ABC can consider a simple test program to determine whether it is right for them.

Douglas T. Hicks is one expert who feels that the time is right for small businesses to implement activity-based costing. In a 1999 *Journal of Accountancy* article entitled "Yes, ABC is for Small Business, Too," Hicks presented a case study for one of his clients, a small manufacturer that builds components for the automobile industry. Hicks detailed how they were able to triple sales and increase profits fivefold in a four-year span after adopting ABC. "Much of this improvement came from a profitable mix of contracts generated by a costing/quoting process that more closely reflects the actual cost structure of the company," Hicks stated. "This has enabled the company to improve the management of its contracts." Isolating and measuring the cost of material movement and using the data to justify many operational changes were other factors Hicks cited for the success his client had with ABC.

Hicks also noted a change in management's attitude after the success of ABC: "On an important but less tangible level, management's knowledge of and attitude toward cost information have undergone a substantial change. Where once managers had their own way of measuring the cost impact of management actions, they now measure those costs in a formal, uniform way. When managers contemplate changes, they have a mental model that directs them toward changes that truly benefit the organization."

POTENTIAL PITFALLS OF ACTIVITY-BASED COSTING

Companies that implement activity-based costing programs run the risk of spending far too much time, effort, and even money on gathering and going over the collected data. Too many details can prove frustrating. On the other hand, too light a touch means lack of actionable information. Another obvious factor that tends to contribute to the downfall of activity-based costing is the simple failure to act on the results that the data provide.

In early 2005 the proponent of activity-based costing, Professor Robert S. Kaplan, published an article in the *Harvard Business School Working Knowledge* entitled "Rethinking Activity-Based Costing." The article acknowledges problems with implementing ABC programs. It appears ABC has proven to be too much work for many and too complicated for many companies to use and maintain over time. The author insists that "the solution to problems with ABC is not to abandon the concept." He goes on to outline a new ABC program which he and his co-author, Steven R. Anderson, call time-driven ABC. Although not fully developed in this article, the new time-driven ABC method is described as a simplification of the original ABC method.

Time-driven ABC requires, for each group of resources, estimates of only two parameters. First, the entire overhead expenditure of a single department divided by the total number of minutes of employee time available. Second, an estimate of how much time it takes to carry out one unit of each kind of activity, for example, the time it takes to process one order. This simplifies greatly the work required t set up an ABC system and may make its implementation more feasible for smaller companies.

As the ways in which we make things change, so too will the systems and methods used to track costs and properly associate them with the products and services being produced. In order to efficiently produce goods and services it is important to know the price of the inputs to the system, both direct and indirect. The more accurately we are able to track these costs, the more efficiently we will be able to make our processes.

SEE ALSO *Overhead Costs; Product Costing*

BIBLIOGRAPHY
Cokins, Gary. "Learning to Love ABC." *Journal of Accountancy.* August 1999.

Cokins, Gary. "Overcoming the Obstacles to Implementing Activity-Based Costing." *Bank Accounting and Finance.* Fall 2000.

Chutchain-Ferranti, Joyce. "Activity-Based Costing." *Computerworld.* August 1999.

Henricks, Mark. "Beneath the Surface." *Entrepreneur.* October 1999.

Hicks, Douglas T. *Activity-Based Costing: Making it Work for Small and Mid-Sized Companies.* 2nd. Edition, John Wiley & Sons, 2002.

Hicks, Douglas T. "Yes, ABC Is for Small Business, Too." *Journal of Accountancy.* August 1999.

Kaplan, Robert S. "Measure Costs Right: Making the Right Decision." *The CPA Journal.* February 1990.

Kaplan, Robert S. and Steven R. Anderson "Rethinking Activity-Based Costing." *Harvard Business School, Working Knowledge.* January 2005.

Lobo, Yane R.O., and Paulo C. Lima. "A New Approach to Product Development Costing." *CMA—The Management Accounting Magazine.* March 1998.

Hillstrom, Northern Lights
updated by Magee, ECDI

ADVERTISING AGENCIES

Advertising agencies are full-service businesses able to manage every aspect of an advertising campaign. They vary widely in size and scope and cater to different kinds of customers. Some agencies have only one or two major clients whose accounts they manage. Others have hundreds of clients spread throughout the country or the world serviced from many field offices. In general, an advertising agency will be able to manage an account, provide creative services, and purchase media access for a client.

STRUCTURE OF ADVERTISING AGENCIES

An agency, depending on its size, will likely have different departments which work on the separate aspects of an account. An account manager or the account planning department will coordinate the work of these departments to ensure that all the client's needs are met. The departments within a full-service agency will typically include:

Research The research department will be able to provide clients with some details about the prospective audience of the final advertising campaign as well as information about the market for the product being advertised. This should include specific market research which leads to a very focused ad campaign, with advertising directed to the ideal target audience.

Creative Services Advertising agencies employ experts in many creative fields that provide quality, professional services. Copywriters provide the text for print ads, and scripts for television or radio advertising. Graphic designers are responsible for the presentation of print ads, and the art department is responsible for providing the necessary images for whatever format advertisement is decided upon. Most advertising agencies also have a technical staff with expertise in web design and implementing an online advertising campaign. Some agencies have in-house photographers and printers; others regularly employ the services of contractors.

The individuals involved in creative services are responsible for developing the advertising platform, which sets the theme and tone of the ad campaign. The advertising platform should draw upon specific, positive features of the product advertised and extrapolate the benefits the consumer could expect to receive as a result of using the product. The campaign, through the development of this platform, should prove to be eye-catching, memorable, and in some way unique. The ads consumers remember stand out from the rest; it is the advertising agency's (and specifically the creative services department's) responsibility to provide this quality for clients.

The final advertising provided by an agency should be fully developed and polished. Television commercials should be produced with professionalism. Print ads should be attractive, informational, and attention-getting. Radio spots should be focused and of high audio quality. Online ads should be well placed and drive traffic to the clients own web site or a site through which the client's products or services are offered.

Media Buying An important function of the agency (and a major source of its revenues) is the placement of the ad in various media. The activity is aimed at achieving the largest targeted audience at the lowest cost. The research conducted by the agency will inform any media-buying decisions.

An agency will be able to negotiate the terms of any contracts made for placing ads in any of various media. A full-service agency will deal confidently with television, radio, newspapers, magazines, and on the World Wide Web. Some agencies are also branching into direct mail marketing and point of purchase incentives. Another area in which agencies will look for ad placements is in the local yellow pages, on outdoor advertising locations which can include billboards, and commercial signs on public buses, subways or trains.

The media-buying staff draws on its experience and research. Some factors to be considered in the development of the media plan include:

Cost Per Thousand: This refers to the cost of an advertisement per one thousand potential customers reached. Media-buyers use this method to compare the various media avenues they must choose between. For example, television ads are considerably more expensive than newspaper ads, but they also reach many more people. Cost per thousand is a straightforward way to

evaluate how to best spend advertising dollars: if a newspaper ad costs $100 and potentially reaches 2,000 customers, the cost per thousand is $50. If a television ad costs $1,000 to produce and place in suitable television spots and reaches a potential of 40,000 viewers, the cost per thousand is only $25.

Cost Per Click and *Click: Through Rate* are new measurement methods used in assessing the cost of accessing potential customers on the Internet. Agreements are often made today under which a company places a small ad on another entity's web site. There is often no fee for placing this ad; rather a fee is assessed only if and when the visitor to the host site clicks on the ad. Sophisticated systems are used to track the number of clicks an ad generates and the owner of the ad is charged on a weekly, monthly, or quarterly basis for resulting service of forwarding potential clients. The fees are based on a prearranged cost per click basis. This also referred to by many as a pay-per-click agreement. Unlike the more widely applicable cost per thousand figure, cost per click measurements are only useful in assessing online ad campaign activity levels.

Reach: This term is used when discussing the scope of an advertisement. The reach of an ad is the number of households which can safely be assumed will be affected by the client's message. This is usually expressed as a percentage of total households. For example, if there are 1,000 households in a town and 200 receive the daily paper, the reach of a well-placed newspaper ad could be expressed as 20 percent: one-fifth of the households in the community can be expected to see the advertisement.

Frequency: The frequency of a message refers to how often a household can be expected to be exposed to the client's message. Frequency differs widely between media and even within the same medium. Newspapers, for example, are read less often on Saturdays and by many more households (and more thoroughly) on Sundays. Fluctuation like this occurs in all media.

Continuity: The media-buyer will also need to consider the timing of advertisements. Depending on the client's product, the ads can be evenly spread out over the course of a day (for radio or television advertisements), a week (for radio, television, or print advertisements), or a month (radio, television, print, or other media). Of course, seasonal realities influence the placement of advertisements as well. Clothing retailers may need to run more advertisements as a new school year approaches or when new summer merchandise appears. Hardware stores may want to emphasize their wares in the weeks preceding the Christmas holiday. Grocery stores or pharmacies, however, might benefit from more evenly distributed advertising, such as weekly advertisements that emphasize the year-round needs of consumers.

SETTING AN ADVERTISING BUDGET

Deciding on an advertising budget is highly subjective; it depends on the type of business, the competitive atmosphere, and the available funds. It will also depend on how well established the business is and what the goal of the advertising is. Trade publications are often good resources to consult in pondering this matter; many provide information on industry standards for advertising budgets.

Price Structures Advertising agencies charge their clients for all the itemized expenses involved in creating finished ads, including hiring outside contractors to complete necessary work. The client should receive invoices for all such expenses. For example, the client may receive an invoice for a television ad that includes a photographer's fee, a recording studio's fee, an actor's fee, and the cost of the film itself. The client will also be charged for the cost of placing the final advertisement in whatever media the agency has chosen (and the client has agreed to, of course).

Beyond these expenses, easily invoiced and itemized for the client, advertising agencies include a charge for their services. This fee pays for the extensive account management, creative services, research, and media placement provided by the agency, all the hidden costs involved in the production of a quality advertising campaign, and profit margin.

When working with a new client, and particularly with a small business, an agency may ask that the client put the agency on a retainer. This retainer will consist of the full advertising budget agreed upon, and will be used to pay all production expenses and media buying costs, as well as provide the agency with its fee. The client should still insist on detailed and accurate invoices for expenses taken from the retainer.

DECIDING TO USE AN AGENCY

Depending upon how important advertising is to the overall health of the particular business, and the amount of resources available for use in advertising, the small business owner should consider whether an investment in the services of advertising agency will yield meaningful benefit.

Benefits of Advertising Agencies Advertising agencies provide a valuable resource for any enterprise seeking to increase its customer base or its sales. They bring together professionals with expertise in a wide array of communication fields, and often—though not always—produce polished, quality ads that are well beyond the capacities of the client. Agencies are generally knowledgeable about business strategy and media placement as well. The media-buying experts at an agency will develop a strategic, targeted media plan for their clients, drawing upon years of experience and close relationships with media professionals. This experience and these connections are likely not available to the small business owner, and can be important factors in launching a successful media campaign.

Drawbacks of Advertising Agencies One drawback to using an agency, of course, is the added stress of dealing with unfamiliar people and unknown territory. Choosing the right agency will take time; the process of reaching a satisfactory ad campaign can be taxing and time-consuming (especially if the client is vague about his or her desires or expects a top-dollar campaign at a bargain-basement price). Work will have to be reviewed, changed, and reviewed again. And the account will have to be monitored closely. As with any outside contractor, the small business owner will need to keep careful tabs on what is received for his or her hard-earned dollar.

Cost is another factor that must be weighed carefully by the small business owner. Although advertising agency campaigns are often extremely valuable in terms of shaping market share, product recognition, and public image, the small business owner will have to carefully consider the potential benefits against the costs associated with hiring an agency of any size. When deciding whether or not to use an agency, the small business owner should consider if the advertising he or she envisions really requires a team of experts working on it. If the ads will be fairly simple, or if they will be placed only in one medium (such as a local newspaper), the owner should probably attempt to create the ads without the aid of an agency. It will be more economical to hire one expert, such as a graphic designer, and to place the ads personally than to hire an agency.

SELECTING A PARTICULAR ADVERTISING AGENCY

It is important for a small business to work with an agency able to devote the time needed to insure a successful ad campaign. Smaller, local agencies can usually offer more one-on-one attention. Large agencies with a stable of large corporate clients may not pay the small business owner the attention he or she thinks needed. Difficult choices arise when a business is mid-sized and needs the "heavy hitters" before it has become one itself.

Ideally, an agency should be familiar with the specific set of concerns shared by most small businesses: a limited advertising budget, finding a niche in a community, and establishing a loyal customer base. Finding a well-informed agency experienced in the customer's line is very helpful. If the potential client's business is a bookstore, for example, and the agency has never promoted a bookstore before, it does not mean they will necessarily be a poor choice to create and manage an advertising campaign. They may have done work for other local retail stores that have faced the same obstacles and challenges.

In an article for *Entrepreneur,* Kim T. Gordon outlined a series of questions for small business owners should ask in picking an agency. First, they should ascertain whether the agency is familiar with the target audience and knows how to reach them. Second, the small business should make sure that the agency has done extensive work in the media they plan to use most extensively. Third, small business owners should ask potential agencies about the results the agency has achieved in working with similar clients. Finally, the business owner should ask for a clear picture of what they should expect to accomplish with their specific advertising budget.

One of the best ways to choose an agency is the same way you would choose a bank, a doctor, or a housepainter: ask others you trust whom they are using. If your friends, neighbors, or fellow business owners have used an agency they were pleased with, it is worth further inquiry. If you see advertising you really like, call the business and compliment them on their good taste; then ask who prepares their ad copy. The agency-client relationship is very much trust-based; the creative work agencies do is subjective. You should work with an agency whose collective personality and creative work make you feel comfortable. These services will cost a considerable amount; starting off with a firm you feel optimistic about will help insure your satisfaction throughout the relationship. The American Association of Advertising Agencies (AAAA) helps match agencies and clients through their New Business Web site, located at www.aaaa.org.

During the introductory meeting, the agency will be prepared to show samples of their work. These are called case histories; they should be relevant to your business. These samples should reflect the agency's understanding of the needs of your small business—including who your customer base is—and a working knowledge of the kind of marketing necessary to sell your product. As a potential client, you should feel free to ask many questions concerning the approach of the advertisements, the audience reached by certain media, and what media plans have been developed for businesses similar to yours. An agency, though, should never be asked to do work "on

spec." Advertising agencies cannot afford to use their considerable creative resources doing free work for potential clients. The case histories they provide, along with the answers to any questions you may have, should be sufficient to decide whether to give them your business.

Once you have found an agency you feel comfortable with, and you have together agreed upon a budget and a timeline for the advertising, the agency will begin producing copy for you to approve. Laying a strong foundation, including asking all the questions you have as they arise, will pave the way for a productive, mutually beneficial relationship.

SEE ALSO *Marketing*

BIBLIOGRAPHY

Adams, Richard. *Www.Advertising.* Watson-Guptill, March 2003.

"Checking the Local Market, Asking Media Can Help Start Long-Term Relationship." *Arkansas Business.* December 27, 1999.

Gordon, Kim T. "Call in the Pros." *Entrepreneur.* December 2000.

Larry, D. Kelly and Donald W. Jugenheimer. *Advertising Media Planning.* M.E. Sharpe, September 2003.

Peppers, Don. *Life's a Pitch and Then You Buy.* Doubleday, 1995.

Poteet, G. Howard (editor). *Making Your Small Business a Success: More Expert Advice from the U.S. Small Business Administration.* Liberty Hall Press, 1991.

"Select an Advertising Agency." *Milwaukee Business Journal.* February 11, 2000.

Hillstrom, Northern Lights
updated by Magee, ECDI

ADVERTISING BUDGET

The advertising budget of a business is typically a subset of the larger sales budget and, within that, the marketing budget. Advertising is a part of the sales and marketing effort. Money spent on advertising can also be seen as an investment in building up the business.

In order to keep the advertising budget in line with promotional and marketing goals, a business owner should start by answering several important questions:

1. Who is the target consumer? Who is interested in purchasing the product or service, and what are the specific demographics of this consumer (age, employment, sex, attitudes, etc.)? Often it is useful to compose a consumer profile to give the abstract idea of a "target consumer" a face and a personality

that can then be used to shape the advertising message.

2. What media type will be most useful in reaching the target consumer?

3. What is required to get the target consumer to purchase the product? Does the product lend itself to rational or emotional appeals? Which appeals are most likely to persuade the target consumer?

4. What is the relationship between advertising expenditures and the impact of advertising campaigns on product or service purchases? In other words, how much profit is likely to be earned for each dollar spent on advertising?

Answering these questions will help to define the market conditions that are anticipated and identify specific goals the company wishes to reach with an advertising campaign. Once this analysis of the market situation is complete, a business must decide how best to budget for the task and how best to allocate budgeted funds.

BUDGETING METHODS

There are several allocation methods used in developing a budget. The most common are listed below:

- Percentage of Sales method
- Objective and Task method
- Competitive Parity method
- Market Share method
- Unit Sales method
- All Available Funds method
- Affordable method

It is important to notice that most of these methods are often combined in any number of ways, depending on the situation. Because of this, these methods should not be seen as rigid but as building blocks that can be combined, modified, or discarded as necessary. Remember, a business must be flexible—ready to change course, goals, and philosophy when the market and the consumer demand such a change.

Percentage of Sales Method Due to its simplicity, the percentage of sales method is the most commonly used by small businesses. When using this method an advertiser takes a percentage of either past or anticipated sales and allocates that percentage of the overall budget to advertising. But critics of this method charge that using past sales for figuring the advertising budget is too conservative, that it can stunt growth. However, it might be safer for a small business to use this method if the own-ership feels that future returns cannot be safely anticipated. On the other hand, an established business, with well-established profit trends, will tend to use anticipated sales when figuring advertising expenditures. This method can be especially effective if the business compares its sales with those of the competition (if available) when figuring its budget.

Objective and Task Method Because of the importance of objectives in business, the task and objective method is considered by many to make the most sense and is therefore used by most large businesses. The benefit of this method is that it allows the advertiser to correlate advertising expenditures with overall marketing objectives. This correlation is important because it keeps spending focused on primary business goals.

With this method, a business needs to first establish concrete marketing objectives, often articulated in the "selling proposal," and then develop complementary advertising objectives articulated in the "positioning statement." After these objectives have been established, the advertiser determines how much it will cost to meet them. Of course, fiscal realities need to be figured into this methodology as well. Some objectives (expansion of area market share by 15 percent within a year, for instance) may only be reachable through advertising expenditures beyond the capacity of a small business. In such cases, small business owners must scale down their objectives so that they reflect the financial situation under which they are operating.

Competitive Parity Method While keeping one's own objectives in mind, it is often useful for a business to compare its advertising spending with that of its competitors. The theory here is that if a business is aware of how much its competitors are spending to advertise their products and services, the business may wish to budget a similar amount on its own advertising by way of staying competitive. Doing as one's competitor does is not, of course, always the wisest course. And matching another's advertising budget dollar for dollar does not necessarily buy one the same marketing outcome. Much depends on how that money is spent. However, gauging one's advertising budget on other participants' in the same market is a reasonable starting point.

Market Share Method Similar to competitive parity, the market share method bases its budgeting strategy on external market trends. With this method a business equates its market share with its advertising expenditures. Critics of this method contend that companies that use market share numbers to arrive at an advertising budget are ultimately predicating their advertising on an arbitrary guideline that does not adequately reflect future goals.

Unit Sales Method This method takes the cost of advertising an individual item and multiplies it by the number of units the business wishes to sell. This method is only effective, of course, when the cost of advertising a single unit can be reasonably determined.

All Available Funds Method This aggressive method involves the allocation of all available profits to advertising purposes. This can be risky for a business of any size it means that no money is being used to help the business grow in other ways (purchasing new technologies, expanding the work force, etc.). Yet this aggressive approach is sometimes useful when a start-up business is trying to increase consumer awareness of its products or services. However, a business using this approach needs to make sure that its advertising strategy is an effective one and that funds which could help the business expand are not being wasted.

Affordable Method With this method, advertisers base their budgets on what they can afford. Of course, arriving at a conclusion about what a small business can afford in the realm of advertising is often a difficult task, one that needs to incorporate overall objectives and goals, competition, presence in the market, unit sales, sales trends, operating costs, and other factors.

MEDIA SCHEDULING

Once a business decides how much money it can allocate for advertising, it must then decide where it should spend that money. Certainly the options are many, including print media (newspapers, magazines, direct mail), radio, television (ranging from 30-second ads to 30-minute infomercials), and the Internet. The mix of media that is eventually chosen to carry the business's message is really the heart of the advertising strategy.

Selecting Media The target consumer, the product or service being advertised, and cost are the three main factors that dictate what media vehicles are selected. Additional factors may include overall business objectives, desired geographic coverage, and availability (or lack thereof) of media options.

Kim T. Gordon, author, marketing coach and media spokesperson offers three general rules to follow when trying to select a media vehicle for advertising in an article entitled "Selecting the Best Media for Your Ad."

Rule number 1: eliminate waste. The key to selecting the right media source is to choose the source "that reaches the largest percentage of your particular target audience with the least amount of waste." Paying to reach a larger number of people may not serve well if the audience reached has only a small percentage of likely customers of your product. It may be preferable to advertise in a paper or magazine with a smaller distribution if the readers of that paper or magazine are more likely to be in the market for your product or service.

Rule number 2: follow your customer. Here again, the objective is to go to the sources used most by your target market, especially a source that that audience looks to for information about your type of product or service. Gordon explains that advertising "in search corridors—such as the Yellow Pages and other directories—is often a cost-efficient solutions. They're the media customers turn to when they've made a decision to buy something."

Rule number 3: buy enough frequency. We are constantly bombarded with advertisements and images and in order to penetrate the consciousness it is important to be seen with some frequency. Gordon emphasizes that it is "essential to advertise consistently over a protracted period of time to achieve enough frequency to drive your message home."

Scheduling Criteria The timing of advertisements and the duration of an advertising campaign are two crucial factors in designing a successful campaign. There are three methods generally used by advertisers in scheduling advertising. Each is listed below with a brief explanation.

- Continuity—This type of scheduling spreads advertising at a steady level over the entire planning period (often month or year, rarely week), and is most often used when demand for a product is relatively even.

- Flighting—This type of scheduling is used when there are peaks and valleys in product demand. To match this uneven demand a stop-and-go advertising pace is used. Notice that, unlike "massed" scheduling, "flighting" continues to advertise over the entire planning period, but at different levels. Another kind of flighting is the pulse method, which is essentially tied to the pulse or quick spurts experienced in otherwise consistent purchasing trends.

- Massed—This type of scheduling places advertising only during specific periods, and is most often used when demand is seasonal, such as at Christmas or Halloween.

ADVERTISING NEGOTIATIONS AND DISCOUNTS

No matter what allocation method, media, and campaign strategy that advertisers choose, there are still ways small businesses can make their advertising as cost effective as possible. Writing in *The Entrepreneur and Small Business Problem Solver,* author William Cohen put together a list of "special negotiation possibilities and discounts" that can be helpful to small businesses in maximizing their advertising dollar:

- Mail order discounts—Many magazines will offer significant discounts to businesses that use mail order advertising.

- Per Inquiry deals—Television, radio, and magazines sometimes only charge advertisers for advertisements that actually lead to a response or sale.

- Frequency discounts—Some media may offer lower rates to businesses that commit to a certain amount of advertising with them.

- Stand-by rates—Some businesses will buy the right to wait for an opening in a vehicle's broadcasting schedule; this is an option that carries considerable uncertainty, for one never knows when a cancellation or other event will provide them with an opening, but this option often allows advertisers to save between 40 and 50 percent on usual rates.

- Help if necessary—Under this agreement, a mail order outfit will run an advertiser's ad until that advertiser breaks even.

- Remnants and regional editions—Regional advertising space in magazines is often unsold and can, therefore, be purchased at a reduced rate.

- Barter—Some businesses may be able to offer products and services in return for reduced advertising rates.

- Seasonal discounts—Many media reduce the cost of advertising with them during certain parts of the year.

- Spread discounts—Some magazines or newspapers may be willing to offer lower rates to advertisers who regularly purchase space for large (two to three page) advertisements.

- An in-house agency—If a business has the expertise, it can develop its own advertising agency and enjoy the discounts that other agencies receive.

- Cost discounts—Some media, especially smaller outfits, are willing to offer discounts to those businesses that pay for their advertising in cash.

Of course, small business owners must resist the temptation to choose an advertising medium only because it is cost effective. In addition to providing a good value, the medium must be able to deliver the advertiser's message to present and potential customers.

RELATIONSHIP OF ADVERTISING TO OTHER PROMOTIONAL TOOLS

Advertising is only part of a larger promotional mix that also includes publicity, sales promotion, and personal selling. When developing an advertising budget, the amount spent on these other tools needs to be considered. A promotional mix, like a media mix, is necessary to reach as much of the target audience as possible.

The choice of promotional tools depends on what the business owner is attempting to communicate to the target audience. Public relations-oriented promotions, for instance, may be more effective at building credibility within a community or market than advertising, which many people see as inherently deceptive. Sales promotion allows the business owner to target both the consumer as well as the retailer, which is often necessary for the business to get its products stocked. Personal selling allows the business owner to get immediate feedback regarding the reception of the business' product. And as Hills pointed out, personal selling allows the business owner "to collect information on competitive products, prices, and service and delivery problems."

BIBLIOGRAPHY
Advertising Your Business. Small Business Administration, n.a.

Clark, Scott. "Do the Two-Step with Advertising Budget." *Memphis Business Journal.* March 3, 2000.

Gordon, Kim T. "Call in the Pros." *Entrepreneur.* December 2000.

Gordon, Kim T. "Selecting the Best Media for Your Ad." *Entrepreneur.* September 2003.

Pinson, Linda and Jerry Jinnett *Steps to Small Business Start-Up.* October 2003.

Rasmussen, Erika. "Big Advertising, Small Budget." *Sales and Marketing Management.* December 1999.

Silver, Jonathan. "Advertising Doesn't Have to Break Your Budget." *Washington Business Journal.* May 1, 1998.

Hillstrom, Northern Lights
updated by Magee, ECDI

ADVERTISING, EVALUATION OF RESULTS

Once the small business owner has successfully designed and placed an ad (or had that ad successfully designed and placed by an agency), he or she will be eagerly awaiting the increased sales that advertising promises. While advertising can be an effective means of increasing profitability, measurable increases in sales may not be immediately forthcoming. But if the advertising was well-planned, well-placed, and well-executed, it will likely produce positive results eventually.

CUMULATIVE EFFECTS

It is widely accepted among advertising experts that one major benefit of advertising any business is the cumulative effect of the message on consumers. This effect occurs as consumers are repeatedly exposed to advertising that may not have an immediate impact, but becomes familiar and remains in the memory. This message will be recalled when the need arises for the advertised product or service. The consumer, because of the cumulative effects of advertising, will already be familiar with the business's name, as well as the image that it has cultivated through its advertising campaigns. For example, a consumer has heard a carpet cleaning company's ads for months, but until the need arises to have his or her carpets cleaned, there is no reason to contact the company. When that need does arise, however, he or she will already know the name of the company and feel familiar enough with it to engage its services.

Consistency One trap that advertisers sometimes fall into is that of restlessness or boredom with a long-running campaign. The owners of a small business may feel a need to change a long-running advertisement simply because of a desire to try a new, more exciting avenue. There are certainly valid reasons for doing so (stagnant sales, changing competitive dynamics, etc.) at times, but advertising experts discourage businesses from yanking advertisements that continue to be effective just for the sake of change. "If it ain't broke, don't fix it," is the guiding principle behind this caution. They note that consumers learn to associate businesses with certain advertisements, design elements, or themes, but that these associations sometimes take time to sink in. Similarly, industry observers counsel small business owners to maintain a level of consistency with the advertising media they utilize (provided those media are effective, of course).

By choosing an appropriate style and theme, and carefully placing ads in effective media, the small business owner begins to create a lasting foundation for his or her company. Maintaining an advertising campaign in itself advertises the stability, dependability, and tone of a business. If customers are finding the ads useful, then the advertising is working; changing the ads could diminish their effectiveness.

STRATEGIES FOR TRACKING ADVERTISING'S EFFECTIVENESS

Before the advertiser decides to stick with one advertising plan for the next several years, however, he or she wants to be sure that the advertising is having some effect. Because of the cumulative effect of advertising, this can sometimes be difficult to ascertain. The following are suggestions for the often vague science of tracking the effectiveness of advertising:

Monitoring Sales Figures This strategy involves tracking sales from a period before the current advertising was used, and then comparing those figures to sales made during the time the advertising is active. One pitfall of this strategy is not choosing a representative time period. One month's worth of sales figures may not be enough to fully gauge the effectiveness of an ad. Ideally, the business owner could compare figures from long periods of sales to exclude changes due to factors other than advertising, such as seasonal fluctuations and holiday sales.

Running a Coupon One satisfyingly concrete way of tracking how many customers were exposed to advertising is to use coupons. These coupons, which will typically provide a discount of some kind or some other incentive to customers to use them, can be easily tabulated, providing businesses with tangible evidence of the advertising campaign's level of effectiveness. Such measurements, however, are limited to print campaigns. Another coupon-type offer, effective across media types, is to encourage customers to mention their exposure to an ad in return for a bonus. For example, a radio ad might include the sentence, "Mention this ad for an additional 5 percent off your purchase!"

Surveying Customers Perhaps the most accurate and easiest method of tracking the effectiveness of a media campaign is simply asking customers how they were directed to you. You can ask if a customer saw a particular ad, or more generally ask how they came to know about the shop or service. Consumers are generally pleased to be asked for their input, and they can give you firsthand accounts of how advertising is affecting your business.

Internet Ad Tracking One of the unique aspects to using the Internet for advertising is the fact that it is easier to track the number of people who actually see and register the ad. Because of the interactive nature of the Internet and the methods used to advertise online, a company can actually track the number of people who both see their ad and take some resulting action, like clicking on a hypertext link. However, knowing how many people have seen an ad does not automatically translate to knowing what percentage of new sales are the result of this exposure. Assessing the value of this Internet exposure must be done in the same ways that advertising generally is assessed, through careful tracking and monitoring.

BIBLIOGRAPHY

East, Robert. *The Effect of Advertising and Display.* Springer, July 2003.

Nucifora, Alf. "Getting the Most from Your Media Purchase." *LI Business News.* 23 October 1998.

United States Small Business Administration. *Advertising Your Business.*n.d.

Hillstrom, Northern Lights
updated by Magee, ECDI

ADVERTISING MEDIA— AUDIO

The most common audio advertising medium is FM radio. Placement of an advertisement on FM radio costs about as much as an advertisement placed in a metropolitan newspaper. However, radio is more dynamic than print alternatives because it allows the advertiser essentially to talk with the consumer. As a result, many small business consultants believe that an entertaining and informative radio advertising campaign can be a major asset. They usually temper this view by adding that a reliance on radio advertising alone is not recommended. Most businesses incorporate a media mix when attempting to sell their products or services, utilizing radio advertising in concert with print and other advertising media. The key for small business owners is to study what types of advertising best suit their products and services and to use that media to spearhead their advertising campaign.

ADVANTAGES AND DISADVANTAGES OF RADIO

Radio stations feature many different programming emphases or categories. These categories range from music-oriented formats such as country, adult contemporary, classic rock, and alternative rock to news- or talk-oriented formats. Since these different formats attract different demographic segments of the total audience, business owners can reach their target audience simply by buying time on appropriate stations and within specified programming categories.

Another major advantage of radio advertising is that it is inexpensive to place and to produce, allowing small business owners to place advertisements on more than one station in a given market. In addition, radio advertising content can be changed quickly to meet changes in the market or to reflect new business objectives. Finally,

radio reaches large numbers of commuters, income-generating people who often pay more attention to radio advertising than to other advertising media, especially if they are driving alone.

The costs associated with purchasing radio advertising time reflect this emphasis on reaching the commuter audience. The four time slots, or "dayparts," offered for advertisers by most radio stations are the morning drive, daytime, afternoon drive, and evening. The two most expensive—but also most effective advertising slots—are the morning and afternoon drive times.

Although radio advertising is effective, there are drawbacks to consider when deciding whether to create and place a radio spot. Aspects to consider include competitor clutter, the cumulative costs associated with long-term radio spots, and the fleeting nature of a radio message. In addition to these drawbacks, several other legal and procedural guidelines need to be considered. These include:

1. Be sure a clear disclaimer is used within the advertisement if celebrity soundalikes are used.

2. Always work with a contract in place when working with a station or advertising agency to create a radio spot.

3. Treat the competition fairly, always avoid slanderous statements. Federal law mandates that advertisers must accurately depict the competition.

4. Be prepared to run a radio advertisement often. Industry analysts agree that an advertisement needs to be heard by a consumer on several occasions before it is likely to generate a response.

5. Be cautious about excessive reliance on one station. On rare occasions the products and services a business offers may be best promoted on a single station. For example, a dealer in sports paraphernalia may want to limit radio spots to the lone sports-talk station in town. Usually, however, small businesses are better served by maximizing exposure and using more than one radio station for their audio advertising.

AM RADIO

AM radio is a curious anomaly for most young adults who grew up with FM radio, cassettes, and CDs. Yet AM radio still exists, has a folksy charm, and is listened to by a significant percentage of the population. AM offers alternative programming to the predominantly music formats broadcast on FM stations. AM stations, which suffered serious declines in the 1960s and 1970s, now broadcast talk shows, sporting events, news programs, and traffic and weather reports. In addition, AM radio broadcasts can reach remote locations, such as those found in many western states—places that truckers and summer vacationers traverse.

BIBLIOGRAPHY

Barber, Mark, and Andrew Ingram. *Advanced Level Radio Advertising.* John Wiley & Sons, Inc., May 2005.

Drexler, Michael D. "Future for Media Requires Interaction; To Stay in Game, Old Media Must Involve Audience." *Advertising Age.* 20 November 2000.

Parry, Caroline. "Analysis: Is In-Store In Danger of Going Out of Fashion?" *Marketing Week.* 8 December 2005.

Hillstrom, Northern Lights
updated by Magee, ECDI

ADVERTISING MEDIA—INFOMERCIALS

Infomercials are long TV commercials, usually lasting about half an hour. They are often hosted by celebrities and are designed to look like celebrity talk shows or light and entertaining news shows. Another term used to refer to infomercials is "direct response TV." Even though infomercials are often considered annoying, they have gained an undeniable reputation for effectiveness that has gained them respectability within the business community. Research over the past 20 years—the time period in which infomercials became an advertising superpower—has shown that most people who make purchase decisions while watching infomercials are between the ages of 25 and 44, a sought after demographic.

In the words of Thomas Burke, president of the infomercial division of Saatchi & Saatchi Advertising, infomercials are "the most powerful form of advertising ever created." A recent article in *Forbes* entitled "So Long, Suzanne Somers," explains that what started off as a much-mocked advertising method has gained respectability and has become lucrative enough to attract large corporations and the so called "A-list celebs."

Much of this success is due to the creativity of infomercial advertisers who use the infomercial's marginality to create a kind of cultural or sub-cultural symbol, giving a voice in the form of purchasing power to the late night and early morning consumer. These consumers are likely to be homemakers, blue-collar workers, and salespeople. This demographic information is an essential component in determining which products are selected for infomercial treatment.

One sign that the legitimacy of infomercials as an effective marketing tool has been recognized in recent years is the growing attention that larger companies have

paid to the practice. As more companies, and larger companies get involved with infomercials prices for ad spots on cable stations has risen. Nonetheless, according to *AdWeek,* infomercials are still a more efficient and flexible way to acquire ad time and target prospective customers. "Direct response inventory tends to sell for 50-70 percent cheaper than tranditional spots and can be used for the same purpose as conventional ads." The ability to incorporate tranditonal media tools like Nielsen and MRI ratings with an infomercial campaign is proving to be both powerful and cost effective.

Infomercials usually work best with products that are easy to demonstrate, so that an interaction with the viewing audience can be achieved. This interaction is quite often that of teacher to student, so that infomercials become a medium for instruction, teaching people (or supposing to teach) how to better their social lives or their bodies. Such an approach creates a dialogue that the viewer can take part in, which often leads to a viewer inquiry for more information or to a purchase.

Another useful approach is to create a "storymercial," in which the infomercial sells its product by encasing it—and the targeted consumer—within a story. These "storymercials" often look and feel like documentaries in which a family or businessperson go about their daily lives aided tremendously by the advertiser's product. Testimonials, or little product specific anecdotes, are similar, both pulling viewers into a world where the product is essential to success and happiness. All in all, these infomercials are attempting to show the consumer how to answer the question "How can this product help me?"

When planning an approach, advertisers often consider several criteria, such as how similar products have fared in other markets, time slots, and seasons. Most infomercial producers believe that even small television ratings for an infomercial can translate into strong returns.

BIBLIOGRAPHY

"Advanced Results Marketing Goes Upscale." *AdWeek.* October 17, 2005.

Bieler, Peter. *This Book Has Legs.* November 6, 1998.

Dworman, Steven. *$12 Billion of Inside Marketing Secrets Discovered Through Direct Response Television Sales.* SDE, Inc., December 2003.

Lattman, Peter. "So Long, Suzanne Somers." *Forbes.* July 4, 2005.

Whitelaw, Kevin. "Not Just Slicing and Dicing." *U.S. News & World Report.* September 9, 1996.

Hillstrom, Northern Lights
updated by Magee, ECDI

ADVERTISING MEDIA— INTERNET

The invention of the World Wide Web created a new way to reach out to people—and for business to reach its customers. The World Wide Web is a communications network; as such, it is a natural venue for communicating advertising messages. Early on people needed computer know-how and command of communications protocols to use the Web. In the mid-1990s this began to change rapidly.

In the early 1990s came the first graphical browser. With that and the later spread of high-speed connections to the network, the World Wide Web, the Internet, became an powerful economic engine. The volatility associated with the early days of Internet growth has settled a bit; but fifteen years later it is still a enormous economic and cultural force; it is changing the ways in which we work and communicate.

Advertising on the Internet, online advertising, has seen many ups and downs. Exactly how best to use the Internet as an advertising medium is still a subject of debate. What is certain is that more and more people are using the Internet more and more regularly. The Internet has "the eyeballs." Advertising is about the eyeballs.

Small businesses may have a unique opportunity for advertising success on the Internet. There are many ways to do so. The sophistication of online advertising campaigns has grown with the proliferation of techniques, from banner ads and pop-ups to direct e-mail and paid search terms. The key to a successful campaign is getting the proper mix of techniques.

MEANS OF ADVERTISING ON THE WEB

To get started involves an initial investment. It is the cost of building an online presence, a web page or web site. This is necessary because most Internet advertising involves bringing users to a web site, "generating traffic." The web site itself may consist primarily of a simple presentation of information about a company, its products and services. The site may also be a more interactive display with e-commerce capabilities allowing a visitor to read about and see pictures of products, to place an order or even to purchase and pay for items online. An e-commerce capable site is often referred to as a cyberstore. The cost of building a web site will depend on the complexity of the resulting web site.

The first questions to ask when deciding on the best way to advertise on the web are the same questions one would pose in launching an ad campaign.

- Who is the target consumer? Who is interested in purchasing the product or service? What are the specific demographics of this consumer (age, employment, sex, attitudes, etc.)?

- How does the targeted customer like to buy? How does she/he use the Internet?

- What is required to get the target consumer to purchase the product? Does the product lend itself to rational or emotional appeals?

- How much profit is likely to be generated for each dollar spent on ads?

Once these questions are answered, planning and designing a web site and online advertising campaign can begin.

ADVERTISING TOOLS

Paid Search Terms Internet users usually navigate the web by starting their session at one of the Internet's search engines: AltaVista, AOLsearch, Dogpile, Excite, Google, HotPot, Lycos, MSN, and Yahoo— , to name but a few. The goal of an advertiser is to capture those users who may be interested in his or her product or service.

Google was one of the first search engines to offer advertisers the opportunity to do just that. Today, many search engine businesses offer this opportunity by selling terms. The practice is called paid search terms, or pay-per-click search-engine advertising, or, in the case of Google, AdWords. By purchasing a term through a search engine, you purchase the right to have a hypertext link appear on the result page of any search phrase that included the term you purchase. For example, a user types the words "air filtration system" into a search engine. The company that has purchased the term "air filtration system" from the search engine will appear on the list of results for that search and the user will have the opportunity to link directly to the advertising company's web site. The advertising air filtering company only pays if and when the user actually clicks through to its web site. This is called pay-per-click.

The use of paid search terms is the fastest growing method of online advertising; it represents 40% of the approximately $12 billion spend on online advertising in the U.S. in 2005. It's also the most potentially powerful online advertising tools for the small business, according to Seth Stevenson in his article entitled "Words That Sell." This is particularly true for companies dealing with specialized items. "Do a search for 'sling-back shoes,' for example, and you will find small e-commerce sites competing head-to-head with major retail chains" explains Stevenson. This form of advertising helps to level the playing field.

Paid search terms are an evolving advertising model. With popularity, the cost for terms will increase since they are sold in an auction format. Nonetheless, a carefully tailored advertising plan can maximize the traffic generated from the purchase of just a few words. And, if nobody clicks through to your site, you pay nothing.

Search Engine Optimization Before the advent of paid search terms, search engine optimization (SEO) was the primary means of capturing the attention of web users as they began an Internet session with a search engine query. It is still a useful method for gaining exposure.

Through the use of SEO, companies can use a combination of HTML design elements (meta tags, links to and from other sites), text and keywords to ensure that their web sites are picked up by the search engines and appear high on a search results page. If done properly, this can increase traffic to the company's web site without paying a pay-per-click fee. However, implementing a successful SEO plan takes a great deal of expertise. That must be acquired or purchased; either way a cost is involved.

Banner Ads Banner advertisements are graphic advertisements that appear on a web site and are intended to build brand awareness or generate traffic for the advertiser's web site. Banner ads were once the leading form of advertising online. They are still an important advertising method, representing 20% of the market in 2004.

Often banners are part of a "link exchange," or cooperative advertising arrangement, in which two businesses with complimentary products and services advertise each other on their respective sites in order to reach a large segment of a given market. However, some Web advertising agencies claim that few people access web pages through banners; these agencies are now trying new motion and graphic technologies to make the banners more inviting. Some experts suggest that businesses consider advertising banners as just one part of an online marketing mix.

E-mail Advertising Sending advertisements by e-mail is another method of using the Internet as an advertising vehicle. The use of mass direct e-mail, in which businesses send unsolicited mail messages to a list of e-mail accounts, has fallen out of favor and in many cases breaks new laws designed to crack down on spamming.

An online newsletter sent out by e-mail is a more sophisticated way in which to reach actual and potential customers. An increasing numbers of businesses have supplemented their general customer satisfaction surveys with queries concerning customers' feelings about being put on a direct mailing list. Online surveys are also a way

to build up an e-mail address mailing list that can be used to send out company information relatively inexpensively. When this is well done, the newsletter or promotional piece will include hypertext links to the company's web page and will encourage the reader to pass the newsletter on to other interested parties.

In addition to the online advertising methods listed here, there are many others. Companies use referral services through which link exchanges are managed. Some companies sponsor web sites for other groups in exchange for links to their own web site. Some publication sites sell classified advertisement space, much as it is done on more traditional print advertising. The list of options is lengthy and the field of online advertising is still quite dynamic.

The key to success is to build a web site that will serve your clients and customers well. This is not always an easy to achieve but essential to the success of any online ad campaign. Once the site is built, the task becomes generating traffic to that site. The methods described above are some of the more successful methods developed for that purpose, so far.

SEE ALSO *Advertising Strategy*

BIBLIOGRAPHY

Bruner, Rick E. *The Decade in Online Advertising, 1994–2004.* DoubleClick, April 2005.

Fass, Allison. "Banner Ads Still Dominate." *New York Times.* August 15, 2000.

Lazaroff, Leon. "Internet Advertising, Markets rely less on 30-second spots as they press full-speed into online ads." *Chicago Tribune.* December 4, 2005.

Stafford, Marla R. and Ronald J. Faber. *Advertising, Promotion, and New Media.* M.E. Sharpe, October 2004.

Stevenson, Seth. "Words That Sell." *Fortune Small Business.* June 2005.

Streitfeld, David. "Ads Fail to Click with Online Users." *International Herald Tribune.* October 31, 2000.

"Time to Set a Standard." *Marketing.* November 16, 2000.

Hillstrom, Northern Lights
updated by Magee, ECDI

ADVERTISING MEDIA—PRINT

The two most common print media are newspapers and magazines, but print media also include outdoor billboards, transit posters, the yellow pages, and direct mail. Print media is important because it can reach such a large audience, and the great number of specialized publications on the market enable businesses to focus on a target audience with a specific set of characteristics. Print media are allowed to advertise most anything, other than products intended for children and sold to children. All other publications may advertise most anything sold legally like cigarettes, liquor, and contraceptives; however, many publications will not accept what they consider to be controversial ads.

TYPES OF PRINT MEDIA

Newspapers When deciding upon a newspaper in which to advertise, there are three physical criteria to consider: distribution, size, and audience. Newspapers are either daily or weekly, come in a standard or tabloid size, and reach a large percentage of the reading public. Because of the broad demographic reach of most newspapers it is difficult to target a specific audience; however, newspapers are effective in increasing awareness of a business' products and services in a specific geographical area.

Types of ads placed in newspapers include: display ads, classified ads, public notes, and preprinted inserts. Newspaper ads have some flexibility in their size. For instance, some are small boxes that take up only a small portion of a page, while others might span one or two full pages (the latter, however, are typically only bought by larger corporations). Regardless of this flexibility, newspaper ads can only use limited special effects, such as font size and color. These limitations lead to advertising "clutter" in newspapers because all the ads look very similar. Therefore, advertisers must use original copy and headings to differentiate their ads from those of their competitors. The quick turnover of newspapers also allows the advertiser to adjust ads to meet new market conditions; however, this turnover means that the same ad may need to be inserted over a significant period of time in order to reach its target audience.

Magazines With magazines an advertiser can focus on a specific target audience. As the Small Business Administration pointed out in *Advertising Your Business:* "Audiences can be reached by placing ads in magazines which have [a] well-defined geographic, demographic, or lifestyle focus." An attractive option for many small businesses may be placing an ad in the localized edition of a national magazine. But magazine advertisements often have a lag time of a couple of months between the purchase of ad space and the publication of the issue in question. Magazines, then, are sometimes not the optimum option for businesses seeking to target fast-changing market trends.

In addition to the above factors, it is also important to consider the nature of the magazine ad copy. Magazines allow elaborate graphics and colors, which give advertisers more creative options than do newspapers. Also, recent surveys have indicated that informative ads are the most persuasive. Therefore, it is important to include copy and art work that are direct and that present important product information to the consumer, such as how the product works, how it benefits the consumer, and where it can be purchased.

Direct Mail Many consultants feel that direct mail is the best way for a small business to begin developing awareness in its target consumers. Mailing lists can be generated (even though they are often difficult to maintain) with the names of those people most likely to purchase the advertiser's products or services. However, direct mail is not always cost effective. A direct mailing campaign can cost as much as $1,000 to reach 1,000 people, whereas television can reach a similar number of potential customers at a fraction of that cost. But business experts indicate that direct mail does tend to generate more purchasing responses than does television, and they observe that the products of many small businesses are often more suited to a direct mailing campaign than to indirect, image advertising.

Yellow Pages The Small Business Administration stated in "Advertising Your Business" that a yellow page ad is often used to "complement or extend the effects of advertising placed in other media." Such an ad has permanence and can be used to target a specific geographic area or community. Essentially, a yellow page ad gives the consumer information needed to make a purchase. Therefore the key information to include in such an ad includes: the products and services available; location; phone number; business hours; special features, such as the acceptable kinds of payment (i.e., credit cards, checks); parking availability; discounts; and delivery policies and emergency services. The best way to arrange this information is in a list, so that the consumer will be able to scan the ad for the desired information.

A major consideration with a yellow page ad is where to place it, which primarily depends on the directory (or category) under which businesses choose to locate their ads. Central to this choice are the products or services that the company wishes to emphasize. The ad copy should compliment the directory, indicating the main products and services for sale, so that the ad will emerge from the similar looking ads that surround it.

Outdoor Advertising Outdoor advertising usually comes in two forms: billboards and transit posters. Like yellow page ads, outdoor advertising is usually used to support advertisements placed in other media. One of the greatest strengths of outdoor advertising is as a directional marker to point customers toward your business. Since the prospective consumer often has only fleeting exposure to billboards and transit posters, the advertising copy written for these media needs to be brief with the ability to communicate ideas at a glance. To do this well one must use graphics and headings efficiently and artfully.

SEE ALSO *Advertising Media—Internet; Advertising Budget*

BIBLIOGRAPHY

Addis, Jim. "How the Net and Print Media Can Help Each Other." *Marketing.* November 1999.

Gordon, Kim T. "Selecting the Best Media for Your Ad." *Entrepreneur.* September 2003.

Ries, Al, and Laura Ries. *The Fall of Advertising and the Rise of PR.* HarperCollins, May 2004.

Stafford, Marla R., and Ronald J. Faber. *Advertising, Promotion, and New Media.* M.E. Sharpe, October 2004.

United States Small Business Administration. *Advertising Your Business,* n.d.

Hillstrom, Northern Lights
updated by Magee, ECDI

ADVERTISING MEDIA— VIDEO

Video advertising can be an effective avenue for reaching an audience. The term *video advertising* is used, here, to refer to all full-motion visual presentations of information. Most such presentations include audio and text elements but what differentiates video advertising from other forms of advertising is its full-motion video aspect. The use of video advertising has grown with the proliferation of video-ready equipment in American homes— televisions, cable channels, VCRs, DVDs, and computers connected to the Internet via broadband or high-speed connections.

In the past, video gave advertisers the ability to reach primarily a broad audience and was, therefore, oriented toward consumers. This has begun to change. The market for video advertising is growing as high-speed connections to the Internet make video viable online. Many new technologies are making video presentations viable in unexpected places (AdsOnFeet, wearable flat-screen LCD TV vests) and on small new devices like video cell phones, iPods, and rCards, a credit card size media player. These increased outlets for video advertising both increase the size of the market and increase the advertiser's ability to target a message to a very particular audience.

Ongoing developments with video advertising are making this form of advertising ever more useful to the small business. When video was primarily used to reach a broad consumer audience, it was not idea for a small business or one operating in a niche market. With the ability to focus the message and the distribution of the message through new video advertising outlets, small businesses can put video to use effectively. Although video advertising can still be very expensive, by focusing the message for a well-defined audience it can also be very effective. There are several video options that can be used effectively by small businesses of modest financial means.

TYPES OF VIDEO ADVERTISING

Network Television Network television reaches the largest audience of all advertising media. As the Small Business Administration noted in *Advertising Your Business,* most small businesses use "spot television," which is an ad "placed on one station in one market." Placing such a spot ad on one of the national networks can be rather expensive, depending on the size of the audience reached and the demand of the specific time slot desired. In any case, such network television spots are often priced well beyond the financial means of small businesses.

Local television, on the other hand, is much more affordable, and many small businesses use it to reach local consumers. Local network advertising time is usually purchased as 30-second "spot announcements," which are similar to the network spot ads. The time slots for local ads begin in the early morning and continue up until the network news broadcasts begin. As with network television, the cost for such a spot depends on the size of the audience determined to be watching and the demand for the particular time slot.

Cable and Satellite Television Cable and satellite stations offer selectivity, low cost, and flexibility. Since many cable stations, like *ESPN* and the *History Channel,* broadcast specific kinds of programs that appeal to certain demographic groups, a defined audience can be targeted. Spot ads are purchased from either a national cable network or from a local cable station. The cost depends on the cable penetration in the area and the channel's viewership. For example, most infomercials are broadcast on cable stations, such as the *Lifetime Network,* because of the programming flexibility and comparatively low advertising costs.

Drawbacks associated with the purchase of advertising time on cable television include fragmentation (which refers to the wide range of viewing options available on cable—and thus the dilution of impact that any one ad may have) and image. The latter factor is primarily associated with local cable stations, which typically have low budgets and viewerships. Moreover, some locally produced cable shows are amateurish and/or feature offensive content.

Streaming Video for the Internet The use of video on the Internet was made possible by the increased speed of data transmission. If data can be sent at a very fast speed from an Internet site to an end user's PC then video can be sent and viewed almost simultaneously. The sending of such video material on the Internet is often referred to as streaming video.

The use of video online is often part of an existing Internet advertising campaign in which video is added to Web sites or existing banner ads. The inclusion of video material on a company's own Web site is a relatively simple matter. Online applications in which this sort of video usage is being seen a great deal include:

- Real estate brokers using streaming video and interactive video to offer prospective buyers a virtual tour of properties on the market.

- Entertainment sites using streaming video to present previews for movies and music.

- Television sites using streaming video to offer their programs, or excerpts of their programs, to Web visitors.

- Online consultants and advertising agencies using streaming video by way of demonstrating their expertise in this producing online ads.

Outlets for online video advertising, beyond a company's own Web site, are multiplying. Services that offer to aggregate video advertising spots and manage their distribution online are appearing. These services are somewhat like online advertising agencies. They bring together the videos from a large number of advertisers. They have agreements with Web entities willing to host ads. Then, they match up the host sites with suitable advertisements and handle all tracking and financial arrangements for the host sites and the advertisers. One such service, Instream, Inc., launched in late 2005, expects to reach "500 million monthly streams per month by early 2006," according to Aimee Irwin, an executive with the firm.

All the ways in which video will expand on the Internet are not clear. The technology upon which the Internet rests is developing rapidly and making things possible today that were not possible just a year ago. What the Internet offers is a unique chance to reach out to a very well-defined audience and not only pass along a message, but interact almost immediately with that portion of the audience for whom your products or

services are of interest. This is a powerful tool for businesses of any size.

SEE ALSO *Advertising Media–Internet*

BIBLIOGRAPHY
Berkowitz, Ira. *Vault Career Guide to Advertising.* Vault, Inc., April 2004.

Instream, The Video Advertising Network, Launches. PR Newswire, 16 November 2005.

Klaassen, Abbey. "Media Morph: Unexpected Video." *Advertising Age.* 3 October 2005.

United States Small Business Administration. *Advertising Your Business,* n.d.

Vickers, Amy. "Being at One with the Consumer: The New Art of Interactive Advertising." *New TV Strategies.* June 2000.

Hillstrom, Northern Lights
updated by Magee, ECDI

ADVERTISING STRATEGY

An advertising strategy is a plan to reach and persuade a customer to buy a product or a service. The basic elements of the plan are 1) the product itself and its advantages, 2) the customer and his or her characteristics, 3) the relative advantages of alternative routes whereby the customer can be informed of the product, and 4) the optimization of resulting choices given budgetary constraints. In effect this means that aims must be clear, the environment must be understood, the means must be ranked, and choices must be made based on available resources. Effective product assessment, market definition, media analysis, and budgetary choices result in an optimum plan—never the perfect plan because resources are always limited.

DEVELOPING THE STRATEGY

Positioning Statement. Formal advertising strategies are based on a "positioning statement," a technical term the meaning of which, simply, is what the company's product or service *is,* how it is differentiated from competing products and services, and by which means it will reach the customer. The positioning statement covers the first two items in the listing above.

Implicit in a good positioning statement is what the industry calls the *product concept,* namely a cluster of values that the product or service represents and the associational frameworks in which it fits. A hunting knife will thus have a very different product concept than a pair of pink silk slippers that glow in the dark. The product concept will later guide the choice of copy, images, and message content to be used in actual ads (the "copy platform"). The positioning statement must also implicitly include the profile of the targeted customer and the reasons why he or she would buy this product or this service. At a later stage, more data on the "target consumer" is then developed as the strategy is fleshed out.

Target Consumer. The target consumer is a complex combination of persons. First of all, it includes the person who ultimately buys the product. Next it includes those who, in certain circumstances, decide what product will be bought (but do not physically buy it). Finally, it includes those who influence product purchases (children, spouse, and friends). In practice the small business owner, being close to his or her customers, probably knows exactly how to advise the advertising agency on the target consumer.

Communication Media. Once the product and its environment are understood and the target consumer has been specified, the routes of reaching the consumer must be assessed—the media of communication. Five major channels are available to the business owner:

- Print—Primarily newspapers (both weekly and daily) and magazines.

- Audio—FM and AM radio.

- Video—Promotional videos, infomercials.

- World Wide Web.

- Direct mail.

- Outdoor advertising—Billboards, advertisements on public transportation (cabs, buses).

Each of the channels available has its advantages, disadvantages, and cost patterns. A crucial stage in developing the advertising strategy, therefore, is the fourth point made at the outset: how to choose the optimum means, given budgetary constraints, to reach the largest number of target consumers with the appropriately formulated message.

Implementation The advertising campaign itself is distinct from the strategy, but the strategy is meant to guide implementation. Therefore across-the-board consistency is highly desirable. Copy, artwork, images, music—indeed all aspects of the campaign—should reflect the strategy throughout. This is especially important when multiple channels are used: print, television, and direct mail, for instance. To achieve a maximum coherence, many effective advertisers develop a unifying thematic expressed as an image, a slogan, or a combination which

is central to all the elements that ultimately reach the consumer.

SEE ALSO *Advertising, Evaluation of Results; Marketing*

BIBLIOGRAPHY
Berkowitz, Ira. *Vault Career Guide to Advertising.* Vault, Inc., April 2004.

Gordon, Kim T. "Selecting the Best Media for Your Ad." *Entrepreneur.* September 2003.

Ries, Al,and Laura Ries. *The Fall of Advertising and the Rise of PR.* HarperCollins, May 2004.

Stafford, Marla R., and Ronald J. Faber. *Advertising, Promotion, and New Media.* M.E. Sharpe, October 2004.

United States Small Business Administration. *Advertising Your Business,* n.d.

Hillstrom, Northern Lights
updated by Magee, ECDI

AFFIRMATIVE ACTION

Affirmative action refers to concrete steps that are taken not only to eliminate discrimination—whether in employment, education, or contracting—but also to attempt to redress the effects of past discrimination. The underlying motive for affirmative action is the Constitutional principle of equal opportunity, which holds that all persons have the right to equal access to self-development. In other words, persons with equal abilities should have equal opportunities.

The extent to which affirmative action programs attempt to overturn discrimination differs widely. Some programs simply institute reviews of the hiring process for women, minorities, and other affected groups. Other affirmative action programs explicitly prefer members of affected groups. In such programs, minimum job requirements are used to create a pool of qualified applicants from which members of affected groups are given preference.

Affirmative action affects small businesses in two main ways. First, it prevents businesses with 15 or more employees from discriminating on the basis of race, color, sex, religion, national origin, and physical capability in practices relating to hiring, compensating, promoting, training, and firing employees. Second, it allows the state and federal governments to favor women-owned and minority-owned businesses when awarding contracts, and to reject bids from businesses that do not make good faith efforts to include minority-owned businesses among their subcontractors.

The interpretation and implementation of affirmative action have been contested since their origins in the

1960s. A central issue of contention was the definition of discriminatory employment practices. As the interpretation of affirmative action evolved, employment practices that were not intentionally discriminatory but that nevertheless had a "disparate impact" on affected groups were considered a violation of affirmative action regulations.

Another central issue of contention is whether members of affected groups may receive preferential treatment and, if so, the means by which they are to be preferred. This issue is sometimes referred to as the debate over quotas. Though affirmative action programs came under heavy attack during the Reagan and Bush administrations, the principles of affirmative action were reaffirmed by the Civil Rights Act of 1991. In 1997, however, California's Proposition 209 banned affirmative action in that state. In 2003 a group of affirmative action opponents began a campaign to challenge its use in Michigan. Ward Connerly, a California businessman and national leader in the campaign to end affirmative action, has pushed for the Michigan Civil Rights Initiative, which would bar the use of race and gender in government hiring, contracting, and university admissions. As of early 2006, and barring legal appeals to the contrary, the Michigan Civil Rights Initiative will be on the November 2006 Michigan ballot. The legal battles over affirmative action and how it may and may not be used continue. On a state-by-state basis, challenges to affirmative action programs are being made.

HISTORY OF AFFIRMATIVE ACTION

Affirmative action has its roots in the civil rights movement. In March of 1961, President John F. Kennedy signed Executive Order 10925, which established the President's Commission on Equal Employment Opportunity. The order stated that contractors doing business with the government "will take affirmative action to ensure that applicants are employed, and employees are treated during their employment, without regard to their race, creed, color, or national origin." The order did not advocate preferential treatment of affected groups but rather sought to eliminate discrimination in the traditional sense.

The legal status of affirmative action was solidified by the Civil Rights Act of 1964. This landmark legislation prohibited discrimination in voting, public education and accommodations, and employment in firms with more than fifteen employees. Title VII of the Civil Rights Act offered a similar understanding of affirmative action as Executive Order 10925, stating that the act was not designed "to grant preferential treatment to any group because of race, color, religion, sex, or national origin." The act's sponsors, Senators Joseph Clark and Clifford Case, emphasized this non-preferential

interpretation of affirmative action when they wrote: "There is no requirement in Title VII that an employer maintain a racial balance in his workforce. On the contrary, any deliberate attempt to maintain a racial balance, whatever such a balance may be, would involve a violation of Title VII, because maintaining such a balance would require an employer to hire or refuse to hire on the basis of race."

The Civil Rights Act did not provide criminal penalties for employers that discriminated, nor did the civil remedies established by the act include compensation for pain and suffering or punitive damages. Rather, the act sought to establish a conciliation process by which victims would be restored to the situation they would have had in the absence of discrimination. To carry out the conciliation process, the act created a new federal agency as a branch of the U.S. Department of Labor, the Equal Employment Opportunity Commission (EEOC). The EEOC acts as a facilitator between plaintiffs and private employers and also pressures violating employers to provide compensation, whether in the form of back pay or restitution. The EEOC also provides legal support for plaintiffs should the plaintiffs pursue their grievances in court.

Two important issues were contested in the wake of the Civil Rights Act of 1964: whether unintentional or structural discrimination constituted violation of the principle of equal opportunity; and the extent to which preferential treatment should be given to affected groups. These issues came to the forefront during the Johnson administration. In a 1965 commencement speech, President Johnson argued that equality of opportunity required more than simply ending discrimination. Rather, he argued for a more active interpretation of affirmative action that would assure "equality as a result."

In 1966, the U.S. Department of Labor began collecting employment records with breakdowns by race in order to evaluate hiring practices, overturning earlier policies of the Eisenhower and Kennedy administrations. In 1968, the Office of Federal Contract Compliance issued regulations which required, for the first time, that specific targets be set by which the effects of affirmative action programs could be evaluated. The regulations stated that "the contractor's program shall provide in detail for specific steps to guarantee equal employment opportunity keyed to the problems and needs of minority groups, including, when there are deficiencies, the development of specific goals and timetables for the prompt achievement of full and equal employment opportunity." It was in these regulations and analogous measures by the EEOC that the debate over affirmative action quotas had its origins.

Goals and timetables were established by the U.S. Department of Labor using "utilization analysis," which statistically compared the proportion of employed women and minorities in a firm with the proportion of women and minorities in the regional workforce, deriving a measure of what the department called "disparate impact." In the absence of discrimination, it was assumed that these proportions would and should be roughly equal. Since these regulations focused on results and not intent, the structural nature of discrimination was officially recognized. In addition, these regulations provided an official and measurable basis for the preferential treatment of affected groups.

In the landmark *Griggs v. Duke Power Co.* case of 1971, the Supreme Court unanimously ruled against Duke's requirement of high school diplomas or IQ tests for those applying for unskilled jobs. The decision held that "Title VII forbids not only practices adopted with a discriminatory motive, but also practices which, though adopted without discriminatory intent, have a discriminatory effect on minorities and women." The ruling provided a legal foundation for cases of "disparate impact," asserting that employers may not use job requirements that adversely affect women and minorities unless required by what it termed "business necessity." (For example, in the case of serious health or safety threats to co-workers or customers.)

The EEOC was strengthened by the Equal Employment Opportunity Act of 1972, which enabled the Commission to file class action suits. Under the Carter administration, the Uniform Guidelines on Employee Selection established the "four-fifths rule." This rule was significant in that it provided an explicit benchmark to determine disparate impact, which had been left vague in earlier U.S. Department of Labor regulations. The four-fifths rule held that firms contracting with the federal government should not be allowed to hire any race, sex, or ethnic group at a rate below four-fifths that of any other group.

Another significant Supreme Court ruling on affirmative action came in a 1978 case, *Regents of the University of California v. Bakke.* Under the University of California at Davis's admission policies, 16 of 100 places were set aside for minority applicants. Allan Bakke was a white applicant who was denied enrollment to Davis's medical school, even though his test scores were higher than the minority students who were admitted. Casting the deciding vote, Justice Lewis Powell held that Bakke should be admitted to the program since Davis's policies constituted a rigid quota, but that, nonetheless, Davis could continue to favor minorities in its admission practices and that it had a "compelling state interest" to attain a diversified educational environment.

The tide favoring affirmative action began to turn in the 1980s during the Reagan and Bush administrations. In his 1980 campaign, Reagan stated, "We must not allow the noble concept of equal opportunity to be distorted into federal guidelines or quotas which require race, ethnicity, or sex—rather than ability and qualifications—to be the principal factor in hiring or education." Through court appointments, hiring and firing decisions, and budget cuts, the Reagan administration sought to end affirmative action as it had evolved since the Johnson administration. Between 1981 and 1983, the budget of the EEOC was cut by 10 percent and the staff by 12 percent. The Office of Federal Contract Compliance was hit harder yet, with budget cuts of 24 percent and staff cuts of 34 percent during these same years.

Two important Supreme Court rulings in the late-1980s also acted to substantially weaken affirmative action. The 1988 case, *Watson v. Fort Worth Bank and Trust* overturned the landmark 1971 case, *Griggs v. Duke Power Co.,* shifting the burden of proof in employment discrimination cases from employers to plaintiffs. In the 1989 case *Wards Cove Packing Company v. Antonio,* the Court ruled that a plaintiff could not simply show disparate impact to prove discrimination, but must demonstrate that a specific employment practice created the existing disparity.

AFFIRMATIVE ACTION IN THE 1990S AND 2000S

In an effort to fight the dramatic rollback of affirmative action, Congress passed the Civil Rights Act of 1991. The Act returned the burden of proof to employers in disparate impact cases, requiring employers to prove that employment practices that resulted in disparate impact were "job related" and "consistent with business necessity." The act thus overturned the Supreme Court's rulings in *Watson v. Fort Worth Bank and Trust* and *Wards Cove Packing Company v. Antonio.* In addition, the Civil Rights Act of 1991 addressed issues of unlawful harassment and intentional discrimination, allowing minority and female victims of intentional discrimination to be awarded up to $300,000 in compensatory damages in addition to back pay and restitution.

In 1994, the Federal Communications Commission (FCC) initiated one of the largest affirmative action programs ever. The FCC voted unanimously to earmark 1,000 of 2,000 new radio licenses for small businesses owned by women and minorities. These licenses are for businesses serving the rapidly growing number of users of pocket-sized telephones, fax machines, pagers, and hand-held computers. Small companies owned by women or minorities could receive up to a 60 percent discount on the cost of these licenses, which federal officials estimated have a total market value of $10 billion. One of the concerns expressed about the FCC ruling is that it would enable the rise of companies that were only nominally headed by women or minorities. This could occur as a result of the acquisition provisions of the ruling, which allow up to 75 percent of the equity and 49.9 percent of the voting stock of a small firm to be acquired by a larger firm, and yet the small firm still qualifies for licensing discounts.

Despite such efforts, the mid-1990s saw affirmative action programs continue to be rolled back by the Republican-controlled U.S. Congress, as well as by state legislatures and court decisions. Critics charged that affirmative action was a form of "reverse discrimination," meaning that by favoring minorities and women it discriminated against white males. In addition, they argued that affirmative action sometimes prevented companies from hiring the best available worker, and in so doing caused resentment toward minority workers on the job.

In 1996, California voters passed Proposition 209, which banned preferential treatment on the basis of gender or race in public employment, education, and contracting in the state. In effect, the measure eliminated affirmative action programs in California, except as necessary to comply with federal law. Although civil rights groups quickly blocked the measure with a court injunction, it took effect in August 1997 when the injunction was overturned on appeal. It was widely believed that if the U.S. Supreme Court upheld Proposition 209, many states would follow California's lead and make dramatic changes to their affirmative action programs.

Two important cases were decided by the U.S. Supreme Court in 2003—*Gratz v. Bollinger* and *Grutter v. Bollinger*. In the latter case, the Court upheld the right of the University of Michigan Law School to consider race and ethnicity in admissions. The Court ruled that although affirmative action was no longer justified as a way to redress past oppression and injustice, it promoted a "compelling state interest" in diversity at all levels of society. In the former case, the Court invalidated a particular admissions policy used by the University of Michigan's College of Literature, Science, and the Arts. In this case the race-conscious admissions policy was deemed to be rigid and to fail to provide for individual consideration of applicants. This decision is seen as a rejection of the use of quotas in admission policies at public institutions of higher education.

Although recent court cases have addressed state use of affirmative action policies, and not their use in the private sector, they demonstrate the direction in which this wide and ongoing social debate is tending. Lisa Chang, in an article she wrote for *Employee Relations Law Journal* discusses how corporate America can learn

from recent U.S. Supreme Court rulings on the subject of affirmative action. "American companies recognize the need for and benefits from tapping into [the strengths of] that diversity, and the Supreme Court has cast an approving eye on those efforts, at least for the moment."

SEE ALSO *Racial Discrimination; Employee Hiring*

BIBLIOGRAPHY
Bell, Dawson. "Court Orders Affirmative Action Put on 2006 Ballot." *Detroit Free Press.* 21 December 2005.

Chang, Lisa E. "Grutter v. Bollinger, et al.: Affirmative Action Lessons for the Private Employer." *Employee Relations Law Journal.* Summer 2004.

Chung, Kim-Sau. "Role Models and Arguments for Affirmative Action." *American Economic Review.* June 2000.

Katznelson, Ira. *When Affirmative Action was White.* W. W. Norton & Company, August 2005.

Nye, David. "Affirmative Action and the Stigma of Incompetence." *Academy of Management Executives.* February 1998.

Rundles, Jeff. "Affirm Affirmative Action." *Colorado Business Magazine.* April 1998.

Sowell, Thomas. *Affirmative Action Around the World.* Yale University Press, 2005.

Hillstrom, Northern Lights
updated by Magee, ECDI

AGE DISCRIMINATION

Age discrimination is the practice of letting a person's age unfairly become a factor when deciding who receives a new job, a promotion, or other job benefit. It most commonly affects older workers who feel they have been discriminated against in favor of younger workers, but there have been cases involving younger workers being displaced by older workers. A 2005 survey of 2,600 human resource professionals and managers, published jointly by the Chartered Institute of Personnel and Development and the Chartered Management Institute, found that 60 percent of the respondents claimed to have experienced some form of age-related discrimination. However, the survey also showed that much progress has been made over the last decade on reducing age-related discrimination. The number of respondents in the survey who reported having been passed over for promotion based on age dropped by 50 percent since the same question was asked in the 1995 survey.

One factor that may be involved in the changing perception of age-related discrimination is the changing demographic picture of the U.S. workforce. "With 76 million baby boomers approaching retirement age, retaining older workers is not so much a choice as a necessity," explains Alicia Barker, vice president of human resources for the firm Hudson North America. She discusses, in an article entitled "Age Discrimination Visible, But U.S. Businesses Urge Older Workers to Stay on the Job," the need for companies to establish policies that encourage older workers to stay on the job. The need for such policies is not only in order to avoid costly discrimination lawsuits but also by way of preparing for the coming shift in the labor force that will occur as baby boomers retire.

THE ADEA

Age discrimination has officially been a major employment issue since 1967, when the U.S. government passed the Age Discrimination in Employment Act (ADEA). The act's stated purpose is "to promote employment of older persons based on their ability rather than age; to prohibit arbitrary age discrimination in employment; to help employers and workers find ways of meeting problems arising from the impact of age on employment." Specifically, the act prevents employees over the age of 40 from being unfairly fired, demoted, or offered reduced pay or benefits, and it makes it illegal to discriminate against a person on the basis of age in regard to any employment benefits. Older and younger workers must receive access to equal benefits, which generally include: the same payment options; the same type of benefits, such as health care and pension; and the same amount of benefits. The ADEA applies to companies with more than 20 employees that are "engaged in industry affecting commerce." Only true employees are covered; independent contractors are not.

There are exceptions to these rules, but they are few in number and closely monitored. For example, companies are allowed to offer early retirement incentives to older workers without penalty. But the early retirement benefits can only be offered if participation in the plan is voluntary and all other parts of the plan are nondiscriminatory. A company cannot force its workers to accept an early retirement offer, nor can it offer an early retirement plan that reduces benefits as a worker's age increases.

There are also some exemptions regarding the employees who are covered. Jobs that involve public safety, such as police and firefighters, are allowed to have age restriction clauses. Top-level executives who meet certain criteria are excluded from the ADEA. In addition, a company may still utilize an official seniority system, which has long been an accepted practice in the American workplace. The ADEA has strict rules about how a seniority system is to be administered, however, and requires that such systems include merit factors as

well as years of employment as determining factors. Finally, if faced with an age discrimination suit, employers may argue that the job in question had a "bona fide occupation qualification (BFOQ)" that required a younger worker. If challenged in court, the company must prove that the BFOQ was legitimate and not just a ruse to skirt the law. Generally, this means proving that *all* people above the age limit for the position can be shown to be inappropriate for the job. This is extremely difficult to prove, so most companies do not try to challenge the ADEA in this manner.

Employers must prominently display notices about the ADEA and the protection it offers older workers. They must also maintain detailed records as required by the Equal Employment Opportunity Commission (EEOC), which can take action against an employer if it feels discrimination has occurred. Individuals may also file civil suits on their own. The plaintiff may sue to recover back pay, front pay, and liquidated damages from the employer. If an employee proves that the age discrimination was "willful," then back pay damages are doubled. State laws also permit punitive damages to be assessed, which can add millions of dollars to a judgement. To prove his or her case, the plaintiff can present direct evidence of discrimination (such as when the person was plainly told they were being fired because they are too old for the job), prove that a pattern of discrimination exists through the use of statistical analysis, or provide circumstantial evidence that discrimination occurred.

Since it was first written, the ADEA has been updated a number of times. The Older Workers Benefit Protection Act was passed in October 1990. Among its provisions were clear requirements that had to be met if a company wished to settle an ADEA lawsuit brought by an employee. The employee must sign a waiver releasing his or her claim. The waiver must:

- Be "knowing and voluntary," meaning that it must be in writing

- Refer to the specific portions of the ADEA that were applicable to this case

- Provide the employee with some form of compensation, or "consideration," over and above what he or she would have normally received if they had not signed the waiver

- Recommend, in writing, that the employee has the right to consult an attorney

- Indicate that the employee has 21 days to sign the waiver

- Be revocable for seven days after being signed by the employee

- Make certain information available to the employee if the case involves employment termination

While not a direct update of the ADEA, a 1993 court case has proven to be extremely important in the field of age discrimination. In *Hazen Paper Co. v. Biggins,* the U.S. Supreme Court ruled that, even though a decision by the paper company adversely affected older workers more than younger workers, the decision did not constitute age discrimination. In the case in question, the company claimed that money was the basis for its decision, not the age of the employees affected, and the court accepted its defense. In cases since that time, the "cost, not age" defense has been widely accepted by the courts.

WHO IS PROTECTED

Recent court rulings have affirmed the idea that retirees are also protected from age discrimination. A recent Supreme Court case called *Robinson v. Shell Oil Co.* that was primarily about race issues determined that "employee benefits" encompass benefits provided to a company's current employees and to its retirees. As a result, there have been more court cases involving retirees and age discrimination under the ADEA's equal cost or equal benefit provisions. In the case *Erie County Retirees Association v. County of Erie,* the U.S. Third Circuit court ruled that, while companies could continue the common practice of reducing company-provided medical benefits once a retiree qualified for Medicare medical benefits, the companies had to follow the equal cost, equal benefit standards and could not reduce the benefits more than those standards allowed. Employers are also barred by the ADEA from retaliating against employees who have participated in ADEA litigation against the company in any way, be it filing a claim themselves or testifying at someone else's trial.

One of the tools an employee can use to prove age discrimination is through comments made at the workplace. These comments, under certain circumstances, can come from the employee's supervisor, other management personnel, co-workers, or even the company's chief executive officer. Comments that are directly related to the job and the employee in question and that show bias are always admissible in court, while other comments face different qualifying standards. Comments from the CEO are almost always allowed because they are indicative of the company's official policy. Remarks made by senior managers and other employees, even if they are a year older or more, can be admissible if they indicate that a pattern of bias is present in the corporate culture.

THE CURRENT STATE OF AGE DISCRIMINATION LAW

In 2000, the U.S. Supreme Court made two important rulings that extended the scope of the ADEA. In *Reeves v. Sanderson Plumbing Products, Inc.,* the plumbing company fired an employee who had been with the firm for 40 years, citing one reason for the firing that turned out to be not true. The employee sued, saying that the false reason offered was really just a pretext for the real reason—that the company wanted a younger worker. A jury agreed with the employee, but an appeals court overruled the jury, stating that the employee had to offer additional proof that he was discriminated against—just proving that the company lied about why they fired him was not enough to prove age discrimination. The U.S. Supreme Court disagreed, reinstating the original verdict that the employee was discriminated against. The court ruled that all the employee had to do to prove discrimination was prove that the company's original reason for firing him was false. He did not have to provide "pretext plus," as the rule requiring additional evidence of discrimination was called.

An even more significant case was *Kimel v. Florida Board of Regents,* in which the court sided with the employers. In the Kimel case, the court ruled by a 5-4 vote that under the 11th Amendment to the Constitution, state governments were shielded from age discrimination suits. In other words, no state employee could sue his employer for age discrimination. This does not totally wipe out an older employee's right to seek recourse, but it does make it tougher for employees. Every state has its own laws making age discrimination illegal, and employees may still take action under those state laws. But each state law is different and, in general, not as tough as federal laws.

In March 2005, the U.S. Supreme Court's decision in the case *Smith v. City of Jackson, Mississippi,* answered an important question: Must a plaintiff prove discriminatory intent or is proof of disparate impact enough? The ruling in this case, although in favor of the defendant (the employer), was a victory for civil rights plaintiffs. The ruling laid out a rationale by which disparate impact may be used in cases brought under the ADEA, supporting the use of disparate impact as an alternative to employer intent. The requirement that a plaintiff prove that there was discriminatory intent on the part of an employer, when bringing a discrimination case under the ADEA, has long been an obstacle for plaintiffs. The decision in *Smith v. City of Jackson, Mississippi* reduces the obstacle and clears the way for claims that rest on proof that there was a disparate impact on older employees regardless of the employer's intentions. The practical reality is that it is much easier for a plaintiff to prove disparate impact than discriminatory intent.

The ruling in Smith v. City of Jackson, Mississippi highlights the need for employers to establish strong anti-discrimination policies and to have demonstrated business reasons for employment decisions that may adversely affect older workers.

BIBLIOGRAPHY

"Age Discrimination: Past, Present, Prologue." *Trial.* December 2000.

"Age Discrimination Visible, but U.S. Businesses Urge Older Workers to Stay on the Job." PR Newswire, 16 November 2005.

"Aging Angst." *Association Management.* November 2000.

Chemerinsky, Erwin. "Age Discrimination Claims Get Boost from the Court." *Trial.* July 2005.

Spero, Donal J. "An Overview of the Age Discrimination in Employment Act." Florida Mediation Group, 27 September 2000. Available from http://www.floridamediationgroup.com/articles/ADEA.html.

"Suspect Age Bias? Try to Prove It." *Fortune.* 1 February 1999.

Tackling Age Discrimination in the Workplace. Chartered Management Institute, October 2005.

Hillstrom, Northern Lights
updated by Magee, ECDI

AGE DISCRIMINATION IN EMPLOYMENT ACT

The Age Discrimination in Employment Act (ADEA) prohibits any employer from refusing to hire, discharge, or otherwise discriminate against any individual because of age. The act covers compensation, terms, conditions and other privileges of employment including health care benefits. This act specifically prohibits age-based discrimination against employees who are at least 40 years of age. The purpose of the act is to promote the employment of older persons and to prohibit any arbitrary age discrimination in employment.

The Age Discrimination in Employment Act became law in 1967 but its roots can be traced back to 1964, when the U.S. government enacted Title VII of the 1964 Civil Rights Act. This act radically changed working life in the United States. The core of Title VII was to prohibit discrimination in employment based on race, color, sex, national origin, or religion. This statute provided a way for women and minorities, in particular, to challenge barriers that limited equal opportunities in organizations. States adopted similar legislation as well. One variable noticeably missing from Title VII was age discrimination.

Three years later, the U.S. Senate and the House of Representatives enacted the 1967 Age Discrimination in Employment Act (ADEA).

SCOPE OF COVERAGE

The ADEA covers individuals, partnerships, labor organizations and employment agencies, and corporations that: 1) engage in an industry affecting interstate commerce and 2) employ at least 20 individuals. The act also controls state and local governments. Referrals by an employment agency to a covered employer are within the ADEA's scope regardless of the agency's size. In addition, the ADEA covers labor union practices affecting union members; usually, unions with at least 25 members are covered. The ADEA protects against age discrimination in many employment contexts, including hiring, firing, pay scales, job assignments, and fringe benefits.

Under the act, employers are forbidden to refuse to hire, to discharge, or to discriminate against anyone with respect to the terms, conditions, or privileges of employment because of a person's age. The act also forbids employers from limiting, segregating, or classifying an individual in a way that adversely affects his or her employment because of age. The act states that all job requirements must be truly job-related and forbids employers to reduce the wage rate of an employee to comply with the act. It forbids seniority systems or benefits plans that call for involuntary requirements due to age and also makes it illegal for employees to indicate any issue related to age in advertisements for job opportunities.

The ADEA was enacted to promote the employment of older persons based on ability rather than age and to help employers and employees find ways to work around problems that arise from the impact of age on employment. As a result, the act authorizes the Secretary of Labor to perform studies and provide information to labor unions, management, and the public about the abilities and needs of older workers and their employment potential and varied contributions to the economy.

PROCEDURAL REQUIREMENTS AND DEFENSES UNDER ADEA

The procedural requirements for an ADEA suit are complicated. Before an individual can sue in his/her own right, a private plaintiff must file charges with the Equal Employment Opportunity Commission (EEOC) or with an appropriate state agency. The EEOC may also sue to enforce the ADEA. A three-year statute of limitations exists for both government and private suits starting from the date of an alleged willful violation. For cases of nonwillful violations, the statute of limitations is two years from the date of the alleged violation.

The plaintiff does not need to prove that age was the *only* factor motivating the employer's decision, but must establish that age was one of the determining factors guiding the employer's discriminatory actions. Once the plaintiff establishes a prima facie case, the burden of evidence shifts to the employer. The employer must provide a legitimate, nondiscriminatory reason for the employee's demotion or discharge. Charges filed and resolved under the ADEA are tracked by the Office of Research, Information, and Planning which gets its data from the EEOC's Charge Data System.

The ADEA allows employers to discharge or otherwise discipline an employee for good cause, and to use reasonable factors other than age in their employment decisions. It also allows employers to observe the terms of a bona fide seniority system, except where such a system is used to require or permit the involuntary retirement of anyone age 40 or over.

In addition, the ADEA provides for a bona fide occupational qualification (BFOQ) defense. In general, an employer seeking to use this defense must show that its age classification is reasonably necessary to the safe and proper performance of the job in question. Specifically, the employer must show either: 1) that it is reasonable to believe that all or most employees of a certain age cannot perform the job safely, or 2) that it is impossible or highly impractical to test employees' abilities to tackle all tasks associated with the job on an individualized basis. For example, an employer that refuses to hire anyone over the age of 60 as a pilot has a potential BFOQ defense if it has a reasonable basis for concluding that 60-and-over pilots pose significant safety risks, or that it is not feasible to test older pilots individually.

CURRENT ADEA ISSUES

Age discrimination cases will be of increasing concern to businesses in the future as the work force in the US and in many developed countries continues to mature. In addition, changes in Social Security laws are pushing up the age at which a person may begin to draw full Social Security benefits and this will cause many more workers to stay on the job until later in life. In *Supervision,* Mary-Katheryn Zachary warns that plaintiffs in age discrimination cases typically receive more empathy than other discrimination plaintiffs and judges hearing such cases are likely to be in the protected class themselves. Damages can be substantial and may take the form of back pay, front pay, overtime pay, emotional distress pay, liquidated damages, and multipliers for intentional violations of the law. Remedies can also include equitable relief,

hiring, reinstatement, and promotion. Employers are cautioned to consider ADEA laws when restructuring the workplace.

Another important issue facing employers in this realm is the legal interpretation of the ADEA as it relates to retirees. Federal court rulings in mid-2000 indicated that under the Age Discrimination in Employment Act, employers had to provide the same health care benefits to Medicare-eligible retirees that they do to younger retirees who do not yet qualify for Medicare. Critics of this interpretation within the business world claim that the practical result of such a ruling, if not addressed by Congress, will be a dramatic drop in the percentage of businesses offering comprehensive health care benefits to retired workers.

Amidst a flood of protests from employers and labor organizations, the EEOC reviewed the question of differential health care benefits for retirees of different ages, those under and those over the age of Medicare-eligibility. In 2003 the EEOC proposed a rule to exempt retiree health care plans from the ADEA and adopted the new rule in 2004. The rule was almost immediately challenged in a law suit, brought by the American Association of Retired Persons (AARP), late in 2004. A initial ruling in the case found in favor of the AARP. However, the ruling was reviewed in light of a mid-2005 U.S. Supreme Court ruling on another case. According to an article in *Business Insurance* dated October 3, 2005, Judge Anita Brody of the U.S. District Court for the Eastern District of Pennsylvania "stated last week the EEOC has the authority to implement a rule that would exempt from the Age Discrimination in Employment Act changes to health plans that affect retired workers when they become eligible for Medicare."

This ruling, if it withstands appeal, leaves employers free to provide a two-tiered system of retiree health care coverage, with younger retirees receiving more generous benefits than their older and Medicare-eligible counterparts, without running afoul of the ADEA.

As health care costs rise and the workforce ages with the steady march of the baby boom generation, issues of age discrimination on both ends of the age spectrum are likely to remain an issue of importance for all employers.

BIBLIOGRAPHY
"EEOC Rule on Lower Benefits for Retirees Violates the ADEA." *HR Focus.* May 2005.

Geisel, Jerry. "Court Blocks EEOC Rule Exempting Retiree Health Plans from ADEA." *Business Insurance.* 4 April 2005.

Geisel, Jerry. "EEOC Can Issue Rule on Retiree Benefits." *Business Insurance.* 3 October 2005.

Lindemann, Barbara. *American Discrimination in Employment Law.* January 2003.

Zachary, Mary-Kathryn. "Age Discrimination-Part II: The Private Employee." *Supervision.* September 2000.

Zachary, Mary-Kathryn. "Age Discrimination-Part I: The State Employee." *Supervision.* July 2000.

Zall, Milton. "Age Discrimination-What Is It Besides Illegal?" *Fleet Equipment.* April 2000.

Hillstrom, Northern Lights
updated by Magee, ECDI

AIDS IN THE WORKPLACE

Acquired immune deficiency syndrome (AIDS) is a disease that impairs the human immune system and renders it susceptible to infections that would be repelled by a functioning immune system. The terminal stage of the human immuno-deficiency virus (HIV), AIDS is transmitted by contamination of the bloodstream with HIV-infected body fluids, specifically blood, semen, breast milk, and vaginal fluid. The virus is principally spread through vaginal or anal intercourse, by the transfusion of virus-contaminated blood, by the sharing of HIV-infected intravenous needles, or by mothers to fetuses during pregnancy. U.S. Centers for Disease Control (CDC) literature emphasizes that "no additional routes of transmission have been recorded, despite a national sentinel system designed to detect just such an occurrence." AIDS is not spread by casual physical contact (biting insects, or airborne means) and transmission through body fluids such as saliva and tears has never occurred. Once a person becomes infected with HIV, the incubation period averages eight years before AIDS symptoms appear.

Given a supportive work environment and early detection, people with HIV and AIDS can continue to be productive members of the workforce. Studies have shown that for half of the people who contract HIV, it takes more than a decade to develop AIDS. With medical treatment, many of them can manage the infection as a chronic, long-term condition, similar to many other medical disorders. The numbers of people with HIV and their extended life expectancy means there will be more employees on the job with HIV in the future. This, in turn, means that most, if not all, businesses will eventually have to deal directly with HIV-infected and AIDS-afflicted employees.

GOVERNMENT AGENCIES AND POLICIES RELATING TO AIDS

The Business Responds to AIDS (BRTA) program was formed in 1992 as a public-private partnership among the CDC, the public health sector, other organizations and agencies, and business and labor to provide workplace education and community services in order to prevent the spread of HIV. The BRTA program assists businesses of all sizes in the creation and implementation of workplace-based HIV and AIDS policies. In addition to education, service, and prevention of the spread of HIV, the program's goals are to prevent discrimination and foster community service and volunteerism both in the workplace and in the community. In order to achieve these goals, the BRTA has developed materials and technical assistance to help businesses form comprehensive HIV and AIDS programs, including training for management and labor leaders and education for employees and their families.

Corporate HIV and AIDS policies and practices should comply with federal, state, and local legislation and Occupational Safety and Health Administration (OSHA) guidelines. Federal laws regarding AIDS in the workplace include: the Occupational Safety and Health Act of 1970; the Vocational Rehabilitation Act of 1973 (VRA); the Employee Retirement Income Security Act of 1974 (ERISA); the U.S. Consolidated Omnibus Budget Reconciliation Act of 1986 (COBRA); and the Americans with Disabilities Act (ADA) of 1990.

The ADA, which applies to any company with 15 or more employees, forbids discrimination against any employee affected by a disability or chronic disease, including AIDS. It defends people who are infected, people perceived to be at high risk, and relatives and caregivers of people with AIDS in matters ranging from hiring and promotion to resignation and retirement. Basically, employers cannot treat employees who are affected by AIDS any differently than other employees, and they are required to provide appropriate accommodations whenever possible. The ADA does make a slight exception for restaurants, however, in that they are permitted to reassign employees with HIV or AIDS to positions in which they are not required to handle food.

In 1998 the U.S. Supreme Court also stipulated that asymptomatic HIV patients (those without visible signs of illness) should be included under the Americans with Disabilities Act. The Court ruled in a 5-4 decision (in *Bragdon v. Abbott*) that asymptomatic patients should still be covered by the ADA because HIV infection interferes with "major life activities"—in this case, the major life activity of reproduction.

PROACTIVE AIDS POLICIES FOR BUSINESSES

Despite the growing impact of AIDS and AIDS-related illnesses on American businesses, very few companies are aware of their legal obligations to affected employees or have enacted policies to ensure compliance with the law.

The Centers for Disease Control (CDC) has a program called Business Responds to AIDS, that provides detailed recommendations for companies on how they can establish and implement a simple AIDS policy.

An AIDS policy is used to clarify a company's consistent response to issues of HIV/AIDS in the workplace. The CDC strongly recommends having an employee HIV education program available to all employees. Such an educational program can reduce fear, prevent discriminatory behavior which may invite lawsuits, and prevent loss of productivity if trouble erupts when an employee discloses his or her HIV or AIDS status.

In its relatively short history, AIDS has become the most litigated health concern in American legal history. The majority of these lawsuits are employment related. Having a well designed AIDS policy can help clarify a company's position for all parties and can help to avoid the situations that arise and often lead to litigation. A good policy will assist with management questions, HIV-infected employees, and all of his or her co-workers. The following are five actions which should be covered and documented in a solid AIDS policy.

- **Show compliance with the law.** State that your company adheres to the Americans with Disabilities Act and its protections for people with HIV, including acceptable performance standards, non-discrimination and reasonable accommodation.

- **Provide educational materials on HIV/AIDS.** Policies should contain a component stating that HIV/AIDS is not transmitted through casual contact, and that employees with HIV/AIDS are not a health risk to their co-workers. Invite employees to receive more information on HIV through human resources, or state there will be regular employee education.

- **Protect all employees.** Assure employees that their individual health status is confidential, private and not to be disclosed. Also state that the safety of all employees is of utmost importance.

- **Give clear direction.** State where employees should go with questions about HIV transmission, and from whom supervisors should get direction on dealing with HIV issues in their department.

- **Disseminate policy information.** Be certain all employees at all levels read and understand your AIDS policy.

The prevalence of HIV and AIDS in the U.S. population was estimated by the CDC in 2002 to be 1 in every 268 people. The prevalence is highest in the age group 25 to 44 years of age and AIDS has surpassed cancer and accidents as the leading cause of death for persons in this age group. It is clear that most companies will at some time deal with an employee who is HIV-positive or has full-blown AIDS. Having a clear and well-publicized AIDS policy in place in companies of any size is desirable in avoiding misunderstandings and legal liability that may arise in the absence of an established policy.

BIBLIOGRAPHY

"AIDS Presents New Challenges for Employers." *Employee Benefit Plan Review.* March 1998.

Alcamo, I. Edward. *AIDS in the Modern World.* Blackwell Publishing, 2002.

American College of Occupational and Environmental Medicine. *HIV and AIDS in the Workplace.* 2002.

Barnett, Tony, and Alan Whiteside. *AIDS in the Twenty-First Century.* Palgrave, 2002.

Zachary, Mary-Kathryn. "Supreme Court Resolves Questions, Raises Others, with HIV Ruling." *Supervision.* November 1998.

Hillstrom, Northern Lights
updated by Magee, ECDI

ALIEN EMPLOYEES

An alien employee is any employee working in the United States who is not a citizen of the United States. Those employees who enter the country and secure employment legally do so by first obtaining employment visas. Employment visas are classified into two categories: immigrant visas and nonimmigrant visas. Immigrant visas are used by aliens who are approved for permanent residency in the U.S., while nonimmigrant visas provide for temporary stays in the country of up to seven years.

The subject of alien employees is often complicated by the issue of illegal aliens. Foreigners may enter the U.S. legally, on, for example, a tourist visa, and then seek employment illegally. Or, foreigners may enter the country illegally. Employers must be very careful when hiring to establish that a prospective foreign employee is eligible to work in the U.S.

Immigration law has often been characterized as the second most complicated field of U.S. law, second only to tax law. As a result, it is advisable for any business wishing to employ foreign nationals or alien employees to either develop an in-house expertise in immigration law or consult with an expert in the field. For many businesses, alien employees are of great value, bringing unique talents and knowledge to the business and thereby justifying the additional work involved in hiring them.

IMMIGRANT AND NONIMMIGRANT VISAS

Immigrant visas are given to aliens who are granted permanent residency in the United States. These individuals tend to be highly educated persons with experience and skills that are in high demand by companies in the United States. Immigrant visas that are most frequently granted are in the following employment areas: business executives and managers; notable professors, researchers, and other academics; advanced degree professionals; professionals with bachelor's degrees; investors in new business ventures; and aliens "of exceptional beauty." Skilled and unskilled workers are also sometimes granted immigrant visas.

Nonimmigrant visas are issued to foreigners whose stay in the U.S. will be temporary, though may extend to a length of seven years. There are 20 nonimmigrant visa classifications, of which only 6 normally allow for work while in the U.S. These nonimmigrant visas are frequently bestowed upon aliens working in the following areas: students engaged in educational pursuits (work authorization is available for practical training after they complete their course of study); registered nurses; temporary agricultural workers; workers in the service sector; trainees; intra-company transfers; artists and entertainers; athletes; and aliens of "distinguished merit" or "extraordinary ability," especially in such fields as the sciences, high technology, education, the arts, business, or athletics.

KEY LEGAL CONSIDERATIONS PERTAINING TO ALIEN EMPLOYEES

The regulatory picture for employing alien workers is an ever-changing one in the United States. The 1990s was a period of economic growth and saw U.S. corporations turn strongly to alien employees to fill positions in specialized areas, high technology in particular. With the slowing of the economy in the first decade of the new century, and the terrorist attacks in the U.S. in the middle of 2001, the general mood regarding alien workers has changed.

The U.S. government passed major laws during the last 15 years related to immigration. Among them were the Immigration Act of 1990, the Illegal Immigration Reform and Immigrant Responsibility Act of 1996, the American Competitiveness and Workforce Improvement Act of 1998 (ACWIA) and the Enhanced Border Security and Visa Entry Reform Act of 2002. Each of these has had a direct impact on the hiring and work environment for businesses and immigrants alike. These laws are interpreted and enforced by U.S. agencies such as the Department of Labor (DOL) and the Immigration and Naturalization Service (INS).

In 2004 President George W. Bush proposed legislation that would both strengthen efforts along the U.S. border to halt the entry of illegal aliens and establish a temporary or guest worker program. Under the proposed plan, undocumented immigrants would be allowed to get a three-year work visa, extendable for an additional three years. This proposed legislation has met with little support and as of the end of 2005 has failed to gain traction.

Two additional proposed bills await action by Congress in 2006. They are the Secure America and Orderly Immigration Act and the Comprehensive Enforcement and Immigration Reform Act of 2005. Each of these proposed bills would alter existing visa requirements, annual quotas, and the penalties imposed on employers who hire illegal workers.

HIRING ALIEN EMPLOYEES

The restrictions on alien hiring place a lot of requirements on employers. Companies should make sure that they are familiar with the basics of utilizing alien employees in their workplaces. There are a few steps that all small business owners should take when hiring new employees to minimize the likelihood of employing an unauthorized worker and possibly incurring legal penalties.

First, employers should ask all job applicants if they are authorized to work in the United States. It is discriminatory to ask whether applicants for employment are U.S. citizens, however, all employment applications can—and should—ask prospective employees whether they are authorized to work in the United States and if so, establish the basis of this authorization—citizenship or an employment visa. In an article entitled "The Visa Maze," Bill Reilly, unit chief for the office of investigations at the U.S. Immigration and Customs Enforcement (ICE), talks about a program that small businesses can join that will help them comply with the law. Reilly suggests that entrepreneurs join Basic Pilot, an employment-verification system run by ICE that determines whether or not a non-citizen is eligible to work in the U.S. by searching databases at the Social Security Administration and the Homeland Security Department.

For prospective employees who do have visas, it is sometimes necessary for employers to file appropriate documentation with the INS before the person in question can begin work. Requirements vary considerably from situation to situation, so it is often a good idea for small businesses to secure the services of an attorney with experience in immigration law for guidance. While companies are obviously under no obligation to hire a person who has the appropriate authorization to work in the United States, they also may not discriminate against an alien authorized to work in America on the basis of his or her citizenship. Given this situation, a company should determine its policy of sponsoring work visas and apply it equally to all employees. Such a policy need only oblige a company to sign the visa forms for alien employees and complying with wage and hiring requirements.

It is also important for employers to be aware of prevailing wage structures for positions that may be filled by alien workers. By law, employers are required to compensate immigrant workers at roughly the same levels that non-aliens in the same positions and in the same geographic region earn. These laws were passed so that alien employees would be fairly compensated for their work. Businesses that neglect to meet minimum standards of compensation may be assessed fines and penalties by the DOL. Small business owners seeking "prevailing wage" information can contact their state's Bureau of Employment Services or secure a wage survey compiled by an authoritative source, such as an employment agency.

Small business owners also have to make certain that they file all the appropriate documentation before hiring an alien employee. An alien's visa application can be approved by the INS only after his or her would-be employer has filed the appropriate forms with the DOL. A Labor Certification Application is the most common one for employment-based visa classifications, while Labor Condition Applications are used for professional applicants, such as attorneys and doctors. Presuming that the application is approved, the employer may then proceed with the visa application. Visa applications can be filed with the nearest regional INS office. "It's mandatory that you include documentation, such as a diploma, verifying that the employee has the necessary educational requirements and is otherwise qualified for the position," wrote Reid. (The INS also will accept work experience in lieu of a degree in a particular field as long as the candidate proves that he or she has achieved a certain level of general education or technical expertise.) "The INS will review the visa application and the supporting documents for accuracy. Depending on the type of visa application, the INS review process can take anywhere from one to six months." Finally, small business owners should be aware that Labor Certification and Labor Condition Applications have to be revalidated every two years.

Illegal Immigration Reform and Immigrant Responsibility Act of 1996 This legislation, which included new sanctions for companies found in violation of alien labor regulations, should be consulted before making any hiring decisions regarding alien workers. Basically, the law states that American employers have to make sure that all of their employees are eligible to work in the United States when they begin their work. Immigration experts recommend that businesses conduct an INS Form I-9 audit to make sure that they are in full compliance with all pertinent immigration laws. Such audits not only help employers meet all legal obligations, but also may be regarded as evidence that they made good-faith attempts to follow employer verification requirements.

ALIEN EMPLOYEES AND AMERICAN CULTURE

Business owners who hire alien employees also may face challenges outside of the legal realm. Managing a culturally diverse work force can be a difficult process at times, although successful integration of people from different cultural and ethnic backgrounds can be a tremendously rewarding experience for a business on a wide range of levels, both socially and economically.

One key to creating a strong multicultural environment in the workplace is anticipating the difficulties that alien employees sometimes have with various aspects of American culture. Depictions of American culture are commonplace around the world, but as any American viewer can tell you, these depictions are often exaggerated or slanted, and they may provide aliens with fundamentally erroneous impressions of life in the United States. And, of course, immersion into any society, let alone one as complex and fast-moving as America's, can be a disorienting experience.

There are myriad aspects of life to which alien employees will have to adjust themselves, including a new language in many cases, recognition of the regional dialects, a new culture, different ways of shopping, banking, obtaining medical attention, commuting, to name but a few.

Another difficult adjustment for non-Americans has to do with socializing and a sense of community. If work interactions do not lead to corresponding social interactions, alien employees may view it as rejection. "One barrier to acceptance for international employees is the failure to follow U.S. workplace culture," one business consultant told Carla Joinson for her *HR Magazine* article on the subject. "For instance, in a brainstorming or solution-oriented meeting, it is our way to jump in, talk and solve the problem. However, folks from other cultures may feel this is a waste of time because we haven't thought it all through and are throwing out various solutions that may not work. We then say, 'What's wrong with them? Why don't they speak up?' Then, there's a domino effect: They get invited to meetings less and less." In addition, "inpat" employees may also struggle to adjust to the so-called "benefit gap" that exists between the United States and many other countries in such realms as annual paid vacation, length of lunch hour, and subsidies for commuting costs.

Experts agree that business owners who want to ease the transition for alien employees into the American workplace (and the larger community) can do so by establishing a system of education, mentoring, and training. "Companies that do a good job of accommodating diversity and are willing to locate and use specialized expertise find that the addition of international workers adds to their success," stated Joinson.

SEE ALSO *Cross-Cultural/International Communication*

BIBLIOGRAPHY

Canter, Laurence A., and Martha S. Seigel *U.S. Immigration Made Easy.* Nolo Press, August 2004.

Gurchiek, Kathy, "H-1B Visas Not Only Foreign Worker Option." *HRMagazine.* November 2005.

Joinson, Carla. "The Impact of 'Inpats.'" *HR Magazine.* April 1999.

Powell, Gary N. *Managing a Diverse Work Force.* Second edition, Sage Publishing, Inc. 2004.

Quittner, Jeremy. "The Visa Maze." *BusinessWeek.* 19 September 2005.

Thibodeau, Patrick. "IT Groups Push Congress to Raise H-1B Visa Limits."*Computerworld.*October 2005.

Woodard, Kathy L. "Not All Green Cards Need to Be Green to Hire Employees." *Business First-Columbus.* 9 June 2000.

Hillstrom, Northern Lights
updated by Magee, ECDI

ALTERNATIVE DISPUTE RESOLUTION (ADR)

Alternative dispute resolution (ADR) is a term that refers to several different methods of resolving disputes outside traditional legal and administrative forums. These philosophically similar methodologies, which include various types of arbitration and mediation, have surged in popularity in recent years because companies and courts became extremely frustrated over the expense, time, and emotional toll involved in resolving disputes through the usual legal avenues. "The adversarial system is expensive, disruptive, and protracted. More significantly, by its very nature, it tends to drive the parties further apart, weakening their relationship, often irreparably" pointed out Whayne Hoagland in *Business Insurance.* ADR programs emerged as an alternative, litigation-free method of resolving business disputes.

Analysts also trace the rise of ADR methods to changing attitudes within the American judicial system. *Business Horizons* contributor Stephen L. Hayford

observed that until the 1980s, "attempts by business firms to avoid litigation ... were frustrated by a long-standing hostility on the part of the courts toward any devices that infringed on their jurisdiction." But during the 1980s, Hayford noted that a new body of case law emerged that sanctioned the use of binding arbitration provisions in commercial contracts between companies, business partners, employees and employers, etc. This body of law continued to evolve in the late 1990s. For example, the Alternative Dispute Resolution Act of 1998 extended ADR mechanisms throughout the federal district court system. As Simeon Baum stated in *CPA Journal,* "the act recognizes that ADR, when properly accepted, practiced, and administered, can not only save time and money and reduce court burdens, but also 'provide a variety of benefits, including greater satisfaction of the parties, innovative methods of resolving disputes, and greater efficiency in achieving settlements.'"

Today, legal and corporate acceptance of alternative dispute resolution as a legitimate remedy for addressing business disagreements is reflected in the language of business contracts. ADR contingencies have become a standard element in many contracts between companies and their employees, partners, customers, and suppliers. As *U.S. News & World Report* noted, "virtually every state has experimented with some form of ADR." With the growth of ADR has come a growing number of organizations and associations designed to assist commercial entities in the use of these alternative dispute resolution methods.

Arbitration Associations and Organizations There are several U.S. organizations and agencies that are directly involved in arbitration and arbitration issues. These include the National Academy of Arbitrators (NAA), the American Arbitration Association (AAA), and the Federal Mediation Conciliation Service (FMCS). The NAA was founded in 1947 as a non-profit organization to foster high standards for arbitration and arbitrators and to promote the process. The NAA works to attain these objectives through seminars, annual conferences, and educational programs. The non-profit AAA offers its services for voluntary arbitration as part of its mandate to promote the use of arbitration in all fields. The FMCS, meanwhile, maintains a roster from which arbitrators can be selected and champions procedures and guidelines designed to enhance the arbitration process.

PRIMARY FORMS OF ADR

Arbitration Arbitration is the procedure by which parties agree to submit their disputes to an independent neutral third party, known as an arbitrator, who considers arguments and evidence from both sides, then hands down a final and binding decision. This alternative, which can be used to adjudicate business-to-business, business-to-employee, or business-to-customer disputes, can utilize a permanent arbitrator, an independent arbitrator selected by the two parties to resolve a particular grievance, or an arbitrator selected through the procedures of the AAA or FMCS. A board of arbitrators can also be used in a hearing.

After the arbitrator is selected, both sides are given the opportunity to present their perspectives on the issue or issues in dispute. These presentations include testimony and evidence that are provided in much the same way as a court proceeding, although formal rules of evidence do not apply. Upon completion of the arbitration hearing, the arbitrator reviews the evidence, testimony, and the collective bargaining agreement, considers principles of arbitration, and makes a decision. The arbitrator's decision is generally rendered within 60 days. Hayford noted that "[binding arbitration] minimizes pre-hearing machinations with regard to discovery, motion practice, and the other preliminary skirmishes that extend the time, expense, and consternation of court litigation. In exchange, the parties to a contractual binding arbitration provision agree to accept the risk of being stuck with an unacceptable decision."

Other forms of arbitration include the following:

- Expedited arbitration is a process intended to speed up the arbitration process with an informal hearing. Under this process, decisions are generally rendered within five days. It was first used in 1971 in settling disputes in the steel industry.

- Interest arbitration is the use of an arbitrator or board of arbitrators to render a binding decision in resolving a dispute over new contract terms.

- Final offer selection arbitration is an interest arbitration process in which the arbitrator or board of arbitrators selects either the union or management proposal to the solution. There can be no compromised decisions. This process is also termed either-or arbitration.

- Tripartite arbitration is a process wherein a three-member panel of arbitrators is used to reach a decision. Both labor and management select an arbitrator and the third is selected by the other two arbitrators or the parties to the dispute as a neutral participant.

Mediation In contrast to arbitration, mediation is a process whereby the parties involved utilize an outside party to help them reach a mutually agreeable settlement. Rather than dictate a solution to the dispute between labor and management, the mediator—who maintains scrupulous neutrality throughout—suggests various proposals to help the two parties reach a mutually agreeable solution. In mediation, the various needs of the conflicting sides of an issue are identified, and ideas and concepts are exchanged until a viable solution is proposed by either of the parties or the mediator. Rarely does the mediator exert pressure on either party to accept a solution. Instead, the mediator's role is to encourage clear communication and compromise in order to resolve the dispute. The terms "arbitration" and "mediation" are sometimes used interchangeably, but this mixing of terminology is careless and inaccurate. While the mediator *suggests* possible solutions to the disputing parties, the arbitrator makes a final decision on the labor dispute which is *binding* on the parties.

Mediation can be a tremendously effective tool in resolving disputes without destroying business relationships. It allows parties to work toward a resolution out of the public eye (the courts) without spending large sums on legal expenses. Its precepts also ensure that a company will not become trapped in a settlement that it finds unacceptable (unlike an arbitration decision that goes against the company). But Hayford commented that "mediation only works when the parties employing it are willing to go all out in the attempt to achieve settlement," and he warned that "the mediator must be selected carefully, with an eye toward the critical attributes of neutrality, subject matter and process expertise, and previous track record." Finally, he noted that with mediation, there is a "lack of finality inherent in a voluntary, conciliation-based procedure."

Other forms of mediation often employed in labor disputes include "grievance mediation" and "preventive mediation." Grievance mediation is an attempt to ward off arbitration through a course of fact-finding that is ultimately aimed at promoting dialogue between the two parties. Preventive mediation dates to the Taft-Hartley Act (1947) and is an FMCS program intended to avoid deeper divisions between labor and management over labor issues. Also termed technical assistance, the program encompasses training, education, consultation, and analysis of union-management disputes.

Ombuds An ombudsman is a high-ranking company manager or executive whose reputation throughout the company enables him/her to facilitate internal dispute resolutions between the company and employees. Hayford points to several benefits of ombud-based ADR: "It provides a confidential, typically low-key approach to dispute resolution that keeps conflicts 'in the family.'.... Properly effected, the ombuds mechanism can do much to enhance the perception that the company is concerned and eager to address the problems of its employees by providing them with an accessible, nonthreatening avenue for seeking redress when they believe they have been wronged." The primary drawback of ADR by the ombud process, however, is that many companies—whether large or small—do not have an individual equipped with the reputation, skills, or training to take on such a task.

Neutral Evaluation In neutral evaluations, a neutral individual, with a background in ADR, listens to each party lay out its version of events. After their perspectives have been considered, the neutral evaluator offers his/her opinion on the disagreement. This opinion is not binding in any way, but if the neutral party is respected and trusted by both sides, it can help the parties reassess their negotiating positions with an eye toward finding common ground.

UTILIZING ADR

The popularity of alternative dispute resolution has increased dramatically in recent years. Small- and medium-sized businesses have contributed to this surge in use, drawn by the promise of cost and time savings. But ADR provisions need to be weighed carefully before they are incorporated into any business agreement with partners, employees, vendors, or clients. The questions to ask are: when is an ADR resolution method preferable to litigation; when is it to be avoided; and, if ADR is preferred, what form of ADR should be pursued? Legal assistance is particularly vital for small business owners who wish to fully answer these questions and incorporate ADR provisions into their contracts and agreements.

BIBLIOGRAPHY

Baum, Simeon H. "The ADR Act of 1998 Offers Opportunities for Accountants." *CPA Journal.* March 1999.

Elkouri, Frank. *How Arbitration Works.* BNA Books, January 2003.

Ford, Hunter. "Arbitration Pits Business vs. Consumers." *Birmingham Business Journal.* 1 September 2000.

Hayford, Stephen L. "Alternative Dispute Resolution." *Business Horizons.* January 2000.

Hoagland, Wayne. "Keep Employment Disputes Out of Court." *Business Insurance.* 29 August 2005.

Jacobs-Meadway, Roberta. "Alternatives to Litigating IP Disputes." *New Jersey Law Journal.* 18 July 2005.

Jasper, Margaret C. *The Law of Alternative Dispute Resolution.* Oceana Publications, 2000.

Kleiner, Carolyn. "The Action Out of Court." *U.S. News & World Report.* 29 May 1999.

Phillips, Gerald F. "What Your Client Needs to Know about ADR." *Dispute Resolution Journal.* February 2000.

Rendell, Marjorie O. "ADR Versus Litigation." *Dispute Resolution Journal.* February 2000.

Stein, Harry. *How ADR Works.* BNA Books, January 2002.

Wall, Michael. "Settlements Rise as Way to Avoid Court Wrangling." *Atlanta Business Chronicle.* 9 June 2000.

Woodard, Kathy L. "Arbitration Growing in Popularity for Its Cost Benefits, Efficiency." *Business First-Columbus.* 16 June 2000.

Hillstrom, Northern Lights
updated by Magee, ECDI

AMERICANS WITH DISABILITIES ACT (ADA)

The Americans with Disabilities Act (ADA) is a revolutionary piece of legislation designed to protect the civil rights of people who have physical and mental disabilities, in a manner similar to that in which previous civil rights laws have protected people of various races, religions, and ethnic backgrounds. The ADA mandates changes in the way that both private businesses and the government conduct business to ensure that all Americans have full access to and can fully participate in every aspect of society. The ADA requires the removal of barriers that deny individuals with disabilities equal opportunity and access to jobs, public accommodations, government services, public transportation, and telecommunications. The law applies to small companies as well as to large ones, so small business owners must be aware of its provisions and how they affect their companies' employment practices, facilities, and products. The Equal Employment Opportunity Commission (EEOC) is the federal agency charged with enforcing the various aspects of the ADA.

It is estimated that 50 million Americans, or one out of every five, have a disability. As defined in the ADA, the term "disability" applies to three categories of individuals: 1) people who have a physical or mental impairment that substantially limits one or more major life activities; 2) people who have a record of an impairment which substantially limits major life activities; and 3) people who may be regarded by others as having such an impairment. For an employee or job applicant to be protected by the ADA, an individual must be "disabled" in one or more of the above manners, be "otherwise qualified" for the position, and be able to perform the essential functions of the job, "with or without accommodation."

PROVISIONS OF THE ADA

President George H. Bush signed the ADA into law on July 26, 1990. The legal structure of the ADA is based on the Civil Rights Act of 1964 and the Rehabilitation Act of 1973. The ADA uses concepts of disability, accessibility, and employment which were introduced in the Architectural Barriers Act of 1968 and the Rehabilitation Act of 1973. These two federal laws were the predecessors of the ADA that mandated a level of accessibility in federally funded buildings and programs. The ADA expanded the requirements of accessibility to the new and existing facilities of privately funded companies for the first time.

The ADA consists of five separate parts or titles: Title I relates to employment; Title II concerns public services; Title III pertains to public accommodations and commercial facilities; Title IV refers to telecommunications; and Title V covers miscellaneous other items.

Title I of the ADA prohibits discrimination in employment against qualified individuals with disabilities. For companies with 25 or more employees, the requirements became effective on July 26, 1992. For employers with between 15 and 24 workers, the requirements became effective on July 26, 1994.

Title II of the ADA prohibits discrimination in programs, services, or activities of public entities (state and local governments), including public transportation operated by public entities. The provisions of Title II which do not involve public transportation became effective on January 26, 1992.

Title III, pertaining to public accommodations and commercial facilities, requires that private businesses that are places of "public accommodation"—including restaurants, health clubs, department stores, convenience stores and specialty shops, and hotels and motels—allow individuals with disabilities to participate equally in the goods and services that they offer. This title also requires that all future construction of commercial facilities—including office buildings, factories, and warehouses—and places of public accommodation be constructed so that the building is accessible to individuals with disabilities.

Title III also mandates modifications in policies, practices, and procedures. Commercial businesses and places of public accommodation are required to provide auxiliary aids and services, and to make accessible transportation available when transportation services are offered. In addition, companies are required to remove architectural and communications barriers and to comply with ADA in any ongoing or new construction. The Act stipulates that all fixed-route or on-demand transportation services—such as hotel-to-airport and other shuttle services—be accessible to persons in wheelchairs and other disabled individuals.

Title IV of the ADA requires telephone companies to make relay services available for persons with hearing and speech impairments.

Title V ties the ADA to the Civil Rights Act of 1974 and its amendments. It includes a variety of miscellaneous legal and technical provisions, including one that stipulates that the ADA does not override or limit the remedies, rights, or procedures of any federal, state, or local law which provides greater or equal protection for the rights of individuals with disabilities.

The ADA draws an important distinction between the terms "reasonable accommodations" and "readily achievable." For small businesses and other employers, no modifications to their facilities must be undertaken to fulfill the requirements of the ADA until a qualified individual with a disability has been hired. At that point, "reasonable accommodations" must be made unless they impose a significant difficulty or expense. In contrast, the terminology "readily achievable" refers to business obligations to clients or guests and applies to actions that can be accomplished without much difficulty or expense. "Readily achievable" modifications must be made in anticipation of a disabled guest's or client's needs, before he or she ever arrives on the premises.

Compliance with the various provisions of the Americans with Disabilities Act also lies with both landlord and tenant, so either or both parties may be held legally liable for violations of the ADA. Assignation of ADA responsibilities is generally made via the lease agreement. Small business owners who lease their office space or other place of business, then, should examine these agreements closely.

THE ADA AND THE MENTALLY DISABLED

The fastest-growing area of legal activity relating to the Americans with Disabilities Act concerns mentally disabled employees. Claims that businesses failed to accommodate their employees' psychological problems according to the provisions of the ADA grew rapidly in the late 1990s but stabilized in the early years of the 2000s at around 13 to 14 percent of all ADA claims received by the Equal Employment Opportunity Commission. Under the original language of the ADA, the Act applied a higher standard for legal redress to individuals whose disabilities stemmed from "any mental or psychological disorder." But legislative efforts to eliminate this higher standard have intensified in recent years.

Problems associated with mentally disabled employees may include workplace socialization difficulties, limited stamina, irregular attendance, difficulty dealing with stress or criticism, and limited attention spans. But many experts in both the mental health and business fields insist that the mentally disabled can be valuable additions to the workforce if companies provide appropriate accommodations.

One valuable tool that business owners and managers can utilize in establishing and maintaining a productive work environment for mentally disabled employees is the EEOC Enforcement Guidance, a comprehensive legal guidebook issued in 1997. As *Business Horizons* points out, the Guidance stipulates that "traits or behaviors are not, in themselves, mental impairments. This means that stress does not automatically indicate a mental impairment, although it may be a symptom. Similarly, such traits as irritability, chronic lateness, and poor judgement are not, in themselves, mental impairments, although they may be linked to them." Legitimate mental disabilities do, however, include major depression, bipolar disorder, various anxiety disorders, schizophrenia, mental retardation, and special learning disorders.

Under the ADA, companies employing mentally disabled individuals are not responsible for every aspect of the employees' behavior. For instance, they are not required to relieve employees of work responsibilities or excuse them from violations of established work policies. Nor are they required to employ workers who are deemed a safety threat. Moreover, employers are not legally responsible for mental disabilities of which they are unaware.

But employers are required under ADA law to make "reasonable accommodations" for mentally disabled employees. These may include leaves of absence; minor modifications in work policy, supervision, or job position; or flexible work schedules. "Although the nature or form of accommodation is up to the employer, and is only 'reasonable' if it helps the employee do a better job, in some instances the employer might wish to consider professional assistance in the communication process," wrote Robert Schwartz, Frederick Post, and Jack Simonetti in *Business Horizons*. "Managers should also verify that the condition qualifies as a psychiatric disability and whether the person can perform the job's essential functions with or without accommodation. Management can request reasonable documentation from a health care professional about the disability and the need for accommodations."

Compliance with the ADA's mental disability provisions can help companies retain productive employees and protect themselves from legal peril. But "even beyond mere compliance, socially responsible businesses may elect to embrace these legal mandates as changes that advance the common good of society," noted Schwartz, Post, and Simonetti. "By doing so, they would be helping millions of mentally ill citizens become gainfully employed and saving society billions of government dollars spent supporting the presently unemployed mentally ill."

THE ADA IN PRACTICE

Since the Americans with Disabilities Act was signed into law in 1990, its provisions, enforcement measures, and effectiveness have all come under scrutiny. Supporters have credited the ADA with improving the quality of life of millions of disabled citizens and opening new economic opportunities for disabled workers across the nation. In addition, C.C. Sullivan noted in *Building Design and Construction* that "the landmark civil rights law changed the way U.S. businesses and institutions understand the rights and abilities of disabled citizens." But Sullivan also voiced a common lament among business owners and managers that "the ADA's open-ended, murky language has been a decade-long minefield of confusion and litigation." Indeed, even supporters of the Act admit that efforts to clarify various provisions of the ADA—now underway—are needed to reduce litigation.

Critics of the ADA—in its current incarnation at least—also note that employment among people with disabilities was lower in the late 1990s, a period of great economic expansion in the United States, than it was when it was passed in 1990. Measuring unemployment is a difficult task in the best of conditions. Measuring the unemployment rate for disabled people is more difficult yet. People often stop looking for employment after an extended and unsuccessful search. The act of giving up on job searching removes a person from the roles of the unemployed. The most recent data available on the unemployment rate for disabled people dates back to 2000 when, according to the U.S. Department of Labor, the rate at which disabled Americans were unemployed stood at approximately 30 percent, more than six times higher than the nation's overall unemployment rate.

Some observers attribute these high rates of unemployment, a decade after the ADA passed, to lax ADA compliance and enforcement efforts by federal agencies charged with seeing that the Act's provisions are carried out. Another factor contributing to the seemingly negligible impact of the ADA on employment rates for disabled people has to do with demographics. As the large baby boom generation ages, many of its members are dropping out of the workforce before the age of retirement. Of these, a very large percentage is departing the workforce based on disability, according to a 2004 Congressional Budget Office report on the subject entitled *Disability and Retirement: The Early Exit of Baby Boomers from the Labor Force.*

Whatever difficulties exist in tracking and measuring the benefits that the ADA has had on increasing accessibility for disabled Americans, attention has been drawn to the subject of disability in American. Across the society, efforts to comply with the law are being made, in the private sector as well as the public sector, by small organizations as well as large. As time passes and data are collected, more analysis of how effective efforts have been to more thoroughly integrate disabled Americans into all aspects of social life will be possible.

SEE ALSO *Disabled Customers*

BIBLIOGRAPHY
Colker, Ruth *Disability Pendulum.* NYU Press, May 2005.

DeLeire, Thomas. "The Unintended Consequences of the Americans with Disabilities Act." *Regulation.* Winter 2000.

"Finding Mediation for ADA Disputes." *Dallas Business Journal.* 8 September 2000.

Hofius, Julie. "Guidelines Define Discrimination Against the Disabled." *Tampa Bay Business Journal.* 8 September 2000.

Holtz-Eakin, Douglas. *Disability and Retirement: The Early Exit of Baby Boomers from the Labor Force.* November 2004.

Leonard, Bill. "New Report Criticizes ADA Enforcement Efforts." *HRMagazine.* September 2000.

National Council on Disability. *Promises to Keep: A Decade of Federal Enforcement of the Americans with Disabilities Act.* 2000.

"Navigating the ADA and Disability Maze." *HR Focus.* July 2000.

Office on the Americans with Disabilities Act.U.S. Department of Justice. Civil Rights Division. *The Americans with Disabilities Act–Title II Technical Assistance Manual.* n.d.

Schwartz, Robert H. et. al. "The ADA and the Mentally Disabled: What Must Firms Do?" *Business Horizons.* July 2000.

"Special Report ADA: The Case for Unlimited Access." *Market Event.* 15 June 2005.

Sullivan, C.C. "ADA's Contentious Decade." *Building Design and Construction.* September 2000.

"Work for All." *T&D.* January 2003.

Hillstrom, Northern Lights
updated by Magee, ECDI

AMORTIZATION

Amortization is an accounting practice whereby expenses or charges are accounted for as the useful life of the asset is consumed or used rather than at the time they are incurred. Amortization includes such practices as depreciation, depletion, write-off of intangibles, prepaid expenses and deferred charges. By amortizing an asset or liability the value of the item is reduced gradually over time by some periodic amount (i.e., via installment payments). In the case of an asset, it involves expensing the item over the "life" of the item—the time period over which it can be used. For a liability, the amortization takes place over the time period that the item is repaid or earned. Amortization is essentially a means to allocate categories of assets and liabilities to their pertinent time period.

The key difference between depreciation and amortization is the nature of the items to which the terms apply. The former is generally used in the context of tangible assets, such as buildings, machinery, and equipment. The latter is more commonly associated with intangible assets, such as copyrights, goodwill, patents, and capitalized costs (e.g., product development costs). On the liability side, amortization is commonly applied to deferred revenue items such as premium income or subscription revenue (wherein cash payments are often received in advance of delivery of goods or services), and therefore must be recognized as income distributed over some future period of time.

Amortization is a means by which accountants apply the period concept in accrual-based financial statements: income and expenses are recorded in the periods affected, rather than when the cash actually changes hands. The importance of spreading transactions across several periods becomes clearer when considering long-lived assets of substantial cost. Just as it would be inappropriate to expense the entire cost of a new facility in the year of its acquisition since its life would extend over many years, it would be wrong to fully expense an intangible asset only in the first year. Intangible assets such as copyrights, patents, and goodwill can be of benefit to a business for many years, so the cost of accruing such assets should be spread over the entire time period that the company is likely to use the asset or generate revenue from it.

The periods over which intangible assets are amortized vary widely, from a few years to as many as 40 years. The costs incurred with establishing and protecting patent rights, for example, are generally amortized over 17 years. The general rule is that the asset should be amortized over its useful life. Small business owners should realize, however, that not all assets are consumed by their use or by the passage of time, and thus are not subject to amortization or depreciation. The value of land, for example, is generally not degraded by time or use. In fact, the value of land often increases with time. This applies to intangible assets as well; trademarks can have indefinite lives and can increase in value over time, and thus are not subject to amortization.

The term amortization is also used in connection with loans. The amortization of a loan is the rate at which the principal balance will be paid down over time, given the term and interest rate of the note. Shorter note periods will have higher amounts amortized with each payment or period.

SEE ALSO *Accounting Methods; Assets; Loans*

BIBLIOGRAPHY

Cornwall, Dr. Jeffrey R., David Vang, and Jean Hartman. *Entrepreneurial Financial Management.* Prentice Hall, 13 May 2003.

Davis, Jon E. "Amortization of Start-Up Costs." *The Tax Adviser.* April 1999.

Mueller, Jennifer L. "Amortization of Certain Intangible Assets: Companies Should Question the Treatment of Assets with Contractual or Legal Lives." *Journal of Accountancy.* December 2004.

Pinson, Linda. *Keeping the Books: Basic Record Keeping and Accounting for the Successful Small Business.* Business & Economics, 2004.

Hillstrom, Northern Lights
updated by Magee, ECDI

"ANGEL" INVESTORS

Angel investors are wealthy individuals who provide capital to help entrepreneurs and small businesses succeed. They are known as "angels" because they often invest in risky, unproven business ventures for which other sources of funds—such as bank loans and formal venture capital—are not available. New startup companies often turn to the private equity market for seed money because the formal equity market is reluctant to fund risky undertakings. In addition to their willingness to invest in a startup, angel investors may bring other assets to the partnership. They are often a source of encouragement, they may be mentors in how best to guide a new business through the startup phase and they are often willing to do this while staying out of the day-to-day management of the business.

Wealthy private investors provide American small businesses with the majority of their seed money. These individuals want to invest in up-and-coming new companies not only to earn money, but also to provide a resource that would have been helpful to them in the early stages of their own businesses. In many cases, the investors sit on the boards of the companies they fund and provide valuable, firsthand management advice.

Like other providers of venture capital, angel investors generally tend to invest in private startup companies with a high profit potential. In exchange for their funds, they usually require a percentage of equity ownership of the company and some measure of control over its strategic planning. Due to the highly speculative nature of their investments, angels eventually hope to achieve a high rate of return.

For many entrepreneurs, angels include friends, relatives, acquaintances, and business associates. Nearly 90 percent of small businesses are started with this type of financial help. Some entrepreneurs gain access to angel investors through venture capital networks—informal organizations that exist specifically to help small businesses connect with potential investors, and visa versa. The networks—which may take the form of computer databases or document clearinghouses—basically provide "matchmaking" services between people with good business ideas and people with money to invest.

In January 2004, the Angel Capital Association (ACA) was founded. It is a peer organization of angel investing groups from across North America. The ACA has a Web site that provides information about best practices and offers links to local angel investor groups.

TYPES OF ANGELS

Although an angel can seem like the answer for an entrepreneur who is desperate for capital, it is important to evaluate the person's motives for investing and need for involvement in the day-to-day operations of the business before entering into a deal. Knowing how to recruit the right angel, one who shares the entrepreneur's goals and objectives, and maintaining an open, communicative relationship with the angel can mean the difference between a solid financial foundation and a failing venture.

In an article for *Entrepreneur,* David R. Evanson and Art Beroff described several basic personality types that tend to characterize angel investors. "Corporate angels" are former executives from large companies who have been downsized or have taken early retirement. In many cases, these angels invest in only one company and hope to turn their investment into a paid position. "Entrepreneurial angels" are individuals who own and operate their own successful businesses. In many cases, they look to invest in companies that provide some sort of synergy with their own company. They rarely want to take an active role in management, but often can help strengthen a small business in indirect ways.

"Enthusiast angels" are older, independently wealthy individuals who invest as a hobby. As a result, they tend to invest small amounts in a number of different companies and not become overly involved in any of them. "Micromanagement angels," in contrast, usually invest a large amount in one company and then seek as much control over its operations as possible. "Professional angels" are individuals employed in a profession such as law, medicine, or accounting who tend to invest in companies related to their areas of expertise. They may be able to provide services to the company at a reduced fee, but they may also tend to be impatient investors. Evanson and Beroff stress that understanding the needs of various types of investors can help entrepreneurs to develop positive working relationships.

ANGEL GROUPS OR FUNDS

Although angel investors usually work on an individual basis there has been a trend towards the formation of angel investor groups within the last decade. These groups usually meet on a regular basis and invite prospective entrepreneurs to present their business ideas for consideration. David Worrell discusses what such a presentation may involve in his article entitled "Taking Flight: Angel Investors are Flocking Together to Your Advantage." If invited to present ideas before an angel investor group, "expect to be one of two or three presenters, each given 10 to 30 minutes to showcase an investment opportunity. Speak loudly, as most groups mix presentations with a meal."

Despite the potential for funding through an angel investor group, according to Worrell, individual angels are still likely to be the best source of seed and early stage money for a small business or startup. "Angel groups can bring more money and other resources, which makes them more effective at later stages."

AVOIDING POTENTIAL PROBLEMS

Regardless of the type of angel a small business owner is able to recruit, there are a number of methods available to help avoid potential problems in the relationship. Entrepreneurs should, for example, be very frank and honest when describing their business idea to a potential investor. Entrepreneurs should also interview potential investors to be sure that their goals, needs, and styles are a good fit with the small business. It is important to ask questions of potential investors and listen to their answers in order to gauge their needs and interests. Ideally, the angels' investment approach will be compatible with the entrepreneur's needs. A partnership between angels and entrepreneurs is much like a marriage involving issues of compatibility, cash, and shared goals.

SEE ALSO *Venture Capital; Seed Money*

BIBLIOGRAPHY

Angel Capital Association, January 2006, Available from http://www.angelcapitalassociation.org/. "About ACA."

Benjamin, Gerald A., and Joel Margulis. *The Angel Investor's Handbook.* Bloomberg Press, January 2001.

Chung, Joe. "Panning Out." *Technology Review.* October 2004.

Evanson, David R., and Art Beroff. "Heaven Sent: Seeking an Angel Investor? Here's How to Find a Match Made in Heaven." *Entrepreneur.* January 1998.

Gallagher, Kathleen. "Your Guide to Finding an Angel Investor." *The Milwaukee Journal Sentinel.* 4 July 2005.

Phalon, Richard. *Forbes Greatest Investing Stories.* John Wiley & Sons, April 2004.

Worrell, David. "Taking Flight: Angel Investors are Flocking Together to Your Advantage." *Entrepreneur.* October 2004.

Hillstrom, Northern Lights
updated by Magee, ECDI

ANNUAL PERCENTAGE RATE (APR)

The annual percentage rate (APR) is the effective rate of interest that is charged on an installment loan, such as those provided by banks, retail stores, and other lenders. Since the enactment of the Truth in Lending Act in 1969, lenders have been required to report the APR in boldface type on the first page of all loan contracts. The truth in lending law requires lenders to disclose in great detail the terms and conditions that apply to consumers when they borrow. Its purpose is to allow consumers who are shopping for credit to compare different offers on the same basis, to compare apples with apples. In the absence of legal requirements to clearly state interest rate calculations on all loan contracts, it would be possible for a lender to misrepresent the interest rate of a loan through the use of different compounding periods. By insisting upon a clear statement of the APR on loan contracts, the truth in lending law has gone a long way towards eliminating interest rate confusion. However, the APR can be calculated in different ways and can sometimes cause rather than eliminate confusion.

LOANS AND INTEREST RATES

A loan is the purchase of the present use of money with the promise to repay the amount in the future according to a pre-arranged schedule and at a specified rate of interest. Loan contracts formally spell out the terms and obligations between the lender and borrower. Loans are by far the most common type of debt financing used by small businesses. The interest rate charged on the borrowed funds reflects the level of risk that the lender undertakes by providing the money. For example, a lender might charge a startup company a higher interest rate than it would a company that had shown a profit for several years. The interest rate also tends to be higher on smaller loans, since lenders must be able to cover the fixed costs involved in making the loans.

The lowest interest rate charged by lenders—which is offered only to firms that qualify on the basis of their size and financial strength—is known as the prime rate. All other types of loans feature interest rates that are scaled upward from the prime rate. Interest rates vary greatly over time, depending on lending policies set forth by the Federal Reserve Board as well as prevailing economic conditions in the nation. For all but the simplest of loans, the nominal or stated rate of interest may differ from the annual percentage rate or effective rate of interest. These differences occur because loans take many forms and cover various time periods. The effect of compounding and the addition of fees may also affect the APR of a loan.

CALCULATING THE APR

The effective rate of interest on a loan can be defined as the total interest paid divided by the amount of money received. For simple interest loans—in which the borrower receives the face value of the loan and repays the principal plus interest at maturity—the effective rate and the nominal rate are usually the same. As an example, say that a small business owner borrows $10,000 at 12 percent for 1 year. The effective rate would thus be $1,200 / $10,000 = 12 percent, the same as the stated rate.

But the effective rate would be slightly different for a discount interest loan, wherein the interest is deducted in advance so the borrower actually receives less than the face value. Using the same example, the small business owner would pay the $1,200 interest up front and receive $8,800 upon signing the loan contract. In this case, the effective interest rate would be $1,200 / $8,800 = 13.64 percent.

The most problematic differences between the nominal and effective rates of interest occur with installment loans. In this type of loan, the interest is calculated based on the nominal rate and added back in to get the face value of the loan. The loan amount is then repaid in equal installments during the loan period. Using the same example, the small business owner would sign for a loan with a face value of $11,200 and would receive $10,000. Since the loan is repaid in monthly installments, however, the business owner would not actually have use of the full loan amount over the course of the year. Instead, assuming 12 equal installments, the business owner would actually have average usable funds from the loan of $5,000. The effective rate of the loan is thus $1,200 / $5,000 = 24 percent, twice the stated rate of the loan.

True APR calculations should also include any up-front fees or penalties that are applied to a loan. These amounts are totaled and added to the interest figure. In the case of mortgage loans, such charges can be signifi-cant. They might, for example, include a mortgage insurance premium, points, lost interest earnings on escrow accounts, and prepayment penalties.

BIBLIOGRAPHY

Eaglesham, Jean. "APRs Daze and Confuse." *Financial Times.* 16 April 1997.

Glanz, Morton. *Managing Bank Risk.* Elsevier, December 2002.

Lee, Jinkook, and Jeanne M. Hogarth. "The Price of Money: Consumers' Understanding of APRs and Contract Interest Rates." *Journal of Public Policy and Marketing.* Spring 1999.

Pinson, Linda. *Keeping the Books: Basic Record Keeping and Accounting for the Successful Small Business.* Business & Economics, 2004.

Price, Derek V. *Borrowing Inequality.* Lynne Rienner Publishers, January 2004.

Hillstrom, Northern Lights
updated by Magee, ECDI

ANNUAL REPORTS

Annual reports are formal financial statements that are published yearly and sent to company stockholders and various other interested parties. The reports assess the year's operations and discuss the companies' view of the upcoming year and the companies' place and prospects. Both for-profit and not-for-profit organizations produce annual reports.

Annual reports have been a Securities and Exchange Commission (SEC) requirement for businesses owned by the public since 1934. Companies meet this requirement in many ways. At its most basic, an annual report includes:

- General description of the industry or industries in which the company is involved.

- Audited statements of income, financial position, cash flow, and notes to the statements providing details for various line items.

- A management's discussion and analysis (MD&A) of the business's financial condition and the results that the company has posted over the previous two years.

- A brief description of the company's business in the most recent year.

- Information related to the company's various business segments.

- Listing of the company's directors and executive officers, as well as their principal occupations, and, if a director, the principal business of the company that employs him or her.

- Market price of the company's stock and dividends paid.

Some companies provide only this minimum amount of information. Annual reports of this type usually are only a few pages in length and produced in an inexpensive fashion. The final product often closely resembles a photocopied document. For these companies, the primary purpose of an annual report is simply to meet legal requirements.

ANNUAL REPORT AS MARKETING TOOL

Many other companies, however, view their annual report as a potentially effective marketing tool to disseminate their perspective on company fortunes. With this in mind, many medium-sized and large companies devote large sums of money to making their annual reports as attractive and informative as possible. In such instances the annual report becomes a forum through which a company can relate, influence, preach, opine, and discuss any number of issues and topics.

An opening "Letter to Shareholders" often sets the tone of annual reports prepared for publicly held companies. The contents of such letters typically focus on topics such as the past year's results, strategies, market conditions, significant business events, new management and directors, and company initiatives. The chairman of the board of directors, the chief executive officer, the president, the chief operating officer or a combination of these four usually sign the letter on behalf of company management. Some of these letters may run a dozen or more pages and include photographs of the CEO in different poses (some even expound on topics that, while perhaps of only tangential interest to stockholders and other readers, are of importance to the CEO). More often, however, these letters are significantly shorter, amounting to 3,000 words or fewer.

Annual reports usually advance a theme or concept that has been embraced by company management and/or its marketing wings. Catch phrases such as "Poised for the Twenty-first century" or "Meeting the Needs of the Information Age" can unify a company's annual report message. In addition, particular events or economic conditions of a given year may be incorporated into the themes advanced in an annual report. Companies also use milestone anniversaries—including industry as well as company anniversaries—in their annual reports. Promoting a long, successful track record is often appealing to shareholders and various audiences, for it connotes reliability and quality. Still other companies have developed a tried-and-true format that they use year after year with little change except updating the data. Whatever the theme, concept, or format, the most successful reports are ones that clearly delineate a company's strategies for profitable growth and cast the firm in a favorable light.

TARGET AUDIENCES FOR ANNUAL REPORTS

Current shareholders and potential investors remain the primary audiences for annual reports. Employees (who today are also likely to be shareholders), customers, suppliers, community leaders, and the community-at-large are also targeted audiences.

Employees The annual report serves many purposes with employees. It provides management with an opportunity to praise employee innovation, quality, teamwork, and commitment, all of which are critical components in overall business success. In addition, an annual report can also be used as a vehicle to relate those company successes—a new contract, a new product, cost-saving initiatives, new applications of products, expansions into new geographies—that have an impact on its work force. Seeing a successful project or initiative profiled in the annual report gives reinforcement to the employees responsible for the success.

The annual report can help increase employee understanding of the different parts of the company. Many manufacturing locations are in remote areas, and an employee's understanding of the company often does not go beyond the facility where he or she works. An annual report can be a source for learning about each of a company's product lines, its operating locations, and who is leading the various operations. The annual report can show employees how they fit into the "big picture."

Employees also are often shareholders. So, like other shareholders, these employees can use the annual report to help gauge their investment in the company. In this case, the annual report can serve as a reminder to employees of the impact that the work they do has on the value of the company's stock value.

Customers Customers want to work with quality suppliers of goods and services, and an annual report can help a company promote its image with customers by highlighting its corporate mission and core values. Describing company initiatives designed to improve manufacturing processes, reduce costs, create quality, or enhance service can also illustrate a company's customer orientation. Finally, the annual report can also show the company's financial strength. Customers are reducing their number of suppliers, and one evaluation criterion is financial strength. They want committed and capable suppliers that are going to be around for the long term.

Suppliers A company's abilities to meet its customers' requirements will be seriously compromised if it is saddled with inept or undependable suppliers. Successful companies today quickly weed out such companies. By highlighting internal measurements of quality, innovation, and commitment, annual reports can send an implicit message to suppliers about the company's expectations of outside vendors. Sometimes an annual report will even offer a profile of a supplier that the company has found exemplary. Such a profile serves two purposes. First, it rewards the supplier for its work and serves to further cement the business relationship. Second, it provides the company's other suppliers with a better understanding of the level of service desired (and the rewards that can be reaped from such service).

The Community Companies invariably pay a great deal of attention to their reputation in the community or communities in which they operate, for their reputations as corporate citizens can have a decisive impact on bottom-line financial performance. A company would much rather be known for its sponsorship of a benefit charity event than for poisoning a local river, whatever its other attributes. Annual reports, then, can be invaluable tools in burnishing a company's public image. Many annual reports discuss community initiatives undertaken by the company, including community renovation projects, charitable contributions, volunteer efforts, and programs to help protect the environment. The objective is to present the company as a proactive member of the community.

This sort of publicity also can be valuable when a company is making plans to move into a new community. Companies seek warm welcomes in new communities (including tax breaks and other incentives). Communities will woo a company perceived as a "good" corporate citizen more zealously than one that is not. The good corporate citizen also will receive less resistance from local interest groups. The company's annual report will be one document that all affected parties will pore over in evaluating the business.

READING AN ANNUAL REPORT

People read annual reports for widely different purposes and at dramatically different levels. Generalizations, however, are difficult. The stockholder with five shares might be as careful and discriminating a reader of an annual report as the financial analyst representing a firm owning one million shares.

It may require an MBA to understand all the details buried in an annual report's footnotes. Nevertheless, a good understanding of a company is possible by focusing on some key sections of the report.

Company Description Most companies will include a description of their business segments that includes products and markets served. Formats vary from a separate fold-out descriptive section to a few words on the inside front cover. A review of this section provides readers with at least a basic understanding of what the company does.

The Letter Whether contained under the heading of Letter to Shareholders, Chairman's Message, or some other banner, the typical executive message can often provide some informative data on the company's fortunes during the previous year and its prospects for the future. Readers should always bear in mind that it is invariably in the executive's best interests to maintain a fundamentally upbeat tone, no matter how troubled the company may be. This is often the most widely read portion of the entire annual report, so business owners and managers should make a special effort to make it both informative and engaging.

Management's Discussion and Analysis (MD&A) This section of an annual report provides, in a fairly succinct form, an overview of the company's performance over the previous three years. It makes a comparison of the most recent year with prior years. It discusses sales, profit margins, operating income, and net income. Factors that influenced business trends are outlined. Other portions discuss capital expenditures, cash flow, changes in working capital, and anything "special" that happened during the years under examination. The MD&A is also supposed to be forward-looking, discussing anything the company may be aware of that could affect results either positively or negatively. An MD&A can be written at all different levels of comprehension, but business consultants generally urge companies to make the information—from balance sheets to management analysis—comprehensible and accessible to a general readership. This means forsaking jargon and hyperbole in favor of clear and concise communication.

Financial Summary Most companies will include a five-, six-, ten-, or eleven-year summary of financial data. Sales, income, dividends paid, shareholders' equity, number of employees, and many other balance sheet items are included in this summary. This section summarizes key data from the statements of income, financial position, and cash flow for a number of years.

Management/Directors A page or more of an annual report will list the management of the company and its board of directors, including their backgrounds and business experience.

Investor Information There almost always is a page that lists the company's address and phone number, the stock transfer agent, dividend and stock price information, and the next annual meeting date. This information is helpful for anyone wanting additional data on the company or more information about stock ownership.

PACKAGING THE ANNUAL REPORT

For most companies, large or small, the financial information and the corporate message are the most important aspects of an annual report. Many companies also want to be sure, however, that their targeted audiences are going to read and understand the message. This is less essential for privately owned businesses that do not need to impress or soothe investors, but they too recognize that disseminating a dry, monotonous report is not in the company's best interests.

The challenge for producers of annual reports is to disseminate pertinent information in a comprehensible fashion while simultaneously communicating the company's primary message. In many ways the annual report serves as an advertisement for the company, a reality that is reflected in the fact that leading business magazines now present awards to company reports deemed to be of particular merit. In recent years, companies have also chosen to make their annual reports available in a variety of electronic media that lend themselves to creative, visually interesting treatments.

Of course, the personality of the company—and perhaps most importantly, the industry in which it operates—will go a long way toward dictating the design format of the annual report. The owner of a manufacturer of hospital equipment is far less likely to present a visually dramatic annual report to the public than are the owners of a chain of suntanning salons. The key is choosing a design that will best convey the company's message.

SUMMARY ANNUAL REPORTS

Few major trends have shaken the tradition of annual reports, but one is the "summary annual report." In 1987, the SEC eased its annual reporting requirements. It allowed companies to produce a summary annual report, rather than the traditional report with audited statements and footnotes. Public disclosure of financial information was still required, but with the new rulings, filing a Form 10-K—provided it contained this information and included audited financial data and other

required material within a company's proxy statement (another SEC-mandated document for shareholders)—met SEC requirements. Promoters of the summary annual report see it as a way to make the annual report a true marketing publication without the cumbersome, detailed financial data. Financial data are still included, but in a condensed form in a supporting role. Since its use was approved, however, the summary annual report has not gained widespread support.

In some respects, annual reports are like fashions. Certain techniques, formats, and designs are popular for a few years and then new ideas displace the old. Several years later, the old ideas are back in vogue again. Other formats are "classic," never seeming to go out of style or lose their power. A key to a successful annual report is not getting caught up in a trend, and instead deciding what works best for conveying the message.

SEE ALSO *Balance Sheets; Income Statement; Financial Statement*

BIBLIOGRAPHY
Parks, Paula Lynn. "Satisfy Stockholders." *Black Enterprise.* April 2000.
Stittle, John *Annual Reports.* Gower Publishing Ltd., 2004.

Hillstrom, Northern Lights
updated by Magee, ECDI

ANNUITIES

An annuity is an interest-bearing financial contract that combines the tax-deferred savings and investment properties of retirement accounts with the guaranteed-income aspects of insurance. Annuities can be described as the flip side of life insurance. Life insurance is designed to provide financial protection against dying too soon. Annuities provide a hedge against outliving your retirement savings. While life insurance plans are designed to create principal, an annuity is designed to liquidate principal that has been created, usually in the form of regular payments over a number of years.

Annuities can be purchased from insurance providers, banks, mutual fund companies, stockbrokers, and other financial institutions. They come in several different forms, including immediate and deferred annuities, and fixed and variable annuities. Each form has different properties and involves different costs. Although the money placed in an annuity is first subject to taxation at the same rate as ordinary income, it is then invested and allowed to grow tax-deferred until it is withdrawn. Distribution is flexible and can take the form of a lump sum, a systematic payout over a specified period, or a guaranteed income spread over the remainder of a person's life. In most cases annuities are a long-term investment vehicle, since the costs involved make it necessary to hold an annuity for a number of years in order to reap financial benefits. Because of their flexibility, annuities can be a good choice for small business owners in planning for their own retirement or in providing an extra reward or incentive for valued employees.

TYPES OF ANNUITIES

There are several different types of annuities available, each with different properties and costs that should be taken into consideration as business owners put together their retirement investment portfolio. The two basic forms that annuities take are immediate and deferred.

An immediate annuity, as the name suggests, begins providing payouts at once. Payouts may continue either for a specific period or for life, depending on the contract terms. Immediate annuities—which are generally purchased with a one-time deposit, with a minimum of around $10,000—are not very common. They tend to appeal to people who wish to roll over a lump-sum amount from a pension or inheritance and begin drawing income from it. The immediate annuity would be preferable to a regular bank account because the principal grows more quickly through investment and because the amount and duration of payouts are guaranteed by contract. Immediate annuities are also known by the name income annuities. What is important to remember when considering an immediate annuity is that "at the end of the day, you've got to remember what you're buying is insurance, not an investment vehicle like a stock or mutual fund," explains Rob Nestor in an article by Murray Coleman in *Investor's Business Daily.*

Deferred annuities delay payouts until a specific future date. The principal amount is invested and allowed to grow tax-deferred over time. More common than immediate annuities, deferred annuities appeal to people who want a tax-deferred investment vehicle in order to save for retirement.

There are also two basic types of deferred annuity: fixed and variable. Fixed annuities provide a guaranteed interest rate over a certain period, usually between one and five years. In this way, fixed annuities are comparable to certificates of deposit (CDs) and bonds, with the main benefit that the sponsor guarantees the return of the principal. Fixed annuities generally offer a slightly higher interest rate than CDs and bonds, while the risk is also slightly higher. In addition, like other types of annuities, the principal is allowed to grow tax-deferred until it is withdrawn.

The more popular of the deferred annuity types is the variable annuity which offers an interest rate that changes based on the value of the underlying investment. Purchasers of variable annuities can usually choose from a range of stock, bond, and money market funds for investment purposes in order to diversify their portfolios and manage risk. Some of these funds are created and managed specifically for the annuity, while others are similar to those that may be purchased directly from mutual fund companies. The minimum investment usually ranges from $500 to $5,000, depending on the sponsor, and the investments (or subaccounts) usually feature varying levels of risk, from aggressive growth to conservative fixed income. In most cases, the annuity principal can be transferred from one investment to another without being subject to taxation. Variable annuities are subject to market fluctuations, however, and investors also must accept a slight risk of losing their principal if the sponsor company encounters financial difficulties.

FEATURES OF ANNUITIES

Variable annuities have a number of features that differentiate them from common retirement accounts, such as 401(k)s and IRAs, and from common equity investments, such as mutual funds. One of the main points of differentiation involves tax deferral. Unlike 401(k)s or IRAs, variable annuities are funded with after-tax money—meaning that contributions are subject to taxation at the same rate as ordinary income prior to being placed in the annuity. In contrast, individuals are allowed to make contributions to the other types of retirement accounts using pre-tax dollars. That is why financial specialists usually instruct people to first maximize their contributions to 401(k) plans and IRAs before considering annuities. On the plus side, there is no limit on the amount that an individual may contribute to a variable annuity, while contributions to the other types of accounts are limited by the federal government. Unlike the dividends and capital gains that accrue to mutual funds, however, which are taxable in the year they are received, the money invested in annuities is allowed to grow tax free until it is withdrawn.

Another feature that differentiates variable annuities from other types of financial products is the death benefit. Most annuity contracts include a clause guaranteeing that the investor's heirs will receive either the full amount of principal invested or the current market value of the contract, whichever is greater, in the event that the investor dies before receiving full distribution of the assets. However, any earnings are taxable for the heirs.

Another benefit of variable annuities is that they offer greater withdrawal flexibility than other retirement accounts. Investors are able to customize the distribution of their assets in a number of ways, ranging from a lump-sum payment to a guaranteed lifetime income. Some limitations, however, do apply. For example, the federal government imposes a 10 percent penalty on withdrawals taken by anyone before they reach the age of 59½ years. But contributors to variable annuities are not required to begin taking distributions until age 85, whereas contributors to IRAs and 401(k)s are required to begin taking distributions by age 70½.

COSTS ASSOCIATED WITH ANNUITIES

In exchange for the various features offered by annuities, investors must pay a number of costs. Many of the costs are due to the insurance aspects of annuities, although they vary among different sponsors. One common type of cost associated with annuities is the insurance cost, which averages 1.25 percent and pays for the guaranteed death benefit in addition to the insurance agent's commission. There are also usually management fees, averaging 1 percent, which compensate the sponsor for taking care of the investments and generating reports. Many annuities also charge modest administrative or contract fees.

One of the more problematic costs of annuities, in the eyes of their critics, is the surrender charge for early removal of the principal. In most cases, this fee begins at around 7 percent but then phases out over time. However, the surrender fee is charged in addition to the 10 percent government penalty for early withdrawal if the investor is under age 59½.

All of the costs associated with variable annuities detract somewhat from their attractiveness as a financial product when one compares them to mutual funds. The costs also mean that there are no quick profits associated with annuities; instead, they must be held as a long-term investment. In fact, it can take as long as 17 years for the benefits of tax deferral to outpace the administrative expenses of an annuity. For investors who wish to put money away for an extended period, a variable annuity may be a very good investment vehicle.

DISTRIBUTION OPTIONS

On the positive side, investors in annuities have a number of options for receiving the distribution of their funds. The three most common forms of distribution— all of which have various costs deducted—are lump sum, lifetime income, and systematic payout. Some investors who have contributed to a variable annuity over many years may elect to take a lump-sum withdrawal. The main drawback to this approach is that all the taxes are due immediately. Other investors may decide upon a systematic payout of the accumulated assets over a specified time period. In this approach, the investor can determine the amount of payments as well as the intervals

at which payments will be received. Finally, some investors choose the option of receiving a guaranteed lifetime income. This option is the most expensive for the investor, and does not provide any money for heirs, but the sponsor of the annuity must continue to make payouts even if the investor outlives his or her assets. A similar distribution arrangement is joint-and-last-survivor, which is an annuity that keeps providing income as long as one person in a couple is alive.

Annuities are rather complex financial products, and as such they have become the subject of considerable debate among experts in financial planning. As mentioned earlier, many experts claim that the special features of annuities are not great enough to make up for their cost as compared to other investment options. As a result, financial advisors commonly suggest that individuals maximize their contributions to IRAs, 401(k)s, or other pre-tax retirement accounts before considering annuities (investors should avoid placing annuities into IRAs or other tax-sheltered accounts because the tax shelter then becomes redundant and the investor pays large annuity fees for nothing). Some experts also prefer mutual funds tied to a stock market index to annuities, because such funds typically cost less and often provide a more favorable tax situation. Contributions to annuities are taxed at the same rate as ordinary income, for instance, while long-term capital gains from stock investments are taxed at a special, lower rate—usually 20 percent. Still other financial advisors note that, given the costs involved, annuities require a very long-term financial commitment in order to provide benefits. It may not be possible for some individuals to tie up funds for the 17 to 20 years it takes to benefit from the purchase of an annuity.

Despite the drawbacks, however, annuities can be beneficial for individuals in a number of different situations. For example, annuities provide an extra source of income and an added margin of safety for individuals who have contributed the limit allowed under other retirement savings options. In addition, some kinds of annuities can be valuable for individuals who want to protect their assets from creditors in the event of bankruptcy. An annuity can provide a good shelter for a retirement nest egg for someone in a risky profession, such as medicine. Annuities are also recommended for people who plan to spend the principal during their lifetime rather than leaving it for their heirs. Finally, annuities may be more beneficial for individuals who expect that their tax bracket will be 28 percent or lower at the time they begin making withdrawals.

Annuities may also hold a great deal of appeal for small businesses. For example, annuities can be used as a retirement savings plan on top of a 401(k). They can be structured in various ways to reward employees for meeting company goals. In addition, annuities can provide a nice counterpart to life insurance, since the longer the investor lives, the better an annuity will turn out to be as an investment. Finally, some annuities allow investors to take out loans against the principal without paying penalties for early withdrawal. Overall, some financial experts claim that annuities are actually worth more than comparable investments because of such features as the death benefit, guaranteed lifetime income, and investment services.

A small business owner considering setting up an annuity should consider all options, look carefully at both the costs and the returns, and be prepared to put money away for many years. It is also important to shop around for the best possible product and sponsor before committing funds. "Before investing in an annuity, make sure the insurance company that will sponsor the contract is financially healthy," counseled Mel Poteshman in *Los Angeles Business Journal.* "Also, find out from the sponsoring company the interest rates that have been paid out over the last five to ten years and how interest rate changes are calculated. This will give you an idea of the annuity's overall performance and help you identify the annuity that provides the best long-range financial security.

SEE ALSO *Retirement Planning; Life Insurance*

BIBLIOGRAPHY
Baldwin, Ben *The New Life Insurance Investment Advisor.* Second Edition. McGraw-Hill, 2001.

Chandler, Darlene K. *The Annuity Handbook: A Guide to Nonqualified Annuities.* Third Edition. National Underwriter Company, 2002.

Clements, Jonathan. "Ensuring Your Nest Egg Doesn't Crack." *Wall Street Journal.* 8 February 2000.

Coleman, Murray. "Immediate Annuities: Wave of Future?" *Investor's Business Daily.* 8 November 2004.

Hillstrom, Northern Lights
updated by Magee, ECDI

APPLICATION SERVICE PROVIDERS

According to the Information Technology Association of America, an application service provider (ASP) is "a company that provides a collection of IT resources to clients or subscribers who access those resources via the Internet or other networking arrangements." With the many challenges that businesses face every day, the last thing they need to worry about are a lot of technological issues that are beyond their area of expertise. Many busi-

nesses that run their own applications are forced to increase their staffs to include information technology experts who maintain and upgrade application software. Over time, this can become an expensive endeavor.

Many businesses are deciding to outsource the management of the applications to an application service provider. While cost is usually the main reason for a company to enlist the help of an ASP, other benefits include saving time, gaining access to top-tier software, and providing scalability. The speed at which advances are made in the field of computerization means that a significant investment must be made to remain knowledgeable and informed about the newest applications in the field. The cost benefit assessment of this investment for a single user is often not favorable. Quite simply, an ASP allows managers the opportunity to do what they do best and invest in acquiring knowledge about their own industry and not the computer systems industry.

An application service provider can handle many aspects of a business. ASPs manage and deliver application capabilities to multiple entities from a single data center across the private or public Internet on a rental basis. Typical of the sorts of hosted applications that ASPs offer include: enterprise resource planning applications (human resources, financials, manufacturing, supply chain management); e-commerce applications; customer relationship management packages, (sales automation, customer services and other front-office applications); productivity applications (collaboration, workflow management, project management office); and e-mail and messaging services.

Some businesses have concerns about using ASPs. Security and reliability are just two of the issues that have made businesses reluctant to turn over full control of their applications to an outside source. The ASP industry as a whole is working diligently to address these concerns and prove that their services are valid and cost efficient. Overall, their efforts appear to be successful. As Samuel Greengard stated in *Workforce:* "Where there was once fear and distrust, there's now growing acceptance of the idea that outside companies can manage hardware, software, and telecommunications remotely. And, make no mistake, these so-called application service providers are forever changing the way companies view technology and how they use it to gain a competitive advantage."

Before entering into a formal relationship with an application service provider, businesses should make sure they fully understand the service level agreement (SLA). The SLA is a document that protects the interests of both the business and the ASP, and usually guarantees performance levels in areas such as uptime, bandwidth, and interapplication communication. By taking the time to understand the SLA up front, a business cuts down on the number of potential problems and headaches later.

Small businesses are one sector that stands to benefit from the expertise of an application service provider. It is a quick and affordable way to acquire the necessary applications to run a successful business, especially if the business is a dot-com startup with no in-house staff or technology. Still, a small business (or any business, for that matter) should always make sure that the ASP is specific to their industry, offers a full line of business applications, is able to scale as the business grows, and can manage custom applications and solutions that are unique to the company. The ability of the ASP to integrate with the company's customers, suppliers, and partners can also be a crucial element in the business relationship.

BIBLIOGRAPHY

Bansal, Parveen. "Grasping ASPs." *The Banker*. March 2001.

Borck, James R. "Enterprise Strategies: Customers Really Can Find Happiness with the Application Service Provider Model." *InfoWorld*. 11 December 2000.

Cameron, Preston. "Slaying the Competition Dragon: Selecting an Application Service Provider." *CMA Management*. March 2001.

Greengard, Samuel. "Handing Off Your HRMS: What You Need to Know." *Workforce*. February 2001.

Grevstad, Eric. "ASP Versus PC." *Home Office Computing*. March 2001.

Jossi, Frank. "ASP Trend Hits Home." *Minneapolis-St. Paul City Business*. 8 December 2000.

Lee, Mie-Yun. "Choose or Lose." *Entrepreneur*. December 2000.

Paul, Lauren Gibbons. "The ASP Dilemma." *Electronic Business*. January 2001.

Shutovich, Christina A. "ASP Model Can Reduce Short- and Long-Term Costs." *Aftermarket Business*. March 2001.

Umar, Amjad, and Paula Lynn Parks. "Satisfy Stockholders." *e-Business and Distributed Systems Handbook: Applications Module*. Business & Economics, 2003.

Hillstrom, Northern Lights
updated by Magee, ECDI

APPRENTICESHIP PROGRAMS

Apprenticeship programs are occupational training programs that combine on-the-job work experience with technical or classroom study. Such programs are designed to develop useful job skills in individuals entering the work force. These programs, which are designed to address the need for better trained entry-level workers and help young people make the transition from school to the work world, can also serve as a good source of labor for businesses of all shapes and sizes.

Many U.S. industries maintain thriving apprenticeship programs. These programs can be found in the skilled trades and crafts, notably in occupations related to the construction industry. Indeed, in many states, apprenticeship programs are required to obtain occupational licensing or certification. The United States does not currently maintain a national apprenticeship program. The U.S. Department of Labor, Bureau of Apprenticeship and Training, maintains a registry of apprenticeship programs and the occupations that are covered throughout the country.

Apprenticeship programs may be sponsored by individual employers, a group of employers, or a union. Trade and other nonprofit organizations also sponsor apprenticeship programs within certain industries. Unions and employers often form joint apprenticeship committees to administer the programs. Such committees are concerned with determining an industry's particular needs and developing standards for the apprenticeship programs. Apprenticeship programs are usually registered with the federal or state government to ensure that the programs meet standards relating to job duties, instruction, wages, and safety and health conditions.

Individuals who are interested in entering an apprenticeship program must meet certain qualifications. Because of child labor laws in the United States, most apprenticeship programs in the United States require applicants to be at least 16 or 18 years of age. While some states have apprenticeship programs for high school juniors and seniors, most apprenticeship programs require a high school diploma. Other requirements relate to aptitude and physical condition.

Once an individual has been accepted into an apprenticeship program, he or she usually signs an agreement with the program's sponsor. The agreement covers such matters as the sponsor's compliance with the program's standards and the apprentice's performance of the required work and completion of the necessary studies. While enrolled in the program the apprentice works under the supervision of a fully qualified journeyperson as a paid, full-time employee (apprentices are usually paid about half of what a journeyperson makes). They also receive relevant instruction outside of regular working hours, either in a classroom or through at-home study. The program may last from one to six years, depending on the occupation and other requirements. Certification is usually granted upon successful completion of an apprenticeship program.

In recent years, growing numbers of economists and industry experts have called for the establishment of some type of national apprenticeship program in the United States. Supporters contend that such a program, which would provide apprenticeship training and job skills certification at the national level, would help to reduce the wage gap between college graduates and those who do not attend college, and would nourish better-trained entry-level workers.

In the meantime, the most significant legislation in this realm in recent years has been the 1994 School-to-Work Opportunities Act. This federal legislation encouraged educators and local businesses to join together to provide students with information and opportunities to explore various careers. Apprenticeship programs quickly emerged as an important part of this legislation, which distributed approximately $1.5 billion to academic and business participants between 1994 and 1998. But seed funding for "school-to-work," "school-to-career," or "career prep" programs expired in 2001, and was not renewed.

SEE ALSO *Training and Development*

BIBLIOGRAPHY

Jacobs, Ronald L. *Structured On-The-Job Training.* Berrett-Koehler Publishers, 2003.

Kiser, Kim. "Tapped Out." *Training.* July 1999.

Zipf, Karen L. *Labor of Innocents.* LSU Press, May 2005.

Hillstrom, Northern Lights
updated by Magee, ECDI

ARTICLES OF INCORPORATION

For small businesses that decide to incorporate, one of the first steps they must take is filing the articles of incorporation (sometimes called certificates of incorporation, articles of association, or charters) at a Secretary of State's Office or with the Department of Commerce. A company can file in the state in which it does business or in any other state of its choosing. In the past, businesses were often advised to incorporate in Delaware because of its simple and advantageous corporate laws. More recently, though, there is less agreement on the subject. Many other states have reformed their tax codes in order to keep businesses at home, thus muting the advantages previously associated with incorporating in Delaware.

In most states, the Secretary of State can provide blank forms by mail and most also make these forms available online. These differ from state to state, but they are fairly straightforward and only require you to fill in the blanks. In a few states, no forms are available, and you will have to draw up the articles of incorporation from scratch. You may prepare the articles of incorporation on your own (there are many guides available, some of which are specifically created for a certain state and include sample forms), or you may hire a lawyer to do this for you. But even if you take on the task yourself, it is a good idea to ask an attorney to look over the form.

Generally, the articles of incorporation include the following sections:

- Corporate Name.

- Initial agent (sometimes called a registered agent or resident agent) and office—This is usually the corporate president or one of the directors. In any case, this is the contact person to whom all legal notices and official mailings will be sent.

- Purpose for which the Corporation is organized—In most states, this section does not need to be filled in. It will already contain a statement to the effect that the Corporation can do anything that's legal for a corporation to do in that state. If you have to fill it in yourself, it is best to leave the language as general as possible. That way, if you later change the nature of your business, you will not need to amend the articles of incorporation.

- The Duration of the Company—This is usually listed as perpetual.

- Authorized Shares, Issued Shares, and Classification of Stock—The amount of information about authorized or issued shares required in this section varies by state. You may be asked to list the total number of shares authorized to be issued, the number of shares actually issued, the class of stock (common, preferred or both), the value per share, or the consideration received for the shares.

- Directors of the Corporation and their Addresses

- Name(s) and Address(es) of Incorporator(s)—This section should list the names of those individuals who have performed the incorporation and prepared the articles of incorporation (attorneys, directors, or owners).

- Estimated Property and Gross Revenue—This section, which is optional in some states, may include an estimate of the business's property value and the estimated gross amount of business which will be transacted during the following year.

Once the form is complete, it should be mailed to the Secretary of State or Department of Commerce in the state in which the business will operate. Any fees that are due should be sent along at this time as well. Each state has a filing fee, and there are usually other fees such as a franchise tax (usually based on your capitalization), a fee for designating a registered agent, or an organization tax based on the number and value of stock. These fees vary dramatically from state to state.

When the articles of incorporation are returned to the business owner after being accepted by the Secretary of State, they will probably need to be filed with the Recorder of Deeds in the county where the corporation's home office is located. The articles of incorporation, now the company's charter, then become public record.

SEE ALSO *Incorporation*

BIBLIOGRAPHY

Diamond, Michael R., and Julie L. Williams. *How to Incorporate: A Handbook for Entrepreneurs and Professionals.* Fourth Edition. John Wiley & Sons, 2000.

"Don't Underestimate the Legal Clout of Your Bylaws and Corporate Charter." *The Business Owner.* May-June 1999.

Steingold, Fred S., and Ilona M. Bray. *The Legal Guide for Starting and Running a Small Business.* Seventh Edition. Nolo Press, 2003.

Hillstrom, Northern Lights
updated by Magee, ECDI

ASSEMBLY LINE METHODS

An assembly line is a manufacturing process in which interchangeable parts are added to a product in a sequential manner to create an end product. In most cases, a manufacturing assembly line is a semi-automated system through which a product moves. At each station along the line some part of the production process takes place. The workers and machinery used to produce the item are stationary along the line and the product moves through the cycle, from start to finish.

Assembly line methods were originally introduced to increase factory productivity and efficiency. Advances in assembly line methods are made regularly as new and more efficient ways of achieving the goal of increased throughput (the number of products produced in a given period of time) are found. While assembly line methods apply primarily to manufacturing processes, business experts have also been known to apply these principles to other areas of business, from product development to management.

The introduction of the assembly line to American manufacturing floors in the early part of the twentieth century fundamentally transformed the character of pro-

duction facilities and businesses throughout the nation. Thanks to the assembly line, production periods shortened, equipment costs accelerated, and labor and management alike endeavored to keep up with the changes. Today, using modern assembly line methods, manufacturing has become a highly refined process in which value is added to parts along the line. Increasingly, assembly line manufacturing is characterized by "concurrent processes"—multiple parallel activities that feed into a final assembly stage. These processes require sophisticated communications systems, material flow plans, and production schedules. The fact that the assembly line system is a single, large system means that failures at one point in the "line" cause slowdowns and repercussions from that point forward. Keeping the entire system running smoothly requires a great deal of coordination between the parts of the system.

Computer power has enabled tracking systems to become more sophisticated and this, in turn, has made it possible to reduce the costs associated with holding inventories. Just-in-time (JIT) manufacturing methods have been developed to reduce the cost of carrying parts and supplies as inventory. Under a JIT system, manufacturing plants carry only one or a few days' worth of inventory in the plant, relying on suppliers to provide parts and materials on an "as needed" basis. Future developments in this area may include suppliers establishing operations within the manufacturing facility itself or increased electronic links between manufacturers and suppliers to provide for a more efficient supply of materials and parts.

VARIATIONS IN ASSEMBLY LINE METHODOLOGIES

The passage of years has brought numerous variations in assembly line methodologies. These new wrinkles can be traced back not only to general improvements in technology and planning, but to factors that are unique to each company or industry. Capital limitations, for example, can have a big impact on a small business's blueprint for introducing or improving assembly line production methods, while changes in international competition, operating regulations, and availability of materials can all influence the assembly line picture of entire industries. Following are brief descriptions of assembly line methods that are currently enjoying some degree of popularity in the manufacturing world.

- Modular Assembly—This is an advanced assembly line method that is designed to improve throughput by increasing the efficiency of parallel subassembly lines feeding into the final assembly line. As applied to automobile manufacturing, modular assembly would involve assembling separate modules—chassis, interior, body—on their own assembly lines, then joining them together on a final assembly line.

- Cell Manufacturing—This production method has evolved out of increased ability of machines to perform multiple tasks. Cell operators can handle three or four tasks, and robots are used for such operations as materials handling and welding. Cells of machines can be run by one operator or a multi-person work cell. In these machine cells it is possible to link older machines with newer ones, thus reducing the amount of investment required for new machinery.

- Team Production—Team-oriented production is another development in assembly line methods. Where workers used to work at one- or two-person work stations and perform repetitive tasks, now teams of workers can follow a job down the assembly line through its final quality checks. The team production approach has been hailed by supporters as one that creates greater worker involvement in the manufacturing process and knowledge of the system.

- U-shaped assembly "line"— A line may not be the most efficient shape in which to organize an assembly line. On a U-shaped line, or curve, workers are collected on the inside of the curve and communication is easier than along the length of a straight line. Assemblers can see each process; what is coming and how fast; and one person can perform multiple operations. Also, workstations along the "line" are able to produce multiple product designs simultaneously, making the facility as a whole more flexible. Changeovers are easier in a U-shaped line as well and, with better communication between workers, cross-training is also simplified. The benefits of the U-shaped line have served to increase their use widely.

As new assembly line methods are introduced into manufacturing processes, business managers look at the techniques for possible application to other areas of business. One such application is called Joint Application Development, or JAD. It is a process originally developed for designing a computer-based system. It brings together those working in business areas and those working in the information technology area into a single workshop. The advantages of JAD include a dramatic shortening of the time it takes to complete a project. The JAD process does for computer systems development what Henry Ford did for the manufacture of automobiles (a method of organizing machinery, materials, and labor so that a car could be put together much faster and cheaper than ever before – the assembly line).

In a similar way the fundamentals of assembly line theory have been applied to business processes with success. These new methods of organizing work all share the common goal of improving throughput by reducing the amount of time individual workers and their machines spend on specific tasks. By reducing the amount of time required to produce an item, assembly line methods have made it possible to produce more with less.

SEE ALSO *Productivity; Automation*

BIBLIOGRAPHY

Croci, F., M. Perona, and A. Pozzetti. "Work Force Management in Automated Assembly Systems." *International Journal of Production Economics.* 1 March 2000.

Maloney, David. "New Roots." *Modern Materials Handling.* October 2003.

Nieble, Benjamin, and Andris Freivalds. *Methods, Standards, and Work Design.* July 2002.

Whitfield, Kermit. "Assembly: How Standard Can You Get?" *Automotive Design & Production.* March 2004.

Umble, Michael, Van Gray, and Elisabeth Umble. "Improving Production Line Performance." *IIE Solutions.* November 2000.

Hillstrom, Northern Lights
updated by Magee, ECDI

ASSETS

Assets are anything of value that is owned by a company, whether fully paid for or not. These range from cash, inventory, and other "current assets" to real estate, equipment, and other "fixed assets." Intangible items of value to a company, such as exclusive use contracts, copyrights, and patents, are also regarded as assets.

CURRENT ASSETS

Also known as soft or liquid assets, current assets include cash, government securities, marketable securities, notes receivable, accounts receivable, inventories, raw materials, prepaid expenses, and any other item that could be converted to cash in the normal course of business within one year.

Cash is, of course, the most liquid of assets. But in business circles, the definition of cash is expanded beyond currency (coins and paper money) to include checks, drafts, and money orders; the balance in any company checking account (provided there are no restrictions attached to the account); and even less liquid assets that are nonetheless commonly regarded as cash equivalents. These include certificates of deposit (CDs) with maturities of less than a year, money market funds, and Treasury bills.

For many small businesses, cash comprises the bulk of their current assets. Cash is flexible and can be quickly and easily converted into needed goods or services. But the very ease with which it can be used makes it attractive for disreputable people both within and outside the business, so small business owners need to make sure that they take the appropriate precautions when handling such assets. Consultants often recommend that their clients take out insurance policies to protect themselves from financial losses as a result of employee theft or error; this practice is commonly known as "bonding."

Another important practice that helps to safeguard current assets has to do with dividing up tasks. To reduce the likelihood of any one malicious individual being able to rob or embezzle from a company it is useful to have different people in charge of tracking both receipts and disbursements. Splitting up the responsibilities for handling cash, bookkeeping, and bank statement reconciliation is an easy way to be sure that various people are all monitoring current assets. In small businesses these tasks are often, and understandably, handled by one individual. Having at least two people involved in these tasks on a regular basis increases the chances that errors, whether intentional or not, are found and remedied in a timely fashion.

The use of a petty cash fund is a practical way to provide for small outlays without exposing a larger percentage of a company's current liabilities. While small businesses may not be able to institute the elaborate systems used in larger enterprises, cash control is important.

Accounts receivable is another type of current asset. Accounts receivables are sums owed to the company for services or goods rendered. Inventories are important current assets as well, particularly for business firms engaged in manufacturing and merchandising. Inventories typically held by merchandisers include finished goods ready for sale or resale, while the inventories of manufacturing establishments can include raw materials, supplies used in manufacture, partially completed work, and finished goods.

FIXED ASSETS

Also known as hard assets, fixed assets include real estate, physical plants and facilities, leasehold improvements, equipment (from office equipment to heavy operating machinery), vehicles, fixtures, and other assets that can reasonably be assumed to have a life expectancy of several years. Most fixed assets, with the notable exception of real estate, will lose value over time. This is known as depreciation, and is typically figured into a business's various financial documents (the expense of real estate purchases can also be depreciated when figuring taxes).

Small business consultants note, however, that this depreciation can be figured by several different formulas. The smart business owner should take the time to figure out which formula is most advantageous for his or her company.

Fixed assets are among the most important assets that a company holds, for they represent major investments of financial resources. Indeed, fixed assets usually comprise the majority of a business's total assets. Intelligent allocation of resources to meet a business's land, facility, and large equipment needs can bring it assets that will serve as cornerstones of successful operation for years to come. Conversely, a company saddled with ill-considered or substandard fixed assets will find it much more difficult to be successful. This is especially true for small businesses, which have a smaller margin of error.

Fixed assets are also very important to small business owners because they are one of the things that are examined most closely by prospective lenders. When a bank or other lending institution is approached by a small business owner who is seeking a loan to establish or expand a company, loaning agents will always undertake a close study of the prospective borrower's hard assets. Bankers view these fixed assets as a decisive indicator of a business's financial health.

When examining a business's fixed assets, lenders are typically most concerned with the following factors: 1) The type, age, and condition of equipment and facilities; 2) The depreciation schedules for those assets; 3) The nature of the company's mortgage and lease arrangements; and 4) Likely future fixed asset expenditures.

RISKY VS. RISKLESS ASSETS

The monetary flow that a business owner receives from an asset can vary because of many different factors. When comparing the value of various assets, the monetary flow of an asset is an important consideration, especially relative to the asset's value or price. A risky asset provides a monetary flow that is at least in part random, in other words, the monetary flow isn't known with in advance. A "riskless" asset, on the other hand, is one that features a known level of monetary flow to its owner. Bank savings accounts, certificates of deposit (CDs), and Treasury bills all qualify as riskless assets because the monetary flow of the asset to the owner is known. Finally, the "return" on an asset—whether risky or riskless—is the total monetary reward it yields as a fraction of its price.

ASSET UTILIZATION RATIOS

A financial ratio is a simple mathematical comparison of two or more entries from a company's financial statements. Business owners and managers use ratios of all sorts to chart a company's progress, uncover trends and point to potential problems. Bankers and investors look at a company's ratios when they are trying to decide whether or not to invest or lend to the company.

The asset utilization ratio is a measure of the speed at which a business is able to turn assets into sales, and thus, revenue. The use of ratio analysis, especially with a small company, is of greatest value when done over time to chart changes in the company's performance and compare the company's performance with others within the same industry.

The four primary asset utilization ratios are: 1) Receivables turnover, which studies the number of times that receivable balances are collected annually; 2) Inventory turnover, which is determined by dividing the annual cost of sales by the average inventory at both the beginning and the end of the period being studied; 3) Fixed asset turnover; and 4) Total asset turnover. Asset turnover ratios measure the efficiency with which a company uses its assets to generate sales. The higher the turnover ratio, the more efficient the company. Fixed asset turnover ratios are not particularly useful to compute if the company under examination does not have a significant amount of hard assets, frequently true with small, new and/or service-oriented businesses.

SEE ALSO *Liabilities*

BIBLIOGRAPHY

Bannister, Anthony. *Bookkeeping and Accounts for Small Business.* Straightforward Company Ltd., 1 April 2004.

Cornwall, Dr. Jeffrey R., David Vang, and Jean Hartman. *Entrepreneurial Financial Management.* Prentice Hall, 13 May 2003.

Epstein, Lita. *Reading Financial Reports for Dummies.* December 2004.

Lunt, Henry. "The Fab Four's Solo Careers." *Accountancy.* March 2000.

Pinson, Linda. *Keeping the Books: Basic Record Keeping and Accounting for Successful Small Business.* Business & Economics, 2004.

Strassmann, Paul A. "GAAP Helps Whom?" *Computerworld.* 6 December 1999.

Taylor, Peter. *Book-Keeping & Accounting for Small Business.* Business & Economics, 2003.

Tuller, Lawrence W. *Finance for Non-Financial Managers and Small Business Owners.* Adams Media, 1997.

Hillstrom, Northern Lights
updated by Magee, ECDI

ASSUMPTIONS

An assumption is a statement that is presumed to be true without concrete evidence to support it. In the business world, assumptions are used in a wide variety of situations to enable companies to plan and make decisions in the face of uncertainty. Perhaps the most common use of assumptions is in the accounting function, which uses assumptions to facilitate financial measurement, forecasting, and reporting.

There are four basic types of assumptions used regularly in accounting. They are:

- The separate-entity assumption, which holds that the particular business entity being measured is distinct and separate from similar and related entities for accounting purposes.

- The continuity or going concern assumption. This assumption holds that the entity will not cease operations or liquidate its assets during the accounting period.

- The time-period assumption. According to this assumption, accounting reports are assumed to apply to a short time period, usually one year.

- The unit-of-measure assumption which is sometimes referred to as the stable monetary unit assumption. This assumption holds that the U.S. dollar is the common denominator or measuring stick for all accounting measurements taken for American companies.

In addition to these underlying accounting assumptions, there are also a number of smaller assumptions that are commonly made in certain calculations. For example, companies must make several assumptions in computing the value of pension and medical benefits that will be provided to retirees in the future. These funds—which are built up over time and held as investments until needed, but are actually owed to employees at some future point—are reported by companies as assets and liabilities on their financial statements. The assumptions made by a company help determine the monetary amounts that are reported, and thus may affect the company's current reported earnings and tax liability.

In the case of pensions that are provided to employees following retirement, companies must make assumptions regarding the likely rate of wage inflation and the discount rate to be applied to projected future payments. Similarly, the calculation of health care benefits provided to retirees includes assumptions about the discount rate and medical cost trend rate, as well as demographic assumptions such as the employee turnover rate, the average age of employees at retirement, and the percentage of married retirees. Changing one of these assumptions can have a marked effect on a company's results.

For example, increasing the discount rate reduces the present value of the company's liabilities and the amount of annual contributions that must be made to fund the retirement accounts, and therefore increases the company's current earnings.

The ease with which a company's current earnings may be "improved" by changed assumptions in forecasting highlights the need to avoid the natural inclination towards overly optimistic assumptions. The early 2000s have exposed serious problems for many companies and public institutions because of the overly optimistic assumptions made in the 1990s about pension fund financing.

Edward Siedle, a former Securities and Exchange Commission attorney, discusses assumption in the pension field in a *Fort Worth Star-Telegram* article. "In my experience, every pension fund I've ever seen has an actuarial assumption that is more akin to wishful thinking than what is reasonably foreseeable. You just want to laugh out loud." Assumptions about pension fund obligations may be somewhat more difficult than forecasting other obligations because of the long time period over which they must extend. Nonetheless, the mass failure of companies to accurately assess pension fund requirements in the 1990s shows just how important it is to base assumptions on as sound a footing as possible and avoid overly optimistic forecasts.

Experts recommend that companies review their accounting assumptions every few years to see whether making a change would be beneficial and to verify that assumptions about the economy generally are still accurate.

SEE ALSO *Forecasting*

BIBLIOGRAPHY
Allen, Steve L. *Financial Risk Management*. John Wiley & Sons, 2003.

Berard, Yamil. "Overly Optimistic Assumption About Public Pension Plans Haunts Officials." *Fort Worth Star-Telegram.* 16 February 2005.

Gilman, Joan, and Sarah White. *Business Plans that Work*. Adams Media, 2001.

Pison, Linda. *Anatomy of a Business Plan*. Fifth Edition. Dearborn Trade Publishing, 2001.

Hillstrom, Northern Lights
updated by Magee, ECDI

AUDITS, EXTERNAL

An audit is a systematic process of objectively obtaining and evaluating the accounts or financial records of a governmental, business, or other entity. Whereas some businesses rely on audits conducted by employees—these are called internal audits—others utilize external or independent auditors to handle this task (some businesses rely on both types of audits in some combination).

External auditors are authorized by law to examine and publicly issue an opinion on the reliability of corporate financial reports. Dennis Applegate describes the history of the external audits in an article appearing in the magazine *Internal Auditor* as follows. "The U.S. Congress shaped the external auditing profession and created its primary audit objective with the passage of the Securities Act of 1933 and the Securities Exchange Act of 1934. This combined legislation requires independent financial audits of all firms whose capital stock is bought and sold in open markets. Its purpose, in part, is to ensure that the financial status and operating performance of publicly traded companies are fairly presented and disclosed." Firms not obliged by law to perform external audits often contract for such accounting services nonetheless. Smaller businesses, for example, that do not have the resources or inclination to maintain internal audit systems will often have external audits done on a regular basis as a sort of safeguard against errors or fraud.

The primary goal of external auditing is to determine the extent to which the organization adheres to managerial policies, procedures, and requirements. The independent or external auditor is not an employee of the organization. He or she performs an examination with the objective of issuing a report containing an opinion on a client's financial statements. The attest function of external auditing refers to the auditor's expression of an opinion on a company's financial statements. The typical independent audit leads to an attestation regarding the fairness and dependability of the statements. This is communicated to the officials of the audited entity in the form of a written report accompanying the statements (an oral presentation of findings may sometimes be requested as well). During the course of an audit study, the external auditor also becomes well-acquainted with the virtues and flaws of the client's accounting procedures. As a result, the auditor's final report to management often includes recommendations on methodologies of improving internal controls that are in place.

Major types of audits conducted by external auditors include the financial statements audit, the operational audit, and the compliance audit. A financial statement audit (or attest audit) examines financial statements, records, and related operations to ascertain adherence to generally accepted accounting principles. An operational audit examines an organization's activities in order to assess performances and develop recommendations for improvements, or further action. Auditors perform statutory audits which are performed to comply with the requirements of a governing body, such as a federal, state, or city government or agency. A compliance audit has as its objective the determination of whether an organization is following established procedures or rules.

The rules that must be followed by publicly traded companies changed in 2002 with the passage of the Sarbanes-Oxley Act. This act came about in the wake of the 2001 bankruptcy filing by Enron, and subsequent revelations about fraudulent accounting practices within the company. Enron was only the first in a string of high-profile bankruptcies. Serious allegations of accounting fraud followed and extended beyond the bankrupt firms to their accounting firms. The legislature acted quickly to fortify financial reporting requirements and stem the decline in confidence that resulted from the wave of bankruptcies.

The Sarbanes-Oxley Act is a wide-reaching and complex law that imposes heavy reporting requirements on all publicly traded companies. Meeting the requirements of this law has increased the workload of auditing firms. In particular, Section 404 of the Sarbanes-Oxley Act requires that a company's annual report include an official write-up by management about the effectiveness of the company's internal controls. The section also requires that outside auditors attest to management's report on internal controls. An external audit is required in order to attest to the management report.

INDEPENDENT AUDITING STANDARDS

The auditing process is based on standards, concepts, procedures, and reporting practices that are primarily imposed by the American Institute of Certified Public Accountants (AICPA). The auditing process relies on evidence, analysis, conventions, and informed professional judgment. General standards are brief statements relating to such matters as training, independence, and professional care. AICPA general standards declare that:

- External audits should be performed by a person or persons having adequate technical training and proficiency as an auditor.

- The auditor or auditors maintain complete independence in all matters relating to the assignment.

- The independent auditor or auditors should make sure that all aspects of the examination and the preparation of the audit report are carried out with a high standard of professionalism.

Standards of fieldwork provide basic planning standards to be followed during audits. The AICPA's standards for fieldwork stipulate that:

- The work is to be adequately planned and assistants, if any, are to be properly supervised.

- Independent auditors will carry out proper study and evaluation of the existing internal controls to determine their reliability and suitability for conducting all necessary auditing procedures.

- External auditors will make certain that they are able to review all relevant evidential materials, whether obtained through inspection, observation, inquiries, or confirmation, so that they can form an informed and reasonable opinion regarding the quality of the financial statements under examination.

Standards of reporting describe auditing standards relating to the audit report and its requirements. AICPA standards of reporting stipulate that the auditor indicate whether the financial statements examined were presented in accordance with generally accepted accounting principles; whether such principles were consistently observed in the current period in relation to the preceding period; and whether informative disclosures to the financial statements were adequate. Finally, the external auditor's report should include 1) an opinion about the financial statements/records that were examined, or 2) a disclaimer of opinion, which typically is included in instances where, for one reason or another, the auditor is unable to render an opinion on the state of the business's records.

THE EXTERNAL AUDITING PROCESS

The independent auditor generally proceeds with an audit according to a set process with three steps: planning, gathering evidence, and issuing a report.

In planning the audit, the auditor develops an audit program that identifies and schedules audit procedures that are to be performed to obtain the evidence. Audit evidence is proof obtained to support the audit's conclusions. Audit procedures include those activities undertaken by the auditor to obtain the evidence. Evidence-gathering procedures include observation, confirmation, calculations, analysis, inquiry, inspection, and comparison. An audit trail is a chronological record of economic events or transactions that have been experienced by an organization. The audit trail enables an auditor to evaluate the strengths and weaknesses of internal controls, system designs, and company policies and procedures.

The Audit Report The independent audit report sets forth the independent auditor's findings about the business's financial statements and their level of conformity with generally accepted accounting principles. A check is made to verify that representations over a period of years are consistent. A fair presentation of financial statements is generally understood by accountants to refer to whether the accounting principles used in the statements have general acceptability. This includes such things as 1) the accounting principles are appropriate in the circumstances; 2) the financial statements are prepared so they can be used, understood, and interpreted; 3) the information presented in the financial statements is classified and summarized in a reasonable manner; and 4) the financial statements reflect the underlying events and transactions in a way that presents an accurate portrait of financial operations and cash flows within reasonable and practical limits.

The auditor's unqualified report contains three paragraphs. The *introductory* paragraph identifies the financial statements audited, states that management is responsible for those statements, and asserts that the auditor is responsible for expressing an opinion on them. The *scope* paragraph describes what the auditor has done and specifically states that the auditor has examined the financial statements in accordance with generally accepted auditing standards and has performed appropriate tests. The *opinion* paragraph expresses the auditor's opinion (or formally announces his or her lack of opinion and why) on whether the statements are in accordance with generally accepted accounting principles.

Various audit opinions are defined by the AICPA's Auditing Standards Board as follows:

- Unqualified opinion—This opinion means that all materials were made available, found to be in order, and met all auditing requirements. This is the most favorable opinion that can be rendered by an external auditor about a company's operations and records.

- Explanatory language added—Circumstances may require that the auditor add an explanatory paragraph (or other explanatory language) to his or her report. When this is done the opinion is prefaced with the term, explanatory language added.

- Qualified opinion—This type of opinion is used for instances in which most of the company's financial materials were in order, with the exception of a certain account or transaction.

- Adverse opinion—An adverse opinion states that the financial statements do not accurately or completely represent the company's financial position, results of operations, or cash flows in conformity with generally accepted accounting principles. Such an opinion is obviously not good news for the business being audited.

- Disclaimer of opinion—A disclaimer of opinion states that the auditor does not express an opinion on the financial statements, generally because he or she feels that the company did not present sufficient information. Again, this opinion casts an unfavorable light on the business being audited.

The fair presentation of financial statements does not mean that the statements are fraud-proof. The independent auditor has the responsibility to search for errors or irregularities within the recognized limitations of the auditing process. Investors should examine the auditor's report for citations of problems such as debt-agreement violations or unresolved lawsuits. "Going-concern" references can suggest that the company may not be able to survive as a functioning operation. If an "except for" statement appears in the report, the investor should understand that there are certain problems or departures from generally accepted accounting principles in the statements, and that these problems may call into question whether the statements fairly depict the company's financial situation. These statements typically require the company to resolve the problem or somehow make the accounting treatment acceptable.

DETECTING FRAUD

Detection of potentially fraudulent financial record keeping and reporting is one of the central charges of the external auditor. According to *Fraudulent Financial Reporting, 1987-1997,* a study published by the Committee of Sponsoring Organizations of the Treadway Commission, most companies charged with financial fraud by the Securities and Exchange Commission (SEC) posted far less than $100 million in assets and revenues in the year preceding the fraud. Not surprisingly, fraud cropped up most often in companies in the grips of financial stress, and it was perpetrated most often by top-level executives or managers. According to the study, more than 50 percent of fraudulent acts uncovered by the SEC involved overstatements of revenue by recording revenues prematurely or fictitiously.

As the study's authors, Mark Beasley, Joseph Carcello, and Dana Hermanson, noted in *Strategic Finance,* fraudulent techniques in this area included false sales, recording revenues before all terms were satisfied, recording conditional sales, improper cutoffs of transactions at period end, improper use of percentage of completion, unauthorized shipments, and recording of consignment sales as completed sales. In addition, many firms overstated asset values such as inventory, accounts receivable, property, equipment, investments, and patent accounts. Other types of fraud detailed in the study included misappropriation of assets (12 percent of charged companies) and understatement of liabilities and expenses (18 percent).

Accidental misstatements are almost always detected in audits. But these errors should not be confused with fraudulent activity. Errors can occur at any time, in any place with unpredictable financial statement effects. Fraud, on the other hand, is intentional and is often more difficult to detect than are errors. Part of the job of an external auditor is to recognize when conditions indicate potentially higher risks of employee or management fraud and then increase the scrutiny of all records accordingly.

WORKING WITH EXTERNAL AUDITORS

Experts urge business owners to establish proactive working relationships with external auditors. In order to accomplish this, companies should make sure that they:

- Select an auditing firm with expertise in their industry and a proven track record.

- Establish and maintain efficient record keeping systems to ease the task of the auditor.

- Make sure that owners, executives, and managers know the basics of financial reporting requirements.

- Establish effective lines of communication and work processes between external auditors and internal auditors (if any).

- Recognize the value that external auditors can have as objective reviewers of existing and proposed operational processes.

- Focus on high-risk areas of operations, such as inventory levels.

- Focus on periods of change and expansion, such as transitions to public ownership or expansion into new markets.

- Build an effective audit committee that can provide cogent financial and operational analysis based on audit results.

ACCOUNTING FIRMS AND CONSULTING SERVICES

The 1980s and 90s saw an increase in the types of service offered by accounting firms. The situation became so prevalent that, according to an article on the subject in *Internal Auditor,* 307 of the Standard & Poor's 500 companies paid their audit firms, on average, almost three times as much in fees for non-auditing services as for auditing itself. Many analysts believe that it was the resulting conflict of interest that was at least partially responsible for the rash of bankruptcies of large corpo-

rations which occurred in the early 2000s. How important accounting firm collaboration was in the accounting fraud of the early 2000s has yet to be fully determined. However, passage of the Sarbanes-Oxley Act in 2002 put into place increased restrictions on the consulting services that an accounting firm can offer the clients for which it performs audits.

SEE ALSO *Audits, Internal; Accounting Methods*

BIBLIOGRAPHY

Beasley, Mark S., Joseph V. Carcello, and Dana R. Hermanson. "Just Say No." *Strategic Finance.* May 1999.

Hake, Eric R. "Financial Illusion: Accounting for Profits in an Enron World." *Journal of Economic Issues.* September 2005.

Pearlman, Laura. "They Can Have the Leftovers." *Corporate Counsel.* July 2001.

Pilla, Daniel J. *The IRS Problem Solver.* HarperCollins, 2004.

Reed, A. "Companies Pay More for Nonaudit Services." *Internal Auditor.* June 2001.

Reinstein, Alan, and Gregory A. Coursen. "Considering the Risk of Fraud: Understanding the Auditor's New Requirements." *National Public Accountant.* March-April 1999.

Yee, Ho Siew, "Accounting Fraud Cases Up Globally." *Business Times.* 14 December 2005.

Hillstrom, Northern Lights
updated by Magee, ECDI

AUDITS, INTERNAL

Internal auditing is an independent appraisal function that is performed in a wide variety of companies, institutions, and governments. What distinguishes internal auditors from governmental auditors and public accountants is the fact that they are employees of the same organizations they audit. Their allegiance is to their organization, not to an external authority. Because internal auditing has evolved only within the last few decades, the roles and responsibilities of internal auditors vary greatly from one organization to another. Internal audit functions have been structured based on the differing perceptions and objectives of owners, directors, and managers. Since the passage in 2002 of the Public Company Accounting Reform and Investor Protection Act, commonly called the Sarbanes-Oxley Act, the function of the auditor has been highlighted in compliance with the new regulations. In publicly held corporations, the internal auditing function has been greatly expanded as a part of fulfilling the requirements of Sarbanes-Oxley.

The structure given to the internal auditing function within a company depends to a great extent on four things: 1) the size of the company; 2) the type of business it carries out; 3) the philosophy of the management group, and 4) the level of interest or concern placed on auditing by the chief executive and the board of directors. In a very small business, the owner-manager will usually perform the role of internal auditor by continuously monitoring all of the business's activities. In larger companies, employees who fulfill internal auditing functions are known by a wide variety of titles—control analysts, systems analysts, business analysts, internal consultants, evaluators, and operations analysts.

The Institute of Internal Auditors (IIA) is an international governing body for internal auditors that brings some uniformity and consistency to the practice. The IIA provides general standards for performing internal audits and serves as a source for education and information. In its *Standards for the Professional Practice of Internal Auditing,* the IIA defines the internal auditing function as "an independent appraisal function established within an organization to examine and evaluate its activities as a service to the organization. The objective of internal auditing is to assist members of the organization in the effective discharge of their responsibilities. To this end, internal auditing furnishes them analysis, appraisals, recommendations, counsel, and information concerning activities reviewed."

There is theoretically no restriction on what internal auditors can review and report about within an organization. In practice, internal auditors work within the parameters of the company's overall strategic plan, performing internal auditing functions so that they are coordinated with the larger goals and objectives of the organization. Internal auditors perform a variety of audits, including compliance audits, operational audits, program audits, financial audits, and information systems audits. Internal audit reports provide management with advice and information for making decisions or improving operations. When problems are discovered, the internal auditor serves the organization by finding ways to prevent them from recurring. Internal audits can also be used in a preventative fashion. For example, if the internal auditor communicates potential problems and risks in business operations during his/her review, management can take preemptive action to prevent the potential problem from developing.

DEVELOPMENT AND CURRENT STATUS OF INTERNAL AUDITING PRACTICES

Prior to the twentieth century, companies and other institutions relied on external auditing practices for financial and other information on their operations. The growing complexity of American companies after World War I, however, required better techniques for planning, directing, and evaluating business activities. These needs, coupled with the stock market crash of 1929 and increased evidence of questionable accounting practices by corporations, led to the creation of the Securities and Exchange Act of 1934. This legislation established the Securities and Exchange Commission (SEC) as a monitor of corporate financial reporting. In the wake of these developments, the new thrust for internal auditing was to verify financial statements, as well as to continue testing transactions. World War II led internal auditors into the assurance of compliance with government regulations. The boom that followed, with the growth of conglomerates and international subsidiaries, imposed further responsibility upon the auditors requiring them to review the adequacy of corporate procedures and practices in operational evaluations, as well as performing the financial audit.

The importance of quality internal auditing was further underlined with the passage of the Foreign Corrupt Practices Act and the establishment of the Financial Accounting Standards Board. While these developments did not specifically call for an internal auditing function, internal auditors were poised to help management fulfill the additional requirements implicit therein. In the 1980s, highly publicized business failures and fraudulent financial statements that went undetected by external auditing firms gave further merit to the concept of internal auditing.

In December of 2001, the Enron Corporation, which had ranked as the seventh largest U.S. corporation in terms of revenue just one year earlier, filed for bankruptcy protection. A string of similar high-profile bankruptcies of very large corporations followed. Serious allegations of accounting fraud were made and extended well beyond the bankrupt corporations to include some of the nation's largest and most reputable accounting firms. Confidence was shaken, the country was still reeling in the aftermath of the terrorist attacks of 9/11, and the stock market was dropping. The SEC acted by proposing regulations requiring enhanced certification of the financial statements of all publicly traded companies by their CEOs and CFOs. The U.S. Congress was quick to follow suit and passed the Sarbanes-Oxley Act, which was signed by President George W. Bush in July of 2002.

The Sarbanes-Oxley Act is a wide-reaching and complex law that imposes heavy reporting requirements on all publicly traded companies. Meeting the requirements of this law has increased the workload of auditing firms and increased the need for internal audits and controls in publicly held companies. In particular, Section 404 of the Sarbanes-Oxley Act requires that a company's annual report include an official write-up by management about the effectiveness of the company's internal controls. The section also requires that outside auditors attest to management's report on internal controls.

Private companies are not covered by the Sarbanes-Oxley Act. However, analysts suggest that even private firms should be aware of the law and how it may impact them under specific circumstances. For example, if a private company anticipates being acquired by a public company, it will need to comply with Sarbanes-Oxley's requirements on internal controls for several quarters before the acquisition date in order to reassure the acquiring company's CEO and CFO that they may certify the consolidated financials. In general, Sarbanes-Oxley has raised the bar in terms of expectations regarding internal controls and corporate governance.

INTERNAL AUDITING AND INTERNAL CONTROL

The manner in which internal auditing has evolved has linked it directly to the concepts and objectives of internal control. The IIA clearly advocates an internal control focus when it defines the scope of internal auditing: "The scope of internal auditing should encompass the examination and evaluation of the adequacy and effectiveness of the organization's system of internal control and the quality of performance in carrying out assigned responsibilities." At the most basic level, internal controls can be identified as individual preventive, detective, corrective, or directive actions that keep operations functioning as intended. These basic controls are aggregated to create whole networks and systems of control procedures which are known as the organization's overall system of internal control.

The IIA's *Standards of Professional Practice* outlines five key objectives for an organization's system of internal control: 1) reliability and integrity of information; 2) compliance with policies, plans, procedures, laws and regulations; 3) safeguarding of assets; 4) economical and efficient use of resources; and 5) accomplishment of established objectives and goals for operations or programs. It is these five internal control objectives that provide the internal auditing function with its conceptual foundation and focus for evaluating an organization's diverse operations and programs.

KEY ASSUMPTIONS ABOUT THE INTERNAL AUDIT FUNCTION

There are three important assumptions implicit in the definition, objectives, and scope of internal auditing: Independence, competence, and confidentiality.

Independence Internal auditors have to be independent from the activities they audit so that they can evaluate them objectively. Internal auditing is an advisory func-

tion, not an operational one. Therefore, internal auditors should not be given responsibility or authority over any activities they audit. They should not be positioned in the organization where they would be subject to political or monetary pressures that could inhibit their audit process, sway their opinions, or compromise their recommendations. Independence and objectivity of internal auditors must exist in both appearance and in fact; otherwise the credibility of the internal auditing work product is jeopardized.

Related to independence is the assumption that internal auditors have unrestricted access to whatever they might need to complete an appraisal. That includes unrestricted access to plans, forecasts, people, data, products, facilities, and records necessary to perform their independent evaluations.

Competence A business's internal auditors have to be people who possess the necessary education, experience, and proficiency to complete their work competently, in accordance with accepted internal auditing standards. An understanding of good business practices is essential for internal auditors. They must have the capability to apply broad knowledge to new situations, to recognize and evaluate the impact of actual or potential problems, and to perform adequate research as a basis for judgments. They must also be skilled communicators and be able to deal with people at various levels throughout the organization.

Confidentiality Evaluations and conclusions contained in internal auditing reports are directed internally to management and the board, not to stockholders, regulators, or the public. Presumably, management and the board can resolve issues that have surfaced through internal auditing and implement solutions privately, before problems get out of hand. Management is expected to acknowledge facts as stated in reports, but has no obligation to agree with an internal auditor's evaluations, conclusions, or recommendations. After internal auditors report their conclusions, management and the board have responsibility for subsequent operating decisions—to act or not to act. If action is taken, management has the responsibility to ensure that satisfactory progress is made and internal auditors later can determine whether the actions taken have the desired results. If no action is taken, internal auditors have the responsibility to determine that management and the board understand and have assumed any risks of inaction. Under all circumstances, internal auditors have the direct responsibility to apprise management and the board of any significant developments that the auditors believe warrant ownership/management consideration or action.

It should be noted, however, that the "confidential" aspect of the internal audit function is not absolute. According to the Securities and Exchange Commission (SEC), internal audit reports must be made available for review in case of regulatory inquiries. Business owners dislike this state of affairs because of an understandable reluctance to divulge sensitive business information. But the SEC cites Section 21 of the Securities and Exchange Act, which grants the agency the power to subpoena financial records as part of investigations. The United States' major stock exchanges, NASDAQ and the New York Stock Exchange (NYSE), have adopted similar positions regarding their own inquiries into alleged misdeeds, seeing internal audits as key indicators of supervision, policies, and controls within the firm in question. These exchanges generally regard failure to produce internal audit reports or other records when demanded as violations of their basic tenets.

Under some circumstances, however, experts contend that a firm may be able to claim a legal foundation for withholding particular internal audit reports. According to *Compliance Reporter,* "If a specific report has been prepared under the supervision of legal counsel and for the purpose of providing legal advice to the firm and not for more routine business purposes, or the report has been specifically prepared at the direction of attorneys in anticipation of threatened litigation, then the report may be protected by either the attorney-client privilege or the attorney work product doctrine."

DIFFERENCES BETWEEN INTERNAL AND EXTERNAL AUDITING

Internal auditors and external auditors both audit, but have different objectives and a different focus. Internal auditors generally consider operations as a whole with respect to the five key internal control objectives, not just the financial aspects. External auditors focus primarily on financial control systems that have a direct, significant effect on the figures reported in financial statements. Internal auditors are generally concerned with even small incidents of fraud, waste, and abuse as symptoms of underlying operational issues. But the external auditor may not be concerned if the incidents do not materially affect the financial statements—which is reasonable given the fact that external auditors are engaged to form an opinion only of the organization's financial statements. The external auditor does perform services for management, including making recommendations for improvement in systems and controls. By and large, however, these are financially oriented, and often are not based on the same level of understanding of an organization's systems, people, and objectives that an internal auditor would have. It should be recognized, however, that the traditionally limited role of the external auditor has broadened in recent years to include an increased operational review facet.

This comparison of internal auditing to external auditing considers only the external auditors' traditional role of attesting to financial statements. During the 1990s a number of the large public accounting firms began establishing divisions offering "internal auditing" services in addition to existing tax, actuarial, external auditing, and management consulting services. Predictably, the event has caused a flurry of debate among auditors about independence, objectivity, depth of organizational knowledge, operational effectiveness, and true costs to the organization.

One option available to small business enterprises is to investigate the possibility of "co-sourcing" its internal audit functions with an outside vendor. "Co-sourcing arrangements with outside vendors allow the in-house auditors to retain responsibility for the internal audit process while relying on the outside entity for specialized technical skills and personnel," wrote C. William Thomas and John T. Parish in *Journal of Accountancy.* "By contract, a company that outsources loses day-to-day control over its activities to the vendor—usually a professional service firm."

As Thomas and Parish note, the relative autonomy of the internal audit function makes it an ideal candidate for co-sourcing. Under such an arrangement, the outside vendor can attend to specialized elements of the internal audit function, such as "reconciliation of specialized accounts; valuation, disclosure and Environmental Protection Agency compliance issues for certain types of inventory; and reconciliation of foreign accounts where business customs pose review problems." In return, the company saves expenses on permanent staff, gains greater in-house flexibility in evaluating projects and practices, and garners the ability to maximize its access to specialized knowledge by selecting vendors for each functional area.

There are potential drawbacks to the co-sourcing arrangement, however. Thomas and Parish cite staff worries over long-term job security, the possibility of "turf battles" between in-house auditors and vendors, and loss of in-house focus on "big picture" issues of company-wide profitability and efficiency as stumbling blocks. But they charge that "a cost-conscious, proactive internal audit group with custom-designed co-sourcing programs retains the advantages of outsourcing along with the benefits of having an in-house internal audit staff, such as knowledge of management methods, accessibility, responsiveness, loyalty, and a shared vision for the organization's strategic business goals."

TYPES OF INTERNAL AUDITS

Various types of audits are used to achieve particular objectives. The types of audits briefly described below illustrate a few approaches internal auditing may take.

Operational Audit An operational audit is a systematic review and evaluation of an organizational unit to determine whether it is functioning effectively and efficiently, whether it is accomplishing established objectives and goals, and whether it is using all of its resources appropriately. Resources in this context include funds, personnel, property, equipment, materials, information, space, and whatever else may be used by that unit. Operational audits can include evaluations of the work flow and propriety of performance measurements. These audits are tailored to fit the nature of the operations being reviewed. "Carefully done, operational auditing is a cost-effective way of getting a higher return from the audit function by making it helpful to operating management," wrote Hubert D.Vos in *What Every Manager Needs to Know About Finance.*

System Audit A system analysis and internal control review is an analysis of systems and procedures for an entire function such as information services or purchasing.

Ethical Practices Audit An ethical business practices audit assesses the extent to which a company and its employees follow established codes of conduct, policies, and standards of ethical practices. Policies that may fall within the scope of such an audit include adherence to specified guidelines in such areas as procurement, conflicts of interest, gifts and gratuities, entertainment, political lobbying, ownership of patents and licenses, use of organization name, speaking engagements, fair trade practices, and environmentally sensitive practices.

Compliance Audit A compliance audit determines whether the organizational unit or function is following particular rules or directives. Such rules or directives can originate internally or externally and can include one or more of the following: organizational policies; performance plans; established procedures; required authorizations; applicable external regulations; relevant contractual provisions; and federal, state, and local laws.

Financial Audit A financial audit is an examination of the financial planning and reporting process, the conduct of financial operations, the reliability and integrity of financial records, and the preparation of financial statements. Such a review includes an appraisal of the system of internal controls related to financial functions.

Information Systems Audit A systems development and life cycle review is a unique type of information systems audit conducted in partnership with operating personnel who are designing and installing new information systems. The objective is to appraise the new system from an internal control perspective and independently test the system at various stages throughout its design, development, and implementation. This approach intends to identify and correct internal control problems before systems are actually put in place because modifications made during the developmental stages are less costly. Sometimes problems can be avoided altogether. There is risk in this approach that the internal auditor could lose objectivity and independence with considerable participation in the design and installation process.

Program Audit A program audit evaluates whether the stated goals or objectives of a certain program or project have been achieved. It may include an appraisal of whether an alternative approach can achieve the desired results at a lower cost. These types of audits are also called performance audits, project audits, or management audits.

Fraud Audit A fraud audit investigates whether the organization has suffered a loss through misappropriation of assets, manipulation of data, omission of information, or any illegal or irregular acts. It assumes that intentional deception has occurred.

INTERNAL AUDIT PLANNING

Business consultants strongly encourage small business owners to establish self-auditing practices. "Not many years ago a company measured its success by how much of its product it was able to sell," stated Jeffrey Davidson and Charles Dean in *Cash Traps: Small Business Secrets for Reducing Costs and Improving Cash Flow.* "Today success is heavily influenced by the ability to keep costs under control and, of course, to maintain a healthy cash flow. Volatile interest rates, shrinking profit margins, and increasing operational costs are causing many businesses to reassess and upgrade their internal control procedures."

For a small business owner, knowing what areas to audit and where to commit resources is an integral part of the internal audit function. A long-range audit plan provides a complete view of audit strategy and coverage in relation to the relative significance of functions to be audited. The goal is to plan an audit strategy that is cost-effective and emphasizes audit projects that have high impact or address areas of significant risk. An in-depth understanding of the organization and how it operates is a prerequisite for the audit planning process. Developing the plan first requires identifying and listing all auditable units or functions. (This is frequently called the "audit universe.") Next, a rational system must be devised to assign significance and risk to each auditable unit or function. Based on perceived significance and estimated risk, the audit priorities and strategies are documented in the audit plan.

Business owners and managers, however, should recognize that the internal audit process is not a static one. Its character and emphasis should adapt to the changes that take place in the organization over time. Departure of key people, changes in markets, new demographics, new competitors, and other factors can dramatically affect the operations of small businesses and other organizations. Organizational processes and existing internal control systems may become obsolete with new technology. Legal and regulatory environments change with the political winds. Consequently, risks and significance rankings, the audit universe, and audit strategies will change. The successful small business owner, though, will learn to anticipate such changes, and adjust his or her internal auditing strategies accordingly.

SEE ALSO *Accounting Methods*

BIBLIOGRAPHY

Braiotta, Louis, Richard Hickok, and Main Hurdman *The Audit Committee Handbook.* 4th edition, John Wiley & Sons, 2004.

"Customer Documentation, Internal Audits." *Compliance Reporter.* 9 October 2000.

Hake, Eric R. "Financial Illusion: Accounting for Profits in an Enron World." *Journal of Economic Issues.* September 2005.

Moeller, Robert, and Herbert Witt. *Brink's Modern Internal Auditing.* 6th edition, John Wiley & Sons, 2005.

Pickett, K. H. Spencer. *The Internal Audit Handbook.* John Wiley & Sons, 2003.

Thomas, C. William, and John T. Parish. "Co-Sourcing: What's In It for Me?" *Journal of Accountancy.* May 1999.

Hillstrom, Northern Lights
updated by Magee, ECDI

AUTOMATED GUIDED VEHICLE (AGV)

The term "automated guided vehicle" (AGV) is a general one that encompasses all transport systems capable of functioning without driver operation. The term "driverless" is often used in the context of automated guided vehicles to describe industrial trucks, used primarily in manufacturing and distribution settings, that would conventionally have been driver-operated.

Since their introduction in 1955, automated guided vehicles have found widespread industrial applications. AGVs are now found in all types of industries, with the only restrictions on their use mainly resulting from the dimensions of the goods to be transported or spatial considerations. Many applications of AGVs are technically feasible, but the purchase and implementation of such systems is usually based on economic considerations.

The uses of AGVs can be divided into four main areas of application: 1) supply and disposal at storage and production areas, 2) production-integrated application of AGV trucks as assembly platforms, 3) retrieval, especially in wholesale trade, and 4) supply and disposal in special areas, such as hospitals and offices. In all of these settings, AGVs have been found to reduce the damage to inventory, make production scheduling more flexible, and reduce staffing needs. But, as with any other major capital decision, implementation of these systems must be undertaken cautiously.

AGVs AS PART OF A FLEXIBLE MANUFACTURING SYSTEM

AGV usage is growing. One reason is that as manufacturers strive to become more competitive, they are adopting flexible manufacturing systems (FMS). These systems integrate automated material handling systems, robots, numerically controlled machine tools, and automated inspection stations. Flexible manufacturing systems offer a high capital utilization and reduced direct labor costs. They also reduce work-in-process inventories and make it possible to work with shorter lead times. Because the systems are flexible, they are more responsive to changes in production requirements. These systems offer high product quality and increased productivity.

Flexible manufacturing systems can benefit from the linkage with AGVs. While robots are often highlighted as saving billions in production costs, at some plants—including steel and other metals plants—automated material-handling systems have made the biggest inroads. Today, there are hundreds of instances of computer-controlled systems designed to handle and transport materials, many of which have replaced conventional human-driven platform trucks. Although only a single component of a flexible manufacturing system, automated material handling systems have advantages of their own. These include a reduction in damage to in-process materials, simplified inventory tracking and production scheduling, increased safety, and the need for fewer personnel than in conventional systems.

ECONOMIC VIABILITY OF AGVs

United States Steel-Posco, I/N Tek and I/N Kote, Allegheny Ludlum, Logan Aluminum, Alcoa, and Kennecott Copper all use automated guided vehicles to move steel, aluminum, and copper coils within their mills. Although the choice of a transport system is often viewed as a technical issue, like every capital decision it demands a comparative economic study. When selecting an investment calculation procedure one should bear in mind that transport systems provide assistance only in achieving the actual production performance of the organization (i.e., the application of a transport system has no actual market value).

Writing in *Industrial Management Principles of Automated Data Processing*, B. Hartmann suggests following a simple investment formula to compare the costs of AGV systems, which is the cash value of savings from the AGV divided by the cash value of extra costs (compared to the old system) plus the difference in initial outlay (which sets the cash value difference of the extra costs and the cash value difference of the initial outlay against the savings). Obviously, the larger the comparison factor, the more favorable the investment. In performing this calculation, a business must consider both the fixed and variable costs. Fixed costs are incurred independently of the degree of loading, while variable costs depend on the degree of loading the AGVs.

PLANNING FOR AGV IMPLEMENTATION

It is difficult to improve the material flow in existing organizations, since in most cases there are relatively few opportunities to reorganize existing installations or to recover the costs involved. Once the decision to restructure material flow using AGVs has been made, however, certain criteria need to be examined to achieve the full advantages of an automated, yet flexible system.

The first criterion is the physical material flow. By examining the type of goods transported (or load units), the order of transport operations, the quantity framework of the material flow, and the distances of connections within the network, the organization can begin to outline the type of transportation best suited for its material handling requirements. Once the type of transportation is identified, the space and floor conditions need to be addressed. The width of the transport lanes or gangways, any gradients that have to be negotiated, and the type of floor installation required for specific types of trucks all need to be considered carefully. Finally, the choice of AGV can be made. Again, close consideration must be given to transport function, the material flow densities, and the overall process organization.

Computer simulations are often used in planning complex transportation systems. Facilities may require pathways, wire-guidance systems, automatic cranes, and additional computer software and hardware to run the entire AGV system. Some AGV systems even use laser

scanners as guidance systems. AGV systems can reduce manual handling damage, and the vehicles are always available, alleviating problems associated with scheduling employees on nights, weekends, and holidays.

UNUSUAL APPLICATIONS

Two unique applications of a very customized AGV system are the two Mars rovers, Spirit and Opportunity. These are automated guided vehicles that are operated on Mars and are directed via radio transmitted instructions from Earth by a team at the National Aeronautics and Space Administration (NASA). They have spent nearly two years (originally landing in January 2003) on Mars, traveling several miles and frequently stopping to collect materials and do scientific analysis. Their mission is a big success for NASA and represents one of the more unusual applications of AGV to date.

SEE ALSO *Robotics; Automation*

BIBLIOGRAPHY
"Automated Guided Vehicle Suites Pallitizing Application." *Product News Network.* 7 October 2005.

Hartmann, B. *Industrial Management Principles of Automated Data Processing.* Verlag, 1961.

"Portal Aids in AGV System Design." *Transportation & Distribution.* November 2002.

Hillstrom, Northern Lights
updated by Magee, ECDI

AUTOMATED STORAGE AND RETRIEVAL SYSTEMS (AS/RS)

Automated storage and retrieval systems (AS/RS) are inventory management systems that are widely used in manufacturing facilities, distribution centers, and warehouses throughout the United States and the world. AS/RS systems generally consist of machines that move up and down one or multiple parallel storage aisles, storing and retrieving products and materials for dissemination to internal and external destinations alike.

The advantages of these systems are numerous. They provide users with increased inventory control and tracking, including greater flexibility to accommodate changing business conditions. These AS/RS systems are comprised of modular subsystems that can be easily replaced to minimize downtime and extend the service life of the overall system. They also reduce labor costs, lowering necessary workforce requirements, increasing workplace safety, and removing personnel from difficult working conditions (such as cold food storage environments). Perhaps most significantly, however, AS/RS systems can produce major savings in inventory storage costs, as vastly improved warehouse space utilization—both vertically and horizontally—creates greater storage density.

CONDITIONS THAT ARE FAVORABLE TO AS/RS

The facilities in which AS/RS are used vary greatly but Howard Zollinger discusses some of the more favorable operational conditions and environments into which these systems have been successfully installed in an article that appeared in *Material Handling Management.* The environments in which AS/RS can offer the greatest benefit are cold storage, frozen foods, and those in which very strict item tracking is necessary. In terms of the conditions into which an AS/RS installation may be most successfully installed, Zollinger lists the following ten conditions:

- Two or three shifts
- Critical inventory levels
- Production flexibility is essential
- Joint storage of parts and tools
- High land cost areas
- No limit on building height
- Skilled technicians are on-staff or available
- High value parts or assemblies are used
- The number of stock keeping units (SKUs) in not large
- Tight existing site space in which an AS/RS installation may eliminate the need to move

Every situation is different but these guidelines provide an overview of the sorts of applications that are best suited to AS/RS.

INSTALLATION CONCERNS

Automated storage and retrieval systems do require a considerable up-front investment to install and an ongoing financial commitment to maintain. "Maintaining highly integrated systems requires training and experience and is not without occasional frustrations," noted Michael Wigington in *Plant Engineering.* "Even the most experienced AS/RS user struggles to support the changing requirements of maintaining aging technology and tired mechanization." The cost of purchasing and implementing an effective automated storage/retrieval system is significant as well, encompassing everything from pre-purchase analysis of supply chain and inventory management needs to the actual purchase price of AS/RS equipment and software. In addition, experts in the use and maintenance of AS/RS systems note that companies often experience significant ongoing costs for maintenance and updating of various subsystems.

These capital expenses can tempt some business owners to cut financial corners, buying "bargain" systems that are ill-equipped for extensive, long-term use. In many cases, such decisions can end up costing far more in the long run. "A long and reliable service life [for an AS/RS system] begins with procurement, not maintenance," wrote Wigington. "Light-duty storage systems are particularly vulnerable by failing to deliver well-engineered equipment and software. These systems require a high level of upkeep and experience a sticky, entangled web of mechanical, electrical, and software problems." When such disruptions occur, the impact can be devastating to small and mid-sized businesses. The toll of interrupted AS/RS service extends from the measurable (lost production and shipping revenue, increased labor costs for repair) to the intangible (diminished workforce confidence in the company's operations, downgraded client confidence). As a result, businesses are urged to examine the long-term implications of their choices when they incorporate an automated storage and retrieval system into their operations.

SEE ALSO *Inventory Control Systems*

BIBLIOGRAPHY
Feare, Tom. "Staging/Storing: Up, Down, and All Around." *Modern Materials Handling.* February 2001.

Muller, Max. *Essentials of Inventory Management.* AMACOM a Division of American Management Association. 2002

Poirier, Charles C. *Advanced Supply Chain Management.* Berrett-Koehler, 1999.

"State of the Art in Automated Warehousing." *Dairy Foods.* March 1999.

Van Denberg, Jeroen, and A. Gademann. "Optimal Routing in an Automated Storage/Retrieval System with Dedicated Storage." *IIE Transactions.* May 1999.

Wild, Tony. *Best Practice in Inventory Management.* Wiley, 1998.

Zollinger, Howard. "How to Shop for AS/RS and VNA Systems." *Material Handling Management.* October 2001.

Hillstrom, Northern Lights
updated by Magee, ECDI

AUTOMATION

Automation is the art of making processes or machines self-acting or self-moving. Automation also means the technique of making a device, machine, process, or procedure more fully automatic. Automated machinery may range from simple sensing devices to autonomous robots and other sophisticated equipment. Automation of operations may encompass the automation of a single operation or the automation of an entire facility.

There are many different reasons to automate. Increased productivity is normally the major reason for many companies desiring a competitive advantage. Automation also offers low operational variability. Variability is directly related to quality and productivity. Other reasons to automate include the presence of a hazardous working environment and the high cost of human labor. Some businesses automate processes in order to reduce production time, increase manufacturing flexibility, reduce costs, eliminate human error, or make up for a labor shortage. Decisions associated with automation are usually concerned with some or all of these economic and social considerations.

For small business owners, weighing the pros and cons of automation can be a daunting task. The speed with which technology is advancing combined with a natural resistance to change makes it easy for a business owner to put off changes in the hope that by waiting he or she will be able to acquire more powerful automation equipment for less in the near future. But consultants contend that it is important not to put off implementation of new and more efficient technologies.

TYPES OF AUTOMATION

Although automation can play a major role in increasing productivity and reducing costs in service industries—as in the example of a retail store that installs bar code scanners in its checkout lanes—automation is most prevalent in manufacturing industries. In recent years, the manufacturing field has witnessed the development of major automation alternatives. Some of these types of automation include:

- Information technology (IT)
- Computer-aided manufacturing (CAM)
- Numerically controlled (NC) equipment
- Robots
- Flexible manufacturing systems (FMS)
- Computer integrated manufacturing (CIM)

Information technology (IT) encompasses a broad spectrum of computer technologies used to create, store, retrieve, and disseminate information. It is in the area of information technology where most of the more flexible and non-industry-specific advances are now being made.

Computer-aided manufacturing (CAM) refers to the use of computers in the different functions of production

planning and control. CAM includes the use of numerically controlled machines, robots, and other automated systems in the manufacturing process. Computer-aided manufacturing also includes computer-aided process planning (CAPP), group technology (GT), production scheduling, and manufacturing flow analysis. Computer-aided process planning (CAPP) means the use of computers to generate process plans for the manufacture of different products. Group technology (GT) is a manufacturing philosophy that aims at grouping different products and creating different manufacturing cells for the manufacture of each group.

Numerically controlled (NC) machines are programmed versions of machine tools that execute operations in sequence on parts or products. Individual machines may have their own computers for that purpose; such tools are commonly referred to as computerized numerically controlled (CNC) machines. In other cases, many machines may share the same computer; these are called direct numerically controlled machines.

Robots are a type of automated equipment that may execute different tasks that are normally handled by a human operator. In manufacturing, robots are used to handle a wide range of tasks, including assembly, welding, painting, loading and unloading of heavy or hazardous materials, inspection and testing, and finishing operations.

Flexible manufacturing systems (FMS) are comprehensive systems that may include numerically controlled machine tools, robots, and automated material handling systems in the manufacture of similar products or components using different routings among the machines.

A computer-integrated manufacturing (CIM) system is one in which many manufacturing functions are linked through an integrated computer network. These manufacturing or manufacturing-related functions include production planning and control, shop floor control, quality control, computer-aided manufacturing, computer-aided design, purchasing, marketing, and other functions. The objective of a computer-integrated manufacturing system is to allow changes in product design, to reduce costs, and to optimize production requirements.

AUTOMATION AND THE SMALL BUSINESS OWNER

Understanding and making use of automation-oriented strategic alternatives is essential for manufacturing firms of all shapes and sizes. It is particularly important for smaller companies, which, due to their inherent advantage of being more flexible, are able to implement changes somewhat more quickly and thus gain competitive advantage more quickly. But experts note that whatever your company's size, automation of production processes is no longer sufficient in many industries.

The computer has made it possible to control manufacturing more precisely and to assemble more quickly. Today, with the aid of the computer, companies must move to the next logical step in automation—the automatic analysis of data into information that is useful to employees in implementing on-the-fly changes to production processes. Opportunities now lie primarily in the automation of information and not in automation of labor. The work that is being done now in advanced manufacturing is work to manage and control the process.

Small business owners face challenges in several distinct areas as they prepare their enterprises for the technology-oriented environment in which the vast majority of them will operate. Three primary issues are employee training, management philosophy, and financial issues.

Employee Training Many business owners and managers operate under the assumption that acquisition of fancy automated production equipment or data processing systems will instantaneously bring about measurable improvements in company performance. But as countless consultants and industry experts have noted, even if these systems eliminate work previously done by employees, they ultimately function in accordance with the instructions and guidance of other employees. Therefore, if those latter workers receive inadequate training in system operation, the business will not realize the full benefits of new system put into place.

An essential key to automation success for small business owners is the establishment of a thorough education program for employees. It is also useful to set up a framework through which workers can provide input on the positive and negative aspects of new automation technology. The application of automation technology is growing but it is the human factor that remains essential in assuring the effective installation and use of these new technologies.

Management Philosophy Many productive business automation systems, whether in the realm of manufacturing or data processing, call for a high degree of decision-making responsibility on the part of those who operate the systems. As both processes and equipment become more automatically controlled, the need for human management of these automated systems does not diminish. These new technologies—enabler tools, if you will—are changing the employee's job from one of physically laboring to one of monitoring and supervising an entire process.

But many organizations are reluctant to empower employees to this degree, either because of legitimate concerns about worker capabilities or a simple inability to relinquish power. In the former instance, training and/or workforce additions may be necessary; in the latter, management needs to recognize that such practices ultimately hinder the effectiveness of the company. Part of implementing automating systems includes the reworking of the entire process, including the roles and tasks held by all members of an organization.

Financial Issues It is essential for small businesses to anticipate and plan for the various ways in which new automation systems can impact on bottom-line financial figures. Factors that need to be weighed include tax laws, long-term budgeting, and current financial health.

Depreciation tax laws for software and hardware are complex, which leads many consultants to recommend that business owners use appropriate accounting assistance in investigating their impact. Budgeting for automation costs can be complex as well, but as with tax matters, business owners are encouraged to educate themselves for this ongoing process. With the relatively short life of most new technology it is critical that annual reinvestments on technology become a part of all business plans. Deciding upon an affordable spending level requires a strategic look at the business to determine the role that new technologies play in the success of the business.

Once new automation systems are in operation, business owners and managers should closely monitor financial performance for clues about their impact on operations. As with any potentially cost saving or time saving process, the savings are only achieved if the process is correctly implemented. Proper monitoring of the new systems helps to identify problems with their implementation and make corrections so that the anticipated savings can be obtained.

The accelerating pace of automation in various areas of business can be dizzying. It will be a challenge for small businesses to keep pace—or stay ahead—of such changes. But the forward-thinking business owner will plan ahead, both strategically and financially, to ensure that the ever-more automated world of business does not leave him or her behind. The key is careful implementation of the proper tools, not rapid acceptance of all new technologies.

SEE ALSO *Robotics*

BIBLIOGRAPHY
Bartholomew, Doug. "Automation Advance." *Industry Week.* 15 May 2000.

Burgess, Stephen. *Managing Information Technology in Small Business.* Idea Group Inc., 2002.

"Hot Trends in Automation." *Instrumentation and Automation News.* June 2005.

"Improving Productivity through Automation." *Automation.* May 2004.

Marks, Gene. *Outfoxing the Small Business Owner.* Adams Media, 2005.

Merker, Renate, and Wolfgang Schwartz. *System Design Automation.* Springer, 2001.

Hillstrom, Northern Lights
updated by Magee, ECDI

AUTOMOBILE LEASING

Leasing an automobile is an alternative to purchasing that usually enables consumers to pay lower up-front costs and make affordable monthly payments. At the end of the lease period, however, the consumer does not own the vehicle. Instead, consumers opting for automobile leasing arrangements pay for the use and depreciation of the vehicle over the duration of the lease. Purchasing a vehicle for cash is usually the most cost-effective option, followed by financing a purchase and, finally, leasing. The best option depends to a large extent on the individual consumer's situation. In many cases, leasing enables people to drive a more expensive car or to pay a lower amount per month than they would under a purchase arrangement. Leasing can be an attractive option for small business owners because of the tax deductibility of lease payments on cars used for business purposes. In recent years, many special lease deals have been established with small business owners in mind.

BUY OR LEASE?

The decision of whether to buy or lease an automobile depends upon a number of factors. First, it depends upon how long the consumer tends to keep cars before obtaining new ones. Leasing tends to make more sense when the consumer changes cars at least every four years, because then monthly car payments are a basic part of his or her budget. Second, the buy-or-lease decision depends upon the amount of annual mileage the consumer tends to put on cars. Leasing is less attractive for people who regularly drive long distances, since most leases impose mileage limits (generally 12,000-15,000 miles annually) and charge a high fee for excess mileage. However, many car dealers allow consumers to purchase extra miles at a reduced rate at the time the lease is signed. Finally, the decision depends upon the consumer's budget. Leasing is a good way for people on a limited budget to minimize up-front costs, since they are usually required to pay a down payment consisting only of the first month's lease rate plus a security deposit.

It is also important to note, however, that there can be hidden costs associated with leasing. For example, many dealers charge a variety of lease-end fees. A disposition fee of several hundred dollars is common for consumers who do not wish to purchase the car. In addition, dealers often levy "excessive wear and tear" charges against customers when they turn in their vehicle (typical charges are for significant paint scratches, large windshield cracks and chips, upholstery and carpet burns, mismatched or bald tires, etc.). According to *Business Week,* dealers dun customers for such charges on nearly 30 percent of leased vehicles, charging an average of $1,600 per vehicle. In addition, some dealers establish maintenance rules for leased vehicles and charge fees when consumers fail to perform the required maintenance. In some cases, there are higher liability insurance requirements for leased vehicles than for those acquired through a purchase arrangement, which also costs consumers more money. Finally, most dealers include a premature termination clause in the lease contract and charge consumers a disposition fee, the car's residual value, and the remaining lease payments to end the lease early.

HOW AUTOMOBILE LEASES WORK

Like financed purchases, automobile leases require consumers to make monthly payments. Rather than covering the principal and interest on a loan, however, these payments cover the use and depreciation of the car over the lease period. The amount of the payment is calculated using the purchase price (capitalized cost) of the vehicle, its expected residual value (cost less expected depreciation) at the end of the lease, a fraction of the going interest rate (called the leasing factor), and applicable taxes. In some lease agreements an additional fee is included to cover all regular maintenance requirements.

The first step in calculating the monthly payment is to determine the monthly lease rate. This rate is equal to the capitalized cost, plus the residual value, multiplied by the leasing factor. The next step is to find the monthly cost of depreciation on the vehicle by subtracting the residual value from the capitalized cost, then dividing by the number of months in the lease.

A closed-end lease—the most common kind—means that the dealer assumes the risk that the car's residual value will be lower than expected at the end of the lease period. In this type of lease, the consumer can either buy the car for the residual value or walk away. In contrast, an open-end lease means that the consumer assumes the risk that the residual value will be lower than expected, and must make up the difference if this is the case. In exchange for accepting greater risk, the consumer usually makes lower payments in this type of lease. In general, two- or three-year leases tend to be the most cost-effective for consumers. Shorter leases do not justify the added taxes, while longer leases mean that the car will require too many repairs.

TAX BENEFITS OF LEASING

Leasing rather than buying an automobile often holds some tax benefits for small businesses. "Leasing may beat buying when it comes to tax benefits," Donald J. Korn wrote in *Black Enterprise*. "Under current law, the interest you pay on a car loan is usually not deductible. However, when you lease, the finance charges are included in the monthly payment. If you get to deduct three-quarters of your lease payment, you're actually deducting three-quarters of the interest as well."

Small business owners can deduct a percentage of their automobile lease payments—as well as fuel, maintenance, and insurance costs—from their federal income taxes. To calculate the deduction on a leased vehicle, a small business owner would use the actual-expense approach. This approach adds up all the costs of operating the car for a year and multiplies that total by the percentage of the annual mileage that was attributable to business purposes. It is necessary to maintain an accurate mileage log and associated automobile expenses in order to support the deduction.

The mileage deduction is a better deal for self-employed people than for those who work for companies. Self-employed persons merely report the leasing expense with their other business expenses. Employees, on the other hand, must report leasing expenses with other miscellaneous itemized deductions; the deduction is only allowed for the amount by which the expense exceeds 2 percent of their adjusted gross income. It is also important to note that commuting to and from work is considered personal rather than business mileage for employees.

SEE ALSO *Equipment Leasing*

BIBLIOGRAPHY

Coulombe, Charles A. "Little Fleet: A New Approach to Leasing Lets Small Businesses Zoom into High Gear." *Success.* October 1997.

Edgerton, Jerry. *Car Shopping Made Easy.* Warner Brothers, 2001.

Fisherman, Stephen. *Deduct It.* Nolo Press, 2004.

"Leases: Dings to Watch." *Business Week.* 24 April 2000.

Sykes, Tanisha Ann. "Is Car Leasing for You?" *Black Enterprise.* April 2000.

Hillstrom, Northern Lights
updated by Magee, ECDI

B

BABY BONDS

Baby bonds are savings-type securities that are available in small dollar denominations, typically $5000 or less. In the past, small dollar bonds were common in the United States, especially during wartime. During the Civil War, for example, the Union government financed most of the costs of fighting the war by selling baby bonds, often in amounts of $50 or less. During World War I, bonds again helped pay for U.S. war efforts; the popular Liberty Bonds were available in denominations as low as 25 cents.

In 1935, the U.S. government issued a series of bonds that are also commonly referred to as baby bonds. Launched in March of that year, the bonds were the first savings-type bond to be offered to the average, everyday investor. Bonds issued that year were known as A bonds, with B bonds following in 1936, C bonds in 1937 and 1938, and D bonds from 1938 to 1941. The bonds were a huge success, as the government raised a total of $3.9 billion selling the low-denomination bonds to citizens.

The bonds were sold at 75 percent of face value in denominations that ranged from $75 to $1000. They had a 10-year maturity period, and if they were held for the entire 10-year period, they accrued interest at 2.9 percent, compounded semi-annually. Available across the country at every branch of the U.S. Post Office (or from the U.S. Treasurer's office), the bonds featured tax-free interest. While most of the baby bonds have already been cashed in, they still pop up from time to time today when elderly customers of the early savings bonds pass away. The government still honors the bonds and will pay up to the full face value of $1,000 if they are cashed in.

In the current bond market, the term baby bonds does not usually refer to those early U.S. government bonds, but instead to small denomination municipal bonds issued by cities and states to fund construction and other high-cost projects. The bonds typically have maturity periods of 8 to 15 years and are zero coupon bonds, usually rated A or better on the bond market. There is no purchase commission on the bonds, and they are typically bought by the small investor directly from the issuing city or state treasurer's office. An example of a baby bond would be one purchased for $975 with a $5000 face value if redeemed at full-term in 2019, yielding interest at 6.4 percent. In recent years "baby" corporate bonds have also made their appearance.

Buyers can either manage such bonds themselves (keep them safe, track their maturity, and cash them in) or use a management service. The first such service was offered in 1993 by the Midwest Securities Trust Company, a subsidiary of the Chicago Stock Exchange.

In the late 1990s, another type of bond gained popularity under the "baby bond" name. First launched in the United Kingdom, this type of baby bond is a savings instrument parents can use to build a nest egg for their child. Under the plan parents contribute money to a tax-free bond fund that guarantees a minimum lump sum payment when the child turns 18. The plan has to last a minimum of 10 years; during that time the parents can make monthly contributions ranging from £10 to £25 ($17 to $43). Participants are not required to pay income tax or capital gains taxes on the baby bond investments.

The United Kingdom's Child Trust Fund, approved in April of 2005, is the latest incarnation of this program. It applies to children born after September 1, 2002; each such child receives a voucher worth £250 ($430) to start the account. The most recent new program was launched in Hungary. Late in 2005, the Hungarian Parliament approved baby bonds for children born after December 31, 2005. Each bond will be worth 40,000 forints ($190), will be tax free, and will reach maturity with the 18th birthday of the child.

SEE ALSO *Bonds*

BIBLIOGRAPHY
"Child Trust Fund: What Will Yours Grow Into?" *HM Revenue & Customs* 30 December 2005.

"Hungary's Parliament OKs Special Bonds." *Business Week.* 28 December 2005.

U.S. Department of the Treasury, Bureau of the Public Debt. "Series A, B, C, and D." Available from http://www.publicdebt.treas.gov/sav/savold.htm. Retrieved on 7 January 2005.

Hillstrom, Northern Lights
updated by Magee, ECDI

BALANCE SHEET

A balance sheet is a financial report that provides a snapshot of a business's position at a given point in time, including its assets (economic resources), its liabilities (debts or obligations), and its total or net worth (assets less liabilities). "A balance sheet does not aim to depict ongoing company activities," wrote Joseph Peter Simini in *Balance Sheet Basics for Nonfinancial Managers.* "It is not a movie but a freeze-frame. Its purpose is to depict the dollar value of various components of a business at a moment in time." Balance sheets are also sometimes referred to as statements of financial position or statements of financial condition.

Balance sheets are typically presented in two different forms. In the report form, asset accounts are listed first, with the liability and owners' equity accounts listed in sequential order directly below the assets. In the account form, the balance sheet is organized in a horizontal manner, with the asset accounts listed on the left side and the liabilities and owners' equity accounts listed on the right side. The term "balance sheet" originates from this latter form: when the left and right sides have been completed, they should sum to the same dollar amounts—in other words, they should balance.

CONTENTS OF THE BALANCE SHEET

Most of the contents of a business's balance sheet are classified under one of three categories: assets, liabilities, and owner equity. Some balance sheets also include a "notes" section that holds relevant information that does not fit under any of the above accounting categories. Information that might be included in the notes section would include mentions of pending lawsuits that might impact future liabilities or changes in the business's accounting practices.

Assets Assets are items owned by the business, whether fully paid for or not. These items can range from cash—the most liquid of all assets—to inventories, equipment, patents, and deposits held by other businesses. Assets are further categorized into the following classifications: current assets, fixed assets, and miscellaneous or other assets. How assets are divided into these categories, and how they match corresponding liability categories, are important indicators of a company's health.

Current assets include cash, government securities, marketable securities, notes receivable, accounts receivable, inventories, prepaid expenses, and any other item that could be converted to cash in the normal course of business within one year.

Current assets should reasonably balance current liabilities. Current assets divided by current liabilities produce one of the "health indicators" of a company, the "Current Ratio." If that ratio is unfavorable, the company may lack liquidity—meaning the necessary resources to meet its cash obligations. Since inventories are sometimes difficult to turn into cash, the "Acid Test" is another ratio used. It includes Current Assets less Inventory divided by Current Liabilities. The company's "Working Capital" is determined by deducting Current Liabilities from Current Assets. Rather than being a ratio, it is a dollar-denominated indicator of a company's health.

Fixed assets include real estate, physical plant, leasehold improvements, equipment (from office equipment to heavy operating machinery), vehicles, fixtures, and other assets that can reasonably be assumed to have a life expectancy of several years. In practice most fixed assets—excluding land—will lose value over time in a process called depreciation. Fixed assets are reported *net of depreciation* in an attempt to claim only their current value.

Fixed assets also include intangibles like the value of trademarks, copyrights, and a difficult category known as "good will." When someone buys a company and pays more for it than the worth of current and fixed assets combined, the difference is written into the books of the acquired entity as "good will." The value of this good will cannot be extracted again unless by sale to another willing buyer.

Fixed assets, of course, should be in some reasonable balance with long-term liabilities. If a company owes more for capital purchases than those purchases are worth on its books, that is an indicator of potential problems.

Liabilities Liabilities are the business's obligations to other entities as a result of past transactions. These entities range from employees (who have provided work in exchange for salary) to investors (who have provided loans in exchange for the value of that loan plus interest) to other companies (who have supplied goods or services in exchange for agreed-upon compensation). Liabilities are typically divided into two categories: short-term or current liabilities and long-term liabilities.

Current Liabilities are due to be paid within a year. These include payments to vendors, payable taxes, notes due, and accrued expenses (wages, salaries, withholding taxes, and FICA taxes). Current liabilities also include the "current" portion of long-term debt payable during the coming year. *Long-term liabilities* are debts to lenders, mortgage holders, and other creditors payable over a longer span of time.

Owners' Equity Once a business has determined its assets and liabilities, it can then determine owners' equity, the book value of the business: the remainder after liabilities are deducted from assets. Owners' equity, also called stockholders' equity if stockholders are involved in the business, is in essence the company's net worth.

A company's "leverage" is calculated using its total equity. "Leverage" is long-term debt divided by total equity. The higher the leverage, the more a company is financed by borrowing. People then say that it is "highly leveraged," i.e., it is more vulnerable to market shifts which make it difficult for it to service its debt. If leverage is small or modest, the company is able to control its own destiny with greater certainty.

BALANCE SHEETS AND SMALL BUSINESSES

As shown above, the balance sheet, if studied closely, can tell the small business owner much about the enterprise's health. In *Balance Sheet for Nonfinancial Managers,* for instance, Simini points out that "in a well-run company current assets should be approximately double current liabilities." He goes on: "By analyzing a succession of balance sheets and income statements, managers and owners can spot both problems and opportunities. Could the company make more profitable use of its assets? Does inventory turnover indicate the most effi-

cient possible use of inventory in sales? How does the company's administrative expense compare to that of its competition? For the experienced and well-informed reader, then, the balance sheet can be an immensely useful aid in an analysis of the company's overall financial picture."

The small business owner, by mastering the concepts hidden in the balance sheet, can also effectively foresee what a bank or other lender will see when looking at the company's balance sheet—and what to do in anticipation to make the numbers look better by changes in purchasing, collections, prepayments, and by other management actions within the owner's competence.

SEE ALSO *Annual Report*

BIBLIOGRAPHY

"Analyzing Company Reports."Ameritrade, Inc. Available from www.ameritrade.com/educationv2/fhtml/learning/balsheet analysis.fhtml. Updated in 2003 to reflect changes in the Internal Revenue Code enacted by Congress.

Atrill, Peter. *Accounting and Finance for Nonspecialists.* Prentice Hall, 1997.

Bangs, David H., Jr., and Robert Gruber. *Finance: Mastering Your Small Business.* Upstart, 1996.

Simini, Joseph Peter. *Balance Sheet Basics for Nonfinancial Managers.* Wiley, 1990.

Hillstrom, Northern Lights
updated by Magee, ECDI

BANKRUPTCY

Bankruptcy is a legal proceeding, guided by federal law, designed to address situations where a debtor—either an individual or a business—has accumulated obligations so great that he or she is unable to pay them off. Bankruptcy law does not require filers to be financially insolvent at the time of the filing. Rather, it applies a criterion in which approval is granted if the filer is "unable to pay debts as they come due." Once a company is granted bankruptcy protection, it can terminate contractual obligations with workers and clients, avoid litigation claims, and explore possible avenues for reorganization.

Bankruptcy laws are designed to distribute the debtor's assets as equitably as possible among his or her creditors. Most of the time, with some exceptions, bankruptcy also frees the debtor from further liability. Bankruptcy proceedings may be initiated either by the debtor—a voluntary process—or may be forced by creditors.

According to the Administrative Office of the U.S. Courts, in Fiscal Year 2005, 1.637 million bankruptcies were filed in federal courts, up from 1.277 million in FY

2000. Of these 32,406 were business bankruptcies (down from 36,910 in FY 2000). Bankruptcy statistics are dominated by personal filings; these have been increasing sharply in recent years due in large part to rapidly increasing levels of personal indebtedness.

This phenomenon has been responsible for a major overhaul of bankruptcy law in 2005. The legislation, known as The Bankruptcy Abuse Prevention and Consumer Protection Act of 2005 (BAPCPA) was signed into law on April 20, 2005 and became effective October 17 of the same year. The law was designed, in part, to eliminate the practice of serial bankruptcy filings by individuals to escape carelessly accumulated debt.

Types of bankruptcy are named after chapters of the bankruptcy code. Individuals may file under the provisions of Chapter 7 or Chapter 13.

CHAPTER 7 BANKRUPTCY

Under Chapter 7 bankruptcy law, all of the debtor's assets—including any unincorporated businesses that he or she may own—are fully liquidated. Assets deemed necessary to support the debtor and his/her dependents, such as a residence, may be exempted. This "liquidation bankruptcy" is the most common filing for business failures, accounting for about 75 percent of all business bankruptcy filings.

The federal bankruptcy court develops a full listing of the debtor's assets and liabilities. The court identifies assets deemed to be exempted, such as a family home, and then divides remaining assets among the various creditors; a trustee is appointed to oversee distribution of proceeds. Unpaid taxes receive top priority; secured creditors are usually considered next. After all assets are liquidated and distributed, the debtor is freed of all further obligations. John Pearce II and Samuel DiLullo note the pluses and minuses of this procedure in *Business Horizons* as follows: "This type of filing is critically important to sole proprietors or partnerships, whose owners are personally liable for all business debts not covered by the sale of the assets unless they can secure a Chapter 7 bankruptcy allowing them to cancel any debt in excess of exempt assets. Although they will be left with little personal property, the liquidated debtor is discharged from paying the remaining debt." The debts thus discharged exclude certain items which the debtor is required to pay despite the Chapter 7 filing. These include child support, alimony, recent income taxes, and student loans guaranteed by government.

The recently passed BAPCPA limits the ability of a debtor to file under Chapter 7. The debtor can only file for "liquidation bankruptcy" if his or her median income is below the state median income; if it is higher, and the person can afford to pay out $100 monthly to liquidate debt, he or she may only file under Chapter 13. The new law also mandates credit counseling ahead of filing in a government-approved program.

CHAPTER 13 BANKRUPTCY

An individual or business filing under Chapter 13 turns over his or her finances to the bankruptcy court and is then obliged to make payments at the court's direction. Whereas Chapter 7 is characterized by full discharge of debt, Chapter 13 results in a repayment plan. Debtors prefer Chapter 7 because it usually allows them to hold on to their equity but, after a brief time, all obligations except such as listed above (child support, alimony, etc.) are eliminated. Courts prefer filings under Chapter 13 if the individual has any ability to satisfy the debt over time, and BAPCPA now codifies this leaning of the courts by defining a "threshold"—the state median income and an ability to pay $100 a month toward the indebtedness.

Provisions of BAPCPA have made Chapter 13 filings more burdensome for filers. Under the old dispensation, Chapter 13 filers enjoyed more protection against legal actions by litigants intending to recover funds or to impose new costs. Filers were protected against evictions; under BAPCPA they no longer are. They may lose their driver's licenses. They must continue to respond to divorce and child-support actions. BAPCPA has also moved family members with financial claims (e.g., for child support, alimony) to the first rank of recipients, ahead of secured creditors. Like Chapter 7 filers, Chapter 13 filers are also required to participate in mandatory financial management education.

CHAPTER 11 BANKRUPTCY

In a bulletin titled *Corporate Bankruptcy,* the U.S. Securities and Exchange Commission summarizes why corporations file for bankruptcy under Chapter 11: "Most publicly-held companies will file under Chapter 11 rather than Chapter 7 because they can still run their business and control the bankruptcy process. Chapter 11 provides a process for rehabilitating the company's faltering business. Sometimes the company successfully works out a plan to return to profitability; sometimes, in the end, it liquidates. Under a Chapter 11 reorganization, a company usually keeps doing business and its stock and bonds may continue to trade in our securities markets."

Companies generally turn to Chapter 11 protection after they are no longer able to pay their creditors. Once a company has filed under Chapter 11, its creditors are notified that they cannot press suits for repayment (although secured creditors may ask the court for a "hardship" exemption from the general debt freeze that is imposed). Creditors are, however, permitted to appear before the court to discuss their claims and provide data on the debtor's ability to reorganize. In addition, unsecured creditors may appoint representatives to negotiate a settlement with the debtor company. Finally, creditors who feel that the debtor company's financial straits are due to mismanagement or fraud may ask the court to appoint an examiner to look into such possibilities.

Once a company asks for Chapter 11 protection, it provides the court, lenders, and creditors with a wide range of financial information on its operations for analysis even as it continues with its day-to-day operations; during this period, major business expenditures must be approved by the court. The business will also prepare a reorganization plan, which, according to *CPA Journal* contributor Nancy Baldiga, "details the amount and timing of all creditor payments, the means for effectuating such payments (such as the sale of assets, refinancing, or compromise of disputed claims), and the essential legal and business structure of the debtor as it emerges from Chapter 11 protection." Another important component of this plan is the disclosure statement, which presents projected business fortunes, proposed financial settlements with creditors and equity holders, and estimates of the liquidation value of the company. "The information included in the disclosure statement is critical to a creditor's evaluation of the reorganization plans offered for acceptance, as compared to possible other plans or even liquidation," wrote Baldiga.

The reorganization plan, if approved by the court and a majority of creditors, becomes the blueprint for the company's future. Principal factors considered in determining the feasibility of reorganization proposals include:

- Status of the company's capital structure
- Availability of financing and credit
- Potential earnings of the company after reorganization
- Ability to make creditor payments
- Management stability
- General economic conditions in the industry
- General economic conditions in geographic regions of operation

BAPCPA has also introduced a number of changes governing Chapter 11 filings related to leases, payments made immediately prior to the bankruptcy filing, improved ability of creditors to reclaim products, caps on wage claims applicable to the pre-filing period, and other matters.

SMALL BUSINESS CREDITORS

Small businesses facing a bankrupt client have few options to protect themselves. If the debtor is engaged in questionable or fraudulent business activities, the small business may use legal actions beyond simply waiting patiently for a bankruptcy court to act. In situations where the debtor has incurred debt only a short time before filing before bankruptcy, creditors can sometimes obtain judgments that put added pressure on the debtor to make good on that liability. In addition, noted the *Entrepreneur Magazine Small Business Advisor,* "the law provides for a '60-day preference' rule. This rule is designed to prevent debtors from paying off their friends right before they file bankruptcy while leaving others stiffed. The 60-day rule allows the court to set aside any payments made up to 60 days before the actual filing of bankruptcy. Creditors who have been paid must return the money to the bankruptcy court for it to be placed in the pot. Business owners should keep in close contact with their ongoing customers so that they will have a good enough relationship to know far in advance to avoid being caught up in this rule." Indeed, small business owners in particular should always be watching for clients/customers who show signs of being in financial distress. If such indications become present, the owner needs to determine the depth of that distress and whether his or her small business can withstand the likely financial repercussions if that client/customer declares bankruptcy. If a bankruptcy declaration would be a significant blow, then the business owner should weigh various alternatives to protect his/her business, such as cutting back on business dealings with the endangered company or tightening up credit arrangements with the firm.

Finally, advisors typically counsel small business creditors to file confirmations of debt with the court even if it seems highly unlikely that they will ever be compensated. This filing allows creditors to write off bad debts on their taxes.

ALTERNATIVES TO BANKRUPTCY

A company that runs into serious financial difficulties has alternatives to bankruptcy. It can liquidate the business on its own and make payments to its creditors. "Such action may be achieved efficiently if [the business's] creditors... are few... and the assets... can readily be converted to cash," wrote Pearce and DiLullo. "If the number of creditors is large and the assets are numerous and difficult or time-consuming to sell (such as real estate), the protection, structure, and authority of the court may be needed."

Another option is for the company to place liquidation of assets in the hands of a trustee who subsequently pays creditors. The principal advantage of this avenue, say Pearce and DiLullo, is that the assets are thus protected from individual creditors who might otherwise file liens on the assets. "Composition agreements," meanwhile, can be used in situations where creditors agree to receive proportional (pro rata) payments of their claims in return for freeing the debtor company from the remainder of its debts.

These alternative strategies may enable some business owners to avoid the stigma of bankruptcy. But Pearce and DiLullo note that pursuing these options involves considerable risk: "astute creditors will recognize such actions as precursors to bankruptcy and may modify their relationships with [the company], which could precipitate a bankruptcy filing. If creditors believe that continuing in business will result in reduced assets, they may force a bankruptcy in order to stop operations and preserve the existing assets to pay outstanding debts."

SEE ALSO *Business Failure/Dissolution*

BIBLIOGRAPHY

Administrative Office of the U.S. Courts."Number of Bankruptcy Cases Filed in Federal Courts." Press Release, 24 August 2005.

Baldiga, Nancy R. "Practice Opportunities in Chapter 11."*CPA Journal.* May 1998.

"Checklist of Key Changes."*FindLaw.* Available from http://bankruptcy.findlaw.com/bankruptcy/bankruptcy-basics/key-changes.html. January 2006.

Pearce II, John A., and Samuel A. DiLullo. "When a Strategic Plan Includes Bankruptcy." *Business Horizons.* September/October 1998.

U.S. Securities and Exchange Commission."Corporate Bankruptcy."Available from http://www.sec.gov/investor/pubs/bankrupt.htm. 8 December 2005.

Hillstrom, Northern Lights
updated by Magee, ECDI

BANKS AND BANKING

The banking sector of the economy can be viewed bottom-up or top-down. The top-down view shows central banks overseeing financial activities for the entire nation. Beneath them full-service national commercial banks conduct business. At the bottom of the system are small full-service community banks and specialized savings and loan institutions. Other specialized institutions, some regional, some local, fill in the fabric of banking. These include trusts and credit unions. Of greatest interest to the small business is the local community bank or the local branch of a national commercial bank.

THE FEDERAL RESERVE

Our central bank, the U.S. Federal Reserve, operates through 12 regional banks. The Fed, as it is known, provides services like check clearing; more importantly, it regulates the banking sector and sets monetary policy by managing credit and the money supply. Its principal aim is to hold inflation in check. The Fed uses three major tools to do this job. First, it sets the rate at which banks can borrow from the Federal Reserve. High rates discourage and low rates encourage economic activity. Second, under law the Federal Reserve sets "reserve requirements." The nation's banks must place a portion of their deposits with the Federal Reserve, e.g., 20 percent; they may only lend out the remainder. If the Fed increases the reserve requirement, that takes money out of the economy. Lowering reserve requirements makes money available. Third, the Federal Reserve engages in open market operations that indirectly affect reserves. It either sells or buys Treasury securities on the open market. Holding a Treasury bill is, in effect, a savings: it takes money out of circulation. Thus the Fed sells securities to "cool" and buys securities to "heat up" a sluggish economy. The Fed thus decreases or increases the money supply. Such activities are reflected in interest rate levels which, of course, affect the small business. In this manner even a very small business feels the activity of the Fed's activities.

COMMERCIAL BANKS

Full-service commercial banks accept deposits from customers; the interest paid on such deposits is relatively low, but the funds up to a maximum of $100,000 are insured by the Federal Deposit Insurance Corporation, an entity created by Congress in 1933 to restore faith in the banking system during the Depression. The bank places a portion of its deposits with the Fed (the "reserve requirement," see above) and lends the rest to others at a higher rate of interest—be these loans to purchase cars, homes, or to finance business activities. Commercial banks also generate revenues from services such as asset management, investment sales, and mortgage loan maintenance. By their very nature, banks are conservative. Most of their lending is secured. So-called "investment bankers" that finance start-ups are not to be confused with commercial banks. They are other types of financial entities. A commercial bank may operate an investment banking business, but not as part of its regulated activities. Small businesses should not look to banks to obtain start-up capital.

Most commercial banks are operated as corporate holding companies that own one or several banks. Because of regulatory constraints, banks that are not associated with holding companies must operate under restrictions that often put them at a disadvantage compared with other financial institutions. Holding companies are often used as vehicles to circumvent legal restrictions and to raise capital by otherwise unavailable means. For instance, many banks can indirectly operate branches in other states by organizing their entity as a holding company. Banks are also able to enter, and often effectively compete in, related industries through holding company subsidiaries. In addition, holding companies are able to raise capital using methods from which banks are restricted, such as issuing commercial paper. Multibank holding companies may also create various economies of scale related to advertising, bookkeeping, and reporting.

Commercial banking in the United States has been characterized by: 1) a proliferation of competition from other financial service industries, such as mutual funds and leasing companies; 2) the growth of multibank holding companies; and 3) new technology that has changed the way that banks conduct business. The first two developments are closely related. Indeed, as new types of financial institutions have emerged to meet specialized needs, banks have increasingly turned to the holding company structure to increase their competitiveness. In addition, a number of laws passed since the 1960s have favored the multibank holding company format. As a result the U.S. banking industry had become highly concentrated in the hands of bank holding companies by the early 1990s.

Electronic information technology, the third major factor in the recent evolution of banking, is evidenced most visibly by the proliferation of electronic transactions. Electronic fund transfer systems, automated teller machines (ATMs), and computerized home-banking services all combined to transform the way that banks conduct business. Such technological gains have served to reduce labor demands and intensify the trend toward larger and more centralized banking organizations. They have also diminished the role that banks have traditionally played as personal financial service organizations. Finally, electronic systems have paved the way for national and global banking systems.

THRIFTS AND OTHER BANK-LIKE INSTITUTIONS

Savings banks, savings and loan associations (S&Ls), and credit unions are known as thrift institutions or simply as "thrifts." Like commercial banks, they are depository institutions but, under law, deal with individuals rather than businesses. Small businesses are unlikely to do business with thrifts.

Trust companies act as trustees, managing assets that they transfer between two parties according to the wishes of the trustor. Trust services are often offered by departments of commercial banks. Insurance companies and pension funds, which are really outside the banking sector strictly viewed, fulfill some bank-like functions such as the management of savings. They typically invest their assets but are not good sources of small business financing.

BANKS AND SMALL BUSINESSES

Small business is the fastest-growing segment of the American business economy. As a result, more and more commercial banks are creating special products and programs designed to attract small business customers. The small business owner looking for funds is best advised to seek out a local community bank. Tom Henderson, writing in *Crain's Detroit Business,* sums up the situation: "Name changes and consolidations among the area's biggest banks capture headlines, but industry and government analysts say the activity also creates big opportunities for community banks. Those banks continue to carve out a niche by providing loans and lines of credit to small and medium-sized businesses." Citing a 2004 report by the Federal Deposit Insurance Corporation, Henderson says that "small banks have an advantage in small-business lending because it requires 'local expertise that is both characteristic of community banks and more favorable to some small-business borrowers, such as new or young firms with limited credit history.'"

There are a number of factors a small business owner should consider when selecting a bank, including its accessibility, compatibility, lending limit, loan approval process, general services provided, and fees charged. Perhaps the best way to approach banks is to obtain referrals to business representatives or loan officers at three to five banks. This approach aids the small business owner by providing a recommendation or association from a known customer, and also by providing the name of a specific banker to talk to. The company's accountant, business advisors, and professional contacts will most likely be good sources of referrals.

The next step in forming a positive banking relationship is to arrange for a preliminary interview at each bank to get a feel for its particular personnel and services. It may be helpful to bring a brief summary of the business and a list of questions. The small business owner should also be prepared to answer the bankers' questions, including general information about the business, its primary goods/services, its financial condition, its banking needs, and the status of the industry in which it operates. All of these queries are designed to solicit information that will enable the institution to evaluate the small business as a potential client. After all the face-to-face meetings have taken place, the small business owner should compare each bank to the list of preferred criteria, and consult with his or her business advisors as needed. It is important to notify all the candidates once a decision has been made.

Ideally, a small business's banking relationship should feature open communication. Consultants recommend regular appointments to keep the banker updated on the business's condition, including potential problems on the horizon, as well as to give the banker an opportunity to update the small business owner on new services. The banker can be a good source of information about financing, organization, and record keeping. He or she may also be able to provide the small business owner with referrals to other business professionals, special seminars or programs, and networking opportunities.

BIBLIOGRAPHY

The Federal Reserve Bank of St. Louis. "In Plain English: Making Sense of the Federal Reserve." Available from http://www. stls.frb.org/publications/pleng/default.html. Retrieved on 4 January 2006.

Henderson, Tom. "Banking on Small Business; Increased Lending to Small Business Lays the Groundwork for Growth of Community Banking." *Crain's Detroit Business.* 12 December 2005.

Koehler, Dan M. *Insider's Guide to Small Business Loans.* PSI Research, 2000.

Hillstrom, Northern Lights
updated by Magee, ECDI

BANNER ADVERTISEMENTS

"Banners" are graphic advertisements that appear on World Wide Web sites intended to build brand awareness or to generate traffic for the advertiser's site. The term "banner" comes from the general shape for such ads: a short, wide strip usually placed at the top of a page. The first advertisements appeared on the Web in 1993. In 2005, according to the Interactive Advertisement Bureau (IAB), ad revenues could exceed $12 billion, up from $9.6 billion in 2004, another record year. According to Ann M. Mack, writing in *Adweek* in 2000 and citing IAB estimates, banner advertising accounted for 52 percent of activity, down slightly from the late 1990s when its share was around 56 percent. Banner advertisement competes with contextually generated ads, direct e-mail advertising, sponsorship arrangements, and other forms of publicity.

Although ad space on Web sites can be expensive, it is an increasingly important marketing tool for small businesses seeking to establish a presence online. Experts suggest that Internet advertising—whether through banners or through smaller "sponsored by" notes on Web sites—is the easiest and most effective way to encourage potential customers to visit a company's site. In addition, sophisticated new Web technology allows small businesses to focus their advertising dollars on specific geographic or demographic groups.

COST CONSIDERATIONS

According to Vince Emery in *How to Grow Your Business on the Internet,* banner advertisements can be quite expensive for small businesses. For example, it may cost several thousand dollars per month to place an ad on a site with high traffic. The cost is determined by the number of people who either see the ad or follow through to visit the advertised site. Some Web sites charge per thousand *impressions,* meaning people who visit the Web site and see the advertiser's banner there. A more relevant number is the *clickthrough rate*— the percentage of people viewing the banner who actually click on it to visit the advertiser's site. The clickthrough rate helps quantify the success of banner advertisements. Emery noted that a clickthrough rate of 1 percent is about normal; a 10 percent rate is outstanding.

Ideally, small businesses will want to pay only for fully delivered banners. Between 20 and 30 percent of people surfing the Web do so with the graphics feature of their browsers disabled. Turned off graphics help speed Web page transfers but also transform fancy banners into empty boxes on the user's screen. Other Web surfers use their browser's stop button feature to interrupt the up-loading of banners. These people save time but avoid looking at the advertiser's message. For this reason, Emery recommends that advertisers arrange to pay only for banners potential customers actually see.

Paying for "impressions" can also cause problems for the small business advertiser. A certain Web site may boast that it attracts 100,000 visitors; the number may only mean 10,000 unique users who visit the site 10 times each. At the same time, many sellers of ad space on the Web are reluctant to accept payment based on clickthroughs. This arrangement can leave the seller vulnerable to poorly designed advertising banners unlikely to generate clickthroughs. As a result, many sellers will only agree to clickthrough deals with large advertisers who purchase a log of space. For small businesses, the best way to determine the true cost of Internet advertising is probably neither impressions nor clickthroughs. Instead, Emery recommends calculating cost per sale or cost per lead, generated through Web advertising, in order to gauge the banner's effectiveness.

DECIDING WHERE TO RAISE BANNERS

But where should the banners be displayed? Emery notes that space is sold by content and by search sites. Internet users visit content sites to find information, e.g., ESPN SportZone for sports stories, Travelocity for airline flight information. Thousands of lesser known sites specialize in every conceivable business topic or hobby. Advertising on most content sites requires small businesses to rent space for a banner with payment based on impressions, clickthroughs, or the time period in which the ad appears.

Advertising on search engines like Yahoo or AltaVista tends to be more expensive but also gives advertisers more options. For example, small businesses can buy space for a banner within a certain search category or even tied to a specific search term. If an Internet user searches for information on "fishing," the banner advertisement for a fishing tackle or sporting goods retailer can thus appear on the screen with the search results.

Many producers of Web browser software also allow advertising on their sites. As Dowling wrote in *Web Advertising and Marketing,* these sites can be a good place for a business to start building brand awareness. Many new Internet users receive browser software free with their PCs; they may not be technically sophisticated enough to change the default screen as it arrives. These users see the browser Web site every time they log on to the Internet; advertisers can take advantage of this fact to gain the attention of new surfers. A form of free advertising is also available from browser sites. Small businesses with exceptionally useful Web sites may be listed on the "what's new" or "what's cool" pages for a certain browser; such listing translates to immediate increases in traffic for featured sites. It may also be helpful to establish links to your site on other, related sites.

Another option for small businesses is to place banner advertisements on the sites operated by Internet Service Providers (ISPs). Some providers, known as free ISPs, depend on advertising revenue—rather than user fees—to operate. Many of these companies provide free Internet access in exchange for detailed information about subscribers; advertisers may gain access to such data. But as Brown noted in *Tele.com,* advertising on established, fee-for-service ISPs like America Online remains popular as well. By charging users a monthly fee for access, these companies ensure that subscribers are likely to use the service regularly. Yet another option for advertisers is online magazines, e-zines. Most e-zines serve highly specialized niche markets that may provide a good fit for a small business's offerings.

In *The E-Commerce Book,* Steffano Korper and Juanita Ellis provide several suggestions for small business owners. They recommend brainstorming to create a list of all the potential options. An important aspect of this process is viewing the company's product or service from a customer's perspective. Korper and Ellis suggest putting yourself in the position of a potential buyer and trying to figure out how you might look for such offerings on the Internet. Another way to target promising Web sites for banner advertisements is to input likely search terms into various search engines and look over the list of matching sites. Most Web pages that accept advertising include contact information for advertisers.

CREATING EFFECTIVE BANNERS

The final step is creating an effective banner. Even a well-placed banner will fail to attract the customer if it is ill-designed. Emery noted that the best banners arouse people's curiosity and urge some action. A banner for an accounting service might say, "Click here to reduce your tax bill."

Emery also emphasized that the banner should generate traffic to the advertiser's Web site. He suggested focusing the banner's message on the single most compelling reason for a visit. In this context it is well to mention additions or changes in the site the potential customer may have missed. Emery also wrote that many companies have been successful using contests and "free" offers. Finally, he noted that advertisers need to recognize that banner advertisements typically have a short useful life. Most people will only clickthrough in their first few exposures; after that the banner becomes wallpaper and is ignored.

Even the most effective banner advertisement will not generate customers or sales for a small business if the company's site itself is poorly designed. The site should be attractive and fully functional before it's advertised. "If your company plans to spend a lot on advertising, make sure the investment is proportionate to your investment in the Web site itself," Dowling wrote. "Site content must be dynamic and informative to keep surfers coming back. Spending lots of money on advertising does no good if people leave your home page as soon as they see it."

A number of Internet sites provide helpful information for small businesses interested in advertising on the Web. It is important to keep in mind that Internet technology continues to change at a rapid pace; banner ads will likely be around for a long time, but they yield to more interactive means of reaching the customer as Web techniques evolve. In addition to banner ads, small businesses can increase traffic using other means as well. You might, for instance, include the company's Web address on brochures, letterhead, product packaging. And the "old" media (TV, billboards, and paper magazine) can point people your way as well.

SEE ALSO *Reciprocal Marketing*

BIBLIOGRAPHY
"Banner Years Ahead." Mack, Ann M. *Adweek Eastern Edition.* 25 September 2000

Emery, Vince. *How to Grow Your Business on the Internet.* Third Edition. Coriolis Group, 1997.

Freeman, Laurie. "Web Ad Revenue Up Sharply." *B to B.* 8 May 2000.

Interactive Advertising Bureau. 21 November 2005. Available from http://www.iab.net/news/pr_2005_11_21.asp.

Korper, Steffano, and Juanita Ellis. *The E-Commerce Book: Building the E-Empire.* Academic Press, 2000.

Hillstrom, Northern Lights
updated by Magee, ECDI

BAR CODING

Bar coding is an automatic identification technology that allows data to be collected rapidly and accurately from all aspects of a company's operations, including manufacturing, inspection, transportation, and inventory elements. Because of these attributes, bar coding is used for a wide range of applications in almost every aspect of business. Indeed, it is the most commonly used tool for automated data entry worldwide, and is widely regarded as one of the most important business innovations of the twentieth century.

Bar codes provide a simple method of encoding text information that can be easily read by inexpensive electronic scanners. The code itself consists of a series of adjacent parallel bars of differing widths similarly spaced apart. This pattern of bars and spaces—sometimes referred to as the Universal Product Code—represents alphabetic characters or numbers that are the unique identification for a certain product. First utilized in supermarkets and libraries, bar coding identification has grown over the years to have applications in many fields.

Today's retail businesses use bar codes elements in complicated electronic point-of-sale (POS) systems. These systems enable businesses to capture information about inventory levels on a continuous basis. For example, a seller of health and beauty aids can scan the bar codes on merchandise as it leaves the store and transmit that data via an Electronic Data Interchange (EDI) system to its main suppliers. The supplier can then replenish the store's inventory automatically. Internally, the retailer can study the point-of-sale data to determine more effective ways of marketing and merchandising its offerings.

Manufacturers, meanwhile, utilize bar code technology in work process control, property management, job costing, maintenance, inventory control, and in tracking shipping and receiving activities. In the latter instance, for example, "scanners located at receiving and shipping areas can be used to record product movement," remarked W. H. Weiss in *Supervision.* "In addition, captured information at the point of transaction permits invoices to be verified and bills of lading generated that are based on actual quantities shipped. Back orders can be immediately routed to the shipping dock."

Users tabulate bar code information with reading devices called scanners. "Contact" scanners are handheld devices that must either touch or come into close proximity to the bar code symbol to read it; these scanners are used in situations where bar codes are difficult to get at or are attached to heavy or large items that cannot easily pass across stationary scanners. "Non-contact" readers, by contrast, are usually stationary scanners permanently installed (at checkout counters, etc.) Some handheld scanners may also use non-contact technology. Whatever the choice, a non-contact scanner does not have to come in contact with the bar code in order to register its contents. It uses reflected beams of light to read the bar code.

A small business planning to use bar codes should familiarize itself with the appropriate symbology to be used on its products. A website of the Measurement Equipment Corporation lists more than 230 national and international standards organizations able to assist the would-be user of bar codes depending on the kind of product to be coded. Examples are the Group of Terrestrial Freight Forwarders (GTF), the Chemical Industry Data Exchange (CIDX), and National Hardware Retail Organization (NHRO). Those looking for some general orientation may wish first to visit the Web site of the Uniform Code Council, (renamed GS1 U.S. on June 7, 2005 but still referred to by many as UCC) one of the leading umbrella organizations in bar coding. Part of the preparation is to ensure that the bar codes the business produces meet certain standards of print quality. "Print quality standards state the minimum levels of reflectance, contrast, and other critical measures of printed bar code symbol readability," explained Weiss. "Information requirements covered by standards vary by industry. A serial number is important for some while a product weight is important for others."

Today, bar coding technology stands as a ubiquitous part of nearly every industry of any size or economic significance. This state of affairs is unlikely to change any time soon, according to experts. Analysts do note that use of Optical Character Recognition (OCR) technology has grown in the field of document image processing in recent years. But bar coding technology remains superior to OCR in terms of expense, accuracy, and ease of operator use, and its users continue to find new and innovative uses for its still-developing technology.

BIBLIOGRAPHY

Alpert, Mark. "Building a Better Bar Code." *Fortune.* 15 June 1992.

"Does It Mean 'Toothpaste' or 'Rat Poison'?" *Fortune.* 17 February 1997.

GS1 U.S. (Uniform Code Council). "GS1 US." Available from http://www.gs1us.org/gs1usnamechange.html. Retrieved on 31 December 2005.

Mack, Stephen L. "Making a Read on Bar Codes." *Managing Office Technology.* January-February 1998.

Mark, Teri J. "Decoding the Bar Code." *Records Management Quarterly.* January 1994.

Snell, Ned. "Bar Codes Break Out: Once You Learn What Bar Codes Do Today, You May Find Uses You Never Thought of Before." *Datamation.* 1 April 1992.

"Sources for Standards and Specifications." Measurement Equipment Corporation. Available from http://www.mecsw.com/stdorg/orgs.html. Retrieved on 2 January 2006.

Weiss, W.H. "The Multi-functions of Bar Coding." *Supervision.* March 1997.

"What Matters Most." *Modern Materials Handling.* 31 January 2000.

Hillstrom, Northern Lights
updated by Magee, ECDI

BARRIERS TO MARKET ENTRY

Entry into a market is always in some way possible yet also constrained in some ways—except in purely theoretical descriptions. The two extremes are described by a state-supported absolute monopoly on the one hand (an insurmountable barrier to a new entrant) and a market on the other hand where entry has zero cost (a totally barrier-free market).

In actual practice, barriers to entry are always present to a new entrant in the very nature of things: some investment is always required, however minimal it may be. If the market already exists, some unusual effort to convince existing customers to buy, and channels to carry the goods will be required. The subject of barriers, therefore, in academic or policy contexts, turns on the concept of maintaining a healthy degree of competition or, in international contexts, fair access to markets. Economic theory asserts that competition holds down prices and thus contributes to the common good. The natural tendency of competitors in the market is to limit competition in order to raise profits to a maximum. A conflict is inherent. Given the great complexity of markets and the presence of all manner of historical, locational, technical, and other advantages, sorting out "natural" and "artificial" barriers to entry or international trade is a never-ending activity.

The major categories that translate into barriers are cost, capital, know-how, location, and state power. These factors are complexly intertwined. To give a few examples: A company with an absolute cost advantage may have acquired it by investing large amounts of capital, by ownership of patents no one can use except at a high cost, by being located in a region of extremely low labor cost, or because it is highly subsidized by the state. Know-how is often based on patents; patent protection is provided under state laws. A current controversy concerning growing Chinese imports involves very low wage rates in China and Chinese governmental manipulations of currency to keep costs in the U.S. low. These actions are said to create barriers to entry into markets by American entrepreneurs who have high labor costs.

In a recent paper published in the *Journal of Business and Industrial Marketing,* Fahri Karakaya reported the findings of a literature search aimed at determining barriers to entry by all kinds of enterprises. Karakaya found the following top-ranked barriers: 1) absolute cost advantages enjoyed by the incumbent, 2) economies of scale, 3) product differentiation, 4) the degree of firm concentration, 5) capital requirements to enter a market, 6) customers' cost of switching, 7) access to distribution channels, and 8) government policy.

Economies of scale are another form of cost advantage, specifically lower acquisition costs for raw materials (bulk purchasing) and lower overhead (overhead absorbed by more operations). Product differentiation, similarly, represents the consequences of investment in new and specialized products. Firm concentration is another way of saying that oligarchic structures prevent entry. In such cases, often, access to distribution channels is also difficult. The cost of switching customers occurs frequently in modern industrial times in which highly integrated technical products play a role. It is difficult, for example, to cause a customer to replace a well-established computer system with a new one. The cost savings must be very high. Anyone who has ever installed a new operating system will understand.

Karakaya also conducted his own survey of executives, concentrating on industrial enterprises. His survey disclosed similar but slightly different rankings. The first eight barriers cited by his respondents were 1) absolute cost advantages, 2) capital requirements, 3) incumbents with superior production processes, 4) capital intensity of the market, 5) incumbents with proprietary product technology, 6) customer loyalty advantage held by the incumbent, 7) incumbents with economies of scale, and 8) amount of sunk cost involved in entering the market.

All of the above applies equally to very large would-be entrants to a market and the aspiring small-business entrepreneur. The small business owner will benefit by entering a market poorly served locally, especially if he or she has a special cost advantage, an unusually good location, and product differentiation sufficient to attract new customers easily. Ultimately "barriers to market entry" can be translated into another phrase: "stiff competition."

SEE ALSO *Competitive Analysis*

BIBLIOGRAPHY

Karakaya, Fahri. "Barriers to entry in industrial markets." *Journal of Business & Industrial Marketing.* Vol. 17, No. 5, 2002

Rhoda, Chris. "Contestable Markets." *Economics for International Students.* 2001. Available from: http://www.cr1.dircon.co.uk/TB/2/monopoly/contestablemarkets.htm.

Hillstrom, Northern Lights
updated by Magee, ECDI

BARTERING

Bartering is the exchange of goods and services among businesses. The practice is as old as time, but since about the late 1970s it has taken on a new life of its own and has grown into a major national and international activity, more recently mediated by means of the Internet. Bartering organizations and networks have come into being. In what amounts to a revival of mediaeval practices, these organizations have created and maintained new forms of money in the form of "trading credits." Trading profits are taxable; in turn, also, trading costs are deductible from taxes like any other costs. The principal justification of barter trading is three-fold: barter exchanges offer new ways of finding markets, new ways of obtaining goods at lower costs, and barter lowers participating companies' cash-flow requirements. The last of these justifications usually acts as the driving force.

The International Reciprocal Trade Association (IRTA) reports World Trade Organization figures to the effect that 15 percent of international trade is now conducted on a non-cash basis. In North and Latin America, some 500 commercial trade exchange companies operated and accounted for $2.3 billion in barter trade in 2004, the most recent data. IRTA's own survey indicates a world market of $8.25 billion in 2004. IRTA is one of the leading associations of companies engaged in barter trade; the National Association of Trade Exchanges is another.

BARTERING BASICS

Traditional bartering took the form of simple exchanges: I mow your lawn, you cut my hair. Modern bartering is much more complex. A company wishing to barter first joins a trading exchange. Sign-up fees ranging from $200 to $600 and monthly membership costs are usually involved. A broker may be assigned to the company. The goods or services to be bartered are priced by negotiation. In exchange for these the company receives trading credits. These credits work exactly like money but must be exchanged for goods/services available through the exchange the company has joined or other exchanges with which that exchange is affiliated. Each transaction has its own costs (10 to 15 percent of the transaction's face value)—in addition to the assessed membership fees. Bartering exchanges, in effect, "make a new market" and also maintain a "currency" (the trading credits) to be used within that market.

Tina Traster, writing in *Crain's New York Business* provides some valuable tips for those wishing to participate. She points out that barter transactions take more time; those in a hurry had better use cash. It is best to investigate, in advance, if the exchange has what the would-be participant needs. She reminds the would-be trader that taxes are due on all barter exchanges and the exchange will report them to the IRS on Form 1099B. She suggests that bartering is potentially a way of networking with new customers and should not be viewed as a one-time transaction.

Joanne Sammer, writing in the *New Jersey Law Journal,* shows the manner in which a small business used barter to get going. The story involves a two-lawyer startup. The new law-firm's principal joined two barter exchanges to kick-start the business. Sammer quotes the principal as saying: "As a small firm, we needed opportunities to find clients we ordinarily would not get." The law-firm encounters 20 potential barter clients yearly. Many of these contacts eventually become cash-paying clients and also refer other paying customers.

TRENDS AND DIRECTIONS

Web-based barter trading appears to be the next major development in the barter industry. As Gabriel Landriault put it in a 1999 article in *Computer Dealer News,* "Internet-based barter exchanges are growing in popularity and could represent the last true e-commerce revolution." New entities are announced at regular intervals and have features designed to increase participation—lower or no fees and a huge variety of difficult-to-find products (on the model of e-Bay). Established "brick and mortar" operations (which have warehouses, brokers, and usually charge substantial fees) as well as established e-traders are carefully watching development now. Landriault reported that consolidation was both anticipated and resisted by many of those involved.

The barter business appears above all to depend on participants who are low on cash and using barter as a way to get around these problems. This fact is hinted at by IRTA's own web site. On IRTA's page titled *Joining an Exchange* (see http://www.irta.com) the first bulleted item reads as follows: "First things first, make sure that your business is stable with cash flow. If your business is already experiencing cash flow problems, don't assume that barter is going to solve them." If cash problems are the driving force, the ultimate expansion of this business will be indirectly governed by economic conditions—unless other factors, such as networking and finding new clients, come to trump the primary motive for participation.

EVALUATING BARTER NETWORKS

Small businesses interested in exploring membership in a local, national, or international barter exchange should consider the following factors when examining networks:

- Examine the roster of network participants/members to ensure that they have goods and/or services of value to your small business.

- Study the number of members and the frequency with which they trade. Some exchanges are much more active than others, depending on the trading philosophy of participants and the rules of the network itself.

- Examine the attractiveness of ancillary network services (consulting, member mixers, information newsletters, etc.) for your company.

- Study the size of the trades made within the network. Companies that are interested primarily in bartering expensive goods or services may find it difficult to find parties willing to engage in a barter agreement.

- Compare pricing structure and other financial aspects of the network to ensure that bartering makes financial sense for your business. Origination, monthly, and transaction fees can all vary significantly from network to network. In addition, entrepreneurs should attempt to gauge the level of sincere interest that the exchange has in helping their business. For example, some bartering networks limit the number of businesses offering the same goods or services so that benefits of membership are not diluted among too many companies.

- Study the geographic location of other businesses within the barter exchange. For some businesses, close proximity to other network participants is essential for membership to be financially viable.

BIBLIOGRAPHY

"Internet-based bartering service launched." *Internet Business News.* September 30, 2005.

Katz-Stone, Adam. "Trading Off." *Baltimore Business Journal.* August 25, 2000.

Kooser, Amanda C. "Swap hop. (BUZZ) (SwapThing.com)." *Entrepreneur.* December 2005.

Ladriault, Gabriel. "E-barter set for explosion." *Computer Dealer News.* 29 October 1999.

McClellan, Steve. "Old Business of Bartering Finds New Life in Media." *AdWEEK.* 4 April 2005.

Sammer, Joanne. "Bartering for Business." *New Jersey Law Journal.* 21 March 2005.

Traster, Tina. "Five steps to bartering unused goods or services." *Crain's New York Business.* 13 June 2005.

Hillstrom, Northern Lights
updated by Magee, ECDI

BENCHMARKING

Benchmarking is a management technique aimed at detecting "best practice" in other organizations and then adopting it in one's own.

According to Keith Session and his associates, writing in an occasional paper titled "All Benchmarkers Now?," the practice has its roots in Japanese reverse engineering efforts in the 1950s and in *kaizen,* meaning *continuous improvement,* a practice introduced by Toyota. Benchmarking, in other words, is a competitive response: "Others are doing a better job. How do they do it? Let's do the same thing." According to Session et. al., the practice is "very much associated with Xerox in the USA, leading to the first book on the subject by the company's head of benchmarking in the 1980s.... Initially, in the late 1970s and early 1980s, Xerox focused on the activities of its Japanese competitors. This 'competitive benchmarking' was quickly joined by 'generic benchmarking', in which Xerox looked beyond immediate competitors, to include companies with strong practices wherever they were to be found—railways, insurance and electricity generation, for example."

Since that time benchmarking has been applied in a formal fashion (following strict rules) to all manner of technical and administrative procedures. The phrase has also come to be used somewhat loosely to indicate any kind of comparisons between companies, departments, and discrete processes. It may be applied very narrowly to such matters as Internet download time performance and as broadly as comparing marketing campaigns.

Benchmarking has become a well-accepted management tool among larger corporations, both as a means of remaining competitive and in justifying their own performance. Richard T. Roth, writing in *Financial Executive,* leads off his article on benchmarking by saying: "The benchmarking concept, a familiar one to most executives, keeps gaining converts. Bain & Co.'s most recent Management Tools study, which charts the tools that companies use to set strategic direction, finds that for the past four years, benchmarking has held steady in second place, with 84 percent of all surveyed companies using it. Only formal strategic planning surpassed benchmarking in the ranking." Benchmarking picked up with the onset of the recession in the late 1990s: it helps document a business unit's contribution to corporate performance no matter which way the economy moves. Benchmarking also helps to make the case for necessary but painful change.

HOW IT WORKS

Benchmarking is a study of best practices elsewhere and the implementation of findings "back home." Studies may be very broad (generic benchmarking), industry-wide (industry benchmarking), specific to a business function like purchasing (functional benchmarking), or aimed at a particular process (performance benchmarking).

The general procedure involves selection of a target, identifying best practitioners, surveying best practices by interview and other means, analyzing the results, and making whatever changes are needed internally to apply the discoveries made.

Unless the practice is well-integrated and institutionalized, barriers to effective benchmarking abound, especially in smaller organizations. Formal programs usually require a substantial commitment of staff time and direct expenditures. For maximum effect, therefore, top management involvement is vital but not always forthcoming: benchmarking initiatives may arise at lower levels in order to "nudge" upper management. Identifying best practice may prove difficult and may involve extra costs. It is obviously most difficult to benchmark direct competitors: they tend to shy from sharing the secret of their success. Once best practices have been identified, their analysis can present serious difficulties. Frequently "best practice" is due to unique circumstances, sometimes intangible qualities like a leading personality, and are therefore very difficult to adopt. Finally, implementation of best practice may be fiercely resisted within the company slated for improvement.

For these reasons, benchmarking programs are most successful when their aims are fairly narrow and quantifiable, awareness of the problem within the company is widespread and shared, best practice is reasonably accessible, and implementation is well rewarded.

BENCHMARKING AND SMALL BUSINESS

Benchmarking tends to be a method most suited to large, centralized, and bureaucratically organized institutions. Smaller companies sometimes attempt it, but success appears to require effective top management participation. James Dodd and Mark Turner, writing in *National Public Accountant,* accurately assess small business attitudes toward this management technique: "Most regard their businesses as too unique to warrant detailed comparison across industries," they write. "They see no valid comparisons and, therefore, do not recognize any meaningful benefit from examining practices outside their own industries." There is also the further consideration that small businesses have better uses for their money than visiting scores of distant companies to learn how they collect debt or display merchandise. The functional equivalent to benchmarking, however, does take place when small business owners interact with competitors and peers in the marketplace—and keep eyes and ears open.

SEE ALSO *Best Practices*

BIBLIOGRAPHY
Ackoff, Russell L. "The Trouble with Benchmarking." *Across the Board.* January 2000.

"All Benchmarkers Now? Benchmarking and the 'Europeanisation' of Industrial Relations." Sussex European Institute, 2002.

Bogan, Christopher E., and Michael J. English. *Benchmarking for Best Practices: Winning through Innovative Adaptation.* McGraw-Hill, 1994.

Dodd, James L., and Mark A. Turner. "Is Benchmarking Appropriate for Small Businesses?" *National Public Accountant.* August 2000.

"Main Obstacles to Benchmarking." *Modern Materials Handling.* 29 February 2000.

Roth, Richard T. "Best Practice Benchmarking." *Financial Executive.* July-August 2005.

Wieder, Tamara. "E-Commerce Benchmarking." *Computerworld.* 7 August 2000.

Hillstrom, Northern Lights
updated by Magee, ECDI

BEST PRACTICES

The phrase "best practices" or, in the singular, "best practice" is business jargon arising from the management tool known as "benchmarking." The assumption underlying this term is that production and management processes are uniform enough so that a "best practice" can be identified and then adopted more or less "as is" by another entity. This is obviously the case in technical areas, the adoption of "best practice" by others blocked only by patent protection. When the concept is applied to management procedures however, the transferability of "best practices" may be more difficult to accomplish. Benchmarking programs attempt to identify best practices in a sector, an industry, or a cluster of competitors. Best practices are quantified to the extent possible by developing measurements ("metrics") and then comparing the numbers to similarly developed values inside the surveying operation.

According to the consulting firm Best Practices LLC, companies exhibiting a best practice may not be best-in-class in every area. But due to industry forces or the firm's goal of excellence, practices have been implemented and developed that have brought the firm recognition in a certain area. Typically the best practices result in higher profits.

IDENTIFYING BEST PRACTICES

Some firms are so well known for best practices in certain areas that it is not necessary to consult books, magazines, libraries, or the Internet to find the information. For example, Federal Express is often cited as having best practices among competitors in the expedited small package industry for their on-time delivery and package tracking services. Microsoft, the computer software developer, is cited as being innovative and creative, while the L. L. Bean outdoor products and clothing company is frequently lauded for its customer service practices and return policy guarantees.

When a firm is benchmarking to learn about the best practices of others, often these superior methods are found in companies outside the firm's key industry segment. Thus it is important to research and observe companies in a wide variety of settings, countries, industries, and even in the not-for-profit sector to learn better ways to improve continuously.

Information on best practices and innovative technologies can also be found on the Best Manufacturing Practices (BMP) Web site at http://www.bmpcoe.org/. This site has as its goal to increase the quality, reliability, and maintainability of goods produced by American firms. One way BMP accomplishes this goal is to identify best practices, document them, and share the information across industry segments. They believe that by sharing best practices, they allow companies to learn from others' attempts and to avoid costly and time-consuming duplication of efforts. Companies profiled have submitted abstracts of what their organization does well and they include previous practices, changes to new processes, and information on implementation as well as quantitative details and lessons learned.

An example of best practice outside the manufacturing sector is provided by Richard T. Roth in a recent article in *Financial Executive*. Roth writes: "An analysis of the most recent finance benchmarks in the 2005 Hackett Book of Numbers finds that world-class performers spend 42 percent less than typical companies on their finance operations as a percentage of revenue... and operate with less than half the staff of their peers. At the same time, they close their books more quickly each month, and historically have generated significant additional savings through reducing effective tax rates and days sales outstanding." The example illustrates how a well-quantified "best practice" can become a corporate goal elsewhere.

LEARNING FROM AWARD WINNERS

Other ways to identify best practices include observing businesses as a consumer or as a mystery shopper. It is also possible to identify best practices by examining professional journals and business periodicals. Companies that win various awards often exhibit best practices to emulate. The Malcolm Baldrige National Quality Award winners are a good group of companies to benchmark for best practices. They have met the rigorous award criteria and have had success that allowed them to win this prestigious award. The Malcolm Baldrige National Quality Award is given to U.S. organizations that have shown achievements and improvements in seven areas: leadership, strategic planning, customer and market focus, information and analysis, human resource focus, process management, and business results. For information about the award and profiles of past winners, see http://www.quality.nist.gov/.

Industry Week, a publication aimed at manufacturers, has since 1990 set out to find and share stories of America's best plants. They later extended their coverage to include Europe's best plants. They have set out to define the best practices of world-class competition and highlight quality approaches, lean manufacturing, and employee empowerment. The publication stresses the fact that these practices can be implemented in a wide range of industries to improve competitiveness and productivity.

Learning about the best practices of others is a valuable way for firms to gather fresh insights into possible methods of improving a myriad of aspects of their operations. It should be an important part of an organization's strategic planning activities.

SEE ALSO *Benchmarking*

BIBLIOGRAPHY

Panchak, Patricia. "The Never-Ending Search for Excellence." *Industry Week.* 16 October 2000.

Patton, Susannah. "By the Numbers." *CIO.* 1 October 2000.

Roth, Richard T. "Best practice benchmarking." *Financial Executive.* July-August 2005.

Hillstrom, Northern Lights
updated by Magee, ECDI

BETTER BUSINESS BUREAUS (BBBs)

Better Business Bureaus (BBBs) are private non-profit organizations that collect and report information to help consumers make informed decisions when dealing with businesses or charitable organizations. The BBB is not a government or law enforcement agency; it does not have the power to collect money, administer sanctions, or impose other penalties against companies or individuals that engage in poor business practices. But its ability to disseminate a company's operating track record makes it a force to be reckoned with. Faced with the prospect of losing customers because of unfavorable BBB rankings, companies have a significant incentive to adhere to proper business practices and address customer complaints. In addition to their information-gathering activities, local BBBs also provide mediation services when disputes arise between customers and businesses, promote ethical business standards, maintain standards for truthful advertising, and share pertinent information (about possible fraudulent activity, etc.) with local and national law enforcement agencies. With the rise of e-commerce in the late 1990s, they have also become involved in efforts to address business fraud on the Internet. BBBs are licensed by the Council of Better Business Bureaus (CBBB) and governed by their own local boards of directors.

The most widely-used service of the Better Business Bureau is its inquiry and information service; it features information updated on a daily basis. In fact, the BBB receives as many as 1,000 inquiries a day from consumers and businesses seeking reports on firms. These reliability reports are limited to marketplace practices; they do not provide information on either individual or business credit information. BBB reliability reports contain information about the nature of the business, its principal officers, a three-year summary of any complaints processed, and any government action involving the company's marketplace practices. Most Bureaus also note BBB membership (if any) in its public report and indicate whether the firm in question participates in any special BBB programs to improve customer satisfaction. In addition, the BBB issues reports on products, services, and general business topics to promote educated comparison shopping by consumers and businesses alike. These reports are available on the Better Business Bureau website (www.bbb.org), which also provides businesses and consumers with the ability to file complaints.

Many small businesses and consumers also utilize the BBB's arbitration program. This system was instituted in 1973 as a way to help businesses and customers avoid litigation. "[It] uses trained volunteer arbitrators from the community," noted *Business First-Columbus.* "[They] perform their duties as a public service, the arbitration process is provided at no cost to the consumer and, in most instances, at no cost to the business. Depending on the dollar amount in dispute, the arbitration is either conducted by a single arbitrator or by a panel of three. The arbitrators' decisions are rendered within 10 days after the close of the hearing, and most cases are completed within 45 days after the process has been chosen by the parties."

The most recent data on complaints received by BBB early in 2006 were statistics for the year 2004. In that year the business categories receiving the most complaints were, in this order, Cell Phone Services, Equipment and Supplies; New Car Dealers; Credit Cards and Plans; Collection Agencies; Internet Services; Furniture Retailers; Internet Shopping Services; Telephone Companies; Auto Repair and Service Companies; and Electronic Equipment Suppliers and Dealers.

BBB MEMBERSHIP

Each Better Business Bureau is independently supported by businesses that operate within their designated service area. BBBs receive their operating funds from the membership dues that are paid by business and professional groups in those service areas. Companies that become members of their local Better Business Bureau receive several benefits in return. These usually include: 1) membership identification on the company's place of business; 2) access to all BBB publications, programs, and services; 3) right to participate in BBB training programs in such areas as arbitration, customer service, and mediation; 4) affiliation with other member businesses.

But the BBB maintains certain standards for membership to ensure that the organization's integrity remains unquestioned. Companies with bad track records are not accepted, and companies that do become members have to adhere to certain rules. For example, BBB members must respond to consumer complaints presented by the BBB; if they do not do so, they lose their membership. In addition, it should be noted that the BBB attaches a number of conditions to ensure that companies do not join simply for the purpose of trumpeting their membership. BBBs do not endorse or recommend businesses or what they sell. Moreover, they do not allow members to advertise their membership, because the public could conceivably reach the erroneous conclusion that such advertising means that the BBB is endorsing the member's business. In addition, BBB membership dues are not tax deductible for federal income tax purposes, though they may be tax deductible as an ordinary and necessary business expense. Finally, the CBBB has noted that membership does not confer any advantages when complaints arise: "The BBB's integrity is on the line every time we review and process a complaint. If a Bureau were to favor members over non-members in a complaint, such action would destroy our most valuable asset—the public trust that we have held for over 80 years."

In addition, a branch of the Council of Better Business Bureaus known as the Philanthropic Advisory Service maintains information on various charitable organizations. These reports, which are maintained by the national Council but updated by local BBBs, cover all sorts of charitable and other nonprofit organizations. Information typically included in these reports includes the group's background, its current programs (if any), the structure of its governing body, its tax-exempt status, its fund-raising practices, its financial standing, and notification as to whether the organization complies with the CBBB's "Standards for Charitable Solicitations."

These reliability reports can be invaluable to both individual and business customers who want to make sure that they are conducting business with an ethical company. The BBB cautions, however, that it does not maintain reports on every business operating in a given area. The reasons for this vary. In some cases, the business is relatively new. In other instances, the company may simply operate in such a manner that customers see no reason to file a complaint.

BIBLIOGRAPHY

"2004 Complaint & Inquiry Stats." Better Business Bureau. Available from http://www.bbb.org/about/stat2004.asp. Retrieved on 2 January 2006.

"BBB Dispute Resolution: Common-Sense Alternative." *Business First-Columbus.* 22 October 1999.

"BBB History and Traditions." Better Business Bureau Consumer Information Series, n.d.

"Before You Buy: BBB Offers Inquiry, Information Services." *Business First-Columbus.* 22 October 1999.

Cohen, Alan. "Meet the Watchdogs." *PC Magazine.* 14 December 1999.

"Dissatisfied Consumers Who Complain to the Better Business Bureau." *Journal of Consumer Marketing.* September-October 1999.

"Frequently Asked Questions About the Better Business Bureau." Better Business Bureau Consumer Information Series, n.d.

Hillstrom, Northern Lights
updated by Magee, ECDI

BIOMETRICS

Biometrics is a field of science that uses computer technology to identify people based on physical or behavioral characteristics such as fingerprints or voice scans. "Bio" in the name refers to the physiological traits measured; "metrics" refers to the quantitative analysis that provides a positive identification of an individual. Biometrics is gaining widespread use in the business world as means to make the workplace more secure and efficient. The technology promises almost foolproof security for facilities and computer networks. It also helps employees increase their productivity by providing instant identification for time cards, payroll processing, computer logins, phone or copy machine usage, and myriad other purposes. In the age of terrorism, biometrics is increasingly recruited to help in tracking potentially dangerous individuals.

"The biometrics industry, which produces technologies to identify people by their natural biological features, such as fingerprints, the patterns in the eye's iris, and facial characteristics—the stuff of *Mission Impossible*—is sensing the chance to break out of high-tech security doors and enter the mainstream of daily life," Julian Perkin wrote in the *Financial Times.* "Biometrics are enjoying good reviews from the businesses that have integrated them into their systems to date," Sheila Smith Drapeau added in the *Westchester County Business Journal.* "They are proving themselves reliable, time efficient, affordable, and easy to use—another nod to shaving a few dollars off the office payroll. And their popularity is expected to skyrocket as aging baby boomers concerned with memory loss eagerly seek an alternative to remembering passwords, numerical systems, and their car keys." The U.S. Government is deploying biometrics as well. On January 1, 2006, the U.S. State Department announced the installation of biometric "entry systems" at U.S. land ports. According to the State Department release, "The program compares biometric data such as digital and inkless fingerscans and digital photos, as well as biographical information collected by the Department of State, against U.S. terrorist and criminal watch lists to identify and intercept criminals and violators who try to enter the United States."

One benefit of biometrics is that it relieves people from the burden of remembering dozens of different passwords to company computer networks, e-mail systems, Web sites, etc. In addition to creating distinct passwords for each system they use or Web site they visit, people are expected to change their passwords frequently. Employees who have trouble remembering their passwords may be more likely to keep a written list in a desk drawer or posted on a bulletin board, thus creating a security risk. But biometrics offers an easy solution to this problem. "An employee may not be able to remember a dozen passwords and PINs, but is very unlikely to forget or misplace his or her thumb," P.J. Connolly wrote in *InfoWorld.*

A related problem with passwords is that they do not provide reliable security. In fact, hackers can download password-cracking software for free on the Internet that will test the most obvious combinations of characters for each user on a system and often find a way in. Electronic retailers have found that their prospective customers are aware of the unreliable nature of password-based security systems. A survey conducted by Yankelovich Partners and reported in *Entrepreneur* indicated that security concerns prevent 31 percent of Internet users from making purchases online. Installing a biometrics-based security system is likely to impress customers who are concerned about Web site security. "You may already have the solution to all your security needs right in the palm of your hand—or, more likely, at your fingertips," Mike Hogan noted in *Entrepreneur.* "That's because biometrics offers an answer to all security and authorization issues."

Biometrics systems—which once cost tens of thousands of dollars to install—were originally used only by large corporations and the government. But now less expensive systems—costing as little as a few hundred dollars per desktop—are making the technology available to smaller businesses and individual consumers. As a result, analysts believe that the usage of biometrics will grow over the next few years, so that the technology will become prevalent on the Internet as well as in businesses. Several recent developments have helped assure the future of biometrics. For example, digital signature legislation passed in 2000 provided for biometric authentication to be accepted in place of a written signature and considered legally binding on documents. In addition, Microsoft announced that it would support biometric technology in future versions of Windows, making it easier to build Internet and network servers that can accept the biometric identifications. Before long, biometric scanning devices may be bundled into every new PC sold.

One of the first general applications of biometric technology may be in the health care industry. The Health Insurance Portability and Accountability Act recommended biometric authentication for health care facilities and insurance providers and set high penalties for improper or negligent disclosure of medical information. At some time in the future, every U.S. citizen's medical records may be available online and accessible with biometric authentication. This would allow individuals to access their records from a pharmacy or an emergency room far from home. It would also allow physicians to share case information and expertise online. However, many people still have concerns about privacy and worry that the online availability of medical records might affect their ability to change jobs or obtain insurance.

HOW BIOMETRICS SYSTEMS WORK

The main biometrics systems on the market work by scanning an individual's fingerprints, hands, face, iris, retina, voice pattern, signature, or strokes on a keyboard. According to Hogan, finger scanning accounts for 34 percent of biometric system sales, followed by hand scanning with 26 percent, face scanning with 15 percent, voice scanning and eye scanning with 11 percent each, and signature scanning with 3 percent. Retinal scanning—which reads the blood vessels in the back of the eye and requires the user to be within six inches of the scanning device—is the most accurate system but also the least likely to enjoy widespread use because of people's natural protectiveness toward their eyes.

Once the scanner reads the user's physiological information, the computer begins analyzing it. "The system reads the physical or behavioral characteristic, looks for telltale minutiae, and applies an algorithm that uniquely expresses those minutiae as a very large alphanumeric key," Bill Orr explained in the *ABA Banking Journal.* "This sample key then goes to a repository where it is compared with a key (called a template) that was created by the approved user when she enrolled in the system. This in turn generates a score based on how closely the two samples match."

Some experts suggest that the various types of biometric technologies will be combined as needed to fit different user applications. "If you already have a telephone in your hand, the most natural thing in the world is to use voice scanning for identification," Samir Nanavati of the International Biometric Group told Hogan. "If you're already typing at a keyboard, the unique pattern of how you type makes the most sense. And if you need an electronic signature anyway, why not do a biometric match for identification purposes?"

For companies hoping to incorporate some form of biometrics into their facility or computer security systems, the most difficult aspect of the process might be making various systems work together. "The tough part of implementing a biometric method isn't choosing between face, fingerprint, and voice pattern recognition but integrating the chosen method with your existing applications," Connolly acknowledged in *InfoWorld.* Even though biometric scanners are becoming more affordable, Web site operators still have to buy authentication and authorization servers that can accept the biometric identifications. However, some vendors are beginning to offer these services for companies that are unable to maintain a biometric server in-house.

Perhaps the most difficult obstacle to overcome in adopting biometric technology is employee or customer concern about its invasiveness. For example, many people think the technology could be used to collect fingerprints for a huge database. "But that's not how it works," Hogan noted. "While biometrics may make you more efficient at matching your Web site visitors to the customer profiles you keep of them, it doesn't provide any more information about the user at the point of access than the typical password system."

SEE ALSO *Data Encryption; Internet Security; Counter terrorism*

BIBLIOGRAPHY
Connolly, P.J. "Biometrics Comforts Customers while Securing Assets." *InfoWorld.* 2 April 2001.

Connolly, P.J. "Future Security May Be in the Hands, or Eyes, of Users—By Eliminating the Need for User Passwords, Biometrics Will Tighten Networks and Save Big IT Money." *InfoWorld.* 16 October 2000.

Connolly, P.J. "Security Steps into the Spotlight." *InfoWorld.* 29 January 2001.

Drapeau, Sheila Smith. "Biometrics: Where Science Meets the Company Payroll." *Westchester County Business Journal.* 5 February 2001.

Fonseca, Brian. "Biometrics Eye the Mainstream Markets." *InfoWorld.* 15 January 2001.

Hogan, Mike. "Body Language." *Entrepreneur.* March 2001.

Orr, Bill. "Time to Start Planning for Biometrics." *ABA Banking Journal.* October 2000.

Perkin, Julian. "New Services Will Keep an Eye on Security: Biometrics." *Financial Times.* 21 February 2001.

United States Department of State, Press Release. "Biometric Entry System Installed at Final U.S. Land Ports." 1 January 2006

Hillstrom, Northern Lights
updated by Magee, ECDI

BLUE CHIP

A "blue chip" is the stock of a well-established, financially sound, and historically secure corporation. According to Ken Kurson, writing in *MONEY Magazine,* the term itself comes from the early 20th century and was borrowed from the game of poker: blue chips had the highest value. In the investment world, however, blue chip companies are far from being a gamble. They are companies with a history of posting earnings and paying dividends, all while continuing to increase profits. While markets always fluctuate and all companies go though occasional downturns, blue chips are known for strong executive management teams that make intelligent growth decisions and for their high-quality products and services. Blue chip stocks, also known as large cap stocks (because the companies have a high market capitalization of $1 billion or more), tend to rise and fall in conjunction with the stock market in general.

Examples of blue chip stocks include Coca-Cola, Disney, Intel, and IBM. Because the return on blue chip stocks is close to a sure thing, the stocks tend to be expensive and to have a low dividend yield. These drawbacks are offset by the earnings and dividends paid. Most blue chip stocks are offered by companies that have been around for decades, or even longer, but new companies can break into the blue chip ranks if analysts expect the company to last.

Recent example of this phenomenon are Yahoo! and Google, two World Wide Web search engines which may eventually enter the ranks of blue chips. Yahoo! was the highest flyer among Web stocks in the late 1990s. Google is the current sensation (2006). Only time will tell if these companies will eventually take on the permanence and stature of an Intel or an IBM. Meanwhile once unquestionable pillars of the Blue Chip temple, like General Motors and Ford, are fighting battles of survival. Thus even in the world of blue chips, change is the only certainty.

BLUE CHIPS OUTPERFORM OTHER INVESTMENTS

While some people continue to doubt the ultimate financial security of stocks, blue chips are the closest to a sure thing on the stock market—provided that you carefully maintain your list by additions and subtractions. In a 1996 study outlined in his book, *Stocks for the Long Run,* Jeremy Siegel found that blue chip stocks are quite possibly the best financial investment a consumer can make. Siegel analyzed financial data from 1802 to the present; he found that blue chip stocks were a better investment than gold, bonds, or Treasury bills.

According to a report in *Forbes,* one dollar invested in stocks in 1802 would have been worth more than $350,000 in 1995. In comparison, a dollar in T-bills grew to only $261, which is only 0.0007 percent of the rate of return on stocks. Treasury bonds did not fare much better, finishing with $752, while gold did even worse, although figures were not available. Inflation and taxes hurt all of the investments, but it hurt bonds worst. Not available until after World War II, bonds would have wiped out many an investor who chose them for his or her only investment. Accounting for inflation and taxes, Siegel found that $1 million invested in bonds immediately after the war would be worth only $218,000 in real purchasing power in 1995. This stretch of history does show that blue chips are a good investment for the long run. But in the financial field, nothing is certain. It should be noted that Siegel's study was completed before the stock market soared to record highs in 1998 and 1999; had such results been included, his case would have been stronger. But a market crash in the intervening time would have changed the conclusions in the other direction.

Financial advisor John Campbell of the firm Goldman Sachs reaffirmed Siegel's buy recommendation in 1998. At that time, Campbell maintained a list of 20 to 25 blue chip stocks that had returned 36.42 percent annually for the three years he managed the list compared with a return of 30.2 percent for the Standard and Poor's 500. Campbell's advice about buying blue chips, which he discussed in *Fortune,* was to "invest in the best businesses and the best managements, pay a fair price, and over the course of your life your stocks will do better than the market."

POSITIVE AND NEGATIVE ASPECTS OF BLUE CHIPS

As with any stock, there are positives and negatives with blue chips. Because blue chips are the oldest and best-known companies, they are easy to follow, often ending up on the front page instead of just in the financial section of the local newspaper. Investors can thus track these companies and evaluate their advertising and marketing strategies. Finally, they are a great tool for teaching kids about the stock market by using brand names they recognize, like McDonald's or Walt Disney.

The negatives associated with blue chips are basically the same as for other stocks. Even blue chips can take a nosedive. And as the old saying goes, "the bigger they are, the harder they fall." The more you have invested in a company, the worse its mistakes can be for your portfolio. In addition, blue chip stocks often pay smaller dividends than even the 4 percent yield associated with income stocks. This puts off some investors.

Most blue chip stocks are traded on the New York Stock Exchange and make up a significant portion of the Dow Jones Industrial Average and the S & P 500 Index. They can be purchased through brokers or online. The best time to buy blue chip stocks is after a disappointing earnings report or after a particularly bad public relations blunder: the stock is sure to dip then, making it more likely that you will buy low and be able to sell high later. If you divide the company's net assets by the number of shares it has outstanding, and the stock is selling for less than that number, consider buying because it is a very good value at that point. Also, try to avoid companies that have accrued a large amount of long-term debt.

SEE ALSO *Fortune 500*

BIBLIOGRAPHY
Dreman, David. "A (Very) Simple Truth." *Forbes.* 14 October 1996.

Kurson, Ken, "Where have all the blue chips gone?"*MONEY Magazine.* 2 December 2002.

Morris, Kenneth M., Virginia B. Morris, and Alan M. Siegel. *The Wall Street Journal Guide to Understanding Money & Investing.* Fireside, 1999.

Siegel, Jeremy J., and Peter L. Bernstein. *Stocks for the Long Run.* McGraw-Hill Professional Publishing, 1998.

Hillstrom, Northern Lights
updated by Magee, ECDI

BOARD OF DIRECTORS

A corporation is a legal entity created ("chartered") either under federal or state law. The corporation is an artificial "person" distinct from the individuals who own it. This prompted a jurist once to remark that a corporation has "neither a soul to damn nor a body to kick" (as recalled by Barron's *Dictionary of Finance and Investment Terms.*) This legal person is nevertheless entitled to own property, borrow money, bring law suits, and to have its communications protected under the First Amendment. The charter of this institution is its "constitution," the shareholders are its "people," the management is its "executive," and the board of directors is its "legislature." In theory stockholders elect board members and board members elect the chief executive. Thus a "board of directors" is associated with companies organized as corporations. Partnerships and sole proprietorships do not have boards. The minimum and maximum number of board members is usually specified by state law; three is a typical minimum membership; the maximum may not exceed the number of shareholders. The board's duties are defined by the corporate charter which, in turn, is structured by state and/or federal law.

HISTORICAL PERSPECTIVE

In discussing boards generally, it is important at the outset to note that all boards are different. Despite major trends over time, specific boards have exhibited every variety of function associated with such bodies, often in defiance of prevailing custom.

By historic origin, boards initially *were* the investors—the three or four wealthy people who funded an energetic entrepreneur. The distinction between investors and boards developed over time as the number of investors grew large and, in more modern times, enormous; boards then took on the role of bodies representing stockholders. The presence on the board of major stockholders, however, in person or by proxy, has never disappeared. Through much of the sustained growth period that followed World War II, boards retained their governance functions but often exercised them weakly ("rubber stamp boards"), especially in successful, growing corporations led by dominant executives. In the opening years of the 21st century, in response to major corporate scandals, a strong role for boards has reemerged, mandated by federal law. But these changes are strictly speaking specific only to publicly traded companies. The role of boards in privately held corporations continues to be shaped by other factors, most prominently by the degree to which major stockholders alone or in groups wish to be involved. Private boards may be quite active in some companies and may exercise supervisory powers; in others board members are chiefly used as resources and as ambassadors to other interests; in yet others boards are a mere formality required by law.

BOARDS AND THEIR ORGANIZATION

Corporate boards have members, usually called "directors," who are elected by the stockholders. In the ordinary course of events, a privately held corporation has board members selected by the consensus of the company's founders without a formal election. When the company goes public and stockholder numbers increase substantially, the company prepares slates of board candidates and submits these to stockholders for a vote. The stockholder may accept the recommended slate, choose one of the alternatives, name others who do not appear on the list, or give his or her vote ("proxy") to the company itself to exercise.

Board members are called *inside directors* if they are members of the management or *outside directors* if they have no direct role in the company itself. Outside directors are typically well-known figures in the business community recruited for service on the board to provide valuable advice and counsel; they may not be executives of competitors or sit on competitors' boards. Outside directors may also be drawn from community organizations sometimes representing academia, law, labor, or other large constituencies or interests. Outside directors are also called independent directors because they are not under the influence of the chief executive of the corporation. In publicly held companies directors receive compensation for their services. Compensation may also be paid in privately held organizations.

Under the rules of the Securities and Exchange Commission (SEC), directors of either category are held to be "insiders" and therefore prohibited from trading stock based on "inside knowledge."

In large corporations the board is frequently subdivided into committees with functional roles such as Executive, Finance, Compensation, Strategy, Audit, etc. Board members are assigned to committees and these, in turn, develop positions on issues pertinent to the functional matter assigned to the committee. They make recommendations to the full board. Under legislation passed in 2002, audit committees are mandatory and their functions and membership are precisely defined.

Boards set their own rules of operation. If the corporation's bylaws or charter specify that Robert's Rules of Order will be followed, procedures may take the parliamentary form—or do so if conflicts arise.

In large corporations the board—and its committees—will have full-time staffs engaged in preparatory and administrative work related to board activities. Employees of such staffs are also considered to be insiders because of their unique access to sensitive data.

THE EVOLUTION OF A BOARD

In a small privately held corporation the board will typically be a so-called "working board," with its members all engaged in the business. In addition one or two additional family members may be on the board but inactive in operations. Board meetings tend to be rather informal in such situations because operational and board decisions coincide. The paper-work connected with the board activity—recording legally mandated board meetings, for instance—will be seen as rather a nuisance. If and when the business begins to grow, the board will tend to evolve.

A growing business tends to enlarge its board by inviting new investors to serve—or may have to welcome a new investor (or his or her representative) willingly or not. The owners also often see great benefit in drawing in people who can bring new points of view and important skills and knowledge in guiding the company as it expands, often into unfamiliar territories. An "advisory board" thus develops. Board meetings take on a real value at this stage. They serve to clarify directions and to gather information. Management learns to view itself more clearly and consciously by explaining the business to others at board meetings. Board members bring suggestions, make contacts, redirect efforts by good advice, identify opportunities, and otherwise participate in consulting capacities.

The board may finally develop into a "governing board" at the next stage when the company, seeking either to cash out its assets for the owners or to raise funds for the next stage of expansion, "goes public" and becomes a publicly traded entity. At that point the company comes under the regulatory aegis of the SEC. Its board members now are exposed to the colder and harsher winds of securities law. The character of the board will change automatically even if its inside management remains in control by retaining more than half the outstanding shares. The most important duties of a public board are the selection of senior executives, approving issuance of additional shares, declaring dividends, and overseeing financial activities through its auditing committee. Under securities laws, board members are held responsible for the lawful discharge of their duties; failing to do so may result in heavy fines and imprisonment.

PUBLIC COMPANIES AND SOX

The spectacular collapse of Enron Corporation, the energy trader, on December 1, 2001 added the largest bankruptcy ever in U.S. history to the national woes in a year of shock after the terrorist attack on 9/11 of that year. This bankruptcy, ultimately traced back to hidden and suspicious off-balance-sheet transactions, fraudulently overstated earnings, and failures in formal external audits brought into laser-like focus a long-building and widespread critique not only of top management but also of cozy boards of directors viewed as cheerleaders for flamboyant chief executives willing to approve actions without exercising due diligence. Long before Enron, pressure was building to enlist boards of directors into a fight for more disciplined and publicly responsible corporate behavior. Enron brought a very energetic legislative response in the form of the Sarbanes-Oxley Act of 2002, abbreviated as SOX. The subject is discussed in some detail elsewhere in this volume. Here it is only necessary to note that SOX overhauled financial reporting requirements, created a national Public Accounting Oversight Board to reform all auditing procedures, and criminalized a number of executive and director actions. An important provision of Sarbanes-Oxley was the requirement that every public board must have an audit committee made up exclusively of outside (independent) directors. Securities laws had always regulated insider trading activities, which affect directors. More regulations were introduced by SOX; the act unambiguously conveyed the sense of Congress that directors on boards are personally responsible for active supervision of the companies they serve.

SEE ALSO *Sarbanes-Oxley*

BIBLIOGRAPHY

Hellriegel, Don, Susan E. Jackson, and John W. Slocum, Jr. *Management: A Competency-Based Approach.* Thomson South-Western, 2005.

Hitt, Michael A., R. Edward Freeman, and Jeffrey S. Harrison, eds. *The Blackwell Handbook of Strategic Management.* Blackwell Publishers, 2001.

Monks, A.G., and Neil Minow. *Corporate Governance.* Blackwell Publishing, 2004.

Robert III, Henry M. et al. *Robert's Rules of Order Newly Revised, 10th Edition.* Perseus Publishing, 2000.

Shultz, Susan F. *The Board Book: Making your corporate board a strategic force in your company's success.* AMACOM, 2001.

U.S. Congress. *Sarbanes-Oxley Act of 2002.* Available from http://www.law.uc.edu/CCL/SOact/soact.pdf. Retrieved on 20 April 2006.

Darnay, ECDI

BONDS

Bonds are tradeable instruments of debt issued by institutions to finance their activities. Bonds have a face or par value (e.g., $1,000), a fixed interest rate also known as the coupon rate (e.g., 8 percent a year), and a maturity (e.g., 10 years). Bonds are routinely traded, i.e., sold and bought after the initial acquisition from the bond issuer. When a bond is sold at a rate higher than its face value, it is sold "at a premium"; when sold below face value, it is sold "at a discount." Trading in bonds is motivated by the coupon value of the bond in comparison with currently prevailing rates of interest, as discussed below.

Bonds are named after the issuing institutions. Best known are "treasuries," issued by the U.S. Treasury, "municipals," issued by municipalities and other levels of government, and "corporate bonds," issued by corporations. Municipals are tax-free; their earnings are not taxed, a special advantage. Other major categories are "mortgage bonds" issued by such agencies as the Government National Mortgage Association and the Federal Home Loan Mortgage Corporation, "federal agency bonds" issued by departments other than Treasury, "money market bonds" such as bankers' acceptances and commercial paper, and large time deposits, and "asset-backed bonds" where the bonds, issued by either private or public bodies, are tied to a specific object or activity.

Based on data assembled by the Bond Market Association, as of the end of the Third Quarter of 2005, total bonds outstanding amounted to $24.7 trillion. Bond categories in rank order were 1) mortgage bonds: 23.3 percent; 2) corporate bonds: 20.2 percent; 3) U.S. Treasury bonds: 16.4 percent; 4) money market bonds: 13.2 percent; 5) Federal Agency bonds: 10.3 percent; 6) municipal bonds: 8.8 percent; and 7) asset-backed bonds: 7.8 percent. The federal government, Treasury and other agencies combined, represented 26.7 percent; all government (municipals thrown in) 35.5 percent or somewhat over one-third of total.

TRADING IN BONDS

Just like stocks, bonds are actively traded. Why would a person holding a bond with a par value of $1,000 sell it for $800? Why would a person purchase a bond, par value $1,000, for $1,200? The determining factors are the components of the bonds (face value, coupon rate, and maturity) and the characteristics of competing securities and their fluctuating values.

To take "maturity" first, a ten-year bond ties up the invested amount for a ten-year period. An individual who, because of changing circumstances, needs to have cash now ("liquidity") can sell the bond to someone else. The purchaser will take advantage of the seller's situation by bidding less than the face value of the bond. The seller realizes cash immediately; the seller has a bond with a higher yield.

The yield of a bond is calculated by dividing its interest rate (which is fixed) by its face value (which can change when it is sold). When initially purchased, a $1,000 bond yielding $80 a year in interest has an 8 percent yield. If the bond is sold for $800, the yield becomes 10 percent (80 divided by 800). Conversely, if the bond is sold for $1,200, the yield drops to 6.7 percent (80 divided by 1200). Trading in bonds is based on a more complex formula called "yield to maturity." The calculation involves summing up all future yields until maturity, discounting future earnings to current value by using currently achievable interest rates, and deriving a new value. (The calculation is based on the general assumption that future earnings are worth less than cash in hand.) If the resulting "YTM" is higher than the owner of the bond can achieve by other means, he or she holds on to the bond; if not, the bond can be sold at a discount and the money reinvested elsewhere.

Because bonds have a par value and a fixed coupon rate, they are inherently safer than stocks. For this reason, bond prices tend to rise as stock prices drop and vice versa. A downturn in stocks brings money into the bond market; bonds with the most desirable features based on bond ratings, YTM, and tax-exempt status of earnings, tend to go up most. When stock surge, money tends to leave the bond market because greater appreciation is possible holding stocks than is possible to achieve by a combination of bond par values and yields.

BOND RATINGS

Bonds are rated by Moody's Investor Service, Standard & Poor's, Fitch Bond Rating Agency, and others. Using Moody's ratings, similar to S&P/Fitch ratings, Aaa is the highest quality rating, Aa is high quality, A is strong, and Baa is medium grade; all of the above are "investment grade." Ba, B is a speculative "junk grade" bond, Caa/Ca/C is a highly speculative junk bond, and a rating of C means a junk bond in default. S&P and Fitch use D to indicate a bond in default. The label "junk" in all cases indicates that the bond holder is in some kind of financial difficulty.

The higher a bond's rating, the lower will be its coupon rate. Junk bond issuers, by contrast, attempt to attract buyers by paying a high rate in compensation for the greater risks.

SEE ALSO *Baby Bond*

BIBLIOGRAPHY
Cooper, James C. "The Bond Market: Don't Watch This Curve Too Closely." *Business Week.* 9 January 2006.

"Outstanding Level of Public & Private Bond Market Debt." The Bond Market Association. Available from http://www.bondmarkets.com/story.asp?id=323. Retrieved on 7 January 2006.

Hillstrom, Northern Lights
updated by Magee, ECDI

BOOKKEEPING

Bookkeeping is the task of recording all business transactions—amounts, dates, and sources of all business revenue, gain, expense, and loss transactions. Bookkeeping is the starting point of the accounting process. Having accurate financial records helps managers and business owners answer important questions. Is the business making money, or losing it? How much? Is the business on sound financial ground, or are troubling trends in cash flow pointing to an instability of some kind? A sound bookkeeping system is the foundation for gathering the information necessary to answer these questions.

Bookkeeping involves keeping track of a business's financial transactions and making entries to specific accounts using the debit and credit system. Each entry represents a different business transaction. Every accounting system has a chart of accounts that lists actual accounts as well as account categories. There is usually at least one account for every item on a company's balance sheet and income statement. In theory, there is no limit to the number of accounts that can be created, although the total number of accounts is usually determined by management's need for information.

The process of bookkeeping involves four basic steps: 1) analyzing financial transactions and assigning them to specific accounts; 2) writing original journal entries that credit and debit the appropriate accounts; 3) posting entries to ledger accounts; and 4) adjusting entries at the end of each accounting period. Bookkeeping is based on two basic principles. One is that every debit must have an equal credit. The second, that all accounts must balance, follows from the first.

A chronological record of all transactions is kept in a journal used to track all bookkeeping entries. Journal entries are typically made into a computer from paper documents that contain information about the transaction to be recorded. Journal entries can be made from invoices, purchase orders, sales receipts, and similar documents, which are usually kept on file for a specified length of time. For example, the journal entry for a transaction involving a cash payment for a new stapler might debit the cash account by the amount paid and credit the office supplies account for the value of the stapler.

Journal entries assign each transaction to a specific account and record changes in those accounts using debits and credits. Information contained in the journal entries is then posted to ledger accounts. A ledger is a collection of related accounts and may be called an Accounts Payable Ledger, Accounts Receivable Ledger, or a General Ledger, for example. Posting is the process by which account balances in the appropriate ledger are changed. While account balances may be recorded and computed periodically, the only time account balances are changed in the ledger is when a journal entry indicates such a change is necessary. Information that appears chronologically in the journal becomes reclassified and summarized in the ledger on an account-by-account basis.

Bookkeepers may take trial balances occasionally to ensure that the journal entries have been posted accurately to every account. A trial balance simply means that totals are taken of all of the debit balances and credit balances in the ledger accounts. The debit and credit balances should match; if they do not, then one or more errors have been made and must be found.

Reconciling bank statements on a monthly basis, of crucial importance in the management of cash flow, is another important task for the bookkeeper. Other aspects of bookkeeping include making adjusting entries that modify account balances so that they more accurately reflect the actual situation at the end of an accounting period. Adjusting entries usually involves unrecorded costs and revenues associated with continuous transactions, or costs and revenues that must be apportioned among two or more accounting periods.

Another bookkeeping procedure involves closing accounts. Most companies have temporary revenue and expense accounts that are used to provide information for the company's income statement. These accounts are periodically closed to owners' equity to determine the profit or loss associated with all revenue and expense transactions. An account called Income Summary (or Profit and Loss) is created to show the net income or loss for a particular accounting period. Closing entries means reducing the balance of the temporary accounts to zero, while debiting or crediting the income summary account.

Good bookkeeping is an essential part of good business management. Bookkeeping enables the small business owner to support expenditures made for the business in order to claim all available tax credits and deductions. It also provides detailed, accurate, and timely records that can prove invaluable to management decision-making, or in the event of an audit.

BIBLIOGRAPHY

Bannester, Anthony. *Bookkeeping and Accounting for Small Business.* Straighforward Co. Ltd., April 2004.

Pinson, Linda. *Keeping the Books.* Dearborn Trade Publishing, 2004.

Ragan, Robert C. *Step-By-Step Bookkeeping.* Sterling Publishing Company, Inc., 2001.

Rohr, Ellen. "The Best Beekkeeper." *Reefing Contractor.* March 2005.

Taylor, Peter. *Book-Keeping and Accounting for the Small Business.* How To Books, Ltd., 2003.

Hillstrom, Northern Lights
updated by Magee, ECDI

BOUNDARYLESS

"Boundaryless" is a neologism that has become a slogan of sorts in business practice, usually in the form of "a boundaryless organization." Such an organization is supposed to transcend the rigid lines of bureaucracy and divisional boundaries within a corporation and ignore the borders where the corporation itself is separated from its markets, customers, and "stakeholders." The emphasis of the boundaryless organization is on fluid and adaptive behavior modeled on organic structures rather than mechanical. Change is a welcomed constant. Professionals inside the organization form networks and links and emphasize collaboration on projects. Business relationships are informal and people come together when they share a common need or problem. Employees are grouped by competencies centered around technology, information, and expertise. Global operations and, indeed, the outsourcing of labor, are implicit in the concept and, for some, have negative connotations.

According to Russell H. Mouritsen writing in *American Salesman*—and others—Jack Welch coined the term. Welch was the larger-than-life Chairman and Chief Executive of General Electric between 1981 and 2001, now retired. His immense popularity, in turn based on GE's performance during his tenure, have made him a management guru. Not surprisingly, a Google *Book Search* conducted early in 2006 identified 288 books which carry at least some reference to the "boundaryless organization."

THE CHANGING ROLE OF EMPLOYEES

To be successful in the new boundaryless world of business requires a person to be a team player. Employees must feel at ease in free-form work structures and situations that may border on the chaotic. The tremendous networking and linking that occur changes the role of employees to that of consultants. Employees no longer work in isolation but work as part of a team on broad, company-wide projects, like quality management, just-in-time methods, lean production, and supply-chain management. Strategic alliances and collaborative arrangements, often between competitors and vendors, are another facet of the boundaryless organization.

Because technology plays a major role as a communication medium in the boundaryless organization, much work is done from a distance via e-mail, phone, and fax. Less work is done in traditional face-to-face settings. Virtual collaboration makes it easier to use the expertise of a broader range of individuals. With telecommuting, international employees are more easily made a part of all business processes. Employees often like the freedom that boundaryless work offers them, particularly with virtual teams and more flexible work plans, arrangements, and schedules.

Boundaries and organizational affiliations are also blurring as large organizations are teaming up with small businesses and consultants, as well as with other informal networks of groups, professional organizations, and businesses. The emphasis is on expertise and not location or affiliation. Employees may be part of multiple networks and organizations in the new workplace. Because employees change roles and affiliations, the responsibility for training, education, and development now rests more with the employee and not specifically with the organization.

Research suggests that even in a boundaryless organization, some boundary-spanning activities must take place. These include creating and maintaining a common task and group climate to focus groups and teams on the tasks at hand and on overall strategies. As organizations restructure, these boundary-spanning activities change as well.

BIBLIOGRAPHY
Cross, Robert L., Amin Yan, and Reis Louis. "Boundary Activities in Boundaryless Organizations: A Case of a Transformation to a Team-Based Structure." *Human Relations.* June 2000.

Mouritsen, Russell H. "Boundaryless Thinking." *American Salesman.* August 2004.

Taylor, Marilyn, and John Lansley. "Relating the Central and the Local: Options for Organizational Structure." *Nonprofit Management and Leadership.* Summer 2000.

Hillstrom, Northern Lights updated by Magee, ECDI

BRAINSTORMING

Brainstorming is a problem-solving technique in which a group of people freely and spontaneously present their ideas, build upon each other's visions and intuitions, until something new and unique emerges. The technique is designed so that critical and negative thinking, usual in group settings, is temporarily suspended so that ideas can flow freely and may be expressed without embarrassment.

A.F. Osborne is credited with inventing the technique in 1941. Osborne published his ideas in 1957 in a book entitled *Applied Imagination.* The well-known author Arthur Koestler (famous for his *Darkness at Noon*) laid out the manner in which humor, invention, and artistic creativity all result from unsuspected linkages between seemingly different ideas and images—a phenomenon used in brainstorming. That book was entitled *The Act of Creation.*

Brainstorming is widely applicable to the solution of any problem whatever it might be. It is used in problems related to concrete physical objects as well as very abstract administrative procedures.

Three critical factors determine the success of a brainstorming effort. First, the group must strive to produce a large quantity of ideas to increase the likelihood that the best solution will emerge. Second, the group must be certain to withhold judgment of the ideas as they are expressed. Third, the group leader must create a positive environment for the brainstorming session and channel the creative energies of all the members in the same direction.

During the brainstorming session, meanwhile, participants should keep in mind the following:

- The aim of the session is to generate a large quantity of ideas. Self-censorship is counterproductive. A brainstorming session is successful when the sheer quantity of ideas forces participants to move beyond preconceived notions and explore new territory.

- Discussions of the relative merits of ideas should not be undertaken as they are voiced; this slows the process and discourages creativity.

- Seniority and rank should be ignored during the session so that all participants feel equal and feel encouraged to be creative.

- A lively atmosphere should be maintained, and when activity lags, someone should strive to introduce a novel and surprising perspective. A brainstorming team might, for example, shift the viewpoint and ask: How would a five-year old look at this problem...?

After the brainstorming portion of the meeting has been completed, the leader or group should arrange all the ideas into related categories to prioritize and evaluate them. These lists can then be evaluated and modified by the group as needed in order to settle on a course of action to pursue. After the conclusion of the meeting, it may be helpful to send participants a copy of the idea lists to keep them thinking about the issue under discussion. The group moderator may ask members to report back later on ideas they considered worthy of action, and to offer any ideas they might have about implementation.

There are a number of variations on the basic theme of brainstorming. In "brainwriting" the members of a group write their ideas down on paper and then exchange their lists with others. When group members expand upon each other's ideas in this way, it frequently leads to innovative new approaches. Another possibility is to brainstorm via a bulletin board, which can be hung in a central office location or posted on a computer network. The bulletin board centers upon a basic topic or question, and people are encouraged to read others' responses and add their own. One benefit of this approach is that it keeps the problem at the forefront of people's minds. Finally, it is also possible to perform solo brainstorming. In this approach, a person writes down at least one idea per day on an index card. Eventually he or she can look at all the cards, shuffle them around, and combine the ideas.

BIBLIOGRAPHY

Correl, Linda Conway. *Brainstorming Reinvented: a corporate communications guide to ideation.* Response Books, 2004.

Cory, Timothy. *Brainstorming.* IUniverse, December 2003.

Hurt, Floyd. "Beating Brainstorming Blues." *Association Management.* April 2000.

Koestler, Arthur. *The Act of Creation.* Penguin Group, 1964, reissued in 1989.

Osborne, A.F. *Applied Imagination.* Scribner, 1957.

Rasiel, Ethan M. "Some Brainstorming Exercises." *Across the Board.* June 2000.

Hillstrom, Northern Lights
updated by Magee, ECDI

BRAND EQUITY

When people speak of "brand equity" they mean the public's valuation of a brand. Brand equity is associated with wide recognition, customer loyalty, and the market share enjoyed by the branded product or service. Wide familiarity, strong loyalty, and a dominant share tend in the long run to be the consequences of consistently favorable performance by the owner of the brand. A very strong bond equity of long standing may also result in that brand being used as the name of an entire category. Thus people talk of "hoovering," "cola" is a generic for a soft drink, and people say, "Let me get you a Xerox of that" even when the copier used is of another brand. In these situations the brand equity of the Hoover vacuum cleaner, of Coca-Cola, and of Xerox copiers is clearly evident. As discussed elsewhere in this volume (see *Brands and Brand Names*) Coca-Cola's brand equity is the highest in the world.

Brand equity, however, can also turn negative. Examples are communications services that get a reputation for wretched customer service, automobiles with a dangerous design defect, or a widely-used pharmaceutical that is discovered, later, to cause heart problems. Unless corrected, negative brand equity soon means oblivion.

To be sure, brand equity is just one way of saying that a product or service has superior features and is therefore profitable for the company that owns the brand. This profitability may be due to market share and/or to the price commanded by the product because of its brand equity. Branded products invariably command a higher price than so-called "generic" or "store brands"—even when the product is itself a commodity like sugar. In such cases the higher price is due almost entirely to the power of the brand. Quite evidently, therefore, "brand," as such, is separable from the product or service narrowly viewed. Brands can be bought and sold. The buyer acquires the brand equity and attempts, thereafter, to maintain it by selling a product that measures up to the brand's reputation. Similarly, the owner of a famous brand can put on the market an inferior product and at least temporarily enjoy benefits brought by the brand's equity—until the customer becomes wise.

MEASURING AND PROTECTING BRAND EQUITY

For these reasons, brand equity management has become a business specialty complete with competing "brand equity models" and "brand strategies." Models are built from formulae in which elements of brand equity are assigned different values (market share and price, for instance) or built out of very extensive surveys on how customers perceive the brand. The models are then modified in order to increase brand equity. All of these techniques, in effect, are attempts better to understand why a product performs better than another.

An example of such modeling is presented in a recent article in *Nilewide Marketing* entitled "Mind and market share?". The anonymous author starts out by saying: "While some believe that brand equity is a function of its market share, others believe that it is how the brand is held in the customer's mind." It is possible for a brand to have a higher "mind share" than "market share." One reason for this might be that the brand is held in high regard but its pricing is just out of reach for many who admire it. Modifying the pricing component of the model could therefore potentially bring "mind share" into better balance with "market share."

Brand equity is also recognized to be complexly related to many other factors beyond the product and service on the one hand and customer perceptions on the other. Measurement of brand equity, therefore, involves a holistic attention to all the factors, including the channel through which the product flows and services rendered to the channel. Improved relations with the wholesaling and retail channels, for example, could result in much more or more attractive shelf-space for the product.

Brand management also has a defensive component. As Alan Mitchell wrote in *Marketing Week,* "Companies which develop good measures of their brand equity have an early warning indicator of likely future profit trends .... If brand equity is falling, you're storing up trouble for yourself ... If brand equity is rising, you're investing in future performance, even if it's not showing through in profits today. Real business performance therefore equals short-term results plus shifts in brand equity."

TRANSFERRING BRAND EQUITY ONLINE

Companies often seek to leverage their brand equity by transferring consumers' positive associations with a brand to a related product or service. In the late 1990s, many companies attempted to extend their brands into electronic commerce. Doing business online proved difficult even for established businesses with popular brands. "Think branding an offline business is tough? It's nothing compared with creating a brand for your company's electronic offshoot," Rochelle Garner declared in an article for *Sales and Marketing Management.* "That's because b-to-b [business-to-business] brands are built brick by independent brick with customer service, support, and quality—and are cemented by personal relationships. In the offline world, those relationships are forged by a sales force that calls on customers face-to-face. Successful online brands must deliver those same elements, and more, through the use of technology."

Garner outlined a series of steps for companies to take in creating a successful online brand. First, the company must decide whether or not to use its offline brand name in its new online venture. This strategy may prove effective in cases where the online business is a straightforward extension of the existing brand, but it may also have the effect of diluting the brand equity. Second, Garner says that companies should develop an understanding of the benefits they want to deliver through the online business and assess how technology can help in this mission. Third, she emphasizes that companies should try to understand customers' expectations for the online business and the brand. Finally, she recommends that companies find ways to use Internet technology to create a rewarding shopping or purchasing experience for their customers.

Overall, according to Garner, the key to extending a brand online is using technology to enhance the buying experience for customers. After all, the Internet offers sellers a number of new ways to service their customers' needs, including bringing together buyers and sellers from all over the world, offering instant electronic customer support, creating new production efficiencies, and reducing order time and costs. When companies can take advantage of Internet technology to improve their relationships with their customers, moving the business online can only increase their brand equity.

BIBLIOGRAPHY

Berry, Leonard L. "Cultivating Service Brand Equity." *Journal of the Academy of Marketing Science.* Winter 2000.

"Finding a Holistic Brand Value." *Nilewide Marketing Review.* 18 December 2005.

Garner, Rochelle. "A Brand by Any Other Name." *Sales and Marketing Management.* October 2000.

"Mind and Market Share?" *Nilewide Marketing Review.* 25 September 2005.

Mitchell, Alan. "Why Brand Equity Is the True Measure of Success." *Marketing Week.* 3 August 2000.

Hillstrom, Northern Lights
updated by Magee, ECDI

BRANDS AND BRAND NAMES

A brand is a name and/or a symbol that uniquely identifies a seller's goods or services in the market. Nielsen Media Research lists more than 500,000 brands worldwide in more than 2,000 product categories. Brands enable customers rapidly to recognize the makers of goods or providers of services. Over time, and with consumer experience, brands acquire reputations for quality, value, price-level, reliability, and many other traits that help consumers choose among competing offerings. They are convenient and highly abbreviated tools of communication.

Brands have been used since ancient times. Cattle-branding crossed the Atlantic from Spain, for example, but "trademarks" had been used long before that time by potters and silversmiths to identify their products. In legalese, in fact, a brand *is* a trademark. Ornate signs hung on inns and taverns served the same purpose. Since the second half of the nineteenth century, branding has evolved into an advanced marketing tool. The industrial revolution, new communication systems, and improved modes of transporting goods made it both easier and more necessary for companies to advertise brands over larger regions. As manufacturers gained access to national markets, numerous brand names were born that would achieve legendary U.S. and global status.

Based on a *Business Week* scoreboard of the 100 top global brands, eight brands in 2005 were U.S. in origin. In rank order these were Coca-Cola, Microsoft, IBM, GE, Intel, Nokia (Finland), Disney, McDonald's, Toyota (Japan), and Marlboro. To make the *Business Week* "top 100" a company must sell 20 percent or more of its product outside its home country. Among U.S. automakers only Ford makes the list (ranked 22nd); but motorcycle aficionados will be pleased to learn that Harley-Davidson is present (ranked 46th). The last five on the list were Levi's (96th), LG (97th, Japan), Nivea (98th, Germany), Starbucks (99th), and Heineken (100th, Netherlands).

THE BRAND CONCEPT

A brand is backed by an intangible agreement between a consumer and the company selling the brand. A consumer elects to buy a brand, rather than a competitor's, based primarily on the brand's reputation. He or she may stray from the brand occasionally because of price, accessibility, or other factors, but some degree of allegiance will continue to exist until a different brand gains the customer's loyalty. Until then the consumer will reward the owner of the brand with dollars, almost assuring future cash flows to the company.

Price and brand are complexly related. Branded goods are always more expensive than "store" or "generic" brands. Some products have a "brand equity" so high that they always command a premium. In some cases high price itself may be a defining aspect of the brand—and consumption of that brand may signal to others the consumer's wealth or social status. In more competitive environments, brand commands loyalty only when the price is right.

There are two major categories of brands: manufacturer and dealer. Manufacturer brands, such as Ford, are owned by the producer or service provider. The best-known brands are held by large corporations that sell multiple products or services affiliated with the brand. Dealer brands, like Die-Hard batteries, are usually owned by a middleman, such as a wholesaler or retailer. These brand names often are applied to the products of smaller manufacturers that make a distribution arrangement with the middleman rather than trying to establish a brand of their own. Manufacturers or service providers may sell their offerings under their own brands, a dealer brand, or as a combination of the two types, called a mixed brand. Under the latter arrangement, part of the goods are sold under the manufacturer's brand and part are sold under the dealer brand.

BRAND STRATEGY

In launching new products into the market, start-ups have fewer options than companies with one or more established brands. Start-ups must first decide if the product is likely to reach a wide enough market to merit the costs of formally establishing a brand; if yes, they have to select a name and launch a marketing program to build recognition for the brand. An intermediate position is possible and frequently used. The brand is named and money is spent on suitable packaging and limited advertising. Then the brand is allowed to establish itself slowly by word of mouth. Many brands have been established in this way.

An established company may choose to follow the same strategy. But because it has one or more brands already recognized, it may elect, instead, to launch the new product under an existing name. The down-side of this strategy is that it may dilute the equity of the established brand if the new product proves to be unpopular.

Launching new products under a new brand name is in many ways identical to starting a new operation—with the difference that many of the basic business operations are already in place. New launches cost more money and are avoided where possible. An Ernst and Young study conducted in 1998 bears this out. Ernst and Young found that 78 percent of product launches in that year were line extensions; their owners risked brand dilution rather than bear the higher costs of establishing new identities.

Strategies of maintaining the value of brands are discussed in another article in this volume. See *Brand Equity*.

LEGAL ASPECTS

By legal definition, a brand is a trademark, also called a service mark when the brand is associated with a service. Trademarks may be protected by virtue of their original use. Most U.S. trademarks are registered with the federal government through the Patent and Trademark Office of the U.S. Department of Commerce. Federal trademark registration helps to secure protection related to exclusive use, although additional measures may be necessary to achieve complete exclusivity. The Lanham Act of 1946 established U.S. regulations for registering brand names and marks. They are protected for 20 years from the date of registration. Various international agreements protect trademarks from abuse in foreign countries.

Trademarks have suffered from infringement and counterfeiting since their inception. The U.S. government, in fact, does not police trademark infringement; it leaves that task to registrants. In FY 2004, U.S. Customs seized $138.8 million worth of so-called "gray goods" in violation of intellectual property rights, up from $45.3 million in FY 2000. Data available for mid-FY 2005 suggest that FY 2005 seizures will be around $95.3 million, down from FY 2004. In any case very substantial sums are involved in *seizures alone.* Data on total goods reaching the market are not collected. Gray goods do substantial damage to owners of actual brands by depriving them of the extra profits earned by years of high-level performance—and also by damaging the brand reputations if the counterfeited goods are of slip shod quality.

SEE ALSO *Private Labels*

BIBLIOGRAPHY
Aaker, David. *Brand Portfolio Strategy.* Free Press, 2004.

"Nielsen Monitor-Plus Launches Quick*Views." Nielsen Media Research. Press Release, 21 August 2003.

Simms, Jane. "Stretching Core Value." *Marketing.* 19 October 2000.

"Top 100 Global Brands Scoreboard." *Business Week Online.* Available from http://bwnt.businessweek.com/brand/2005/. Retrieved on 10 January 2006.

U.S. Department of Homeland Security. U.S. Customs Bureau. "Yearly Comparisons: Seizure Statistics of Intellectual Property Rights." Available from www.cbp.gov/xp/cgov/import/commercial_enforcement/ipr/seizure/seizure_stats.xml. Retrieved on 10 January 2006.

Volkert, Lora. "Changes in Federal Patent Law Loom: Legislation may generate rush of applications." *Idaho Business Review.* 3 October 2005.

Hillstrom, Northern Lights
updated by Magee, ECDI

BREAK-EVEN ANALYSIS

The Weatherhead School of Management, part of Case Western Reserve University, provides a succinct definition of break-even analysis on its Web site of the same name: "On the surface, break-even analysis is a tool to calculate at which sales volume the variable and fixed costs of producing your product will be recovered. Another way to look at it is that the break-even point is the point at which your product stops costing you money to produce and sell, and starts to generate a profit for your company." They continue to say that break-even analysis can also be used to solve other management problems, including setting prices, "targeting optimal variable/fixed cost combinations," and evaluating the best strategies to follow.

The basic formula for break-even analysis, sometimes abbreviated as BEA, is as follows:

BEQ = FC / (P-VC)

Where BEQ = Break-even quantity

FC = Total fixed costs

P = Average price per unit, and

VC = Variable costs per unit.

Fixed costs are costs that never change no matter how much or little a company produces: administrative salaries, rent or mortgage payments, insurance, interest on borrowed funds, and similar costs sometimes also labeled fixed overhead. *Variable costs* are directly tied to product manufacturing or service provision: direct labor, raw materials, sales commissions, delivery expenses, and more.

In the formula shown above, BEQ, the "quantity," refers to a single unit sold, whatever it might be. It may be a product like a teddy-bear (including its packaging) or something more complicated such a "carpet cleaning job" (including travel to and from the site). BEQ always refers to the actual entity sold (teddy-bear or carpet cleaning job) rather than something that goes into the entity (e.g., teddy-bear stuffing or vacuum cleaner bags). BEQ is the entity the company puts a price on, "the unit." Total sales of this unit, divided by the number of units sold, produces P, the average price. All costs associated with the unit, divided by number of units sold, yields VC, the cost per unit. Note that fixed cost is *not* included in VC.

Price per unit less variable cost per unit produces a surplus if the price is set correctly. In accounting terminology, this is called the "contribution margin." It is the amount the sale of each unit contributes to the ultimate profitability of a corporation. When enough such chunks of contribution have been produced to *equal* fixed costs, the business has reached its break-even point. It isn't profitable yet, but all of the overhead has been "absorbed."

Supposing that fixed costs are $150,000. Price per unit is $85 and variable cost per unit is $75. The contribution margin will then be $10. Fixed cost divided by $10 results in 15,000. Therefore this company must sell

15,000 units just to break even. The next unit sold thereafter is the first contribution to profit. This company must sell 15,001 units to make a tiny profit of $10.

This example illustrates how changes can affect break-even. Fixed costs can be lowered, price can be increased, variable costs can be shaved. Conversely, if variable costs rise and cannot be lowered, contribution margin will sink and break-even will require more sales—unless, for example, price is hiked or the company moves to cheaper space and lowers its rent substantially.

DIFFICULTIES AND APPLICABILITY

BEA is easiest to use in situations where the product or service is uniform and variable costs can be very clearly calculated and assigned to the "unit." Significant analytical problems arise with complexity. In a medical practice, for example, the "unit" may be easy to determine: it is a single patient-visit to the practice. But variable cost associated with every visit will vary with the patient's condition, needs, medical insurance policies, the payments those policies cover depending on the diagnosis, the percentage of charges the patient must pay directly, and the variable costs of collecting that contribution. Administrative personnel dealing with insurance companies must maintain exacting records to tie their time not only to patients but to specific visits by each patient. Doctors, similarly, must be meticulous in dividing time between administrative duties (fixed costs) and patient-related activities (variable costs); these activities often extend beyond the visit itself, e.g., to time spent reviewing test results or studying recent literature on a disease or medication. Very substantial data must be gathered over a long time to arrive at precise data. Unless this is done, the break-even analysis will be too broad to serve informed management decisions.

An example of the difficulties is presented by Merry J. McBryde-Foster writing in *Nursing Economics* about BEA as practiced in a hypothetical nurse-managed center. "[P]rices for visits will vary according to the type of visit billed," writes McBryde-Foster. "The variable costs of visits will vary according to the type of visit." She shows how, in this hypothetical center, contribution margins for each type of visit must be calculated using Current Procedural Terminology (CPT) codes. CPT was developed by the American Medical Association and is a complex structure that frequently changes based on Medicare Payment Schedules.

Similar difficulties arise in many contracting businesses where the size and complexity of the contract—which is the "unit"—and the great variability of inputs make it very difficult to produce a single number that means break-even.

Despite these difficulties, BEA is universally applicable. Attempts to apply it will bring out deficiencies in accounting and cost-tracking practices and will indirectly improve the management of the business.

BIBLIOGRAPHY

Bohinc, Michael A. "Math for Contractors or . . . Yes, Your Teacher Was Correct: All too often, hard-working contractors are shortchanging themselves by making mistakes in math and accounting." *Plumbing & Mechanical.* October 2004.

Hilton, Ronald W. *Managerial Accounting.* McGraw-Hill, 1991.

LeFever, Steve and Laurie Owen. "Break Even, Part II: Know thy costs . . . and manage the 'creepers'." *Jewelers Circular Keystone.* January 2005.

McBryde-Foster, Merry J. "Break-Even Analysis in a Nurse-Managed Center." *Nursing Economics.* January-February 2005.

Peterson, Ken W. "Break-Even Analysis Boosts Dealer Profitability." *Kitchen & Bath Design News.* March 2005.

Hillstrom, Northern Lights
updated by Darnay, ECDI

BUDGET DEFICIT

The phrase, "budget deficit," is normally applied to situations where, at the end of a calendar or fiscal year, a public entity turns out to have spent more money than it has been able to collect in taxes, fees, and other impositions. Individuals, businesses, not-for-profit entities, and public bodies all operate under budgets too, of course. But when a business has a "budget deficit" the phrase means that it has experienced a "loss." Individuals "overspend." When contractors spend more than their contracts provide, they have "overruns."

Public sector deficits are of substantial interest to the public, not least to the commercial sector. Deficits are invariably covered by borrowing. When governments borrow money they compete for available national savings with the commercial institutions that also wish to borrow money to finance their operations. The Federal Government, particularly, enjoys an advantage because its treasury bills are of the highest quality and are preferred to any other kinds of bonds. A shortage of available money hampers economic activity.

THE U.S. BUDGET DEFICIT

Based on the estimates of the Congressional Budget Office, the FY 2005 budget deficit was $331 billion, down from $412 billion in FY 2004. In the 40-year span from FY 1965 to FY 2005, the Federal Government has had a budget surplus only five times, in FY 1969 and in the period FY 1998-2001 inclusive. In all other years, the government ran in the red. The FY 2004 deficit was the highest ever in U.S. history.

INDIVIDUALS AND HOUSEHOLDS

According to the Bureau of Economic Analysis (BEA), an element of the U.S. Department of Commerce, the personal savings rate in FY 2004 stood at 1.8 percent (savings as a percent of disposable income); this rate stood at 7.7 percent in FY 1992 and has been on a steady decline in the intervening years. Household data indicate a slightly lower rate, 1.6 percent in FY 2004 and 7.5 percent in FY 1992. In FY 2005, according to the BEA, the savings rate had turned negative (-0.2 percent in November, but it had been as low as –3.4 percent in August), suggesting that individuals were experiencing a "budget deficit" too.

BIBLIOGRAPHY

Congressional Budget Office. "Historical Budget Data." *The Budget and Economic Outlook: Fiscal Years 2006 to 2015.* 25 January 2005.

Hornyak, Steve. "Budgeting Made Easy." *Management Accounting.* October 1998.

Reason, Tim. "Building Better Budgets." *CFO.* December 2000.

U.S. Department of Commerce. "Personal Income and Outlays: November 2005." Bureau of Economic Analysis. 22 December 2005.

Hillstrom, Northern Lights
updated by Magee, ECDI

BUDGET SURPLUS

When a governmental entity has revenues from taxes, fees, and other impositions which exceed its budgeted outlays, it is said to have a budget surplus. When a business under-spends its budget but all else remains the same, i.e., sales are at projected levels, it is said to have "improved profits" rather than experienced a surplus. Both the phrases "budget surplus" and "budget deficit" are usually applied to public entities.

Surpluses are almost always the consequence of two interacting forces: on the one hand efforts to contain costs or spending have been successful; and, on the other hand, revenues (over which government rarely has any genuine control except by raising or cutting taxes) have exceeded expectations.

THE U.S. FEDERAL BUDGET

In the 40-year period from FY 1965 to FY 2005, the Federal Government experienced a budget surplus in only five fiscal years. The government had a modest surplus of $3.2 billion in FY 1969. In fiscal years 1998 through 2001, the government had surpluses of $69.2, $125.5, $236.2, and $128.2 billion respectively. In all other years of the 1965-2005 period, the government experienced deficits, reaching a record deficit of $412 billion in 2004 (and a projected deficit of $331 billion in FY 2005).

The government's exceptional performance between FY 1998-2001 was due to a combination of deliberate cuts in expenditures, particularly in the defense sector, and a booming economy due to the expansion of the Internet. The terrorist attack of 9/11 and an already softening economy changed the economic landscape. A recession began in FY 2002.

THE U.S. HOUSEHOLD BUDGET

Although households rarely operate on a formal budget, the Bureau of Economic Analysis (BEA), an agency of the U.S. Department of Commerce, calculates the "surplus" or "deficit" experienced by U.S. individuals and households as part of its National Income and Product Accounts. National Income and Product Account (NIPA) data are used to build Gross Domestic Product estimates. BEA collects data on total and disposable income and total outlays. Disposable income less outlays produces savings. The savings rate (savings divided by disposable income) is positive to indicate a surplus and negative when households, collectively, experience a deficit.

In fiscal years 1992 through 2004, according to data available from BEA, U.S. households had a positive savings rate but with a steadily declining trend. The savings rate was 7.5 percent of disposable income in FY 1992 but had declined to a 1.6 percent rate by FY 2004. Negative savings rates began to appear in FY 2005 in the "personal income" category; data for personal income tend always to be higher than the household data, suggesting that household saving rate has also turned negative; but in early 2006 no data had as yet been published for households for 2005 by BEA.

BIBLIOGRAPHY

Alesina, Alverto. "The Political Economy of the Budget Surplus in the U.S." *National Bureau of Economic Research Working Paper Series.* January 2000.

Bohn, Henning, and Robert P. Inman. *Balanced Budget Rules and Public Deficits: Evidence from the U.S. States.* April 1996.

Congressional Budget Office. "Historical Budget Data." *The Budget and Economic Outlook: Fiscal Years 2006 to 2015.* 25 January 2005.

Fearon, Craig. "The Budgeting Nightmare." *CMA Management.* May 2000.

Reason, Tim. "Building Better Budgets." *CFO.* December 2000.

U.S. Department of Commerce. "Personal Income and Outlays: November 2005." Bureau of Economic Analysis. 22 December 2005.

Hillstrom, Northern Lights
updated by Magee, ECDI

BUDGETS AND BUDGETING

In the broadest sense, a budget is an allocation of money for some purpose. The word once used to mean "pouch" or "purse"; a budget therefore is "what's in the pouch." Budgeting as an activity ranges in extent from managing household finances on up to the preparation of the Budget of the United States, undertaken yearly by Congress; that document is rarely less than 1,000 pages in length. This article will focus principally on "formal budgeting" as practiced in corporations, sometimes called the "budget process."

Budgeting has always been part of the activities of any business organization of any size, but formal budgeting in its present form, using modern budgeting disciplines, emerged in the 1950s as the numerical underpinning of corporate planning. Modern corporate planning owes much to operations research and systems theory. A pioneer in that field, Russell L. Ackoff, worked closely with General Electric, Anheuser-Busch, and other major corporations. His first book on the subject, the first of four, *A Concept of Corporate Planning*, had a major impact.

Modern formal budgets not only limit expenditures; they also predict income, profits, and returns on investment a year ahead. They have evolved into tools of control and are also used as a means of determining such rewards as profit-sharing and bonuses. Unless the budgetary process is managed with extreme skill and care, the very virtues of budgeting can turn into negatives—and have, of late, emerged into a movement actively working to change this process.

BUDGETING AS A PROCESS

In large corporations, budgeting is a collective process in which operating units prepare their plans in conformity with corporate goals published by top management. Each unit plan is intended to contribute to the achievement of the corporate goals. Unit managers prepare projections of sales, operating costs, overhead costs, and capital requirements. They calculate operating profits and returns on the investment they intend to use. The budget itself is the projection of these values for the next calendar or fiscal year. As part of this process, each unit presents its plans and budget to a reviewing upper management panel and may, thereafter, make whatever changes result from instructions from or negotiations with the higher level. Texts presenting, documenting, and defending the rationales underlying the numbers are usually part of the planning document. Approved budgets then become the road-map for operations in the coming year. Ideally monthly or quarterly budget reviews track performance against the budget. As part of such reviews, changes to the budget may be approved. At year-end managers are judged by their performance against the budget.

While budgets are developed bottom up, managers must strive to meet top-down corporate goals (e.g., "Annual growth in after-tax profits of 39 percent."). Because performance is measured based on meeting or exceeding positive projections (of sales, returns, and profits) and meeting or coming in below negative projections (fixed and variable costs and capital expenditures) managers have strong incentives for projecting the lowest possible "positive" and the highest possible "negative" results. The more successful they are in understating sales and profits and overestimating costs, the higher the likelihood of "meeting the budget." Top management's incentives, by contrast, are to do the opposite. Therefore the budgeting process is inherently marked by potential conflict.

Such difficulties can be, and usually are, mitigated by rational policies, good will on both sides, and straight forward implementation. Projections should be as realistic and quantifiable as possible. If projections are out of line with historical patterns, up or down, management must question the planning. Thus, for instance, a sharply rising projection of costs must have some real-world justification. Overly ambitious revenue projections must also be questioned. Conversely, managers must resist pressures sharply to raise revenue targets unless tangible changes in the market or compensating raises in sales expenditures are present. If the negotiating levels are honest and realistic, the right projections will result. Ideally, operating units should not be measured on activities over which they lack full control. An operation which does not operate its own debt collection, for example, should not be measured on how rapidly invoices are collected. Since budgets are often at least 50 percent guess-work, formal budgetary review at reasonable intervals and realistic adjustments based on actual events must be part of a well-functioning process. All too often, the spring budgeting event is rapidly forgotten.

BENEFITS AND COSTS

The single-most potential benefit of formal budgeting lies in ensuring that responsible managers take time each year (and then at fixed intervals throughout the year) in thinking about their operation by looking at all of its aspects. Budgeting creates a comprehensive picture of the future and makes both opportunities and barriers conscious. This foreknowledge then helps guide day-to-day activities.

The chief cost of the budget process is time. In some corporations the process takes on a life of its own and becomes a convoluted exercise of excessive complexity which, moreover, prevents unit managers from doing any thinking: their time is consumed in efforts to comply with a vast array of requirements dictated from above. Much of the negative attitude that has developed concerning this activity has its roots in unnecessary bureaucratic impositions on the one hand and unreliability because of rapid change a few months out.

TYPES OF BUDGETS

The two dominant forms of budgeting are traditional and zero-based. Business planning is usually a combination of the two. *Traditional* budgeting is based on a review of historical performance and then the projection of such findings to the future with modifications. If inflation is high, for instance, cost trends of the last several years are projected forward but with adjustments both for inflation and for projected growth or decline in business activity. Historical sales patterns, using established trends in sales growth, are projected; new sales from planned new product introductions are then added. *Zero-based* budgeting is the creation of a completely new budget from the ground up—as if no history existed. When using this method, the operation must justify and document every item of expenditure and income anew. Brand-new operations will utilize zero-based methods.

In government planning, but only very rarely in business, *performance* budgeting is used as a third alternative. Under this method, the budget is fixed at the outset. The planning activity is to determine exactly what activities will be carried out using the allocated funds. Performance budgeting is sometimes used in the corporate setting when the advertising budget is arbitrarily set as such-and-such a percent to projected sales. The advertising function then uses performance budgeting to allocate the budget to various products and media.

CRITIQUES OF THE PROCESS

As early as 1992, the famous guru of management, Peter Drucker, wrote in *The Wall Street Journal*: "Uncertainty—in the economy, society, politics—has become so great as to render futile, if not counterproductive, the kind of planning most companies still practice: forecasting based on probabilities."

Uncertainty has, if anything, grown since 1992 with the expansion of the Internet, the reality of terrorism, pressures on hydrocarbon fuels, the threat of global warming, and worldwide epidemics. In addition to uncertainty, formal budgeting has also come under fire for impeding trust and empowerment, two new concepts in the evolving corporate culture, as well as for stifling innovation. As David Marginson and Stuart Ogden recently wrote in *Financial Management (UK)*, "Budgets have long had a bad press, but they have attracted even more flak recently for being at best inappropriate to modern business practice and at worst potentially harmful.... The Beyond Budgeting Round Table (BBRT) has been one of their most vociferous critics. It argues, for example, that the necessary conditions of trust and empowerment in today's organizations are not possible with budgets still in place, because the entire system perpetuates central command and control." Innovation is vital for economic survival. But "budgeting stifles trust and empowerment, according to its critics, which in turn stifles innovation."

The BBRT is an element of The Player Group, a management advisory firm; the Round Table has 29 major corporate members. On its homepage, BBRT advocates a set of principles which include, among others, continuous planning and controls (rather than an annual budget process), resource allocation as needed (rather than based on annual allocations and plans), high performance standards (rather than detailed rules and budgets), and freedom of action by small front-line teams (rather than direct control of operations from the center).

The high costs of the budget process and its poor adaptability to stock market perceptions is another force working to bring about change in the budgetary process as it has been practiced over the last 50 years or so. An article in *The Practical Accountant* put the matter as follows, citing Herman Heyns of Accenture/Cranfield School of Management: "[T]he budget process is obsolete given today's economy, resulting in documents that are time-consuming to produce, of little predictive value, subject to gamesmanship and, quite frankly, out of date by the time they're implemented." Among the new approaches advocated by Heyns is the *rolling budget*. Under a rolling budget, performance of the operation over the last 12 months is evaluated on an on-going basis; projections for the next three months are generated every month.

Budgeting appears to be on the cusp of a change. How long it will take to transform itself is difficult to predict. In a new book titled *Beyond Budgeting*, Jeremy Hope and Robert Fraser start off by sketching the ambivalence felt by top and middle management toward formal, traditional budgeting. Then they go on: "Though this ambivalence toward budgeting has existed for decades, the balance of opinion has swung decidedly in favor of the 'very dissatisfied.' Even within the financial management community, nine of ten have expressed their dissatisfaction, finding the budgeting process too 'unreliable' and 'cumbersome.'"

The changes, as they evolve, will impact large corporations first and foremost. For the small business owner, budgeting in the traditional sense will continue to be a sensible, necessary, and valuable tool practiced, in essence, by examining current resources, eyeing the future, and making rational allocations for the immediate future.

SEE ALSO *Business Planning*

BIBLIOGRAPHY

Ackoff, R. L. *A Concept of Corporate Planning.* Wiley-Interscience, 1969.

Drucker, Peter. "Planning for Uncertainty." *Wall Street Journal.* 22 July 1992.

Fearon, Craig. "The Budgeting Nightmare." *CMA Management.* May 2000.

Hope, Jeremy, and Robin Fraser. *Beyond Budgeting.* Harvard Business School Press, 11 April 2003.

Marginson, David and Stuart Ogden. "Budgeting and Innovation: Do budgets stifle creativity?" *Financial Management (UK).* April 2005.

Reason, Tim. "Building Better Budgets." *CFO.* December 2000.

"Throwing Out the Annual Budget." *The Practical Accountant.* February 2002.

Hillstrom, Northern Lights
updated by Magee, ECDI

BUSINESS APPRAISERS

Appraisers are agents who establish the value of businesses, personal property, intellectual property (such as patents, trademarks, and copyrights), and real estate through a process known as valuation or appraisal. The demand for valuation of business enterprises has increased in the last several years in many industry sectors for a variety of reasons, including the rise in corporate restructuring, rising incidences of litigation (such as divorce, in which value and possession of closely held businesses may be hotly contested), changing employee-compensation packages, continued purchases of existing businesses, and the proliferation of employee stock ownership plans (ESOPs), which require annual appraisals of value. Indeed, the dramatic surge in popularity of ESOP plans accounts for a significant portion of the increase in appraisal/valuation activity across the American business landscape.

Problems in the Business Appraisal Industry Beginning in the late 1990s but continuing still, the appraisal industry began a process of change and consolidation driven primarily by changes in the real estate sector. Steve Bergsman, writing in *Valuation Insights & Perspectives,* provides a summary: "There was a time not so very long ago, at least as recent as the early 1990s, when the appraisal industry—residential and commercial—was reliant on the mortgage lending business. By the middle of the last decade, however, a number of crosscurrents began to buffet that type of work...competition from other appraisers and technology. First, competition caused pricing to flatten; even banks admit there have not been rate increases in a number of years. Second, new technologies, particularly automated valuation models, appeared, and more and more data, i.e., historical records of home sales and multiple listing services, became widely available on the Internet." As a consequence of these developments, real estate appraisal has become a much less profitable part of this business. Survivors of the shake-out, however, have found new opportunities in business valuation and litigation.

Finding a Qualified Appraiser But while the business appraisal industry is in a state of transformation, consultants hasten to add that many qualified appraisers do exist—and can be of valuable service to small business owners who take the trouble to investigate the merits of various appraisers. Keys to finding a good appraiser include the following:

- Network—As one tax and estate-planning attorney told *Inc.,* "Ask around, and then ask around some more. Talk to people in your geographical area, even if their businesses aren't just like yours; talk to people with similar businesses, even if they're not in your geographical area. Appraisal is a fraternity, and once you know who's in the fraternity, who's respected, you'll know who to go to. And, very importantly, if the reason you're looking for a valuation has anything to do with taxes, or is likely to somewhere down the line, find out who's respected by the Internal Revenue Service—who do they use to do their valuation work?"

- Look for experience and education—Appraisers with significant experience and a good educational background (MBA or CPA) are far preferable to those who are limited in either area. Moreover, some analysts believe that the appraisal industry is moving towards increased specialization (office buildings, hotels, professional practices, retail outlets, etc.); if possible, find an appraiser who is familiar with your business area.

- Recognize that valuations vary from client to client. Appraisals of business can vary significantly in terms of their cost, both in terms of time and money. Learn about standard fees imposed on business that most resemble yours in terms of size, health, and situation. "The vicissitudes of most projects—the standard ESOP valuation being an exception—often make it impossible to charge on a flat-fee basis, or even give a responsible estimate of hourlies," warned Nell Margolis in *Inc.*

- Find a licensed appraiser—The relative ease with which people are able to secure certification in the appraisal business has drawn fire, but it does establish a ground floor of presumed competence.

SEE ALSO *Buying An Existing Business; Selling A Business*

BIBLIOGRAPHY

Bergsman, Steve. "The Changing Composition of Your Overall Client Base." *Valuation Insights & Perspectives.* Winter 2003.

Mobley III, T. Alvin. "Defining and Allocating Going Concern Value Components." *Appraisal Journal.* October 1997.

Semanik, Michael K., and John H. Wade. *The Complete Guide to Selling a Business.* AMACOM, 1994.

Tuller, Lawrence W. *Getting Out: A Step-by-Step Guide to Selling a Business or Professional Practice.* Liberty Hall, 1990.

Yegge, Wilbur M. *A Basic Guide to Buying and Selling a Company.* Wiley, 1996.

*Hillstrom, Northern Lights
updated by Magee, ECDI*

BUSINESS ASSOCIATIONS

Business associations are membership organizations engaged in promoting the business interests of their members. These associations typically perform activities that would be unduly costly or time-consuming for an individual company to perform by itself, including lobbying, information gathering, research, and setting industry standards. Association spokespeople contend that by combining their voices under one banner, companies are able to establish a strong and unified presence and effectively protect their shared interests. Leading business associations in the United States include the U.S. Chambers of Commerce, the Better Business Bureau, the National Restaurant Association, the National Retail Federation, and the National Manufacturers Association, but there are tens of thousands more that operate at local, state, regional, and national levels all over America.

Large firms have long been active participants in business associations, using the organization to advance their goals in a wide range of areas, from regulatory issues to research to industry image improvement. But smaller companies can benefit from association memberships as well, provided they find an organization that adequately reflects their priorities and needs, which may be dramatically different from those of big corporations. For example, a small business owner may value an association that provides education, peer contact, and networking opportunities more than one that is focusing its resources on eliminating an OSHA regulation that pertains primarily to large companies.

Before entrepreneurs and small business owners begin shopping around for an association, they should first compile a chart of specific business and personal goals, as well as a list of talents that they have that would be welcomed by an association. "All too often," explained Robert Davis in *Black Enterprise,* "contact-hungry entrepreneurs and professionals join networking organizations before investigating them thoroughly. Does this sound familiar? You hastily join an organization, only to discover later that it's disorganized, poorly attended and moreover, doesn't meet your needs."

In order to avoid such a scenario, small business owners should undertake a serious information-gathering effort before committing to an association. People considering an association should first request a brochure or information packet on the group that adequately covers its background, philosophy, structure, services, and affiliations, then request a meeting with an association representative or attend an organization meeting or event to get more detailed information. Current and former members of the association under consideration are also potentially valuable sources of information. "Ask them about the level of commitment needed for worthwhile membership," said Davis. "Also ask them to compare the benefits they have received from this organization with benefits received from other groups."

Associations can be a positive force for a small business. Many join local or regional chambers of commerce as a means of providing health insurance to their employees. But all associations are not created equal. Some are poorly organized, poorly attended, and offer little benefit to ambitious entrepreneurs. Moreover, some entrepreneurs, already struggling to find time to attend to both business and family needs, are simply unable to invest the necessary time to make association membership worthwhile for them or their company.

SEE ALSO *Chambers of Commerce*

BIBLIOGRAPHY

Bovet, Susan Fry. "Leading Companies Turn to Trade Associations for Lobbying." *Public Relations Journal.* August-September 1994.

Davis, Robert. "Look Before You Leap." *Black Enterprise.* September 1992.

Eby, Deborah. "Who Needs Associations?" *America's Network.* 1 December 1995.

Engquist, Erik. "Cheap B'klyn health plans: GHI, Chamber sharply cut cost of coverage for needy, small firms." *Crain's New York Business.* 1 August 2005.

Fisher, William. "The Value of Professional Associations." *Library Trends.* Fall 1997.

Holding, Robert L. "Leveraged Investment—Your Association Advantage." *Appliance Manufacturer.* April 1998.

Stybel, Laurence J., and Maryanne Peabody. "Association Membership: A Strategic Perspective." *Compensation & Benefits Management.* Autumn 1995.

Hillstrom, Northern Lights
updated by Magee, ECDI

BUSINESS BROKERS

Business brokers act as intermediaries between buyers and sellers of a business. They may represent either party in the transaction. They do not take possession of goods or property or deal on their own account.

Brokers differ from dealers in that the latter transact on their own account and may have a vested interest in the transaction. Brokers fill the important marketing function of bringing buyers and sellers together and helping them negotiate mutually beneficial agreements. In addition, they facilitate transactions by providing expertise and advice. As Richie Lowe Areinz points out succinctly in *NZ Business,* "[B]usiness brokers generally sell an intangible, such as the expected profits or in some cases the losses of a business. Real estate agents sell bricks and mortar. Put another way, agents sell land and buildings while business brokers usually sell an entity or business activity leasing space within a building."

Brokers supply numerous benefits to both buyers and sellers. Sellers benefit because they do not have to spend time and money searching for buyers. Qualified brokers have access to people in the market to purchase a company; they know how to attract and screen potential buyers much more quickly than do typical business owners. The broker may also be able to help the seller place value on his enterprise accurately; he or she can devise a strategy to transfer ownership over time, address necessary paperwork, and overcome legal hurdles related to taxes.

The buyer also benefits. A broker may be able to find a business that suits the buyer's abilities, wants, and financial situation much more quickly. Moreover, good business brokers will not accept overpriced properties, those based on illegal activities, or businesses otherwise fatally flawed. They save buyers the legwork of qualifying prospects. A good brokerage firm typically turns down as many as half of the businesses offered it for sale. In addition to screening, the broker can help the buyer determine what he or she can afford and may be able to assist in arranging financing to purchase the business. And, as with sellers, business brokers can provide help with licenses, permits, and other paperwork. In addition, it is the broker's duty to ensure that the interests of the buyer (and the seller) are protected by any contracts or agreements relating to the sale.

All of these services can be of great value to business buyers and sellers, but perhaps none is as valuable as the broker's status as a buffer between the two sides. The skilled business broker will diplomatically field and address sensitive questions and concerns that, were they delivered directly between the buyer and seller, might damage or ruin the prospects for completing a deal. Brokers that can address the concerns of one side without ruffling the feathers of the other are invaluable to the negotiating process.

For their services, brokers typically receive in compensation a percentage of the total value of the transaction. The fee may be paid by the buyer, seller, or both parties, depending on the nature of the transaction. Commissions vary widely, usually depending on the size of the transaction and the level of service provided by the broker.

THE BROKERAGE PROCESS

Although it is a broker's chief function, bringing buyer and seller together is often the easiest part of his/her job. Closing the transaction, however, is often a complicated process, colored by a spectrum of factors that are unique to each situation. For instance, the seller of a business often views the enterprise as his or her "baby," and subsequently places a value on it that may be greater than its actual worth. Similarly, a buyer may fail to appreciate the amount of work involved in building a business to a certain point. Other major factors that can complicate an agent's task include financing, which can become very complicated, and problems related to employees and/or clients of the business being sold.

As Susan Pravda and Gabor Garai observed in *Mergers and Acquisitions,* the process of securing an agreement typically is a multi-faceted one. Once a business broker brings an interested buyer and seller together, he or she often attempts to set a target date for completion of the transaction. This is usually accomplished by means of a letter of intent in which the buyer and seller agree to move toward a deal. The importance of the letter of intent is that it serves as a framework around which to structure negotiations. The letter also reduces ambiguity and misunderstanding, and ensures that both parties are serious about pursuing the transaction. Finally, establishing a deadline through a letter of intent helps to keep the buyer and seller focused on the big issues, rather than on minor details that can drag the deal out for months on end or kill the sale.

After setting a target date, the broker's next task is to close the price gap between what the seller wants and what the buyer is offering to pay. A wide range of considerations have to be taken into account here, including value of inventory, value of accounts receivables, value of community goodwill, inclusion or exclusion of equipment in final purchase price, tax issues for both buyer and seller, etc. Another possible obstacle to a sale that often crops up around this time is "seller's remorse." Seller's remorse commonly occurs during the latter stages of negotiations, when the seller suddenly realizes that he/she is relinquishing control of the company that has been a cornerstone of his/her life (and often the life of his/her entire family) for many years. Seller's remorse can kill the deal if the broker fails to confront it early in the negotiations by assuaging the seller's concerns.

After the framework for an agreement has been reached, the business brokering process moves on to due diligence, wherein various legal technicalities which could thwart an otherwise legal arrangement are identified and addressed. For example, the buyer might want to ensure that he or she was procuring the legal rights to all patents held by the firm. It is the broker's job to facilitate due diligence to protect parties on both sides of the deal.

In the final stage, the broker helps the buyer and seller iron out and sign a final contract. This stage is the one most likely to entail the use of attorneys on both sides, even for smaller transactions. The best way for the broker to reduce the chance that the deal will fail at this critical juncture is to try to address all questions and concerns in the letter of intent and due diligence stages. Despite his best efforts, one or both parties may employ brinkmanship tactics that threaten to scrap the entire deal, such as significantly raising the asking price or demanding that some new contingency be added to the agreement. At this point, the broker's expertise as mediator and peacemaker is key to ensuring that the transaction goes through.

BUSINESS BROKERS AND THE ENTREPRENEUR

Business brokers can be invaluable to both buyers and sellers of small businesses, but the quality of these agents can vary tremendously. Business brokerage firms have traditionally been a notoriously unregulated group, and while there have been some improvements in this regard in recent years, complaints about incompetence and/or questionable business practices still crop up. Whether an entrepreneur is looking to start a business through a purchase or sell an existing business to start on a new idea, it is essential that he/she take steps to ensure that the services of a skilled and qualified broker have been secured.

There are, of course, certain basic kinds of information that any buyer or seller should obtain when shopping for a business broker. "When you're looking for a broker to help you buy or sell a business, ask about the broker's level of experience and pursuit of continuing education," counseled *Nation's Business*. "When getting references, ask for the names of not only buyers and sellers but also attorneys, accountants, and commercial bankers." Another basic aspect of an agent's operation that should be checked is its exclusivity policy (some brokers will list businesses only if they can do so exclusively, a requirement that limits the business's visibility). But there are other steps that can be taken as well. For example, a broker's record of sales as a proportion of total listings can provide significant insight into his or her abilities. Brokers who are unable to deliver sales on more than 50% of listings on the market for six months to a year should probably be avoided. Not surprisingly, a broker who can document a successful track record of sales to listings is preferable to one who can not.

Other recommendations that Pratt gave to *Inc.* included the following:

- Determine how often the broker's listing price corresponds to the eventual sales price—"I'd be much more favorably inclined to work with a brokerage if its average selling price is within at least 20% of the average listing price," remarked Pratt.

- Inquire about the broker's affiliation with highly regarded industry groups, like the International Business Brokers Association, which maintains rigid standards for its members.

- Inquire whether the broker specializes in specific geographic regions or industries—A broker who has primarily dealt with manufacturing firms may not be the best choice to help a business owner sell his or her restaurant.

- Look for tell-tale signs of unethical or incompetent behavior—Does the broker accept bogus listings (those that are listed at ridiculously inflated prices or owned by owners uncertain of their desire to sell)? Has the agent prematurely leaked private information about your company to potential buyers? Is the broker favorably adjusting a company's income statement to an excessive degree? Unfortunately, these signs often become apparent only after a buyer or seller has established a relationship with the agent. In such cases, business experts counsel entrepreneurs to sever all ties and move on to another broker or method of purchase/ sale.

BIBLIOGRAPHY

Areinz, Richie Low. "Business Brokers Know the Ropes." *NZ Business* August 2005.

Bianchi, Alessandra. "The American Dream Revisited: Why You Won't Sell Your Business," *Inc.* August 1992.

Coleman, Bob. *Guide to Business Start-Ups.* Entrepreneur Magazine Group, 1993.

Garai, Gabor, and Susan Pravda. "The Critical Line Between Dealmakers and Deal Breakers." *Mergers and Acquisitions.* March/April 1994.

Maynard, Roberta. "Business Brokers." *Nation's Business.* July 1997.

Rosenbloom, Joe, III. "Brokers for Hire." *Inc.* March 1987.

Hillstrom, Northern Lights
updated by Magee, ECDI

BUSINESS CYCLES

The business cycle is the periodic but irregular up-and-down movement in economic activity, measured by fluctuations in real gross domestic product (GDP) and other macroeconomic variables. A business cycle is typically characterized by four phases—recession, recovery, growth, and decline—that repeat themselves over time. Economists note, however, that complete business cycles vary in length. The duration of business cycles can be anywhere from about two to twelve years, with most cycles averaging six years in length. Some business analysts use the business cycle model and terminology to study and explain fluctuations in business inventory and other individual elements of corporate operations. But the term "business cycle" is still primarily associated with larger (industry-wide, regional, national, or even international) business trends.

STAGES OF A BUSINESS CYCLE

Recession A recession—also sometimes referred to as a trough—is a period of reduced economic activity in which levels of buying, selling, production, and employment typically diminish. This is the most unwelcome stage of the business cycle for business owners and consumers alike. A particularly severe recession is known as a depression.

Recovery Also known as an upturn, the recovery stage of the business cycle is the point at which the economy "troughs" out and starts working its way up to better financial footing.

Growth Economic growth is in essence a period of sustained expansion. Hallmarks of this part of the business cycle include increased consumer confidence, which translates into higher levels of business activity. Because the economy tends to operate at or near full capacity during periods of prosperity, growth periods are generally accompanied by inflationary pressures.

Decline Also referred to as a contraction or downturn, a decline basically marks the end of the period of growth in the business cycle. Declines are characterized by decreased levels of consumer purchases (especially of durable goods) and, subsequently, reduced production by businesses.

FACTORS THAT SHAPE BUSINESS CYCLES

For centuries, economists in both the United States and Europe regarded economic downturns as "diseases" that had to be treated; it followed, then, that economies characterized by growth and affluence were regarded as "healthy" economies. By the end of the 19th century, however, many economists had begun to recognize that economies were cyclical by their very nature, and studies increasingly turned to determining which factors were primarily responsible for shaping the direction and disposition of national, regional, and industry-specific economies. Today, economists, corporate executives, and business owners cite several factors as particularly important in shaping the complexion of business environments.

Volatility of Investment Spending Variations in investment spending is one of the important factors in business cycles. Investment spending is considered the most volatile component of the aggregate or total demand (it varies much more from year to year than the largest component of the aggregate demand, the consumption spending), and empirical studies by economists have revealed that the volatility of the investment component is an important factor in explaining business cycles in the United States. According to these studies, increases in investment spur a subsequent increase in aggregate demand, leading to economic expansion. Decreases in investment have the opposite effect. Indeed, economists can point to several points in American history in which the importance of investment spending was made quite evident. The Great Depression, for instance, was caused by a collapse in investment spending in the aftermath of the stock market crash of 1929. Similarly, the prosperity of the late 1950s was attributed to a capital goods boom.

There are several reasons for the volatility that can often be seen in investment spending. One generic reason is the pace at which investment accelerates in response to upward trends in sales. This linkage, which is called the acceleration principle by economists, can be briefly explained as follows. Suppose a firm is operating at full capacity. When sales of its goods increase, output will have to be increased by increasing plant capacity through further investment. As a result, changes in sales result in magnified percentage changes in investment expenditures. This accelerates the pace of economic expansion, which generates greater income in the economy, leading to further increases in sales. Thus, once the expansion starts, the pace of investment spending accelerates. In more concrete terms, the response of the investment spending is related to the *rate* at which sales are increasing. In general, if an increase in sales is expanding, investment spending rises, and if an increase in sales has peaked and is beginning to slow, investment spending falls. Thus, the pace of investment spending is influenced by changes in the rate of sales.

Momentum Many economists cite a certain "follow-the-leader" mentality in consumer spending. In situations where consumer confidence is high and people adopt more free-spending habits, other customers are deemed to be more likely to increase their spending as well. Conversely, downturns in spending tend to be imitated as well.

Technological Innovations Technological innovations can have an acute impact on business cycles. Indeed, technological breakthroughs in communication, transportation, manufacturing, and other operational areas can have a ripple effect throughout an industry or an economy. Technological innovations may relate to production and use of a new product or production of an existing product using a new process. The video imaging and personal computer industries, for instance, have undergone immense technological innovations in recent years, and the latter industry in particular has had a pronounced impact on the business operations of countless organizations. However, technological innovations—and consequent increases in investment—take place at irregular intervals. Fluctuating investments, due to variations in the pace of technological innovations, lead to business fluctuations in the economy.

There are many reasons why the pace of technological innovation varies. Major innovations do not occur every day. Nor do they take place at a constant rate. Chance factors greatly influence the timing of major innovations, as well as the number of innovations in a particular year. Economists consider the variations in technological innovation as random (with no systematic pattern). Thus, irregularity in the pace of innovations in new products or processes becomes a source of business fluctuations.

Variations in Inventories Variations in inventories—expansion and contraction in the level of inventories of goods kept by businesses—also contribute to business cycles. Inventories are the stocks of goods firms keep on hand to meet demand for their products. How do variations in the level of inventories trigger changes in a business cycle? Usually, during a business downturn, firms let their inventories decline. As inventories dwindle, businesses eventually use down their inventories to the point where they are short. This, in turn, starts an increase in inventory levels as companies begin to produce more than is sold, leading to an economic expansion. This expansion continues as long as the rate of increase in sales holds up and producers continue to increase inventories at the preceding rate. However, as the rate of increase in sales slows, firms begin to cut back on their inventory accumulation. The subsequent reduction in inventory investment dampens the economic expansion, and eventually causes an economic downturn. The process then repeats itself all over again. It should be noted that while variations in inventory levels impact overall rates of economic growth, the resulting business cycles are not really long. The business cycles generated by fluctuations in inventories are called *minor* or *short* business cycles. These periods, which usually last about two to four years, are sometimes also called inventory cycles.

Fluctuations in Government Spending Variations in government spending are yet another source of business fluctuations. This may appear to be an unlikely source, as the government is widely considered to be a stabilizing force in the economy rather than a source of economic fluctuations or instability. Nevertheless, government spending has been a major destabilizing force on several occasions, especially during and after wars. Government spending increased by an enormous amount during World War II, leading to an economic expansion that continued for several years after the war. Government spending also increased, though to a smaller extent compared to World War II, during the Korean and Vietnam Wars. These also led to economic expansions. However, government spending not only contributes to economic expansions, but economic contractions as well. In fact, the recession of 1953-54 was caused by the reduction in government spending after the Korean War ended. More recently, the end of the Cold War resulted in a reduction in defense spending by the United States that had a pronounced impact on certain defense-dependent industries and geographic regions.

Politically Generated Business Cycles Many economists have hypothesized that business cycles are the result of the politically motivated use of macroeconomic policies (monetary and fiscal policies) that are designed to serve the interest of politicians running for re-election. The theory of political business cycles is predicated on the belief that elected officials (the president, members of

Congress, governors, etc.) have a tendency to engineer expansionary macroeconomic policies in order to aid their re-election efforts.

Monetary Policies Variations in the nation's monetary policies, independent of changes induced by political pressures, are an important influence in business cycles as well. Use of fiscal policy—increased government spending and/or tax cuts—is the most common way of boosting aggregate demand, causing an economic expansion. The Central Bank, in the case of the United States, the Federal Reserve Bank, has two legislated goals—price stability and full employment. Its role in monetary policy is a key to managing business cycles and has an important impact on consumer and investor confidence as well.

Fluctuations in Exports and Imports The difference between exports and imports is the net foreign demand for goods and services, also called net exports. Because net exports are a component of the aggregate demand in the economy, variations in exports and imports can lead to business fluctuations as well. There are many reasons for variations in exports and imports over time. Growth in the gross domestic product of an economy is the most important determinant of its demand for imported goods—as people's incomes grow, their appetite for additional goods and services, including goods produced abroad, increases. The opposite holds when foreign economies are growing—growth in incomes in foreign countries also leads to an increased demand for imported goods by the residents of these countries. This, in turn, causes U.S. exports to grow. Currency exchange rates can also have a dramatic impact on international trade—and hence, domestic business cycles—as well.

BUSINESS CYCLE VARIANTS, STAGFLATION AND THE JOBLESS RECOVERY

Business cycles are difficult to anticipate accurately, in part because of the number of variables involved in large economic systems. Nonetheless, the importance of tracking and understanding business cycles has lead to a great deal of study of the subject and knowledge about the subject. It was as a result somewhat surprising when, in the 1970s, the nation found itself stuck in a period of seemingly contradictory economic conditions, slow economic growth and rising inflation. The condition was named stagflation and paralyzed the U.S. economy from the mid-1970s through the early 1980s.

Another somewhat unexpected business cycle phenomenon has occurred in the early 2000s. It is what has come to be known as the "jobless recovery." According to the National Bureau of Economic Research's Business Cycle Dating Committee, in a late 2003 report, "the most recent economic peak occurred in March 2001, ending a record-long expansion that began in 1991. The most recent trough occurred in November 2001, inaugurating an expansion." The problem with the expansion has been that it has not included a rise in employment or real personal income, something seen in all previous recoveries.

The reasons for the jobless recovery are not fully understood but are the cause of much debate within the economic and political circles. Within this debate there are four leading explanations that analysts have given for the jobless recovery. According to a study published in *Economic Perspectives* in the summer of 2004, these four explanations are:

- An imbalance in labor available by sector.
- The emergence of just-in-time hiring practices.
- The rising cost of health care benefits.
- Rapidly increasing productivity not being off-set by aggregate demand.
- Only time and further analysis will show which of these factors, or which combination of factors explains the advent of a jobless recovery. Neil Shister, editorial director of the *World Trade* summarizes a discussion of the jobless recovery this way, "The culprit is ourselves. We have become dramatically more productive." This assessment suggests that much more will need to be understood about modern business cycles before we can again anticipate them and plan for their effects on the economy generally.

KEYS TO SUCCESSFUL BUSINESS CYCLE MANAGEMENT

Small business owners can take several steps to help ensure that their establishments weather business cycles with a minimum of uncertainty and damage. The concept of cycle management is earning adherents who agree that strategies that work at the bottom of a cycle need to be adopted as much as those which work at the top of a cycle. While there is no definitive formula for every company, the approaches generally emphasize a long-term view focused on a company's core strengths and stressing the need to plan with greater discretion at all times. Essentially, efforts are made to adjust a company's operations in such a manner that it maintains an even keel through the ups and downs of a business cycle.

Specific tips for managing business cycle downturns include the following:

- Flexibility—Having a flexible business plan allows for development times that span the entire cycle and includes various recession-resistant funding structures.

- Long-term Planning—Consultants encourage small businesses to adopt a moderate stance in their long-range forecasting.

- Attention to Customers—This can be an especially important factor for businesses seeking to emerge from an economic downturn. Maintaining close relations and open communication with customers is a tough discipline to maintain in good times, but it is especially crucial coming out of bad times. Customers are the best gauges of when a company is likely to begin recovering from an economic slowdown.

- Objectivity—Small business owners need to maintain a high level of objectivity when riding business cycles. Operational decisions based on hopes and desires rather than a sober examination of the facts can devastate a business, especially in economic down periods.

- Study—Timing any action for an upturn is tricky. The consequences of getting the timing wrong, of being early or late, can be serious. How, then, does a company strike the right balance between being early or late? Listening to economists, politicians, and media to get a sense of what is happening is useful. The best route, however, is to avoid trying to predict the upturn. Instead, listen to your customers and know your own response-time requirements.

BIBLIOGRAPHY

Aaronson, Daniel, and Ellen R. Rissman; Daniel G. Sullivan. "Assessing the Jobless Recovery." *Economic Perspectives.* Summer 2004.

Arnold, Lutz G. *Business Cycle Theory.* Oxford University Press, 2002.

Bonamici, Kate. "Why You Shouldn't be Scared of Stagflation." *Fortune.* 31 October 2005.

Hall, Robert, and Martin Feldstein. *The NBER's Business-Cycle Dating Procedures.* National Bureau of Economic Research, 21 October 2003.

Hendrix, Craig, and Jan Amonette. "It's Time to Determine Your E-Business Cycle." *Indianapolis Business Journal.* 8 May 2000.

Marshall, Randi F. "Is Stagflation Back?" *Newsday.* 29 April 2005.

Nardi Spiller, Christina. *The Dynamics of the Price Structure and the Business Cycle.* Business & Economics, August 2003.

Shister, Neil. "Global Trade and the 'Jobless Recovery'." *World Trade.* October 2004.

Walsh, Max. "Goldilocks and the Business Cycle." *The Bulletin with Newsweek.* 7 December 1999.

Hillstrom, Northern Lights
updated by Magee, ECDI

BUSINESS EDUCATION

Business education is a term that encompasses a number of methods used to teach students the fundamentals of business practices. These methods range from formal educational degree programs, such as the Master of Business Administration (MBA), to school-to-work opportunity systems or cooperative education. Business education programs are designed to provide students with the basic theories of management and production. The main goals of business education programs are to teach the processes of decision making; the philosophy, theory, and psychology of management; practical applications; and business start-up and operational procedures.

TYPES OF BUSINESS EDUCATION PROGRAMS

Traditional academic programs for business education include college courses that teach students the fundamentals of management, marketing, business ethics, accounting, and other relevant topics. These have been supplemented in recent years with extensive course offerings in computer skills, e-commerce management, and other factors in managing a business within the global economy. Students can earn degrees ranging from an Associate degree in business to a Ph.D (Doctor of Philosophy) in business administration. Some programs may consist of classwork only, while others—such as tech-prep and cooperative education programs, internships, and school-to work opportunities—combine academics with on-the-job training.

Tech-Prep Programs A tech-prep program is a four-year planned sequence of study for a technical field which students begin in their junior year of high school. The program extends through either two years of college in occupational education, or a minimum two-year apprenticeship. Students who complete the program earn either certificates or Associate degrees.

Co-ops Cooperative education (co-op) is a program which offers students a combination of college courses and work experience related to their majors. Co-op programs are available in a wide range of business disciplines, e.g., information systems, accounting, and sales. Participants enroll in a postsecondary educational program while employed in a related job. Most co-op participants are paid by their employers. The co-op program provides students with the work experience they need to obtain full-time employment after graduation. More than 1,000 postsecondary educational institutions and 50,000 employers participate in co-op programs throughout the United States.

Internships Internships are related closely to co-op programs. The main difference, however, is that those who participate in internship programs are not paid, as internships are designed specifically to provide participants with work experience. Often, interns will complete the program separately from their academic setting, rather than combining the two.

School-to-Work Programs School-to-work opportunity programs focus on career awareness for students. They provide participants with work mastery certificates and furnish them with links to technical colleges. In these programs, all participants have jobs, apprenticeships, or further schooling after finishing high school.

Career Academies Career academies are occupationally focused high schools that contain "schools within schools." Primarily, they train high school juniors and seniors in such areas as environmental technology, applied electrical science, horticulture, and engineering. In addition to these schools, there are also privately operated business schools that grant certificates to students who complete their programs.

All of these types of business education programs provide participants with career paths for high-skill technical and professional occupations by formally linking secondary and post-secondary education, and by integrating academic and occupational learning. Students who complete such programs gain an advantage over people who concentrate solely on the academic part of business education. Whichever route students use to acquire a basic knowledge of business skills and principles, there exist ample opportunities to prepare them for business careers.

ENTREPRENEURS AND THE MBA

In the past, many entrepreneurs viewed the Master of Business Administration (MBA) degree as unnecessary to small business success, and some believed that it stifled the creativity that allowed small businesses to develop and grow. Most entrepreneurs counted on their energy, work experience, industry knowledge, and business connections rather than on their formal business education. In the late 1990s this attitude began to change and increasing numbers of entrepreneurs chose to pursue an MBA degree. Two reasons for this change are often cited. First, today's business world often requires small companies to compete for the same customers as much larger, professionally managed corporations. Second, entrepreneurs are finding that even their smaller competitors are likely to be run by MBAs, as more downsized executives decide to start their own companies. And the appeal of the MBA to entrepreneurs seems to runs in both

directions. According to Della Bradshaw in an article appearing in *The Financial Times,* "while the dotcom boom caused frenzy in MBA ranks, business schools themselves report that the 1998 to 2001 boom was just a blip in the sustained interest students have shown in entrepreneurship over the years."

The MBA degree offers entrepreneurs a set of sophisticated management tools that can be brought to bear on the challenges of running a small business, including economic analysis, marketing knowledge, strategic planning, and negotiating skills. In addition, a business education can help many small business owners to broaden their viewpoints and recognize trends within their business or industry.

Yet another reason for the increase in entrepreneurs pursuing MBA degrees is that most such programs have become more practical in recent years. In addition to teaching theory, MBA programs are increasingly emphasizing teamwork, hands-on experience, and cross-disciplinary thinking. This approach makes the MBA much more applicable to the entrepreneur's interests and experience.

BIBLIOGRAPHY

Alon, Ilan, and John R. McIntyre, *Business Education and Emerging Market Economies.* Stringer, 2004.

Avis, Ed. "Plugged-in Professors: Business Schools Must Balance Traditional Lessons with Tech Trends." *Crain's Chicago Business.* 2 October 2000.

Bradshaw, Della. "Entrepreneurs are Back in the Classroom." *The Financial Times.* 21 April 2003.

Cashill, Jack. "Capitalizing on Business Education." *Ingram's.* July 2000.

Mitchell, Meg. "A Difference of Degree." *CIO.* September 2000.

Hillstrom, Northern Lights
updated by Magee, ECDI

BUSINESS ETHICS

Caveat emptor. This ancient Latin proverb, *let the buyer beware,* tells us that business ethics has been a societal concern going back a long ways indeed. Richard T. De George, a distinguished student of the subject, dates the modern interest in business ethics to the 1960s when changing attitudes toward business began to manifest in environmental concerns, the rise in consumerism, and criticism of multinationals—and large corporations began to embrace the idea of social responsibility as a business value. Since that time business ethics has also been associated with civil rights, women's rights, the international fight against Apartheid, and many other issues on which *Moral Man and Immoral Society* (title of a book by Reinhold Niebuhr, the theologian) collide.

DEFINITIONS

Webster's defines ethics as "the discipline dealing with what is good and bad or right and wrong or with moral duty and obligation." (Unabridged, 1961.) The word derives from the Greek word meaning "moral," a Latin word with roots in "mores" or "customs"—in other words the values held by society. Ethicists point out that law represents an ethical minimum and that ethical behavior is something more than being within the law. Individuals—and by extension institutions—obtain their values from religion, philosophy, culture, law, and the special requirements of particular professions. An individual may hold that morality is absolute (what is wrong is always wrong) or may hold that morality is relative (the good is defined in part by other factors). In either case, all but the tiniest minorities assert that good and bad exist and can be determined. Very sophisticated theories exist which assert a hierarchy of good even when morality is held to be absolute; thus, for instance, lying is always wrong, but to lie to save the life of a fugitive Jew during the Nazi era was good: it prevented a worse evil. Given these definitions, business ethics is at minimum something more than operating a business under existing laws; the values to be applied arise from values currently held by society; but the ethics a company may define as its own may hold to an even higher standard.

ETHICS IN A COMPETITIVE ENVIRONMENT

The key difficulty surrounding business ethics is that ethics, by definition, goes beyond the merely legal—but how far beyond? No institutionalized rules exist defining an upper limit. Public opinion is not a very good guide. It is subject to change. Opinions even on environmental issues are subject to change depending on such pocketbook issues as the cost of gas. By its very nature, therefore, business ethics is embroiled in philosophical and operational difficulties.

The traditional concept of business based on Adam Smith's imagery of the market's "hidden hand" assumes that business entities bring about social goods by maximizing profits while operating within the law. Social goods are thus a by-product of market forces—not an objective assigned to corporate management to meet. This viewpoint has been long asserted by free market economists like Milton Friedman. Friedman, in *The New York Times Magazine,* criticized those who insisted that executives and business owners had a social responsibility beyond serving the interests or their stockholders, saying that such views showed "a fundamental misconception of the character and nature of a free economy. In such an economy, there is one and only one social responsibility of business—to use its resources and engage in activities designed to increase its profits, so long as it stays within the rules of the game, which is to say, engages in open and free competition, without deception or fraud."

Thus the movement to embrace social responsibility has an ambiguous character. It is not formally mandated but may be rewarded by customer and/or employee loyalty; it may also, indirectly, fend off intrusive legislation. But while it may be easy to be moral when all is going well, it gets tougher when markets shrink. An article in *Nilewide Marketing* ("Fat profits and slim pickings") puts the matter succinctly: "While the majority of companies claim that employees are their most important asset, they seem to act as though they can do without them, or pay the ones they have a minute proportion of the top salary."

On the face of it, the business that avoids extra costs associated with ethical behavior, and bears only costs necessary to meet the law, will be more profitable, all things equal. A more complex approach to this subject, used by many corporations, is based on the insight that high ethical values have positive consequences (in consumer acceptance, brand valuation, employee loyalty, and so on) which may be difficult to measure but are real. In line with this insight, corporations have invented the notion of a Return on Values (ROV) but find it difficult to give it a numerical expression. At the same time, there is an awareness abroad these days that corporations that set their sights no higher than bare legality may foster an environment where managers may slip across the border of legality and create disasters like the Enron bankruptcy in 2002.

BUSINESS AND EMPLOYEE VALUES

Aside from the structural problems presented by the societal roles of business, corporate policies based on well-formulated ethical principles appear to produce real benefits. A. Millage recently reported in *Internal Auditor,* about the findings of the "2005 National Business Ethics Survey" (NBES), conducted by the Ethics Resource Center. "Seventy percent of employees from organizations with a weak ethical culture," wrote Millage, "reported observing at least one type of ethical wrongdoing, whereas only 34 percent of employees from organizations with a strong ethical culture said they have witnessed misconduct." Problems listed included abusive or intimidating behavior toward employees; lying to employees, customers, vendors, or the public; violations of safety regulations; misreporting of time worked; theft; sexual harassment; and other problems. Undoubtedly such unethical activities ultimately translate into lost sales, higher turnover, and lower profits. Internally, therefore, ethical behavior is efficient, all else being equal. Whether measurable or not business ethics has a positive "ROV."

BUSINESS ETHICS IN SMALL BUSINESS

Business experts and ethicists alike point to a number of actions that owners and managers can take to help steer their company down the path of ethical business behavior. Establishing a statement of organizational values, for example, can provide employees—and the company as a whole—with a specific framework of expected behavior. Such statements offer employees, business associates, and the larger community alike a consistent portrait of the company's operating principles—why it exists, what it believes, and how it intends to act to make sure that its activities dovetail with its professed beliefs. Active reviews of strategic plans and objectives can also be undertaken to make certain that they are not in conflict with the company's basic ethical standards. In addition, business owners and managers should review standard operating procedures and performance measurements within the company to ensure that they are not structured in a way that encourages unethical behavior. As Ben & Jerry's Ice Cream founders Ben Cohen and Jerry Greenfield stated, "a values-led business seeks to maximize its impact by integrating socially beneficial actions into as many of its day-to-day activities as possible. In order to do that, values must lead and be right up there in a company's mission statement, strategy and operating plan."

Most importantly, business owners and managers lead by example. If a business owner treats employees, customers, and competitors in a fair and honest manner—and suitably penalizes those who do not perform in a similar fashion—he or she is far more likely to have an ethical work force of which he or she can be proud.

BIBLIOGRAPHY

Di Norcia, Vincent, and Joyce Tigner. "Mixed Motives and Ethical Decisions in Business." *Journal of Business Ethics.* 1 May 2000.

Fandray, Dayton. "The Ethical Company." *Workforce.* December 2000.

"Fat Profits and Slim Pickings." *Nilewide Marketing Review.* 12 December 2005.

Felsher, Louise M. "Improving Workplace Ethics: How to become a better manager, employee or co-worker." *Meetings & Conventions.* December 2005.

Friedman, Milton. "The Social Responsibility of Business is to Increase its Profits." *The New York Times Magazine.* 13 September 1970.

Kaler, John. "Reasons To Be Ethical: Self-Interest and Ethical Business." *Journal of Business Ethics.* September 2000.

Millage, A. "Ethical misconduct prevalent in workplace." *Internal Auditor.* December 2005.

Torres, Nicole L. "Ethically Speaking: What are today's students learning about business ethics." *Entrepreneur.* December 2005.

Verschoor, Curtis C. "Benchmarking Ethics and Compliance Programs." *Strategic Finance.* August 2005.

Williams, David and Todd Dewett. "Yes, You Can Teach Business Ethics: A review and research agenda." *Journal of Leadership & Organizational Studies.* Winter 2005.

Hillstrom, Northern Lights
updated by Magee, ECDI

BUSINESS EXPANSION

The economy is notoriously cyclical. It expanded forcefully in the 1990s reaching a peak growth of 7.3 percent in the fourth quarter (Q4) of 1999. Growth then dipped to 1 percent in the Q1 of 2000 and hit a negative growth rate of -0.5 percent by Q3 of that year. Growth remained anemic until late 2003 but has not, since, matched "irrational exuberance" as Alan Greenspan, the outgoing Chairman of the Federal Reserve, labeled market behavior late in 1996. Expansions and contractions are thus a normal part of economic life; most businesses expand in good times and contract somewhat in bad. Not surprisingly, a look at business literature for the late 1990s shows scores of articles dealing with the "problems of expansion" and how to deal with them. In 2005 and 2006, such articles were conspicuous by absence. Instead, here and there, an article appeared suggesting how a business might plan to trigger its own growth.

Business expansion thus has two aspects. One is planned and carefully managed expansion at the business owner's initiative. The other, which can be much more problematical, is sudden and involuntary expansion that simply happens for various reasons—among them economic expansion or simply because the business caught the market's eye with a novel product or service. Careful management of such good fortune may be even more vital than planned growth. Somewhat surprisingly for the layman, the Small Business Administration lists "unexpected growth" as one of 10 causes of business failure. Expansion carries risks, whether it is planned or involuntary.

PLANNED EXPANSION

Especially in small business, not all owners wish to expand—sometimes because they started their small business precisely to maintain what they wished to have in the first place: close contact with customers, employees, or the product/service itself, freedom from the burdens of administrative management, and the autonomy that sole-proprietorship often provides. Those who plan expansion tend to have a different vision of the business, one in which "smallness" is not in itself a goal but a necessary starting point. Others plan to expand because the very logic of the business indicates that a larger size is desirable to achieve the full potential of the enterprise. Every situation is unique, of course, but in broad strokes the methods will largely involve one or the other of the following categories of actions: 1) sell more of the same, 2) expand the range of products or services sold, 3) sell something very different, and/or 4) change the underlying business concept. These strategies are listed roughly in the order in which most small businesses consider them. As we move from 1 to 4, each step is more difficult and requires more comprehensive changes and larger investments.

Each strategy, of course, implies additional alternatives some of which may be quite risky. By way of an example, the first choice, to *sell more of the same,* may involve one or a combination of the following: a) regional expansion of outlets, b) significant expansion of production facilities, c) vertical integration whereby more of the product is made in-house, d) revamping the distribution system, and more.

In one of the few recent articles on planned expansion, Julie Monahan, writing in *Entrepreneur,* lists seven expansion strategies with very similar characteristics. These are 1) introduction of a new product, 2) taking existing product to a new market, 3) licensing the product for others to make, 4) starting a chain, 5) turning the business into a franchise, 6) growing through acquisition or merger, and 7) seeking foreign markets.

In essence, planned expansion—particularly one based on more complex strategies—is essentially the same as starting a business from scratch with the exception that a running business provides the owner with a minimum base from which to start. Important administrative structures are already in place—even if they have to be expanded. For these reasons the same financial, planning, and business skills are needed as were necessary to found the original business. On the whole business owners who stay closest to their experience will have the fewest regrets.

MANAGING UNEXPECTED GROWTH

Along with much positive reinforcement, unexpected growth also brings danger: it is exuberance. Unless kept in check, it may lead to careless decisions and a temporary relaxation of the very disciplines that made the business successful in the first place. For this reason, management experts counsel caution when sales suddenly surge. Furthermore, unexpected growth is a challenge that may be unavoidable: the business choosing deliberately not to respond to strong demand may, as a conse-

quence, be left behind and find itself contracting. Growth must be managed. Paul Hawken in his popular book, *Growing A Business* [Simon and Schuster, 1986], says that problems are normal to business. "What's the difference between a good business and a bad one?" Hawken asks. "A good business has interesting problems," he answers, "a bad business has boring ones." Unexpected growth is a business problem, but it is an "interesting problem." Most business owners would rather face growth than empty stores or silent phones.

The chief challenge presented by surging growth tends to be financial. Capacity may have to be expanded and money must be spent to purchase inventory way above normal levels. Capital for either purpose may be difficult to find—or expensive to borrow. In service-providing businesses, new people must be hired rapidly and as rapidly trained. At the same time, the business may be able quite accurately to calculate its immediate financial needs but be less able to assess the sudden demand. Will it continue? Is this a flash? The business owner must retain a certain sobriety and look at the situation—which may involve talking to a lot of people—before deciding to invest.

Most business failures due to unexpected growth are triggered by cash-flow problems. The business will have great sales and high profits, but cash in hand may be inadequate because of the time lag between sales and cash collections from the customer. Customers will expect to purchase on credit; commercial customers may be slow in paying. In a rapid growth situation cash receipts tend to lag sales and deliveries in any case. If growth continues to expand, the business may find itself unable to pay bills even though it has more than adequate resources coming in—later. This can lead to bankruptcies.

Added to potential cash-flow problems are a host of other managerial problems that can occur simply because the business is operating now at greater speed, with more people (many not yet fully trained), and a stressed management less likely to find time to examine financial control systems which, in their turn, may be over-taxed. Some problems, caused by intense activity, may show up later to cause trouble. Thus customer service may be neglected and brand equity may be damaged as a consequence. Minor disagreements—perhaps even simply temperamental differences—may intensify into outright disagreements and divided loyalties within. The small business owner, accustomed to a hands-on-operation, may find himself or herself pushed into a much more distant and corporate role without adequate preparation or willingness to change.

Problems of this nature have no simple or single formulaic solution. Management experts universally counsel a "go it slow" approach to the situation, the maintenance of established disciplines, openness and flexibility in meeting problems, close work with employees, drawing in expert help and using its recommendations, and, if necessary, "leaving money on the table" today so that it can be safely picked up tomorrow.

CHOOSING NOT TO GROW

Given the dynamics of specific markets, choosing not to grow may sometimes be another way of deciding to close the business. Most often a rich variety of alternatives remains open—permitting the business to stay small, in fact, to increase its reputation and its profits in the process. Such adaptiveness, however, also requires action.

Unwelcome rapid growth is, in fact, just another business challenge similar to the sudden appearance of a formidable competitor. Many successful businesses adapt to stay small. Invariably, however, they will also change. For example, management may decide that, rather than trying to handle the new demand, it will cut back on its product line and retain a portion of it in a new niche. The adjustment of the business may take the form of concentrating on one kind of customer, for example the household market, whereas the company formerly also worked with corporations. It may mean staying in the high end of a market and repositioning the enterprise accordingly (through changed advertising, signage, sales strategy) while letting others serve the larger but lower-priced segments.

The analogy to competition is apt in this situation because the small business, unwilling to sell a suddenly popular product in much greater quantity *will* see competition. The new demand will create its own expanded supply. The new suppliers will then draw business from the reluctant laggard unless the company adapts by differentiation along the lines outlined above.

BIBLIOGRAPHY

Koppel, Nathan. "Churn: the Dark Downside of Expansion." *New Jersey Law Journal.* 14 March 2005.

McCoy-Pinderhughes, Paula. "Capital Expansion." *Black Enterprise.* December 2000.

Monahan, Julie. "All Systems Grow." *Entrepreneur.* March 2005.

Morrow, Aubrey. "What steps to take to finance expansion." *San Diego Business Journal.* 25 August 2003.

U.S. Small Business Administration. "Firm Size Data." Available from http://www.sba.gov/advo/research/data.html. Retrieved 19 January 2006.

Weinzimmer, Laurence G. *Fast Growth: How to Attain It, How to Sustain It.* Dearborn, 2001.

Hillstrom, Northern Lights
updated by Magee, ECDI

BUSINESS FAILURE AND DISSOLUTION

CLOSURES AND FAILURES: THE NUMBERS

In 2002, 22.98 million businesses operated in the United States, but the overwhelming majority of these were enterprises without employees. The U.S. Census Bureau maintains data on the closure of businesses with employees (a universe of 5.66 million firms) but without specifying the *cause* of the closure. Dun & Bradstreet Corporation tracks business failures, but its database clearly includes some one-person corporations.

The Census Bureau data, available from the U.S. Small Business Administration on its Web page titled "Firm Size Data," shows that in 2002, 586,890 firms with employees closed their doors; 569,750 businesses were launched. The Census refers to these as "deaths" and "birth." In most years births outnumber deaths by a small margin; 2002 was an unusual year. In 2001, a much more typical year, 553,291 firms closed their doors and 585,140 were started, a net gain of 31,849.

The terminology employed by statistical agencies does not make it easy to distinguish between business closures or dissolutions for whatever cause and business *failures* more narrowly defined as involuntary closures due to financial or legal failure. Some indication is provided by bankruptcy data. In 2002 38,540 business bankruptcies were equivalent to 6.6 percent of closures; in 2001, 40,099 bankruptcies were equivalent to 7.2 percent of "deaths." Brian Headd, a researcher for the Census Bureau's Center for Economic Studies looked closely at closure rates of small businesses. He found that 66 percent of small businesses that close are "unsuccessful"; the rest close for other reasons. Bankruptcy, of course, is an extreme form of being unsuccessful.

Another source of statistical data, maintained by Dun & Bradstreet Corporation and reported by the U.S. Census Bureau (see "Business Enterprise" under references), identifies business failures explicitly. "Failures" are due to insolvency, bankruptcy, or legal action. But these data, while explicit, are difficult to compare with federal data: the number of business concerns D&B uses as its base is much larger, almost certainly because the company includes some firms without employees; such firms are excluded from Census Bureau data. In D&B's report for 1994, for instance, 707,000 new incorporations are shown against 71,529 failures, a ratio of nearly 10 startups to 1 failure. The Census ratio for the same year was 570,587 startups for 503,563 "deaths," a ratio of 1.1 to 1.

The logical conclusion from these data, insufficient though they are, is that business *failures* are a subset of total business *closures*—and closures are much more common. Most businesses are dissolved voluntarily while still successful because owners close shop for whatever reason or sell their businesses to others who merge them into existing entities.

REASONS FOR BUSINESS FAILURE

Businesses almost always fail for reasons that are complex and intertwined. The Small Business Administration, citing two well-known authors (Michael Ames and Gustav Berle) provides a ten point list for consideration. SBA's list includes 1) lack of experience, 2) insufficient capital, 3) poor location, 4) poor inventory management, 5) over-investment in fixed assets, 6) poor credit arrangements, 7) personal use of business funds, 8) unexpected growth, 9) competition, and 10) low sales.

The first item in SBA's list is not only the most important cause of failure. In a way it includes all of the others. Robert Fairlie and Alicia Robb found, for instance, in a study published by the Census Bureau, that individuals who had acquired experience in working in a family business were much more likely to succeed in another enterprise—but their own. They had acquired what the authors called "human capital," i.e., experience.

The literature provides many lists like SBA's, and longer ones at that. They all touch on the same matters but in more detail. In a more systemic way, one might assign the causes of failure to poor planning, poor controls, incompetent execution, and slow adaptability. Planning, which relies on experience, of course, will correctly assess the market environment, including demand, competition, location, and availability of capital and credit. Operational planning will determine the efficiency of the enterprise and will ensure that financial controls are in place and are used to provide early warnings of trouble. Controls are vital to match purchasing to inventory and to trigger timely discounts when inventories become too old or too large. The business must not be started if capital is unavailable or credit arrangements are still too loose. Prospective entrepreneurs must cultivate a certain humility and realism about the competition. No matter how promising one's own product or service, the competition is not likely just to melt away. It may respond.

"Unexpected growth" may appear to be an unusual cause of business failure. It is relatively common because the owners are dizzied and confused by sudden success and fail to maintain discipline in dealing with a rush of orders. The growth may be temporary—but they overextend themselves in anticipation of its continuing. They may expand too soon. They cannot get the financing to meet the demand. The market, disappointed, may suddenly turn away and leave them with very high commitments to vendors.

BANKRUPTCY

Bankruptcy is a legal proceeding, guided by federal law, designed to address situations wherein a debtor—either an individual or a business—has accumulated debts so great that the individual or business is unable to pay them off. It is designed to distribute those assets held by the debtor as equitably as possible among creditors. Bankruptcy proceedings may be initiated either by the debtor—a voluntary process—or by creditors—an involuntary process.

Chapter 7 Bankruptcy. Individuals are allowed to file for bankruptcy under either Chapter 7 or Chapter 13 law. Under Chapter 7 bankruptcy law, all of the debtor's assets—including any unincorporated businesses that he or she owns—are totally liquidated, and the assets are divided by a bankruptcy court among the individual's creditors.

Chapter 13 Bankruptcy. This is a less severe bankruptcy option for individuals. Under the laws of Chapter 13 bankruptcy, debtors turn over their finances to the court, which distributes funds and payment plans at its discretion.

Chapter 11 Bankruptcy. Chapter 11 bankruptcy law is designed to provide businesses with the opportunity to restructure their finances and debt obligations so that they can continue to operate. Companies usually turn to Chapter 11 protection after they are no longer able to pay their creditors, but in some instances, businesses have been known to act proactively in anticipation of future liabilities.

RECOVERING FROM BUSINESS FAILURE

Business failure is usually a demoralizing event in a person's life. It impacts both professional and personal self-esteem. Indeed, many experts believe that the entrepreneur who experiences a business failure goes through many of the same stages as individuals who suffer from the loss of a friend or loved one—shock, denial, anger, depression, and acceptance. But observers are quick to point out that people who experience business failure can still go on to lead rewarding professional lives, either as part of another company or—down the line—in another entrepreneurial venture.

Many analysts believe that chances of subsequent success in the business world often hinge on the entrepreneur's activities in the first year or two after the failure has occurred. The best response, after the initial shock has passed, is a realistic look at the reasons for the failure. This assessment, carried out by the individual with some help from uninvolved friends or mentors, may pinpoint the fatal turn which, if corrected, could lead in the future to a more successful run. For some, of course, the conclusion might be that life as an entrepreneur is not what they are seeking. Paul Hawken, a very successful small businessman and author of *Growing A Business* [Simon and Schuster, 1987], makes the important point that business is*about* problems; they cannot be avoided. The art of management is a knack for turning bad problems into good ones so that they stimulate creative responses—and new problems which challenge rather than overwhelm us.

SEE ALSO *Bankruptcy; Liquidation*

BIBLIOGRAPHY

"Are You Ready?" U.S. Small Business Administration. Available from http://www.sba.gov/starting_business/startup/ areyouready.html. Accessed on 19 January 2006.

Business Enterprise U.S. Bureau of the Census. Available from www.census.gov/prod/2/gen/96statab/business.pdf. Accessed 19 January 2005.

Fairlie, Robert W. and Alicia Robb. "Families, Human Capital, and Small Business: Evidence from the Characteristics of Business Owners Survey." Center for Economic Studies. U.S. Census Bureau. September 2003.

"Firm Size Data." U.S. Small Business Administration. Available from http://www.sba.gov/advo/research/data.html. Accessed 19 January 2006.

Headd, Brian. "Business Success: Factors leading to surviving and closing successfully." Center for Economic Studies. U.S. Census Bureau. November 2000.

Hillstrom, Northern Lights
updated by Magee, ECDI

BUSINESS HOURS

The term "business hours" refers to the "open" and "closed" schedule that a business determines for its operations. Small and large businesses adhere to a wide range of business hours depending on such factors as customer expectations, technology, and seasonal fluctuations in business. The rise in online shopping has expanded the concept to "24/7," as we now say. To some extent in response to Internet pressure and expanding hours worked by the public, a relatively recent development has been the growth in businesses that have expanded their hours. As George Russell observed in the *Fairfield County Business Journal*, "The business community is not in a 24/7 work mode—yet—but we're no longer in a 9 to 5, Monday through Friday world. Business owners and their employees work past dinner-time, on weekends and often into the early hours of the morning. And more—much more—pre-9 a.m. and post-5 p.m. working hours are in our immediate futures." As this observation illus-

trates, the issue of business hours has two aspects: the time during which a business is open—and the amount of time employees must work.

Principal Determinants of Business Hours Business owners point to several factors important in determining what hours their business will be open. The nature of the business is the principal driving force. A nightclub will be open when bakeries are shut. The last young people leaving as the nightclub closes may be present, however, as the breakfast-serving bagel-shop turns on its lights. Companies serving other businesses will match their hours to the customer's. The continuing and still growing participation by women in the workforce has greatly contributed to the expansion of retail hours as women have shifted shopping from daytime hours to the night.

Among many and continuously dynamic factors that impact working hours are the following:

- Non-traditional lifestyles—Increasing numbers of customers, and especially retail customers, keep non-traditional work hours themselves as mentioned above. Some work overtime, while others are employed on a part-time basis or work two or even three jobs to support their families. These potential customers will likely be lost to stores that do not keep extended hours. Moreover, some consumers simply prefer to shop late at night to avoid long checkout lines and hassles associated with busy aisleways and parking lots.

- Seasonal considerations—Some businesses are highly seasonal in nature. Retail establishments based in regions that are highly dependent on tourist dollars, for example, often scale back their hours (or even close entirely) during the off-season.

- Technology—The emergence of e-mail, fax machines, cellular phones, and other trappings of the modern business world has accelerated the pace of the entire commercial environment in the U.S. and around the world, in part because they have made it so easy for people and businesses to communicate with one another, no matter the time of day.

- Competitive pressures—Analysts point out that simple economics have played a large part in the surge in expanded business hours for many companies. "The ceaseless search for efficiencies and the high cost of adding capacity are compelling many small companies to squeeze more out of existing facilities by adding second and third shifts," said Dale Buss in a *Nation's Business* article entitled "A Wake-Up Call for Companies."

Members of the business community agree that for many companies, hours of operation are likely to continue to expand, as demands for convenience on the part of both individual and corporate customers do not appear likely to abate any time soon. But small business owners should make sure that they lay the appropriate groundwork for an expansion of operating hours before committing to it. Thorny issues will almost inevitably crop up, whether they take the form of logistical worries about restocking shelves in the presence of customers or difficulties in finding employees to work that fledgling second shift. But the business owner who takes the time to study these issues in advance will be much better equipped to handle them in an effective fashion than the owner who tackles each issue as it rears its head.

FLEX TIME

A corollary to expanding business hours has been the rise in "flex time," a policy that permits employees to set their own hours of work within certain limits. Flex time tends to increase in times of economic expansion and to contract in times of high unemployment. "Across all industries," reported Celeste Ward recently in *ADWEEK,* "the use of flex time has dropped in the past several years, as workers are more skittish about asking for it and fewer companies are offering it. According to a July [2005] report from the Department of Labor, the number of full-time workers age 16 and older who are on flexible schedules dropped from 29 million in May 2001 to 27.4 million in 2004. And the proportion of companies that offer flex time fell from 64 percent in 2002 to 56 percent this year, according to the Society for Human Resource Management." George Russell's complaint about "more—much more" work is therefore on target. In the current environment, economic and competitive conditions are increasing the hours—and decreasing the worker's flexibility.

BIBLIOGRAPHY

Buss, Dale D. "A Wake-Up Call for Companies." *Nation's Business.* March 1998.

Russell, George. "24/7 Workweek Hovers on Horizon." *Fairfield County Business Journal.* 27 December 2004.

Stewart, Thomas A. "It's 10 p.m. Do You Know Where Your Business Is?" *Fortune.* 3 April 2000.

"24-Hour Businesses Have Unique Practices." *HR Focus.* October 1999.

Ward, Celeste. "Make Your Own Hours: How some staffers bend the work week with flex time." *ADWEEK.* 19 September 2005.

Weeks, Linton. "In U.S., Nighttime is the Right Time: 24-Hour Businesses are Making Odd Hours Ideal for Doing Errands." *Washington Post.* 20 July 1997.

Hillstrom, Northern Lights
updated by Magee, ECDI

BUSINESS INCUBATORS

As the phrase itself implies, business incubators are programs intended to help small businesses get off the ground. They almost always provide both services and rental space to fledglings. The services typically include administrative help, consulting, and referral. Incubator programs are managed by public and private agencies. According to the National Business Incubation Association (NBIA), around 5,000 incubators were operating around the world in 2006; 1,000 of these were located in North America (http://www.nbia.org/).

In its Web-site article titled "The History of Business Incubation," NBIA names the Batavia Industrial Center (Batavia, NY) as the first incubator, founded in 1959. "But the concept of providing business assistance services to early-stage companies in shared facilities did not catch on with many communities until at least the late 1970s," NBIA reports. "In 1980, approximately 12 business incubators were operating in the United States—all of them in the industrial Northeast, which had been hard-hit by plant closures in the previous decade." Other important influences were promotional efforts by the U.S. Small Business Administration (mid-1980s), a program enacted by the Pennsylvania legislature in 1982, and the efforts of Control Data Corporation (Minneapolis) under the leadership of its founder, William Norris.

NBIA provides a profile of the incubator movement in 2006 on its Web site. Ninety percent of incubators are not-for-profit, the rest are for-profit entities hoping to benefit from start-up growth. Nearly half (47 percent) have a mix of clients; 37 percent focus on technology businesses, 7 percent serve manufacturers, 6 percent serve service organizations, and 3 percent serve niche markets and concentrate on community revitalization projects. Forty-four percent of incubators draw clients from urban, 31 percent from rural, and 16 percent from suburban locations.

The sponsorship of incubators in 2006 was 25 percent academic institutions, 16 percent government agencies, 15 percent economic development agencies, 10 percent for-profit entities, 10 percent other, and 5 percent hybrids. The remainder had no formal host or sponsor.

ADVANTAGES OF INCUBATORS

Given the myriad advantages associated with membership in an incubator program, small business consultants often counsel their clients to at least investigate the possibility of securing a spot in one. Strengths of incubators include the following:

Shared Basic Operating Costs Tenants in a business incubator share a wide range of overhead costs, including utilities, office equipment, computer services, conference rooms, laboratories, and receptionist services. In addition, basic rent costs are usually below normal for the region in which the fledgling business is operating, which allows entrepreneurs to realize additional savings. It is worth noting, however, that incubators do not allow tenants to remain in the program forever; most lease agreements at incubator facilities run for three years, with some programs offering one or two one-year renewal options.

Consulting and Administrative Assistance Incubator managers and staff members can often provide insightful advice and/or information on a broad spectrum of business issues, from marketing to business expansion financing. Small business owners should remember that the people that are responsible for overseeing the incubator program are usually quite knowledgeable about various aspects of the business world. They are a resource that should be fully utilized.

Access to Capital Many business incubators help entrepreneurs acquire capital by means of revolving loan and microloan funds, according to NBIA. They link businesses to investors by referral. They assist entrepreneurs in preparing presentations to venture capitalists, and assist companies in applying for loans. Start-ups are helped in raising capital merely by having been accepted by an incubator program. These programs act as a qualifying filter. Those who are accepted gain legitimacy in the business community.

Universality of Incubator Concept One of the key advantages of incubators is that the concept works in all communities of all shapes, sizes, demographic segments, and industries. In many cases, the incubator naturally takes on some of the characteristics of the community in which it is located. For example, rural-based incubators may launch companies based on the agriculture present in the area. But whether based in a small town in the Midwest or a large urban area on the West Coast, proponents of incubator programs contend that the small business people in the community would know more about how to start and operate such businesses than major corporations that focus on mass production.

Comradeship of Fellow Entrepreneurs Many small business owners that have launched successful ventures from incubators cite the presence of fellow entrepreneurs as a key element in their success. They note that by gathering entrepreneurs together under one roof, incubators create a dynamic wherein business owners can 1) provide encouragement to one another in their endeavors; 2) share information on business-related subjects; and 3) establish networks of communication that can serve them well for years to come.

FACTORS TO WEIGH IN CHOOSING AN INCUBATOR

Many incubators have been pivotal in nourishing small businesses to the point where they can make it on their own. But observers note that the programs are not foolproof. Some small businesses fail despite their membership in such programs; incubators themselves sometimes fold, crippled by any number of factors. Entrepreneurs, then, need to recognize that some incubators are better suited to meet their needs than others. Considerations to weigh when choosing an incubator include the following:

- Is It a True Incubator?—Some office building owners falsely advertise themselves as incubators in order to lure tenants. Entrepreneurs need to study the details of each offer to determine whether such claims are legitimate.
- Length of Operation—Incubators take some time to establish their reputation in an area unless they are sponsored by a very high-profile corporation or a well-funded government agency.
- Incubator Leadership—Many analysts contend that entrepreneurs can learn a great deal about the fundamental quality of an incubator program simply by studying the program's leadership. Is the incubator managed by people with backgrounds in business, or by general college or agency administrators? Can the managers provide long-term business plans that show how they intend to guide the incubator to financial independence?
- Location—Does the incubator's setting adequately address your fledgling company's needs in terms of target market, transportation, competition, and future growth plans?
- Financing—Is the incubator's financial base a reliable one, or is it on shaky ground?

Entrepreneurs interested in exploring the incubator concept can request information from several sources, including the Small Business Administration, area economic development agencies, area educational institutions, or the National Business Incubation Association.

Would-be small business owners should have a complete business plan in hand before applying for entrance into an incubator program. Most incubators maintain a stringent screening process to ensure that their resources are put to the best possible use.

RECENT INCUBATOR INNOVATIONS

Internet Incubators "Internet incubators—a for-profit variant of the old-time government- or academic-supported not-for-profit entities—are sprouting up like dandelions in summer," wrote Thea Singer in *Inc.* As with traditional incubators, Internet versions provide dot-com startups with office space, business information and advice, financial assistance (either directly or by connecting them to potential sources of seed money), and management, accounting, and other infrastructure services. According to Internet incubators, these kinds of assistance can provide entrepreneurs with essential tools to accelerate their all-important "speed-to-market" in the fast-paced Internet economy. The price of membership in an Internet incubator can be steep, however. In return for providing their various services and funding, incubators receive a percentage (anywhere from 5 to more than 50 percent) of the dot-com's equity.

Entrepreneurs who are considering membership in an Internet incubator should study the benefits and drawbacks closely before making a final decision. Potential other sources of funding and assistance should be explored, as well as the level of autonomy that is present in the program. In addition, entrepreneurs should examine whether their e-business is prepared to take advantage of the incubator's ability to accelerate the launch process. Analysts note that speed-to-market is of little benefit if you do not have a complete, focused business plan in place. Finally, entrepreneurs need to objectively weigh whether increased speed-to-market is worth giving up a piece of the company.

Internalized Business Incubators Another recent wrinkle in incubator creation has emerged in the corporate world in recent years. Weary of mass defections of valuable employees who decide to launch entrepreneurial ventures of their own, some companies have established business incubators within their own corporate structures. In these programs, employees can use the company's resources (including their already established name and reputation) to build and promote their own new business ideas. "The company will provide the management guidance, infrastructure, and financial support to 'incubate' these ventures," explained David Cutbill in *Los Angeles Business Journal.* "The outcome is a clear win-win. Existing companies stem the hemorrhaging of top talent to Internet start-ups, while profiting from the high multiples investors are willing to pay for a share in Internet ventures.... And entrepreneurial employees get the challenge—and the profits—of creating their own 'companies' with little of the risk they would face on their own."

BIBLIOGRAPHY

Brandt, Jerry. "To Incubate or Not to Incubate, That is the Question." *Los Angeles Business Journal.* 27 March 2000.

Cutbill, David. "Incubators: The Blueprint for New Economy Companies." *Los Angeles Business Journal.* 27 March 2000.

"Due Diligence Advised in Picking Biz Incubator." *Business First-Columbus.* 1 September 2000.

"How to Benefit from a Business Incubator." *Northern Ontario Business.* January 2005.

Krizner, Ken. "Incubators: help startup companies get off the ground." *Expansion Management.* July 2005.

Singer, Thea. "When It's Time to Market that Matters Most, the Extra Heat of an Incubator can be a Lifesaver." *Inc.* July 2000.

Temes, Judy. "Incubators Enter Intensive Care." *Crain's New York.* 6 September 2004.

Totterman, Henrik and Jan Sten. "Start-Ups: Business Incubation and Social Capital." *International Small Business Journal.* October 2005.

Trask, Mike, "Business Incubators Form Association to Increase Awareness." *Daily Record.* 19 November 2005.

Watson, Stuart. "Organic Growth." *Property Week.* 17 June 2005.

Hillstrom, Northern Lights
updated by Magee, ECDI

BUSINESS INFORMATION SOURCES

Business information comes in general surveys, data, articles, books, references, search-engines, and internal records that a business can use to guide its planning, operations, and the evaluation of its activities. Such information also comes from friends, customers, associates, and vendors. Published sources may be daily newspapers; financial, trade, and association magazines; databases, government statistics, directories, technical manuals, and much else. In effect, since "information" is defined more by context than by content, business information is whatever information helps a business know its environment.

Writing in his book *Business Information: How to Find It, How to Use It,* Michael R. Lavin commented that business information is of tremendous value in problem solving and strategic planning: "Information can be used to evaluate the marketplace by surveying changing tastes and needs, monitoring buyers' intentions and attitudes, and assessing the characteristics of the market. Information is critical in keeping tabs on the competition by watching new product developments, shifts in market share, individual company performance, and overall industry trends. Intelligence helps managers anticipate legal and political changes, and monitor economic conditions in the United States and abroad. In short, intelligence can provide answers to two key business questions: How am I doing? and Where am I headed?"

Business analysts cite two primary sources of business information: external information, in which documentation is made available to the public from a third party; and internal information, which consists of data created for the sole use of the company that produces it, such as personnel files, trade secrets, and minutes of board meetings.

EXTERNAL BUSINESS INFORMATION

External information comes in a variety of forms—from printed material to broadcast reports to online dissemination.

Print Information The category of print covers not only a vast array of books and periodicals, but also includes microfilm and microfiche, newsletters, and other subcategories. State and federal government reports also fit into this category; indeed, Lavin described the U.S. Government Printing Office as "the largest publisher in the free world; its products can be purchased by mail, telephone or through GPO bookstores in major cities."

Perhaps the most accessible documents in the print category are books and periodicals. Certainly business owners have a wide array of book titles to choose from, many of which find their way onto the shelves of public, business, and university libraries every year. In addition to books that provide general reference information on human resources management, start-up financing, product development, establishing a home-based business, and a plethora of other topics of interest to small business owners, the publishing industry has seen a surge of books that tackle more philosophical issues, such as balancing work and family life, establishing healthy personal interactions with co-workers and employees, the nature of entrepreneurial activity, and many others.

Many other small business owners, meanwhile, get a considerable amount of their business information from print sources. As with books, entrepreneurs and established business owners (as well as corporate executives, human resource managers, and nearly every other category of person involved in business) can turn to a variety of periodical sources, each with its own target niche. Some magazines and newspapers, such as *Business Week* and *Wall Street Journal,* provide general interest coverage, while others (*Forbes, Fortune, Inc.*) provide more of an emphasis on subjects of interest to investors and executives in large firms. Still others—most notably *Entrepreneur, Small Business Start-Ups,* and *Nation's Business* (published by the U.S. Chamber of Commerce)—publish information specifically targeted at small business owners. These magazines can provide entrepreneurs with helpful information on every aspect of

operations, from creating a good business plan to determining which computer system is most appropriate for your enterprise.

Then there are the trade journals, an enormous subsection of print aimed at very select audiences. These trade journals, which typically provide narrow coverage of specific industries (journals targeted at owners of bakeries, amusement parks, real estate businesses, grocery stores, and a variety of other businesses can all be found), often contain valuable industry-specific information. Another subcategory of the specialized print category is the material published through business research services and associations such as Commerce Clearing House, the Bureau of National Affairs, and Dun & Bradstreet.

Finally, both government agencies and educational institutions publish a wide variety of pamphlets, brochures, and newsletters on a range of issues of interest to small business owners and would-be entrepreneurs. While government brochures and reports have long been a favored source of business information—in some measure because many of these documents are available free of charge—consultants indicate that valuable studies and reports compiled by educational institutions are often underutilized by large and small companies alike.

Television and Radio Media This source of business information is perhaps the least helpful of the various external sources available to small business owners. Programs devoted to general investment strategies and the changing fortunes of large companies can be found, of course, but the broad-based nature of broadcasting makes it difficult, if not impossible, to launch programs aimed at narrow niche audiences (like dental instrument manufacturers or accounting firms, for example).

Online Information As we advance into the first decade of the 21st century, the ever-greater speed and scope of the Internet is beginning to turn the Web into the most powerful source of information for the small business. With appropriate subscription services like InfoTrac, even access to print sources is easier to achieve than actually searching newspapers or trade magazines. Search skills, of course, must be developed, but the small business owner can practice this art in the evenings when libraries and bookstores are closed.

Many of these databases offer information pertinent to the activities of business owners. As Ying Xu and Ken Ryan observed in *Business Forum,* the Internet includes data on demographics and markets, economics and business, finance and banking, international trade, foreign statistics, economic trends, investment information, and government regulations and laws. This information is provided by Internet news groups, online versions of newspapers and magazines, and trade associations. In addition, "many colleges, universities, libraries, research groups, and public bodies make information freely available to anyone with an Internet connection," stated Robert Fabian in *CMA—The Management Accounting Magazine.* "Often, the motivation is to make information available to people within the institution. But it can be less costly to provide general access than to screen access." He also noted that "increasingly, governments are publishing information on the Internet and insisting that organizations they fund also publish on the Internet. It's a practical way to move towards open government, and does make information, which is paid for by the taxpayers, far more accessible to those taxpayers (and any others with Internet access). The range of available information is impressive."

CD-ROM Information CD-ROM (compact disc read-only memory) is an alternative to online services. As the name implies, CD-ROM is not so much an interactive system; in usage it is close to traditional print. In fact, CD-ROM versions of such print staples as the *Oxford English Dictionary* are now commonly available. Business applications for CD-ROM include corporate directories such as Dun & Bradstreet's *Million Dollar Disk* and demographic statistics such as Slater Hall Information Products' *Population Statistics.* The primary drawback associated with business CD-ROM products is the absence of current information, although many publishers of CD-ROM products offer updates on an annual—or even more frequent—basis.

The CD-ROM as an information delivery system is now facing increasing competition from subscription-based online services. The growing speed of the Internet when accessed by cable or DSL lines is making large down-loads from the Web less of a frustration; at the same time very rapid updates to the databases consulted are available to the user.

OTHER SOURCES OF BUSINESS INFORMATION

External sources of business information can be invaluable in helping a small business owner or entrepreneur determine appropriate courses of action and plan for the future. But researchers note that members of the business community often rely on personal contact for a great deal of their information.

"Common experience and the result of numerous research studies show quite clearly that managers, and indeed all seekers of information, frequently prefer personal and informal contacts and sources to published documents and formal sources generally," wrote David Kaye in *Management Decision.* "The reasons are well understood. A knowledgeable friend or colleague will often provide, not only the facts requested, but also advice, encouragement, and moral support. He or she may be able to evaluate the information supplied, indicate the best choice where there are options, relate the information to the enquirer's needs and situation, and support the enquirer's action or decision. Many such personal contacts will of course be found within the manager's own organization, which is for many people the prime source of facts, knowledge, and expertise.... Any organization is a complex information processing system in which actions and decisions are underpinned by an array of oral and written instructions, reports, regulations, information, and advice. Accordingly, many managers seldom look beyond the organization's boundaries in their search for information."

Business analysts note, however, that companies that do rely exclusively on internal information sources run the risk of 1) remaining uninformed about important trends in the larger industry—including new products/services and competitor moves—until it is too late to respond effectively; and 2) receiving skewed information from employees whose goals and opinions may not exactly coincide with the best interests of the business.

BIBLIOGRAPHY
Daniells, Lorna M. *Business Information Sources.* Berkeley: University of California Press, 1993.

Fabian, Robert. "Business Information and the Internet," *CMA—The Management Accounting Magazine.* November 1994.

Haynes, David. *Metadata for Information Management and Retrieval.* Facet Publishing. 2004.

Kaye, David. "Sources of Information, Formal and Informal." *Management Decision.* September 1995.

Lavin, Michael. *Business Information: How to Find It, How to Use It.* 2nd ed. Phoenix, AZ: Oryx Press, 1992.

McCollum, Tim. "All the News That's Fit to Net." *Nation's Business.* June 1998.

Ying Xu and Ken Ryan. "Business Travelers on the Infobahn: Fee Vs. Free Access to Internet Business Resources." *Business Forum.* Summer-Fall 1995.

Hillstrom, Northern Lights
updated by Magee, ECDI

BUSINESS INSURANCE

Business insurance is a risk management tool that enables businesses to transfer the risk of a loss to an insurance company. By paying a relatively small premium to the insurance company, the business can protect itself against the possibility of sustaining a much larger financial loss. All businesses need to insure against risks—such as fire, theft, natural disaster, legal liability, automobile accidents, and the death or disability of key employees—but it is especially important for small businesses. Oftentimes, the life savings of the small business owner are tied up in the company, so the owner must take steps to protect his or her family from the financial consequences of events that could disrupt operations, reduce profits, or even cause the business to go bankrupt. Insurance can help a small business be successful by reducing the uncertainties under which it operates. It places the economic burden of risk elsewhere so that managers can focus their attention on running the business. In addition, the premiums paid for many types of insurance are considered tax deductible business expenses.

Many large corporations employ a full-time risk management expert to identify and develop strategies to deal with the risks faced by the firm, but small business owners usually must assume responsibility for risk management themselves. Though it is possible to avoid, reduce, or assume some risks, very few companies can afford to protect themselves fully without purchasing insurance. Yet many small businesses are either underinsured or uninsured.

COMMON TYPES OF LOSSES AND INSURANCE

Small business owners seeking insurance protection should first identify their companies' main areas of exposure to risk. A risk analysis survey or questionnaire, available through many insurance companies and agents, can be a useful tool in this process. Next, the business owner can evaluate the probability of each risk and determine the potential severity of the loss associated with it. Armed with this information, the owner can decide which risks to insure against and the amount of coverage needed. According to the Small Business Administration, the most common types of risks encountered by small businesses involve: property losses; legal liability for property, products, or services; the injury, illness, disability, or death of key employees; and the interruption of business operations and income due to the occurrence of these other losses. Each category of loss can be managed with a corresponding type of insurance.

Property The types of property losses that can befall a small business include theft, physical damage, and loss of use. Losses from theft can result from the criminal activity of outsiders, as in the case of burglary, or from the illegal activities of employees, including fraud, embezzlement, and forgery. Physical damage can occur due to fire, severe weather, accidents, or vandalism. In analyzing the risk of physical property damage, it is important for the small business owner to consider the potential for damage to the contents of a building as well as to the

structure itself. For example, a manufacturing company might lose expensive raw materials in a fire, a retail store might lose valuable inventory in a flood, and any type of business could lose important records to computer vandalism. Although loss of use of property usually results from another covered event, in some instances it can occur without actual physical damage to the property. For example, an office building may be closed for several days due to a gas leak, or a restaurant may be shut down by a health inspector for unsanitary practices.

In insuring against property losses, experts recommend that small business owners purchase a comprehensive policy that will cover them against all risks, rather than just the ones specifically mentioned in the policy. Comprehensive property insurance policies help small business owners avoid gaps in coverage and the expense of duplicating coverage. In addition, they usually allow for speedier settlements of claims. Still, additional insurance may be needed to adequately cover a specific calamity that is particularly likely in the business's geographic area—such as a hurricane in Florida or an earthquake in California. Experts also recommend that business owners purchase a policy that covers the full replacement cost of materials and equipment in order to protect themselves against inflation.

Small businesses may be able to improve their property insurance rates by implementing a variety of safety measures and programs. For example, installing locks, alarm systems, sprinkler systems, and smoke vents may help lower premiums. In addition, some companies can improve their rates by joining a highly protected risk (HPR) classification that is preferred by insurers. The HPR designation is based on stringent property protection programs and involves routine compliance checks.

Legal Liability A small business's legal liability usually comes in two forms: general liability and product liability. General liability covers business-related injuries to employees, customers, or vendors, on the company premises or off, that occur due to the company's negligence. Product liability covers problems that occur due to defective merchandise or inadequately performed services. In both the manufacturing and retail sectors, a company is legally responsible for knowing if a product is defective. This responsibility lasts long after the product leaves the company's control. Indeed, a company that bases its legal defense for a faulty product on the fact that it met safety standards at the time it was sold may still be vulnerable to crippling financial judgments or penalties. Even in the service sector, the service provider may be held liable under certain circumstances—for example, if a repair later causes an injury, or if a poorly prepared tax return leads to an IRS audit.

Whether the determination of the company's liability results from a court decision, a legal statute, or a violation of the terms of a contract, litigation can be time-consuming and expensive. Basic liability insurance is available to protect small businesses against the costs associated with these and other sources of liability. A comprehensive general liability policy, which is recommended for nearly every sort of business, covers accidents and injuries that may occur on the company's premises, or off the premises when they involve a company employee. Such policies generally cover the medical expenses, attorney fees, and court fees associated with the liability. These policies do not, however, cover product liability or automobile accidents. A separate policy can cover product liability, though producers of some types of products—such as children's toys or food products—may find it difficult or expensive to obtain coverage.

Workers' Compensation A special category of liability coverage pertains to workers' compensation. This type of insurance is mandatory in most states and provides medical and disability coverage for all job-related injuries to employees, whether they occur on company property or not. A few states provide workers' compensation through state-run funds, and companies simply pay a mandatory premium per employee, depending on their line of business. Other states allow private insurers to compete for companies' workers' compensation dollars. Another option available to some businesses is self-insurance, in which the company creates a special reserve fund to use in case a workers' compensation claim is filed against it. In effect, these companies assume the risk themselves rather than transferring it to an insurer. A company's workers' compensation rates depend on its line of business and accident record. The best way to reduce rates is to reduce the risk of employee injuries by improving safety standards.

Company Vehicle Company vehicles must be insured, just like vehicles that are intended for personal use. Automobile insurance is usually handled separately from other property and liability coverage. Experts recommend that business owners be sure to list all employees on the insurance policies for company vehicles. In order to determine needed coverage and obtain the most favorable rates, small businesses can consult an insurance watchdog agency.

Key Person Loss Small businesses often depend on a few key people (owners, partners, managers, etc.) to keep operations running smoothly. Even though it is unpleasant to think about the possibility of a key employee becoming disabled or dying, it is important to prepare so that the business may survive and the tax implications

may be minimized. In the case of a partnership, the business is formally dissolved when one partner dies. In the case of a corporation, the death of a major stockholder can throw the business into disarray. In the absence of a specific agreement, the person's estate or heirs may choose to vote the shares or sell them. This uncertainty could undermine the company's management, impair its credit, cause the flight of customers, and damage employee morale.

Small businesses can protect themselves against the loss of a key person in a number of ways. One is to institute a buy-sell agreement, which gives the surviving partner(s) or stockholders the right to purchase the deceased person's portion of the business. Another way a business can protect itself is by purchasing a key person insurance policy. This type of insurance can provide an ill or disabled person with a source of income, and can facilitate financial arrangements so that the business can continue operations in his or her absence. Partnership insurance basically involves each partner acting as beneficiary of a life insurance policy taken on the other partner. In this way, the surviving partner is protected against a financial loss when the business ends. Similarly, corporate plans can ensure the continuity of the business under the same management, and possibly fund a repurchase of stock, if a major stockholder dies.

Life and Health Some experts claim that since the most valuable asset in many businesses is the employees, ensuring employee welfare is a vital form of coverage. Group life and health insurance are common methods companies use to provide for employee welfare. This type of coverage falls under the category of employee benefits, along with disability and retirement income. It can help small businesses compete with larger ones to attract and retain qualified employees. Life insurance is generally inexpensive and is often packaged with health insurance for a small additional fee. Specialized plans are available to provide survivors with income upon an employee's death. Other plans can protect the firm against financial losses due to the death or disability of a key employee. It is important to note, however, that when the company is named as beneficiary of a life insurance policy taken on an employee, the cost is not tax deductible for the business.

In recent years, many health insurance providers have begun offering affordable plans for small businesses. In some states, businesses are required to provide health insurance if they employ more than five workers. The type of coverage a business needs depends upon its work force. For example, a company with a work force consisting primarily of married people with dependent children will need more comprehensive coverage than a company with a mostly unmarried, childless work force.

Many insurance companies offer computer models that enable small businesses to determine the most economical insurance plan for them. Another option that can reduce premiums is pooling insurance with other small businesses through trade associations, chambers of commerce, and other organizations.

The two basic health insurance options are fee-for-service arrangements and managed care plans. In a fee-for-service arrangement, employees can go to the hospital or doctor of their choice. The plan reimburses costs at a set rate—for example, the insurance company might pay 80 percent and the company or employee might pay 20 percent—for all services rendered. This type of plan declined in popularity during the 1990s in favor of managed care plans. These plans, the most common of which are run by Health Maintenance Organizations (HMOs) and Preferred Provider Organizations (PPOs), require participants to use an approved network of doctors and hospitals. They pay the health care providers a predetermined price for each covered service. The employee may have a deductible and a small co-pay amount. It is important to note that a company that employs more than twenty people and provides group health insurance to its employees is obliged to offer an employee who leaves the company the option to continue that coverage for a certain period of time at his or her own expense under the terms of the Consolidated Omnibus Budget Reconciliation Act (COBRA).

Business Interruption Though property, liability, and other types of insurance can provide businesses with protection against specific risks, most policies do not cover the indirect costs associated with losses. When a small business suffers a loss, as in the case of property damage in a fire, it may be forced to shut down for some time or move to a temporary location. A typical property damage policy will cover the cost to repair or replace buildings and equipment, but it will not cover the loss of income the business is likely to experience during its downtime. The business thus may be forced to tap cash reserves in order to pay expenses that continue—such as taxes, salaries, loan payments, etc.—even when the company has no income. In addition, the company may face extra expenses in a crisis, such as employee overtime or rent on a temporary location. Business interruption insurance provides a company with the difference between its normal income and its income during a forced shutdown. The prior year's records or tax returns are usually used to determine the payment amount.

Business Opportunity Plans A wide variety of specialized insurance packages that cover a custom combination of

risks are available to small businesses. One popular option is a Business Opportunity Plan or BOP, which acts as a starting point for many small businesses that require insurance. A BOP provides basic property coverage for computers and other office equipment, plus liability protection for work-related accidents. In some cases, a BOP might also include business interruption coverage that will maintain the company's income stream for up to a year if a catastrophe disrupts business. Many BOPs also offer optional coverage against power failures and mechanical breakdowns, liability for workplace practices (including discrimination, sexual harassment, and compliance with the Americans with Disabilities Act), professional liability, and other risks.

Many people who work out of their homes assume that their homeowner's insurance will cover them against property and liability losses. But in reality, a typical homeowner's policy is not sufficient to cover business equipment and liability. In fact, many homeowner insurance policies limit the amount paid for the loss of electronic equipment to $2,500, and will not cover the business's liability if a client trips and falls on the property. Additional protection is required, although it may be possible to add a rider to the homeowner's policy for business equipment and liability.

E-Commerce Insurance In recent years, the Internet has emerged as a major business tool for companies large and small. This has led some insurers to introduce policies that protect businesses in the event that their Internet presence is disrupted by hackers or other problems. Hacker attacks, known as "denial of service" among insurance professionals, are a particular cause of concern for companies that rely exclusively on Internet sales. "The business interruption portion of an e-commerce insurance policy usually will cover the cost of sending consultants to the company to help stop the attack and determine how to prevent future attacks," stated Rose-Robin Lamb in *LI Business News*. "It also covers loss of income for the time that an e-commerce site was down and unable to accept business."

PROFESSIONAL ASSISTANCE WITH INSURANCE NEEDS

A small business owner involved in risk management should 1) identify the risks faced by the company; 2) seek ways to reduce or eliminate the risks; 3) decide which risks the business can assume; 4) determine which risks should be transferred to an insurance company; and 5) shop around for the best insurance coverage for the money. Obtaining the assistance of a professional insurance agent with all of these steps is highly recommended. To gain the most benefit from a relationship with an insurance agent or broker, experts recommend that business owners write down their needs and expectations ahead of time, avoid withholding information, check the credentials of the agents and their firms, obtain competitive bids, and keep careful records of coverages and losses.

Insurance agents often work independently and may select among the offerings of a variety of different insurance companies. They may be able to offer expertise on the regulations that apply in the small business's home state and tailor a policy to meet the unique needs of a particular business. Many large insurance companies have also begun to focus on the needs of small businesses. These companies offer the advantage of being able to provide legal assistance with liability claims, rehabilitation programs for injured workers, and inspection of facilities for safety. Experts recommend that a small business owner select an insurance professional who offers experience working with small businesses, a knowledge of the particular industry, and an ability to provide needed coverage at a competitive price.

Other helpful hints for small business owners include covering the largest area of exposure first, then adding other coverage as the budget permits; selecting the largest affordable deductible in order to save money on premiums; and reviewing costs and coverages periodically or whenever the company's location or situation changes. Experts also warn small business owners against self-insurance. Although it may be tempting to simply keep some funds in reserve in case problems occur, the pool of funds needed to provide adequate coverage is well beyond the capacity of most small businesses. In contrast, insurance premiums are relatively small, and their cost is often offset by a tax deduction.

BIBLIOGRAPHY

Anastasio, Susan. *Small Business Insurance and Risk Management Guide.* U.S. Small Business Administration, n.d.

"Better Business: Insurance – Prepare for the Worst." *Print Week.* 8 December 2005.

Gardner, Eileen. "Disaster Preparedness Pays Dividends." *Business Insurance.* 5 December 2005.

Lamb, Rose-Robin. "Biz Insurance: An Evolving Realm." *LI Business News.* 28 July 2000.

Luxenberg, Stan. "Sponsors embrace insurance to cut risk." *Crain's New York Business.* 28 November 2005.

Pasich, Kirk. "Don't get shortchanged on Katrina cover." *Business Insurance.* 14 November 2005.

Hillstrom, Northern Lights
updated by Magee, ECDI

BUSINESS INTERRUPTION INSURANCE

Business interruption insurance compensates a business for certain specified categories of costs in the event of catastrophic events. Three categories that may be covered are 1) profits that would have been realized if the disaster had not occurred; 2) operating expenses that must be paid despite inability to operate; and 3) expenses incurred because business operations had to be moved while damaged original premises were restored for use. This type of protection is also known as business income protection, profit protection, and out-of-business coverage. Free-standing business interruption policies are rarely sold. They tend to be provisions that are part of property insurance policies and so-called "business owners policies" (BOPs).

What is Covered Interruption insurance clauses are not uniform. Clauses that trigger coverage may be limited by category and further delimited within the category. Excluded categories may include public unrest or riots; water damage or flooding; firestorms, tornadoes, or simply "storm damage"; earthquakes; and war and terrorist acts. The business owner is well-advised to review such clauses to ensure that he or she is covered. Exclusions may be present because the business is located in an area such as a flood plain or in some location where annual firestorms are common. Coverage for such events, of course, will tend to be costly.

In the modern electronic environment, interruptions in Internet services or hacker attacks may interrupt or severely damage a business that depends significantly on Web trade or, for instance, is involved in software development for others. Such businesses should be especially careful to ensure that disruptions from such sources are covered.

Record Keeping and Security In many cases a business must have good records to collect on such a policy. It may have to prove, for instance, that it has actually earned profits, at a particular level, in the year preceding the catastrophic event; it may similarly have to document its operating expenses. If records are burned or destroyed in a flood, collection of amounts due may be problematical. For this reason those purchasing business interruption insurance should implement policies to keep copies of records at locations other than the main business site. Carol Schroeder, writing in *Gifts & Decorative Accessories,* described a minimum policy: "[A] backup copy of your computer files should routinely be stored off-site. Our bookkeeper keeps a zip disk of financial data in the trunk of her car, and once a week she brings it in to make a copy of the latest numbers. That's somewhat low-tech, but it works! Those who keep records on paper should keep copies at home, or store them safely elsewhere. You may also want to take photos of your shop's exterior and interior in case you ever file a claim."

Keeping Coverage Up to Date Insurance policies tend to be forgotten after they are purchased; they will cover the business status as it was at the time of purchase—but in the meantime the business may grow. Schroeder provides another example: "[I]f you wrote the policy when your inventory was valued at $100,000, you may not be fully covered if you have $200,000 in stock. Also find out if the coverage for your furniture, fixtures, and building (if you own it) reflect[s] their current value."

Other Related Coverage Business interruption insurance can also provide a small business with income protection in the event an accident or injury causes the disability of an owner or key employee. This type of policy is usually combined with basic individual disability coverage. Basic disability benefits generally begin one month to one year after the onset of the disability, can last between two years and the remainder of the person's life, and pay between 60 and 70 percent of the individual's usual income during the period when he or she is unable to work. Though this type of policy is important to help an owner or key employee cover living expenses, additional benefits—in the form of a business interruption insurance policy—are often needed to keep the business running in his or her absence.

Yet another type of insurance that fits into this category is called *extra expense insurance*. Such insurance, sometimes used in lieu of business interruption insurance, reimburses a business owner for special expenses incurred, over and above normal operating costs, to keep a business from shutting down during a period of recovery from a disaster.

Continuity Programs Small business experts urge entrepreneurs to research their options in the realm of business interruption insurance and select the one that works best for them. But they also caution small business owners that such policies, while extremely valuable in terms of preserving the financial viability of an enterprise, are often not, in and of themselves, sufficient to keep a business afloat during difficult times. Business interruption insurance should be only one element in an overall "business continuity" program. These programs, which can be developed in conjunction with many insurers, seek to address all company functionalities in the event of a business interruption. Their principal aim is to help the company resume operations in as timely and efficient a

manner as possible. Interruption insurance is usually the cornerstone of such programs, but it is hardly the only element. Business continuity programs also seek to minimize a company's financial and operational vulnerabilities and protect its customer base, work force, and assets in the event of an interruption. They also help companies adopt training programs and preventive policies to minimize the likelihood of a business interruption in the first place.

Events such as the terrorist attack in September of 2001 and the Katrina and Rita hurricanes of 2005 acted as wake-up-calls for businesses large and small. Thoughtful entrepreneurs will keep a checklist handy to remind them, even in quiet times, to give thought, occasionally, to the completely unforeseen.

BIBLIOGRAPHY

Alexander, Robert H. Jr. "Loss of business income may be covered by insurance." *Mississippi Business Journal.* 21 November 2005.

Anastasio, Susan. *Small Business Insurance and Risk Management Guide.* U.S. Small Business Administration, n.d.

Blakely, Stephen. "Finding Coverage for Small Offices." *Nation's Business.* June 1997.

"Business Interruption Insurance Necessary." *Construction Contractor.* November 2005.

Hudson, Roderick. "Business Continuation Demands Planning." *Business Insurance.* 19 June 2000.

Jervey, Gay. "Cash Flow, Covered: One firm is bailed out by heavy-duty business interruption insurance." *FSB.* 1 November 2005.

Quinley, Kevin M. "Business Interruption, Technology Concern Risk Managers." *Claims.* June 2005.

Schroeder, Carol L. "Planning for Emergencies." *Gifts & Decorative Accessories.* November 2005.

Zolkos, Rodd. "To Rebound from Disaster Requires Advance Plans." *Business Insurance.* 28 February 2000.

Hillstrom, Northern Lights
updated by Magee, ECDI

BUSINESS NAME

A business name is any name, other than that of the owner, under which a company conducts business. One of the first decisions entrepreneurs must make when starting a new business involves coming up with an appropriate and marketable business name. Although some entrepreneurs simply conduct business under their own names, most opt to create a distinctive business name that provides a good fit with the aims of their companies. The emergence of Internet commerce—with its attendant need for participating businesses to choose effective domain names—is another recent wrinkle in this realm. However, it is important for entrepreneurs to choose business and domain names that will not be confused with those of other businesses or infringe on their rights. The procedures that businesses use to register and protect their names depend to a large extent on the way that they are organized.

Entrepreneurs organizing as a corporation, limited liability company, or limited partnership are creating a distinct entity when they form their businesses. The entity comes into existence through filing a charter with the state in which the entity will operate. At this point, the state checks to see if the name chosen for the new business will be "confusingly similar" to that of an entity already registered in the state. Even if the state gives the business clearance to use the name, that does not necessarily mean that no other business is using or can use it. A similar business may be using the name in another state, for example. A sole proprietorship or partnership may be using the name in the home state; such entities need not register the name with the state. To avoid this situation, entrepreneurs can check a variety of databases that include the names used by a wide range of entities. These databases are accessible at many business libraries; most attorneys have access to them as well.

Although sole proprietorships and partnerships are not usually required to file charters with the state in which they operate, they are subject to certain rules if they plan to do business under any name other than the owner's own. The procedures for registering a "fictitious name" for a sole proprietorship or partnership vary by state. In some cases, the small business owner simply fills out a form—known as a "doing business as" form or DBA—available at its city or county offices, has the form notarized, and pays a registration fee ranging from $10 to $100. In other cases, the small business owner is required to print a legal notice announcing the fictitious name in a local newspaper. Perhaps the easiest way for the owner of a sole proprietorship or partnership to determine the appropriate procedure is to call his or her bank and inquire whether it requires registration of the business name to open a commercial account. It is important to note that corporations, as distinct entities, do not have to file a DBA unless they plan to do business under a name other than the corporate name for some reason. The documents of incorporation and the charter filed with the state serve the same purpose as a DBA.

Businesses can protect their names in a number of different ways. One option involves filing the name, along with any associated logo or slogan, with the trademark (or servicemark in the case of a service business) registry of any state in which it will do business. Although the protection is limited—because state registration can be preempted by federal registration—it does provide valuable evidence of prior use of the name in that state. Federal registration with the U.S. Patent Office is the strongest protection available for a business name. Federal registration prevents any person or business from using the name in the future within a relevant class of goods. However, people or businesses that have established rights through prior use of the name are usually allowed to continue to use it. Federal protection for a business name is generally difficult to obtain. It will ordinarily be denied if the name is already in use or if it is deemed too generic—applying to a class of goods rather than a specific product. In most cases, however, small businesses can obtain a comfortable level of protection by registering their names according to the procedures set forth by their home state.

BIBLIOGRAPHY

Elias, Stephen, and Kate McGrath. *Trademark: Legal Care for Your Business and Product Name.* Nolo Press, 1999.

Lofton, Lynn. "What's in a (Business) Name? Plenty it Turns Out." *Mississippi Business Journal.* 11 July 2005.

Malandruccolo, Kris. "What's In a Name?" *EventDV.* November 2005.

"Q&A. What's In a Name?" *Printing World.* November 2005.

Williams, Phillip G. *Naming Your Business and Its Products and Services.* P. Gaines, 1991.

Hillstrom, Northern Lights
updated by Magee, ECDI

BUSINESS PLAN

Most business plans produced each year are prepared by operating elements of corporations. These plans contribute to a broader corporate strategic or long-range plan which may itself never be widely disseminated. Plans may be elaborate and detailed or may be little more than projections of revenues and estimates of costs ("the budget").

Management gurus and management writers strongly urge every business to prepare an annual business plan, but small businesses rarely do so except under certain circumstances. By their very nature, small businesses tend to be in touch with their markets. Their two or three principals interact constantly; they are always, in a sense, planning. And small businesses have fewer resources to expend on formalities. But small businesses also prepare plans when selling the business or when they seek funding—be that at start-up or when trying to obtain second-tier financing. These plans are, if anything, more complete than annual corporate plans. In addition to the usual content, they will contain a thorough description of the business (rarely included in corporate plans) and also argue that the management team, which is presented in the plan complete with resumes of individuals, is well-suited to achieve the goals of the enterprise.

Aside from these differences, all business plans have the same general content. They discuss the environment, they formulate objectives based on changes in the environment, they lay out alternative actions and the chosen strategy, they estimate outcomes by forecasting revenues, costs, and returns; they specify capital expenditures that will be necessary; finally, they lay out benchmarks over time to measure progress toward achievement of the goals.

It is well to remember that most business plans are written by someone seeking funding—from top management, a bank, the Small Business Administration, a rich individual, or a venture capitalist. Business plans therefore, are documents intended to persuade. For this reason, plans focus on important issues and leave out what might be called "boiler plate." The boiler plate is present, but usually only in the budget details.

PLAN DEVELOPMENT

Environmental Assessment Business planning, like all planning, is an attempt to deal with change. Elements of the business likely to operate pretty much as they did the year before do not need special focus.

Business planning therefore begins with an assessment of the environment: the market itself and trends in that market, the competition the business faces and what competitors might do; changes in the supply chain on which the business depends, including technology; changes in the distribution channel by means of which the business sends its product to the customer; and finally changes in the business itself, including its products, its labor, housing, and so on. Sometimes changes in the legal structure are an important issue. The focus of the planning is on *change* and how change produces opportunities or threats. The environmental assessment results in a few important issues that should be addressed by the plan. Change is a constant; some issues, therefore, should always emerge.

A new business intending to enter a market will, of course, focus on features of the market poorly served by existing suppliers, features of the company's own products that differentiate it, innovations in distribution it intends to exploit, and so on. In such a situation, an important part of the environmental assessment is the business itself—and how it will fit into the environment.

Formulating Objectives The "issues" that emerge from the environmental assessment are next translated into objectives. A nursery might discover that its revenues

are threatened by the repaving of the urban artery on which it sits. The producer of an attractive composting system may discover that price hikes to its popular system will be resisted by its wholesalers. The nursery may set as its objectives at minimum matching its last year's sales. The compost system producer may plan to roll back its price hike.

Broad objectives may be imposed from above. The corporate goal, for instance, may be to increase return on investment (ROI) by minimally 2 percent. This case illustrates the manner in which the "environment" may be an internal factor—namely the parent corporation itself.

Evaluating Alternatives and Making Choices Once the environment has been evaluated and objectives have been formulated, alternative actions will be considered to reach the objective. The nursery, for instance, may consider substantially increasing advertising, providing deep discounts to attract customers despite traffic delays, or setting up auxiliary "tent sales" in parking lots, by special arrangements, to give its customers easier access elsewhere. The compost system producer may look at cutting costs through reengineering, changed materials, or a new painting system. The corporate element reaching for higher ROI may look at its inventory levels and seek ways to reduce these by "just in time" procurement and/or by speeding up collection of payables: both of which would lift ROI.

All such choices imply variable costs and benefits that must be calculated and compared; they have further intangible costs which have to be assessed. The optimum alternatives are selected for implementation.

In the very nature of things, alternative actions may fall into any of the known categories of business and often into several at the same time: marketing, sales, distribution, warehousing, engineering, patents, production, procurement, distribution, finance, law, personnel, and so on. Manuals and books on the subject tend to focus on major activities, but in practice everything is always on the table.

Budgeting and Implementation By the time actions to be taken have been decided, the basic planning is virtually done. But business planning tends to be an iterative activity. In the next phase, budgeting, plans are more fully developed. All costs are calculated and revenue forecasts are refined. Quite frequently, in this process, new discoveries are made. If necessary, the process is repeated and actions are modified. Such might be the case, for instance, if the compost system producer discovers that its new painting system will take much longer to install and therefore it must use some other route to cut costs.

Benchmarking The final step in the business plan is to establish benchmarks by which achievement of the objectives can be measured—internally as well as by the source of funding. Benchmarks are often a combination of financial goals by quarter and particular achievements such as, for instance, leasing parking lot space for the nursery's "tent sales."

BUSINESS PLANS AND PLANNING DOCUMENTS

Every business operates under a plan: the absence of a plan is itself a kind of plan. In the small business environment plans tend to be informal: they arise from periodic discussions between the principals and are understood as a kind of consensus in which all individuals involved will be aware of the important issues and expectations. Active planning tends to take place when change is perceived and "something must be done." The transition to formal planning tends to evolve with increasing size—when management realizes that formal communication of intentions will be beneficial and necessary to obtain everyone's cooperation. At first such plans may be in the form of memoranda with the subject "The Year Ahead." They may take the form of a Mission Statement that, in part, specifies goals and broadly outlines the means to their achievement. Later such plans will become ever more structured.

Planning documents come in two forms. One is the "business plan" entrepreneurs use to obtain funding. The other is the "annual plan" that business elements submit to the next level of management for approval. Annual plans may take the form of budget requests with minimal descriptive text or they may be structured documents with "required" rubrics such as "competitive analysis" and "human resources." In many corporations, the planning process is highly structured; planning staff may distribute spreadsheet templates in which budgets must be elaborated and outlines which must be filled in with appropriate text.

The ideal business plan, whether written or merely "understood" will be 1) comprehensive, covering all relevant aspects of the business; 2) structured around changes in the internal and external environment; 3) realistic rather than promotional or defensive in nature; thus it will attempt to document facts; 4) analytical in that it presents alternatives each of which is weighted; and 5) within the competence of the planner to implement and control.

BIBLIOGRAPHY

Abrams, Rhonda. *The Successful Business Plan: Secretes & Strategies.* The Planning Shop. 2003.

Belkin, Lisa. "The Art of Making a Plan and Making It Happen." *New York Times.* 18 December 2000.

De George, Richard T. "A History of Business Ethics." Paper presented at the Third Biennial Global Business Ethics Conference, Markkula Center for Applied Ethics. 19 February 2005.

Jones, Rebecca. "Business Plans: Roadmaps for Growth and Success." *Information Outlook.* December 2000.

McKeever, Mike *How To Write A Business Plan.* Nolo. 1 January 2005.

"Your Business Plan." *Phoenix Business Journal.* 29 September 2000.

Hillstrom, Northern Lights
updated by Magee, ECDI

BUSINESS PLANNING

Business planning in the modern sense has a fairly long history. Henry Mintzberg, in *The Rise and Fall of Strategic Planning*, pointed out that business planning with modern characteristics (10-year horizon, five-year reviews) was already practiced in the mining industry in France in the 19th century. The current form took hold in the U.S. in the 1950s as an extension of budgeting processes. It became a very major corporate activity and continues so to this day.

With the twenty-first century underway, corporate planning (also known as long-range planning and strategic planning) may become transformed beyond recognition. Resistance to it became visible in the early 1990s. Peter Drucker, the renowned management guru, wrote in 1992 in *The Wall Street Journal* as follows: "Uncertainty—in the economy, society, politics—has become so great as to render futile, if not counterproductive, the kind of planning most companies still practice: forecasting based on probabilities." Since then uncertainty has increased (terrorism, potential problems of global warming, a looming shortage of hydrocarbon fuels, and waves of epidemics); the electronics age has vastly increased the speed of communications and the Internet has created a vast, global theater of activity. The chorus of critics has also grown louder. Despite these signs of a changing "planning culture," formal planning is still practiced in many if not all major corporations.

WHAT IS BUSINESS PLANNING?

A corporate plan may be a simple statement of objectives, including indications of methods to be used to achieve them—or it may be a very extensive planning process in which every element of the corporation routinely takes part: a formal planning cycle.

An example of the first category might be a simple statement such as the following: "Increase market share by 30 percent within five years by acquiring and integrating two of our smaller competitors, increasing our own sales by exploiting the cost advantages of the triploid valve, and divesting our holdings in toys and children's furniture by spinning them off."

Much more common are formal plans built from the bottom-up by the synthesis of projections and plans produced by the operating element (divisions, wholly-owned subsidiaries). In these cases the corporate expression of objectives will tend to be more abstract and financial, e.g., a projected growth rate for revenues, profits, and return on investment. Communication of such financial goals to operating elements may kick off the process. Each business manager then attempts to make his or her contribution to the corporate objective.

The fundamental elements of formal planning are 1) corporate goals to be met; 2) projections of earnings, costs, and returns; 3) actions to be carried out in light of opportunities and barriers (e.g., competition); and 4) a fixed time horizon. In most corporate environments, plans are for the next twelve months but will have projections out five, 10, or even 15 years. Time horizons in retail industries are typically much shorter: a long-range plan may be a year; the operational plan may be for the next quarter. The corporate budget, including not just cost projections but every aspect of future financial outcomes, is the skeletal framework of the corporate plan. *The numbers* are used to measure the performance of operational managers; the stock price is used as the way to judge top management.

The complex process is by far the most common. It has become deeply institutionalized. The planning cycle is usually referred to tongue-in-cheek as the "silly season." In many corporations a substantial bureaucratic structure ("the planning staff") has developed; it runs the exercise, coordinates inputs from operating elements, and synthesizes the evolving plan in successive waves. A major draw-back of formal planning is that operating units benefit by promising as little as possible to make it easier to *meet plan.* Top management objectives are to incentivize operating units to *stretch* themselves as much as possible. Conflicts are inherent in the process. In recent decades, accelerating change has made it ever more difficult accurately to predict what will happen six months out, much less a year out. Planning structures have grown very large, ritualized, and rigid. Information systems have improved to such an extent that constant adjustment to the environment is somewhat easier. "Rolling" budgets are becoming more popular and resistance to fixed long-range budgets is stiffening. All of these factors are playing a role in the foreseeable transformation of business planning in the years ahead.

PROS AND CONS OF BUSINESS PLANNING

As Henry Mintzberg pointed out in his 1994 book, nothing ever really happens without planning; we cannot even make a sandwich without "looking ahead" a little. He wrote, concerning this subject, that as far back as the late 1960s the business community could no longer come up with a single coherent definition of what "planning" and "long-range forecasting" meant. These phrases had taken on special meanings in every corporation.

It appears, therefore, that business planning, in the modern sense, as described above, is a technique of management in which routine planning (which goes with any kind of activity) is carried out *consciously,* formally, and with the deliberate projection of *measurable* outcomes based on a fixed future date.

At the time when this management technique came into widespread use (the 1950s and 1960s), it was well-adapted to business conditions generally. In many industries long-time horizons are required to build new capacity (e.g., the process industries like power, chemicals, and petroleum); in such operations long-range planning remains unquestionably superior to "doing what comes naturally." Even in industries where change has accelerated, a periodic, formal look ahead provides valuable insights. Well-conceived future goals always clarify current decisions. The principal benefit of formal business planning is therefore unlikely to be changed by changes in the environment. Looking ahead is good; looking ahead with concentration and some effort to understand a wide variety of forces that impinge upon our actions is even better. What is likely to change is the frequency with which this will be done and the methods used to arrive at the plans.

The primary negatives associated with modern business planning (the annual cycle), arise chiefly from three factors: 1) the bureaucratization of the process and the resulting high costs associated with it, 2) uncertainty brought about by rapid change, and 3) performance evaluation issues which, many claim, stifle innovation and result in unproductive gamesmanship. To this list some add a fourth issue: namely that the planning process poorly matches the quarterly stock market cycle. Such observers advocate a 3-month rolling planning cycle which matches plans to quarterly reports; such reports influence stock analysts who, in turn, influence stock price.

Business plan contents will be discussed elsewhere in this volume (see *Business Plan.*) What follows here is a discussion of two of the problem areas in modern planning that will likely undergo change.

FORECASTING UNCERTAINTIES

Forecasting the future is the very essence of modern business planning. It provides the measurements that justify the planning effort. The operating manager planning for his or her unit makes the best possible projections about future costs, sales, capital needs, and returns. Some of these will be relatively easy to document. Others will be mere guesses. But after a plan has been approved, these forecasts tend to be transformed into something much more solid than they actually are: they turn into numbers which will determine promotions, bonuses, even the future of a job.

In times of rapid change, ability to forecast far ahead becomes more difficult. Pressures increase, therefore, to shorten the time horizon. An unforeseen flu epidemic or terrorist action may severely restrict travel, soften demand, and disrupt supplies. In the 1960s a competing retailer may have had to find and furnish retail outlets and establish warehouse distribution sites; in the 2000s he or she may enter the market suddenly with Internet distribution and a flurry of publicity. In a global market where much specialized labor is outsourced, international conflicts, well beyond a manager's control, can instantly put labor resources out of reach without much warning. Not surprisingly, therefore, pressures are now mounting to replace long-range planning with rolling budgets adjusted monthly or quarterly after brief assessments of changes in the environment.

PERFORMANCE TIED TO ANNUAL PLANS

In today's ever more uncertain business environment, the concepts of trust, empowerment, flexibility, and small, innovative front-line teams capable of rapid adaptation have become popular approaches for gaining a competitive edge. The Planning Group, a major management advisory group, has established the Beyond Budgeting Round Table (BBRT) of which 29 major corporations are currently members (2006). David Marginson and Stuart Ogden recently wrote in *Financial Management, (UK)* citing BBRT sources, that the necessary conditions of trust and empowerment in today's organizations "are not possible with budgets still in place, because the entire system perpetuates central command and control." Innovation is vital for economic survival. But "budgeting stifles trust and empowerment, according to its critics, which in turn stifles innovation."

Rapid changes in plans and flexible responses to competitive pressure—or to take advantage of suddenly appearing opportunities—are very difficult if individual managers' performances are measured based on formal plans. Long-range plans, out of time-phase with the rhythm of current events, are viewed as obsolete in today's environment. In addition to this emerging factual situation, *gaming* the system by carefully adjusting projections so that they can be met—in order to achieve bonuses, stock-options, or other benefits—has weakened the originally rational structure of formal business planning.

SUMMARY

Business planning, in some form, is here to stay. Highly evolved and complex planning cycles are in use in most corporations. In many sectors which are somewhat immune to rapid changes in the business environment—for structural reasons, above all, such as the long lead time necessary to plan and to build a power plant, for instance—the established form of planning (the annual cycle) will continue to be used as a major management technique. Elsewhere signs are present that business planning will undergo a radical change soon. The annual cycle is already being abandoned by some. The new style of planning will most likely introduce much shorter time horizons, more fluid budgetary methods, and restructure managerial rewards to provide incentives for flexibility and innovation.

SEE ALSO *Budgets and Budgeting; Strategy*

BIBLIOGRAPHY

Ackoff, R. L. *A Concept of Corporate Planning.* Wiley-Interscience. 1969.

Drucker, Peter. "Planning for Uncertainty." *Wall Street Journal* 22 July 1992.

Hope, Jeremy and Robin Fraser. *Beyond Budgeting.* Harvard Business School Press, 11 April 2003.

Marginson, David and Stuart Ogden. "Budgeting and Innovation: Do budgets stifle creativity?" *Financial Management (UK).* April 2005.

Mintzberg, Henry. *The Rise and Fall of Strategic Planning.* The Free Press, 1994.

Hillstrom, Northern Lights
updated by Magee, ECDI

BUSINESS PROPOSALS

A business proposal is a written document sent to a prospective client in order to obtain a specific job. Proposals may be solicited or unsolicited. A client may simply request a proposal on a project in the course of a sales call by saying: "You know, that sounds interesting. Why don't you send me a proposal on that." In other cases the proposal may be a formal solicitation, usually called an RFP (request for proposal). RFPs are almost always documents, too. They specify the product or service to be provided, the qualifications sought, and the deadline for submission. Solicited proposals, obviously, mean that the client has already decided to make a purchase. Only the selection of a vendor remains to be done. An unsolicited proposal, by contrast, is often a sales presentation dressed in another cloak—but the proposal is specifically aimed at a well-defined and limited activity. An example of an unsolicited proposal is the submission of the outline of a book to a publisher arguing the popularity of the subject, the novelty of the approach, and the merits of the author.

Business proposals must be distinguished from *estimates*. In many fields where small business is active, estimates serve the same purpose as a proposal. They are the document that clinches the sale of a roofing or a paving job or a monthly house-cleaning service. But where estimates are used, the qualifications of the seller and his or her method of accomplishing the job are also established, but by other means—typically by an interview or sales call. Sometimes the seller is assumed to fit the job because the business already enjoys a good reputation. Proposals, on the other hand, usually involve complex or unusual one-time services like landscaping a park, surveying a market, or building a refinery. In these cases the approach to the job, the design, the implementation, the schedule, and even the aesthetics require more than simply a dollar estimate.

Many service businesses operate entirely on the basis of proposal. In other cases a proposal is sometimes required, sometimes not. In highly technical fields, the proposal may be filled with dry listings of engineering specifications and/or process details. But it is vital to remember that proposals are always first and foremost *sales documents*.

ELEMENTS OF THE BUSINESS PROPOSAL

In most industries proposals have a well-defined format specific to the field. Examples might be providing electrical wiring services to a major high-rise or pouring foundations for a suburban development. In such cases the bidder should first obtain old proposals and follow the structure typically used by his trade in that market. In professions such as architecture and landscaping a visual presentation, sometimes even a model, is central to the sale. The same holds for an advertising proposal. In these three areas—there are others as well—the actual presentation is usually a meeting. Any document is supplemental and tends to summarize the presentation with additional so-called "boiler plate," i.e., administrative details.

What follows here is a discussion of more general proposals, usually associated with studies, surveys, or service activities (e.g., protective services for a warehouse complex). In such proposals the following general structure applies.

All proposals have at least two distinct pieces: a cover letter and the proposal document itself. In addition, sometimes, one or more appendices may be provided with charts, graphs, photographs, maps, and so on. Brief proposals, also sometimes known as "letter proposals," combine the first two pieces into a single submission usually of a maximum of six to eight pages.

The *cover letter* serves as a transmittal document. Many bidders also use the cover letter to provide the essence of the proposal in very abbreviated form, highlight the bidder's qualifications, name the price, and ask for the order.

The *proposal document* usually has the following structure:

- Title Page. This part typically includes your name and the name of your company, the name of the person or company to whom the proposal is submitted, and the date of submission.

- Table of Contents. While usually not necessary for shorter proposals, these are sometimes used for complex formal proposals. In cases where different departments of the client will separately review parts of the document, the table of contents is a helpful means of rapidly guiding the reader to such topics as Electrical, Structural, Heating & Cooling (in a building project)... or Food Services, Music, Entertainment, Transportation Services (in a project to organize a festival).

- Executive Summary. A summary may be included here or may be conveyed in the cover letter.

- Statement of the Problem/Issue/Job. This section repeats, in a rephrased manner, the client's objectives and goals as interpreted by the bidder. Including this restatement of the issue is valuable in showing the client that the bidder understands the issue correctly.

- Approach. In this section the bidder summarizes his or her proposed approach to solving the client's problem or carrying out the necessary task. The proposed approach is often the key to winning the job—if the price is right—because it shows unique means, modes of thought, or techniques, why they will solve the problem, and why they are superior to alternatives. The section need not be detailed. Details are left to the Methodology. But it presents the strategic elements of the proposal and argues in their favor.

- Methodology. This section develops in some detail how the Approach will be carried out. Level of detail should be just sufficient to convey to the client convincingly what will happen without becoming entangled in minutiae.

- Bidder's Qualifications. The section presents documentation why this bidder should be chosen on the basis of qualifications, past history, and successful accomplishment of similar jobs in the past.

- Schedule and Benchmarks. Major elements of the job are here displayed against a time line. If necessary, specific benchmarks are identified to indicate successful accomplishment of intermediate objectives.

- Cost Proposal, Payment Schedules, and Legal Matters. The bidder concludes by presenting the price in as much detail as required in the RFP. It is always wise to specifically pin-point when the bidder expects to obtain partial payments as the work proceeds. If legal matters are involved, they can be placed here. If they are lengthy, they may merit a section of their own.

SUCCESSFUL PROPOSALS

Successful proposals are, above all, what clients describe as "responsive," meaning that the bidder has done his or her homework, is thoroughly familiar with the client's needs and aspirations, and has carefully responded to all aspects of an RFP. Responsiveness is ultimately much more important, all else equal, than the visual appeal of the presentation or even the fluidity of its writing. A beautiful and well-written proposal that misses or ignores key elements of the client's project will lose to a dull proposal that is otherwise responsive. Writing in the *Los Angeles Business Journal*, Sharon Berman noted that "Doing your homework and making the required preparations can make all the difference. This is especially important in light of the enormous time and effort required to craft a professional proposal." Meeting with key decision-makers ahead of time and asking probing questions to determine exactly what they are looking for is minimum preparation. Needless to say, a competitive price is invariably the final determinant between equal contenders.

BIBLIOGRAPHY

Berman, Sharon. "How to Craft Business Proposals That Sway Clients." *Los Angeles Business Journal.* 3 January 2000.

Gilliam, Stacy. "Power up your Proposal." *Black Enterprise.* June 2005.

Sant, Tom. *Persuasive Business Proposals.* AMACOM, 1 December 2003.

Hillstrom, Northern Lights
updated by Magee, ECDI

BUSINESS TRAVEL

Business travel is a significant expense for companies of all shapes and sizes. Indeed, business observers cite travel costs as one of the largest cost categories for many companies, sometimes close to payroll, data processing, and a few others. Given this reality, business surveys often cite cost containment as the single most important element of travel management.

Certainly, several American industries rely on business travelers for their continued existence. But while business travel is commonly associated with huge corporations, many small businesses rely on the practice as well to make sales, keep in contact with vendors, market their products or services, and keep up with industry trends (via trade shows, conventions, etc.). Indeed, intelligent choices in the realm of business travel can be a major boon to small businesses hoping to curb spending without sacrificing in other business areas.

With this in mind, business consultants urge companies to implement written policies on all aspects of business travel, including spending limits on lodging, meals, entertainment, transportation, etc. Businesses are also urged to establish a person or department responsible for coordination of travel needs and to consolidate their travel needs with one agency. By implementing such steps, companies can register savings in a number of areas while still attending to their basic business needs.

HOTELS

Several factors are typically taken into account when a hotel is selected for business travel. Convenience of location (proximity to client, field office, or airport), quality of room, and quality of service are all major considerations. But price is often the paramount consideration, especially if other elements of the hotel—location, etc.—are acceptable.

Small businesses can pursue a couple of different strategies to cut down on lodging expenses. Writing in *Nation's Business,* Peter Weaver noted that "you can sometimes cut one-half off quoted room rates by getting your reservations through a hotel broker. Hotels often designate 10 to 15 percent of their rooms to be sold by brokers at deeply discounted rates because these specialized travel companies can guarantee the hotels business in the low season and can bring in new customers all year... Hotel brokers generally find the biggest discounts among the largest chains in major metropolitan areas and resort spots. But you can often get even lower rates by staying at budget hotels." In addition, surveys and studies indicate that small business owners are often able to cut their lodging expenses by negotiating discounts of as much as 30 percent if they provide a large volume of business to a particular hotel. Finally, business travelers should keep in mind that many airlines will pay for overnight lodging in the event of a cancellation or major delay (more than four hours) if they receive a request for such assistance.

AIR TRAVEL

Small businesses can save huge amounts of money on air fare if they are able to plan trips in advance. This is not always possible, of course, and there may be instances in which the company may simply have to bite the bullet and pay full price for a short-notice trip. As one travel expert admitted to *Nation's Business,* "You always pay top dollar to the airlines by making your plans, or changing them, at the last minute." But experts claim that companies can cut as much as 50 percent of their airline expenses through judicious timing of out-of-town meeting dates. Tuesdays and Wednesdays are cited as particularly good travel days for obtaining discount fares. Savings can also be realized by choosing mid-day or evening flights rather than morning flights. However, statistics indicate that morning flights are less likely to be delayed or canceled than afternoon or evening flights.

Other tactics that can be used by small business to cut their air travel expenses include the following: 1) If a company's business requires regular travel (a minimum of 40 flights a month on the same airline) between the same two cities, it may be able to secure a "city-pair" discount of up to 10 percent; 2) Business travelers who choose flights that include stops in a carrier's "hub city" can sometimes secure discounts; 3) Some airports have greater levels of competition—and hence, a greater likelihood of discounted fares—than others. Some metropolitan areas of the eastern United States support two airports within an hour's drive of one another, which gives business travelers an opportunity to explore this possibility; 4) Smaller, budget airlines may offer better fares (and service) than the giants of the industry; 5) Frequent-flier points can sometimes be utilized to register significant savings.

In addition to cost considerations, convenience is another important factor to consider when planning a business flight. To this end, usage of electronic ticketing increased dramatically in the 2000s. "E-ticketing" is popular with airlines because it enables them to register savings in ticket distribution and handling and simplifies their accounting procedures. It is popular with travelers because it enables them to go straight to the boarding gate, bypassing long lines at the ticket counter. Electronic tickets are identical to paper tickets in practical terms, as they provide each user with a reservation and a seat assignment. But airlines require photo ID before they will hand over a boarding pass, so make sure you have one on hand when going the e-ticket route.

Finally, savvy business travelers can take easy steps to increase their chances for a comfortable and successful flight. For example, early check-ins enable travelers to ask for seats in emergency exit rows, which have considerably higher volume of leg room than do the rows in the rest of the cabin. And frequent-flier status generally confers preferential treatment in several areas, including likelihood of receiving upgrades or new flights in the event of cancellation.

CAR RENTALS

As with other aspects of business travel, advance planning in securing car rentals can help reduce costs, sometimes by significant amounts. In addition to making advance reservations, business travelers should use discount coupons from travel agents, membership organizations, or airline frequent-flyer clubs when securing a rental car.

TRAVEL AGENTS

According to the American Society of Travel Agents (see "Frequently Asked Questions" on http://www.astanet.com/about/faq.asp#1), long before airlines were hard-hit by the events following the 9/11 terrorist attack, airlines began capping or reducing commissions paid to travel agents. The process began in 1995. In March 2002, U.S. carriers eliminated commissions altogether. As a consequence, travel agencies—which, up to that point provided a service largely paid for by the airlines—began to charge fees for services in order to stay in business. Fees have increased from around $13 per airline ticket in 2001 to $27 per ticket in the mid-2000s. The industry is also undergoing major restructuring, with many agents becoming specialists in destinations or specific kinds of travel. In the late 1990s they sold 80 percent of all domestic and 90 percent of all international airline tickets; in 2004, according to ASTA, they sold 51 percent of all airline tickets.

The upshot of these dramatic changes is that the small business, intending to take advantage of the skills of travel agents and to save on travel as a consequence must now undertake first to find the right agent for the job. With a good agent secured, the help of a professional in navigating through the maze of travel options will be eased for the small business owner—who can more profitably spend his or her time on the business.

TRAVEL DEDUCTIONS

Provided that the representative of the firm incurs his or her costs while engaged in "company business," many costs of business travel can be deducted. Travel deductions are permitted for the cost of transportation, whether by automobile, train, bus, or plane; lodging; meals; and other miscellaneous costs such as baggage fees, facsimile calls, dry cleaning, tips, and public transportation (bus service, taxicab service). Business travelers should note, however, that these miscellaneous deductions are only permitted if the person in question stays overnight.

Deduction rules for travel to foreign countries are somewhat more complicated, especially for self-employed business owners and major shareholders of small corporations. While many deductions still apply, the Internal Revenue Service (IRS) does have some additional stipulations; contact the agency for more information.

SEE ALSO *Expense Accounts; Standard Mileage Rate*

BIBLIOGRAPHY

Applegate, Jane. "Business Travel Can Be Fun If You Negotiate Good Deals." *Los Angeles Business Journal.* 11 December 2000.

Cohen, Amon. "How to Ease the Burden." *The Financial Times.* 23 June 1997.

Dix, Sally. "Hanging Pigs, Angry Cats, and Fake Plants: Loving, Hating, and Coping with Business Travel." *Internal Auditor.* June 1997.

Jordan, Archie. "Family Considerations While on the Road." *American Salesman.* February 1997.

McGinnis, Chris. "Return of The Agent: Online booking doesn't always cut it. Know when to call the pros." *Entrepreneur.* January 2006.

Miller, Lisa. "Why Business Travel is Such Hard Work." *Wall Street Journal.* 30 October 1996.

Morris, Hal. "It Pays to Review Travel Coverage." *Nation's Business.* September 1997.

"Select a Travel Agency." *Business Journal-Milwaukee.* 11 February 2000.

Ward, Angela. "Planes, Trains, and Automobiles…" *Acquisitions Monthly.* November 1996.

Weaver, Peter. "Cutting Costs Before Takeoff." *Nation's Business.* November 1997.

Hillstrom, Northern Lights
updated by Magee, ECDI

BUSINESS-TO-BUSINESS

"Business-to-business," as a phrase—together with abbreviations like "B-to-B" and "B2B"—arose in the 1990s in the context of the Internet to divide web-based commerce into two categories. The second category was business-to-consumer, abbreviated B-to-C or B2C. Most people associate electronic commerce with the latter, with consumer purchasing on the Internet. Amazon.com, initially a book seller, and E-bay, the auction house, are almost emblematic of e-commerce in general, although they take a business-to-consumer form. Most people do not know, however, that the overwhelming majority of commercial electronic transactions on the Web—and the money-flows that they represent—are business-to-business transactions. In fact, electronic sales predate the appearance of the Internet by decades. They were based, and to some extent continue to be based, on large computers and leased high-speed, proprietary cable connections. A typical old-fashioned electronic connection between businesses was that between a manufacturer and a distributor (or dealer) with a proprietary computer linkage used to order product and replacement parts, the credits and debits thus created leading to account adjustments or billings. With the rise and speed-improvements of the Internet, business rapidly embraced the new medium well ahead of consumers.

The expansion of the Internet had—and still to some extent retains—a heady sense of excitement. The new phrase therefore "developed legs." Needless to say, business-to-business relationships are as old as business itself but once went by such boring tags as "industrial sales" or "industry-to-industry." In current practice B-to-B has come to be applied to any and all transactions between corporations, even if the Internet does not play a significant or, indeed, any role. This seems somewhat to irk the people who first coined and deployed the phrase to designate a newly evolving phase of business communications—new because the visual interface of the Web provided additional resources for business. Formal definitions of B-to-B thus strongly underline and emphasize the *electronic* aspects of the interactions and the sophistication of these. But the genie is out of the bottle, and the phrase now serves a much more general purpose.

Narrowly conceived, B-to-B involves one or more of the following:

1. Formal, contractual arrangements to do business over the Internet. An example of this might be an electronic relationship between a bank and several of its industrial customers in which all manner of financial transactions take place in automated form.

2. Software and systems specifically designed to serve such business relationships. For full-fledged B2B, data transfer must be safe and private and such systems therefore feature WAC (for Web Authorization and Control), and have features that enable parties to exchange technical information and to conduct online negotiations.

3. Electronic catalogs and displays access to which is restricted to qualifying industrial shoppers. An example of this is a supplier of sophisticated components who gives access to the catalog to established customers who, using the displays, can get very detailed technical data far transcending simple

descriptions. Amazon.com, which is B-to-C, provides an analog here by allowing customers to "look inside" a book and examine some of its content and index.

4. Systems that automate the actual distribution function so that the buyer can trigger shipments automatically to designated locations based on automatic inventory levels; and the automated ordering then, in turn, triggers automatic payment orders based on similarly automated price look-ups and discount calculations. And,

5. Advanced computerized lead generation by Web searches based on customer profiles sometimes involving Web crawlers—software routines that "crawl" the Web and automatically collect information on site contents. Using one such technique, for example, as reported by Brian Quinton in *Direct,* a marketer ordered a crawling survey looking for "the presence of Secure Socket Layer (SSL) transaction security." SSL is only present when a site uses credit cards and thus sells to customers. The marketer's crawlers, therefore, were identifying potential *business* customers—the target of the marketer's search.

More broadly conceived, B-to-B is simply a category identifying both electronic and conventional interactions between commercial/industrial buyers and business sellers. Typical B2B news stories are apt to feature marketing techniques that mix lead generation by electronic means, direct mail, Web site and trade journal advertising, and telephone contact. Other stories deal with the growth of B-to-B as contrasted to that of "dot-coms," the latter viewed as ordinary business-to-consumer commerce. B-to-B is also used to headline or to discuss traditional industrial sales transactions and relationships. Here, for instance, is a quote from a story in *Marketing* headlined "B2B: Business practice": "Direct mail is at the heart of many B2B campaigns, but it should not work in isolation. With direct mail, if you do the planning, you can get your message across in a more succinct and relevant way than you can with broadcast advertising. Well-targeted direct mail is still the best route to catching these decision-makers when they are at work and very busy. The combination of direct mail with follow-up telemarketing can also drive conversion and make the campaign work harder." The article *does* mention Internet-based methods but is largely about ordinary industrial sales approaches.

B-TO-B DOMINATES E

The new phrase, evidently, is here to stay. The U.S. Census Bureau has adopted both B-to-B and B-to-C as terms under which it collects data. The Bureau uses the traditional meaning but highlights those portions of business taking place by electronic and other forms of commerce.

As reported by the Census Bureau for 2003, the total value of shipments, sales, or revenues for B-to-B and B-to-C were almost equal, $8,296 billion for the first, $8,352 for the second. But the *electronic* component of this number greatly favored B-to-B. In 2003, business-to-business electronic commerce was $1,573 billion (19 percent of total B-to-B) and electronic business-to-consumer sales were $106 billion (1.3 percent of B-to-C). The dominance of B-to-B may be put another way: it represented 93.7 percent of all e-commerce transactions.

Electronically conducted business-to-business transactions broke down further as follows in 2003: direct manufacturing sales represented 53.6 percent of B-to-B e-transactions; merchant wholesale activities, which include manufacturers' branches and branch offices, represented 46.4 percent. In the B-to-C category, the much smaller electronic volume broke down into retail sales (52.8 percent) and selected services deliveries (47.2 percent). The growth rate in e-commerce between 2002 and 2003 was significantly lower for business-to-business at 10.9 percent than for business-to-consumer at 23.3 percent. Growth rates in part reflect the fact that overall B-to-B sales grew less (2.9 percent) than B-to-C (4.3 percent) and also suggest that the business sector itself, with less noise and trumpeting than the consumer sector, has long been engaged in electronic forms of distribution and is thus more mature and that the business sector is also easier to serve electronically; e-commerce, therefore, is better developed in the B-to-B category. Business migration to the Internet often takes the form of transitioning an electronic system from leased cable to the public network.

The chief reasons for B-to-B dominance of electronic sales is that industrial sales tend to be technical, contracts tend to be longer-term, and deliveries are typically routine and continuing. For these reasons arrangements are well-suited to computerization; many of these arrangements were made pre-Web in order to exploit the advantages of automation and speed available. The rise of the Internet in turn enlarged the capacity for this type of transaction. It provided a common system for exchanging visual data and a very widespread network by means of which even quite small businesses could be brought into electronic systems—as buyers, sellers, or both.

Some 70 percent of all manufacturers' electronic shipments fell into five categories. In order of importance they were transportation equipment (autos, in other words), chemicals, computers and related electronic products, food products, and petroleum and coal products. Just over 60 percent of e-sales of wholesalers, excluding manufacturers' branches, were in the categories of drugs and druggists' sundries, motor vehicle parts and supplies, and professional and commercial equipment. Manufacturers' branches were also substantially involved with drugs and druggists' sundries; other major categories were miscellaneous nondurable goods and groceries.

DOING BUSINESS B-TO-B

Ignoring for the moment the fact that all businesses tend to *buy* from other businesses, in the sales category most small businesses either serve consumers directly through retail operations or service businesses or they are and have always been in B-to-B. Some, of course, will have both kinds of customers.

The chief difference between these markets tends to lie in the size of the transaction and in the characteristics of the sales effort. B-to-B transactions are typically larger and therefore entail proportionally less administrative work per transaction; the sales effort, however, will tend to be more complicated and costly: business sales frequently require selling to multiple levels of a customer simultaneously, e.g., to management in order to gain recognition, to engineering departments to determine technical specifications, and then to purchasers in order to negotiate the price. Business sales can be costly in that they frequently require the preparation of written proposals. On the whole business buyers are more demanding technically, exert more pressure on price, and are almost never moved by emotions or to purchase impulsively.

Businesses can be very good customers for the small operation—indeed, sometimes, too good. Depending on the size of the small business, it may put itself in danger by having too few business customers. Many small businesses can often get more than enough business from a single corporate buyer to carry their business. This sometimes happens when a company is formed by former employees to serve that employer as outside suppliers: the owners have great advantages by knowing the customer inside and out. But yielding to this strategy exposes them to the risk of serious problems if the "big" client fails, changes its internal arrangements, or one of its influential buyers takes a dislike to the seller. For these reasons, ideally, the small business will strive to balance its income so that the "big" client is balanced by others.

The small business engaged in B-to-B will be able to enter the electronic forms of that type of commerce almost seamlessly, sometimes, because the buyer will be as interested in buying electronically as the seller may be to sell. And once such a system is established with one customer's assistance, it may be expandable to others.

SEE ALSO *Business-to-Consumer*

BIBLIOGRAPHY

"B2B: Business practice." *Marketing.* 8 March 2006.

Copeland, Michael V. "Everyone's Investing in B-to-B. Business 2.0." April 2006.

Kremer, Dennis B. "Vive La Difference: Consumer vs. Business Sales." *Westchester County Business Journal.* 3 October 2005.

Quinton, Brian. "Live from Chicago: B-to-B Must be Innovative to Find Leads." *Direct.* 29 March 2006.

Stewart, Al. "What I Learned About My Dad's Business from our Survey on Technology." *National Floor Trends.* May 2005.

U.S. Department of Commerce. "E-Stats." 11 May 2005. Available from http://www.census.gov/eos/www/papers/2003/2003finaltext.pdf. Retrieved on 29 April 2006.

Darnay, ECDI

BUSINESS-TO-BUSINESS MARKETING

Commercial transactions between businesses are covered more generally in this volume in the article called *Business-to-Business.* Here the intention is to characterize the marketing aspects of business-to-business relationships. The current abbreviations commonly applied to these transactions, B2B or B-to-B, are closely associated with Internet activities. But the underlying reality is very old (businesses have always sold to other businesses) and, significantly, electronic transactions between enterprises predate the emergence of the World Wide Web by many decades. Long before the Internet's dramatic appearance and continuing to this day, B-to-B commerce by electronic means operated and still operates by privately maintained electronic data interchange (EDI) channels. For this reason, B-to-B electronic commerce was nearly 15 times greater than business-to-consumer e-trade in 2003, the most recent year for which data are available. Most of the heavy B-to-B commerce began over private channels, but new and emerging business-to-business electronic transactions are coming to rely on the Internet.

MARKETING AND SALES

Marketing in the modern sense covers a vast range of activities including advertising, public relations, promotion, all types of sales, and aspects of distribution—including also specialties within this field such as market research, strategy, and planning. In those corporations predominantly engaged in selling to the consumer, marketing and sales are typically separate functions, but with sales subordinated to and managed by the more prestigious marketing function. Marketing thus represents the overall strategic, intelligence, and communications function whereas sales are detail-oriented implementations obeying and carrying out a general marketing strategy.

The chief difference between business-to-business and business-to-consumer marketing is that the roles of marketing and sales are largely reversed. A business dealing with another business relies much less on image-based forms of mass persuasion and heavily on technical and commercial communications, product demonstrations, and cultivation of relationships through industrial channels. The basic reason for this is that B-to-B sales are in their very nature much more influenced by price, by product performance, by timely and reliable deliveries, and effective and swift services—than by perceptions or emotions. Image marketing in B-to-B plays a definite but subordinated role; occasionally it uses mass media, but generally the message is channeled through magazines, journals, and newspapers (such as *Barron's* or the *Wall Street Journal*) intended to reach decision makers in business.

Virtually all businesses selling to the ultimate consumer also sell to the "channel," namely distributors and retailers. Thus their sales have a multi-tiered aspect. In these situations the broad marketing aimed at the ultimate consumer is, of course, of great interest to the business buyer too. The retailer is much more likely to stock a heavily and effectively advertised consumer product for which the producer also provides lucrative incentives for joint advertising at the local level—than the retailer is likely to stock a brand with low recognition value. In such contexts marketing in the traditional sense also plays a major role in selling to the business customer.

CATEGORIES OF RELATIONSHIPS

B-to-B sales activities differ by the nature of the relationship. Sales categories take three major forms; most businesses belong predominantly to one type of distribution. The categories are industry specialists, institutional generalists, and channel-sales specialists.

Industry Specialists A business may typically sell all of its products or services to participants in the same narrowly defined industry or activity. Classical examples are defense contractors who rarely sell anything except to the U.S. Department of Defense or other such entities abroad with federal government approval. Process engineering firms are likely to be concentrated in the petrochemicals industries: their job is to build refineries and chemicals plant. Such firms occasionally also build power plants for utilities, compressor stations for pipelines, etc. Major categories, like autos, produce an array of suppliers that work exclusively for the category. Golf cart producers sell principally to golf courses.

A subgrouping of the specialist category is formed by companies that sell to a narrow category within a single industry. Specialized equipment companies serving medicine or laboratory research fall into this category—selling only to certain kinds of hospitals or clinics, for example.

Institutional Generalists At the other extreme are businesses that sell products to every kind of business and similar institutions and to virtually every element of such client operations. Examples are office supply producers, manufacturers of file cabinets, and makers of office furniture. Advertising agencies and public relations firms may be similarly in the generalist category—but many will develop special clienteles. Subsets of this "generalist" category are producers who sell to one sector in preference to others—thus, for instance, tool makers or steel producers who sell to virtually all manufacturers but very rarely to wholesalers, retailers, or financial companies.

Yet another but narrower generalist category is the producer who, by the nature of its product or services, deals exclusively with a well-defined department but one almost always present in a business or an institution. Payroll or health insurance companies are an example in that their clients are finance departments or human resources functionalities. Most large computer companies deal with information system (IT) departments even when selling stand-alone computers.

Channel Specialists All companies that use a multi-tier distribution channel concentrate their selling effort (but not necessarily their marketing efforts) on distributors specializing in their products. The actual selling may take place at annual or seasonal meetings at which the company hosts its distributors, makes presentations, and uses two or three days to negotiate orders with the distributors. When distributors must be added or changed, the company often engages in a complex process of recruitment to line up the right candidate. In some industries, e.g., recreational boat sales, dealings are directly with the retail channel. Automotive companies deal directly with dealers through intermediate, company-owned "zone" administrations.

Other Variants The three broad categories outlined do not present an exhaustive description. All kinds of variants and specializations exist—and, of course, within large companies different divisions may use different methods to reach their markets. Some producers also deliberately target only large, midsized, or small business clients again using the broad approaches outlined.

These categorizations illustrate the rather extensive specializations that characterize B-to-B marketing. The single-buyer company faces quite a different challenge than the company selling to virtually everyone. But the defense contractor, selling only to DOD, must, nevertheless, also cultivate relations with other political decision makers to maintain its reputation and visibility. A single client does not mean a single relationship. Many narrowly defined product or systems sales are heavily technical, with both buyers and sellers being midlevel technical people who, internally, interact with their own managements, over time, to make a project happen. In major acquisitions, like the production of a new power plant, interactions at the highest executive levels are as necessary as the bidding process that takes place at the technical level. But a company selling office supplies typically operates at a low level with clerical people or purchasing departments.

VENUES AND METHODS

B-to-B marketing and sales take all the forms used in business-to-consumer sales as well, not least catalog sales commonly used for many types of technical components as well as such standard products as office supplies and furniture. Highly differentiated sales organizations are common.

Businesses of all sizes use their own sales forces organized in many different ways: from headquarters, from branch locations, and as separate sales divisions. The use of manufacturer's representatives—independent sales organizations—is exclusive to B-to-B. The subject is covered in detail under *Manufacturers' Agents*. In multi-tier marketing, of course, the sales function is mediated by distributors and retailers between the producer and the consumer.

Important venues in business-to-business marketing are conventions and trade shows where a company may participate in two different forms. The company may have its display booth and show off its own equipment, and its representatives may also participate as speakers or presenters in technical sessions. Such appearances, while in content and form far removed from what is conventionally viewed as marketing, are in effect valuable means of reaching potential business customers with information of use to this clientele. Conventions are also opportunities for companies to gain visibility from attendees by hosting entertainment events, hospitality suites, and providing services like shuttles or organizing tours. Such activities, of course, build good will.

Not least, businesses engage in conventional forms of marketing by advertising. When ads appear in industry journals and technical publications, their basic purpose is to promote the company's products and services to business buyers. When a company runs ads in the mass media, however, its objective may be to reach actual and potential investors. It is engaging in what is labeled "institutional advertising": the aim is simply to make its name visible to the public.

BASIC ELEMENTS OF B-TO-B MARKETING

The most important characteristics of business-to-business marketing are 1) building relationships, 2) candid technical interactions, 3) intensive commercial negotiations, and 4) close attention to after-sale services.

Individual transactions between businesses are typically larger as measured in dollars and fewer in number than in business-to-consumer sales. The contract or sale is more difficult to get, but once a relationship is established successfully, repeat business is almost guaranteed if performance is acceptable—the seller being helped by the buyer's desire to avoid the time, effort, and occasionally the hassle required to find a new supplier. For this reason, establishing and building a good relationship with a business client is vital. Ideally it will be established at all levels of the client—with its leaders, its management, and also with the working level using the product. Unhappiness at any of these levels can jeopardize the relationship. Periodic efforts to touch base with all of these levels is an important aspect of marketing. Both marketing and sales take a direct form—face-to-face—rather than by advertising. Advertising is used as a reminder of a relationship maintained by other means.

Technical interactions are ideally open and candid. The business client will always discover flaws or shortcomings in the product—and is usually also able to accommodate awkward features if all else works well. The seller is wise both to discuss difficulties openly and yet not to overstate them. Such approaches are, of course, just as beneficial in *all* sales but businesses tend to be more distant and engage in more "games" with ordinary off-the-street clients than with the industrial buyer who is typically much more knowledgeable and less moved by emotions. A converse of this general rule is that the business owner encountering a game-playing industrial buyer should be prepared to walk. The relationship must be two-way. The client who behaves in bureaucratic ways is a special problem for the B-to-B seller. Such behavior can sometimes be exploited and sometimes neutralized by developing better relationships with higher levels.

The very openness ideal in reaching agreement on the product itself makes commercial negotiations difficult. Business buyers tend to be hard customers generally; they will tend to know or be in a position to guess the real costs of the seller. They may also be under management pressure to push prices down. In price negotiations, therefore, games tend to be played unless a good relationship exists and the buyer is not under severe pressure. Here effective, flexible, and, if at all possible, open dealing is best. The buyer must sometimes yield—but should do so while openly stating that this particular easing of the price is for this case only, in order to accommodate the buyer *this time,* and not to set a precedent. Living up to this assertion later, by refusing to continue to sell at the low price, is, of course, part of keeping the deal going.

Business-to-business sales have a tendency sometimes never to close. This is wrong, that is wrong. The seller must be prepared to service the product. Too much after-sale service, amounting to extra services, can be avoided in the future by negotiating more stringent contract terms. But, under the usual circumstances, the business buyer calls only when something is really wrong. In that case swift and effective corrective action is the right response to maintain the relationship and, in effect, to sell the next contract.

B-to-B can often be the best kind of business for any kind of company, large or small. Large transactions, low cost of selling, a reliable market, and often an attractive price are inherent aspects of this type of transaction. The biggest danger of B-to-B for the small business is to become reliant on one or two clients for which it is just a small supplier. B-to-B is best practiced by the small business by cultivating several such customers, the favor or disfavor of no *one* of which will threaten the company's own survival.

BIBLIOGRAPHY

Ackerman, Elise. "The World of Internet Exchanges." *Detroit Free Press.* 26 February 2001.

"B2B: Business Practice." *Marketing.* 8 March 2006.

Coe, John M. *The Fundamentals of Business-to-Business Sales & Marketing.* McGraw–Hill, 2004.

Quinton, Brian. "Live from Chicago: B-to-B Must be Innovative to Find Leads." *Direct.* 29 March 2006.

U.S. Department of Commerce. "E-Stats." 11 May 2005. Available from http://www.census.gov/eos/www/papers/2003/2003finaltext.pdf. Retrieved on 29 April 2006.

Vitale, Rob, and Joe Giglierano. *Busines to Business Marketing: Analysis and Practice in a Dynamic Environment.* South-Western College Publishing, 2001.

Darnay, ECDI

BUSINESS-TO-CONSUMER

"Business-to-Consumer," usually abbreviated B2C, is a phrase that has become attached to electronic business activities that focus on *retail* transactions rather than activities conducted between two businesses; the latter, business-to-business, is called B2B. These uses appeared along with Internet commerce in the 1990s and have been current since then. The usage has expanded so that, in the mid-2000s, B2C is also used as a handy abbreviation in talking about retail trade where electronics is just one component of the transaction and other cases where simply "retail trade" is meant. Combined forms are also referred to by other catchy phrases such as "bricks-and-clicks," "click-and-mortar," and "clicks-and-bricks."

SIZE AND PRODUCTS

Curiously, retail activity on the Internet is by far the best known new business model of the Information Age—yet it is a rather small proportion of total electronic commerce. The U.S. Census Bureau began collecting and tabulating data on electronic commerce in 1999, with the first comprehensive tabulations available for 2000. The data capture all economic exchanges for major economic sectors whether they take place over the Internet or by means of privately maintained electronic data interchange (EDI) channels.

Between 2000 and 2003 (the last year available), electronic trade as a whole increased from 7.2 percent of total trade activity to 10.1 percent. During this four-year period, B2C has represented a small fraction of total e-trade: 6.1 percent in 2000 and 6.3 percent in 2003 (including both retail sales and services); but in 2002, the B2C's share dropped temporarily to 5.7 percent.

In light of the rather extensive publicity regarding Internet business activity, these results may appear surprising. But the reasons for this lie in the fact that business-to-business electronic transactions predate the rise of the Internet by many decades; they were already massive when the Internet appeared; and businesses were also first in exploiting the Internet for B-to-B trading.

In 2003, B2C volume was, nevertheless, a respectable $106 billion and represented 1.3 percent of all business-to-consumer sales. B2C was also growing more rapidly than its more massive B-to-B electronic counterpart, reflecting its relative novelty and immaturity. The B2C activity was further subdivided into retail sales of products (52.8 percent of total) and services delivered by electronic means (47.2 percent).

Electronic Retail As reported by the Census Bureau, and using the Bureau's industrial categories, B2C retail sales in 2003 were dominated by Nonstore Retailers, more specifically by Electronic Shopping and Mail Order Houses, a subdivision of Nonstore: 72.4 percent of all B2C retail flowed through the category. Other major participants and their shares were Motor Vehicle and Parts Dealers (17.1 percent); Other Nonstore Retailers (2.1); Miscellaneous Retailers (1.7); Sporting Goods, Hobby, Book, and Music Stores (1.5); Electronics and Appliance Stores (1.4), Clothing and Clothing Accessories Stores

(1.3); and Building Materials and Garden Equipment and Supplies Stores (0.8 percent).

Within the largest category, Electronic Shopping and Mail Order Houses (those that do not have physical "stores"), the top five subdivisions (ignoring the large miscellaneous category), were Computer Hardware (12.1 percent of B2C retail), Clothing and Accessories, including Footwear (9.9); Office Equipment and Supplies (6.2); Furniture and Home Furnishings (6.2); and Electronics and Appliances (5.2 percent of B2C retail).

Based on these data, in electronic retailing the winners are ... Autos, Computers, and Clothing, together claiming more than a third of all sales. And pure electronic retailing wins over brick-and-click by a long country mile.

Electronic Services Within the services categories delivered by electronic means, all of which the Census Bureau classifies as B2C, the biggest categories, arranged by share of total e-services delivered, were Travel Arrangements and Reservation Services (13.5 percent of total e-services); Publishing Industry (12.0); Computer Services (10.9); Stock Transactions (8.8); Truck Transportation (6.6). The last category, somewhat puzzling, is presumably centered on the truck rental business.

The biggest industrial *grouping* within services is Information (24.8), which includes Publishing but also Broadcasting and Telecommunications and Online Information Services. Second is Administrative Support (23.2) which holds Travel Arrangements and many other linking services. Third is Professional, Scientific, and Technical Services (16.4 percent of all e-services); it includes computer-based but also laboratory, legal, tax preparation, and other similar services.

TYPES OF B2C

In its article on "Business-to-consumer electronic commerce," based in part on the work of Sandeep Krishnamurthy, Wikipedia divides B2C commerce into five major categories: 1) direct sellers, 2) online intermediaries, 3) advertising-based models, 4) community-based models, and 5) fee-based models. These categorizations somewhat mix apples and oranges in that they put side-by-side strategies of distribution, positions in the sales channel, and strategies aimed at reaching particular audiences. Thus the categories present views of B2C that are not necessarily mutually exclusive.

Direct sellers are further subdivided into e-tailers and manufacturers. E-tailers ship product from their own warehouse and also, as Amazon.com does, from other's stocks by triggering deliveries. Manufacturers (e.g., of software, computers) use the Internet as a sales channel

and thus entirely or in part avoid intermediaries. The Internet thus becomes a manufacturer's catalog.

Intermediaries perform a brokerage function. In these cases the B2C business fulfills the role of a middleman between consumers who visit its site and businesses whom it represents. Brokers provide a variety of services to buyers by assembling attractive arrays of products and to sellers by, for instance, facilitating the financial side of the transactions.

Advertising-based models make use of high-traffic or specialized sites in order to attract consumers by advertising placed at these sites. Advertising itself may be the "business." These approaches are identical to traditional marketing but are specifically adapted to the Web. The high-traffic approach emphasizes sheer numbers and thus offers products of wide interest at median price-point. Those using the niche approach are willing to pay substantially for a pre-qualified audience with specific income and/or interest profiles (sports aficionados, conservatives, executives, etc.).

The community-based model may be seen as a hybrid of the two advertising approaches. The communities in question are "chat groups" and interest groups with specific preoccupations. Thus sites used by computer programmers for exchanging information—or by gardeners trading advice—are good venues for advertising software and hardware product to one group, tools and seeds to another.

Fee-based models rely on the value of the content that they present on the Internet. Paid subscription services or pay-as-you-buy services are differentiations within the category. The latter approach is used, for example, by sellers of single articles of which they show parts or a summary as teasers; the former approach is used to sell on-line subscriptions to journals.

THE FUTURE

The future of B2C appears to be bright. This type of commerce may still only be in its infancy and likely to grow simply because it is a convenient form of purchasing and also because looming storm clouds on the energy horizon may soon cause a quick trip to the store cost consumers a tidy sum. Leaves in the wind, suggesting the trend, are provided by the recent history of electronic retailing, more than half of all B2C.

Total retail sales in the U.S. (overwhelmingly "brick") experienced an annual compounded rate of growth of 4.8 percent between 2000 and 2005—yet in that same period the electronic portion grew at an annual rate of 26 percent each year. In 2005 e-retail was just a small fraction of total retail at 2.3 percent of total—but it was almost zero in 2000 (0.9 percent). These results were achieved during the time and in the quite visible presence of the so-called dot-com bust. It came early in 2000 as the tech-heavy NASDAQ Composite Index reached its all-time high and then dropped sharply. This meant that new B2C startups could no longer count on deep investment pockets—but the dot-coms that survived the bust have been doing very well. Many of them are small businesses—some of which are pure B2Cs serving niche markets very effectively. For a closer look at the factors that spell success, see another entry in this volume, *Dot coms.*

SEE ALSO *Business to Business; Dot-coms*

BIBLIOGRAPHY

"Business-to-Consumer Electronic Commerce." Wikipedia. Available from http://en.wikipedia.org/wiki/Business-to-consumer_electronic_commerce. Retrieved on 3 May 2006.

"Data Clinic: How to buy … B2C lists." *Direct Response.* 6 February 2006.

Kremer, Dennis B. "Vive La Difference: Consumer vs. Business Sales." *Westchester County Business Journal.* 3 October 2005.

Krishnamurthy, Sandeep. *E-Commerce Management.* Thomson South-Western, 2003.

Margolis, Nik. "Why is B2B So Far Ahead of B2C in the Digital Marketing Arena?" *Precision Marketing.* 20 May 2005.

"Minding Our Business." *Multichannel Merchant.* 1 March 2006.

U.S. Department of Commerce. "E-Stats." 11 May 2005. Available from http://www.census.gov/eos/www/papers/2003/2003finaltext.pdf. Retrieved on 29 April 2006.

Darnay, ECDI

BUYING AN EXISTING BUSINESS

Most businesses are purchased by companies as a means of diversification or expansion. In these situations several of the ingredients of success are usually present: the business has good reasons for the acquisition, it has experience in the industry to be entered through long contact, it has skilled people to evaluate acquisition candidates, it has the means to make the purchase in cash or through contact with funding sources, and it has the ability to run the purchased business. Nevertheless, many acquisitions flounder. Similarly, the prospective buyer may be a wealthy individual with many years of business experience but presently no corporate base. Such an individual is functionally equivalent to a company in means and in experience. Buying an existing business is also, finally, one of the alternatives available to the would-be entrepreneur. He or she faces the same decision manufacturers call the "make or buy" decision: Should we tool up to make this product or buy it from someone else? To make some-

thing from scratch usually takes longer but offers opportunities to shape the product exactly as the builder intends it to function. To buy the product usually gets the buyer to the starting line much faster but limits his or her choice to a preexisting design.

The individual entering business must keep in mind that buying a business is not a way to avoid initial fund-raising chores. In its summary of the issue, for example, the U.S. Small Business Administration (on its site titled "Buying a Business") makes the following somewhat erroneous statement: "Many find the idea of running a small business appealing, but lose their motivation after dealing with business plans, investors, and legal issues associated with new start-ups. For those disheartened by such risky undertakings, buying an existing business is often a simpler and safer alternative." The reason entrepreneurs worry over business plans and talk to investors is because they want to raise money they don't have. A person lacking funds but wishing to buy an existing business must *also* project the business into the future, have a plan, and undergo the process of raising funds. Books exist that boldly promise to teach the entrepreneur how to buy a business with not a penny down—but few people actually have the persuasive powers or profiles of experience to make that sort of thing happen. Buying rather than building a business is a decision to be reached *after* the funding effort has at least been started and looks reasonably promising.

KEY ELEMENTS

Once the funding issues are resolved sufficiently to turn the entrepreneur into an actual buyer, meaning that at least a portion of the down payment is in hand, the key elements of buying a business are 1) formulation of clear objectives (homework), 2) search and contact, 3) evaluation of the target (sometimes called due-diligence), and 4) negotiation and purchase.

These elements are very frequently iterated in an actual acquisition program, meaning that failure to close deals and the learning that has taken place while getting to an unsatisfactory result will cause the entrepreneur to rethink the process, sometimes from the beginning. Initial homework consists of exploring the industry or specialty that looks most suitable to the talents and experience of the buyer. A part of that homework is to learn the going price for different types of enterprises. That, in turn, may cause changes—and even require additional fundraising efforts. A search for candidates may reveal that not too many businesses are available or available in the right locations, that prices may be high or most candidates in trouble. Evaluation of businesses after contact may generate wrong assumptions about the real returns possible. Negotiations may fail. Buying a company is almost always a learning process unless the buyer is very experienced, (perhaps even working in the business already) the business to be purchased and its ownership are well known (possibly in the extended family), and everything is easily negotiated because of previous relationships.

Objectives A buyer's earlier experience (business or avocational) usually sets the stage for formulating goals. Buyers rarely set out to buy into altogether unknown industries, but they may not know the business at its highest levels. For example, a person may know a business from an operational but not from a marketing point of view—or the reverse. Some kind of homework is usually involved.

Search Sellers of businesses will advertise themselves or engage the services of a business broker. Finding candidates is thus similar to recruiting employees. Sources of leads are newspaper ads, the Internet, or brokers who also advertise themselves. Well-developed Internet resources usually enable a buyer to locate businesses within a state or zip code zone further subdivided by type of business and even asset-size categories. Brokers specializing in different regions or nationally are relatively easy to find. Substantial searching around is, of course, implied—but provides a great deal of information on what is available, what asking prices are, and where the nearest targets are located. Searching can be handed to a broker who will then call or e-mail the buyer with suggestions. Examples of sites, including one that advertises businesses for sale directly (cityfeetBiz) and of brokers (United Business Brokers, serving cities in Utah, Nevada, California, and Idaho), are provided in the references; there are many more.

Evaluation Once contact has been established with a candidate, a process of mutual exploration begins, usually with a visit to the candidate's place of business where, following a tour of the place, preliminary discussions begin. The motivations of buyers and sellers are essentially the same. Each wishes to establish the qualifications of the other—and the buyer must therefore be prepared to give as much as he/she gets, namely to display his or her abilities to buy the business. If the buyer has no business identity, the seller will usually ask for references and not make financial disclosures beyond those advertised until the buyer's status and net worth have been carefully checked. In the normal course of events several contacts will take place before the buyer can obtain information sufficient to study the targeted business closely. That process is described further later in this entry. Evaluation of a business is central to price nego-

tiations later and must be carried out with care and diligence in order to avoid legal and financial problems later.

Negotiations and Purchase Assuming that the evaluation has produced satisfactory results, negotiations may become necessary to resolve remaining open issues. These can take many forms and may deal with just about any aspect of the business, from the handling of certain liabilities to employment contracts for key employees or executives. Eventually a purchase agreement will be drawn up, usually involving legal professionals, and the purchase finalized with signatures and transfers of funds.

EVALUATION OF A BUSINESSES

The evaluation of a business can be divided into four clusters: the seller's history and motivations, legal matters affecting the operation, the financial status of the business, and the condition and prospects of the business in its market (its products, services, and future).

The buyer, of course, will want to know the history of the business, how it came about, how it developed, and why the seller is now willing to sell. The usual reason for the sale of a small business is the age of the seller: he or she wishes to retire and does not have children or relatives willing to take over. A business is also often for sale because it is being spun off from a larger operation because it no longer fits. Why it no longer fits then becomes a matter of interest to the buyer—who is, above all, interested in discovering weaknesses in the business.

Legal matters concern pending lawsuits or regulatory problems some of which may have to be dealt with by the new owner. Leases and other long-term legal obligations are usually reviewed in this context—ideally with the help of the buyer's own legal advisor.

Financial evaluation is based on the thorough review of the company's books—its balance sheet and income statement going back at least five years or to the beginning of the business, whichever is earlier. Ideally, again, audited financial returns are best or, if the seller is unwilling to pay for an audit, tax filings with the IRS can be used for a separate view of finances. Sole proprietorships and partnerships do not have stock and therefore sales of the businesses are always based on assets; the level of attention to assets will therefore depend on their character and value. Depending on the situation, the buyer may wish to undertake an inventory of assets at his or her own expense or to engage the services of an appraiser. Such detailed checking of physical assets is not usual, however, but inspections by knowledgeable people (if the buyer lacks personal expertise) are usually arranged. Normally the books of a well-run business will accurately reflect asset values. If the business is poorly run, the offered price can hedge against risks.

Most careful buyers will use the company's financial data to develop an alternative valuation of the business using discounted cash flow analysis. For more detail on this subject, please see the entries titled *Discounted Cash Flow* and *Mergers & Acquisitions* in this volume. Such valuation typically involves projecting operating results of the business out in time, which requires a good grasp of the company's products, processes, and likely futures sales and profits in an evolving market—the last category of evaluation. The value of the business as calculated using such analysis is then compared to the asking price. If the two values are reasonably close, an agreement is likely. If far apart, negotiations need to ensue or the buyer may elect to stop discussions.

Finally, the buyer must strive to understand the business thoroughly enough to have confidence to run it in the future. From an internal perspective this means a good grasp of how the company is run internally, who its suppliers are, how processes run—and above all the state and morale of the employees. Looked at from the outside, the buyer must understand the company's distribution channel(s), major customers or categories of customers, the market itself, and forces that impact on that market. In fact, direct contact with the customers of the company being sold is highly advisable—being, in effect, an early effort of marketing to the buyer's future customers. Some businesses operate in very tricky environments. An example may be an environmental services provider whose business absolutely demands strict government enforcement to underpin sales. In such a case careful examination of regulatory trends—and their easing or tightening in good and bad economic times—may reveal hidden weaknesses in a business. This broad analysis, delving deeply into details that invite a closer look, is invaluable in making projections into the future.

FINANCING

Whether the buyer and seller ultimately agree to an installment sale, a leveraged buyout, a stock exchange, or an earn-out to transfer ownership of the company (see the entry *Selling a Company* for descriptions of these options), the sale cannot proceed if the buyer is unable to secure adequate financing.

Most small businesses are acquired by buyers who finance a considerable portion of the purchase price themselves. Even so, the buyer must still make sure that he or she has enough money to make a down payment and cover the business's capital requirements. Sometimes, then, buyers are forced to secure financing from outside sources. The level of these will depend on the buyer's personal investment. Lenders or investors like to see the

buyer deeply committed before they come to the table pen in hand.

Lending institutions like banks and consumer finance companies are more open to borrowers involved in purchasing larger companies, but even in these instances, the institutions often ask buyers to put up the company's inventory, machinery, real estate, and accounts receivable as collateral. Sensible buyers in need of outside financing will make certain that they approach potential lenders with a comprehensive and well-considered loan proposal (including a good business plan). Thus the entrepreneur is unlikely to avoid that task even when buying an existing business.

CLOSING THE DEAL

Closings are generally done either by means of an escrow settlement or through the services of an attorney who performs settlement. In an escrow settlement, the money to be deposited, the bill of sale, and other relevant documents are placed with a neutral third party known as an escrow agent until all conditions of sale have been met. After that, the escrow agent disburses the held documents and funds in accordance with the terms of the contract.

If an attorney performs settlement, meanwhile, he/she—acting on behalf of both buyer or seller, or for the buyer—draws up a contract and acts as an escrow agent until all stipulated conditions of sale have been met. Whereas escrow settlements do not require the buyer and the seller to get together to sign the final documents, attorney-performed settlements do include this step.

Several documents are required to complete the transaction between business seller and business buyer. The purchase and sale agreement is the most important of these, but other documents often used in closings include the escrow agreement; bill of sale; promissory note; security agreement; settlement sheet; financing statement; and employment agreement.

SEE ALSO *Discounted Cash Flow; Business Appraisers; Franchising; Selling a Company*

BIBLIOGRAPHY
cityfeetBiz. Web Site. Available from http://www.cityfeetbusinessesforsale.com/. Retrieved on 26 May 2006.

Ennico, Cliff. "Buying a Business; Getting a Private Mailbox." *Entrepreneur.* 17 June 2003.

Hollander, Linda. *Bags to Riches: Success Secrets for Women in Business.* Celestial Arts, 2003.

"How to Buy a Business." *Entrepreneur.* 6 September 2005.

Klueger, Robert F. *Buying and Selling a Business: A Step-by-Step Guide.* John Wiley & Sons, 2004.

Steingold, Fred, and Emily Dostow. *The Complete Guide to Buying a Business.* Nolo, 2005.

Tuttle, Samuel S. *Small Business Primer: How To Buy, Sell, and Evaluate a Business.* streetsmartbooks, 2002.

United Business Brokers. Web Site. Available from http://unitedbusinessbrokers.com/. Retrieved on 26 May 2006.

U.S. Small Business Administration. "Buying a Business." Available from http://www.sba.gov/starting_business/startup/buy.html. Retrieved on 25 May 2006.

Hillstrom, Northern Lights
updated by Magee, ECDI

C

C CORPORATION

When a small business incorporates, it is automatically a C corporation, also called a regular corporation. The most basic characteristic of the corporation is that it is legally viewed as an individual entity, separate from its owners, who are now shareholders. This means that when the corporation is sued, shareholders are only liable to the extent of their investments in the corporation. Their personal assets are not on the line, as they would be if the business was a partnership or sole proprietorship. Any debts that the corporation may acquire are also viewed as the corporation's responsibility. In other words, once the business is incorporated, shareholders are protected by the corporate veil, or limited liability.

Because the corporation is a separate entity, it is viewed as an individual taxpayer by the Internal Revenue Service (IRS). As a result, corporations are subject to double taxation, which means that the profits are taxed once on the corporate level and a second time when they are distributed as dividends to the shareholders. If a business is eligible, it may elect S corporation status upon incorporating to avoid this negative characteristic of C corporations.

ADVANTAGES

Limited Liability Most small businesses that consider incorporating do so for the limited liability that corporate status affords. The greatest fear of the sole proprietor or partner—that his or her life's savings could be jeopardized by a law suit against his or her business or by sudden overwhelming debts—disappears once the business becomes a corporation. Although the shareholders are liable up to the amount they have invested in the corporation, their personal assets cannot be touched. Rather than purchase expensive liability insurance, then, many small business owners choose to incorporate to protect themselves.

Raising Capital It can be much easier for a corporation to raise capital than it is for a partnership or sole proprietorship, because the corporation has stocks to sell. Investors can be lured with the prospect of dividends if the corporation makes a profit, avoiding the necessity of taking out loans and paying high interest rates in order to secure capital. However, from a banker's perspective, a newly formed corporation is a more risky loan applicant than an individual with a home and other assets.

Attracting Top-Notch Employees Corporations may find it easier to attract the best employees, who may be lured by stock options and fringe benefits.

Fringe Benefits One advantage C corporations have over unincorporated businesses and S corporations is that they may deduct fringe benefits (such as group term life insurance, health and disability insurance, death benefits payments to $5,000, and employee medical expenses not paid by insurance) from their taxes as a business expense. In addition, shareholder-employees are exempt from paying taxes on the fringe benefits they receive. To be eligible for this tax break the corporation must not design a plan that benefits only the shareholders/owners. A good portion of the employees (usually 70 percent) must also be able to take advantage of the benefits. For many small businesses, providing fringe benefits for all employees is too expensive, so in these cases the tax break is not a particular advantage.

Continuance of Existence Transfer of stock or death of an owner does not alter the corporation, which exists perpetually, regardless of owners, until it is dissolved. While this is usually considered an advantage, Fred Steingold argues in *The Legal Guide for Starting and Running a Small Business* that, in reality, "You don't need to incorporate to ensure that your business will continue after your death. A sole proprietor can use a living trust or will to transfer the business to heirs. Partners frequently have insurance-funded buy-sell agreements that allow the remaining partners to continue the business."

DISADVANTAGES

Double Taxation After they deduct all business expenses, such as salaries, fringe benefits, and interest payments, C corporations pay a tax on their profits at the corporate level. If any of those profits are then distributed as dividends to the shareholders, those individuals must also pay a tax on the money when they file their personal tax returns. For companies that expect to reinvest much of the profits back into the business, double taxation may not affect them enough to be a serious drawback. In the case of the small business, most if not all of the company's profits are used to pay salaries and fringe benefits, which are deductible, and double taxation may be avoided because no money is left over for distributing dividends.

Bureaucracy and Expense Corporations are governed by state and federal statutes. In order to abide by all of the sometimes complex regulations related to C corporations, it is often necessary to hire lawyers and accountants to assist with tax preparation. Regular stockholder and board of directors meetings must be held and detailed minutes of those meetings must be kept. All of the actions taken by a corporation are to be approved by its directors and this necessity can reduce a company's ability to take quick action on pressing matters. Another difference between a sole proprietor and a C corporation that imposes a bureaucratic burden arises if and when a corporation wishes to bring a case in small claims court. The corporation is required to be represented by a lawyer, whereas sole proprietors or partners can represent themselves. In addition, if the corporation does interstate business, it is subject to taxes in other states.

Rules Governing Dividend Distribution A corporation's profits are divided on the basis of stockholdings, whereas a partnership may divide its profits on the basis of capital investment or employment in the firm. In other words, if a stockholder owns 10 percent of the corporation's stock, she may only receive 10 percent of the profits. However, if that same person was a partner in an unincorporated firm to which she had contributed 10 percent of the company's capital, she might be eligible to receive more than 10 percent of the business's profits if such an agreement had been made with the other partners. Strict rules, though, govern the way corporations divide their profits, even to the point, in some states, of determining how much can be distributed in dividends. Usually, all past operations must be paid for before a dividend can be declared by the corporation's directors. If this is not done, and the corporation's financial stability is put in jeopardy by the payment of dividends, the directors can, in most states, be held personally liable to creditors.

STRUCTURE OF A CORPORATION

In small businesses, the owners often hold more than one or all of the following positions, which are required of all corporations:

- Shareholders: They own the company's stock and are responsible for electing the directors, amending the bylaws and articles of incorporation, and approving major actions taken by the corporation like mergers and the sale of corporate assets. They alone are allowed to dissolve the corporation.

- Directors: They manage the corporation and are responsible for issuing stock, electing officers, and making the corporation's major decisions.

- Officers: The corporation must have a president, secretary, and treasurer. These officers are responsible for making the day-to-day decisions that govern the corporation's operation.

- Employees: They receive a salary in return for their work for the corporation.

FINANCING A CORPORATION

Financing the operations of a corporation may involve selling stock (equity financing), taking out loans (debt financing), or reinvesting profits for growth.

Equity This is cash, property, or services exchanged for stock in the company. Generally, each stock is equivalent to one dollar of investment. If the small business owner is planning to exchange property to the corporation for stock, then a tax advisor should be consulted; if the property has appreciated, taxes may be due on the exchange.

Debt This is money lent by banks or shareholders. In the former case, a personal guarantee by the corporation's principals is usually required, which makes an exception to the limited liability rule. The owner of a corporation who personally guarantees a loan is also personally responsible for paying it back if the corporation goes under. Many corporations have preferred to fund the corporation with shareholder money in exchange for promissory notes because unlike dividends, the repayment of debts is not taxable. The Internal Revenue Service monitors such debt closely, though, to make sure it is not excessive and that adequate interest is paid. It should be noted that the interest accrued on money borrowed is taxable when paid to the lender.

PAYING C CORPORATION TAXES

After the C corporation deducts all business expenses, such as salaries, fringe benefits, and interest payments, it pays a tax on its profits at the corporate level. Then dividends may be distributed to the shareholders who must pay a tax on the money when they file their personal tax returns. In the case of the small business, though, double taxation may not be a consideration, because most, if not all of the company's profits are reinvested in the business or go to pay salaries and fringe benefits, which are deductible, and no money is left over for distributing dividends.

To avoid double taxation, corporations sometimes pay their shareholder-employees higher salaries instead of distributing income as dividends. The IRS, however, watches out for such tax avoidance measures and often audits corporations, claiming that executive salaries are not "reasonable" compensation. To prevent this charge, then, the corporation should consider the duties performed, the experience and/or special abilities of the employee, and how much other corporations pay for similar positions before determining "reasonable" compensation. A corporation should keep salaries somewhat consistent over time as fluctuating salaries—high salaries in high earning years and low salaries in lean years—will attract a review of salary payments by the Internal Revenue Service. A charge might be made, for example, that the high salary payments were in fact dividend payments.

RUNNING A CORPORATION

Once a small business has been incorporated, the day-to-day management of business affairs should not be that much different than it was beforehand. It is important, though, that the business is treated like a corporation. The courts have been known on occasion to overlook a business's corporate status and find the shareholders/owners liable because the business was run as if it were

still a sole proprietorship or partnership. Simply filing the articles of incorporation does not guarantee limited liability. In order to maintain corporate status in the law's eyes, these guidelines should be followed:

Act Like a Corporation Before doing business, stock certificates should be issued to all stockholders, and a corporate record book should be established to hold the articles of incorporation, records of stock holdings, the corporation's bylaws, and the minutes of board and shareholder meetings. In addition, such meetings should be held regularly (once a year is the minimum requirement). In this way, the corporation can record all important actions taken and show that such actions were approved by a vote. It is also important to treat the corporation like the separate entity it is by keeping personal and corporate accounts separate. Whereas a small business owner may have previously used one account to pay the company's accounts and personal expenses, as a corporate shareholder, he now needs to receive a regular salary from the corporation, deposit it in a separate account, and pay his personal expenses from that account. In all respects, the corporation and owner must be treated as distinct individuals. Fred Steingold advises, "document all transactions as if you were strangers. If the corporation leases property to you, sign a lease." In addition, the corporation's full name (which should indicate the company's corporate status through use of "Inc." or an equivalent) must be used on all correspondence, stationery, advertising, phone listings, and signs.

Act Like a Corporate Officer When the corporation's owner signs her name to checks, contracts, or correspondence for the corporation, she must always indicate that she is the president to show that she is not acting on her own but as an agent of the corporation.

Adequate Capital Investment and Insurance Coverage It is important to protect the corporation against failure due to debts and lawsuits. In other words, simply trying to protect the owners' assets by becoming a corporation and neglecting to fortify the business can be viewed as reason to disregard a business's corporate status in a lawsuit. Therefore, enough capital should be invested in the corporation to handle all business activities. Likewise, if business activities pose a risk to employees or customers and reasonably priced insurance is available to protect against such risks, such coverage should be secured.

SEE ALSO *Incorporation; S Corporation*

BIBLIOGRAPHY
Byrd, Stephen, and Brett Richey. "The Choice of Entity for the Small Business Owner." *Mid-Atlantic Journal of Business.* 1 December 1998.

Cornwall, Dr. Jeffrey R., David Vang, and Jean Hartman. *Entrepreneurial Financial Management.* Prentice Hall, 13 May 2003.

Epstein, Lita. *Reading Financial Reports for Dummies.* December 2004.

"New Ventures and Start-Ups: Which Form of Business Is Best for You?" *Business Owner.* January-February 1999.

Selecting the Legal Structure for Your Business. Small Business Administration. n.d.

Steingold, Fred S. *The Legal Guide for Starting and Running a Small Business* Fifth Edition. Nolo Press, 2005.

Taylor, Peter. *Book-Keeping & Accounting for Small Business.* Business & Economics, 2003.

Hillstrom, Northern Lights
updated by Magee, ECDI

CAPITAL

Capital is the money or wealth needed to produce goods and services. In the most basic terms, it is money. All businesses must have capital in order to purchase assets and maintain their operations. Business capital comes in two main forms: debt and equity. Debt refers to loans and other types of credit that must be repaid in the future, usually with interest. Equity, on the other hand, generally does not involve a direct obligation to repay the funds. Instead, equity investors receive an ownership position in the company which usually takes the form of stock, and thus the term "stock equity."

The capital formation process describes the various means through which capital is transferred from people who save money to businesses that require funds. Such transfers may take place directly, meaning that a business sells its stocks or bonds directly to savers who provide the business with capital in exchange. Transfers of capital may also take place indirectly through an investment banking house or through a financial intermediary, such as a bank, mutual fund, or insurance company. In the case of an indirect transfer using an investment bank, the business sells securities to the bank, which in turn sells them to clients who wish to invest their funds. In other words, the capital simply flows through the investment bank. In the case of an indirect transfer using a financial intermediary, however, a new form of capital is actually created. The intermediary bank or mutual fund receives capital from savers and issues its own securities in exchange. Then the intermediary uses the capital to purchase stocks or bonds from businesses.

THE COST OF CAPITAL

"Capital is a necessary factor of production and, like any other factor, it has a cost," according to Eugene F. Brigham in his book *Fundamentals of Financial Management.* In the case of debt capital, the cost is the interest rate that the firm must pay in order to borrow funds. For equity capital, the cost is the returns that must be paid to investors in the form of dividends and capital gains. Since the amount of capital available is often limited, it is allocated among various businesses on the basis of price. "Firms with the most profitable investment opportunities are willing and able to pay the most for capital, so they tend to attract it away from inefficient firms or from those whose products are not in demand," Brigham explained. But "the federal government has agencies which help individuals or groups, as stipulated by Congress, to obtain credit on favorable terms. Among those eligible for this kind of assistance are small businesses, certain minorities, and firms willing to build plants in areas with high unemployment."

Despite these federal government programs, the cost of capital for small businesses tends to be higher than it is for large, established businesses. Given the higher risk involved, both debt and equity providers charge a higher price for their funds. "A number of researchers have observed that portfolios of small-firm stocks have earned consistently higher average returns than those of large-firm stocks; this is called the 'small-firm effect,'" Brigham wrote. "In reality, it is bad news for the small firm; what the small-firm effect means is that the capital market demands higher returns on stocks of small firms than on otherwise similar stocks of large firms. Therefore, the cost of equity capital is higher for small firms." The cost of capital for a company is "a weighted average of the returns that investors expect from the various debt and equity securities issued by the firm," according to Richard A. Brealey and Stewart C. Myers in their book *Principles of Corporate Finance.*

CAPITAL STRUCTURE

Since capital is expensive for small businesses, it is particularly important for small business owners to determine a target capital structure for their firms. The capital structure concerns the proportion of capital that is obtained through debt and that obtained through equity. There are tradeoffs involved: using debt capital increases the risk associated with the firm's earnings, which tends to decrease the firm's stock prices. At the same time, however, debt can lead to a higher expected rate of return, which tends to increase a firm's stock price. As Brigham explained, "The optimal capital structure is the one that strikes a balance between risk and return and thereby maximizes the price of the stock and simultaneously minimizes the cost of capital."

Capital structure decisions depend upon several factors. One is the firm's business risk—the risk pertaining to the line of business in which the company is involved. Firms in risky industries, such as high technology, have lower optimal debt levels than other firms. Another factor in determining capital structure involves a firm's tax position. Since the interest paid on debt is tax deductible, using debt tends to be more advantageous for companies that are subject to a high tax rate and are not able to shelter much of their income from taxation.

A third important factor is a firm's financial flexibility, or its ability to raise capital under less than ideal conditions. Companies that are able to maintain a strong balance sheet will generally be able to obtain funds under more reasonable terms than other companies during an economic downturn. Brigham recommended that all firms maintain a reserve borrowing capacity to protect themselves for the future. In general, companies that tend to have stable sales levels, assets that make good collateral for loans, and a high growth rate can use debt more heavily than other companies. On the other hand, companies that have conservative management, high profitability, or poor credit ratings may wish to rely on equity capital instead.

SOURCES OF CAPITAL

Debt Capital Small businesses can obtain debt capital from a number of different sources. These sources can be broken down into two general categories, private and public sources. Private sources of debt financing include friends and relatives, banks, credit unions, consumer finance companies, commercial finance companies, trade credit, insurance companies, factor companies, and leasing companies. Public sources of debt financing include a number of loan programs provided by the state and federal governments to support small businesses.

Types of debt financing available to small businesses included private placement of bonds, convertible debentures, industrial development bonds, leveraged buyouts, and, by far the most common type of debt financing, a regular loan. Loans can be classified as long-term (with a maturity longer than one year), short-term (with a maturity shorter than two years), or a credit line (for more immediate borrowing needs). They can be endorsed by co-signers, guaranteed by the government, or secured by collateral—such as real estate, accounts receivable, inventory, savings, life insurance, stocks and bonds, or the item purchased with the loan.

When evaluating a small business for a loan, lenders like to see a two-year operating history, a stable management group, a desirable niche in the industry, a growth in market share, a strong cash flow, and an ability to obtain short-term financing from other sources as a supplement to the loan. Most lenders will require a small business owner to prepare a loan proposal or complete a loan application. The lender will then evaluate the request by considering a variety of factors. For example, the lender will examine the small business's credit rating and look for evidence of its ability to repay the loan, in the form of past earnings or income projections. The lender will also inquire into the amount of equity in the business, as well as whether management has sufficient experience and competence to run the business effectively. Finally, the lender will try to ascertain whether the small business can provide a reasonable amount of collateral to secure the loan.

Equity Capital Equity capital can be secured from a wide variety of sources. Some possible sources of equity financing include the entrepreneur's friends and family, private investors (from the family physician to groups of local business owners to wealthy entrepreneurs known as "angels"), employees, customers and suppliers, former employees, venture capital firms, investment banking firms, insurance companies, large corporations, and government-backed Small Business Investment Corporations (SBICs).

There are two primary methods that small businesses use to obtain equity financing: the private placement of stock with investors or venture capital firms; and public stock offerings. Private placement is simpler and more common for young companies or startup firms. Although the private placement of stock still involves compliance with several federal and state securities laws, it does not require formal registration with the Securities and Exchange Commission. The main requirements for private placement of stock are that the company cannot advertise the offering and must make the transaction directly with the purchaser.

In contrast, public stock offerings entail a lengthy and expensive registration process. In fact, the costs associated with a public stock offering can account for more than 20 percent of the amount of capital raised. As a result, public stock offerings are generally a better option for mature companies than for startup firms. Nonetheless, public stock offerings may offer advantages in terms of maintaining control of a small business by spreading ownership over a diverse group of investors rather than concentrating it in the hands of a venture capital firm.

BIBLIOGRAPHY

Bierman, Harold. *The Capital Structure Decision.* Springer, 2002.

Brealey, Richard A., and Stewart C. Myers. *Principles of Corporate Finance.* 6th ed. McGraw Hill, 2002.

Brigham, Eugene F., and Joel F. Houston. *Fundamentals of Financial Management.* 5th ed. South-Western College Publishing, 2003.

Caselli, S. and S. Gatti. *Venture Capital.* Springer, 2003.

Culp, Christopher L. *The Art of Risk Management.* John Wiley & Sons, 2002.

Downes, John, and Jordan Elliot Goodman. *Finance & Investment Handbook.* Barron's Educational Series, 2003.

"Strategies for Effective Capital Structure Management: Executive Summary." *Healthcare Financial Management.* August 2005.

*Hillstrom, Northern Lights
updated by Magee, ECDI*

CAPITAL GAIN/LOSS

A capital gain or loss results from the sale, trade, or exchange of a capital asset. Simply stated, when the resulting transaction nets an amount lower than the original purchase value of the capital asset, a capital loss occurs. When the resulting transaction nets an amount greater than the original value at purchase, a capital gain occurs. Capital gains and losses can either be short-term (when the transaction is completed within one year) or long-term (when the transaction is completed in more than one year). The period is determined from the day after acquisition of the asset to the day of its disposal. Capital gain/loss is a concept that affects small business owners in a number of ways—from the decisions they must make regarding their personal property and investments to the attractiveness of their businesses to outside investors. The factors relevant to capital gain/loss are the capital asset, the transactional event, and time.

The subject of capital gain/loss is the source of debate among analysts and in government and economic circles generally. The current philosophy centers on the benefits and efficiencies of capital accumulation and utilization. To encourage capital formation and investment, the federal tax codes tax capital gains at lower rates than ordinary income. In 2005, the maximum tax rate on a long-term capital gain was lowered from 20 percent to 15 percent, compared to the maximum income tax rate of 35 percent. Two somewhat higher capital gains rates do apply to gains resulting from the sale of very specific items—a 25 percent rate applies to part of the gain from selling depreciated real estate, and a 28 percent rate applies to gains from the sale of small business stock and/or collectibles.

Tax rate changes that were made in 2003 were based on the theory that a lower capital gains tax will encourage people to sell stock and other assets. This, in turn, is expected to increase the federal government's tax revenues. Many believe that lower capital gains tax rates have a beneficial effect on investments in small businesses. Such investments tend to provide investors with income via an appreciation in stock price (which is taxed as a capital gain) rather than via dividends (which are taxed as ordinary income).

CAPITAL ASSETS

Everything one owns for personal use, pleasure, or investment is a capital asset. This includes: securities; a residence; household furnishings; a personal car; coin and stamp collections; gems and jewelry; and precious metals. Since property held for personal use is considered a capital asset, the sale or exchange of that property at a price above its purchase price, or basis, thus results in a capital gain, which is taxable. If one incurs a loss on that property from a sale or exchange, however, the loss cannot be taken as a tax deduction unless it resulted from a personal casualty loss, such as fire, flood, tornado, or hurricane. Other types of property and investments also have some irregularities in their treatment as capital gains or losses for tax purposes.

Investment Property, Collectibles, Precious Metals, and Gems All investment property is also considered a capital asset. Therefore, any gain or loss is generally a capital gain or loss, but only when it is realized—that is, upon completion of the sales transaction. For example, a person who owns stock in a growing technology company may see the price of that stock appreciate considerably over time. For a gain to be realized, however, the investor must actually sell shares at a market price higher than their original purchase price (or lower, in the case of a capital loss). Section 1244 of the federal revenue code treats losses on certain small business stocks differently. If a loss is realized, the investor can deduct the amount as an ordinary loss, while he or she must report any gain as a capital gain.

Sale of a Home The sale of a personal residence enjoys special tax treatment in order to minimize the impact of long-term inflation. For most people, a residence is the largest asset they own. While some appreciation is expected, residences are not primarily used as investment vehicles. Inflation may cause the value of a home to increase substantially while the constant-dollar value may increase very little. In addition, the growth in family size may encourage a family to step up to a larger home. To minimize the impact of inflation and to subsidize the purchase of new homes, the tax code does not require reporting a capital gain if the individual purchases a more expensive house within two years. In addition, individuals are entitled to exclude for tax purposes up to $250,000 and married couples up to $500,000 of capital gains from the sale of a home, provided they have lived in the home as a principal residence in two out of the previous five years. As of 2005, this exclusion was available to taxpayers every two years.

DETERMINING THE BASIS

Capital gain/loss is calculated on the cost basis, which is the amount of cash and debt obligation used to pay for a property, along with the fair market value of other property or services the purchaser provided in the transaction. The purchase price of a property may also include the following charges and fees, which are added to the basis to arrive at the adjusted basis:

1. Sales tax

2. Freight charges

3. Installment and testing fees

4. Excise taxes

5. Legal and accounting fees that are capitalized rather than expensed

6. Revenue stamps

7. Recording fees

8. Real estate taxes where applicable

9. Settlement fees in real estate transactions

The basis may be increased by the value of capital improvements, assessments for site improvements (such as the public infrastructure), and the restoration of damaged property. A basis is reduced by transactional events that recoup part of the original purchase price through tax savings, tax credits, and other transactions. These include depreciation, nontaxable corporate distributions, various environmental and energy credits, reimbursed casualty or theft losses, and the sale of an easement. After adjusting the basis for these various factors, the individual subtracts the adjusted basis from the net proceeds of the sale to determine capital gain/loss.

NET GAIN OR LOSS

To calculate the net gain/loss, the individual first determines the long-term gain/loss and short-term gain/loss separately. The net short-term gain/loss is the difference between short-term gains and short-term losses. Likewise, net long-term gain/loss is the difference between long-term gains and losses. If the individual's total capital gain is more than the total capital loss, the excess is taxable generally at the same rate as the ordinary income. However, the part of the capital gain which is the same amount as the net capital gain is taxed only at the capital

gains tax rate, a maximum of 15 percent (5 percent for those whose income tax rate is either 10 or 15 percent). If the individual's capital losses are more than the total capital gains, the excess is deductible up to $3,000 per year from ordinary income. The remaining loss is carried forward and deducted at a rate up to $3,000 a year until the entire capital loss is written off.

BIBLIOGRAPHY

Bhattacharya, Sudipto, and George M. Constantinides. *Theory of Valuation.* World Scientific, 2005.

Dixon, Daryl. "Gaining on the Capital Gains Tax." *The Bulletin with Newsweek.* 13 April 1999.

Dixon, Daryl. "Two for the Money: Plans to Reduce Taxes on Capital Gains." *The Bulletin with Newsweek.* 22 June 1999.

Goold, Linda. "How Low Can You Go? New capital gains tax rates pose interesting choices for exchangers." *Journal of Property Management.* January-February 2004.

Kadlec, Daniel. "Capital Gain = Market Pain?" *Time.* 18 August 1997.

Murphy, Kevin E. and Mark Higgins *Concepts in Federal Taxation 2005.* Thomson West, 2004.

Santoli, Michael. "Profiting from Losses: These Tax Moves Can Help You Play Scrooge to the IRS." *Barron's.* December 6, 1999.

Yeager, Holly. "House Passes Bill to Extend Tax Cuts Capital Gains." *The Financial Times.* 9 December 2005.

Hillstrom, Northern Lights
updated by Magee, ECDI

CAPITAL STRUCTURE

Capital structure is a term that describes the proportion of a company's capital, or operating money, that is obtained through debt versus the proportion obtained through equity. Debt includes loans and other types of credit that must be repaid in the future, usually with interest. Equity involves selling a partial interest in the company to investors, usually in the form of stock. In contrast to debt financing, equity financing does not involve a direct obligation to repay the funds. Instead, equity investors become part-owners and partners in the business, and thus earn a return on their investment as well as exercising some degree of control over how the business is run.

Since capital is expensive for small businesses, it is particularly important for small business owners to determine a target capital structure for their firms. Capital structure decisions are complex ones that involve weighing a variety of factors. In general, companies that tend to have stable sales levels, assets that make good collateral for loans, and a high growth rate can use debt more heavily than other companies. On the other hand, companies that have conservative management, high profitability, or poor credit ratings may wish to rely on equity capital instead.

ADVANTAGES AND DISADVANTAGES OF FINANCING OPTIONS

Both debt and equity financing offer small businesses a number of advantages and disadvantages. The key for small business owners is to evaluate their company's particular situation and determine its optimal capital structure. An optimal capital structure is one that strikes a balance between risk and return and maximizes the price of the stock while simultaneously minimizing the cost of capital.

Advantages of Debt Financing The primary advantage of debt financing is that it allows the founders to retain ownership and control of the company. In contrast to equity financing, debt financing allows an entrepreneur to make key strategic decisions and also to keep and reinvest more company profits. Another advantage of debt financing is that it provides small business owners with a greater degree of financial freedom than equity financing. Debt obligations are limited to the loan repayment period, after which the lender has no further claim on the business, whereas an equity investor's claim does not end until his or her stock is sold. Debt financing is also easy to administer, as it generally lacks the complex reporting requirements that accompany some forms of equity financing. Finally, debt financing tends to be less expensive for small businesses over the long term than equity financing. Over the short term, however, debt financing is far more expensive.

Disadvantages of Debt Financing The main disadvantage of debt financing is that it requires a small business to make regular monthly payments of principal and interest. Very young companies often experience shortages in cash flow that may make such regular payments difficult, and most lenders provide severe penalties for late or missed payments. Another disadvantage associated with debt financing is that its availability is often limited to established businesses. Since lenders primarily seek security for their funds, it can be difficult for unproven businesses to obtain loans without a personal guarantee from one of the principals in the business.

Advantages of Equity Financing The main advantage of equity financing for small businesses, which are likely to struggle with cash flow initially, is that there is no obligation to repay the money. Equity financing is also easier to acquire than debt financing for early-stage or start-up

businesses. Equity investors seek growth opportunities, so they are often willing to take a chance on a good idea. But debt financiers seek security, so they usually require the business to have some sort of track record before they will consider making a loan. Another advantage of equity financing is that investors often prove to be good sources of advice and contacts for small business owners.

Disadvantages of Equity Financing The main disadvantage of equity financing is that the founders must give up some control of the business. If investors have different ideas about the company's strategic direction or day-to-day operations, they can pose problems for the entrepreneur. In addition, some sales of equity, such as initial public offerings, can be very complex and expensive to administer. Such equity financing may require complicated legal filings and a great deal of paperwork to comply with various regulations. For many small businesses, therefore, equity financing may necessitate enlisting the help of attorneys and accountants.

SEE ALSO *Debt Financing; Equity Financing*

BIBLIOGRAPHY
Bierman, Harold. *The Capital Structure Decision.* Springer, 2002.

Brealey, Richard A., and Stewart C. Myers. *Principles of Corporate Finance.* Sixth Edition. McGraw Hill, 2002.

Brigham, Eugene F., and Joel F. Houston. *Fundamentals of Financial Management.* 5th ed. South-Western College Publishing, 2003.

Caselli, S., and S. Gatti. *Venture Capital.* Springer, 2003.

Culp, Christopher L. *The Art of Risk Management.* John Wiley & Sons, 2002.

Downes, John, and Jordan Elliot Goodman. *Finance & Investment Handbook.* Barron's Educational Series, 2003.

Romano, Claudio A., et al. "Capital Structure Decision Making: A Model for Family Business." *Journal of Business Venturing.* May 2001.

"Strategies for Effective Capital Structure Management: Executive Summary." *Healthcare Financial Management.* August 2005.

Hillstrom, Northern Lights
updated by Magee, ECDI

CAREER AND FAMILY

Over the past several decades, American society has undergone significant changes in its attitudes toward balancing work and family life. These attitudes have been influenced by changing demographics; a dramatic increase in the percentage of women who choose to work in non-household related areas; rising costs in the realm of housing, transportation, clothing, and food; changing societal and personal priorities; and a host of other factors. Today, both employer and employee are grappling with the challenges of balancing career and family obligations and desires in a more visible way than ever before. American media outlets (television, radio, newspapers, etc.), for instance, simultaneously extol the virtues of those who excel in the business world and lament the impact that such ambition allegedly can have on the psychological health of the individual, his or her partner, and their children.

This concern with the issue of career/family balance is reflected in the barrage of media attention that accompanies any small trend in this area. Among the trends documented in numerous articles in newspapers and magazines are such things as an increase in the number of professional women leaving work to become full-time mothers. The general society-wide movement toward simplification of life is another such trend, typically characterized as symbolic of an increased emphasis on family happiness and growth at the expense of career development.

Indeed, the debate over what constitutes an appropriate balance between family and career is livelier than ever. For example, proponents of recent trends toward attitudes that are typically characterized as "family-friendly" laud the decisions of those who choose less time-consuming careers or institute flexible work rules to increase family time. Others, though, resent the assumption that is sometimes made that people who are ambitious and driven in their chosen profession, and thus spend significant amounts of time involved in such endeavors, must have their priorities screwed up. For example, Joseph Nocera wrote in *Fortune* that "without question, it's unhealthy to be so consumed by work that the kids feel abandoned. But there is also something unhealthy about so sanctifying family time that we diminish the importance of work. Yet that is precisely the judgment our culture now renders on a regular basis." Nocera went on to critique the widespread assumption that "no matter what's going on at the office, it can't be more important than coaching your kid's basketball team. Well, sometimes it isn't, and sometimes it is. Sometimes other people's jobs are at stake, or a crisis has to be averted. Sometimes you need to accomplish something in your work for the sheer satisfaction of it, and sometimes that means staying late or working on weekends. Why should it be such a sin to admit this out loud?"

For the small business owner, achieving a reasonable balance between work and family obligations can be a particularly daunting task. The challenge of striking this appropriate balance can be especially acute for women entrepreneurs, who, despite tremendous changes in societal acceptance of their right to make their mark in the business world, still face disapproval in some quarters for making such a choice.

For both men and women, the demands of establishing and maintaining a profitable business are numerous and time-consuming in most instances. After all, it is the entrepreneur who is ultimately responsible for realizing his or her vision of the business, and who has typically invested a great deal of time, thought, and energy into nourishing that vision. The entrepreneur or small business owner is often the chief decision maker within the business, and is frequently the primary producer of the company's goods and/or services as well. This latter element is particularly true of smaller businesses, whether the enterprise is concerned with silk screening, freelance writing, portrait photography, carpentry, or some other area of endeavor.

Life partners and children, of course, have needs as well. Successful entrepreneurs and family counselors alike warn that a person who establishes a profitable business is likely to find that his or her victory is a hollow one if his or her relationship with a spouse or child is irreparably damaged in the process. Balancing home and career can be a bit like a juggling act and just like a juggler, if you try to juggle too many balls at once, you're bound to drop one of them. Deciding what one's goals are and setting priorities is essential for all small business owners.

Finally, small business owners have to recognize that the career/family issue is one that impacts on employees as well. Indeed, "family-friendly" policies have proliferated in many industries in recent years, as various sectors respond to general societal perceptions that the work/family balance had become unevenly weighted toward work over the past few decades. In many cases, it has become essential for small business owners to recognize the changing expectations of their employees in this area.

FAMILY LEAVE LEGISLATION

In an attempt to address some of the difficulties that employees were having in balancing work and family, legislation was passed in 1993. The law, entitled Family and Medical Leave Act (FMLA), covers all employers with 50 employees or more. Those employers must grant an eligible employee up to a total of 12 workweeks of unpaid leave during any 12-month period for one or more of the following reasons:

- The birth and care of the newborn child of the employee
- Placement with the employee of a son or daughter for adoption or foster care

- The care for an immediate family member (spouse, child, or parent) with a serious health condition

- Inability to work because of a serious health condition

The FMLA has had wide acceptance. According to a 2000 survey carried out by the U.S. Bureau of Labor, 84 percent of employers found that the benefits of providing family or medical leave offset or outweighed the costs.

HELPING EMPLOYEES ESTABLISH AN APPROPRIATE WORK/FAMILY BALANCE

Increasingly, small businesses have shown an interest in helping their work forces manage the challenges of addressing both work and family obligations. Their ability to do so is dictated somewhat by financial health, workload, competitive pressures, and a host of other factors, but many small business owners have come to the conclusion that workplaces that insist on long hours from their employees may be sacrificing long-term health for short-term gains. "Many experts in the field of management have argued that family-responsive policies and programs will be necessary to attract and retain needed employees and to build competitive advantages," wrote Teresa Joyce Covin and Christina C. Brush in *Review of Business*. "Research also suggests that conflicts between work and family are related to decreased productivity, lost work time, job dissatisfaction, increased health risks for employed parents, poorer performance of the parenting role, absenteeism, poor morale, reduced life satisfaction, and depression. While work-family conflict is commonly viewed as a woman's problem, more companies are beginning to recognize that both men and women feel the impact of work-family conflicts."

There are several steps that small business owners can take to help employees manage their obligations both in the office and at home. "A number of external, structural innovations help people immeasurably in balancing work and family," stated Deborah Lee in *Having It All/ Having Enough: How to Create a Career/Family Balance that Works for You*. These include "flexible work schedule, the availability of part-time work that is taken seriously and is respected by employers, the option of working at home or bringing a child to work. However, these options won't help much unless people also adjust their attitudes about work and unless employers adjust their expectations about what people can produce. A part-time schedule doesn't help if it contains a full-time equivalent workload or penalties such as loss of health benefits or loss of advancement opportunities." Of course, some small business owners contend that a person who takes on a part-time schedule does not warrant the

same consideration for advancement as does a full-time employee, and that providing health benefits to all part-time employees puts the business at an unacceptable competitive disadvantage. Each individual business faces challenges and considerations that are unique; thus, each business owner has to decide for himself or herself what family-friendly policies (and attitudes) can be put in place.

BALANCING WORK AND FAMILY IN HOME-BASED BUSINESSES

Owners of home-based businesses face unique challenges in the realm of achieving a desired work/family balance. Whereas small business owners who commute to their place of business every day are usually freed from child-rearing responsibilities for the duration of their time there, entrepreneurs who work out of their home often have to devise methods in which they can both attend to the needs of their business and provide adequate attention to their children. Researchers and home-based business owners tout several steps that can be taken to assist entrepreneurs in meeting these twin challenges.

- Establish a family-friendly business—This sounds simple, but in reality all home-based businesses are not created equal. Some may provide a parent with significant freedom in structuring business around his or her children's schedule, while others may not provide nearly the same level of flexibility.

- Communicate with spouse and/or others— Establishing and maintaining a home-based business requires changes in the routines of all family members, not just the entrepreneur. Changes in travel schedules, household chore allocation, and other areas of family life may all need to be made. The key to making sure that such changes are made with a minimum of disruption and/or resentment is open, honest communication.

- Make maximum use of free time—Home-based entrepreneurs can dramatically increase their productivity—and keep a lid on feelings of frustration—by scheduling demanding and/or important work obligations for times when child supervision obligations are minimal. Nap times, pre-school sessions, extracurricular programs, etc. can all provide parents with valuable windows of opportunity to attend to vital work-related matters.

- Prioritize and establish a daily schedule—Business owners who work out of their home should avoid falling into a routine in which tasks—both family- and work-related—are addressed in a haphazard, "as they come up" fashion. Instead, they should try to establish a daily or weekly schedule. Work discipline can be difficult to maintain at home even without children; their presence further compounds the challenge.

- Establish an office area that is physically removed from the rest of the house—People who attempt to take care of work while situated in the heart of a child's play area are apt to experience high levels of frustration. Instead, home-based entrepreneurs should consider establishing an office in a separate area that includes all necessary equipment to conduct business. Moreover, children should be taught to respect the importance of that area. Another option which may be more popular with parents of toddlers and young children is to create a "child-friendly" office with a corner that is set aside for their needs.

- Communicate the importance of your work to children—In *How to Raise a Family and a Career Under One Roof,* Lisa Roberts noted that home-based entrepreneurs should make a special effort to educate their children about the importance of the work they are doing. She counseled parents to "share your victories, challenges and rewards as often as possible. If your children feel like they're a part of what you're doing, they'll be much more supportive than if they see your business as something that's just taking you away from them."

- Enjoy your family—Many home-based business owners may create a situation for themselves for the express purpose of spending greater time with their mates or children, yet find themselves feeling frustrated with the demands on time and energy that those people inevitably make during the course of every day. Counselors urge home-based entrepreneurs not to lose sight of why they made the decision to operate out of the home in the first place.

Overall, experts stress that owning a business is not something to take lightly. It requires planning to achieve an appropriate balance between work and family that all interested parties can live with. "Make time for family," Michelle Prather wrote in *Entrepreneur.* "Acknowledge you're taking them on the wildest ride of their lives. Find a mentor to help you through the tough times. Know your limits. Know that unhealthy relationships will worsen, and solid ones could waver."

SEE ALSO *Child Care; Eldercare*

BIBLIOGRAPHY
"Completing the Package: Balancing Work and Family as You Press Ahead." *InfoWorld.* 23 August 1999.

Covin, Teresa Joyce, and Christina C. Brush. "Attitudes Toward Work-Family Issues: The Human Resource Professional Perspective." *Review of Business.* Winter 1993.

Lee, Deborah. *Having It All/Having Enough: How to Create a Career/Family Balance that Works for You.* AMACOM, 1997.

Levine, James A., and Todd L. Pittinsky. *Working Fathers: New Strategies for Balancing Work and Family.* 1997.

Murray, Katherine. *The Working Parents' Handbook: How to Succeed at Work, Raise Your Kids, Maintain a Home, and Still Have Time for You.* Park Avenue, 1996.

"New FMLA Certification OK in DOL Opinion Letter." *HR Focus.* December 2005.

Nocera, Joseph. "Oh, Quit Whining and Get Back to Work!" *Fortune.* 17 March 1997.

Prather, Michelle. "Sacrificial Rites." *Entrepreneur.* February 2001.

Roberts, Lisa. *How to Raise a Family and a Career Under One Roof.* Brookhaven Press, 1996.

Rose, Karol L. "Assessing Work/Family Needs." *Compensation and Benefits Management.* Summer 1995.

Shellenbarger, Sue. "Work-Family Issues Go Way Beyond Missed Ball Games." *Wall Street Journal.* 28 May 1997.

Thomas, Marian. *Balancing Career and Family: Overcoming the Superwoman Syndrome.* National Seminars, 1991.

Hillstrom, Northern Lights
updated by Magee, ECDI

CAREER PLANNING AND CHANGING

According to the U.S. Department of Labor, those born between 1957 and 1964 (the end of the baby boom generation) held 10.2 jobs on average during their first 20 years in the work force. Changing jobs is more frequently necessary in recent periods than in earlier eras. People therefore either do or *should* spend more time planning flexible careers. The greater dynamism in the labor market is due to many factors. Increases in productivity have been mirrored by down-sizing of production and service forces. Modern means of data handling and communications have changed the manner in which sales and administrative work are done. In parallel with the growth of many new employment benefits have come increased costs—which many corporations have begun to shed by transferring labor from full-time employees (who get such benefits) to independent contractors, temporary employees, and outsourced laborers (who do not). Many people face new careers—abruptly and involuntarily. They have been downsized or laid off.

At the same time, and in parallel with these broad trends, the educational attainment of individuals entering the work force is much higher. The workforce is not only better trained but much better informed. The same dynamics that cause contractions in many traditional industries create opportunities in emerging fields. Individuals see opportunities that draw them. They change careers—voluntarily. They are drawn by greener pastures and shimmering rainbows.

Changing jobs is most stressful for those who must do so involuntarily. Richard Ream, writing in *Information Today* recently counseled such people as follows: "Careers are linear in foresight but circuitous in hindsight, and chance favors the prepared mind. What you need as you plan yours is to sustain curiosity, optimism, flexibility, and open-mindedness."

ALTERNATIVES

Persons facing involuntary changes in making a living typically follow a sequence of activities which, in another sense, represent the available options. They 1) attempt to find another, similar job in the same or related industry or sector doing essentially what they have done before. Or, 2), they make use of a secondary skill or previous experience to change industry/sector. Or, 3), they return to school to acquire a new or enhanced set of skills drawn either by inclination or by studying the job market. Or, 4), they choose to obtain work in the same or related specialty as a self-employed person; this is often relatively easy for some—sometimes even with the old employer. Or, 5) they opt to start a business of their own.

To some extent these five alternatives may be pursued in parallel. Thus a person may get another job but, anticipating further problems, may stay in an exploratory posture, enroll in some courses of study, and engage in a serious reassessment of his or her career path. A self-employed person may decide, after a while, that with a little more effort, investment from friends, and joining with a friend or two, the "self-employment" may be turned into a small business.

When these activities are undertaken with a certain heightened consciousness, the search for "what to do next" may evolve into career planning and, sometimes, a change in careers.

THE ELEMENTS OF A PLAN

Like any planning activity, in business as in personal life, a change in careers begins with 1) environmental assessment, internal and external, 2) goal setting, 3) evaluation of alternatives, 4) cost assessment, and 5) implementation.

In addition to the mechanics, career planning requires self-knowledge, honesty, and systematic work. Perhaps the most important aspect of a career change not listed above is drive. As Jessica Jarvis pointed out in a recent article in *Personnel Today*, research carried out by the Chartered Institute of Personnel Development "shows [that] it is critical to be proactive in your career. The single most important factor in getting to the top…, the research found, was personal drive and ambition."

The *environmental assessment* must begin with a list of the person's skills and the extent to which these are certifiable (through degrees or experience). High levels of skill in an activity the person hates are useless. Therefore the assessment should focus on a combination of skills and personal inclination. This effort should result in a listing of activities, jobs, or involvements the career planner would be happy and able to do. This is the "internal" part of the environmental survey. The next step is study of the labor market for activities that match the person's profile. *Goal setting* is the consequence of this initial match of internal resources and external opportunities. Experts in the field suggest that the person should "enlist expert counsel." Thus John Lees recently wrote in *Personnel Today:* "Seek advice from senior colleagues or a mentor to help you create an action plan and clarify your performance objectives. This will help you keep focused and motivated."

Evaluation of alternatives may, all depending, involve studying companies to interview, curricula to pursue in school, or even looking at potential sites for starting up a store. At this point the career seeker is still only *evaluating* choices, not making decisions. Each alternative will have a monetary, time, and possibly also an emotional cost. *Cost assessment* follows. Here the career seeker may be required to make hard choices. He or she may accept two years' of study and a low income, meanwhile, from a part-time job, in order to achieve the highest goal—or an immediate job campaign to get a start at a lower level now. Whatever the choice, its success will depend on consciously carrying out the last step, *implementation*.

CONTINUOUS CAREER PLANNING

Statistics on the number of businesses there are in the U.S. each year provide an interesting glimpse into trends in our economy. What these data from the U.S. Bureau of the Census show is that the number of single-person firms grew rapidly between 1997 and 2003. In fact, they grew at a rate of 21 percent. This is a growth rate 6 percent higher than the growth rate for all firms and more than twice as fast a growth rate as was seen for all firms with three or more employees. People are clearly working on their own in greater numbers and in many case they are establishing single-person businesses in which to do so. The very meaning of "career" for most people is changing from being a single more or less continuous activity to a succession of different activities in a rapidly changing environment. Career planning, therefore, will for most forward-looking individuals become a continuous activity repeated at regular intervals.

BIBLIOGRAPHY

Bolles, Richard. *What Color Is Your Parachute?* Ten Speed Press, 1999.

Jarvis, Jessica. "Trends in Career Planning." *Personnel Today.* 17 January 2006.

Kanchier, Carole. *Dare to Change Your Job—And Your Life.* Jist Works, 1995.

Komisar, Randy. "Goodbye Career, Hello Success." *Harvard Business Review.* March 2000.

Lees, John. "How to Plan Your Career in 2006." *Personnel Today.* 31 December 2005.

Randall, Iris. "Take In the Whole Picture." *Black Enterprise.* February 2000.

Ream, Richard. "Changing Jobs? It's a Changing Market." *Information Today.* February 2000.

U.S. Department of Commerce. Bureau of the Census. *Nonemployer Statistics: 2003.* October 2005.

U.S. Department of Labor. Bureau of Labor Statistics. *Number of Jobs Held, Labor Market Activity, and Earnings Growth Among Younger Boomers.* 25 August 2004.

Hillstrom, Northern Lights
updated by Magee, ECDI

CASH CONVERSION CYCLE

The cash conversion cycle (CCC) is a key measurement of small business liquidity. The cash conversion cycle is the number of days between paying for raw materials or goods to be resold and receiving the cash from the sale of the goods either made from that raw material or purchased for resale. The cash conversion cycle measures the time between outlay of cash and the cash recovery. The cycle is a measure of the time that funds are tied up in the cycle. The CCC measure illustrates how quickly a company can convert its products into cash through sales. The shorter the cycle, the more working capital a business generates, and the less it has to borrow.

Effective management of the cash conversion cycle is imperative for small business owners. Indeed, the CCC is cited by economists and business consultants as one of the truest measures of business's health, particularly during periods of growth. Other often used ratios and measures of a company's activity may not provide advance notice of a cash flow problem as well as the CCC. For example, the current and quick ratios are popular with companies and their bankers. However, in a period when collections have slowed, asset turns have become sluggish and vendors have not extended terms beyond previously agreed limits, a clearly worrisome combination, the current ratio would probably look good. At the same time, the quick ratio

may even show improvement or remain steady, even though the company is actually in substantial need of working capital. This happens because of the balance-sheet-oriented limitations of current and quick ratios. These often used ratios do not work well on a company going through a period of rapid and dynamic change.

Instead of the potentially misleading measurements mentioned above, small business owners should consider using the cash conversion cycle, which provides a more accurate reading of working capital pressure on cash flow. The objective is to keep the CCC as low as possible. During periods of growth, the goal should be to strive to maintain a constant CCC. Unless inventory, credit, or vendor policies change, rapid growth should not cause the CCC to increase. The ease with which this ratio can be calculated makes it an even more attractive measure for tracking a business's operations and managing cash flow.

Cash conversion cycles for small businesses are predicated on four central factors: 1) the number of days it takes customers to pay what they owe; 2) the number of days it takes the business to make its product (or complete its service); 3) the number of days the product (or service) sits in inventory before it is sold; 4) the length of time that the small business has to pay its vendors. The following formulas may be used to determine these factors:

- Accounts receivable days – divide the receivables balance by the last 12 months' sales, then multiply the result by 365 (the number of days in a year).

- Inventory days – take the inventory balance, divide it by the last 12 months' cost of goods sold, and then multiply the result by 365.

- Accounts payable days – take the company's payables balance, divide it by the last 12 months' cost of goods sold, and then multiply the resulting figure by 365.

Once a small business owner has these figures in hand, he or she can determine the company's cash conversion cycle by adding the receivable days to the production and inventory days and then subtracting the payables days. That will render the number of days a company's cash is tied up and is the first step in calculating how much money the company will want to secure for its revolving line of credit.

BIBLIOGRAPHY

Costa, John. "Challenging Growth: How to Keep Your Company's Rapid Expansion on Track." *Outlook.* September 1997.

Neely, Andrew. *Business Performance Measures.* Cambridge University Press, 2002.

Sawyers, Roby, and Greg Jenkins, Steve Jackson. *Managerial Accounting*. Thomson South-Western, 2005.

"The Numbers You'll Need." *Inc.* August 1999.

Hillstrom, Northern Lights
updated by Magee, ECDI

CASH FLOW STATEMENT

A cash flow statement is a financial report that describes the sources of a company's cash and how that cash was spent over a specified time period. It does not include non-cash items such as depreciation. This makes it useful for determining the short-term viability of a company, particularly its ability to pay bills. Because the management of cash flow is so crucial for businesses and small businesses in particular, most analysts recommend that an entrepreneur study a cash flow statement at least every quarter.

The cash flow statement is similar to the income statement in that it records a company's performance over a specified period of time. The difference between the two is that the income statement also takes into account some non-cash accounting items such as depreciation. The cash flow statement strips away all of this and shows exactly how much actual money the company has generated. Cash flow statements show how companies have performed in managing inflows and outflows of cash. It provides a sharper picture of a company's ability to pay creditors, and finance growth.

It is perfectly possible for a company that is shown to be profitable according to accounting standards to go under if there isn't enough cash on hand to pay bills. Comparing amount of cash generated to outstanding debt, known as the "operating cash flow ratio," illustrates the company's ability to service its loans and interest payments. If a slight drop in a company's quarterly cash flow would jeopardize its ability to make loan payments, that company is in a riskier position than one with less net income but a stronger cash flow level.

Unlike the many ways in which reported earnings can be presented, there is little a company can do to manipulate its cash situation. Barring any outright fraud, the cash flow statement tells the whole story. The company either has cash or it does not. Analysts will look closely at the cash flow statement of any company in order to understand its overall health.

PARTS OF THE CASH FLOW STATEMENT

Cash flow statements classify cash receipts and payments according to whether they stem from operating, investing, or financing activities. A cash flow statement is divided into sections by these same three functional areas within the business:

- **Cash from Operations** - this is cash generated from day-to-day business operations.
- **Cash from Investing** - cash used for investing in assets, as well as the proceeds from the sale of other businesses, equipment, or other long-term assets.
- **Cash from Financing** - cash paid or received from issuing and borrowing of funds. This section also includes dividends paid. (Although it is sometimes listed under cash from operations.)
- **Net Increase or Decrease in Cash** - increases in cash from previous year will be written normally, and decreases in cash are typically written in (brackets).

Although cash flow statements may vary slightly, they all present data in the four sections listed here.

CLASSIFICATIONS OF CASH RECEIPTS AND PAYMENTS

Cash from Financing At the beginning of a company's life cycle, a person or group of people come up with an idea for a new company. The initial money comes from the owners or is borrowed by the owners. This is how the new company is "financed." The money that owners put into the company is classified as a financing activity. Generally, any item that would be classified on the balance sheet as either a long-term liability or an equity would be a candidate for classification as a financing activity.

Cash from Investing The owners or managers of the business use the initial funds to buy equipment or other assets they need to run the business. In other words, they invest it. The purchase of property, plant, equipment, and other productive assets is classified as an investing activity. Sometimes a company has enough cash of its own that it can lend money to another enterprise. This, too, would be classified as an investing activity. Generally, any item that would be classified on the balance sheet as a long-term asset would be a candidate for classification as an investing activity.

Cash from Operations Now the company can start doing business. It has procured the funds and purchased the equipment and other assets it needs to operate. It starts to sell merchandise or services and make payments for rent, supplies, taxes, and all of the other costs of doing business. All of the cash inflows and outflows associated with doing the work for which the company was established would be classified as an operating activity. In general, if an activity appears on the company's income statement, it is a candidate for the operating section of the cash flow statement.

Methods of Preparing the Cash Flow Statement In November 1987, the Financial Accounting Standards Board (FASB) issued a "Statement of Financial Accounting Standards" which required businesses to issue a statement of cash flow rather than a statement of changes in financial position. There are two methods for preparing and presenting this statement, the direct method and the indirect method. The FASB encourages, but does not require, the use of the direct method for reporting. The two methods of reporting affect the presentation of the operating section only. The investing and financing sections are presented in the same way regardless of presentation methods.

Direct Method The direct method, also called the income statement method, reports major classes of operating cash receipts and payments. Using this method of preparing a cash statement starts with money received and then subtracts money spent, to calculate net cash flow. Depreciation is excluded altogether because, although it is an expense that affects net profits, it is not money spent or received.

Indirect Method This method, also called the reconciliation method, focuses on net income and the net cash flow from operations. Using this method one starts with net income, adds back depreciation, then calculates changes in balance sheet items. The end result is the same net cash flow produced by the direct method. The indirect method adds depreciation into the equation because it started with net profits, from which depreciation was subtracted as an expense.

Regardless of whether the direct or the indirect method is used, the operating section of the cash flow statement ends with net cash provided (used) by operating activities. This is the most important line item on the cash flow statement. A company has to generate enough cash from operations to sustain its business activity. If a company continually needs to borrow or obtain additional investor capitalization to survive, the company's long-term existence is in jeopardy.

FINANCING AND INVESTING SECTIONS

The cash flows, in and out, resulting from financing and investing activities are listed in the same way whether the direct or indirect method of presentation is employed.

Cash Flows from Investing The major line items in this section of the cash flow statement are as follows:

- Capital Expenditures. This figure represents money spent on items that last a long time such as property, plant, and equipment. When capital spending increases, it often means the company is expanding.

- Investment Proceeds. Companies will often take some of their excess cash and invest it in an effort to get a better return than they could in a savings account or money market fund. This figure shows how much the company has made or lost on these investments.

- Purchases or Sales of Businesses. This figure includes any money the company made from buying or selling subsidiary businesses and will sometimes appear in the cash flows from operating activities section, rather than here.

Cash Flows from Financing The major line items in this section of the cash flow statement include such things as:

- Dividends Paid. This figure is the total dollar amount the company paid out in dividends over the specified time period.

- Issuance/Purchase of Common Stock. This is an important number because it indicates how a company is financing its activities. New, rapidly growing companies will often issue new stock and dilutes the value of existing shares in so doing. This practice does, however, give a company cash for expansion. Later, when the company is more established it will be in a position to buy back its own stock and in this way increase the value of existing shares.

- Issuance/Repayments of Debt. This number tells you whether the company has borrowed money during the period or repaid money it previously borrowed. Borrowing is the main alternative to issuing stock as a way for companies to raise capital.

The cash flow statement is the newest of the three fundamental financial statements prepared by most companies and required to be filed with the Securities and Exchange Commission by all publicly traded companies. Most of the components it presents are also reported, although often in a different format, in one of the other statements, either the Income Statement or the Balance Sheet. Nonetheless, it offers the manager, investor, lender, and supplier of a company a view into how it is doing in meeting its short-term obligations, regardless of whether or not the company is generating income.

SEE ALSO *Financial Statements*

BIBLIOGRAPHY

Brahmasrene, Tantatape, and C. David Strupeck, Donna Whitten. "Examining Preferences in Cash Flow Statement Format." *The CPA Journal.* October 2004.

Hey-Cunningham, David. *Financial Statements Demystified.* Allen & Unwin, 2002.

O'Connor, Tricia. "The Formula for Determining Cash Flow." *Denver Business Journal.* 2 June 2000.

Taulli, Tom. *The Edgar Online Guide to Decoding Financial Statements.* J. Ross Publishing, 2004.

"Ten Ways to Improve Small Business Cash Flow." *Journal of Accountancy.* March 2000.

Hillstrom, Northern Lights
updated by Magee, ECDI

CASH MANAGEMENT

Cash management is a broad term that refers to the collection, concentration, and disbursement of cash. The goal is to manage the cash balances of an enterprise in such a way as to maximize the availability of cash not invested in fixed assets or inventories and to do so in such a way as to avoid the risk of insolvency. Factors monitored as a part of cash management include a company's level of liquidity, its management of cash balances, and its short-term investment strategies.

In some ways, managing cash flow is the most important job of business managers. If at any time a company fails to pay an obligation when it is due because of the lack of cash, the company is insolvent. Insolvency is the primary reason firms go bankrupt. Obviously, the prospect of such a dire consequence should compel companies to manage their cash with care. Moreover, efficient cash management means more than just preventing bankruptcy. It improves the profitability and reduces the risk to which the firm is exposed.

Cash management is particularly important for new and growing businesses. Cash flow can be a problem even when a small business has numerous clients, offers a product superior to that offered by its competitors, and enjoys a sterling reputation in its industry. Companies suffering from cash flow problems have no margin of safety in case of unanticipated expenses. They also may experience trouble in finding the funds for innovation or expansion. It is, somewhat ironically, easier to borrow money when you have money. Finally, poor cash flow makes it difficult to hire and retain good employees.

It is only natural that major business expenses are incurred in the production of goods or the provision of services. In most cases, a business incurs such expenses before the corresponding payment is received from customers. In addition, employee salaries and other expenses drain considerable funds from most businesses. These factors make effective cash management an essential part of any business's financial planning. Cash is the lifeblood of a business. Managing it efficiently is essential for success.

When cash is received in exchange for products or services rendered, many small business owners, intent on growing their company and tamping down debt, spend most or all of these funds. But while such priorities are laudable, they should leave room for businesses to absorb lean financial times down the line. The key to successful cash management, therefore, lies in tabulating realistic projections, monitoring collections and disbursements, establishing effective billing and collection measures, and adhering to budgetary restrictions.

CASH COLLECTION AND DISBURSEMENT

Cash collection systems aim to reduce the time it takes to collect the cash that is owed to a firm. Some of the sources of time delays are mail float, processing float, and bank float. Obviously, an envelope mailed by a customer containing payment to a supplier firm does not arrive at its destination instantly. Likewise, the payment is not processed and deposited into a bank account the moment it is received by the supplier firm. And finally, when the payment is deposited in the bank account oftentimes the bank does not give immediate availability of the funds. These three "floats" are time delays that add up quickly, and they can force struggling or new firms to find other sources of cash to pay their bills.

Cash management attempts, among other things, to decrease the length and impact of these "float" periods. A collection receipt point closer to the customer—perhaps with an outside third-party vendor to receive, process, and deposit the payment (check)—is one way to speed up the collection. The effectiveness of this method depends on the location of the customer; the size and schedule of its payments; the firm's method of collecting payments; the costs of processing payments; the time delays involved for mail, processing, and banking; and the prevailing interest rate that can be earned on excess funds. The most important element in ensuring good cash flow from customers, however, is establishing strong billing and collection practices.

Once the money has been collected, most firms then proceed to concentrate the cash into one center. The rationale for such a move is to have complete control of the cash and to provide greater investment opportunities with larger sums of money available as surplus. There are numerous mechanisms that can be employed to concentrate the cash, such as wire transfers, automated clearinghouse (ACH) transfers, and checks. The tradeoff is between cost and time.

Another aspect of cash management is knowing a company's optimal cash balance. There are a number of methods that try to determine this magical cash balance, which is the precise amount needed to minimize costs yet provide adequate liquidity to ensure bills are paid on time (hopefully with something left over for emergency purposes). One of the first steps in managing the cash balance is measuring liquidity, or the amount of money on hand to meet current obligations. There are numerous ways to measure this, including: the Cash to Total Assets ratio, the Current ratio (current assets divided by current liabilities), the Quick ratio (current assets less inventory, divided by current liabilities), and the Net Liquid Balance (cash plus marketable securities less short-term notes payable, divided by total assets). The higher the number generated by the liquidity measure, the greater the liquidity—and vice versa. However, there is a tradeoff between liquidity and profitability which discourages firms from having excessive liquidity.

CASH MANAGEMENT IN TROUBLED TIMES

Many small businesses experience cash flow difficulties, especially during their first years of operation. But entrepreneurs and managers can take steps to minimize the impact of such problems and help maintain the continued viability of the business. Suggested steps to address temporary cash flow problems include:

- Create a *realistic* cash flow budget that charts finances for both the short term (30-60 days) and longer term (1-2 years).

- Redouble efforts to collect outstanding payments owed to the company. "Bill promptly and accurately," counseled the *Journal of Accountancy*. "The faster you mail an invoice, the faster you will be paid. . . . If deliveries do not automatically trigger an invoice, establish a set billing schedule, preferably weekly." Businesses should also include a payment due date.

- Offer small discounts for prompt payment.

- Consider compromising on some billing disputes with clients. Small business owners are understandably reluctant to consider this step, but in certain cases, obtaining *some* cash—even if your company is not at fault in the dispute—for products sold/services rendered may be required to pay basic expenses.

- Closely monitor and prioritize all cash disbursements.

- Contact creditors (vendors, lenders, landlords) and attempt to negotiate mutually satisfactory arrangements that will enable the business to weather its cash shortage (provided it is a temporary one). In some cases, you may be able to arrange better payment terms from suppliers or banks. "Better credit terms translate into borrowing money interest-free," states the *Journal of Accountancy*.

- Liquidate superfluous inventory.

- Assess other areas where operational expenses may be cut without permanently disabling the business, such as payroll or non-strategic goods and/or services with small profit margins.

BIBLIOGRAPHY

Bee, Judy. "Keeping Tabs on Cash Flow: If you're not, your office could be leaking money." *Medical Economics*. 2 December 2005.

Gage, Jack. "Living Within Your Means." *Forbes*. 26 December 2005.

Hommel, Ulrich, and Michael Frenkel, Markus Rudolf, eds. *Risk Management*. Springer, 2005.

Kono, Clyde. "Bank on It: Managing Your Cash Flow." *Hawaii Business*. August 2004.

"Ten Ways to Improve Small Business Cash Flow." *Journal of Accountancy*. March 2000.

Hillstrom, Northern Lights
updated by Magee, ECDI

CASUAL BUSINESS ATTIRE

Casual business attire—also known as the "business casual" style of dress—revolutionized the American office environment in the 1990s. According to the Society for Human Resource Management, 95 percent of U.S. companies had some sort of casual day policy in place in 1999, compared to 24 percent in 1992. In fact, casual clothing manufacturer Levi Strauss claimed that 75 percent of American workers dressed casually every day in 1999, compared to 7 percent in 1992.

The trend toward casual business attire began in the high-technology companies of California's Silicon Valley, where young computer and Internet entrepreneurs refused to wear business suits and often showed up at work in denim jeans and cotton T-shirts. The trend spread across the country to various types of businesses throughout the 1990s, until it finally struck even the most buttoned-down, old-school firms. Most companies moved toward casual attire gradually, beginning with a "casual Fridays" policy, then conceding the heat of summer to casual dress, and finally allowing business casual in the office at all times. Over time, many businesses found that they had to allow casual dress in order to compete for talented employees in a shrinking labor pool.

As the fast growing economy of the 1990s cooled in 2001 the trend towards casual business attire began to change. In an article on this subject that appeared in the *San Francisco Business Times,* James Ammeen, president of the Men's Apparel Alliance, attributed the shift away from casual wear in the workplace to the state of the economy. "You're in a tough market, so if you want people to trust you, invest with you, you'd better look like a pretty serious person," said Ammeen. In a survey commissioned by the Men's Apparel Alliance the reversal of trend was seen clearly. Of the companies surveyed with revenues over $500 million, 19 percent had reinstated more formal dress codes during 2001 or early 2002. The threat of being the next person laid off has motivated some to return to suits before their companies even formalize a change in dress code, added Ammeen.

ADVANTAGES AND DISADVANTAGES OF CASUAL DRESS POLICIES

The majority of American workers view casual office attire as a perk that creates a less stratified work environment and puts the emphasis on employees' contributions rather than their wardrobes. "While the goals of a corporate casual dress code include improving morale, enhancing productivity, lowering status barriers, and fitting in with the corporate climate of customers, the wrong code can undermine a company's credibility," wrote Brian Anderson in an article for *Wearables Business.*

Although casual business attire tends to be a popular option among employees, some companies encounter problems implementing casual dress policies. Many problems arise when companies describe their dress codes using vague words like "appropriate," "professional," and "businesslike" without spelling out a specific policy. This can create confusion among workers and make people feel uncomfortable trying to interpret the right way to dress for work. "The biggest problems employers face with these policies may be how to modify them, enforce them, and adapt the corporate-dress culture to a changing workforce," Anderson noted. "A clear, definitive explanation of a corporate casual dress code is rare. What is acceptable at one mortgage broker's office may be completely unacceptable at another—even if they are different branch offices of the same company."

Unclear dress code policies can also contribute to problems with employees taking advantage of the situation by wearing sloppy rather than casual attire to the office. In fact, there were cases in California in the late 1990s dotcom boom when some employees took things to a real extreme. One in particular, a gentleman who wished to work in the nude, inspired the title for a book about Silicon Valley by Po Bronson; *The Nudist on the Late Shift.* Although this example is extreme, many companies have been forced to issue specific guidelines describing appropriate attire after they have adopted casual dress policies. There is, as the old saying goes, no accounting for taste. Banned items that frequently appear on corporate dress code policy amendments are halter-tops, stretch pants, jeans, shorts, sandals, and shirts without collars. In order to avoid a situation in which amendments must be added to a new dress code policy, small business owners should make their dress codes as specific as possible. In fact, it may be helpful to communicate the policies by including photos of employees wearing appropriate attire on bulletin boards, in company publications, on Web sites, and in employee manuals.

Another potential problem with casual office attire is that employees may tend to take work less seriously when they are dressed casually. A survey of managers conducted by the employment law firm Jackson Lewis and cited in *Entrepreneur* indicated that 44 percent noticed an increase in employee absenteeism and tardiness when casual dress policies were introduced. The managers also noted a rise in inappropriate, flirtatious behavior. "Some employers and workers say they don't like the way dress-down day has turned into leisure day, affecting not only attire but behavior," Patricia Wen explained in *Knight-Ridder/Tribune Business News.*

Some office workers prefer traditional, "business formal" attire because they believe it provides an equalizing factor for people of different ages or levels of the corporate hierarchy. After all, if everyone is wearing a suit and tie, it can be difficult to tell the difference between a CEO and a new hire. As a result, younger people may be more likely to be taken seriously in business meetings. Formal business attire is particularly valued by some minority professionals, who feel that the corporate "uniform" helps them overcome prejudices.

Of course, some people believe wearing a suit and tie simply makes dressing for work easier. Older men, in particular, tend to have trouble making the transition to casual dress. "Men have clearly struggled more with casual day than women, who have never stuck to a corporate uniform and who have a wider selection when it comes to choosing attire," Wen wrote. "Psychologists say many men, to some degree, see casual day as yet another arena where they have to compete. Indeed the jungle of casual fashion requires a mix-and-match ability and a fashion sense that many men say they do not possess." However, some experts argue that the rapid increase in casual office environments during the 1990s forced most people to update their wardrobes. "By now, most former white-collar office workers have business casual wardrobes, which are often the same clothes they go out to dinner in, go to the mall in, or travel in," according to Anderson.

Another reason people resist the movement toward casual office attire is worry about losing their credibility. Bosses are afraid they might lose the respect of their employees by dressing casually, for example, while employees are afraid they might lose out on promotions to better dressed co-workers. In the meantime, salespeople and others involved in relationships with clients often live in fear that a client will drop by the office and find them dressed casually. "How you look goes a long way toward establishing your identity. What you wear says much about your character and credibility," said a writer for *Sales and Marketing Management*. "As the saying goes, you never get a second chance to make a first impression—and there's nothing casual about that."

In some industries, formal office attire has remained the standard. These industries did not embrace the trend towards casual dress. For the most part these are industries in which employees deal regularly and extensively with clients and need to project a professional, serious image. The banking and legal fields are among those industries that never fully embraced casual business attire and are leading a trend back towards more formal business attire.

As Sherry Maysonave explained in her book *Casual Power*, the goal in choosing casual attire for the office is to exude the same power, credibility, and authority as if you were wearing a suit. It is also important that the way you dress shows respect for your workplace and reflects your career goals. After all, Maysonave argued, dressing too sloppily can erode your self-confidence and make you appear unprofessional in the eyes of clients and employees.

Trends in clothing fashion are ever changing. This is as true for the work environment as it is generally. The lasting effect that the 1990s trend towards casual business attire seems to have had in the business world is to eliminate a single standard for business attire. Now, companies from different industries and different regions tend to establish dress code policies that suit their particular situations. Finding the right mix in the line from formal and professional to informal and comfortable is the key.

BIBLIOGRAPHY

Anderson, Brian. "The Code of Corporate." *Wearables Business.* January 2000.

"Birthday Suit Still Isn't Appropriate Office Wear: In the 21st century, dress codes remain a minefield at work." *The America's Intelligence Wire.* 16 July 2005.

Bronson, Po. *The Nudist on the Late Shift.* Random House, 1999.

Garbato Stankevitch, Debby. "Now It's Business Attire 'Chic'." *Retail Merchandiser.* April 2002.

Griffin, Cynthia E. "Dressed for Distress: Is Business Casual in for a Backlash?" *Entrepreneur.* March 2001.

"Hot Tips." *Sales and Marketing Management.* August 2000.

Maysonave, Sherry. *Casual Power: How to Power Up Your Nonverbal Communication and Dress Down for Success.* Bright Books, 1999.

Temple, James. "Old Economy Makes a Comeback; So Does Its Traditional Uniform." *San Francisco Business Times.* 22 February 2002.

"Too Sexy for this Office? Dress code study finds managers in mini skirts get short shrift from staff." *Europe Intelligence Wire.* 2 December 2005.

Wangensteen, Betsy. "Casually Climbing the Corporate Ladder." *Crain's Chicago Business.* 16 October 1995.

Wen, Patricia. "Office Casual-Dress Policies Spark Confusion, Even a Backlash." *Knight-Ridder/Tribune Business News.* 28 July 2000.

Hillstrom, Northern Lights
updated by Magee, ECDI

CENSUS DATA

The U.S. Constitution (Article I, Section 2) mandates that a census ("enumeration") of the population be conducted at 10-year intervals. The first census took place in 1790; U.S. marshals went door to door to get the count.

To streamline and speed up the process, Congress established a census office within the Department of the Interior in 1880 for that year's census; it was staffed by professionals for the first time rather than U.S. marshals' agents. In 1902 Congress created a permanent Census Office in the Department of Commerce and Labor. When the Department of Labor split from this department in 1913, the Bureau of the Census stayed in "Commerce." As an element of the Department of Commerce, the Bureau of the Census was also charged by Congress to conduct the Economic Census which takes place at five-year intervals (years ending in 2 and 7). Commerce tracks the economy as a whole and publishes the Gross Domestic Product (GDP) data at quarterly intervals.

After Congress created the Department of Labor, DOL established its own extensive statistical element, the Bureau of Labor Statistics (BLS). BLS tracks labor issues, compensation, and pricing. It is the agency which publishes the Consumer Price Index (CPI). Other federal departments have developed substantial, formal statistical organizations as well, among them notably the departments of Agriculture, Education, Energy, Interior, Justice, Health and Human Services, and Transportation. Statistics in some form are available from virtually all other federal agencies as well, but these are somewhat less formally managed and offered and may be more difficult for the small business owner to find.

Federal statistics are the most complete and comprehensive sources of data available to the small business at the right price: free. Some costs are involved for the publication itself (which may take the form of a printed book, pamphlet, CD, or computer tape), but no payment is required for the substantial work that goes into every survey. Virtually all published data are available for the nation as a whole, for states, for counties, and (for the population census) down to the census tract level, an area of a few blocks. Data are reasonably current. The Bureau of the Census (as well as BLS) conduct a partial survey in between census years. These are used to extrapolate data for the U.S. as a whole.

USEFULNESS OF DATA TO SMALL BUSINESSES

Many advertising, architectural, consulting, economic research, educational, engineering, market research, polling, surveying, and training organizations are small businesses themselves. For this community of users, census data and their counterparts in other agencies are often a major input to—or the very raw material of—the work product that they create. Such businesses, of course, make it their business to understand the data sources, the many intricate problems of data and how to work around them, and, of course, where to get what in what format.

A small business in some other line of work may, however, with relatively low investment in learning, begin to use census data in assessing its market and competition. A starting point might be the Census Bureau's annual County Business Patterns series. The CBP provides data at the county, metropolitan, or zip code level on a number of establishments by industry, employment, and payroll data. Several years' worth of data are usually available so that comparisons can be made year to year. The most recent data will be three years old. Using his or her own county, town, or zip code, the business owner can rapidly get a feel for the competition, the average number of people it employs, and what employees are paid on average. The only requirement is that the owner must know the numerical code for his or her business. Industries are classified using the North American Industry Classification System (NAICS). Getting data on one's NAICS code—and downloading data on one's own industry—can be easily done on the Internet. Internet "fluency," however, is a requirement. The alternative to online searching is to obtain data on paper from the nearest large public library with a department for federal documents.

Data on the size of the market, the housing and income characteristic of one's area, on growth or decline trends in an industry, on money spent on labor, supplies, or capital investments—all this and considerably more are available. It is a law of information science that information is defined by context. Federal data are richly available. Which source might help the small business will depend on the context of its search. Questions about pricing, for instance, can be answered by exploring BLS data. Questions on transportation can be explored using Department of Transportation statistics.

LIMITATIONS

The business seeking information about another company specifically or on a range of companies *by name* will discover that census data hide any and all information that may reveal the particular operational numbers for a single business. Thus if a zip code has only *one* participant in a NAICS industry, the County Business Patterns, for instance, will "hide" the results in a higher NAICS code rather than let the public know how many employees ABC Inc. has and what it pays them. Federal data are most useful for discovering broader trends in markets, prices, employment, output, and purchasing. Specific company-level intelligence may also be available, but only if the company is publicly traded and falls under the regulation of the Securities and Exchange Commission. In such a case, the small business can obtain the filings of that company with the SEC.

Many people, encountering federal data for the first time, also complain that "the statistics are old." Indeed, it takes substantial effort and time to collect statistics from millions of businesses or individuals, to process these data, and then to make them available in printed or electronic forms. Thus three- or four-year-old federal data are "fresh," indeed the most up-to-date available anywhere. Whenever more recent data are cited, they are based on extrapolations and estimates, not genuine *enumeration* such as the Constitution requires.

BIBLIOGRAPHY

U.S. Bureau of the Census. *200 Years of Census Taking: Population and Housing Questions, 1790-1990.* 1989.

U.S. Bureau of the Census. County Business Patterns. Available from http://www.census.gov/epcd/cbp/view/cbpview.html. Retrieved on 27 January 2006.

U.S. Bureau of the Census. Available from http://www.census.gov/index.html. Retrieved on 27 January 2006.

U.S. Department of Labor. Bureau of Labor Statistics. Available from http://www.bls.gov/. Retrieved on 27 January 2006.

Hillstrom, Northern Lights
updated by Magee, ECDI

CERTIFIED LENDERS

Certified lenders are banking institutions that qualify for inclusion in a streamlined lending program maintained by the Small Business Administration. Certified lenders are institutions that have been heavily involved in regular SBA loan-guaranty processing and have met other criteria stipulated by the SBA. When a lender is approved as a SBA certified lender, its applications are given priority by the Small Business Administration. The lender receives a partial delegation of authority and is given a three-day turnaround by the SBA on the loan applications (they also have the option of using regular SBA loan processing). In the mid-2000s, according to the SBA, 10 percent of all SBA business loans passed through certified lenders.

A lending institution can become a part of the SBA's Certified Lender Program (CLP) in one of two ways: 1) It may make a request to an SBA field office for consideration for the program, or 2) An SBA field office may nominate the lender without prompting from the institution. SBA district directors approve and renew a lender's status as part of the CLP. Primary considerations in determining whether the lender will qualify include:

- Whether the applicant has the ability to process, close, service, and liquidate loans.

- Whether the applicant has a good performance history with the SBA (i.e., has it submitted complete and accurate loan guarantee application packages in the past?).

- Whether the applicant has an acceptable SBA purchase rate.

- Whether the applicant seems able to work amicably with the local SBA office.

If a lending institution makes an application for inclusion in the CLP, only to be turned down, it may make an appeal to the AA/FA, whose decision is final.

According to the Small Business Administration, the AA/FA may suspend or revoke CLP status upon written notice providing the reasons are given at least 10 business days prior to the effective date of the suspension or revocation. Lending institutions may lose their status for a variety of reasons, including a poor loan performance record; failure to make the required number of loans; violations of applicable statutes, regulations, or published SBA policies.

Similar to certified lenders are preferred lenders. Banks that qualify as preferred lenders are among the best SBA lenders and enjoy full delegation of lending authority in exchange for a lower rate of guaranty. In other words, they do not have to run an SBA loan past the SBA before approving it. This lending authority has to be renewed every two years, and the lender's portfolio is examined by the SBA on an annual basis. Preferred lenders are also required to employ two SBA-trained loan officers. Preferred loans accounts for about ten percent of all SBA loans.

BIBLIOGRAPHY

Buchanan, Doug. "SBA Fretting Over Adequacy of Credit to Small Companies." *Business First-Columbus.* 17 September 1999.

Heath, Gibson. *Doing Business with Banks: A Common Sense Guide for Small Business Borrowers.* DBA/USA Press, 1991.

Olson, Scott. "Certified Lenders Will Soon Compete: Feds hope changes will boost demand for loans." *Indianapolis Business Journal.* 27 October 2003.

U.S. Small Business Administration. "SBA Assistance." Available from http://www.sba.gov/starting_business/startup/guide5.html. Retrieved on 27 January 2006.

Hillstrom, Northern Lights
updated by Magee, ECDI

CERTIFIED PUBLIC ACCOUNTANTS

Certified public accountants (CPAs) provide a broad range of financial services to small businesses. These services include preparation of financial statements and tax returns, providing advice on various aspects of business (operations, management, etc.), and assisting in the development and installation of effective accounting systems.

Unlike large corporate enterprises, small business owners may not need continuous accounting services. Still, small business owners need to ensure that their enterprise operates in accordance with the complexities of modern finance, and that they have an informed understanding of the business's financial health in order to ensure that they can make sound business decisions. Many entrepreneurs and business owners turn to CPAs for help in these areas. For a small business, financial mismanagement can spell failure; choosing and using the services of a CPA are critical to business success.

QUALIFICATIONS

The CPA has a comprehensive educational background. Each candidate must attend a four-year program in accounting at an accredited institution. A CPA must also pass a standard test for competency in the field. The CPA exam covers four main areas: Law and Professional Responsibility; Auditing Procedures; Accounting and Reporting (taxation and accounting); and Financial Accounting and Reporting. This exam is administered in every state by a state board of accounting.

Individual state boards also set up state regulations for professional licensing standards. This often means that CPAs are required to have professional experience. Each state has requirements that are peculiar to the state, and regulatory efforts are continuous. Recently, for instance, the Katrina hurricane and the devastation it caused has produced changes in CPA practices in Louisiana; in Michigan, new rules were instituted requiring that CPAs submit past work product for peer review in order to have their licenses renewed. A small business wishing to keep up-to-date with current practice can do so by contacting its state board.

There are several organizations for CPAs which also provide information and educate the public on the role of the CPA. The major national organization is the American Institute of Certified Public Accountants (AICPA). Its goals are to provide members with resources and information and to promote public awareness about the CPA profession. The AICPA sets a code of professional standards which serve as guidelines for CPAs in conduct and professional responsibility.

SERVICES

CPAs provide financial services to the general public—which can encompass both private citizens and business enterprises—rather than to one single company. They can act individually or as members of a public accounting firm. A CPA may provide service in one or more areas in which they have been trained, including the following:

- Financial Planning—A CPA may analyze assets, income, and spending in order to give a person a clear picture of his or her financial status. This can be done on an individual basis (retirement planning or investment planning) or on the business level (preparation of pension plans and business investments).

- Tax Preparation—A CPA can be a valuable resource to entrepreneurs seeking help in unraveling various tax codes and their impact on business. This function includes areas such as tax regulation compliance, consultation, and planning and representation.

- Management Advisory Services—Small business owners may need advice on anything from how to file for a business loan to the preparation of a budget. A CPA can assist businesses in preparing financial statements, budgets, strategic planning, and other financial advice.

- Accounting and Auditing—This involves verification of a company's accounting processes, documentation, and data to be certain they conform to accounting principles. In this function, the CPA makes sure that financial statements are in order.

CPAs often specialize in specific areas of the accounting practice, such as auditing and accounting, tax law, or management advisory. They may also specialize in certain industry areas, such as retail, health care, or restaurant businesses.

ENTREPRENEURS AND THE CPA

Entrepreneurs seeking a CPA should look for the following:

- Reasonable Prices—Most CPAs charge competitive rates, but it makes sense to check pricing to be sure that the CPA an entrepreneur is considering is not charging rates exorbitantly higher than his or her competitors. It is always advisable to request a letter from the firm or individual CPA that explicitly states the CPA's fee or billing rate. This letter may also specify the billing and payment methods.

- Good Reputation—Does the CPA come well recommended? Integrity is something people discuss when talking about people who work with financial information. Listening to other business owners can provide valuable information in making your own choices. In addition, trade associations, local business resource centers, and business organizations (such as a local chamber of commerce) are also potentially valuable sources of information when selecting a CPA. As you narrow the field of candidates down, ask for the names of other businesses they serve and follow up with those references.

- Quality and Timeliness of Service—A CPA who does not deliver quality services in a prompt and reliable fashion is of little use to a small business. "Although it seems that all CPAs are similar, they don't all provide the same level of service," noted Thomas Murray in *LI Business News*. "And while price is a factor in any business decision, your choice should be primarily based upon the added value you receive from your relationship with your CPA."

- Flexibility and Adaptability—Can the CPA's business or firm fit your needs? Some CPAs provide only auditing or tax services, while others offer a host of financial planning, retirement, pension, and other services. A business should choose a CPA which can grow as its needs change.

- Communicate—Business owners should be prepared to outline all the services that they believe they will need from their CPA. In some instances, a CPA may realize that the business owner is asking for a scope of services or a level of specialization that he/she cannot provide. If these obstacles can be identified early, both the entrepreneur and the accountant can save themselves a great deal of time and pursue other business opportunities.

Once a CPA has been selected, entrepreneurs should prepare to do some footwork to make the relationship a valuable one. The business owner should be prepared to keep accurate records, including invoices, payments, and amounts spent on business-related expenses. A little bookkeeping goes a long way to improving the service a CPA can provide.

BIBLIOGRAPHY

Lane, Amy. "New Laws Tighten Rules, Penalties for Accountants." *Crain's Detroit Business.* 16 January 2006.

LaRose, Greg. "Louisiana CPA Board Adapts to Post-Katrina Conditions." *New Orleans CityBusiness.* 16 January 2006.

Murray, Thomas J. "Choosing Your Accountant." *LI Business News.* 12 May 2000.

"Net Not Always the Best for Choosing Advisors." *LI Business News.* 23 October 1998.

Shapiro, Leslie. "Future Services of Accountants—an AICPA Perspective." *National Public Accountant.* January/February 1997.

Hillstrom, Northern Lights
updated by Magee, ECDI

CHAMBERS OF COMMERCE

A chamber of commerce is a voluntary association whose membership is comprised of companies, civic leaders, and individual business people. Its members seek to promote the interests of business, typically in a broad-based way. Chambers of commerce exist on municipal, state, regional, national, and even international levels. Today, chambers of commerce—sometimes called boards of trade or commercial associations—can be found in most of the world's industrialized countries.

In the United States, the first chamber of commerce was created in 1768 in New York City. Its stated objectives encompassed "encouraging commerce, supporting industry, adjusting disputes relative to trade and navigation, and producing such laws and regulations as may be found necessary for the benefit of trade in general." Soon other chambers of commerce formed in other major cities. Arising in quick succession during the 19th century, chambers of commerce spread throughout the land and today number in the thousands.

At the local level, chambers of commerce strive to develop and publicize business opportunities in their communities, as well as work for the betterment of local schools and other community institutions. Local chambers of commerce offer a range of programs and services to their members, including information and advice on timely business matters, opportunities for networking, and a variety of publications. Local chambers of commerce also provide their members with numerous forums—task forces, committees, special events, and so on—in which to express their specific views and concerns, whether pertaining to the challenges facing small businesses or to the issues surrounding international commerce. Depending on their geographic settings, local chambers of commerce can be small or large in terms of their membership and scope of activities.

At the national level, chambers of commerce function as a unified voice for their affiliates. The U.S. Chamber of Commerce, for example, counts individual companies, affiliate chambers of commerce, and trade and professional associations among its members. Through them, it represents more than three million business organizations and individuals. Members include business of all sizes, from the Fortune 500 companies to home-based, one-person operations. In fact, 96 percent of the U.S. Chamber of Commerce's membership is made up of companies with fewer than 100 employees.

Founded as a national federation in 1912 and headquartered in Washington, D.C., the national chamber was instrumental in persuading the federal government to institute a national budget and in gaining passage of the Federal Reserve Act. Its chief aims are to: stop perceived over-regulation; push down business taxes; improve labor relations; increase production, develop new markets; provide more jobs; raise educational levels; build better cities; and keep organized business strong and increasingly effective.

To carry out its mission, the national chamber maintains a large staff that engages in a broad spectrum of activities, ranging from informing and counseling its members on key government developments to conducting policy studies and issuing reports, bulletins, booklets, and periodicals. In addition, the national chamber maintains a vigorous stance in making its policies and members' viewpoints known to federal agency personnel, members of Congress, and other public officials. Augmenting the national chamber are four regional offices and 50 foreign-based American chambers of commerce.

At the global level is the International Chamber of Commerce, founded in 1920. This organization constitutes an international federation of business organizations and individuals and as such serves as a powerful voice for business interests worldwide. It holds the highest-ranking status afforded to organizations the United Nations calls on in a consultative capacity. It also operates a prominent court of arbitration to settle international business disputes; utilizes teams of experts to formulate solutions to problems in such areas as communications, law, and financial relations; and issues a quarterly publication entitled *World Trade.* Headquartered in Paris, the International Chamber of Commerce functions as a vital mechanism for articulating global business concerns to world opinion leaders and the public at large.

Junior chambers of commerce, known as the Jaycees, also originated in the 1920s. These associations, evolving from the larger chamber of commerce movement, are composed of young business people in their twenties and thirties. Prevalent throughout the United States and in many other countries as well, junior chambers of commerce principally devote their energies to projects of community improvement.

SEE ALSO *Business Associations; U.S. Chamber of Commerce*

BIBLIOGRAPHY

Cashill, Jack. "When Your Chamber Becomes Your Competitor." *Ingram's.* January 2000.

Pierce, Jan, ed. *World Chamber of Commerce Directory, 2000.* International Chamber of Commerce, 2000.

U.S. Chamber of Commerce. "Business Competitiveness Platform: Recommendations to the Parties." July 2004.

Hillstrom, Northern Lights
updated by Magee, ECDI

CHARITABLE GIVING

Many small business owners engage in charitable giving, either as private individuals or in their corporate capacity. This charitable giving can take many forms, including sponsorship of local charitable events, donations of excess inventory, and sustained philanthropy in one or more areas through the establishment of a formal foundation or council. Whatever form the charitable giving takes, experts and entrepreneurs agree that such activity can have a beneficial impact on the company as well as the charities and institutions it supports.

CONTRIBUTIONS OF GOODS AND SERVICES

Charitable giving by small businesses most often takes the form of contributions of goods and, less often, services. Indeed, many companies have made donations of obsolete, excess, erroneously packaged, or slow-moving inventory. The bottom-line advantages of such donations are considerable for small companies. "Not only can you get rid of that inventory and free up warehouse space, but you also can get a hefty tax deduction—often, more than your production costs—and at the same time help a not-for-profit organization," wrote Marsha Bertrand in *Nation's Business.* Indeed, some companies that donate goods to charitable causes can reap tax deductions that equal the cost of producing those goods plus half the difference between that cost and the fair market value of those goods. The amount of the deduction for which companies are eligible will vary with their legal status. Partnerships, S corporations, and sole proprietorships will only be able to claim deductions amounting to the production cost of the donated goods. But for C corporations, the deduction can be two times the production cost.

Bertrand and others point out, however, that the donated goods will entitle businesses to a deduction only if they meet requirements laid out in the Internal Revenue Service's tax code. For instance, the donor business will qualify for a deduction only if it hands over its goods to a qualified non-profit organization. Moreover, products that are donated must be targeted at helping disadvantaged or otherwise legitimate groups, such as children, the needy, and people who are ill. Finally, donated goods must be handed over unconditionally; the donor business is not allowed to receive compensation in any form for its largess. Despite these restrictions, analysts and companies that have established charitable giving programs agree that making such donations can have a potent positive impact for the participating business.

In addition to the tax deduction and the reduced inventory-carrying costs, companies realize tremendous public relations benefits from corporate giving. According to the "Cone Corporate Citizenship Study" conducted by Boston-based Cone Inc., 8 in 10 Americans say corporate support of causes helps earn their loyalty to a business. C. J. Prince explains in an *Entrepreneur* article on the subject that to many entrepreneurs focused "on keeping costs down and milking every cash-flow dollar, corporate giving sounds like a luxury they just can't afford. But in today's competitive environment, corporate charitable programs and partnerships may be the cheapest strategic competitive edge you can get—not to mention the satisfaction they can bring."

Many businesses that choose to direct their excess inventory toward philanthropic targets have come to realize that there are a number of agencies that can help them in this task. In addition to non-profit organizations themselves, which typically try to make the donation process as easy as possible for donor companies, companies interested in handing over goods can enlist the help of organizations known as exchanges. These organizations serve as middlemen, accepting products from companies and then distributing them to various deserving charitable groups. "In addition to finding an outlet for your goods, exchanges supply you with the proper tax documentation, handle distribution, and ensure that the recipient qualifies under the tax code," stated Bertrand.

ORGANIZED GIVING IN SMALL FAMILY ENTERPRISES

Business experts agree that charitable giving is an activity that, when considered by small family-owned businesses, is particularly rife with both opportunities and challenges. The chief pitfall of charitable giving by members of family businesses is lack of communication. All too often each member of a family involved in a business writes out checks to charities of his or her choosing. One may donate to the cancer society, another to the arts, and a third to yet a different worthy non-profit. When the donations are tallied up a lack of direction and consistency in support is often the result. Analysts encourage owners of family businesses to organize their charitable giving in a cohesive way that can benefit both deserving non-profit organizations and the business itself.

Organizing a Strategy for Philanthropic Giving There is no one organized giving plan that all family-owned businesses should adhere to. Indeed, small and mid-sized family businesses utilize a broad range of charitable strategies, many of which are tremendously effective despite their differences in emphasis, direction, and execution. But most successful giving programs share a common characteristic that is also a hallmark of success in the business arena: proper research and planning. Family businesses seeking to establish a program of charitable giving need to recognize that such policies are predicated on three major issues—choice of charities, size of donations, and the vehicle that will be used to execute donations.

Choice of Charity or Charities—Some family businesses choose to provide financial support only to causes that are personally important to family members, regardless of their influence on the business or industry in which the family is involved. Other families, meanwhile, may choose to steer their charitable giving toward areas that also impact on the family business. A publisher who supports literacy causes, for example, can publicize that connection and boost its public image. A paper manufacturer that supports environmental and deforestation causes may, likewise, create good will in the community.

Of course, many families will discover that agreeing on the primary recipients of a charitable giving program is no easy matter. Some family members may be enthu-

siastic supporters of a non-profit organization, only to find to their dismay that other members are lukewarm or even hostile to that organization's goals and mission. In such instances, consultants urge individuals not to adopt an intransigent position or engage in "tit-for-tat" negotiations in which approval of a charity is withheld until family members agree to provide financial support to a cause of which they may not be enamored. There are plenty of charities out there to which everyone should be able to agree to donate. In instances where disagreements break down along generational lines, another option is to create a three- to five-year plan in which the causes favored by one generation give way over time to those favored by the next generation.

Deciding How Much to Give The size of charitable donations that family-owned businesses give is, of course, directly linked to the size and fortunes of the family business. A family-owned lumber business with several locations and a host of reliable corporate clients is obviously going to be able to make larger donations, if it is so inclined, than are the owners of a single sporting goods store. But no matter what the sum total of donations is, family members should make sure that they arrive at the total together and in an informed fashion. That is, organized giving totals should be arrived at with an eye toward the business's current financial standing and its future business plans and prospects. A company poised on the brink of a major expansion effort, for example, may adopt a more modest strategy of organized giving than would a mature business that requires less reinvestment.

Another consideration that members of family-owned businesses need to weigh is their allocation of time to charities. Certain individuals may be enthusiastic supporters of a charity, giving considerable amounts of time and talent to the organization in order to advance its work. Such selflessness is laudable, but it can also give rise to resentments among fellow family members if they begin to feel they are taking on an unfair share of the company's workload as a result. For this reason, family members should make sure that they communicate the needs of the business as well as the charity to one another through regular meetings. Of course, sometimes a business may find that extensive involvement in charitable work can also pay dividends for the company. A hands-on involvement in charitable work demonstrates a tangible commitment to the cause while also allowing for networking with others in the business community.

Choosing a Vehicle for Giving Many a family-owned business has chosen to establish a philanthropic foundation to guide its charitable activities. This is especially true of families that own larger businesses that can afford to make donations of considerable size. If you intend to donate a very large sum, more than $250,000, there are advantages to setting up a foundation, which is a legal entity recognized under state law and by the IRS as a non-profit corporation. Such foundations are subject to complex rules. Nonetheless, contributions to the foundation are generally tax-deductible, whether they're made by family members or by non-family members who support the foundation's goals. Before committing to a foundation, however, small business owners should consider the various restrictions that apply (foundations are required by law to distribute a minimum of five percent of their net worth to charities every year, for example) and the legal and accounting fees associated with running it.

Another option that some small businesses pursue is the formation of a charitable council. Like individuals, the council can give tax-deductible donations to charities. However, councils are not recognized by or accountable to the IRS and as a result contributors do not receive a tax break on any direct contributions to the council's funds.

BIBLIOGRAPHY
Bertrand, Marsha. "Donations for Deductions." *Nation's Business.* January 1996.

Kahan, Stuart. "Strategies of Charitable Giving." *Accounting Technology.* January 2000.

Prince, C. J. "Give and Receive: When done right, corporate charitable giving can boost company morale and exposure—as well as your bottom line." *Entrepreneur.* November 2005.

Saxe, Douglas S. "Discussing Charitable Giving." *Business First-Columbus.* 22 September 2000.

Stockman, Farah. "For-Profit Businesses Market 'Experience' of Charitable Giving." *Knight-Ridder/Tribune Business News.* 14 December 2000.

Wilkinson Troy, Carol. "Commentary: Breakdown of Charitable Giving in the U.S." *Daily Record, Kansas City, MO.* 6 January 2006.

Hillstrom, Northern Lights
updated by Magee, ECDI

CHILD CARE

Child care has emerged as an important issue for both employers and employees in recent decades. The statistics are telling. In a publication by the U.S. Department of Health and Human Services, Health Resources and Services Administration, Maternal and Child Health Bureau, entitled *Child Health 2004,* the following facts about working mothers are presented. "In 2003, 63 percent of mothers with preschool-aged children

(younger than 6 years) were in the labor force (either employed or looking for work), and 58 percent were actually employed. Of those mothers, 70 percent worked full-time and 30 percent worked part-time. Of women with children ages 6-17, 78 percent were in the labor force in 2003 and nearly all of those were actually employed. Among these employed mothers, 77 percent worked full-time and 23 percent worked part-time." Parents in the U.S. are working outside the home in greater numbers than ever before and the issue of how best to bring up the next generation is one that touches us all.

As early as the mid-1990s a U.S. Department of Labor study observed that, "America has become a society in which everyone is expected to work—including women with young children. But many of society's institutions were designed during an era of male breadwinners and female homemakers. What is needed is a . . . reform of the institutions and policies that govern the workplace to ensure that women can participate fully in the economy and that men and women have the time and resources to invest in their children." Researchers, child care experts, and working parents have been heartened by the success that some businesses have experienced in their efforts to assist their employees in this area, but the consensus remains that many child care arrangements are inadequate for working parents.

This problem is even more acute for single parents who do not have partners who can carry the childcare load in emergency situations. It is also more prevalent in certain industries; studies indicate that working women in professional occupations (typified by high levels of education and salary) are two or three times more likely to receive child care benefits from their employers than are women who work in service, production, and agricultural occupations.

Child Care Policies in the Workplace Child care problems have repercussions for employers as well as employees. Analysts have pointed out that problems with child care can be a significant drain on worker productivity, and in some cases can even result in the permanent loss of valued employees. According to some experts, small businesses are particularly vulnerable to such losses, since they often do not have the financial resources to install the on-site child care centers that have proven beneficial to some larger companies in addressing this issue. But observers contend that small business enterprises have a variety of options at their disposal to help their employees deal with the child care issue.

Of course, the first priority for working parents is ensuring that their children are placed in a child care environment that protects them and attends to their physical and emotional needs. Working parents may have different family situations and child care needs but they all voice the same concerns. Parents want their children to be in a safe environment, shielded from the potential dangers and abuses about which they hear so much in the media. When parents believe their children are safe and secure in another person's care, they feel a sense of relief and are able to attend to other matters more fully.

While safety is the paramount concern in selecting a child care provider, parents also look at other tangible quality factors like cleanliness, licensing, staff certification, and curriculum. Many parents expect the day care environment in which they leave their children to be an enriching environment as well, one in which the children learn. Unfortunately, the state of professional child care in the United States all too often leaves much to be desired. As David Whitman remarked in *U.S. News & World Report,* "the warped dynamic of the child care market is all too plain: There are too many parents chasing too few day-care openings in settings where there is too much turnover of providers who receive too little training and pay." This state of affairs naturally serves to further exacerbate the concerns of working parents seeking to juggle home and office responsibilities.

Intergenerational Care Changing demographics in the United States have also created a situation wherein increasing numbers of working people find themselves dividing their time, energy, and financial resources between two sets of care demands. On one end are small children, while on the other can be found elderly parents. This phenomenon has given rise to the still modest but growing success of so-called "intergenerational care" centers, in which working parents who also have obligations to care for their own elderly parents can place both categories of dependents in a single facility, where they will be cared for. Most experts expect that, given the continued rise in participation by women in the work place—and the track record of success enjoyed by intergenerational care programs in hospitals, nursing homes, and child care centers—the concept of intergenerational care will continue to increase in popularity in the business world. In fact, some studies indicate that demographic trends practically ensure the continued growth of intergenerational care facilities.

Given all of these considerations, observers believe that businesses looking to provide some measure of child care assistance to their employees will factor the elder care issue into their analysis of options with increasing frequency. "Companies that aren't doing anything at all probably could not envision doing on-site intergenerational care, or even elder care," admitted one executive—whose company opened an intergenerational care facility

for its employees—in an interview with *HR Focus.* "But we're finding that companies that are either planning or thinking about on-site child care now are rethinking their space [to accommodate elder care in the future]."

BENEFITS OF CHILD CARE FOR EMPLOYERS

Discussions of child care nearly always center on the desired benefits of such programs for working parents and their children. But some analysts believe that employers can also reap significant benefits from good child care arrangements. This accounts for the steady growth in the percentage of companies that offer some manner of child care assistance to their employees. In 1999, for instance, Hewitt Associates conducted a survey of U.S. employers that indicated that 90 percent of respondents offer child care assistance to workers.

This increase in child care assistance can be directly traced to concerns that employees who are grappling with child care issues are less productive than those who are unencumbered. These workers spend sometimes large amounts of company time on the issue (calling about possible providers, checking on the well-being of sick children, etc.), may fall victim to tardiness, and typically miss several days of work each year due to child care situations. Indeed, studies conducted in the early 1990s indicated that one out of three sick days taken by a working parent is actually due to child-related illnesses that preclude the child's presence at school or his or her usual day-care provider, and that other child care problems can siphon off another seven or eight days of employee attendance on an annual basis.

Some businesses, meanwhile, allow parents to occasionally bring their children to work with them when child care plans fall through. In some business environments, this may not result in dramatic reductions in productivity, but in other settings—such as office environments—this can result in significant productivity downturns for both the parent (who has to divide his or her time between work and child supervision) and co-workers, who are often distracted by the presence of the youngster. Finally, some businesses permanently lose valuable workers who decide, after having a child, that the expense and hassles associated with day care make returning to the workplace a questionable strategy.

Given the above factors, many experts believe that small and large businesses alike should investigate ways in which they can help their employees secure acceptable child care arrangements. By doing so, they may well reap increased benefits in the realm of worker productivity. In addition, they are likely to find that having a program of child care assistance in place can be a tremendous boon in recruiting efforts, and that child care provisions can help companies retain employees who might otherwise stay at home or leave for a competitor that offers meaningful child care benefits.

Finally, companies may find that providing child care programs to workers is not nearly as expensive as they believed, since the provision of child care assistance is tax-deductible to employers. From a company standpoint, assisting employees with their child care needs is good business. A well administered child care program can save a company more money than any other employee benefit. It allows a company to recruit employees more effectively, to reduce turnover and absenteeism, and to increase the productivity of employees.

RESEARCHING EMPLOYEES' CHILD CARE NEEDS

Prior to settling on a methodology by which to help working parents in their employ, businesses should first do some research to learn which alternatives will do the best job of meeting the needs of both the company and its workers. The first step in establishing a sound child care plan is to determine what a company's goals are, what type of corporate culture exists, and how much money it is willing to spend. A child care plan that does not adequately integrate these considerations will almost certainly perform inadequately or fail. In addition, small business owners should make sure that child care is a pressing issue before investing time and money into finding solutions for it. "Make sure that you have a problem in the first place," wrote Dayton Fandray in *Workforce.* "And if you find that a problem exists, measure its dimensions in terms that you can quantify—before you try to fix it."

Employers should consider disseminating a questionnaire or find some other means of assessing the needs and desires of their work force. In addition, business owners and managers should take a good look at the demographic make-up of their employee roster. After all, a company that employs relatively few people under the age of 40 is far less likely to need a comprehensive child care assistance plan than is a business that employs large numbers of women under the age of 35. "Ask how many would be involved in some kind of child care arrangement, the ages of their children and their current arrangements for having those children taken care of," one management consultant told *Nation's Business.* Employee impressions of various child care options and the amounts they are willing to contribute to employer-assisted child care programs should also be solicited.

From there, businesses should investigate the community in which they operate. By checking out what programs the surrounding communities already have to offer, as well as determining both the resources and

barriers to starting new ones, a company can be sure not to overlook existing services. Taking advantage of existing services and possibly subsidizing those services is a more economical solution than try to start from scratch. Finally, companies should try to find ways to accurately evaluate return on investment in their child care policies. This return on investment can take many forms, from increased loyalty and productivity to growth in employee retention rates.

CHILD CARE ASSISTANCE OPTIONS FOR SMALL BUSINESSES

In the past, business enterprises have associated child care almost exclusively in terms of on-site centers, which have been viewed as excessively expensive to build and operate. But proponents of such facilities contend that those opinions are based partly on misconceptions. In addition, child care experts and business consultants alike point to several other options that may be viable for employers, including those of small size. These options include company consortiums, outside referral services, salary reduction plans, and reimbursement plans.

On-Site Facilities Providing on-site child care facilities is the most expensive option for businesses. It requires significant up-front costs and in some cases increased operating costs in such areas as payroll (states have various guidelines on the necessary qualifications of day care facility managers/professionals, which may necessitate hiring new personnel), utilities, and liability insurance (although companies in some areas may be able to avoid increases in this area). But this option also usually provides the greatest peace of mind to employees, who can visit their children during lunch breaks, etc., and dramatically reduces logistics complications that workers face with off-site facilities (routine drop-offs and pick-ups, picking up kids who are sick, etc.). Moreover, the presence of an on-site day care facility is a terrific attraction to prospective employees. And as mentioned above, the expense of establishing an on-site facility can be deducted from taxes. Understandably, however, most of these types of arrangements have been established by larger companies with healthy bottom lines rather than smaller businesses with more modest assets.

Consortiums Consortiums are among the most popular child care alternatives for small businesses with limited resources that nonetheless want to assist their workers in securing good care for their youngsters.

In these programs, several small companies in a geographic region pool their resources to support an off-site day-care center that is operated by a qualified day-care provider. By combining resources, companies can realize significant cost savings while also meeting the child care needs of their employees. They simply pay for a certain number of slots and make the openings available to their employees (unused slots are usually made available to parents who are employed outside the consortium).

Outside Referrals Companies that pursue this option contract with an outside agency to provide their employees with community day care information. This information includes rates, locations, and openings at various licensed facilities. This "information clearinghouse" approach is obviously the least expensive option for businesses, but it may also be the least satisfactory for parents who must still research these various options.

Salary Reduction and Reimbursement Plans A favorite of business owners, who like its minimal expense, salary reduction plans call for the establishment of a flexible spending account that permits employees to reduce their pre-tax incomes by a specified amount and place that money in an account that is used to reimburse them for child care expenses. Reimbursement plans, meanwhile, call for tax-deductible payments that are either paid directly to the child care provider or to the working parents by the company.

In addition to these child care assistance options, business owners can institute other policies that can have a beneficial impact on their employees' ability to balance work and family responsibilities. Flextime, job sharing, work-at-home options, and extended maternity or paternity leaves have all been touted as policies that can be helpful to working parents.

BACKLASH AGAINST CHILD CARE BENEFITS

In recent years, American companies have discovered that new child care (and other family-oriented) policies for working parents have not been universally embraced by their employees. Certainly, these sorts of programs have been applauded by workers who benefit from them, and they are increasingly popular in virtually every industry. But some single and childless employees have expressed resentment over this state of affairs. In fact, a 1996 Conference Board survey of companies with "family-friendly" policies in child care, etc., reported that 56 percent of the companies admitted that childless employees feel resentment about perceived bias in favor of employees with children.

The primary complaint of these single/childless employees is that they are expected to work longer hours and accept lower levels of compensation (in the form of fringe benefits) than co-workers with children. As Dan Seligman explained in *Forbes*, "The tales are of singles who have plans for the evening but are expected to alter

them and cover for the mother whose child has a temperature, and are expected not to ask for the prime-time summer vacation slots, and don't benefit from day care centers, and take it for granted that the money invested in the centers is ultimately coming out of their own pockets." Crafting personnel policies that help working people deal with all types of family obligations is important and making sure that they are fully understood by all employees is equally important.

SEE ALSO *Career and Family; Flexible Spending Accounts*

BIBLIOGRAPHY

Allen, Eugenie. "Home Sick No More: When Mom and Dad Simply Have to Be at Work, Where Do Their Sick Children Spend the Day?" *Time*. 24 April 2000.

Center for American Progress. "Working Mothers Caught in a Bind." Available from http://www.americanprogress.org/ July 2004.

Fandray, Dayton. "What is Work/Life Worth?" *Workforce*. May 2000.

"Few Employers Provide Direct Childcare Help." *IRS Employment Trends*. 15 September 1997.

Seligman, Dan. "Who Needs Family-Friendly Companies?" *Forbes*. 11 January 1999.

U.S. Department of Health and Human Services, Health Resources and Services Administration, Maternal and Child Health Bureau. *Child Health 2004*. 2004.

Vaeth, Elizabeth. "Child-care Presents Challenge, Expense for Working Parents." *Atlanta Business Chronicle*. 6 September 1996.

Whitman, David. "Waiting for Mary Poppins." *U.S. News & World Report*. 24 November 1997.

Hillstrom, Northern Lights
updated by Magee, ECDI

CHILDREN'S ONLINE PRIVACY PROTECTION ACT (COPPA)

The Children's Online Privacy Protection Act (COPPA) is a U.S. federal law designed to limit the collection and use of personal information about children by the operators of Internet services and Web sites. Passed by the U.S. Congress in 1998, the law took effect in April 2000. It is administered and enforced by the Federal Trade Commission (FTC). COPPA is "the first U.S. privacy law written for the Internet," Melissa Campanelli wrote in *Entrepreneur*. "It was written specifically for Internet marketers that operate Web sites visited by children under the age of 13 and collect personal information from those kids. Its purpose is to regulate that collection."

The FTC conducted a survey of 212 Web sites in 1998 and found that 89 percent of them collected personal information from children. Of those that collected data from children, 46 percent did not disclose this fact or explain how the information was used. The law was intended to address this potential problem by requiring Web sites and other online services directed toward children under the age of 13—as well as general audience sites that collect personal information from children—to obtain verifiable consent from the children's parents. "Its stated purpose is to protect children from micro-targeting by advertisers and to minimize the potential for contact with dangerous individuals through chat rooms, e-mail, and bulletin boards by involving parents in kids' online activities," Monica Rogers explained in *Crain's Chicago Business.*

REQUIREMENTS OF COPPA

COPPA applies to a variety of Web sites and services with content that may appeal to children. "In determining whether a Web site is directed toward children, the FTC will consider, among other things, the site's content, language, advertising and intended audience, as well as the use of child-oriented graphics or features," Antony Marks and Keith Klein noted in the *Los Angeles Business Journal.*

But the law also affects general interest sites that collect information from children, whether the site's operators intend to do so or not. "The arm of COPPA is very long because it also applies to general audience Web sites that have actual knowledge that they are collecting personal information from children," Robert Carson Godbey wrote in *Hawaii Business.* "You can easily, and inadvertently, fall into this category. If you invite browsers of your Web site to submit individually identifiable information—which can include name, address, e-mail address, hobbies, interests, information collected through cookies, basically anything that can be individually identified to the person responding, for a variety of reasons, and that information includes age— then you may have 'actual knowledge' that you have collected personal information from children if anyone under 13 responds to your invitation."

COPPA requires the operators of these types of Web sites to include a clearly written privacy notice on their home page and anywhere on their site where user data are collected. The privacy policy must reveal who is collecting and maintaining the information children supply to the Web site and provide information about how to contact them; explain how the children's personal information will be used; and state whether it will be made available to third parties. In addition, COPPA requires Web site operators to obtain "verifiable parental con-

sent" in advance of collecting or using personal information from children. Even when parental consent has been granted once, the site operators must seek consent again any time they make changes in their privacy policies. Exceptions to COPPA's parental consent requirements are allowed for the collection of e-mail addresses in order to seek consent, protect the safety of a child, or respond to a child's one-time request (provided that the e-mail address is deleted immediately afterwards).

The FTC rules cite several acceptable methods for Web site operators to verify parental consent, including a signed form sent via fax or regular mail, a credit card number provided online, calls made on a toll-free telephone staffed by trained personnel, and e-mail accompanied by a digital signature or password. The method used by a certain Web site depends on the type of information collected from children and the way it is used. For example, e-mail consent is acceptable for Web sites that collect personal information only for internal purposes, like marketing to a child based on his or her preferences. Stricter methods are required when the information is made available to third parties.

COPPA COMPLIANCE

The FTC applies penalties for noncompliance ranging up to $11,000 per incident. Although the financial penalty is stiff, a business that failed to comply with the law would likely suffer even worse consequences as a result of negative publicity. After all, who would want their Web site to be known as one that put children at risk? Unfortunately, COPPA compliance can be complicated. "The goals of COPPA are no doubt admirable. The implementation, however, can be daunting," Godbey noted. "The difficulty comes from the requirement of 'verifiable consent' from a parent... How do you obtain verifiable parental consent? How do you verify parental consent in an online environment where the children probably know more about the family computer than their parents do?"

Many online businesses have also complained that COPPA compliance is expensive. According to Campanelli, some of the major costs of compliance include employing staff to compose and maintain the online privacy policy statements, hiring attorneys to review the policies, and coordinating the collection and secure storage of parental consent forms. Experts estimate that these costs would amount to between fifty cents and three dollars per child interaction, or up to $100,000 per year, for a medium-sized Web site. Faced with these potential costs, some sites were forced to limit access to children over the age of 13. Other sites—like the popular United Kingdom-based site for the "Thomas the Tank Engine" series of books and toys—decided to eliminate their e-mail and chat room features because they could not afford to comply with COPPA.

In response to complaints from Web site operators about the cost of compliance, the FTC noted that COPPA was not intended to block kids' access to information on the Internet. Instead, the law's objective is to involve parents in the decision about whether to release children's personal information. Lawmakers argue that children under 13 are not sophisticated enough to make such decisions on their own.

Like all Internet laws, COPPA is somewhat difficult to enforce. For example, tech-savvy youngsters may find ways to forge parental consent. In addition, the law only applies to companies doing business in the United States, whereas the Internet is global in scope. Some entrepreneurs resent the restrictions imposed by COPPA, arguing that the government should not become involved in regulating the Internet. "One of the beauties of the Internet is that an entrepreneur can begin his or her business with minimal investment and regulatory scrutiny," Campanelli noted. They argue that regulation increases costs for small business owners. But other operators of small Web sites for children believe it is their responsibility to protect their users' privacy, even though it can be expensive. "If you're going to play in the kids' arena, you've got to offer safety, even if it costs," Alison Pohn, marketing director for a children's Web site, told Rogers. "If you operate a school or a camp, you invest in having the safest playground equipment and the best lifeguard at the pool. This is no different."

In any case, it is important for small business owners involved in online commerce to be aware of the provisions of COPPA. The full text of the Children's Online Privacy Protection Act is available on the FTC Web site, at www.ftc.gov. In addition, the Direct Marketing Association (DMA) offers a guide to COPPA compliance and a "privacy policy generator" that walks users through the process of creating a compliant policy. Both are available on the DMA Web site, at www.the-dma.org/library/privacy.

BIBLIOGRAPHY

Bagner, Jessica, Amanda Evansburg, Vanessa Kaye Watson, and J. Brooke Welch. "Largest COPPA Civil Penalties to Date in FTC Settlements with Mrs. Fields Cookies and Hershey Food Corporation." *Intellectual Property & Technology Law Journal.* June 2003.

Campanelli, Melissa. "The Wizard of Laws." *Entrepreneur.* February 2001.

DiSabatino, Jennifer. "FTC OKs Self-Regulation to Protect Children's Privacy." *Computerworld.* 12 February 2001.

"Firms May Need to Examine Kid-Oriented Privacy." *Financial Net News.* 31 July 2000.

Godbey, Robert Carson. "The Law of the Line." *Hawaii Business.* November 2000.

Jarvis, Steve. "COPPA Minefield." *Marketing News.* 4 December 2000.

Marks, Antony, and Keith Klein. "Coping with COPPA." *Los Angeles Business Journal.* 31 July 2000.

Retsky, Maxine Lans. "Sites Find COPPA Compliance Mandatory." *Marketing News.* 28 August 2000.

Rogers, Monica. "Kids' Privacy Act Stings Web Sites; New Guidelines Limit Sharing of Data with Others." *Crain's Chicago Business.* 15 May 2000.

Rosencrance, Linda. "FTC Warns Sites to Comply with Children's Privacy Law." *Computerworld.* 24 July 2000.

Hillstrom, Northern Lights
updated by Magee, ECDI

CHOOSING A SMALL BUSINESS

The individual who decides to establish his or her own small business stands on the cusp of an exciting and potentially rewarding period of life. But he or she also faces a number of decisions that will likely have a considerable impact not only on the ultimate success of the entrepreneurial venture, but also the very character of the individual's life. Of these decisions, perhaps none is more significant than choosing the type of small business that they will establish and maintain.

Factors that should be considered before choosing a small business are numerous, ranging from financial and family issues to those of personal fulfillment and work background. Most consultants recommend that before embarking on an entrepreneurial venture, would-be small business owners start by taking the time to examine their personal strengths and weaknesses, a seemingly fundamental step that, amazingly enough, is sometimes given short shrift in the decision-making process.

Yet a self-examination of positive and negative attributes is of little use to the prospective entrepreneur if he or she rationalizes or discounts negative qualities and overstates positive qualities. Honesty is essential, after all, because these good and bad qualities are going to be the foundation of your business. It is better to find out that the base is insufficiently strong to support your enterprise before you begin building it rather than after. The list should be a comprehensive one, including both personal and professional attributes.

The personal attributes will tend to cover characteristics like your ability to get along with others, your level of self-motivation, your talent for written and oral communication, your temperament, your organizational abilities, and your capacity for forcefully dealing with unpleasant people (customers, employees, vendors, etc.). An assessment of your professional attributes should include your expertise in various business tasks that you will need to attend to yourself or through oversight of another's work. These business tasks include bookkeeping, marketing/advertising, sales, financial planning, project management, research, and computers/technology. Once a would-be entrepreneur has taken the time to list his or her attributes, she will be able to glean not only what qualities she already has, but also what areas need shoring up (via training, assistance from employees, etc.). As countless entrepreneurs and researchers can attest, the strengths and weaknesses of the establishment's owner are, more often than not, reflected in the business itself.

In addition, such an exercise allows the prospective entrepreneur to match his or her personality with a business whose inherent characteristics are compatible. If there is a mutual attraction between what a person enjoys and the type of business he or she intends to operate, it will greatly enhance the likelihood of success. In other words, doing what one likes to do will allow one to work to full potential.

Of course, some people are not well-suited, either in terms of skills or temperament, to run any kind of small business. Successful small business owners are often characterized by self-confidence, energy, and creativity; those who lack some or all of these qualities should think long and hard before launching a business enterprise. Indeed, confidence, determination, and creativity are perhaps the most important personal characteristics necessary for success. During the early years of any new business there will be day when everything will go wrong. An ability to keep striving through times like these, to start every days with confidence that obstacles will be overcome, is important to success.

WEIGHING THE ALTERNATIVES

Most people who start a successful business have an idea for the business before they even think of it as a business. Typically, new business ideas are inspired by one of four sources: 1) previous work experience; 2) education or training; 3) hobbies, talents, or other personal interests; or 4) recognition of an unanswered need. Whatever the inspiration, potential small business owners need to consider a broad spectrum of factors when choosing whether or not to follow that inspiration and start a new business.

OBJECTIVES

People establish businesses for themselves for a wide variety of reasons. Some entrepreneurs simply tire of being a cog in a larger business enterprise and pine for greater independence, while others are determined to carve out a life for themselves in which they can make a living doing something that they already love to do in their spare time. And, of course, many people take the small business ownership plunge in hopes of improving their financial fortunes or creating a more compatible lifestyle for themselves.

Identifying clearly what you want from a business is essential since what is desired may conflict directly with the realities of the requirements of the business one intends to start. For example, someone who hopes to spend more time with his or her family in the evenings should not decide to open a restaurant or bar. An article in the *San Diego Business Journal* describes the potential pitfalls to be avoided when starting a new business. "If you have a hobby you enjoy, don't assume you can turn it into a business, and 'work and play' at the same time. The hobby may stop being fun if it becomes an obligation, or, if you continue pursuing your hobby, you may ignore the business issues, and your company may never reach its full potential." Matching up one's goals with the likely requirements of running a particular business is essential to success.

RISK ASSESSMENT

Once a prospective entrepreneur has taken stock of his or her personal and professional talents and areas of interest, consideration of compatible small business options can begin. But even after the entrepreneur has settled on a business idea that seems like an ideal match, a diligent period of risk assessment should be undertaken. After all, starting a new business usually has significant repercussions in various areas of the entrepreneur's life (and the lives of the entrepreneur's family members).

Factors that need to be studied include the following:

- Financial Situation—This is usually the single most important factor to consider. Not only do would-be entrepreneurs need to assess their current financial standing, they also need to undertake a comprehensive examination of business start-up costs (including initial operating expenses) and likely—not hoped for—business financial fortunes in the first few years of operation. Quantitative financial analysis is a must.

- Impact on Friends and Family—Family members and friends can often provide valuable insights into the pros and cons of various new business proposals. Starting a business is an endeavor that will involve family and friends, indirectly if not directly. Having their support from the beginning is very helpful.

- Market for Business's Products or Services—Would-be entrepreneurs need to research the potential market for their business, and the various steps needed to reach and expand on that audience.

- Industry Health and State of Competition—A business does not operate in a vacuum. Generally, a company is subject to the same conditions that affect the overall industry. If consumer spending declines and retail industries as a whole suffer, there's a good chance that a neighborhood boutique will not be immune and will suffer poor sales. While it is certainly possible to make money in an industry that is experiencing hard times, one can only do so if a conscious effort is made to position the company appropriately. In addition, start-up businesses often find that raising capital is a considerably more difficult task if the business is in a struggling business sector.

- Choice of Partners and/or Managers—Selecting partners and/or key personnel for your new business venture is a task that is both fraught with peril and bursting with possibility. The addition of a talented, enthusiastic business partner or experienced, trustworthy management staff can help get your business off to a sound, promising start. However, taking on an unreliable partner because this person can bring along a big up-front investment can put a swift end to entrepreneurial dreams.

- Franchising Option—Many entrepreneurs choose to make their first venture into the world of small business ownership with a franchise. The franchise market offers opportunities in market segments. The initial entry may be higher with a franchising arrangement. These arrangements also provide a proven business plan and usually offer training for a new entrepreneur as well. This support is comforting to many new business owners and well worth the cost.

Prospective small business owners also need to take precautions to make sure that they are basing their decision to open a new business or buy an existing one on sound business criteria rather than emotionalism, which often strikes hardest during periods of personal stress. For example, some consultants and researchers warn would-be entrepreneurs of the hazards of making huge career decisions during a divorce. Others note that the period right after losing a job is usually not the best time to open a new business. Having thought through things and planned thoroughly before launching a new business enterprise can help to avoid the sort of problems that can arise if the decision to start a business is made too quickly or impulsively.

BIBLIOGRAPHY

Friedman, Caitlin, and Kimberly Yorio. *The Girl's Guide to Starting Your Own Business.* HarperCollins. 1 January 2004.

Moltz, Barry J. *You Need to Be a Little Crazy: The Truth About Starting and Running Your Own Business.* Dearborn Trade Publishing. 2003.

"Pitfalls to Avoid When Starting Up a New Business." *San Diego Business Journal.* 9 June 2003.

Steingold, Fred. *Legal Forms for Starting and Running a Small Business.* Nolo Press, 1 February 2004.

"Ten Myths and Realities about Becoming an Entrepreneur." *Phoenix Business Journal.* 29 September 2000.

*Hillstrom, Northern Lights
updated by Magee, ECDI*

CLEAN AIR ACT

The Clean Air Act of 1970 is a U.S. federal law intended to reduce air pollution and protect air quality. The act—which underwent major revisions in 1990 and 2003—deals with ambient air pollution (that which is present in the open air) as well as source-specific air pollution (that which can be traced to identifiable sources, such as factories and automobiles). The Clean Air Act sets standards for air quality that limit the amount of various pollutants to specified levels. The Clean Air Act also sets deadlines for governments and industries to meet the standards. The federal Environmental Protection Agency (EPA) is ultimately responsible for establishing standards and enforcing the Clean Air Act, although much of the daily business of fighting air pollution takes place at the state and local levels.

The Clean Air Act affects American businesses in a number of ways. Polluting industries may be forced to control air pollution through end-of-pipe methods, which capture pollution that has already been created and remove it from the air. Or businesses may be required to implement preventative measures, which limit the quantity of pollutants produced in the course of their operations. The cost of compliance with Clean Air Act regulations can be high for companies but the cost to society of air pollution is also quite high. What is clear is that the Clean Air Act has been largely successful in reducing air pollution. According to a report by the National Center for Public Policy Research entitled *Earth Day 2004 Fact Sheet,* it has contributed to a reduction in total emissions of major air pollutants in the United States of 25 percent between 1970 and 2004, and this despite the fact that U.S. gross domestic product increased 42 percent during the same period.

MAJOR PROVISIONS OF THE ACT

The original version of the Clean Air Act, which was passed by the U.S. Congress in 1970, was fairly straightforward. It placed the Environmental Protection Agency in charge of monitoring and improving the nation's air quality. The EPA's powers under the act included establishing research programs, setting clean air standards, enforcing regulations, and providing technical and financial assistance to state and local government efforts toward reducing air pollution. The 1970 act also directed the EPA to establish National Ambient Air Quality Standards (NAAQS) to control the emission of a number of substances that threatened air quality. The NAAQS divided pollutants into two categories: primary pollutants, or those directly affecting human health; and secondary pollutants, or those indirectly affecting human welfare.

The Clean Air Act underwent significant changes and amendments in 1990. The amendments brought widespread reform to the government's methods of dealing with all kinds of air pollution. For example, the 1990 revisions specifically targeted acid rain, with the goal of reducing the emissions of sulfur dioxide and nitrogen oxides by half. The reforms also established new limits on ozone—a prime contributor to smog—in urban areas. Cities that failed to meet the regulations were divided into five different categories of non-attainment areas, with specific ozone emission goals for each category. Another change to the act addressed the depletion of the protective ozone layer in the earth's atmosphere. It mandated the gradual phasing out of chlorofluorocarbons (CFCs) and other ozone-depleting chemicals.

The Clean Air Act of 1990 also placed new regulations on automobile emissions. It set targets for reducing the emissions of hydrocarbons and nitrogen oxides by vehicles and assembly plants. It also required new automobiles to meet stricter pollution standards, whether by installing pollution control equipment like catalytic converters or by burning cleaner fuels. Another major provision of the Clean Air Act dealt with toxic air pollutants. The 1990 amendments expanded the number of regulated substances from 7 to 189, set safety standards for factories where toxic chemicals were used or emitted, and required polluters to install the best available pollution control equipment.

In early 2003 a new law to amend the Clean Air Act was introduced before the Senate. The proposed law, entitled the Clear Skies Act of 2003, is based on an initiative by the same name put forward by President George W. Bush. The Clear Skies Act is controversial because it proposes amending the Clean Air Act substantially, changing many of the mandated emission reduction goals and altering the way in which emission controls would be implemented. According to one of the bill's sponsors, Senator James Inhofe, Republican of Oklahoma, "Moving beyond the confusing, command-and-control mandates of the past, Clear Skies cap-and-trade system harnesses the power of technology and innovation to bring about significant reductions in harmful pollutants." As of early 2006, the Clean Air Act remains in committee, having failed to garner enough support to be passed into law.

ACT FACES COURT CHALLENGES

In 1997, the EPA established strict new regulations to control the release of ozone and particulates, two dangerous pollutants that agency experts believed are responsible for killing thousands of Americans each year. In fact, *Business Week* reported that EPA estimates showed that the new rules could prevent 15,000 premature deaths, 350,000 cases of asthma, and one million cases of impaired lung function annually, in addition to saving billions of dollars in health care costs.

But business groups felt that the new regulations were too broad and would impose excessive compliance costs on industry. Associations representing a number of different industries joined in suing to overturn the EPA rules. They argued that the agency had overstepped its authority in imposing the restrictions under the Clean Air Act, and had thus infringed on the constitutional power of Congress to pass laws. The industry groups also argued that the EPA should be forced to consider the costs as well as the benefits of such actions.

The lawsuit, *Browner v. American Trucking Associations,* went before the U.S. Supreme Court in the fall of 2000. In arguments before the court, the EPA claimed that it was banned by a 20-year-old federal court ruling from considering costs when imposing new regulations. In 2001 the Supreme Court upheld this argument, ruling in favor of the EPA.

SEE ALSO *Environmental Law and Business*

BIBLIOGRAPHY
Bassett, Susan. "Clean Air Act Update." *Pollution Engineering.* July 2000.

"Earth Day 2004 Fact Sheet." The National Center for Public Policy Research. Available from http://www.nationalcenter.org/EarthDay04Progress.html Retrieved on 24 January 2006.

Hess, Glenn. "Supreme Court Examines Arguments Concerning Clean Air Act Regulations." *Chemical Market Reporter.* 13 November 2000.

Kilian, Michael. "Bush Administration Pushes Plan to Change Air Pollution Regulation." *Chemical Market Reporter.* Chicago Tribune, 27 January 2005.

Marriott, Betty Bowers. *Environmental Impact Assessment: A Practical Guide.* McGraw-Hill, 1997.

"Regulators: By Whose Authority?" *Business Week.* 16 October 2000.

Trzupek, Richard. *Air Quality Compliance and Permitting Manual.* McGraw-Hill Professional, 2002.

Varva, Bob. "The 1970 Clean Air Act Changes Rules on Fuels and the Environment." *National Petroleum News.* August 2000.

*Hillstrom, Northern Lights
updated by Magee, ECDI*

CLEAN WATER ACT

The Clean Water Act is a U.S. federal law that regulates the discharge of pollutants into the nation's surface waters, including lakes, rivers, streams, wetlands, and coastal areas. Passed in 1972 and amended in 1977 and 1987, the Clean Water Act was originally known as the Federal Water Pollution Control Act. The Clean Water Act is administered by the U.S. Environmental Protection Agency (EPA), which sets water quality standards, handles enforcement, and helps state and local governments develop their own pollution control plans.

The original goal of the Clean Water Act was to eliminate the discharge of untreated waste water from municipal and industrial sources and thus make American waterways safe for swimming and fishing (the use of surface water for drinking purposes is covered under separate legislation, the Safe Drinking Water Act). Toward this end, the federal government provided billions of dollars in grants to finance the building of sewage treatment facilities around the country. The Clean Water Act also required businesses to apply for federal permits to discharge pollutants into waterways, as well as to reduce the amount of their discharges over time.

The Clean Water Act has been credited with significantly reducing the amount of pollution that enters the nation's waterways from "point sources," or municipal and industrial discharges. As of 1998, 60 percent of American lakes, rivers, and shoreline were considered clean enough for swimming and fishing. "In the years following passage of the Clean Water Act, the EPA largely succeeded in stemming the 'point source' discharges of big industrial and municipal offenders, whose pipes spewed chemicals directly into oceans, rivers, lakes, and streams," wrote Jeff Glasser and Kenneth T. Walsh in *U.S. News & World Report.* "It has become clear, however, that 'point source' pollution is only part of the problem."

By the late 1990s, the EPA had changed its focus under the Clean Water Act to emphasize eliminating nonpoint source pollution, like chemicals from agricultural runoff or erosion from logging or construction activities. In a 2000 report to Congress, the EPA cited these diffuse sources of pollution as the top factors making the remaining 40 percent of the nation's waterways too polluted for swimming or fishing. As scientists increasingly recognized the value of wetlands in filtering out pollution, the EPA also began to emphasize wetlands protection under the Clean Water Act. Businesses must be aware of the expanding applications of the Clean Water Act. The law can affect not only discharges of pollution from factory pipes, but also incidental pollution resulting from the activities of smaller enterprises, such as residential development or the construction of a golf course or office building.

PROVISIONS CREATE CONTROVERSY

Under the Clean Water Act, the EPA sets national water quality criteria and specifies levels of various chemical pollutants that are allowable under these criteria. The discharge of regulated chemicals into surface waters is controlled by the National Pollutant Discharge Elimination System (NPDES), which requires polluters to obtain federal permits for every chemical they discharge. The permits, which can be issued by the EPA or by state government agencies, gives a business or municipality the right to discharge a limited amount of a specific pollutant. The NPDES has been criticized by industry groups for issuing ambiguous regulatory policies and causing long delays in granting permits. In 2000, the EPA sought to address these concerns through a number of initiatives designed to streamline the permit process for municipal and industrial discharges of wastewater.

The EPA also took steps toward cleaning up polluted waterways and regulating nonpoint source pollution in 2000. The agency introduced new rules that encouraged individual states to identify dirty waterways and establish standards to help eliminate sources of pollution. The states were required to come up with a maximum amount of pollution that each waterway could absorb. This measurement was known as the Total Maximum Daily Load (TMDL). Then the states had to decide which local landowners or businesses needed to reduce their pollution levels to meet the TMDL. The states were also required to evaluate future development plans near the waterways to make sure they would not increase pollution levels.

It soon became clear that the TMDL program would be very controversial. "At the heart of the controversy is a long-neglected provision of the Clean Water Act that requires states to identify rivers and lakes too polluted to meet water-quality standards for fishing and swimming," Margaret Kriz explained in *National Journal.* "Under the watchful eye of the EPA, each state must rank its waterways for cleanup and develop site-specific plans for curbing pollution flowing into the water body."

Some cities and industry groups worried that the new provisions would discourage development along already-polluted waterways and restrict the rights of property owners. Others complained that compliance with the new regulations would be too expensive. Finally, some people claimed that the new regulations served only to expand the EPA's influence over state and local government matters. But former EPA director Carol Browner disagreed with this assessment. "There's been a certain amount of misinformation about this being a top-down, one-size-fits-all approach. That's not true," Browner told Kriz. "The TMDL approach is led by the states. They assess the pollution levels of their own waters, and they make the key decisions about reducing pollution in each body of water based on state water-quality standards."

Another area of controversy involves the regulation of wetlands and the need to obtain federal permits to build on a wetland. Under the provisions of the Clean Water Act, the U.S. Army Corps of Engineers has jurisdiction over navigable waterways and associated wetlands. Two consolidated law suits—Carabelli v. United States Army Corp of Engineers and United States v. Rapanos—are scheduled to be heard by the U.S. Supreme Court in the summer of 2006. In each case there is a dispute as to whether a particular wetland falls under the jurisdiction of the Clean Water Act. The ruling in these cases will determine whether and when a non-navigable and even man-made waterway, such as a ditch or storm-sewer system, can be considered a "navigable water" under the Clean Water Act and thus be subject to federal permitting requirements. These cases are being watched very closely by builders, developers, and municipalities since their outcome will have a bearing on the permitting requirements for all future developments on and/or near wetlands.

As with most regulatory laws, clarifications of the law are ongoing. Businesses involved in any way with more than a limited, non-industrial use of water must follow developments related to the protection of waterways.

SEE ALSO *Environmental Law and Business*

BIBLIOGRAPHY

Agnese, Braulio. "Legal Action." *Builder.* January 2006.

Glasser, Jeff, and Kenneth T. Walsh. "A New War over the Nation's Dirty Water." *U.S. News and World Report.* 17 July 2000.

Hoover, Kent. "Builders: 'Clarification' of Wetlands Law Illegal." *Business First of Buffalo.* 21 August 2000.

Kriz, Margaret. "Testing the Waters at the EPA." *National Journal.* 22 April 2000.

Marriott, Betty Bowers. *Environmental Impact Assessment: A Practical Guide.* McGraw-Hill, 1997.

O'Reilly, Brendan. "EPA, Lawmakers, and Timber Fight to the End." *Arkansas Business.* 11 December 2000.

Steinway, Daniel M. "Court Case Offers Prospect of Liability Protection under the Clean Water Act." *Corporate Counsel.* October 2000.

Hillstrom, Northern Lights
updated by Magee, ECDI

CLOSELY HELD CORPORATIONS

Closely held firms are those in which a small group of shareholders control the operating and managerial policies of the firm. Over 90 percent of all businesses in the United States are closely held. These firms differ from most publicly traded firms, in which ownership is widely disbursed and the firm is administered by professional managers. Most—but not all—closely held firms are also family businesses. Family businesses may be defined as those companies where the link between the family and the business has a mutual influence on company policy and on the interests and objectives of the family. Families control the operating policies at many large, publicly traded companies. In many of these firms, families remain dominant by holding senior management positions, seats on the board, and preferential voting privileges even though their shareholdings are significantly less than 50 percent.

VALUATION ISSUES

One of the major concerns associated with closely held firms is the determination of their value. This uncertainty is largely due to the fact that shares of a closely held business are owned by a small number of stockholders, and often by members of a family. Because there is no established market for the shares, it is difficult to establish the value of the shares in an estate or gift tax situation.

In preparing a valuation report, the Internal Revenue Service has established a set of major guidelines to follow. According to the IRS, the proper estimate of value should be based on the price at which a property would change hands between a willing buyer and a willing seller, with neither party under any compulsion to buy or sell and with all relevant facts available to both parties (the fair market value standard). The IRS provides valuation criteria for closely held businesses that are generally accepted by appraisers and the courts. The criteria include the history of the business, economic outlook, book value, earning capacity, dividend-paying capacity, goodwill and other intangibles, past sales of company stock, and stock of comparable businesses.

Without a marketplace that reflects the price arrived at by both buyer and seller, the security prices of a closely held firm must be set by calculation, comparison, and the use of financial ratios. Valuation techniques that have evolved fall into three principal categories: 1) market (price-earnings) methods, 2) cash flow methods, and 3) book value (balance sheet) methods. Another area of concern when addressing valuation issues is the notion of discounts for minority interests and lack of marketability.

BUY/SELL AGREEMENTS

It is important to have detailed plans and procedures for the sale or transfer of stock at the time of the death, disability, or retirement of a shareholder in a closely held firm. Without such procedures, the departure of one major shareholder could also signal the end of a business. Buy/sell agreements, also known as Shareholder Agreements, spell out the terms governing sale of company stock to an outsider and thus protect control of the company. In many instances, these agreements allow co-owners to buy out heirs or other shareholders in the event of death or disability. In order to be considered valid for estate tax purposes, a stock buy/sell agreement must meet several conditions, including a "full and adequate consideration" provision. Life insurance is often used to provide the funds to purchase the shares of a closely held company if one of the owners dies.

There are two basic types of buy/sell agreements: cross-purchase agreements and redemption agreements. With a cross-purchase agreement, one owner separately purchases a policy on the other owner (or owners). With a redemption agreement, the corporation is obligated to redeem the stock at a price set in the agreement if any of the business owners dies. Typically, the buy/sell agreements are funded with life insurance; the life insurance proceeds provide the necessary funds for the purchase of the business.

The prolonged disability of a principal can also present serious difficulties for closely held firms. A long-term disability buy/sell agreement can provide a cushion to protect the disabled principal's interests during recovery. The first step in implementing such an agreement is to determine how long the company should be without the disabled partner's services before a buyout is activated. It is recommended that an actual buyout of ownership interest be postponed at least 12 months but not more than 24 months after the infirmity occurs.

SEE ALSO *Family Business*

BIBLIOGRAPHY

Bennedsen, Morten, and Daniel Wolfenzon. "The Balance of Power in Closely Held Corporations." *Journal of Financial Economics.* October-November 2000.

Einhorn, Stephen. "Selling the Valued Family Business." *Adhesives Age.* June-July 2003.

Green, Charles H. *Streetwise Financing the Small Business.* Adams Media, 2003.

Linton, Heather. *Streetwise Business Valuation.* Adams Media, 2004.

McEvoy, Michael R., and Christopher M. Potash. "Dividing a Closely Held Corporation When a Couple Divorce." *Estate Planning.* February 1996.

Stronzniak, Peter. "Who Will Succeed You?" *Inside Business.* December 2002.

Schnee, Edward J. "Challenging Excess Compensation." *Journal of Accountancy.* December 1998.

Hillstrom, Northern Lights
updated by Magee, ECDI

CLUSTERS

Clusters are geographic concentrations of interconnected companies or institutions that manufacture products or deliver services to a particular field or industry. Clusters arise because they increase the productivity with which companies within their sphere can compete. Clusters typically include companies in the same industry or technology area that share infrastructure, suppliers, and distribution networks. Supporting firms that provide components, support services, and raw materials come together with like-minded firms in related industries to develop joint solutions and combine resources to take advantage of market opportunities. These are groups of related businesses and organizations—sometimes direct competitors, but more often operating in a complementary manner. They may comprise more than just one industry and a true cluster is more than just a supplier-producer-buyer model.

An economic cluster, or several clusters, serves as the driving force in most regional economies. Examples include Detroit's auto industry concentration, computer chip production in California's Silicon Valley, London's financial sector, the Napa Valley's wine production, and Hollywood's movie production industry. Because clusters are a vibrant economic force, the development and upgrading of clusters is an important economic development objective for governments and other organizations involved in regional economic development efforts.

The clustering concept was popularized by Harvard Business School Professor Michael Porter (1990). His techniques teach communities to analyze their existing business and industrial bases and build their economic development on those strengths. From the identified clusters in an area, the next step is to develop a marketing plan for industry.

By developing a massive database of companies, county by county, Dr. Porter's research has statistically grouped businesses together in clusters. A strong cluster will include the suppliers of raw materials and the distributors, as well as the primary producers. But it will also include specialized services in finance, marketing, packaging, education, and more, including specialized trade associations. In general, the broader the base of related businesses, the better for the cluster, for that often reflects the specialization that comes with concentrated resources.

Related firms and industries have tended to locate in close geographical proximity for a number of reasons. In his 1916 economic text, Alfred Marshall was one of the first to identify the benefits of spatial clustering. These benefits include: the existence of a pooled market for specialized workers; the provision of specialized inputs from suppliers and service providers; and the rapid flow of business-related knowledge among firms, which results in technological spillovers. It may be difficult to predict where clusters will emerge beforehand, but once established their growth is predictable due to the benefits gained from the strategy and the economies of scale produced. A variety of terms are synonymous to a cluster; these include co-location, industrial districts, and innovative milieus.

BENEFITS OF CLUSTERING

A well-developed concentration of related business spurs three important activities: increased productivity (through specialized inputs, access to information, synergies, and access to public goods), more rapid innovation (through cooperative research and competitive striving), and new business formation (filling in niches and expanding the boundaries of the cluster map).

Clusters are always changing. They respond to the constant shifting of the marketplace. They usually begin through entrepreneurship. Silicon Valley is a relatively new cluster of computer-related industries; in the past, Detroit was the same for automobiles. Nothing sparks productive innovation better than having your competitor across the street.

Clustering helps cities and counties direct their economic development and recruiting efforts. It also encourages communities to refocus efforts on existing industries. Communities understand that the best way to expand their own economies and those of the surrounding region is to support a cluster of firms rather than to try to attract companies one at a time to an area. Chambers of Commerce, business incubators, and some universities work with companies to develop clusters and synergies in business communities.

Strong domestic clusters also help attract foreign investment. If clusters are leading centers for their industries, they will attract all the key players from both home and abroad. In fact, foreign-owned companies can enhance the leadership of the cluster and contribute to its upgrading, according to research by Julian Birkinshaw (2000), Chair and Professor of Strategic and International Management at the London Business School.

For small and developing businesses, locating in a cluster near competitors and related industries may aid the firm in faster growth, recognition, and status within the market. Economies of scale can be gained by group purchasing within the cluster. There can be discussions among cluster members about their unique competitive advantages and future challenges. Linked supply chain networks can naturally be created within a tightly-linked cluster. Informal day-to-day contact with similar companies is also important and physical location proximity is not always required to be a cluster. Many firms, including retailers and publishers, can be grouped together in "cyberspace" by sharing an Internet site.

Potential Downside of Clusters A concentrated industrial base has one potential downside if the concentration is oriented too closely to a single industry. A community that has reaped the benefits of a cluster for a long period of time may also find it very difficult to adjust during a time of downturn for the industry central to their cluster. The difficulties being experienced by the State of Michigan during the early 2000s is an example of this phenomenon. The decline of the American automobile manufacturing industry has had an especially profound impact on metropolitan Detroit and its surroundings, areas that have consistently had the highest unemployment rates in the country during the first decade of the new century. In an early 2006 *New York Times* article entitled "Putting the Motor City Back in Gear," the decline of the "Big Three" American automakers was described as the sad story of armies in retreat and a retreat that is feeling more and more like a rout. Some diversity within an industrial concentration is desirable. The most promising clusters are those that include more than a single industry because diversity provides the flexibility necessary to change with evolving market trends and broader economic transitions.

A CLUSTER EXAMPLE: "THE CARPET CAPITAL OF THE WORLD"

The city of Dalton, Georgia—located between Atlanta, Georgia, and Chattanooga, Tennessee—is unrivaled in its production of carpet. Almost 90 percent of the functional carpet produced worldwide is made within a 25-mile radius of Dalton. In their 1999 book about the industry, Randall L. Patton and David B. Parker note that Dalton has evolved in much the same way as California's Silicon Valley, through a rapid expansion of new firms started by entrepreneurs and through cooperation among owners, mills, and local government. It was only after World War II that the carpet industry came to be identified with this region. Entrepreneurs developed a new tufting technology and captured the carpet industry previously dominated by woven-wool carpet manufacturers in the Northeast.

The six largest carpet companies and 18 of the largest 35 carpet companies are headquartered in Georgia. The carpet cluster includes the carpet tufting mills, yarn mills, finishers, backing manufacturers, machinery suppliers, maintenance services, and sample companies that directly support the carpet industry. Seventy-five to eighty percent of the yarn used by the carpet industry is produced and processed in Georgia. Over 50,000 employees in Dalton are engaged in carpet manufacturing, and seventy-two interstate trucking companies are utilized to transport carpet and raw materials, in addition to fleets owned by many carpet companies.

A CLUSTERING MODEL IN PROGRESS

Porter recently applied his work in industry clusters and economic analysis to the community that includes the carpet cluster. His data is available at the county level and organizes businesses into some 50 industry clusters producing non-local goods and services. Many familiar businesses are excluded. Fast-food restaurants, automobile dealers, and newspapers, for instance, are spread rather evenly across the country, for they serve basically local customers.

Porter also helped the city of Chattanooga, Tennessee, to perform a cluster analysis. To implement a regional growth initiative, the city appointed two groups: a steering committee of 25 members, including prominent business and government leaders, to provide guidance and policy direction; and a core team of business and academic leaders to research local conditions and manage cluster team meetings. The region for study was based on geographic features, political boundaries, local sentiments, economic strengths, and even commuting patterns. For each cluster, a "location quotient" was developed and defined as the cluster's strength here compared to what might be expected if that industry were spread evenly across the country.

The "Textiles and Floor Coverings Cluster," centered in Dalton but with related businesses elsewhere in the region, was by far the strongest cluster. The carpeting businesses also accounted for most of the strength in the second strongest cluster, "Construction Materials." Three additional clusters emerged: "Confectionery and Baked Goods," "Tourism and Hospitality," and "Medical Devices and Health Services."

Leaders in each field, and others from lists generated by Standard Industry Classification code numbers, were invited to become part of the cluster team and attend a series of meetings over four weeks. The agenda for the teams included a discussion of conditions in the cluster; issues holding the cluster back; opportunities for creating better inputs, sharper demand, and high-quality related institutions; and problems with regulation, the labor pool, and the physical infrastructure. The meetings also included a discussion of what cluster team members could do about these issues; what types of legislation or change in processes could make the cluster better; cooperative efforts toward applied research; and ways to attract complementary businesses to the region.

The immediate goal was a plan for action that went well beyond analysis. The ultimate goal was to accomplish change. The core or "diamond" of the cluster included: factor input conditions (labor, capital, resources, etc.); demand conditions (nature of the home market, including any special conditions or expertise locally); related and supporting industries (from service industries to trade associations); and context for firm strategy and rivalry (the level of entrepreneurship, and tradition of united actions). The team in Chattanooga learned that concentrated competition leads to greater prosperity, and the best strategy means not trying to do all things but focusing on your cluster. There was also a more general appreciation that the cluster process could, indeed, lead to more and better-paying jobs and that a strong cluster would enhance the general economic situation for its members. In the end, the Chattanooga region should see a shift in its own business culture. It should move away from traditional reliance on fixed endowments, and move toward real competition, true productivity, effective collaboration and greater prosperity.

BIBLIOGRAPHY

Birkinshaw, Julian. "Upgrading of Industry Clusters and Foreign Investment." *International Studies of Management and Organizations.* Summer 2000.

Edidin, Peter. "Putting the Motor City Back in Gear." *New York Times.* 29 January 2006.

Muktarsingh, Natasha. "In Search of Ghetto Heaven." *Director* 2000.

Patton, Randall L., and David B. Parker. *Carpet Capital: The Rise of a New South Industry.* University of Georgia Press, 1999.

Porter, Michael E. *Locations, Clusters, and Company Strategy.* Oxford University Press, 2000.

"Regions Should Muster Cluster." *Business North Carolina.* September 2004.

Sickinger, Ted. "Harvard Professor Suggests Industry Clusters." *The Oregonian.* 10 January 2006.

Hillstrom, Northern Lights
updated by Magee, ECDI

CODE OF ETHICS

A code of ethics issued by a business is a particular kind of policy statement. A properly framed code is, in effect, a form of legislation within the company binding on its employees, with specific sanctions for violation of the code. If such sanctions are absent, the code is just a list of pieties. The most severe sanction is usually dismissal—unless a crime has been committed.

Business ethics emerged as a specialty in the 1960s in the wake of the "social responsibility" movement embraced by some large corporations; that movement itself was stimulated by rising public interest in consumerism and the environment. An important distinction exists between law and ethics. Obeying the law is the minimum level of ethical conduct enforced in society; ethical behavior includes more than simply legal behavior. It is unethical to lie, for instance; but lying is against the law only under certain limited circumstances: lying under oath is perjury. Business ethics, and the codes that formally define it, always include elements that go beyond strict legality; they demand adherence to a *higher* standard. In the wake of the Enron and Worldcom corporate scandals, codes of ethics have taken on yet another dimension. Legislation passed in 2002, the Sarbanes-Oxley Act ("SOX"), requires that corporations whose stock is traded under the provisions of the Securities Exchange Act of 1934 must publish their codes of ethics, if these exist, and also publish any changes to these codes as they are made. This requirement has given corporations strong incentives to formulate codes of ethics in order to win investor confidence. Most small businesses, of course, are not regulated by the Securities and Exchange Commission (SEC) because they do not issue publicly traded stock; thus they are not affected by SOX.

Perhaps the best-known code of ethics in history is the Hippocratic Oath taken by all doctors. Contrary to common belief, that oath does not include the phrase "First, do no harm." The actual language, in the third paragraph of the classical version, states: "I will apply dietetic measures for the benefit of the sick according to my ability and judgment; I will keep them from harm and injustice." According to *Bartlett's Familiar Quotations,* the more famous phrase comes from Hippocrates' *Epidemics:* "As to diseases make a habit of two things—to help, or at least, to do no harm."

THE DOCUMENT

A code of ethics is a formal document rather than merely an "environment," an "understanding," a consensus, "unwritten rule," or just an aspect of "corporate culture." It is at minimum a published document. In many organizations employees are also required to sign a statement to the effect that they have read and understood it. Variations on this theme exist. In very large corporations or corporations reacting to recent scandals, sometimes only corporate officers or only financial officers are required to sign. In other cases multiple codes of ethics may exist tailor-made to such functions as purchasing, sales, accounting, etc.

Codes of ethics are free-standing expressions of corporate will even when they are published as chapters or sections in a document which may contain a mission statement, a listing of corporate values, and general policies relating to operations.

CONTENT

Codes typically divide into three distinct elements: 1) an introduction or preamble, 2) a statement of purposes and values, 3) specific rules of conduct which may be subdivided in various ways, and 4) implementation of the code, which will define administrative processes, reporting, and sanctions.

Introduction: Management Sponsorship The introduction or preamble to a code of ethics ideally carries a statement by the top-ranked officer of the corporation indicating his or her personal commitment to and backing of the code. Experts on and scholars of business ethics never fail to underline the importance of top management leadership, including by example. Codes of ethics published pro forma, possibly in the context of some rumors of scandals, carry little weight with employees unless tangible signs of corporate commitment are given. The preamble of a code of ethics provides an opportunity for sending such a signal.

Purposes and Values The leading section of the code typically provides an abbreviated mission statement followed by values. This section states what the company is all about, what it does, why it exists. Ideally the code will state practical financial objectives as well as less precise social and professional aspirations. The statement of values, similarly, will begin with narrowly defined statements and expand on these. Obeying all pertinent laws and regulations may be the initial value; adherence to higher ethical values will be spelled out next. Corporations engaged in some professional specialty (engineering, medicine, law, etc.) may explicitly refer to professional standards and standard-setting bodies.

Rules of Conduct Rules of conduct are typically subdivided. The Institute of Business Ethics (IBE), a London-based organization, provides a list easily adaptable by a small business formulating its own code. IBE divides the central presentation into codes of conduct adopted by the business toward its employees, customers, shareholders and other funding agents, suppliers, and then the wider society. In the subsection dealing with employees, an effective code will be further subdivided into the corporation's conduct toward employees and, separately, conduct expected from its employees.

In the language of business, the groups named above constitute the "stakeholders," those who have a stake in the well-being (and also in the ethical behavior) of the business. These groups typically define all those with whom the corporation has an interaction. In many cases, all depending on the range and activities of the corporation, other areas will get special emphasis. Thus rules of conduct may be spelled out in relation to the physical environment; ethnic, gender, and race relations; realms such a law and justice or medical practice. Codes of ethics may also specifically address areas of difficulty such as campaign contributions or compliance with specific laws. Examples of such rules are provided by FindLaw for Small Business, of instance, relating to antitrust statutes.

Within subdivisions, the code may specify categories of problems such as conflicts of interest; taking or offering bribes, gifts, favors, etc.; rules relating to information such as disclosures, withholding data, insider trading, and so forth; preferential treatment, discrimination; interpersonal relations including sexual harassment; resolving quality versus cost conflicts; and potentially endlessly more issues. Well-executed codes of ethics will be concise, as brief as possible, yet will contain vivid examples to make each point as clear as possible.

Implementation, Reporting, and Sanctions The final section of a code will deal with administrative implementation of the code and sanctions against code violations. The simplest code will require reporting of code infractions up the management chain, including what action to take if the next level up fails to take action. In larger organizations an office or function may be expressly charged with handling code violations. Ombudsmen may be named. Sanctions will be spelled out and their administration defined, including a transparent process for establishing facts, the issuance of warnings, requirements for counseling or reeducation, consequences of repeat offences, on up to discharge or even, if appropriate, litigation.

For obvious reasons, a code of ethics without sanctions and a rational process for its implementation will be viewed by employees as merely a gesture without "teeth."

Conversely, the business owner must be alert to the fact that *ethical* violations are not necessarily be *legal infringements*; therefore sanctions such as firing an employee may be problematical unless the business has an "employment at will" hiring and firing policy and its exercise is backed by state and federal law under the circumstances.

ETHICS CODES AND SMALL BUSINESS

One of the advantages of small business is that it can avoid what are sometimes time-consuming upheavals in the business world. By any measure, traditional or modern, ethics is an important issue. Observation and studies show that ethical behavior is efficient. A. Millage recently wrote in *Internal Auditor* about the findings of the "2005 National Business Ethics Survey" (NBES). The NBES is conducted by the Ethics Resource Center. The survey showed that 70 percent of employees in companies with a "weak" ethical culture (as measured by NBES) observed ethical wrong-doing in their companies. Only 34 percent of employees in organizations with "strong" ethical culture did so. Employees observed morale-destroying behavior such as discrimination and sexual harassment; lying internally, to vendors, customers, and the public; misreporting of time; direct thievery; and other problems. By any measure such activities translate into higher costs, lost reputation, poor performance, etc. Ethics matters.

At the same time, the current preoccupation with codes of ethics is producing very large documents, sometimes reaching the length of books. A Google search on the phrase "code of ethics" yielded 17,900,000 hits in January 2006, a Yahoo search 12,000,000. Much of the current interest may be due to recent corporate scandals and the requirements of the Sarbanes-Oxley Act of 2002. Does the current interest mean that a small business must formulate its own code of ethics? In most cases, it will do no harm.

To publish such a code is relatively easy. Many hundreds of sample codes are available on the Internet, many of them specifically designed for the small business. The small business owner can easily write a one-page code and distribute it to employees if he or she sees the need for this. Many small businesses have found it useful in the past to publish policy statements that deal with personnel policy, including business hours, vacations, accrual of personal time, and so forth. A code of ethics along the same lines may be easy to produce and serve an important purpose: to underline the owner's commitment to ethical behavior.

Many very small businesses of 10 to 20 employees operate more like families. Ethical behavior is part of the culture—as it is in a family. In such situations the sudden appearance of a code of ethics may be rather jarring.

Discussion of the matter in a staff meeting may serve the purpose better: to alert employees to this issue and what is happening "out there."

BIBLIOGRAPHY

Di Norcia, Vincent, and Joyce Tigner. "Mixed Motives and Ethical Decisions in Business." *Journal of Business Ethics.* 1 May 2000.

Fandray, Dayton. "The Ethical Company." *Workforce.* December 2000.

"Fat Profits and Slim Pickings." *Nilewide Marketing Review.* 12 December 2005.

Felsher, Louise M. "Improving Workplace Ethics: how to become a better manager, employee or co-worker." *Meetings&Conventions.* December 2005.

Millage, A. "Ethical misconduct prevalent in workplace." *Internal Auditor.* December 2005.

"Sample Code of Ethics Policy Statement." FindLaw for Small Business. Available on http://smallbusiness.findlaw.com/business-forms-contracts/form2-1.html. Retrieved on 22 January 2006.

Verschoor, Curtis C. "Benchmarking ethics and compliance programs." *Strategic Finance.* August 2005.

Webley, Simon. "Outline of the content of a code of business practice and ethics." Institute of Business Ethics. Available on http://www.ibe.org.uk/contentcode.html. Retrieved on 22 January 2006.

Darnay, ECDI

COLLATERAL

Collateral is an item of value that is pledged to guarantee repayment of a loan. Collateral items are generally of significant value—property and equipment are often used as collateral, for example—but the range varies considerably, depending on the lending institution and variables in the borrower's situation. The value of collateral is not based on the market value. It is discounted to take into account the value that would be lost if the assets had to be liquidated in order to pay off the bank loan.

A business that has a long history of profitable operations may be able to obtain an unsecured loan, a loan without collateral. A new or a small business wishing to expand is almost always going to be asked to secure a loan with collateral. Unlike unsecured loans, in which a borrower is able to get a loan solely on the strength of its credit reputation, secured loans require borrowing companies to put up at least a portion of their assets as additional assurance that the loan will be repaid. Fail to repay the loan and the bank takes the items identified as collateral. Many start-up businesses turn to collateral-based loans to get their start.

Types of Collateral Many different types of collateral arrangements can be made by companies, whether they are experiencing a financial crunch or making plans for expansion. Common types of collateral include the following:

Purchase Money Security Interest (PMSI). Also known as a chattel mortgage, this option allows the borrower to secure a loan by borrowing against the value of the equipment being purchased.

Real Estate. Businesses that utilize real estate—usually a personal residence—as collateral are generally requesting long-term loans of significant size (the company has plenty of other collateral options for smaller loans). The size of the loan under this arrangement is predicated in large measure on the market and foreclosure value of the property, as well as the amount of insurance coverage that the company has taken out on it.

Endorser. Under this form of collateral, a company secures a loan by convincing another person to sign a note that backs up the promises of the borrower. "This endorser is then liable for the note," stated Mark Van Note in *ABCs of Borrowing.* "If the borrower fails to pay, the bank expects the endorser to pay. Sometimes the endorser may also be asked to pledge assets." A guarantor loan security is similar to the endorser arrangement, except that the guarantor is not required to post collateral.

Warehouse Receipts. Another option for borrowers is to put up a portion of their warehouse commodities as collateral. Van Note explained that with warehouse receipts, "the receipt is usually delivered directly to the bank and shows that the merchandise has either been placed in a public warehouse or has been left on your premises under the control of one of your employees who is bonded. Such loans are generally made on staple or standard merchandise that can be readily marketed. The typical loan is for a percentage of the cost of the merchandise."

Display Merchandise. This method of borrowing, which is also sometimes referred to as "floor planning," is similar to warehouse inventory. Under this plan, display merchandise such as furniture, automobiles, boats, large appliances, and electronic equipment can be used as collateral to secure loans.

Inventory. This encompasses all the various assets (merchandise, property, equipment, etc.) owned by the borrowing business that could be liquidated to repay the loan.

Accounts Receivable. "Many banks lend money against accounts receivable; in effect, counting on your customers to pay your loan," explained Van Note. "The bank may take accounts receivable on a notification or nonnotification plan. Under the notification plan, the purchaser of the goods is informed by the bank that the account has been assigned and is asked to make payments directly to the bank. Under the nonnotification plan, customers continue to pay you and you pay the bank." Under this collateral agreement, lenders sometimes advance up to 80 percent of the value of the receivables once the goods are shipped. Typically, a lender will buy or advance 70 to 80 percent of a company's accounts receivable balance and in turn assess a finance charge or "discount" on the total amount of the receivable. That discount is usually between 4 and 5 percent.

Savings accounts and certificates of deposit.

Stocks and bonds. Publicly held companies have the option of offering stocks and bonds within the company as security.

Life insurance. Some lenders are willing to accept the cash value of a life insurance policy as collateral on a loan.

SEE ALSO *Assets; Cash Management; Loans*

BIBLIOGRAPHY

Brealey, Richard A., and Stewart C. Myers. *Principles of Corporate Finance.* McGraw-Hill, 1991.

Linton, Heather. *Streetwise Business Valuation.* Adams Media, 2004.

Pinton, Linda, and Jerry Jinnett. *Steps to Small Business Start-Up.* Dearborn Trade Publishing, 2003.

U. S. Small Business Administration. *Financing for the Small Business.* n.d.

U. S. Small Business Administration. Van Note, Mark. *ABCs of Borrowing.* n.d.

Walter, Robert. *Financing Your Small Business.* Barron's Educational Series, 15 March 2005.

Hillstrom, Northern Lights
updated by Magee, ECDI

COLLEGIATE ENTREPRENEURIAL ORGANIZATIONS

In 1997, the first Collegiate Entrepreneurs' Organization was launched. It grew out of a meeting of entrepreneur-minded business students in 1983. They met in Chicago and organized the Collegiate Entrepreneurs of Illinois Conference in 1984, a conference which far exceeded expectations and exposed the high level of interest among young entrepreneurs in connecting with one another. Out of these events has grown a network of collegiate entrepreneurial organizations (CEOs) in colleges and universities around the United States.

Collegiate entrepreneurial organizations (CEOs) are comprised of students, primarily from graduate level business schools, who form groups for the purpose of educating members on small business matters, such as running a start-up and obtaining financing. They hold meetings, sponsor speakers and educational events, and serve as a storehouse of information on entrepreneurial matters. Their primary goal is to develop and support creative and competent entrepreneurs across industries and the world. They also serve as an important source for networking between prospective entrepreneurs. According to Eric Hansen in *Entrepreneurship: Theory and Practice,* the growth of an entrepreneurial enterprise is dependent on these types of relationships.

CEOs provide entrepreneurial students with a wide variety of resources to support their own start-up. These include opportunities to meet with business executives, information support, and in some cases, financial support. Many collegiate entrepreneurial organizations, such as the Berkeley Solutions Group, work hand in hand with the business school itself to provide opportunities for students to put their education to work in summer internship programs. Participants in collegiate entrepreneurial organizations at top business school programs are heavily recruited by leading companies. However, some entrepreneurial organizations seek to place MBA students with start-up companies. Depending on the organization, the interns may help to improve a company's information systems, investigate new markets and sales channels, or develop business plans.

In addition to these services provided to student entrepreneurs, many collegiate entrepreneurial organizations provide consulting services to small businesses and non-profit organizations unable to afford the fees of a professional consultant. MBA students primarily provide the services. A small business taking advantage of these services has the benefit of both a no- or low-cost consultation as well as the latest research on business management. Students may work alone or in groups to assist the small business with such tasks as feasibility studies, market research programs, and the development of an operational structure. In most cases, this support is offered during the academic year, with internship programs providing additional service or overlap where needed.

The Collegiate Entrepreneurial Organization (www.c-e-o.org) serves as a national organization for many university entrepreneurial groups and can be used as a starting point to research some of these organizations. Further information on these groups can frequently be found on the Web site of a university's business school.

SEE ALSO *Business Incubators; Entrepreneurial Networks; Mentoring*

BIBLIOGRAPHY

International Schumptners Society. *Entrepreneurship, the New Economy, and Public Policy.* Springer, 2005.

Kushnell, Jennifer. *The Young Entrepreneur's Edge: Using Your Ambition, Independence, and Youth to Launch a Successful Business.* Random House, 1999.

Luscher, Keith F. *Don't Wait Until You Graduate!: How to "Jump-Start" Your Career While Still in School.* New Horizon Press, 1998.

Lynn, Jacquelyn. "Need Start-Up Help? Give Your Business Some Class." *Entrepreneur.* December 1999.

Poe, Richard. "Generation E." *Success.* November 1993.

Price, Courtney, and Kathleen Allen. *Tips and Traps for Entrepreneurs.* McGraw Hill, 1998.

Hillstrom, Northern Lights
updated by Magee, ECDI

COMMUNICATION SYSTEMS

Communication systems are the various processes, both formal and informal, by which information is passed between the managers and employees within a business, or between the business itself and outsiders. Communication—whether written, verbal, nonverbal, visual, or electronic—has a significant impact on the way business is conducted. The basic process of communication begins when a fact or idea is observed by one person. That person (the sender) may decide to translate the observation into a message, and then transmit the message through some communication medium to another person (the receiver). The receiver then must interpret the message and provide feedback to the sender indicating that the message has been understood and appropriate action taken.

The goal of any form of communication is to promote complete understanding of a message. But breakdowns in communication can occur at any step in the process. Business managers need to understand and eliminate the common obstacles that prevent effective communication. Some of the causes of communication problems in business settings include:

- A lack of basic language skills

- Differing expectations and perceptions on the part of senders and receivers

- Selectivity or the tendency for individuals to pick and choose what they retain when they receive a message from another person

- Distractions such as ringing telephones, scheduled meetings, and unfinished reports

According to Herta A. Murphy and Herbert W. Hildebrandt in their book *Effective Business Communications*, good communication should be complete, concise, clear, concrete, correct, considerate, and courteous. More specifically, this means that communication should: answer basic questions like who, what, when, where; be relevant and not overly wordy; focus on the receiver and his or her interests; use specific facts and figures and active verbs; use a conversational tone for readability; include examples and visual aids when needed; be tactful and good-natured; and be accurate and nondiscriminatory.

Unclear, inaccurate, or inconsiderate business communication can waste valuable time, alienate employees or customers, and destroy goodwill toward management or the overall business. In fact, according to a 2004 study by the National Commission on Writing, entitled *Writing: A Ticket to Work... Or a Ticket Out,* "it appears that remedial deficiencies in writing may cost American firms as much as $3.1 billion annually." As we enter the information age, the importance of communicating clearly grows and the emphasis on written communication increases. Brent Staples explains how the change to an information age economy is increasing the need for good writing skills in his *New York Times* article, "The Fine Art of Getting it Down on Paper, Fast." "Companies once covered for poor writers by surrounding them with people who could translate their thoughts onto paper. But this strategy has proved less practical in the bottom-line-driven information age, which requires more high-quality writing from more categories of employees than ever before. Instead of covering for non-writers, companies are increasingly looking for ways to screen them out at the door."

HISTORY OF BUSINESS COMMUNICATIONS

In the early years of corporate America, business managers operated on a strict basis of top-down communications. Whatever the boss or owner of the company said was the law. In most cases, strategies for doing everything from selling product to dealing with employees would be discussed behind closed doors. Once those decisions were made by managers, lower-level employees were expected to put them into effect. Employees had little input; they did as they were told or found work elsewhere. Such management attitudes, particularly when they applied to worker safety issues in such places as coal and steel mines, led to the growth of labor unions. If nothing else, unions had the power in many cases to slow or shut down production until management listened to the demands of the workers.

In reaction to union demands, corporations eventually set up communication systems where rank-and-file members could speak their minds through union representatives. Although the unions provided the impetus for corporate managers to implement such systems, managers eventually realized that employees could have meaningful input into solving company problems. When presented with the opportunity to contribute, many employees jumped at the chance. This sort of feedback came to be called bottom-up communication.

In today's business environment, most corporations encourage employees to take an active role in the company. Employees who notice ways to improve production are encouraged, and usually rewarded, for passing those ideas on to managers. Employees who submit ideas that withstand intense study can be rewarded with a percentage of the savings to the company. Employees who are harassed on the job are strongly encouraged to report such harassment as far up the chain of management as necessary to stop it. Regular employee meetings are held where the lowest-level employee can stand up and ask the highest-level manager a direct question with the full expectation that a direct answer will be offered in return.

Business managers have also developed a method of monitoring how the company is running while meeting employees halfway. Sometimes called "management by walking around," this method of communication calls for top managers to get out of their offices and see what is happening at the level where the work is performed. Instead of simply reading reports from subordinates, business owners visit factories or service centers, observe employees on the job, and ask their opinions. Although the practice is both praised and denigrated regularly by business management experts, this form of communications does serve to keep the boss in touch.

PREPARING EFFECTIVE MESSAGES

Perhaps the most important part of business communication is taking the time to prepare an effective and understandable message. According to Murphy and Hildebrandt, the first step is to know the main purpose of the message. For example, a message to a supplier might have the purpose of obtaining a replacement for a defective part. The next step is to analyze the audience so that the message can be adapted to fit their views and needs. It may be helpful to picture the recipient and think about which areas of the message they might find positive or negative, interesting or boring, pleasing or displeasing. After that, the sender must choose the ideas to include and collect all the necessary facts. The next step involves organizing the message, since a poorly organized message will fail to elicit the required response.

It may be helpful to prepare an outline beforehand, paying particular attention to the beginning and ending portions. Finally, before transmitting the message it is important to edit and proofread.

COMMUNICATION MEDIA

There are two main media used for communication: written and oral. Nonverbal communications are also an element of communication systems. Each of these types of communication is described below.

Written Communication Written communication is the most common form of business communication and ever more so in the information age and spread of electronic communications tools. It is essential for small business owners and managers to develop effective written communication skills and to encourage the same in all of its employees. The information age has altered the ways in which we communicate and placed an increasing emphasis on written versus oral communications.

The ever-increasing use of computers and computer networks to organize and transmit information means the need for competent writing skills is rising. Dr. Craig Hogan, a former university professor who now heads an online school for business writing, receives hundreds of inquiries each month from managers and executives requesting help with improving their own and their employees' writing skills. Dr. Hogan explains, in an article entitled "What Corporate America Can't Build: A Sentence," that millions of people previously not required to do a lot of writing on the job are now expected to write frequently and rapidly. According to Dr. Hogan, many of them are not up to the task. "E-mail is a party to which English teachers have not been invited. It has companies tearing their hair out." Survey results from The National Commission on Writing study back up this assessment. They found that a third of employees in the nation's "blue chip" companies write poorly and are in need of remedial writing instruction.

The most basic principles of written communication are similar to those for overall communication. Experts within the growing industry of remedial writing agree that there are five minimal requirements for good writing. They are:

1. Know your audience

2. Keep sentences short and simple

3. Avoid jargon and cliches

4. Distinguish between facts and opinions

5. Always double-check spelling, grammar, and punctuation

The key is, of course, to convey meaning in as accurate and concise a manner as possible. People do not read business memoranda for the pleasure of reading. They do so in order to receive instructions or information upon which to base decisions or take action. Therefore, highly literary prose is not desirable in business writing. Overly formal prose may also be counterproductive by seeming stand-offish or simply wordy. A style of writing that is too informal can also convey an unintended message, namely that the subject matter is not serious or not taken seriously by the sender. A straightforward, courteous tone is usually the best choice but one that may not come naturally without practice.

Business correspondence should start with an outright statement about the purpose of the message and should be followed with simple and clear details in support of the purpose. The recipients of correspondence need information in order to act appropriately. They also need reasons that convince them to act or think in the way the sender intends. If the message conveys its meaning with clear arguments that identify reasons and provide evidence it should achieve that goal.

Special concern should be taken in all external correspondence since it reflects on the business as a whole. For example, letters intended to persuade somebody to either invest in a project or purchase from a company have a special organization. According to Murphy and Hildebrandt, they should: 1) attract favorable attention from the reader; 2) arouse interest; 3) convince the reader and create desire; and 4) describe the action the reader should take. When the purpose of the letter is to make a sale, it is also important to include facts about the product and a clear central selling point. Above all, it is important that any type of written communication that originates from a business create or enhance goodwill.

Oral Communication Small business owners and managers are frequently called upon to make presentations, conduct interviews, or lead meetings, so oral communication skills are another important area for development. Presentations might be made to employees for training purposes, or to potential customers for sales purposes. In either case, good presentation techniques can generate interest and create confidence. Interviewing skills might be needed for hiring new employees, conducting performance appraisals, or doing market research. Meetings or conferences can be important tools for relating to employees or to interested parties outside of the organization in order to solve problems or set goals.

The same principles that apply to other forms of oral communication also apply to telephone calling. It is important to plan business calls by determining the purpose, considering the audience (including the best time to call), and deciding the ideas to be included and the questions to be asked. When answering the telephone in a business setting, it is important to answer promptly and to state your name and department in a clear, pleasant voice. Communication over the telephone can create impressions that are vital to small business success.

An often overlooked element of oral communication is listening. Good listening skills can be vital in finding a solution to grievances or even in making sales calls. Listening involves showing an interest in the speaker, concentrating on the message, and asking questions to ensure understanding. It helps to be prepared for the discussion, to avoid arguing or interrupting, to take notes as needed, and to summarize the speaker's statements.

Nonverbal Communication Nonverbal communication—such as facial expressions, gestures, posture, and tone of voice—can aid in the successful interpretation of a message. "Sometimes nonverbal messages contradict the verbal; often they express true feelings more accurately than the spoken or written language," Murphy and Hildebrandt noted. In fact, studies have shown that between 60 and 90 percent of a message's effect may come from nonverbal clues. Therefore, small business owners and managers should also be aware of the nonverbal clues in their own behavior and develop the skill of reading nonverbal forms of communication in the behavior of others.

There are three main elements of nonverbal communication: appearance, body language, and sound. The appearance of both the speaker and the surroundings are vital in oral communications, while the appearance of written communications can either convey importance or cause a letter to be thrown out as junk mail. Body language, and particularly facial expressions, can provide important information that may not be contained in the verbal portion of the communication. Finally, the tone, rate, and volume of a speaker's voice can convey different meanings, as can sounds like laughing, throat clearing, or humming.

COMMUNICATIONS TECHNOLOGIES

Advances in technology over the last 20 years have dramatically changed the way in which business communications take place. In fact, in many ways communication technologies have changed the way in which business is done. The expanded use of electronic mail and of the Internet generally have enabled businesses to more easily move work from one location to another, establish remote and/or mobile offices, even to create virtual offices. New communication technology has also speeded up the turn-around time for decision making and blurred the line between work hours and personal hours. All of these developments challenge companies to adapt to a faster business environment. This is both an opportunity for companies to become more productive and efficient and a test of their adaptability.

Although changes in electronic communication technology are occurring at a phenomenal pace, they are not radical changes in the basic forms of communication. They are, rather, enhancements to traditional communication techniques. These technologies have made two basic enhancements in how we can communicate.

Mobility and Reach. Wireless and cellular technology have greatly expanded the places from which we can communicate and the distance over which we communicate easily. A manager on the way to work anywhere in the U.S. can easily call and chat with a colleague or supplier in Singapore as she makes her way home in the evening there.

Speed and Power. High-speed fiber optic phone lines and reasonably priced high-speed satellite transmissions have created a situation in which it is as easy to transfer large data files from one department to another in a single building as it is to transfer those files to a location anywhere in the world.

Both of these enhancements to communications have influenced how business is done. They each have upsides and downsides. The ease with which colleagues can stay in touch with one another is helpful in coordinating a company's activities. Staying in close contact with suppliers is also beneficial. For a particular employee, however, being available at any time may also be a burden.

Cell phones, lap top computers, and hand-held messaging devices of various kinds are all valuable tools for business communications. They enhance our ability to communicate and stay in touch but to benefit from their potential a company must use them wisely and efficiently and establish rules that prevent the devices from becoming burdensome to the user. With ease may also come complacency. For example, just because a sales representative can call Joan in production—easily, quickly, and from almost anywhere—to clarify and answer questions about a sloppily placed order does not mean that making and answering many calls about the order is efficient. An emphasis on clear and accurate communications is needed for efficiency, regardless of the ease or speed with which communication devices operate.

Internal Communications Intranets, or internal organizational computer networks, have become the media of choice for most companies when it comes to keeping employees informed. The company intranet can be used like an electronic bulletin board and when paired with e-mail can serve to disseminate information quickly and efficiently.

Since an intranet may be used to easily connect people working in various locations, it can help to establish or maintain a sense of community in an organization that is geographically dispersed. In fact, intranets make it possible for groups of people to work together closely in what is known commonly as a virtual office. Many small service businesses are started as virtual offices in which each person within the group works at his or her own home or place of choosing. What unites the group are two things: a common goal, and a computer network of some sort through which information and software tools are shared.

External Communications The growth of the Internet has made it almost essential for a business to have an online presence, simple though it may be. On a simple Internet Web site a company can provide potential customers, clients, employees, and/or investors with contact information and a picture of the company. For those wishing to use the Internet as a sales and marketing vehicle, a more sophisticated (and expensive) site can be developed. Often called e-Commerce Web sites, these sites are used for advertising, displaying merchandise, taking and processing orders, tracking orders, and/or performing many customer service tasks.

Small businesses may have a unique opportunity for benefiting from a Web presence. The outreach that is possible through a well-marketed Web site is much greater than would be possible through any other media at a similar cost. According to some analysts, for businesses one of the most powerful aspects of an interactive medium like the Internet is the ability to develop a true two-way conversation with clients and customers. The Internet is a powerful communications tool and one that businesses of all sizes now use regularly.

INFORMAL COMMUNICATIONS

Informal methods of communication, such as rumors and "the company grapevine," can be outside of management's control. The grapevine is a bottom-up form of communication in which employees try to understand what is happening around them when there is no official word from management. When management is silent, employees fill the void with guesses about what is happening. Although there is no way the grapevine can be stopped, it can be influenced. When dealing with questions that cannot, or should not, be answered, managers should take the initiative before negative rumors get started. If it is obvious to employees that the company will soon undergo major changes, for example, management should confirm that it will. Employees should be informed that management recognizes they have legitimate concerns, which will be addressed when possible. If official talk would damage the company, that should be made clear to the employees.

THE IMPORTANCE OF GOOD COMMUNICATION

All forms of communication, even the lack of it, can have a significant impact on business dealings. A stiffly-worded, official-sounding memo to employees telling them not to talk to the press about impending litigation could be interpreted as admitting that the company did something wrong. Management's repeated "no comments" to employees and the press on a rumored merger may launch dozens of informal discussions about company suitors, how much the company will sell for, and how many employees will be laid off.

In order to avoid the negative effects of such scenarios, small business owners should make it a practice to communicate as much and as openly as possible. They should think twice before eliminating the company newsletter as a cost-saving measure, keep electronic bulletin boards up-to-date, and hold meetings in which employees can ask questions of management. In addition, they should develop their skills so that all business communications are easily understandable. Management terms and jargon, stiff or flowery language may contribute to the impression among employees that management is talking down to them. It is also helpful to obtain and analyze feedback. Asking employees if they feel informed or not and what would make them feel more informed about the company can open valuable channels of communication.

BIBLIOGRAPHY

Bonner, William H., and Lillian H. Chaney. *Communicating Effectively in an Information Age.* Second Edition, Dame Publishing, 2003.

Holz, Shel. "Establishing Connections: Today's Communications Technologies Have Shifted the Dynamic." *Communication World.* May-June 2005.

Irwin, David. *Effective Business Communications.* Thorogood Publishing, 2001.

Murphy, Herta A., and Herbert W. Hildebrandt. *Effective Business Communications.* Seventh Edition. McGraw-Hill, 1997.

Olkkonen, Rami, Henrikkie Tikkanen, and Kimmo Alajoutsijarvi. "The Role of Communication in Business Relationships and Networks." *Management Decision.* May-June 2000.

Ross-Larson, Bruce. *Writing for the Information Age.* W.W. Norton & Company, 2002.

Staples, Brent. "The Fine Art of Getting It Down on Paper, Fast." *New York Times.* 15 May 2005.

Writing: A Ticket to Work... Or a Ticket Out. National Commission on Writing, The College Board. September 2004.

Hillstrom, Northern Lights
updated by Magee, ECDI

COMMUNITY DEVELOPMENT CORPORATIONS

Community development corporations (CDCs) are locally based nonprofit organizations that work to help the residents of impoverished areas to improve their quality of life. Such organizations exist in virtually every major urban area of the United States today. CDCs provide residents with a variety of different benefits, including housing, day care for children, nursing home care for the elderly, employment opportunities, job training, and health care facilities. Some CDCs act as part-owners of vital businesses within their neighborhoods, like supermarkets and shopping centers, while others assist residents in starting their own small businesses.

"Community development corporations function somewhat like private developers but are governed by the community," Gustav Spohn explained in an article for the *San Diego Business Journal.* "Their boards of directors are typically composed of community residents together with experts who advise them on the technical aspects of fund-raising and development projects. They depend heavily on government and private philanthropic funds, which in turn leverage financing from banks and other investors. Their goal is not to turn a profit but to generate economic renewal in poor communities."

As recently as the early 1990s, CDCs were being dismissed as small-time players unable to make a real contribution to solving urban problems. Banks were rarely willing to provide them with financing or any other assistance. But today CDCs are viewed as "key components of public strategies to fight poverty in cities across the country," according to Spohn. Nearly every major bank in the country is now actively involved in community development in at least one city. According to the National Congress for Community Economic Development, there were more than 2,200 CDCs operating in the United States in 2005. CDCs are a driving force in many reviving poor places because they refurbish housing, restore enterprise to ruined commercial districts, and work to make life difficult for those standing in the way of progress, from junkies to zoning bureaucrats.

Although CDCs have had an increasing impact on the fight to reclaim urban neighborhoods, they are still the subject of some skepticism. Critics believe that CDCs cannot operate on a large-enough scale to overcome a 40-year lack of investment in many inner cities. Others believe that community improvement efforts in impoverished neighborhoods are pointless, claiming that residents will simply choose to leave as soon as they are able to raise their incomes to a certain level. Finally, some people worry that CDCs—which receive major funding from the federal government through the Community Development Block Grant and other programs—will not be able to remain effective in the face of inevitable budget cuts.

In his article, Spohn outlined some of the functions of a successful CDC. First, it must make local residents feel that they have an investment in the neighborhood. Second, it must serve a mediating role between the differing interests of various neighborhood groups. Third, it must not polarize the interests of the community and the interests of government and outside private-sector institutions. Finally, it must continually battle the forces that act to return the inner cities to a state of disorder. Overall, CDCs can have a significant impact on the communities they serve. "Nationally there's a feeling that nothing can work in the cities—they have no hope—that there's nothing the society can do," Roland Anglin of the Ford Foundation told Spohn. "It's not true. There is a movement there. There is a structure there in inner cities. There is a strategy that can help."

OTHER COMMUNITY INITIATIVES TO ATTRACT SMALL BUSINESSES

In the late 1990s, as Internet technology made location less important for many small businesses, a number of communities began enacting programs designed to attract entrepreneurs to their areas. These cities and towns "are appealing directly to a new breed of 'lone eagles,' self-employed professionals who can do their work any time, any place, and who don't need the security of a regular paycheck," David Stamps wrote in *Training.* For instance, some communities chose to upgrade their telephone systems to offer high-speed connections for computer modems, while others began providing inexpensive Internet access and hosting services for small business Web sites.

In a study for *Business Horizons,* William M. Shanklin and John K. Rayns, Jr. found that "economic development initiatives designed to invigorate entrepreneurial growth have become centerpieces of state and community efforts. Indeed, political entities spend billions of dollars and untold hours on stimulating their economies." Numerous communities have begun offering a wide variety of assistance programs for entrepreneurs and small businesses. In the course of their research, Shanklin and Rayns found that such programs were most successful when the communities first conducted a realistic self-assessment to uncover the unique benefits they had to offer developing businesses. "Neglecting to complete this strategic first step is precisely why some communities set missions that are unrealistic," the authors noted. "Concisely stated, without a strategic compass there is no way a community can

design programs and policies that are effective in boosting entrepreneurship."

Shanklin and Rayns also surveyed small business owners and entrepreneurs to see what components of community assistance programs they found most helpful. The respondents particularly valued community assistance in obtaining loans to begin operations, developing pro-forma financial statements, conducting market research, obtaining equity capital, and finding a suitable location for their businesses. Communities that provide assistance in these areas—for example, by creating enterprise development boards staffed by knowledgeable local business people—were most likely to boost entrepreneurship in their areas. "Results from states and communities throughout the United States show that economic development efforts can and do boost entrepreneurial performance," Shanklin and Rayns wrote. "By creating a climate that encourages small business and by offering competent managerial and technical assistance to aspiring and growth-oriented entrepreneurs, economic development officials can make a difference."

BIBLIOGRAPHY

"Community Development Corporations Emerge as Major Generators of Economic Development in Urban Neighborhoods." Ford Foundation. Available from http://www.fordfound.org/news/view_news_detail.cfm?news_index=8. Retrieved on 27 January 2006.

De Paula, Matthew. "Grants to Poor Entrepreneurs Nurture Future Business." *US Bank.* September 2004.

Murphy, Patricia W., and James V Cunningham. *Organizing for Community Controlled Development.* Sage Publications, Inc., 23 January 2003.

Shanklin, William M., and John K. Rayns, Jr. "Stoking the Small Business Engine." *Business Horizons.* January-February 1998.

Spohn, Gustav. "Engines for Rebuilding Communities Make Headway." *San Diego Business Journal.* 16 June 1997.

Stamps, David. "Social Capital." *Training.* November 1998.

Hillstrom, Northern Lights
updated by Magee, ECDI

COMMUNITY RELATIONS

The phrase "community relations," narrowly understood, simply describes a company's interactions with the community in which it resides. The use of this phrase by businesses, the media, and students of business, however, almost always signifies something more than ordinary relationships and includes voluntary actions that either are (or can be interpreted as) done just for the good of the community. This produces ambiguities and conflicts. A strictly "free market" view of business defines a company as working for its stockholders under law; any charitable work or contributions are thus shorting what stockholders are due. A more modern view, which arose in the 1960s under the rubric of "social responsibility," defines corporations as involved in, indeed responsible for, achieving social goods over and above profits. Ambiguity also arises from the fact that many businesses are small and, in effect, the extensions of one or two individuals who are viewed as autonomous persons—while large corporations are collectives managed by hired functionaries. Two definitions of community relations are thus equally correct. One defines community relations as the corporation's unforced contributions to the community. The other makes community relations a branch of public relations—a form of communications.

A SPECTRUM OF ACTIVITIES

"Community relations" may be the consequence of a generous corporate culture in which relations just happen to be helpful. Thus a company may have acquired a good reputation because it is always ready to help when asked in different ways—through people, money, or providing equipment. Managers at all levels understand in advance that this is sanctioned and approved. It is a corporate tradition, the way that things are done.

In another company, community relations may take a much more publicly visible form. The company will be proactively generous. It may sponsor an annual festival, for instance; it may be the chief support of a famous hospital or research center; or it may be well-known for lending executives to civic causes or for taking a leadership role in fund-raising activities for the orchestra or the community theater. Such behavior is often the long, institutionalized shadow of a famous founder who set such activities going. They are still pursued with energy, at high cost, with a high level of public recognition. In the very nature of things, it is always difficult, in such cases, to distinguish "generosity" from "corporate pride."

Yet another form that community relations takes is that of a communications program the purpose of which is to improve or maintain a company's reputation at least cost; here the underlying idea is that good community relations are good for business, but the community must be "educated" to the values the company brings to it. Under such a program, the company publicizes information about its activities. If it expands, it presents adding jobs in a favorable light. If it closes an operation, it presents its out-placement and employee counseling activities in the most favorable light. Anything even remotely associated with the community is interpreted

as a contribution whether it is or not. The driving force in these cases is "perception," and the philosophical underpinning is that "perception is reality."

Community relations may also take a very proactive form but arising as parts of defensive strategies. Thus companies sometimes engage in or even initiate program activities, exploited to the maximum by using public relations, in order to counter a single unfavorable event or a chronic problem. A major fire blamed on poor supervision may be the triggering event; the chronic problem may be the production of toxic wastes or a strong odor that occasionally rises from its factory.

This description clearly shows that community relations is a conscious expression of corporate will and that the motives behind it become visible to the public over time. The more free the activity is, i.e., the less it is necessitated by unfavorable events, the more the community will value it; similarly, the less credit the company seeks, the more credit it will get.

JUSTIFICATIONS AND MOTIVATIONS

Commenting on a survey of 255 business executives, The Boston College Center for Corporate Community Relations stated in a 2000 press release: "Half of manufacturing executives say corporate citizenship will become more important in the next three to five years and 95 percent agree that a positive reputation in the community will help them achieve business objectives." A few lines later the press release continues: "Survey respondents agree that companies should organize volunteer programs, give grants to nonprofit organizations, and help to solve society's problems. Despite their good intentions, however, some 70 percent of survey respondents admit they fail to consider community goals in business unit plans."

Many hundreds of other releases, Web pages, brochures, speeches, papers, and exhortations state over and over again that community relations is "good for business." Promoters of community relations programs link business benefits to participation thinking perhaps that businesses require a pragmatic reason to share resources. The discontinuity between beliefs and actual behavior, however, as reported by Boston College, may be due to two factors. First, businesses may be principally motivated to participate in programs by the personal and humanitarian inclinations of owners and executives—not for business reasons (unless some problem needs to be addressed). Second, data are very difficult to find that produce immediate and direct linkages between, say, charitable contributions, organizing volunteer programs, providing vehicles for a clean-up event, or the establishment of a scholarship program—and the bottom line.

SEE ALSO *Public Relations*

BIBLIOGRAPHY

Burke, Edmund M. *Corporate Community Relations: the principle of the neighbor of choice.* Quorum Books. 1999.

Desatnik, Lisa. "Corporate Volunteering Is Good Business." *Cincinnati Business Journal.* 1 September 2000.

Joyner, Fredricka. "Bridge Building: Enhancing the Possibility of Partnerships." *Journal for Quality and Participation.* May-June 2000.

Kiser, Cheryl. "Companies Say Corporate Citizenship Good for Business, But Many Don't Invest in Their Communities." Press Release. Center for Corporate Citizenship at Boston College. 3 October 2000.

Hillstrom, Northern Lights
updated by Magee, ECDI

COMP TIME

Comp Time, or Compensatory Time, is an alternate way of rewarding overtime work. Instead of paying an hourly employee time-and-a-half for work done over the time allotted in the normal work week, employers would allow an hour and a half of time off for each hour of overtime worked. This time could be used in emergencies, or scheduled for personal use. Comp time should not be confused with "flex-time." Flex-time allows employees to schedule their regular working hours in a way that accommodates their personal preferences and family commitments. Comp time strictly refers to compensation for overtime work.

Federal legislation, embodied in the Fair Labor Standards Act of 1938 (FLSA) governs the compensation of hourly employees. Under FLSA employees are assigned to either "exempt" or "non-exempt" status, i.e., those who are exempt from the requirements of FLSA and those who are not. Non-exempt employees are paid by the hour, exempt employees receive a salary. FLSA mandates that non-exempt employees be paid at the rate of 1.5 times the hourly wage for every hour over 40 worked in a week. Non-exempts must be paid in dollars for their overtime and cannot receive compensatory time instead. In 1978, Congress passed the Federal Employees Flexible and Compressed Work Schedules Act. This enabled the Federal Government to pay its employees comp time instead of overtime pay. In 1985, this provision was extended to state and local employees as well at the employee's option. In 2000 the Supreme Court ruled (in *Christensen v. Harris County* that local government can compel employees to take accumulated comp time rather than take it at any time of their choosing. FLSA, however, continues to require overtime compensation in dollars for private sector hourly workers.

Since that time a major effort began in Congress to amend the FLSA to liberalize comp time rules for private sector hourly workers. The effort has thus far failed because of opposition from labor unions and their allies. The last event in this process was the withdrawal in 2003 of H.R. 1119, the House of Representatives' bill called "Comp-Time Reform Bill" for lack of votes.

THE CURRENT DEBATE

The movement to pass comp time legislation has been led primarily by Republicans, who argue that comp time will provide employees with greater freedom to schedule their work around family commitments. Supporters also contend that broadening use of comp time into the private sector will give a financial boost to businesses. But opposition is strong from the Democratic Party and labor unions. Primary reasons for contesting the use of comp time are questions over the actual scheduling of time off, and whether employees will be free to choose either comp time or payment in return for overtime work. Those opposing legislation suggest that employees in practice will not be allowed to freely schedule the use of their comp time but will be restricted by employers. This would result in an option much less valuable to employees, limiting the prospect of "emergency" time, and restricting time off at certain points during the year. Concerns have also been expressed over possible pressure from businesses on employees to accept comp time over monetary compensation for overtime work, and whether voluntary overtime could be offered only in exchange for comp time. Finally, unions object to proposed comp time arrangements in which hours do not count toward pension benefits.

COMP TIME IN SMALL BUSINESSES

Some business experts believe that employers who do not offer large benefits packages, significant vacation time, or paid time off should seriously consider offering comp time as a kind of perk for employees. These observers contend that comp time can be a sensitive (and economical) way of rewarding employees for extra help at crunch times, especially since many workers have come to value time off even more than increased pay.

But small businesses, which may not be in a position to offer employees elaborate benefits, may also not be able to support a comp time system. Whether the system is regimented or informal, the small business may not be able to afford the lost productivity and additional paperwork involved in keeping track of comp time accrued and taken. There may also arise scheduling problems, especially for very small businesses that rely on only a few employees for their entire function. If a business is necessarily inflexible when it comes to scheduling time off, comp time may not be a valid alternative to regular overtime compensation.

SEE ALSO *Flexible Employment*

BIBLIOGRAPHY
"Comp-Time and Flex Time: Giving Employees a Say." RPC Backgrounder. Republican Policy Committee. 24 February 2005.

Eisenbrey, Ross. "The Naked Truth About Comp Time." EPI Issue Brief #190. Economic Policy Institute. 31 March 2003.

"H.R. 1119, the Comp-Time Reform Bill." *Motor Age.* August 2003.

"Legalize Comp Time." *Crain's Detroit Business.* 31 July 2000.

Rosenfeld, Larry. "The Rules on Comp Time." *Entrepreneur.* 24 March 2003.

U.S. Small Business Administration, n.a. *Employees: How to Find and Pay Them.*

Hillstrom, Northern Lights
updated by Magee, ECDI

COMPETITIVE ANALYSIS

Small businesses keep track of the competition. In large corporations the activity is formalized. Operating managers within large companies usually conduct competitive analysis as part of preparing annual plans. Competitive analysis may also involve elaborate brand studies from time to time; some industries practice reverse-engineering to discover how a competitor's technology or software works. Indeed, competitive analysis can reach a staggeringly high level of sophistication. However, as many sectors of the U.S. economy illustrate—autos are a recent example—high sophistication may not be sufficient to save an industry from competitive impacts. Both small and large businesses must go beyond analysis and do something to protect their operations. As Peter Drucker, the late management guru, never tired of pointing out, effective business practice and sophisticated business practice do not necessarily mean the same thing.

THE CONTEXT OF ANALYSIS

Key aspects of this activity are when to do it and what to look at. Consultants, writers, and business schools uniformly urge that competitive analysis must be routine—much as dentists urge flossing thrice daily. In the usual environment of small business, concentrated competitive analysis tends to start after a triggering event produces awareness of trouble—the actual or looming loss of sales. Until then the tracking of competition will be low-key and routine. Once early signs of trouble appear, analysis

begins with looking for causes. These may be complex. "Competition" may take many different forms. The following list identifies some of the things to look at:

- *Direct Competition.* This may take several forms. A known competitor may have initiated changes in pricing, product, or services. One or more new competitors may have appeared and are bidding prices down. A new buyer in the client's organization may have shifted contracts to his or her favored suppliers. Finally, the customer may have decided to make the product or to do the job in-house.

- *Indirect Competition.* A new technology or class of products may have appeared functionally matching what this business sells. In our technology-driven market, for instance, television initially and the VCRs and DVDs later transformed the movie business.

- *Market Contraction.* Recessionary forces may be pressuring the customer so that he or she is simply not buying our product which may be in the highly discretionary category.

- *Self-inflicted Wounds.* A business may sometimes overlook that *it* is causing customers to shift their business elsewhere because of unwarranted price hikes, deteriorating service, aging technology, and countless other reasons.

The foregoing reveals that competitive analysis is in a way indistinguishable from effective management, which means keeping in close touch with the market and all those factors that influence it. Competitors need to be known and watched attentively. It is important to keep oneself informed of the internal affairs and plans of a commercial or institutional customer. Trends need watching; products and services must be kept up to date; and fall-back positions must be prepared if the economy can deprive a business of its core earnings. All this must be done continuously and with the right level of intensity. For the small business formal competitive analysis may be a luxury, but the activities that enter into it must be carried out.

THE PROCESS ITSELF

The U.S. Small Business Administration, on its Web site entitled "Competitive Analysis," provides an excellent list of fundamentals. SBA suggests that small businesses answer six questions: 1) Who are your five nearest direct competitors? 2) Who are your indirect competitors? 3) Is their business growing, steady, or declining? 4) What can you learn from their operations or from their advertising? 5) What are their strengths and weaknesses? and 6) How does their product or service differ from yours?

The SBA's emphasis is on competitors, which is appropriate but may be too narrow. The small business needs to expand this list to include data on the internal operations of its commercial customers and vendors as well and include information on trends in the market.

Many of the questions posed by SBA are very difficult to answer. Appropriately the agency suggests a process which is well adapted to the operation of a small business. SBA recommends that owners establish and keep files on competitors and that they review these from time to time. Precise answers may never be available to all the questions, but a general pattern will emerge. It is important consciously to make time for looking at what data are available by way of feeding one's awareness.

Important sources for information recommended by SBA are the following:

- Internet searches on appropriate topics.

- Personal visits to competitors' locations.

- Customers. "Your sales staff," SBA says, "is in regular contact with customers and prospects, as is your competition. Learn what your customers and prospects are saying about your competitors."

- Competitors' ads.

- Speeches and presentations. "Attend speeches or presentations made by representatives of your competitors."

- Trade show displays.

- Written sources such as trade publications, newspapers, industry surveys, and computer databases.

To this list might be added two or three other classes of informants. First are sales reps who call on the small business organization. The same sales people who call on this business also call on the owner's competitors. Gossip flows and will invariably contain interesting matters which, combined with other information, will produce new insights into trends, competitive plans, and even the kinds of problems competitors are struggling to solve. Principals of vendor organizations are an excellent source of broader market trends. The vendors sell to the entire range of people participating in a market and, as such, watch the health of all competitors. Finally, and this is easiest to achieve at trade shows, competitors themselves are an excellent source of information on what they do—and what others are doing. It is a truism of all intelligence work that information begets information. Sharing problems can result in gaining solutions.

SEE ALSO *Barriers to Market Entry*

BIBLIOGRAPHY

Cohen, Heidi. "Competitive Intelligence: What You Don't Know *Can* Hurt You." ClickZ Network. Available from http://www.clickz.com/experts/crm/actionable_analysis/article.php/3511216. 9 June 2005.

U.S. Small Business Administration. "Competitive Analysis." Available from http://www.sba.gov/starting_business/marketing/analysis.html. Retrieved on 23 January 2006.

Hillstrom, Northern Lights
updated by Magee, ECDI

COMPETITIVE BIDS

In many sectors of industry and almost invariably in government, procurement of goods and services takes place by competitive bidding. Vendors are solicited to present a proposal to meet the specifications published by the buyer. Such solicitations are referred to as requests for proposal (RFPs) or requests for quote (RFQs). Sellers present their bids in written form either routinely or, if the job bid is of some complexity, after discussions with the buyer. In many instances purchasing is from a pre-approved list of vendors; vendors get on these lists by answering requests for qualifications. In yet other instances, particularly in connection with preferential purchasing from women-owned or minority-owned enterprises, a frequently complicated bureaucratic process must first be followed to get on the list of qualified bidders; similar processes are involved in procurements under the Federal Government's small-business set-aside programs.

Bidding is common practice in selling at retail in some sectors, especially construction services. Roof-replacements, new windows, new gutters, and siding are sold to the homeowner directly usually in a competitive environment by presenting quotes. The careful buyer will obtain at least three bids before selecting the supplier.

People who start up small businesses in one of the sectors that uses competitive bidding tend to have prior experience of the process acquired as employees or managers while working for someone else in the industry. Occasionally, however, small business owners who sell in other ways may have opportunities to garner sales by competitive bidding as well. This tends to happen when the buyer is a large institution calling on a retail vendor. An example might be a rental business receiving a solicitation from an event organizer for massive stocks of chairs, tables, and tents. The owner may also come across an advertised solicitation which happens to fit the company's capabilities. The bidding process may be quite easy to discern from the solicitation. In other cases the small business may have to educate itself to what are frequently complicated procurement cultures. Resources for learning, however, are available. The U.S. Small Business Administration (SBA), for instance, is an excellent resource for learning how to bid for government contracts.

MAJOR ELEMENTS OF THE PROCESS

For the Buyer From the viewpoint of the buyer, competitive bidding is a way to identify the best supplier based on a combination of qualifications, history of achievement, timeliness, responsiveness, and cost. All things equal, the low bidder will get the job, but all things are rarely equal. The buyer's process will consist of 1) finding qualified bidders, 2) preparing a concise but complete RFP, 3) publishing the solicitation, 4) evaluating the proposals received, which may involve interviews with bidders, and 5) selecting the winner and notifying the losers.

Precisely because evaluating proposals can be time-consuming, especially when proposals are for some unusual program and are complex, buyers frequently begin with a formal qualification under which vendors are invited to submit packages defining their experience, personnel, and history of performance. The buyer then selects from among those submitting packages vendors it will invite to bid on a job. In more routine situations, the buyer will tend to develop a list of trusted suppliers and will only ask those people to bid. In such a situation the solicitation is sent directly and is not published. Evaluation of proposals is often difficult unless the job is well-defined and standard. A research study may require original approaches, and the buyer must choose from among often equally innovative methodologies. To resolve such issues, the buyer may invite leading bidders to make presentations as well. Often proposals are "unresponsive," meaning that the bidder has failed evidently to grasp the buyer's full intentions. When many bidders are unresponsive, the fault may lie in the RFP itself: it may have been poorly constructed. In a well-managed buying process, both winners and losers are notified of the buyer's final decision. This decision may follow additional discussions with the tentative winner to work out final problems.

Buyers are looking for bidders who have internalized the buyer's problems, are responsive to special issues in the RFP, match their capabilities closely to elements of the job, show that they have the capacity to do the job on time, and are neither "greedy" nor "trying to buy the job." The last phrase is a red flag. It means that the vendor may be "too hungry" and is bidding too low—and may later fail to perform.

For the Seller The seller does no business until it has been invited to bid and has been selected as a winner. The seller's tasks are 1) pre-solicitation sales activities,

2) getting qualified, 3) reviewing the RFP in light of all available intelligence, 4) deciding to bid or not to bid, 5) being fully responsive to the proposal, 6) differentiating its offer from competitors, 6) accurately to estimate cost, and 7) effectively sell the job in the post-quote period.

The effective seller routinely calls on the buyer and makes itself fully aware of buyer's plans, culture, and ways of doing business. As the saying has it, nothing propinqus like propinquity. In most company-to-company or company-to-agency transactions, known sellers tend to win jobs not necessarily because they are best qualified but because they are most knowledgeable about the buyer's needs. Sales activity works in the other direction too. The buyer will get to know the seller and getting qualified will therefore be easier.

Successful sellers will frequently decline to bid a job because, based on their knowledge of themselves, of the client, sometimes of the buyer's budget, they judge in advance that they have a low probability of winning. Skills in making such decisions grow with experience. Some buyers always shift business to certain sellers; in the jargon of the trade, the "contracts are wired." These buyers may cultivate vendors they do not intend to buy from but still need in order to have "three bids." Skillful sellers know how to assess buyers and to act accordingly. Deciding *not* to bid is sometimes as useful for profitability as to bid and win.

It is the seller's responsibility to understand the RFP fully and, if need be, to seek clarifications before bidding. Such interaction may produce valuable information— and also indicate the seller's seriousness to the buyer. Buyers value responsive bidding. Sellers, similarly, need to know exactly what the buyer wants in order properly to price the proposal. All else being equal, the most unique proposal will win the contract. In many cases involving standard services or goods, original methodology may be impossible to present, but unusual ways of delivering services or providing back-up may differentiate the seller from other bidders. Cost is of primary importance. However, a high-priced proposal may sometimes win the contract if the work is unique, the methodology recognizably superior, or the seller's qualifications unusual. Sometimes the real sale is made in interviews and presentations *after* the proposal has been presented. The seller should be prepared to make a strong follow-up if so requested.

A Great Diversity of Applications Competitive bidding is used in an enormous range of commercial activities each of which will have its special features. No generic description can capture all of the subtleties of bidding. A company bidding prepared meals for an airline will do quite different things than a company offering insurance services to a franchise seller. The important concepts will still be present, however: know your customer, bid to your capabilities, be responsive, price as low as possible, and be prepared to follow up. Finally, and most importantly, be prepared to deliver what you bid.

SMALL-BUSINESS SET-ASIDES

The U.S. Small Business Administration, on its site concerned with Federal Procurement, "Defining the Market," states as follows: "By law, federal agencies are required to establish contracting goals, such that 23% of all government buys are intended to go to small businesses. In addition, contract goals are established for women-owned businesses, small disadvantaged businesses, firms located in HUBZones and service disabled veteran-owned businesses. These government-wide goals, which are not always achieved, are 5%, 5%, 3% and 3%, respectively. They are important, however, because federal agencies have a statutory obligation to reach-out and consider small businesses for procurement opportunities. It is up to you to market and match your business products and services to the buying needs of federal agencies."

A HUBZone is a "Historically Underutilized Business Zone" as established in the Small Business Reauthorization Act of 1997. Information about HUBZone locations is available through the SBA.

Small business set-asides are established under Part 19 of the Federal Acquisition Regulations. Contracts under $2,500 are not eligible. Most small business set-asides relate to contracts between $2,500 and $100,000 in size. Such contracts are *intended* to be performed by small business organizations provided that government procurement officers have a reasonable expectation of getting bids from two or more qualified bidders. At their option, in order to meet federal contracting goals, procurement officers may also set aside larger contracts under the same rules. There are additional provisions whereby small businesses can participate in large contracts as subcontractors.

Participation in such programs will require substantial study and preparation for a small business not as yet engaged in Federal Procurement. It may well be a way to develop new business opportunities or to increase sales. An excellent starting point for self-familiarization is the SBA at Web sites provided in the bibliography.

SEE ALSO *Request for Proposals*

BIBLIOGRAPHY
Berman, Sharon. "How to Craft Business Proposals That Sway Clients." *Los Angeles Business Journal.* 3 January 2000.

FirstGov. "Federal Acquisition Regulations." Available from http://www.arnet.gov/far/. Retrieved on 24 January 2006.

Gilliam, Stacy. "Power up your Proposal." *Black Enterprise.* June 2005.

Luman, Stuart. "Want City Work? Red Tape Awaits." *Crain's Chicago Business.* 1 August 2005.

Sant, Tom. *Persuasive Business Proposals.* AMACOM. 1 December 2003.

U.S. Small Business Administration. "The Basics." Available from http://www.sba.gov/businessop/index.html. Retrieved on 24 January 2006.

U.S. Small Business Administration. "Defining the Market." Available from http://www.sba.gov/businessop/basics/defining.html. Retrieved on 24 January 2006.

Hillstrom, Northern Lights
updated by Magee, ECDI

COMPREHENSIVE ENVIRONMENTAL RESPONSE CLEANUP AND LIABILITY ACT (CERCLA)

The Comprehensive Environmental Response Cleanup and Liability Act (CERCLA), better known to the general public as the Superfund program, was passed by Congress on December 11, 1980. Under CERCLA, the Environmental Protection Agency (EPA) was given the authority to respond directly to the release or threatened release of hazardous substances onto sites which could endanger the public health or the environment. Superfund established requirements regarding these - contaminated sites as well as the liability of individuals and businesses responsible for the site contamination. In order to pay for the environmental cleanup of abandoned or uncontrolled hazardous waste sites, the government began taxing chemical and petroleum industries over a period of five years. The resulting $1.6 billion created a trust fund or Superfund to pay for these cleanups.

Later legislation, such as the Superfund Amendments and Reauthorization Act (SARA) in 1986, underlined the need for permanent and creative solutions in cleaning up hazardous waste sites by providing methods for settlement between responsible parties and the government. SARA also ensured CERCLA was in line with other federal and state environmental legal standards and requirements and increased state involvement in the Superfund program. It revised the Hazards Ranking System in order to ensure it focused on the human health issues associated with the sites. Finally, SARA brought another $8.5 billion into the fund for cleanup. Additional funds have been appropriated since.

There have been some legislative attempts at reducing or eliminating the liability of small businesses under CERCLA. In 2002, President George W. Bush signed into law the Small Business Liability Relief and Brownfield Revitalization Act which modified CERCLA.

However, in the wake of expensive cleanup efforts and increased environmental legislation, most large companies have dramatically improved their operations in order to avoid future remedial action. Unfortunately, the EPA has found that many small businesses tend to be among the most egregious polluters.

POTENTIALLY RESPONSIBLE PARTIES (PRPs)

Liability for contamination under CERCLA extends to a number of individuals or groups it terms "potentially responsible parties" (PRPs). These include the current owner or operator of the site; previous owners or operators of the site during the time of contamination or after it; companies or individuals handling the waste disposal or transportation; and other parties connected to the sale or lease of the property such as title companies or real estate agents.

The impact of this legislation for the small business owner can be devastating. Essentially, if a site is found to be contaminated, the landowner or operator and other parties connected to the property are responsible for environmental cleanup costs. This liability extends to the owner/operator, even if the site was contaminated by previous owners/operators and, in most cases, even if the current owner/operator was unaware of the contamination.

When considering the purchase of real estate, a small business should attempt to avoid contaminated sites both from the perspective of unwanted liability and costs for cleanup as well as the adverse impacts on business that a cleanup (also known as a remediation project) can bring. These include the stigma associated with a contaminated site and the cleanup's probable interference with business operations.

Therefore, a thorough assessment of the site in question (also known as "due diligence") should be conducted *prior* to purchasing it. This can, in some instances, protect the purchaser from liability for contamination. In order to be covered under the "innocent purchaser exemption" of CERCLA, however, a landowner must prove that s/he "did not know and had no reason to know" of the problem at the time of purchase. Since there is so much at stake, hiring a professional to do an environmental site assessment can (but does not guarantee) that you qualify for the exemption if the property turns out to be contaminated.

ENVIRONMENTAL SITE ASSESSMENTS

An environmental site assessment (ESA) performed by an environmental auditing company can ensure that a property is not contaminated. There are two forms of environmental site assessments. The first, known as a Phase I ESA, examines public records such as aerial photographs, EPA documents, and other public documents of the property in question, in order to determine whether the site had previous uses such as manufacturing operations or hazardous materials storage which may cause contamination. If any data found during the Phase I ESA prove questionable or suspicious, a Phase II ESA is called for. In a Phase II ESA, the environmental consulting firm takes soil and other samples from the site. The type and location of the samples will be determined by information found in the Phase I ESA.

Environmental site assessments (primarily Phase I ESAs) of property may also be required by banks when a business seeks to borrow against the equity of the property. This is because a possible cleanup could severely diminish the value of the site. Depending on the lending institution, this may be required for large loans, such as those over $500,000; consultants in the business, however, say that more and more banks are requiring a Phase I ESA on smaller projects as well.

According to the Small Business Administration, the cost of a Phase I Environmental Site Assessment can begin around $1,000 and rises with the size of the property and detail of the assessment. Since this is a crucial investment, it pays to secure a reputable firm. Look for an environmental consulting firm with a proven track record and actual experience in performing ESAs, as well as one that is insured. Be sure to check references. Phase II ESAs begin around $8,000 for the simplest studies (no groundwater sampling) and will run to $12,000 or higher if groundwater must be sampled or contamination is high.

LIABILITY

What happens if a business already owns a contaminated site or, despite its best efforts, purchases a site which is later found to have contamination? Under CERCLA, liability for cleanup is difficult to avoid. In legal terms, CERCLA liability is strict, several, and joint. Strict liability does not require intent or negligence or a specified amount of precaution on the part of the potentially responsible party. If the PRP is within one of the categories established by CERCLA, that party can be held strictly liable for all costs associated with an environmental cleanup of the site. Liability for the cleanup is also joint and several. This means, according to Martin McCrory in *American Business Law Journal,* that all of the

PRPs "are liable as a group or that each contributor is individually liable for the entire harm at the site." In layman's terms, a business's responsibility for costs incurred in the site cleanup is not necessarily proportional to those of its actions that lead to the site's contamination.

Once the liability of a PRP is established, escaping the burden of costs is only defensible under a few scenarios. Defensible scenarios include an act of God, an act of war, an act or the lack of action by a third party, or any combination of these. The defense that the release was caused by an act or lack of action by a third party is the most often used defense. It also frequently fails, according to McCrory.

RESPONSE ACTIONS OR SITE CLEANUP

Under CERCLA, there are two types of governmental responses that can take place in regard to contamination. The first is known as a short-term removal or removal action, in which the EPA takes immediate action in order to prevent or eliminate the release of hazardous materials in the case of an environmental emergency. A removal action cannot take more than one year from start to finish, and cannot cost more than $2 million. The second, known as a long-term remedial action, works to "permanently and significantly" lower the dangers connected to releases or threats of releases. This kind of action is meant to be much more comprehensive and therefore can continue over several years and, according to McCrory, can average over $30 million per site. Long-term remedial response actions occur only at sites listed on the EPA's National Priorities List (those sites which rate highest on the Hazards Ranking System).

Prior to the start of the cleanup, a remedial investigation and feasibility study (RI/FS) is done on the site in order to determine the level of contamination and select a method for removal or neutralization of the hazardous materials. The RI portion of the study collects information needed to establish the nature and extent of the contamination at the site. It also characterizes the environmental risks of the contamination and establishes the goals of cleanup. Using this information, the FS develops a number of possible cleanup scenarios for the contaminated site. Finally, the RI/FS forms the basis of the Record of Decision (ROD), which evaluates these scenarios and selects the appropriate one. Frequently, the cleanup proposal will be phased with separate remedies to address different problems on the site.

A PRP may settle with the EPA to handle all of these remedies (known as a global settlement) or some of them. The business may also come to an agreement with the EPA to pay for the RI/FS or the removal of the contamination. In some cases, the business/PRP may actually perform the site cleanup, rather than reimburse the EPA. It should be noted, however, that a settlement with the EPA does not necessarily protect a PRP from future liability.

Given the potential for liability, the best method for avoiding costly litigation and cleanup is prevention. When purchasing real estate, a company should work to avoid previously contaminated properties by engaging professionals to do thorough site evaluations. Companies whose business operations generate or deal with hazardous waste should work to prevent disasters. An environmental plan is crucial for this. A company needs to determine which regulations impact them, develop a comprehensive plan for dealing with hazardous waste, and work closely with local authorities where needed to execute it.

The EPA has established a toll-free number for assistance on hazardous waste issues: the RCRA/Superfund Hotline. Callers can get information on storage and transportation procedures, local contractors and governmental agencies, and other information pertinent to hazardous waste. The RCRA/Superfund Hotline number is (800) 424-9346. Additional information is available on the EPA Web site at http://www.epa.gov/superfund/. If contamination is discovered, the most important action a business can take is to stay involved in the process and take responsibility early in the hopes of a settlement rather than become involved in an EPA-led cleanup.

SEE ALSO *Environmental Law and Business*

BIBLIOGRAPHY

Hoover, Kent. "Smith Believes Superfund Needs More Than Small-Business Relief." *Sacramento Business Journal.* 17 December 1999.

Hoover, Kent. "Small Businesses Contest Superfund Fines." *Baltimore Business Journal.* 22 October 1999.

McCrory Martin A. "Who's On First: CERCLA Cost Recovery, Contribution, and Protection." *American Business Law Journal.* Fall 1999.

Mester, Zoltan C. "The Role of Environmental Due Diligence in Property Transactions." *Pollution.* November 2000.

Powell, Fiona M. "Current Issues in Environmental Management." *Business Horizons.* January-February 1998.

"State Order is Not A Civil Action Under CERCLA." *Hazardous Waste Consultant.* June 2005.

Hillstrom, Northern Lights
updated by Magee, ECDI

COMPUTER APPLICATIONS

According to The History of Computing Project, the prototype of the first microcomputer was introduced by the aptly named Micro Computer Inc., Los Angeles, in 1968. ARPANET, a defense contractors' information exchange and the precursor of the Internet, was born a year later. Commercial microcomputers (Apple, Commodore, Tandy, Sinclair, and Texas Instruments) appeared in 1977. Apple Computer introduced the first graphical interface with the Macintosh; Microsoft followed with the first version of Windows in 1985. The Internet evolved from ARPANET over a period of 18 years and, by 1987, it was a world-wide network. By 1990 it was beginning to appear in small businesses, usually in text mode. The first well-known microcomputer software applications were the VisiCalc spreadsheet and the word processors Applewriter and WordStar, all dating to the 1978-1979 period.

A few small businesses used computers before the micros appeared, but primarily in professional applications rather than as business tools. Minicomputers like the Honeywell (used in engineering) and the Wang (a dedicated word processor much used by law-firms and here and there by a successful author) were in the small business price range. Since then the three related strands of computing—hardware, software, and networks—have produced something of an avalanche of change in business administration and communications, every year bringing changes. Not surprisingly, four months before 2006 began, *PC Magazine* published a forecast entitled "2006: The Year Everything Changes." More or less the same theme has been sounded every year since 1980. But changes in computing and related software applications have shifted toward cell-phone-sized devices. In the traditional areas of office computing, the emerging issues of the mid-2000s are 1) centralization and decentralization: should the information technology (IT) staff have more or less control; 2) renewal or adaptation: should aging applications be brought up to date or should the business intelligently integrate old and new and save money; and 3) Web-related expansion and exploitation.

Small business has taken an active part both in the use and provision of computer applications. Once computers became affordable, they have been widely deployed in small business and, whether stand-alone or networked, have provided much the same administrative support service they do in larger enterprises. Small businesses have also participated actively in providing computer services, the production of custom software, the writing of such software for their own operations, in consulting with clients and systems integration, and in Web-consulting and Web-page design and development. By the very nature of the small business environment, small operations have found it easy to adapt and to respond rapidly to change in what was a dynamic environment.

CATEGORIES OF APPLICATIONS

Operating Systems All computers run under the control of operating system software (OS) designed for the hard-

ware platform. The OS provides the basic environment in which everything takes place. Windows is the most widely-used OS on small computers followed by the Apple's Mac OS; only a small minority of small computers run on Unix, developed in 1969 at Bell Laboratories, or its derivates, e.g., LINUX. The choice of operating systems in small businesses is often driven by the type of work done and/or the operating systems used by clients. Many operations based on the graphic arts use Macintosh computers; in other cases the need easily to exchange data with clients may dictate choice of the OS. All else being equal, small businesses will tend to use the most cost-effective system in-house, typically a Windows-based or a Macintosh system.

Office Applications Word processing for written communications, spreadsheets for analysis, databases for inventory control, bookkeeping software for accounting, and software for tax preparation have become reasonably priced for even small businesses that have only one computer. Payroll software has now emerged for smaller operations too, sometimes free-standing and sometimes as extensions of popular bookkeeping packages. In the mid-2000s, most small businesses were computerized and, in addition, enjoyed data management at levels of sophistication unimaginable in the mid-1990s.

Professional Software Computer-assisted software development, design, and manufacturing systems (CAS, CAD, and CAM) are perhaps the best-known examples of professional software. Such systems, however, are also available for just about any professional activity that is based on symbol manipulation, data storage, and data processing. The Apple Macintosh, an early entrant into the graphical environment, continues to dominate graphic arts operations. Computer-based page design and typesetting packages have become affordable and are widely used in the small organization. Virtually all medical practices use computer-based patient scheduling and billing systems; the goal of completely automated and digitalized patient record-keeping, however, is still in the future; systems are being installed here and there but are not yet widely used.

Business Communications and Outreach The introduction of computer faxes and especially e-mail systems has revolutionized the way that businesses communicate with one another and employees interact within the company. Long-distance telephone costs and postage costs are saved in the process, and faster communications also speed up decision-making. Of greatest importance, perhaps, for the small business is its ability to communicate with potential customers through its own Web-site. Web-based marketing is very widespread.

FACTORS TO WEIGH WHEN CONSIDERING NEW COMPUTER APPLICATIONS

Many small business owners have embraced computers as tools in doing business—and have done so early enough so that at present, in many places, hardware and applications both are becoming old. Amanda Kooser, writing in *Entrepreneur,* summed up the situation as follows: "A recent report by the Business Performance Management Forum took a look at this neglected issue [obsolete programs]. They surveyed a cross section of businesses and found more than 70 percent of respondents were convinced there were redundant, deficient or obsolete applications being maintained and supported on their networks. Forty percent estimated unwanted programs consumed more than 10 percent of their IT budgets. That can add up to a lot of unnecessary costs." IT in this context stands for Information Technology. Kooser recommends that companies conduct disciplined IT audits followed by systematic culling of old technology and its replacement with more modern software.

Another view is taken by Joe Tedesco, writing in *Database.* Tedesco's title signals the strategy: "Out With The Old? Not So Fast." Tedesco asks: "Is it time, simply, to buy new stuff? Again?" He goes on to spell out the downside: "Investing anew in software is not an especially appealing option, for a variety of reasons. How can [companies] leverage proven tools for new challenges such as increased functionality, heightened security and better data and subject-matter management? More and more companies are finding new value in the software already in use in their organizations."

These two views—replace the old or rationalize the old—have a counterpart in movements to centralize systems that have grown up throughout the company without coordination (on the one hand) and creating order by networking or rearranging existing systems to fit a more orderly situation easier for computer staffs to oversee and to maintain (on the other).

These kinds of arguments, common in the trade press, may signal that computer use is beginning to mature in organizations and that, at least in the immediate future, much more attention will be paid to cost-effective management of existing resources and cautious acquisition of the new.

Despite conflicting views, peer pressure and anxiety often influence buyers, not least small business buyers. In an article for *Fortune,* Joel Dreyfuss wrote as follows: "If you don't have the latest and (always) greatest software and hardware on your business computers, your vendors and employees can make you feel that you're just one step away from quill pens and parchment. The truth is that most small businesses, and consumers for that matter, get cajoled into upgrades that give them more headaches than benefits."

Dreyfuss suggested that small business owners have employees figure out the cost of installation, debugging, and training associated with new computer equipment before consenting to a purchase. He also mentioned that Usenet discussion groups and technical bulletin boards on the Internet can provide valuable analysis of new products. "Seeing the comments about installation problems, upgrade issues, and reported incompatibilities with other products can cool the ardor of any technology fanatic," he noted.

Another factor for small business owners to keep in mind is that a variety of computer applications are available online over the Internet. A number of companies have established small business portals on the Internet to give companies access to software and services—such as payroll processing, legal services, online banking, or assistance in building a Web site for E-commerce. In addition, application service providers (ASPs) offer companies the opportunity to test and use software over the Internet without having to purchase it. These options may eventually reduce the cost and improve the accessibility of computer applications for small businesses.

BIBLIOGRAPHY

Cohen, Alan. "Within Striking Distance: Small Business Web Portals Struggle to Attract Customers with the Right Mix of Content and Services." *FSB.* 1 April 2001.

Cullen, Cheryl Dangel. "Software for Designers: What Do They Want? What Are They Getting?" *Digital Output.* August 2005.

Dreyfuss, Joel. "The Latest and Greatest Disease: Even Big Companies, with Pricey Evaluation Staffs, Find It Hard to Resist the Allure of the Bigger and Better Hardware and Software Products. But Do You Need All Those Newfangled Features?" *Fortune.* 16 October 2000.

Kooser, Amanda C. "Spring cleaning: Old Software Draining Your IT Budget? Here's How to Clean Up." *Entrepreneur.* May 2005.

Loehr, Mark. "Right Size IT." *Database.* May 2005.

Miller, Michael J. "2006: The Year Everything Changes." *PC Magazine.* 9 August 2005.

Tedesco, Joe. "Out With The Old? Not So Fast." *Database.* May 2005.

The History of Computing Project. Available from www.thocp.net. Retrieved on 26 January 2006.

Hillstrom, Northern Lights
updated by Magee, ECDI

COMPUTER CRIMES

DEFINITIONS

The U.S. Department of Justice (DOJ), in its manual on computer crime, defines such crime as "any violations of criminal law that involve a knowledge of computer technology for their perpetration, investigation, or prosecution." Being very broad, the definition, dating to 1989, remains valid. In its elaborations on the subject, DOJ divides computer crime into three categories: 1) crimes in which computer hardware, peripherals, and software are the target of a crime; the criminal is obtaining these objects illegally; 2) crimes in which the computer is the immediate "subject" or "victim" of a crime, i.e., the crime consists of attacks on a computer or a system, destruction or disrupting of which is the damage caused; and 3) crimes in which computers and related systems are the means or "instrument" by which ordinary crimes are committed, such as theft of identities, data, or money or the distribution of child pornography.

Computer Crime: Broad Focus The first category is part of computer crime no doubt because computers are still surrounded by a halo of novelty. In the course of time, the theft of computers or software will no more be remarked upon than the theft of groceries or horses (e.g., "grocery crime" or "horse crime.") In the third category the computer is the principal means of obtaining other things and is thus analogous to "armed" robbery—where a weapon is the means of achieving the criminal end. The rapid spread of computers and computer systems, interconnected by wired or wireless means, has opened a new field in which criminals could operate. But all the crimes covered by the third category existed before computers.

Computer Crime: Narrow Focus The second of DOJ's categories is the one most people associate with computer crime and also with "computer annoyance" in the form of "spam." These disruptions began innocently enough. The first virus, known as Elk Clone, was written by Rich Skrenta as a boy in the 9th grade around 1982. The virus resided on an Apple II disk and, on the 50th booting of the computer with that disk, displayed a little poem, entitled "Elk Cloner: the program with a personality," which said in part: *It will get on all your disks / It will infiltrate your chips / Yes it's Cloner!* Rich Skrenta has, since, gone on to become the co-founder and CEO of Topix.net, an Internet news service. Viruses have differentiated into other categories. Major forms and definitions are listed below as outlined by Ryan P. Wallace and associates writing in *American Criminal Law Review:*

- *Viruses.* These are programs that modify other computer programs so that they carry out functions intended by the creator of the virus. The Melissa Virus, for example (March 1999), disrupted e-mail service around the world.

- *Worms.* Worms have the functionality of viruses but spread by human action by way of the Internet hitch-hiking on mail.

- *Trojan horses.* As their name implies, these intruders pretend to be innocent programs. Users are persuaded to install something innocent-seeming on their computer. The Trojan horse then activates a more destructive program embedded in the innocent code.

- *Logic bombs.* Are destructive programs activated by some event or a specific date or time. Elk Cloner fit this category because it activated its message on the 50th booting of a disk. The same concept is used legally by companies that distribute time-limited samples of their software. The software disables itself after the passage, say, of 30 or 60 days.

- *Sniffers.* These are legitimate programs used to monitor and analyze networks. They can be deployed in a criminal fashion to steal passwords, credit card information, identities, or to spy on network activity.

- *Distributed denial of service attacks.* Such attacks are directed at Web sites by illegitimately causing multiple computers to send barrages of connection requests to the target site, thus causing it to crash.

The "Hacker" The term "hacker" came to be applied to computer hobbyists who spent their spare time creating video games and other basic computer programs. The term acquired negative connotations in the 1980s when computer experts illegally accessed several high-profile databanks. Databases at the Los Alamos National Laboratory (a center of nuclear weapons research) and the Sloan-Kettering Cancer Center in New York City were among their targets. Access to systems by telephone linkage from any computer increased such attacks. Over time, the "hacker" label came to be applied to programmers and disseminators of viruses. The public perception of hackers continues to be that of a lone expert with a taste for mischief. But "hacking" has come to encompass a wide range of computer crimes motivated by financial gain. Indeed, the vital information kept in computers has made them a target for corporate espionage, fraud, and embezzlement efforts. With the growing sophistication in computer security programs and law-enforcement efforts has come the insight that many apparent "hacker" attacks come from well-informed insiders intent on spoil or, occasionally, on vengeance.

Spam Since the spread of the Internet, "spam" has acquired the meaning of "unsolicited e-mail." Spam came under relatively mild regulation with the passage of the Controlling the Assault of Non-Solicited Pornography and Marketing Act, also officially called the CAN-SPAM Act of 2003 (Public Law 108-197). It became effective in December of 2003 and took effect on January 1, 2004. The Act requires that senders of unsolicited commercial e-mail label their messages, but Congress did not require a standard labeling language. Such messages are required to carry instructions on how to opt-out of receiving such mail; the sender must also provide its actual physical address. Misleading headers and titles are prohibited. Congress authorized the Federal Trade Commission to establish a "do-not-mail" registry but did not require that FTC do so. CAN-SPAM also prevents states from outlawing commercial e-mail or to require their own labeling. Since 2003 other bills have been proposed but have not been enacted.

In effect, based on the provisions of CAN-SPAM, spam is not a computer crime unless, according to U.S. Code, Title 18, No. 1037, violation is committed "in furtherance of any felony under the laws of the United States or of any State." Despite its legal status, spam is both a major annoyance and extracts a cost. According to Ryan P. Wallace et. al., "Estimates put the total cost of spam to American businesses in 2003 at more than $10 million in lost productivity and anti-spam measures."

INCIDENCE AND COSTS

The FBI Survey As reported by the Federal Bureau of Investigation in its *2005 FBI Computer Crime Survey,* 64.1 percent of 2,066 companies surveyed reported some kind of computer crime incident in 2005 resulting in financial loss; all told, 5,389 incidents were reported. Small businesses were well-represented in the survey: more than half of the respondents (51.2 percent) had a range of 10 to 99 employees. Responding organizations experienced 2.75 incidents on average. Half of the respondents had 1 to 4 incidents, 19 percent had 20 or more incidents, the rest fell in between. Large organizations tended to have the most incidents.

The total cost of incidents reported by this group of companies was $31.7 million. The largest losses, amounting to $12 million, were associated with viruses, worms, and Trojan horses. The next four categories, in order, were thefts of laptops, desktops, and personal digital assistants ($3.5 million), financial fraud ($3.2 million), and network intrusion ($2.6 million). The smallest category, with a cost of $52,500, was Web-site defacement.

As already stated, slightly over 64 percent experienced financial losses. The FBI extrapolated this result to the nation as a whole but intentionally made its assumptions conservative. The agency assumed that only 20 percent of a total population of 13 million companies would have experienced losses rather than 64 percent, as in its sample. The downward shift was in part based on the likelihood that respondents to the FBI survey may have done so because they were more aware of problems through experience. But the FBI also recognized that actual victimization rate may have been much higher than the 20 percent assumed. In any case, the conservative assumption used produced a total loss for the nation of $67.2 billion in 2005.

The CSI/FBI Survey The Computer Security Institute (CSI) describes itself as "the world's leading membership organization specifically dedicated to serving and training the information, computer and network security professional." With FBI cooperation, CSI has been conducting the *CSI/FBI Computer Crime and Security Survey* every year for a decade; its 2005 survey was the tenth. It is both a smaller and a larger survey than the FBI survey summarized above in that it looks at fewer but larger organizations. In 2005 CSI surveyed 699 organizations; these included governmental entities and universities as well as businesses; only 20 percent of survey respondents were organizations in the 1 to 99 employee category. Ninety-one percent of respondents reported financial losses; these amounted to $130.1 million (over against $31.7 million by 2006 organizations in FBI's 2005 survey). CSI made no attempt to extrapolate its loss figure to the nation as a whole.

The pattern of losses reported in the CSI/FBI survey shows up some interesting differences. The top loss category was also from viruses ($42.8 million); second ranked was unauthorized access ($31.2 million); third was theft of proprietary information ($30.9 million). These three categories accounted for 80.6 percent of all damages.

Only 20 percent of respondents reported incidents to law-enforcement agencies, an all-time low level already reached in 2004. The principal reasons given for not reporting incidents was that such information, reaching the public, would hurt stock price or aid competitors. Based on the survey results, "inside jobs" are as frequent as attacks by hackers or criminals from the outside.

INTERNAL AND EXTERNAL THREATS

Andrew Harbinson, an expert in computer crime working for Ernst & Young in Ireland wrote recently in *Accountancy Ireland* that for every external attack there are 3 or 4 attacks on the inside. "This is for obvious enough reasons," wrote Harbinson. "To carry out a crime you need knowledge, motive and opportunity. An outsider may have a lot of motive and a degree of knowledge (depending on the internal security of the network) but an insider is likely to have all three." Harbinson also finds it notable that "in some surveys in the last couple of years the proportion of internal to external frauds has miraculously 'flipped,' with external frauds now stated as being more common." The most likely reason for this, in Harbinson's view, is a new regulatory climate produced by scandals like those involving Enron and Worldcom. "Companies are much more reluctant to admit to fraud, as to do so might have regulatory consequences. It is a matter of some concern that, instead of dealing with such issues, most companies appear to want to sweep them under the carpet." The CSI/FBI survey discussed above appears to substantiate this view by showing a decline in the reporting of such incidents in order to protect the stock price.

SECURITY MEASURES

Computer security is concerned with preventing information stored in or used by computers from being altered, stolen, or used to commit crimes. The field includes the protection of electronic funds transfers, proprietary information (product designs, client lists, etc.), computer programs, and other communications, as well as the prevention of computer viruses. It can be difficult to place a dollar value on these assets, especially when such factors as potential loss of reputation or liability issues are considered. In some cases (e.g., military and hospital applications) there is a potential for loss of life due to misplaced or destroyed data; this cannot be adequately conveyed by risk analysis formulas.

The question most companies face is not whether to practice computer security measures but how much time and effort to invest. Fortunately, companies looking to protect themselves from computer crime can choose from a broad range of security options. Some of these measures are specifically designed to counter internal threats, while others are shaped to stop outside dangers. Some are relatively inexpensive to put in place, while others require significant outlays of money. But many security experts believe that the single greatest defense that any business can bring to bear is simply a mindset in which issues of security are of paramount concern.

Protection from Internal Threats Whereas big corporations typically have entire departments devoted to computer system management, small businesses often do not have such a luxury. But common-sense measures that can be taken by managers and/or system administrators to minimize the danger of internal tampering with computer systems include the following:

- Notify employees that their use of the company's personal computers, computer networks, and Internet connections will be monitored. Then do it.

- Physical access to computers can be limited in various ways, including imposition of passwords; magnetic card readers; and biometrics, which verify the user's identity through matching patterns in hand geometry, signature or keystroke dynamics, neural networks (the pattern of nerves in the face), DNA fingerprinting, retinal imaging, or voice recognition. More traditional site control methods such as sign-in logs and security badges can also be useful.

- Classify information based on its importance, assigning security clearances to employees as needed.

- Eliminate nonessential modems that could be used to transmit information.

- Monitor activities of employees who keep non-traditional hours at the office.

- Make certain that the company's hiring process includes extensive background checks, especially in cases where the employee would be handling sensitive information.

- Stress the importance of confidential passwords to employees.

Protection from External Threats Small businesses also need to protect their systems against outside attack. Firewalls may be expensive but may be worth the cost. The single greatest scourge from the outside are viruses of one kind or another. Business owners can do much to minimize this threat by heeding the following basic steps:

- Install and use anti-virus software programs that scan PCs, computer networks, CD-ROMs, tape drives, diskettes, and Internet material, and destroy viruses when found.

- Update anti-virus programs on a regular basis.

- Ensure that all individual computers are equipped with anti-virus programs.

- Forbid employees from putting programs on their office computers without company approval.

- Make sure that the company has a regular policy of backing up (copying) important files and storing them in a safe place, so that the impact of corrupted files is minimized. Having a source of clean (i.e., uninfected by viruses) backup copies for data files and programs is as important as it is elementary.

A variety of sources exist to assist small business owners with virus protection and Internet security measures. For example, several Web sites provide free virus warnings and downloadable antivirus patches for Web browsers, including www.symantec.com/avcenter and www.ciac.org. The Computer Security Institute provides annual surveys on security breaches at www.gocsi.com. Another useful resource is the National Computer Security Association (www.ncsa.com), which provides tips on Internet security for business owners and supplies definitions of high-tech terms.

Small businesses seeking to establish Internet security policies and procedures might begin by contacting CERT. This U.S. government organization, formed in 1988, works with the Internet community to raise awareness of security issues and organize the response to security threats. The CERT web site (www.cert.org) posts the latest security alerts and also provides security-related documents, tools, and training seminars. Finally, CERT offers 24-hour technical assistance in the event of Internet security breaches. Small business owners who contact CERT about a security problem will be asked to provide their company's Internet address, the computer models affected, the types of operating systems and software used, and the security measures that were in place.

HARDWARE THEFT

Although computer viruses and theft of information pose the greatest financial threats to large organizations, loss of hardware by simple thievery is the second-ranking loss category for small business. Common-sense measures such as supervising entrances and locking up easily transported equipment at night are obvious enough. Many laptops are lost to thieves-of-opportunity who, standing in an unattended lobby, see a laptop on a desk while distantly laughter sounds from an office birthday party.

Business travelers, of course, must keep a close eye on their notebook and laptop computers. The allure of portables is so great that thieves sometimes work in teams to get their hands on them. Airports and hotels are favorite haunts of thieves. Security experts counsel travelers to be especially vigilant in high-traffic areas, to carry computer serial numbers separately from the hardware, and to consider installing locks, alarms, or tracking software.

SEE ALSO *Internet Security*

BIBLIOGRAPHY

Federal Bureau of Investigation. *2005 FBI Computer Crime Survey.* Available from www.fbi.gov/publications/ ccc2005.pdf. Retrieved on 28 January 2006.

Gordon, Lawrence A., Martin P. Loeb, William Lucyshyn, and Robert Richardson. *2005 CSI/FBI Computer Crime and Security Survey.* Computer Security Institute. Available from www.gocsi.com. Retrieved on 29 January 2006.

Gibson, Stan. "Hacking: It's a Mad, Mad, Mad New World." *eWeek.* 1 January 2001.

Harbinson, Andrew. "Understanding Computer Crime: A Beginner's Guide." *Accountancy Ireland.* August 2005.

Karp, Josh. "Small Businesses Often Target of Cybercrime; Lack of IT Expertise Leads to Vulnerability." *Crain's Chicago Business.* 19 February 2001.

Morgan, Lisa. "Be Afraid . . . Be Very Afraid—Malicious Attacks Are on the Rise, and Trends Are Harder to Predict." *Internet Week.* 8 January 2001.

Rich Skrenta Home Page Available from http:// www.skrenta.com/. Retrieved on 28 January 2006.

Wallace, Ryan P., Adam M. Lusthaus, and Jong Hwan Kim. "Computer Crimes." *American Criminal Law Review.* Spring 2005.

U.S. Department of Justice. National Institute of Justice. *Computer Crime: Criminal Justice Resource Manual.* 1989.

Hillstrom, Northern Lights
updated by Magee, ECDI

COMPUTER-AIDED DESIGN (CAD) AND COMPUTER-AIDED MANUFACTURING (CAM)

Computer-aided design (CAD) involves creating computer models defined by geometrical parameters. These models typically appear on a computer monitor as a three-dimensional representation of a part or a system of parts, which can be readily altered by changing relevant parameters. CAD systems enable designers to view objects under a wide variety of representations and to test these objects by simulating real-world conditions.

Computer-aided manufacturing (CAM) uses geometrical design data to control automated machinery. CAM systems are associated with computer numerical control (CNC) or direct numerical control (DNC) systems. These systems differ from older forms of numerical control (NC) in that geometrical data are encoded mechanically. Since both CAD and CAM use computer-based methods for encoding geometrical data, it is possible for the processes of design and manufacture to be highly integrated. Computer-aided design and manufacturing systems are commonly referred to as CAD/CAM.

THE ORIGINS OF CAD/CAM

CAD had its origins in three separate sources, which also serve to highlight the basic operations that CAD systems provide. The first source of CAD resulted from attempts to automate the drafting process. These developments were pioneered by the General Motors Research Laboratories in the early 1960s. One of the important time-saving advantages of computer modeling over traditional drafting methods is that the former can be quickly corrected or manipulated by changing a model's parameters. The second source of CAD was in the testing of designs by simulation. The use of computer modeling to test products was pioneered by high-tech industries like aerospace and semiconductors. The third source of CAD development resulted from efforts to facilitate the flow from the design process to the manufacturing process using numerical control (NC) technologies, which enjoyed widespread use in many applications by the mid-1960s. It was this source that resulted in the linkage between CAD and CAM. One of the most important trends in CAD/CAM technologies is the ever-tighter integration between the design and manufacturing stages of CAD/CAM-based production processes.

The development of CAD and CAM and particularly the linkage between the two overcame traditional NC shortcomings in expense, ease of use, and speed by enabling the design and manufacture of a part to be undertaken using the same system of encoding geometrical data. This innovation greatly shortened the period between design and manufacture and greatly expanded the scope of production processes for which automated machinery could be economically used. Just as important, CAD/CAM gave the designer much more direct control over the production process, creating the possibility of completely integrated design and manufacturing processes.

The rapid growth in the use of CAD/CAM technologies after the early 1970s was made possible by the development of mass-produced silicon chips and the microprocessor, resulting in more readily affordable computers. As the price of computers continued to decline and their processing power improved, the use of CAD/CAM broadened from large firms using large-scale mass production techniques to firms of all sizes. The scope of operations to which CAD/CAM was applied broadened as well. In addition to parts-shaping by traditional machine tool processes such as stamping, drilling, milling, and grinding, CAD/CAM has come to be used by firms involved in producing consumer electronics, electronic components, molded plastics, and a host of other products. Computers are also used to control a number of manufacturing processes (such as chemical processing) that are not strictly defined as CAM because the control data are not based on geometrical parameters.

Using CAD, it is possible to simulate in three dimensions the movement of a part through a production process. This process can simulate feed rates, angles and speeds of machine tools, the position of part-holding clamps, as well as range and other constraints limiting the operations of a machine. The continuing development of the simulation of various manufacturing processes is one of the key means by which CAD and CAM systems are becoming increasingly integrated. CAD/CAM systems also facilitate communication among those involved in design, manufacturing, and other processes. This is of particular importance when one firm contracts another to either design or produce a component.

ADVANTAGES AND DISADVANTAGES

Modeling with CAD systems offers a number of advantages over traditional drafting methods that use rulers, squares, and compasses. For example, designs can be altered without erasing and redrawing. CAD systems also offer "zoom" features analogous to a camera lens, whereby a designer can magnify certain elements of a model to facilitate inspection. Computer models are typically three dimensional and can be rotated on any axis, much as one could rotate an actual three dimensional model in one's hand, enabling the designer to gain a fuller sense of the object. CAD systems also lend themselves to modeling cutaway drawings, in which the internal shape of a part is revealed, and to illustrating the spatial relationships among a system of parts.

To understand CAD it is also useful to understand what CAD cannot do. CAD systems have no means of comprehending real-world concepts, such as the nature of the object being designed or the function that object will serve. CAD systems function by their capacity to codify geometrical concepts. Thus the design process using CAD involves transferring a designer's idea into a formal geometrical model. Efforts to develop computer-based "artificial intelligence" (AI) have not yet succeeded in penetrating beyond the mechanical—represented by geometrical (rule-based) modeling.

Other limitations to CAD are being addressed by research and development in the field of expert systems. This field is derived from research done in AI. One example of an expert system involves incorporating information about the nature of materials—their weight, tensile strength, flexibility, and so on—into CAD software. By including this and other information, the CAD system could then "know" what an expert engineer knows when that engineer creates a design. The system could then mimic the engineer's thought pattern and actually "create" more of the design. Expert systems might involve the implementation of more abstract principles, such as the nature of gravity and friction, or the function and relation of commonly used parts, such as levers or nuts and bolts. Expert systems might also come to change the way data are stored and retrieved in CAD/CAM systems, supplanting the hierarchical system with one that offers greater flexibility. Such futuristic concepts, however, are all highly dependent on our abilities to analyze human decision processes and to translate these into mechanical equivalents if possible.

One of the key areas of development in CAD technologies is the simulation of performance. Among the most common types of simulation are testing for response to stress and modeling the process by which a part might be manufactured or the dynamic relationships among a system of parts. In stress tests, model surfaces are shown by a grid or mesh, that distort as the part comes under simulated physical or thermal stress. Dynamics tests function as a complement or substitute for building working prototypes. The ease with which a part's specifications can be changed facilitates the development of optimal dynamic efficiencies, both as regards the functioning of a system of parts and the manufacture of any given part. Simulation is also used in electronic design automation, in which simulated flow of current through a circuit enables the rapid testing of various component configurations.

The processes of design and manufacture are, in some sense, conceptually separable. Yet the design process must be undertaken with an understanding of the nature of the production process. It is necessary, for example, for a designer to know the properties of the materials with which the part might be built, the various techniques by which the part might be shaped, and the scale of production that is economically viable. The conceptual overlap between design and manufacture is suggestive of the potential benefits of CAD and CAM and the reason they are generally considered together as a system.

Recent technical developments have fundamentally impacted the utility of CAD/CAM systems. For example, the ever-increasing processing power of personal computers has given them viability as a vehicle for CAD/CAM application. Another important trend is toward the establishment of a single CAD-CAM standard, so that different data packages can be exchanged without manufacturing and delivery delays, unnecessary design revisions, and other problems that continue to bedevil some CAD-CAM initiatives. Finally, CAD-CAM software continues to evolve in such realms as visual representation and integration of modeling and testing applications.

THE CASE FOR CAS AND CAS/CAM

A conceptually and functionally parallel development to CAD/CAM is CAS or CASE, computer-aided software engineering. As defined by SearchSMB.com in its article on "CASE," "CASE ... is the use of a computer-assisted method to organize and control the development of software, especially on large, complex projects involving many software components and people." CASE dates back to the 1970s when computer companies began to apply concepts from the CAD/CAM experience to introduce more discipline into the software development process.

Another abbreviation inspired by the ubiquitous presence of CAD/CAM in the manufacturing sector is CAS/CAM. This phrase stands for Computer-Aided Selling/Computer-Aided Marketing software. In the case of CASE as well as CAS/CAM, the core of such technologies is integration of work flows and application of proven rules to a repeating process.

BIBLIOGRAPHY

Ames, Benjamin B. "How CAD Keeps It Simple." *Design News.* 19 June 2000.

"CAD Software Works with Symbols from CADDetails.com." *Product News Network.* 11 January 2006.

"CASE." SearchSMB.com. Available from http://searchsmb.techtarget.com/sDefinition/0,sid44_gci213838,00.html. Retrieved on 27 January 2006.

Christman, Alan. "Technology Trends in CAM Software." *Modern Machine Shop.* December 2005.

Leondes, Cornelius, ed. "Computer-Aided Design, Engineering, and Manufacturing." Vol. 5 of *The Design of Manufacturing Systems.* CRC Press, 2001.

"What Do You Mean?" *Mechanical Engineering-CIME.* November 2005.

Hillstrom, Northern Lights
updated by Magee, ECDI

COMPUTERS AND COMPUTER SYSTEMS

A computer is a programmable device that can automatically perform a sequence of calculations or other operations on data once programmed for the task. It can store, retrieve, and process data according to internal instructions. A computer may be either digital, analog, or hybrid, although most in operation today are digital. Digital computers express variables as numbers, usually in the binary system. They are used for general purposes, whereas analog computers are built for specific tasks, typically scientific or technical. The term "computer" is usually synonymous with digital computer, and computers for business are exclusively digital.

ELEMENTS OF THE COMPUTER SYSTEM

The core, computing part of a computer is its central processing unit (CPU), or processor. It comprises an arithmetic-logic unit to carry out calculations, main memory to temporarily store data for processing, and a control unit to control the transfer of data between memory, input and output sources, and the arithmetic-logic unit. A computer is not fully functional without various peripheral devices, however. These are typically connected to a computer through cables, although some may be built into the same unit with the CPU. These include devices for the input of data, such as keyboards, mice, trackballs, scanners, light pens, modems, magnetic strip card readers, and microphones, as well as items for the output of data, such as monitors, printers, plotters, loudspeakers, earphones, and modems. In addition to these input/output devices, other types of peripherals include computer data storage devices for auxiliary memory storage, where data is saved even when the computer is turned off. These devices most often are magnetic tape drives, magnetic disk drives, or optical disk drives.

Finally, for a digital computer to function automatically, it requires programs, or sets of instructions written in computer-readable code. To be distinguished from the physical or hardware components of a computer, programs are collectively referred to as software.

A computer *system,* therefore, is a computer combined with peripheral equipment and software so that it can perform desired functions. Often the terms "computer" and "computer system" are used interchangeably, especially when peripheral devices are built into the same unit as the computer or when a system is sold and installed as a package. The term "computer system," however, may also refer to a configuration of hardware and software designed for a specific purpose, such as a manufacturing control system, a library automation system, or an accounting system. Or it may refer to a network of multiple computers linked together so that they can share software, data, and peripheral equipment.

Computers tend to be categorized by size and power, although advancements in computers' processing power have blurred the distinctions between traditional categories. Power and speed are influenced by the size of a computer's internal storage units, called words, which determine the amount of data it can process at once and is measured in bits (binary digits). Computer speed is also determined by its clock speed, which is measured in megahertz. Additionally, the amount of main memory a computer has, which is measured in bytes (or more precisely, kilobytes, megabytes, or gigabytes) of RAM (random access memory), plays a role in determining how much data it can process. The amount of memory that auxiliary storage devices can hold also determines the capabilities of a computer system.

THE MICROCOMPUTER

The development of the microprocessor, a CPU on a single integrated-circuit chip, enabled the development of affordable single-user microcomputers for the first time. The slow processing power of the early microcomputers, however, made them attractive only to hobbyists and not to the business market. In 1977, however, the personal

computer industry got under way with the introduction of off-the-shelf home computers from three manufacturers.

The term "personal computer" (PC) was coined by IBM with the launch of its PC in 1981. This model became an instant success and set the standard for the microcomputer industry. By the early 1990s personal computers had become the fastest-growing category of computers. This was largely due to the adoption of their use in businesses of all sizes. The availability of these small, inexpensive computers brought computer technology to even the smallest of enterprises.

The most recent category of microcomputer to enter the business world is the portable computer. These small and light—but increasingly powerful—computers are commonly known as laptop or notebook computers. Laptop computers have the same power as desktop personal computers, but are built more compactly and use flat screen monitors, usually using liquid crystal display, that fold down to form a slim unit that fits in a briefcase and usually weigh under 15 pounds. A notebook computer is one that weighs under 6 pounds and may or may not have a full-size keyboard. A pocket computer is a hand-held calculator-size computer. A personal digital assistant is a pocket computer that uses a pen and tablet for input, has a fax/modem card, and is combined with the capabilities of a cellular telephone for remote data communications. Portable computers are increasingly popular among businesspeople who travel, such as executives or sales representatives.

Open Systems Today, most computer systems are "open"—compatible with computer hardware and software from different manufacturers. In the past, all components of a computer system originated from the same manufacturer. There were no industry-wide standards. As a result, printers, monitors, and other peripheral equipment from one manufacturer would not operate when matched with the computer of another manufacturer. More significantly, software could only run on the specific computer brand for which it was designed. Today, however, "open systems," wherein various equipment from different manufacturers can be matched together, is common. Open systems are especially popular among small business owners because they allow enterprises to upgrade or expand their computer systems more easily and cheaply. Open systems provide business owners with more buying options, enable them to minimize expenses of employee retraining on new systems, and give them greater freedom to share computer files with outside clients or vendors.

Networking Computers on a network are physically linked by cables and use network software in conjunction with the operating system software. Depending on the hardware and software used, different types of computers may be put on the same network. This may involve computers of different sizes—such as mainframes, midranges, and microcomputers—or computers and peripherals of different manufacturers, which the trend toward open systems has facilitated. Local area networks (LANs) link computers within a limited geographical area, while Wide area networks (WANs) connect computers in different geographic regions. Networks may have various architectures which determine whether computers on the network can act independently. A commonly used system architecture is client-server, whereby a server computer is designated as the one storing and processing data and is accessed by multiple users each at a client computer.

LANs have transformed how employees within an organization use computers. In organizations where employees formerly accessed midrange computers through "dumb" terminals, these employees now typically have more capabilities. These users have their own personal computers at their desks, but are still able to access needed data from a midrange or other server through the network. Whereas smaller businesses typically favor LANs, WANs are often used by companies with multiple facilities located over a wide geographic area. After all, under a WAN system, a company's databases can be accessed at headquarters in one city, at a manufacturing plant in other city, and at sales offices in other locations.

BUSINESS USAGE OF COMPUTERS

Computers are used in government, industry, nonprofit and nongovernmental organizations, and in the home, but their impact has been greatest in business and industry. The competitive nature of business has created demands for continuous advances in computer technology and systems design. Meanwhile, the declining prices of computer systems and their increasing power and utility has led more and more enterprises to invest in computer systems for an ever-widening range of business functions. Today, computers are used to process data in all aspects of a business enterprise: product design and development, manufacturing, inventory control and distribution, quality control, sales and marketing, service data, accounting, and personnel management. They are also used in businesses of all sizes and in all industry segments, including manufacturing, wholesale, retail, services, mining, agriculture, transportation, and communications.

The most common business uses of a computer system are database management, financial management and accounting, and word processing. Companies use database management systems to keep track of changing information in databases on such subjects as clients, vendors, employees, inventory, supplies, product orders, and service requests. Financial and accounting systems are used for a variety of mathematical calculations on large volumes of numeric data, whether in the basic functions of financial service companies or in the accounting activities of firms. Computers equipped with spreadsheet or database management software, meanwhile, are used by accounts payable, accounts receivable, and payroll departments to process and tabulate financial data and analyze their cash flow situations. Finally, word processing is ubiquitous and is used to create a wide range of documents, including internal memos, correspondence with outside entities, public relations materials, and products (in publishing, advertising, and other industries).

Databases may also be used to help make strategic decisions through the use of software based on artificial intelligence. A database system may include—in addition to records and statistics of products, services, clients, etc.—information about past human experience within a specific field. This is referred to as a knowledge base. Examples of expert system usage include business forecasting activities such as investment analysis, financial planning, insurance underwriting, and fraud risk prediction. Expert systems are also used in activities associated with regulatory compliance, contract bidding, complex production control, customer support, and training.

COMPUTER SYSTEMS AND SMALL BUSINESS

For most small businesses, jumping into the world of computers is a competitive requirement, especially with the advent of the Internet. But computer system purchases can be daunting for entrepreneurs and established business owners alike. After all, small business enterprises typically have less margin for error than their big business brethren. Given this reality, it is very important for owners and managers to make wise choices when choosing and maintaining computers and computer systems. Four major areas that business owners and managers need to consider when weighing computer options are: 1) your company's overall business strategy; 2) the needs of your customers; 3) the needs of your workforce; and 3) the technology's total cost of ownership (TCO).

Company Strategy "It is common to view computer systems technology as a stand-alone entity when, in fact, it should be regarded as one of the larger-scale and more widely-used business tools," wrote Richard Hensley in *Cincinnati Business Courier*. "[Computer systems technology is] a tool that is critical for achieving the overall corporate strategy.... Although it may well exist in the owner's mind, many small and mid-sized companies have no detailed written system strategy. It is not surprising then, that many of the systems technology implementation decisions are more reactive than they are strategically based. Competitive pressures, the need to catch up to the marketplace, and internal growth tend to force buying decisions." Instead, system purchasing decisions should be used proactively as an opportunity to evaluate overall strategies and assess the effectiveness of current operational processes.

Customer Needs Business owners also need to ensure that their chosen computer system meets the needs of customers. Is ongoing communication with clients a critical component of your business? If so, then your system should be equipped with features that allow you and your client to communicate via computer in a timely and effective fashion. Does your business's health hinge on processing customer orders and generating invoices? If so, make sure your system can easily handle such requirements.

Workforce Needs Whether introducing a new computer system or making changes to an existing system, businesses inevitably change the ways in which their employees work, and this factor must be taken into consideration. "It is not unusual to experience some resistance from employees who are reluctant to accept departure from the status quo," said Hensley. "Such resistance can often be greatly reduced by involving the affected employees in the development of, or modification to, the system. They can provide practical information on what works well within the current system and what doesn't. Once the changes have been implemented, establish a training program and support structure for all users. This will maximize the benefits of the system and better equip employees to achieve the results expected from the change." In addition, companies need to make sure that computer technology is distributed in an intelligent fashion. Computers should be allocated according to need, not ranking.

Total Cost of Ownership Many small businesses neglect to consider the accumulated costs associated with various computer systems when making their hardware decisions. In addition to the original price tag, companies need to weigh hidden information technology costs associated with the purchase. These costs, known as total cost of ownership (TCO), include technical support, administrative costs, wasteful user operations, and supplementary expenses (printer ink and paper costs, electricity, etc.). Another factor that should be considered is the equipment's useful life. After all, as Hensley noted, "to assure the capability to produce relevant information, technology systems require scheduled investments." Business owners that ignore this reality do so at their peril, suggest experts. "When it comes to cutting costs, one of your first instincts may be to hold on to your PCs as long as

you can, thinking the less money you spend on new technology, the better," wrote Heather Page in *Entrepreneur.* Actually, though, such reasoning ultimately raises business costs. "Having several generations of hardware, software and operating systems increases the complexity of your PC environment, thus increasing your costs," explained Page. "Not only do you have to maintain technical expertise in older technologies, but you also have to find ways for older equipment to work with the new technologies and develop all your custom applications to support multiple environments."

Given today's fast-changing business environment, then, system upgrades are a fact of life. As Joel Dreyfuss noted in *Fortune,* "if you don't have the latest and (always) greatest software and hardware on your business computers, your vendors and employees can make you feel that you're just one step away from quill pens and parchment." But upgrade initiatives should not be approved impulsively. Instead, business owners and managers should conduct appropriate cost-benefit analysis, weighing such issues as installation and training costs, compatibility with other systems, usefulness of new features, and current ability to meet business needs, before investing in major computer system upgrades.

BIBLIOGRAPHY

Codkind, Alan. "Automating The Business Process." *CMA - The Management Accounting Magazine.* October 1993.

Dreyfuss, Joel. "FSB/Small Businesses." *Fortune.* 13 November 2000.

Hensley, Richard. "Owner Quandary: How Much to Spend on New Technology?" *Cincinnati Business Courier.* 3 March 1997.

Page, Heather. "What Price PC?" *Entrepreneur.* October 1997.

"Small Firm's Usage Patterns." *Nation's Business.* August 1993.

Smith, Sandi. "The Smart Way to Invest in Computers." *Journal of Accountancy.* May 1997.

*Hillstrom, Northern Lights
updated by Magee, ECDI*

CONSOLIDATED OMNIBUS BUDGET RECONCILIATION ACT (COBRA)

The Consolidated Omnibus Budget Reconciliation Act (COBRA), first enacted in 1985 and revised in 1999, is a federal law that requires most employers to provide continuing health insurance coverage to employees and their dependents who are no longer eligible for the company's health insurance program. Employees can lose eligibility for coverage by terminating their employment, reducing their working hours, becoming eligible for Medicare, or in a number of other ways. Under the terms of COBRA, all businesses that employ more than 20 people and offer a group health insurance plan must give employees the option of continuing coverage at their own expense for a limited period of time when they lose eligibility for company-provided benefits. In addition, 44 states have their own laws regarding continuation coverage, some of which apply to smaller businesses and to benefits in addition to health insurance.

COBRA and similar health insurance continuation laws affect small businesses in two ways. First, many entrepreneurs start their own businesses after leaving their jobs with larger companies. These entrepreneurs may wish to take advantage of continuation coverage for themselves and their dependents until they are able to arrange their own health insurance plans. Second, many small business owners must comply with COBRA or other applicable state laws and offer continuation coverage to their employees. Although workers must pay the actual cost of the insurance themselves, the administration of COBRA can be time-consuming and expensive for businesses. There are severe financial penalties for noncompliance, including a fine of $100 per day for failure to notify an employee of his or her COBRA rights, or even the revocation of a company's tax deduction for its group health insurance plan. Employers can also be held liable for damages, including workers' medical costs and legal fees. As a result, many companies outsource the activities associated with COBRA compliance to experienced independent administrators and management programs. For a business with 50 employees, such services are estimated to cost around $1,000 per year.

COBRA SPECIFICS

COBRA applies to nearly all businesses that have more than 20 employees and offer a group health care plan. The only exceptions are churches, church-related tax-exempt organizations, and some federal employees. Companies that are subject to COBRA are required to offer continuation coverage to all "qualified beneficiaries," a category which includes employees, spouses, dependents, and retirees who were covered under the company's group health insurance plan up until they lost eligibility for coverage through a "qualifying event." Companies are not required to offer COBRA benefits to those employees who were not eligible for or declined to participate in the group health plan, or who were eligible for Medicare benefits.

The qualifying events that activate COBRA provisions include a voluntary or involuntary termination of employment, a reduction in hours from full to part-time, a failure to return to work after taking family or medical leave, a call for active military duty, or the bankruptcy of the business. An employee's spouse or dependents can qualify for COBRA benefits—provided they were covered by the company's group health plan—upon the employee's death, the couple's separation or divorce, or a dependent's change in eligibility status (i.e., a child reaches an age at which he or she no longer qualifies for coverage under the employee's insurance). The company may deny COBRA coverage to an employee who was involuntarily terminated from employment due to willful, job-related misconduct. But since these cases often end up in federal court, the company should weigh the expense of court costs against the expense of providing continuation coverage.

When a qualifying event occurs and COBRA is triggered, the company is required to offer a qualified beneficiary the option to continue coverage under all health care plans, medical spending accounts, dental, vision, and hearing plans, prescription drug programs, substance abuse plans, and mental health programs that are offered to regular employees. However, the company is not required to offer continuation coverage for life insurance, disability insurance, retirement plans, or vacation plans. Under normal circumstances, COBRA coverage lasts a maximum of eighteen months. This time limit is extended to twenty-nine months for dependents, or in cases where the employee becomes disabled. If the employee qualifies for COBRA for a reason other than termination of employment or reduction of hours, or experiences a second qualifying event during the regular COBRA coverage period, then the time limit may be extended to thirty-six months.

The employee pays 100 percent of the costs of health insurance coverage under COBRA, plus a 2 percent surcharge to help the employer cover administrative expenses. The employer is entitled to terminate coverage if payments are late, but must allow a 30-day grace period. This time lag may pose a problem for some small businesses, since most insurance companies require payment for COBRA coverage in advance.

Notifications Another component of COBRA involves communication with affected employees. A company is required to explain the right to continue benefits to the each employee when they first join the company group health insurance plan, and again when a qualifying event occurs. When an employee qualifies for COBRA, the company has 30 days [changed to 90 days in 2004, see below] to notify the insurance company of that person's eligibility, and the insurance company then has 14 days to provide the employee with information regarding the costs and benefits of their health care continuation coverage. The employee has 60 days to decide whether he or she wants to continue coverage. If so, the coverage is retroactive to the time of the qualifying event so that no lapses occur.

THE 1999 REVISION OF COBRA REGULATIONS

On February 3, 1999, the Internal Revenue Service (IRS) issued a set of revised and updated guidelines for the administration of COBRA. These new regulations took effect on January 1, 2000, meaning that they applied to all qualifying events occurring on or after that date. Although the new guidelines themselves required some interpretation, many tax and human resources professionals claimed that the rules would ultimately clarify and simplify several aspects of COBRA administration for businesses. Some of the major changes to COBRA are outlined below:

- The new regulations specifically address how COBRA applies to employers and employees when a company is involved in a merger or acquisition. The two companies involved in the transaction are allowed to determine who is responsible for the seller's COBRA liability by contract. If no other arrangements are made, the buyer will assume liability for COBRA coverage if it also assumes the acquisition's health care plan. If the seller terminates all of its health care plans prior to the date of the sale, however, the buyer may avoid COBRA liability.

- The new guidelines prevent employers from terminating a qualified employee's COBRA benefits because of other health care coverage the employee had before electing COBRA. However, the employer can terminate COBRA coverage early if the employee fails to pay premiums on time or becomes covered under another group health care plan or Medicare, or if the employer terminates all of its group health care plans.

- The IRS rules give employers more flexibility in determining how many health care plans they offer under COBRA. Previously, each separate benefit plan (i.e., dental, eye care, or prescription drug benefits) had to be offered separately to employees eligible for COBRA. Under the new guidelines, employers can combine all of their health care benefits into one group plan and offer employees an all-or-nothing package of benefits under COBRA. This provision was expected to greatly simplify COBRA administration for employers.

- The 1999 guidelines limit the application of COBRA to employees covered by flexible spending accounts (FSA) for health care. For employees who maintain an FSA, employers only have to offer COBRA coverage during the year of the qualifying event. In addition, employers are not required to offer COBRA coverage if the amount an employee could receive under the FSA exceeds the amount they would pay for COBRA coverage for the same time period.

- The new regulations eliminate the requirement that employers offer "core coverage" as a separate option for COBRA-eligible employees. Previously, employers who provided an extensive health care benefit package were required to allow employees to elect to continue only the major medical portion, or core coverage, under COBRA, and opt out of additional coverage, like prescription drugs or dental care. Now employees may be required to elect to receive either all the coverage in a plan or no coverage at all. Although this provision may raise the expense for employees, it is also expected to simplify COBRA administration for employers.

- The revised guidelines also clarify an employer's responsibility under the law when an employee who wants COBRA coverage moves to a new geographic area outside the normal boundaries of the group health care plan. If the company's group health care plan is region-specific, the employer is only required to provide COBRA coverage if there are other employees covered in the new geographic region. Employers are not required to make alternative coverage available if none exists in that region.

- Finally, the new rules clarify the small employer exception to COBRA. Under normal circumstances, COBRA does not apply to companies with fewer than twenty employees. But it does apply in cases where a company with fewer than twenty employees pools its health care benefits in a multiple-employer plan under which another company has greater than twenty employees. The new regulations also state that employers cannot terminate COBRA coverage for existing beneficiaries because the number of employees later drops below twenty.

2004 NOTIFICATION RULES CHANGES

The most recent changes to the implementation of COBRA took place on May 26, 2004, with the issuance by the U.S. Department of Labor of its revised rule implementing notification requirements under the law. The information was published in the Federal Register of that date, as "29 CFR Part 2590, Health Care

Continuation Coverage; Final Rule." DOL introduced this rule change on May 28, 2003 in order to update notification requirements. The main change introduced by this regulation was to extended by 30 days (from 60 to 90) the time available for an employer to notify an employee of his or her COBRA rights after the employee was enrolled in a group health program.

Overall, compliance with COBRA and the various state laws governing health insurance continuation can be tricky and expensive. Although the revised COBRA regulations clarify some matters, they also add new rules for employers to be aware of and follow. "To ensure compliance with the new regulations, employers should review their COBRA procedures, COBRA notices, and group health plans and summary plan descriptions, including health FSA plan documents," Mark Bogart wrote in *The CPA Journal*. "Employers should also consider implementing new options permitted under the new rules that could help alleviate some of the complexities in COBRA administration." The U.S. Department of Labor and the U.S. Public Health Service offer free information on how the laws affect businesses.

SEE ALSO *Family and Medical Leave Act*

BIBLIOGRAPHY

Anastasio, Susan. *Small Business Insurance and Risk Management Guide.* U.S. Small Business Administration, n.d.

Bates, Steve. "Benefits Experts Welcome Final COBRA Rules." *HRMagazine.* July 2004.

Bogart, Mark. "New COBRA Regulations Issued." *CPA Journal.* June 1999.

"DOL Releases Final COBRA Notice Rule." *HR Focus.* September 2004.

"How to Comply with the Newly Revised COBRA Regulations." *HR Focus.* August 2000.

"IRS Releases Final COBRA Guidelines." *Journal of Accountancy.* July 1999.

Kilgour, John G. "COBRA: Managing the New Problems." *Employee Benefits Journal.* March 2000.

Manning, Margie. "COBRA Can Create Potholes for Employers, Workers." *St. Louis Business Journal.* 20 November 2000.

Hillstrom, Northern Lights
updated by Magee, ECDI

CONSTRUCTION

Many successful small businesses decide to expand their operations either by purchasing, leasing, or building a new facility. In some instances, the business in question relocates its entire operation to the new facility. In other cases, the business may use the new facility to house excess inventory, maintain equipment, relieve office overcrowding, or open a new store.

For those companies that decide to expand via new construction, the experience can be an unsettling one, full of uncertainties. In fact, relatively few start-up businesses choose construction as their mode of entry due to the higher costs associated with it and the greater length of time involved from the breaking ground stage to the day when the establishment opens its doors for business. Established small- and mid-sized businesses are likely to be in a better position financially to launch a new construction project. Such firms have a proven track record—which can help them with financing—and already-productive operations that bring in revenue that can be used to defray the costs of construction.

A full assessment of the advantages and disadvantages of new construction should be undertaken before any decision is made to build new. Designing and building a new facility has the advantage of providing a company with exactly the space and arrangements to meet its needs. The obvious disadvantages are the delay in occupancy while land acquisition, design work, and building are going on, and the cost of overruns, common in large projects. Oversight responsibilities are essential but can also be very time consuming and distract from the primary business of a company.

Certainly, there are risks associated with construction. But for small- and mid-sized business owners that choose this method of expansion and/or growth—and plan wisely before, during, and after the construction phase—it can also mark the beginning of a bright new chapter in the company's history. A well-designed and built property can allow a company to generate additional revenue, reduce expenses, and/or increase efficiency.

SECURING A BUILDING CONTRACTOR

Some sources of potential building contractors include professional association databases, referrals from architects or fellow small business owners, and a competitive bidding process. "It is important to find a contractor that can build in your specific industry, whether it's a restaurant, health care facility, industrial plant, or technology center," Amanda Strickland wrote in the *Dallas Business Journal.* "Contractors tend to have niches."

A small business owner seeking to secure a good building contractor should concentrate on three factors:

- The contractor's reputation in the community.
- The financial condition of the contractor.
- The status of currently uncompleted jobs by the contractor.

There are many warning signs to watch for when assessing potential contractors. Is the contractor known for subcontracting out large percentages of the total construction work? Does the contractor have a history of clashes with subcontractors? How long has the contractor done business in the area? What percentage of jobs does she complete on schedule? Does his previous work experience adequately match the sort of renovation or construction that your company needs? Does the contractor have a backlog of projects that could hurt her ability to meet your timetable? What sort of references can he provide? The answers to all of these questions can be either reassuring or cause for further investigation. In either case, the key is to make sure that you ask them.

One way in which small business owners can learn the answers to some of these questions is by requiring bidding contractors to submit a surety bond, which is basically a three-party contract between the contractor, the project owner, and the underwriting surety company. Surety companies will make an extensive review of the construction company before issuing such a bond. In addition, if the contractor signs the bond, he is basically guaranteeing his ability to complete the project on which he is bidding.

MONITORING THE CONSTRUCTION PROCESS

After the bidding process is completed and the building contract awarded, the successful contractor should be asked to provide a performance bond. Such a bond guarantees that the project's contractual provisions will be carried out. In addition, a payment bond should be secured which certifies that suppliers and subcontractors will be paid. Ensuring that the contractor and all of his subcontractors have adequate insurance (workers' compensation, general and umbrella liability, equipment, builders' risk, etc.) to address problems is another key to attaining peace of mind for the small business owner. Finally, the project owner needs to make sure that he or she continuously monitors the performance of the contractor.

SEE ALSO *Buying an Existing Business; Comprehensive Environmental Response Cleanup and Liability Act*

BIBLIOGRAPHY

Bolles, Dennis. *Building Project Management Centers of Excellence.* AMACOM Division of the American Management Association, April 2002.

Campbell, Melissa. "10 Steps Towards Getting the Right Contractor." *Alaska Business Monthly.* August 2002.

Lorenz, Daniel E. "Reduce Construction Risk with Management Systems." *Memphis Business Journal.* 20 October 2000.

Strickland, Amanda. "Choosing the Right Contractor for Your Project." *Dallas Business Journal.* 7 April 2000.

Hillstrom, Northern Lights
updated by Magee, ECDI

CONSTRUCTIVE DISCHARGE

"Constructive discharge" is a legal doctrine originating in labor disputes going back to the 1930s. Originator of the doctrine was the National Labor Relations Board (NLRB) which was attempting to deal with situations in which employers forced employees to resign by creating intolerable working conditions, usually because the employees were engaged in union activities. The first use of the phrase was in an NLRB case in 1938 called *In re Sterling Corset Co.,* 9 N.L.R.B. 858, 865. The doctrine has been frequently applied in cases brought under Title VII of the Civil Rights Act of 1964, initially in racial discrimination contexts. In recent decades constructive discharge has figured as a doctrine in dealing with sexual harassment cases.

Unemployment compensation is paid employees only when the employee is discharged involuntarily for no fault of his or her own or if the employee resigns but with a qualifying cause. An employee who simply resigns without a qualifying cause is not eligible; neither is an employee discharged for misconduct. Constructive discharge because of an intolerable working environment is one of the qualifying causes, along with illness and other causes. An employee who quits because of sexual harassment or other hostile conditions is constructively discharged; he or she may be found to be eligible for unemployment benefits and will have the right to sue the company for wrongful termination as well—although in this case, the employee took the action on his or her own initiative.

LEGAL HISTORY

In the case of constructive discharge for sexual harassment, the direct involvement of the employer—and thus the employer's liability—has been clarified in three Supreme Court judgments rendered in 1998 and 2004. The issue arises because sexual harassment is seen to arise from the personal desires of the harassing party. Unlike the cases arising from an employer's desire to keep unions out, sexual harassment carries no benefit for the employer. Thus the question arises: if one or more supervisors engage in sexual harassment of an employee, is the employer as such liable for such activity?

The courts, relying on long-established law, had held that if a supervisor uses his powers as an agent of the corporation in attempts to get sexual favors, the mere use of such powers by a supervisor automatically involves the employer in the harassment because those powers are delegated. Thus if a supervisor uses assignments, demotions, promotions, hiring or threat of discharge, and similar means in connection with sexual harassment, the employer is also implicated. But what if the sexual harassment "stands alone," as it were, and does not involve "employment actions"?

Faragher/Ellerth Two such cases were decided by the Supreme Court in 1998. In one (*Faragher* v. *Boca Raton*) the plaintiff, Beth Ann Faragher sued the City of Boca Raton. She had resigned as a lifeguard in protest at the sexual harassment of two supervisors (Bill Terry and David Silverman) who had created a hostile environment by inappropriately touching and making lewd remarks. The District Court agreed with Faragher, but the Eleventh Circuit Court reversed the District Court's decision arguing that the two supervisors were just acting on their own, not as agents of the city. No "employment actions" were involved, in other words.

In the second case, with very similar facts, the District Court and the appellate court reached diametrically opposed conclusions. In this case (*Burlington Industries, Inc.* v. *Ellerth*) Kimberly Ellerth quit a job as a sales employee after claiming to have endured constant sexual harassment by a single supervisor (Ted Slowik). Ellerth claimed that he had on three occasions made remarks which she interpreted as threats that he would deny her certain job benefits. But this did not actually happen. In fact she was promoted. At the same time, she never filed a complaint against the supervisor although she knew that her employer, Burlington Industries, had a policy against sexual harassment. The District Court ruled against Ellerth but the Seventh Circuit Court reversed the ruling but in a confusing manner: eight separate opinions were rendered which did not result in a clear rationale for reversing the lower court.

The Supreme Court accepted these cases in an effort to make order and reached conclusions later referred to as *Faragher/Ellerth*. The Court held in essence that 1) the employer was strictly liable for a supervisor's actions if the action culminated in a tangible employment action, such as discharge, demotion, or undesirable reassignment; 2) in the absence of such a direct linkage, the employee may sue the employer anyway, but the employer has a right to a defense on the basis of having responsibly attempted to prevent such conduct; and 3) that the actions of the employee in using or not using

available internal channels of reporting abuses should be part of the consideration.

Pennsylvania State Police v. Suders The most recent event in this legal history was the Supreme Court judgment in the case of *Pennsylvania State Police* v. *Suders* decided in 2004 (hereafter *Suders*). The nature of this case was to draw the lines sharper than they had been drawn in *Faragher/Ellerth*.

The case involved Nancy Sue Suders who, while working for the Pennsylvania State Police (PSP), was subjected to sexual harassment by three supervisors (Eric D. Easton, William D. Baker, and Eric B. Prendergast). Suders talked to the PSP Equal Employment Opportunity Officer, Virginia Smith-Elliott, but while told to file a complaint, Smith-Elliott did not provide Suders the form necessary to file the complaint.

In this case the District Court ruled in favor of the PSP without trial on the grounds that Suders had failed to file a compliant and therefore, under the *Faragher/Ellerth* precedent Suders' hostile work environment claim was untenable as a matter of law. The appeals court in this case, the Third Circuit Court, sent the case back for trial on the grounds that issues of material fact existed about the effectiveness of PSP's program to deal with sexual harassment. The court also held that if Suders proved constructive discharge, that alone would constitute an employment action and would deprive PSP of a defense under *Faragher/Ellerth*.

The Supreme Court, under *Suders,* agreed with the Third Circuit that the case should be tried. But the Supreme Court also held that PSP nonetheless had a right to an affirmative defense unless the plaintiff quit "in reasonable response to an adverse action officially changing her employment status or situation, e.g., a humiliating demotion, extreme cut in pay, or transfer to a position in which she would face unbearable working conditions."

The upshot of *Suders* therefore was that sexual harassment as such suffices as grounds for constructive discharge, whether or not the employee makes use of complaint procedures that may be in place. On the other hand, the employer has a right to an affirmative defense unless the employee quit after employment actions such as those named above. If such actions were shown to have taken place, the employer is strictly liable.

IMPLICATIONS FOR SMALL BUSINESS

The evolving doctrine of constructive discharge makes it clear that reasonable policies and their active enforcement will go a long way toward avoiding the creation of hostile environments and lawsuits that may result from them.

Small business owners have the advantage of being closer to their employees than the management of large firms. The disadvantage in small businesses arises from the same cause: informality. Ideally a small business will have:

- A clear policy on sexual harassment signed by every employee. The policy should outline the procedure for filing a complaint and should include at least two names with telephone numbers: the individual who is to receive complaints and a second individual who may be contacted if no action is taken by the first; the second person, ideally, will be outside the company and an objective third party.

- Periodic scheduled discussions of this policy, ideally led by top management people to give it weight.

- A watchful management attitude and close supervision especially in situations where individuals are isolated.

- A personnel review procedure in which the subject is raised by the reviewing manager.

- An action plan for dealing with complaints, for establishing facts, and for resolving the issues, ideally involving a third party if possible outside the company.

SEE ALSO *Employee Termination*

BIBLIOGRAPHY
Clark, Margaret M. "Ruling Allows Defense in Harassment Cases." *HRMagazine*. August 2004.

Mesritz, George D. "Constructive Discharge and Employer Intent: Are the Courts Split over a Distinction without a Difference?" *Employee Relations Law Journal*. Spring 1996.

Nagle, Mark E. "Suders: the Supreme Court Reaffirms Value of an Anti-Harassment Policy." *Employee Relations Law Journal*. Winter 2004.

United States Supreme Court. *Burlington Industries, Inc. v. Ellerth*. No. 97-569. 26 June 1998.

United States Supreme Court. *Faragher v. City of Boca Raton*. No. 97-282. 26 June 1998.

United States Supreme Court. *Pennsylvania State Police v. Suders*. No. 03-95. 14 June 2004.

Darnay, ECDI

CONSULTANTS

A consultant is an individual who possesses special knowledge or skills and provides that expertise to a client for a fee. Consultants help all sorts of businesses find and implement solutions to a wide variety of problems, including those related to business start-up, marketing, manufacturing, strategy, organization structure, environmental compliance, health and safety, technology, and communications. Some consultants are self-employed, independent contractors who offer specialized skills in a certain field; other consultants work for large consulting firms, such as Anderson Consulting or Gemini Consulting, that offer expertise in a wide range of business areas; and still other consultants hail from academia.

The consulting industry has grown rapidly since its origins in the 1960s. In fact, *Business Week* reported that the ten largest consulting firms in the United States averaged growth of 10 percent annually in the late 1990s and achieved 14 percent growth in 2000. Several factors have contributed to the growth of consulting. First, as a result of the trend toward corporate downsizing, many companies have found that they lack the internal manpower to complete all necessary tasks. Second, the complexity of today's business climate—as a result of deregulation, globalization, and technology advancements—has outpaced many companies' levels of expertise. Finally, consultants provide a way for companies to get special projects done without adding employees to the payroll.

The decision to hire a consultant is not one that a small business should take lightly. Consultants can be very expensive, although their expertise can prove invaluable. The small business owner must first decide whether the situation facing the company requires the input of a consultant. If it does, then advance preparation should be done to ensure a successful consulting experience. The small business owner is then ready to find and negotiate a contract with the right consultant. An important part of this process is understanding the ways in which consultants charge for their services. Hopefully, after completing the consulting process, the small business will emerge with a successfully implemented solution to its problem.

DECIDING WHETHER TO USE A CONSULTANT

In deciding whether or not to hire a consultant, the small business owner should consider the nature of the problem, the reasons why internal resources cannot be used to solve it, and the possible advantages a consultant could offer. In her article "Do's and Don'ts of Hiring Consultants," Joan Adams describes several situations in which a consultant's services are likely to be required. "You want to call a consultant when you feel like your business is 'stuck.' Your revenues are flat or growing very slowly. Your costs are growing at a faster rate than revenue... Something isn't working but you don't quite know what it is—or what to do about it." A small business should not hire a consultant simply in order to have someone else implement unpopular decisions.

MAKING THE CONSULTING EXPERIENCE WORK

Once the decision has been made to enlist the help of a consultant, there are several steps the small business owner can take in advance to increase the likelihood that the consulting experience will be successful. First and foremost, the company's managers should define the problem they need the consultant to address. Using probing questions to go beyond superficial symptoms to underlying causes, the managers should attempt to state the problem in writing. Next, they should define the expected results of the consulting experience. The objectives the managers come up with should be clear, realistic, and measurable.

Another important step in preparing for a successful consulting experience is to communicate with employees. The small business owner should explain the problem fully and honestly, in as positive terms as possible, and ask employees for their understanding and cooperation. When employees feel surprised or threatened, they may hamper the consultant's efforts by withholding information or not providing honest opinions. It is also helpful to gather all important company documents relating to the problem in order to make them available to the consultant. The consultant's job will be easier if he or she has ample information about both the company and the problem at hand.

Once the consulting project begins, there are several other steps a small business owner can take to help ensure its success. For example, it is important to manage the project from the top in order to give it the visibility and priority it deserves. The small business owner should appoint a liaison to assist the consultant in gathering information, and should receive regular progress reports about the project. In the implementation stage, the small business owner should adequately staff the project and empower those involved to make any necessary changes.

HOW TO SELECT A CONSULTANT

Selecting the right consultant for the company and the type of problem at hand is a vital part of the process. The first step is to assemble a list of candidates by getting recommendations from people in the same line of business, contacting consulting associations or consultant brokers that represent the same industry. Trade and professional journals are also a source of potential consulting firms and a place where such firms advertise. Several library reference books, such as Thomson Gale's *Consultants and Consulting Organizations Directory,* provide contact information for consultants in a variety of fields. It is important to avoid selecting a consultant based upon a current management fad; instead, the decision should be based upon the company's particular needs.

The next step is to determine, based on the nature of the problem, what type of consultant is needed. An advisory consultant analyzes the problem and turns recommendations over to the client, but is not involved in implementation of the solution. In contrast, an operational consultant remains on hand to assist the client in proper implementation, or in some cases handles the implementation without the client's assistance. Part-time consultants are generally employed full-time within their field of expertise—marketing, for example—but also offer their services to other companies on the side. They usually charge less money than full-time consultants, but they also cannot devote their undivided time and energy to the client.

Process consultants are skills-oriented generalists. With expertise in one or more technical areas, these consultants can apply their skills to any industry or organization. In contrast, functional consultants apply their skills to a particular environment; for example, a hospital facilities planner would concentrate on consulting to hospitals, rather than to other types of businesses that require facilities planning. Another distinction between consultants is based on the size of their operation. Consultants can work for large firms, small firms, or even independently. Large firms offer greater resources, but also have higher overhead and thus charge higher fees. Small firms or independent consultants may offer more attentive service, but may not have access to the precise type of talent that is required. Finally, consultants can be academically or commercially based. In general, academic consultants may be most helpful with problems requiring research or a background in theory, while commercial consultants may be able to offer more practical experience.

Once a small business owner has determined what type of consultant would be best suited to handle the company's problem and assembled a list of candidates, the next step is to interview the candidates. Some of the traits to consider include experience with the company or industry, availability, knowledge of the problem at hand, communication skills, flexibility, and compatibility. Since consultants are usually required to work within the corporate culture, often in times of crisis, it is important that their style is compatible with that of the firm.

After discussing the problem in detail with the leading candidates, the small business owner may opt to ask each consultant to submit a written proposal to aid in the selection process. In some cases, the contents of these proposals may convince the small business owner that the problem could be better handled using in-house resources. After deciding to hire a specific consultant, the small business owner should ask that consultant to draw up a contract, or at least a formal letter, confirming their arrangements. It is important to note that the contract should be based on negotiations between the two parties, so the small business owner may wish to add, delete, or clarify the information included. There are several peripheral issues that the small business owner may want to address in the contract, including the consultant's proposed methods of handling conflicts of interest, subcontractors, insurance/liability, expenses, confidentiality, and nonperformance.

WEB CONSULTANTS

Recent growth in Internet applications for businesses has created a simultaneous growth in the number of E-commerce and Web consultants. Many of the same general guidelines that apply to choosing a traditional business consultant also apply to choosing a Web consultant. As Tara Teichgraeber wrote in an article for the *Dallas Business Journal,* the first step in selecting a Web consultant is deciding what goals the company hopes to achieve by establishing a presence on the Internet. For example, some companies want to set up an interactive online store in order to sell products or services over the Internet, while others may just want a basic Web site to enhance the company's image. "Deciding what a consultant should do helps narrow down a candidate with similar experience and proven success, as well as helps the business owner stick to a financial plan," Teichgraeber noted.

Many different types of Web consultants exist, each offering various types of services and charging widely disparate fees. "In hiring a consultant, you can choose from among independent site developers, Web design shops, technology consulting firms, traditional advertising and public relations agencies, and interactive agencies," Reid Goldsborough explained in an article for *Link-Up.* "A Web consultant can build you a Web site from scratch or enhance an existing one. Costs are all over the place, from several hundred dollars for a simple site consisting of a few pages, to a million dollars or more for an e-commerce site with product databases that are easily updated, a search engine, animated product demonstrations, secure online transactions, and audio and video enhancements."

Goldsborough suggested that small business owners looking to hire a Web consultant contact their Internet Service Provider for referrals. It may also be helpful to look online for sites you like and then find out who designed them. Upon contacting potential consultants, it is important to ask to see a list of sites they have designed. Goldsborough also recommended that small business owners be sure to ask about arrangements for maintaining the site once it is up and running. Some consultants provide this service to their clients, while others supply the tools and training for in-house personnel to take over site maintenance tasks.

HOW CONSULTANTS CHARGE CLIENTS

Most consultants use the same basic formula to determine the fees charged for their services, but clients are asked to pay these fees in a wide variety of ways. All consultants' fees are based on a daily billing rate, which reflects the value they place on one day's labor plus expected overhead expenses. In some cases, this daily billing rate—multiplied by the amount of time the consultant spends on the project—is the amount the company actually pays. But other consultants may estimate the amount of time needed and quote the client a fixed fee. Other consultants may provide a bracket quotation, or a range within which the total fee will fall. Another way in which consultants charge clients is a monthly retainer, which covers all the necessary services for that month. Finally, some consultants—especially in high-technology fields—charge on the basis of the company's performance linking payments to measurable outcomes.

THE CONSULTING PROCESS

The consulting process begins when the client company decides to enlist the services of a consultant. The consultant then analyzes the company's problem and provides recommendations about how to fix it. Small business owners should avoid the temptation to blindly follow a consultant's recommendations; instead, they should seek to understand the diagnosis and be prepared to negotiate any necessary changes. The consulting process should not be mysterious or unusual, but rather a mutually beneficial business arrangement between consultant and client. Finally, after implementing the consultant's recommendations, the client company should formally evaluate the success of the consulting experience so that those lessons can be applied to future problems.

BIBLIOGRAPHY

Adams, Joan. "Do's & Don'ts of Hiring Consultants." *Supply House Times.* March 2005.

"Avoid Hiring Consultants with Conflicts of Interest." *Managing Benefits Plans.* August 2005.

Goldsborough, Reid. "How to Hire a Web Consultant." *Link-Up.* July-August 1999.

"It's Getting Quieter in the Advice Business." *Business Week.* 26 February 2001.

Lewis, Harold. *Consultants and Advisers.* Kogan Page, August 2004.

Teichgraeber, Tara. "What to Look For: E-Commerce Consultants." *Dallas Business Journal.* 14 July 2000.

Zahn, David. *The Quintessential Guide to Using Consultants.* HDR Press, Inc., January 2004.

Hillstrom, Northern Lights
updated by Magee, ECDI

CONSULTING

Consulting is the business of providing advice to clients for a fee in order to help them solve a particular problem or range of problems within a certain area of business. Consulting services are provided by consultants, a majority of whom have gained their expertise from previous employment. Some consultants work for large consulting firms, such as Accenture or Bain & Company, that offer expertise in a wide range of business areas; other consultants hail from academia and assist companies with problems relating to research or theory; and still other consultants are self-employed, independent contractors who offer specialized skills in a very specific area of expertise. For example, a former stockbroker might become a financial consultant; a computer scientist might become a computer consultant; a former employee in a non-profit organization might open a business as a fundraising consultant; and an accountant might become a tax consultant.

Expertise alone, however, does not make someone a consultant—at least not a full-time one. To be a consultant requires applying that expertise to practical problem solving. Consulting is a business. Consequently, it requires the application of marketing skills and the ability to reach out and establish job contacts. Personality also plays a role in consulting success. In fact, many experts advise those looking to hire a consultant to trust their instincts about personality. Joan Adams, in an article entitled "Do's and Don'ts of Hiring a Consultant" replies this way to the question How do I select the right consultant? "Go with your gut. The starting point for selection is you really have to like, respect and trust this person or it just won't work...Change is tough. I don't care how brilliant a consultant is—it is not going to work if you don't like the person."

In general, the kind of person who is most likely to succeed as a consultant is one who can put the needs and interests of clients before her own, who is not condescending, and who is unfailingly courteous and patient. A small minority of consultants work as internal consultants for one firm, usually a very large one. The majority, however, work independently and with no partners, often from their own homes, or run their own small consulting firms.

Consultants constitute a growing number (as yet undetermined, since there are no licensing requirements for consultants) of the self-employed. This growth began in the early 1990s, when the trend toward corporate downsizing left many skilled professionals without jobs. Many of these "downsized" professionals struck out on their own to do consulting work, often for the very firms that used to employ them. Those who succeed in building viable consulting businesses may earn as much if not more than they did in their former employment.

Reasons for failure often involve a combination of such factors as poor initial planning, careless marketing of one's business, and intense competition. The successful consultants are usually those who find a market niche for themselves through research, intensive marketing, and locale. Charging the right fee and avoiding falling into the trap of "free" consulting (for instance, when a client whose contract with a consultant has ended insists upon additional "feedback" or "follow up") requires business sense. Consulting fees can vary from almost nothing to thousands of dollars per assignment, depending on the assignment, market conditions, and the standard rate for that type of work.

Since most consultants are self-employed professionals, consulting can often involve inconsistent workflow, long hours and a great deal of pressure. Consultants must study their fields of expertise continuously to keep abreast of developments. To the millions of entrepreneurs who enter the consulting profession, however, the attraction and challenge of creative, independent work performed in a comfortable environment together outweigh the difficulties. And while competition is great, the number of large firms that dominate this profession are few. While some consulting fields have become saturated—such as the computer and environmental fields—there are always new trends emerging. For instance, with the unexpected fall of communism, the demand for eastern European specialists and "free market" consultants skyrocketed. As the need for business information grows and changes, the demand for consultants should continue to escalate.

TYPES OF CONSULTANTS

Consultants help all sorts of businesses find and implement solutions to a wide variety of problems, including those related to business start-up, marketing, manufacturing, strategy, organization structure, environmental compliance, health and safety, technology, and communications. In addition to size of the operation and field of specialty, consultants can be categorized in a number of other ways. For example, an advisory consultant analyzes the problem and turns recommendations over to the client, but is not involved in implementation of the solution. In contrast, an operational consultant remains on hand to assist the client in proper implementation, or in some cases handles the implementation without the client's assistance.

Part-time consultants are generally employed full-time within their field of expertise—marketing, for example—but also offer their services to other companies on the side. Although they are not usually able to charge as much money as full-time consultants, they also are not expected to devote their undivided time and energy to the client. Process consultants are skills-oriented generalists. With expertise in one or more technical areas, these consultants can apply their skills to any industry or organization. In contrast, functional consultants apply their skills to a particular environment; for example, a hospital facilities planner would concentrate on consulting to hospitals, rather than to other types of businesses that require facilities planning.

ESTABLISHING A CONSULTING BUSINESS

Start-Up An entrepreneur starting up a consulting business must go through many of the same processes as those starting other types of businesses. The first step should be completing an honest assessment of skills. The aspiring consultant should identify both content skills—the technical expertise that clients will be willing to pay for—and process skills—the qualities that would enable someone to run a successful consulting business. Some of the more important process skills include communication, problem-solving, and interpersonal skills. In addition, independent consultants must have the ability to manage, market, and grow their own businesses. A good starting point is to make a list of all one's relevant skills and qualities, and then work from that list to create a short mission statement to guide the consulting business.

Like other entrepreneurs, consultants also must determine the most appropriate structure, location, and name for their businesses. The form or structure of the business depends upon the new consultant's tax situation, willingness to assume liability, and interest in taking on partners. A consultant who operates as a sole proprietorship, for example, is taxed as an individual and holds all personal and business liability. In a partnership of two or more consultants, each partner is taxed as an individual and shares in the liability. A consultant who organizes as a corporation enjoys limited liability, and the business is taxed as a separate entity. Preparing a detailed business plan can help aspiring consultants to think about how their business should be financed, where it should be positioned in relation to its competition, and what its most effective forms of marketing might be.

Setting Fees However interesting or fulfilling it may be, most consultants ultimately view their work as a money-making venture. To avoid confusion, each service the consultant performs should have a clearly defined fee. But deciding how much to charge for various services can be a challenge for a new consultant. The first step should be examining the costs relating to the consulting business itself. In addition to direct costs—expenses that can be directly attributed to a specific project and thus billed to the client in question—the consultant must also

consider indirect costs—overhead expenses associated with running the business. Some common indirect costs include rent, utilities, insurance, office supplies and equipment, marketing costs, postage, automobile expenses, accounting or legal fees, dues to professional associations, and entertainment. The next step in developing a fee structure is to determine the cost of the consultant's labor. Some new consultants might use their previous salary as a starting point, or the salary of a comparable position. The most important factor to consider is whether the figure reflects the market value of the consultant's skills and experience.

Finally, the estimates of indirect costs and labor should be converted to daily values, taking any expected non-working days into consideration (including vacations, administrative time, business development time, and downtime). For example, a consultant hoping to earn $100,000 over the course of a year, expecting to pay $30,000 in indirect costs, and planning to perform 200 days of billable work would have a daily rate of $100,000 + $30,000 / 200, or $650 per day. This does not take a profit margin into account, which can range from 10 to 30 percent of daily expenses. A consultant's daily rate only provides a starting point for determining his or her fees for various types of services. The fee also depends on the kind of assignment, the prevailing rate in the industry or marketplace, the client's budget, and whether the consultant may need to establish a relationship with a new client or develop a reputation in a new industry. In addition, a consultant's fees may be structured in a number of ways. Some consultants charge by the hour, for example, while others charge a fixed price for specific services, receive a monthly retainer, or are paid on a contingency basis.

Marketing Potential clients cannot take advantage of a consultant's services if they are unaware of them. Therefore, in order to remain in business, new consultants must be able to market their services effectively. Analysts recommend that consultants use a variety of direct and indirect marketing techniques to gain clients and grow their businesses. One possible direct marketing technique is telemarketing, which involves calling potential clients on the telephone. Telemarketing is most effective if the consultant making the call is armed with knowledge about the company ahead of time, uses a prepared script, describes the benefits he or she offers, and mentions successful projects with other clients.

In some cases, telemarketing can be augmented with a direct mail marketing campaign. Although direct mail can be expensive, it is flexible and allows responses to be tracked. Experts suggest increasing the success rate of direct mail campaigns by making them specific, easy to read and understand, and aesthetically pleasing, and by including testimonials and business reply cards. Other possible direct marketing methods for consulting businesses include magazine and newspaper advertisements, association directories, networking, and referrals from other clients.

Indirect marketing techniques, while less likely to lead to immediate client relationships, are invaluable in helping new consultants increase their name recognition and credibility over the long term. Giving seminars, speaking before groups, joining professional associations, and writing articles or books are all good ways for consultants to build their reputations as sought-after experts in a given field. Another important means of publicizing a new business is through news releases, which can be sent to local media or trade journals to announce client relationships, successful projects, upcoming seminars, or other important happenings related to the business.

Evaluating Consulting Opportunities New consultants may be tempted to jump at any business opportunity that comes along. A new consultant should, however, gather information about the client in order to make an informed decision about pursuing a consulting opportunity. This process, called qualifying the client, involves considering the nature, scope, and urgency of the project, as well as the client's budget. It is also helpful to find out about the client's desired outcomes and decision-making process. In addition, it may be useful to know whether the client has had successful experiences with consultants in the past, and what they feel the major obstacles to success would be for the project under consideration. A face-to-face interview and a formal request for proposal are the two main tools companies use in selecting consultants. Consultants can use these tools as a way to find out more about their clients, as well.

Proposals and Contracts Proposals are an important part of the consulting business. Sometimes proposals serve to introduce consultants and their services to prospective clients, while other times proposals serve to finalize the arrangements between a consultant and a client. Prospective clients may request a formal proposal in order to compare several possible consultants, make decisions related to budgets or scheduling, or simply to collect ideas about how to solve a particular problem using in-house resources. Though companies sometimes ask for proposals and then do not end up hiring a consultant, companies that make a habit of such behavior are simply looking for "free consulting." Most experienced consultants try to discern the motives of potential clients ahead of time in order to avoid committing excessive time and resources to "free consulting."

Prior to submitting a proposal, a consultant needs to gather information about the company and its problem from interviews and outside sources. When writing a proposal, it is important for a consultant to demonstrate a strong understanding of the client's needs, describe his or her own ability to meet those needs, and detail a plan of action toward that end. Many successful consulting proposals are divided into three sections: the introduction, the methodology section, and the timing and cost section. The introduction provides an overview of the proposal, and should be used to demonstrate the consultant's understanding of the client's needs and desired outcomes. The methodology section is the main part of the proposal, and specifies the actions the consultant plans to take in order to provide a focused solution to the client's problem. It may also be helpful for the consultant to mention any unique services or expertise he or she can offer, in order to differentiate the proposal from those submitted by other consultants. The timing and cost section provides a realistic and specific fee structure and schedule for completion of the project. In addition, the consultant may wish to outline what effect, if any, the consulting process will have on the client's internal resources.

Proposals should be written in a conversational tone, without excessive use of technical jargon, and with the prospective client's needs in mind. The consultant may benefit from keeping in touch with the client while writing the proposal, as this helps avoid misunderstandings or incomplete information. If the consultant receives the assignment, the proposal then serves as the basis for a formal contract. Although some clients may simply sign the proposal to authorize the consultant to begin work, many consultants prefer to clarify the arrangements in a separate document. At a minimum, the contract should outline the scope of the project, the consultant's fees, and the proposed time frame. There are several other issues that the consultant may wish to address, including conflicts of interest, subcontractors, insurance/liability, expenses, confidentiality, and cancellation.

BIBLIOGRAPHY

Adams, Joan. "Do's & Don'ts of Hiring Consultants." *Supply House Times.* March 2005.

"Avoid Hiring Consultants with Conflicts of Interest." *Managing Benefits Plans.* August 2005.

Goldsborough, Reid. "How to Hire a Web Consultant." *Link-Up.* July-August 1999.

Holtz, Herman, and David Zahn. *How to Succeed as an Independent Consultant.* John Wiley & Sons, August 2004.

"It's Getting Quieter in the Advice Business." *Business Week.* 26 February 2001.

Lewis, Harold. *Consultants and Advisers.* Kogan Page, August 2004.

Teichgraeber, Tara. "What to Look For: E-Commerce Consultants." *Dallas Business Journal.* 14 July 2000.

Weiss, Alan. *Getting Started in Consulting.* John Wiley & Sons, December 2003.

Zahn, David. *The Quintessential Guide to Using Consultants.* HDR Press, Inc., January 2004.

Hillstrom, Northern Lights
updated by Magee, ECDI

CONSUMER ADVOCACY

Consumer advocacy refers to actions taken by individuals or groups to promote and protect the interests of the buying public. Historically, consumer advocates have assumed a somewhat adversarial role in exposing unfair business practices or unsafe products that threaten the welfare of the general public. Consumer advocates use tactics like publicity, boycotts, letter-writing campaigns, and lawsuits to raise awareness of issues affecting consumers and to counteract the financial and political power of the organizations they target. Since even large businesses can be visibly wounded when their mistreatment of consumers or other constituencies arouses the ire of consumer advocacy organizations, it should be obvious to small business owners that they can ill-afford to engage in business practices that might draw the attention of consumer advocates.

Periods of vocal consumer advocacy around the turn of the twentieth century and in the late 1960s have left a legacy of federal legislation and agencies intended to protect consumers in the United States. The rights of consumers have expanded to include product safety, the legitimacy of advertising claims, the satisfactory resolution of grievances, and a say in government decisions. In the early days of industry, companies could afford to ignore consumers' wishes because there was so much demand for their goods and services. As a result, they were often able to command high prices for products of poor quality. The earliest consumer advocates to point out such abuses were called "muckrakers," and their revelations of underhanded business practices spurred the creation of several federal agencies and a flurry of legislation designed to curb some of the most serious abuses. At the same time, increased competition began to provide consumers with more choices among a variety of products of higher quality. Still, some notable cases of corporations neglecting the public welfare for their own gain continued, and corporate influence in American politics enabled many businesses to resist calls for reform in advertising, worker or consumer safety, and pollution control.

This situation led to the consumer movement of the 1960s. One of the country's most outspoken and controversial consumer advocates, lawyer Ralph Nader, came to the forefront during this time. Nader's effective and well-publicized denunciations of the American automobile industry included class-action lawsuits and calls for recalls of allegedly defective products, and many of his actions served as a tactical model for future advocacy organizations.

The efforts of Nader and other activists led to the formation of several federal agencies designed to protect consumer interests. The U.S. Office of Consumer Affairs, created in 1971, investigates and resolves consumer complaints, conducts consumer surveys, and disseminates product information to the public. The Consumer Product Safety Commission, formed in 1972, sets national standards for product safety and testing procedures, coordinates product recalls, and ensures that companies respond to valid consumer complaints. Many other government agencies have responsibilities that include the safety of consumers, among their many responsibilities. They include such agencies as the Federal Communications Commission (FCC), the Food and Drug Administration (FDA), the Federal Aviation Administration (FAA), the U.S. Department of Agriculture (USDA), and the Federal Trade Commission (FTC). Some state-level agencies are also involved in the regulation of products and services in order to assure the safety of the public. And the Better Business Bureau is an organization strongly involved in monitoring safety issues related to business activity.

The Consumer Federation of America is the largest consumer advocacy group in the United States, consisting of about 220 member organizations. The International Organization of Consumers Unions, based in the Netherlands, actively promotes consumer interests on a global scale. In the late 1990s, the widespread networking of home computers advanced consumer advocacy by making it easier for citizens to gather information and make their views known. Indeed, by the end of the twentieth century, the Internet had emerged as an important weapon in the arsenal of consumer advocates. Its usefulness as a vehicle for spreading consumer information quickly and widely has made it one of the primary means by which public interest advocates mobilize opposition to corporate policies.

The use of computers, the Internet, and the spread of e-commerce have all contributed to new areas of concern for consumer advocates. Identity theft is on the rise and the safety of children working on the Internet is of concern to many parents, law enforcement officers, legislators and consumer advocates.

BIBLIOGRAPHY

Brabbs, Cordelia. "Web Fuels Consumer Activism." *Marketing.* 21 September 2000.

Cook, Gareth G. "The Case for (Some) Regulation." *Washington Monthly.* March 1995.

"Is Lawsuit Reform Good for Consumers?" *Consumer Reports.* May 1995.

Levin, Carol. "Privacy, Please—Opt-In or Opt-Out?" *PC Magazine.* 20 March 2001.

Orisewezie, Ignatius. "Trends in Consumer Protection Advocacy." *Africa News Service.* 13 January 2006.

Stingley, Ruth Nauss. "It Pays to Complain." *Reader's Digest.* October 1993.

Hillstrom, Northern Lights
updated by Magee, ECDI

CONSUMER PRICE INDEX (CPI)

The Consumer Price Index (CPI), sometimes called the cost-of-living index, measures the average change in prices that typical American wage earners pay for basic goods and services, such as food, clothing, shelter, transportation, and medical care. It is expressed as a percentage of the cost of the same goods and services in a base period. For example, using the years 1982 to 1984 as a base period with a value of 100, the CPI for December 2005 was 198.6, meaning that prices had increased by an average of 98.6 percent over time. The CPI is often used to measure inflation, so it is closely monitored by government policymakers and by individuals whose wages vary with the purchasing power of money. The practice of indexing wages to the CPI is known as a cost-of-living adjustment (COLA). The term "cost of living" is often applied to the numerical result of the CPI. Loosely defined, it refers to the average cost to an individual of purchasing the various goods and services needed to maintain a reasonable living standard.

The U.S. Bureau of Labor Statistics (BLS) began calculating the CPI in 1917, and over the years it has become an important economic statistic. The CPI is calculated monthly and is usually reported within the first two weeks of the following month. In order to calculate the CPI, the BLS surveys about 24,000 households to find out where families shop regularly and what types of goods and services they purchase. It then contacts about 21,000 retail businesses in 85 major metropolitan areas to obtain prices for 90,000 items. All of this information is combined in the CPI, which represents the average price of a "market basket" of goods and services.

The selection of items in the basket can not be held absolutely fixed for a very long period, of course, since the mix of items people buy changes over time. For example, the weight on tobacco in the CPI basket has fallen over the years as the number of smokers in the population has fallen. Personal computers were not part of the CPI in the 1970s but are a part of the basket today. To address these changes in purchasing patterns the BLS tries to incorporate any new developments in the market by changing 20 percent of the retail outlets and items in its survey every year on a rotating basis.

A separate CPI is calculated for different income levels, geographical areas, and types of goods and services. For example, the CPI-U is calculated for all urban households, which includes about 80 percent of the U.S. population. In contrast, the CPI-W measures average price increases for the 32 percent of Americans who derive their primary income as wage earners or clerical workers. The BLS also publishes a CPI for each of seven major categories of items: food and beverages, housing, apparel, transportation, medical care, entertainment, and other goods and services. In addition, it compiles individual indexes for 200 different items and combined indexes for 120 smaller categories of items. Separate CPI measurements are also released for four major geographical regions of the United States—Northeast, North Central, South, and West—as well as 29 large metropolitan areas.

The CPI influences the American economy in several ways. A high annual percentage increase in the CPI reflects a high rate of inflation. The Federal Reserve Board, which controls the nation's money supply, often reacts to such increases by raising interest rates. This makes it more expensive for individuals and businesses to borrow money, which usually slows spending, encourages saving, and helps to curb inflation in the economy. The CPI also determines the percentage of annual increase or decrease in income for many Americans. For example, COLA formulas based on the CPI are built into many employment contracts. The federal government also uses the CPI to adjust Social Security and disability benefits, to determine the income level at which people become eligible for assistance, and to establish tax brackets. In addition, the CPI is often used to compare prices for certain goods within a set of years, and to calculate constant dollar values for two points in time.

Some economists believe that the CPI overstates actual increases in the cost of living by 1 percent or more annually. They generally attribute the discrepancy to some combination of the following four factors: improvements in the quality of goods; the introduction of new goods; substitution by consumers of different goods or retail outlets; and the difficulty of measuring the prices consumers actually pay for goods.

BIBLIOGRAPHY

Boskin, Michael J. "The CPI Commission." *Business Economics.* April 1997.

"Cost-of-Living Lesson." *American Demographics.* December 1994.

Reinsdorf, Marshall. "The Effect of Price Dispersion on Cost of Living Indexes." *International Economic Review.* February 1994.

U.S. Census Bureau, Current Population Reports. *Income in the United States: 2002.* September 2003.

Hillstrom, Northern Lights
updated by Magee, ECDI

CONSUMER PRODUCT SAFETY COMMISSION (CPSC)

The Consumer Product Safety Commission (CPSC) was established in 1972 with the passage of the Consumer Product Safety Act. The primary responsibility of the CPSC is to protect the public from unreasonable risks of injury that could occur during the use of consumer products. The CPSC also promotes the evaluation of consumer products for potential hazards, establishes uniform safety standards for consumer products, eases conflicting state and local regulations concerned with consumer safety, works to recall hazardous products from the marketplace, and selectively conducts research on potentially hazardous products. The CPSC promotes the development of voluntary safety standards and under certain circumstances has the authority to issue and enforce standards and ban unsafe products. In all its activities the CPSC strives to work closely with private consumer groups, industry, the media, and agencies of various state and local governments.

Although the CPSC is an independent federal regulatory agency it does not have jurisdiction over all consumer products. Safety standards for trucks, automobiles, and motorcycles are set by the U.S. Department of Transportation; standards for drugs and cosmetics are handled by the U.S. Food and Drug Administration (FDA); and standards for alcohol, tobacco, and firearms fall under the authority of the U.S. Department of the Treasury. Nevertheless, approximately 15,000 types of consumer products are regulated by the CPSC.

CONSUMER SAFETY LEGISLATIVE HISTORY

Early federal consumer safety legislation dealt primarily with foods, drugs, and cosmetics. The Federal Food and Drugs Act of 1906 (also known as the Wiley Pure Food

and Drug Act) forbade the adulteration and fraudulent misbranding of foods and drugs sold through interstate commerce. Other early consumer legislation included the Meat Inspection Act of 1907 (amended in 1967 by the Wholesome Meat Act). In 1933 legislation was introduced to strengthen the Federal Food and Drugs Act of 1906. This legislation mandated the standardized labeling of food products, required that manufacturers prove drugs are safe for the purpose for which they are sold, and established a pre-market clearance procedure for new drug products. Many drug companies opposed this bill; they were joined by much of the nation's print media, which feared the loss of corporate advertising revenue. After a five-year battle in Congress, however, the bill was passed in 1938 as the Food, Drug, and Cosmetic Act. Amendments to the bill in 1962 established biennial factory inspections, disclosure through labeling of dangerous side effects, FDA approval of all new drugs, FDA power to remove dangerous drugs from the market, and the requirement that a manufacturer prove that its drugs are not only safe but also effective for their stated purpose.

The scope of federal consumer safety legislation broadened throughout the 1950s and 1960s. The Flammable Fabrics Act of 1953 established safety standards for fabrics used in clothing. The Refrigerator Safety Act of 1956 required that refrigerator doors have inside release mechanisms. The 1962 National Traffic and Motor Vehicle Safety Act established federal jurisdiction over motor vehicle safety, while the 1965 Federal Cigarette Labeling and Advertising Act required the famous "Caution: Cigarette Smoking May Be Hazardous to Your Health" label. Other pre-1972 consumer product safety legislation included the Radiation Control for Health and Safety Act of 1968, which dealt with radiation emission levels of electronic products, and the Poison Prevention Packaging Act of 1970, which established packaging standards to protect children from potentially hazardous substances.

In 1967 the National Commission on Product Safety was established. It was believed at that time that federal consumer safety legislation was ineffective because it took a piecemeal approach, targeting only specific products for regulation. Supporters of the commission contended that the government needed to establish legislative authority over broad categories of potentially hazardous goods and products. The National Commission on Product Safety was charged with identifying these broad categories of potentially hazardous goods and evaluating existing legal and voluntary methods for securing consumer product safety. The commission subsequently found that "the exposure of consumers to unreasonable product hazards is excessive by any standards of measurement." The commission also asserted that even though consumers must take some responsibility for their own safety, industry must also assume responsibility for the design and manufacturing of safe consumer products.

On the basis of their inquiry the commission recommended the creation of an independent federal regulatory agency and a presidential appointee to the commission to serve as a consumer advocate before the new agency. The commission also recommended that the new agency have the authority to issue safety regulations and standards. Thus, the Consumer Product Safety Commission was created in 1972.

RECENT DEVELOPMENTS

During its first decades, limited by budgetary realities, the CPSC was slow to establish a significant and active role in regulating consumer safety nationwide. In recent years, however, the CPSC has emerged as a more visible and vigorous protector of public safety. In 2004, for example, the agency (armed with a budget of $59.6 million) issued more than 350 product recalls, including recalls of more than 30 million toys that were deemed to be a potential health hazard to children. That same year it levied approximately ten times the amount of fines on companies that it had assessed a decade earlier. And *Manufacturing News* reported that the CPSC has dramatically cut its customer complaint response time in recent years. In 2004, for example, its average response time was less than 6 days. In the late 1980s, by contrast, the agency's typical response time was nearly 50 days. In 2004 the CPSC also launched new initiatives designed to address the explosion in e-commerce. The most visible of these efforts is Operation SOS—Safe Online Shopping, in which agency representatives investigate unsafe and/or illegal consumer goods that are made available over the Internet. Finally, in 2004 the CPSC established a Small Business Ombudsman to help small companies comply more easily with product safety regulations by providing them with a single point of contact for obtaining information and assistance.

The CPSC consists of five commissioners, each appointed by the President of the United States with the advice and consent of Congress. One of the commissioners is appointed chairman. The CPSC is headquartered in Bethesda, Maryland, with regional offices in Chicago, New York, and San Francisco, and field offices in various cities across the country. The CPSC also maintains a toll-free Consumer Product Safety Hotline (1-800-638-CPSC).

BIBLIOGRAPHY

"Consumer Product Safety Commission is Back On Track." *Manufacturing News*. 12 January 2000.

Gooden, Randall. "Reduce the Potential Impact of Product Liability on Your Organization." *Quality Progress*. January 1995.

Postrel, Virginia. "When You're In the Danger Business." *Forbes*. 25 January 1999.

U.S. Consumer Product Safety Commission. *2005 Performance Budget (Operating Plan)*. March 2005.

Hillstrom, Northern Lights
updated by Magee, ECDI

CONTRACTS

A contract is a legally enforceable promise. Contracts are vital to society because they facilitate cooperation and trust. Rather than relying on fear of reprisal or the hope of reciprocity to get others to meet their obligations, people can enlist other people to pursue common purposes by submitting to contracts that are backed by impartial authority. Without contracts and their supporting institutions, promises would be much more vulnerable to ill will, misunderstanding, forgetfulness, and other human flaws. Indeed, contracts allow people who have never even met to reach agreements, such as lending/borrowing money to buy a house, that they would never consider making outside of a legal framework. Discussed below are characteristics and types of contracts.

CONTRACT ELEMENTS

As a legally enforceable promise, a contract differs from a simple verbal promise in that either party may ask the state to force the other party to honor its promise. To distinguish contracts from other types of promises and agreements, courts have established basic elements that are necessary for a contract to exist. A contract may be legally defined as a voluntary, legal, written agreement made by persons with the proper capacity. It should include: 1) an offer; 2) an acceptance; and 3) consideration, or an exchange of value. There are legal exceptions to most of these conditions, and all of them are subject to interpretation in the courts. Furthermore, some contracts do not meet these requirements, such as implied contracts and those created under promissory estoppel, both of which are discussed later.

Contracts not entered into voluntarily are voidable. For example, a company might tell a supplier that it was considering ending their business relationship if, within the next ten minutes, the supplier did not sign a contract to provide materials at a certain cost. If the supplier signed the agreement, it might be able to convince the courts that it did so under duress or undue influence, and therefore was not bound by its terms. In general, contracts created under duress, undue influence, fraud, and misrepresentation are voidable by the injured party.

Contracts are also void if they involve a promise that is illegal or violates public policy. For instance, a contract regarding the sale of illegal drugs is unenforceable. Likewise, contracts that are legal but are not in the public interest may be rendered null. For example, a contract in which a company requires a customer to pay an extremely high rate of interest on borrowed funds could be deemed invalid by the courts. Similarly, a retail company that required an employee to sign an agreement that he would never work for another retailer would likely not be able to enforce the contract because it had unreasonable restrictions or imposed undue hardship on the worker.

Contracts do not have to be written to be enforceable in court. In fact, most oral contracts are legally enforceable. However, they are obviously much more difficult to prove. Furthermore, most states have adopted "statutes of frauds" which specify certain types of contracts that must be in writing. Examples of contracts that typically fall under the statues of frauds include agreements related to the sale of real estate, contracts for the sale of goods above $500, and contracts in which one person agrees to perform the obligation of another person. Such contracts need not be overly long or involved. In fact, a simple memo or receipt may satisfy all legal requirements. There are exceptions in this area, however. For instance, when one party will suffer serious losses as a result of reliance on an oral agreement, the statute of frauds may be waived (see promissory estoppel below).

An otherwise acceptable contract may also be voided if one (or both) of the parties making the agreement does not have the mental or legal capacity to do so. Obviously, a mentally retarded individual or a child could not be bound by a contract. But a contract signed by a person exceeding his authority to make an agreement may also be voided.

In addition to being voluntary, legal, written, and made by persons with proper capacity, contracts usually must possess three basic components: an offer, an acceptance, and consideration. An offer is a promise to perform an act conditioned on a return promise of performance by another party. It is recognized by a specific proposal communicated to another party. Once a legal offer has been made, the offering party is bound to its terms if the other party accepts. Therefore, the offering party must clearly indicate whether the proposal is an offer or some other communique, such as an invitation to negotiate. The offering party, however, may stipulate certain terms of acceptance, such as time limits, and even withdraw the offer before the other party accepts.

Acceptance, the second basic requirement for the existence of a contract, is legally defined as "a manifestation of assent to the terms [of the offer] made by the offeree in the manner invited or required by the offeror." As with offers and offerors, the courts look for an intent to contract on the part of the acceptor. The difference is that the offeror may stipulate terms of acceptance with which the other party must comply. If the offeree attempts to change the terms of the offer in any way, a rejection is implied and the response is considered a counteroffer, which the original offeror may reject or counter. As with most rules regarding contracts, exceptions exist. For example, the Uniform Commercial Code includes a "Battle of the Forms" provision whereby an offeree may imply acceptance under certain circumstances even if it changes or alters the offer.

Even if an offer is accepted, it must be consummated by consideration for a legally enforceable contract to exist. Consideration entails doing something that you were not previously bound to do outside of the agreement. In other words, promisees must pay the price (consideration) that they agreed to pay the promisor in order to gain the right to enforce the promisor's obligation.

The requirement of consideration serves an important purpose. It protects the promisor from being liable for granting, or relying on, gratuitous promises. For example, suppose that a person told her roommate that she would always pay the entire rent for their apartment. If she later changed her mind, she could not be held liable for the rent because she had neither asked for, nor received, anything in exchange for the promise. Had the other roommate promised to clean the apartment in exchange for the roommate's promise to pay the rent, an enforceable contract would exist (assuming other requirements were met).

CONTRACT TYPES

The two primary categories of contracts are "unilateral" and "bilateral." In a unilateral contract only one party promises something. For instance, if a car dealer tells a customer, "I will give you that car if you give me $15,000," he has made an offer for a unilateral contract—the contract will only be created if the customer accepts the offer by paying the $15,000. If the dealer says, "I will promise to give you the car if you promise to pay me $15,000," a bilateral contract has been proposed because both parties must make a promise. The concept of unilateral contracts is important because it has been used by courts to hold a party liable for a promise even when consideration was not given by the other party. For instance, an employer may be liable for providing pension benefits that it promised to an employee, even if the worker gave no promise and did nothing in return.

Contracts may also be classified as "express" or "implied." Express contracts are those in which both parties have explicitly stated the terms of their bargain, either orally or in writing, at the time that the contract was created. In contrast, implied contracts result from surrounding facts and circumstances that suggest an agreement. For instance, when a person takes a car to a repair shop he expects the shop to exercise reasonable care and good faith in fixing the car and charging for repairs. Likewise, the shop expects the customer to pay for its services. Although no formal agreement is created, an implied contract exists.

In addition to express and implied contracts are "quasi-contracts," which arise from unique circumstances. Quasi-contracts are obligations imposed by law to avoid injustice. For instance, suppose that a man hires a woman to paint his house. By accident, she paints the wrong house. The owner of the house knows that she is painting it by mistake but, happy to have a free paint job, says nothing. The painter would likely be able to collect something from the homeowner because he knowingly was "unjustly enriched" at her expense. Had she painted his house while he was on vacation, he would be under no obligation to her.

Contracts may also be categorized as valid, unenforceable, voidable, and void. Valid contracts are simply those that meet all legal requirements. Unenforceable contracts are those that meet the basic requirements but fail to fulfill some other law. For instance, if a state has special requirements for contracts related to lending money, failure to comply could make the contract unenforceable. Voidable contracts occur when one or both parties have a legal right to cancel their obligations. A contract entered into under duress, for example, would be voidable at the request of the injured party. Void contracts are those that fail to meet basic criteria, and are therefore not contracts at all. An illegal contract, for example, is void.

A separate type of contract, and one which overtly exemplifies the trend away from strict interpretation and toward fairness, is created by promissory estoppel. Under the theory of promissory estoppel, a party can rely on a promise made by another party despite the nonexistence of a formal, or even implied, contract. Promissory estoppel can be evoked if allowing a promisor to claim freedom from liability because of a lack of consideration (or some other contractual element) would result in injustice. Suppose that a business owner promised an employee that he would eventually give her the business if she worked there until he (the owner) retired. Then, after 20 years of faithful service by the employee, the owner decides to give the business to his son-in-law. The owner could be "estopped" from claiming in court that a true contract did not exist, because the worker relied on the owner's promise.

CONTRACTS AND SMALL BUSINESSES

Contracts are a necessary part of all sorts of small business transactions—office and equipment leases, bank loan agreements, employment contracts, independent contractor agreements, supplier and customer contracts, agreements for professional services, and product warranties, to name a few. Even the process of writing a contract can be helpful, because it forces the parties to think through contingencies and decide in advance how to handle them. Small business owners should thus be careful of the standard legal terminology that appears in some types of contracts. It is important to understand and agree with all aspects of a contract before signing it. A good rule to apply is that contracts above a certain amount—that amount to be set by the business owner—should be reviewed by the business owner's own law firm. The cost may well be worth it.

BIBLIOGRAPHY

Butler, Susan. "The Art of the Deal: 2005." *Billboard.* 8 January 2005.

"Get It In Writing!" *Commercial Motor.* 6 May 2004.

Howe, Jonathan T. "Do You Have a Binding Agreement? Planners Might Think They've Made a Deal, but Basic Contract Law Often Proves Otherwise." Meetings & Conventions. September 2004.

"Perspectives on Contract Law. 3d ed." *Reference & Research Book News.* August 2005.

Petrillo, Joseph J. "New Buying Regulations: The Never-Ending Story." *Government Computer News.* 19 September 2005.

"Remoteness of Damages." *Contract Journal.* 16 February 2005.

"Rochester Legal Briefs: October 6, 2005." *Daily Record.* 6 October 2005.

Hillstrom, Northern Lights
updated by Magee, ECDI

COOPERATIVE ADVERTISING

Cooperative advertising is the sharing of costs for locally placed advertising between a retailer or wholesaler and a manufacturer. Many manufacturers have a set amount of cooperative advertising funds available per year, distributed as opportunities for collaboration arise. Manufacturers report, however, that much of this money goes unspent, as relatively few retailers and wholesalers pursue cooperative agreements.

Cooperative advertising can be a very powerful tool for the small business owner, especially one with limited means to support the kind of advertising campaign which can be vital to the survival and success of a business enterprise. The added funds from such a cooperative agreement can improve the quality of advertising or broaden the scope of its distribution. It can create important links between products and the small wholesaler or retailer who handles the product for the manufacturer. Above all, it can attract customers loyal to a certain product to a vendor whose name had not before been associated with that product.

Cooperative advertising can take many forms, as Gail Smith explained in *Industrial Distribution:* "There are many devices with which a manufacturer can assist a distributor in product promotion, including product flyers, catalog and trade magazine ads, direct mail flyers and direct mail campaigns, electronic data for CD-ROM, trade show booth materials for customer appreciation/open house or sports events, and giveaway items, such as clothing, mugs, or sports gear. Any one or combination of the above, used with a marketing program, can effectively assist a distributor with making their customer base aware of a product."

BUSINESS NICHES AND COOPERATIVE ADVERTISING

Any small business that deals with the products of a major manufacturer (tennis shoes, perfume, ice cream, propane, computers, etc.) and engages in national—as opposed to local—advertising can benefit from cooperative advertising ventures. These terms can be deceptive, because frequently national advertising is done through local media. But there do exist clear differences between local and national advertising.

Local advertising refers strictly to the advertisement of local shops and services that are not available nationwide or over large regional areas. Small businesses that would engage solely in local advertising, for example, would be small groceries and specialty stores, or small service providers which are not linked to any national chain, such as a local dry cleaner.

National advertising, on the other hand, is advertising that focuses on nationally recognized and available goods and services. Most brand-name items would fall into this category: automobiles and machinery, designer clothes and jewelry, some services. But the actual advertisements are likely to be run only locally, to draw attention to the local provider of these national goods and services—the small dealership, for example, which sells John Deere tractors. It is with this type of advertising that the small business owner can seek a cooperative agreement with a national manufacturer.

BENEFITS OF COOPERATIVE ADVERTISING

The biggest benefit of cooperative advertising for small business owners, of course, is that such arrangements can dramatically cut advertising costs. Manufacturers will sometimes provide anywhere from 50 to 100 percent of the cost of placing local ads. These corporate advertising dollars can make it possible for small businesses to establish a far stronger presence in the community than would otherwise be possible.

Another benefit that sometimes results from such agreements is valuable creative and media-buying guidance. Some large manufacturers will provide help for the small business owner in refining the look and message of the advertisement, and in effectively placing the ad in a mutually beneficial way.

Finally, cooperative advertising can lend an air of legitimacy to small business enterprises. Small companies that are able to link their name with that of a nationally recognized product or service should work hard to maintain such ties, particularly if the product or service in question already has strong user loyalty.

Cooperative advertising also benefits manufacturers and service providers. Enlisting small business allies diminishes the cost of advertising for these larger companies, especially if they encourage cooperative advertising arrangements in several communities. In addition, just as local businesses can benefit from associations with established national corporations, these large manufacturers and service providers may also enjoy benefits associated with having their products or services aligned with leading businesses in a given community. For example, a designer brand of clothing may benefit from cooperative advertising with an exclusive neighborhood boutique: the personality of the shop itself will reflect positively on the product.

DRAWBACKS TO COOPERATIVE ADVERTISING

The small business owner must be careful that he or she completely understands the commitment involved when seeking a cooperative advertising agreement. Many manufacturers demand a certain style of advertising, or a high level of quality that may be difficult to achieve with a limited budget. There may be hidden requirements which must be met, or limits on the kind of advertising which can be funded by manufacturers' dollars. The specific demands involved in an advertising cooperation will vary widely between manufacturers; business consultants recommend that small business owners consult an attorney before signing any such agreements.

SEE ALSO *Cost Sharing*

BIBLIOGRAPHY
Alisau, Patricia. "Co-op Deals Help Boost Properties' Visibility." *Hotel & Motel Management.* 16 May 2005.

Bergen, Mark, and George John. "Understanding Cooperative Advertising Participation Rates in Conventional Channels." *Journal of Marketing Research.* August 1997.

Gruner, Stephanie. "The Secrets of Cross-Promotion: Done Well, Marketing Partnerships Can Stretch Your Budget." *Inc.* June 1997.

Smith, Gail. "Cooperative Advertising: An Untapped Resource." *Industrial Distribution.* August 1997.

Hillstrom, Northern Lights
updated by Magee, ECDI

COOPERATIVES

A cooperative in its simplest sense is formed when individuals organize together around a common, usually economic, goal. For business purposes, a cooperative refers to the creation of a nonprofit enterprise for the benefit of those individuals using its services. According to the National Association of Business Cooperatives, roughly 100 million Americans belong to one of the 47,000 existing cooperatives. Of these cooperatives, 10,500 credit unions make up the largest segment. Other types of goods and services that can be provided by working under cooperative principles include agricultural products, utilities, child care/preschools, insurance, health care, legal services, food, equipment, and employment services.

THE ROCHDALE PRINCIPLES

The modern cooperative dates back to 1844, when the Rochdale Equitable Pioneers Society was established in Great Britain. According to the National Rural Electric Collective Association, the Rochdale Principles are still followed by every cooperative business. First is the principle of a voluntary and open membership. Cooperatives are open to all individuals who are able to use their services and are willing to accept the responsibilities of membership.

The next principle is that of a democratic organization, operated by its members. The board of directors is comprised of members and is accountable to them. Members actively participate in the co-op by developing policy and making decisions. In a primary cooperative, each member has one vote. Other cooperatives are organized in a different but democratic manner. Members also contribute equally to the economic capital of the cooperative. Part, if not all, of the capital becomes the common property of the collective. Surpluses can be used for development of the organization, as reserves, to benefit members according to their use of or contributions to the cooperative, or to support other member-approved works.

A cooperative is autonomous and independent from other organizations. If it enters into a working relationship with another organization, the arrangement must

"ensure the democratic control" of its members and maintain the independence of the organization. Cooperatives provide training and education to members and employees of the organization in order for them to contribute effectively to the cooperative. They also provide information on the benefits of cooperation to the public. Cooperatives work with other cooperatives in order to strengthen the cooperative movement locally and abroad. Although cooperatives exist for the benefit of their members, they work towards the sustainable development of their communities in accordance with membership policies.

The basic operating principles used by cooperatives are simple. The member-owners share equally in the control of their cooperative. They meet on a regular basis, monitor the business closely using a variety of tools, and elect a board of directors from among themselves. The board in turn hires managers to oversee the daily affairs of the cooperative in a way that serves the members' interests. The initial capital for a cooperative comes from membership investment. After the cooperative's costs are covered and money is designated for operations and improvements to the cooperative, the remaining surplus or profit (in a for-profit enterprise) is returned to the membership. For a small business, membership in a cooperative may provide greater purchasing power or access to a wider distribution of goods or services than the business would have on its own.

A related concept is that of a collective. A collective is comprised of a group of individuals pooling together their intellectual and financial resources in order to operate a business enterprise for their mutual benefit. Frequently, members have no specific job but rather contribute to projects if they have free time or specific strengths to add to a job. Members of the collective share equally in any monies left over after paying bills. This alternative method of working has lately found favor with creative businesses such as advertising and design groups. Collectives may remain intact or be of a more fluid nature with members joining and dropping out regularly.

CONSUMERS' COOPERATIVES

Cooperatives may be consumer-owned, producer-owned, or worker-owned. A consumers' cooperative is one in which individuals combine their buying power, usually for the purchase and wholesale or retail distribution of agricultural or other products. Cost savings are achieved by buying directly from the producer or farmer. A form of commonly known consumers' cooperative is a food or grocery cooperative. Membership is open to anyone, with goods sold at market price to members and non-members alike, with any surplus over expenses going back to members. According to Aliza Earnshaw in *Business Journal-Portland,* "[Food] co-ops must pay out at least

20 percent of the surplus in cash, but may reinvest 80 percent in the business for the good of members." The benefits to members of this reinvestment may include reduced prices, a larger store, or extra services.

Management of the food co-op works with members to determine these benefits. Some members may desire a discount when purchasing their goods. Other co-ops may use a patronage system in which members receive dividends at the end of the year, based on how much they have purchased at the co-op. This method keeps members involved and also helps to ensure the viability of the cooperative.

A credit union is a cooperative financial institution, which is owned and controlled by the consumer members who use its services. Typically, they serve groups that share something in common, such as where they work, live, or go to church. They are closely regulated, with deposits insured by the National Credit Union Share Insurance Fund. Unlike banks and savings-and-loans, they are not-for-profit enterprises.

A utility cooperative, such as an electric cooperative, is another consumer-owned cooperative. They are private, independent utilities established to provide electric, natural gas, or telephone service at-cost to their member-owners who are primarily in rural areas. Many utility cooperatives are also involved in community development projects.

Another type of consumers' cooperative is a preschool or child care cooperative. The most common type of cooperative preschool is the parent-based one in which parents come together to provide care and schooling for their children. Newer versions of cooperative preschools may be initiated by a business or group of businesses. In this case, a business may provide a space, initial capital, and assistance to a child care program but gives ownership and operation responsibilities to the parents/employees who use it.

Likewise, a business consortium comprised of businesses or organizations form a cooperative to be operated and owned by their collective employee groups. Organizations generate the dollars needed to fund the program initially, provide space for the program, and possibly hire a management group. The board of directors for the consortium cooperative preschool consists of both parent-members as well as representatives of the business or sponsoring organizations.

PRODUCERS' COOPERATIVES

A producers' cooperative is typically operated by farmers, producers of goods, or small businesses. Farmers and producers organize cooperatives in order to process and market their goods as well as to acquire credit, equipment, and production supplies. This provides them with greater economies of scale. For example, members of an agricultural cooperative, such as a dairy cooperative, will combine their efforts in order to purchase equipment and supplies at a discount, process their milk products in a combined fashion, and then market and distribute those products as a group. Unlike a collective farm, however, a member of an agricultural cooperative retains the ownership rights to his or her land. Similarly, small businesses can organize cooperatives to provide their membership with supplies or common services at a reduced rate. Crafts people frequently come together in the form of a cooperative in order to purchase supplies inexpensively and then to sell their goods to a larger market.

Just as non-members may take advantage of the benefits of consumers' cooperatives such as food co-ops, producers' cooperatives such as small businesses may employ non-members. However, according to John Murray in *Review of Social Economy,* studies done on the use of non-member labor within a producers' cooperative show this generally has a negative impact on the cooperative, such as reduced productivity. It may also spur the evolution of the cooperative into a more conventional form of business "in which the owners [are] employers rather than employees."

BUYING COOPERATIVES

A buyers' cooperative is an association of businesses that gather together so that they may obtain economies of scale by combining their purchasing power and negotiating wholesale prices as a group. Claude Solnik describes the benefits of buying cooperatives this way in his article in the *Long Island Business News,* "Whether they're small or large operations, in the electronics industry or in health care, education or government, many managers reduce costs through joining a good, old-fashioned buying cooperative.... A big reason that smaller outfits join these cooperatives is that they save them some real money." Small businesses that join a buying cooperative are able to get the same pricing on merchandise from vendors as larger retails or "big box" stores. Better service on delivery and exchanges as well as greater selection are also benefits touted by co-op members. In an era of proliferating big-box stores buying cooperatives are gaining popularity among small- and mid-size retail organizations.

WORKERS' COOPERATIVES

A worker-owned cooperative is a business that is commonly owned and managed by its workers. By organizing a business as a cooperative, the owner/employees make the initial investment in the enterprise, work for its success, and reap any benefits. They also share in the risks of the business. Another method of developing a worker-owned cooperative is when a labor union purchases a failing or failed privately owned business and operates it using the principles of cooperation. Some types of businesses which are often owned and controlled by their employees include restaurants, manufacturing and distribution enterprises, and taxi companies.

More information about cooperatives is available from the International Cooperative Alliance at www.coop.org, or from the National Business Cooperative Association at www.nbca.org.

BIBLIOGRAPHY

Colvin, Robert. "Buying Cooperatives Are a Useful Weapon." *Modern Plastics.* January 2001.

Diekmann, Frank J. "CUs May Cooperate, but Cooperative? Not at First." *Credit Union Journal.* 18 September 2000.

Earnshaw, Aliza. "Remember Food Co-Ops? Portland's Still Flourishes." *Business Journal-Portland.* 25 August 2000.

"Group Dynamics." *Creative Review.* September 2000.

Murray, John E. "Communal Viability and Employment of Non-Member Labor: Testing Hypotheses with Historical Data." *Review of Social Economy.* March 2000.

Solnik, Claude. "Old Fashioned Buying Cooperatives Are Catching On." *Long Island Business News.* 6 January 2006.

Stevens Hume, Lynn. "Indiana Cooperatives Not Political Subdivisions and Can't Issue Tax-Exempts, IRS Ruling Says." *The Bond Buyer.* 16 December 1991.

Hillstrom, Northern Lights
updated by Magee, ECDI

COPYRIGHT

Copyright is a kind of protection offered by the laws of the United States to the authors of "original works of authorship," including literary, musical, dramatic, artistic, and other intellectual works. Copyright law thus protects a wide variety of creative compositions, including books, magazine articles, songs (both lyrics and music), plays (and any accompanying music), choreography, photographs, drawings, sculptures, and films and other audiovisual works. This protection is extended to both published and unpublished works. Copyright experts note that the definition of "intellectual works" should be interpreted quite broadly in this regard. For example, computer software programs can be registered as "literary works," and maps and architectural blueprints can be registered as "pictorial, graphic, and sculptural works."

Once the author or creator of an intellectual work secures a copyright for that work, he or she has exclusive rights to do whatever he or she wishes with it. The owner can reproduce and/or distribute copies of it for sale; transfer ownership via sale, lease, rental, or lending; prepare derivative works based on the copyrighted work; or provide public displays or performances of the work.

Several categories of material are generally not eligible for copyright protection. These include ideas, methods, concepts, principles, titles, names, slogans, familiar symbols or designs, listings of ingredients or contents, coloring, and variations of typographic ornamentation. Other material not eligible for copyright include works consisting entirely of information that is common property and contains no original authorship (standard calendars, height and weight charts, tables taken from public documents) and works that, in the words of the Copyright Office, "have not been fixed in a tangible form of expression." Examples of the latter include improvisational performances or choreographic works that have not been written or recorded.

CORNERSTONES OF COPYRIGHT LAW

The basic philosophy underlying American copyright law can be found in Article 1, Section 8 of the Constitution, which stipulates that "Congress shall have Power... To promote the Progress of Science and useful Arts, by securing for limited Times to Authors and Inventors the exclusive Right to their respective Writings and Discoveries." The sentiments embodied in this proclamation were given added legal heft in 1909 and 1976, years that saw major copyright legislation become law.

A major change in American copyright law came in the late 1970s, as Congress passed new laws addressing the length and character of copyright protection. As a result of that legislation, which took effect on January 1, 1978, all works created on or after that date automatically receive legal protection from the moment of their creation (before then a work did not receive copyright protection until it had been published or registered with the Copyright Office). The new legislation expanded the duration of copyright protection as well. It provided authors with legal protection that ordinarily lasts for the entire life of the author, plus an additional 50 years after the author's death. In the case of "joint works" (works created by two or more authors under circumstances that were not "for hire"), the copyright protection lasts for 50 years after the last surviving author's death. For works made for hire, anonymous works, and pseudonymous works (unless the author's identity is revealed in Copyright Office records), the copyright on the work in question last for 75 years from publication or 100 years from creation, whichever is shorter. Creative works that came into being prior to January 1, 1978, but had not yet been published or registered by that date are given similar protection under the terms of the statute.

Copyright protection is somewhat different for works originally created and published or registered prior to

January 1, 1978. For such works authors could secure copyright protection for 28 years, with an option to renew that protection for another 28 years as the initial term expired. The new copyright law extended the length of that second term from 28 years to 47 years, thus making pre-1978 works eligible for a total of 75 years of copyright protection. In addition, a 1992 amendment to the Copyright Act of 1976 automatically extended the term of copyrights obtained from January 1, 1964, through December 31, 1977, to the full renewal limit of 47 years.

American copyright law underwent another change in 1989, when copyright notices on copyrighted material become optional. Prior to March 1, 1989, copyright notices had been mandatory on all published works; any works not carrying a copyright notice risked loss of copyright protection. After March 1, 1989, however, that notice was no longer required—although it was still highly recommended—because works created after that date were automatically copyrighted the moment they were presented in a fixed form (generally print, audio, or video).

Notice is not required legally but may be useful practically. Kelly James-Enger, writing in *The Writer,* advised as follows: "To get the most protection from the copyright law . . . you have to register your work with the U.S. Library of Congress. Properly registered, you're entitled to statutory monetary damages and attorney's fees if you prevail in a copyright infringement lawsuit; if you haven't registered, you'll have to prove not only that your copyright was infringed, but that you lost a certain amount of money as a result." James-Enger suggests that writers begin online at www.loc.gov/copyright.

The most recent significant legislation impacting copyright protection was signed into law by President Clinton in October 1998. This legislation, called the Digital Millennium Copyright Act, included a number of significant provisions, including the following:

- Made it illegal to circumvent anti-piracy measures in commercial software.

- Outlawed the manufacture, sale, or distribution of devices used illegally to copy software.

- Placed limits on the copyright infringement liability of Internet service providers who transmit information over the Internet (although the Act also called for ISPs to remove materials that infringe on legitimate copyright claims).

- Limits liabilities of nonprofit institutions of higher learning for acts of copyright infringement committed by student or faculty.

- Requires payment of licensing fees to record companies for "webcasting."

Despite the changes that have taken place in American copyright rules over the past 200 years, in many respects copyright protection has always been—and continues to be—fairly simple. If you create something and record that creation in a tangible manner, you own it. The exceptions are materials in the public domain and others' right to so-called "fair use."

Public Domain Once the term of a copyright (or a patent) expires, it is said to become a part of the "public domain." In essence, this means that it becomes community property. Anyone may use it. Photographs, magazine articles, and books are among the most common "public domain" materials used today.

Another potentially valuable source of public domain material is works produced by the United States government. While state and local governments often copyright their documents, reports, and other publications, the federal government does not do so.

"Fair Use" Section 107 of the U.S. Copyright Act, in one paragraph that embeds a list of four items, describes "fair use" as follows:

"Notwithstanding the provisions of sections 106 and 106A [dealing with copyright itself], the fair use of a copyrighted work, including such use by reproduction in copies or phonorecords or by any other means specified by that section, for purposes such as criticism, comment, news reporting, teaching (including multiple copies for classroom use), scholarship, or research, is not an infringement of copyright. In determining whether the use made of a work in any particular case is a fair use the factors to be considered shall include—

1. "the purpose and character of the use, including whether such use is of a commercial nature or is for nonprofit educational purposes;

2. "the nature of the copyrighted work;

3. "the amount and substantiality of the portion used in relation to the copyrighted work as a whole; and

4. "the effect of the use upon the potential market for or value of the copyrighted work.

"The fact that a work is unpublished shall not itself bar a finding of fair use if such finding is made upon consideration of all the above factors."

The language of the law clearly leaves matters somewhat ambiguous, but the intent is not that difficult to discern. The law wishes to give reviewers and scholars the right to quote small portions of the work, teachers and researchers the right to use the work in actual practice, while protecting the income of the copyright holder.

Freelancers and small businesses using copyrighted material will sensibly protect themselves against lawsuits by quoting copyrighted materials very sparingly and in the contexts specified by the law itself. If large parts of the publication or the musical composition or whatever other form the object takes are needed, the user should make the necessary efforts to obtain formal permission and pay whatever fees the copyright owner charges.

WORK FOR HIRE AND COPYRIGHT

In situations where a work—a software program, an essay, a mural, an advertising design, or another intellectual work—has been produced for someone who is working for someone else, the copyright for the work may belong to the person or business that arranged to have the work done, rather than the creator of the work itself. Such arrangements are known as work for hire. Copyright law defines "work for hire" as either: 1) a work prepared by an employee within the scope of his or her employment, or 2) a work specially ordered or commissioned for use as a contribution to a collective work, as a part of a motion picture or other audiovisual work, as a translation, as a supplementary work, as a compilation, as an instructional text, as a test, as answer material for a test, or as an atlas, provided that the parties involved expressly agree in a written contract signed by both of them that the work shall be considered a work made for hire. Indeed, contracts that specifically define copyright ownership for work performed are essential, especially for small business owners who contract work out to freelancers.

COPYRIGHT NOTICE

Although attaching a formal notice of copyright to a work is no longer required by law (it was required prior to March 1, 1989), it is still a good idea. "Use of the notice is recommended because it informs the public that the work is protected by copyright, identifies the copyright owner, and shows the year of first publication," stated the Copyright Office. "Furthermore, in the event that a work is infringed, if the work carries a proper notice, the court will not allow a defendant to claim 'innocent infringement'—that is, that he or she did not realize that the work is protected. (A successful innocent infringement claim may result in a reduction in damages that the copyright owner would otherwise receive.)"

According to the Copyright Office, forms of notice vary for different kinds of intellectual works. For books, articles, sheet music, architectural plans, designs, and other kinds of "visually perceptible" works, copyright notice should contain all of the following three elements:

1. The copyright symbol (the letter "C" in a circle) or the word "Copyright," or the abbreviation "Copr."

2. The year of first publication of the work (in cases where the work is a compilation or derivation that incorporates previously published material, the year date of first publication of the compilation or derivation is acceptable). The year date may be omitted in instances where a pictorial, graphic, or sculptural work, with accompany text (if any) is reproduced in or on greeting cards, postcards, stationery, jewelry, dolls, toys, or any useful article.

3. The name of the owner of copyright in the work, or an abbreviation by which the name can be recognized, or a generally known alternative designation of the owner.

For works that are fixed through audio means—cassette tapes, CDs, "books-on-tape," etc.—the requirements for copyright notice are somewhat different. Copyright notice for these types of works should contain all of the following:

1. The sound recording copyright symbol (the letter "P" in a circle).

2. The year of first publication of the sound recording.

3. The name of the owner of copyright in the sound recording, or an abbreviation by which the name can be recognized, or a generally known alternative designation of the owner. In addition, if the producer of the recording is named on the label or containers of the work, and if no other name appears in conjunction with the notice, the producer's name shall be considered a part of the notice.

Notice of copyright can also be extended to unpublished works. Finally, when affixing notice of copyright to intellectual works of any kind, it is important to make sure that the notice is plainly visible.

COPYRIGHT REGISTRATION

Registration of copyrighted material may be made at any time during the life of the copyright. It is no longer required under American copyright law, but there are advantages associated with taking such a step.

- Registration establishes a public record of the copyright claim

- Certificates of registration are required if the copyright owner wants to file an infringement suit

- Registration establishes *prima facie* evidence in court of the validity of the copyright and of the facts stated in the certificate in instances where the registration is made within five years of original publication

- Registrations made within three months of the work's publication—or prior to any infringement of the work—entitle the copyright owner to statutory damages and coverage of attorney's fees in court; otherwise, only an award of actual damages and profits is available to the copyright holder

- Registration gives the copyright owner additional protection against the importation of infringing copies

To register a copyright, the Copyright Office must receive a properly completed application form, a non-refundable filing fee for each work that is being registered, and a non-returnable copy of the work that is being registered. There are variations to the above rules depending on the kind of work that is being registered, so registration seekers should contact the Office beforehand to get a full rundown on what is required for their particular work. The Copyright Office uses a variety of forms for the various intellectual works that people register; copyright owners need to make sure that they use the correct one. Form TX, for example, covers published and unpublished non-dramatic literary works such as board game instructions, computer programs, and books, while Form VA is intended for use in registering published and unpublished visual works such as photographs, sculptures, and architectural designs.

All applications and materials related to copyright registration should be addressed to the Registrar of Copyrights, Copyright Office, Library of Congress, Washington, DC 20559-6000. The Copyright Office also maintains an Internet site at lcweb.loc.gov/copyright/.

INTERNATIONAL COPYRIGHT PROTECTION

As the Copyright Office itself admits, "there is no such thing as an 'international copyright' that will automatically protect an author's writings throughout the entire world. Protection against unauthorized use in a particular country depends, basically, on the national laws of that country. However, most countries do offer protection to foreign works under certain conditions, and these conditions have been greatly simplified by international copyright treaties and conventions."

The two major copyright treaties to which the United States belongs are the Universal Copyright Convention (UCC) and the Berne Convention for the Protection of Literary and Artistic Works. The United States was actually a founding member of the UCC,

which came into being in September 1955. Under the rules of the UCC, a work by a citizen or resident of a member nation or a work first published in a member nation may claim protection.

The Berne Convention, meanwhile, was first established more than a century ago, in 1886. The central feature of the Berne Convention is the automatic copyright protection that it extends to all citizens of member nations. If a country is a signatory to the Berne Convention, it must extend to nationals of other member nations the same copyright protection and copyright restrictions afforded to its own citizens. The United States joined the Berne Convention—which is regarded as the wellspring of most other national and international copyright regulations—in 1989, becoming its 77th member. In recent years, the United States has also entered into international copyright agreements enacted by the World Intellectual Property Organization (WIPO).

COPYRIGHT LAW AND THE INTERNET

The emergence of electronic commerce and digital technology triggered a fundamental reevaluation of U.S. copyright law in the 1990s. The Copyright Office has firmly supported the rights of companies to limit access to their Internet content, and the government has passed laws that make it illegal for Internet users to negate copyright protection mechanisms meant to protect Internet content. However, libraries, universities, research institutions, and other critics have charged that the Copyright Office position will unduly impede fair-use access to content in its zeal to protect owners of copyrighted material on the Internet.

In the meantime, companies are gearing up to protect electronic copyrighted material from illegal distribution. They are doing so through a variety of schemes collectively known as Digital Rights Management (DRM). These content control measures include: locking access to content through encryption schemes, plug-ins, and new markup languages. Other options include the traditional "honor system," in which permissions and payments are provided by the Copyright Clearance Center or other similar entities. Prosecution of copyright violators is another option.

The Copyright Office's response to growing Internet use is not limited to policymaking. In recognition of the growing reliance on and use of the Internet, the Copyright Office is also in the process of installing an electronic registration, recordation and deposit system, dubbed CORDS. This program will ultimately provide users with the ability to register copyrights and deposit dissertations online. According to the Library of Congress, "creators will register their works electronically, transmitting both the application and the works in digital form, with registration information then incorporated into the centralized online database of copyright registration records." In addition, the program will enable copyright owners and agents to record transfers of copyright ownership (including assignments, licenses, and security interests) on an online database.

COPYRIGHT OFFICE

In July 1999 the Copyright Office increased its fees for a variety of services it provides, including basic registration, document recordation, supplementary and/or renewal registration, search services (including reference and bibliographic reports), and certificates. But these increases do not provide full-cost recovery for its various services. Since the Copyright Office is not self-supporting, it relies on assistance from the Library of Congress general budget to fulfill its many obligations.

All correspondence intended for the Office should be addressed to the Registrar of Copyrights, Copyright Office, Library of Congress, Washington, DC 20559-6000. In addition, you can contact the Copyright Office through its Internet web site: lcweb.loc.gov/copyright/.

SEE ALSO *Trademarks*

BIBLIOGRAPHY

Albiniak, Paige. "Do Not Bypass Go." *Broadcasting and Cable.* 6 November 2000.

Butler, Susan. "Piracy a Fight for All." Billboard. 14 January 2006.

"Buying Books One Page At a Time." *New York Times Upfront.* 9 January 2006.

Copyright Basics From the U.S. Copyright Office. Copyright Office, n.d.

Harmon, Amy. "Copyright and Copying Wrongs: A Web Rebalancing Act." *New York Times.* 10 September 2000.

James-Enger, Kelly. "Dear Writer." *The Writer.* February 2006.

Matthews, Anna Wilde. "Copyrights on Web Content are Backed." *Wall Street Journal.* 27 October 2000.

Miller, Michael J. "Why Google Print is More Important Than You Think." *PC Magazine.* 27 December 2995.

Peek, Robin. "The Digital Rights Management Dilemma." *Information Today.* November 2000.

"Politicians In No Mood to Change Copyright Law." *Broadcast Engineering.* 13 December 2005.

Hillstrom, Northern Lights
updated by Magee, ECDI

CORPORATE CULTURE

Corporate culture refers to the shared values, attitudes, standards, and beliefs that characterize members of an organization and define its nature. Corporate culture is rooted in an organization's goals, strategies, structure, and approaches to labor, customers, investors, and the greater community. As such, it is an essential component in any business's ultimate success or failure. Closely related concepts, discussed elsewhere in this volume, are corporate ethics (which formally state the company's values) and corporate image (which is the public perception of the corporate culture). The concept is somewhat complex, abstract, and difficult to grasp. A good way to define it is by indirection. The Hagberg Consulting Group does just that on its Web page on the subject. HCG suggests five questions that, if answered, get at the essence:

- What 10 words would you use to describe your company?
- Around here what's really important?
- Around here who gets promoted?
- Around here what behaviors get rewarded?
- Around here who fits in and who doesn't?

As these questions suggest, every company has a culture—but not all cultures (or aspects of them) help a company reach its goals. The questions also suggest that companies may have a "real culture," discernible by answering these questions, and another one which may sound better but may not be the true one.

EMERGENCE AND CHARACTERISTICS

The concept of corporate culture emerged as a consciously cultivated reality in the 1960s along-side related developments like the social responsibility movement—itself the consequence of environmentalism, consumerism, and public hostility to multinationals. Awareness of corporate culture was undoubtedly also a consequence of growth, not least expansion overseas—where corporations found themselves competing in other national cultures. The U.S. competition with Japan, with its unique corporate culture, was yet another influence. So was the rise to prominence of management gurus the dean of whom was Peter Drucker. As corporations became aware of themselves as actors on the social scene, corporate culture became yet another aspect of the business to watch and to evaluate—alongside the "hard" measures of assets, revenues, profits, and shareholder return.

Corporate culture by definition affects a firm's operations. It is also, by definition, something that flows from management downward and outward. In many corporations, the "culture" was set very early on by the charismatic activity and leadership of a founder. But as major tendencies become deeply institutionalized, corporate culture also becomes an institutional habit that newcomers acquire. In actual practice "reinventing" the corporation from the top down, therefore, is difficult to achieve, takes time, and happens only under strong leadership.

Observers and analysts of the phenomenon tend to subdivide culture into its various expressions related either to major constituencies (employees and workers, customers, vendors, government, the community) or to methods or styles of operation (cautious, conservative, risk-taking, aggressive, innovative). A corporate culture may also, by overstepping certain bounds, become suicidal—as the case of Enron Corporation, the energy trader, illustrates. In the Enron culture an aggressive, creative, high-risk style led to fraud and ultimate collapse. Analysis is helpful in understanding how a corporate culture expresses itself in specific areas. However, the concept is social and culture, as the phrase itself implies. It does not lend itself to reorganization by a rearrangement of standard building blocks.

CULTURE IN SMALL BUSINESSES

Culture can be a particularly important consideration for small businesses. A healthy company culture may increase employees' commitment and productivity, while an unhealthy culture may inhibit a company's growth or even contribute to business failure. Many entrepreneurs, when they first start a new business, quite naturally tend to take on a great deal of responsibility themselves. As the company grows and adds employees, however, the authoritarian management style that the business owner used successfully in a very small company can become detrimental. Instead of attempting to retain control over all aspects of the business, the small business owner should, as consultant Morty Lefcoe told *Nation's Business,* strive to "get everybody else in the organization to do your job, while you create an environment so that they can do it."

In a healthy culture, employees view themselves as part of a team and gain satisfaction from helping the overall company succeed. When employees sense that they are contributing to a successful group effort, their level of commitment and productivity, and thus the quality of the company's products or services, are likely to improve. In contrast, employees in an unhealthy culture tend to view themselves as individuals, distinct from the company, and focus upon their own needs. They only perform the most basic requirements of their jobs, and their main—and perhaps only—motivation is their paycheck.

Since every company is different, there are many ways to develop a culture that works. Following are several main principles that small business owners should consider in order to create a healthy corporate culture:

Prevailing corporate culture begins at the top. Entrepreneurs need to explain and share their vision of the company's future with their workers. "Let your vision for the company become their vision for the company," stated John O'Malley in his article "How to Create a Winning Corporate Culture." He goes on to say that "a company without a vision is reactive in nature, and its management is seldom confident addressing competitive threats and stepping into the future." In addition, small business owners should be aware that their own behavior and attitudes set the standard for the entire workforce. Small business owners who set poor examples in areas such as lifestyle, dedication to quality, business or personal ethics, and dealings with others (customers, vendors, and employees) will almost certainly find their companies defined by such characteristics.

Treat all employees equally. Entrepreneurs should treat all employees equally. This does not mean that business owners can not bestow extra rewards on workers who excel, but it does mean that interactions with all employees should be based on a foundation of respect for them. One particular pitfall in this area for many small business owners is nepotism. Many small businesses are family-owned and operated. But bloodlines should be irrelevant in daily operations. "Successful . . . businesses constantly place 'you are no different' expectations on family members they employ," noted O'Malley. "Doing otherwise quickly undermines employees' morale. . . . Showing favoritism in the workplace is like swimming with sharks—you are destined to get bitten."

Hiring decisions should reflect desired corporate culture. The wise small business owner will hire workers who will treat clients and fellow employees well and dedicate themselves to mastering the tasks for which they are responsible. After all, "good attitude" is an essential component of any healthy corporate culture. But entrepreneurs and their managers also need to make sure that hiring decisions are not based upon ethnic, racial, or gender issues. Besides, businesses typically benefit from having a diverse workforce rather than one that is overly homogeneous.

Two-way communication is essential. Small business owners who discuss problems realistically with their workforce and enlist employees' help in solving them will likely be rewarded with a healthy internal environment. This can be an important asset, for once a participatory and engaging culture has been established, it can help propel a small business ahead of its competition.

On the other hand, problems with the corporate culture can play a major role in small business failures. When employees only perform the tasks necessary to their own jobs, rather than putting out extra effort on behalf of the overall business, productivity declines and growth comes to a halt. Unfortunately, many entrepreneurs tend to ignore the developing cultures within their businesses until it is too late to make needed changes.

In an article for *Entrepreneur,* Robert McGarvey outlined some warning signs of trouble with the company culture, including: increased turnover; difficulty in hiring talented people; employees arriving at work and leaving for home right on time; low attendance at company events; a lack of honest communication and understanding of the company mission; an "us-versus-them" mentality between employees and management; and declining quality and customer satisfaction. A small business exhibiting one or more of these warning signs should consider whether the problems stem from the company culture. If so, the small business owner should take steps to improve the culture, including reaffirming the company's mission and goals and establishing a more open relationship with employees.

SEE ALSO *Corporate Ethics; Corporate Image*

BIBLIOGRAPHY

Barrier, Michael. "Building a Healthy Company Culture." *Nation's Business.* September 1997.

"Corporate Culture: Telling the CEO the Baby is Ugly." Hagenberg Consulting Group. Available from http://www.hcgnet.com/research.asp?id=6. Retrieved on 2 February 2006.

Grensing-Pophal, Lin. "Hiring to Fit Your Corporate Culture." *HRMagazine.* August 1999.

Hindle, Tim. *Field Guide to Strategy.* Boston: Harvard Business/The Economist Reference Series, 1994.

McGarvey, Robert. "Culture Clash." *Entrepreneur.* November 1997.

O'Malley, John. "How to Create a Winning Corporate Culture." *Birmingham Business Journal.* 11 August 2000.

Phegan, Barry. *Developing Your Company Culture: The Joy of Leadership.* Context Press, 1996.

Hillstrom, Northern Lights
updated by Magee, ECDI

CORPORATE IMAGE

"Corporate image" was once advertising jargon but is today a common phrase referring to a company's reputation. The "image" is what the public is supposed to *see* when the corporation is mentioned. The ordinary man and woman on the street usually have a wry view of public relations, advertising, hype, hoopla, and therefore also of corporate image—and this often for good reasons. But a good corporate image is a genuine asset; it translates into dollars at the counter and higher stock valuation.

The concept is usually associated with large corporations, but small businesses also have a corporate image even if neither their owners nor customers think of it that way. In the absence of active efforts, corporate image "simply happens": it is how a company is perceived. Management, however, may actively attempt to shape the image by communications, brand selection and promotion, use of symbols, and by publicizing its actions. Corporations trying to shape their image are analogous to individuals who will dress appropriately, cultivate courteous manners, and choose their words carefully in order to come across competent, likeable, and reliable. In the personal as in the corporate case, the image should match reality. When it does not, the consequence will be the opposite of the one intended.

THE ELEMENTS OF IMAGE

A corporate image is, of course, the sum total of impressions left on the company's many publics. In many instances a brief, casual act by an employee can either lift or damage the corporate image in the eyes of a single customer or caller on the phone. But the overall image is a composite of many thousands of impressions and facts. The major elements are 1) the core business and financial performance of the company, 2) the reputation and performance of its brands ("brand equity"), 3) its reputation for innovation or technological prowess, usually based on concrete events, 4) its policies toward its salaried employees and workers, 5) its external relations with customers, stockholders, and the community, and 6) the perceived trends in the markets in which it operates as seen by the public. Sometimes a charismatic leader becomes so widely known that he or she adds a personal luster to the company.

Image versus Images Only in the best of cases does a corporation enjoy a *single* reputation. Different publics may have different views of the corporation depending on their different interests. A company's brand image may be very good but its reputation among suppliers poor—because it bargains very hard, pays late, and shows no loyalty to vendors. A company may be highly regarded on Wall Street but may be disliked on the Main Street of cities where it has closed plants. A company may be valued for providing very low prices yet disliked for its employment practices or indifferent environmental performance. It is much more likely that a small business will have an all-around reputation for excellence than that a very large conglomerate will merit all-around praise. Smallness has its advantages.

At the Core: Business Performance The single most important factor in the corporate image is a company's core business performance; performance, by definition, includes financial results. A growing, profitable corporation with a steady earnings history will, for these reasons alone, please its customers, investors, and the community in which it operates. A profitable company that, nevertheless, exhibits huge gyrations in earnings will fare worse: its earnings and dividends will be unpredictable; it will have layoffs; its stock will fluctuate; its vendors will be more uneasy; its employees nervous. When a business fails in its core function, its reputation heads straight south. Enron Corp., an energy trader, had a stellar reputation as the 7th largest corporation measured in revenues. It fell into bankruptcy almost abruptly on December 2, 2001; the Justice Department began to investigate it for fraud. Suddenly every aspect of the company that had been admired and lauded—its audacity, energy, profitability, innovativeness, entrepreneurial spirit, and so on—took on opposite and negative connotations. The core business had failed; Enron's reputation imploded. No amount of corporate image polishing could have saved Enron's reputation after that.

MEASURING THE CORPORATE IMAGE

Corporations evaluate their image, much as politicians do, by survey. They employ the methodology of marketing surveys used both in polling and in support of advertising. The investigators select appropriate samples of the public and interview them; telephone surveys are the most common. They use statistical methods of extrapolation to project from the sample what the public as a whole (or selected publics) think. Corporations, of course, also rely on the much "harder" measures such as sales and stock performance. Surveys of the corporate image are sometimes motivated by sagging sales and a miserable press.

The theory of the corporate image holds that, all things equal, a well-informed public will help a company achieve higher sales and profits, whereas a forgetful or poorly informed public may come to hold negative impressions about the company and may ultimately shift more of its patronage toward competitors.

A recent campaign launched by Toyota Motor North America Inc. illustrates measurement and a response to it. As reported by Jamie LaReau in *Automotive News,* "Toyota periodically surveys U.S. consumers' perceptions of the automaker. The surveys suggested [that] Americans' awareness of Toyota's U.S. presence had declined since 2000 . . . even as the company was building and expanding plants." The company launched a print and TV program to highlight the company's contributions to the U.S. economy.

WORDS AND ACTION

The example of Toyota is a case in which Toyota felt the need to communicate ("words") something about its investments ("action") in the United States. Ideally words and actions are always closely linked in building

or repairing the corporate image. Ideally, also, the two will correspond. To achieve a close alignment of words and deeds is often difficult in practice. Who has not observed with a knowing eye the difference between the cheerful, helpful clerks in the TV ads of a company and the surly indifference of that same company's actual clerks? Expert advisors to the corporate world, such as Roger Hayward writing in *Accountancy Age* emphasize the need for consistent follow-through—so that employees become "a vast army of goodwill ambassadors."

Whether the objective is to make the most of a good thing or to turn around an adverse situation, good management practice will ensure that action is accomplished before the words are spoken. A case of that sort is presented by the Rite Aid chain store. The company went through a financial scandal in the late 1990s; its former chief executive and others were convicted and jailed. A new management team first turned the chain around before, as reported in *Chain Drug Review,* it launched a campaign to tell the world that "the turnaround is complete and we are a stable, healthy company focusing on growth," as *Chain Drug Review* quotes Karen Rugen, Rite Aid's senior vice president of communications and public affairs, a newcomer to the company.

ATTENTION TO DETAIL

The management of the corporate image also involves management of the more mundane side of image, the corporation's logo, its brand images, the look and feel of its retail outlets, its offices, signage, even its stationery and the look of its calling cards. Good management implies ensuring that all spokespersons for the company say the same thing in the same way for a consistent message. Furthermore, in pays attention to consistent self-presentation in the look of its facilities.

SMALL BUSINESS AND CORPORATE IMAGE

Every small business will have the equivalent of a corporate image because it will have a reputation among its employees, customers, vendors, neighbors, and the government agencies with which it deals. The first action of the owner, in choosing the name of enterprise, is an exercise in building a corporate image. The process continues in many ways: in the choice of brand names to be used, the location of leased space, office decorations and/ or store equipment selected, the company's Web site design if the business has an Internet presence, its sales literature, and so on. As the business begins to operate, it will build its visibility in its market by outward symbols; the quality of its products or services; the knowledge, skill, and friendliness of its employees; its promptness in paying bills; its effectiveness in mounting promotions; and the list goes on.

By their very nature, small businesses tend to be closer to all of their constituencies. As a consequence, the business will enjoy rapid feedback from the public when it begins to make mistakes or has some bad luck. If that should happen, the small business, like the major corporation, will engage in the actions—followed by words—which will be necessary to recover losses or make the most of unusual success.

SEE ALSO *Brand Equity*

BIBLIOGRAPHY
"Analysis: Corporate Case Study – Schering-Plough Looks to Remedy An Ailing Image." *PR Week.* 12 December 2005.

Brady, Diane, Michael Arndt and Amy Barrett. "When Your Name is Mud, Advertise; Companies in Crisis Used to Lie Low. The New Response to Bad Press is Positive Spin." *Business Week.* 4 July 2005.

"Explaining the Enron bankruptcy." *CNN.com/U.S.* Available from http://archives.cnn.com/2002/US/01/12/enron.qanda.focus/. 13 January 2002.

Hayward, Roger. "Insight: Corporate Reputation" *Accountancy Age.* 30 June 2005.

LaReau, Jamie. "Toyota Polishes Corporate Image in TV Campaign." *Automotive News.* 28 February 2005.

"Maintaining Corporate Image." *Automotive Industries.* May 2005.

"Retailer Burnishes Its Image as 'Stable, Healthy Company'." *Chain Drug Review.* 20 December 2004.

"What's in a Name?" *Industry Week.* September 2005.

Darnay, ECDI

CORPORATE LOGO

A logotype, commonly referred to as a logo, is a graphical symbol created for an individual company or product. It is designed to communicate quickly, and to be a distinctive and easily recognizable symbol. Logos often include a special typeface or font used to spell out the company name or initials. They also tend to include specific colors and graphical shapes. Corporate logos appear on a wide range of materials distributed or maintained by companies, including store signs, business cards, company Web sites, major equipment, stationery, marketing materials, packaging, uniforms, etc. Effective company logos have been cited as important elements in corporate image-building efforts. Conversely, many marketing experts believe that poorly conceived or unattractive logos can have a negative impact on a business's appeal and hence, its performance in the marketplace.

As small business owners and CEOs of major multinational firms alike are aware, corporate image is an important factor in business success. Companies that are thought of as innovative, smart, or stable in the marketplace have achieved that status in part because of the way in which they present themselves to clients and competitors alike. Corporate logos are one of the tools that businesses have at their disposal in shaping that image. As Anne McGregor Parsons argued in *Colorado Business Magazine,* corporate logos are potentially valuable visual symbols because they can express both the personality and the mission of a company.

Issues in Corporate Logo Creation Business consultants, entrepreneurs, and designers that specialize in logo creation all agree that several factors have to be weighed when creating a logo for a company:

1. Desired Image—This is far and away the most important consideration, and it can be of even greater importance to business start-ups that may not have the financial wherewithal to recover from early slips in logo choice and other marketing areas. Entrepreneurs seeking to make or update a logo, then, should make sure that specific business objectives, target markets, and competitor image are all factored into the logo's creation. For example, a new microbrewery would probably be more inclined to go with a creative, bold logo that features a stylized image of its product than would an independent insurance agency, which would place greater value on logo characteristics that connote stability and trustworthiness.

2. Industry—Many companies sport logos that reflect the industry in which they operate. Providing such associations often makes it easier to attract prime customers.

3. Cost—Creating a logo, or updating an existing logo, "can be an expensive proposition," wrote McGregor Parsons, "affecting a company's entire range of visual communications from business cards to truck fleets." Opinions vary about the financial emphasis that start-ups and established small businesses should place on logos and slogans. Some analysts believe that entrepreneurs sometimes devote too much energy and money to creating a distinctive logo at the expense of addressing basic financial and operational needs. Other consultants and experienced small business owners, however, believe that a visually interesting logo can not only attract much needed attention to fledgling businesses, but can also present businesses with opportunities to make additional sales, by making available clothing, gear,

and other merchandise in which the logo is prominently featured. This phenomenon has been most evident on the national stage, as athletic shoe manufacturers and professional sports teams have proven quite adept at selling such wares to customers, but it can also be seen with local logos that are deemed trendy by young consumers.

4. Impact on Current Customers—Owners of established businesses who are considering changing their logo should weigh the potential negative impact that such a switch could have on existing clients/customers. As Raymond Snoddy observed in *Marketing*, redesigning familiar corporate logos can be disturbing to customers who have established a certain comfort level with the old logo.

5. Longevity—Entrepreneurs should beware of using logos that are overly reliant on passing fads or marketing gimmicks. "Communications cost a lot of money for a company, so they need to have the greatest longevity that they can," one logo designer told *Colorado Business Magazine*. "That's why we try to focus on timeless, classic design [when making logos], leaving the trendier things to the more short-term tactical type of advertising media." Another designer agreed, remarking that a logo "must stand the test of time."

6. Distinctive—Experts urge business owners not to use gimmicky logos, but they also tout the benefits of logos that are unique in some fashion. Not only do such logos enjoy a certain level of legal protection from infringement, they also catch the eye of the customer.

7. Flexible—Logo designs should be made so that they can be used on a wide variety of promotional materials, from billboards and the sides of trucks to letterheads and shirt insignias.

BIBLIOGRAPHY

Haig, Bill. "Great Logos and Why." *Designnews*. 29 July 2003.

Love, Kenneth D., and Kenneth J. Roberts. "Your Company's Identity Crisis." *Management Review*. October 1997.

McGregor Parsons, Anne. "Making Your Mark." *Colorado Business Magazine*. August 1994.

Morioka, Noreen, and Sean Adams. *Logo Design Workbook*. Rockport Publishers, 2004.

Snoddy, Raymond. "Familiarity with Design Kills Off Shock of the New." *Marketing*. 23 October 1997.

Ten Kate, Nancy. "Graphic Design for the Bottom Line." *American Demographics*. April 1994.

Underwood, Elaine. "Proper I.D.: With Brand Values Under Increasing Attack, Companies are Keener Than Ever to Devise Memorable, Meaningful Corporate Identities." *Brandweek*. 8 August 1994.

Williams, Hugh Aldersey. "You are Your Logo." *Management Today*. January 1998.

Hillstrom, Northern Lights
updated by Magee, ECDI

CORPORATE SPONSORSHIP

Corporate sponsorship is a form of advertising in which companies pay to be associated with certain events. When the sponsorship of a nonprofit or charitable event is involved, the sponsorship activity is often referred to as event marketing or cause marketing. Corporate sponsorship has been growing rapidly in recent years, faster, in fact, than the growth in overall corporate advertising in the late 1990s. According to Trevor Hartland, writing in the *International Journal of Sports Marketing & Sponsorship*, "global sponsorship reached an all-time high of $26.2 billion in 2003."

Most of the sponsors of large events are, of course, large companies. However, part of the increase in corporate sponsorship worldwide is attributable to the number of small- and medium-sized firms that are becoming involved. Not long ago, only large entities could afford to sponsor large events as a way of building goodwill and boosting revenue. But in today's business environment, small companies have embraced sponsorship of everything from local softball and volleyball teams to festivals, fairs, and park cleanups as an effective means of increasing their visibility in their home community. Many of these kinds of sponsorships enable small companies to increase their public profile in a relatively cost-effective manner.

A company can benefit in many ways from sponsorship. *Nation's Business* contributor Harvey Meyer touts a wide range of potential benefits: "[Sponsorships] can enhance a company's image and visibility; differentiate the company from competitors; help develop closer relationships with current and prospective customers; showcase products and services; unload obsolete inventory; and allow the company to compete more effectively against bigger firms that have much larger advertising budgets. In addition, tickets to sponsored events can be used as incentives for employees, vendors, and customers and to promote worker loyalty. And proponents say that if sponsorships are well-conceived and strategic, they can boost sales—both long-term and short-term—as they improve the community through the events they support."

In an article that discusses recent trends in corporate sponsorship entitled "Why Sponsors Sponsor," author Jim Karrh lists the four criteria that not-for-profit fundraisers expect to be used by most companies in assessing the request to become involved as a sponsor. The four criteria are as follows:

- Relevance—the cause must be relevant to the company's products or service.

- Branding Fit—there must be a good fit with the overall company brand.

- Mission Alignment—the partnership must align with a company's mission.

- Business Result—the company must believe it can achieve some measurable business result through the partnership.

In addition to the advertising and promotional aspects of corporate sponsorship, it also provides benefits in the realm of community relations. A comprehensive, ongoing community relations program—including event sponsorship—can help virtually any organization achieve visibility as a good community citizen. Organizations are recognized as good community citizens when they support programs that improve the quality of life in their community, including crime prevention, employment, environmental programs, clean-up and beautification, recycling, and restoration. Some other examples of ongoing programs might include scholarship programs, urban renewal projects, performing arts programs, social and educational programs, children's activities, community organizations, and construction projects. These kinds of sponsorships—also sometimes referred to as "cause-related marketing"—may also be linked to national or even international social causes. For example, a kayak manufacturer who donates a percentage of its boat sales directly to a national river conservation organization not only supports a worthwhile cause, but also creates an effective marketing tool for itself.

Good community relations programs give employees a reason to be proud of the company, which increases loyalty and may help to reduce labor and production costs. Furthermore, a company with happy employees and a good reputation in the community is likely to attract highly qualified new employees. A small company may also generate new business through the contacts and leads it generates in its community relations activities. Such contacts might also make it easier for the company to obtain financing for expansion, find promising new locations, or gain favorable treatment in terms of taxes, ordinances, or utilities. Good community relations can also be beneficial in times of crisis, such as a fire or a plant closing, by rallying the community around the affected business.

Event sponsorship, in particular, is an attractive option because it provides a business with access to various audiences, including employees, business decision makers, and government regulators as well as consumers. It can be an especially good marketing tool for companies that participate in international trade, because sponsorship transcends language and cultural barriers. Many marketers feel that corporate sponsorship is superior to other methods because it allows for an immediate customer response to new product offerings. Events provide business managers with an opportunity to come face-to-face with their customers. They also provide customers with an opportunity to try a company's products out firsthand. By comparison, marketing research tools like focus groups can be expensive and may not target the right people, while market questionnaires or surveys generally do not give potential customers a chance to try the product.

Corporate sponsorship also provides marketers with a unique opportunity to position their products in the marketplace. With corporate sponsorship—unlike conventional marketing techniques—the company, the product, and the event or cause being sponsored tend to become linked in consumers' minds. By sponsoring an event or funding the broadcast of an event, a sponsor is able to gain visibility while simultaneously creating an association to itself with the event's values. The event generates the audience while projecting values associated with the activities of the event. Each sponsorship vehicle has certain associated images in the consumer's mind that transfer to the sponsor.

Given this tendency for consumers to associate sponsors with events, it is important for sponsoring companies to choose events that fit well with the image of their products. Indeed, small businesses should not associate themselves with any cause or event without first undertaking a serious examination of the potential drawbacks of a sponsorship opportunity. For example, effective sponsorships often require active participation on the part of companies and segments of their workforces. In addition, some companies shy away from sponsorship because of fears that they will be exposed to litigation or bothered by organizers of other events. Finally, affiliation with a community event that is poorly organized or violates local standards of good taste can be quite costly to a small business. With this in mind, small business owners should always undertake a background check on events or organizations they are considering sponsoring. Talking with current and past sponsors is one good way to learn more about the event from someone other than its promoters. It is worth noting that the growing popularity of corporate sponsorship has spurred many market research firms to aid businesses in the selection, implementation, and evaluation of sponsorship opportunities. But these services may be prohibitively expensive for smaller companies.

Even when there is a good fit between sponsor and event, it is still vital for a company to promote the event and its involvement in order to gain benefits. After all, sponsorship is a form of advertising, even when it is of a nonprofit venture or charitable event. Possible ways to promote events sponsorship include billboards, print and broadcast advertisements, and direct mail. Sponsoring companies may also find it helpful to issue press releases about the event to the media, as well as to contribute articles and editorials to publications that reach the target audience. Marketers of consumer products may also engage in joint promotions with retailers, such as coupons and tie-ins.

The fees involved in event marketing can range from a few hundred dollars to hundreds of thousands of dollars, depending on the scale of the event and the level of the sponsor's involvement. In addition to the cost of staging the event itself, there are also associated advertising, publicity, and administrative costs to consider. Many small businesses choose to begin as a co-sponsor of an existing event, which allows them to take advantage of the other sponsors' experience. It may also be possible for a small business to underwrite a new event and share advertising costs with a co-sponsor. Some businesses find it difficult to justify the expense of corporate sponsorship because it can be difficult to gauge the results in monetary terms. But it is often possible to conduct before-and-after interviews with attendees of the event, or to give away coupons and then track redemption rates. Some businesses also attempt to gauge the success of an event by providing a toll-free telephone number for attendees to call for more information about their products or services.

AMBUSH MARKETING

The benefits provided by corporate sponsorship can be decreased significantly by competitive tactics known as "ambush marketing," which occurs when competitors take steps to deflect an event audience's attention away from the sponsor and toward themselves. Ambush marketing tactics include sponsoring the media coverage of an event rather than the event itself, sponsoring a subcategory of an event, sponsoring individual athletes or teams involved in an event, or planning advertising to coincide with the event. Although the practice is considered unethical by paid sponsors and event owners, others consider it a normal part of competitive advertising.

There are several preemptive measures corporate sponsors can take to reduce the chances of being hit with ambush marketing. Sponsor companies should try to anticipate competitive promotions and establish those specific rights with the event owner, identify related avenues for promotion and block them, and seek legal remedies when their sponsorship rights are infringed

upon. But perhaps the most effective way for sponsor companies to reduce the effectiveness of ambush marketing tactics is to promote their involvement effectively.

SEE ALSO *Charitable Giving*

BIBLIOGRAPHY

Fry, Andy. "Sponsors Play to Win." *Marketing.* 7 August 1997.

Hartland, Trevor, and Heather Skinner. "What Is Being Done to Deter Ambush Marketing? Are These Attempts Working?" *International Journal of Sports Marketing & Sponsorship.* July 2005.

Karrh, Jim. "Why Sponsors Sponsor." *Arkansas Business.* 12 December 2005.

Kasrel, Deni. "Corporate Sponsorship Grows." *Philadelphia Business Journal.* 2 May 1997.

Meyer, Harvey. "And Now, Some Words About Sponsors." *Nation's Business.* March 1999.

Moore, Paula. "Companies Unearth a Gold Mine of Goodwill: Using Generosity as a Marketing Strategy." *Denver Business Journal.* 22 August 1997.

Hillstrom, Northern Lights
updated by Magee, ECDI

COST CONTROL AND REDUCTION

Cost control and reduction refers to the efforts business managers make to monitor, evaluate, and trim expenditures. These efforts might be part of a formal, company-wide program or might be informal in nature and limited to a single individual or department. In either case, however, cost control is a particularly important area of focus for small businesses, which often have limited amounts of time and money. In a small business the focus is often on selling and servicing the customer. This leaves the task of purchasing slightly sidetracked. Even seemingly insignificant expenditures—for items like office supplies, telephone bills, or overnight delivery services—can add up for small businesses. On the plus side, these minor expenditures can often provide sources of cost savings.

PLANNING AND CONTROL

Cost control refers to management's effort to influence the actions of individuals who are responsible for performing tasks, incurring costs, and generating revenues. First managers plan the way they want people to perform, then they implement procedures to determine whether actual performance complies with these plans. Cost control is a continuous process that begins with the annual budget. As the fiscal year progresses, management compares actual results to those projected in the budget and incorporates into the new plan the lessons learned from its evaluation of current operations. Through the budget process and accounting controls, management establishes overall company objectives, defines the centers of responsibility, determines specific objectives for each responsibility center, and designs procedures and standards for reporting and evaluation.

A budget segments the business into its components, or centers, where the responsible party initiates and controls action. *Responsibility centers* represent applicable organizational units, functions, departments, and divisions. Generally a single individual heads the responsibility center exercising substantial, if not complete, control over the activities of people or processes within the center, as well as the results of their activity. *Cost centers* are accountable only for expenses. *Revenue centers* primarily generate revenues. *Profit centers* accept responsibility for both revenues and expenses. The use of responsibility centers allows management to design control reports and pinpoint accountability. A budget also sets standards to indicate the level of activity expected from each responsible person or decision unit, and the amount of resources that a responsible party should use in achieving that level of activity.

The planning process, then, provides for two types of control mechanisms: feedforward, which provides a basis for control at the point of action (the decision point); and feedback, which provides a basis for measuring the effectiveness of control after implementation. Management's role is to feedforward a futuristic vision of where the company is going and how it is to get there, and to make clear decisions coordinating and directing employee activities. Management also oversees the development of procedures to collect, record, and evaluate feedback.

CONTROL REPORTS

Control reports are informational reports that tell management about a company's activities. Control reports are only for internal use, and therefore management directs the accounting department to develop tailor-made reporting formats. Accounting provides management with a format designed to detect variations that need investigating. In addition, management also refers to conventional reports such as the income statement and balance sheet, and to external reports on the general economy and the specific industry.

Control reports need to provide an adequate amount of information so that management may determine the reasons for any cost variances from the original budget. A good control report highlights significant information by focusing management's attention on those items in which actual performance significantly differs from the standard.

Managers perform effectively when they attain the goals and objectives set by the budget. With respect to profits, managers succeed by the degree to which revenues continually exceed expenses. In applying the following simple formula, Net Profit = Revenue − Expenses, managers realize that they exercise more control over expenses than they do over revenues. While they cannot predict the timing and volume of actual sales, they can determine the utilization rate of most of their resources; that is, they can influence the cost side. Hence, the evaluation of management's performance and the company's operations is cost control.

STANDARDS

For cost control purposes, a budget provides standard costs. As management constructs budgets, it lays out a road map to guide its efforts. It states a number of assumptions about the relationships and interaction among the economy, market dynamics, the abilities of its sales force, and its capacity to provide the proper quantity and quality of products demanded. An examination of the details of the budget calculations and assumptions reveals that management expects operations to produce the required amount of units within a certain cost range. Management bases its expectations and projections on the best historical and current information, as well as its best business judgment.

For example, when calculating budget expenses, management's review of the historic and current data may strongly suggest that the production of 1,000 units of a certain luxury item will cost $100,000, or $100 per unit. In addition, management might determine that the sales force will expend about $80,000 to sell the 1,000 units. This is a sales expenditure of $80 per unit. With total expenditures of $180, management sets the selling price of $500 for this luxury item. At the close of a month, management compares the actual results of that month to the standard costs to determine the degree and direction of any variance. The purpose for analyzing variances is to identify areas where costs need containment.

In the above illustration, accounting indicates to management that the sales force sold 100 units for a gross revenue of $50,000. Accounting's data also show that the sales force spent $7,000 that month, and that production incurred $12,000 in expenses. While revenue was on target, actual sales expense came in less than the projected, with a per unit cost of $70. This is a *favorable* variance. But production expenses registered an *unfavorable* variance since actual expenditures exceeded the projected. The company produced units at $120 per item, $20 more than projected. This variance of 20 percent significantly differs from the standard costs of $100 and would likely cause management to take corrective action.

As part of the control function, management compares actual performance to predetermined standards and makes changes when necessary to correct variances from the standards. The preparation of budgets and control reports, and the resulting analysis of variances from performance standards, give managers an idea of where to focus their attention to achieve cost reductions.

COST CUTTING FOR SMALL BUSINESSES

A variety of techniques can be employed to help a small business cut its costs. One method of cost reduction available to small businesses is hiring an outside analyst or consultant. These individuals may be independent consultants or accountants who analyze costs as a special service to their clients. They generally undertake an in-depth, objective review of a company's expenditures and make recommendations about where costs can be better controlled or reduced. Some expense-reduction analysts charge a basic, up-front fee, while others collect a percentage of the savings that accrue to the company as a result of their work. Still others contract with specific vendors and then pool the orders of their client companies to obtain a discount. Some of the potential benefits of using a consultant include saving time for the small business owner, raising awareness of costs in the company, and negotiating more favorable contracts with vendors and suppliers.

Steps that a small business can take relatively quickly and can start them down the path of cost reduction include such things as printing or photocopying on both sides of the paper whenever possible. Securing supplies to which employees have access, like locking the office supply cabinet, to better track usage of these items. Canceling insurance policies on unused equipment and vehicles is another way to check unnecessary costs. Establishing a regular cost-cutting program can be done by setting aside time to review several months' worth of checks and invoices and make a detailed list of all monthly expenses. Then, decide upon a few areas that might benefit from comparison-shopping for better prices. If the small business owner is not inclined to undertake the comparison-shopping personally, a responsible employee can be assigned to the task.

Despite the importance of cost control to small businesses, and the potential for cost savings, cost reduction alone cannot guarantee success. For cost cutting to be effective, the sales and revenue end of the business must be healthy. "Only the most exceptional leaders of the most exceptional companies avoid getting sucked into a period of heady growth followed by desperate cutbacks," Alan Mitchell wrote in *Management Today*.

"These companies have learned the hard way that cost cutting alone doesn't guarantee customer preference."

Mitchell went on to explain that every business reaches a point in its growth when management recognizes a need to cut costs, usually in the face of a crisis. "Over time, you get a cost cutting culture," consultant Paul Taffinder told Mitchell. "Once you have, the types of people who are good at building things—creating new values, new products, new services—are driven out of the business because it is unpleasant for them to work there. Then, once boom time arrives again, the organization piles on capacity but doesn't solve the problem of creating innovative potential. It has to hire talented new people again." Many companies repeat this process of inefficient growth several times.

The effective implementation of a cost control and reduction program takes planning and time. It should be seen as a continuous process and one that will need ongoing attention. Instead of blindly trying to cut costs in the face of a crisis, Mitchell recommended that managers embrace cost cutting as a strategic issue and approach the task from a marketing perspective. "If you are going to talk about waste, you need to define what value is, because the opposite of waste is value," business school professor Dan Jones told Mitchell. "And you can only define value from the end customer's perspective. If you can really do this—if you really know what it is that doesn't add value to the customer—then you can start asking 'How can we get rid of that?' Otherwise, we are just saying 'Let's cut costs.'"

BIBLIOGRAPHY

"Bain Study Outlines Strategic Importance of Continuous Cost-Reduction Program." *The Controller's Report.* February 2004.

Cost Reduction and Control Best Practices: The Best Ways for a Financial Manager to Save Money. Second Edition. Institute of Management and Administration (IOMA), 2005.

Covington, Donna. "Cost Reduction Essential to Competition: A Global Look at Costs Gives the Big Picture and a Big Advantage." *Industry Week.* 16 December 2005.

Horngren, Charles T., George Foster, and Srikant M. Datar. *Cost Accounting: A Managerial Emphasis.* Prentice Hall, 1999.

Meigs, Robert F., and Walter B. Meigs. *Accounting: The Basis for Business Decisions.* Ninth Edition. McGraw-Hill, 1998.

Mitchell, Alan. "Corporate Dieting Can Make Your Company Fat." *Management Today.* May 1998.

Patterson, Perry. *Cost Reduction and Control Best Practices: The Best Ways for a Financial Manager to Save Money.* John Wiley & Sons, 2002.

Hillstrom, Northern Lights
updated by Magee, ECDI

COST SHARING

Cost sharing is a process wherein two or more entities work together to secure savings that one alone would be unable to obtain. Such partnerships may be pursued in order to realize any number of business objectives—increased marketplace exposure, access to technology, reduce expenses through economies of size in purchasing or reducing costs, etc.—but cost savings is usually a central component of these arrangements. Cost-sharing partnerships can be implemented in many different operating areas, from marketing to transportation to research and development. It is a favorite tool of many small business enterprises with limited financial resources.

Cost sharing partnerships can be entered into by a business with other businesses, with its own employees, and/or with its clients and customers. Each of these cost sharing types is discussed below.

COST SHARING BUSINESS TO BUSINESS

Traditionally, the meaning of cost-sharing partnerships has been an arrangement in which one or more businesses partner to secure savings of some kind. Relatively few cost-sharing arrangements have been implemented for the actual manufacture of goods or execution of services. Instead, the majority of cost-sharing plans are in the area of marketing and advertising. "Today's direct marketing partnerships achieve impressive cost-benefit results," stated Myron Gould in *Direct Marketing*. He cited three primary advantages associated with cost-sharing partnerships in this operational area:

- They enable marketers to address the competitive challenges of the rising cost of direct marketing essentials, such as postage and paper.

- They help marketers reduce direct mail expenses because costs are shared.

- Their effectiveness is enhanced by the development of technology tools and media outlet alternatives.

Gould cited the latter factor as particularly important for businesses seeking to engage in effective cost-sharing. "Computers have transformed [the marketing] industry and given birth to partnership opportunities. Today's computer-driven partnerships empower us to target qualified recipients and segment lists as never before. Many of our alternative direct marketing programs have traditionally taken a broadcast approach—reaching broadly defined segments. Now, partnerships offer qualified segmentation, targeting narrower, clearly defined lifestyle and demographic segments. Technical advances in imprinting and inserting also offer enhanced ability to customize the package and the offer."

Finding a Cost-Sharing Partner "There are no rules, standards, or boundaries that should restrict your vision when seeking a partner. Rather, shared goals should guide your 'vision quest,'" wrote Gould. "Partnership can be formed in the profit and nonprofit sectors, in the same or different industries, within different divisions of the same company, and in similar market segments/demographics in non-competitive industries."

Many small business owners seek out allies for the exclusive purpose of registering savings in their operating costs. This is a perfectly legitimate course of action, but entrepreneurs should make certain that the final agreement is a fair one that explicitly delineates the terms of the agreement. Indeed, written partnership agreements that define each partner's spending obligations should be insisted on. In addition to discussing cost-sharing matters, these documents can also provide details on agreed-upon procedures and work flow, parameters for responsibilities, and mechanisms to measure results both during and after the project. As Gould observed, carefully crafted proposals "will help you mitigate concerns about loss of control and structuring the partnership for mutual benefit. When a partnership fulfills the consumers' needs with a new, exciting, or value-added offer or program, risks are minimized for all involved."

In addition to ensuring that cost-sharing agreements are sufficiently documented, small business owners should weigh possible other benefits associated with partner alternatives when making their decision. Gould noted, for example, that a larger company might be able to provide a small business with valuable access to technology and training, while a smaller business might be blessed with a much-coveted contemporary market image. Ideally, a small business owner will be able to find a partner who not only can help him or her secure savings in one or more aspects of business operations, but also provide additional benefits.

Cost-Sharing Arrangements and the Internal Revenue Service The Internal Revenue Service (IRS) maintains certain rules concerning how cost-sharing agreements within business groups should allocate costs. According to the IRS, a cost-sharing arrangement is defined as an agreement under which costs to develop intangibles are shared in proportion to reasonably anticipated benefits that each entity will reap. Such arrangements must include two or more participants; provide a method to calculate each controlled participant's share of intangible development costs, based on factors that can reasonably be expected to reflect each participant's share of anticipated benefits; provide for adjustments to the controlled participant's shares of intangible development costs to account for changes in economic conditions and the business operations and practices of the participants; and be recorded in an up-to-date document that provides detailed information on specifics of the arrangement.

The IRS established a "safe harbor" for actual benefits that diverge from estimates, but only if the difference is less than 20 percent. In allocating intangible development costs under a cost-sharing agreement, it is necessary to project the participant's share of anticipated benefits. That share is then compared to the participant's allocated share of the total costs. If these shares are not equal, the IRS has the authority to adjust accordingly. Benefits include additional income generated and costs saved by the use of the intangible.

COST SHARING WITH EMPLOYEES

The economic slowdown of the early 2000s combined with nearly 10 percent annual increases in the cost of health care benefits have created a situation in which many companies feel forced into passing long a greater and greater portion of health insurance costs to employees. This cost shifting is referred to in the business world as health care cost sharing. In an attempt to reduce the cost of employee benefits, many companies have begun to increase the percentage of premium costs that must be born by the employee. This is often done by increasing the amount of co-pays that employees are asked to pay for doctor visits and prescription drugs. It may also be done by an outright increase in the percentage of the premium paid directly by the employee for his or her coverage. Either way, it is a cost-sharing measure that reduces a company's costs by passing them on to employees.

COST SHARING WITH CUSTOMERS

Anyone who has put together a swing-set or computer table, pumped gasoline into his or her car, or downloaded a computer software patch has participated in a cost-sharing arrangement. A *CIO Magazine* article discussing the rules for successful self-service explains the trend this way: "...companies have been eager to tap into the free labor pool of customers who can be convinced to help themselves. Through self service, organizations have been able to reduce labor costs, increase revenue from orders of out-of-stock items or increase the loyalty of customers who appreciate speedier service."

The increasing use of self-serve arrangements in retail establishments and financial institutions represents the rising popularity of cost-sharing measures that share costs with customers. In order to be effective these arrangements must be seen by the customer to be beneficial in some way, at least in their early stages. The customer may be offered a reduced price for booking his or her own airline ticket, or for assembling a piece of furniture. A customer may save time by using a self

check-out lane and feel that this compensates for the effort. The tools offered a customer for performing these self-service tasks are also important. They must be intuitive. "If the interface is confusing, people are not going to stand there and figure it out. They're just gone," explained Francie Mendelsohn, president of Summit Research Associates, in the *CIO Magazine* article. If the transaction is made easy and the customer is convinced that he or she is receiving value equal to or greater than the effort expended, cost-sharing partnerships with customers can be a means for companies to save.

SEE ALSO *Barter; Cooperative Advertising; Cooperatives; Shared Services*

BIBLIOGRAPHY

Baldwin III, Arthur L. "The Price of Illness: Cost Sharing and Health Plan Benefits." *Medical Benefits*. 15 November 2005.

Clift, Vicki. "Small Firms Benefit from a Promotional Partner." *Marketing News*. 23 September 1996.

Dicker, Adrian J. W. "Final Cost-Sharing Regulations." *Tax Advisor*. May 1996.

Dragoon, Alice. "Six Simple Rules For Successful Self-Service." *CIO Magazine*. 15 October 2005.

Fitzgerald, Kevin R. "Proprietary Information—Should Suppliers Share It?" *Purchasing*. 3 October 1996.

Gould, Myron. "Partnering for Profit—How to Achieve Impressive Cost-Benefit Results." *Direct Marketing*. February 1997.

Hanson, Don R., and Maryanne M. Mowen. *Cost Management*. Fifth Edition. Thomson South-Western, 2005

"Health Care Cost Sharing." *The Controller's Report*. August 2005.

Kaplan, Todd R., and David Wettstein. "Cost Sharing: Efficiency and Implementation." *Journal of Mathematical Economics*. December 1999.

Hillstrom, Northern Lights
updated by Magee, ECDI

COST-BENEFIT ANALYSIS

Cost-benefit analysis is the exercise of evaluating a planned action by determining what net value it will have for the company. Basically, a cost-benefit analysis finds, quantifies, and adds all the positive factors. These are the benefits. Then it identifies, quantifies, and subtracts all the negatives, the costs. The difference between the two indicates whether the planned action is advisable. The real key to doing a successful cost-benefit analysis is making sure to include all the costs and all the benefits and properly quantify them. It is the fundamental assessment behind virtually every business decision, due to the simple fact that business managers do not want to spend money unless the benefits that derive from the expenditure are expected to exceed the costs. As companies increasingly seek to cut costs and improve productivity, cost-benefit analysis has become a valuable tool for evaluating a wide range of business opportunities, such as major purchases, organizational changes, and expansions.

Some examples of the types of business decisions that may be facilitated by cost-benefit analysis include whether or not to add employees, introduce a new technology, purchase equipment, change vendors, implement new procedures, and remodel or relocate facilities. In evaluating such opportunities, managers can justify their decisions by applying cost-benefit analysis. This type of analysis can identify the hard dollar savings (actual, quantitative savings), soft dollar savings (from such things as management time or facility space), and cost avoidance (the elimination of a future cost, like overtime or equipment leasing) associated with the opportunity.

Although its name seems simple, there is often a degree of complexity, and subjectivity, to the actual implementation of cost-benefit analysis. This is because not all costs or benefits are obvious upon initial assessment. Take, for example, a situation in which a company is trying to decide if it should make or buy a certain subcomponent of a larger assembly it manufactures. A quick review of the accounting numbers may suggest that the cost to manufacture the component, at $5 per piece, can easily be beaten by an outside vendor who will sell it to the company for only $4. But there are several other factors that need to be considered and quantified (if possible):

1. When production of a subcomponent is contracted to an outside vendor, the company's own factory will become less utilized, and therefore its fixed overhead costs have less components over which to be spread. As a result, other parts it continues to manufacture may show an increase in costs, consuming some or possibly all of the apparent gain.

2. The labor force may be concerned about outsourcing of work to which they feel an entitlement. Resulting morale problems and labor unrest could quickly cost the company far more than it expected to save.

3. The consequences of a loss of control over the subcomponent must be weighed. Once the part is outsourced, the company no longer has direct control over the quality, timeliness, or reliability of the product delivered.

4. Unforeseen benefits may be attained. For example, the newly freed factory space may be deployed in a more productive manner, enabling the company to make more of the main assembly or even another product altogether.

This list is not meant to be comprehensive, but rather illustrative of the ripple effect that occurs in response to changes made in a real business setting. The cost-benefit analyst needs to be cognizant of the subtle interactions of other events with the action under consideration in order to fully evaluate its impact. In fact, accuracy in quantifying the costs and benefits in this sort of analysis is essential in producing information useful for the decision-making process.

The time value of money is a central concept in doing a cost-benefit analysis. The reason is that an amount of money received today has greater value than getting that same amount of money in the future. Compensating for this difference between the present value and the future value of money is essential if a cost-benefit analysis is to accurately quantify the costs and benefits of the action being studied.

Capital budgeting is essentially a cost-benefit analysis that extends the evaluation of costs and benefits into a longer timeframe and therefore greater emphasis is placed on considerations of the time value of money. When the inputs and outputs related to a capital expenditure are quantified by year, they can then be discounted to present value to determine the net present value of the opportunity at the time of the decision.

A formal cost-benefit analysis is a multi-step process which includes a preliminary survey, a feasibility study, and a final report. At the conclusion of each step, the party responsible for performing the analysis can decide whether continuing on to the next step is warranted. The preliminary survey is an initial evaluation that involves gathering information on both the opportunity and the existing situation. The feasibility study involves completing the information gathering as needed and evaluating the data to gauge the short- and long-term impact of the opportunity. Finally, the formal cost-benefit analysis report should provide decision makers with all the pertinent information they need to take appropriate action on the opportunity. It should include an executive summary and introduction; information about the scope, purpose, and methodology of the study; recommendations, along with factual justification; and factors concerning implementation.

Cost-benefit analysis is a decision support method used to help answer questions that often start with "what if" or "should we." It is a mathematical method to measure the benefits of a course of action. It is a powerful tool that can be used to thoroughly analyze the likely net effect to a business of buying new equipment, expanding into a new service area, or outsourcing a task now handled internally. Feeling confident that the benefits derived from an action taken will outweigh the costs of implementing that action makes the decision to proceed much easier.

BIBLIOGRAPHY

Bhemani, Alnoor. *Management Accounting in the Digital Economy.* Oxford University Press, 2004.

Campbell, Harry F., and Richard P.C. Brown. *Benefit-Cost Analysis, Financial and Economic Appraisal Using Spreadsheets.* Cambridge University Press, 2003.

Dmytrenko, April L. "Cost-Benefit Analysis." *Records Management Quarterly.* January 1997.

Dompere, Kofi K. *Cost-Benefit Analysis and the Theory of Fuzzy Decisions.* Springer, 2004.

Hoque, Zahirul. *Handbook of Cost and Management Accounting.* Spiramus Press, Ltd., 2005.

Shein, Esther. "Formula for ROI." *PC Week.* 28 September 1998.

Hillstrom, Northern Lights
updated by Magee, ECDI

COSTS

Costs are the necessary expenditures that must be made in order to run a business. Every factor of production has an associated cost. The cost of labor, for example, used in the production of goods and services is measured in terms of wages and benefits. The cost of a fixed asset used in production is measured in terms of depreciation. The cost of capital used to purchase fixed assets is measured in terms of the interest expense associated with raising the capital.

Businesses are vitally interested in measuring their costs. Many types of costs are observable and easily quantifiable. In such cases there is a direct relationship between cost of input and quantity of output. Other types of costs must be estimated or allocated. That is, the relationship between costs of input and units of output may not be directly observable or quantifiable. In the delivery of professional services, for example, the quality of the output is usually more significant than the quantity, and output cannot simply be measured in terms of the number of patients treated or students taught. In such instances where qualitative factors play an important role in measuring output, there is no direct relationship between costs incurred and output achieved.

DIFFERENT WAYS TO CATEGORIZE COSTS

Costs can have different relationships to output. Costs also are used in different business applications, such as financial accounting, cost accounting, budgeting, capital budgeting, and valuation. Consequently, there are different ways of categorizing costs according to their relationship to output as well as according to the context in which they are used. Following this summary of the different types of costs are some examples of how costs are used in different business applications.

Fixed and Variable Costs The two basic types of costs incurred by businesses are fixed and variable. Fixed costs do not vary with output, while variable costs do. Fixed costs are sometimes called overhead costs. They are incurred whether a firm manufactures 100 widgets or 1,000 widgets. In preparing a budget, fixed costs may include rent, depreciation, and supervisors' salaries. Manufacturing overhead may include such items as property taxes and insurance. These fixed costs remain constant in spite of changes in output.

Variable costs, on the other hand, fluctuate in direct proportion to changes in output. In a production facility, labor and material costs are usually variable costs that increase as the volume of production increases. It takes more labor and material to produce more output, so the cost of labor and material varies in direct proportion to the volume of output.

For many companies in the service sector, the traditional division of costs into fixed and variable does not work. Typically, variable costs have been defined primarily as "labor and materials." However, in a service industry labor is usually salaried by contract or by managerial policy and thus does not fluctuate with production. It is, therefore, a fixed and not a variable cost for these companies. There is no hard and firm rule about what category (fixed or variable) is appropriate for particular costs. The cost of office paper in one company, for example, may be an overhead or fixed cost since the paper is used in the administrative offices for administrative tasks. For another company, that same office paper may well be a variable cost because the business produces printing as a service to other businesses, like Kinkos, for example. Each business must determine based on its own uses whether an expense is a fixed or variable cost to the business.

In addition to variable and fixed costs, some costs are considered mixed. That is, they contain elements of fixed and variable costs. In some cases the cost of supervision and inspection are considered mixed costs.

Direct and Indirect Costs Direct costs are similar to variable costs. They can be directly attributed to the production of output. The system of valuing inventories called direct costing is also known as variable costing. Under this accounting system only those costs that vary directly with the volume of production are charged to products as they are manufactured. The value of inventory is the sum of direct material, direct labor, and all variable manufacturing costs.

Indirect costs, on the other hand, are similar to fixed costs. They are not directly related to the volume of output. Indirect costs in a manufacturing plant may include supervisors' salaries, indirect labor, factory supplies used, taxes, utilities, depreciation on building and equipment, factory rent, tools expense, and patent expense. These indirect costs are sometimes referred to as manufacturing overhead.

Under the accounting system known as full costing or absorption costing, all of the indirect costs in manufacturing overhead as well as direct costs are included in determining the cost of inventory. They are considered part of the cost of the products being manufactured.

Product and Period Costs The concepts of product and period costs are similar to direct and indirect costs. Product costs are those that the firm's accounting system associates directly with output and that are used to value inventory. Period costs are charged as expenses to the current period. Under direct costing, period costs are not viewed as costs of the products being manufactured, so they are not associated with valuing inventories.

If the firm uses a full cost accounting system, however, then all manufacturing costs—including fixed manufacturing overhead costs and variable costs—become product costs. They are considered part of the cost of manufacturing and are charged against inventory.

Other Types of Costs These are the basic types of costs as they are used in different accounting systems.

Controllable and Uncontrollable Costs— In budgeting it is useful to identify controllable and uncontrollable costs. This simply means that managers with budgetary responsibility should not be held accountable for costs they cannot control.

Out-of-pocket and Sunk Costs— Financial managers often use the concepts of out-of-pocket costs and sunk costs when evaluating the financial merits of specific proposals. Out-of-pocket costs are those that require the use of current resources, usually cash. Sunk costs have already been incurred. In evaluating whether or not to increase production, for example, financial managers may take into account the sunk costs associated with tools and machinery as well as the out-of-pocket costs associated with adding more material and labor.

Incremental and Opportunity Costs— Financial planning efforts utilize the concepts of incremental and opportunity costs. Incremental costs are those associated with switching from one level of activity or course of action to another. Incremental costs represent the differ-

ence between two alternatives. Opportunity costs represent the sacrifice that is made when the means of production are used for one task rather than another, or when capital is used for one investment rather than another. Nothing can be produced or invested without incurring an opportunity cost. By making one investment or production decision using limited resources, one necessarily forgoes the opportunity to use those resources for a different purpose. Consequently, opportunity costs are not usually factored into investment and production decisions involving resource allocation.

Imputed Costs— Also of use to financial planners are imputed costs. These are costs that are not actually incurred, but are associated with internal transactions. When work in process is transferred from one department to another within an organization, a method of transfer pricing may be needed for budgetary reasons. Although there is no actual purchase or sale of goods and materials, the receiving department may be charged with imputed costs for the work it has received. When a company rents itself a building that it could have rented to an outside party, the rent may be considered an imputed cost.

BUSINESS APPLICATIONS USE DIFFERENT TYPES OF COSTS

Costs as a business concept are useful in measuring performance and determining profitability. What follows are brief discussions of some business applications in which costs play an important role.

Financial Accounting One of the major objectives of financial accounting is to determine the periodic income of the business. In manufacturing firms a major component of the income statement is the cost of goods sold (COGS). COGS is that part of the cost of inventory that can be considered an expense of the period because the goods were sold. It appears as an expense on the firm's periodic income statement. COGS is calculated as beginning inventory plus net purchases minus ending inventory.

Depreciation is another cost that becomes a periodic expense on the income statement. Every asset is initially valued at its cost. Accountants charge the cost of the asset to depreciation expense over the useful life of the asset. This cost allocation approach attempts to match costs with revenues and is more reliable than attempting to periodically determine the fair market value of the asset.

In financial accounting, costs represent assets rather than expenses. Costs only become expenses when they are charged against current income. Costs may be allocated as expenses against income over time, as in the case of depreciation, or they may be charged as expenses when revenues are generated, as in the case of COGS.

Cost Accounting Cost accounting, also sometimes known as management accounting, provides appropriate cost information for budgeting systems and management decision making. Using the principles of general accounting, cost accounting records and determines costs associated with various functions of the business. These data are used by management to improve operations and make them more efficient, economical, and profitable.

Two major systems can be used to record the costs of manufactured products. They are known as job costing and process costing. A job cost system, or job order cost system, collects costs for each physically identifiable job or batch of work as it moves through the manufacturing facility and disregards the accounting period in which the work is done. With a process cost system, on the other hand, costs are collected for all of the products worked on during a specific accounting period. Unit costs are then determined by dividing the total costs by the number of units worked on during the period. Process cost systems are most appropriate for continuous operations, when like products are produced, or when several departments cooperate and participate in one or more operations. Job costing, on the other hand, is used when labor is a chief element of cost, when diversified lines or unlike products are manufactured, or when products are built to customer specifications.

When costs are easily observable and quantifiable, cost standards are usually developed. Also known as engineered standards, they are developed for each physical input at each step of the production process. At that point an engineered cost per unit of production can be determined. By documenting variable costs and fairly allocating fixed costs to different departments, a cost accounting system can provide management with the accountability and cost controls it needs to improve operations.

Budgeting Systems Budgeting systems rely on accurate cost accounting systems. Using cost data collected by the business's cost accounting system, budgets can be developed for each department at different levels of output. Different units within the business can be designated cost centers, profit centers, or departments. Budgets are then used as a management tool to measure performance, among other things. Performance is measured by the extent to which actual figures deviate from budgeted amounts.

In using budgets as measures of performance, it is important to distinguish between controllable and uncontrollable costs. Managers should not be held accountable for costs they cannot control. In the short run, fixed costs can rarely be controlled. Consequently, a typical budget statement will show sales revenue as forecast and the variable costs associated with that level of production. The difference between sales revenue and variable costs is the contribution margin. Fixed costs are then deducted from the contribution margin to obtain a figure for operating income. Managers and departments are then evaluated on the basis of costs and those elements of production they are expected to control.

Cost of Capital Capital budgeting and other business decisions—such as lease-buy decisions, bond refunding, and working capital policies—require estimates of a company's cost of capital. Capital budgeting decisions revolve around deciding whether or not to purchase a particular capital asset. Such decisions are based on a cost-benefit analysis, an estimate of the net present value of future revenues that would be generated by a particular capital asset. An important factor in such decisions is the company's cost of capital.

Cost of capital is a percentage that represents the interest rate the company would pay for the funds being raised. Each capital component— debt, equity, and retained earnings—has its own cost. Each type of debt or equity also has a different cost. While a particular purchase or project may be funded by only one kind of capital, companies are likely to use a weighted average cost of capital when making financial decisions. Such practice takes into account the fact that the company is an ongoing concern that will need to raise capital at different rates in the future as well as at the present rate.

Other Applications Costs are sometimes used in the valuation of assets that are being bought or sold. Buyers and sellers may agree that the value of an asset can be determined by estimating the costs associated with building or creating an asset that could perform similar functions and provide similar benefits as the existing asset. Using the cost approach to value an asset contrasts with the income approach, which attempts to identify the present value of the revenues the asset is expected to generate.

Finally, costs are used in making pricing decisions. Manufacturing firms refer to the ratio between prices and costs as their markup, which represents the difference between the selling price and the direct cost of the goods being sold. For retailers and wholesalers, the gross margin is the difference between their invoice cost and their selling price. While costs form the basis for pricing decisions, they are only a starting point, with market conditions and other factors usually determining the most profitable price.

BIBLIOGRAPHY

Albrecht, W. Steve, and James D. Stice, Earl Kay Stice, Monte Swain. *Financial Accounting.* Thomson South-Western, 2004.

Cooper, Robin, and Regine Slagmulder. "Introduction to Enterprise-Wide Cost Management." *Management Accounting.* August 1998.

Horngren, Charles T., George Foster, and Srikant M. Datar. *Cost Accounting: A Managerial Emphasis.* Prentice Hall, 1999.

Kimmel, Paul, and Leslie Kren. "Dual-Rate Cost Assignment to Evaluate Performance." *The CPA Journal.* July 2002.

Sands, Jack. *Accounting for Business, What the Numbers Mean and How to Use Them.* Arena Books, Inc., 2003.

Hillstrom, Northern Lights
updated by Magee, ECDI

COUPONS

Coupons are certificates that provide consumers with discounts on goods or services when they are redeemed with retailers or manufacturers. Offered mainly by retailers and manufacturers as sales promotion tools to accomplish specific sales and marketing goals, they are very popular with small business owners because they are so inexpensive to disseminate and because of their historical effectiveness. Consumers are attracted to coupons because they offer immediate value and savings, but in recent years the proliferation of coupon distribution programs has produced a decided excess in the marketplace. This flood of coupon offers, commonly known as "coupon clutter," has resulted in falling redemption rates in recent years.

Advantages and Disadvantages Like other sales promotion tools, coupons have their advantages as well as their problems. On the plus side, they have the advantage of passing along savings directly to consumers, as opposed to trade allowances given to retailers by producers. Consumers perceive coupons as a temporary special offer rather than a price reduction, so the withdrawal of coupons usually does not have an adverse effect on sales. In addition, coupons often create added traffic for retailers, who have the option of doubling or even tripling the value of manufacturers coupons at their own expense to create even more store traffic. Moreover, retailers often receive additional compensation from manufacturers for handling the coupons.

Critics of coupon-oriented sales promotions argue that coupon clutter has dramatically reduced their effectiveness. They question whether coupons actually generate incremental business from new users, pointing out that the increased quantity of distributed coupons has been paralleled by falling redemption rates. In addition, excessive coupon distribution also increases the likelihood of fraud and misredemption. Coupons that are issued for established brands, say critics, tend to be redeemed primarily by loyal users who would have purchased the product without a coupon.

Coupon Objectives Coupons may be issued to serve a variety of different strategic marketing objectives. One use is to encourage consumers to try new products; coupons have historically been fairly efficient at getting consumers to try new products by reducing the risk of trying something new. Coupons are also issued to convert trial users into regular customers, such as when a product sample includes a cents-off coupon. In addition, coupons can be used to convince consumers to make purchases of new sizes, flavors, or forms of an established product.

Other objectives served by issuing coupons include building retail distribution and support, moving out-of-balance inventories, targeting different markets, cushioning price increases, and enhancing other promotional efforts with coupon add-ons. Coupons are frequently used by manufacturers because of competitive pressure. When used offensively against the competition, coupons are issued to get users of a competitive product to try a new brand. When used defensively, manufacturers provide coupons to current users to keep them from purchasing a competing brand.

Coupon Distribution There are several ways in which small businesses can distribute coupons, including direct mail, in-store or central location, by electronic mail, print media, in-pack and on-pack, and through retailer advertising. Because of its targeted distribution, coupons sent by direct mail historically offer higher redemption rates than coupons distributed by print media. Freestanding inserts (FSIs) in newspapers, which accounted for the vast majority of all coupon distribution throughout the 1990s, are generally regarded as more effective than other coupon distribution methods.

Perhaps the most popular coupon distribution method for small businesses is the coupon mailer. This is a strategy wherein a group of retail businesses in a community send out a mailing of individual coupons together; consumers within the community thus receive a variety of coupons for area businesses in one envelope. Sometimes the mailing will consist of an actual booklet of coupons for participating businesses, but most are sent out in loose-leaf fashion. Many business communities house businesses that specialize in putting such coupon mailers together. These companies charge a fee for their production and distribution services.

Finally, the Internet has grown as a distribution network for coupons and other similar promotional pieces. According to Jeanette Best, writing in *Brandweek*, "The Internet is making this a possibility by transforming the way coupons are distributed and opening a new world for marketers to communicate with consumers in a highly interactive way. Smart marketers need to take note and be aware of the advantages and benefits of using online coupons." Even newspapers are taking their coupon section online, adding these sections to their Web sites. Individual companies are using the Internet for coupon distribution as well. A company may post coupons on its Web site or it may send coupons directly to customers who are already signed up to receive an e-newsletter. The coupons are usually redeemable through online purchases or by printing a copy of the coupon and bringing it along when shopping at a retail outlet.

SEE ALSO *Rebates*

BIBLIOGRAPHY

Best, Jeanette. "Online Coupons: An Engaging Idea." *Brandweek*. 2 May 2005.

"Don't Discount the Coupon." *Prepared Foods*. May 1997.

Fields, Laura. "Making Coupons Count." *Marketing*. July 10, 1997.

Lisanti, Tony. "The Almighty Coupon, Redux." *Discount Store News*. 21 September 1998.

Reese, Shelly. "Declining Use, Costs Spur Hard Look at Coupons." *Stores*. March 1997.

Hillstrom, Northern Lights
updated by Magee, ECDI

CREDIT

Credit is a transaction between two parties in which one, acting as creditor or lender, supplies the other, the debtor or borrower, with money, goods, services, or securities in return for the promise of future payment. As a financial transaction, credit is the purchase of the present use of money with the promise to pay in the future according to a pre-arranged schedule and at a specified cost defined by the interest rate. In modern economies, the use of credit is pervasive and the volume enormous. Electronic transfer technology moves vast amounts of capital instantaneously around the globe irrespective of geopolitical demarcations.

In a production economy, credit bridges the time gap between the commencement of production and the final sale of goods in the marketplace. In order to pay labor and secure materials from vendors, the producer secures a constant source of credit to fund production expenses, i.e., working capital. The promise or expect-

ation of continued economic growth motivates the producer to expand production facilities, increase labor, and purchase additional materials. These create a need for long-term financing.

To accumulate adequate reserves from which to lend large sums of money, banks and insurance companies act as intermediaries between those with excess reserves and those in need of financing. These institutions collect excess money (short-term assets) through deposits and redirect it through loans into capital (long-term) assets.

REASONS FOR PURCHASING CREDIT

In a production economy, credit is widely available and extensively used. Because credit includes a promise to pay, the credit purchaser accepts a certain amount of financial and personal risk. Three strategies summarize the reasons for purchasing credit:

1. The lack of liquidity prevents profitable investments at advantageous times.

2. Favorable borrowing costs make it less expensive to borrow in the present than in the future. Borrowers may have expectations of rising rates, tight credit supplies, growing inflation, and decreasing economic activity. Conversely, profit expectations may be sufficiently favorable to justify present investments that require financing.

3. Tax incentives, which expense or deduct some interest costs, decrease the cost of borrowing and assist in capital formation.

USES FOR CREDIT

There are three major reasons why businesses borrow. The first and most common reason to borrow is to purchase assets. A loan to acquire assets may be for buying short-term, or current, assets such as inventory. This sort of loan will be repaid once the new inventory is sold to customers. The purchase of long-term or fixed assets also falls into this first category.

The second reason to borrow is to replace other types of credit. For example, if your business is already up and running, it may be time to take out a bank loan to repay the money borrowed from a relative.

The third business reason for acquiring credit is to replace equity. The desire to buy out a partner who no longer wishes to be involved with a business may be a good reason to consider borrowing.

PROMISE TO PAY

The credit contract defines the terms of the agreement between lender and borrower. The terms of the contract delineate the borrower's obligation to repay the principal according to a schedule and at a specified cost or interest rate. The lender reserves the right to require collateral to secure a loan and to enforce payment through the courts.

The lender may levy a small charge for originating or participating in a loan placement. This charge, measured in percentage points, covers administrative costs. This immediate cash infusion decreases the costs of the loan to the lender, thereby reducing the risk. The lender may also require the borrower to provide protection against nonpayment or default by securing insurance, by establishing a repayment fund, or by assigning collateral assets.

A promissory note is an unconditional written promise to pay money at a specified time or on demand. The maker of the note is primarily liable for settlement. No collateral is required. A lien agreement, however, holds property as security for payment of debt. A specific lien identifies a specific property, as in a mortgage. A general lien has no specific assignment.

CREDIT TERMS

The terms of the credit contract deal with the repayment schedule, interest rate, necessity of collateral, and debt retirement.

Repayment Schedules Credit contracts vary in maturity. Short-term debt is from overnight to less than one year. Long-term debt is more than one year, up to 30 or 40 years. Payments may be required at the end of the contract or at set intervals, usually on a monthly basis. The payment is generally comprised of two parts: a portion of the outstanding principal and the interest costs. With the passage of time, the principal amount of the loan is amortized, or repaid little by little, until completely retired. As the principal balance diminishes, the interest on the remaining balance also declines. Interest on loans do not pay down the principal.

Revolving credit has no fixed date for retirement. The lender provides a maximum line of credit and expects monthly payment according to an amortization schedule. The borrower decides the degree to which to use the line of credit. The borrower may increase debt anytime the outstanding amount is below the maximum credit line. The borrower may retire the debt at will, or may continue a cycle of paying down and increasing the debt.

Interest Rates Interest is the cost of purchasing the use of money, i.e., borrowing. The interest rate charged by lending institutions must be sufficient to cover the lender's operating costs, administrative costs, and an acceptable rate of return. Interest rates may be fixed for the term of the loan, or adjusted to reflect changing market conditions. A credit contract may adjust rates daily, annually, or at intervals of three, five, and ten years.

Collateral Assets pledged as security against a failure to repay a loan are known as collateral. Credit backed by collateral is secured. The asset purchased by the loan often serves as the only collateral. In other cases the borrower puts other assets, including cash, aside as collateral. Real estate or land serve as the collateral for securing mortgages.

Unsecured debt relies on the earning power of the borrower. A debenture is a written acknowledgment of a debt similar to a promissory note in that it is unsecured, relying only on the full faith and credit of the issuer. Corporations often issue debentures as bonds. With no collateral, these debentures are subordinate to mortgages.

A bond is a contract held in trust obligating a borrower to repay a sum of money. A debenture bond is unsecured, while a mortgage bond holds specific property in lien. A bond may contain safety measures to provide for repayment. An indenture is a legal document specifying the terms of a bond issue, including the principal, maturity date, interest rates, any qualifications and duties of the trustees, and the rights and obligations of the issuers and holders. Corporations and government entities issue bonds in a form attractive to both public and private investors.

Debt Retirement & Types of Credit Debt retirement is the term used for the paying off of a debt. The credit contract defines the terms under which credit is issued and usually this contract also outlines how debt is to be retired or paid off. Different types of debt have different means of debt retirement.

Overnight funds are lent among banks to temporarily lift their reserves to mandated levels. A special commitment is a single purpose loan with a maturity of less than one year. Its purpose is to cover cash shortages resulting from a one-time increase in current assets, such as a special inventory purchase, an unexpected increase in accounts receivable, or a need for interim financing.

Trade credit is extended by a vendor who allows the purchaser up to three months to settle a bill. In the past it was common practice for vendors to discount trade bills by one or two percentage points as an incentive for quick payment. A seasonal line of credit of less than one year is used to finance inventory purchases or production. The successful sale of inventory repays the line of credit. A permanent working capital loan provides a business with financing from one to five years during times when cash flow from earnings does not coincide with the timing or volume of expenditures. Creditors expect future earnings to be sufficient to retire the loan.

Commercial papers are short-term, unsecured notes issued by corporations in a form that can be traded in the public money market. Commercial paper finances inventory and production needs. A letter of credit ("l/c") is a financing instrument that acts more like credit money than a loan. An l/c is used to facilitate a transaction, especially in trade, by guaranteeing payment at a future date. Unlike a loan, which invokes two primary parties, an l/c involves three parties: the bank, the customer, and the beneficiary. The bank issues, based on its own credibility, an l/c on behalf of its customer, promising to pay the beneficiary upon satisfactory completion of some predetermined conditions. A bank's acceptance is another short-term trade financing vehicle. A bank issues a time draft promising to pay on or after a future date on behalf of its customer. The bank rests its guarantee on the expectation that its customer will collect payment for goods previously sold.

Term loans finance the purchase of furniture, fixtures, vehicles, and plant and office equipment. Maturity generally runs more than one year and less than five. A large equipment purchase may have longer terms, matched to its useful production life. Mortgage loans are used to purchase real estate and are secured by the asset itself. Mortgages generally run 10 to 40 years. When creditors provide a mortgage to finance the purchase of a property without retiring an existing mortgage, they wrap the new mortgage around the existing debt. The interest payment of the wraparound mortgage pays the debt service of the underlying mortgage.

Treasury bills are short-term debt instruments of the U.S. government issued weekly and on a discounted basis with the full face value due on maturity. T-bill maturities range from 91 to 359 days and are issued in denominations of $10,000. Treasury notes are intermediate-term debt instruments ranging in maturity from one to ten years. Issued at par, full-face value, in denominations of $5,000 and $10,000, T-notes pay interest semiannually. Treasury bonds are long-term debt instruments. Issued at par values of $1,000 and up, T-bonds pay interest semi-annually, and may have call dates (retirement) prior to maturity.

CREDIT WORTHINESS

The granting of credit depends on the confidence the lender has in the borrower's credit worthiness. Generally defined as a debtor's ability to pay, credit worthiness is one of many factors defining a lender's credit policies. Creditors and lenders utilize a number of financial tools to evaluate the credit worthiness of a potential borrower. Much of the evaluation relies on analyzing the borrower's balance sheet, cash flow statements, inventory turnover rates, debt structure, management performance, and market conditions. Creditors favor borrowers who generate net earnings in excess of debt obligations and contingencies that may arise. Following are some of the factors lenders consider when evaluating an individual or business that is seeking credit:

Credit worthiness. A history of trustworthiness, a moral character, and expectations of continued performance demonstrate a debtor's ability to pay. Creditors give more favorable terms to those with high credit ratings via lower point structures and interest costs.

Size of debt burden. Creditors seek borrowers whose earning power exceeds the demands of the payment schedule. The size of the debt is necessarily limited by the available resources. Creditors prefer to maintain a safe ratio of debt to capital.

Loan size. Creditors prefer large loans because the administrative costs decrease proportionately to the size of the loan. However, legal and practical limitations recognize the need to spread the risk either by making a larger number of loans, or by having other lenders participate. Participating lenders must have adequate resources to entertain large loan applications. In addition, the borrower must have the capacity to ingest a large sum of money.

Frequency of borrowing. Customers who are frequent borrowers establish a reputation which directly impacts on their ability to secure debt at advantageous terms. A history of timely loan payments creates a positive credit picture whereas a history of slow payments will work against a borrower on later credit applications.

Length of commitment. Lenders accept additional risk as the time horizon increases. To cover some of the risk, lenders charge higher interest rates for longer term loans.

Social community considerations. Lenders may accept an unusual level of risk because of the social good resulting from the use of the loan. Examples might include banks participating in low income housing projects or business incubator programs.

INTEREST RATES AND RISK

Lenders use both subjective and objective guidelines to evaluate risk and to establish a) a general rate structure reflective of market conditions, and b) borrower-specific terms based on individual credit analysis. To be profitable, lenders charge interest rates that cover perceived risks as well as the costs of doing business. The risks calculated into the interest rate include the following:

Opportunity cost risk. The lender fixes interest costs at a level sufficient to justify making a loan in the present rather than waiting for more advantageous terms in the future. The lender focuses on a desired rate of return rather than the credit worthiness of the borrower.

Credit risk or repayment risk. The borrower may not be able to make scheduled payments nor repay the debt at all. The greater the credit risk, the higher the interest rate. Creditors charge lower interest rates to those with the highest credit ratings, and those who are the most able to pay. In other words, those least able to pay find themselves paying the highest rates.

Interest rate risk and prepayment risk. These risks arise when the payment or prepayment of outstanding debt does not match the terms and pricing of current debt, thus exposing the lender to a "mismatch" in the costs of doing business and the terms of lending.

Inflation risk. Inflation decreases the purchasing power of money. Lenders anticipate these losses with higher interest rates.

Currency risk. International trade and money markets may devalue the currency, decreasing its purchasing power abroad even during times of low inflationary expectations at home. Since currency devaluation heightens inflationary expectations in a global economy, interest rates rise.

FINANCIAL INTERMEDIATION

Financial intermediation is the process of channeling funds from financial sectors with excesses to those with deficiencies. The primary suppliers of funds are households, businesses, and governments. They are also the primary borrowers. Financial intermediaries, such as banks, finance companies, and insurance companies, collect excess funds from these sectors and redistribute them in the form of credit. Financial intermediaries accumulate reserves of funds through investment and savings instruments.

Banks provide savings and checking accounts, certificates of deposit, and other time accounts for customers willing to loan the bank their funds for the payment of interest. Insurance companies gather funds through various investments and through the collecting of premiums. Banks, finance, and insurance companies also raise cash by selling equity positions or borrowing money from private or public investors. Pension funds utilize available funds from participant contributions and from investment earnings. Federally sponsored credit intermediaries capitalize themselves in a manner similar to banks.

Financial intermediation provides an efficient and practical method of redistributing purchasing power to qualified borrowers. Banks aggregate many small deposits to finance a single family home mortgage, for example. Finance companies break large pools of cash down to sizes appropriate for the purchase of an automobile. The pooling of funds from many sources and the distribution of credit to a large number of creditors spreads the risks.

In essence, financial intermediaries are reducing risk by qualifying borrowers and directing funds into creditworthy situations. Furthermore, financial intermediation increases liquidity in the system, acting as a buffer against cash shortages resulting from unexpected increases in deposit withdrawals.

CREDIT SECURITIZATION

Credit securitization is one of the most recent and important developments in financing and capital formation. Securitization is, very basically, the process of pooling various categories of assets and creating securities that derive their value from the asset pool and income streams derived therefrom. "Securitization is a complex series of financial transactions designed to maximize the cash flow and cash out options for loan originators," explains the American Bar Association in a report entitled *Mortgage Securitization, Servicing, and Consumer Bankruptcy.* "To securitize an asset, the loan originator creates a pool of financial assets ... It then uses one or more [special purpose vehicle] SPV corporations to convert the large pools of these mortgages into complex investment certificates, backed or securitized by valid liens on the transferred collateral. These certificates are then rated and offered for sale to asset capital investors, foreign investors and life insurance companies to name a few. The certificates are normally split into various types, each of which has predetermined cash flow or equity positions in the underlying collateral."

In many instances the underlying debt is mortgages, secured by real estate, and guaranteed by an agency or insurance company. For example, an underwriter may place into securitization only mortgages guaranteed by the Veterans Administration of maturities no less than 20 years, with interest rates of not less than 9 percent, and with a cumulative principal (face) value of $10 million. The underwriter sells shares in this pool of mortgages to the public. In addition to mortgages, credit instruments securitized in this way include auto loans, credit card receivables, and trade receivables.

Credit securitization supports the viability of financial intermediaries by a) spreading the risk over a broader range of investors who purchase the securities, and b) increasing liquidity through an immediate cash infusion for the securitized debt. This process is helpful to investors and borrowers alike. The large volume and efficiency of the system puts downward pressure on interest rates. The pooling of loans into large, homogeneous securities facilitates the actuarial and financial analyses of their risks.

Investors may participate in a portion of the cash flow generated by the interest and/or principal payments made by borrowers of the underlying debt. Investor participation may be limited to the cash flow of a set number of years, or to a portion of the principal when the underlying debt is retired. Investors also choose to participate at a point suitable to their risk/reward ratio.

SEE ALSO *Cash Management; Collateral; Equity Financing; Loans*

BIBLIOGRAPHY
Allen, Steve L. *Financial Risk Management.* John Wiley & Sons, 2003.

de Servigny, Arnaud, and Olivier Renault. *Measuring and Managing Credit Risk.* McGraw-Hill Professional, 2004.

Gardner III, O. Max. "Mortgage Securitization, Servicing, and Consumer Bankruptcy." *GP Solo Law Trends & News.* American Bar Association, September 2005.

"New Technology Makes Small Business Credit More Available." *Financial Update.* July-September 2005.

U.S. Federal Reserve Bank of New York. "The Credit Process: A Guide for Small Business Owners." Available from http://www.newyorkfed.org/education/addpub/credit.html. Retrieved on 3 February 2006.

Hillstrom, Northern Lights
updated by Magee, ECDI

CREDIT BUREAUS

A credit bureau is an agency that collects and sells information about the credit-worthiness, or the ability to meet debt obligations, of individuals and companies. Consumer credit bureaus maintain and report on this information for individuals, while commercial credit bureaus collect and distribute this information for businesses. A synonym for a credit bureau is a credit reporting agency. Credit bureaus provide information to a number of clients, including merchants that extend credit to consumers and businesses that extend credit to other businesses. Credit bureaus may be private enterprises or may be operated as cooperatives by merchants in a particular geographic area. Users of the services typically pay either a fee based on their amount of usage or a flat membership charge.

Credit bureaus serve as a clearinghouse for credit history information. Credit grantors provide the bureaus with information about how credit customers pay their bills, and the bureaus assemble this information into a file on every consumer or business. Credit grantors can obtain credit reports about potential customers who wish to open accounts. There are over 1,000 local and regional consumer credit bureaus throughout the United States, and most are either owned or under contract with one of the nation's three major consumer credit reporting agencies: Trans Union, Equifax, and Experian.

The largest player in the commercial credit reporting business is Dun and Bradstreet Corporation. According to Elayne Robertson Demby in *Collections and Credit Risk,* Dun and Bradstreet maintains a database on nearly 60 million public and private businesses worldwide, including 12 million American firms. But the rapid increase in e-commerce has changed the commercial credit reporting business in a number of ways. Customers have begun to demand information more quickly and in condensed, ready-to-use form, and a number of Internet-based credit bureaus have developed to meet these needs.

THE HISTORY OF CREDIT BUREAUS

Cooperative credit bureaus were known in some countries from the early 1860s, but the industry experienced rapid growth only after World War I. They were originally organized to facilitate the exchange of credit information among merchants. Until the arrival of credit bureaus, the very small amount of credit granted was based on the merchant's own knowledge of the customer.

The earliest credit bureaus just maintained lists of customers who were considered by the merchants to be poor risks. After World War I, however, the U.S. population became more mobile and credit bureaus expanded to serve a wider audience of dispersed merchants. The bureaus filled a void by providing these merchants with information that could be used to make decisions on whether to grant credit. The development of high speed computing capacity has increased the data processing power of credit bureaus and made it possible to keep more updated information on individuals and businesses alike.

CONSUMER CREDIT BUREAUS TODAY

The three major consumer credit bureaus in the U.S. are affiliated with the Associated Credit Bureaus, Inc. This international trade association, founded in 1906, provides its members with fraud prevention and risk management products, credit and mortgage reports, tenant and employment screening services, check fraud and verification services, and collection services. The Associated Credit Bureaus, Inc. represents the consumer credit reporting information industry before state and federal legislators. It also represents the industry before the media in consumer credit reporting matters. Over 500 American credit reporting agencies, mortgage reporting companies, collection services, and tenant screening and employment reporting companies are members.

Consumer credit bureaus are important and growing because some one billion credit cards are in use in the United States today. A similar number of consumer credit reports are issued annually in the United States. Two billion pieces of data are entered monthly into credit records. Each of the three major consumer credit reporting systems—Equifax, Experian, and Trans Union—maintains 190 million credit files, which are used by independent credit reporting agencies across the United States.

The power of credit bureaus grew as they became the primary source through which a consumer's creditworthiness was judged. If an individual's credit information with a bureau was incorrect, she was at risk of being denied credit, insurance, or even employment based on the erroneous information. Worse yet, the individual may not have known why she was denied. The credit scoring systems used by credit bureaus was a closely held secret.

In the 1990s and early 2000s the country saw a rise in consumer fraud and in particular, identity theft. The victims of identity theft often find themselves struggling with credit bureaus to repair their credit scores in the wake of the crime. This effort is made more difficult by the secrecy of the credit scoring process. A flurry of state and federal legislation has been passed, aimed at protecting the privacy of personal data while also granting consumers access to their own credit information. In late 2003 the Fair and Accurate Credit Transactions Act was passed. This law is designed to improve the quality of credit information and protect consumers from identity theft schemes. Some of the provisions of the law include:

- Giving Americans the right to their credit report free of charge every year. Consumers will be able to review a free report every year for unauthorized activity, including activity that might be the result of identity theft.

- Helping prevent identity theft by requiring merchants to leave all but the last five digits of a credit card number off store receipts.

- Creating a national system of fraud detection to make identity thieves more likely to be caught. Previously, victims would have to make phone calls to all of their credit card companies and three major credit rating agencies to alert them to the crime. Now consumers will only need to make one call to receive advice, set off a nationwide fraud alert, and protect their credit standing.

- Establishing a nationwide system of fraud alerts for consumers to place on their credit files. Credit reporting agencies that receive such alerts from customers will now be obliged to follow procedures to ensure that any future requests are by the true consumer, not an identity thief posing as the consumer.

- Requiring regulators to devise a list of red flag indicators of identity theft, drawn from the patterns and practices of identity thieves.

- Requiring lenders and credit agencies to take action before a victim even knows a crime has occurred. With oversight by bank regulators, the credit agencies will draw up a set of guidelines to identify patterns common to identity theft, and develop methods to stop it.

THE THREE MAJOR CONSUMER CREDIT BUREAUS

Equifax Equifax serves the financial services, retail, credit card, telecommunications/utilities, transportation, information technology, and health care industries, as well as government. Global operations include consumer and commercial credit information services, payment services, software, modeling, analytics, consulting and direct-to-consumer services. Equifax provides services and systems that help grant credit, authorize and process credit card and check transactions, manage receivables, authenticate, identify and manage digital certificates, predict consumer behavior, market products, and manage risk. Equifax serves the U.S., Chile, Argentina, U.K., Spain, Portugal, Canada, Peru, El Salvador, and Brazil.

Experian According to its mission statement, Experian uses the power of information to help its clients target prospective customers, manage existing customer relationships, and identify opportunities for profitable growth. Through its Web-based products and services, Experian enables clients to conduct secure and profitable e-commerce. Experian is a subsidiary of The Great Universal Stores PLC and has headquarters in Nottingham, U.K., and Orange, California. Its 12,000 employees support clients in over 50 countries and annual company sales are $1.5 billion.

Trans Union Trans Union is the third primary source of consumer credit information and also offers risk and portfolio management services. They serve a broad range of industries that routinely evaluate credit risk or verify information about their customers, which includes financial and banking services, insurance agencies, retailers, collection agencies, communication and energy companies, and hospitals. Trans Union operates nationwide through a network of offices and independent credit bureaus. They have many subsidiaries and divisions in the U.S. and abroad.

COMMERCIAL CREDIT BUREAUS

The Internet has created a number of changes in the commercial credit reporting business. Electronic commerce and online business-to-business (B2B) transactions have expanded the need for commercial credit checks to include small businesses and foreign firms. In the meantime, the instantaneous transfer of information over the Internet has caused client companies to expand their expectations about the manner in which they receive credit reports. "With more companies doing business with smaller firms and companies overseas, obtaining credit information on those businesses is more important today than ever," Demby noted. "Customers are demanding more information faster, and in a format that allows them to make rapid-fire decisions about whether or not to grant credit."

The changing demands of client companies has increased competition among commercial credit bureaus. Many new players have sprung up online, where they are collecting newly available data and distributing it at a lower cost than traditional reporting firms. For example, CreditRiskMonitor.com, established in 1997, is an Internet-based credit reporting agency that provides up-to-the-minute data and credit analysis on 35,000 public U.S. companies worldwide.

In addition to increased competition from Internet-based reporting agencies, commercial credit bureaus face several new business trends in the twenty-first century. For example, more commercial credit reporting agencies are beginning to offer information on small businesses, which represent an increasing share of the overall market. Consumer credit expert Experian has begun offering a commercial credit service that combines a small business's financial information with personal information about the small business owner to create a risk score. Another emerging trend involves providing credit information in real time in order to assist clients in making quick decisions about whether or not to extend credit. Instead of providing a mass of financial information, many commercial credit bureaus are moving toward evaluating the information in advance and providing clients with credit scores.

BIBLIOGRAPHY

Bennett, Andrea. "Credit Scores Are Due to Go Public." *Money.* 1 August 2000.

"Check Your Credit." *Phoenix Business Journal.* 22 September 2000.

Demby, Elayne Robertson. "Getting a Line on Lending." *Collections and Credit Risk.* January 2001.

Goodman, Jordan Elliot. *Everyone's Money Book on Credit.* Dearborn Trade Publishing, 2002.

Hill, Sidney, Jr. "Hungry for Credit Data?" *Collections and Credit Risk.* 31 August 2000.

Mitchel, Leslie. "Credit Bureaus Big on Errors, Small on Fixes." *The Salt Lake Tribune.* 3 November 2005.

The White House *Fact Sheet: President Bush Signs the Fair and Accurate Credit Transactions Act of 2003.* Available from http://www.whitehouse.gov/news/releases/2003/12/20031204-3.html. Retrieved on 4 January 2006.

Hillstrom, Northern Lights
updated by Magee, ECDI

CREDIT CARD FINANCING

Increasing numbers of entrepreneurs have turned to credit cards to finance their business ventures in recent years. Often, these credit cards were originally secured for personal use, but credit card issuers are targeting business owners for corporate cards as well. Credit cards are one resource available to small businesses with few other options to obtain start-up capital. It is by no means a desirable means of financing a start-up. Most credit cards charge extremely high interest rates making this form of financing very expensive. In terms of using a credit card as a primary means of paying bills monthly, a credit card offers small businesses the administrative benefit of providing detailed records of all charges that may be easily transferred to an accounting process.

Studies indicate that use of credit cards for small business purposes has surged dramatically in recent years. An online article published by *About, Inc.*, part of The New York Times Company, states that two-thirds of small businesses use a credit card for expenses. Of these, 40 percent use business credit cards exclusively and the remaining 60 percent use a personal card for at least part of their credit card purchasing transactions. This represents a growing trend and one that has not been overlooked by credit card issuing companies.

Credit-card issuers are beginning to aggressively pursue small business owners in the hopes of selling them on corporate credit cards. According to Visa USA in a brief article in *Cardline*, commercial payment volume on Visa cards grew 20.4 percent in the year ending in the middle of 2004. Visa USA expects that these rates of growth are likely to continue through 2010 and they are launching a variety of marketing efforts to try and capture more of this growing commercial business. From the credit card companies' perspective, commercial accounts have several advantages over personal accounts. They include the standard use of annual fees with commercial credit card accounts, the opportunity to establish long-term relationships with commercial customers, and the proceeds they are able to make from extra fees for multiple cards on a single commercial account.

The reasons for the increase in credit card financing vary. Surely the single biggest factor is the explosion in overall credit card use throughout the United States during the 1990s, when overall economic expansion surged. But there are other reasons for the growing use of plastic by entrepreneurs. For one thing, many entrepreneurs contend that large banks habitually steer businesses that are looking for less than $10,000 to consumer loan departments. In addition, entrepreneurs commonly blame their use of credit cards on the reluctance of banks to provide loans. Moreover, using personal or corporate credit cards allows small business owners to skirt the bureaucratic paperwork associated with obtaining loans from banks or the Small Business Administration (SBA). Also, stories of entrepreneurial success that started with the use of credit card financing were common in the late 1990s, providing further encouragement to business owners weighing whether or not to take the plunge. Finally, small business owners who use credit cards to pay off business expenses can also use them to stretch their payment periods or earn significant points in frequent-flyer programs.

Nonetheless, using credit cards is a riskier-than-usual way to finance a company. Every month there is a huge bill instead of several smaller ones that can be juggled. Once a credit line is spent, one can not pay bills and it is a very short trip from cash flow trouble to general weakness to bankruptcy. Entrepreneurs who have parlayed their credit cards into business success caution fellow business owners to pursue other financing options before turning to credit card financing. If credit card financing is the only or best alternative for getting the necessary money to start a business, there are ways in which to minimize the potential downside of this sort of expensive financing. The following six credit card management techniques were presented in the *About, Inc.* article.

1. Apply with Those You Know: Always consider applying for a small business credit card at the financial institution you already use. Your banking relationship may aid with the approval process. When you need an extension of credit you will have a relationship established with your lender helping with credit applications over $100,000 not using automated scoring systems.

2. Limit Card Hopping: Signing up for multiple cards in an attempt to take advantage of deals can have a negative impact on your credit rating. It is also more difficult to manage many cards well.

3. Use Grace Periods: The majority of small business credit cards offers a 21-day grace period before you have to make payment on your purchases. Improve your cash flow using a credit card instead of checks.

4. Pay Online: When possible save time and extra costs by paying your small business credit card online versus paying by teller at a branch or mailing in your payment.

5. No Cash Advance: Reduce credit card fees and interest costs by not using the cash advance feature on your card. Cash advances incur more fees and costs. Use your business account debit when you need immediate funds.

6. Avoid Late Payments: Late fees and high interest rates quickly erode the merits of using your small business credit card. Be responsible by paying off as much of your balance as possible each month.

SEE ALSO *Banks and Banking; Capital Structure; Cash Flow Management*

BIBLIOGRAPHY

"6 Steps to Effective Small Business Credit Card Management." *About, Inc.* Available from http://sbinformation.about.com/od/creditloans/a/creditcard_p.htm. Retrieved on 6 February 2006.

Green, Charles H. *SBA Loan Book.* Adams Media, 2005.

Hise, Phaedra. "Don't Start a Business Without One." *Inc.* February 1998.

Pinson, Linda, and Jerry Jinnett. *Steps to Small Business Start-Up.* Dearborn Trade Publishing, 2003.

Snavely, Brent. "Credit Card Financing: Tempting but Risky for Small Businesses." *Crain's Detroit Business.* 14 August 2000.

Walter, Robert. *Financing Your Small Business.* Barron's Educational Series, 2004.

Hillstrom, Northern Lights
updated by Magee, ECDI

CREDIT EVALUATION AND APPROVAL

Credit evaluation and approval is the process a business or an individual must go through to become eligible for a loan or to pay for goods and services over an extended period. It also refers to the process businesses or lenders undertake when evaluating a request for credit. Granting credit approval depends on the willingness of the creditor to lend money in the current economy and that same lender's assessment of the ability and willingness of the borrower to return the money or pay for the goods obtained—plus interest—in a timely fashion. Typically, small businesses must seek credit approval to obtain funds from lenders, investors, and vendors, and also grant credit approval to their customers.

EVALUATING CREDIT WORTHINESS

In general, the granting of credit depends on the confidence the lender has in the borrower's credit worthiness. Credit worthiness—which encompasses the borrower's ability and willingness to pay—is one of many factors defining a lender's credit policies. Creditors and lenders utilize a number of financial tools to evaluate the credit worthiness of a potential borrower. When both lender and borrower are businesses, much of the evaluation relies on analyzing the borrower's balance sheet, cash flow statements, inventory turnover rates, debt structure, management performance, and market conditions. Creditors favor borrowers who generate net earnings in excess of debt obligations and any contingencies that may arise. Following are some of the factors lenders consider when evaluating an individual or business that is seeking credit:

Credit worthiness. A history of trustworthiness, a moral character, and expectations of continued performance demonstrate a debtor's ability to pay. Creditors give more favorable terms to those with high credit ratings via lower point structures and interest costs.

Size of debt burden. Creditors seek borrowers whose earning power exceeds the demands of the payment schedule. The size of the debt is necessarily limited by the available resources. Creditors prefer to maintain a safe ratio of debt to capital.

Loan size. Creditors prefer large loans because the administrative costs decrease proportionately to the size of the loan. However, legal and practical limitations recognize the need to spread the risk either by making a larger number of loans, or by having other lenders participate. Participating lenders must have adequate resources to entertain large loan applications. In addition, the borrower must have the capacity to ingest a large sum of money.

Frequency of borrowing. Customers who are frequent borrowers establish a reputation which directly impacts on their ability to secure debt at advantageous terms.

Length of commitment. Lenders accept additional risk as the time horizon increases. To cover some of the risk, lenders charge higher interest rates for longer term loans.

Social and community considerations. Lenders may accept an unusual level of risk because of the social good resulting from the use of the loan. Examples might include banks participating in low-income housing projects or business incubator programs.

OBTAINING CREDIT APPROVAL FROM LENDERS

Many small businesses must rely on loans or other forms of credit to finance day-to-day purchases or long-term

investments in facilities and equipment. Credit is one of the foundations of the American economy, and small businesses often must obtain credit in order to compete. To establish credentials for any credit approval process, from short-term loans to equity funding, a small business needs to have a business plan and a good credit history. The company must be able to show that it can repay the loan at the established interest rate. It must also demonstrate that the outlook for its type of business supports planned future projects and the reasons for borrowing.

In applying for credit, small business owners should realize that potential creditors—whether banks, vendors, or investors—will seek to evaluate both their ability and willingness to pay the amount owed. This means that the creditor will examine the character of the borrower as well as his or her ability to run a successful business. Creditors will also look at the size of the loan needed, the company's purpose in obtaining funds, and the means of repayment. Ideally, lenders evaluating a small business for credit approval like to see up-to-date books and business records, a large customer base, a history of prompt payment of obligations, and adequate insurance coverage.

The process of granting loans to businesses is regulated by the Federal Trade Commission (FTC) to ensure fairness and guarantee nondiscrimination and disclosure of all aspects of the process. The Small Business Administration (SBA) publishes a series of pamphlets and other information designed to assist businesses in obtaining loans. These publications advise businesses on a range of credit approval topics, including describing assets, preparing a business plan, and determining what questions to expect and how to prepare responses to those questions.

GRANTING CREDIT APPROVAL TO CUSTOMERS

Credit approval is also something that a small business is likely to provide for its customers, whether those customers are primarily individual consumers or other businesses. The process by which a small business grants credit to individuals is governed by a series of laws administered by the Federal Trade Commission that guarantee nondiscrimination and other benefits. These laws include the Equal Credit Opportunity Act, Fair Credit Reporting Act, Truth in Lending Act, Fair Debt Collection Practices Act, and Fair and Accurate Credit Transactions Act.

Experts recommend that small businesses develop credit policies that are consistent with overall company goals. In other words, a company's approach toward extending credit should be as conservative as its approach toward other business activities. While granting credit to customers can offer a small business a number of advantages, and in fact is a necessary arrangement for many types of business enterprises, it also involves risks. Some of the disadvantages of providing customers with credit include increasing the cost of operations and tying up capital that could be used elsewhere. There is also the risk of incurring losses due to nonpayment, and of eroding cash flow to an extent that requires borrowing. But granting credit does offer the advantage of creating a strong base of regular customers. In addition, credit applications provide important information about these customers that can be used in mailing lists and promotional activities. In the retail trade, furthermore, credit purchasers have proven to be less concerned with prices and inclined to buy more goods at one time.

When developing credit policies, small businesses must consider the cost involved in granting credit and the impact allowing credit purchases will have on cash flow. Before beginning to grant credit to customers, companies need to be sure that they can maintain enough working capital to pay operating expenses while carrying accounts receivable. If a small business does decide to grant credit, it should not merely adopt the policies that are typical of its industry. Blindly using the same credit policies as competitors does not offer a small business any advantage, and can even prove harmful if the company's situation is atypical. Instead, small businesses should develop a detailed credit policy that is compatible with their long-term goals.

The decision about whether to grant credit to a certain customer must be evaluated on a case-by-case basis. Each small business that grapples with this issue needs to gather and evaluate financial information, decide whether to grant credit and if so how much, and communicate the decision to the customer in a timely manner. At a minimum, the information gathered about a credit applicant should include its name and address, Social Security number (for individuals), bank and/or trade references, employment and income information (for individuals), and financial statements (for companies). The goal is to form an assessment of the character, reputation, financial situation, and collateral circumstances of the applicant.

Credit Programs for Business Customers There are many avenues available to small businesses for gathering information about credit applicants. In the case of business customers, a small business's sales force can often collect trade references and financial statements from potential customers. The small business can also contact local attorneys to find out about liens, claims, or actions pending against the applicant, and can hire independent accountants to verify financial information. An analysis of a company's debts, assets, and investments can provide

a solid picture of its credit worthiness, particularly when the data are compared to a composite of companies of similar size in similar industries. It is important to note that all information gathered in the credit approval process should be held strictly confidential.

Credit Programs for Individual Consumers Consumer credit bureaus are a useful resource for small businesses in evaluating the credit worthiness of individual customers. These bureaus maintain records of consumers' experiences with banks, retailers, doctors, hospitals, finance companies, automobile dealers, etc. They are able to provide this information in the form of a computerized credit report, often with a weighted score. Still, credit bureau reports do have some potential for error, so small businesses should not necessarily use them as the only source of consumer credit information. It is also important to note that credit granted to consumers is subject to the federal Truth in Lending Law, as well as a number of other federal statutes.

Many small businesses, particularly in the retail trade, choose to participate in major credit card plans. Allowing customers to pay with credit cards offers businesses a number of advantages. Since most large retailers provide this service to customers, accepting credit cards helps small businesses compete for new customers and retain old ones. In addition, customers are often tempted to spend more when they do not have to pay cash. The convenience of credit card purchases may also attract new business from travelers who do not wish to carry large sums of cash. Finally, credit card programs enable small businesses to receive payment more quickly than they could with an individual credit account system. The main disadvantage to participating in credit card plans is cost, which may include card reading and verification machinery, fees, and a percentage of sales. Credit cards also make it easier for customers to return merchandise or refuse to pay for items with which they are dissatisfied. Still, in this technological age, few small businesses (or large ones, for that matter) can afford to forsake membership in some sort of credit card plan.

Another common type of consumer credit is an installment plan, which is commonly offered by sellers of durable goods such as furniture or appliances. After credit approval, the customer makes a down payment and takes delivery of the merchandise, then makes monthly payments to pay off the balance. The down payment should always be large enough to make the purchaser feel like an owner rather than a renter, and the payments should be timed so that the item is paid off at a faster rate than it is likely to depreciate from use. The merchandise acts as collateral and can be repossessed in the case of nonpayment. Although installment plans can tie up a small business's capital for a relatively long period of time, it is possible to transfer such contracts to a sales finance company for cash.

SEE ALSO *Cash Flow Management*

BIBLIOGRAPHY

Anderson, Roger. "Rewards for the Way You Run Your Account." *New Statesman (1996).* 18 September 2000.

Finegold, Martin. "Credit Where It's Due." *Money Marketing.* 8 June 2000.

Green, Charles H. *SBA Loan Book.* Adams Media, 2005.

"Money Monitor." *Money.* 1 March 2000.

Prince, C.J. "Extending Credit to Your Customers Can be a Boon to Your Business, but Only if You Do it Wisely." *Entrepreneur.* April 2004.

Siskos, Catherine. "Blazing New Trails." *Kiplinger's Personal Finance Magazine.* January 2000.

U.S. Federal Trade Commission. *A Guide to Building a Better Credit Record.* n.d.

Hillstrom, Northern Lights
updated by Magee, ECDI

CREDIT HISTORY

A credit history is a record of an individual or company's past borrowing and repaying behavior. In the case of individuals, these records are collected and maintained by several large credit reporting agencies on behalf of companies that extend credit to consumers. These agencies gather and sell information about individual consumers, including whether a person pays his or her bills on time or has filed for bankruptcy. Whenever a bank, retailer, car dealer, or other business needs to decide whether to extend credit to a certain individual, they can access that person's credit history through the reporting agencies.

The Fair Credit Reporting Act is the federal law that gives individuals the right to examine their credit histories. It is designed to promote accuracy, fairness, and privacy of information in the files of every consumer credit reporting agency. There are three major bureaus that report credit information for individuals: Trans Union, Equifax, and Experian. At an individual's request, these bureaus or agencies must provide the information in the individual credit file as well as a list of everyone who has recently requested the file. Individuals are entitled to one free report every twelve months upon request.

It is important for both individuals and businesses to have a solid credit history and to periodically examine their credit reports to protect that credit history. For an individual, beginning to establish a credit history might entail opening a checking or savings account, applying for a credit card from a local department store, or taking out a small bank loan and making regular, on-time payments. A small business can obtain a favorable credit history in the same way. Credit issuers typically look at an individual or business's debt-to-income ratio to determine whether the borrower is a good or bad credit risk.

USE OF THE CREDIT HISTORY BY EMPLOYERS

For an employer, reviewing a job applicant's credit report may be a helpful step in pre-employment screening, retention, promotion, and even job re-assignment. Every employer has the right to review the credit history of all job applicants, as long as they have obtained a signed release from the potential employee for this phase of the background check.

In the past, employers were only concerned with a potential employee's credit history if they were going to handle money as part of the job. This is no longer strictly true. According to research by the Society of Human Resource Managers, published in an *HR Focus* article, 35 percent of employers now check credit history as part of the hiring process. Only 19 percent of companies reported doing so in 1996. A person's credit report offers a company a way to verifying an applicant's name, address (both current and prior), birth date, and social security number. Credit reports provide a detailed history of payments, liabilities, and total debts and financial obligations as well. Howard Dvorkin explained to Chris Penttila in an Entrepreneur article, "Credit history says a lot about a person, including whether or not they [sic] would make a good employee... People who have financial pressures are less productive than those who have none."

Using credit histories in the hiring process may be very useful but should be used with a full understanding of the number of errors that experts have shown appear in credit reports. Chris Penttila explains that more than 50 percent of credit reports were shown to contain errors of some kind in a 2000 study. With the chance of error so high, many employment attorneys are discouraging business owners from rejecting applicants based solely on his or her credit report.

Human resource managers recommend that an employer look at credit troubles that arose from causes beyond a person's control differently than credit troubles that result from seemingly reckless spending. The former may be due to a layoff followed by medical bills, or they may be due to identity theft. Credit trouble caused by such events may not be held against a potential hire if they can explain the circumstances and emphasize progress in paying the debts. The latter circumstances, however, may lead an employer to question a potential employee's overall judgment.

Finally, if an applicant is rejected for employment based on his or her credit history, the prospective employer is required by law to do the following: notify the applicant of the denial and reasons; send the applicant a copy of his or her credit report, and send the applicant a summary of his or her rights under the Fair Credit Reporting Act. The applicant must also be given 60 days in which to dispute any inaccuracies in the credit report upon which the rejection of employment was made.

BIBLIOGRAPHY

Fisher, Anne. "Staying Smart/Managing/Careers." *Fortune.* 26 October 1998.

"How To Do Background Checks Properly." *HR Focus.* August 2004.

Lank, Avrum D. "Poor Credit May Be Worse for Your Wallet." *The Milwaukee Journal Sentinel.* 15 September 2006.

Penttila, Chris. "Risky Business: Staff Smarts: Should a prospective employee's credit history determine whether he or she gets the job?" *Entrepreneur.* September 2003.

Hillstrom, Northern Lights
updated by Magee, ECDI

CRISIS MANAGEMENT

Crisis management is the task for creating and implementing a business plan that can be implemented quickly in the face of a crisis. Events that would qualify as crises include a wide range of potential threats; natural disasters like hurricanes, earthquakes, tornadoes and floods; terrorist attacks; power blackouts; workplace violence; cyber crimes; product tampering; bomb threats, and the unexpected death or illness of key leaders to name but a few. The speed with which a company recovers after a crisis tomorrow depends upon the plans established today. "Though each situation is unique, any organization can be better prepared if it plans carefully, puts emergency procedures in place, and practices for emergencies of all kinds." This is how the U.S. Department of Homeland Security emphasizes the importance of crisis management planning in its Web site entitled "Preparing Makes Business Sense."

The first 5 years of the 21st century have provided a number of unsettling examples of crisis that have befallen large numbers of people, communities, and businesses. The terrorist attacks of 9/11, the anthrax scare of 2001, the Northeast blackout of 2003, and the devastating hurricanes that hit the Gulf Coast in the summer of 2005 each had wide impact. These events have focused

the attention of leaders at all levels on the need to have a crisis management plan.

One commentator, writing for *PR News* in 2005, shortly after Hurricane Katrina slammed into the Gulf Coast, discussed the way in which this catastrophic incident caused public relations professionals to reassess their crisis management responsibilities. "For PR pros, dealing with the day-to-day challenge of trying to rehabilitate a company after a fit of corporate chicanery in the C-suite or of assuaging consumer concerns after launching what turns out to be a faulty product simply can't compare with dealing with the aftermath of what looks to be the worst natural disaster in U.S. history." The events of this decade so far have refocused the national attention on the need for robust crisis management in organizations of all sizes.

CREATING AND IMPLEMENTING A CRISIS MANAGEMENT PLAN

An effective crisis management plan incorporates emergency response, disaster recovery, contingency communications, business continuity, and a clear delineation of key personnel and their spheres of responsibility.

Assess the Threats Risk assessment is a sophisticated area of expertise that can range from self-assessment to an extensive engineering study. The specific industry, size, and scope of a particular business will determine the organization's risk assessment needs. The first step is determining what kinds of emergencies might affect a particular company both internally and externally. Find out which natural disasters are most common in the region or regions of operations. Ideally a list of threats is produced so that they may be categorized. Overall emergency plans will likely be useful in a number of different sorts of scenarios with only slight modification.

It is important to find out what community-level emergency procedures are in place for different sorts of incidents. Knowing the existing public safety protocols is key in coordinating rescue activities and evacuation plans. Local authorities are also a useful source of information about what actions to take and not take in the case of a biological, chemical, explosive, nuclear or radiological attack. Tenants in a commercial building or office/industrial complex may also wish to coordinate with the owners and/or managers of the facility so that company procedures work in tandem with the procedures in place for the larger entity.

Emergency Procedures In any crisis that has the potential to take life, the physical well being and safety of all personnel is, of course, the first priority. One of the first questions in a crisis is whether to shelter in place or to evacuate. Guidelines should be established in advance to help make this decision quickly. For example, a fire is one situation in which there is no decision needed about whether to shelter in place or evacuate. Fires are the most common of all business disasters. A fire plan should be in place and practices with evacuation drills should be held periodically.

On the other hand, a tornado siren signals an emergency plan of another kind, in this case, again, no decision about whether to shelter in place or evacuate is necessary. Clearly, sheltering in place is the right decision when under threat of a tornado and provisions for a safe place in which to seek protection from such a storm should be in place and known to all employees.

Instructions for assisting disabled personnel, visitors, customers, and vendors in any emergency procedure should be a part of the crisis management plan. With the exception of disabled co-workers, for whom plans should be in place, these visitors will not know company procedures. Arrangements should be spelled out for assisting outsiders in the case of emergency.

Emergency Supplies When preparing for emergency situations, it is usually best to think first about the basics of survival: fresh water, food, clean air, and warmth. For small businesses it is a good idea to talk with everyone about what emergency supplies the company can feasibly provide, if any, and which ones individuals should consider keeping on hand. Encouraging everyone to have a basic emergency kit is wise. Such a kit need not contain more than bottled water and anything else the individual may need, like essential medications. A can of tuna fish and a candy bar would not be out of place in such a kit either.

At the company level, the following list of suggested items is provided by the U.S. Homeland Security Department Web site mentioned above:

- Water, amounts for portable kits will vary. Individuals should determine what amount they are able to both store comfortably and to transport to other locations

- Food, at least a three-day supply of non-perishable food

- Battery-powered radio and extra batteries

- Flashlight and extra batteries

- First Aid kit

- Whistle to signal for help

- Dust or filter masks, readily available in hardware stores, which are rated based on how small a particle they filter

- Moist towelettes for sanitation

- Wrench or pliers to turn off utilities

- Can opener for food (if kit contains canned food)

- Plastic sheeting and duct tape to "seal the room"

- Garbage bags and plastic ties for personal sanitation

Back-ups of Essential Information A company's essential documents and information should be backed up as a part of the normal business practice. Crisis management plans should include periodic inspection of these back-up procedures and verification that all essential information is being included in the normal back-up routine. Electronic data back-ups are a norm in today's business environment but any and all important paper documents too should be safeguarded in such a way that they could be recreated if necessary. The back-ups themselves need to be stored off-site.

Communications The key in any crisis is communications. A contingency plan for working around the failure of communications infrastructure is important. Initially, it is important to have access phone numbers or e-mail addresses for all personnel. Preparing for several alternative methods for communicating with emergency personnel, co-workers, and the families of employees is recommended. In the post-crisis period it may be necessary to have similar information in a mobile format on insurance agents, vendors, suppliers, and bankers.

The Department of Homeland Security recommends providing all employees with a wallet-size card detailing instructions on how to get company information in an emergency situation. This is preemptive action that can prove very helpful. Such a card should include telephone numbers, Internet addresses and passwords, as well as a special out-of-town phone number that can be used to leave "I'm Okay" messages in case of a region-wide catastrophe. Ensure that established staff members know that they are responsible for communicating regularly with employees throughout the crisis.

In the case of severe dislocations, the continuity of a company may rest on its ability to effectively communicate with employees, suppliers, and customers during a relocation period.

Continuity Planning Securing property and planning for business continuation is another responsibility of those in charge of crisis planning. In the case of machinery, equipment, and other physical property, a crisis management plan of action will depend on the type of threat anticipated. In the case of a hurricane, for example, some warning is available and therefore a crisis management plan should provide guidelines for what needs to be moved and to where, as well as what should be secured and how that is to be done. In situations where a threat

276

can be anticipated, most insurance policies will require that an entity take some actions to try and mitigate the likely damage. Many property and business interruption insurance policies specifically state that the insured has an obligation to mitigate damage. Writing in *Business Insurance,* Judy Greenwald interviewed an insurance company vice president about how he advises clients who call in a panic after a loss. He starts with the stark advice; forget you have insurance. "The best approach, in terms of ultimately submitting a successful business interruption policy claim, is to go ahead and make the best decisions possible to keep the business going."

In crisis situations for which no warning is available—an earthquake, a chemical explosion nearby—rapid implementation of a well-designed crisis management plan is the first step. Thereafter, most of the business continuity efforts are the same whether there was or was not warning about the original cause of the crisis.

A crisis management plan that does not include planning for business continuity is incomplete. Once the initial crisis has been met the plan should lay out a path to bringing the company back to full operations. Having thought through in advance what will be necessary if a company must relocate makes a difficult process easier. The uncertainly surrounding post-crisis periods can be greatly diminished by having a detailed plan to follow.

In preparing the business continuity portion of a crisis management plan, it may be useful to use the following 7-point checklist to be sure that each broad area has been addressed.

1. Carefully assess how your company functions, both internally and externally, to determine which staff, materials, procedures, and equipment are absolutely necessary to keep the business operating.

2. Identify your suppliers, shippers, resources, and other businesses you must interact with on a daily basis. Develop relationships with more than one company to use in case your primary contractor cannot service your needs or supply essential materials. A disaster that shuts down a key supplier can be devastating to your business. Create a contact list for existing critical business contractors and others you plan to use in an emergency. Keep this list with other important documents.

3. Plan what you will do if your building, plant, or store is not accessible. This type of planning is often referred to as a continuity of operations plan, or COOP, and includes all facets of your business.

4. Plan for payroll continuity.

5. Specify exactly who will be responsible for each area of the business.

6. Coordinate with others by meeting with businesses in your building or industrial complex. Talk with first responders, emergency managers, community organizations, and utility providers. Plan with your suppliers, shippers, and others you regularly do business with. Share your plans and encourage other businesses to set in motion their own continuity planning and offer to help others.

7. Review and update your crisis management plan annually.

PUBLIC RELATIONS CRISIS

Threats to a company's public relations (PR) are a different sort of crisis. They may occur in conjunction with a broader crisis or may be the result of some non-life threatening incident, like a boycott or accusations of the mismanagement of funds. In either case, planning for how best to manage the PR side of a crisis is an important part of the overall crisis management plan. Small businesses that are faced with public relations crises are far more likely to escape relatively unscathed if they can bring two weapons to bear: 1) a solid record as a good citizen, and 2) an already established crisis management strategy.

The most important factor in managing and resolving the public relations side of a crisis is communications. When a crisis does erupt, prompt and proactive communication should be a cornerstone of any business's crisis containment strategy. A single individual should be designated as the official spokesperson during a crisis if at all possible. By controlling the information that is released, a company can assure both a greater degree of accuracy and a consistent message. "Pick someone who is cool under pressure, credible, good on camera, and adept at presenting a positive image for your business," wrote Kim Gordon in an article for *Entrepreneur.* It may be helpful for this person to attend media training in order to practice interview techniques... Small businesses should prepare positive messages about their operations that can be disseminated to media contacts in the event of a crisis. These messages may include any points you want the public to keep in mind during the negative publicity, such as an impressive safety or environmental record.

In order to ensure that your company's perspective is heard, it is vital that you do all you can to make sure that your message is accurately presented to any media providing coverage of the crisis. The media establish the perception of most companies and organizations and whether accurate or not, they must be dealt with. So, dealing with the media in an organized, aggressive, and timely fashion is essential if one is to at least help mold the overall perception.

Effective communication with media, then, is an essential element of any crisis management plan. But consultants offer other tips as well. Following are a list of other actions that small businesses should take when confronted with a crisis management situation:

1. Be open and honest with media and customers alike—Such a stance may well garner sympathy with customers and consumers, particularly if the crisis is one over which the company has little control, such as malicious product tampering.

2. React quickly—A company's actions in the early stages of a crisis will often determine how the media coverage portrays the company.

3. Utilize only one spokesperson—Consultants can cite countless instances in which companies faced with a business crisis compounded their problems by using multiple spokespeople who gave conflicting statements. A single, clear, and accurate story is best served up by a single spokesperson.

4. Arm yourself with the facts—Companies can hurt themselves terribly when they make public statements based on incomplete knowledge of events.

5. Stay on message—Engaging in speculation and/or rambling discourses does not help your company's cause. Spokespeople should be candid without being unduly negative.

6. Do not lie or mislead the media, the public, or investigating agencies—This may seem obvious but history shows that it is worth noting. The discovery of one single lie casts every statement that your company makes into doubt.

7. Establish and maintain contact with other important groups—Depending on the nature of the crisis, communication with employee, industry, and community groups can be a valuable part of a crisis response plan. Is the crisis likely to have an impact on the company's labor union or general work force? If so, arrange a meeting with representatives so that they can be kept informed and ask questions, and so that you can get your message across. Are your company's production processes arousing the ire of local civic or environmental groups (and the growing interest of local media)? Arranging a meeting in which they could register their concerns might relieve the situation somewhat (again, provided that your company shows a genuine interest in hearing them out and responding to legitimate concerns).

Advanced planning is important for all aspects of managing a business. But sometimes, things will occur that can simply not be reasonably anticipated. In these situations, the best public relations advice is to manage the situation ethically, with good grace, humility, and if at all possible, some humor.

Establishing a flexible and fine-tuned crisis management plan is important for any organization. If nothing else, it will enable the leaders of such organizations to lead more easily during the most difficult of times. The anxiety and fear that arise during a crisis can best be combated by clarity, calm, and a plan of action.

SEE ALSO *Business Insurance; Disaster Planning; Public Relations*

BIBLIOGRAPHY
Coccia, Regis. "Proven Crisis Management Needs Testing in Advance." *Business Insurance.* 17 October 2005.

"Crisis Management In A Post Katrina World." *PR News.* 14 September 2005.

Crisis Management: Master the Skills to Prevent Disaster. Harvard Business School Press, September 2004.

Gordon, Kim. "Under Fire: Will a Crisis Take Your Company Down? Here's How Deft Handling Can Turn Public Opinion Around." *Entrepreneur.* April 2001.

Greenwald, Judy. "When Losses Can't be Prevented, Produce Records to Back Up Claims." *Business Insurance.* 21 March 2005.

Keating, Lauren. "Proactive Approach Minimizes Damage to Image." *Atlanta Business Chronicle.* November 10, 2000.

Lagadec, Patrick, and Erwann Michel-Kerjan. "A New Era Calls for a New Model: Crisis Management." *International Herald Tribune.* 2 November 2005.

Lockwood, Nancy R. "Crisis Management in Today's Business Environment: HR's Strategic Role." *HRMagazine.* December 2005.

Meisinger, Susan. "Crisis Management and HR's Role." *HRMagazine.* February 2006.

Simms, Jane. "Controlling a Crisis." *Marketing.* 9 November 2000.

Magee, ECDI

CROSS-CULTURAL/ INTERNATIONAL COMMUNICATION

Business is not conducted in an identical fashion from culture to culture. Consequently, business relations are enhanced when managerial, sales, and technical personnel are trained to be aware of areas likely to create communication difficulties and conflict across cultures.

Similarly, international communication is strengthened when businesspeople can anticipate areas of commonality. Finally, business in general is enhanced when people from different cultures find new approaches to old problems, creating solutions by combining cultural perspectives and learning to see issues from the viewpoint of others.

ETHNOCENTRISM

Problems in business communication conducted across cultures often arise when participants from one culture are unable to understand culturally determined differences in communication practices, traditions, and thought processing. At the most fundamental level, problems may occur when one or more of the people involved clings to an ethnocentric view of how to conduct business. Ethnocentrism is the belief that one's own cultural group is somehow innately superior to others.

It is easy to say that ethnocentrism only affects the bigoted or those ignorant of other cultures, and so is unlikely to be a major factor in one's own business communication. Yet difficulties due to a misunderstanding of elements in cross-cultural communication may affect even enlightened people. Ethnocentrism is deceptive precisely because members of any culture perceive their own behavior as logical, since that behavior works for them. People tend to accept the values of the culture around them as absolute values. Since each culture has its own set of values, often quite divergent from those values held in other cultures, the concept of proper and improper, foolish and wise, and even right and wrong become blurred. In international business, questions arise regarding what is proper by which culture's values, what is wise by which culture's view of the world, and what is right by whose standards.

Since no one individual is likely to recognize the subtle forms of ethnocentrism that shape who he or she is, international business practitioners must be especially careful in conducting business communication across cultures. It is necessary to try to rise above culturally imbued ways of viewing the world. To do this, one needs to understand how the perception of a given message changes depending on the culturally determined viewpoint of those communicating.

FACTORS AFFECTING CROSS-CULTURAL BUSINESS COMMUNICATION

The communication process in international business settings is filtered through a range of variables, each of which can color perceptions on the part of both parties. These include language, environment, technology, social organization, social history and mores, conceptions of authority, and nonverbal communication behavior.

By assessing in advance the roles these variables play in business communication, one can improve one's ability to convey messages and conduct business with individuals in a wide range of cultures.

Language Among the most often cited barriers to conflict-free cross-cultural business communication is the use of different languages. It is difficult to underestimate the importance that an understanding of linguistic differences plays in international business communication. Given this reality, business consultants counsel clients to take the necessary steps to enlist the services of a good translator. Language failures between cultures typically fall into three categories: 1) gross translation problems; 2) subtle distinctions from language to language; and 3) culturally-based variations among speakers of the same language.

Gross translation errors, though frequent, may be less likely to cause conflict between parties than other language difficulties for two reasons. Indeed, the nonsensical nature of many gross translation errors often raise warning flags that are hard to miss. The parties can then backtrack and revisit the communication area that prompted the error. Even if they are easily detected in most cases, however, gross translation errors waste time and wear on the patience of the parties involved. Additionally, for some, such errors imply a form of disrespect for the party into whose language the message is translated.

The subtle shadings that are often crucial to business negotiations are also weakened when the parties do not share a similar control of the same language. Indeed, misunderstandings may arise because of dialectical differences within the same language. When other parties with full control over the language with whom the nonnative speaker communicates assume that knowledge of this distinction exists, conflict deriving from misunderstanding is likely.

Attitudes toward accents and dialects also create barriers in international business communication. The view that a particular accent suggests loyalty or familiarity to a nation or region is widespread in many languages. The use of Parisian French in Quebec, of Mexican Spanish in Spain, or subcontinental Indian English in the United States are all noticeable, and may suggest a lack of familiarity, even if the user is fluent. More importantly, regional ties or tensions in such nations as Italy, France, or Germany among others can be suggested by the dialect a native speaker uses.

Finally, national prejudices and class distinctions are often reinforced through sociolinguistics—the social patterning of language. For example, due to regional prejudice and racism certain accents in the United States associated with urban areas, rural regions, or minorities may reinforce negative stereotypes in areas like business ability, education level, or intelligence. Similarly, some cultures use sociolinguistics to differentiate one economic class from another. Thus, in England, distinct accents are associated with the aristocracy and the middle and lower classes. These distinctions are often unknown by foreigners.

Environment and Technology The ways in which people use the resources available to them may vary considerably from culture to culture. Culturally-ingrained biases regarding the natural and technological environment can create communication barriers.

Many environmental factors can have a heavy influence on the development and character of cultures. Indeed, climate, topography, population size and density, and the relative availability of natural resources all contribute to the history and current conditions of individual nations or regions. After all, notions of transportation and logistics, settlement, and territorial organization are affected by topography and climate. For example, a mountainous country with an abundance of natural waterways will almost certainly develop different dominant modes of transportation than a dry, land-locked region marked by relatively flat terrain. Whereas the first nation would undoubtedly develop shipping-oriented transportation methods, the latter would concentrate on roadways, railroads, and other surface-oriented options.

Population size and density and the availability of natural resources influence each nation's view toward export or domestic markets as well. Nations with large domestic markets and plentiful natural resources, for example, are likely to view some industries quite differently than regions that have only one (or none) of those characteristics.

Some businesspeople fail to modify their cross-cultural communications to accommodate environmental differences because of inflexibility toward culturally learned views of technology. Indeed, cultures have widely divergent views of technology and its role in the world. In *control cultures,* such as those in much of Europe and North America, technology is customarily viewed as an innately positive means for controlling the environment. In *subjugation cultures,* such as those of central Africa and southwestern Asia, the existing environment is viewed as innately positive, and technology is viewed with some skepticism. In *harmonization cultures,* such as those common in many Native American cultures and some East Asian nations, a balance is attempted between the use of technology and the existing environment. In these cul-

tures, neither technology nor the environment are innately good and members of such cultures see themselves as part of the environment in which they live, being neither subject to it nor master of it. Of course, it is dangerous to over-generalize about the guiding philosophies of societies as well. For example, while the United States may historically be viewed as a control culture that holds that technology is a positive that improves society, there are certainly a sizable number of voices within that culture that do not subscribe to that point of view.

Social Organization and History Social organization, as it affects the workplace, is often culturally determined. One must take care not to assume that the view held in one's own culture is universal on such issues as nepotism and kinship ties, educational values, class structure and social mobility, job status and economic stratification, religious ties, political affiliation, gender differences, racism and other prejudices, attitudes toward work, and recreational or work institutions.

All of these areas have far-reaching implications for business practice. Choosing employees based on résumés, for example, is considered a primary means of selection in the United States, Canada, and much of northern Europe—all nations with comparatively weak concepts of familial relationships and kinship ties. In these cultures, nepotism is seen as subjective and likely to protect less qualified workers through familial intervention. By contrast, it would seem anywhere from mildly to highly inappropriate to suggest to members of many Arabic, central African, Latin American, or southern European cultures to skip over hiring relatives to hire a stranger. For people in these cultures, nepotism both fulfills personal obligations and ensures a predictable level of trust and accountability. The fact that a stranger appears to be better qualified based on a superior résumés and a relatively brief interview would not necessarily affect that belief. Similarly, the nature of praise and employee motivation can be socially determined, for different cultures have settled upon a wide array of employee reward systems, each of which reflect the social histories and values of those cultures.

Finally, it is often difficult to rid business communication of a judgmental bias when social organization varies markedly. For example, those from the United States may find it difficult to remain neutral on cultural class structures that do not reflect American values of equality. For instance, the socially determined inferior role of women in much of the Islamic world, or of lower castes in India—to name just two—may puzzle or anger Western citizens. Nevertheless, if the Western businessperson cannot eliminate the attendant condemnation from his or her business communication, then he or she cannot expect to function effectively in that society. An individual may personally believe that a country's social system is inefficient or incorrect. Nevertheless, in the way that individual conducts business on a daily basis, it is necessary to work within the restraints of that culture to succeed. One may choose not to do business with people from such a culture, but one cannot easily impose one's own values on them and expect to succeed in the business arena.

Conceptions of Authority Different cultures often view the distribution of authority in their society differently. Views of authority in a given society affect communication in the business environment significantly, since they shape the view of how a message will be received based on the relative status or rank of the message's sender to its receiver. In other words, conceptions of authority influence the forms that managerial and other business communications take. In working with cultures such as Israel and Sweden, which have a relatively decentralized authority conception or small "power distance," one might anticipate greater acceptance of a participative communication management model than in cultures such as France and Belgium, which generally make less use of participative management models, relying instead on authority-based decision making.

Nonverbal Communication Among the most markedly varying dimensions of intercultural communication is nonverbal behavior. Knowledge of a culture conveyed through what a person says represents only a portion of what that person has communicated. Indeed, body language, clothing choices, eye contact, touching behavior, and conceptions of personal space all communicate information, no matter what the culture. A prudent business person will take the time to learn what the prevailing attitudes are in such areas before conducting businesses in an unfamiliar culture (or with a representative of that culture).

SMALL BUSINESS AND INTERNATIONAL COMMUNICATION

As business has turned more and more to an integrated world market to meet its needs, the difficulties of communicating at a global level have become increasingly widespread. Lack of understanding deriving from ethnocentrism or ignorance of culturally based assumptions erroneously believed to be universal can readily escalate to unproductive conflict among people of differing cultural orientation. This may occur on the domestic front as well. With the increasing numbers of immigrants to the U.S. our "melting pot" society leads to cultural diversity in the workplace. In combination with a growing emphasis on global markets and an interdependent and internationalized economy, the need for dealing with intercultural differences and cross-cultural communication barriers has grown.

Small business owners and representatives face a sometimes dizzying array of communication considerations when they decide to move into the international arena, but most issues can be satisfactorily addressed by 1) respectfulness toward all people you meet; 2) thinking before speaking; and 3) research on current business etiquette, cultural and customer sensitivities, current events, and relevant history.

SEE ALSO *Alien Employees; Communication Systems; Globalization; International Markets*

BIBLIOGRAPHY
"Cross Cultural Training Seen as Essential for Foreign Operations." *Asia Africa Intellegence Wire.* 8 August 2005.

Gardenswartz, Lee, and Anita Rowe. "Cross-Cultural Awareness." *HRMagazine.* March 2001.

Jandt, Fred E. *Intercultural Communications.* Sage Publications, Inc., 2003.

Lieberman, Simma, Kate Berardo, and George F. Simons. *Putting Diversity to Work.* Thomson Crisp Learning, 2003.

Moon, Chris J., and Peter Wooliams. "Managing Cross-Cultural Business Ethics." *Journal of Business Ethics.* September 2000.

Zakaria, Norhayati. "The Effects of Cross-Cultural Training on the Acculturation Process of the Global Workforce." *International Journal of Manpower.* June 2000.

Hillstrom, Northern Lights
updated by Magee, ECDI

CROSS-FUNCTIONAL TEAMS

The most simple definition of cross-functional teams (or CFTs) is groups that are made up of people from different functional areas within a company—marketing, engineering, sales, and human resources, for example. These teams take many forms, but they are most often set up as working groups that are designed to make decisions at a lower level than is customary in a given company. They can be either a company's primary form of organizational structure, or they can exist in addition to the company's main hierarchical structure.

Cross-functional teams have become more popular in recent years for three primary reasons: they improve coordination and integration, span organizational boundaries, and reduce the production cycle time in new product development. Bringing people together from different disciplines can improve problem solving and lead to more thorough decision making. The teams foster a spirit of cooperation that can make it easier to achieve customer satisfaction and corporate goals at the same time.

Cross-functional teams are not new. Northwestern Mutual Life insurance company pioneered their use in the 1950s when the CEO of the company brought together people from the financial, investment, actuarial, and other departments to study the impact that computers would have on the business world. As a result of that first CFT, Northwestern was among the first companies in the country to create an information systems department that gave the company a large competitive advantage as computers gained in popularity. The company now relies on cross-functional teams in almost every facet of its organization. Based on success stories like this one, CFTs slowly grew in popularity throughout the 1960s and 1970s before exploding in popularity in the 1980s when faster production time and increased organizational performance became critical in almost every industry.

Cross-functional teams are similar to conventional work teams, but they differ in several important ways. First, they are usually composed of members who have competing loyalties and obligations to their primary subunit within the company (for example, a marketing person serving on a cross-functional team has strong ties to his or her home department that may conflict with the role he or she is being asked to play on the CFT). Second, in companies where CFTs are being used on a part-time basis as opposed to a permanent organizational structure, they are often temporary groups organized for one important purpose, which means group members are often under considerable pressure. On these temporary teams, the early development of stable and effective group interaction is imperative. Finally, CFTs are often held to higher performance standards than conventional teams. Not only are they expected to perform a task or produce a product, they are also expected to reduce cycle time, create knowledge about the CFT process, and disseminate that knowledge throughout the organization.

For cross-functional teams to succeed, several factors have been identified that are imperative:

- Team members must be open-minded and highly motivated.

- Team members must come from the correct functional areas.

- A strong team leader with excellent communication skills and a position of authority is needed.

- The team must have both the authority and the accountability to accomplish the mission it has been given.

- Management must provide adequate resources and support for the team, both moral and financial.

- Adequate communications must exist.

Without any one of these elements, any cross-functional team will be fighting an uphill battle to succeed.

CROSS-FUNCTIONAL TEAMS AND NEW PRODUCT DEVELOPMENT

Many businesses have been able to use cross-functional teams to reduce the cycle time in new product development. As a result, CFTs have become a common tool in new product development at many companies, especially those in industries in which rapid change and innovation is the norm. CFTs have shown the flexibility to adapt to changing market needs and the ability to more quickly develop innovative products.

In the past, new product development invariably meant gathering data sequentially from a number of departments before a new product was given the green light. First, the idea would be conceptualized. Then, it would be handed off to the marketing department, which would conduct market research to see if the product was viable. The product might then be passed on to the sales department, which would be asked to create a sales estimate. From there, the idea would move on to engineering or manufacturing, which would determine the costs to produce the product. Finally, with all those numbers gathered over the course of months, or even years, the product would move to an executive committee which would either approve or kill the project. By that time, market conditions sometimes had shifted sufficiently to render the product obsolete.

Cross-functional teams eliminate the "throw it over the wall" mentality that passes a product off from department to department. Instead, a member of each of the above functional areas would have a representative on the new product team. Team members would learn of the new product at the same time and would begin working on estimates together. If part of the product simply could not be manufactured cheaply enough, the team member from that area could immediately sit down with the engineering rep and come up with a new production method. The two of them could then meet with the marketing and sales team members and discuss new ways to position the product on the market. The result, say proponents, is a vastly improved product that is manufactured and released to the market in far less time than was achieved using traditional methods.

ESTABLISHING A CROSS-FUNCTIONAL TEAM

Set Goals When CFTs are first convened, conflict may be the result. There is a good chance that some of the members of the new team have bumped heads in the past when their functional areas clashed over a project. Additionally, some CFT members may think that their area of specialty is the most important on the team and thus assume an inflated sense of value to the team. Finally, since CFTs often bring together people who have vastly different ranks in the organizational hierarchy, there can be power plays by members who are high-ranking employees off the team but are actually less important stakeholders on the team. Those high-ranking team members may try to assert authority over the team in a situation when they should be deferring to lower-ranking team members.

The best way to solve these conflicts is to set clear goals for the team. It is important to start with a general goal, such as improving quality, but more specific goals should be set almost immediately to give the group a common bond and to ensure that everyone is working together towards the goal. Goals are easier to establish if research has been conducted by someone in the organization before the team is convened. This allows the team to jump right into goal-setting and problem-solving without getting bogged down in background research.

When setting goals, it is important to clearly define the problem that needs to be solved, not the solution that needs to be achieved. If the desired solution is held up at the outcome, then the group's focus becomes too narrow—the range of options is narrowed to fit that solution before the team even begins its work. Also, when setting goals, the team should determine if there are operating limits that it faces. For example, are there time or budget limitations that have to be considered? Are there some solutions that have been deemed undesirable by the company's officers? The team must recognize these limitations and work around them if it hopes to be successful in reaching its goal.

The final thing to do when goal-setting is to be sure to identify key interdependencies on the team—does one team member have to finish his or her part of the project before another team member can get started? It is essential to know these sequential steps before a team gets too deep into its project.

Work with Key Stakeholders Stakeholders are those people who stand to benefit or lose from the work of the team. Every stakeholder should be represented on the team, and it is these stakeholders who can make or break the team. For example, if a key department head does not believe that the team is needed, he or she can withhold his or her best employees from participating on the team, thus depriving the team of resources. Or, that department head can choose to ignore the work of the team, conducting business as usual because the team threatens his or her traditional role in the company. It is up to the business ownership, management, and key CFT mem-

bers to make all stakeholders understand the importance of the team and its purpose and priorities.

Customers, whether internal or external, are also stakeholders. Teams should spend the maximum allowable time interacting with customers to learn their needs and what outcomes they expect from the team. Some CFTs find it works best if one person is named to act as customer liaison because it makes it easier for customers to provide the team with feedback and it allows the team to have one person go through training in client management skills. Other businesses have had success in letting customers either join the team or attend team meetings as an observer.

When identifying all stakeholders, determine what level of representation each needs on the team. Some groups will need permanent members, others may only need to participate in certain areas of the project. Communicate with all stakeholders and anyone else in the company who is affected by the team's work. Do not spring surprises—this will make people resistant to the work that the team is trying to achieve. Communication steps should be decided upon up front and planned as carefully as any other part of the project.

Northwestern Mutual Life, one of the leaders in CFTs, has expanded the stakeholder idea. When it used to create a CFT, Northwestern followed the traditional model and appointed only those people whose roles were crucial to the process at hand. That is no longer the case. Now, Northwestern is experimenting with appointing one person to each CFT who is not a stakeholder at all. Colleen Stenholt, director of human resources at Northwestern, was quoted in *Getting Results* magazine as saying that "One of our goals is to break out of the box, and the stakeholders are the people who built the box." She went on to note that outsiders are desirable because they are not locked into an established way of thinking and are often thus able to bring a fresh perspective to a problem.

Deal with Team Conflict CFTs often face regular conflict situations. This is especially true of cross-functional teams that are relatively new. Business owners and managers should be aware, however, that important steps can be taken to manage and reduce conflict, including:

- Provide all team members with conflict resolution training. Conflicts can have value if managed properly, so improving team members' listening and consensus building skills is necessary.

- Make sure that the company's human resources personnel are involved in the team-building process to help teach facilitation and group dynamics skills.

- Disregard the rank or perceived status of each group member and have standards in place that put value on what every team member brings to the CFT.

- Co-locate the team members. Putting team members together on an everyday basis strengthens communication and breaks down barriers.

CROSS-FUNCTIONAL TEAMS AND SMALL BUSINESS

Many people think that cross-functional teams are only successful in large companies. Conventional wisdom dictates that small companies are probably already operating cross-functionally out of necessity—i.e., the company is so small that people have to perform multiple tasks and work together with everyone else in the company. While that may be true in start-up operations, it is certainly not true of the majority of small businesses. Most small operations have to weigh the pros and cons just like their larger counterparts when deciding whether or not to use CFTs. Those that have chosen to adopt CFTs have been largely pleased with the results.

For example, *Getting Results* magazine documented the use of CFTs by Reprint Management Services of Lancaster, Pennsylvania, a small company with fewer than 30 employees. The owner of the business originally arranged his company into functional units, but found that he had an odd assortment of employees left over who did not fit into any of the existing teams. As a result, he created a permanent cross-functional team to handle special projects at the company. The results were immediate and impressive. He claimed that since adopting the cross-functional team concept:

- Employees in support roles are more concerned with profits and ways to increase sales. They now realize that the more the company succeeds, the more they benefit directly.

- People communicate more openly and are more helpful to each other. There is a far greater sense of teamwork instead of each person looking out for number one.

- Employees' problem-solving skills have improved dramatically, and it is easier to build consensus for a given solution.

- People are more likely to speak up and point out problems. Before the CFT, people were more likely to be passive and quiet, reasoning that the problem was not their responsibility.

- People recognize that there is strength in diversity—that not everyone has to agree on an issue. They know they are being understood, but that some people may still choose to disagree with them, and that such differences are acceptable.

Staff members have also benefited from the CFT arrangement. Employees now understand the different processes that occur throughout the organization and understand the interrelationships between different functional areas. Instead of looking only at their one "silo" of operations, employees now see the big picture. Indeed, according to CFT supporters, participating employees often improve their interpersonal and problem-solving skills, which make them better employees and makes them more attractive in the job market should they choose to pursue other opportunities. Finally, proponents say that employees are less likely to become bored with their own job when they are given the opportunity to learn new skills on the CFT.

COMPENSATION AND CROSS-FUNCTIONAL TEAMS

The overall goal of cross-functional teams is increased organizational profits through teamwork. As a result, companies have had to develop new compensation systems to reward members of cross-functional teams. One example of this is team incentive pay. Instead of individual merit increases, team members instead earn rewards based on overall team performance. The incentive pool is funded by increased profits and new business that are created as a result of using teams. The amount of compensation that can be earned in the team incentive model is actually far greater than that which can be obtained in the standard individual merit pay system.

Another system that has proven popular in organizations that utilize CFTs is the system called Pay for Applied Services (PAS). Under this system, employees who learn and apply new skills have their base pay increased. In addition, performance bonuses are available if their teams and the company perform better than expected. PAS works this way: employees identify their "primary service," i.e., their basic job skill or title. This primary service determines the person's entry-level salary. A salary range is determined for all people who provide that primary service, ranging from entry-level to maximum based on experience and performance. Employees can increase their salary the traditional way, by gaining increases within their service range, or they can learn new services and qualify for bonuses or increases. In addition to individual increases, employees can earn team incentive bonuses that total up to 10 percent of base pay. Team incentives are paid out once per year.

DRAWBACKS TO CROSS-FUNCTIONAL TEAMS

Cross-functional teams have become an integral part of the business landscape in many industries in recent years. But observers point out that their use can have unintended drawbacks if companies are not watchful.

For example, analysts note that CFTs can actually limit the professional growth of team members because they have a narrow focus in one area. As a result, some companies have had success by shaking things up periodically. After two years of serving on the same team, team members may become bored and feel that they are learning only about the clients or the business categories handled by their team. The solution? Team members should be rotated onto other teams periodically. This can help to prevent a sense of stagnation and help to keep the innovative aspects of the cross-functional team alive with new members.

Some companies try to hand off projects to CFTs that are simply too large in scope and are essentially doomed to failure from the start. Such large projects lack the focus needed for CFT success, and trying to make such a project work in that environment can sour an entire organization on using CFTs for other projects. Another sure pitfall is to establish a CFT without imposing either project deadlines or interim reporting deadlines. Without a sense of urgency to complete a project, the project will almost certainly stall and fail.

Converting employees to a new compensation system when CFTs are implemented can be difficult as well. When team incentives replace individual merit increases, team members often complain, even though more money can be earned in the team-based system. Employees often feel that they have very little control over whether or not the company's profits actually increase, therefore they have no control over earning a raise. Additionally, many employees balk at giving up their own merit increase for the sake of the team. They may see the team plan as a way to demand more from teams than from individuals without giving anything back in return.

BIBLIOGRAPHY

Alexander, Jeffrey A., Richard Lichtenstein, Kimberly Jinnett, Rebecca Wells, James Zazzali, and Dawei Liu. "Cross-Functional Team Processes and Patient Functional Improvement." *Health Services Research.* October 2005.

Berns, Evan. "Cross-Functional Teams Spawn Excellence." *Design News.* 16 October 2000.

Lafasto, Frank M. J., and Carl E. Larson. *When Teams Work Best.* Sage Publications, Inc., August 2001.

Levi, Daniel. *Group Dynamics for Teams.* Sage Publications, Inc., 2001.

Maynard, Roberta. "A Client-Centered Firm's Lesson in Team Work." *Nation's Business.* March 1997.

"Recipe for Success: Cross-Functional Teams + Project Management Skills." *Getting Results.* October 1996.

Scholtes, Peter R., and Brian L. Joiner, Barbara J. Streibelmart, Karl L., and Carol Barnum. *The Team Handbook.* Oriel Incorporated, 2003.

Smart, Karl L., and Carol Barnum. "Communication in Cross-Functional Teams." *Technical Communication.* February 2000.

Hillstrom, Northern Lights
updated by Magee, ECDI

CROSS-TRAINING

Cross-training involves teaching an employee who was hired to perform one job function the skills required to perform other job functions. In the world of sports, the benefits of cross training are clear. By mixing different activities into a regular workout routine one can avoid overuse injuries, balance the development between muscle groups, and prevent boredom. The same may be said of cross-training in the workplace. Employees involved in cross-training programs become skilled at tasks outside the usual parameters of their jobs and thus become greater assets for the company while gaining knowledge and skills that benefit them personally.

Many small businesses use cross-training practices regularly, although in a less formal manner than is usually written about in business journals. When an entrepreneur starts a business and makes those first hiring decisions, he or she will naturally look for candidates who appear to possess the flexibility to handle multiple and often unrelated jobs. A welder, for example, who has taken college courses in engineering or a bookkeeper with people skills who is willing to help with human resource tasks. In a small business it is often the norm to wear more than one hat.

Cross-training programs are a way to more formally organize the process of getting employees prepared to be able to do more than a single job. These programs offer a wide variety of benefits for businesses. For example, a well-designed program can help reduce costs, improve employee morale, reduce turnover, and increase productivity. It can also give a company greater scheduling flexibility, and may even lead to operational improvements. Perhaps the most important benefit that accrues to companies that implement cross-training programs, however, is greater job satisfaction among employees. Cross-training demonstrates that the company has faith in employees' abilities and wants to provide them with opportunities for career growth. In an age when companies are always trying to accomplish more work with fewer workers, anything that helps to motivate and retain employees can be worthwhile. Cross-trained employees often feel that their jobs have been enriched, and they are often able to contribute more to a firm by coming up with creative solutions based on drawing upon their knowledge of different company systems.

Another benefit of cross-training is increased workforce flexibility. The ability of cross-trained employees to fill in during absences, vacations, and peak demand periods can reduce the costs involved in hiring and training temporary workers or new employees.

Cross-training programs may also improve the overall work atmosphere in a business, which may in turn improve the bottom line. Employees are a valuable asset in small businesses, which often must maintain only a bare bones staff in order to remain competitive. This makes it even more important to make maximum use of employees' skills and talents. Investing in on-the-job training shows all those involved that individual career growth is a valuable and necessary part of the company's overall growth. If employees believe they have the potential to improve within the company, they will be generally happier with their jobs and more willing to go the extra mile when needed. Employees will be more productive and feel more a part of the overall mission of the company. This usually leads to a high overall morale.

IMPLEMENTING A CROSS-TRAINING PROGRAM

To be effective, a cross-training program must be carefully planned and organized. It cannot be implemented all of a sudden during a crisis. For one thing, there are a number of decisions that a company must make before the program can get started. It is important, for example, to decide who will be eligible for training, whether the training will be mandatory or voluntary, whether the training will be restricted within job classifications or open to other classifications, and whether it will be administered internally or externally. Prior to implementation, it might be helpful to set up a task force consisting of both management and employees to research the pros and cons of cross-training for the business, assess the feasibility of setting up a program, work out the implementation issues, and set up a realistic schedule for each position.

One of the first steps to setting up a cross-training program is having each different area or department draw up a list of functions and tasks that are necessary to its day-to-day operations. Then the various tasks can be prioritized to decide which should be included in the cross-training program. This helps match staff members to the tasks that need cross-training coverage. It is always important to have participating employees review the lists of functions and tasks. This way each can identify the functions/tasks they already know how to do, those they would like to learn, and those they would be willing to learn if necessary. Having their feedback allows the pro-

gram manager to consider both competence and interest in the matching process.

Rather than simply training one employee to perform another one's job—which would not really solve the problem if the first employee experienced a long absence—it may be better to train several employees in various components of the first one's job so that they can all pitch in as needed. Training can take place through an on-the-job buddy system, or supervisors can be asked to conduct all the training. It is important to note that those selected as trainers may need to receive instruction in how to teach others. Finally, cross-trained employees must be given the time they need to absorb the new information. Their workload should be reduced both during the training and during later practice sessions so that they will not feel as if they are being penalized for participating in the program. It may also be helpful to evaluate newly trained employees' progress on a regular basis.

SUCCESS FACTORS

One of the most important factors in the success of any cross-training initiative is gaining the full support of top management. To be truly dedicated to cross-training, the traditional idea of one job per person must be replaced with a broader definition. It is also vital to involve employees who are already performing the job in the training process. Making all those who will be impacted by a cross-training program feel included from the outset, involving them in training will help avoid fears that their job may be in jeopardy. It is extremely important to communicate to employees that cross-training is not a management scheme designed to eliminate jobs. These programs benefit both the company and the individuals involved and this fact must be emphasized when implementing such a program.

Creating a successful cross-training program is not necessarily easy, and small business owners should expect to encounter some resistance from employees. One way to help ease acceptance of such a program is to address compensation issues ahead of time. Companies must be willing to compensate employees for increasing their skills. In some cases, instituting pay-for-skill or pay-for-knowledge programs may help encourage people to participate. It may also be helpful to promote people who learn new skills to a new grade in a graded-pay system, or to attach a dollar value to specific skills and then pay employees for the time they spend cross-training on a higher-paying skill. Employees must be made to feel that their efforts are being recognized for a cross-training program to be successful.

There are several potential pitfalls that companies need to avoid in order to implement a successful cross-training initiative. One of the major pitfalls is trying to establish a program without taking a systematic approach. Some other potential pitfalls include failure to include employees in planning the program, trying to coerce the participation of reluctant employees, assuming that employees are familiar with the techniques needed to train others, penalizing employees who take part in cross-training by not reducing their workload accordingly, and not recognizing the value of new skills with appropriate changes in compensation.

In the "new global economy," which Thomas L. Friedman calls flat in his best selling book *The World is Flat,* we are all encouraged to prepare for a future in which we will have many jobs and need to embrace "lifelong learning" and not "lifelong employment." Cross-training certainly fits into this view of the future.

SEE ALSO *Flexible Work Arrangements; Training and Development*

BIBLIOGRAPHY
Berta, Dina. "Cross-Training Seen as the Way to Work Out Staffing Shortage Problems." *Nation's Restaurant News.* 9 October 2000.

Friedman, Thomas L. *The World is Flat.* Farrar, Straus and Giroux, 2005.

Karp, David. "Taking Cross-Training Too Far." *Medical Economics.* 4 November 2005.

Lien, Judy. "Human Resources Planning: Building a Case for Cross-Training." *Medical Laboratory Observer.* February 2000.

Senese, Tony. "Are You Cross-Training Your Employees?" *CircuiTree.* December 2004.

Hillstrom, Northern Lights
updated by Magee, ECDI

CUSTOMER RETENTION

Customer retention refers to the percentage of customer relationships that, once established, a business is able to maintain on a long-term basis. Customer retention is a simple concept—happy customers who feel important and are regularly communicated with in the right way will keep coming back. It is a major contributing factor in the net growth rate of businesses. For example, a company that increases its number of new customers by 20 percent in a year but retains only 85 percent of its existing customers will have a net growth rate of only 5 percent (20 percent increase less 15 percent decrease). But the company could triple that rate by retaining 95 percent of its clients.

Of course, growth is just one of the benefits that superior customer retention can offer a company. Increased profits are another. The cost of acquiring customers and putting them on the books generally exceeds by several times the annual cost of serving existing customers. So the longer customers are kept, the more years over which the initial cost of acquisition can be spread.

A variety of strategies are available to small business owners seeking to improve their customer retention rates. Of course, the most basic tools for retaining customers are providing superior product and service quality. High-quality products and services minimize the problems experienced by customers and create goodwill toward the company, which in turn increases customers' resistance to competitors' overtures. However, it is important that small business owners not blindly seek to improve their customer retention rate. Instead, they must make sure that they are targeting and retaining the right customers—the ones who generate high profits. In short, customer retention should not be a stand-alone program but should be seen as part of an overall customer relations management.

The first step in establishing a customer retention program is to create a time line of a typical customer relationship, outlining all the key events and interactions that occur between the first contact with and the eventual loss of the customer. The next step is to analyze the company's trends in losing customers. Customer defections may be related to price increases or to a certain point in the relationship life cycle, for example. Finally, small business owners can use the information gathered to identify warning signs of customer loss and develop retention programs to counteract it.

STRATEGIES FOR RETAINING CUSTOMERS

One basic customer retention strategy available to small business owners involves focusing on employee retention and satisfaction. A company with a high turnover rate may not be able to maintain strong personal relationships with its customers. Even if relationships are established, the customer may decide to take its business to a new company when its contact person leaves. At the very least, high turnover creates a negative environment and reduces the quality of service provided to customers. In order to reduce turnover, it is important to provide employees with career development opportunities and high degrees of involvement in the business.

Another possible strategy for retaining customers involves institutionalizing customer relationships. Rather than just providing contact with individual employees, a small business can provide value to customers through the entire company. For example, it could send newsletters or provide training programs in order to become a source of information and education for customers. It may also be possible to establish membership cards or frequent-buyer programs as direct incentives for customer retention.

Some companies may be able to use electronic links to improve the service they provide to customers. For example, e-mail connections could be used to provide updates on the status of accounts, electronic order systems could be used to simplify reordering and reduce costs, and online services could be used to provide general information.

Customer retention programs are particularly important in volatile industries—those characterized by fluctuating prices and product values. In this situation, superior service may discourage but not prevent customer defections. Some strategies that may be useful to companies in volatile industries include providing stable prices over the customer life cycle, basing prices on the overall cost and profitability of the customer relationship, and cross-selling additional products and services. All of these strategies are intended to minimize the changes and problems customers experience, thus making them want to maintain the business relationship.

SEE ALSO *Difficult Customers*

BIBLIOGRAPHY

Bernstal, Janet Bingham. "Riding Herd on Attrition: Here's one approach to maintaining your grip on customers in the 'top-tier,' 'mature' and 'business banking' segments." *ABA Bank Marketing.* May 2005.

Bland, Vikki. "Keeping the Customer (Satisfied): In an age where brand loyalty is only as good as the next promotion and people use the internet to compare goods from near and far, customer retention is more important than ever." *NZ Business.* September 2004.

Buttle, Francis. *Customer Relations Management.* 3 December 2003.

Schreiber, David. "Customer Retention Is All in the Customer Service." *Atlanta Business Chronicle.* 10 November 2000.

Snell, Bridget Ryan. "Customer Retention 101." *Motor Age.* October 2000.

Zemke, Ron. "Customer Retention Hinges on Service Experience." *Minneapolis-St. Paul City Business.* 2 March 2001.

Hillstrom, Northern Lights
updated by Magee, ECDI

CUSTOMER SERVICE

The term "customer service" encompasses a variety of techniques used by businesses to ensure the satisfaction of a customer, from friendly and attentive staff to prompt response when confronted with product defects. Successful small business owners often cite customer service as the factor most important in establishing and maintaining a prosperous company. A strong emphasis on customer service throughout a business will help to produce the sort of environment conducive to loyal customers. This is true for companies that sell to other businesses and to companies that sell to individual consumers.

The U.S. Small Business Administration provides, on its Web site, a variety of reports useful to small businesses. In one simply entitled *Customer Service,* the administration summarizes the importance of customer service to the small business this way: "The growing significance of meeting—or exceeding—customer demands for quality service has special implications for small business. For it is in this arena that small companies can, in the least expensive way, set themselves apart from the competition. In fact, a recent three-year study by the National Federation of Independent Business (NFIB) in Washington, D.C., showed that small businesses which put heavy emphasis on customer service were more likely to survive and succeed than competitors who emphasized such advantages as lower prices or type of product."

DEVELOPING A CUSTOMER-ORIENTED COMPANY CULTURE

In order to assure that there is a positive customer service attitude within every department or area of a company it is important to establish customer service goals for the company as a whole. Customers have contact with companies at many levels and at each they should meet courteous, friendly, and knowledgeable people willing to work with them. Customer service can be seen to be like a three-legged stool. The three legs of the stool are employees, sound practices, and training.

Employees Many business observers contend that the most critical facet of ensuring good customer service lies in simply hiring personable and responsible employees. The use of pre-employment screening tests can enhance the hiring procedure by helping employers measure the skills and characteristics needed for success in customer service jobs before hiring a new employee. There are a variety of valid tests available, and consistently hiring people who score highest on these tests will ensure that new hires will represent the business in a positive light. In addition, business owners are urged to make sure that they adequately inform potential employees of any customer-relations obligations that they might have. This is typically accomplished through training programs.

Training Employee training is an important component of customer service. Customer service principles should be put in writing, and it should be made clear that all employees are expected to be familiar with them and be prepared to live up to them. Small business owners also need to recognize that customer service training should be extended to all employees who interact with clients, not just those in high-profile sales positions. Service technicians, for example, often regularly interact with customers, but all too often they receive little or no customer service training. "More companies are asking their technicians to fill gaps in sales efforts and to repair communication breakdowns," noted Roberta Maynard in *Nation's Business.* "Some companies are cultivating their technicians' abilities to clarify customer needs and identify and capitalize on sales opportunities.... Some managers are giving technicians greater authority to do what it takes to keep customers happy, such as occasionally not charging for a service call or a part."

Sound Practices Finally, businesses need to make sure that they work hard to ensure customer satisfaction on a daily basis. Customer service should be ingrained in the company, commented one entrepreneur in an interview with Michael Barrier in a *Nation's Business* article: "It has to be part of the organization's mission and vision, right from Day One. Then the rest tends to be simple—it carries over to your products, your advertising, your staffing, and everything else."

INSTILLING CUSTOMER LOYALTY

Business experts cite several tangible steps that small business owners can take to ensure that they provide top-notch service to their customers. These include:

- Build quality support systems—Companies armed with tangible, easily understood guidelines for establishing and maintaining quality customer service will go far toward satisfying clients.

- Communicate with customers—Communication with customers can often be accomplished more easily by smaller businesses than larger companies that are often slowed by layers of bureaucracy. Methods of communication can include telephone calls, postcards, newsletters, and surveys as well as face-to-face conversation. By keeping in touch with customers one is able to more quickly address problems that arise and anticipate some before they are even serious. And while such steps are perhaps most helpful when dealing with regular customers, consultants counsel business owners who specialize in making big-ticket sales to try and maintain communications with their customers as well. Such customers may not make a purchase every month, noted Frederick F. Reichheld, author of *The Loyalty*

Effect, but those purchases that they do make carry a lot of weight. Reichheld notes that big-ticket purchases typically have a fair amount of service and financing associated with them, both of which provide small businesses with opportunities to nourish their relationship with the customer. In addition, consultants observe that communication with ex-customers can be helpful as well. "A defecting customer may offer a reason that points to a potentially serious problem [within your company]," wrote Barrier.

- Communicate with front-line employees—Employees who are kept apprised of changes in company products and services are far more likely to be able to satisfy customers than those who are armed with outdated or incomplete information.

- Retain employees—Many customers establish a certain comfort level over time with individual employees—a salesman, a project coordinator, etc.—and these relationships should be valued and nurtured by the small business owner. "Each customer has special needs," observed Barrier, "and the longer that employee and customer work together, the more easily those needs can be met. Companies that want long-term relationships with their customers need equally healthy relationships with their employees. In particular, they must encourage employee involvement."

- Invest in technology that aids customer service—Small businesses should choose voice mail systems that make it easy for customers to contact the person or department that they wish to reach. Technology systems can also help small businesses gather information about their customers.

- Cultivate an atmosphere of courtesy—Small gestures such as friendly smiles, use of the customer's first name, and minor favors can have a disproportionate impact on the way that a business is viewed. "Remember that small kindnesses can carry a lot of weight," said Barrier.

- Address mistakes promptly and honorably—No business is infallible. Errors inevitably occur within any business framework, and sooner or later a customer is apt to be impacted. But business experts contend that in many instances, these incidents can actually help strengthen the bond between a company and its customers. "In the normal course of a business relationship, the depth of a vendor's commitment will not be put to the test," wrote Barrier, "but a serious mistake will reveal quickly just how trustworthy that vendor is."

- Avoid equating price with customer service—Many small businesses find it difficult to compete with larger, high-volume competitors in the realm of price, but most analysts insist that this reality should not be construed as a failure in the realm of customer service. Moreover, most experts indicate that many small businesses can triumph over price differences, provided that they are relatively minor, by putting an extra emphasis on service. "For some customers, of course, price is all that matters," admitted Barrier. "Those are customers you probably can live without."

- Create a user-friendly physical environment—Writing in *Entrepreneur,* Jay Conrad Levinson counseled small business owners to "design your company's physical layout for efficiency, clarity of signage, lighting, accessibility for the disabled and simplicity. Everything should be easy to find."

By crafting a customer service policy that combines the practices listed above, a company is likely to leave a positive impression with customers. Over time, the cumulative effect of this positive impression will build loyalty.

CUTTING TIES WITH BAD CUSTOMERS

Although smart entrepreneurs and business managers recognize that customer service is an important element in ensuring company success, it is a reality of life that a small percentage of customers are simply incapable of being satisfied with the service they receive. Small business owners are generally averse to letting any customers go, but consultants contend that some clients can simply become more trouble than they are worth for any number of reasons. The solution to determining whether a business owner should sever ties with a problematic customer, observed *Nation's Business,* "may lie in defining the word 'customer' properly: Someone who costs you money isn't a customer but rather a liability."

Entrepreneur's Jacquelyn Lynn listed several scenarios in which consultants recommend that small businesses consider ending their relationship with a troublesome client. Client attitudes and actions that should prompt an honest assessment include:

- Lack of respect or appreciation for the small business owner's work.

- Excessive demands, either on company or individual staff members.

- Unreasonable expectations in terms of monetary arrangements for work or goods provided.

- Proclivity for imposing difficult or unrealistic deadlines.

- Tendency to pay bills late (or not at all).

- Treats company as a commodity that can be discarded as soon as it ceases to be useful to the client.

Lynn noted that, in some instances, honest communication with the client can salvage a deteriorating relationship, but this does not always work. "If your attempts to make the relationship a mutually productive one don't work," said Lynn, "it may be time to move on and focus on more profitable clients or prospective clients. Calculate what you will lose in gross revenue, and decide if your business can stand the financial hit." If the business is able to withstand the loss of revenue, move forward to terminate the relationship in a professional manner. If not, then the company's leadership needs to develop a strategy to expand existing business relationships or garner new clients so that the company can sever relations with the offending customer down the line.

BIBLIOGRAPHY

Barrier, Michael. "Ties that Bind." *Nation's Business.* August 1997.

Brown, Stanley E., ed. *Customer Relationship Management: A Strategic Imperative in the World of E-Business.* Wiley, 2000.

"Customers You Want to Lose." *Nation's Business.* August 1997.

Friedman, J. Roger. "Quality Service Is the Key to Earning Repeat Customers." *Nation's Restaurant News.* 1 September 1997.

Lee, Dick. *The Customer Relationship Management Survival Guide.* High Yield Marketing Press, 2000.

Levinson, Jay Conrad. "Taking Care: 17 Ways to Show Your Customers You Care." *Entrepreneur.* October 1997.

Lynn, Jacquelyn. "Good Riddance." *Entrepreneur.* October 1997.

Maynard, Roberta. "Are Your Technicians Customer-Friendly?" *Nation's Business.* August 1997.

Paajanen, George. "Customer Service: Training, Sound Practices, and the Right Employee." *Discount Store News.* 15 September 1997.

Reichheld, Frederick F. *The Loyalty Effect.* Harvard Business School Press, September 2001.

Stewart, Thomas A. "A Satisfied Customer Isn't Enough." *Fortune.* 21 July 1997.

Tschohl, John. "How to Succeed in Business by Really Trying." *Canadian Manager.* Spring 1997.

U.S. Small Business Administration. *Customer Service.* Available from http://www.sba.gov/managing/marketing/customer.html. Retrieved on 6 February 2006.

Wilhelm, Wayne, and Bill Rossello. "The Care and Feeding of Customers." *Management Review.* March 1997.

Zemke, Ron, and John A. Woods. *Best Practices in Customer Service.* AMACOM, 1999.

Hillstrom, Northern Lights
updated by Magee, ECDI

D

DATA ENCRYPTION

Data encryption refers to the process of transforming electronic information into a scrambled form that can only be read by someone who knows how to translate the code. Encryption was already used by Julius Caesar in the days of the Roman Empire to scramble letters and messages. It played a major role in many wars and in military circles generally. Encryption has turned electronic in modern times. It is today very important in the business world as well. It is the easiest and most practical method of protecting data stored, processed, or transmitted electronically. It makes electronic commerce possible by protecting credit card and personal information. It is also commonly used to scramble the contents of contracts, sensitive documents, and personal messages sent over the Internet. More and more institutions, including small businesses with data to protect, also use encryption to protect data on their computer in-house.

BASICS

Encryption comes from the science of cryptography, which involves the coding and decoding of messages in order to protect their contents. One of the most ancient forms of it is letter substitution—thus, for instance, sending the next letter in the alphabet instead of the actual letter in the text. *Ifmmp xpsme/* thus spells out *Hello world.*. In the electronic environment, every symbol has a numerical value expressible in binary notation. Thus the letter *A* is 01000001 and the letter *a* is 01100001. Humans cannot make out a vast stream of zeroes and ones, but it is child's play for a computer. Patterns of letters are therefore transformed before trans-

mission by using an arbitrary key; the key may be used in arithmetic, logical, or other ways to make the underlying meaning inaccessible to anyone who does not know the key. The more binary digit the key has, the more difficult the code is to crack—meaning that the longer it takes a computer system, attempting to break the code, to find the key by trial and error. Very safe encryption methods in the mid-2000s made use of 128-bit keys; such keys were used in financial transactions; but newer systems were being fielded using 168 and 256 bits.

TYPES OF ENCRYPTION PROGRAMS

Single Key There are two main types of data encryption systems. In the first—which is variously known as private key, single key, secret key, or symmetric encryption—the sender and the recipient of the data both hold the same key for translation. This single key is used both to code and to decode information exchanged between two parties. Since the same key is used to encrypt and decrypt messages, the parties involved must exchange the key secretly and keep it secure from outsiders. Private key encryption systems are usually faster than other types; they can be cumbersome when more than two parties need to exchange information.

Public Key The second, and more commonly used, type of data encryption system is known as a public key system. This approach involves two separate keys: a public key for encoding information; and a private key for decoding information. The public key can be held and used by any number of individuals and businesses, whereas only one party holds the private key. The system is particularly useful in electronic commerce: the merchant holds the private key and all customers have access to the public key. The public key can be posted on a Web page or stored in an easily accessible key repository. Public key encryption systems are widely available on the Internet and heavily used by large companies.

The best-known data encryption program is called RSA. It was developed in the late 1970s by three graduates of the Massachusetts Institute of Technology—Ronald Rivest, Adi Shamir, and Leonard Adleman. As of the mid-2000, there were more than a billion installations of RSA encryption programs on computer systems worldwide. RSA scrambles data based on the product of two prime numbers, each of which is 100 digits long. RSA is known as a public key encryption system, meaning that many people can use it to encode information, but only the person who holds the key (or knows the value of the two prime numbers) can decode it again. RSA is embedded in hundreds of popular software products, including Windows, Netscape Navigator, Quicken, and Lotus Notes. It is also available as a free download from the World Wide Web.

A number of other data encryption programs enjoy wide use as well. Examples include Pretty Good Privacy (PGP), which is considered easy to use; Secure Sockets Layer (SSL), which is used by many companies that accept online credit card orders; Secure Electronic Transactions (SET), another popular method of handling credit card purchases that is backed by Visa, Mastercard, Microsoft, IBM, and other major players in electronic commerce; and Data Encryption Standard (DES), which was invented by IBM in the mid-1970s and became the U.S. government standard.

DES is a good example of the life-cycle of encryption systems. Unlike diamonds, they are not forever. More powerful and faster computers are able to tackle and break the best the older codes. Thus in 1998, as reported by James Swann in *Community Banker,* the Electronic Frontier Foundation cracked a DES code in less than three days; the year after, another network comprised of 100,000 computers cracked the key in 22 hours and 15 minutes. For this reason The National Institute of Standards and Technology proposed in 2005 that DES be decertified for government work. It will most likely be replaced by Triple DES, also an IBM product. 3DES, as it is known, makes the code much harder to crack by using a 168-bit key.

MOTIVATION FOR ENCRYPTION

Encryption systems cost money in the form of software and greater computer capacity. Processing of encrypted data in and out also adds time to all procedures. But the money is well spent. Betsy Spethmann, writing in 2005

for *Promo* magazine, reports that security breaches of systems holding customer data cost their owners on average $14 million per incident. In addition, once such breaches become known, the database owner typically loses at least 20 percent of its customers. Shedding troubled customers in large numbers is likely to accelerate. At present, Spethmann reports, 21 states "have laws requiring marketers to notify customers or employees when security of personal data has been breached. The federal legislature is considering at least five bills on data security and notification."

TRENDS IN ENCRYPTION PRACTICES

In the early 2000s, many corporations materially strengthened their defenses against the interception of transmitted data by encryption; they also fortified their information systems with ever better firewalls against intruders. Trends in the mid-2000s have been to focus on *internal* security. More and more companies, as reported elsewhere in this volume (see "Computer Crime"), have begun to focus on the enemy within. As one article in *Information Week* put it in its title, "You Know These Security Threats—You Hired Them."

In many companies data are routinely encrypted before transmission to another site—but remain in clear, unencrypted language on the computer itself, protected only by a system of passwords. When these machines are backed up at night on tape, vital proprietary data are simply hanging on a rack, stored on magnetic tape—tapes small enough to fit comfortably into a generously sized canvas shopping bag. These data are all too frequently simply stolen.

More and more companies in consequence are extending encryption to storage tapes used for backup. They are also exploring off-site storage of back-up data on distant computers where they reside in encrypted form. Even such methods are not sufficient to protect data from individuals who, by the very nature of their jobs, have access to the sensitive data. Thus, at the boundaries of encryption other techniques of supervision and control must be devised to protect information where scrambling, however effective and however well protected by keys of ever increasing digits, still do not provide protection.

SEE ALSO *Biometrics; Internet Security*

BIBLIOGRAPHY

Angwin, Julia. "Internet Encryption's Password is 'Slow.'" *Wall Street Journal.* 28 March 2000.

Britt, Phillip. "Encryption Key to Data Security." *Information Today.* November 2005.

"Internet Security Gateway Targets Small Network Environments." *Product News Network.* 16 December 2005.

Komiega, Kevin. "Tape Encryption Not a Security Cure-All." *InfoStor.* January 2006.

Korper, Steffano, and Juanita Ellis. *The E-Commerce Book: Building the E-Empire.* Academic Press, 2000.

MacVittie, Don. "Don't Be The Next Data Debacle— Implement tape encryption now, before you find yourself in the white-hot spotlight for all the wrong reasons." *Network Computing.* 24 November 2005.

"No One-Stop Shopping to Stop Database Pilferages." *eWeek.* 21 December 2005.

Spethmann, Betsy. "Data Security Mistakes Cost an Average $14 Million." *Promo.* 23 November 2005.

Swann, James. "Preparing for Triple DES security." *Community Banker.* December 2005.

"You Know These Security Threats—You Hired Them: New products are designed to stop threats that come from the inside." *Information Week.* 31 October 2005.

Hillstrom, Northern Lights
updated by Magee, ECDI

DATABASE ADMINISTRATION

Database administration is simply maintaining records of any type—customer lists, vendor histories, or addresses, for example—using computer software known as a database management system (DBMS). As Anne Kerven said in *Colorado Business Magazine,* "Database management means the transferring of file cabinet contents to an electronic file." Out of that simple statement has sprung a multimillion dollar computer software industry and a thriving database administration consulting niche. Almost every company has records of one type or another to maintain, which means that almost every company is affected by DBMS in some way or another.

Databases can range in size from a few hundred addresses maintained on a user's hard drive to hundreds of terabytes of data maintained on huge corporate mainframe computers. One of the benefits of using a database management system, however, is that even if the data is vast and is stored on a remote mainframe, end-users throughout a company can all access the data from their desktop using computer networking technology. Reports that in the past had to be requested days or even weeks in advance and created by computer technicians can be generated in minutes by the average user with today's database management systems.

The most common type of system is the relational database management system (RDBMS). It is found in almost every company data center. An RDBMS sorts data into unique fields and allows users to retrieve that data by each field and by linking fields between related records. Relational databases can sort the fielded data any number of ways and generate reports in a matter of minutes. Data can often be output in any form the end-user desires. In addition, a RDBMS can serve as the front-end program that brings data together from several individual databases and produces data tables that combine the information from the various databases.

Database management technology is improving every year, however, and relational databases are starting to be replaced by more sophisticated database management systems. This movement was spurred in large part by companies that realized that they had more than simple records to maintain—they had complicated files, with sounds and images; they had brochures, photographs, time-series inputs, and 3-D coordinates—all of which could be more easily maintained if they were organized and stored in a database. In response to this growing need, software developers have created new object-oriented database management systems (OODBMS) and object-relational database management systems (ORDBMS).

It is expected that ORDBMS will become the most popular type because the need to store disparate types of information is growing. An example of the type of data that might be stored in an object-relation system is a human resources file on an employee. In the past, the database record might have only included text information about the employee—birth date, address, starting date, etc. With an object-relational system, the record could also include the employee's photo or voice sample. Or, a company could maintain geospatial information that would allow it to query the database to locate all customers who made more than $50,000 and lived within 10 miles of the company's location.

SELECTING A SYSTEM FOR A SMALL BUSINESS

For small business owners who are entertaining thoughts about purchasing a database management system, experts say that the first thing they need to do is determine what they hope to get out of the system—what type of reports do they need, etc. Once the output is known, it is easier to know what type of database is needed, what information will be gathered, and what fields will be created. It is a good idea to start small—such as with a mailing list— to get used to the software. Once the first database is mastered, it is easy to set up additional ones for order tracking, inventory, or other purposes.

Most databases are one of two types—transactional or warehouse. Transactional databases are easier to build and are ideal for tracking simple things, such as the availability of a product or part. Warehouse databases collect company data of any type, such as sales histories or hiring statistics, and produce reports that can identify trends or group information in new and relevant ways. Small businesses use both types of databases.

Once you know what you hope to get out of a system and what type of database you will be building, you can move on to selecting the right software for the job. If you are a computer savvy user who is experienced with personal computers, and the database is simple, then you may be able to study the available software packages yourself and choose the one that is best for you. If you are not, or you expect the job to be complex, it is best to locate a consultant in your area and work with them to select your system.

The simpler the system you can get away with, the better. "If you can buy off-the-shelf, that's fantastic because it's less expensive," said Larry Skaff, owner of Junction Software Services, in *Colorado Business Magazine.* "But it will have tradeoffs. If they don't do business exactly the way that database is written, can they live with that?" The most common off-the-shelf system is Microsoft Access, which is sold separately and as part of Microsoft Office and Microsoft Small Office. Access allows users to build databases out of a number of templates so that they do not have to start from scratch. At the same time, it does allow advanced users to build custom databases, and it features fairly powerful sort and reporting options.

More adventurous users may opt for packages that are a notch or two above Access, such as Filemaker Pro, Borland's Paradox, or Microsoft's SQL Server. These are more robust than Access and allow users to define fields and create intricate databases. If you do not feel comfortable creating a database yourself but still need the additional features that these higher-level packages provide, then a consultant is once again the place to turn. Most will charge anywhere from $50 to $250 per hour to create a custom database. Be warned—this can be a time-consuming project and can cost tens of thousands of dollars.

For small businesses that have even more extensive database needs, consultants and computer professionals will undoubtedly be required. High-level products from one of the big three database management systems companies—Oracle, Informix, or Sybase—can manage huge amounts of complex data on either a stand-alone machine or a local- or wide-area network.

MAINTAINING A DATABASE MANAGEMENT SYSTEM

There is one important fact about databases that some people seem to forget—no matter how good the software is, no matter how expensive the computers are, they are only as good as the data that is put into them.

Information must be loaded into the system via data entry work or some other form of input, and it is up to the business owner or manager of information systems to make sure that records are accurate and kept up to date.

Letting records slip from time to time may seem like a small thing, but especially for a small business enterprises, poor database maintenance can reflect poorly on the business and make clients think twice about doing business there. Database managers estimate that more than half of small businesses do not maintain their databases once they are created. Examples of the kinds of mistakes that can occur include failing to bill an account, mailing literature to someone who is deceased, or indicating that there is plenty of a particular product in stock when in fact the supply was exhausted weeks ago. Such situations can give rise to business disasters for owners of small businesses.

Writing in *Colorado Business Magazine,* Anne Kerven outlined some of the other common maintenance mistakes that are made:

- Collecting too much or too little data. Collecting too much information slows down the system, clutters screens with unnecessary fields, and inflates the costs of gathering data. Recording too little data can render the database worthless for compiling reports that can help the business grow; instead, money spent on inputting the little data that is there is wasted.

- Poorly conceived data fields. The most common mistake is putting too much information in one field—the computer can only sort by field, not by what is in the field. The best rule of thumb is to put each unique record element—ZIP code, phone number, fax number, address—in its own searchable field.

- Try to avoid using personal names as the key identifier of a record or as a link between records. Instead, use numbers, assigning a unique number to each record. Personal names cause problems when two or more people have the same name; additionally, if the name is not entered exactly the same way every time it is used as a link—a middle initial is included in one instance and left out in another, for example—the records will not link properly.

- Check the database integrity at least once a month. Corrupted links or other problems can creep in over time. Utility programs are available for this function.

- Back up information and store it in a separate location, preferably someplace that is fireproof and waterproof.

- Set strict standards that must be followed whenever data is input into the system to ensure consistency. This is especially important if multiple departments will be adding data to the system.

- Periodically clean out the database, weeding out records that are inactive or no longer relevant. If you do not want to lose those records permanently, create an archive database and move the records into that file.

COMMON USES OF DATABASE MANAGEMENT SYSTEMS

As discussed, database management systems store company information and allow users to easily retrieve that information. But what does that mean in the business world? How exactly are database management systems being put to use so that companies get the most bang for their buck? Currently, there are two primary uses that are gaining in popularity—data marts and data warehouses, and the use of DBMS together with a company's Internet site or intranet.

Data Marts and Data Warehouses Data marts and data warehouses refer to the information repositories that companies create with their database management software. Data marts are simply smaller versions of data warehouses, storing information on a department-by-department basis. Data warehouses are huge, centralized databases that unify information across an entire company. These huge databases can be used to improve customer service, profitability measurement, and product sales.

Data marts gained popularity before data warehouses. They were seen as a way for departments to achieve one of their main goals—getting information into the hands of all their users quickly and at the same time. However, as DBMS technology improves and larger databases become possible, the flaws in using data marts are being exposed. Data marts do not unify data across an organization—in fact, they can fragment it because every department might be doing things a little differently. Each department's data becomes an island that yields different answers to the same query.

That is not to say that data marts *cannot* work, however. They can, *if* they are built *after* a main data warehouse is built. Most people think it is better to start small with data marts and build up to the big data warehouse, but many experts contend that the opposite is true. If the data marts are built first, then fragmented data held in uniquely structured databases that cannot be accessed by all employees are created.

Instead, small business owners should build the warehouse first. Look at the types of information that are gathered in each department around the company and select the key data from each area. Use this as the starting point for the warehouse. Do not try to build an all-purpose warehouse right from the start. Do what makes sense, then add historical data and other information as time goes by. If information is simply gathered and stored with no allowance made for cross-departmental analysis, then the warehouse is useless. Those considering building a database should understand that if, upon examination, the current processes a company uses do not allow for such cross-departmental analysis, then fundamental changes will have to be made to those processes if the warehouse is to work. This is a significant point that too many managers or business owners do not understand when they decide to build a warehouse.

Small businesses also have to make sure that end-users from every department are actively involved in the design of the data warehouse. Without that type of feedback, the database may turn out to be useless because it does not store the right type of information, or it stores it in the wrong way. Those end-users involved in the design can learn how to use the system first and then serve as trainers in their department. Once the main warehouse is built, it then becomes easy for each department to build its own data marts by pulling out the fields from the main database that it needs.

The initial costs of building a data warehouse are high—software, hardware, and consulting fees add up quickly. However, most businesses, from supermarkets to banks, are finding that having a data warehouse is a competitive necessity. One example of how data warehouses are being used is a practice called "data mining." Data mining is the technique of creating statistical and predictive models of the real world based on patterns that are discovered as a result of complex queries performed on the huge amounts of data stored in a warehouse. When data mining is done right, it can produce amazing results, spotting trends before they happen or identifying new sales prospects, for instance. When done incorrectly, however, data mining can produce false correlations and misleading results. Companies should not rely too heavily on data mining and should ensure that they hire professionals who fully understand statistical analysis to perform the task.

DATABASE MANAGEMENT AND THE INTERNET OR INTRANETS

Data warehouses started out as internal projects, but now they are being seen as the next logical step on the Internet. Companies that need to gather data from customers and pass information down the line to business customers are finding it beneficial to make their data warehouse available over the World Wide Web. This means that either HTML or Java-based client servers need to be created to allow Web users to search the database. If the company desires to gather information on customers, it might make the warehouse available to the public over the Web. If the main purpose is to pass information on to business customers, then the company will make the warehouse available as part of its corporate intranet, which is available only to selected individuals.

At first, only basic queries could be run easily over the Web, but observers note that the situation has changed rapidly. Each of the major database management systems companies has scrambled to enable their databases to work closely with Web servers. Using new technology known as online analytical processing (OLAP), high-level, intricate queries of data warehouses will be possible. At the same time, consumers looking to data mine corporate information should be able to run simple queries.

There are risks associated with making such huge amounts of data available over the Web. Security is the paramount issue, since opening data warehouses to users around the world means that internal systems are exposed to outside interference or hacking. A second issue is the drain on system resources that unlimited access to the data warehouses would cause. Popular databases visited and searched by large numbers of users would need extremely powerful servers to keep up with demand. The servers would have to ensure that the employees and clients of a company would not be hindered by the excess traffic on the system. Finally, there is the issue of cost. As with any new technology, opening databases to the Web costs money. In addition to development costs associated with creating the search engines and OLAP tools, businesses will also have to weigh the cost of the powerful servers needed to meet the increased demand for information.

BIBLIOGRAPHY

Atre, Shaku. "Achieving Unity of Data." *Computerworld.* 15 September 1997.

Cummins, Caroline. "Below the Surface: New tools—and savvy librarians—are turning the ILS into a gold mine for making more informed decisions." *Library Journal.* 1 January 2006.

Dessoff, Alan. "Learning How to Use Data." *District Administration.* October 2005.

English, Larry P. *Improving Data Warehouse and Business Information Quality.* Wiley, 1999.

Karp, Mike. "Data Size Is About to Get Out of Control." *Network World.* 30 August 2005.

Kerven, Anne. "Database Management Keys." *Colorado Business Magazine.* March 1997.

Kerven, Anne. "Keep Files Clean." *Colorado Business Magazine.* April 1997.

Mullins, Craig S. "Openness Complicates Database Management." *Computing Canada.* 26 January 1998.

Shaklet, Mary E. "A Place for Your Stuff: Networked storage solutions tailor-made for your small business." *Computer User.* November 2005.

Stedman, Craig. "Data Vaults Unlocked." *Computerworld.* 2 June 1997.

Wells, Stephen. "Hands On—Spreadsheets—Grand openings. Customising functions in Excel workbooks is simple—just follow these tips." *Personal Computer World.* 1 January 2006.

Hillstrom, Northern Lights
updated by Magee, ECDI

DAY TRADING

The Securities and Exchange Commission (SEC) defines day trading as follows: "Day traders rapidly buy and sell stocks throughout the day in the hope that their stocks will continue climbing or falling in value for the seconds to minutes they own the stock, allowing them to lock in quick profits. Day trading is extremely risky and can result in substantial financial losses in a very short period of time."

In its investigation of the practice, which arose in its most modern form with the Internet, the U.S. Senate Permanent Subcommittee on Investigations defined day trading as "placing multiple buy and sell orders for securities and holding positions for a very short period of time, usually minutes or a few hours, but rarely longer than a day. Day traders seek profits in small increments from momentary fluctuations in stock prices after paying commissions." In the more technical language of the National Association of Securities Dealers (NASD), day trading is "an overall trading strategy characterized by the regular transmission by a customer of intra-day orders to effect both purchase and sale transactions in the same security or securities."

Canada and the World magazine, in an article titled "Rolling the dice," saw analogies to day trading in the "bucket shops" of the 1920s. "They were storefront businesses where traders gathered to buy and sell stocks. Many were illegal and not unlike off-track bettering shops. Customers were doing no more than placing a bet on whether certain stocks would rise or fall. In the Roaring Twenties, just about everyone could score in a bucket shop. Buy your stock, any stock, in the morning; by evening you could be confident you could sell it at a profit." Most of the bucket shops, according to the magazine, disappeared in the stock market crash of 1929—only to resurface as Internet-based day trading programs in the bull market of the 1990s. As air rushed out of *that* bubble, day trading almost collapsed. With the market strengthening again in the mid-2000s, market analysts, here and there, see day trading reviving again.

DAY TRADING AS GAMBLING

Ever since the emergence of stock and currency markets in the 16th and 17th centuries in Europe, an element of chance has been a strong component of trading in stock so that, around the world's stock exchanges, the movement of stock prices, up and down, has become the main focus of traders' attention and the original (and still central) goal of selling stock—namely raising capital for a business—is mentioned only in the context of "prudent" investing for the "long term."

As Larry Williams pointed out in an article on day trading in *Futures*, today's markets still behave as they always have. What has changed, above all, is volatility and speed. "Virtually every day-trading system offered for sale for the last 30 years," Williams wrote, "has *not* been a hard and tight mechanical system.... So, if you what you want is a fail-safe purely mechanical system, I'd suggest you turn your attention to real estate investing or bank accounts." [Emphasis added.]

Day trading differs radically from "prudent investment" in that it is based on very brief movements in the price of stocks. These movements are exploited (or attempted to be exploited) in the most modern form of day trading by using very rapid communications techniques provided by the Internet. Stock is not held for any length of time at all. The transactions are based on watching one or many trend lines conveyed to the trader's screen electronically. Buying and selling is based on a pattern of change. Actual information about the company whose stock is bought or sold is therefore less important than any kind of rumor, be it true or false, which will change that pattern for a few minutes or hours. For these very reasons, day trading is more akin to gambling than investment. Not surprisingly, promoters of day trading and those claiming expertise in it emphasize techniques of trading all of which have the flavor of "systems" used in gambling, e.g., counting cards or statistically evaluating the frequency of black or red on the roulette wheel—and knowing when to hold or fold.

WINNERS AND LOSERS

Statistical data on the performance of day traders are largely anecdotal, but the conclusion is that most people lose money, some in a spectacular way. *Canada and the World* magazine cited one such spectacular case, that of Mark Barton. "He lost hundreds of thousands of dollars day trading in an Atlanta branch of the All-Tech Investment Group. Shortly after that, in July 1999, he walked into the All-Tech offices and shot and killed nine people."

One comprehensive study of day trading was conducted by four scholars (Brad Barber, Yi-Tsung Lee, Yu-Jane Liu, and Terrance Odean) focusing on the Taiwanese stock exchange. They studied 130,000 day traders over a five-year period, 1995 to 1999. Barber et. al. discovered that most day trading is done by a few. "About one percent of individual investors account for half of day trading and one forth of total trading by individual investors." Do these heavy traders make a lot of money? The authors go on: "Heavy day traders earn gross profits, but their profits are not sufficient to cover transaction costs. Moreover, in the typical six month period, more than eight out of ten [actually 82 percent] of day traders lose money." Only a tiny handful, according to the authors, made a strong return. It is worth noting that the period of the authors' study coincided with an expanding market.

ELECTRONIC DAY TRADING

Day trading in its current form has its origins in the birth of the computerized, over-the-counter NASD, which occurred in 1971. Fourteen years later, NASD created the Small-Order Execution System (SOES). SOES made it easy for individuals to execute stock trades automatically so long as the orders were for 1,000 shares or less. Trades placed through SOES bypassed the phone lines used to make most trades and placed orders in a matter of seconds, instead of minutes. While SOES users may not buy or sell the same stock during a five-minute period, there were still a group of daring investors who thought they could use SOES to make rapid stock transactions to make a great deal of money. Thus day trading was born.

The modern day trader is no longer limited to SOES. Indeed, the most popular tool for the day trader today is electronic communication networks, or ECNs; they are internal networks set up to handle groups of customers who make large blocks of stock trades. All the members of one ECN may trade directly with other members of their network, placing buy or sell orders electronically. This has become the main tool of the day trader. To best use that tool, day traders watch the NASDAQ Level II screen religiously on their computers. The best bid on any given stock is displayed on the NASDAQ Level I screen, while the Level II screen displays *all* bid prices for a selected stock. This increased amount of information allows the trader better to gauge what is happening with the stock: What are the high and low bids? How many bids have been made? Are the number of bids increasing or decreasing? This information is invaluable as the day trader decides which stock to buy.

With the growth of any money-making activity come the hangers-on—true for day trading as well.

Book and newsletter publishers, authors, commentators, and consultant stand ready to share their wisdom with the would-be day trader. Anyone tempted to participate in this activity might, however, begin by carefully reading what the SEC see has to say on the subject at its Web site, http://www.sec.gov/answers/daytrading.htm.

BIBLIOGRAPHY

Anuff, Joey, and Gary Wolf. *Dumb Money: Adventures of a Day Trader.* Random, 2000.

Barber, Brad and Yi-Tsung Lee, Yu-Jane Liu, and Terrance Odean. "Do Individual Day Traders Make Money? Evidence from Taiwan." *Social Science Research Network.* Available from http://papers.ssrn.com/sol3/papers.cfm?abstract_id=529063. January 2005.

Barker, Robert. "Day Trading: It's Not Always A Fool's Game." *Business Week.* 16 August 2005.

Bresiger, Gregory. "The Return of The Day Trader: But Is Another Disaster Around the Corner?" *Traders.* 1 February 2004.

Catton, Grant. "NASD Seen Moving Toward Limiting Day Trading." *Compliance Reporter.* 31 May 2004.

"Credit Extension/Day Trading Requirements." Notice to Members. National Association of Security Dealers (NASD). May 2004.

D'Souza, Patricia. "Day Trader's Blues." *Canadian Business.* 16 October 2000.

Kitchens, Susan and Michael K. Ozanian. "Last Man Standing." *Forbes.* 23 May 2005.

Maiello, Michael. "Day Trading Eldorado." *Forbes.* 12 June 2000.

McGinn, Daniel. "Do-It-Yourself Isn't Dead Yet: Day trading was all the rage during the bull run. But even with stocks falling, many are still at it, and adding new recruits. Just don't call them 'day traders' now." *Newsweek.* 3 February 2003.

"Rolling the dice." *Canada and the World Backgrounder.* May 2003.

Schwartz, Nelson D. "Meet The New Market Makers: They're Young, They're Rich, and They Couldn't Care Less about Graham & Dodd. But They're the Ones Driving Those Insane Tech Stocks, and They're Not Going Away." *Fortune.* 21 February 2000.

U.S. Securities and Exchange Commission. "Day Trading." Available from http://www.sec.gov/answers/daytrading.htm. 11 October 2005.

U.S. Securities and Exchange Commission. "Day Trading: Your Dollars at Risk." Available from http://www.sec.gov/answers/daytrading.htm. 20 April 2005.

U.S. Senate Permanent Subcommittee on Investigations. "Day Trading: Everyone Gambles but the House." 24 February 2000.

Williams, Larry. "Day-Trading modern markets." *Futures.* 15 September 2001.

Darnay, ECDI

DEBT COLLECTION

Debt collection is a deliberate attempt by a business to collect an obligation that has become past due. In normal transactions between two businesses, an invoice is rendered and payment is due within 30 days—unless, by special arrangement, a more generous schedule of payments has been agreed upon. Retail customers usually pay cash at time of purchase or, common in medical practices, are billed for portions not covered by insurance; payment is due some reasonable time after billing, e.g., five days or a week. After these time periods have passed, the payment is past due. In normal accounting practice, overdue payables are classified as 30-, 60-, and 90-day past due, and the accounting department routinely sends out "past-due" notices. Once an account is more than 90 days overdue, it becomes problematical and requires special action. In effect the buyer is now using the seller's money without compensation.

Debt collection, in another sense, may be the *main business* of a small enterprise; it may have been formed to collect money owed to others for a percentage of the debt owed. The small business, in yet another sense, may be the *subject* of debt collection activity, either because the business has been careless in paying bills or because the owner refuses to pay for a cause: perhaps the product shipped was deficient, etc.

INHERENT CONFLICTS OF INTEREST

A business expends considerable resources contacting, courting, pleasing, and servicing its clientele. Under normal circumstances, the overwhelming majority of customers pay reasonably promptly so that the payment pattern will have the shape of a bell curve: a few prepay or pay early, the majority pay on time, a few persistently pay late. The very few who fall beyond this pattern may do so because of unusual circumstances. Real "deadbeats" are difficult initially to identify. For this reason most businesses, small or large, treat persistent late-payers with much more courtesy than they deserve. Collecting receivables and paying payables are inherently in conflict. In many business-to-business situations, the customer may have a *policy* of paying late in order to show a better return on assets to its parent: it will be energetic in collecting, a laggard in paying. Debt collection, for this reason, is a difficult area of management for any business. The business, after all, *also* benefits from early collections and late payments. But if it is too aggressive collecting outstanding obligations, it may damage its standing with a valued customer.

ELEMENT OF A GOOD COLLECTION SYSTEM

Whatever its size, a business should pursue collections using a consciously formulated policy with well-defined triggering milestones for actions and an intelligent review process to protect the company's overall posture. Even in a business where the owner is simultaneously chief administrator, salesperson, and accountant, the collection policy should be capable of being written down under a few bullets. Long before collection begins, the company, of course, should have done its homework and established the customer's credit-worthiness. Effective collection systems 1) emphasize and highlight payment conditions in proposals and contracts, 2) kick in promptly, 3) have built-in flexibility and management review, 4) follow a systematic sequence of escalation, 5) are characterized by consistency and persistence, 6) match debtor's behavior to seller's behavior rationally, and 7) work toward definite closure within a preset timeframe.

Emphasis on Payment Where at all possible, the business should strive to highlight payment term in its proposals and contracts in such a manner that the buyer is aware of the seller's policies—and its *emphasis* on being paid promptly. Michelle Dunn, an expert and popular writer on the subject, for instance, advocates that businesses should strive for written payment agreements. Even if a business cannot prevail in getting a particular contract clause, *trying* to do so may be remembered and may be helpful later.

Timing Experts in the field agree that acting promptly on overdue obligations is of primary importance. Michael Giusti, writing for *New Orleans CityBusiness*, gave this issue a memorable formulation: "Debt collectors tell clients [that] overdue bills are not like fine wine—they only worsen with age." Citing Dave Duggins of the Duggins Law Firm in New Orleans, Giusti points out that "after an overdue account becomes 1 year old, the chances of collecting have all but evaporated." In a well-designed system, every overdue account will receive attention on a predefined trigger date; the action taken, however, may be governemed by additional considerations.

Flexible Review A sensible collection policy will recognize up front that knowledge of the customer is all-important both in selling and collecting. Therefore collection activity should be organized to pool information about a late- or non-paying client to discover early what the situation "over there" may be like. Action, including the initial action, should have inputs from all those involved with the debtor. This process may uncover problems which, once fixed, will cause prompt payment and thus avoid unnecessary spinning of wheels.

Reviewing the problem in some detail and then, if indicated, working with the delinquent client may provide the business unexpected opportunities. The client may be going through a temporary problem in which the company can help, perhaps merely through patience. The contact involved in working with the client may create new bonds that, later, will benefit the company. Such effort may also yield partial payments as the customer shows his or her good faith. Flexibility is thus very useful, all things equal. If the situation is hopeless, time can be saved. A rigid policy is never indicated unless the debt is too small to merit the effort required to turn corporate cartwheels in its resolution.

Systematic Sequence As already indicated, most debtors will have received past-due billings before collection activity even begins, and even such billings, highlighting the amount of time a bill is overdue, have a built-in feature of escalation. Similarly, collection effort should proceed in stages that give the debtor a certain benefit of the doubt initially. These stages may involve letters, then calls, and finally visits or—given other circumstances—precisely the reverse of this sequence. Which style of escalation is best will be well-known to the company.

A mature and businesslike approach is, of course, understood. Large outstanding obligations, especially those that significantly affect the seller, produce emotional situations in which, in unguarded moments, the management is inclined to threaten the deadbeat. If an action is threatened, it should have been considered carefully in advance. And management should be committed actually to follow through. If such commitment is lacking, silence is better.

Consistency and Persistence Throughout the collection process, the debtor should clearly understand, at every stage in the process, that the business intends to get paid in full and now. For this to be credible, the seller, of course, must promptly take whatever steps are necessary to deal with the legitimate problems of the debtor and then immediately press for payment. As Michelle Dunn puts it in the title of her most recent book, *Become the Squeaky Wheel*.

Matching the Debtor's Behavior The business intent on collecting its debt must be disciplined and consistent enough to match its own behavior to that of the reluctant client. In many situations of unequal power (large debtor, small company) the business, for instance, will continue work on a contract (a study, a landscaping job) even though a partial payment is long overdue. In situations of this sort, the business must stop working until it has been paid. This is often very painful to do. Similarly, the debtor should be refused any additional product until the matter of payment is settled. The conflict of interest between buyer and seller is here obvious and visible. All buyers would like to get something for nothing. The deep habit of pleasing the customer must sometimes be checked.

Closure Sometimes a debt cannot be collected short of a lawsuit. And in many cases, the amount may not be large enough to merit litigation. A good collection policy will anticipate such situations and describe, in advance, how closure will be handled. Writing off the debt or turning the account over to a collection agency may be the options; having the debt hanging around maybe a third—but holds little promise of return while simply being there as a reminder of failure.

USING THIRD PARTIES

Outside collection agencies or the services of an attorney are the usual venues for collecting the money without doing it in house. Key considerations in following either of these routes are the amount of the debt and its age. Collection agencies and attorneys generally take a percentage (usually one-third of the total amount) of the debt collected as payment for their services. Even with professional help, however, some debts will inevitably be impossible to collect due to bankruptcy, customers who move without notice ("skip"), or the high expense required to collect them. For more information on securing a professional collection agency, contact the Association of Credit and Collection Professionals, P.O. Box 390106, Minneapolis, MN 55439, (952) 926-6547 or http://www.acainternational.org/.

Whatever combination of collection methods a business eventually chooses, the owner needs to remain aware of the limitations that state and federal laws place on debt collection under the Fair Debt Collection and Practices Act—which governs collections from "natural persons," meaning individuals. For example, it is illegal to make continual phone calls, to use profane or threatening language, to threaten repossession when in fact the article cannot be repossessed, or to threaten to damage a customer's credit report or have their wages garnished. It is also illegal to discuss a customer's collection problem in public. In addition, businesses have to desist with collection efforts if the target declares bankruptcy. Given the thicket of legal issues that surround many aspects of collection, small business owners should consult an attorney before initiating aggressive approaches to collect on delinquent accounts.

ELECTRONIC BILL PRESENTMENT AND PAYMENT

Business analysts expect that in coming years, electronic bill presentment and payment (EBPP) will revolutionize

debt collection for large and small businesses alike. In the mid-2000s, electronic bill payment is still under slow development, in part because concerns over Internet security and privacy abound. But most experts believe that electronic bill collection systems will eventually become dominant. According to some EBPP vendors, conversion to such systems could reduce many business's billing costs by 50 to 75 percent once electronic bill payment becomes the norm for companies and individual consumers.

EBPP methodologies are, however, already in use to bill customers. Some businesses post bills on their home page. Others outsource the billing process to a consolidator who maintains its own page for posting electronic billings. Yet others secure the services of vendors who use e-mail to send bills directly to your customers. This method is favored by many; it is characterized by immediacy and convenience for the customer absent in the former options.

SEE ALSO *Credit Evaluation and Approval*

BIBLIOGRAPHY
Burtka, Allison Torres. "Man May Sue Over Billing Mistake That Damaged His Credit." *Trial.* August 2005.

Dunn, Michelle. *Become the Squeaky Wheel.* Never Dunn Publishing LLC, 1 June 2005.

Giusti, Michael. "Debt Collection Companies Advise Business Owners About Recovering Unpaid Accounts." *New Orleans CityBusiness.* 17 May 2004.

Hermann, Hans. "Analysis – Credit and Finance – Debt collection: too important to neglect." *Computer Reseller News.* 23 January 2006.

Lucas, Laurie A. and Alvin C. Harrell. "The Federal Fair Debt Collection Practices Act: 2004 review of appellate decisions." *Business Lawyer.* February 2005.

Palmeri, Christopher. "Debt Collection Puts On a Suit." *Business Week.* 14 November 2005.

Stern, Gary. "Digital Dunning." *CFO, the Magazine for Senior Financial Executives.* 15 April 2000.

"Taking Stock – An Ode to Debt." *Accountancy Age.* 30 June 2005.

Darnay, ECDI

DEBT FINANCING

A business can finance its operations either through equity or debt. *Equity* is cash paid into the business by investors; the business owner is usually one of these investors; investors receive a share of the company, in effect a percentage of it proportional to total investment paid in. The share or stock may appreciate in value in proportion to the increase in the business's net worth—or it may evaporate to nothing at all if the business fails. Investors put cash into a company in the hope of stock appreciation and the yield of dividends which the business may (but need not) pay to the investor; dividends are a portion of the net profits of the business; if the business does not realize a profit, it cannot pay a dividend. The investor can get his or her investment back only by selling the share to someone else. In a privately held company, investors have less "liquidity" because the shares are not traded on the open market and a purchaser may be difficult to find. This is one reason why successful and rapidly growing small businesses are under pressure by stockholders to "go public"—and thus to create an easy way for investors to cash out.

Debt financing, by contrast, is cash borrowed from a lender at a fixed rate of interest and with a predetermined maturity date. The principal must be paid back in full by the maturity date, but periodic repayments of principal may be part of the loan arrangement. Debt may take the form of a loan or the sale of bonds; the form itself does not change the principle of the transaction: the lender retains a right to the money lent and may demand it back under conditions specified in the borrowing arrangement.

Lending to a company is thus at least in theory more safe, but the amount the lender can realize in return is fixed to the principal and to the interest charged. Investment is more risky, but if the company is very successful, the upward potential for the investor may be very attractive; the downside is total loss of the investment.

DEBT/EQUITY RATIO

The character of a company's financing is expressed by its debt to equity ratio. Lenders like to see a low debt/equity ratio; it means that much more of the company's fortunes are based on investments, which in turn means that investors have a high level of confidence in the company. If the debt/equity ratio is high, it means that the business has borrowed a lot of money on a small base of investments. It is then said that the business is highly leveraged—which in turn means that lenders are more exposed to potential problems than investors. These relationships ultimately highlight a certain ambiguity in the relations between lenders and investors: their aims are in conflict but also in mutual support. Investors like to use a small investment and leverage it into a lot of activity by borrowing; lenders like to lend a small amount secured by a large investment. In usual business practice these motivations result in a negotiated equilibrium which shifts this way and that based on market forces and performance.

The U.S. Small Business Administration, on its Web page titled "Financing Basics," draws the following con-clusion for the small business: "The more money owners have invested in their business, the easier it is to attract [debt] financing. If your firm has a high ratio of equity to debt, you should probably seek debt financing. However, if your company has a high proportion of debt to equity, experts advise that you should increase your ownership capital (equity investment) for additional funds. That way you won't be over-leveraged to the point of jeopardizing your company's survival."

CASH FLOW TO DEBT RATIO

The cash flow of a company in relation to its debt serves lenders as another way to measure whether or not to provide debt financing to a business. A company's profitability, as measured on its books, may be better or worse than its cash generation. In calculating cash flow, only actual cash coming in and going out in a given period is used to calculate net cash available for servicing debt.

The sales of a company for a given period, for example, may be considerably higher than its cash receipts; the reason for this may simply be that the company's customers may paying late or may have favorable "stretched out" payment arrangements. Similarly, the costs of a company, as recorded on its books, may be lower than its actual cash payments in a period; the company, for instance, may be prepaying insurance for the next six months this month; it's books will only show one sixth of that payment as cost but six times as much going out as cash. For these reasons, a company may be profitable based on its books but may be short on cash at any given time. Lenders therefore like to look at the amount of cash available to service the current portions of any new debt. If this amount is minimally 1.25 times the debt service required, the business is at least in the ballpark to receive a loan. The higher this ratio, the more inclined the lender will be to lend.

Rules of thumb along these lines are subject to adjustment based on the availability of money. As Daniel Rome Levine pointed out early in 2006, commenting on the money market in Chicago, writing for *Crain's Chicago Business,* "[S]ince the 2001 recession, many entrepreneurs have learned to do more with fewer resources and pared down their debt." Interest rates were low and banks were loosening their terms. "These days," Levine wrote, "[banks] are going as low as 1.1 times debt for companies with strong balance sheets." A tightening of money and less favorable small business profiles will once more push the ratio up.

SOURCES OF DEBT FINANCING

Small businesses can obtain debt financing from a number of different sources. Private sources of debt financing include friends and relatives, banks, credit unions, consumer finance companies, commercial finance companies, trade credit, insurance companies, factor companies, and leasing companies. Public sources of debt financing include a number of loan programs provided by the state and federal governments to support small businesses.

Private Sources Many entrepreneurs begin their enterprises by borrowing money from friends and relatives. Such individuals are more likely to provide flexible terms of repayment than banks or other lenders and may be more willing to invest in an unproven business idea, based upon their personal knowledge and relationship with the entrepreneur. A potential disadvantage is that friends and relatives may try to become involved in the management of the business. Business owners who wish to avoid such complications must use the same formal arrangements with relatives and friends as with more distant business associates.

Banks are the most obvious sources of borrowed funds. Commercial banks usually have more experience in making business loans than do regular savings banks. Credit unions are another common source of business loans; these financial institutions are intended to aid the members of a group—such as employees of a company or members of a labor union—they often provide funds more readily and under more favorable terms than banks. However, the size of the loan available may be relatively small.

Finance companies generally charge higher interest rates than banks and credit unions. Most loans obtained through finance companies are secured by a specific asset as collateral—and the lender can seize the asset if the small business defaults on the loan. Consumer finance companies make small loans against personal assets and provide an option for individuals with poor credit ratings. Commercial finance companies provide small businesses with loans for inventory and equipment purchases and are a good resource for manufacturing enterprises. Insurance companies often make commercial loans as a way of reinvesting their income. They usually provide payment terms and interest rates comparable to a commercial bank but require a business to have more assets available as collateral.

Trade credit is another common form of debt financing. Whenever a supplier allows a small business to delay payment on the products or services it purchases, the small business has obtained trade credit from that supplier. Trade credit is readily available to most small businesses, if not immediately then certainly after a few orders. But the payment terms may differ between suppliers. A small business's customers may also be interested in offering a form of trade credit—for example, by

paying in advance for delivery of products they will need on a future date—in order to establish a good relationship with a new supplier.

Factor companies help small businesses to free up cash on a timely basis by purchasing their accounts receivable. Rather than waiting for customers to pay invoices, the small business can receive payment for sales immediately. Factor companies can either provide recourse financing, in which the small business is ultimately responsible if its customers do not pay, and nonrecourse financing, in which the factor company bears that risk. Although factor companies can be a useful source of funds for existing businesses, they are not an option for startups that do not have accounts receivable. Leasing companies can also help small businesses to free up cash by renting various types of equipment instead of making large capital expenditures to purchase it. Equipment leases usually involve only a small monthly payment, plus they may enable a small business to upgrade its equipment quickly and easily.

Entrepreneurs and owners of startup businesses must almost always resort to personal debt in order to fund their enterprises. Some entrepreneurs choose to arrange their initial investment in the business as a loan, with a specific repayment period and interest rate. The entrepreneur then uses the proceeds of the business to repay himself or herself over time. Other small business owners borrow the cash value of their personal life insurance policies to provide funds for their business. These funds are usually available at a relatively low interest rate. Still others borrow money against the equity in their personal residences to cover business expenses. Mortgage loans can be risky: the home is used as collateral. Finally, some fledgling business people use personal credit cards fund their businesses. Credit card companies charge high interest rates, which increases the risk of piling up additional debt, but they can make cash available quickly.

Public Sources The state and federal governments sponsor a wide variety of programs that provide funding to promote the formation and growth of small businesses. Many of these programs are handled by the U.S. Small Business Administration (SBA) and involve debt financing. The SBA helps small businesses obtain funds from banks and other lenders by guaranteeing loans up to $750,000, to a maximum of 70-90 percent of the loan value, for only 2.75 percentage points above the prime lending rate. In order to qualify for an SBA guaranteed loan, an entrepreneur must first be turned down for a loan through regular channels. He or she must also demonstrate good character and a reasonable ability to run a successful business and repay a loan. SBA guaranteed loan funds can be used for business expansion or for purchases of inventory, equipment, and real estate. In addition to guaranteeing loans provided by other lenders, the SBA also offers direct loans of up to $150,000, as well as seasonal loans, handicapped assistance loans, disaster loans, and pollution control financing.

Small Business Investment Companies (SBICs) are government-backed firms that make direct loans or equity investments in small businesses. SBICs tend to be less risk-averse than banks, so funds are more likely to be available for startup companies. Another advantage is that SBICs are often able to provide technical assistance to small business borrowers. The Economic Development Commission (EDC), a branch of the U.S. Department of Commerce, makes loans to small businesses that provide jobs in economically disadvantaged regions. Small businesses hoping to qualify for EDC loans must meet a number of conditions.

SEE ALSO *Capital Structure; Equity Financing*

BIBLIOGRAPHY
Brown, Carolyn M. "Borrowing From Dad: Financing from relatives and friends has risks and rewards." *Black Enterprise.* January 2005.

Burk, James E. and Richard P. Lehmann. *Financing Your Small Business.* Sphinx Publishing, 2004.

Condon, Bernard. "Junk Gets Junkier." *Forbes.* 17 October 2005.

Even-Zohar, Chaim. "Credit Is Not Forever . . . " *Diamond Intelligence Briefs.* 8 June 2005.

Garcia, Shelly. "Financing Loosens Up While New Banks Proliferate in Area." *San Fernando Valley Business Journal.* 2 January 2006.

Hibbard, Justin. "Bring On The Battered Debt; Wilbur Ross and other investors are betting on a wave of bankruptcies." *Business Week.* 12 September 2005.

Levine, Daniel Rome. "Who Says Beggars Can't Be Choosers? Shopping around." *Crain's Chicago Business.* 10 October 2005.

Marshall, Jeffrey. "Inside A Steel Deal: A new, state-of-the-art mill is starting to rise in Mississippi. A look at the complex financing behind it." *Financial Executive.* December 2005.

Nakamura, Galen. "Choosing Debt or Equity Financing." *Hawaii Business.* December 2005.

Sherefkin, Robert. "Ross on Running Up Debt: Forget it." *Automotive News.* 19 December 2005.

U.S. Small Business Administration. "Financing Basics." Available from http://www.sba.gov/starting_business/financing/basics.html. Retrieved on 6 February 2006.

Hillstrom, Northern Lights
updated by Magee, ECDI

DECISION MAKING

Decision making is a vital component of small business success. Decisions based on a foundation of knowledge and sound reasoning can lead the company into long-term prosperity; conversely, decisions made on the basis of flawed logic, emotionalism, or incomplete information can quickly put a small business out of commission (indeed, bad decisions can cripple even big, capital-rich corporations over time). All businesspeople recognize the painful necessity of choice. Furthermore, making these choices must be done in a timely fashion, for as most people recognize, indecision is in essence a choice in and of itself—a choice to take no action. Ultimately, what drives business success is the quality of decisions and their implementation. Good decisions mean good business.

The concept of decision making has a long history; choosing among alternatives has always been a part of life. But sustained research attention to business decision making has developed only in recent years. Contemporary advances in the field include progress in such elements of decision making as the problem context; the processes of problem finding, problem solving, and legitimation; and procedural and technical aids.

THE ELEMENTS OF DECISION MAKING

The Problem Context All decisions are about problems, and problems shape context at three levels. The *macrocontext* draws attention to global issues (exchange rates, for example), national concerns (the cultural orientations toward decision processes of different countries), and provincial and state laws and cultures within nations. The *mesocontext* attends to organizational cultures and structure. The *microcontext* addresses the immediate decision environment—the organization's employees, board, or office.

Decision processes differ from company to company. But all companies need to take these three context levels into consideration when a decision needs to be made. Fortunately, economical ways to obtain this information are available and keep the cost of preparing for decisions from becoming prohibitive.

Problem Finding and Agenda Setting An important difficulty in decision making is failure to act until one is too close to the decision point—when information and options are greatly limited. Organizations usually work in a "reactive" mode. Problems are "found" only after the issue has begun to have a negative impact on the business. Nevertheless, processes of environmental scanning and strategic planning are designed to perform problem reconnaissance to alert business people to problems that will need attention down the line. Proactivity can be a great strength in decision making, but it requires a decision intelligence process that is absent from many organizations.

Moreover, problem identification is of limited use if the business is slow to heed or resolve the issue. Once a problem has been identified, information is needed about the exact nature of the problem and potential actions that can be taken to rectify it. Unfortunately, small business owners and other key decision makers too often rely on information sources that "edit" the data—either intentionally or unintentionally—in misleading fashion. Information from business managers and other employees, vendors, and customers alike has to be regarded with a discerning eye, then.

Another kind of information gathering reflects the array and priority of solution preferences. What is selected as possible or not possible, acceptable or unacceptable, negotiable or non-negotiable depends upon the culture of the firm itself and its environment. A third area of information gathering involves determining the possible scope and impact that the problem and its consequent decision might have. Knowledge about impact may alter the decision preferences. To some extent, knowledge about scope dictates who will need to be involved in the decision process.

PROBLEM SOLVING

Problem solving—also sometimes referred to as problem management—can be divided into two parts—process and decision. The process of problem solving is predicated on the existence of a system designed to address issues as they crop up. In many organizations, there does not seem to be any system. In such businesses, owners, executives, and managers are apparently content to operate with an ultimately fatalistic philosophy—what happens, happens. Business experts contend that such an attitude is simply unacceptable, especially for smaller businesses that wish to expand, let alone survive. The second part of the problem management equation is the decision, or choice, itself. Several sets of elements need to be considered in looking at the decision process. One set refers to the rationales used for decisions. Others emphasize the setting, the scope and level of the decision, and the use of procedural and technical aids.

Rationales Organizational decision makers have adopted a variety of styles in their decision making processes. For example, some business leaders embrace processes wherein every conceivable response to an issue is examined before settling on a final response, while others adopt more flexible philosophies. The legitimacy of each style varies in accordance with individual business real-

ities in such realms as market competitiveness, business owner personality, acuteness of the problem, etc.

Settings Certainly, some entrepreneurs/owners make business decisions without a significant amount of input or feedback from others. Home-based business owners without any employees, for example, are likely to take a far different approach to problem-solving than will business owners who have dozens of employees and/or several distinct internal departments. The latter owners will be much more likely to include findings of meetings, task forces, and other information gathering efforts in their decision making process. Of course, even a business owner who has no partners or employees may find it useful to seek information from outside sources (accountants, fellow businesspeople, attorneys, etc.) before making important business decisions. "Since the owner makes all the key decisions for the small business, he or she is responsible for its success or failure," wrote David Karlson in *Avoiding Mistakes in Your Small Business*. "Marketing and finance are two of several areas in which small business owners frequently lack sufficient experience, since they previously worked as specialists for other people before they started their own businesses. As a result, they generally do not have the experience needed to make well-informed decisions in the areas with which they are unfamiliar. The demands of running and growing a small business will soon expose any Achilles heel in a president/owner. It is best to find out your weaknesses early, so you can develop expertise or get help in these areas."

Scope and Level Finally, attention must be paid to problem scope and organizational level. Problems of large scope need to be dealt with by top levels of the organization. Similarly, problems of smaller scope can be handled by lower levels of the organization. This is a failing of many organizations, large and small. Typically, top level groups spend much too much time deciding low-level, low-impact problems, while issues of high importance and organizational impact linger on without being addressed or resolved.

Procedural and Technical Aids In recent years, a number of procedural and technical aids have been developed to help business managers in their decision making processes. Most of these have taken the form of software programs that guide individuals or groups through the various elements of the decision making process in a wide variety of operational areas (budgeting, marketing, inventory control, etc.). Leadership seminars and management training offer guidance in the decision making process as well.

Outcome Whatever decision making process is utilized, those involved in making the decision need to make sure that a response has actually been arrived at. All too often, meetings and other efforts to resolve outstanding business issues adjourn under an atmosphere of uncertainty. Participants in decision making meetings are sometimes unsure about various facets of the decision arrived at. Some meeting participants, for example, may leave a meeting still unsure about how the agreed-upon response to a problem is going to be implemented, while others may not even be sure what the agreed-upon response is. Indeed, business researchers indicate that on many occasions, meeting participants depart with fundamentally different understandings of what took place. It is up to the small business owner to make sure that all participants in the decision making process fully understand all aspects of the final decision.

Implementation The final step in the decision making process is the implementation of the decision. This is an extremely important element of decision making; after all, the benefits associated with even the most intelligent decision can be severely compromised if implementation is slow or flawed.

FACTORS IN POOR DECISION MAKING

Several factors in flawed decision making are commonly cited by business experts, including the following: limited organizational capacity; limited information; the costliness of analysis; interdependencies between fact and value; the openness of the system(s) to be analyzed; and the diversity of forms on which business decisions actually arise. Moreover, time constraints, personal distractions, low levels of decision making skill, conflict over business goals, and interpersonal factors can also have a deleterious impact on the decision making capacities of a small (or large) business.

A second category of difficulties is captured in a number of common pitfalls of the decision procedure. One such pitfall is "decision avoidance psychosis," which occurs when organizations put off making decisions that need to be made until the very last minute. A second problem is decision randomness. This process was outlined in the famous paper called "A Garbage Can Model of Organizational Choice" by Cohen, March and Olsen. They argued that organizations have four roles or vectors within them: problem knowers (people who know the difficulties the organization faces): solution providers (people who can provide solutions but do not know the problems); resource controllers (people who do not know problems and do not have solutions but control the allocation of people and money in the organization)

and a group of "decision makers looking for work" (or decision opportunities). For effective decision making, all these elements must be in the same room at the same time. In reality, most organizations combine them at random, as if tossing them into a garbage can.

Decision drift is another malady that can strike at a business with potentially crippling results. This term, also sometimes known as the Abilene Paradox in recognition of a famous model of this behavior, refers to group actions that take place under the impression that the action is the will of the majority, when in reality, there never really was a decision to take that action.

Decision coercion, also known as groupthink, is another very well known decision problem. In this flawed decision making process, decisions are actually coerced by figures in power. This phenomenon can most commonly be seen in instances where a business owner or top executive creates an atmosphere where objections or concerns about a decision favored by the owner/executive are muted because of fears about owner/executive reaction.

IMPROVING DECISION MAKING

Business consultants and experts agree that small business owners and managers can take several basic steps to improve the decision making process at their establishments.

Improve the setting. Organizing better meetings (focused agenda, clear questions, current and detailed information, necessary personnel) can be a very helpful step in effective decision making. Avoid the garbage can; get the relevant people in the same room at the same time. Pay attention to planning and seek closure.

Use Logical Techniques. Decision making is a simple process when approached in a logical and purposeful manner. Small businesses that are able to perceive the problem, gather and present data, intelligently discuss the data, and implement the decision without succumbing to emotionalism are apt to make good ones that will launch the firm on a prosperous course.

Evaluate decisions and decision making patterns. Evaluation tends to focus the attention, and make individuals and teams more sensitive to what they are actually doing in their decision making tasks. Evaluation is especially helpful in today's business environment because of the interdependency of individuals and departments in executing tasks and addressing goals.

Determine appropriate levels of decision making. Business enterprises need to make sure that operational decisions are being made at the right level. Keys to avoiding micromanagement and other decision making pitfalls include: giving problems their proper level of importance and context; addressing problems in an appropriate time frame; and establishing and shifting decision criteria in accordance with business goals.

BIBLIOGRAPHY

Burke, Lisa A., and Monica K. Miller. "Taking the Mystery Out of Intuitive Decision Making." *Academy of Management Executive.* November 1999.

Cohen, M. James, G. March, and J. Olsen. "A Garbage Can Model of Organizational Choice." *Administrative Science Quarterly.* March 1972.

Graham, John R. "Avoiding Dumb and Dumber Business Decisions: Why Even the Experts Make Mistakes." *American Salesman.* April 1997.

Gunn, Bob. "Decisions, Decisions." *Strategic Finance.* January 2000.

Karlson, David. *Avoiding Mistakes in Your Small Business.* Crisp, 1994.

Magasin, Michael, and Frieda L. Gehlen. "Unwise Decisions and Unanticipated Consequences." *Sloan Management Review.* Fall 1999.

Roe, Amy. "One of the Most Ticklish Jobs is Decision Making." *The Business Journal.* 2 June 1997.

Selin, Cynthia. "Trust and The Illusive Force of Scenarios." *Futures.* February 2006.

Hillstrom, Northern Lights
updated by Darnay, ECDI

DECISION SUPPORT SYSTEMS

Broadly speaking, decision support systems are a set of manual or computer-based tools that assist in some decision-making activity. In today's business environment, however, decision support systems (DSS) are commonly understood to be computerized management information systems designed to help business owners, executives, and managers resolve complicated business problems and/or questions. Good decision support systems can help business people perform a wide variety of functions, including cash flow analysis, concept ranking, multistage forecasting, product performance improvement, and resource allocation analysis. Previously regarded as primarily a tool for big companies, DSS has in recent years come to be recognized as a potentially valuable tool for small business enterprises as well.

THE STRUCTURE OF DECISIONS

In order to discuss the support of decisions and what DSS tools can or should do, it is necessary to have a perspective on the nature of the decision process and the various requirements of supporting it. One way of looking at a decision is in terms of its key components. The first component is the data collected by a decision maker to be used in making the decision. The second is the process selected by the decision maker to combine this

data. Finally, there is an evaluation or learning component that compares decisions and examines them to see if there is a need to change either the data being used or the process that combines the data. These components of a decision interact with the characteristics of the decision being made.

Structured Decisions Many analysts categorize decisions according to the degree of structure involved in the decision-making activity. Business analysts describe a structured decision as one in which all three components of a decision—the data, process, and evaluation—are determined. Since structured decisions are made on a regular basis in business environments, it makes sense to place a comparatively rigid framework around the decision and the people making it.

Structured decision support systems may simply use a checklist or form to ensure that all necessary data are collected and that the decision making process is not skewed by the absence of data. If the choice is also to support the procedural or process component of the decision, then it is quite possible to develop a program either as part of the checklist or form. In fact, it is also possible and desirable to develop computer programs that collect and combine the data, thus giving the process a high degree of consistency or structure. When there is a desire to make a decision more structured, the support system for that decision is designed to ensure consistency. Many firms that hire individuals without a great deal of experience provide them with detailed guidelines on their decision making activities and support them by giving them little flexibility. One interesting consequence of making a decision more structured is that the liability for inappropriate decisions is shifted from individual decision makers to the larger company or organization.

Unstructured Decisions At the other end of the continuum are unstructured decisions. While these have the same components as structured ones—data, process, and evaluation—there is little agreement on their nature. With unstructured decisions, for example, each decision maker may use different data and processes to reach a conclusion. In addition, because of the nature of the decision there may only a limited number of people within the organization qualified to evaluate the decision.

Generally, unstructured decisions are made in instances in which all elements of the business environment—customer expectations, competitor response, cost of securing raw materials, etc.—are not completely understood (new product and marketing strategy decisions commonly fit into this category). Unstructured decision systems typically focus on the individual who or the team that will make the decision. These decision makers are usually entrusted with decisions that are unstructured because of their experience or expertise; it is their individual ability that is of value. One approach to support systems in this area is to construct a program that simulates the process used by a particular individual. In essence, these systems—commonly referred to as "expert systems"—prompt the user with a series of questions regarding a decision situation. "Once the expert system has sufficient information about the decision scenario, it uses an inference engine which draws upon a data base of expertise in this decision area to provide the manager with the best possible alternative for the problem," explained Jatinder N. D. Gupta and Thomas M. Harris in the *Journal of Systems Management.* "The purported advantage of this decision aid is that it allows the manager the use of the collective knowledge of experts in this decision realm. Some of the current DSS applications have included long-range and strategic planning policy setting, new product planning, market planning, cash flow management, operational planning and budgeting, and portfolio management."

Another approach is to monitor and document the process used so that the decision maker(s) can readily review what has already been examined and concluded. An even more novel approach used is to provide environments specially designed to give these decision makers an atmosphere conducive to their particular tastes. The key to support of unstructured decisions is to understand the role that individuals experience or expertise plays in the decision and to allow for individual approaches.

Semi-Structured Decisions In the middle of the continuum are semi-structured decisions—where most of what are considered to be true decision support systems are focused. Decisions of this type are characterized as having some agreement on the data, process, and/or evaluation to be used, but are also typified by efforts to retain some level of human judgment in the decision making process. An initial step in analyzing which support system is required is to understand where the limitations of the decision maker may be manifested (i.e., the data acquisition portion, the process component, or the evaluation of outcomes).

Grappling with the latter two types of decisions—unstructured and semi-structured—can be particularly problematic for small businesses, which often have limited technological or work force resources. As Gupta and Harris indicated, "many decision situations faced by executives in small business are one-of-a-kind, one-shot occurrences requiring specifically tailored solution approaches without the benefit of any previously available rules or procedures. This unstructured or semi-structured nature of these decisions situations aggravates the

problem of limited resources and staff expertise available to a small business executive to analyze important decisions appropriately. Faced with this difficulty, an executive in a small business must seek tools and techniques that do not demand too much of his time and resources and are useful to make his life easier." Subsequently, small businesses have increasingly turned to DSS to provide them with assistance in business guidance and management.

KEY DSS FUNCTIONS

Gupta and Harris observed that DSS is predicated on the effective performance of three functions: information management, data quantification, and model manipulation. "Information management refers to the storage, retrieval, and reporting of information in a structured format convenient to the user. Data quantification is the process by which large amounts of information are condensed and analytically manipulated into a few core indicators that extract the essence of data. Model manipulation refers to the construction and resolution of various scenarios to answer 'what if' questions. It includes the processes of model formulation, alternatives generation and solution of the proposed models, often through the use of several operations research/management science approaches."

Entrepreneurs and owners of established enterprises are urged to make certain that their business needs a DSS before buying the various computer systems and software necessary to create one. Some small businesses, of course, have no need of a DSS. The owner of a car washing establishment, for instance, would be highly unlikely to make such an investment. But for those business owners who are guiding a complex operation, a decision support system can be a valuable tool. Another key consideration is whether the business's key personnel will ensure that the necessary time and effort is spent to incorporate DSS into the establishment's operations. After all, even the best decision support system is of little use if the business does not possess the training and knowledge necessary to use it effectively. If, after careful study of questions of DSS utility, the small business owner decides that DSS can help his or her company, the necessary investment can be made, and the key managers of the business can begin the process of developing their own DSS applications using available spreadsheet software.

DSS UNCERTAINTIES AND LIMITATIONS

While decision support systems have been embraced by small business operators in a wide range of industries in recent years, entrepreneurs, programmers, and business consultants all agree that such systems are not perfect.

Level of "User-Friendliness" Some observers contend that although decision support systems have become much more user-friendly in recent years, it remains an issue, especially for small business operations that do not have significant resources in terms of technological knowledge.

Hard-to-Quantify Factors Another limitation that decision makers confront has to do with combining or processing the information that they obtain. In many cases these limitations are due to the number of mathematical calculations required. For instance, a manufacturer pondering the introduction of a new product can not do so without first deciding on a price for the product. In order to make this decision, the effect of different variables (including price) on demand for the product and the subsequent profit must be evaluated. The manufacturer's perceptions of the demand for the product can be captured in a mathematical formula that portrays the relationship between profit, price, and other variables considered important. Once the relationships have been expressed, the decision maker may now want to change the values for different variables and see what the effect on profits would be. The ability to save mathematical relationships and then obtain results for different values is a feature of many decision support systems. This is called "what-if" analysis, and today's spreadsheet software packages are fully equipped to support this decision-making activity. Of course, additional factors must be taken into consideration as well when making business decisions. Hard-to-quantify factors such as future interest rates, new legislation, and hunches about product shelf life may all be considered. So even though the calculations may indicate that a certain demand for the product will be achieved at a certain price, the decision maker must use his or her judgment in making the final decision.

If the decision maker simply follows the output of a process model, then the decision is being moved toward the structured end of the continuum. In certain corporate environments, it may be easier for the decision maker to follow the prescriptions of the DSS; users of support systems are usually aware of the risks associated with certain choices. If decision makers feel that there is more risk associated with exercising judgment and opposing the suggestion of the DSS than there is in simply supporting the process, the DSS is moving the decision more toward the structured end of the spectrum. Therefore, the way in which a DSS will be used must be considered within the decision-making environment.

Processing Model Limitations Another problem with the use of support systems that perform calculations is that the user/decision maker may not be fully aware of the limitations or assumptions of the particular processing model. There may be instances in which the decision maker has an idea of the knowledge that is desired, but not necessarily the best way to get that knowledge. This problem may be seen in the use of statistical analysis to support a decision. Most statistical packages provide a variety of tests and will perform them on whatever data is presented, regardless of whether or not it is appropriate. This problem has been recognized by designers of support systems and has resulted in the development of DSS that support the choice of the type of analysis.

BIBLIOGRAPHY

Carlson, John R., Dawn S. Carlson, and Lori L. Wadsworth. "On the Relationship Between DSS Design Characteristics and Ethical Decision Making." *Journal of Managerial Issues.* Summer 1999.

Chaudhry, Sohail S., Linda Salchenberger, and Mahdi Beheshtian. "A Small Business Inventory DSS: Design, Development, and Implementation Issues." *Computers & Operations Research.* January 1996.

Gupta, Jatinder N. D., and Thomas M. Harris. "Decision Support Systems for Small Business." *Journal of Systems Management.* February 1989.

Kimball, Ralph, and Kevin Strahlo. "Why Decision Support Fails and How to Fix It." *Datamation.* 1 June 1994.

Kumar, Ram L. "Understanding DSS Value." *Omega.* June 1999.

Laudon, Kenneth C., and Jane Price Laudon. *Management Information Systems: A Contemporary Perspective.* Macmillan, 1991.

Muller-Boling, Detlef, and Susanne Kirchhoff. "Expert Systems for Decision Support in Business Start-Ups." *Journal of Small Business Management.* April 1991.

Parkinson, Chris. "What If? Decision Shaping Systems." *CMA— The Management Accounting Magazine.* March 1995.

Raggad, Bel G. "Decision Support System: Use It or Skip It." *Industrial Management and Data Systems.* January 1997.

Raymond, Louis, and Francois Bergeron. "Personal DSS Success in Small Enterprises." *Information and Management.* May 1992.

Hillstrom, Northern Lights
updated by Magee, ECDI

DELEGATION

Delegation is the practice of turning over work-related tasks and/or authority to employees or subordinates. Small business owners often have difficulty with delegation for a variety of reasons, from concerns about the abilities of subordinates to long-standing "hands-on" management habits (a common characteristic of successful entrepreneurs). Indeed, "businesses founded on the creative talents of the owner often struggle with [delegation] because the success of the enterprise depends on the owner's style," wrote Linda Formichelli in *Nation's Business*. But small business consultants warn that owners who do not learn to delegate responsibilities and tasks often end up stunting their company's growth.

The Need for Effective Delegation Practices "Many managers think of delegation as a task—an activity to be carried out and forgotten. In reality, delegation is a process that makes up a critical component of successful management," wrote Janet Houser Carter in *Supervisory Management*. "To get work done with and through others, a manager must regularly give authority to his or her staffers. This shows staffers that the manager has faith in their abilities—which is what makes delegation such a powerful motivational tool."

A propensity for micromanagement—or nanomanagement, as it is sometimes called when applied to a small business firm—can have a deleterious impact on a company in a variety of ways. Moreover, many analysts contend that a lack of delegation can be particularly detrimental to the fortunes of smaller businesses. "In small, entrepreneurial companies, micromanagement by one person—typically the owner—can be especially growth-inhibiting because it can have a proportionately larger sweep through the firm than micro-management by one executive in a large company," wrote Formichelli. Business consultants thus counsel their clients to practice sensible delegation of tasks to their employees—even in instances where they might not do as good a job initially. "Employees can't learn unfamiliar tasks if they never get the chance to learn and practice them," noted Carter. "In the short term, it may make sense to do it yourself; over the long term, however, you save more time by showing others how to do the job."

Of course, not all tasks or responsibilities should be delegated to employees. Small business owners need to take care of basic strategic and planning issues themselves, and other management duties—conflict resolution, performance evaluations, etc.—should be delegated judiciously.

Business experts cite a number of specific problems that are often associated with companies that do not effectively delegate. These include:

- Poor employee morale—An inability or refusal to delegate can have a corrosive impact on the morale of good employees that want to contribute their talents to the business in a meaningful way. "Delegating work to subordinates helps to develop them for their own career advancement as well as improve their management skills," wrote W.H. Weiss in *Supervision*.

- Burnout—Even the most talented, ambitious, and energetic entrepreneurs are apt to run out of gas if they insist on tackling all major aspects of a company's operation. Some small business owners can manage all or most important tasks for the early life of a company. Indeed, some small businesses—especially single-person enterprises like freelance graphics design or editorial services—may be able to handle all significant aspects of a company's operation for years on end. But for the vast majority of small and mid-sized businesses enjoying a measure of growth, owners sooner or later must face the reality that they cannot undertake all duties and responsibilities.

- Misallocation of Personal Resources—Small business owners and entrepreneurs who do not delegate often run the risk of using too much of their time on routine tasks and not enough time on vital aspects of the company's future, such as strategic planning, long-range budgeting, and marketing campaigns.

- Damage to Company Image—Business owners who do not empower their employees, insisting instead on attending to all relevant aspects of his or her business themselves, run the risk of inadvertently suggesting to customers and vendors that the company's workforce is not competent and/or trustworthy.

- Damage to Company Health—This should be the bottom-line consideration of all entrepreneurs running their own business. If micromanagement is slowing processing of work orders, hindering development of new marketing efforts, or otherwise causing bottlenecks in any areas of a company's operation, then it may be eating away at the company's fundamental financial well-being.

Small business owners are encouraged to evaluate whether they are perhaps falling into the trap of micromanagement. Consultants and entrepreneurs cite the following as major warning signs:

- Taking work home in the evening or working long hours of overtime

- Failure to give important tasks the amount of attention that they warrant

- Basic company documents (like business plans) are not updated for long periods

- Excessive amounts of time spent going over work already completed by employees

- Completing important tasks with little time to spare (or a day or two late)

- Spending inordinate amounts of time on relatively unimportant or routine jobs

- Vacations assume mythic status

- Unhappy employees

- Unhappy family members

Keys to Effective Delegation Effective delegation is ultimately predicated on ensuring that the company's workforce is sufficiently talented and motivated to take on the responsibilities that are delegated to them. "New entrepreneurs often have difficulty figuring out what kind of workers to hire," remarked Formichelli. "If the wrong people are hired, they require more training and supervision, which invites nanomanagement." Sound hiring practices and adequate training are thus universally regarded as major factors in establishing a healthy system of delegation. Once those aspects have been addressed, there are other considerations that can be studied as well. These include:

- Work Environment—Establish a positive work environment where employees are not paralyzed by fear of failure or dismissive of tasks that they think is beneath them. Owners and managers need to emphasize tools of motivation and communication to nourish employee enthusiasm.

- Plan for Delegation—A company that is armed with a strong, clear vision of its future—and the role that its employees will play in that future—is far more likely to be successful than the business that does not plan ahead.

- Review Responsibilities—Business owners and managers need to objectively examine which tasks that they have previously taken care of can be delegated to others. "Reserve for yourself those tasks which require the experience, skill, and training which only you possess," wrote W.H. Weiss in the *Supervisor's Standard Reference Handbook.*

- Selection of Appropriate Employees for New Responsibilities—As every personnel manager knows, some members of the work force are better suited to take on new responsibilities than others. When reviewing potential candidates to take on additional responsibilities, business owners should consider level of employee motivation and ambition, skill sets, level of allegiance to the company, and emotional maturity.

- Established Policies—Detailed manuals of policies and procedures can go far toward eliminating the uncertainties that hamstring some delegation efforts.

- Prepare for Bumps in the Road—Even the best-planned delegation efforts can go awry, leading to short-term productivity/profitability losses. Indeed, risk is an inherent element of the delegation process, and some errors or misjudgments may occur as workers adjust to their new responsibilities. "Employees need to be reassured that the manager will be there to offer assistance or clarification, and that mistakes during the learning period are to be expected," said Carter. "Mistakes should be viewed as opportunities to teach, not punish."

- Training—Delegation of tasks and responsibilities is far more likely to be successful if the employees have the knowledge necessary to fulfill their new duties. "The fact that no one has the skills to complete a task you are handling doesn't mean you should avoid delegation—it means you should train," wrote Alice Bredin in *Los Angeles Business Journal.* "While building the skills of an employee requires an investment of time, that investment will pay off."

- Communication—"Be clear and concise when delegating," said Weiss. "Right from the beginning you must clarify what decisions you are delegating and what you are reserving for yourself. Delegating fails when the person to whom you have delegated a task fails to perform it or makes a decision beyond the scope of authority granted." Conversely, delegation can also fail if the business owner hands off a responsibility, but does not give his or her employee the necessary level of authority to execute that responsibility. "If you overlook this, you may cause the person delegated to suffer frustration and stress because he or she was given an assignment yet not given the authority and power needed to accomplish it properly," wrote Weiss in *Supervision.*

- Provide advisory role—Small business owners should make sure that they keep lines of communication open at all times after delegating responsibilities. Employee questions and uncertainties about their new responsibilities are perfectly natural, so owners should make themselves available for questions and maintain a nonjudgmental, helpful stance.

Ultimately, small business owners need to recognize that delegation can help a business grow and prosper, and that good employees, when used intelligently, can be a significant advantage in the marketplace. "The manager who wants to learn to delegate more should remember this distinction," wrote Thomas S. Bateman and Carl P. Zeithaml in *Management: Function and Strategy.* "If you are not delegating, you are merely doing things; the more you delegate, the more you are truly *building* and *managing* an organization."

SEE ALSO *Span of Control*

BIBLIOGRAPHY

Bateman, Thomas S., and Carl P. Zeithaml. *Management: Function and Strategy.* Irwin, 1990.

Bredin, Alice. "Delegating Tasks Can Free Up Time to Pursue Growth." *Los Angeles Business Journal.* 20 November 2000.

Carter, Janet Houser. "Minimizing the Risks from Delegation." *Supervisory Management.* February 1993.

Formichelli, Linda. "Letting Go of the Details." *Nation's Business.* November 1997.

Kelly, Kevin. "Sharing the Load: Sure, I Needed to Delegate More. But I Had to Learn How Far I Could Go." *Fortune.* 28 November 2005.

Pollock, Ted. "Delegation." *Supervision.* August 2005.

Weiss, W.H. "The Art and Skill of Delegating." *Supervision.* September 2000.

Hillstrom, Northern Lights
updated by Darnay, ECDI

DELIVERY SERVICES

The U.S. Postal Service was established by the Continental Congress in America on July 26, 1775—thus before the U.S. had had its official start. The first Postmaster General was Benjamin Franklin. The USPS has had a colorful history since, delivering mail and packages by steamboat, railroad, pony express, and air. In 2005 the service carried 98.1 billion pieces of mail and 1.2 billion packages. Throughout our history, it has been and remains the largest delivery service. Private delivery services of limited geographical coverage have always existed side by side with postal service from early times as well. Today's largest private carrier, United Parcel Service (UPS) began in Seattle as American Messenger Service, founded by 19-year old James E. Casey on a borrowed $100. Casey had worked for other delivery services before. The company underwent several name changes before it became UPS. In 2005, the company delivered 3.75 billion packages, more than three times the volume carried by the U.S. Post Office.

More recent major entrants into the delivery business were Federal Express and DHL, both originating in the late 1960s and early 1970s. DHL was founded in 1969 by Adrian *D*alsey, Larry *H*illblom, and Robert *L*ynn. DHL began in international carriage of bills of lading. FedEx began with a term paper written by Frederick W. Smith in 1965. Smith became the founder of FedEx, incorporating the company in 1971 and launching operations in 1973. Smith's critique of air-freight shippers was that they were piggybacking on passenger routes; he saw a better solution: company-operated major air hubs based on traffic volume. Both DHL and FedEx expanded both by providing competitive services and by acquiring smaller organizations.

WEIGHING DELIVERY OPTIONS

When selecting a delivery service today, the small business owner has many choices but must consider a wide range of factors to reach a cost-effective solution. Small businesses that do a lot of shipping but have not analyzed all of their options may be able to cut costs by a little attention to the multiplicity of services and incentives available. Some issues to consider are:

Speed vs. Cost Private delivery services have created their place in the market by providing rapid services but at a premium cost. In the mid-2000s the Postal Service has, largely in response to this competitive pressure, established express mail and package services as well. The USPS is rarely as convenient as private carriers, but the price will be more attractive. Overnight deliver is immensely popular because it produces certainty. But if the business ships many items overnight, a look at this policy may uncover savings.

Incentives Parcel carriers have optimized their operations around parcel sizes that represent the bulk of their carriage. Two weight ranges that are incentivized are small packages at or below five pounds and packages of 20 to 30 pounds. Carriers will provide the best service and lowest prices in these ranges. If a business can redesign its shipping system to move more packages into these ranges, cost savings may be realized.

Destination Some carriers specialize in cross-country or overseas delivery and offer "single-zone" pricing structures. Others offer attractive rates for shipments within smaller regions. The small business might gain advantages by analyzing the destination of its shipments and selecting carriers based on the most attractive destination zone pricing.

Drop Off or Pickup Many small businesses have trucks or vans on the road which, with a little administrative effort, may be used to drop off packages to private delivery services rather than using pickup at the business site. Investigation of savings possible by doing its own drop off may provide slightly lower costs to the business and optimize the use of its own fleet of vehicles.

Tracking What degree of parcel/document tracking capability does the company require? Companies that deliver materials to rural/remote locales typically look to major carriers offering tracking services. In addition, businesses that ship time- or content-sensitive materials also typically enlist the services of companies like UPS or Federal Express, which can provide clients with detailed information on shipment data.

Integration If a business is well-satisfied with the services of a carrier, it might find it useful to explore additional services offered by the service company, such as inventory management directly tied to in-bound and out-bound shipments. Major carriers offer such services designed, of course, to lock the customer into their system. If such "intimacy" is not a problem, the service may add to efficiency and reduce costs.

BIBLIOGRAPHY

Brown, Ann. "Saving on Next-Day Delivery: The Right Mailing Service Can Reduce Your Office Expenses." *Black Enterprise.* December 1996.

"FedEx Corporate History." FedEx. Available from http://www.fedex.com/us/about/today/history/?link=2. Retrieved on 10 February 2006.

"History." DHL. Available from http://www.dhl-usa.com/Company/History.asp?nav=companyInfo/History. Retrieved on 10 February 2006.

Sigworth, Dwight. "How to Choose a Package Carrier." *Air Cargo World.* March 1998.

U.S. Postal Service. *The United States Postal Service: An American History, 1775-2002.* 2002.

Darnay, ECDI

DEMOGRAPHICS

Demography is the statistical study of populations; the roots of the word come from the Greek for people (*demos*) and picture (*graphy*). Demographics, thus, are pictures of the people derived from statistics. The largest single, consistent collection of data on the population is the U.S. census conducted every ten years under the auspices of the U.S. Census Bureau. The Bureau also collects partial data every year, published as "population estimates." The census itself is at least theoretically a 100 percent count, although controversies about "undercounted" elements of the population break out every decade. This national count covers numbers, gender, age, family relationships, ethnicity and/or race, location, income, occupation, and data on housing patterns. The geographical coverage is down to the census tract level (just a few blocks in extent), so that, for census years, anyway, data can be obtained down to the zip-code level.

All demographics are ultimately based on the census, although the data are extended by many other surveys,

many conducted by government agencies. The U.S. Department of Health and Human Services (HHS), for instance, tracks health issues; U.S. Department of Labor follows employment trends; U.S. Department of Education captures data on educational levels; U.S. Department of Agriculture collects and publishes data on farmers; and state vehicle registration offices collect data on driving. And so on.

Added to this are many, many private surveys which attempt to track consumer preferences, buying habits, attitudes, opinions, and so on *ad infinitum*. The best-known private survey is probably the TV-rating service provided by Nielsen Media Research. People who use discount cards at major grocery or other retail stores are supplying demographic data every time they purchase something. Every subscriber to any kind of print publication is generating demographic information for the publisher—which the publisher uses to set advertising rates. In the mid-2000s the Internet has become a major engine for collecting demographic information if the user bothers to fill out brief questionnaires in which he or she supplies a home address. That home address—plus demographic data from the census—reveal much about the person filling in the boxes: his or her likely ethnicity, age, income, and more. The values obtained are approximate because the census does not reveal individual household data, but people with similar profiles tend to live together.

It is simply to state the obvious that in the modern American culture data collection in some form or another accompanies most commercial transactions done using credit cards. Vast amounts of information come to be stored in countless computers. Techniques of "data mining" from such stores have developed over the years providing companies information better to target their customers.

The public sector (defined to include the academic) is also a major generator and user of demographic information. Health surveys, for instance, are based on doctors' patients' records. Voter registration records trigger selection of juries. HHS tracks birth and death records to generate projections of life expectancy—which in turn serve commercial purposes, e.g., life insurance. Companies and agencies can, if they make the effort, construct quite accurate "pictures" of many different aggregations of people—Superbowl attendees, large boat buyers, first-time voters, and adherents to religions or parties. Demographics is simply an aspect of modern life.

TECHNIQUES AND TRENDS

Extensive collection of demographic data by virtually all larger institutions is both necessitated and motivated by a mass culture. In contrast to Colonial times when sellers knew their customers and principals knew their students, information could be left to ordinary human memory. The gradual evolution of very large institutions far removed from what we are pleased to call "the action," the actual interchange between people, has produced disconnects between decision makers and their constituencies.

The costs of collecting precise demographic data are high, even when in part subsidized by public services like the census. A major trend in this field is to automate data collection using computers and incentives. Free information on the Internet (but you must *register*) or small discounts available when you use a discount card (but you had to *tell* something about yourself to get it) are two examples of incentives provided. The data collected are then consulted using specialized analytical software the reports from which are integrated into the decision stream.

Indirect marketing by mail or advertising are notoriously hit and miss. Producing ever better profiles of people who watch a show or people who live in a zip code helps advertisers and marketers to pinpoint the right "venue" on which to spend money to reach its most desired audience, be that that the "young" or the "young-at-heart."

The high costs of mass marketing can be made more effective by ever more precisely targeted marketing aimed at pre-qualified buyers. But for this method to work, it must remain automated. The highest costs are associated with actual contact between a researcher and a would-be customer; and for this contact to yield any meaningful results, it will require 20 minutes of interaction. Such contacts are only made with tiny samples.

THE PRIVACY DEBATE

The vast stocks of demographic data held by many thousands of institutions in easily searchable and correlatable forms has spawned a debate about privacy. The issue has heated up since Internet browsing became widespread and techniques were developed, through search engines or Internet portals, to track and to record the interests of a user. Articles appear at regular intervals in which a savvy investigator shows just how rapidly he or she can determine intimate details about the life of a celebrity. The issue will continue to evolve, of course. The simple fact is that privacy is attainable, if attainable at all, only by opting out of any and all transactions that require electronic mechanisms or filling in forms. The real protection consumers have is that the exploitation of the data by marketer or others is costly and difficult. As anyone leafing through the day's mail can attest, despite a vast amount of information out there, many people

sending letters to us are aiming at an altogether wrong profile.

SMALL BUSINESS AND DEMOGRAPHICS

It is something of a truism that the business close to its clientele can do without fancy demographics to reach its market. Some small businesses, of course, are *in business* precisely to provide such data to their customers. They will, therefore, be very knowledgeable about demographics; they are still not likely to use such data to reach *their* markets. Other small businesses may be servicing a national market through a Web site, for instance, and, through that web site, may have access to data on their customers that might be exploitable. For most small businesses thinking of turning demographic data to good use for expansion, through a direct mailing for instance, might explore the field by using the services of an advertising agency. The agency will have knowledge of and access to much of the tooling required, including existing and well-honed mailing lists.

SEE ALSO *Market Segmentation*

BIBLIOGRAPHY
Alarcon, Camille. "No More Demographics?" *B&T Weekly.* 2 December 2005.

Berkenfeld, Diane. "The Hispanic Market." *Photo Trade News.* November 2005.

"Changing Demographics Set to Ratchet Up Pressure with Only Migrants to Ease Threat." *Financial Adviser.* 3 November 2005.

Lindsay, Greg. "Control Freak Consumers Reinventing Media Usage; Demographics Plays Key Role in Companies' Rate to Supply Content, Attract Viewers." *Television Week.* 9 January 2006.

Miller, Berna. "A Beginner's Guide to Demographics." *Marketing Tools.* October 1995.

"Naw 2006." *Electrical Wholesaling.* 6 February 2006.

Sheehan, Robert J. "Annual Survey Details Apartment Demographics." *Units.* January 2006.

Zoler, Mitchel L. "Cancer Survival Lags in African American Patients." *Family Practice News.* 15 September 2004.

Darnay, ECDI

DEPRECIATION

"Depreciation" literally means the lowering of the value of something—and specifically of fixed or capital assets. In accounting terminology the word refers to an entry on the balance sheet which records the amount of money deducted from total assets because the assets have aged. All capital assets are subject to depreciation except land.

The current year's depreciation of capital assets may be deducted from income for tax purposes. A business purchasing a van for deliveries must put the acquisition cost of the van, say $36,000, on its books as a capital asset. Tax law permits depreciation of the van over five years. Using a straight-line method of depreciation, the annual depreciation of the van would be $7,200. In actuality the small business may handle depreciation in another way under current tax law, to be discussed below, but this example illustrates the concept. The annual depreciation of $7,200 is treated as a cost, deductible from profits, and therefore it reduces income taxes.

The traditional treatment of capital assets—their depreciation over a number of years—is based on the simple fact that buildings, machinery, vehicles, roads, and other improvements of this type have a life of multiple years. In theory they are paid for from savings accumulated over multiple years and are depreciated (written off) over their useful life. Land is not depreciated because it never wears out. Bookkeeping is aimed at accurately reflecting on-going operations—in the current year. For this reason capital inflows are not reflected in income and depreciation is spread out over the life of the asset.

THE BALANCE SHEET PERSPECTIVE

Company balance sheets are divided into Assets and Liabilities. On the Asset side, the ledger shows current and fixed assets. *Fixed Assets* are subdivided into such categories as Vehicles, Furniture and Fixtures, Equipment, and Buildings. As such assets are acquired, their actual costs of acquisition are entered under these categories. Each of these categories, however, is followed by a line which says: "Less: Accumulated Depreciation." Each year a portion of the asset is added to the depreciation line. The net of these two values (acquisition costs less accumulated depreciation) is what is counted as "fixed assets." The role of depreciation in the accounting sense, therefore, is to keep the books honest: only the actual*remaining* value of fixed assets is counted on the books.

Accountants calculate how much of each category of assets to depreciate every year by using Generally Accepted Accounting Principles (GAAP) established by Financial Accounting Standards Board. Within a single category, such as buildings, for instance, the life of a structure may vary from 10 years for a tool shed to 80 years for fire-resistant bearing walls, beams, decks, and floors. The acquisition cost is divided by the appropriate number of years. Very complex schedules are used to determine "life."

THE TAX PERSPECTIVE

Depreciation is treated as a cost category in tax calculations. It is not a "cash cost" because no actual disbursement of cash takes place; depreciation is simply an entry in the books. But for tax purposes depreciation has a "cash consequence": it reduces the actual tax liability of a company. From a tax perspective, therefore, any law that permits higher deductions of depreciation than accounting principles specify are favorable for the corporation: no cash payment is involved in so-called "accelerated depreciation" but real cash benefits result: lower taxes.

Letting companies speed up depreciation has, for this reason, become a popular technique of lowering taxes and thus, by giving more money to companies, stimulating the economy. Regulating depreciation in the tax code is also a relatively precise instrument. Congress can aim its policy at certain categories of expenditures. It can, for instance, stimulate purchases of vehicles by letting businesses write them off more quickly; or it can favor a broad category such as computers. Congress has done both. It could also, at its discretion, stimulate industrial construction, for instance, by letting companies write off buildings or land improvements quickly.

In the example presented at the beginning, for instance—the $36,000 van—under the rules in force during the 2004 tax year, a small business could write off a substantial portion of that van ($24,000) in the year of acquisition, the remainder over five years. In these situations a maximum cap usually applies. In 2004 tax years, for example, the cap was $102,000.

CASH FLOW CALCULATION

Businesses calculate the cash flow of their business—usually in the context of justifying loans. Cash flow is simply the netting out, for a given period (a quarter, a year, multiple years) of all cash coming in from sales and cash flowing out for purchases and payments on debt and interest. In this context, however, depreciation is often mentioned as part of the cash flow calculation: depreciation is said to be "added back." The phrasing produces confusion. Cash flow calculations are often automated so that all current income and current costs are cumulated; costs are then deducted from income to derive the cash flow. But in this process some costs are not cash costs. Depreciation is one of those. Therefore, to get an accurate cash flow, depreciation must be added back in because it was not a cash cost in the first place.

ALTERNATIVE METHODS USED

Depreciation may be calculated in a variety of ways all of which are specified in law and elaborated in the Generally Accepted Accounting Principles. Major categories are 1) the straight-line method, 2) units-of-production method, 3) declining-balance method, and 4) sum-of-the-years-digits method.

Straight-Line The residual (salvage) value of the asset is first estimated. Thereafter the asset, minus salvage value, is divided by the useful life of the asset. The resulting value is deducted for each year of the asset's life.

Units-of-Production This method is used when the usage of the asset varies from year to year and its use can be determined by some measure such as miles driven, tonnage hauled, cuts made, etc. Again, salvage value is deducted. Next, the remaining value is divided by the total units the asset is estimated to be able to produce. Units produced are recorded for every year. Depreciation for each year is calculated based on the units. Thus depreciation may be very high one year, low in another year—until the total count of units has been used up.

Declining-Balance This method, also known as double-declining-balance, is an accelerated method of depreciation because depreciation is highest in the first year and then declines with each year. The formula requires dividing 2 by the years of life to get a percentage and then applying that percentage to the balance of the asset. Assuming a three-year life for a $5,000 asset, the first year of depreciation will be 5,000 x (2/3) = $3,333. The asset is then reduced by that amount and becomes $1,667. The second year, the depreciation is 1,667 x (2/3) or .66667 = $1,111. Again, the asset is reduced by that amount, leaving $556. The procedure is repeated again. Under this method, however, the asset may not be depreciated below its salvage value; for this reason, the third year operation may not be possible.

Sum-of-the-Years-Digits Supposing that the life of an asset is five years. In that case the sum of the year's digits will be 1+2+3+4+5 = 15. The asset value less its salvage value is calculated. Let us assume that the result is $8,750. In the first year the net asset value will be multiplied by the fraction 5/15 (0.333), in the second by 4/15 (0.2667), in the third by 3/15 (0.2), and so on, yielding depreciations streams of $2,914, $2,333, $1,750, and son on. After five years, the total depreciation streams will sum to $8,750.

It is worthwhile to know about such fascinating things as sum-of-the-years-digits, but most small business owners have better things to do. Those with substantial fixed assets typically seek the advise of a certified public accountant (CPA) and profit by his or her professional experience. In the mid-2000s, when government appeared intent on cutting taxes first and then asking questions later—and the environment was favorable to small business, seen as the only generator of new jobs—substantial tax savings and incentives to invest were avail-

able in an ever changing tax code to which the CPA was an invaluable guide.

BIBLIOGRAPHY

Battersby, Mark. "Take Advantage of New Tax Write-Offs for Fleet Vans and Light Trucks." *Aftermarket Business.* October 2004.

Baxter, William. "Depreciation and Interest." *Accountancy.* October 2000.

Cummings, Jack. "Depreciation Is Out of Favor, But It Matters." *Triangle Business Journal.* 25 February 2000.

"How Cost Segregation Can Save Your Client's Money." *Real Estate Weekly.* 28 September 2005.

O'Bannon, Isaac M. "Fixed Assets Software Replaces Duct Tape Spreadsheets." *The CPA Technology Advisor.* December 2005.

Russ, Don. "Real Estate Depreciation: Be aware of the details." *San Fernando Valley Business Journal.* 12 September 2005.

Whitson, Alan. "Depreciation Without the Headache." *Fairfield County Business Journal.* 19 December 2005.

Vorster, Mike. "Let's Sideline Straight-Line Depreciation." *Construction.* 1 October 2005.

Darnay, ECDI

DESKTOP PUBLISHING

Desktop publishing, sometimes abbreviated as DTP, is a technique for preparing and printing professional quality products using microcomputers, software, and printers. Articles on the subject, presumably by authors who haven't tried to use the technique, still occasionally suggest that DTP is easy, fast, and cheap. Unless the product is a one-page flyer announcing a gutter-cleaning special, DTP is none of those things. It represents the latest level of automation in an industry that marked the dawn of modernity: typesetting.

BACKGROUND

The invention of movable type by Gutenberg dates back to 1450. This technology, therefore, had a developmental period of more than 525 years before the first microcomputers saw wide use in the mid-1970s. Many different kinds of fonts were designed and refined in this period in variants of which, today, bold and italic are well known to everyone. Terminology and rules related to type size (measured in points), kerning (the space between characters), and leading (the space between lines) developed. In 1884, almost exactly 100 years before the first DTP system introduced by Apple Computer, Ottman Mergenthaler introduced linotype, a technique that cast metal type on the fly, one line at a time, using brass patterns for characters; a person working a keyboard-type device selected the characters to be cast. A year later came Tolbert Lanston's monotype, capable of producing one letter at a time, also from raw metal. Monotype made it much easier to space characters in novel ways. Intertype, which came later, was another line-by-line typesetting system. In all of these cases, the cast metal could be remelted for reuse. These systems are still in use but are driven today by computerized interfaces.

The Standard Generalized Markup Language (SGML) began to be developed in 1960 and is available as International Standards Organization 8879:1986. SGML is a convention for embedding markers in text to be read and interpreted by typesetting programs. SGML is the progenitor of XML (Extensible Markup Language) and also of HTML (Hyper Text Markup Language) the language underneath web pages. SGML was developed in order to automate typesetting and standardize formatting; it is widely used by the Federal Government.

In none of these systems leading up to DTP was page composition itself automated so that the insertion of photographs and other graphics was done at other points in the production process. Printing in true color still requires four passes through a printing press to put down yellow, cyan, magenta, and black—unless the printing process used is color Xerography and the closely related color laser printers.

EMERGENCE OF DTP

Computerization of typesetting came before microcomputers themselves arrived. The first DTP systems were scaled-down versions of typesetting and composition software running on larger and much more expensive minicomputers. Operators sat facing multiple monitors and formatted pages using the same computer's services. These were effective and attractive systems—but they cost a lot of money. No small business could afford such systems unless it was itself in the business of providing typesetting services.

Apple Computer introduced the first full-fledged micro-based DTP system in 1984 but did not effectively get it on the market until 1985; in the mid-2000s, therefore, DTP is just 15 years old. The three major components of the first system were the Macintosh computer, the Aldus PageMaker software system, and a LaserWriter printer with the embedded PostScript software developed by Adobe Systems. The user of this system could sit at the screen and, using a keyboard and a mouse, create a document on screen. As people later said: "What You See Is What You Get," WYSIWYG. At the click of the mouse, the image on the screen would come out on the LaserWriter printer. PageMaker was said to be incredibly

easy to use, but not all those who actually used it in the 1980s would agree. The same is true of today's much more sophisticated systems.

Apple was the first commercially sold graphical computer. (Xerox pioneered the concept but did not take it to market.) The graphical interfaced required the use of complex geometrical techniques to render characters and images by vector graphics, namely by a description of drawing directions. Raster graphics, which are static images made up of dots, do not scale satisfactorily, but a vector description of a letter or a drawing can be executed at any scale with very fine precision. The PostScript language developed by Adobe was very compact and efficient—it took up very little space on the printer; at the same time, it could render the picture of a screen perfectly. At this time technology to render color and advanced techniques for handling photograph were still in the future.

MODERN DTP

Some 15 years later and counting, DTP has reached a certain maturity. Many different software packages are on the market; Aldus PageMaker remains a factor, but the two leading producers in the mid-2000s were QuarkXpress and Adobe's InDesign. Adobe is also a leader in photographic manipulation (PhotoShop) and has become the de facto standard for web-based publishing using PDF, the Portable Document Format. Adobe Acrobat can be used to make PDF files; Adobe distributes the Acrobat Reader free of charge, used for reading (but not for editing or creating) PDF files. A PDF file printed on an appropriate device can, in fact, be a professionally typeset document if its preparer had the requisite skills. A competitive see-saw in the software market has been the rule. At present, David Blatner, a leading expert on both QuarkXpress and InDesign (he has written extensive books on how to use both) believes, according to a recent article in *eWeek*, that InDesign has the competitive edge. Such judgments, of course, are always merely snapshots at a given point in time.

DTP systems are today available for every type of operating system, not merely Macintosh operating system (MacOS). Memory installed in computers and in printers, and disk drives in computers with many gigabytes of storage, make it possible to handle very large publications with many hundreds of photographs.

In the 1980s printers came with a resolution of 300 dots per inch (dpi) and handled 8.5 by 11 inch paper; and color printers were not available. In the mid-2000s printers in the price range of $4,500 and up come with minimally 600 and as high as 4,800 dpi—well above the most exacting commercial requirements. They also handle commercial-size sheets of up to 13 by 19 inches. And, of course, they print in full color. Printers in these categories are widely available, moreover, from producers like Canon, Hewlett-Packard, Ricoh, and others.

For an investment of around $25,000, a small business can install a genuinely state-of-the-art DTP system. The investment may be justified if the company is selling typesetting services—or such services are a necessary element of a larger business, e.g., manual preparation or publishing. Costs are significantly lower than in pre-DTP days; back in the early 1980s a single high-end printer could run $20,000. Nevertheless, the investment is substantial. It is also worth-while noting that DTP, in today's market, still excludes important elements of "finishing" printed products: this involves trimming, folding, sewing, stapling, binding, and packaging the brochure, book, magazine, manual, or whatever. High-end DTP is therefore no less a *commercial* decision today for the small business than before micros came with fancy layout software. To be sure, much less cost is involved in a workable DTP system capable of putting out attractive color brochures occasionally.

INTERNAL SKILL SETS

The broad expansion of small computers since the 1970s has been accompanied by a steady drumbeat emphasizing ease of use. In actual fact the industry has leapfrogged ahead in a competitive frenzy to gain or maintain market share and has not delivered on ease and rational perfection of its products.

This is the view taken by William R. Howard, writing in *PC Magazine*. Howard wrote: "Bah, humbug. My feelings of good will toward the technology provider portion of humankind took a dive during the holiday season. My computer just didn't perform many of the tasks that it should have done easily. In the realm of technology, even people who think they're smart can be brought to their knees." In documenting his tale of woe, Howard also touched on DTP. He wrote: "For my wife, I produced a photo book of our summer vacation... The finished product was spectacular. The process was a horror show: Tiny on-screen work area, equally small page preview, limited page layouts that were too small to let you read the text, fixed photo aspect ratios, 38-character caption limits for vertical photos, no spell-checker. I spent close to 10 hours creating 30 pages; half that time was wasted dealing with the clumsy interface."

Almost no one actually engaged in DTP would disagree with Howard. Practiced at the professional level, DTP requires substantial skills acquired over a longer period of time. Skill sets rapidly age unless the art is continuously practiced. A business that only rarely uses DTP faces re-learning cycles each time—for a loss of

efficiency. Sending the job out may be more cost-effective.

Professional level DTP requires the same know-how that the typesetters and page-designers of old also possessed. The difference is that operations that once required cutting, measuring, and pasting are done today by mouse. The software packages dutifully import from the past measurement system and terminology—which must be learned. The great complexity involved in handling a document that may be on several overlaid "layers" (for colors, for pictures, for text of various kinds) mean mastery of sometimes baffling, uninformative, and unintuitive menu systems. Their meanings have to worked out gradually by trial and error. Manuals provided by the software producer rarely cover matters well, are rarely up-to-date, and, these days, may not come on paper. Operators are often required to buy and to use simultaneously several third-party references to solve a single problem.

These points are made in the cause of clarity—not to imply that DTP does not have quite superb values for the enterprise that makes an effort to master and use it. DTP is truly excellent tooling—especially for those who come to DTP already skilled in the underlying arts of photo-composition, layout, and typesetting. Thus it enhances existing skill sets—but imposes training burdens on the small business anticipating ease of use. Therefore a commitment to this type of production, for these reasons, must be a deliberate and commercial decision reached, ideally, after thoughtful testing of alternatives.

BIBLIOGRAPHY

Blatner, David. Real World QuarkXPress 6. Peachpit Press. 22 September 2003.

Blatner, David. "Blatner: InDesign, Not Quark, Is the Future of DTP." *eWeek*. 22 June 2005.

Borden, Mark. "How Adobe is Pushing Quark Off the Page: When the leader in desktop publishing software got lazy, a nimbler competitor grabbed market share." *Business 2.0*. September 2005.

Howard, William R. "Tech humbug." *PC Magazine*. 22 February 2005.

"HP Color LaserJet 5550dtn." *PC Magazine Online*. 23 November 2004.

Hutchenreuther, Mark S. "Background Checks." *Mechanical Engineering-CIME*. December 2005.

Kvern, Olav Martin, and David Blatner. *Real World Adobe InDesign CS2*. Peachpit Press. 17 January 2006.

Lake, Susan E. L. *Destop Publishing*. South-Western College Publishing, 2006.

McGoon, Cliff. "Desktop Publishing: Communicators' Best Friend or Worst Enemy?" *Communication World*. November 1993.

"Quark XPress 7 to Offer Extra Design Edge." *Printing World*. 11 August 2005.

Rosenberg, Jim. "E&P Technical: Weekly's Waxer Runs Cold." *Editor & Publisher.* 1 February 2006.

Stonely, Dorothy. "Desktop Publishing Industry Evolves with Demand." *The Business Journal.* 17 March 1997.

"When DTP Came of Age." *Print Week.* 7 July 2005.

Darnay, ECDI

DIFFICULT CUSTOMERS

Successful small business owners recognize that customer satisfaction is one of the essential elements of organizational prosperity. After all, providing quality service that clients appreciate not only ensures repeat business from them but also encourages future "word-of-mouth" sales. But virtually all small business operations will sooner or later encounter customers who prove troublesome. Customer service experts counsel small business owners who encounter this situation to: 1) determine whether the difficult customer actually has a legitimate complaint; 2) determine whether the business can take steps to mollify the client's concerns (regardless of their legitimacy) and improve the relationship; and 3) in cases where the customer is being unreasonable, decide whether the customer's value is sufficient to warrant continuance of service.

In most industry sectors, the vast majority of customers are fairly easy to work with. They understand the basic rules of commerce, in which they pay your business an agreed-upon amount to render a service or provide a product to them under certain terms that are also mutually agreed upon. But a minority of customers—experts place the number at anywhere from 5 to 10 percent—qualify as difficult. Sometimes these customers seem more prevalent, however, simply because they can take up so much of a business's time and energy.

Nonetheless, small businesses need to learn to differentiate between truly difficult customers who are ultimately of questionable value to their operations and those who may be annoying for one reason or another but who are ultimately solid, valuable clients worth keeping. Often, the difficult customer is someone who has simply taken an annoying habit to an extreme. For example, Richard F. Gerson, author of *Great Customer Service for Your Small Business,* listed ten types of customer behaviors, only one of which—The Perfect Customer—was wholly desirable to the small business owner. But the others—customers that are "know-it-alls," unduly dependent, argumentative, indecisive, chronic complainers, monopolizers of time, etc.—sometimes comprise the majority of customer types. These are the individuals who your establishment depends on for long-term success, and as long as their quirks do not become formidable obstacles to business transactions, your business should continue to do its best to satisfy them. It is when these and other characteristics become excessive that the small business owner needs to intercede and decide how his or her business will interact with that customer—if at all—in the future.

DETERMINING IF THE DIFFICULT CUSTOMER HAS A LEGITIMATE GRIPE

Customer service experts contend that many difficult customers are behaving in that manner because they have a legitimate gripe with the product or service they have received. Indeed, the chances are very good that a poorly run business operation is apt to encounter a far greater number of so-called "difficult" customers than will an establishment that is efficient, competent, and dedicated to ideals of customer service. "Many 'bad' customers are the result of a bad situation," stated Jenny McCune in *Nation's Business.* "A salesclerk is surly; your company doesn't respond quickly enough to a request; a product defect ruins the customer's day; or an order promised for Wednesday doesn't arrive until Friday."

Small business owners and managers, then, need to determine whether the customer has a legitimate complaint before taking any other action. The client is obviously the individual who is best equipped to explain the reasons for his or her dissatisfaction, so he or she should have a full opportunity to express the grievance. From there—provided that it is determined that the customer was poorly served in one respect or another—the small business manager should gather all the pertinent facts from his or her staff to determine where the error occurred and to figure out how best to mollify the client and prevent the problem from occurring again. If the customer—who, after all, may have provided a service to your company by alerting it to an operational weakness or personnel problem—is convinced that you are genuinely sorry for the slip-up and genuinely interested in solving the problem, preservation of the business relationship is often possible.

In addition to making apologies and moving to address problems in performance, small business owners can take several other steps to improve their relationships with difficult customers. For example, firms that take preventive measures—such as regular inquiries into customer satisfaction—are often able to address minor grievances before they erupt into major spots of contention. Instituting such proactive arrangements gives businesses the opportunity to prevent attitudes that eventually grow into problem attitudes from ever taking root.

LETTING DIFFICULT CUSTOMERS GO

There are occasions, however, when even a company's best efforts to address or anticipate customer complaints are fruitless. In other words, a small but significant percentage of customers that your business deals with may prove to be extremely unpleasant, no matter what measures are taken to satisfy them. Few businesses are exempt from this reality. After all, the convenience store owner confronted with a disruptive customer is essentially grappling with the same problem as the owner of a small manufacturing company who is treated shabbily by a corporate buyer. In both cases, the business owner is dealing with a customer/client who makes conducting business a distinctly unpleasant experience.

When confronted with difficult customers who appear unlikely to change their stripes, then, small business owners have to decide whether their business is worth the aggravation. Several factors should be considered:

Impact on Business. This is generally the single most important consideration in weighing whether to continue doing business with a difficult customer. Is the customer one of your major clients? How difficult would it likely be to replace the revenue from that customer? Is the client a possible conduit to other potentially valuable customers? Is the client a major opinion-shaper in the community or industry in which your company operates? What is the nature of the difficulty? This latter consideration is an important one, say customer service experts. For example, a customer that is an indecisive or impossible-to-please sort, and whose demands result in extensive drains on your business's resources, may be far more problematic than a client who is difficult simply because he is woefully lacking in interpersonal skills. If your business can handle the loss, it is perfectly acceptable to sever ties with a difficult customer. But small business owners should do their best to end the relationship decisively and as civilly as possible. "It is impossible to please unreasonable or marginal customers on all occasions, and it's best to consider leaving them to other vendors," summarized Jack Falvey in *Sales and Marketing Management.* "It's far better to expend your efforts in further satisfying already satisfied accounts. The return on investment is almost always far greater."

Impact on Staff. This consideration is sometimes overlooked by small business owners, to their detriment. Unhappy employees are far more likely to secure employment elsewhere than those that are content, and few things can make an employee unhappy more quickly than the specter of regularly dealing with unpleasant customers. Abusive treatment of staff at the hands of clients must be dealt with firmly and speedily. Otherwise, internal morale—and performance—can deteriorate quickly and dramatically.

Impact on Business Owner. Small business owners are more likely to be personally affected by difficult customers than are corporate executives, who may be insulated from such unpleasantness. And since small businesses tend to rely on their founders for a sizable share of their direction and management, the feelings of those founders need to be considered. A small business owner who approaches encounters with a given customer with dread needs to carefully consider whether such meetings are having an adverse impact on his or her ability to attend to other needs of the business without feeling stressed or distracted.

Mitigating Circumstances. Finally, in some instances there may be reasons for difficult behavior that are not immediately apparent. "Most difficult customer situations are complicated by all kinds of subjective judgments and seemingly mitigating circumstances," said Falvey. For example, changes in personnel at a client company can have a dramatic impact on inter-company relations. If the new representative is insecure about his or her capabilities and knowledge, that may manifest itself in a variety of undesirable ways. If the small business owner takes the time to figure out why the customer has suddenly become a problematic one, he or she may be able to devise a strategy to repair the relationship rather than end it.

SEE ALSO *Customer Retention; Customer Service*

BIBLIOGRAPHY

Evenson, Renee. "How to Deal with a Difficult Customer: A Positive Solution to a Negative Situation." *American Salesman.* July 1998.

Falvey, Jack. "Dealing with Difficult Customers: When Customers Become Unreasonable in Their Demands, It May Be Time to Cut Them Loose." *Sales and Marketing Management.* April 1995.

Gerson, Richard F. *Great Customer Service for Your Small Business.* Crisp, 1996.

Gordon, Josh. *Tough Calls: Selling Strategies to Win Over Your Most Difficult Customers.* AMACOM, 1997.

Kroskey, Carol Meres. "It's Okay to Fire a Customer." *Bakery Production and Marketing.* 15 October 1997.

McCune, Jenny C. "When Customers Are Bad Apples." *Nation's Business.* February 1998.

Plagakis, Jim. "Persona Non Grata." *Drug Topics.* 15 September 1997.

Sewell, Carl. *Customers for Life.* Doubleday, 1990.

Hillstrom, Northern Lights
updated by Magee, ECDI

DIFFICULT EMPLOYEES

The term "difficult employee" is typically used to refer to a worker who fails to conduct him- or herself in a responsible and/or professional manner in the workplace. Effectively dealing with such employees can be among the greatest challenges that face small business owners and managers. Few relish the prospect of disciplining or criticizing others in or outside the work environment. But when difficult employees become an issue, their failings must be addressed quickly and decisively lest they erode morale and efficiency. A natural management response is delay, temporizing, and wishful thought. When such traits are indulged, they just make things worse.

THE WELL-BEHAVING WORKPLACE

Problematic employee behavior is doubly difficult because it may have multiple causes not easily discerned. The causes may be work or home related, behavior- or health-related, may be triggered by other employees or outsiders, by changes of work, others' promotion, rising stress levels, etc. For these very reasons, the small business owner or leading manager will concern him- or herself initially, and always, with ensuring that internal causes are minimized. There will be fewer difficult employees in well-behaving work places than otherwise. As shown elsewhere in this volume (see *Corporate Ethics*) companies with high ethics experience much less unethical behavior. In well run operations, broad policy and structural approaches serve as preventive measures; careful and above all attentive management practices serve diagnostic purposes; and a clear, sequenced, escalating, well-documented "coping" process can rapidly bring closure.

Policy and Work Environment A reasonably formal, reasonable orderly, well-organized, straight-forward, crisp but friendly work environment helps instill the right expectation in the workforce. Such an environment is almost always deliberate created and maintained by management by such means as setting working hours, initiating employees by having them read and sign brief but complete employment policies, and passing on the general "rules of the road." The more explicit, clear, and rational these are—and the more they are observed to be enforced—the more they contribute to the right work ambiance.

Maintenance of an efficient and visibly orderly work environment is only indirectly related to handling difficult employees, but once problems appear, this background is vital to the resolution of the problem. It is of central importance that the workplace *have* rules, that these be *public, uniformly enforced*, and equally applicable to all ranks. A somewhat disorderly work environment with poorly established routines, floating coffee breaks, many privileges, many exceptions to rules, temperamental bosses or tolerated high-jinks (perhaps because the cut-up is a very good salesman) and arbitrary rather than scheduled events make it much more difficult, later, suddenly to "wake up" to the need for discipline. Another way experts put this is that difficult employees are often a product of shoddily-run workplaces.

Management Style Assuming that the policies are good and the work environment is reasonably disciplined, managerial performance in conformity with policy will be consistent, alert, but also flexibly sensitive. In effect this means that that managers in charge of individuals will pay attention to those they supervise, maintain a proper but not a frosty or belligerent distance, apply company policies rather than personal whim, assiduously avoid inappropriate relations (like flirtation or special friendships), and promptly and willingly provide both positive and negative feedback with an objective air. Good management style will always involve clear and prompt communications when changes threaten to disrupt—even when the changes are positive. Good management will represent the next level up in a straightforward way, neither deifying nor bad-mouthing it. Managers will be loyal to their employees and promptly go to bat for them. They will avoid turf-oriented behavior and support collective goals—and will promote such attitudes in word and deed.

Methods of Discipline The emergence of a difficult employee will take place quite early in a well-management operation. Most of the time the "difficulty" will never even surface because it will have been dealt with effectively in it nascent stages. If it persist, the company will have in place a well-planned method of dealing with it in stages. The process will be orderly but escalating, beginning with information exchange and goal setting, followed by reviews, by increasing sanctions such as warnings, opportunities for appeal, notices, and finally discharge. In this entire process, management will behave rationally rather than emotionally. It will briefly but fully document the facts in writing because, in today's environment, that is simply sensible. Such methods will be followed even in operations that have at-will hiring policies—because the difficult employee may sue anyway. Top management will take an appropriate role in supervising such processes to ensure that policies are followed. Rarely if ever will a problem employee, managed in a rational, methodical, and orderly manner succeed in prevailing against the employer.

The pain, generally, of facing up to problems early is almost always negligible compared to the "uproar" that results from neglect and avoidance. Here the famous "Pay me now or pay me later" warning applies in full. The general rule—assuming, again, that good policies are in place and properly implemented—is to insist on rational and sensible behavior, full disclosure of problems on both sides, and clearly spelled out consequences which are actually applied.

SPECIFIC METHODS

Management experts cite several steps that entrepreneurs and managers should take when dealing with a difficult employee.

- *Importance of the Written Word.* Companies should prepare and mainting written policies/guidelines. These should include definitions of poor performance and gross misconduct and detail performance and termination review procedures.

- *Taking Stock and Cutting Slack.* In most business settings, workers spend long hours in close proximity. Inevitably, each employees will exhibit personality traits some of which may annoy coworkers, managers, or the owner of the business. But a mildly overbearing, cocky, or whiny demeanor on the part of an employee is not in itself cause for intervention. An owner who attempts to stamp out every personality manifestation that he/she finds to be mildly unpleasant will quickly alienate his/her workforce and hamper the company's ability to focus its energy on business issues. But when employee behavior begins to have a negative impact on coworkers or the health of the business itself, the business owner must intercede quickly.

- *Taking Control.* If a problem employee emerges, the business owner or supervisor should schedule a meeting to discuss the behavior. This meeting time should be scheduled so that both the supervisor and the employee can focus on the issues at hand and speak without being disturbed. It is unwise to hold such a meeting when emotions are running high; but issues must be addressed in a timely manner. Performance problems, whether they take the form of insubordination, tardiness, poor work performance, or problematic behavior with other employees, may intensify or multiply if not addressed. Employees who do not meet standards—whether knowingly or unknowingly—will continue to do so if their unacceptable behavior is not challenged.

- *Hearing the Other Side.* Small business owners often assume that workers possess the same skills and knowledge that they do. But some meetings with "difficult" employees reveal that their inadequate work performance is rooted in a lack of skills. In such cases, instruction and education, rather than disciplinary measures, are the keys to making the employee a valuable part of the workforce. In other instances, the employee may be grappling with personal issues that have had a deleterious impact on his/her performance. The owner can, at his or her discretion, implement measures that may enable to the employee to weather his/her difficulties and became a valuable member of the workforce.

- *Uniform Rules.* Use the same criteria of performance and behavior evaluation with all employees.

- *The Facts.* When confronting a difficult employee, business owners and supervisors are encouraged to focus on two or three specific instances when the worker exhibited problematic behavior. Whenever possible, use measurable and observable facts to explain the problem from your perspective. Establish the link between the employee's unacceptable behavior and/or performance and the overall health and direction of the company.

- *Avoiding Adversarial Confrontations.* By his or her own natural role, the owner is employees ally and should try to convince the employee that the meeting is in essence an effort to solve a problem both parties share. If bad will is involved, that can be dealt with later.

- *Consequences and Review.* Small business owners and managers need to make it clear to problem employees that consequences will follow continued inappropriate or substandard behavior. Choose these consequences with care, however. "Tell an employee who doesn't give a hoot about climbing the corporate ladder that he or she may lose out on a possible promotion, and you'll get no results," noted *Entrepreneur*'s Robert McGarvey. "For a consequence to matter and actually make a difference, it needs to matter to that employee." One way in which owners and supervisors can serve notice to a difficult employee that they are serious about imposing discipline and correcting behavior is to schedule a follow-up meeting *during* the initial meeting. Scheduling a second meeting puts the employee on notice that his behavior and/or performance is regarded as a serious matter that will be monitored on a regular basis.

- *Acknowledging Improvements.* Finally, business owners and managers need to recognize instances in which a problem employee makes a genuine effort to correct his/her workplace shortcomings. Without such acknowledgements, an employee is more likely to slide back into negative patterns of performance and/or interaction with coworkers.

- *Terminating Problem Employees.* Some difficult employees will resist all management efforts to convince them to change their behavior or attitudes. In these cases, termination of employment may be necessary. This is not a step to be taken lightly, especially if the problem employee provides important services to the company (as in the case of the verbally abusive employee who nonetheless is a good computer programmer). But in some cases, it is necessary in order to maintain—or restore—company morale and efficiency in other areas. If behavior-related termination is warranted, small businesses should make sure that they document the employee's shortcomings in specific, quantifiable terms. Personnel files should include accounts of specific incidents of poor performance; summaries of meetings held with the employee and other company-initiated efforts to correct behavior; and any formal warnings of probation or dismissal.

SEE ALSO *Customer Retention*

BIBLIOGRAPHY

Adkerson, D. Michelle. *How to Manage Problem Employees.* M. Lee Smith Publishers, 2000.

"Ambiguity Obscures Employment-At-Will Issues." *Connecticut Law Tribune.* 23 May 2005.

Darby, Mark. "Good as (un)Golden: A set of tactics and some understanding will help you get through to those difficult employees." *Contemporary Long Term Care.* March-April 2004.

"Disrespect For People is Rife in Construction." *Contract Journal.* 30 November 2005.

Janove, Jathan. "Keep 'em at Will, Treat 'em for Cause: Employment at will preserves needed flexibility, but don't arbitrarily give employees the boot." *HR Magazine.* May 2005.

Langenbacher, Wolfgang. "How to Handle Difficult Employees." *SaskBusiness.* November 2003.

McGarvey, Robert. "Lords of Discipline." *Entrepreneur.* January 2000.

"News." *Personnel Today.* 6 December 2006.

Schachter, Debbie. "Dealing with Difficult Employees." *Information Outlook.* February 2005.

Whitaker, Todd C. "Power Plays of Difficult Employees: A three-question litmus test to gauge the likely effect of your rules to change bad behavior." *School Administrator.* February 2003.

Hillstrom, Northern Lights
updated by Magee, ECDI

DIRECT MAIL

Direct mail is a type of advertising medium in which messages are sent to target customers through the mail. The terms "direct mail" and "mail order" are often used interchangeably. The best way to distinguish these similar, yet different, terms is to remember that direct mail is simply an advertising medium, like print or broadcast media. Print media messages are delivered through the printed word, usually in newspapers or magazines, while broadcast media messages are delivered through the airwaves, on television or radio. In direct mail, advertising and other types of messages are delivered through the mail.

Mail order is a particular way of doing business, like retail or personal selling. A mail order business delivers its products through the mail. It may also use direct mail to send out advertising messages or catalogs. Direct mail is simply one advertising medium that direct marketers employ, although it is among the most frequently used.

Direct mail is a particularly attractive option for small business owners, as it can communicate complete information about a product or service and reach almost any conceivable target group, all for a relatively low cost. Direct mail can provide the basis for a business, or it can be used to supplement a company's traditional sales efforts. For example, a small business could use direct mail to inform potential customers about its offerings, then follow up with a phone call or a visit from a salesperson. Owners of start-up businesses may find direct mail an effective method of creating awareness and interest in a new product, while owners of existing companies may find it useful in generating new business outside of their usual customers or geographic area. Another advantage of direct mail is that it is testable, so that entrepreneurs can try out different sales messages on various audiences in order to find the most profitable market for a new product or service.

USES OF DIRECT MAIL

Direct mail is the most heavily used direct marketing medium, and its popularity continues to grow despite postage increases. While most advertisers use third class mail, a significant number of mailings are sent first class, making it difficult to arrive at accurate statistics about the volume of advertising mail being sent.

The primary application of direct mail is to reach consumers with offers of traditional goods and services. Some of the earliest examples of direct mail were seed catalogs sent to American colonists before the Revolutionary War. More recently, direct mail has been used to offer consumers a range of financial services, coupons for discounts on packaged goods, and requests for donations to a variety of nonprofit organizations.

Direct mail is also an effective medium in business-to-business marketing. Since business orders are usually of larger value than consumer purchases, it often takes more than one mailing to make a sale. Imaginative packages are often used to get through to hard-to-reach executives whose mail is screened by their secretaries. In addition to making sales, business-to-business direct mail can be used to generate sales leads and reinforce the personal selling effort.

ELEMENTS OF DIRECT MAIL

The Offer There are three key elements of successful direct mail: making an offer, selecting the target audience among customer lists and databases, and creating the direct mail package. Making an offer is one element that distinguishes direct marketing from general advertising and other types of marketing. Offers are designed to motivate the reader to take action: place an order, request more information, etc. Writing in *Successful Direct Marketing Methods,* Bob Stone gave the following example of how the same offer could be presented in three different ways: 1) Half-price! 2) Buy one—get one free! 3) 50% off! All three convey the same offer, but statement number two pulled a 40 percent higher response than statements one or three because consumers perceived it to be the most attractive offer.

In direct mail the offer can be tailored to fit the characteristics of the individual recipients. Direct mail allows marketers to target individuals with known purchase histories or particular psychographic or demographic characteristics, all of which affect how an offer should be made. Some basic types of offers include: optional features; a special introductory price or quantity discount; free trial or bill me later; order by mail, phone, or fax; premiums or sweepstakes; and special conditions of sale and types of guarantees.

Mailing Lists and Databases Mailing lists and databases offer direct mail marketers the opportunity for more selectivity and personalization than any other advertising medium. The two basic types of lists are in-house lists and external lists. In-house lists—sometimes called response lists—are those compiled by the company based on responses to its previous mailings or to its advertising in other media. These lists, which represent prime repeat business opportunities, are among a small business's most important assets. They are usually not available to competitors for rental, though they are sometimes exchanged with other companies that offer similar products. In contrast, external lists are typically compiled for rental by sources outside the company. There are thousands of different lists available that classify consumers according to a variety of demographic criteria. External lists may be rented by competitors as well.

Depending on the product being sold through direct mail, lists may consist of the names of consumers or businesses. Some examples of compiled consumer lists available for rental include: buyers of certain vehicle models, collectors of different items, subscribers to various periodicals, organic gardeners, or golf enthusiasts. Business lists are typically categorized according to the North American Industry Classification System (NAICS), which assigns code numbers to different types of businesses.

In direct mail, lists are often rented from a list source for one-time use. When multiple lists are rented, a technique known as merge/purge is used to eliminate duplications. The transaction between a direct mailer hoping to obtain a list and a compiler hoping to rent a list may be facilitated by a list broker or list manager. The list broker's job is to match the list buyer with the most appropriate list for its offerings. Although brokers technically represent both the list buyer and the list owner, they are usually paid by the list owner. Whereas a list broker helps a direct mailer find the right list, a list manager is more like an agent who represents one or more specific lists. List managers handle the rental and billing procedures for the list owners, and also work with list brokers and list compilers as well as with direct mailers to arrange usage for the list.

Another place to find list data is on the Internet. There are a variety of online sources for marketing data, many of which allow small businesses to rent customized lists to fit their limited budgets. List costs tend to vary with specificity. That is, a list of subscribers to a particular magazine may rent for $50 per thousand (lists are typically rented on a "per thousand" basis), while a list of women subscribers who live in certain zip codes may rent for $100 per thousand.

Direct mailers employ a variety of selectivity techniques to better target their mailings. Traditional segmentation techniques look at past behavior, including time since most recent purchase, frequency of purchase, and amounts of purchases. More advanced segmentation techniques employ formulas that help predict future behavior. One such technique is list enhancement, or the process of overlaying social, economic, demographic, or psychographic data obtained from other sources on a mailing list. Adding such data to an in-house list allows mailers to develop a customer profile based on such factors as age, gender, car ownership, dwelling type, and lifestyle factors. Once that process is undertaken, the in-house list becomes an in-house database, or a collection of information about customers and prospects that can be used for marketing purposes. Modeling techniques can then be applied to the in-house database to help predict response rates from externally compiled lists whose individuals share some of the characteristics of the company's customer profile.

The Direct Mail Package Direct mail packages come in all shapes and sizes, which makes direct mail one of the most flexible of the direct marketing media. A standard direct mail package includes an envelope, a letter, a brochure, and a response device. A variation on the classic format is the multi-mailer—a package with a number of flyers each selling a different product. Another popular format is the self-mailer, or any piece that is mailed without an outer envelope. More complex direct mail packages are three-dimensional; that is, they include an object such as a gift or product sample. These three-dimensional mailings can be effective in reaching top executives whose mail is screened by a secretary, and they are practically guaranteed to be opened by consumers at home.

Catalogs ranging from six to more than 100 pages are used to sell a variety of goods. They are also used to sell services, such as seminars. A variation of the catalog is called a magalog, which combines a certain amount of editorial content along with sales content to give the catalog the appearance of a magazine. A specialized field of direct marketing, catalog marketing is a discipline unto itself and accounts for a significant part of all direct mail activity.

Looking more closely at the classic direct mail package, the envelope's job is to motivate the recipient to open the package. The recipient's decision whether to open, set aside, or discard the mailing piece takes just one or two seconds. Regardless of the volume of mail a person receives, whether at home or a place of business, the envelope must distinguish itself from other mail by its size, appearance, and any copy that might be written on it. Envelopes that take on the appearance of an invitation or telegram might grab someone's attention faster than a plain envelope, for example. Other choices that are made concerning envelopes include color and texture, window or closed face, and whether to use a preprinted indicia or a postage stamp.

The letter is a sales letter and provides the opportunity to directly address the interests and concerns of the recipient. In a sense the letter replaces the salesperson in face-to-face selling. The letter typically spells out the benefits of the offer in detail. The more personal the sales letter, the more effective it generally is. The letter writer must be intimately familiar with not only the product or service and its benefits, but also the concerns and needs of the person to whom the letter is addressed. While the letter tells the recipient about the benefits of the offer, the brochure illustrates them. Illustrated brochures are used to sell services as well as products.

Brochures come in a range of sizes and different folds. While the use of color may increase response, the brochure's look should fit the product or service it is selling.

Finally, the package must include a response device, such as a business reply card or coupon, that the recipient can send back. Response rates are generally higher when the response device is separate from, rather than part of, the brochure or letter. Toll-free numbers are often prominently displayed to allow the recipient to respond via telephone. However, since some customers will not use the phone to place an order, a response device should be included in addition to a toll-free number. The key to a successful response device is to keep it simple and easy to fill out. A "lift letter" is often added to the package to "lift" the response rate. The lift letter usually carries a message such as, "Read this only if you've decided not to accept our offer," to grab the recipient's attention one more time.

Other enclosures that may be added to the direct mail package include gift or premium slips, article reprints, a business reply envelope, and a variety of involvement devices. Involvement devices such as stamps, stickers, pencils, and rub-off messages motivate the recipient to become involved with the response device and, hopefully, continue to take the action required to make a purchase.

TESTING DIRECT MAIL

Since large expenditures are involved in mailing to lists of thousands, most direct mailers take advantage of the medium's testing capabilities. Every element of direct mail—the offer, the list, and the package—can easily be tested to avoid committing major resources to unproductive mailings. In *Successful Direct Marketing Methods,* Bob Stone recommended testing in six major areas: products and services, media, propositions made, copy platforms, formats, and timing. The point is that tests should concentrate on meaningful components.

For products and services being sold by mail, pricing and payment options are often tested. A test may reveal that a higher price actually produces a better response. While the product and the price are considered the main offer, premiums and other incentives that enhance the offer are also subject to testing.

List testing is basic to direct mail. Experts recommend testing different segments of a particular list, preferably testing the best segment first. The appropriate size of a test sample is dependent on the anticipated response. The smaller the anticipated response rate, the larger the necessary list sample should be. A rule of thumb is that the list sample should be large enough to generate thirty to forty anticipated responses. While list testing may clearly identify winners and losers, it will also reveal that some lists are marginal, or near break-even. In that case, the list may be discarded, or another test may be conducted using different selection criteria on the list to make it pay out better.

The direct mail package is subject to a variety of tests focusing on format and copy. If the mailer has established a control package, then one element at a time is tested to see if it lifts the response to the package. Another type of creative testing is sometimes called breakthrough testing, where an entirely new approach is developed to sell a product or service.

Lists, offers, and packages can all be tested in one mailing when done properly. A test matrix consisting of individual test cells is constructed. Each test cell contains a unique combination of elements being tested and makes up a portion of the overall mailing. After the entire mailing is dropped, responses from each test cell are tracked to determine the performance of the tested elements.

WHEN DIRECT MAIL WORKS BEST

Direct mail offers marketers several advantages over other advertising media. It provides a high degree of measurability, for example, which in turn allows for extensive testing. Of course, for direct mail to work well the direct marketer must be able to identify the target audience and create or rent the appropriate mailing lists to reach them. Direct mail also gives marketers control over the sales message and allows them to present a great deal of information about a product or service in the sales letter and brochure. Repeat mailings can be done to take advantage of the product's or service's potential for repeat sales as well as to sell related goods and services to the same lists. While direct marketing has grown over the years to employ a variety of advertising media as they became available, such as the telephone, broadcast media, and print media, it is direct mail that remains the most heavily used medium in direct marketing today.

In the late 1990s and early 2000s, some analysts predicted that the growth of Internet retailing and advertising could lead to a decline in the usefulness of direct mail. But a study reported by Debora Toth in *Graphic Arts Monthly* predicted that direct mail expenditures would grow at an estimated rate of 6 percent per year from 1998 to 2008. In addition, the study predicted that direct mail's share of total advertising expenditures would remain stable at 11 percent during this period. "The Internet is only enhancing direct mail," printing company president Rick Powell told Toth. "Corporations still need to send a campaign based on direct mail in order to drive consumers to their Web sites. After the consumer receives a beautifully printed piece, the firm then can follow up with an e-mail message." In fact, the Internet offers some benefits to direct mail marketers, including easy access to database lists and Web sites that automate the direct-mail production process.

BIBLIOGRAPHY

Hudson, Adams. "The Dos and Don'ts of Direct Mail Marketing." *Air Conditioning, Heating, and Refrigeration News.* 23 October 2000.

Hudson, Adams. "How to Select the Most Profitable Direct Mail List." *Air Conditioning, Heating, and Refrigeration News.* 20 November 2000.

Jones, Susan K. *Creative Strategy in Direct Marketing.* NTC Business Books, 1991.

Kleinman, Mark. "Why the Future of Media Is Direct." *Marketing.* 16 November 2000.

Kobs, Jim. *Profitable Direct Marketing.* Second Editon. NTC Business Books, 1992.

Lewis, Herschell Gordon. *Direct Marketing Strategies and Tactics.* Dartnell, 1992.

Miller, Rachel. "Getting Big Results from a Small Spend." *Marketing.* 7 September 2000.

Scott, Howard. "Targeting Prospects with Direct Mail." *Nation's Business.* September 1997.

Stone, Bob. *Successful Direct Marketing Methods.* Fourth Editon. NTC Business Books, 1989.

"Survey Finds Offers in Envelopes Receive More Attention." *Direct.* 7 February 2006.

Toth, Debora. "Direct Mail: Still Marketing's Darling." *Graphic Arts Monthly.* September 2000.

Hillstrom, Northern Lights
updated by Magee, ECDI

DIRECT MARKETING

Direct marketing evolved as a technique to reach pre-qualified customers at a reasonable cost—over against mass marketing in which, for every qualified customer, several hundred totally disinterested people had to be contacted. The Direct Marketing Association (DMA) speaks of an "interactive system of marketing"; direct marketing, however, grew up out of using qualified mailing lists to reach customers. The interactions, therefore, are typically a customer receiving a letter and the sender getting a phone call. Direct marketing, in other words, is as old as the hills. Companies dealing with the same customers on a narrow subject, like bicycles, learned that they could earn extra money by selling their mailing lists to others. The next phases in direct marketing was capturing such lists in computer databases and adding more information about the customer. This was then hyped as "database marketing." Direct marketing has added a proactive function of *building* mailing lists and databases using federal statistical sources, surveys, and telephone queries.

In a way it is easier to say what direct marketing is *not*. It is not direct mail, although it uses direct mail. If direct mail is used, it has to be sharply targeted. It isn't advertising, although it uses advertising—including such media as billboards. Again, specificity is important. A billboard may announce a melon sale at the next highway intersection. This is a form of direct marketing. It isn't telephone selling, although it may use telephone banks. Telephone selling is telemarketing; it is part of direct marketing only if a company is calling precious customers.

Most consumers do not understand anything particularly sophisticated by the phrase or even know what it means in detail. They simply think that direct marketing is like mail or people at the door, whereas mass marketing is on TV and in the magazines.

Indeed, in practice, distinctions are very difficult to make, and statistics on the subject are derived from members of the DMA. However, not everyone engaged in direct marketing is a member. And presumably the members also engage in other type of marketing not quite so direct—as becomes clear in the discussion below. The DMA suggests that its activities represented 10 percent of Gross Domestic Product in 2005 or $1.28 trillion. However there is no way to develop this number by an alternative means because federal sources do not report on a "direct marketing" category.

DIRECT MARKETING MEDIA

While many people associate direct marketing with direct mail, direct mail is only one of several advertising media utilized by direct marketers. Other major direct marketing media include the telephone, magazines, newspapers, television, and radio. Alternative media include card decks, package and bill inserts, and matchbooks. Within the major media, new technological developments are giving direct marketers an expanded range of choices from videocassettes (possibly advertised on television, requested by telephone or interactive computer, and delivered via mail or alternate delivery services) to home-shopping networks, interactive television, and the Internet.

Direct Mail Direct mail is the most heavily used direct marketing medium and the one most direct marketers learn first. Direct mail has been used to sell a wide variety of goods and services to consumers as well as businesses, and it continues to grow despite postage increases. Direct mail offers several advantages over other media, including selectivity, personalization, flexibility, and testability. It allows businesses to target individuals with known pur-

chase histories or particular psychographic or demographic characteristics that match the marketer's customer profile. Direct mail can be targeted to a specific geographic area based on zip codes or other geographic factors. Personalization in direct mail means not only addressing the envelope to a person or family by name, but also perhaps including the recipient's name inside the envelope.

Direct mail packages come in all shapes and sizes, making it one of the most flexible of the direct marketing media. A standard direct mail package includes an envelope, a letter, a brochure, and a response device. The envelope's job is to motivate the recipient to open the package. Regardless of the volume of mail a person receives, the envelope must distinguish itself from other mail by its size, appearance, and any copy that might be written on it. The letter is a sales letter and provides the opportunity to directly address the interests and concerns of the recipient. The letter typically spells out the benefits of the offer in detail. While the letter tells the recipient about the benefits of the offer, the brochure illustrates them. Illustrated brochures are used to sell services as well as products. Finally, the package must include a response device, such as a business reply card, that the recipient can send back. Response rates are generally higher when the response device is separate from, rather than part of, the brochure or letter. Toll-free numbers are often prominently displayed to allow the recipient to respond via telephone.

Direct mail is the most easily tested advertising medium. Every factor in successful direct marketing—the right offer, the right person, the right format, and the right timing—can be tested in direct mail. Computer technologies have made it easier to select a randomized name sample from any list, so that mailers can run a test mailing to determine the response from a list before "rolling out," or mailing, the entire list. Different packages containing different offers can also be tested. Other media allow some degree of testing, but direct mail is the most sophisticated. In relation to the other direct marketing media, direct mail is considered to offer the most cost-effective way of achieving the highest possible response. Telemarketing usually produces a higher response rate, but at a much higher cost per response.

Telephone-Based Direct Marketing (Telemarketing) The use of the telephone in direct marketing has grown dramatically over the past two decades. Expenditures now may equal, or even surpass, those of direct mail. Telephone-based direct marketing may be outbound and/or inbound. Inbound telemarketing is also known as teleservicing and usually involves taking orders and responding to inquiries. Outbound telemarketing for consumers may be used for one-step selling, lead generation, lead qualification or follow-up, and selling and servicing larger and more active customers. In business, telemarketing can be used to reach smaller accounts that do not warrant a personal sales call as well as to generate, qualify, and follow up leads.

Telemarketing has the advantages of being personal and interactive. It is an effective two-way communications medium that enables company representatives to listen to customers. Telephone salespeople typically work from a script, but the medium allows the flexibility of revising the script as needed. It also allows for up- and cross-selling. While customers are on the phone it is possible to increase the size of their orders by offering them additional choices—something that tends to lead to confusion in other direct marketing media.

Telemarketing also has its disadvantages. For example, it is more expensive than direct mail. It also lacks a permanent response device that the prospect can set aside or use later. It is not a visual medium—though the technology to make it one may soon be available. Finally, it is perceived as intrusive, generating consumer complaints that have led to legislative actions to regulate the telemarketing industry.

Magazines Direct response print ads in magazines must make a definite offer or request that asks the reader to do something. Typically, such ads require a reader to send in a coupon or reply card, or call a toll-free number. With well over 2,000 consumer magazines now being published, magazine ads allow direct marketers to reach audiences with identifiable interests. In addition to advertising heavily in special interest magazines, direct marketers utilize mass consumer magazines and take advantage of regional advertising space to target specific audiences.

Unlike general advertisers, who measure the effectiveness of their print ads in terms of reach and frequency, direct marketers measure the effectiveness of their print ads in terms of cost effectiveness—either cost-per-inquiry or cost-per-order. Magazine ads offer the advantages of good color reproduction, a relatively long ad life (especially compared to daily newspapers), and a lower cost. Creative costs for magazine ads are also usually lower than for direct mail. But direct marketers find magazines' long lead times, slower response, and scarcer space than direct mail to be disadvantages.

Newspapers While direct marketers advertise in magazines more than newspapers, newspapers have some distinct advantages. These include the variety of sections offered within a newspaper, shorter closing dates, an immediate response, and broad coverage of a large and diverse audience. Disadvantages include poor ad repro-

duction and the limited availability of color. Editorial content can also have more of an adverse effect on ad response than in magazines. In addition to advertising in the regular pages of a newspaper, direct marketers also advertise in free-standing inserts (FSIs) that are usually distributed with the Sunday editions of newspapers.

Television Direct marketing on television is increasing. Early examples of direct response advertisements on television that should be familiar to viewers include those for knives, garden tools, exercise equipment, records, and books, which ask viewers to call in and order a specific product. More recent developments in direct response television advertising include a return to a lengthier format, commonly known as the infomercial, where a product or other offer is explained in some detail over a time period extending to 30 minutes or more. Advocates of this format point out that the greater length gives the advertiser the opportunity to build a relationship with the viewer and overcome initial viewer skepticism, and at the same time present a convincing story spelling out product features and benefits in detail.

Not all direct response television involves asking for an order. Long-distance telephone companies and automobile manufacturers, among other advertisers, have included 800 telephone numbers with their television ads to get viewers to call and request more information about their product or service. Any television ad that includes an 800 number is asking for a response and qualifies as a direct response advertisement.

Thanks to the growing availability of interactive television, together with developments in the delivery of more cable channels that offer audiences with identifiable interests and demographics, direct response television promises to be a dynamic area in the future of direct marketing. Interactive digital television now includes direct response features that allow viewers to order a pizza, book a test drive for a new automobile, or order a new music CD without leaving their sofas. "It is the ultimate shopping trip for the couch potato," Rachel Miller wrote in *Marketing.* "Instead of walking to the shops, logging onto a computer, or even picking up a phone, they can press a button on the remote they already have in their hands." In addition to the benefits for consumers, interactive TV also offers businesses the opportunity to collect a great deal of data about their potential customers. Some experts predict that this will usher in an era of targeted, highly personalized television advertising.

DIRECT MARKETING LISTS AND DATABASES

Lists are commonly used in direct mail and telemarketing. The two basic types of lists are response lists and compiled lists. Response lists contain the names of all the prospects who have responded to the same offer. These individuals typically share a common interest. Names on a response list may include buyers, inquirers, subscribers, continuity club members, or sweepstakes entrants. They may have responded to an offer from one of several media, including direct mail, television, or a print ad. Response lists are not usually rented; rather, they are an in-house list compiled by a particular business. Compiled lists are often rented by direct marketers. Compiled mass consumer, specialized consumer, and business lists are available for a wide range of interests.

Direct marketing databases are similar to mailing lists in that they contain names and addresses, but they go much further. They are the repository of a wide range of customer information and may also contain psychographic, demographic, and census data compiled from external sources. They form the basis of direct marketing programs whereby companies establish closer ties with their customers.

Database marketing became one of the buzzwords of the direct marketing industry in the 1980s, and it has continued to evolve in the twenty-first century. Whether it is called relationship marketing, relevance marketing, or bonding, the common theme of database marketing is strengthening relationships with existing customers and building relationships with new ones. Databases allow direct marketers to uncover a wealth of relevant information about individual consumers and apply that knowledge to increase the probability of a desired response or purchase.

As with mailing lists, there are two basic types of marketing databases, customer databases and external databases. Customer databases are compiled internally and contain information about a company's customers taken from the relationship-building process. External databases are collections of specific individuals and their characteristics. These external databases may be mass-compiled from public data sources; they may contain financial data based on confidential credit files; they may be compiled from questionnaires; or they may be a combination of all three sources.

Database marketing, and especially the prospect of using confidential information for marketing purposes, has made privacy an important issue in the direct marketing industry. Some states have passed legislation limiting access to previously public data or limiting the use of such data as automobile registrations, credit histories, and medical information. In order to avoid excessive government regulation, the direct marketing industry has attempted to be self-policing with regard to the use of sensitive data. However, the struggle between industry self-regulation and government regulation will probably continue for some time.

SUCCESSFUL DIRECT MARKETING FOR SMALL BUSINESSES

Thanks to its relatively low cost, its ability to reach specialized target markets, and its ability to provide immediate and measurable results, direct marketing can be an important tool for start-up businesses. It can also be used effectively as a supplement to a small business's traditional sales efforts. Entrepreneurs interested in starting a direct marketing program can consult with advertising and direct marketing agencies for help in evaluating their sales potential and preparing materials for a campaign.

In the *Macmillan Small Business Handbook,* Mark Stevens identified three steps for a small business owner to take in initiating a direct marketing effort: 1) create promotional tools (such as catalogs, advertisements, or direct mail pieces) that emphasize the benefits of the product or service; 2) identify the target market and select mailing lists and advertising media to reach it; and 3) monitor the results of each campaign and revise the tactics as needed to find the optimum mix of price, copy, and audience. Stevens noted that entrepreneurs might also find it helpful to give consumers an incentive to act, such as a free gift or special price; promote to existing customers—who usually provide the highest response rate—as well as new prospects; and build on successful promotions by broadening the product line.

There are certain situations where direct marketing is more likely to work than others. First, the direct marketer must be able to identify the target audience in terms of shared characteristics. Are they likely to read a particular magazine? Live in a certain geographic area? Have a certain minimum income? Be a certain age or gender? The more characteristics of the target audience that can be identified, the more likely it is that a direct marketing campaign targeted to those individuals will work.

Since direct marketing relies on one-to-one communications and motivating the recipient to act, it is essential to be able to reach the target audience. It is no use identifying a target market if there is no mailing list or print or broadcast medium available to reach them. Some other situations in which direct marketing works well are when there is a lot to say about a product or service; when the product or service has the potential for repeat sales; and when there is a need to have greater control over the sales message.

The success of a direct marketing program depends on delivering the right offer at the right time to the right person in the right way. Direct marketing is a complex discipline that requires expertise in several areas to achieve success. It involves identifying the target market correctly and selecting the appropriate media and/or lists to reach it. The offer must be presented in the best way, and direct marketers must use the most effective creative execution to successfully motivate customers and prospects. At its most effective, direct marketing is an ongoing process of communication to maintain relationships with existing customers and build relationships with new ones.

BIBLIOGRAPHY

"Executive Summary for 2005." *U.S. Direct Marketing Today.* Direct Marketing Association, Inc. Available on http://www.the-dma.org/research/economicimpact2005ExecSummary.pdf. Retrieved on 13 February 2006.

Kobs, Jim. *Profitable Direct Marketing,* Second Edition. NTC Business Books, 1992.

Lewis, Herschell Gordon. *Direct Marketing Strategies and Tactics.* Dartnell, 1992.

Miller, Rachel. "DM's Place in an iTV Future." *Marketing.* 2 November 2000.

Nash, Edward L., ed. *The Direct Marketing Handbook.* Second Edition. McGraw-Hill, 1992.

Schwartz, David O. "Trends to Track for the Millennium." *Target Marketing.* October 1999.

David Shepard Associates. *The New Direct Marketing: How to Implement a Profit-Driven Database Marketing Strategy.* Business One Irwin, 1990.

Stevens, Mark. *The Macmillan Small Business Handbook.* Macmillan, 1988.

Stone, Bob. *Successful Direct Marketing Methods,* Fourth Edition. NTC Business Books, 1989.

Toth, Debora. "Direct Mail: Still Marketing's Darling." *Graphic Arts Monthly.* September 2000.

Hillstrom, Northern Lights
updated by Darnay, ECDI

DIRECT PUBLIC OFFERINGS

A direct public offering (DPO) is a financial tool that enables a company to sell stock directly to investors—without using an underwriter as an intermediary. The company can thus avoid many of the costs associated with "going public" through an initial public offering or IPO. DPOs are, as it were, IPOs "lite." The business choosing this route is exempted from many of the registration and reporting requirements of the Securities and Exchange Commission (SEC).

DPOs first became available to small businesses in 1976 but only gained some popularity in 1989 when the rules were further simplified. In 1992, SEC established its Small Business Initiatives program; the program eliminated even more of the barriers that had limited the ability of small companies to raise capital by selling stock. The development of the Internet stimulated this route because it promised at least the possibility that companies could sell their stocks directly on the Internet. Thus whereas the demanding structure, the reporting requirements, and high costs of IPOs (average cost in the mind-2000s was $3.5 million) arose in an environment or reform and discipline in the wake of the Depression, DPOs developed during a period of exuberant market expansion.

The principal differences between a full-fledged IPO and a DPO is that 1) DPO stock is not registered and trading in such stock is difficult, 2) amounts of capital that may be raised are delimited in various ways, 3) the costs of a DPO are lower, and 4) the very strict adherence to the requirements of SEC-imposed disclosures, accounting methods, and conformity to requirements of the Sarbanes-Oxley Act (a consequence of Enron) do not apply.

The principal similarity is that in both cases stock is sold to the general public; the business, therefore, is able to reach beyond its intimate circle of friends to raise capital.

Although many small businesses need the capital that an IPO can provide, they often lack the financial strength and reputation to appeal to a broad range of investors—necessary ingredients for a successful IPO. For other small businesses, the loss of control, the strict reporting requirements, or the expense of staging an IPO are prohibitive factors.

ADVANTAGES AND DISADVANTAGES

The primary advantage of DPOs over IPOs is a dramatic reduction in cost. IPO underwriters typically charge a commission of 13 percent of the proceeds of the sale of securities, whereas the costs associated with a DPO are closer to 3 percent. DPOs also can be completed within a shorter time and without extensive disclosure of confidential information. Finally, since the stock sold through a DPO goes to a limited number of investors who tend to have a long-term orientation, there is often less pressure on the company's management to deliver short-term results.

DPOs' disadvantages include limitations on the amount that a company can raise within any 12-month period. The stock is usually sold at a lower price than it might command through an IPO. Stock sold through exempt offerings is not usually freely traded: no market price is established for the shares or for the overall company. This lack of a market price may make it difficult for the company to use equity as loan collateral. Finally, DPO investors are likely to demand a larger share of ownership in the company to offset the lack of liquidity in their position. Investors eventually may pressure the company to go public through an IPO so that they can realize their profits.

TYPES OF DPOs

The most common DPO is known as a Small Corporate Offering Registration, or SCOR. The SEC provided this option to small businesses in 1982 through an amendment to federal securities law known as Regulation D, Rule 504. SCOR gives an exemption to private companies that raise no more than $1 million in any 12-month period through the sale of stock. There are no restrictions on the number or types of investors; the securities can be freely traded. The SCOR process is easy enough for a small business owner to complete with the assistance of a knowledgeable accountant and attorney. It is available in most states.

A related type of DPO is outlined in SEC Regulation D, Rule 505. This option enables a small business to sell up to $5 million in stock during a 12-month period to an unlimited number of *accredited investors*. Accredited investors must be people/institutions of substantial means ($1 million in assets for individuals, $5 million for institutions). The business may sell stock to up to 35 people/institutions who do not meet this test. The SEC's purpose in requiring such qualifications arises from the fact that "accredited" investors are presumed to be knowledgeable and sophisticated enough not to be taken in by a scam.

Another type of DPO is outlined in SEC Regulation A. This option is frequently referred to as a "mini public offering": it follows many of the same procedures as an IPO; the securities may also be freely traded. However, companies choosing this option may only offer up to $5 million in securities in any 12-month period. Regulation A offerings are allowed to bypass federal SEC registration and instead are filed with the Small Business Office of the SEC.

Two further types of DPOs are available to businesses with less than $25 million in annual revenues. A Small Business Type 1 (SB-1) offering enables a company to sell up to $10 million in securities in a 12-month period and has simpler paperwork. A Small Business Type 2 (SB-2) filing enables a company to sell an unlimited amount of securities and has more difficult paperwork.

A final type of DPO is available through the SEC's intrastate filing exemption, Rule 147. This option allows companies to raise unlimited funds through the sale of securities as long as the stock is sold only in the primary state in which they do business. Both the company and all the investors must be residents of the same state. This exemption is intended to provide local businesses with a means of raising capital within their locale.

ONLINE DPOs

In the late-1990s, the "magic hand" of the Internet (as one might call it) was touted as a way taking dot-coms public and selling their DPO stock on the Web. Very little of that actually happened, looking back. According to Jack A. Rosenbloom writing in *Journal of Internet Law,* "During the boom, funding from venture capital was occurring at an astonishing rate, peaking at almost $100 billion in 2000.... Businesses with nothing more than an idea and a half finished business plan were going public at astonishing rates, peaking at 1,017 IPOs filed in 2000.... Businesses simply did not see the need to conduct their own Internet DPOs when more established alternatives were so readily available." By 2003 the venture capital had dried up—and it is venture capital that really comes from "accredited" investors. In that year only 118 IPOs were filed. When IPOs are hard to get, so are DPOs.

In any case, the hang-over after the dot-com collapse has brought it home to many that the Internet is not an amplifier of information as television is but, rather, a multiplier of it. To make a DPO stock offering visible on the Internet, the seller of stock must be assured of a high rate of traffic to begin with. If such traffic does not exist, it is like putting a notice on the backside of a suburban garage.

CAUTIONS

Although DPOs can simplify the process of raising capital, there is no guarantee that an offering will be successful. Robert Lowes noted back in the boom times writing in *Medical Electronics:* "In all types of DPOs, the companies usually declare a minimum amount needed to carry out the business plan. Seven of every ten SCORs fail to reach that target—to 'break escrow,' in the parlance." Small business owners considering a DPO need to realize that there is hard work involved. In fact, the business may suffer during the offering period: management often lacks time both to promote the offering and run the company. For this reason, DPOs are most likely to be successful in companies that are not overly dependent on their top management and that have a sound business plan in place.

DPOs are also more likely to be successful for companies that have an established and loyal customer base. Customers are often the best potential investors. Companies initiating DPOs can advertise their stock to customers on product packaging, through mailing lists, with posted messages in offices or other facilities, or by making the prospectus available on an Internet site. "Experts suggest that any company gauge investor enthusiasm before launching a DPO—because costs for attorneys, accountants, and marketing materials can add up," warned Carol Steinberg in *Success.*

Finally, companies can improve their chances for a successful DPO by availing themselves of expert securities advice. "Whether an offering is properly exempt from registration with the SEC is a matter for competent legal counsel and careful structuring of the offering. Errors must be avoided, since a faulty offering generally gives investors the right to get their money back," according to Zeune and Baer. The fact that a DPO does not have to be registered with the SEC does not release a company from compliance with the antifraud provisions of U.S. securities laws. Potential investors must have ample, accurate information to make an informed decision about whether or not to buy stock in the company. Finally, securities laws vary by state, so it is important that small business owners interested in pursuing a DPO consider the laws applicable to their companies.

SEE ALSO *Initial Public Offerings*

BIBLIOGRAPHY
"Stock Offerings in 2005." *Crain's Detroit Business.* 30 January 2006.

Kinsella, Bridget. "How to Raise $1 Million." *Publishers Weekly.* 2 May 2005.

Lowes, Robert L. "Try a Do-It-Yourself Public Offering." *Medical Economics.* 14 April 1997.

McLean, Bethany. "Direct Public Offerings: Cash for Low-Profile Firms." *FSB.* 1 February 2000.

"Reed's Ginger Brew Announces Direct Public Offering." *Gourmet Retailer.* April 2003.

Rosenbloom, Jack A. "From Spring Street to Main Street: Will the Internet direct public offering (DPO) ever catch on?" *Journal of Internet Law.* May 2004.

Steinberg, Carol. "The DPO Revolution: Direct Public Offerings Turn Customers into Investors." *Success.* March 1997.

"Stock Offerings in 2005." *Crain's Detroit Business.* 30 January 2006.

Zeune, Gary D., and Timothy R. Baer. "Floating a Stock Offering: New Buoyancy from the SEC." *Corporate Cashflow Magazine.* August 1993.

Hillstrom, Northern Lights
updated by Magee, ECDI

DISABILITY INSURANCE

Disability insurance or disability income insurance (abbreviated DI in the industry), is designed to compensate the policy holder for income lost if the holder becomes disabled. DI usually also covers additional serv-

ices such as rehabilitation. DI is one in a spectrum of protection measures available to individuals or groups. Group DI policies may have upper limits on their income protection provisions; sometimes it turns out to be difficult to realize a benefit under such policies because of elaborate and government-imposed review processes. Private DI policies were once available providing very high compensation replacement; insurance companies have changed their products since the 1990s in order to protect themselves against claims losses, but private policies can still be purchased with higher benefits than group policies.

Protection against disability in the workplace takes several forms, some at the option of the employer, some provided under state or federal law: 1) most employees have legally mandated sick leave privileges; 2) many employers offer short-term disability (STD) insurance in addition; private STD insurance is available but said by industry observers to be difficult to get for reasons laid out below; 3) worker's compensation programs are provided by state governments paid for through levies on employers; in most states the compensation is two-thirds of wages earned; other benefits (like retraining) may be provided; 3) Social Security disability insurance becomes available after an individual has been unable to work for a year; only those totally disabled are eligible; and payments begin six months after eligibility has been established; the amount paid, like Social Security itself, is based on past earnings but does not necessarily match them; 4) long term disability (LTD) group plans are offered in about 40 percent of medium to large-sized companies, according to *Kiplinger's Personal Finance;* far fewer small companies offer such insurance.

INDIVIDUAL DI

Individual disability insurance, according to Peter C. Katt, an industry advisor, writing in *Journal of Financial Planning,* ran into turbulent times in the late 1990s because of mistakes made in the 1980. These problems are still affecting DI companies and those wishing to buy policies.

The DI industry developed insurance products for individuals with high income some of which was badly underpriced in the 1980s. These came to be known as "own occupation" policies in which a person was deemed to be totally disabled if he or she could not perform the duties of his or her "own occupation." Thus, using one of Katt's examples, an orthopedic surgeon unable to stand during long operations because of persistent back pain would be deemed "totally disabled" and deemed entitled to collect up to 60 percent of his or her weekly compensation until retirement age—even though this same person could easily, by switching to general practice, earn a very decent income if not at the peak level as a surgeon. Such policies became very popular with physicians, specialists, and lawyers. "DI companies fell all over themselves providing narrower definitions of such occupations." Claims experience later showed that the incidence of such narrowly defined disability was much higher than anticipated, the premiums charged too low to sustain the business, and therefore new DI policies are tailored much more in favor of the insurance companies in the mid-2000s.

"Own occupation" coverage may be limited to some period of time after the disability. Thereafter an "any occupation" clause comes into effect. Thus, for instance, a surgeon who must occasionally sit down is obliged to practice some other branch of medicine rather that sit back and collect high DI payments until age 65.

Costs of Individual DI An individual thinking of purchasing individual DI should anticipate paying around 2 percent of his or her annual gross income in premiums for income benefits equivalent to between 45 and 50 percent of gross income, this benefit beginning 90 days after the disabling event and lasting until retirement at age 65—assuming that the individual has no other work activity that produces income. These data are based on quotations obtained in 2006 for a hypothetical 51-year old non-smoking, non-drinking individual earning $250,000 a year in an administrative position. The average of premiums quoted was $4,620 per annum and the average monthly benefit at $9,797, equivalent to 47 percent of gross income.

Group Long-Term-Disability Packages Group coverage generally replaces 40 to 60 percent of the insured person's income, but usually only up to about $5,000 a month. This compensation is fully taxable if the premium is paid by the employer, but the company is permitted to deduct the premium as a business expense. Group plans are relatively inexpensive but are designed to limit what is covered and to make benefits payable as predictable as possible for the insurance carrier. Definitions of disability are limited, any external income or benefits the claimant receives may be deducted from benefits, and certain conditions are excluded. The claimant's ability to sue the company must take place under the provisions of the Employee Retirement Income Security Act of 1974 (ERISA). As Mark F. Seltzer reported in *Physician's News Digest*, the law surrounding ERISA-managed appeals processes has come to favor the insurance carrier.

DEEP-SEATED CONFLICTS

Insurance works most rationally in a real life situation in which a *particular* claims event (e.g. a death) is very difficult to predict but the *aggregate* of such events can be projected statistically with fair precision. In such circumstances the insurance carrier can rationally calculate a reasonable premium which will ultimately pay the claimant what is contractually defined while permitting the carrier to have a profit.

"Disability" does not seem to fit the insurance model very well because it is less predictable and much more difficult to define and prove. The Social Security Administration states that 3 of 10 individuals may become disabled in their working years before reaching retirement age. But the agency does not have very specific definitions of the nature of disability or its duration, both of which have complex causes and factors.

Human disability may have as its cause what seem to be a nearly infinite number of interacting physical and mental disturbances the onset of which is almost impossible statistically to project to a population. And if the liability of the insurance carrier is, furthermore, income protection, the nature of the disability that may strike a policy holder does not necessarily link closely to the policy holder's earnings. There are definitional problems. Disability to perform one's "own occupation" is contrasted to performing "any occupation." And the literature in the field bristles with complaints about the adequacy of definitions in distinguishing between actual and subjective disability—not least the medical basis of something like chronic fatigue syndrome.

In this situation generally, the natural outworkings of socially provided protection schemes tend toward unsatisfactory outcomes. On the private side, insurance carriers attempt to limit exposure by a combination of high premiums in private policies and delimited benefits in mass policies. On the public side, minimal protection is provided but only in cases of total disability, which is the Social Security disability outcome.

Under the circumstances, DI is one option—and not a very satisfactory one—the small business owner can examine as a hedge against personal disability. An aggressive saving plan may be another. Substantial time in soliciting bids, in using legal resources to examine offered policies, and in researching alternatives to such expenditures are in the picture. In a well-run and profitable small business, an internal legal arrangement which will provide some limited income to the disabled owner at company expense may sometimes be the best solution whether or not it involves DI.

BIBLIOGRAPHY

"Disability Insurance and Women." *WebMD*. Available from http://www.medicinenet.com. Retrieved on 15 February 2006.

"Do You Have Enough Disability Coverage?" *Kiplinger's Personal Finance*. 21 March 2003.

Greenwald, Judy. "Insurers, Regulator Clash Over Disability; Policy Language at Center of Fight." *Business Insurance.* 12 December 2005.

Katt, Peter. "Be Wise About Disability Insurance." *Journal of Financial Planning.* June 1997.

Koco, Linda. "New DI Society Gets Under Way." *National Underwriter Life & Health.* 21 November 2005.

Lynn, Jacquelyn. "What's the Damage?" *Entrepreneur.* July 2000.

Mariski, William G. "Cultural underwriting: a revived disability pricing concept?" *National Underwriter Life & Health.* 14 November 2005.

Panko, Ron. "Group Disability Plan to Help Small Employers." *Best's Review.* January 2006.

"Read the Fine Print." *Kiplinger's Personal Finance.* 21 March 2003.

Schneider, Larry. "Arthritis: Outcomes vary in disability insurance cases." *National Underwriter Life & Health.* 14 November 2005.

Seltzer, Mark F. Esq. "ERISA and Long Term Disability Claims." *Physician's News Digest.* November 2003.

Tinkham, Leo D. "Evidence of Cost Savings Grows for Integrated Disability Management." *Employee Benefit News.* 1 August 2000.

Darnay, ECDI

DISABLED CUSTOMERS

According to 2000 Census data published by the U.S. Census Bureau (available in tabular format on http://www.census.gov/hhes/www/disability/disabstat2k/table1.html), in that year, by actual total tally of the population, 49.7 million people (19.3 percent of the population aged 5 or over) had some kind of disability. A further subdivision showed that 5.8 percent of those aged 5 to 15, 18.6 percent of those 16 through 64, and 41.9 percent of those aged 65 and over had some disability. The census provided four distinct categories of disability. Those with *physical* disabilities were 8.2 percent of the population aged 5 or older (21.2 million physically handicapped); *mentally* disabled were 4.8 percent of population (12.4 million), those with *sensory* handicaps were 3.6 percent (9.3 million), and those unable to provide *self-care* 2.6 percent of the total population (6.8 million actual cases).

In 1990 the passage of the Americans with Disabilities Act (ADA) aimed to provide better access for this segment of the population to employment and services. The U.S. Department of Justice, the principal administrator of this law, sums up the aims and intentions of the ADA in one of its Questions and Answers pages on its home page as follows: "Barriers to employ-ment, transportation, public accommodations, public services, and telecommunications have imposed staggering economic and social costs on American society and have undermined our well-intentioned efforts to educate, rehabilitate, and employ individuals with disabilities. By breaking down these barriers, the Americans with Disabilities Act (ADA) will enable society to benefit from the skills and talents of individuals with disabilities, will allow us all to gain from their increased purchasing power and ability to use it, and will lead to fuller, more productive lives for all Americans."

The portion of the Americans with Disabilities Act that most directly relates to disabled customers is Title III dealing with public accommodations. Title III requires that private businesses open to the public—including retail establishments, restaurants, and hotels and motels—give individuals with disabilities the same access to their goods and services that non-disabled customers enjoy. This section of the ADA also required that all future construction of commercial facilities, including office buildings, factories, and warehouses, as well as places of public accommodation, be constructed so that the building is accessible to individuals with disabilities.

BUSINESS OBLIGATIONS UNDER ADA

ADA places Title III requirements on businesses of all sizes. These, principally, are 1) to modify policies and practices that discriminate against the disabled, 2) to comply with access design standards when modifying existing or building new structures, 3) to remove existing barriers in existing structures where easily achievable, and 4) to provide auxiliary aids and service to ensure effective communication with those who have hearing, sight, or speech impairments.

Modified Policies Examples of a policies that might require change is to accommodate guide dogs in stores that would not otherwise permit pets or always to keep open checkout counters capable of handling wheelchairs. The law specifically mentions specialist in diseases who in the past, evidently, refused to treat disabled persons with those diseases; now such selectivity is prohibited as a policy.

Access Standards Many people still believe that the central issue of ADA is access to buildings. That is certain an important element of the law, but not the only one. Since 1992 building modification has been promulgated as the *ADA Standards for Accessible Design*, a 92 page document which clearly describes accommodations to newly built or altered buildings. The first 58 pages deal in detail with external facilities such as parking accommodations and internal access and accommodation matters applicable to any facilities, such a walkways, support rails, access to shelving, toilet facilities, communications devices, and many more areas of contact between people and structural facets; the remaining pages specify requirements unique to restaurants and cafeterias, medical care facilities, business and mercantile structures, libraries, accessible transient lodgings, and transportation facilities.

Removal of Barriers A public accommodation is required to remove architectural barriers in existing facilities, including communication barriers that are structural in nature, where the removal is readily achievable, i.e., it can be accomplishable easily and able to be carried out without much difficulty or expense. The law lists 20 examples, as follows:

1. Installing ramps;
2. Making curb cuts in sidewalks and entrances;
3. Repositioning shelves;
4. Rearranging tables, chairs, vending machines, display racks, and other furniture;
5. Repositioning telephones;
6. Adding raised markings on elevator control buttons;
7. Installing flashing alarm lights;
8. Widening doors;
9. Installing offset hinges to widen doorways;
10. Eliminating a turnstile or providing an alternative accessible path;
11. Installing accessible door hardware;
12. Installing grab bars in toilet stalls;
13. Rearranging toilet partitions to increase maneuvering space;
14. Insulating lavatory pipes under sinks to prevent burns;
15. Installing a raised toilet seat;
16. Installing a full-length bathroom mirror;
17. Repositioning the paper towel dispenser in a bathroom;
18. Creating designated accessible parking spaces;
19. Installing an accessible paper cup dispenser at an existing inaccessible water fountain;
20. Removing high pile, low density carpeting; or
21. Installing vehicle hand controls.

Where such accommodations are difficult to achieve, work-arounds are permissible. Examples are to provide help for reaching shelves or, in multi-screen theaters where access to all screens is not possible to provide, the movie theater can meet the law by rotating the films shown so that each appears on one of the screens accessible to wheelchair-bound customers.

Auxiliary Aids and Services Auxiliary aids and services are intended to give customers or clients access to commercial and other services despite their disabilities. An example is to provide instructions in Braille and large print, telecommunications devices for the deaf, and other means to help communications. The service provider may be exempted from such requirements if he or she can prove that doing so would fundamentally alter the nature of the enterprise or would impose a significantly large expense.

Litigious Beginnings Businesses have perhaps been slow in fully absorbing the requirements of ADA, managements, perhaps, being too focused on the construction issues imposed by access standards—which, after all, may be left to the next major reconstruction project. Slow response, on the other hand, has gradually resulted in the launch of many large class-action law suits brought by or on behalf of disabled groups. As the lists above show, faults can be found in many hidden places. In some states, like California, where additional state legislation has made it more profitable to sue—because California law permits the collection of damages whereas ADA only allows for attorney's fees—lawsuits have reached quite small business as well and have damaged them severely enough to put some out of business. Lawfirms specializing in ADA cases have formed alliances with disabled groups. In the mid-2000s hundreds of ADA suits were being filed per month.

For these reasons, the small business owner is well advised to make the necessary effort to examine his or her compliance with ADA now. Gathering information on compliance is relatively easy, with the U.S. Department of Justice ADA Home Page (provided below) being a trouble-free point of entry. ADA is the law of the land. Its requirements under Title III are sometimes difficult but certainly achievable. They ultimately relate to making goods on display accessible to all, be they disabled or not. Making them so must, ultimately, be good for business.

SEE ALSO *Americans with Disabilities Act*

BIBLIOGRAPHY
"Advocates File ADA Suits Against Local Hotels, Malls." *Crain's Detroit Business.* 28 June 2004.

"Black Angus Chain Hit with ADA Lawsuit in Utah." *Nation's Restaurant News.* 20 October 2003.

"Bradley Launches Next Generation Lavatory Systems." *Contract.* June 2005.

Jennings, Lisa. "California 'Sheriff' Cites ADA, State Law in Rash of Lawsuits: Wheelchair-bound activist slaps hundreds of operators with complaints." *Nation's Restaurant News.* 27 September 2004.

"Small Stores Tackle Big Challenges." *Chain Store Age.* May 2001.

Thornton, Jeremy. "Disabled Golfers File Suit Against Marriott: Joins with federal move to force ADA rules on golf courses, hotels." *Meeting News.* 21 November 2005.

"Ultimate accessibility." *Building and Construction.* July 2005.

U.S. Department of Justice. 28 CFR Part 36. *ADA Standards for Accessible Design.* 1 July 1994. Available from http://www.usdoj.gov/crt/ada/adastd94.pdf. Retrieved on 17 February 2006.

U.S. Department of Justice. Americans with Disabilities Act ADA Home Page. Accessible from http://www.usdoj.gov/crt/ada/adahom1.htm. Retrieved on 19 February 2006.

Wilson, Marianne. "ADA Myths Remain: There is no such thing as a grandfather clause." *Chain Store Age.* January 2006.

Wilson, Marianne. "Retailers Hit Hard by ADA." *Chain Store Age.* August 2003.

Darnay, ECDI

DISASTER ASSISTANCE LOANS

Disaster assistance loans are utilized by businesses to recover from floods, fires, earthquakes, tornadoes, etc. that damage one or more aspects of their operations, from physical structure to inventory to lost business. Of course, adequate insurance policies offer the best protection for small business owners, but many businesses do not maintain adequate coverage. Small businesses are particularly reliant on disaster loans since they can not draw on the corporate coffers to which larger firms often turn. Some small business owners solicit loans from banks and other lending institutions in the wake of a natural disaster, but many others turn to loan programs offered by the Small Business Administration (SBA) and other federal agencies. Indeed, the SBA is a primary source of funding for businesses seeking to rebuild after a disaster strikes.

Any business that qualifies under SBA definitions as a "small business," is located in a major disaster area, and has suffered damage as a consequence of that disaster may apply for assistance. The assistance is earmarked in two ways. First, as help to repair or replace damaged property. Second, as help to meet those financial obligations that it would have been able to honor had a disaster not taken place. The SBA maintains separate programs for each of these eventualities. The agency notes, however,

that qualification for an SBA disaster relief loan is not a given. "The SBA disaster relief program is not an immediate emergency relief program such as Red Cross assistance, temporary housing assistance, etc.," according to the agency. "It is a loan program to help you in your long-term rebuilding and repairing. To make a loan, we have to know the cost of repairing the damage, be satisfied that you can repay the loan, and take reasonable safeguards to help make sure the loan is paid."

Physical Disaster Business Loans The SBA makes physical disaster loans of up to $1.5 million to qualified businesses, provided that the businesses use this money for the repair or replacement of real property, equipment, machinery, fixtures, inventory, and leasehold improvements. This property may have been insured or uninsured prior to the disaster. "In addition," noted the SBA, "disaster loans to repair or replace real property or leasehold improvements may be increased by as much as 20 percent to protect the damaged real property against possible future disasters of the same type." This latter allowance can be particularly attractive to victims of natural disasters that tend to occur on a cyclical basis. Finally, some businesses can use this money to relocate, although the SBA cautions business owners not to formally commit to such plans before gaining loan approval. The SBA points out that the disaster loan is "made for specific and designated purposes. Remember that the penalty for misusing disaster funds is immediate repayment of one and a half times the original amount of the loan. The SBA requires that you obtain receipts and maintain good records of all loan expenditures as your restore your damaged property, and that you keep these receipts and records for three years."

Applications for these loans require the business to file a variety of financial and other records, including an itemized list of losses (with estimated replacement/repair cost), federal income tax information, history of the business, personal financial statements, and business financial statements. Whereas loans of less than $10,000 require no collateral, loans of amounts greater than that require the pledging of collateral to the extent that it is available. The SBA notes that while it will not decline a loan solely for lack of collateral, it does require businesses to pledge collateral when it is available.

Interest rates on physical disaster loans vary, depending on whether or not the applicant is able to obtain credit with other financial institutions. In instances where the business is not able to obtain credit elsewhere, U.S. law sets a maximum interest rate of 4 percent per year on these loans, with a maximum maturity of 30 years. Businesses that would be able to secure credit elsewhere, however, do not get quite so advantageous terms. For these latter enterprises, the interest rate is either 8 percent or whatever is being charged in the private sector at the time, whichever is less. The maturity of these loans cannot exceed three years. Nonprofit organizations can secure better interest rates and maturity terms through the SBA than can for-profit businesses.

Economic Injury Disaster Loans The EIDL loan program is available to small business and small agricultural cooperatives that have suffered substantial economic injury resulting from a physical disaster or an agricultural production disaster. The SBA defines "substantial economic injury" as "the inability of a business to meet its obligations as they mature and to pay its ordinary and necessary operating expenses." In essence, it gives companies an opportunity to catch their breath in the wake of a disaster.

EIDL assistance is available only to those entities that are unable to secure credit from other private sources (banks, etc.). It is used less often than the physical disaster loan option for several other reasons as well:

1. The SBA limits its total assistance to any one company to $1.5 million, no matter how many programs are utilized. This means that a business that secures a $1.5 million loan for facility repair through the SBA's physical disaster business loan is not eligible for any funds through EIDL.

2. The SBA puts limitations on how EIDL funds can be used. For instance, these funds can not be used to pay cash bonuses or dividends, or for disbursements to owners, partners, officers, or stockholders who are not directly related to the performance of services for the business.

3. Finally, EIDL loans do not give the borrower any leeway in the realms of relocation or physical improvements, both of which are sometimes possible through the SBA's physical disaster loan program.

In many other respects, however—determination of interest rates, penalties for misuse of funds, use of collateral, procedures for securing a loan, etc.—the procedures for EIDLs are largely the same as those for physical disaster business loans.

SBA Loans and Flood Insurance According to the SBA, if damage is caused by flooding, or the business is in a special flood hazard area, the business seeking the SBA loan must have flood insurance before the agency will disburse the loan. If the business was legally required to maintain flood insurance but did not, then the SBA will not grant a disaster loan.

Disaster Loans for Personal Property and Homes The SBA also maintains loan programs for homeowners, renters, and/or personal property owners who are victimized by a disaster. Personal property loans of up to $40,000 are available to individuals, homeowners, or renters to help repair or replace personal goods (boats, automobiles, clothes, appliances, furniture, etc.). Real property loans of up to $200,000, meanwhile, are available to homeowners for replacement or repair of actual homes. These loans may not be used for home upgrades or additions, but can be targeted toward making structural improvements necessary to meet city or county building codes. Second homes and vacation homes are not eligible for these loans.

TERRORISM, ECONOMIC CHANGE, AND NATURAL DISASTERS

The SBA has seen a lot of activity since the 9/11 terrorism attacks of 2001, the economic changes wrought by 9/11 in the airline industry, and increasing hurricane events culminating in the record-breaking 2005 season. Developments in the airline industry caused in large part by the growth in Internet-based online ordering of tickets came to a head early in 2001 when the commercial carriers discontinued paying commission on ticket sales to travel agencies; this shock to that industry, in combination with the drastic slow-down in travel after 9/11 and the on-rush of a recession in the wake of the attack, caused enormous economic hardship for travel agencies. Many travel agencies sought disaster loan assistance from the SBA with little experience in dealing the agency; at the same time, SBA had to master the peculiarities of travel agencies to assess how best to help them.

According to NASA, in an article titled "2005: A Hurricane Season 'On Edge'," "Millions of lives were changed by the record-setting 2005 Atlantic hurricane season—a 'worst case scenario' for the United States. The 27 named tropical storms beat the old record of 21 in 1933. Five hurricanes (Dennis, Katrina, Ophelia, Rita and Wilma) and three tropical storms (Arlene, Cindy and Tammy) directly impacted the country: destroying lives, demolishing homes and wrecking the landscape." Katrina was the costliest hurricane in U.S. history; Wilma and Rita both made the top ten. Tens of thousands of small businesses were affected. Katrina hit on August 29, 2005. As of February 2006, the SBA had approved $1.05 billion in loans to 12,455 Florida and Gulf Coast businesses, on average $84,000 per business. These businesses were at least able to get help. Many others will close their doors forever.

BIBLIOGRAPHY
National Aeronautics and Space Administration. "2005: A Hurricane Season 'On Edge'." Available from http://

www.nasa.gov/vision/earth/lookingatearth/ 2005hurricane_recap.html. Retrieved on 14 February 2006.

"SBA Assistance Tops $1.5 Billion." *Mississippi Business Journal.* 2 January 2006.

U.S. Small Business Administration. "Economic Injury Disaster Loans for Small Business" Available from http:// www.sba.gov/disaster_recov/loaninfo/phydisaster.html. Retrieved on 14 February 2006.

U.S. Small Business Administration. "Home and Personal Property Disaster Loans." Available from http:// www.sba.gov/disaster_recov/loaninfo/property.html. Retrieved on 14 February 2006.

U.S. Small Business Administration. "Physical Disaster Business Loans." Available from http://www.sba.gov/disaster_recov/ loaninfo/phydisaster.html. Retrieved on 14 February 2006.

U.S. Small Business Administration. "SBA Approves Over $1 Billion In Disaster Loans To Businesses Affected By 2005 Hurricanes." Press Release. 13 February 2006.

Hillstrom, Northern Lights
updated by Magee, ECDI

DISASTER PLANNING

Small business owners are strongly encouraged to make contingency plans for responding to and recovering from disasters that may befall them. The motivation for doing so may be more sharply present in the aftermath of the 2005 Katrina hurricane that almost wiped out New Orleans. Analysts note that disasters—whether they take the form of floods, corporate espionage, fires, or power outages—can have a devastating impact on a business's viability. Business experts also insist that the importance of a good disaster and recovery plan has never been as acute as it is today. In large part this is because today so many businesses rely on vulnerable technology (communication networks, management information systems, process control systems, etc.) to execute fundamental business operations.

Yet as Alan M. Levitt reported in *Disaster Planning and Recovery,* "various studies and surveys instruct us that most organizations have not established a comprehensive strategy for disaster planning and recovery. The percentage of organizations that lack any semblance of a plan is, simply put, frighteningly large." Levitt also noted that many disaster contingency plans that do exist are "applicable only to certain specific business processes (put another way, it is designed only to rescue specific bits and pieces of the business, not to save the entire organization!)." Many other companies' disaster planning policies, meanwhile, seem to consist only of disaster insurance. Such coverage is valuable, but it is only of limited usefulness. Indeed, Kenneth N. Myers, author of

Total Contingency Planning for Disasters, described disaster insurance as only one element of a comprehensive disaster contingency plan. "The role of insurance in protecting against loss of physical assets, such as buildings and equipment, is clear," wrote Myers. "However, using insurance policies to protect against the loss of cash flow, the ability to service customers, or the ability to maintain market share is often not practical.... The primary function of business insurance is to provide a hedge against loss or damage. A disaster recovery and business continuation plan, however, has three objectives: 1) Prevent disasters from happening; 2) Provide an organized response to a disaster situation; 3) Ensure business continuity until normal business operations can be resumed."

It is essential, then, that small businesses take the time and effort to construct comprehensive disaster and recovery plans if they hope to weather unwelcome interruptions in business operations in good financial and market condition. "Some call it Crisis Management," remarked *Building Design & Construction* magazine. "Others call it Disaster Management, Emergency Preparedness, Business Resumption, or Contingency Planning. The newest 'buzz word' is Business Continuity Planning. It really doesn't matter what it's called as long as your company does it."

CREATING A DISASTER AND RECOVERY PLAN

"It is not easy to recognize the hundreds of hazards or perils that can lead to an unexpected loss," wrote Susan Anastasio in the SBA's *Small Business Insurance and Risk Management Guide.* "For example, unless you've experienced a fire, you may not realize how extensive fire losses can be. Damage to the building and its contents are obvious, but you should also consider: smoke and water damage; damage to employees' personal property and to others' property (e.g., data-processing equipment you lease or customers' property left with you for inspection or repair) left on the premises; the amount of business you'll lose during the time it takes to return your business to normal; the potential permanent loss of customers to competitors."

Of course, many other types of disasters can strike a business as well, ranging from those triggered by natural events such as floods, tornadoes, earthquakes, or hurricanes, to those that come about as a result of localized environmental problems, like water main breaks, work force strikes, power outages, hazardous materials spills, explosions, and major transportation mishaps (aircraft crash, train derailment, etc.). In addition, damage that is the direct result of premeditated human actions such as vandalism, sabotage, and arson can also be classified as a disaster.

The first step in creating a strategy (or reviewing existing contingency plans) to protect a company from these and other events involves mustering the necessary business will to undertake the challenges associated with the task. However, business observers contend that many companies fail in this regard. "The fact is that the majority of private-sector management is still reluctant to allocate the necessary time, staff, or funds to prepare and plan for the possibility of a disaster that may put them out of business," according to *Building Design & Construction.* Myers agreed that this tendency to give short shrift to disaster planning is a common one, observing that "when the economic climate is favorable, contingency planning is last on the list of things to do; when profits are down, contingency planning is the first item to be cut from the budget."

Small business owners, then, need to make sure that they devote adequate resources to disaster preparedness and recovery planning before beginning the process. Indeed, Levitt said that contingency planning efforts are ultimately doomed if they are undertaken without top management commitment, involvement, and support; participation of front line managers and staff teams in both planning and implementation; and ongoing communication with all constituencies of the business.

Once a business's leadership has decided to invest the necessary time and effort into the creation of a good disaster preparedness and recovery plan, it can proceed with the following steps:

Determining Vulnerabilities "Begin the process of identifying exposures by taking a close look at each of your business operations and asking yourself what could cause a loss," counseled Anastasio. "If there are dozens of exposures you may find dozens of answers.... Many business owners use a risk analysis questionnaire or survey, available from insurance agents, as a checklist." These questionnaires will typically address the business's vulnerability to losses in the areas of property, business interruption, liability, and key personnel, among others.

Obviously, this component of disaster preparedness planning—often referred to as risk management—needs to be comprehensive, covering all aspects of business operations, including telecommunications, computer systems, infrastructure, equipment, and the facility itself.

Gathering Information "The process of creating a disaster planning and recovery strategy is, in reality, the result of determining the organization's goals and objectives for business continuation—the ability to deliver its goods and services in the as-intended manner, utilizing

its as-intended processes, methods, and procedures—whenever any out-of-course event might impair, impact, impede, interrupt, or halt the as-intended workings and operations," stated Levitt. "*A disaster planning and recovery strategy* is not a method; it is a medium to sustain ... the organization." With this in mind, businesses should make an extra effort to solicit the opinions of all functional areas when putting together a disaster and recovery plan. Facility management areas may be most knowledgeable when it comes to the vulnerabilities of computer systems, office areas, etc., but other areas can often provide helpful information about the areas of the business that most need protection or fall-back plans so that the business can continue to operate in the case of a disaster.

Reconciling Findings with Principle Objectives All businesses should be concerned with meeting certain fundamental goals of disaster prevention, safety, and fiscal well-being when working on contingency plans. Analysts offer largely similar assessments of priorities in this regard, although minor differences in nuance and emphasis are inevitable, depending on the industry, the size of the business, and the viewpoint of the analyst. Most experts agree, however, that the primary objectives of a good disaster response plan should include:

- Preventing disasters from occurring whenever possible (through use of annual reviews, disaster prevention devices such as fire detectors and alarm systems, and physical access control procedures).

- Containment of disasters when they do occur.

- Protecting the lives, safety, and health of employers and customers.

- Protecting property and assets.

- Establishing priorities for utilization of internal resources (such as manpower, talent, and materials)

- Providing an organized response to a disaster/incident.

- Minimize risk exposure and financial loss (disruptions to cash flow as a result of canceled orders, etc.) through alternate procedures and practices.

- Prevent a significant long-term loss of market share.

Disaster response strategies will vary from business to business, but in the final analysis, they should all be structured in ways that will best ensure that essential business functions can be maintained until operations can be returned to normal.

Communication of Plan Disaster contingency plans should be widely disseminated throughout the company.

All employees should be cognizant of the business's basic disaster plan, but this is particularly important for managers, who are often called upon to make important operational decisions in the aftermath of crisis events.

Recovery This final stage of contingency planning is concerned with returning the business to its pre-disaster competitive position (or at least returning it as close to the position as is possible) and normal business operations in the event that a crisis event does take place. According to *Industry Week's* Karen G. Strouse, this entails restoring productivity in three primary areas: people, information, and facilities. "People are the priority," stated Strouse. "You need to account for them physically and emotionally, and enlist them in your recovery efforts.... Contact each employee personally; don't be satisfied with an answering-machine connection. Restoring technology is critical for two reasons. First, most companies rely on technology to conduct day-to-day business. Second, technology may represent your only means of giving your employees, customers, and the media important information as soon as they need it." Finally, Strouse observed that while information and employees are portable, "facilities are not. Your central facilities—mailroom, copy center, file room—need to be restored immediately. Office space is often on the critical path to people and information; without it, nothing else can happen." She also warned business owners to ensure that safe practices are followed when searching for and conducting operations in temporary locations.

Levitt, meanwhile, broke the recovery stage down into two elements: "First is the aspect of planning concerned with providing the resources for recovery. This encompasses the resources of a workplace, equipment, facilities, power, communication capabilities, information and data, forms and other supplies, people, food, lodging, transport, and all else that enables to the business processes to continue or to be re-established—within the planned time-line basis—after being impeded, impaired, interrupted, or halted." The other aspect of the recovery phase, wrote Levitt, is "concerned with impact, consequence and affect mitigation, and damage restoration requisite for the return to as-intended functioning."

SEE ALSO *Crisis Management*

BIBLIOGRAPHY

Arend, Mark. "Time to Dust Off Your Contingency Plan." *ABA Banking Journal.* February 1994.

Brunetto, Guy, and Norman L. Harris. "Disaster Recovery." *Strategic Finance.* March 2001.

"Dealing with Disasters Takes Careful Planning Ahead of Time." *Building Design & Construction.* September 1996.

Head, George L., and Stephen Horn II. *Essentials of Risk Management.* Insurance Institute of America, 1991.

Karpiloff, Douglas G. "When Disaster Strikes ... How to Manage a Successful Comeback." *Site Selection.* August/ September 1997.

Levitt, Alan M. *Disaster Planning and Recovery: A Guide for Facility Professionals.* John Wiley, 1997.

Mansdorf, Zack. "Emergency Response and Disaster Planning." *Occupational Hazards.* May 2000.

Murphy, Todd P. "Surviving Katrina—with a Lot of Help." *American Banker.* 20 January 2006.

Myers, Kenneth N. *Total Contingency Planning for Disasters.* John Wiley, 1993.

Strouse, Karen G. "What If Your Office Vanishes? Practical Advice on What to Do if Disaster Strikes." *Industry Week.* 3 July 1995.

Tynan, Dan. "When IT Disasters Really Strike – You can't be blamed for acts of God. At least not if you've got robust disaster recovery plans in place." *InfoWorld.* 30 January 2006.

U.S. Small Business Administration. Anastasio, Susan. *Small Business Insurance and Risk Management Guide.* n.d.

Hillstrom, Northern Lights
updated by Darnay, ECDI

DISCOUNT SALES

Discounts are reductions of the regular price of a product or service in order to obtain or increase sales. These discounts—also commonly referred to as "sales" or markdowns—are utilized in a wide range of industries by both retailers and manufacturers. The merits of discount pricing, however, have been a subject of considerable debate over the past several years as analysts argue about their effects on short-term sales, longer term profits, brand loyalty, and total supply chain costs for retailers and manufacturers.

RETAILER AND MANUFACTURER VIEWS OF DISCOUNTING

Discounts are a staple of business strategy for many retail firms. As Tom Hartley noted in *Business First of Buffalo,* sales remain "the fuel that drives the retail engine." He cited the views of several retail experts who flatly insist that sales promotions are integral to most retailers' success. "The name of the game is promotion," one expert told Hartley. "Sales are the only way to drive the business and retailers have to have them, even if they seem to be going on all the time. Discounting in America has been built into the retail cycle. It is no longer a big deal."

But small retail firms should make sure that they go about the discounting process in an intelligent fashion.

Business consultants cite several considerations that small retailers should weigh when putting together their overall marketing strategy. For example, retailers should beware of overuse. Indeed, according to many economists and business owners, discount periods increase sales volume but also deepen sales troughs between sales. Other analysts contend that frequent sales tend to numb customer response over time; Hartley pointed out that "many retail experts think consumer have become less trustful of retailers who[m] they see running weekly sales, or marking up items so high that they make a profit even after slashing prices 20, 30, or 50 percent."

In addition, retailers should study historic customer response, inventory levels, competitor pricing, seasonal cycles, and other factors in determining the level of discount. Some businesses are able dramatically to increase sales volume through discounts of 20 percent or less, which in many instances enables them to maintain a decent profit margin on sales. Other businesses may have to offer discounts of 40-50 percent (because of seasonal considerations, industry trends, etc.) in order to see meaningful increases in traffic. Of course, some retailers employ a price philosophy that emphasizes every-day low prices in the hopes that the increased volume will make up for the small profit margin achieved on individual sales.

Manufacturers, meanwhile, should be very careful in establishing discounts for their goods. Recent studies have indicated that price promotions offered by manufacturers often set a dangerous precedent; they condition customers to make purchases based on price rather than brand loyalty. "Over the long term," claimed *Management Today* contributor Alan Mitchell, "[discount pricing initiatives] do precious little to improve base-line sales, increase the incidence of repeat buying or attract new customers. They do, however, undermine other marketing initiatives by sensitizing consumers to price." A top manufacturing executive agreed with this analysis, noting that "[manufacturers] are actually training consumers to hunt around, to look for high-value offers. We're either encouraging them to shop up heavily when the offer appears and distort the supply chain, or we're really annoying them if they miss the offer because it's just stopped. Net, we're undermining their loyalty." Finally, ill-considered discount sales can lead to price wars with other competitors and can tarnish the image of the brand in question.

There are other drawbacks often associated with discount sales as well, and these can quickly get an unsuspecting small business owner in serious trouble. *Sales & Marketing Management* contributor Minda Zetlin noted, for example, that "discounts have a way of taking on a life of their own." Indeed, the customer

that receives a 15 percent discount for one purchase may well feel entitled to an identical or even greater discount the following year. Moreover, news of a discount extended to one client is often difficult to keep under wraps, and when one client finds out that his deal is not as good as the one that another client is getting, he is apt to react in ways that are not good for business. "What happens is customers talk," one executive told Zetlin. "You get a call from Fred, who thought he was getting your best deal, and found out last night at the bar that he isn't and is now unhappy with you." One way of minimizing the likelihood of running into such complications, say experts, is to make sure that you adhere to a uniform set of discount rules. Of course, some small business owners have to give customers different deals as part of their efforts to establish and grow their enterprises. Nonetheless, as one businessman recounted to *Sales & Marketing Management,* "[with] indiscriminant discounting ... you wind up giving different deals to different customers based on their negotiating ability rather than some more rational technique."

DISCOUNT SALES AND THE COMPANY SALES FORCE

Many businesses utilize sales representatives to deal with customers and close deals. But whereas sales personnel employed by retail outlets typically do not have the power to offer discounts, many representatives in the manufacturing and service sectors are provided with some leeway in this area. Both existing and prospective customers are well aware of this state of affairs. Small business owners, then, need to pay extra attention to this reality as they build their sales force. For as business experts in all industry areas will attest, many sales representatives are so eager to secure a sale—and thus a commission—that they will offer a discount on a sale at the first hint of a price objection. "Salespeople offer discounts too quickly because they get flustered and fear losing a deal, or because it's easier than making the customer understand why this product is worth more," wrote Zetlin.

To head off scenarios in which salespeople might unnecessarily fritter away profits on a sale with an unnecessary discount offer, business consultants and successful salespeople recommend that entrepreneurs consider the following:

1. Informed salespeople are formidable salespeople— Many requests for discounts are based on ignorance (feigned or not) of the difference between your company's goods and/or services and those of the competition, which may be dangling a lower price. The challenge for the small business owner, then, is to make sure that sales representatives can talk about

non-price benefits authoritatively. "A rep with a thorough knowledge of his product has a greater ability to offer creative solutions to his customers' problems," wrote Barry J. Farber in *Sales & Marketing Management.* "Similarly, a rep must be able to articulate what makes his company different from the competition, and better suited to work with a customer. When a customer asks, 'Why should I pay six dollars for your product when your competitor is selling it to me for three?' the rep had better be prepared to answer: 'I understand your concern. My competitor is a fine company, but let me tell you a few things about our organization that makes us unique.' By going immediately to the company's strengths, the rep automatically colors the competition to look weak."

2. Knowledge of client issues—Knowledge includes not only representative awareness of his or her employer's circumstances (inventory, profit margin, etc.), but also an understanding of the challenges facing current and potential customers. By taking a proactive approach that seeks out answers to customer hopes, strategies, and concerns, many representatives can head off attempts to secure a discount by highlighting customer service advantages that they can secure through your company. In addition, small business owners who are knowledgeable about key customers are better able to offer discounts that ultimately benefit their companies. For example, offering a small discount can be a good way to curry favor with a client that is on the verge of significant growth.

3. Provide guidelines and training to sales staff—Sales personnel should be provided with firm guidelines regarding their authority to negotiate discount prices to customers. Moreover, many business experts counsel entrepreneurs--who often serve as their own sales representatives, especially during a business's formative years--and their sales staff to receive training in negotiation tactics so that they can better differentiate between customers who truly are unhappy with the price and those who are merely angling for a discount.

4. Recognize industry dynamics—Some industries allow participants to adhere to set price guidelines fairly closely, while others--whether because of intense competition, economic problems experienced by target markets, or some other factor--may have to be considerably more flexible in providing discount sales to clients.

5. Talk to the right personnel—Negotiations over price can vary considerably, depending on the personnel that are involved on the customer's side of the table.

"There are a lot of people who impact a large purchasing decision, and some are charged with getting the best price," admitted one consultant in an interview with *Sales & Marketing Management.* But she also added that "some are charged with doing what's good for the organization, and some have to work directly with the results of that decision every day. Who you're talking to will determine how much emphasis there is on price. . . . A lot of people say that if you can show value the customer won't care about the price. But if you're talking to a buy whose job is to get the best price, he or she won't care about value. If you want to show better value, you had better also talk to someone more senior, whose job is to find value for the company's bottom line."

6. Recognize sales representative priorities—Zetlin pointed out that "one of the chief problems with giving salespeople leeway to negotiate prices or offer discounts is that it creates a conflict of interest between many salespeople and their employers. After all, it's to the salesperson's advantage to close every deal--no matter how unprofitable--if she will always earn a commission by doing so." Small business owners who closely monitor the performance of sales personnel can curb such abuses to some degree, as can those who firmly communicate sales margin expectations to their sales force. But consultant Al Hahn suggested to *Sales & Marketing Management* that a better solution might be to tie the salesperson's compensation to the profitability of the sale. "In my experience, salespeople . . . respond very strongly to the incentive systems they're given, and they'll do what the commission plan tells them to do to make money." By linking compensation to the profitability of the sale, representatives are thus rewarded for making *good* deals for the company, not just by the number of sales they make irrespective of incentives that are handed out to the client.

7. Know when to look elsewhere for business—Some customers simply will not agree to terms without unreasonable discounts that cut too great a swath into your profit margin (or obliterate it altogether). In such instances, it is usually better to move on in search of other customers rather than continually butt heads with a single client. Certainly, individual business realities can color an entrepreneur's ability to do this. If the entrepreneur's business is predicating a big marketing push on marketplace legitimacy that it owes to its relationship with the client, for instance, then it may be forced to accede to the client's discount demands. But as Farber indicated, if a customer is unable to get beyond the price issue, it

may be time to look elsewhere for business. "Salespeople waste a lot of time on prospects who are not qualified, don't have the decision-making ability, or are stalling them."

ALTERNATIVES TO TRADITIONAL DISCOUNT STRUCTURES

In addition to traditional discounts, wherein individual goods or services are offered at a given percentage below the original asking price, small business owners also have the option of instituting several different discounting variations, such as "earned" discounts, early-payment discounts, and multi-buy promotions.

"Earned" Discounts Some companies offer their customers discounts if they meet certain requirements. Under this scenario, customers that agree to make large purchases, provide repeat business, or sign multi-year contracts are in essence rewarded for their business by receiving a discount on the price of the goods or services they have purchased.

Early-Payment Discounts Some small business owners offer discounts to customers who pay promptly (within 10 days is a common stipulation). Small businesses that do this are often relatively new firms that are operating under tight financial constraints. Unlike established business owners, who may have a financial cushion from which to draw to meet various business and/or personal obligations, entrepreneurs are often in greater need of securing prompt payment from customers. An early-payment discount provides customers with an incentive for them to make payment quickly. Businesses that utilize this discount option range from manufacturers to freelance writers.

Business consultants warn, however, that some customers may abuse this option by taking the early-payment discount, only to pay off the bill after the discount period has ended. Christopher Caggiano noted in *Inc.* that small business owners can institute a couple of different policies that can curb such abuses. One device that entrepreneurs can use is to make it clear that the early-payment discount will be offered only if collection can be made in person by the entrepreneur himself or a member of his staff. Another option is to charge customers for the difference on the next invoice that they submit. In most cases, the customer will pay the amount without complaint since it did not meet the previously agreed-upon terms.

Multi-Buy Promotions Multi-buy promotions are an increasingly popular alternative to the standard discount pricing strategies, especially for retailers. Rather than knock 25 percent off the price of a product, some companies are choosing to offer "buy one, get one free" or "buy three for the price of two" promotions to consumers. This strategy is driven by statistics that indicate that such promotions are often so tremendously popular that the volume of sales outweighs the cost of the discount given. Business observers point out that many multi-buy promotions are made economical by the hidden savings that can be realized through them. "Supermarkets now have computer systems which recognize a second or third pack and automatically adjust the bill at the till, thereby eliminating most of the administrative hassle," wrote Alan Mitchell in *Management Today*. "And the fact that the goods being promoted come in standard packs eradicates many of the design, manufacture, and transport costs associated with other types of promotional offers."

SEE ALSO *Rebates*

BIBLIOGRAPHY

Caggiano, Christopher. "Customers Take Our Early-Payment Discount—But Pay Late." *Inc.* October 1997.

Coleman, Calmetta. "The Evolution of Gift Giving: Deep Discounts Help to Draw Wary Shoppers." *Wall Street Journal.* 27 November 2000.

Farber, Barry J. "The High Cost of Discounting." *Sales & Marketing Management.* November 1996.

Hartley, Tom. "You Always Hear the Word 'Sale'—But Does It Work?" *Business First of Buffalo.* 23 March 1992.

Marn, M.V., and R.L. Rosiello. "Managing Price, Gaining Profit." *Harvard Business Review.* September-October 1992.

Mitchell, Alan. "Multibuys that Wash." *Management Today.* May 1996.

Peppers, Don, and Martha Rogers. "Avoid Price Dilution By Making Yourself Valuable to Loyal Customers." *Business Marketing.* December 1997.

Rasmussen, Erika. "Leading Edge: The Pitfalls of Price-Cutting." *Sales & Marketing Management.* May 1997.

U.S. Small Business Administration. Walker, Bruce J. *A Pricing Checklist for Small Retailers.* n.d.

Zetlin, Minda. "Kicking the Discount Habit: Teach Your Salespeople to Stop Leaving Money on the Table." *Sales & Marketing Management.* May 1994.

Hillstrom, Northern Lights
updated by Magee, ECDI

DISCOUNTED CASH FLOW

Discounted Cash Flow (DCF) analysis is a technique for determining what a business is worth *today* in light of its cash yields in the *future*. It is routinely used by people buying a business. It is based on **cash flow** because future flow of cash from the business will be added up. It is called **discounted** cash flow because in commercial thinking $100 in your pocket *now* is worth more than $100 in your pocket a year from now. Why? You can at minimum put your $100 in the bank and it will earn you at least 3 to 4 percent interest. A year from now it will be worth $104. Therefore, looked at the other way, $100 received a year from now is worth only $96.15 today if the discount rate is 4 percent (96.15 × 1.04 = 100). If your current cash could earn 10 percent interest, the future $100 would be worth only $90.9 in today's valuation.

CALCULATING DCF

The elements of DCF therefore are 1) the period of time to be used for evaluation, say a business life of 10 years, 2) the flows of cash that will occur every year in that business as best as you can guess, 3) your own internal discount rate or, put another way, what your money could earn if invested in something else of equivalent risk. The calculation itself is very easily done in a spreadsheet with a simple formula (shown below). What is really important in DCF is assessing the business and accurately predicting what flows of cash it will yield.

Obtaining the annual cash flow to be discounted is done as follows:

- Start with Net Income After Tax.

- Add Depreciation for the year (because depreciation is not a cash cost).

- Deduct Change in working capital from the previous year. This change may actually be negative, in which case this operation will add to cash. In a growing operation it will be positive and so will require cash.

- Deduct Capital expenditures.

Working capital is current assets less current liabilities. Unless the DCF is very detailed, the usual items included are the "biggies," receivables and inventories on the asset side and payables on the liabilities side, only changes being counted. If receivables were $100,000 at the beginning of the year and $130,000 at the end, $30,000 is the change. If inventories decreased from $40,000 to $35,000, the change is -$5,000—for a net change in assets of $25,000. Assume payables went from $80,000 to $110,000. The change in liabilities then is $30,000. Change in assets less liabilities is therefore -$5,000. This amount is deducted, from net income after tax, but deducting a negative causes it to be added. In effect the situation in this case means that the *cash*

position of the business has improved. Finally capital expenditures, a flat drain on cash, are deducted.

These estimates of the cash flow are repeated for every year of the forecast period, in this case a ten-year cycle. To derive the crucial starting number, net income after tax, the analyst must, of course, project sales and costs assuming some reasonable growth rate for the operation—usually based on the target company's history. He or she must derive necessary inventory levels to support projected sales—and also calculate additions to capital based on capacity at the beginning of the period.

Most DCFs end by assuming that at the end of the cycle the company will be sold again at some conservative multiple of its after-tax earnings. This number is then plugged in as a "residual value" for the 11th year.

Next, and crucially, the analyst must determine what discount rate to use. Suppose the prospective buyer of the company enjoys a net return on its own, current investments in its own business of 16.7 percent. It may use that rate as a minimum or as an acceptable average return.

Now, with the annual cash flows neatly keyed into a spreadsheet down a column, each row representing a year—and the 11th year carrying the "resale residual," application of a discount formula can be applied. The formula for each row is quite simple:

$$PV = FV \times (1 + dr) \char`\^ -n.$$

In this formula, PV stands for present value, namely right now, in the year of analysis. FV is the cash projected for one of the years in the future. dr is the discount rate. The 16.7 percent would be entered as .167. The caret symbol stands for exponentiation; n is the number of years; the negative n is the negative value of the year. Thus year 1 is −1, year 2 is −2 and so on.

Let us assume that the years begin with 2007 and that these years are in column A, beginning on row 5 of our spreadsheet. The cash flows are in column B, also beginning on row 5. Then, the formula in column C, row 5, will read:

$$=B5*(1+0.167)\char`\^(-(A5-2006))$$

Replicating this formula down to the last row, row 15 (which will start with 2017 and will hold the residual), will automatically transform the projected cash flows into their discounted equivalents. Simply adding them up will result in the discounted cash flow value of the business. Assume that the cash flows in column B are (with 1,000s suppressed) 135, 137, 138, 142, 145, 150, 150, 170, 169, 175 and the last, the residual, is 675, the discounting formula will produce the values 116, 101, 87, 77, 67, 59, 51, 41, 42, 37, and, finally, 123. These values will add to 809. In actual cash, as projected, the business will generate $2,186,000, the sum of the first set of numbers. But by discounting using the 16.7 rate, that value, *today*, is worth $809,000. Thus if the asking price is at or below that value, the deal is good. If it is higher, the prospective buyer should probably pass.

OTHER ISSUES

Discounted cash flow analysis is almost always applied when a company is thinking of purchasing another. As shown above, the technique is ultimately simple enough if applied with care. An ordinary spreadsheet is enough to do the job. But the real job is not really the application of a math formula.

As David Harrison pointed out writing in *Strategic Finance*, "The simplicity of a DCF valuation is probably what contributes most to underestimating the time required for valuation jobs in the first place. Think about it—it isn't the DCF calculations that require any time; they run in an instant. But the DCF is only as good as its inputs, so that old adage, 'you are what you eat;' couldn't be truer with respect to DCF. Good estimates yield good valuations; bad estimates... well, you know the rest. How do we get a reasonable range of estimates for our discounted cash flow? Therein lies the problem—the gremlin that eats away our time, drives us crazy, and makes us feel like plodding amateurs."

DCF, in other words, greatly depends on many much fuzzier issues, the most uncertain of which is how the future will treat the business we are thinking of buying. Here, as always, a thorough knowledge of the industry, conservative assumptions, due diligence in looking at the business in detail, especially visits with its clients and suppliers, and also a certain humility on the buyer's part are of crucial importance. Many owners have great confidence in their own abilities and a low estimate of the seller's. That should be a much bigger red flag than a lackluster DCF number.

BIBLIOGRAPHY

"Discounted Cash Flow." *Chartered Management Institute: Checklists: Managing Information and Finance.* October 2005.

Glasgow, Bo. "Metrics and Measures: Cash flow-based analysis rules the roost." *Chemical Market Reporter.* 25 November 2002.

Harrison, David S. "Business Valuation Made Simple: It's all about cash." *Strategic Finance.* February 2003.

Makholm, Jeff D. "In Defense of the 'Gold Standard': It is hard to foresee abandoning the discounted cash flow method relied upon so heavily for the past couple of decades." *Public Utilities Fortnightly.* 15 May 2003.

"What Are You Worth? For sellers, it's back to the future, but for buyers it's here and now." *Financial Planning.* 1 May 2005.

Darnay, ECDI

DISCRETIONARY INCOME

Discretionary income is a widely used but imprecise definition of that portion of personal income not spent on actual or perceived necessities. Thus discretionary income also includes savings. Perhaps because the definition of "necessities" vary from person to person, the U.S. Census Bureau (which collects such data) and the U.S. Bureau of Labor Statistics (BLS—which publishes the Consumer Expenditure Survey) no longer use the term, but the components from which it can be constructed are available.

Personal income is one of the elements of the Gross Domestic Product and is reported by the Census Bureau at quarterly intervals. Personal income less taxes owed is then defined as *disposable income*. From this the Bureau deducts personal consumption expenditures, personal (non-mortgage) interest payments, and contributions to derive *personal savings*. Some portion of consumption expenditures is discretionary; most of it is not; similarly, some contributions such as union fees are not discretionary.

The Census Bureau also conducts a consumer survey that is published by BLS. For the year 2003, the most recent available, housing led consumption expenditures (32.9 percent) followed by transportation (19.1), food (13.1), insurance and pensions (9.9), healthcare (5.9), apparel and services (4.0), and personal care products and services (1.3). Assuming that these categories fall into the rubric of necessities, this suggests that discretionary income in 2003 was 13.8 percent. Categories excluded from necessities were alcoholic beverages, entertainment, reading, education, tobacco, miscellaneous, and cash contributions.

Knowing the pertinent facts about discretionary income is of vital importance to both business and government. Companies are interested in discretionary income levels of consumers in various geographic areas, age brackets, and socioeconomic backgrounds: consumers with larger amounts are more likely to spend their money on the goods and services they provide. The statistics also provide information about consumer spending habits that can be useful in targeting marketing campaigns. Although the data alone cannot predict how a certain consumer will choose to spend his or her discretionary income, it can provide useful information to help marketers make sound planning decisions.

Discretionary incomes of people in certain age groups are of particular value to business and marketing specialists. For example, those over the age of 50 have half of the total amount of discretionary income in their control, making the 50-plus age category the wealthiest group in the nation. This group also corners three-quarters of the bank deposits in the nation, and accounts for 80 percent of all savings accounts. In short, the "over 50s" have enormous financial clout. Similarly, teenage and young adult consumers have considerable sums of discretionary income—and are thus highly valued by companies—because they are more likely to have their living costs absorbed by other individuals (typically parents) and they are less likely to be in a position where they have to devote resources to support a family.

BIBLIOGRAPHY

Woodard, Kathy L. "Boomers Lead Boom in Home Remodeling." *Business First-Columbus.* 21 April 2000.

U.S. Department of Commerce. Bureau of Economic Analysis. News Release: Personal Income and Outlays. 30 January 2006.

U.S. Department of Labor. Bureau of Labor Statistics. "Consumer Expenditure Survey." Available from http://www.bls.gov/cex/home.htm#overview. Retrieved on 13 February 2006.

Hillstrom, Northern Lights
updated by Magee, ECDI

DISTRIBUTION CHANNELS

Goods produced in factories and/or commodities produced in agriculture must reach consumers. The systems by means of which goods reach the consumer are known as distribution channels. These are organizations that facilitate the sale and movement of products. The totality of all distribution channels forms a distribution network. Distribution is a very complex system but can be conceptually divided into four major categories: 1) market makers, 2) sellers, 3) transporters, and 4) hybrids.

PARTICIPANTS IN DISTRIBUTION

Market Makers Market makers are organizations that provide either a real or virtual place where goods may be bought and sold. Classical example are the farmer's market, considered as the entity that actually rents space to farmers for their stalls, a stock market that controls who may or may not trade by selling seats on its exchange, a shopping mall that makes its money by leasing space to stores at the mall, convention centers like McCormick Place in Chicago that hosts trade fairs, and a franchiser who, in effect, sells a method, a name, and an image. Markets need not be "places." Therefore catalog publishers and web-based sellers are also "market makers." A pure form of a web-based market maker is the

auction house e-bay: e-bay itself does not sell anything; it hosts a selling/buying community. The distribution *function* fulfilled by market makers is the aggregation in a real or virtual place of diverse and competing sellers. Thus market makers provide a convenience to the customer who likes to compare many competing products with the least amount of trouble.

Sellers and Resellers Selling organizations either purchase and own the goods they sell or they fulfill a selling function without ownership. If they are in the first category, they will be called distributors, wholesalers, jobbers, retailers, or dealers. If sellers are in the second category, they will be called brokers, traders, rep organizations, and agents. The distinction between these categories is all important from the producer's point of view. "Purchasing and owning" sellers are the most desirable because they take possession and cannot return the merchandise. Sales agents just represent: they take no ownership risk.

Transporters Central to every distribution system, but usually least talked about, is the community of organizations that physically store and move the goods. These elements may be owned by sellers or producers; most often they are independently owned. The Post Office and commercial freight carriers, or instance, are important players. Transporters operate warehouses and provide ground, water, and air transport services.

Hybrids Some of the functions described above are mutually exclusive. A seller either owns merchandise or does not. Other roles, however, are more easily combined and traditionally have been. A grocery store is thus the merging of an old farmers market and a dry goods market into a single enterprise that now "makes its own market" and also owns all the merchandise it sells. Major grocery chains also tend to own all or part of the transportation system they use. In the modern environment a large shopping mall is a market of markets, each store within it being itself an assembly of many types of merchandise that, once, were sold in separate markets. A restaurant is the best example of a small "hybrid." It creates its own market by offering a diversity of foods; it combines the production function by cooking the food and the selling function by offering it for sale on site. Most diverse stores such a grocery chains, drug stores, department stores, and major discounters are hybrids in that they make a market but also own and sell the merchandise. The ice cream vendors selling in the city from a little truck combines seller and transporter roles in a hybrid distribution mode.

STRUCTURAL FEATURES OF CHANNELS

Economic activity viewed functionally consists of aggregating valuable commodities into centers of production where value is added to the commodities by labor. The products of many suppliers are centralized into manufactories. The structural function of a distribution channel is to invert this movement, causing the transformed commodities to reach end-users again. (At the end of this systems comes another aggregation function, namely waste disposal, which now moves residues to their final resting place in landfills.) Distribution is therefore a logistical function at the physical level modulated by communications activities. Channels have evolved over time—and continue to change as participants attempt to take advantage of change as it occurs. A good example of a recent impact on distribution is the communications revolution introduced by the Internet. Thus many books once purchased in stores are bought online and delivered by UPS, FedEx, and DHL. Many airline tickets once sold by travel agents and picked up by customers are purchased online and picked up at the airport.

Tiers Distribution systems are said to have tiers or levels, the number of tiers being defined by the middleman between the original seller and the ultimate buyer. A single-tier system involves a single intermediary seller, namely the retailer. A two-tier system will have a distributor/wholesaler plus a retailer. More tiers may be present. Imported goods, for instance, may be channeled first through an importer. In some industries smaller wholesalers (jobbers) may be involved as secondary distributors between a major wholesaler and a large number of retailers. Some manufacturers sell directly to customers. This may be viewed as a "tier-less" distribution channel; more correctly the manufacturer simply acts as its own retailer: the retail function is simply kept in-house. Competitive pressures limit the number of tiers possible because every level must be compensated and has its own margin (in effect its own "tax") on the transaction. Hierarchical distribution may be necessitated by capital intensity (manufacturers needing to share the burden of capitalizing the distribution system), by remoteness and distance (producers cannot reach every corner of their market), by technical service requirements (manufacturers need dealers to service technical goods and do not wish to establish hundreds of wholly-owned operations), and other factors.

Differentiation by Customer Distribution channels typically service either the consumer or an industrial/institutional client. Industrial/institutional distribution is frequently highly adapted to specific branches. On the whole industrial distribution activity is less marked by hype and much more technical and price-oriented; the impulse buying element is eliminated by professional purchasing functions; at the same time, occasionally industrial sales produce corruption and kickback scandals because very large transactions are frequently the rule.

Differentiation by Technology A subset of industrial distribution is technological differentiation marked by the employment of sales engineers on the one side and highly skilled technical buyers on the other. The vast spread of computer use in every institution, for example, produced a brand new category of intermediaries, the so-called VARs or value-added resellers, sometimes called integrators. These organizations came into existence as independent entities because the complexity of adapting computer systems and networks into the operations of a buying establishment require many complex skills in the absence of which no product could actually be sold. Very few producers of computers or peripherals are able (never mind willing) to master the intricacies of competing products in order to sell their own. The VARs took on this challenge. The emergence of VARs is an excellent example of the manner in which products and services shape and transform distribution channels.

Recurring Trends In the cyclical relationship between the original producer and the "channel," the existence of a distribution "margin" produces recurring attempts by both sides to capture more of that margin by down- or upward integration or by cutting out the middleman. Producers frequently attempt to eliminate distributors by establishing a wholly-owned "branch" structure—making themselves distributors. Distributors, in turn, attempt to buy manufacturing operations so that they come to own the products that they sell. A similarly recurring trend is to eliminate the retailer by "selling at wholesale" in large, bare discount operations—usually somewhat below the retail level but not quite at the wholesale price. Yet another perennial is represented by the well-established machinery seller who distributes through "servicing dealers" and who, thinking of having it both ways, suddenly shifts a large part of his or her sales to a big discount house that does not offer services. The dealer channel will find itself undersold and burdened by new service business which is *not* subsidized by original equipment sales. The reaction is usually violent, eventually forcing the producer to abandon discount sales. An intermediate position is presented by powerful retailers who offer their customers "home brands" cheaper; these, typically, are of a lower quality than branded merchandise. Such recurring gyrations are accompanied by the ever new (but ancient) practice of starting up membership stores where customers pay a fee to have access to lower prices; eventually membership becomes ever cheaper; in due time no check of membership is made.

DISTRIBUTION AND SMALL BUSINESSES

Small businesses typically inherit a distribution channel. The founding owner may be quite expert in distribution by having worked in the industry before. In the absence of personal knowledge, the best approach to learning about the channel rapidly is by immersion in the trade literature. Trade magazines will rapidly teach the business owner such fundamentals as major shows where the industry regularly meets. Visiting such a show and talking to competitors, buyers, and sellers will soon reveal the opportunities open to the business. The owner will probably encounter sales rep organizations, see retail and wholesale distributors at work, and will learn the one or two major preferred means of reaching the market used by the industry.

The owner will rapidly discover that choices are few and the channels already well developed. Learning exactly how to fit the business's products or services into existing channels will become the primary task. Effective entrance may necessitate a different way of packaging the product than initially envisioned, different methods of pricing, the use of incentives not imagined before but common in the industry, and so on.

Special difficulties face the new business which enters an activity for which distribution channels are poorly developed. Such will often be the case where the business is a new kind of service not yet "commodified." An extreme example might be decorating ceilings with original art. The business owner may have to discard his or her original intent to sell the service through art stores but discover that very high-end furniture dealers are the right distribution venue—and the mode of contact will be to decorate the ceilings of such dealers free of charge to attract the eyes of wealthy shoppers. Another venue may be by working closely with stores that sell special lighting equipment—which would, of course, be an element in ceiling art. Consulting businesses with abstract product, e.g. futures studies in support of marketing strategy, may similarly have to create their own distribution channel by the sheer rock-breaking methods of trial and error. Communication being a central element in the distribution of goods and services, such businesses may attempt to create industry specific futures projections and attempt to publish them in industry journals. This may lead to invitations to a conference. Where there is a will, there is a way... These examples illustrate how finding the distribution channel arises, gradually, from exploring the product or service itself.

SEE ALSO *Transportation*

BIBLIOGRAPHY

Barrow, Andy. "Keeping the Big Boys at Bay." *Computer Reseller News.* 30 January 2006.

"Changing Channels—A Whale Of A Program." *VARBusiness.* 19 December 2005.

Griffith, Kimberly. "More Than Just a Shopping Cart." *Industrial Distribution.* 1 January 2006.

Olsztynski, Jim. "Why the 'Middleman' Hangs Around: Excerpted from an address given to the Ft. Wayne Indiana, ASHRAE Chapter on Oct. 11, 2005." *Supply House Times.* December 2005.

Reinhart, Len. "The Final Frontier: Ultra-Wealthy Clients Demand White-Glove Service During all Phases of the Adviser Relationship." *Financial Planning.* 1 May 2004.

"Work With the Channel Partner." *Rental Equipment Register.* 1 February 2006.

Darnay, ECDI

DISTRIBUTORSHIPS AND DEALERSHIPS

Distributors and dealers are participants in a supply channel, the distributor usually a wholesaler who sells to dealers and dealers usually retailers who sell directly to the public. The dealer-distributor terminology is most common in the distribution of machinery and mechanical goods—thus in automobiles, trucks, farm and construction equipment, yard and garden goods (green goods), appliances (white goods), electronics, and also in the sale of industrial equipment. This basic structure has many variants.

Both distributors and dealers actually purchase the goods they sell—the distributor from the manufacturer, the dealer from the distributor. Distributors maintain parts inventories and the dealers provide service functions to the ultimate consumers ("servicing dealers"). Relationships among manufacturers, distributors, and dealers are typically contractual in nature. Distributors and in turn dealers participate in incentive programs offered by the manufacturers—such as subsidized advertising programs, bonuses, and special discounts. Distributors and dealers have rights to use the manufacturer's trademarks and logos—but not as their own.

Distributor and dealer relationships to manufacturers have many features in common with franchises. Indeed, state laws governing franchises may have clauses that directly relate to distributors and dealers. But the franchise concept is fundamentally different from the distributor-dealer model. Traditional distributors and dealers never pay an up-front fee to the manufacturer for the privilege of selling the producer's goods—but may be contractually required to buy some minimum amount of goods. Distributors and dealers may be relatively strong or relatively weak over against the producer, but in all cases they bring something to the table, namely an established market already developed. It is not unusual for strong distributors and dealers to carry the goods of competing manufacturers, although, in most cases, one of the brands will be dominant, the other serving a smaller customer base.

PARTICIPANTS

The Manufacturer A two-tier distribution system (distributor, dealer) may be the preferred channel used by the manufacturer of one or a whole line of its goods. Using distributorships gives the producer the advantage of dealing with just a few major buyers, the distributors, who then, in turn, take care of selling the product through to the ultimate consumer using dealers. In any kind of major equipment business, substantial capital is involved in carrying and holding merchandise, including parts inventories. Distributorships share the burden by purchasing goods on their own account and freeing up the producer's working capital for the next round in the production cycle. The producer in such a channel participates, nevertheless, down to the retail level, by marketing programs, incentive programs for distributors and dealers, discounts for the consumer, and also by providing technical training programs for distributor and dealer personnel.

The Distributor The distributor is an independent selling agent who has a contract to sell the products of a manufacturer. The distributor cannot represent him- or herself *as* the producer but may display the producer's trade name in signage and in the sales situation. Depending on the relative power of the producer, the distributor may be limited to selling only one brand of a product; in practice the strong distributors will have much more freedom. The distributor usually has an exclusive territory which may be part of a metro area or, depending on the product, may be a large territory including more than one state. Distributors pay wholesale prices for the product and then distribute to dealers who pay dealer price.

Variants to this general pattern exist. One such is the contract distributor who purchases a product from a producer, consolidates it with other products thus adding value, and resells the product. A contract distributor differs from a wholesaler in that a wholesaler merely purchases a product, along with other products from different manufacturers, and resells the product with little if any changes.

Being an independent entity, the distributor's operations are not under the direct managerial control of a producer. Producers, however, influence the distributor by providing common methods for display, for inventory management, producing national advertising and symbolism, and offering incentives. Some of these internal matters may be governed by the general contract under which distributors and producers operate.

The Dealer A dealership is sometimes called a retail distributor. It is similar to a distributorship, except that a dealer usually sells only to the public. Unlike other types of franchisees, including some distributors, a dealer rarely carries a single product line. Even in the auto industry, a major dealer will carry competing products, often on the same site, but these will be differentiated by being each in its own building.

By operating as a dealer for a branded product, the dealership in effect participates, but at second hand, in the producer's total marketing scheme—enjoying national advertising support, receiving training, and taking advantage of incentive programs. By taking part in dealer groups, dealerships also act as a feedback mechanism for the producer conveying insights gained by dealing directly with the customer.

SECURING A DEALERSHIP/ DISTRIBUTORSHIP

In order to determine which business opportunity or franchise to invest in, it is important to do careful research. While the advantage of investing in a business opportunity or franchise is that it can be a "turnkey operation," it is crucial to plan and investigate the investment even more thoroughly than with a traditional entrepreneurial effort.

Begin with an assessment of your own skills and goals for the business. Keep these in mind while reviewing franchise possibilities. Start with a thorough reading of the Uniform Franchise Offerings Circular (UFOC) or the business disclosure statement. If the franchising business does not have one, ask why and be concerned about the dependability of the business. Get copies of the company's financial records, as well as details in writing about what exactly is being offered for the purchase price, including training and support. Find out what other distributors exist and, if possible, talk to them about the success of their franchise, the quality of the product/service, and the support of the franchiser. Test the potential of the product/service with family and friends. Ask yourself, "Would I purchase this product/service?"

Another factor in securing a dealer/distributor business is the large initial investment. There are normally two types of fees associated with franchises and business opportunities: the original start-up fee or purchase price, and ongoing fees or product costs. The purchase price may depend on whether the small businessperson is investing in a "turnkey" operation, such as a car dealership, or a less complete franchise. Prospective franchisees should not be afraid to negotiate the purchase price and terms of the business opportunity.

A franchise territory can be exclusive or non-exclusive. There are pros and cons to each type of territory, but be sure you are aware of the status of your prospective business and determine whether you can work in this environment.

It should be noted that both distribution and dealership agreements tend to have a shorter term than a traditional franchise agreement. Distribution and dealership agreements frequently are renewed on an annual basis, by mutual agreement. A traditional franchise agreement normally covers a minimum of five years.

BENEFITS AND COSTS OF DEALERSHIPS AND DISTRIBUTORSHIPS

There are differences in operating a distributorship and a dealership. A distributorship normally costs more than a dealership and requires leadership capability and a better knowledge of basic business skills. It will most likely have a larger territory than a dealership and may even extend to more than one location. A dealership tends to be local and requires less start-up capital. A dealer can focus his/her efforts on the management and success of one location. The dealer works closely with a distributor so it pays him or her to nurture that relationship as well. In the final analysis, the distributorship can be more lucrative; but it will require different skills and higher investments.

The chief benefit of participation in such a two-tiered channel comes from the brand equity of the products carried—and the support the brands may have from the producer. The relationship, however, is mutual. Well-supported brands will tend to be higher priced. The pressure to stock at high levels will be greater and conformity with the producer's programs will be enforced. In turn a well-run distributorship will ensure selection of excellent dealers who, in turn, by commanding strong locations and providing good service to consumers, contribute substantially to the brand's image.

Producer-distributor-dealer relationships have built-in conflicts as well—the smooth resolution of which is central to profitable long-term operations. Conflicts often take opposite forms: producers may wish to "push"

more product into the channel than the channel really wants; at other times, especially when a product really takes off, the channel can't get enough product to meet demand. Effective participants in this channel pay a good deal of attention to the parties. Producers will cultivate good will down the channel. Distributors will both push and protect their dealers. Dealers will "stretch" to meet producer needs by stocking a little more—and will benefit when product is short by being first in line for shipments.

CHALLENGES FOR DEALERSHIPS AND DISTRIBUTORSHIPS

One recent challenge for dealers and distributors are changes in the relationship with the original manufacturer or franchiser. For example, General Motors in the early 1990s wanted to establish 10 percent of their dealerships as factory-owned, according to Robert Ulrich in *Modern Tire Dealer*. GM was looking to maintain its brand name at its dealerships, many of which had begun selling more than one car line under their roofs. Existing independent dealerships were concerned that factory-owned dealerships would receive preferential treatment in the areas of advertising, service agreements, promotions, and even inventory. Dealerships viewed their ability to sell more than one brand as an opportunity for cross-selling into the GM brand when the buyer may have been initially interested in another brand.

The advent of the Internet has also changed the way that dealerships and distributorships operate. Dealerships and distributorships emerged as businesses when manufacturing companies were new and focusing on production, as opposed to distribution. As production costs diminish with increased pressure for profits, many manufacturing companies are looking for a bigger piece of the pie. Business-to-business selling has increased dramatically. Manufacturers have begun selling their products directly to the public, and the Internet is a relatively inexpensive method of doing so. While this may take away some sales from the distributor, a manufacturer's Web site can also benefit its distributors. Many manufacturers use the site as a storehouse for information on the company and its products, providing prospective sellers with needed information that its distributors cannot deliver to unknown markets or sellers.

While they may engage in direct online sales, it is in the best interest of the manufacturer to also direct visitors to the distributors themselves, providing another channel of opportunity for the distributor. In order to improve their chances at getting that sale, a distributor should establish its own Web presence. While online purchasing capabilities are most likely beyond the resources of a distributor, a site gives the manufacturer something to direct the customer to and provides another marketing opportunity to the distributor.

Dealerships and distributorships can be great business opportunities for the prospective entrepreneur. The benefits of established brands, no manufacturing costs, and marketing and training support from a larger company come at a price, but may mean the difference between success and failure.

BIBLIOGRAPHY

Brack, Ken. "A Direct Hit on Distribution." *Industrial Distribution*. March 1999.

Caffey, Andrew A. "Different Worlds: How to Choose Between a Franchise and a Business Opportunity." *Entrepreneur*. 19 June 2000.

Caffey, Andrew A. "Eight Steps to Choosing the Perfect Business Opportunity." *Business Start-Ups*. September 1998.

Entrepreneur Magazine: Starting a Home-Based Business. John Wiley, 1999.

Estratiades, Anastasius. "Ten Key Questions to Consider Before Your Client Goes Global." *Journal of Accountancy*. February 1997.

Gibbs, Andy. "How to Sell Your Product." *Entrepreneur*. 4 September 2000.

Peterson, Dean D. "In the Beginning." *Doors and Hardware*. August 2000.

Pressman, Arthur L., and Craig R. Tractenberg. "An Introduction to Franchise Law." *The Legal Intelligencer*. 31 May 2000.

Price, Courtney, and Kathleen Allen. *Tips and Traps for Entrepreneurs*. McGraw Hill, 1998.

Ulrich, Robert J. "Alignments Can Help Dealerships." *Modern Tire Dealer*. June 1992.

Hillstrom, Northern Lights
updated by Magee, ECDI

DIVERSIFICATION

In its narrowest meaning, diversification in corporate jargon means participation in multiple industrial activities that do not move in concert as the economy goes up and down. Thus a company that is engaged both in construction and in lumber is *not* said to be diversified. If construction slumps, so will lumber. But a company with activities in travel destinations and in the publishing of romance novels is thought to be much more diversified. A slump that hurts vacation travel may lift the more dreamy activity of curling up with a cheap novel....

In actuality the history of corporations shows a cycle of fashions in which diversification is viewed positively in one part of the cycle and negatively in the other. Arguments are made for either. An environment that favors diversification emphasizes that "management" is a skill independent of *what* is managed; management therefore is seen free to select the playing pieces on its boards to reflects its vision of the future. In an environment that favors "focus" (the popular term in the mid-2000s), emphasis is placed on management knowledge of an industry; the "core" business is emphasized; and diverse holdings are viewed as "distractions." The business environment always offers a sufficient large number of both diversified and concentrated companies so that either mode can be proved to be successful using the right sample. In general, times of exuberance, confidence, and high profits favor a diversifying tendency; times of consolidation favor concentration and the shedding of less than stellar businesses. Generally the attitudes and mindsets associated with diversification or concentration are influenced by corporate and stock performance and far less, if at all, by considerations of market needs and employment. Matters of the latter sort are always much more important to the small business which lives and operates at the community level. Diversification, therefore, has a different meaning for the small business.

Corporate structures, based on the *content* of the business, extend from the polarity of narrow concentration to that of incoherent diversity. There are significant variations at each pole.

CONCENTRATION

Concentration may be quite narrow. An example of such a company may be one that owns a single electric furnace that it operates with purchased scrap. Thus its business is steel-making and nothing else. Its well-being will be governed by such issues as distance of other suppliers, the price of steel globally, the going rate for scrap, for electric power, and the well-being of the companies that purchase its steel. If this company also made steel from iron ore in a Bessemer furnace, it would be more diversified: it would have two sources of raw material. If next it acquired the shipping company that transports its ore on the Great Lakes—and bought a trucking company and several scrap dealers in its next expansion move, it would be more diverse yet. In the event of a softening in steel demand, it might be able to redeploy its transportation lines to carry other products. It might next innovatively transform its Bessemer slag into a gravel product and begin to sell it as road construction fill—supporting this business by its transportation and by adding a wholly-owned plant for making reinforcing bar from its own steel. All of these moves would be considered "diversification," but the company would remain "concentrated" in and around the steel business.

Some of these moves are in the category of *vertical integration*, which is one type of diversification practiced by concentrated companies. Vertical integration brings under the company's own control activities it once purchased. The company now earns the margin produced by the this business. Integration, however, exposes the company to greater risk if the business as a whole has a turn-down. Therefore vertical integration has its reverse implementation, these days called *outsourcing*: outsourcing may or may not be cheaper; it certainly provides greater flexibility.

Concentration is always characterized by close, you might say organic, connections between the elements of a business. The skill-sets of the management are built around understanding these connections deeply enough to exploit them to the optimum.

Diversity At the other end of the spectrum may be the hypothetical IJK company which sells Florida time-share condos, operates a printing company that supports investment banking operations, has a banking subsidiary, owns a AAA ball club, a lumber mill, two construction firms, a cruise line, and a textile importer. It also owns IJK Canning, the original company in the diversification of which all these properties were acquired. Over time IJK has become transformed from a manufacturer to a conglomerate. Its many businesses have so little commonality that the company has become, in effect, a holding operation. The management skills involved in running IJK are almost exclusively financial. It operates as a kind of bank and measures its operations by return on investment. If ROI is growing steadily, IJK stock will be valued. But if the company's overall performance begins to slip, stock analysts will begin to question IJK's "coherence." If problems continue, the company may well begin shedding properties based on some formula. In due time, by keeping its condos, ball club, and cruise line, and adding a cluster or well-chosen multi-screen movie centers in well-known up-scale suburbs across the country, it may emerge into coherence again as an entertainment company—thus completing a cycle from extreme diversification to relative diversification, its management now marked by expertise in identifying major trends in recreational activities.

COMMON THEMES

Aside from diversification moves motivated by the likes, dislikes, or predilections of a leading personality or a management team—and moves that are the result of a period of exuberance—diversification is motivated by four structural issues common both to large and small businesses.

1. Cyclicality—Publicly traded companies typically aim at steady and predictable earnings. If they are in a highly seasonal business or if their performance is tied to economic cycles (like housing), they will attempt to diversify to remove cyclicality from their performance. A small business in the lawn and garden business may thus diversify into offering snow-removal equipment and use some part of its retail space in winter to sell Christmas decoration as a way of steadying employment.

2. Growth or Lack of Growth—A business may be engaged in an industry the nature of which limits growth. As Elizabeth McGowan reports in *Waste Age,* hazardous waste disposal is a current example. The industry is stable but its character is controlled by federal regulation. The industry, therefore, seeks diversification in order to grow. A small business may similarly find itself in a well-served market unable to expand except by adding some related product line to its business.

3. Defense—A business may find itself pressed by the absence of competition in its area for some component that it requires and must virtually sole-source through one vendor. Cost pressures may induce it to enter that business to lower its own costs and also to expand by providing its competitors another source.

4. Unusual Opportunity—Due to unplanned circumstances, a business may find itself in possession of an asset the exploitation of which may require diversification for its full exploitation.

DIVERSIFICATION AS ADAPTABILITY

As the foregoing shows, from the small business perspective diversification is a form of adaptability. Significant size was implied before the word took on its more jargonized meaning of acquisitions and divestitures aimed at major transformations of the corporate profile and its image in the market. For the small business diversification moves will emerge as a natural by-product of operations, announcing themselves as problems (the weakening of a product or service line) or as opportunities (new ways of deploying existing resources). A good general rule for the small business is to diversify in relatively small steps from the well known to the lesser known—until the new itself becomes a firm base for the next steps. Any leap into the radically new should be thoroughly studies and the benefits clearly identified in advance.

BIBLIOGRAPHY
Ahmed, Mojib U., Niazur Rahim, and Muhammad Moshfique Uddin. "The Market Impact of Change in Corporate Diversification: Some new evidence." *Journal of Academy of Business and Economics.* January 2003.

Gutter, Michael S. and Saleem Tabassum. "Financial vulnerability of small business owners." *Financial Services Review.* Summer 2005.

"How Good is This Stock? Ask Jeeves: Must shed unwieldy structure to shine." *Crain's New York Business.* 23 January 2006.

Kaiser, Kevin M.J and Aris Stouraitis. "Reversing Corporate Diversification and the Use of the Proceeds from Asset Sales." *Financial Management.* Winter 2001.

Kwak, Mary. "Maximizing Value Through Diversification: Diversifying can be the best way for companies to match their capabilities to the marketplace." *MIT Sloan Management Review.* Winter 2002.

Lins, Karl V. and Henri Servaes. "Is Corporate Diversification Beneficial in Emerging Markets?" *Financial Management.* Summer 2002.

Lee, Jooh, Ernest H. Hall Jr., and Matthew Rutherford. "A Comparative Study of U.S. and Korean Firms: Changes in diversification and performance." *International Journal of Commerce and Management.* Spring 2003.

McGowan, Elizabeth. "Outlook for Hazardous Waste Industry Called 'Grim'." *Waste News.* 13 February 2006.

"The 'Oops!' Factor: Exceptions will happen, but you can control how dramatically they will affect your supply chain." *Logistics Today.* May 2004.

Skaggs, Bruce C. and Scott B. Droege. "The Performance Effects of Service Diversification by Manufacturing Firms." *Journal of Managerial Issues.* Fall 2004.

Darnay, ECDI

DIVIDENDS

Dividends and stock repurchases are the two major ways that corporations can distribute cash to shareholders. Dividends may also be distributed in the form of stock (stock dividends and stock splits), scrip (a promise to pay at a future date), or property (typically commodities or goods from inventory). By law, dividends must be paid from profits; dividends may not be paid from a corporation's capital. This law, which is designed to protect the corporation's creditors, is known as the impairment of capital rule. The law stipulates that dividend payments may not exceed the corporation's retained earnings as shown on its balance sheet.

Companies usually pay dividends on a quarterly basis. When the company is about to pay a dividend, the company's board of directors makes a dividend announcement that includes the amount of the dividend, the date of record, and the date of payment. The date on which the dividend announcement is made is known as the declaration date.

The date of record is significant for the company's shareholders. All shareholders on the date of record are entitled to receive the dividend. The ex-dividend date is the first day on which the stock is traded without the right to receive the declared dividend. All shares traded before the ex-dividend date are bought and sold with rights to receive the dividend (also known as the cum dividend). Since it usually takes a few business days to settle a stock transaction, the ex-dividend date is usually a few business days before the record date. On the ex-dividend date the trading price of the stock usually falls to account for the fact that the seller rather than the purchaser is entitled to the declared dividend.

Corporate dividend policy is a sometimes under-appreciated element of overall company strategy and financial planning. "It's difficult to generalize about dividend policy because it is usually very company-specific or industry-specific, [but] some general observations are possible," wrote Frederic Escherich in *Directors and Boards.* "Dividend policy's most important uses are to: 1) return excess cash to shareholders; 2) effectively manage the company's cash needs and capital structure; and 3) credibly signal shareholders about future earnings prospects." Indeed, when a company puts together its dividend policy, it must decide whether to distribute a certain amount of earnings to the company's shareholders or retain those earnings for reinvestment. Dividend policy is influenced by a number of factors that include various legal constraints on declaring dividends (bond indentures, impairment of capital rule, availability of cash, and penalty tax on accumulated earnings) as well as the nature of the company's investment opportunities and the effect of dividend policy on the cost of capital of common stock. Most firms have chosen to follow a dividend policy of issuing a stable or continuously increasing dividend. Relatively few firms issue a low regular dividend and declare special dividends when annual earnings are sufficient.

Opinions vary regarding the relationship between dividend policy and corporate taxation. "The usual argument is that since dividends are taxed as income, they have a tax disadvantage with respect to capital gains in a relatively light capital gains tax regime, especially for recipients in high tax brackets," wrote Francesca Cornelli in *The Complete MBA Companion.* "Therefore, other things being equal, companies that pay out high dividends should be valued less than companies that pay out low dividends. In response to this argument, however, economists have argued that the increasing domination of the market by tax-exempt institutions, the reduction of personal marginal income tax rates, the moves in both the UK and US to tax dividends and capital gains at the same rate and the abundance of tax shelters have all combined largely to neutralize the potential tax disadvantage of dividend payments."

SEE ALSO *Stocks*

BIBLIOGRAPHY
Allen, F., and R. Michaely. *Dividend Policy.* N. Holland Handbooks.

Cornelli, Francesca. "The Thinking Behind Dividends." *The Complete MBA Companion.* Pitman Publishing, 1997.

Escherich, Frederic A. "Deliberating on Dividend Policy." *Directors and Boards.* Fall 2000.

Lazo, Shirley A. "The Dividends of Dividends: How Significant are Boosts and Cuts?" *Barron's.* 1 July 1996.

Peskett, Roger. "Deciding Dividends." *Accountancy.* September 1999.

Hillstrom, Northern Lights
updated by Magee, ECDI

DOT-COMS

Commercially operated Web sites have a "com" extension connected to the site-name by a period (.com). This gave the commercial Web sites the "dot-com" name. Every corporation has a dot-com-style Web address, but the name came to be associated more narrowly with organizations hoping to become major Web-based businesses. A dot-com bubble developed during the 1990s in parallel with the rapid expansion of the graphically-based World Wide Web. A huge scramble to be in on the beginnings of limitless wealth caused the launch of tens of thousands of businesses aiming to do what the pioneer of this category, Amazon.com, the bookseller, had been the first to accomplish, namely to become the single or, at minimum, the *dominant* force in a given commercial sector. Alongside these new-born enterprises funded by a tsunami of venture capital hundreds of thousands of other businesses also put Web pages on the Internet. Many of these were also (and still are) selling goods, but typically goods they were and are also selling from brick-and-mortar or mail-order operations. These lesser dot-coms did not borrow money or go public: they just used and are still using the Internet as an additional channel of distribution.

The dot-com bubble became a dot-com bust late in 2000. Wikipedia, in its article on the subject (see http://en.wikipedia.org/wiki/Dot.com_bust) put the date as March 10, 2000. On that day the tech-stock-heavy NASDAQ Composite Index reached an all-time high of 5048.62, which it has not reached again; the dot-com bust deepened as the 2000-2001 recession took hold. Venture capital dried up and many .coms disappeared.

The terrorist attack of 9/11 in a way symbolically put the final period on the first grand wave of commercial expansion on the Internet. But in the view of most industry observers and Web-commerce participants, the 2000 bust was far from signaling the end of dot-commerce. Rather, it marked the end of a major sorting-out and learning phase. As the 2000s keep marching on, the real structure of Internet commerce—indeed its impact on the rest of commerce—is beginning to be better understood. Many of the well-adapted dot-coms survived the bust and continue to be profitable. The market is maturing.

BEHIND THE BUST

The dot-com bust came about because virtually every major participant aimed at replicating the model pioneered by Amazon: namely to become the single, dominant factor in one market by offering an overwhelmingly deep array of products, selling these in such high volume that purchasing power would lower prices to unbeatably low levels, thus, in effect, creating Web monopolies. Once the model was well known, multiple companies attempted to do the same thing in a given sector faced very stiff competition and had to negotiate with a community of original equipment sellers grown sophisticated and careful. Only one such entity could really hope to emerge in each market. Furthermore, the nature of the business had to fit the model equally as well. Books, music, software, arcane electronic components, mechanical parts, and hobby supplies (for example) lent themselves more readily to electronic commerce than commodities like pet supplies. If a particular pet snack could not be found at the store, well, too bad for Pooch. But the same buyer would be persistent in trying to find that rare book, that vital audio card, or that remastered album by Joan Baez.

The early naive view that being on the Internet was the same as "being on" TV—commanding a predictable number of eyeballs—did not last long. To put a Web page on the Internet—without otherwise publicizing or promoting its existence—was equivalent to hanging a notice on the backside of one's garage—in a spot where, at best, utility repairmen might see it once a year. Heavy advertising was required to do the job—or very deep pockets until word-of-mouth established the Web site. Many people, for example, first heard about Amazon.com from a colleague; it took the company a long time to build its massive brand identity. Therefore market entry required not only huge expenditures in assembling saleable merchandise and creating a mirror of these on the Web, with massive hardware behind the pages holding the databases, and effective mass-market payment arrangements with credit-card companies, and, often, real brick-and-mortar warehousing too—it required further splashy, expensive, and persistent promotion by TV and other media.

THE LONG TAIL

In October 2004 the Web expert Chris Anderson wrote an influential article in *Wired Magazine* (of which he is the editor) entitled "The Long Tail." An expanded version of the article was scheduled to appear as a book in 2006. As Anderson himself put it, "The theory of the Long Tail is that our culture and economy is increasingly shifting away from a focus on a relatively small number of 'hits' (mainstream products and markets) at the head of the demand curve and toward a huge number of niches in the tail. As the costs of production and distribution fall, especially online, there is now less need to lump products and consumers into one-size-fits-all containers. In an era without the constraints of physical shelf space and other bottlenecks of distribution, narrowly-targeted goods and services can be as economically attractive as mainstream fare." The "long tail" is becoming an important insight in explaining dot-com businesses.

Put into more concrete terminology, Anderson is saying that a major book chain can only afford to stock in its stores books with predictably high sales, but for every such book there will be many hundreds that will never get shelf-space. Those books are in "the long tail." Using a dot-com like Amazon, the buyer can easily find the obscure book and order it online. It will arrive within days. From the online bookseller's point of view—who need not stock that book in its own warehouse but can order it drop-shipped to the buyer—selling a million different books of this type is equivalent to selling one book a million times. But the same will not be true for the physical retailer who cannot stock the obscure books. What holds for books holds for other similar products where uniqueness matters. The category includes many technical devices and creative products like music, art, and writing. Anderson argues, on the one hand, that Web distribution is helped by its ability to provide virtual access (a picture or a paragraph stands for the product) both to popular and "long tail" products; on the other hand, Anderson suggests that production itself, in the future, will evolve in the direction of more and more diversity. Whether both views hold, the future will show. What is evident is that a symbolical warehouse can hold a lot more goods than a physical one.

THE EMERGING VIEW

In the post-bust era of the later 2000s, dot-commerce emerged more and more clearly as a new type of distribution system with the general characteristics of catalog and mail-order sales—but modernized into a dynamic channel. It is driven by 1) access to all manner of goods,

many not easily found (the "long tail"); 2) the ability of merchants rapidly to update "the catalog" online while avoiding printing and mailing costs; 3) powerful search engines that point consumers to the products and also present contextually generated ads; 4) fierce price competition thanks to easy price comparison; 5) rapid delivery through commercial "postal" services like UPS, FedEx, and DHL; and, most importantly of all, 6) the sheer convenience of online shopping from the desk at home or, for that matter, the desk at the office.

An important element in the rise of dot-commerce is the plain fact that most shopping is done by women—and women are busier than ever. Studies and surveys support this. A Reuters story, for example, headlined the fact as follows: "In terms of purchasing, it's a woman's world." Reuters then cited data from NDP, a market research firm. More women work than ever before. The female workforce participation rate in 1950 was 33.9 percent, had risen to 51.5 percent by 1980, stood at 59.2 percent in 2004, and was projected to 59.7 percent by 2014 by the Bureau of Labor Statistics—but BLS projections in the past have tended to be too conservative. Meanwhile male participation rates have slowly slipped. Pressured by work and family demands, women find it very handy to accomplish particularly seasonal shopping chores online. A consequence of this has been very dramatic growth in e-commerce even as the institutional base of that commerce (the dot-coms themselves) was sorting itself out.

SOARING SALES

The compounded annual growth rate of total retail sales in the U.S. was 4.8 percent a year between 2000 and 2005. In the same period, online retail sales rose at a staggering annual rate of 26 percent *a year*. E-retail is still but a tiny fraction of total retail (2.3 percent in 2005), but it was almost invisible in 2000 (0.9 percent). This sector, which is regularly tracked by the Bureau of the Census (whereas industrial online sales are not), had sales of $27.2 billion in 2000 and $86.3 billion in 2005. The dot-coms that had survived the bust have done very well indeed—as have countless small sellers on the Internet who never tried for high visibility but, instead, simply allowed the search engines to find them.

THE SMALL BUSINESS PERSPECTIVE

Small businesses that create a Web site in anticipation of boosting sales are likely to have one of three kinds of experiences. They may experience no sales at all, hardly even an inquiry—and those few that come are off the mark: the visitors are non-buyers or buyers who didn't bother studying the page. Others may experience sporadic sales activity—but insufficient to organize the channel properly because the transactions are few and far between. Yet others experience a slow start but begin to feel an increase in volume; this motivates them to build up the site, to feature specials, to capture the buyers' particulars in a database, and to spend money on direct mailings to such customers when special promotions provide an opportunity.

Assuming that all things are equal—that all the sites are well-designed, attractive, and have appropriate arrangements for accepting credit cards—success will likely to be due to factors that especially favor the dot-com mode of distribution.

Three factors are most important. First, the product or service should be difficult to find by just hopping in a car or picking up a phone. Consumers won't turn to the Web if they can easily find the product—but difficulty getting what they want will drive them to the Internet these days, and the business they find is likely to make a sale. Second, and alternatively, the product should be seasonal in character to take advantage of the busy shopper's determination to stay out of traffic and crowded malls. If a seasonal product, in addition, is somewhat unique, so much the better. Third, the product or service should be easy to find on the Web—which translates into thoughtful Web design. The price, of course, must also be attractively low.

Unique products need not be mass-market products but they should be difficult to find. Examples are specialized tools and supplies, e.g., caning supplies for someone wishing to refinish a chair; hand-made rag dolls or components for making your own; ethnic clothing, decorations, flags, emblems; unusual musical instruments and sheet music; and many other items of this nature.

The biggest shopping season is Christmas—but Valentines Day, Easter, Mother's Day, Thanksgiving, and Halloween are also busy times for women who then try save time by turning to the Internet. Events such as weddings, Christenings, birthdays, Bar mitzvahs, and funerals may come at any time and present opportunities. It is interesting to note in this context that the flower business, highly seasonal, developed a distribution system based on telegraphic communications long before the Internet was born—and, furthermore, that that business has now migrated to the Internet too.

Search engines gather their information by using so-called Web-crawlers. These crawlers visit new and updated Web-sites and gather information about them automatically. Keywords gathered are then fed to the search engines along with other links used by the site. Some sites are designed in such a fashion that crawlers give the site low rankings for a variety of reasons. Sometimes a site ideal for dot-commerce may be very attractive on the screen but, internally, may be designed so that search engines do not feature it properly. For this reason, expert help in site design is well advised to make sure that the page has optimal visibility.

SEE ALSO *New Economy*

BIBLIOGRAPHY
Anderson, Chris. "Chasing the Long Tail." *Information Age (London, UK).* 20 November 2005.

Anderson, Chris. *The Long Tail: Why the Future of Business is Selling Less of More.* Hyperion. 11 July 2006.

Dieckmann, Heike. "Full circle: Shoplet.com is one of the few profitable survivors of the dot.com boom and bust period of the late 1990s. And the Web as a sales and marketing channel is very much here to stay, says Founder/CEO Tony Ellison." *Office Products International.* October 2005.

Doyle, T.C. "Dot-Coms Woo Channel—Ready To Run." *VARbusiness.* 6 February 2006.

Edwards, Jim. "Dot-Coms Stampede into TV Product Placement." *Brandweek.* 28 November 2005.

Foroohar, Rama. "A Second Dot-Coming: A poor combination of online ads, broadband speed and loyal customers is making content Web sites a hot commodity, and media giants are buying them up." *Newsweek.* 31 October 2005.

"In Terms of Purchasing, It's a Woman's World." *Reuters.* 27 January 2006.

Moschella, David. "IT, Dot-Coms and 'Getting' Business." *Computerworld.* 7 November 2005.

U.S. Census Bureau. "Quarterly Retail E-Commerce." Available from http://www.census.gov/mrts/www/ecomm.html. Retrieved on 5 March 2006.

U.S. Department of Labor. Bureau of Labor Statistics. "Labor Force (Demographic) Data." Available from http://www.bls.gov/emp/emplab1.htm. Retrieved on 5 March 2006.

Zamoiski, John. "Facing an Ad Squeeze, Dot-coms Should Eye New Marketing Solutions." *Brandweek.* 1 May 2000.

Darnay, ECDI

DOUBLE TAXATION

Double taxation is a situation that affects C corporations when business profits are taxed at both the corporate and personal levels. The corporation must pay income tax at the corporate rate before any profits can be paid to shareholders. Then any profits that are distributed to shareholders through dividends are subject to income tax again at the recipient's individual rate. In this way, the corporate profits are subject to income taxes twice. Double taxation does not affect S corporations, which are able to "pass through" earnings directly to shareholders without the intermediate step of paying dividends. In addition, many smaller corporations are able to avoid double taxation by distributing earnings to employee/shareholders as wages. Still, double taxation has long been subject to criticism from accountants, lawyers, and economists.

Critics of double taxation would prefer to integrate the corporate and personal tax systems, arguing that taxes should not affect business and investment decisions. They claim that double taxation places corporations at a disadvantage in comparison with unincorporated businesses, influences corporations to use debt financing rather than equity financing (because interest payments can be deducted and dividend payments cannot), and provides incentives for corporations to retain earnings rather than distributing them to shareholders. Furthermore, critics of the current corporate taxation system argue that integration would simplify the tax code significantly.

AVOIDING DOUBLE TAXATION

There are many ways for corporations to avoid double taxation. For many smaller corporations, all of the major shareholders are also employees of the firm. These corporations are able to avoid double taxation by distributing earnings to employees as wages and fringe benefits. Although the individual employees must pay taxes on their income, the corporation is able to deduct the wages and benefits paid to employees as a business expense, and thus is not required to pay corporate taxes on that amount. For many small businesses, distributions to employee/owners account for all of the corporation's income, and there is nothing left over that is subject to corporate taxes. In cases where income is left in the business, it is usually retained in order to finance future growth. Although this amount is subject to corporate taxes, these tax rates are usually lower than those paid by individuals.

Larger corporations—which are more likely to have shareholders who are not employed by the business and who thus cannot have corporate profits distributed to them in the form of salaries and fringe benefits—are often able to avoid double taxation as well. For example, a non-active shareholder may be called a "consultant," since payments to consultants are considered tax-deductible business expenses rather than dividends. Of course, the shareholder/consultant must pay taxes on his or her compensation. It is also possible to add shareholders to the payroll as members of the board of directors. Finally, tax-exempt investors such as pension funds and charities are often significant shareholders in large corporations. The tax-exempt status of these groups enables them to avoid paying taxes on corporate dividends received.

C VERSUS S

Tax changes introduced by Congress in the 2003 and 2004 Tax Acts have created additional avoidance strategies available to C corporations with 100 or fewer stockholders. First, the laws reduced the top individual income tax rate from 39.5 to 35 percent, making it equivalent to the top corporate rate. Whether in a C or an S, the stockholder pays the same rate now. At the same time, the 2004 Tax Act permitted S corporations to have 100 stockholders, up from 75. Many companies avoided S because they had more than 75 stockholders. With this change, all else equal, C corporations of the right "stockholder size" can convert to an S corporation form, pay the maximum personal and corporate rate on earnings (they are the same) and avoid the dividend levy of the C corporation from.

SEE ALSO *Capital Structure; C Corporation*

BIBLIOGRAPHY
Blackman, Irving L. "C Corporation or S Corporation: What's best for you?" *Pavement Magazine.* August-September 2005.

Smith, Greg W. "C Corps vs. S Corps: How tax law changes may prompt switching." *Financial Executive.* May 2005.

Wolosky, Howard W. "Estate Planning Ramifications of S Corporations: Creating an S Corporation is usually done for income tax considerations. However, the estate planning impact must also be evaluated closely." *The Practical Accountant.* August 2004.

Hillstrom, Northern Lights
updated by Magee, ECDI

DOWNLOADING ISSUES

Downloading issues are the risks and liabilities to which a small business may be exposed as a result of providing Internet access and e-mail service to its employees. Many companies provide Internet access to employees for legitimate business purposes—such as conducting research—and find that such access improves productivity. But connecting employees to the Internet also brings up a number of potential problems for small businesses. "In ever increasing numbers, employers are providing employees with access to voice mail, e-mail, facsimile machines, cellular telephones, the Internet, intranets, laptop computers, and integrated computer networks," Lisa Berg wrote in *South Florida Business Journal.* "While the productivity benefits of an electronic workplace are undisputed, companies must take steps to guard against the enormous risks associated with it."

Many of the potential problems associated with employee Internet access involve downloading of information. For example, employees may download copyrighted software, offensive material, or files that are infected with harmful computer viruses. The small business may be legally liable for damages resulting from claims of copyright infringement, racial discrimination, or sexual harassment based on such downloads. Another potential problem in granting employees access to the Internet is personal use that detracts from productivity. According to Debbie Kelley, writing in *The Gazette* (Colorado Springs, CO), 85 percent of employees use computers at work for fun. "Problems arise when personal activity on the work computer affects employee productivity," Kelley writes. "Websense Inc., a San Diego based seller of Internet –filtering software, estimates that Internet misuse in the workplace costs American companies more than $178 billion annually in lost productivity. That translates to more than $5,000 per employee each year."

A rapidly increasing number of companies are responding to such risks by monitoring their employees' online activities. According to a survey cited in *Training,* 54 percent of companies monitor their employees' Internet connections, while 38 percent monitor their employees' e-mail. "Monitoring is essential," software company CEO Ray Boelig told Sarah Boehle in *Training.* "Organizations need to look at the proper use of their assets." At the same time, however, wholesale monitoring of employees' communications can cause a different set of problems for small businesses. For example, employers can be held liable for invasions of privacy under the Electronic Communications Decency Act of 1996. Furthermore, employers who develop a reputation for excessive monitoring of employee communications may have problems attracting and retaining today's valuable tech-savvy workers. Finally, it takes time to monitor employees communications, time that could be used in any number of more productive tasks.

RISKS ASSOCIATED WITH EMPLOYEE INTERNET USE

In his book *Clicking Through: A Survival Guide for Bringing Your Company Online,* Jonathan Ezor mentioned several risks companies might face as a result of employee Internet use. These risks include liability for copyright infringement resulting from downloads of proprietary documents or software; criminal liability for online gambling, fraudulent acts committed online, or downloads of illegal materials; exposure to sexual harassment or racial discrimination charges based on downloads of offensive materials; and breaches of company confidentiality or security.

Internet users have an implied license to copy the information for the purpose of viewing it on their computer screens. But this implied license applies only to a single user and a one-time use. Many people, failing to understand this condition, save copyrighted documents or software to a hard drive and reuse them without permission. In addition, some Web sites—known as pirate sites—routinely display and distribute information for which they do not hold copyright. A small business's employees might download proprietary software from a pirate site and mistakenly believe that they are allowed to use it. Since the rightful copyright owners have little legal recourse against the pirate sites, which are often operated by poor students, they may instead choose to enforce their rights against larger offenders, like businesses. Small businesses can be held liable for copyright infringement if illegal software is found on company computers, or even if employees use network PCs to play pirated music or watch pirated movies, and the monetary damages can be substantial.

Small businesses may also be exposed to criminal liability resulting from employee Internet use. One such risk involves online gambling. Ezor noted that online casinos are commonplace, which may tempt employees to place bets using company machines during work hours. As with other types of gambling, a wide range of state laws and local regulations apply to this practice. Small businesses may be held liable when employees break these laws. In fact, regulators, casino debt collectors, and affected family members are likely to make the company the target of lawsuits rather than the individual employee.

There are several other ways in which employees' online activities may expose a small business to criminal liability. For example, the company may be implicated if an employee commits stock fraud by posting insider information or misleading data on investment Web sites. Likewise, the company may be responsible if an employee uses the Internet connection to conduct electronic commerce and makes false claims about the products sold. Employees may also use workplace computers to acquire documents or images that are illegal to produce and possess. Examples include child pornography, military secrets, bomb-making instructions, or data encryption algorithms (which cannot legally be sent overseas). Many people are not aware of the distinctions between legal and illegal materials, so downloading from the Internet may put employees at risk of arrest or imprisonment. Furthermore, as Ezor pointed out, companies may be under a legal obligation to report an employee's illegal online activities, regardless of whether doing so might make the company liable to prosecution as well.

Another set of potential problems surrounding employee Internet use involves sexual harassment and racial discrimination. One employee may claim that the material downloaded by another employee—and perhaps distributed via e-mail to other employees—is offensive or degrading. Such material might include pornography, racial jokes, or political cartoons. The company can be held liable if the viewing or distribution of potentially offensive material by employees is allowed to create a hostile working environment for other employees. In 2000, several large companies were embarrassed by news reports of employees accessing adult Internet sites during business hours. This situation has led many other companies to enact policies restricting downloads of questionable material—and to take increased disciplinary action against employees who violate such policies—in an attempt to stave off potential charges of workplace harassment.

As Berg explained in *South Florida Business Review*, employee Internet use can also expose small businesses to breaches of confidentiality and security. For example, employees may download software or documents that introduce viruses to the company's computer network. In addition, online connections and e-mail communications may make confidential data and trade secrets available to computer hackers. Finally, employees' Internet communications could potentially expose the small business to charges of defamation if they appear to represent the company when stating controversial personal opinions online.

CONTROLLING THE RISKS OF DOWNLOADING

Experts recommend that small business owners develop policies regarding employee Internet use. In her article, Berg noted that companies should not only establish comprehensive policies regarding employees' Internet usage, but also obtain employees' written acknowledgment of the policies before offering them Internet access or e-mail accounts. Ezor suggested that employers begin by outlining the various business purposes to be achieved by granting employees Internet access. These purposes may differ depending on each employee's role in the company. For example, one employee may only need to send and receive e-mail, while another may need to surf competitors' Web sites. Next, the small business owner should decide whether or not to monitor employee Internet use and, if so, what Web browser to provide. Many Web browsers are available, and they differ widely in the level of oversight and control they offer. Finally, the small business owner should establish consequences in the event an employee runs afoul of the company's policies. The types of punishment should vary depending on the specific offense and the extent to which it exposes the company to liability.

There are a number of software tools to make enforcement of an Internet usage policy easier for small businesses. Web monitoring software is widely available from such industry leaders as Elron, Net Partners, and SurfControl. These packages allow companies to limit, filter, and monitor the materials employees access on the Internet. Some systems print periodic reports of the sites visited by employees, while others scan for certain words in e-mail messages and domain names. Before starting to monitor employee Internet usage, however, it is important for small business owners to establish guidelines regarding inspections and inform employees about the company policies. Otherwise, employees may challenge the monitoring of e-mail or computer usage by claiming the employer has invaded their privacy. It may be helpful to inform employees in advance that the company offers Internet access for business purposes and reserves the right to monitor the use of its computer system.

As more and more companies have chosen to monitor employee e-mail and Internet usage, increasing numbers of workers have begun to challenge such policies. According to the *Business Week* article, some employees question why employers monitor their electronic communications if there is no cause to believe that their performance is suffering. Other people argue that American workers are spending more time at the office than ever before, and that occasional personal use of company computers is a small price for businesses to pay for the increased productivity this trend has brought. Finally, some people note that excessive monitoring tends to make employees less committed to the company, because they feel that management does not trust them. Strict monitoring policies may also alienate talented young potential hires with valuable computer skills. "The exact kinds of people companies want to attract are the kinds they will turn off with these Internet policies," Chris Christiansen of IDC stated in *Business Week*.

Small business owners must find a balance between the potential risks of improper Internet usage by employees and the potential drawbacks of a strict Internet usage policy. "Turning a blind eye to occasional personal use is acceptable and can even improve employee morale," Lauren M. Bernardi wrote in *Canadian Manager*. "However, other employees may resent the amount of time a co-worker wastes on the Internet if it is excessive. Try to balance those competing interests.... Be reasonable [in monitoring] and do only what you need to do to protect your organization from liability."

SEE ALSO *Internet Security*

BIBLIOGRAPHY
Bernardi, Lauren M. "The Internet at Work: An Employment Danger Zone." *Canadian Manager*. Summer 2000.

Berg, Lisa. "Employers Must Guard Against Electronic Workplace Abuses." *South Florida Business Journal.* 5 May 2000.

Boehle, Sarah. "They're Watching You: Workplace Privacy is Going, Going...." *Training.* August 2000.

Ezor, Jonathan. *Clicking Through: A Survival Guide for Bringing Your Company Online.* Bloomberg, 2000.

"Workers, Surf at Your Own Risk." *Business Week.* 12 June 2000.

Hillstrom, Northern Lights
updated by Magee, ECDI

DRUG TESTING

Drug testing of employees is legally mandated in some occupations; corporations may also require that employees undergo drug testing before employment, at periodic intervals, or after an accident or incident. The usual drug test consists of supplying a sample of urine which is then analyzed in-house or by a commercial laboratory for specified drugs (e.g., marijuana, amphetamines, cocaine, or some other set; almost never are tests exhaustive of all substances because of cost). Testing of the breath, a salivary sample, or a sample of hair are alternatives. Blood tests are almost never used in employee drug tests unless a medical situation has arisen. Drug testing is undertaken and justified for safety reasons. The practice is rarely popular because it is intrusive; opponents also charge that drug testing violates fundamental individual rights and can have a corrosive effect on workplace morale.

FEDERAL DRUG TESTING

Testing of transportation workers was mandated by The Omnibus Transportation Employee Testing Act of 1991. According to the Department of Transportation's Web site, the act "requires drug and alcohol testing of safety-sensitive transportation employees in aviation, trucking, railroads, mass transit, pipelines and other transportation industries." DOT states that roughly 12.1 million people are included under the "safety-sensitive" employee definition, but neither the department nor the regulation (49 Code of Federal Regulations, Part 40) actually spell out what that phrase means. It is left to each DOT element regulating the transportation industry to define such individuals. The phrase refers generally to operating and direct supervisory individuals in the transportation industry. Each regulatory agency also publishes separate regulations of how and when it conducts drug and alcohol tests.

Corporate Drug Testing According to the American Management Association's 2000 survey of testing in the workplace, 47 percent of all companies surveyed conducted drug testing, down from 52 percent of companies in 1991. Testing of new hires was highest in manufacturing companies (78.5 percent conducted tests) and lowest in financial services (35.8 percent conducted tests). Testing of all employees also followed this pattern, with 42.2 percent of manufacturers doing tests but only 18.8 percent of financial services companies doing so in 2000. The Bureau of Labor Statistics had conducted a survey in 1990 but has not conducted such a survey since. In the 1990 survey, BLS had also noted a decline in drug testing.

DRUG USE PATTERNS IN THE POPULATION

According to the Office of National Drug Control Policy (ONDCP, a part of the Executive Office of the President), in 1978 31.3 percent of all persons aged 12 and older had used illicit drugs at least once in their lifetime. By 1998 this figure had gradually increased to 35.8 percent. After that year data collection techniques introduced a change so that subsequent years could not be compared to the 1978-1998 period. But the ratio in 1999 was 39.7 percent of all people. It dropped to 38.9 percent in 2000 and climbed to 41.7 percent in 2001.

Based on data published by the Substance Abuse and Mental Health Services Administration (SAMHSA, an element of the U.S. Department of Health and Human Services), around 110 million people aged 12 or older had used illicit drugs during their lifetime in 2004, nearly 35 million had used drugs in the past year, nearly 19 million in the past month. Year-to-year data show some fluctuations but no strong trend. Thus lifetime use increased between 2002 and 2003 (up 1.95 million) but decreased between 2003 and 2004 (down 148,000). The overwhelming majority of these people used marijuana, 88 percent in lifetime, 73 percent in the past year, 76 percent in the past month. The next major use category was non-medical uses of medicines, with painkillers the largest segment of that category.

As reported in *Social Trends and Indicators USA,* alcohol use was significantly greater than any drug use in the United States. FBI arrest records in 2000, for instance, showed 2.8 million arrests for alcohol-related offenses and 1.6 million arrests for drug-offenses; of these drug offenses 646,000 were arrests for marijuana possession. Around 110,000 deaths annually are related to alcohol use; of these 16,000 are alcohol-related traffic deaths. Total drug-related deaths in 1997, according to ONDCP, were also 16,000.

These data show that 1) a large number of people use or have used drugs, 2) the overwhelmingly dominant drug of choice is marijuana, 3) other forms of drug use are extremely varied, with a very small number only using heroin, and 4) alcohol use produces more arrests and has a higher death toll than drugs.

DRUG TESTING ISSUES

Drug testing may be an appropriate initiative for a small business experiencing problems in its workforce or in order to avoid costly problems in the operation of expensive and sensitive equipment. The business may also, because of contracting regulations, be required to institute such a program. Drug testing may also be a means of lowering insurance costs. Advice in the establishment of such a program is available to the small business through the Substance Abuse and Mental Health Administration which maintains a telephone Helpline at 1-800-967-5752. The main issues to consider in planning such a program are the following:

Legality Drug testing is legal and implicitly supported at the federal level by the 1998 Drug Free Workplace Act; the act creates a right to work in a drug-free work environment. But drug testing may be regulated at the state level. Researching such regulations should be an early step.

Test Criteria The most common form of drug test is a urine test, but use of oral fluids and samples of hair are sometimes used. Testing hair can detect drug use some time in the past, but the method is costly. Oral fluid testing is not presently used in federal testing protocols, possibly because it cannot detect the presence of THC after 24 hours; delta-9-tetrahydrocannabinol is an active cannabinoid. Most testing programs focus on a limited number of drugs in order to avoid the high expenses of multiple tests. LSD, for instance, cannot be detected in urine and requires expensive tests. For these reasons, also, conditions of the test need to be established in such a manner that costs can be predicted. The usual times of administration are 1) before hire, 2) randomly throughout the year, 3) following incidents/accidents. The testing plan needs also to define in advance if all employees will be tested or only certain categories of employees, e.g., heavy equipment operators. The cost of tests, including the acquisition of the sample and its analysis by a lab will range from $15 to $60 dollars.

Promulgation The drug testing program needs to be made a formal part of the company's employment policy and announced so that employees are well aware of the testing program and, above all, how positive results will be handled, before the program is instituted.

The Testing Protocol The drug testing program must have a well-designed protocol which will define where and how the test samples will be collected, how privacy will be preserved, and where the actual tests will be conducted. Lists of certified laboratories are available from SAMHSA. If testing is initially conducted in-house using commercially available testing kits, it is especially important to have arrangements for passing on non-negative results with samples to certified labs which can do more equipment-intensive testing (gas chromatography, mass spectroscopy).

Physician's Review An employee may test positive because of his or her use of prescription medications. The availability of a medical review physician to look into such cases should be planned and made part of the total program.

SEE ALSO *Employee Rights*

BIBLIOGRAPHY

A 2000 AMA Survey: Workplace Testing: Medical Testing: Summary of Key Findings. American Management Association. 2000.

Cadrain, Diane. "Helping Workers Fool Drug Tests is a Big Business." *HRMagazine.* August 2005.

Callaghan, Leo G. "Don't Fault Employer for Firing Drug Users." *HRMagazine.* November 2005.

Cholakis, Peter. "How to Implement a Successful Drug Testing Program." *Risk Management.* November 2005.

Close, Louise. "Drugs in the Workplace An Issue for Industry." *Manufacturers' Monthly.* 28 July 2005.

Fletcher, Meg. "Drug-Test Cheats Frustrate Employer Screening Efforts." *Business Insurance.* 1 August 2005.

Gips, Michael A. "High On the Job: Drug dealers and users are more savvy in workplaces today. Businesses need policies and training to counter these trends." *Security Management.* February 2006.

Kaplan, Dale. "Do I want to be a SAP?" *Addiction Professional.* July 2005.

Lazich, Robert, ed. *Social Trends and Indicators USA, Vol. IV.* Thomson Gale, 2003.

"Mouthing Off for Drug Testing." *Security.* February 2006.

Office of National Drug Control Policy. "Drug Use Trends: October 2002." Available from http://www.whitehousedrugpolicy.gov/publications/factsht/druguse/index.html. Retrieved on 24 February 2006.

"Six-Step Program." *Business Insurance.* 1 August 2005.

Hillstrom, Northern Lights
updated by Magee, ECDI

DUE DILIGENCE

Due diligence is a program of critical analysis that companies undertake prior to making business decisions in such areas as corporate mergers/acquisitions or major product purchases/sales. The due diligence process, whether outsourced or executed in-house, is in essence an attempt to provide business owners and managers with reliable and complete background information on proposed business deals so that they can make informed decisions about whether to go forward with the business action. "The [due diligence] process involves everything from reading the fine print in corporate legal and financial documents such as equity vesting plans and patents to interviewing customers, corporate officers, and key developers," wrote Lee Copeland in *Computerworld.* The ultimate goal of such activities is to make sure that there are no hidden drawbacks or traps associated with the business action under consideration.

Many companies undertake the due diligence process with insufficient vigor. In some cases, the prevailing culture views it as a perfunctory exercise to be checked off quickly. In other instances, the outcome of the due diligence process may be tainted (either consciously or unconsciously) by owners, managers, and researchers who stand to benefit personally or professionally from the proposed activity. Businesses should be vigilant against letting such casual or flawed attitudes impact their own processes: an efficient due diligence process can save companies from making costly mistakes that may have profound consequences for the firm's other operational areas and/or its corporate reputation.

AREAS OF DUE DILIGENCE

The due diligence process is applied in two basic business situations: 1) transactions involving sale and purchase of products or services, and 2) transactions involving mergers, acquisitions, and partnerships of corporate entities. In the former instance, purchase and sales agreements include a series of exhibits that, taken in their entirety, form due diligence of the purchase. These include actual sales contracts, rental contracts, employment contracts, inventory lists, customer lists, and equipment lists. These various "representations" and "warranties" are presented to back up the financial claims of both the buyer and seller. The importance of this kind of due diligence has been heightened in recent years with the emergence of the Internet and other transforming technologies. Indeed, due diligence is a vital tool when a company is confronted with major purchasing decisions in the realm of information technology. "A due diligence investigation should answer pertinent questions such as whether an application is too bulky to run on the mobile devices the marketing plan calls for or whether customers are

right when they complain about a lack of scalability for a high-end system," said Copeland.

In cases of potential mergers and acquisitions, due diligence is a more comprehensive undertaking. "The track record of past operations and the future prospects of the company are needed to know where the company has been and where its potential may carry it," explained William Leonard in *Ohio CPA Journal.* In addition, observers note that the dramatic increase in information technology (IT) in recent years has complicated the task of due diligence for many companies, especially those engaged in negotiations to buy or merge with another company. After all, system incompatibilities can require huge amounts of time, money, and personnel resources to integrate.

Leonard notes that traditional due diligence practices in acquisition/merger scenarios called for detailed examination of financial statements, accounts receivable, inventories, workers compensation, employment practices and employee benefits, pending and potential litigation, tax situation, and intellectual property prior to signing on the dotted line. But in this dynamic business era, other areas should be looked at as well, including (if applicable): intellectual property rights, new products in the production pipeline, status of self-funded insurance programs, compliance with pertinent ordinances and regulations, competition, environmental practices, and background of key executives/personnel.

Many business experts also caution that the due diligence process is incomplete if it does not incorporate an element of objective self-analysis. "Self-analysis is the fundamental first step to realistically determine whether the post-acquisition 'whole' will be greater than the sum of its part," wrote Aaron Lebedow in *Journal of Business Strategy.* A detailed assessment of the market that is the target of the proposed acquisition should also be undertaken prior to closing a deal. Both of these requirements can be completed in a reasonable period of time, even in today's fast-changing business environment, by companies that either 1) outsource the due diligence task to a reputable research firm or 2) build an efficient in-house program within their legal, marketing, or corporate security sectors. "Unquestionably, opportunities for growth through acquisition exist," stated Lebedow. "Exploiting these opportunities has risks, but to those companies that acquire only after a comprehensive and systemic assessment of the marketplace and competition, the rewards justify the risks. Limiting due diligence to financial and managerial review is rarely enough. Successful acquisition strategy depends on the structure and depth of the due diligence process."

SUPPLEMENTING DUE DILIGENCE

Growing numbers of business enterprises are pursuing additional legal protection for themselves so as to shield themselves from harm if their due diligence efforts fail to uncover a serious problem with a merger or purchase transaction. One means of mitigating the risks associated with such major business transactions that has become increasingly popular in recent years is to secure a form of insurance coverage known as "representations and warranties liability insurance." A growing number of insurance underwriters are providing these policies, which call for them to pay insured parties for losses resulting from various "wrongful acts." This umbrella term generally covers errors, misstatements, misleading information, etc., but underwriters do include exclusions, some of which should be noted by potential buyers. These include acts of "fraud" (if adjudicated in the courts), pollution (which is typically covered under separate policies), or situations in which a party has received benefits—financial or otherwise—to which it is not entitled. One significant benefit of "representations and warranties liability" policies, however, is that the coverage can be used in place of reserves, escrow, or indemnity provisions that are included in purchase agreements.

Premiums for such policies can be expensive, especially for small and mid-sized firms with limited financial resources. Moreover, securing such insurance is a time-consuming and painstaking process, for underwriters are putting themselves at considerable financial risk. "Premiums will be determined based on the risk and the comfort level of the underwriter," summarized Leonard. ""It is most important that the process start early and not be left to a time when someone gets a 'feeling' things may not be entirely up to snuff. Although this type of coverage can be purchased after the closing, understandably the most beneficial time to place the coverage is during the due diligence phase preceding the closing."

BIBLIOGRAPHY

Bernstein, Leopold A., and John J. Wild. *Analysis of Financial Statements*. McGraw-Hill, 2000.

Copeland, Lee. "Due Diligence." *Computerworld*. 6 March 2000.

Joukhadar, Kristina. "Faster Due Dilligence." *InformationWeek*. 22 January 2001.

Kroll, Luisa. "Gotcha: Pushing the Limits of Due Diligence." *Forbes*. 30 October 2000.

Lebedow, Aaron L. "Due Diligence: More than a Financial Exercise." *Journal of Business Strategy*. January 1999.

Leonard, William J. "Representation and Warranties—When Due Diligence Fails." *Ohio CPA Journal*. January 2000.

Torrey, Rebecca and Larry Scherzer. "Doing Due Diligence to Uncover 'Bad Apple' Applicants." *Los Angeles Business Journal*. 21 October 2000.

Hillstrom, Northern Lights
updated by Magee, ECDI

E

ECONOMIC ORDER QUANTITY (EOQ)

The Economic Order Quantity (EOQ) is the number of units that a company should add to inventory with each order to minimize the total costs of inventory—such as holding costs, order costs, and shortage costs. The EOQ is used as part of a continuous review inventory system in which the level of inventory is monitored at all times and a fixed quantity is ordered each time the inventory level reaches a specific reorder point. The EOQ provides a model for calculating the appropriate reorder point and the optimal reorder quantity to ensure the instantaneous replenishment of inventory with no shortages. It can be a valuable tool for small business owners who need to make decisions about how much inventory to keep on hand, how many items to order each time, and how often to reorder to incur the lowest possible costs.

The EOQ model assumes that demand is constant, and that inventory is depleted at a fixed rate until it reaches zero. At that point, a specific number of items arrive to return the inventory to its beginning level. Since the model assumes instantaneous replenishment, there are no inventory shortages or associated costs. Therefore, the cost of inventory under the EOQ model involves a tradeoff between inventory holding costs (the cost of storage, as well as the cost of tying up capital in inventory rather than investing it or using it for other purposes) and order costs (any fees associated with placing orders, such as delivery charges). Ordering a large amount at one time will increase a small business's holding costs, while making more frequent orders of fewer items will reduce holding costs but increase order costs.

The EOQ model finds the quantity that minimizes the sum of these costs.

The basic EOQ relationship is shown below. Let us look at it assuming we have a painter using 3,500 gallons of paint per year, paying $5 a gallon, a $15 fixed charge every time he/she orders, and an inventory cost per gallon held averaging $3 per gallon per year.

The relationship is $TC = PD + HQ/2 + SD/Q \ldots$ where

- TC is the total annual inventory cost—to be calculated.
- P is the price per unit paid—assume $5 per unit.
- D is the total number of units purchased in a year—assume 3,500 units.
- H is the holding cost per unit per year—assume $3 per unit per annum.
- Q is the quantity ordered each time an order is placed—initially assume 350 gallons per order.
- S is the fixed cost of each order—assume $15 per order.

Calculating TC with these values, we get a total inventory cost of $18,175 for the year. Notice that the main variable in this equation is the quantity ordered, Q. The painter might decide to purchase a smaller quantity. If he or she does so, more orders will mean more fixed order expenses (represented by S) because more orders are handles—but lower holding charges (represented by H): less room will be required to hold the paint and less money tied up in the paint. Assuming the painter buys 200 gallons at a time instead of 350, the TC will drop to

$18,063 a year for a savings of $112 a year. Encouraged by this, the painter lowers his/her purchases to 150 at a time. But now the results are unfavorable. Total costs are now $18,075. Where is the optimal purchase quantity to be found?

The EOQ formula produces the answer. The ideal order quantity comes about when the two parts of the main relationship (shown above)— "HQ/2" and the "SD/Q"—are equal. We can calculate the order quantity as follows: Multiply total units by the fixed ordering costs (3,500 x $15) and get 52,500; multiply that number by 2 and get 105,000. Divide that number by the holding cost ($3) and get 35,000. Take the square root of that and get 187. That number is then Q.

In the next step, HQ/2 translates to 281, and SD/Q also comes to 281. Using 187 for Q in the main relationship, we get a total annual inventory cost of $18,061, the lowest cost possible with the unit and pricing factors shown in the example above.

Thus EOQ is defined by the formula: EOQ = square root of 2DS/H. The number we get, 187 in this case, divided into 3,500 units, suggests that the painter should purchase paint 19 times in the year, buying 187 gallons at a time.

The EOQ will sometimes change as a result of quantity discounts offered by some suppliers as an incentive to customers who place larger orders. For example, a certain supplier may charge $20 per unit on orders of less than 100 units and only $18 per unit on orders over 100 units. To determine whether it makes sense to take advantage of a quantity discount when reordering inventory, a small business owner must compute the EOQ using the formula (Q = the square root of 2DS/H), compute the total cost of inventory for the EOQ and for all price break points above it, and then select the order quantity that provides the minimum total cost.

For example, say that the painter can order 200 gallons or more for $4.75 per gallon, with all other factors in the computation remaining the same. He must compare the total costs of taking this approach to the total costs under the EOQ. Using the total cost formula outlined above, the painter would find TC = PD + HQ/2 + SD/Q = (5 x 3,500) + (3 x 187)/2 + (15 x 3,500)/187 = $18,061 for the EOQ. Ordering the higher quantity and receiving the price discount would yield a total cost of (4.75 x 3,500) + (3 x 200)/2 + (15 x 3,500)/200 = $17,187. In other words, the painter can save $875 per year by taking advantage of the price break and making 17.5 orders per year of 200 units each.

EOQ calculations are rarely as simple as this example shows. Here the intent is to explain the main principle of the formula. The small business with a large and frequently turning inventory may be well served by look-ing around for inventory software which applies the EOQ concept more complexly to real-world situations to help purchasing decisions more dynamically.

BIBLIOGRAPHY

"Accounting Software." *Financial Executive.* October 2002.

Balakrishnan, Antaram, Michael S. Pangburn, and Euthemia Stavrulaki. "Stack Them High, Let 'Em Fly." *Management Science.* May 2004.

Khouja, Moutaz and Sungjune Park. "Optimal Lot Sizing Under Continuous Price Decrease." *Omega.* December 2003.

Piasecki, Dave. "Optimizing Economic Order Quantity." *IIE Solutions.* January 2001.

Wang, Kung-Jeng, Hui-Ming Wee, Shin-Feng Gao, and Shen-Lian Chung. "Production and Inventory Control with Chaotic Demands." *Omega.* April 2005.

Woolsey, Robert E.D. and Ruth Maurer. *Inventory Control (For People Who Really Have to Do It).* Lionheart Publishing, March 2001.

Hillstrom, Northern Lights
updated by Magee, ECDI

ECONOMIES OF SCALE

Economies of scale refer to economic efficiencies that result from carrying out a process on a larger scale. Scale effects are possible because in most production operations fixed and variable costs are involved; the fixed costs are not related to production volume; variable costs are. Large production runs therefore "absorb" more of the fixed costs. An example is a printing run. Setting up the run requires burning a plate after a photographic process, mounting the plate on the printing press, adjusting ink flow, and running five or six pages to make sure everything is correctly set-up. The cost of setting up will be the same whether the printer produces one copy or 10,000. If the set-up cost is $55 and the printer produces 500 copies, each copy will carry 11 cents worth of set up cost. But if 10,000 pages are printed, each page carries only 0.55 cents of set-up cost. The reduction in cost per unit is an economy due to scale. Very much the same thing happens when an author writes a book and gets it published. Writing the book is the fixed cost. If the publisher pays the author a $10,000 advance and then only sells 25 copies, each book cost the publisher $400 in fixed cost alone—and the publisher will lose a lot of money. If the book sells 5,000 copies, each carries $2 dollars in fixed cost. An effective supervisor can supervise 10 to 12 people as effectively as three; after that the supervisor's "span of control" will be affected. This example shows that economies of scale have limits. A forging press cannot be operated longer than 24 hours a day. A moderately sized accounting department cannot handle a growing volume of transactions indefinitely: it will have to add employees eventually.

Economies of scale are closely tied to systems of production where something standardized is replicated many times—or to fixed facilities that may be utilized for a few hours only or for 24 hours a day. Limitations are thus imposed by equipment capacity, time, and the nature of the product or service. Heart by-pass operations, although many thousands are performed every day, are always unique. A heart surgeon's personal action is involved and cannot be mechanically multiplied. Economies of scale are thus not available in heart surgery. Neither are they available in barber shops. In general, therefore, businesses or activities that provide unique services delivered *in person* are less able to generate economies of scale. People who ultimately sell their time—rather than something that they have made (which can be multiplied)—tend therefore to charge more for their time; the higher the skill level, the more they charge.

SMALL BUSINESS AND SCALE

It is frequently repeated that small businesses have less opportunity to apply economies of scale for the simple reason that they are small and unlikely to be engaged in mass production. The generalization is true enough if economies of scale are viewed narrowly. In effect economies of scale are also available to small businesses—and increasingly so as a consequence of modern developments in the services sectors and in electronics.

Buying Services Many small businesses achieve economies of scale by purchasing their payroll services from a large payroll company; they receive sophisticated services, including annual tax notifications, at a much lower cost than they could achieve by paying a payroll accountant in-house. Accounting services are purchased similarly, often in combination with using a modern software program for keying data in at the company's location and having a professional accountant check and use the software for tax preparation purposes. The small business using the professional accountant only uses a small portion of his or her time—and pays only a small percentage of the accountant's fixed costs. Small business are adept at using services rather than doing the job in-house. Any organization servicing a large number of small businesses (like a payroll service) is, from the small business perspective, an "economy of scale."

Sharing Risks In many locations across the country chambers of commerce or other organizations offer health insurance services to small businesses. In these instances, the chamber becomes the effective "large scale" purchaser of insurance on behalf of its members. It thus creates a large pool of people much more attractive to the insurance carrier; the latter enjoys the scale effect by dealing with a single purchaser; the small business enjoys an attractively low premium unavailable except by this participation—an extension of the concept of economies of scale.

Scaling Through Technology Developments in computers and the spread of the Internet have created economies of scale at low cost to the small business which the small business is able to exploit. In the mid-2000s a small business with a handful of employees, a few computers, and an Internet connection can deliver services that, in the 1950s, would have required 200-some-odd employees. Aspects of this subject are covered under a variety of different contexts throughout this volume. The Internet has enabled small operations to be much more productive in purchasing, marketing, hiring, data collection, accounting, selling for credit, desktop publishing, and in other areas.

Providing an Economy of Scale Overlooked in the general discussion of economies of scale, narrowly construed, is the fact that small businesses are themselves providers of economies of scale. By their very nature they are physically closer to the consumer and therefore efficient outlets for the consumer who wishes to save time. Large retail discount houses attract by low pricing—but they are usually at a substantial distance. Small businesses are nimble, flexible, and creative precisely because they are small and, being small, they are not subject to the massive systems-responses of the giants whose recorded voices assure us that "Your call is important to us." Our call is important but sometimes never answered by a living voice.

BIBLIOGRAPHY

"Corporate E-cycling." *Los Angeles Business Journal.* 9 May 2005.

DeYoung, Robert. "The Performance of Internet-Based Business Models: Evidence from the banking industry." *The Journal of Business.* May 2005.

Henricks, Mark. "Learn To Share." *Entrepreneur.* March 2001.

"No Special Relationship." *Utility Week.* 28 November 2003.

Potter, Donald V. "Scale Matters." *Across the Board.* July 2000.

Sinnock, Bonnie. "Industry Needs to Grapple with Issue of Outsourcing Jobs Overseas." *National Mortgage News.* 15 March 2004.

Taylor, Marcia. "How Big is Enough?" *Top Producer.* December 2003.

"Thinking Locally Acting Globally: That's not an easy concept for a lot of multinational companies, but an Oracle executive argues that the old ways of deferring to local practices need to be abandoned in favor of global standardization." *Financial Executive*. March-April 2003.

Darnay, ECDI

ECONOMIES OF SCOPE

Economies of scope are cost advantages that result when firms provide a variety of products rather than specializing in the production or delivery of a single product or service. Economies of scope also exist if a firm can produce a given level of output of each product line more cheaply than a combination of separate firms, each producing a single product at the given output level. Economies of scope can arise from the sharing or joint utilization of inputs and lead to reductions in unit costs. Scope economies are frequently documented in the business literature and have been found to exist in countries, electronic-based B2B (business-to-business) providers, home healthcare, banking, publishing, distribution, and telecommunications.

METHODS OF ACHIEVING ECONOMIES OF SCOPE

Flexible Manufacturing The use of flexible processes and flexible manufacturing systems has resulted in economies of scope because these systems allow quick, low-cost switching of one product line to another. If a producer can manufacture multiple products with the same equipment and if the equipment allows the flexibility to change as market demands change, the manufacturer can add a variety of new products to their current line. The scope of products increases, offering a barrier to entry for new firms and a competitive synergy for the firm itself.

Related Diversification Economies of scope often result from a related diversification strategy and may even be termed "economies of diversification." This strategy is made operational when a firm builds upon or extends existing capabilities, resources, or areas of expertise for greater competitiveness. According to Hill, Ireland, and Hoskisson in their best selling strategic management textbook, *Strategic Management: Competitiveness and Globalization,* firms select related diversification as their corporate-level strategy in an attempt to exploit economies of scope between their various business units. Cost-savings result when a business transfers expertise in one business to a new business. The businesses can share

operational skills and know-how in manufacturing or even share plant facilities, equipment, or other existing assets. They may also share intangible assets like expertise or a corporate core competence. Such sharing of activities is common and is a way to maximize limited constraints.

As an example, Kleenex Corporation manufactures a number of paper products for a variety of end users, including products targeted specifically for hospitals and health care providers, infants, children, families, and women. Their brands include Kleenex, Viva, Scott, and Cottonelle napkins, paper towels, and facial tissues; Depends and Poise incontinence products; Huggies diapers and wipes; Pull-Ups, Goodnites, and Little Swimmers infant products; Kotex, New Freedom, Litedays, and Security feminine hygiene products; and a number of products for surgical use, infection control, and patient care. All of these product lines utilize similar raw material inputs and/or manufacturing processes as well as distribution and logistics channels.

Mergers The merger wave that swept the United States in the late 1990s and early 2000s is, in part, an attempt to create scope economies. Mergers may be undertaken for any number of reasons. "As a rule of thumb," explained Rob Preston in an article about the trouble with mergers, "'scope' acquisitions—moves that enhance or extend a vendor's product portfolio—succeed more often than those undertaken to increase size and consolidate costs." Pharmaceutical companies, for example, frequently combine forces to share research and development expenses and bring new products to market. Research has shown that firms involved in drug discovery realize economies of scope by sustaining diverse portfolios of research projects that capture both internal and external knowledge spillovers.

Linked Supply Chains Today's linked supply chains among raw material suppliers, other vendors, manufacturers, wholesalers, distributors, retailers, and consumers often bring about economies of scope. Integrating a vertical supply chain results in productivity gains, waste reduction, and cost improvements. These improvements, which arise from the ability to eliminate costs by operating two or more businesses under the same corporate umbrella, exist whenever it is less costly for two or more businesses to operate under centralized management than to function independently.

The opportunity to gain cost savings can arise from interrelationships anywhere along a value chain. As firms become linked in supply chains, particularly as part of the new information economy, there is a growing potential for economies of scope. Scope economies can increase a firm's value and lead to increases in performance and higher returns to shareholders. Building economies of scope can also help a firm to reduce the risks inherent in producing a single product or providing a service to a single industry.

BIBLIOGRAPHY

Banker, R.D., H.H. Chang, and S.K. Majumdar, S. K. "Economies of Scope in the U.S. Telecommunications Industry." *Information Economies and Policy.* June 1998.

Fraquelli, Giovanni, and Massimiliano Piacenzo, Davide Vannoni "Scope and Scale Economies in Multi-Utilities." *Applied Economics.* 10 October 2004.

Henderson, R., and I. Cockburn. "Scale, Scope, and Spillovers: The Determinants of Research Productivity in Drug Discovery." *RAND Journal of Economics.* Spring 1996.

Hill, M.A., R.D. Ireland, and R.E. Hoskisson. *Strategic Management: Competitiveness and Globalization.* Fourth Edition. South-Western College Publishing, 2001.

Kass, D. I. "Economies of Scope and Home Healthcare." *Health Services Research* October 1998.

Ryan, M. J. "The Distribution Problem, the More for Less (Nothing) Paradox and Economies of Scale and Scope." *European Journal of Operational Research.* February 2000.

Preston, Rob. "The Trouble with Mergers." *Network Computing.* 5 March 2005.

Woodall, P. "Survey: The New Economy: Falling Through the Net?" *The Economist* 23 September 2000.

*Hillstrom, Northern Lights
updated by Magee, ECDI*

8(A) PROGRAM

The 8(a) Program is a Small Business Administration (SBA) program intended to provide assistance to economically and/or socially disadvantaged business owners. The initiative, which originated out of Section 8(a) of the Small Business Act—hence its name—provides participants with access to a variety of business development services, including the opportunity to receive federal contracts on a sole-source or limited competition basis. The program has been an important one for thousands of minority entrepreneurs over the past few years.

8(A) PROGRAM ELIGIBILITY REQUIREMENTS

Entrepreneurs seeking to gain entrance into the SBA's 8(a) program must meet a number of criteria in such areas as ownership, management, and likelihood of success.

- An applicant must qualify as a small business enterprise as defined by the Small Business Administration's rules and regulations.

- An applicant firm must be majority-owned (51 percent or more) by an individual or individual(s) who is an American citizen. If the business is a corporation, "at least 51 percent of each class of voting stock and 51 percent of the aggregate of all outstanding shares of stock must be unconditionally owned by an individual(s) determined by SBA to be socially and economically disadvantaged," stated the Small Business Administration.

- Majority owners of the applicant firm have to meet the SBA definition of a socially and economically disadvantaged group. Socially disadvantaged individuals are defined by the SBA as those who have been subjected to racial or ethnic prejudice or cultural bias because of their identification as members of groups without regard to their individual qualities. Economically disadvantaged individuals, meanwhile, are defined by the SBA as socially disadvantaged people whose ability to compete in the free enterprise system has been diminished as a result of lesser capital and credit opportunities. Individuals from a broad array of social/ethnic groups have been found eligible for the 8(a) program under the above criteria, including black Americans, Hispanic Americans, Native Americans, Pacific Americans, and members of other ethnic groups. Individuals who are not members of recognized socially disadvantaged groups may also apply, but the SBA notes that such applicants "must establish social disadvantage on the basis of clear and convincing evidence."

- Stock status is also considered. For example, a business may not claim to be unconditionally owned by socially/economically disadvantaged individuals if they make that claim on the basis of unexercised stock options. Similarly, the SBA considers options to purchase stock held by non-disadvantaged entities when determining ownership.

- One 8(a) firm may not hold more than a 10 percent equity ownership interest in any other 8(a) firm. Moreover, no individual owner of an 8(a) firm, even if he or she qualifies as disadvantaged, may hold an equity ownership interest of more than 10 percent in another firm involved in the 8(a) program.

- According to the SBA, "the management and daily business operations of a firm must be controlled by an owner(s) of the firm who has (have) been determined to be socially and economically disadvantaged. For a disadvantaged individual to control the firm, that individual must have managerial or technical experience and competency directly related to the primary industry in which the firm is seeking 8(a) certification.... for those industries requiring professional licenses, SBA determines that the firm or individuals employed by the firm hold(s) the requisite license(s)."

- At least one full-time manager who qualifies under SBA definitions as a disadvantaged person must hold the position of president or CEO in the company.

- The individual or individuals claiming disadvantage must demonstrate that they personally suffered disadvantage, not just that the group of which they are a member has historically been considered to be disadvantaged. Moreover, the SBA stipulates that social disadvantage must be 1) rooted in treatment received in American society, not other countries; 2) chronic and substantial; 3) and hindered their entrance or progress in the world of business. Applicants can point to several kinds of experiences to demonstrate the above, including denial of equal access to institutions of higher education; exclusion from social and professional associations; denial of educational honors; social pressures that discouraged the individual from pursuing education; and discrimination in efforts to secure employment or secure professional advancement.

- Individuals claiming economic disadvantage can not have a personal net worth in excess of $250,000, no matter what their origins are.

- Applicants have to show that they have been in business in the industry area to which they are applying for at least two years prior to the date of their 8(a) application. They can do this by submitting income tax returns showing revenues for those years.

- Applicants have to be deemed by the SBA to have a good probability of success in the industry in which they are involved. In making this determination, the Small Business Administration considers many factors, including the technical and managerial abilities and experiences of the owners, the financial situation of the applicant firm, and the company's record of performance on prior federal and private sector contracts.

Businesses owned by white women may also be eligible for the program. In the past, these entrepreneurs had to demonstrate in strong terms that they had been discriminated against in the past because of gender, and that this discrimination had been sufficiently egregious to hinder their success in the business world. In the late 1990s, however, the SBA adjusted eligibility requirements to make it easier for white women-owned businesses to gain entrance into the 8(a) program.

Certain kinds of businesses are ineligible for inclusion in the 8(a) program. These include franchises of any kind, nonprofit organizations, brokers and packagers, and businesses owned by other disadvantaged firms. In addition, firms may be denied entry into the program for reasons of character. As defined by the SBA, demonstrations of "lack of character" may include any or all of the following:

- Adverse information regarding possible criminal conduct undertaken by the applicant and/or the firm's principals.

- Violations of SBA regulations.

- Debarment or suspension of firms and/or individuals.

- Evidence of lack of business integrity (such as indictments, pleas of guilt in legal cases, convictions for violations of legal behavior, adverse civil judgements, or out-of-court settlements).

- Evidence that the company knowingly submitted false information during the application process.

- Owners and/or other principals of the firm are currently in prison, on parole, or on probation for criminal activity.

Waivers of the "Two-Years-In-Business" Requirement
Under certain circumstances, the SBA permits small businesses that have not yet been in operation for two years to participate in the 8(a) program. These mitigating circumstances include:

- Individual or individuals making the application have "substantially demonstrated business management experience."

- Applicant has sufficient technical expertise in his or her chosen area of business to make it very likely that he or she will be able to launch and maintain a successful business.

- Applicant had enough capital to carry out his or her business plan.

- Applicant shows that he or she has the ability to obtain the necessary personnel, facilities, equipment, and other requirements to perform all duties and obligations associated with contracts available through the 8(a) program.

- Individual or individuals making the application have a record of successful performance of contract work in the past, provided that those contracts (which may be from either government or private clients) are in the primary industry category in which the applicant is seeking program certification.

APPLYING TO THE 8(A) PROGRAM

Applications to the SBA's 8(a) program can be made through local SBA district offices. Small business owners will be asked to provide a wide range of materials, ranging from personal and business financial statements to organization charts, licenses, and schedules of business insurance. As of September 2004, applications may be made through an electronic online application system that promises to make the process easier, faster and less expensive for small companies.

Rulings on completed applications are generally made within 90 days. Not all applicants are accepted into the 8(a) program, which has been a very popular one since its inception. If an application is turned down, the owner has the right to resubmit the application to the SBA with additional or changed information, but if the resubmitted application is still turned down, the owner may not present a new application until 12 months have passed from the date of the reconsideration decision. Finally, in cases where the applicant has been denied enrollment in the program solely because of questions about the applicant's social or economic disadvantage or majority ownership, then the owner may appeal the SBA's decision to that agency's Office of Hearings and Appeals (OHA). In this case, however, the applicant may not change the application in any way.

If a disadvantaged individual acquires a business that is enrolled in the 8(a) program, he or she may be able to continue to maintain the firm's participation in the program, provided that prior approval was obtained by the SBA.

Companies that are accepted into the 8(a) program are not eligible for 8(a) contracts until they submit and receive approval from the SBA for their business plan. "After the firm has an approved plan, the length of time before the first 8(a) contract is awarded will vary based on the success of the firm's marketing efforts," said the SBA. "While SBA will make every effort to assist a firm with its marketing efforts, the 8(a) program is a self-marketing program and SBA cannot guarantee 8(a) contract awards."

In addition to marketing assistance, participants in the 8(a) program receive help in the following areas during both the developmental stage (first four years) and transitional stage (next five years) of their involvement. During the developmental stage, enrollees can look forward to sole source and competitive 8(a) program support, transfer via grants of technology or surplus property owned by the U.S., and training to enhance entrepreneurial skills in a variety of areas. During the transitional period, meanwhile, small business owners can look forward to continued aid in the above areas, as well as assistance from procuring agents in forming joint ventures and technical assistance in planning for graduation from the 8(a) program.

8(A) BUSINESS DEVELOPMENT MENTOR-PROTÉGÉ PROGRAM

In the late 1990s the SBA introduced a new Business Development Mentor-Protege Program meant to help improve the fortunes of 8(a) participants seeking federal government contracts. Mentors—which may include graduates of the 8(a) program, firms in the transitional stage of that program, or other businesses—are required to demonstrate the ability to assist the protégé company for at least one year. Mentor companies also are required to be in good financial health and be existing federal contractors in good standing.

Companies interested in entering the program as protégé firms, meanwhile, must be in the developmental stage of the 8(a) business development program, unless it has never received an 8(a) contract or is of a size that is less than half the size standard for a small business in its primary industry. It also must be qualified for inclusion in the 8(a) program in all other respects and be current with all reporting requirements.

Ideally, benefits of this special 8(a) program to the protégé firm—which can have only one mentor at a time—will include technical and management assistance; options to enter into joint-venture business agreements with mentor firms to compete for government contracts; financial assistance in the form of equity or loans; and qualification for other SBA assistance programs. The Small Business Administration intends to conduct annual reviews of this program to evaluate its success, with an eye toward possible future expansion (or suspension, if it fails to meet stated goals).

SEE ALSO *Government Procurement; U.S. Small Business Association Guaranteed Loans*

BIBLIOGRAPHY
Bowles, Erskine. "Bite-Sized Loans." *Entrepreneur.* December 1993.

Caplan, Suzanne. *A Piece of the Action: How Women and Minorities Can Launch Their Own Successful Businesses.* AMACOM, 1994.

Mukherjee, Sougata. "SBA Planning Major Overhaul of 8(a) Program." *San Antonio Business Journal.* 25 August 1997.

"SBA Annoucnes 8(a) Online Applications." *St. Charles County Business Record.* 16 September 2004.

U.S. Small Business Administration. *8(a) Business Development.* Available from http://www.sba.gov/med 27 April 2001.

U.S. Small Business Administration. *SBA Profile: Who We Are and What We Do.* 2000.

Hillstrom, Northern Lights
updated by Magee, ECDI

ELASTICITY

Elasticity is a measure of the responsiveness of one economic variable to another. For example, advertising elasticity is the relationship between a change in a firm's advertising budget and the resulting change in product sales. Economists are often interested in the price elasticity of demand, which measures the response of the quantity of an item purchased to a change in the item's price. A good or service is considered to be highly elastic if a slight change in price leads to a sharp change in demand for the product or service. Products and services that are highly elastic are usually more discretionary in nature—readily available in the market and something that a consumer may not necessarily need in his or her daily life. On the other hand, an inelastic good or service is one for which changes in price result in only modest changes to demand. These goods and services tend to be necessities.

Elasticity is usually expressed as a positive number when the sign is already clear from context. Elasticity measures are reported as a proportional or percent change in the variable being studied. The general formula for elasticity, represented by the letter "E" in the equation below, is:

$$E = \text{percent change in x} \,/\, \text{percent change in y.}$$

Elasticity can be zero, one, greater than one, less than one, or infinite. When elasticity is equal to one there is unit elasticity. This means the proportional change in one variable is equal to the proportional change in another variable, or in other words, the two variables are directly related and move together. When elasticity is greater than one, the proportional change in x is greater than the proportional change in y and the situation is said to be elastic.

Inelastic situations result when the proportional change in x is less than the proportional change in y. Perfectly inelastic situations result when any change in y will have an infinite effect on x. Finally, perfectly elastic situations result when any change in y will result in no change in x. A special case known as unitary elasticity of demand occurs if total revenue stays the same when prices change.

ELASTICITY FOR MANAGERIAL DECISION MAKING

Economists compute several different elasticity measures, including the price elasticity of demand, the price elasticity of supply, and the income elasticity of demand. Elasticity is typically defined in terms of changes in total revenue since that is of primary importance to managers, CEOs, and marketers. For managers, a key point in the discussions of demand is what happens when they raise prices for their products and services. It is important to know the extent to which a percentage increase in unit price will affect the demand for a product. With elastic demand, total revenue will decrease if the price is raised. With inelastic demand, however, total revenue will increase if the price is raised.

The possibility of raising prices and increasing dollar sales (total revenue) at the same time is very attractive to managers. This occurs only if the demand curve is inelastic. Here total revenue will increase if the price is raised, but total costs probably will not increase and, in fact, could go down. Since profit is equal to total revenue minus total costs, profit will increase as price is increased when demand for a product is inelastic. It is important to note that an entire demand curve is neither elastic nor inelastic; it only has the particular condition for a change in total revenue between two points on the curve (and not along the whole curve).

Demand elasticity is affected by three things: 1) availability of substitutes; 2) the urgency of need, and 3) the importance of the item in the customer's budget. Substitutes are products that offer the buyer a choice. For example, many consumers see corn chips as a good or homogeneous substitute for potato chips, or see sliced ham as a substitute for sliced turkey. The more substitutes available, the greater will be the elasticity of demand. If consumers see products as extremely different or heterogeneous, however, then a particular need cannot easily be satisfied by substitutes. In contrast to a product with many substitutes, a product with few or no substitutes—like gasoline—will have an inelastic demand curve. Similarly, demand for products that are urgently needed or are very important to a person's budget will tend to be inelastic. It is important for managers to understand the price elasticity of their products and services in order to set prices appropriately to maximize firm profits and revenues.

SEE ALSO *Financial Analysis; Pricing*

BIBLIOGRAPHY

Haines, Leslie. "Elasticity is Back" *Oil and Gas Investor.* November 2005.

Hodrick, Laurie Simon. "Does Price Elasticity Affect Corporate Financial Decisions?" *Journal of Financial Economics.* May 1999.

Montgomery, Alan L., and Peter E. Rossi. "Estimating Price Elasticity with Theory-Based Priors." *Journal of Marketing Research.* November 1999.

Perreault, William E. Jr., and E. Jerome McCarthy. *Basic Marketing: A Global-Managerial Approach.* McGraw-Hill, 1997.

Hillstrom, Northern Lights
updated by Magee, ECDI

ELDERCARE

Eldercare is an important issue for many members of today's work force, and is thus a relevant matter for employers to study as well. Analysts contend that many businesses lose valuable production from the estimated 30 percent of working Americans who have to contend with the needs of elderly parents and other relatives, and they point out that America's changing demographics are likely to make this an even more important issue for employers and employees in the coming years. "Eldercare is the next big wave washing over the workplace," wrote Jill Mazullo in *Minneapolis-St. Paul CityBusiness.* "Many workers are faced with taking on caregiving duties for an aging parent, spouse, or sibling who needs assistance with grocery shopping, medical visits, bathing, and more. Some caregivers spend upwards of 20 hours a week with a family member in need. The emotional toll is difficult to quantify, particularly when care for a loved one with Alzheimer's disease or dementia is involved. Add that to a full-time job, and you've got a career crisis in the making."

Eldercare receives far less publicity than does childcare, another very important issue to workers. But as Elise Feuerstein Karras noted in *Small Business Reports,* "in many ways, eldercare is more complex than childcare because it covers such a wide range of needs. Many elderly people need assistance with routine tasks such as eating, dressing, bathing and obtaining medical care. But as adults, they also need to pay their bills, access Social Security benefits and deal with legal matters such as estate planning. Employees may have to help with these tasks or arrange for others to do it—sometimes for relatives who live far away." Karras added that the level of dependency that older relatives have for caregivers also increases with time, while the opposite is true of childcare. Finally, she pointed out that caregivers for elderly parents and relatives often have to tread a fine, and sometimes exhausting line between diplomacy and control: "The balance of authority between employees and their parents can make the [eldercare] arrangements awkward. An employee with children can simply make any necessary arrangements because he or she has the authority to do so. But the grown son or daughter of an elderly person must obtain the parent's consent before arranging for care."

IMPACT OF ELDERCARE OBLIGATIONS ON EMPLOYEE PERFORMANCE

In many instances, obligations associated with providing eldercare can become a considerable drain on an employee's productivity. According to a 1999 study by the MetLife Mature Market Institute, 16 percent of survey respondents indicated that they had to quit their jobs entirely in order to meet the needs of elderly parents (the percentage is even greater in businesses that have a high percentage of employees who are women, society's traditional caregivers). Many other respondents indicated that they passed up job promotions, training opportunities, or career-advancing projects because of their caregiving obligations. When these sorts of situations develop, small business owners and other employers are faced with the loss or diminished value of a productive, trained employee and—in cases where those obligations force a departure—additional costs associated with finding and training a replacement.

But the obligations associated with eldercare are felt in other ways, too. Workers who provide assistance to their elderly parents or other relatives are likely to take off several days each year to attend to routine care issues. The MetLife survey confirmed this condition, noting that 64 percent of respondents used sick days or vacation time in order to address eldercare issues. Some employers might comfort themselves by observing that those vacation days are not unexcused absences, but they should recognize that losing vacation time for this reason can have a negative impact on employee morale and, ultimately, performance. Moreover, partial absenteeism—late arrivals, long lunch breaks, early departures, etc.—can take a heavy toll as well. But Tibbett L. Speer contended in *American Demographics* that an even bigger problem for employers are "the workday interruptions faced by caregivers who talk on the phone with loved ones and service providers. This situation can arise even with employees who don't physically care for parents or whose parents live elsewhere. Estimated at one hour per week per caregiver, this factor is the biggest drain of all on employee productivity."

SMALL BUSINESS AND ELDERCARE BENEFITS

Many small business owners operate under the assumption that they can provide little assistance to employees who are grappling with eldercare issues. In reality, however, business experts say that both small and large companies can take several relatively inexpensive measures to help their staffers out and, in the long run, help them reach or return to high levels of productivity. Indeed, "by helping employees balance work and family responsibilities, elder care benefits can have a positive effect on employee attendance and productivity," observed *HR Magazine.* "Elder care benefits also support recruitment and retention efforts."

Possible elder care benefits feasible for small businesses include the following:

Information services. A very inexpensive way in which employers can help employees with eldercare problems is to offer resource and referral hotlines for such services and subjects as adult day care, nursing home evaluation, insurance issues, and "meals on wheels." Finding such information can be a time-consuming process for employees, and the establishment of a small in-house resource center that contains contact information can save workers significant hassles. In addition, many resource and referral services offer one-on-one counseling and/or seminars, many of which can be arranged to take place at the business's facilities. These seminars and counseling sessions can provide employees with important information on such diverse issues as nursing home care, Medicare and Medicaid, legal issues, and Alzheimer's disease.

Incorporate Into Existing Assistance Programs. Many companies have chosen to integrate eldercare benefits in with existing employee assistance plans.

*Flexible Work Schedules.*Employers have a variety of options from which to choose here, including job sharing, compressed work weeks, and work-at-home arrangements. In addition, some small business owners have loosened vacation and sick day policies, blending them together into so-called personal days, to better accommodate employees with eldercare obligations.

Financial Benefits. Employers should consider setting up dependent care assistance programs (DCAPs) for their employees. Under this plan, employees who have elderly dependents living with them can gain assistance in paying for various eldercare expenses. Funds are regularly withheld from the paychecks of participating employees, who then bill the plan and receive reimbursements for eldercare expenses. "The result," noted Karras, "is that employees don't pay income or Social Security taxes on the DCAP funds. Your company saves as well because it won't owe Social Security and unemployment taxes on the money they set aside." Business consultants note, however, that businesses that set up DCAP plans do run into administration expenses, whether they choose to administer the program themselves or hire an outside firm to do so.

INTERGENERATIONAL CARE

Another trend that is shaping the way in which employees and employers approach eldercare is the increased popularity of intergenerational care facilities. These programs allow working parents who also have obligations to care for their own parents to place both children and elderly relatives in a single facility, where they will be cared for. Given the steady growth of women in the work place and the success that many hospitals, child care centers, and nursing homes have had with intergenerational care programs, many analysts believe that the availability of such facilities will continue to grow over the next number of years, especially in regions in which competition for labor talent is intense. Indeed, demographic trends would seem to guarantee the continued growth of intergenerational care facilities. A 2004 study conducted by the National Alliance for Caregiving and American Association of Retired Persons (AARP) showed that 21 percent of adults (18 and older) provided unpaid aid to friends and relatives; the caregiving population thus was more than 44 million people. Sixty-one percent of caregivers were women, 39 percent were men. Such statistics indicate that businesses seeking to attract and retain top talent will not only examine child care assistance options in greater depth, but will also factor the elder care issue into their analysis of options with increasing frequency.

ELDERCARE RESOURCES

Employees and employers can turn to a variety of sources for information on dealing with the many financial, medical, and personal aspects of eldercare. Local hospitals, churches, and agencies on aging are often good sources of information on eldercare issues. In addition, several national organizations maintain a variety of services and information on the subject. Notable organizations include the American Association of Retired Persons (202-434-3525), the Alzheimer's Association (800-272-3900), and the American Association of Homes and Services for the Aging (202-783-2242). Another good source of information is the Eldercare Locator (800-677-1116), a federally funded hotline operated by the National Association of State Units on Aging and the National Association of Area Agencies on Aging.

SEE ALSO *Career and Family*

BIBLIOGRAPHY

Aschkenasy, Janet. "Eldercare Grows Up: For your oldest clients—and their children—planning takes on new dimensions." *Financial Planning.* 1 September 2005.

Beerman, Susan, and Judith Rappaport-Musson. *The Eldercare 911 Question and Answer Book.* Prometheus Books, 2005.

Caregiving in the U.S. National Alliance for Caregiving and AARP. April 2004.

Cole, Bob. "It's a Changing and More Challenging World for the Elderly." *Westchester County Business Journal.* 21 November 2005.

Karras, Elise Feuerstein. "Affordable Eldercare Benefits." *Small Business Reports.* November 1994.

Lee, Karen. "Eldercare Benefits are Gaining More Attention." *Employee Benefit News.* 1 May 2000.

Mazullo, Jill. "Eldercare Needs More Participants." *Minneapolis-St. Paul CityBusiness.* 7 July 2000.

Patouhas, Dennis. "Shortage of Geriatricians is Growing." *Fairfield County Business Journal.* 21 November 2005.

"Recognize the Warning Signs of Caregiver Burnout." *Fairfield County Business Journal.* 21 November 2005.

Speer, Tibbett L. "The Unseen Costs of Eldercare: Employers Can Help Employees Help Their Aging Parents, and Save Money in the Process." *American Demographics.* June 1996.

Walsh, Brenda, and Bob Chernow. "Aging and Health Care." *The Futurist.* November-December 2005.

Hillstrom, Northern Lights
updated by Magee, ECDI

ELECTRONIC BULLETIN BOARDS

Electronic bulletin boards (also known as message boards or as computer forums) are online communication systems where one can share, request, or discuss information on just about any subject. E-mail is a way to converse privately with one or more people over the Internet; electronic bulletin boards are public. Any visitor to a message board can read and respond to any message found there, although registration of some kind is usually required before "posting" privileges are granted. A large collection of electronic bulletin boards is known as a newsgroup. Thousands of newsgroups populate the Internet, each dedicated to a single topic. Some are dedicated to roof-repair, some to obscure computer languages, some to skin defects. You name it.

Participation in bulletin boards messaging is simple. Any person can start a discussion on a topic and then wait for replies. The initial message alone—and others responding to it, if any—constitute a "thread." Some threads continue on for days or weeks or months. Sometimes a poster with a question or a statement, however, is completely ignored. The longer threads tend to find people responding not only to the original post but to subsequent replies as well. The latecomer who happens to hit on one of the items in a long thread my have to "unwind" the thread a long ways back to learn what the initial impetus was all about.

Bulletin boards provide a genuine service to the public in that they create an open forum for the discussion of issues and problems of the most diverse nature—but these discussions are easily accessible because search engines will ultimately pinpoint threads of interest to the searcher. Experts are similarly drawn to the BBs. Problems posed on a message board will draw answers from knowledgeable individuals pleased to enlighten the puzzled. To be sure, the answers may not always be correct—or, more likely, complete—but any flaw in a thread will tend to be corrected by others eventually. The initial poster may, indeed, request more detail. The ulti-mate judge of the received information, however, must be the individual asking the question or posing the problem.

On the downside, the accessibility of bulletin boards also attracts those merely seeking stimulation and attention. Troublemakers delight in stirring up controversy, badmouthing everyone and everything in "virtual" sight—and they do so from behind the handy "mask" of user names (handles) which hide their actual identity. In response to such invasions by less-than-helpful visitors, many BBs use editorial functions, some automated, to filter out unwanted material. Spamming is also a bulletin board problem. Very active bulletin boards require mas-sive computer memory resources; for this reason older messages may be scrubbed from the system. BBs there-fore do not always serve archival reference purposes well.

BBS AND SMALL BUSINESS

While many electronic bulletin boards have educational or recreational aims, or serve as forums for professional discussions in arcane fields like physics or philosophy, many are designed around business functions, occupa-tions, or activities—sometimes directly tied to vendor groups, sometimes fielded by university extension serv-ices. The small business owner or self-employed profes-sional will find such bulletin boards frequently extremely valuable in solving specific problems, diagnosing some peculiar problem, finding a suitable vendor for an unusual product or service, and sharing experience on common issues. As Bob Wittkamp pointed out, writing for *ICS Cleaning Specialist,* growing the business is a much favored and discussed topic on bulletin boards.

Although a BB appears to exist for virtually every topic under the sun, from "Amor" in its most graphic forms to "Zen" mediation at its most quiescent, small businesses engaged in complex fields of a technical nature will probably benefit most directly from routinely using message boards. Computer programming, hardware, and wiring problems; construction issues from cesspool seep-age to wallpaper hanging; the seemingly infinite issues in growing anything from vegetables to flowers; the frustrat-ing quest for old brass fixtures in restoration work; and on, and on—are all served by bulletin boards that attract the knowledgeable. Discovering the right BB is relatively easy. Sampling a few threads rapidly reveals the character of the participants and the seriousness of their treatment of issues. Once a BB is qualified, joining it and trying it is the next step—unless the user has already obtained a useful answer just reading a few postings.

Small business owners may also discover bulletin boards that talk about their products and performance. They may be pleasantly or unpleasantly surprised. Negative posts (whether they are true or not) can, of course, seriously affect the company. As Patrick Collinson mentioned in an article that appeared in *Retail Financial Strategies,* a British company called IBNet is about to start marketing software which will alert a company each time any mention of it appears anywhere on the Internet. When the company learns that the information is false, it can request that it be removed and seek to identify who is posting the information.

SEE ALSO *Newsgroups*

BIBLIOGRAPHY
"AMD Hack Points to Widespread Web Forum Flaws, Attacks." *ExtremeTech.com.* 3 February 2006.

Collinson, Patrick. "Collinson on Bulletin Boards." *Retail Financial Strategies.* October 2000.

Whittaker, Jason. "Open Forum: It's easy to add sticky content to your site. Jason Whittaker talks about how to implement bulletin boards." *Australian PC World.* March 2006.

Wittkamp, Bob. "Growing Your Business: A very common topic of discussion in classes and on Internet bulletin boards is how to grow one's business and, inevitably, what programs work best." *ICS Cleaning Specialist.* July 2005.

Hillstrom, Northern Lights
updated by Magee, ECDI

ELECTRONIC DATA INTERCHANGE

In the quest to achieve a paperless society, electronic data interchange (EDI) has long been a leading technology. Ralph W. Notto, a leading chronicler of electronic commerce (see *Challenge and consequence; forcing change to e-Commerce*), has noted that EDI is and has been an essential component in such commerce. EDI predates the emergence of the Internet, now the chief electronic network connecting just about every business to every other. The first implementations of EDI were internal to companies, used private networks, and enabled a multi-location company to use a common accounting system regardless of location. Earliest uses of EDI were also heavily deployed to track parts inventories within a business—but also between a producer, its distributors, and, in turn, the dealers served by the distributors. These private networks were full-grown implementations of EDI in the sense that data were exchanged by means of wired and/or wireless networks and kept data in live format and therefore instantly accessible.

With the spread of small computers, EDI in the less automated form of exchanges of data on tape and on diskettes (and later on CDs) came into widespread use. This technique is still widely used in the exchange of electronic files between systems using the Internet; either e-mail or up/downloading to/from file transfer protocol (FTP) sites is used. Many EDI systems in use in the mid-2000s remain private and move data through private networks; many others utilize proprietary software, but the software uses Internet connections; yet other forms are special arrangements for data sharing making use of standard methods of Internet exchange. Large systems today invariably involve data encryption to ensure data security.

The driving force behind EDI is efficiency made possible by avoiding the handling and rekeying of data on paper. Electronic scanning of bar codes at the point of sale or in inventory taking and document scanning technologies combined with improvements in optical character recognition (OCR) systems have further contributed to EDI by replacing keying of some documents. Data capture, however, is still accomplished predominantly by human keying. A human interface is also typically necessary to check OCR results.

Electronic data interchange had its beginnings in the management of financial data. The technique, however, is rapidly expanding to documentary information and, in such areas as security and law enforcement, also to biometric data.

BENEFITS OF EDI

EDI was developed to solve the problems inherent in paper-based transaction processing and in other forms of electronic communication. In solving these problems, EDI is a tool that enables organizations to reengineer information flows and business processes. It directly addresses several problems long associated with paper-based transaction systems:

- Time delays—Paper documents may take days to transport from one location to another, while manual processing methodologies necessitate steps like keying and filing that are rendered unnecessary through EDI.

- Labor costs—In non-EDI systems, manual processing is required for data keying, document storage and retrieval, sorting, matching, reconciling, envelope stuffing, stamping, signing, etc. While automated equipment can help with some of these processes, most managers will agree that labor costs for document processing represent a significant proportion of their overhead. In general, labor-based processes are much more expensive in the long term than are EDI alternatives.

- Accuracy—EDI systems are more accurate than their manual processing counterparts because there are fewer points at which errors can be introduced into the system.

- Information Access—EDI systems permit myriad users access to a vast amount of detailed transaction data in a timely fashion. In a non-EDI environment, in which information is held in offices and file cabinets, such dissemination of information is possible only with great effort, and it cannot hope to match an EDI system's timeliness. Because EDI data is already in computer-retrievable form, it is subject to automated processing and analysis. It also requires far less storage space.

INFRASTRUCTURE FOR EDI

Several elements of infrastructure must exist in order to introduce an EDI system, including: 1) format standards to facilitate automated processing by all users, 2) translation software to translate from a user's proprietary format for internal data storage into the generic external format and back again, 3) value-added networks to solve the technical problems of sending information between computers, 4) inexpensive microcomputers to bring all potential users—even small ones—into the market, and 5) procedures for complying with legal rules. It has only been in the past several years that all of these ingredients have fallen into place.

Format Standards To permit the efficient use of computers, information must be highly organized into a consistent data format. A format defines how information in a message is organized: what data go where, what data are mandatory, what is optional, how many characters are permitted for each data field, how data fields are ordered, and what codes or abbreviations are permitted.

Early EDI efforts in the 1960s used proprietary formats developed by one firm for exclusive use by its trading partners. This worked well until a firm wanted to exchange EDI documents with other firms who wanted to use their own formats. Since the different formats were not compatible, data exchange was difficult if not impossible. To facilitate the widespread use of EDI, standard formats were developed so that an electronic message sent by one party could be understood by any receiver that subscribes to that format standard. In the United States the Transportation Data Coordinating Committee began in 1968 to design format standards for transportation documents. The first document was approved in 1975. This group pioneered the ideas that are used by all standards organizations today.

North American standards are currently developed and maintained by a volunteer organization called ANSI (American National Standards Institute). The format for a document defined by ANSI is broad enough to satisfy the needs of many different industries. Electronic documents are typically of variable length and most of the information is optional. When a firm sends a standard EDI purchase order to another firm, it is possible for the receiving firm to pass the purchase order data through an EDI translation program directly to a business application without manual intervention. In the mid-2000s, international format standards were in force to facilitate international business activity as well.

Translation Software Translation software makes EDI work by translating data from the sending firm's internal format into a generic EDI format. Translation software also receives a sender's EDI message and translates it from the generic standard into the receiver's internal format. There are currently translation software packages for almost all types of computers and operating systems.

Value-Added Networks (VANs) When firms first began using EDI, most communications of EDI documents were internal or directly between trading partners. Unfortunately, direct computer-to-computer communication requires that both firms 1) use similar communication protocols, 2) have the same transmission speed, 3) have a common proprietary network, and 4) have compatible computer hardware. If these conditions are not met, communication becomes difficult if not impossible. A value-added network (VAN) can solve these problems by providing an electronic mailbox service. By using a VAN, an EDI sender need only learn to send and receive messages to or from one party: the VAN. Since a VAN provides a very flexible computer interface, it can talk to virtually any type of computer. This means that to conduct EDI with hundreds of trading partners, an organization only has to talk to one party. In addition, VANs provide important security elements for dissemination of information between parties.

Inexpensive Computers The fourth building block of EDI is inexpensive computers that permit even small firms to implement EDI. Since microcomputers are now so prevalent, it is possible for firms of all sizes to deal with each other using EDI. Internet protocols, including standard formats such as HTML, have created a standard understood by computers of all makes running different operating systems—all of which are fully enabled to communicate across the Web.

Procedures for Complying with Legal Rules Legal rules apply to the documents that accompany a wide variety of business transactions. For example, some contracts must include a signature or must be an original in order to be legal. If documents are to be transmitted via EDI, companies must establish procedures to verify that messages are authentic and that they comply with the agreed-upon protocol. In addition, EDI requires companies to institute error-checking procedures as well as security measures to prevent unauthorized use of their computer systems. Still, it is important to note that some sorts of business documents—such as warranties or limitations of liability—are difficult to transmit legally using EDI.

An example of a legal requirement is represented by the Public Health Security and Bioterrorism Preparedness and Response Act of 2002, known as the Bioterrorism Act. Manufacturers, processors, packagers, transporters, receivers, holders, and importers of food must establish and maintain records of all such transactions. As reported in *Food Logistics,* the Grocery Manufacturers Association (GMA) examined commonly used EDI systems to ensure that their record-keeping methods comply with the Bioterrorism Act. GMA found that EDI systems meet the challenge.

SMALL BUSINESS AND EDI

In at least some form (such as securing backups to computerized accounting and inventory data), most small businesses participate in EDI actively. Many use online order taking integrated with their own systems through proprietary software. Small businesses serving as suppliers to large organizations may participate in a number of EDI systems tied into their own computer systems using the Internet.

SEE ALSO *Data Encryption.*

BIBLIOGRAPHY
Davino, Margaret M. "Implementing EDI." *Medical Economics.* 6 January 2006.

Dirks, Brent. "High-End Accounting Products Provide Cutting-Edge Technologies." *The CPA Technology Advisor.* December 2005.

"EDI helps meet Bioterrorism regs." *Food Logistics.* November-December 2005.

"EDI Software Streamlines Business-to-Business Transactions." *Product News Network.* 13 February 2006.

"Leslie's Streamlines Its Operations." *Pool & Spa News.* 1 December 2005.

Mortleman, James. "Enterprise—Paint Company Installs Web Link for Customers." *Computing.* 10 November 2005.

Notto, Ralph W. *Challenge and Consequence: Forcing Change to e-Commerce.* Fenestra Books, 2005.

Schuff, Sally. "EDI eases recordkeeping." *Feedstuffs.* 5 December 2005.

"Wal-Mart Tests RFID Data-Sharing Project: Using EDI, the company will be able to know when products are on their way from suppliers." *InformationWeek.* 17 January 2006.

Hillstrom, Northern Lights
updated by Magee, ECDI

ELECTRONIC MAIL

Electronic mail, or e-mail, has in large part displaced internal memoranda in most institutions of any size and has also significantly cut down on telephoning as a way of coordinating business. E-mail requires a network of computers or a single computer linked to the Internet. Messages are generated by and read inside mail software like Microsoft's Outlook Express or Netscape Communications' Netscape program. Mail moves to the recipient's address directly through a corporate mail server or over the Internet using a mail-services provider. Most systems enable the user to attach documents to the e-mail message itself. These may be anything digital, be they word processing documents, spreadsheets, photographs, databases, or other electronic letters. Sending software is designed so that the same letter can be sent to multiple recipients; indeed blind or open copies (what in the old days were labeled bcc's and cc's) can be sent as well. An e-mail is delivered almost instantly and thus is like a phone call—but the e-mail recipient need not be there to receive it. These many benefits have made e-mail ubiquitous. It is doubtful that anyone actually knows how many e-mails are sent, but studied estimates have been made. International Data Corporation, a market research firm, has estimated a more than three-fold increase in e-mail volume between 2000 and 2005, to 35 billion messages in the U.S. in 2005, and volume is still rapidly climbing.

E-MAIL PROS AND CONS

E-mail is a genuinely *new* form of communication combining elements of traditional mail, the telegram, and the telephone. It can be paperless and yet a record is retained; an e-mail can also be printed out. It is very rapid and yet, unlike a telephone call, it is much less intrusive. It can be used at any hour of the day. Once the basic cost of a network or an Internet connection has been justified, e-mail is very cheap. Modern electronic documentation techniques have advanced to such a level that e-mail attachments can be book-sized documents typeset like books, with illustrations embedded. No, we cannot send a baby-rattle with our e-mail, but almost any kind of document is possible.

The negatives of e-mail arise from its very popularity. Virtually all employees in larger organization, especially management employees, complain of overwhelming e-mail volume. Mark Brownstein, writing in *Network Magazine,* noted, citing various sources, that data stored on disk has more than doubled between 1999 and 2002 (according to UC Berkely), that e-mail volume grows at a rate of 20 percent a year (according to the Radacati Group), and that 3 of 4 electronic documents are unprotected and unmanaged (according to Strategic

Research). The management of e-mail alone is absorbing more and more time—so that it appears to be interfering with the very productivity such innovations as e-mail are supposed to be bringing about. Software-based management systems are appearing, but these, of course, add costs. Furthermore, in the wake of corporate scandals like Enron and Worldcom, and legislation aimed at reform such as the Sarbanes-Oxley Act, it has become clear that record keeping practices must be much more disciplined. The courts have found that e-mail must be protected as soon as any kind of investigation begins.

The very volume of e-mail has drawn the attention of legislators who see e-mail as a potentially enormous source of revenue if some kind of e-postage can be imposed. Cost, at present, is not one of the "cons" of e-mail, but, predictably, e-mail will eventually cost more. With a tariff of some kind overlying e-mail (and presumably increasing over time), e-mail may become more manageable but also much less popoular.

Spam E-mail, being real mail, rapidly came to be abused by organizations sending out millions of unsolicited e-mail messages selling everything from drugs to insurance to pornography. Such unwanted mail became known as spam. Spam is one of the negative phenomena associated with e-mail.

Spam came under relatively mild regulation with the passage of the Controlling the Assault of Non-Solicited Pornography and Marketing Act, also officially called the CAN-SPAM Act of 2003 (Public Law 108-197). It became effective in December of 2003 and took effect on January 1, 2004. The act requires that senders of unsolicited commercial e-mail label their messages, but Congress did not require a standard labeling language. Such messages are required to carry instructions on how to opt-out of receiving such mail; the sender must also provide its actual physical address. Misleading headers and titles are prohibited. Congress authorized the Federal Trade Commissioned to establish a "do-not-mail" registry but did not require the FTC do so. CAN-SPAM also has preemptive features: it prohibits states from outlawing commercial e-mail or to require their own labeling. Since 2003 other bills have been proposed but have not been enacted.

With CAN-SPAM in effect, it is at least theoretically possible to curb unsolicited mail by the tedious effort of answering every piece of spam and filling in an "opt-out" form. Software for controlling unsolicited e-mail is also available; the simplest forms of such control require entering addresses from which mail may be accepted; all other mail is rejected; this technique is very effective but, obviously, turns e-mail into a private communications service. E-mail servers also offer effective filtering services.

Nonetheless, a rather negative conclusion must be drawn: with the positive aspects of e-mail go many negative aspects which threaten to erode the effectiveness of this new medium.

MANAGING E-MAIL

The advice offered by organizational experts on handling e-mail boils down to good traditional rules of communication and task management but applied to this medium. Barbara Hemphill, writing in *Business Credit,* advises *senders* of e-mail to be clear and brief, to provide sufficient context, and to avoid sending attachments if at all possible. She advises withholding attachments because people fear opening mail with attachments lest they release a virus; if the recipient knows about the attachment, obviously this rule will be unnecessary. The subject line should be a precise capsule of the e-mails content. When answering mail, the essence of the message being answered should be included so that the receiver knows the context—but the bulk of the incoming message can be deleted first. Hemphill's advice to *receivers* of e-mail deals with sorting and ranking: some mail can be tossed at once, some requires action, some should be filed. If an immediate response is possible, it should be made—immediately. She advises keeping an uncluttered Inbox by keeping messages in separate folders by project.

If the organization is involved in some kind of legal process (as discussed below), deleting e-mail should be done only if its content has nothing whatever to do with the matter under litigation. In this context, and in general, as a matter of good management, important e-mails should be printed and filed in the old, traditional way.

E-MAIL DOCUMENTS ARE RECORDS

Jeanette Burriesci, writing in *Intelligent Enterprise,* has pointed out that fines in the millions of dollars have been assessed by the Securities and Exchange Commission (SEC) on organizations for failure to keep adequate records. She points out that e-mail has become a main feature of record keeping concerns "because it proliferates so quickly." Intense preoccupation with record keeping has come in the wake of the Sarbanes-Oxley Act passed in 2002 ("SOX"). The act was triggered by corporate accounting scandals and has imposed very strict record keeping requirements on publicly traded companies and accounting firms. As a consequence of SOX, corporations have been retooling their archiving methods, including collecting and classifying e-mail by subject matter and reorganizing back-up systems so that back-up tapes are not periodically reused lest old e-mails are erased.

Small privately held business concerns will, of course, rarely be touched by these issues. However, awareness of what is happening in the larger context of the publicly traded companies is valuable and, in any case, effective management of records benefits businesses of any size. E-mails, by their very character (their sheer number and frequently informal tone) may suggest that they are unimportant—like casual conversation. With new attention on records, it is becoming obvious, however, that electronic communications, no less than those on paper, have legal status. Back in the days when the Internet was still in history's womb (1964), Marshal McLuhan, the high priest of pop culture, coined the famous phrase: "The Medium is the Message." It now turns out that, on the contrary, the *message* is the message—and we must manage it regardless of medium.

SEE ALSO *Spam*

BIBLIOGRAPHY

Ball, Craig. "Retention Policies That Work." *Law Technology News.* November 2005.

Brownstein, Mark. "Who's Counting?" *Network Magazine.* 1 November 2004.

Burriesci, Jeanette. "A Record Collection Worth Millions." *Intelligent Enterprise.* August 2005.

Carr, Jim. "Exorcising E-mail Demons—Midwest investment house MJSK tackles electronic communications compliance issues with a context-sensitive e-mail archiving system." *IT Architect.* 1 November 2005.

Federal Trade Commission. "The Can-SPAM Act: Requirements for Commercial E-mailers." Available from http://www.ftc.gov/bcp/conline/pubs/buspubs/canspam.htm. Retrieved on 28 February 2006.

"For This, They Needed a Survey?" *eWeek.* 28 September 2005.

Hemphill, Barbara. "Top 10 Tips for Managing E-Mail More Effectively." *Business Credit.* March 2004.

"Letter: E-mail marketing: say yes to relationships." *Marketing Week.* 8 September 2005.

Mearian, Lucas. "The 100-year Archive Dilemma: As more organizations store more data longer, the IT industry seeks a better way." *Computerworld.* 25 July 2005.

Mook, Bob. "Tips for Dealing with E-Mail Overload." *Denver Business Journal.* 12 January 2001.

Nickson, Stephen. "Spy Mail." *Risk Management.* February 2001.

"Tech Taboos." *Journal of Accountancy.* December 2005.

Darnay, ECDI

ELECTRONIC TAX FILING

Electronic tax filing refers to various systems that enable individuals and small businesses to file their tax returns and make tax payments through electronic data transfer.

In 1996, the Internal Revenue Service (IRS) began requiring businesses that owed more than $47 million in payroll taxes annually to make their monthly payments via telephone or computer through the Electronic Federal Tax Payment System (EFTPS). Development of this general methodology of tax filing culminated in new regulations issued by the U.S. Treasury in January 2005. With that regulation, corporations with assets of $50 million or greater and filing at least 250 returns annually were required to file their income tax returns electronically for years ending after December 31, 2005. After the first effective year is over (thus no later than 2007) the threshold drops to $10 million in assets and 250 returns annually. Smaller corporations—and individuals too—may at their option file taxes electronically as well. In fact 8 million business filed taxes electronically in 2005; 68.5 million individuals filed electronically in the same year, up 11 percent over 2004. Meanwhile telephone-based filing (known as the TeleFile program) was discontinued as of August 16, 2005. The U.S. Treasury is well on its way toward achieving one of its goals—maximum tax filing by electronic means.

Small businesses that utilize a payroll service may already be engaged in filing at least their payroll taxes electronically without being aware of it—because the payroll service may be doing so on their behalf. Those not yet engaged in filing taxes electronically in any way can begin by visiting the IRS site entitled "Approved IRS e-file for Business Providers" accessible at http://www.irs.gov/efile/article/0,,id=118516,00.html. The site is organized by various tax forms and provides the names, telephone numbers, and profiles for organizations approved by IRS to provide e-filing services. Price information is provided in most cases. The small business may be working with an outside public accountant—another point of contact to explore transition from paper to electronic filing. Web addresses sometimes change. Should that be the case, access to the most recent site should be available through www.irs.gov.

PROS AND CONS

The IRS prefers businesses to submit their taxes via electronic means because the costs and error rates for electronic tax filing are dramatically lower than those for paper filing. Critics of this approach have worried in the past (Mike Dries writing in *Milwaukee Business Journal* in the 1990s being an example) citing the very large number of small businesses and the then-anticipated lack of technological sophistication of owners. Since that time, however, market forces, effective technical support by the IRS, and entrepreneurial energy have changed the situation. Low-cost services and very effective software products have emerged to make the process essentially painless for even very small enterprises.

Tax preparation is ultimately algorithmic in nature and therefore very well-suited for computerized methods—especially for small businesses in which complexities are relatively low. Software aiding the business owner in preparing taxes is designed to acquire from the owner those elements of information not automatically captured from the accounting software with which the tax package interacts. Typically, also, the owner is shown intermediate results and can iterate the procedures until the right results are reached. Some packages also provide the user with direct access to tax regulations and definitions so that more fuzzy issues can be resolved. Finally, many small businesses use electronic filing indirectly by having their accountants do the job—so that a highly skilled interface person mediates between the software and the owner.

E-FILING AND STATES

Electronic tax filing is available in every state as well, but, as Kathleen Hunter reported in *Stateline.org*, the rate of electronic filing at the state level lags that experienced by the IRS except in three states, Kansas, Massachusetts, and Ohio. The principal reason for this lag appears to be that fewer states provide advanced services, such as allowing users to check the status of their refunds online. Tax preparation software typically comes with the necessary forms and facilities for filing state taxes at the same time as federal taxes.

SEE ALSO *Tax Preparation Software*

BIBLIOGRAPHY
Dries, Mike. "Dialing for Dollars." *Milwaukee Business Journal.* 7 September 1996.

Higginbotham, Keith. "IRS Expands Electronic Tax Filing." *Knight-Ridder/Tribune Business News.* 5 January 2001.

Hunter, Kathleen. "States Lag Feds in Electronic Tax Filing." Stateline.org. Available from http://www.stateline.org/live/ViewPage.action. 11 April 2005.

Mosquera, Mary. "Snowball Effect: Maine's move to online services picks up speed—and users." *Government Computer News.* 11 October 2004.

United States Department of the Treasury. Internal Revenue Service. "e-file for Business and Self-Employed Taxpayers." Available from http://www.irs.gov/efile/article/0,,id=118520,00.html. Retrieved on 1 March 2006.

Darnay, ECDI

EMERGING MARKETS

The phrase "emerging markets" has two distinct connotations. *First,* it means new and emerging foreign export markets for U.S. companies. The U.S. Commerce Department's International Trade Administration (ITA) uses the phrase in this sense—pointing at markets where U.S. companies might find additional sales. *Second,* the phrase acts as an abbreviation in investment circles and refers to groups of nations, regions of the world, and investment strategies which specialize in buying and selling the stock or debt instruments of "emerging markets." The same countries are often referred to in either context, although U.S. trade promoters sometimes include countries that would not meet the definition of an emerging market as used by Wall Street investors.

Depending on the particular viewpoint of the individual or institution providing the definition, emerging markets are just a few leading countries or include more than 40 countries on all continents. Frequently mentioned emerging markets are China and India in Asia; Argentina, Brazil, and Chile in the Americas; the former Communist European countries and Russia in Europe; Turkey in the Middle East; and Egypt in Africa. An important leading subgroup with the catchy acronym of "the BRICs" includes Brazil, Russia, India, and China—thus the largest of the emerging markets. By common consensus, *the* emerging market in the mid-2000s was China—as in the 1970s it had been Japan.

The defining features of emerging markets include at least the following factors. The markets are actively growing under governmental policies that favor a capitalist-style economy. Governments are predictably stable but not necessarily democratic. Substantial future growth is guaranteed because their internal resources and infrastructure still remain unexploited and undeveloped. They have a large, growing, and prosperous middle class; in China, for instance, the size of this class is equivalent to the total population of the U.S.; in India this class is only slightly smaller. The countries have either abandoned or are in the process of abandoning state control and ownership of major sectors. They have transparent and modern financial systems. They have a skilled but modestly compensated labor force.

THE GLOBAL CONTEXT

Emerging markets may be seen as a global natural phenomenon in which waves of economic development lift different countries in sequence to a higher level. The "economic miracle" of the German economy after World War II marked Germany's recovery from the destruction of Allied bombing with the help of aid and the inflow of foreign investment; Germany lead the recovery of Europe; Japan's rise—and the rise of the Asian "Tigers" (Hong Kong, Taiwan, Singapore, and South Korea)—followed in turn. Latin America developed by exploitation of its agriculture and oil resources. The collapse of Communism led to liberalization of East

European economies and the emergence of new market economies there, initially in Poland, then elsewhere. This process indirectly stimulated Chinese liberalization of its economy (if not its politics) producing the rise of China to economic eminence in the 2000s. The process, however, has not been without its ups and downs. As Gill Tudor documented in her book, *Rollercoaster: The Incredible Story of the Emerging Markets,* a Mexican monetary crisis beginning in 1994 produced a global crisis of confidence in emerging markets which spread throughout Latin America and from there eventually touched all of the emerging markets. But the emerging markets recovered from the panic in part through the intervention of the "mature markets" which adjusted their investments and refinanced emerging market debt.

THE LOCAL CONSEQUENCES

In the context of major international trade agreements, like the North American Free Trade Agreement (NAFTA), emerging markets are presented to the U.S. public as opportunities for export—and therefore a vibrant domestic economy. However, the globalization of modern, technological economies is an adjustment process that has local costs for mature economies which may be higher than benefits achieved.

Emerging markets are "emerging" because they offer advantages, usually lower cost labor, no longer available in mature economies. Thus they induce a flow of capital from developed to developing theaters of economic activity.

As Jeffrey E. Garten pointed out, writing in *Newsweek International,* "emerging markets have moved from the periphery of the global economy to the center. They have become integral to international production, trade, and finance.... [O]ver the last 10 years the emerging-market share of international trade has increased from about 27 percent to more than 33 percent." This translates into a strong flow of direct investment (in plant and equipment) to these markets. Garten, citing IMF figures: "Between 1994 and 1996 net private direct investment ... was 1.5 times greater than investment in stocks and bonds.... Now it is eight times greater. Between 1994 and 2005, net foreign direct investment increased 92 percent, whereas net investment in stocks and bonds actually decreased slightly." He cites a 2005 General Electric announcement that 60 percent of GE's revenue growth would come from China, India, Russia, and Brazil over the next decade. He points out that Wal-Mart, which entered the Brazilian market in 1995, had started 259 stores in that country. Wal-Mart had also opened 51 stores in China since 1996 and was planning dozens more in 2006. These examples, multiplied by the hundreds, indicate growing investments made elsewhere, not in the U.S.

Meanwhile, as Robert Samuelson pointed out (in *Newsweek*), the U.S. economy, seemingly unaware of the broad trends, has been on a shopping spree. "From 1996 to 2005," Samuelson wrote, citing Sara Johnson of Global Insight, "the United States generated almost 45 percent of global growth in consumer spending... That dwarfs the U.S. share of the world economy, [which is] about 20 percent." Not surprisingly the U.S. trade deficit moved from $191 billion in 1996 to $784 billion in 2005.

HALF FULL OR HALF EMPTY

Emerging markets off U.S. shores represent a growing standard of living across the globe. Locally they cause the unwelcome phenomenon of factory closings and layoffs due to outsourcing. Globalists see the glass half full and foresee eventual equilibrium as emerging markets mature. Samuelson put it as follows: "As people [overseas] grow richer, their wants multiply. Industry looks more to meeting their demands than generating ever-larger trade surpluses. The expansion of consumer credit (which is still tiny compared with the United States) encourages the process." Meanwhile American consumers, hurt by high interest rates and very high debts will wean themselves of their consumption addiction. And the gap will close. Pessimists see the glass half empty and advocate, instead, curbing uncontrolled globalization in favor of managed trade that will protect the jobs of U.S. workers.

BIBLIOGRAPHY

Frink, Lyle. "Not East and West, but Simply Europe." *Automotive News Europe.* 20 February 2006.

Garten, Jeffrey E. "Hot Markets, Solid Ground: Why emerging nations are a new force for stability in the world economy, not a new crisis-in-the-making." *Newsweek International.* 9 January 2006.

Goldberg, Steven. "Now's a Good Time to Tiptoe Into Emerging Markets." *Kiplinger's Value Added 0 Column.* 10 January 2006.

"Investing in BRICs." *Money Management (Australia).* 2 February 2006.

Samuelson, Robert. "Will America Pass the Baton? The world is addicted to America's shopping spree. But some experts see emerging markets increasingly driving the world economy." *Newsweek.* 6 March 2006.

"Schroders Shifts Emerging Markets Emphasis to Asia." *Money Marketing.* 16 February 2006.

Tudor, Gill. "Rollercoaster: The Incredible Story of the Emerging Markets." *Financial Times Management.* 6 September 2000.

"US to Rely on World Economies for Wealth." *Investment Adviser.* 30 January 2006.

Darnay, ECDI

EMPLOYEE ASSISTANCE PROGRAMS

Employee assistance programs (EAPs) are plans that help identify and resolve issues facing troubled employees through short-term counseling, referrals to specialized professionals or organizations, and follow-up services. Many EAPs also train business owners and supervisors to recognize and deal with behavioral problems in the workforce. These programs are not designed to provide long-term treatment, but as *Business Week* noted, "they do offer a safe environment where an employee can discuss problems with a counselor who then makes a confidential assessment, and if necessary, gives a referral to a mental-health professional." Indeed, business experts regard them as a potentially valuable tool in reversing declining performance among valued workers. "We're not talking here about employees who turn violent or hear voices," said *Business Week*. "The people a business owner needs to worry about are the...valued workers whose productivity suddenly and mysteriously plummets. From depression to anxiety, from drug abuse to alcohol addiction, common psychiatric disorders take a remarkable, if little-discussed, toll. In lost productivity and absenteeism alone, the cost to business approaches $312 billion annually."

Given these sobering statistics regarding the impact of emotional disorders on business productivity, employee assistance programs have become an increasingly popular element of total benefits packages for small and large employers alike.

First created in response to business concerns about the impact of employee alcohol and drug abuse on bottom-line productivity, employee assistance programs (EAPs) are now designed to deal with a wider range of issues confronting workers today. Modern EAP systems are designed to help workers with other problems as well, such as family and/or marriage counseling, depression, stress, gambling addiction, financial difficulties, crisis planning, illness among family or co-workers, and pre-retirement planning. Many EAPs have also expanded the scope of their counseling to help workers grapple with eldercare issues, natural disasters, and workplace violence. In addition, many employee assistance programs have added proactive elements to their offerings. For example, a number of employee assistance programs have actively promoted AIDS/HIV workplace policies and education efforts.

This expansion in the scope of EAP counseling is commonly attributed to changes in America's larger social fabric. "The prevalence of two-wage-earner families, single parent households, mobility and career change patterns, demographic shifts, and technological change have helped to create new and different types of stress

and mental health crises, which affect the health and productivity of many employees," wrote Jody Osterweil in *Pension World*. "Where individuals formerly sought advice and counsel from a respected cleric, a personal physician, a close family member or a friend, those relationships are increasingly rare and cannot fulfill individuals' needs for crisis intervention. Thus, individuals experiencing a personal or family crisis, or who are under chronic stress, may have no place to turn for advice other than to the benefits (the EAP) offered through their workplace."

In addition, companies have come to realize that a direct link can often be detected between employee well-being and employee productivity, and that the difference in value between happy and unhappy employees can often be quite profound. This is especially true if the troubled person is a manager or supervisor with important responsibilities. In addition, erratic behavior from one employee typically has a ripple effect, producing anxiety and lost efficiency in numerous other employees who have to deal with the troubled individual on a regular basis. "Despite continuing technological advances, today's companies rely on their employees to improve productivity and increase the bottom line," wrote Brian W. Gill in *American Printer*. "Therefore, the relationship between employees' well-being and productivity cannot be ignored. Personal and work-related problems may manifest themselves in poor job performance, which adversely affects the firm's overall productivity." Indeed, consultants contend that few staffers are able to wholly shield their work performance from the negative residue of personal difficulties. Increased absenteeism, higher accident rates, substandard performance on previously mastered tasks, employee theft, and poor morale are just some of the symptoms that may appear if an employee is struggling to handle a problem in his or her personal or professional life.

Finding EAPs nearby is possible using an online service provided by the Employee Assistance Professional Association at http://www.eapassn.org/public/providers/. The Web site enables the user to specify the category or multiple categories of assistance sought and pick a geographical area. EAPs will be presented with contact information.

KEY ADVANTAGES OF EAP IMPLEMENTATION

Perceived costs associated with implementation and maintenance of employee assistance programs looms as the biggest concern for most small business owners. Many owners of small businesses recognize that EAPs can be helpful to the members of their work force, but the specter of yet another operating expenditure may dissuade them. But analysts say that small business owners can institute an employee assistance program for their employees at relatively small expense. Monthly fees for legitimate EAP providers typically range from $2 to $6 per employee, according to some estimates.

Benefits experts and businesses alike cite several important benefits associated with employee assistance programs. Business owners are, of course, concerned with the utility of an EAP as a cost-management tool. To an entrepreneur with a small business, the most important advantage associated with an EAP is likely to be its positive impact on employee productivity and its use in controlling health care costs. But according to many businesses that have adopted employee assistance programs, there are other benefits that may accrue as well. For example, companies that provide for an EAP may be viewed as more employee-supportive in the community in which they operate than will competitors for workers who do not provide such a program. In addition, employee assistance programs have been cited as an effective element in employee retention efforts designed at reducing turnover.

But a less remarked on advantage associated with EAP implementation is that it frees up the company to do what it does best—provide its goods or services to its customers—instead of devoting work time to issues that may not be directly related to meeting production deadlines, etc. Basically, putting together an EAP allows business owners and managers to concentrate on their internal operations. "We have to focus on the job and the ability to do the job," one business executive told the *Pittsburgh Business Times*. "We don't want to play counselor and dive into areas we're not qualified for."

CHOOSING AN EMPLOYEE ASSISTANCE PROGRAM

The characteristics and quality of EAP programs can vary considerably, so small business owners should undertake a careful study of their options before selecting a plan. Factors to consider when comparing programs include:

Appropriate qualifications. The EAP you select for your company should be operated by professionally licensed staff with established relations with local health groups and/or national self-help organizations. They should also be engaged in continuing education initiatives. Check their affiliations and level of EAP experience when reviewing their program.

Find out about cost structure. Roberta Reynes noted in *Nation's Business* that costs can vary considerably from program to program, depending on operation structure, types and extent of services provided, and method of calculating charges. Benefits experts also recommend that small business owners make sure that materials and administration costs incurred by EAP providers are included in their base fee. National services tend to offer more affordable programs than local providers, but this is by no means always the case.

Extent of training services. EAP training programs vary widely in scope and subject matter. The most comprehensive plans provide managers with assistance in confronting troubled employees, developing wellness policies, and arranging seminars on health issues.

Convenience and responsiveness. Business owners should seek out EAP providers with facilities that are in the same geographic region as the company, so that employees can visit the facilities before, during, or after work. The EAP that is ultimately selected should also have a toll-free telephone line that is operational around the clock, since difficulties do not always strike employees during traditional working hours. In addition, business owners should inquire about the program's response time to employee inquiries in nonemergency situations (a wait of more than three days is a warning sign that the program has problems with its central mandate: helping troubled employees).

Communication. "Most providers issue monthly updates," said Karen Carney in an article published in the magazine *Inc.* "But they should also record their own effectiveness in helping you reach agreed-upon productivity goals or implement safety programs. Some providers also supply payroll handouts or "stuffers" on subjects like practical parenting."

NOURISHING YOUR EMPLOYEE ASSISTANCE PROGRAM

Training of managers and other supervisory personnel (including the owner, if he or she is actively involved in supervision) is a vital component of instituting a successful EAP. "Managers who have the most contact with employees will be the first line of defense in recognizing potential problems and correcting them before they reach the termination stage," stated Gill. "Therefore, it is imperative that managers understand the objectives of the EAP to ensure the program's success and reduce any potential employer liability." In addition, management personnel have to be adequately instructed about what Gill termed "the do's and don'ts" of EAPs. They can refer employees to the assistance program, but no one can be forced to seek assistance. Supervisors and employees must understand that these services are strictly confidential and using them will not be cause for disciplinary action. However, being involved in an EAP service does not exempt employees from disciplinary action when company rules are violated. This is a very fine line that must be addressed in supervisory training.

Promotion of the program is another important element for small businesses seeking to maximize the effectiveness of their EAP. "All too often, plan sponsors assume that employees are fully cognizant of the EAP and the services it offers," stated Osterweil. "Employees and dependents must become more aware of the program's existence, the nature of its resources and coverages, and the means of accessing such programs. Employees must develop confidence in the abilities of those providing such services, trust that confidentiality will be assured, and obtain knowledge that their specific needs can be addressed through the resources available from the EAP. Simply publishing an '800' telephone number in a summary plan description, or posting a notice in the workplace, is not likely to effectively communicate the existence of this valuable resource."

Osterweil noted, though, that a coordinated approach that is non-threatening in tone and that indicates that "the sponsor truly desires to meaningfully assist and retain employees and sees them as a valuable resource" can help significantly in reassuring employees about the program's character and purpose. For that reason, benefits experts counsel small businesses to establish a plan in which workers are provided with regular, timely (around the holidays, for instance) reminders of the availability and offerings of their employee assistance program, including assurances that the program is confidential and free.

EVALUATING ESTABLISHED EAPs

Once an employee assistance program has been put in place, it is up to the sponsor to make certain that it is an effective addition to their overall benefits package. After all, an EAP that does not address the primary needs and concerns of a company's employees is essentially a waste of money. Admittedly, determining the effectiveness of an employee assistance program can sometimes be a difficult task, since employee problems like family strife, substance abuse, and workplace stress are impossible to quantify. For example, an EAP provider will not be able to provide statistics to a client stating that over the previous six months, workplace stress dropped by 27 percent and family strife declined by 14 percent. In addition, the confidentiality restrictions associated with employee assistance programs place further limitations on tracking EAP use and effectiveness.

Small business owners looking for information on the effectiveness of their EAP do have other options, however. "Attention to trends in utilization and expenditures by type of service (such as in- or out-patient detoxification, rehabilitation, and aftercare) can help plan sponsors evaluate the cost-effectiveness of their EAP and the efficacy of the vendors providing these services," said

Osterweil. "For example, a successful EAP should show a positive influence on expenditures under the employer's health plan. It should also show lessening absenteeism, tardiness, and disability and improving productivity. And, the evaluation process gives plan sponsors an opportunity to design a system that can capture data that will more readily assess the ongoing cost-effectiveness of the program."

Benefits experts also encourage sponsors of employee assistance programs to look at their EAP within the overall context of its total benefits structure. *Pension World* pointed out that in many instances, employee assistance programs are regarded by workers as being "peripherally attached to the rest of the employee benefits package. This is certainly understandable as the need for employee confidentiality must be preserved, so that a certain degree of arms-length delivery of services is desirable. Because of privacy issues, EAPs may be managed by professional, outside vendors, with services provided at sites away from the workplace." But as much as possible, company sponsors of EAPs should try to integrate their programs with their other efforts to promote wellness for employees and their dependents.

Signs of a Flawed Employee Assistance Program
Employee assistance programs are commonly touted as a valuable cost-management tool, but if the implementation or design of an EAP is flawed, then the purported cost savings of the program will not be realized. Benefits experts counsel small business owners to look out for the following indications that an employee assistance program may need revision:

- General dissatisfaction with the program expressed by employees
- Only a small percentage (less than 5 percent) of eligible employees use the program
- Issues that prompted the initial use of the EAP are not resolved within a reasonable period of time
- EAP referrals indicate an unwarranted bias toward one type of care or treatment
- Employees view the EAP with distrust, seeing it as a possible management tool for doling out punishment or justifying termination
- EAP staff have potential conflicts of interest (for example, a staffer who is found to have financial ties to a provider to whom referrals are made)

All of these warning signs can be addressed, but companies should make sure that they conduct adequate research into the needs and desires of their employees before attempting any sort of shake-up. And when revision of an EAP does occur, employers should take every precaution to ensure that any employees who did benefit from the program's previous incarnation are not left behind.

BIBLIOGRAPHY

Carney, Karen E. "Choosing an EAP." *Inc.* July 1994.

Gaipa, Marilyn. "Compliance, Risk Management, and EAPs: How to build the partnership." *The Journal of Employee Assistance.* January-March 2006.

Gill, Brian W. "Employee Assistance Programs." *American Printer.* June 1997.

Herlihy, Patricia. "Employee Assistance Programs and Work/Family Programs: Obstacles and Opportunities for Organizational Integration." *Compensation & Benefits Management.* Spring 1997.

"It's Your Problem Too." *Business Week.* 28 February 2000.

Osterweil, Jody. "Evaluating and Revising EAPs." *Pension World.* June 1991.

Reynes, Roberta. "Programs that Aid Troubled Workers." *Nation's Business.* June 1998.

Tramer, Harriet. "Small Biz Offering EAPs to Preserve Productivity." *Crain's Cleveland Business.* 25 April 2005.

Wojcik, Joanne. "EAPs Extend Role to Help Employers Recover Too." *Business Insurance.* 12 September 2005.

Hillstrom, Northern Lights
updated by Magee, ECDI

EMPLOYEE BENEFITS

The phrase "employee benefits" is an umbrella term that includes insurance programs, fully compensated absences (vacations, holidays, sick leave), pensions, stock ownership plans, and employer-provided services (such as child care) offered by employers to their employees. Employee benefits are also referred to as fringe benefits. Yet other benefits sometimes are treated by government as forms of income for tax purposes. These include bonuses, profit sharing, and the provision of a leased vehicle or housing. All "fringes" are by definition offered at the employer's option; thus employer contributions to Social Security, Medicaid, basic Medicare, Workers' Compensation, and other programs are not viewed as fringe benefits; they are required under law.

Certain categories of employee benefits may require that the employee pay a part of the cost of the benefit in order to receive the employer's contribution. For this reason, employees who have *access* to benefits outnumber employees who actually *participate* in the benefits offered. Young employees, for instance, may opt out of retirement programs. An employee may choose not to participate in a medical insurance program because he or she may already be covered by the spouse's participation in a family program elsewhere.

THE NATIONAL SURVEY

The U.S. Bureau of Labor Statistics (BLS) conducts an annual compensation survey as part of which it collects data on the major categories of employee benefits. Benefits tracked include paid leave, health insurance, retirement plans, life insurance, and disability benefits. The highlights of the BLS March 2005 survey follow:

- *Paid Leave* was the most common employee benefit offered; 77 percent of employees had both paid holidays and paid vacation time. Sixty-nine percent of workers had paid jury duty leave; 48 percent had paid military leave benefits.

- *Health Care Benefits.* Seventy percent of employees had access to medical care benefits, 46 percent had access to dental care, and 29 percent to vision care. Sixty-four percent had outpatient prescription drug coverage. Because most plans required employee participation, participation rates were much lower: 53 percent of employees participated in medical plans, 36 percent in dental plans, 22 percent in vision care plans, and 48 percent in drug coverage. Employee contributions averaged $273.03 for family plans and $68.96 for single employee coverage.

- *Retirement Benefits.* Sixty percent of employees had access to such benefits; 50 percent participated in such programs.

- *Life Insurance.* Of all private employees, 52 percent had access to such insurance; 49 percent participated.

- *Disability Insurance.* Forty percent of employees had access to short-term and 40 percent to long-term disability benefits. Nearly all employees participated in these programs.

TRENDS IN ACCESS

Trends in access to employee benefits in the six-year period 1999 to 2005 have been generally favorable from the employee's point of view showing either no change or a positive change. Thus access to retirement plans and medical care plans remained the same. The number of employees enjoying paid holidays, paid sick leave, and access to child care services and short-term disability programs increased. Child care access showed the strongest positive increase, from 6 percent of employees having access in 1999 to 14 percent in 2005—an 8 point increase. On the negative side, fewer employees had paid vacations—79 percent in 1999 and 77 percent in 2005. In 1999 67 percent of medical plans required an employee contribution; this number rose to 76 percent in 2005, a 9 point increase reflecting the continuing growth in healthcare—and hence in health-insurance—costs.

SMALL ESTABLISHMENTS

The BLS national survey provides breakdowns in its data by establishment size rather than company size, thus for establishments with 1 to 99 workers and those with 100 workers and more. Data on small businesses available from BLS are rather old; therefore this "small establishment" breakdown is the closest approximation to "small business" we now have available. Across the board, a smaller percentage of employees working for small establishments have access to benefits. Under medical programs, 59 percent of small establishment workers had access (versus 84 percent of large establishment workers); medical coverage was also the top-ranking programmatic benefit (ignoring time off) offered by small establishments. Data for other categories follow showing percent of workers having access in small establishments and, in parentheses, the percent in large establishments: Dental: 31 (65); Vision: 19 (41); Prescription Drugs: 52 (79); Retirement: 44 (78); Life Insurance: 37 (70); Short-Term Disability: 28 (55); and Long-Term Disability: 19 (44).

While small establishments offer fewer employees medical insurance, the costliest of the employee benefits, for single employee coverage small establishments paid nearly as high a proportion of such insurance as did large establishments. In 2005, small enterprises picked up 82 percent of the medical insurance premium; large enterprises 83 percent. Small establishments, however, required more participation from the employee opting for family coverage: they paid 66 percent of such premiums over against 74 percent paid by large establishments.

GOODS PRODUCERS AND SERVICES PROVIDERS

In every programmatic benefit category, goods producers offered more of their employees benefits than did establishments engaged in providing services. Among goods producers the leading category was short-term disability insurance, with 88 percent of employees offered such a benefit; medical coverage was a close second, with 85 percent of employees having access. In these two categories, service providers offered 36 percent of employees short-term disability coverage and 66 percent medical coverage. Data for the other categories follows in abbreviated format showing percent of workers in the goods producing sector having access and, in parentheses, the corresponding percentage for services producers: Dental: 56 (43); Vision: 36 (27); Prescription Drugs: 80 (59); Retirement: 71 (56); Life Insurance: 63 (48); and Long-Term Disability: 31 (30).

Goods producers also paid more of medical premiums than companies in the service sector: 84 percent for single coverage and 75 percent for family coverage.

Corresponding values for service sector companies were 82 and 69 percent.

THE PROS AND CONS OF BENEFITS

A comprehensive benefits package can be an important and useful asset for a company in attracting and holding employees. A company with a reputation for excellent benefits—particularly a long history of offering and *protecting* such fringes—has competitive advantages and, indeed, can in part compensate for the cost of such benefits by paying somewhat lower salaries and wages.

Rich benefits packages, of course, also have a downside. They are costly. Cutting back on benefits in difficult economic environments can produce adverse effects on employee morale and productivity. In the U.S., where such benefits are available to a large percentage of the population and where the benefits (particularly medical care) are funded by the private sector, employee benefits can also reduce competitiveness over against employers overseas who either offer no benefits at all or where such benefits are paid from general taxes.

The two major forces at work affecting employee benefits are thus availability of labor on the one hand, which pushes up benefits in times of rapid growth, and the need to control costs, which causes benefits to be curtailed or their costs to be transferred to employees, on the other. Economic cycles, therefore—and international trade pressures—affect trends in benefits in a see-sawing fashion. Changes between 1999 and 2005, a period generally of economic downturn, illustrate this process: child-care programs were increasing, in part to attract a lower-paid female labor force; at the same time medical costs were being transferred to employees.

Small businesses tend to benefit from economically stressful times because cut-backs and layoffs increase the labor pool and small organizations with minimal benefit programs can compete more effectively for employees. In rapidly growing economies, large organizations improve their benefits programs to attract scare labor resources. These conditions suggest the optimum solution for the small business: it is to offer benefits sufficient to hold employees in good times but to keep benefits always affordable and modest enough to survive the downturns.

SEE ALSO *Employee Reward Systems; Flexible Spending Accounts; Sick Leave and Personal Days*

BIBLIOGRAPHY

"Easier Done than Said." *Employee Benefit News.* 1 December 2000.

EBRI Research Highlights: Retirement Benefits. Employee Benefit Research Institute. 2003.

Michael, Andy. "Playing a Pivotal Role." *Employee Benefits.* December 2000.

Simmons, John G. "Flexible Benefits for Small Employers." *Journal of Accountancy.* March 2001.

"Small Biz Balks." *Crain's New York Business.* 13 February 2006.

U.S. Department of Labor. Bureau of Labor Statistics. *National Compensation Survey: Employee Benefits in Private Industry in the United States, March 2005.* August 2005.

Hillstrom, Northern Lights
updated by Magee, ECDI

EMPLOYEE COMPENSATION

People work in order to earn money, but the structure of compensation is quite diversified. The two broadest categories are salaries and wages. Salaries tend to be paid every other week or monthly; wages are typically calculated by the hour but paid by the week. As a consequence of legislative language, salary-earning employees are sometimes referred to as "exempt" employees and hourly workers as "non-exempt"; in other words the first are exempt from the requirements of Fair Labor Standards Act (discussed below), the latter group are covered. Compensation may also take the form of commissions paid to sales people based entirely on some percent of the goods or services they sell; this type of compensation is often combined with a minimal salary to even out the ups and downs of commission earnings—but people on pure commission who fail to "earn back" their base salary rarely continue in the job long. Piece work, where pay is based on actual performance of some job measured by units produced, is a variant of this approach. People serving as wait-personnel in restaurants are typically compensated by a low wage inadequate to support them: they get the majority of their income from tips. In the so-called New Economy which began emerging in the 1990s, characterized by cutbacks and layoffs of salaried and professional employees, many individuals became self-employed of necessity but, often, continued working in actual "jobs," much as before. The compensation of such people is based on contract revenues, but they receive no fringe benefits and are required to pay their own payroll taxes.

Compensation has a legal status and, once engaged, people can use the courts to enforce the employment agreement. Employee benefits ("fringe benefits") have another status: they are provided at the employer's option and may be withdrawn at will. As such they are not strictly speaking compensation although, in practice, they are viewed as a part of the full compensation "package." The employer's payment of premiums for certain types of fringe benefits, such as health care coverage and insurance

policies (disability, life insurance), are not viewed under tax law as part of the employee's taxable income. Others, such as the provision of an automobile or housing, are taxable and therefore fall under the definition of "compensation."

COMPENSATION AND TIME

For the non-exempt part of the workforce hours spent on the job are the measure of compensation to be paid. Time spent at work is regulated by the government, and laws govern pay scales over and above the specified work week, typically 40 hours. The vast majority of exempt workers are also required to work a fixed number of hours a week—but the hours may be flexible under "flextime" rules set by the employer. For exempt employees, pay for "overtime" is not controlled by law in most cases. In other words, the typical administrative/professional/executive employee is expected to work 40 hours—and as many more as the job may require, the extra hours compensated, if at all, by bonuses or time off. In the case of people working for commissions, time spent on the job is only incidentally related to compensation. Normally, of course, such people spend a lot of time working—but one can imagine the highly charismatic (and lucky) sales person who, in a couple of hours a month, can move a million dollars worth of real estate....

COMPENSATION LAWS

The Fair Labor Standards Act of 1938 (FLSA) is in a sense the basic law controlling employment and compensation issues and, through amendments passed later, the management of benefits packages. FLSA sets minimum wage, overtime pay, equal pay for men and women, controls child labor, and establishes record keeping requirements. On the whole FLSA is aimed at protecting the non-exempt work force—which was the overwhelming majority of all workers at the time of the law's passage. Since that time the profile of the workforce has greatly change; amendments to FLSA have in part reflected these changes. As illustrated by state over-rides of FLSA's minimum wage requirements (see below), states also actively regulate compensation and other aspects of the workplace.

The chief amendment of FLSA was passage of the Equal Pay Act of 1963 (EPA). EPA prohibits unequal compensation of men and women in the same workplace doing similar jobs. EPA makes exceptions for seniority, allows the use of merit systems, and recognizes compensation systems based on performance. EPA requirements do not differentiate between exempt and nonexempt employees.

Other legislation related to employment compensation issues includes: 1) the Consumer Credit Protection Act of 1968 which deals with wage garnishments; 2) the Employee Retirement Income Security Act of 1974 (ERISA), which regulates pension programs; 3) the Old Age, Survivors, Disability and Health Insurance Program (OASDHI), which forms the basis for most benefits programs; and 4) legislation implementing unemployment insurance, equal employment, worker's compensation, Social Security, Medicare, and Medicaid programs and laws.

MAJOR COMPENSATION ISSUES

The two major issues related to compensation are the adequacy of the compensation, addressed by minimum wage laws, and pay equity—between women and men and between racial and ethnic groups—addressed by EPA and social anti-discrimination statutes.

Minimum Wage Non-exempt employees, for whom the definition is intrinsically tied to time, are also guaranteed a minimum wage of $5.15 per hour under federal law. Six states (Alabama, Arizona, Louisiana, Mississippi, South Carolina, and Tennessee) have no minimum wage. Fifteen states have higher minimum wage than the U.S. as a whole: Alaska, California, Connecticut, Delaware, Florida, Hawaii, Illinois, Maine, Massachusetts, Minnesota, New Jersey, New York, Oregon, Washington, and Wisconsin. The highest wage is in Oregon, $7.63 an hour; in 2006 Connecticut had a $7.40 per hour minimum wage to be raised to $7.65 in 2007. The rest of the states have the same minimum wage as the national rate. Under the federal rules, a non-exempt worker is entitled to receive the highest minimum wage available in the place where he or she works. Changes in state law are monitored by the U.S. Department of Labor and may be consulted at http://www.dol.gov/esa/minwage/america.htm.

Equal Pay for Women and Men Detailed data comparing income of men and women in the same occupation are not routinely collected so that the pay-equity issues remains somewhat in the dark, but more general data series give an indication of overall patterns. Based on data published by the U.S. Census Bureau, the average income of a man in 1954, but measured in 2004 dollars, was $20,992 a year. The average income of a woman, using the same method of calculation, was $9,358. On average, in 1954 a woman earned 44.6 percent of what a man earned. Women's earnings were 41.1 percent of men's in 1964, thus showing a decline, 42.2 percent in 1974 (still down from 1954), were up to 49.3 percent in 1984 but dropped again to 43 percent in 1994. In 2004, average male income was $42,832, average female income was $24,998. A gap of $17,834 separated men from women, but women were earning an all time high of 58.4 percent of what men earned on average.

In this 50-year period, women's income grew at a faster rate than men's (1.98 percent a year versus men's income at 1.44 percent). Women's participation rate in the work force grew in this period as well: female participation in the workforce increased from 34 percent to 59.2 percent, 1954 to 2004. At the same time, the difference in male-female income averaged around $17,000 a year in this period, strongly suggesting that women had a competitive advantage in the labor market. This is further substantiated by data, published in *Social Trends and Indicators USA* showing that more men than women (on a percentage basis) are laid off during periods recessions.

In a 2002 survey conducted by the U.S. Bureau of the Census and published in *Current Population Survey* data showing income differentials between men and women of the same educational attainment are presented. This study showed that income differentials were substantial across the board: 2000 data showed women on average earning 57.5 percent of what men earned. The differentials were the following: for less than 9th grade education, 59.9 percent; for high school graduates, 59.3; for bachelor's degree, 56.0; for masters, 59.7; for professional degrees, 55.9; and for doctoral degrees, 60.3 percent of what men with the same education attainment level earned.

Racial and Ethnic Differences The U.S. Bureau of the Census data cited above for all men and women also provide a look at racial and ethnic difference—and difference between men and women in those groups. Data cited are for 2004 only because long-term data are not uniformly available. The highest average earnings are achieved by Asians. Asian women have the highest earnings among all women but earn only 61.1 percent of the income of Asian males. Lowest earnings were reported for Hispanics, again for both males and females. Hispanic females earned 66.5 percent of what Hispanic males earned. Whites had the second highest earnings, but white women lagged farthest behind. They had 56.9 percent of white males' earnings. Black women earned 75.5 percent of black males' earnings. For these four racial and ethnic group comparisons, black women were highest in relation to men.

COMPENSATION IN THE SMALL BUSINESS SECTOR

According to a Wells Fargo press release, announcing the latest Wells Fargo/Gallup Small Business Index, "Sixty percent of small business owners see the amount of compensation they can offer an employee as a critical disadvantage when compared to larger companies."

Are small business owners simply grumbling? No. Data for 2001 from the Census Bureau on firm size measured by employment and payroll show that the smaller the firm, the lower the average payroll per employee. Companies with 10,000 or more employees averaged $39,789 per employee, the smallest firms (1-4 employees) averaged $27,299. With the exception of companies with 5-9 employees, which were even lower than the smallest at $26,706, at each step up the size-scale payroll per employee went up.

Small firms dominate the corporate population. Firms with less than 100 employees were 98 percent of all firms employing people, those with 100 or more employees were 2 percent of companies. But the small firms employed 36 percent of people working for companies in 2001 (41 million) and large firms employed 64 percent (74 million). In 2001 companies with fewer than 100 employees had payroll costs of $29,138 per employee, companies with 100 or more employees had costs of $37,265 per employee, for a differential of $8,127 a year.

In the mid-2000s, indeed in earlier periods as well, small business had certain advantages: it was adding while the large companies were shedding jobs. The small business sector also offers a work environment that is attractive to many individuals and this fact can be turn to an advantage when recruiting—even if with lower salaries. These include hands-on involvement in business activity, absence of bureaucracy, flexible and often more varied job assignments, more rapid and rational decision processes, and the ability of a small business to adapt to the special needs of an employee. Some employees also value closer contact with the customer; yet others, especially those with entrepreneurial ambitions, feel that they can learn more about business in a small enterprise than embedded deep in the structure of a large one.

A practical aid for the small business owner offered by the Bureau of Labor Statistics is an extensive and reasonably up-to-date tabulation of wages actually paid per occupation by area. This is the BLS Wages by Area and Occupation Program, accessible on the internet. Close study of what wages actually are paid often shows that prevailing rates are frequently much more modest than generally believed because of local or regional economic conditions.

SEE ALSO *Employee Benefits; Employee Motivation; Employee Reward Systems*

BIBLIOGRAPHY

"ADP Small Business Services—EasyPayNet" *The CPA Technology Advisor.* August 2005.

Brainfood: Workplace Rights—Gender pay." *Management Today.* 7 February 2006.

Magee, Monique D. ed. "Are Women Better Able to Weather Economic Storms?" *Social Trends and Indicators USA: Work & Leisure.* The Gale Group, 2003.

"Small Businesses Face Tough Competition Attracting Top Talent According to Wells Fargo/Gallup Small Business Index." Press Release. Wells Fargo. 3 May 2005.

"Small Business Index." *Business Record (Des Moines).* 9 May 2005.

U.S. Census Bureau. *Current Population Survey.* 21 March 2002.

U.S. Census Bureau. "Historical Income Tables – People." Available from http://www.census.gov/hhes/www/income/histinc/p03.html. Retrieved on 5 March 2006.

U.S. Department of Labor. "Minimum Wage Laws in the States–January 1, 2006" Available from http://www.dol.gov/esa/minwage/america.htm. Retrieved on 6 March 2006.

U.S. Department of Labor. Bureau of Labor Statistics. "Wages by Area and Occupation." Available from http://www.bls.gov/bls/blswage.htm. Retrieved on 6 March 2006.

Hillstrom, Northern Lights
updated by Magee, ECDI

EMPLOYEE HIRING

Hiring employees invariably involves a certain formality—even if the business is very small and the person hired is a member of the family: at the very least, mandatory forms must be filed with the federal and state government. The bigger the business the more complex it is likely to be; the hiring process will tend to reflect that. The major elements in the process are 1) the definition of the job itself, often a formal job description rendered on paper, an important aspect of which is determination of the compensation to be paid; 2) a process of recruitment; 3) prospective employee interviews; 4) the job offer and related negotiations (if any); 5) registration of the employee and related introductions and orientations; and 6) some kind of job training which may be minimal or may involve formal training programs. The hire may be a permanent or temporary employee; this status will also influence the process.

Employment of individuals is substantially governed by federal and often also by state law touching upon compensation (the minimum wage requirement), the type of job offered (hourly or salaried), and also on matters relating to discrimination and equal pay for men and women. Hourly workers are covered by the Fair Labor Standards Act and are therefore viewed as "non-exempt"—meaning non-exempt from the FLSA rules—whereas salaried workers are exempt. If the business offers fringe benefits, these in turn are regulated by law. Businesses that do government contracting may also be under regulatory requirements that must be known and respected—lest federal contracts are placed in jeopardy.

Only larger businesses will typically have human resources people whose job it is to keep up to date with changing requirements. In the smallest operations hiring is typically done by the owner; in those of some size the task if often managed by the person who handles most of the heavy administrative work load. But the absence of well-developed "machinery" surrounding the hiring of employees in no way changes the general rules that apply. Indeed, it is good practice generally to dot the i's and cross the t's in an activity that may result in time-consuming difficulties if the hiring process misfires for lack of care, attention, and observance of proprieties.

At the same time, hiring employees is a quintessentially *human* activity in which personality, fit, and many intangible qualities play crucial roles. In businesses of any size, a new employee changes the company for the better or the worse: in a small business this fact will tend to emerge sooner. For this reason hiring of employees is one of the business's most important management tasks. Doing it well pays high dividends.

DEFINING THE JOB

Writing a job description is very similar to doing planning work: most managers dislike the job but, having done it, learn that it was worth the time. The effort of creating the description brings out crucial aspects of the job not usually consciously considered—which helps later in the recruiting and in the interviewing process. More importantly, a job description helps a prospective employee picture the work and respond (or fail to respond) to it revealingly. To be sure, many jobs do not appear to require description beyond saying: "Wait on customers and help with the stocking." But if the store's primary customers are elderly, or if this is the midnight shift and the employee will be alone in the store, or if the stocking involves using a forklift—then adding such details adds significantly to the job description. Part of the description, therefore, includes the hours to be worked and other relevant context that will help in the selection of employees.

Crucial to the job's description, even if not part of it, is setting the compensation. This may be easy if the job already exists. If it is new, the business owner may wish to consult data offered by the Bureau of Labor Statistics on wages actually paid for specific occupations in an area. This is the BLS Wages by Area and Occupation Program and is accessible on the Internet.

Even if a job description is not actually written, some kind of conscious process by the team engaged in

hiring will be helpful. And the job should then be described to the applicant in as much detail as necessary.

Recruiting Recruitment typically takes place by word of mouth, by publishing an advertisement in a paper or hanging up a sign, participating in job fairs, contact with state unemployment services, or even the engagement of a recruiting firm. Using third parties can be expensive and run as high has 30 percent of the new employee's first year's earnings. All experts on hiring agree that recruiting simultaneously from within and without is desirable, especially if the job represents potential advancement for current employees. Some managements resist this because it potentially doubles the hiring labor, but openness in personnel policies provides good returns in morale. Often the announcement of an opening will result in employees lending a hand to find good candidates outside.

The content of recruitment ads will typically depend entirely not only on the job but also on the competitive environment. Sometimes quite creative approaches are tried when labor is tight—merely to draw potential candidates' attention. The golden rule, generally, is to be straightforward. The job should be minimally described and the approach specified: should the candidate call, visit, or send a resume? Sometimes it is valuable to show the compensation, sometimes it is best left unrevealed. Small businesses typically pay less than large ones (see *Employee Compensation* in this volume). However, many prospective employees are also scared away by job titles but would apply if they judged the salary within their personal reach. For the small business it is sometimes a very good tactic to add the words "small business" to the language of the ad: this may cause some not to apply while drawing others who *want* to work in a small business.

The chief aim of recruitment is to find the *right* candidate. For this reason, sometimes, recruitment is quite personal: the owner calls a person he or she already knows. However, in most situations getting a reasonable sample of the talent "out there" is the best approach even if it later becomes difficult to pick the right person from several highly qualified applicants.

INTERVIEWS

In the well-managed hiring process, resumes or applications will be filtered and only a selection of promising candidates will be invited for an interview. The well-prepared employer will have read and annotated the resume first and will not spend time at the interview with head bent over paper.

Although the human resources literatures is filled with wisdom on how to conduct interviews, the distillation of the best advice is that the interview be a semi-formal but friendly interchange in which the interviewer makes an effort to cause the candidate to relax so that a *conversation* can ensue. The best interviewers play a nice game of give-and-take. The worst hold lectures for an hour or sit in hostile silence like inquisitors. The clear object of the interview is to elicit information *from* the candidate but in reaction*to* the offered job situation. It is good practice in larger organizations to pass promising candidates to two or three other people each of whom will, in turn, obtain a different view—and also present the company from a different perspective. Objectivity and concentration on the mission are important. Frequently interviewer and candidate will hit it off very well—as people—even when the qualifications are poor. The inverse, of course is possible. The candidate may have a charisma-deficit and yet do a tremendous job.

SELECTION AND JOB OFFER

Every business has a selection process; it may be formal or simply understood. The ultimate decision on who should be selected from the pool of qualified applications ultimately rests with the most senior person involved in the process—or that person should have veto power—even when others make an input. Companies have styles. Some decide swiftly, others tend to do so after long discussions. One blessing of life in a small business is that such enterprises are more natural, organic; they do things their own way and usually get rapid feedback when making mistakes. Thus effective methods evolve. Once selections are made, however, good practice calls for due diligence in checking out the candidate before actually making an offer. This means making every effort to check references. Depending on the nature of the business, this process may be extensive (especially if government contracts are a major part of the business) and may involve checking arrest records, if any, military services, and proactive documentation of the candidate's educational achievements.

A job offer, even when verbally made, can be construed as a contractual agreement. For this reason the offer should be made very clearly and precisely, indicating the type of job it is (hourly or salaried, permanent or temporary), the compensation offered and at what intervals it will be paid, the trial period during which the employer reserves the right to terminate the offer, what benefits are included or excluded ("We have a medical program but no dental or vision care; if you participate, you'll have to pay part of the cost."), and how long the employee has to respond to the offer. These matters should be covered even if already discussed during the interview. If a verbal offer is followed up in writing, the letter should repeat these and other appropriate points.

To be sure, in actual practice small businesses often neglect formalities of this sort because the managers know the kinds of people they are hiring and know what to expect. And in 99 cases out of a hundred, the informal approach works just fine. ("Hey, Joe, you got the job. When can you start?") The formalities are intended for that one case out of a hundred when an employee sues or lodges a formal complaint. Formality, therefore, is a kind of insurance—and costs very little in the way of preparation and effort.

The offer itself may be followed by some negotiation with the prospective employee in the course of which, for example, the manager may agree to accommodate the new employee's night-school hours or fixed times off for eldercare. Once negotiations are done, the offer will be made again with the adjustments built in.

REGISTRATION AND ORIENTATION

Registration of new employees involves, first of all, filling out necessary government forms and their submission. Three types of documents are involved. The *Federal Tax Withholding Form (W-4)* which has an employee and employer version, the *State and/or Local Tax Withholding forms* that correspond to the federal W-4, and the *Employment Eligibility Verification Form (I-9)* required to be filed with the U.S. Citizenship and Immigration Services (successor to the Immigration and Naturalization Service).

The new employee's initial session, at which these forms are filled out, is also an ideal time to collect information for use by the company such as the names and telephone numbers of next of kin for emergency purposes, information on the individual's health status for the files, and other information the company wishes or has to keep.

The session also lends itself to handing over the company's employment and/or operating policies to be read by the employee. Some companies provide two copies, one of which is to be signed and returned to indicate that the employee has read and understood the contents.

Part of the registration process, normally, is a minimal orientation. It may involve providing the employee keys to the business or to toilet facilities, a brief tour that should include pointing out emergency procedures and exits, and passing on important trivialities such as, for instance, under what conditions the copier always jams and how to avoid it...

INTRODUCTION TO THE JOB

The employee registration and orientation typically ends with introductions to co-workers and to the work itself. The new hire will usually be part of a team with its own supervisor. The lines of authority to be followed can be made clear at this stage—with the supervisor then assuming the role of guide and trainer; in many situations, the trainer may also be a co-worker assigned to introduce the new employee to the actual work itself.

In most work situations some training will be required. In well-run operations such training will be administered based on a checklist and will not be allowed to take place casually—with potentially costly consequences if training is neglected. The job might involve working with complex computerized databases or may require the employee to fill customers' propane containers. All manner of equipment training may be involved. In yet other organizations, complex telephone disciplines may be used. If all training cannot be provided immediately, it is always at least possible to alert the new employee to dangers and to instruct him or her to ask for help before using the forklift, the compressor, or the sonic instrument cleaner.

HIRING AND THE LAW

The hiring process is subject to legal guidelines set out by both federal and state governments; these deal with discriminatory hiring practices. Companies that hire people may not discriminate on the basis of sex, age, race, national origin, religion, physical disability, or veteran status—so-called "protected classes." A hiring manager may not screen out any applicant because of membership in a protected class or address topics during the job interview related to the protected class.

The most important laws related to hiring are—

- The Civil Rights Act of 1964 (Title VII)

- Age Discrimination in Employment Act of 1967 (ADEA)

- Americans With Disabilities Act of 1990 (ADA)

- The Uniformed Services Employment Reemployment Rights Act of 1994 (USERRA)

- Immigration Reform and Control Act

Anti-discrimination laws do not require a company to hire an applicant because of membership in a protected class, nor is a manager required to hire applicants from any protected class in proportion to their numbers in the community. But the business owner is required to select the best qualified applicant for the position, based on the critical skills of the job, and is required to make that selection irrespective of whether or not that applicant belongs to a protected class.

The complexity of the laws shown above is rather daunting. Fortunately an excellent booklet is available from the U.S. Small Business Administration to help the small business owner and his or her administrative helpers. It is entitled *An Equal Opportunity Guide for Small Business Employers* and available on the Internet for downloading (see references below). The SBA guide has the merit of being much more than a motivational pamphlet. It is comprehensive, well-organized, and sufficiently detailed to let the business owner translate its requirements to his or her operation. It provides specific guidance on many issues. Obtaining this guide and spending one or two evenings looking it over with a marking pen will probably suffice in most instances to vastly improve a small business's compliance with the many laws relating to protected classes.

SEE ALSO *Employee References; Employee Reinstatement; Employment Applications; Employment Interviews; Resumes*

BIBLIOGRAPHY

Davis, Martin E. "Hiring and Orienting a New Employee." Entrepreneur.com. Available from http://www.entrepreneur.com/article/0,4621,323632,00.html. 28 September 2005.

"Dealer Wants his Workers to Retire Rich." *Automotive News.* 2 February 2004.

Greenwald, Judy. "Web Recruitment Needs More Care." *Business Insurance.* 2 January 2006.

Hall, John R. "Seminar Provides Tips on Hiring Practices." *Air Conditioning, Heating & Refrigeration News.* 20 June 2005.

"HR Directors: keep employer branding real." *Personnel Today.* 14 February 2006.

"Many U.S. Employers Lack Formal Diversity Recruitment Programs." *HR Focus.* January 2006.

Norwood, F. Bailey and Shida Rastegari Henneberry. "Employers Rank What They Seek for a New Hire." *Feedstuffs.* 30 January 2006.

Smith, Marguerite. "Aging Workers: Overlooked no more?" *Public Management.* January-February 2005.

U.S. Department of Labor. Bureau of Labor Statistics. "Wages by Area and Occupation." Available from http://www.bls.gov/bls/blswage.htm. Retrieved on 6 March 2006.

U.S. Department of the Treasury. Internal Revenue Service. "Businesses with Employees – Hiring Employees. Accessible from http://www.irs.gov/businesses/small/article/0,,id=98164,00.html. Retrieved on 7 March 2006.

U.S. Small Business Administration. *An Equal Opportunity Guide for Small Business Employers.* Available from http://www.sba.gov/library/pubs/equalemployguide.html. Retrieved on 7 March 2006.

Darnay, ECDI

EMPLOYEE LEASING PROGRAMS

TERMINOLOGY

To understand what employee leasing programs are it is useful to make some distinctions at the outset. Four arrangements dealing with employees are common. 1) A business handles all relationships with employees and all employment-related activity *inside the business.* These relationships may or may not involve labor unions. If they do, the contents of labor contracts are part and parcel of the administrative implementation. 2) Many small businesses farm out the *payroll function* to a commercial service. The vendor organization keeps records in parallel with the employer but handles the payment of all salaries and wages, makes all the deductions, and submits appropriate payments to federal and state taxing agencies. The vendor performs an administrative service, pure and simple, and has no actual contact with the employees. 3) Some businesses employ a vendor who takes on the entire *human resources administration function,* including the management of benefit programs as well as handling complaints and legal problems. Finally, 4) but usually only in relation to a tiny subgroup of employees, the business may engage *temporary employees* from a vendor like Kelly Services; the people engaged are employees of the temporary service, but for the duration of the assignment they take their direction from the business's management. None of the four arrangements in dealing with employees is an "employee leasing program." That phrase refers to a fifth alternative.

The Professional Employer Organization (PEO) The fifth alternative, and the one in which the phrase "employee leasing" occurs (or at least used to occur), involves a contractual relationship between the business and a professional employer organization. When a business enters into a contract with a PEO, the PEO becomes the co-employer of the business's employees. It takes over all personnel-related administrative activities, including payroll, the administration of benefits programs, the payment of payroll taxes, workers' compensation, etc. Under the co-employment arrangement, the employees of the company come under the PEO's control for personnel-related matters but remain under the business's control for operational matters. The business pays all of the employment costs involved and also pays the PEO a fee based either on payroll (2 to 8 percent) or a fixed fee per employee. The business, in effect, "leases" its employees; thus it participates in an "employee leasing program." In theory, at least, nothing changes at the business except that, in relation to personnel matters, the employee reports to the PEO. But employees still come to work, still take their day-to-day directions from the management, but now, in effect, they work for both the business and the PEO—but their checks come from the PEO.

Employee leasing became a visible economic model in the 1980s, when the phrase "employee leasing" also first occurred. But the phrase is being used less and less in the mid-2000s. In its stead, people refer to "outsourcing human resources" or simply "working with a PEO." Terminology continues to be murky because a milder form of this type of outsourcing (alternative 3 shown above) also exists. It is called "administrative services outsourcing"; companies that offer this service are known as ASOs. An ASO takes over the *administrative* functions only of the human resources activity but does *not* become a co-employer. Businesses also avoid the word "leasing" of late because, apparently, it has negative connotations—you lease a car, not a person....

DRIVING FORCES AND BENEFITS

When ABC Business outsources its employees to XYZ PEO, the employees almost always immediately benefit because ABC did not have such fringes as health insurance but XYZ offers fringes. Since the employees are now "co-employed" by XYZ—and it is in XYZ's interest to keep unemployment costs down, employees laid off by ABC might more easily find work at one of XYZ's other clients.

ABC, as a small business, can now attract employees more easily because its benefits package is as good as that of much larger companies. Furthermore, ABC's management no longer needs to manage its personnel; XYZ takes care of it all. Thus ABC gets intangible benefits, a more attractive employment package, avoids administrative tasks, and, furthermore, its actual payroll costs may also go down because overall unemployment levies and workers' compensation payments may be lower. For all this ABC pays XYZ a fee. If in ABC's calculus the positives outweigh the fee, the deal is attractive.

XYZ is in the business of collecting fees for a service. It achieves low enough costs to offer fringe benefits and a lower payroll cost as a carrot through economies of scale. It buys medical insurance for 80,000 employees as a group—of which ABC's 25 employees are but a drop in a lake. The PEO's unemployment costs will be much lower because its 50,000 employees (pieced together from some 1,700 small businesses) will have a lower layoff experience. These lower unemployment cost savings are passed on to ABC and others, some of whom, alone, would have much higher unemployment and workers' compensation costs. Similarly, XYZ's administrative structure is supported by large numbers and therefore overheads are spread over many employees, not a few. XYZ targets as its market small businesses which have no fringe benefits but would like to offer them.

This hypothetical—but typical—case illustrates the benefits enjoyed by all the parties. These benefits act as the driving force behind this commercial development.

If instead of working with XYZ the owner of ABC had chosen to outsource the administrative labors of dealing with employees to an ASO, it would still have to pay a fee but would not be able to offer a richer benefits package or benefit from lower unemployment insurance or workers' compensation costs of the 50,000 employee group.

DISADVANTAGES

A very real but intangible negative of joining with a PEO is ambiguity created by the "co-employment" clause of PEO contracts. Under such arrangements, both the business and the PEO have equal rights to hire, fire, and direct employees. The employee suddenly has two masters. Looked at from the employee's perspective without too much reflection, one party has brought health benefits and pays the salary; the PEO, furthermore, is a large organization with potential other employment to offer; the other party, the small business, just manages the work—and handles the frictions that arise there. Potentially serious conflicts of loyalty are likely to develop. The small business has, in effect, delegated to others a vital, perhaps a central, aspect of its business. Employees may feel grateful because benefits have increased and yet they may wonder: this form of relationship is rather new. In short, ambiguity is a fundamental problem of the relationship between the business and its people after the PEO has "moved in."

From the business owner's point of view, loss of control, generally, is the chief downside of farming out the people. The PEO industry has seen some notable failures which have left employees stranded without pay and benefits—and the owner holding a huge empty bag. In a number of states litigation by the state is underway to eliminate the benefits PEOs have achieved by pooling the employees of many organizations into one. Unemployment taxes are levied on businesses based on their layoff experience. A company that hasn't laid off anyone in five years pays a much lower rate than one that routinely lets go one or two people every year. The PEOs, in effect, pool not only employees but layoff experience and thus, in the aggregate, lower the payments to state unemployment systems. For this reason, litigation is under way to force PEOs to pay unemployment taxes based on the experience of member businesses, not on the collective.

TRENDS

The PEO industry has been expanding and is in the process of consolidation; companies, of course, benefit substantially from size in spreading risks and absorbing overhead costs; in turn, large size provides greater security to clients. As Mike Vogel reported in *Florida Trend* (Florida being one of the early acceptors of this industry), PEOs anticipated double-digit growth in 2006—based in large part on the hiring activity of their clients. The top 10 companies in the U.S., Vogel reported, citing data from *Staffing Industry Report* had revenues of $19.6 billion in 2003.

The PEOs are, in a sense, a consequence of U.S. industry's fascination with outsourcing. The industry has and continues to concentrate on its primary market, companies in the 50 or fewer employee category. But, as Jessica Marquez reported in *Workforce Management*, ASOs, which target the midsize employer, are feeling increasing competition from PEOs now in their efforts to take over the human resources functions of these larger companies.

Interestingly, as the power of unions continued to wane in the mid-2000s and union membership continued to decrease year after year, another form of labor aggregation into ever larger pools was evolving—but this time under the leadership of the corporate sectors, small and large.

BIBLIOGRAPHY

Clark, Edie. "Working Definition." *Security Management.* August 2005.

Erlam, Alexander N. "Employment Liability." *Security Management.* September 2005.

Genn, Adina. "Outsourcing HR Functions Gains Traction." *Long Island Business News.* 13 August 2004.

Lane, Amy. "Groups Feud Over PEOs in SUTA Dumping." *Crain's Detroit Business.* 7 March 2005.

Marquez, Jessica. "PEOs May Heat Competition in Middle Market." *Workforce Management.* 30 January 2006.

"Outsourcing HR: Advisory firms are growing and staffs are burgeoning. Now there's a way to buy out of your personnel headaches." *Financial Planning.* 1 February 2006.

Vogel, Mike. "Growing Their Base." *Florida Trend.* January 2005.

Yager, Milan P. and Joan Szabo. "The Truth About PEOs." *Entrepreneur.* January 2006.

Zimmer, Matt. "Outsourcing: From soup to nuts or a la carte?" *Club Management.* December 2004.

Hillstrom, Northern Lights
updated by Magee, ECDI

EMPLOYEE MANUALS

The employee manual or handbook can be a valuable tool for any business. Ideally, it should provide detailed guidelines for the employment relationship and document company policies and procedures for both employer and employee. For example, handbooks define an employer's legal responsibilities by putting policies on record; make employees aware of rights, benefits, and policy, providing legal protections to employers; provide background information on the organization; and serve as employee reference tools. Because of its many uses, it is crucial for businesses to craft their employee manuals in a careful and thoughtful fashion.

Indeed, employee manuals have become the focus of considerable employment-related litigation in recent years, as growing numbers of workers and employers became enmeshed in legal tangles over workplace actions, expectations, etc. "Since there is no reason to believe that this flood of litigation will slow any time soon, an employer can help protect itself by drafting a handbook that clearly sets forth its policies and covers the important topics in a way that will not come back to haunt," wrote Paul Berninger in *Business Courier*. "The specific contents will vary widely, depending on the size of the company and the nature of the business, but there are some elements that every employee handbook should contain."

TYPICAL CONTENTS

The contents of employee manuals should be limited to statements of fact, avoiding vague or blanket pronouncements on issues that are generally addressed on a case-by-case basis (such as job security). "Make only statements of fact regarding company policies and procedures, avoiding generalizations, and reiterate the employer's right to change employment practices and procedures at any time without prior notice to employees," Berninger counseled.

Most employee manuals contain these basic sections:

1. A welcome from the president, the company's mission or vision statement, and a brief history of the company.

2. The company's discrimination and harassment policies, including complaint and investigation procedures. By incorporating these policies in the manual, an employee understands that there is no tolerance for such activity. This language helps ensure a productive, efficient workplace, and can protect the company from legal liability. "You must make sure you have a discrimination and harassment policy that's right at the cutting edge of the law," explained one attorney in *Workforce*. "There are a lot of laws

that say the existence of these procedures may well provide the employer with a safe harbor, shielding it from liability."

3. Employee classifications and an explanation of them.

4. General pay and overtime provisions. Often, there are state laws that must be reflected with regard to pay, so this section should be thoroughly reviewed.

5. Hiring and recruiting policy, including a statement regarding equal employment opportunity.

6. Sections on general procedures such as work hours, dress code, and other office-specific policies.

7. Sections describing benefits, including vacation, leaves of absence, insurance, pensions, sick time, etc. Again, because many of these are covered by state as well as federal regulations, it is important to review these carefully before publication. For example, employers covered by the Family and Medical Leave Act must include information about employee rights and obligations under the FMLA.

8. Statement of disciplinary procedures, including a clear list of behaviors that can result in immediate termination. Drug and alcohol policies are typically explained here.

9. Outline of grievance procedures. Company privacy policies, extending from employee lockers to their use of the Internet.

10. An employment-at-will statement, defining the rights of the employer to terminate an employee at any time. This right is also granted the employee, who may resign at any time for any reason. An acknowledgment, to be signed and returned to the employer, stating that an employee has received, read, and understood the information contained in the manual. This is a vital but often overlooked aspect of the handbook creation and distribution process, for it provides significant legal protection for employers.

Disclaimers may also be added, such as a disclaimer stating that the manual does not represent a contract made with the employee, or a disclaimer stating that the list of company rules and procedures is not exhaustive. Such disclaimers protect the company from potential legal action in these areas. Whatever liability shielding language is employed, however, businesses should make sure that all handbook contents are carefully reviewed by legal counsel before publication.

REVIEW

If at all possible, the employee manual should be reviewed by the company's legal counsel to ensure that it conforms to federal and state laws and states legal matters in an appropriate language. As reported by Todd Raphael in *Workforce,* a small private service company in San Diego won the World's Worst Manual contest in 2002 for an employee manual filled with outright errors, including a misstatement of California's overtime rules. As Raphael said in his article, "This isn't the kind of contest you want to win."

MAINTENANCE, DISTRIBUTION, AND UPDATING ISSUES

When constructing or maintaining an employee manual, it is worthwhile to consider using a team approach, bringing in people from all areas of the company who are impacted by the policies embodied in the manual. This group insures that policies are not developed and reviewed solely by human resources representatives (although their input can certainly be valuable) or the owner, but by a representative cross-section of the entire company. If this technique is used, it is critical to assign trustworthy people to manage the project and see to its completion.

An employee manual should be distributed at the time of hire to all incoming employees. This does not mean that the manual does not ever change, however. If revisions are to be made, a manual must first state that the employer has the right to revise the policies in it at any time. It should then be redistributed (in whole or in part, depending on its format) to all employees, with a detailed description of the revisions made. Generally, the manual should be reviewed once per year to see if revisions are necessary. In addition, in instances where federal and state laws materially impact a company's operations or policies, relevant sections should be updated immediately, then disseminated to all affected employees.

BIBLIOGRAPHY

Barrier, Michael. "Going by the Handbook." *Success.* September 2000.

Berninger, Paul. "Employee Handbook Can Work For or Against You." *Business Courier Serving Cincinnati-Northern Kentucky.* 13 October 2000.

Lee, Sean, and Leonard H. Kanterman. "Uncovering Substance Abusers." *Medical Economics.* 2 December 2005.

Raphael, Todd. "Don't Go By this Book." *Workforce.* July 2002.

Steingold, Fred S. Edited by Amy DelPo. *The Employer's Legal Handbook.* Seventh Edition. Nolo Press, 2005.

Williams, Thomas. "How to Write an Employee Manual." *Detroiter.* December 2002.

Hillstrom, Northern Lights
updated by Magee, ECDI

EMPLOYEE MOTIVATION

Employee motivation is the level of energy, commitment, and creativity that a company's workers bring to their jobs. Whether the economy is growing or shrinking, finding ways to motivate employees is always a management concern. Competing theories stress either incentives or employee involvement (empowerment). Employee motivation can sometimes be particularly problematic for small businesses. The owner has often spent years building a company hands-on and therefore finds it difficult to delegate meaningful responsibilities to others. But entrepreneurs should be mindful of such pitfalls: the effects of low employee motivation on small businesses can be harmful. Such problems include complacency, disinterest, even widespread discouragement. Such attitudes can cumulate into crises.

But the small business can also provide an ideal atmosphere for employee motivation: employees see the results of their contributions directly; feedback is swift and visible. A smoothly working and motivated work force also frees the owner from day-to-day chores for thinking of long-term development. Furthermore, tangible and emotional reward can mean retention of desirable employees. People thrive in creative work environments and want to make a difference. Ideally the work result itself will give them a feeling of accomplishment—but well-structured reward and recognition programs can underline this consequence.

WHAT MOTIVATES?

One approach to employee motivation has been to view "add-ins" to an individual's job as the primary factors in improving performance. Endless mixes of employee benefits—such as health care, life insurance, profit sharing, employee stock ownership plans, exercise facilities, subsidized meal plans, child care availability, company cars, and more—have been used by companies in their efforts to maintain happy employees in the belief that happy employees are motivated employees.

Many modern theorists, however, propose that the motivation an employee feels toward his or her job has less to do with material rewards than with the design of the job itself. Studies as far back as 1950 have shown that highly segmented and simplified jobs resulted in lower employee morale and output. Other consequences of low employee motivation include absenteeism and high turnover, both of which are very costly for any company. As a result, "job enlargement" initiatives began to crop up in major companies in the 1950s.

While terminology changes, the tenets of employee motivation remain relatively unchanged from findings over half a century ago. Today's buzzwords include "empowerment," "quality circles," and "teamwork." Empowerment gives autonomy and allows an employee to have ownership of ideas and accomplishments, whether acting alone or in teams. Quality circles and the increasing occurrence of teams in today's work environments give employees opportunities to reinforce the importance of the work accomplished by members as well as receive feedback on the efficacy of that work.

In small businesses, which may lack the resources to enact formal employee motivation programs, managers can nonetheless accomplish the same basic principles. In order to help employees feel that their jobs are meaningful and that their contributions are valuable to the company, the small business owner needs to communicate the company's purpose to employees. This communication should take the form of words as well as actions. In addition, the small business owner should set high standards for employees, but also remain supportive of their efforts when goals cannot be reached. It may also be helpful to allow employees as much autonomy and flexibility as possible in how their jobs are performed. Creativity will be encouraged if honest mistakes are corrected but not punished. Finally, the small business owner should take steps to incorporate the vision of employees for the company with his or her own vision. This will motivate employees to contribute to the small business's goals, as well as help prevent stagnation in its direction and purpose.

MOTIVATION METHODS

There are as many different methods of motivating employees today as there are companies operating in the global business environment. Still, some strategies are prevalent across all organizations striving to improve employee motivation. The best employee motivation efforts will focus on what the employees deem to be important. It may be that employees within the same department of the same organization will have different motivators. Many organizations today find that flexibility in job design and reward systems has resulted in employees' increased longevity with the company, improved productivity, and better morale.

Empowerment Giving employees more responsibility and decision-making authority increases their realm of control over the tasks for which they are held responsible and better equips them to carry out those tasks. As a result, feelings of frustration arising from being held accountable for something one does not have the resources to carry out are diminished. Energy is diverted from self-preservation to improved task accomplishment.

Creativity and Innovation At many companies, employees with creative ideas do not express them to management for fear that their input will be ignored or ridiculed. Company approval and toeing the company line have become so ingrained in some working environments that both the employee and the organization suffer. When the power to create in the organization is pushed down from the top to line personnel, employees who know a job, product, or service best are given the opportunity to use their ideas to improve it. The power to create motivates employees and benefits the organization in having a more flexible work force, using more wisely the experience of its employees, and increasing the exchange of ideas and information among employees and departments. These improvements also create an openness to change that can give a company the ability to respond quickly to market changes and sustain a first mover advantage in the marketplace.

Learning If employees are given the tools and the opportunities to accomplish more, most will take on the challenge. Companies can motivate employees to achieve more by committing to perpetual enhancement of employee skills. Accreditation and licensing programs for employees are an increasingly popular and effective way to bring about growth in employee knowledge and motivation. Often, these programs improve employees' attitudes toward the client and the company, while bolstering self-confidence. Supporting this assertion, an analysis of factors which influence motivation-to-learn found that it is directly related to the extent to which training participants believe that such participation will affect their job or career utility. In other words, if the body of knowledge gained can be applied to the work to be accomplished, then the acquisition of that knowledge will be a worthwhile event for the employee and employer.

Quality of Life The number of hours worked each week by American workers is on the rise, and many families have two adults working those increased hours. Under these circumstances, many workers are left wondering how to meet the demands of their lives beyond the workplace. Often, this concern occurs while at work and may reduce an employee's productivity and morale. Companies that have instituted flexible employee arrangements have gained motivated employees whose productivity has increased. Programs incorporating flextime, condensed workweeks, or job sharing, for example, have been successful in focusing overwhelmed employees toward the work to be done and away from the demands of their private lives.

Monetary Incentive For all the championing of alternative motivators, money still occupies a major place in the mix of motivators. The sharing of a company's profits gives incentive to employees to produce a quality product, perform a quality service, or improve the quality of a process within the company. What benefits the company directly benefits the employee. Monetary and other rewards are being given to employees for generating cost-savings or process-improving ideas, to boost productivity and reduce absenteeism. Money is effective when it is directly tied to an employee's ideas or accomplishments. Nevertheless, if not coupled with other, non-monetary motivators, its motivating effects are short-lived. Further, monetary incentives can prove counterproductive if not made available to all members of the organization.

Other Incentives Study after study has found that the most effective motivators of workers are non-monetary. Monetary systems are insufficient motivators, in part because expectations often exceed results and because disparity between salaried individuals may divide rather than unite employees. Proven non-monetary positive motivators foster team spirit and include recognition, responsibility, and advancement. Managers who recognize the "small wins" of employees, promote participatory environments, and treat employees with fairness and respect will find their employees to be more highly motivated. One company's managers brainstormed to come up with 30 powerful rewards that cost little or nothing to implement. The most effective rewards, such as letters of commendation and time off from work, enhanced personal fulfillment and self-respect. Over the longer term, sincere praise and personal gestures are far more effective and more economical than awards of money alone. In the end, a program that combines monetary reward systems and satisfies intrinsic, self-actualizing needs may be the most potent employee motivator.

SEE ALSO *Employee Benefits; Employee Compensation*

BIBLIOGRAPHY
Battisti, Pete. "Reward to Motivate." *Walls & Ceilings*. December 2005.

Frase-Blunt, Martha. "Driving Home Your Awards Program." *HRMagazine*. February 2001.

Hohman, Kevin M. "A Passion for Success: Employee buy in is the key." *Do-It-Yourself Retailing*. February 2006.

"In Brief: Recognition is greatest motivator." *Employee Benefits*. 10 February 2006.

"Incentive Schemes are Still Failing to Retain Staff." *Employee Benefits*. 4 November 2005.

Parker, Owen. "Pay and Employee Commitment." *Ivey Business Journal*. January 2001.

"Providing Opportunities to Grow." *Computer Weekly*. 7 February 2006.

White, Carol-Ann. "Expert's View on Managing Demotivated Employees." *Personnel Today*. 15 November 2005.

Hillstrom, Northern Lights
updated by Magee, ECDI

EMPLOYEE PERFORMANCE APPRAISALS

An employee performance appraisal is a process—often combining both written and oral elements—whereby management evaluates and provides feedback on employee job performance, including steps to improve or redirect activities as needed. Documenting performance provides a basis for pay increases and promotions. Appraisals are also important to help staff members improve their performance and as an avenue by which they can be rewarded or recognized for a job well done. In addition, they can serve a host of other functions, providing a launching point from which companies can clarify and shape responsibilities in accordance with business trends, clear lines of management-employee communication, and spur re-examinations of potentially hoary business practices. Yet Joel Myers notes in *Memphis Business Journal* that "in many organizations, performance appraisals only occur when management is building a case to terminate someone. It's no wonder that the result is a mutual dread of the performance evaluation session—something to be avoided, if at all possible. This is no way to manage and motivate people. Performance appraisal is supposed to be a developmental experience for the employee and a 'teaching moment' for the manager."

PERFORMANCE APPRAISAL AND DEVELOPMENT

While the term *performance appraisal* has meaning for most small business owners, it might be helpful to consider the goals of an appraisal system. They are as follows:

1. To improve the company's productivity

2. To make informed personnel decisions regarding promotion, job changes, and termination

3. To identify what is required to perform a job (goals and responsibilities of the job)

4. To assess an employee's performance against these goals

5. To work to improve the employee's performance by naming specific areas for improvement, developing a plan aimed at improving these areas, supporting the employee's efforts at improvement via feedback and assistance, and ensuring the employee's involvement and commitment to improving his or her performance.

All of these goals can be more easily realized if the employer makes an effort to establish the performance appraisal process as a dialogue in which the ultimate purpose is the betterment of all parties. To create and maintain this framework, employers need to inform workers of their value, praise them for their accomplishments, establish a track record of fair and honest feedback, be consistent in their treatment of all employees, and canvass workers for their own insights into the company's processes and operations.

A small business with few employees or one that is just starting to appraise its staff may choose to use a pre-packaged appraisal system, consisting of either printed forms or software. Software packages can be customized either by using a firm's existing appraisal methods or by selecting elements from a list of attributes that describe a successful employee's work habits such as effective communication, timeliness, and ability to perform work requested. Eventually, however, many companies choose to develop their own appraisal form and system in order to accurately reflect an employee's performance in light of the business's own unique goals and culture. In developing an appraisal system for a small business, an entrepreneur needs to consider the following:

1. Size of staff
2. Employees on an alternative work schedule
3. Goals of company and desired employee behaviors to help achieve goals
4. Measuring performance/work
5. Pay increases and promotions
6. Communication of appraisal system and individual performance
7. Performance planning

Size of Staff A small business with few employees may choose to use an informal approach with employees. This entails meeting with each employee every six months or once a year and discussing an individual's work performance and progress since the last discussion. Feedback can be provided verbally, without developing or using a standard appraisal form, but in many cases, legal experts counsel employers to maintain written records in order to provide themselves with greater legal protections. As a

company increases its staff, a more formal system using a written appraisal form developed internally or externally should always be used, with the results of the appraisal being tied to salary increases or bonuses. Whether the appraisal is provided verbally or in writing, a small business owner needs to provide consistent feedback on a regular basis so that employees can improve their work performance.

Alternative Work Schedules Employees working alternative work schedules—working at home, working part-time, job-sharing, etc.—will most likely need to have their performance appraised differently than regular full-time staffs in order to be fairly evaluated. An alternative work schedule may require different duties to perform a job and these new responsibilities should be incorporated into the appraisal. A small business owner should also be careful to ensure that these employees are treated fairly with regard to both the appraisal and resulting promotions.

Company Goals and Desired Performance The performance of employees, especially in a smaller firm, is an essential factor in any company's ability to meet its goals. In a one-person business, goal-setting and achieving is a matter of transforming words into action, but moving the business towards its goals in a larger firm means that the employer has to figure out each person's role in that success, communicate that role to him or her, and reward or correct their performance. It also means that the appraisal should incorporate factors such as collaborative ability and sense of teamwork, not just individual performance.

Measuring/Assessing Performance Once a list of tasks and attributes is developed, a small business owner or manager needs to determine how to measure an employee's performance on these tasks. Measurement provides another objective element to the appraisal. Ideally, measurement would be taken against previous performance, whether of the individual employee, the group, or the company at large. If a company is just developing its appraisal system or does not have a baseline performance to measure against, it should develop realistic goals based on business needs or on the similar performance of competitors.

Pay Increases and Promotions When developing an appraisal system, a small business owner needs to consider the connection between the appraisal and pay increases or promotions. While performance feedback for development/improvement purposes may be given verbally, a written summary of the individual's work performance must accompany a pay increase or promotion (or demotion or termination). It is crucial, therefore, that a manager or small business owner regularly document an employee's job performance.

The method of pay increases impacts the appraisal as well. If a small business uses merit-based increases, the appraisal form would include a rating of the employee on certain tasks. If skill-based pay is used, the appraisal would list skills acquired and level of competency. Appraisals and resulting salary increases that take into account group or company performance should include the individual's contributions to those goals.

Communicating the System A performance appraisal system is only effective if it is properly communicated and understood by employees. When devising an appraisal system for his or her company, an entrepreneur may want to consider involving staff in its development. Supporters contend that this promotes buy-in and understanding of the plan, as well as ensuring that the appraisal takes into account all tasks at the company. If the small business owner is unable to involve her staff, she should walk through the system with each employee or manager and have the manager do the same, requesting feedback and making adjustments as necessary.

Communicating Performance and Planning Part of the appraisal system is the actual communication of the performance assessment. While this assessment may be written, it should always be provided verbally as well. This provides an opportunity to answer any questions the employee may have on the assessment, as well as to provide context or further detail for brief assessments. Finally, the employee and the entrepreneur or manager should make plans to meet again to develop a plan aimed at improving performance and reaching agreed-upon goals for the following review period. This planning session should relate company and/or group goals to the individual's tasks and goals for the review period and provide a basis for the next scheduled review.

TYPES OF APPRAISALS AND ASSESSMENT TERMS

Traditional In a traditional appraisal, a manager sits down with an employee and discusses performance for the previous performance period, usually a single year. The discussion is based on the manager's observations of the employee's abilities and performance of tasks as noted in a job description. The performance is rated, with the ratings tied to salary percentage increases. However, as David Antonioni notes in *Compensation & Benefits,* "The traditional merit raise process grants even poor performers an automatic cost of living increase, thereby creating per-

ceived inequity.... In addition, most traditional performance appraisal forms use too many rating categories and distribute ratings using a forced-distribution format." Antonioni suggests the appraisal form use just three rating categories—outstanding, fully competent, and unsatisfactory—as most managers can assess their best and worst employees, with the rest falling in between.

Self-Appraisal Somewhat self-explanatory, the self-appraisal is used in the performance appraisal process to encourage staff members to take responsibility for their own performance by assessing their own achievements or failures and promoting self-management of development goals. It also prepares employees to discuss these points with their manager. It may be used in conjunction with or as a part of other appraisal processes, but does not substitute for an assessment of the employee's performance by a manager.

Employee-Initiated Reviews In an employee-initiated review system, employees are informed that they can ask for a review from their manager. This type of on-demand appraisal is not meant to replace a conventional review process. Rather, it can be used to promote an attitude of self-management among workers. Adherents to this type of review process contend that it promotes regular communication between staff and managers. Detractors, though, note that it is dependent on the employees' initiative, making it a less than ideal alternative for some workers with quiet, retiring personalities or confidence issues.

360-Degree Feedback 360-degree feedback in the performance appraisal process refers to feedback on an employee's performance being provided by the manager, different people or departments an employee interacts with (peer evaluation), external customers, and the employee himself. This type of feedback includes employee-generated feedback on management performance (also known as upward appraisals). As a company grows in size, a small business owner should consider using 360-degree feedback to appraise employees. Communication in a business of ten people varies wildly from that of a company of 100 persons and 360-degree feedback ensures that an employee's performance is observed by those who work most closely with him. Small business owners or managers can either include the feedback in the performance review or choose to provide it informally for development purposes.

LEGAL ISSUES

Given that the results of a performance appraisal are often used to support a promotion, termination, salary increase, or job change, they are looked at very closely in employee discrimination suits. Besides providing a written summary of the appraisal to the employee, a small business owner would be well-advised to ensure the following with regards to the system at large:

- Job expectations as well as the appraisal system and its impact on employee's work status are adequately communicated to all employees

- Performance measures are related to the job being performed

- Managers or co-workers providing input into the appraisal must be sufficiently trained as to be able to provide objective input

- Employees are given timely feedback on performance and a reasonable amount of time and support in improving their performance

Assistance in developing a system is available through a variety of sources including consultants, periodicals and books, and software. In addition, given the legal implications of appraisals, small business owners should have their companies' performance assessment processes, including training of managers and employees, reviewed by a qualified attorney.

BIBLIOGRAPHY

Antonioni, David. "Improve the Performance Management Process Before Discontinuing Performance Appraisals." *Compensation & Benefits, Vol. 26.*

Grote, Dick. "Performance Appraisals: Solving Tough Challenges." *HR Magazine.* July 2000.

"How to Conduct a Performance Review." *Personnel Today.* 14 February 2006.

Koziel, Mark J. "Giving and Receiving Performance Evaluations." *CPA Journal.* December 2000.

Myers, Joel. "How to Evaluate Your Evaluation System." *Memphis Business Journal.* 9 February 2001.

Olsztynski, Jim. "How to Critique, Criticize Important for Supervisors." *Snips.* December 2005.

Thomson, Sally. "Food for Thought: Giving feedback to staff is a great test of a manager's skill." *Nursing Standard.* 23 November 2005.

Hillstrom, Northern Lights
updated by Magee, ECDI

EMPLOYEE PRIVACY

Rights to privacy are anchored fundamentally by the Fourth Amendment of the U.S. Constitution which provides against unreasonable searches and seizures in the citizen's home, but the prohibition applies to govern-

ment and does not cover every and all places where the citizen spends time. This right has been gradually enlarged, particularly in relation to sexual behavior—and government spying on it—but these developments have little or no bearing on the workplace. The citizen as an employee has rather limited rights to privacy in the workplace. During the hiring process, candidates may not be asked questions relating to sex-related issues, age, race, disability, religion, national origin, and veteran's status—prohibitions arising from the Civil Rights Act's anti-discrimination mandates. His or her personnel records at the company are also protected by law and may not be arbitrarily published. With these few exceptions, no rights to privacy exist unless they are actually granted by the employer.

Ever since the wide spread use of the Internet, pressures have been building to expand privacy rights to include private documents and files that may coexist with company files on business computers, but no significant changes in national policy or legislation were on record in the mid-2000s. On the contrary, due to highly publicized corporate scandals (Enron, WorldCom)—and the passage of the Sarbanes-Oxley Act which significantly ratcheted up record-keeping requirements—e-mail had achieved a status as official documentation to be safeguarded for litigation purposes.

ISSUES OF WORKPLACE PRIVACY

Legitimate claims by an employee that his or her privacy has been violated on the job ultimately rest on whether or not the employer, at its option, created a reasonable expectation of privacy by the employee. An employer, for example, who explicitly states in a company policy that all activities on the job must be company-related and private activities must be pursued off-site has by this policy *removed* such expectations. On the other hand, in a company that lacks such a policy and where it is common for employees to use their break time to do personal tasks at their desks—pay bills and such—a reasonable expectation of privacy may be held up in court. The small business wishing to avoid ambiguous situations is well advised to publish a policy; the policy may prohibit or allow private activities, but if it allows them, then the privacy created by this policy must also be respected.

Employees, on the other hand, are most prudent if they recognize that no privacy rights actually exist and act accordingly. Some of the issues are highlighted next.

Searches and Seizures An employer has the right to inspect personal belongings (bags, purses, briefcases, cars, lockers, desks, etc.), except when the employer has created a reasonable expectation of privacy. These expectations can be raised if the employee is given a key to a desk or if the employer has disseminated a written policy explicitly stating that it will not make such inspections.

Monitoring Computer, E-mail, Internet, and Fax Use Businesses have some significant rights in this regard: they own the equipment. But if these resources are knowingly made available for private employee use then a reasonable expectation of privacy has been created. Management must therefore refrain from looking at data the employee claims are private. If criminal activity is suspected, appropriate law enforcement officials will, of course, have access to such data.

Monitoring Telephone Calls Companies are allowed to monitor calls to make sure that they are business-related and to record them for training purposes.

Surveillance and Investigation Many surveillance methods (cameras, ID checkpoints, etc.) are legal; so are investigations of employees provided that they are reasonable and undertaken for work-related purposes.

Drug testing These policies have been validated by the courts, although criticism of the practice remains intense in some quarters. Drug testing is a popular measure in many industries, and it is practiced by perhaps 70 percent of large American companies. Furthermore, it is specifically mandated by legislation in the transportation industries. In other industries and for many small businesses, the attitude towards drug testing is quite different. Drug testing can be expensive, disruptive, and unpopular among employees.

TRENDS AND CYCLES

As Lucas Conley reported in *Fast Company,* "In the 1830s, workers at New England's textile mills lived in company houses, worked in company factories, and worshipped at the company church. Attendance was mandatory. Milton Hershey and Henry Ford are both famous for having hired detectives to keep an eye on their employees outside of work. Ford even created his own sociological department, staffed by 50 inspectors who kept tabs on autoworkers' behavior off the job. Misbehave, and your wallet got a little lighter come payday."

Corporate policies ultimately reflect the general culture on the one hand and changing economic/legal realities on the other—so that permissive and scrutinizing policies have a cyclical nature. The massive economic expansion which began after World War II and has lasted ever since with but a few relatively brief pauses for breath produced an expansive atmosphere with improving benefit packages and the ubiquitous coffee break. Privacy issues have arisen as a consequence of two developments—high rates of illegal drug use since the 1970s and electronic communications since the 1990s. The first led to drug testing, the second—in that it enables employees to use company time to live what amounts to a "virtual" home-life (paying bills, chatting, corresponding, and entertaining themselves with anything at all, including pornography)—to electronic monitoring. Other forms of invasive contact between employees and their employers, namely searches to detect theft of company property, continued unabated during the entire latter half of the 20th century. Such invasions have not been much remarked upon because the public clearly sees the rationale behind them. E-life on company time, however, appears to fall into another category: it is not viewed as theft.

In the mid-2000s, the trend was decidedly toward "scrutiny," especially of e-mail and unwelcome smut-files on business computers. Conley reported on this trend citing data from the American Management Association. In 1997, 15 percent of large U.S. companies monitored the e-mail of their employees; in 1999, the percent had increased to 27, in 2001 to 47, in 2003 to 52 percent. Because of kibitzing on e-mail, more and more companies are installing automated tracking systems that filter sites visited by people using corporate systems—and alerting the powers-that-be when suspicious sites are frequent destinations.

Technology to do this sort of electronic spying was also improving by leaps and bounds in the mid-2000s. But the corporate motivations behind such activities were hard to assign unambiguously to spying: the Sarbanes-Oxley Act has rigorously tightened rules on record keeping; courts have ruled that e-mail has the status of real documents. Many new software packages are designed to search e-mail by content in order to archive it by appropriate categories. If in that process abuses of corporate systems are detected, it is not surprising that some companies take corrective action.

PRIVACY IN THE SMALL BUSINESS

In a very real sense there is less privacy in a small business (as there is less privacy inside a family) than in larger groupings: employees and their managers interact more; everyone knows everyone else; slacking off by employees is more easily noticed, indeed tends to be felt by others immediately, and, often, slackers are corrected by peer pressure before their offenses ever reach the manager's or the owner's attention. In the well-run business, management deals with abuses quickly and effectively. Indeed, from a small business perspective, there is something contemptible about automated tracking systems—or the boss secretly searching through an employee's desk after work. There are more straight forward ways of dealing with problems.

SEE ALSO *Downloading Issues; Employee Rights*

BIBLIOGRAPHY
Conley, Lucas. "The Privacy Arms Race." *Fast Company.* July 2004.

Halbert, Terry, and Elaine Ingulli. *Law & Ethics in the Business Environment.* West, 2006.

Schramm, Jennifer. "Privacy at Work." *HRMagazine.* April 2005.

Volkert, Lora. "Workplace Privacy? Laws give employers wide scope to snoop." *Idaho Business Review, Boise.* 28 November 2005.

Wakefield, Robin L. "Computer Monitoring and Surveillance: Balancing privacy with security." *The CPA Journal.* July 2004.

Wilson, Jeffrey D. "E-privacy: Snoop out problems using your company's e-mail." *Detroiter.* May-June 2005.

Darnay, ECDI

EMPLOYEE REFERENCES

Employee references are the positive or negative comments about an employee's job performance provided to a prospective employer. In most cases, a prospective employer will contact a person's current or former employer to seek references as part of the process of considering that person for a new position. Prospective employers check references during the interview process in order to ensure that a candidate's assertions about his or her job skills and work experience are accurate. In fact, obtaining references is one of the most important parts of the hiring process because it can provide valuable information that sets one candidate apart from others and facilitates a sound hiring decision.

Although seeking references has a number of benefits for the prospective employer, providing references can be a complicated issue for the current or former employer. As Olga Aikin pointed out in *People Management,* companies that provide references have a duty both to the employee who is the subject of the reference and to the prospective employer who is the recipient of the reference. Giving a negative reference may expose the company to legal liability if the former employee does not get a desired job and decides to sue for defamation or slander. But providing a falsely positive reference or failing to disclose potentially damaging information can leave the company open to legal liability as well.

If a candidate is selected for a position on the basis of a reference and then commits a crime or causes harm to another person while on the job, the new employer might sue the provider of the reference. Several court decisions have held a former employer liable for crimes committed by a former employee in a new job because that employer had provided a positive reference and failed to notify the prospective employer about one or more negative aspects of the former employee's performance. As a result of these dual sources of liability, providing references sometimes leaves small business owners stuck in the middle. "The issue of references is always controversial, involving a balance of employers' fears of legal liability, interests in providing relevant information to prospective employers, and concerns for fairness to former employees," Ellen Harshman and Denise R. Chachere wrote in the *Journal of Business Ethics.*

AVOIDING LEGAL LIABILITY WHEN PROVIDING REFERENCES

In recent years, many companies have tried to avoid the legal liability involved in providing employee references by enacting policies that strictly limit the information they are willing to supply. When asked for a reference, these companies will not provide any assessment of an employee's job performance. Instead, they will only confirm the person's job title, dates of employment, and salary. "Due to legal ramifications, corporate executives are increasingly wary of being specific about former employees and their work histories," Max Messmer wrote in *Business Credit.* "Providing references can be a double-edged sword." In fact, Messmer noted that 74 percent of Fortune 1000 companies have a policy limiting employee references to a confirmation of basic employment information. However, half of the executives polled said they were willing to bend the company rules in order to give positive references for their best performers.

According to Robert A. Siegel and Anne E. Garrett in the *Los Angeles Business Journal,* small business owners have two main options in providing employee references without exposing themselves to legal liability. First, as noted above, they can simply verify the candidate's basic employment information without making any positive or negative assessment of his or her performance or qualifications. This is known as a "no comment" reference. It has become the policy at a wide range of companies, despite the fact that the prospective employer gains very little information upon which to base a hiring decision.

The second option open to small business owners is to provide a "full disclosure" reference. This type of reference often consists of a letter containing all the relevant facts of a person's employment, including an appraisal of their performance and potential. Experts suggest that an employer cannot be held liable for defamation in providing this type of reference as long as it is made without malice and the information is based on credible evidence. In fact, several states have enacted laws protecting employers from civil liability when they provide references that include job performance information. But some employers still choose to play it safe by only providing information based on performance appraisals that were signed by the former employee.

"In making a decision between the two alternatives, employers will have to balance the value of full disclosure to prospective employers against the risks of litigation presented by that choice," Siegel and Garrett wrote. "While full disclosure is viewed by many observers as the most desirable course, and it is clear that many employers will decide to select that alternative in the future, employers should do so with care in order to avoid litigation challenges by unhappy employees."

TIPS FOR EMPLOYERS CHECKING REFERENCES

With so many companies limiting the reference information they are willing to provide about former employees, small business owners often face a challenge in obtaining the information they need to make sound hiring decisions. In his article, Messmer supplied a series of suggestions for small business owners to use in obtaining references for prospective employees. First, he noted that companies should inform all prospective employees that their backgrounds will be checked carefully prior to hiring. It may be helpful to obtain written approval from all candidates to check their references, as well as a signed release allowing former employers to speak freely without fear of legal liability.

Messmer also suggested that the small business owner, or the person doing the hiring, call prospective employees' references themselves, rather than delegating the task to a human resources representative. It may be helpful to learn something about the candidate's former employer in advance in order to establish trust during the call. If the former employer is reluctant to provide much information—perhaps due to a company policy limiting employee references—Messmer suggests that the small business owner try to engage him or her in conversation by asking open-ended questions. If all else fails, Messmer recommends at least reading parts of the candidate's resume to the former employer and asking him or her to confirm the information it contains.

Other suggestions for small business owners include making sure the references you check are legitimate by calling a central switchboard number at the former employer's offices and asking for the person providing the reference, and checking several references for each

candidate to be certain you obtain a clear picture of their qualifications. The Internet may offer another source of basic information about some potential employees. However, small business owners should keep in mind that the same anti-discrimination laws apply to checking references that apply to interviewing: you cannot ask about a candidate's age, marital status, race, religion, etc. or use that information in your hiring decisions. In filling sensitive positions, it may be helpful to hire an outside firm to conduct a detailed background check.

Although the process of checking references may be time-consuming, it is a vital part of making good hiring decisions. "In the current low unemployment environment, it can be tempting to skip calling references in favor of making a quick decision," Messmer noted. "However, it is important not to overlook this important step in the employment process, because one poor hiring decision can affect the productivity of an entire department. Reference checking is hard work and not without pitfalls, but with a little extra effort it can be one of the most useful tools in making the right hiring decisions."

SEE ALSO *Employee Hiring*

BIBLIOGRAPHY
Aikin, Olga. "Watch Your Back, Referee." *People Management.* 13 April 2000.

Harshman, Ellen, and Denise R. Chachere. "Employee References: Between the Legal Devil and the Ethical Deep Blue Sea." *Journal of Business Ethics.* 1 January 2000.

Messmer, Max. "The Delicate Art of Reference Checking." *Business Credit.* May 1999.

Rogerson, Pam. "Insider-Insight: Employee References – Putting pen to paper. The fear of litigation and employment tribunals is putting employers off writing a reference for even valued staff. But it doesn't have to be that way." *Accountancy Age.* 14 July 2004.

Siegel, Robert A., and Anne E. Garrett. "Giving Employee References: Potential Pitfalls and Protections." *Los Angeles Business Journal.* 12 January 1998.

Swanson, Sandra. "Rave Reviews." *Crain's Chicago Business.* 3 October 2005.

Hillstrom, Northern Lights
updated by Magee, ECDI

EMPLOYEE REGISTRATION PROCEDURES

When a business hires a new employee, it is legally obligated to make sure that certain information about these new hires is provided to relevant government agencies. This information, which is provided by employees who fill out specific forms on their first day of employment, is used for tax purposes and to ensure that they are legally eligible to work in the United States.

The primary documents necessary for employee registration with the government are the Federal Tax Withholding Form (W-4), state and/or local tax withholding forms, and the Employment Eligibility Verification Form (I-9). Companies may also have specific forms for emergency notification and other critical information. The content of each form, as well as its purpose, should be fully explained to each employee.

Tax Withholding Forms "As an employer you have a tremendous fiduciary responsibility to collect and withhold taxes from employees on virtually every paycheck you issue," wrote Bob Adams in his *Adams Streetwise Small Business Start-Up*. "Throughout the United States, you must withhold an appropriate amount for federal income and other earnings-related taxes. Many states and some municipalities also require the payment of an income or other tax on earnings."

A cornerstone of the federal tax-gathering system is the federal W-4 form. This form, also known as the Employee's Withholding Allowance Certificate, provides the Internal Revenue Service with the filing status and withholding allowances of each employee. Once a new hire has determined his or her filing status and number of withholding allowances, the employer uses IRS tables to determine how much federal income tax should be withheld from the employee's wages (employers should understand that under this arrangement, they are essentially acting as agents for the taxing authority; the money that is withheld belongs to the taxing authority, even if possession has not been formally transferred).

Where applicable, employers also have to withhold state and local income taxes from worker paychecks. States and municipalities have dramatically different arrangements in this regard; some states for instance, have no state income tax, while others have fairly sizable ones. Employers who wish to keep up to speed on their requirements, if any, in this area should contact their local and state tax agencies for information on specific employee registration procedures, etc.

Employee Eligibility The other major employee registration procedure that small business owners need to pay attention to is the completion of the federal Form I-9. This document assures the U.S. Citizenship and Immigration Services (CIS, formerly the U.S. Immigration and Naturalization Service) that the employee is legally eligible to work in America. The Form I-9 is filled out by both the employee and the employer. For further information, consult the CIS web site at http://uscis.gov/graphics/index.htm. CIS is an element of the Department of Homeland Security.

BIBLIOGRAPHY

Adams, Bob. *Adams Streetwise Small Business Start-Up: Your Comprehensive Guide to Starting and Managing a Business.* Adams Media, 1996.

Josefowicz, Barbara. "Worker Classification and Employment Taxes." *Tax Advisor.* February 2001.

U.S. Internal Revenue Service. "Employer's Supplemental Tax Guide." 2000.

Weiss, Donald. *Fair, Square & Legal: Safe Hiring, Managing & Firing Practices.* AMACOM, 1993.

Hillstrom, Northern Lights
updated by Magee, ECDI

EMPLOYEE REINSTATEMENT

In the past, it was a rare occurrence if an employee left a company and then returned to it at a later date, either in the same position or a completely new one. Many companies strictly enforced policies that discouraged this sort of hiring of ex-employees, while the employees themselves would consider it an embarrassment to have to crawl back to their former workplace after failing to achieve success at another job. But times have changed—this type of activity has become a very common practice. In fact, it is so common that the term "boomerang employee" was coined to describe the types of workers who are able to include this type of situation on their resumes. Boomerang employees seem to be most common in technology fields, but can also be found in other work sectors (retail, for instance) as well.

When an employee leaves a company, he or she may have no intention of ever returning. But just to be on the safe side, the employee should make absolutely sure not to burn any bridges with the former employer. In most cases, the last impression can be the strongest one—it can even overshadow years of dedicated service. By leaving on good terms, the employee creates more options for a possible return, especially if the new job isn't all that it was cracked up to be. It is also wise for employees to keep in touch via phone calls, e-mails, or simple friendly letters in order to keep a pulse on the goings-on of the company. The practice of keeping in touch can also benefit the employer, who can use the ex-employee as a network source to find other talent within their particular industry.

There are other ways in which a boomerang employee can be valuable to a company. Many times when the employee leaves, he or she moves on to another company that allows him or her to gain new skills and more experience. In most instances, this allows the employee to perform at a higher level than before, and even can qualify him or her for a different and more skilled position. In addition, the employee's familiarity with the company from their previous tenure can only help make the transition back a positive experience for all involved. The company benefits because it is getting a known commodity rather than a fresh face that may have to undergo extensive training to familiarize itselves with the inner workings of the company.

Furthermore, studies have shown that boomerang employees tend to stick around longer in their second go-around with a company—proving to be more loyal than employees who are in the middle of their first stint with the company. Still, the employer should consider the feelings of his current employees (the ones who never left in the first place) and make sure that the rehire does not cause dissent within the ranks (especially if the boomerang employee gets a hefty raise and better position). In addition, both the employer and employee should be aware of policies that cover things like benefits, vacation time, the restoration of seniority, and other office perks in this type of situation.

SEE ALSO *Employee Hiring*

BIBLIOGRAPHY
Clarke, Robyn D. "Going for Round Two." *Black Enterprise.* June 2000.

Gannon, Joyce. "'Boomerang Employee's Club Grows as More Companies Rehire Former Workers." *Knight Ridder/Tribune Business News.* 18 April 2004.

Herman, Roger, and Joyce Gioia. "The Changing Corporate Landscape: Three trends to watch." *Incentive.* April 2003.

Lynn, Jacquelyn. "Many Happy Returns." *Entrepreneur.* November 2000.

Hillstrom, Northern Lights
updated by Magee, ECDI

EMPLOYEE RETENTION

Employees leave a company to get a better job—and for other reasons. It has cost the business money to hire and to train them; over time they have become more and more useful; to replace them will cost money. It frequently happens that the most effective employees have the most enterprise and initiative and also hold the better jobs. They tend also to be among the first to look for greener pastures—and leave a greater hole behind. For these reasons retaining employees is an issue in every business. At the two poles human resource experts emphasize *benefits* or *meaning* as ways to hold on to valued employees. The first approach sees success in rewards (better pay, fringes) the second in making jobs more valuable (training, advancement, interest). Most observers suggest a blend of approaches.

But retention also arises in the broader context of economic trends and affects different elements of the workforce in different ways. Thus employee retention is not much discussed in times of economic downturn: employees tend to be hunkered down and glad they have a job at all. In times like that "retention" has a kind of inverted aspect. The question becomes: "Whom will the company retain?" In most cases those with lower income tend to be favored. In expansive times companies are beating the bushes for people, and opportunities abound. At different times different skills are greatly in demand and turn-over in these skills is high as companies bid up the jobs. In the 1980s and into the 1990s computer programmers and analysts enjoyed a surge of attention until employers found ways to ease the pressure by outsourcing this type of work to India and elsewhere. Meanwhile, in good times as in bad, the most qualified and enterprising employees are always in demand and always mobile. Small business has a special view of this issue as discussed below.

FOCUSING THE RETENTION EFFORT

Employee retention is usually discussed in a too-narrow context and is therefore treated as an unalloyed good thing, like gold. This view arises because both the hiring and training processes are costly and employees increase in value, from the company's perspective, as they become ever more experienced. But employee turnover can also be a benefit. As *Management Today* reported in 2006, "At least one multinational distinguishes between what it rather elegantly calls 'regretted' and 'non-regretted' types of staff turnover. Bosses in that company worry if regretted turnover is too high—but also worry if non-regretted turnover is too low, suggesting that managers are not pushing the wrong 'uns out of the door fast enough." In the view of most seasoned managers, it is rather a truism that the good ones leave and the not-so-good hang around forever. The unnamed multinational cited by *Management Today* had its finger on the pulse. Retention must not be isolated from good personnel management generally. In well-run organizations, personnel policies will be designed around the mission of the business—recognizing that turn-over is both unavoidable and sometimes necessary.

WHY EMPLOYEES STAY

Employees stay with a company either because the business satisfies their needs and uses their abilities to an optimum extent (the ideal case) or because they just can't find another job (the worst case).

Job satisfaction is a complex consequence of the total corporate identity. It obviously includes compensation and fringe benefits as a minimum, but surveys keep reporting that most employees want to "make a contribution" or want to "make a difference." They will feel that they're achieving this goal if their skills are fully used, if the balance between discipline and freedom is right, and if the overall mission of the company makes good social sense. Ambitious employees also require that some path of advancement be at least visible to them.

Given this general profile, it is fairly obvious that retention policies based simply on reward mechanics (increase health coverage, add a child-care service) will be inadequate. Retention will work best if the company's values are very clear, supportive of employee aspirations, and implemented to provide both "rewards" and "scope" within the means of the business. In actual practice, far too many companies provide excellent reward systems and yet are populated with alienated employees because corporate policies seem irrational, bureaucracy is stifling, the motives of management appear to be pure ambition, and the corporate goal seems to be meaningless growth. Yet, employees stay because they cannot easily replace the rewards. In contrast some businesses—often small ones—offer meager rewards but a meaningful work environment—and yet still manage to keep their employees.

RETENTION IN SMALL BUSINESS

Small businesses on average pay lower salaries than larger firms. Data from the U.S. Census Bureau for 2001, for instance, show that companies with fewer than 100 employees had payrolls of $29,138 per employee; companies with 100 or more employees had payrolls of $37,265 per employee—a difference of $8,127 a year. Data on employee benefits were not provided, but small businesses also offer fewer benefits. Thus small business has a distinct disadvantage in holding on to employees. If employee retention depended entirely on compensation and fringe benefits, small businesses (they employ somewhat over a third of all people in companies) would eventually lose their employees. But retention is based on the total employment situation, and in that context small businesses have advantages over the large employers: 1) employees are closer to management and interact with management more intensively; 2) there are fewer layers; the owners are visible and not "princely" figures you read about; 3) the work situation is more organic (more like a family, less bureaucratic); 4) employees usually have more scope; they are required to do more things, wear more hats, and are therefore more fully utilized; and 5) the mission of small businesses is almost

always clearer, more immediately felt; contact with the customer may be frequent; feedback is good; and therefore employees "make more of a difference." The thoughtful small business owner will do the best to exploit these natural advantages to counter the natural disadvantage of having less to offer.

BIBLIOGRAPHY
"Design Business: Put staff on the career ladder." *Design Week.* 2 March 2006.

"Going Nowhere Slowly." *Management Today.* 7 February 2006.

McClanahan, C.J. "Top employees don't deserve the 'leased car' treatment." *Indianapolis Business Journal.* 30 January 2006.

Piper, Bob. "Retention Tune-Up." *Professional Builder.* 1 March 2006.

U.S. Census Bureau. "Historical Income Tables – People." Available from http://www.census.gov/hhes/www/income/histinc/p03.html. Retrieved on 5 March 2006.

"Walking the Retention Tightrope: Balancing employees' needs and wants." *Supervision.* February 2006.

Darnay, ECDI

EMPLOYEE RETIREMENT INCOME SECURITY ACT (ERISA)

The Employee Retirement Income Security Act of 1974 (ERISA) is a U.S. federal law that regulates most private sector employee benefit plans, including 401(k) plans, profit-sharing plans, simplified employee pension (SEP) plans, and Keogh plans. Originally intended to address the problem of embezzlement from plan funds by trustees, ERISA sets minimum standards to ensure that such plans are established and maintained in a fair and financially sound manner. The law obligates employers to provide plan participants with the benefits they are promised, and establishes strict penalties for those who fail to do so. It also sets forth vesting requirements—time periods over which employees gain full rights to the money invested by employers on their behalf. ERISA governs most employer-sponsored pension plans, but does not apply to those sponsored by businesses with less than 25 employees.

ERISA outlines a number of requirements for administrators of employee benefit plans. For example, those who manage plan funds are required to manage them in the exclusive interest of plan participants and beneficiaries. In other words, employers are not allowed to use retirement funds set aside by employees for their own purposes. ERISA also requires plan administrators to avoid transactions that would create a conflict of interest, and to respect limitations on the percentage of employee benefit plan funds that can be invested in employer securities.

ERISA also sets rules governing the disclosure of information about the financial condition of benefit plans to participants and to the U.S. government. For example, administrators are required to furnish participants with a summary plan description (SPD) covering their rights and benefits under the plan. In addition, employers must file Form 5500 annually with the Internal Revenue Service to report the financial condition and other information about the operation of the plan. ERISA provides for civil and criminal penalties of up to $1000 per day for failing or refusing to comply with these annual reporting requirements.

In 1996 the Health Insurance Portability and Accountability Act (HIPAA) amended ERISA to improve the continuity of health insurance coverage for employees who terminate their employment with a company. The amendment prohibits employers from discriminating against employees on the basis of health status and sets rules regarding preexisting conditions.

The Consolidated Omnibus Budget Reconciliation Act (COBRA), initially passed in 1985 but amended in 1999 and most recently in 2004 also enhanced the provisions of ERISA. The COBRA provisions enable workers to continue health coverage after losing their jobs and other specified conditions. For more detail, see this volume under *Consolidated Omnibus Budget Reconciliation Act (COBRA)*.

For more information about the provisions of ERISA, see the Department of Labor Web site at http://www.dol.gov.

SEE ALSO *Pension Plans; Consolidated Omnibus Budget Reconciliation Act (COBRA)*

BIBLIOGRAPHY
Bates, Steve. "Benefits Experts Welcome Final COBRA Rules." *HRMagazine*. July 2004.

Clifford, Lee. "Getting Over the Hump before You're Over the Hill." *Fortune*. 14 August 2000.

"DOL Releases Final COBRA Notice Rule." *HR Focus*. September 2004.

Infante, Victor D. "Retirement Plan Trends." *Workforce*. November 2000.

Lynn, Jacquelyn. "Request Denied? Protect employees from a health insurance loophole." *Entrepreneur*. March 2006.

Szabo, Joan. "Pension Tension." *Entrepreneur*. November 2000.

U.S. Department of Labor. "Health Plans & Benefits." Available from http://www.dol.gov/dol/topic/health-plans/erisa.htm. Retrieved on 4 March 2006.

U.S. Small Business Administration. Anastasio, Susan. *Small Business Insurance and Risk Management Guide*. n.d.

Hillstrom, Northern Lights
updated by Magee, ECDI

EMPLOYEE REWARD AND RECOGNITION SYSTEMS

In a competitive business climate, more business owners are looking at improvements in quality while reducing costs. Meanwhile, a strong economy has resulted in a tight job market. So while small businesses need to get more from their employees, their employees are looking for more out of them. Employee reward and recognition programs are one method of motivating employees to change work habits and key behaviors to benefit a small business.

REWARD VS. RECOGNITION

Although these terms are often used interchangeably, reward and recognition systems should be considered separately. Employee reward systems refer to programs set up by a company to reward performance and motivate employees on individual and/or group levels. They are normally considered separate from salary but may be monetary in nature or otherwise have a cost to the company. While previously considered the domain of large companies, small businesses have also begun employing them as a tool to lure top employees in a competitive job market as well as to increase employee performance.

As noted, although employee recognition programs are often combined with reward programs they retain a different purpose altogether. They are intended to provide a psychological—rewards a financial—benefit. Although many elements of designing and maintaining reward and recognition systems are the same, it is useful to keep this difference in mind, especially for small business owners interested in motivating staffs while keeping costs low.

DIFFERENTIATING REWARDS FROM MERIT PAY AND THE PERFORMANCE APPRAISAL

In designing a reward program, a small business owner needs to separate the salary or merit pay system from the reward system. Financial rewards, especially those given on a regular basis such as bonuses, profit sharing, etc., should be tied to an employee's or a group's accomplishments and should be considered "pay at risk" in order to distance them from salary. By doing so, a manager can avoid a sense of entitlement on the part of the employee and ensure that the reward emphasizes excellence or achievement rather than basic competency.

Merit pay increases, then, are not part of an employee reward system. Normally, they are an increase for inflation with additional percentages separating employees by competency. They are not particularly motivating since the distinction that is usually made between a good employee and an average one is relatively small. In addition, they increase the fixed costs of a company as opposed to variable pay increases, such as bonuses, which have to be "re-earned" each year. Finally, in many small businesses teamwork is a crucial element of a successful employee's job. Merit increases generally review an individual's job performance, without adequately taking into account the performance within the context of the group or business.

DESIGNING A REWARD PROGRAM

The keys to developing a reward program are as follows:

- Identification of company or group goals that the reward program will support

- Identification of the desired employee performance or behaviors that will reinforce the company's goals

- Determination of key measurements of the performance or behavior, based on the individual or group's previous achievements

- Determination of appropriate rewards

- Communication of program to employees

In order to reap benefits such as increased productivity, the entrepreneur designing a reward program must identify company or group goals to be reached and the behaviors or performance that will contribute to this. While this may seem obvious, companies frequently make the mistake of rewarding behaviors or achievements that either fail to further business goals or actually sabotage them. If teamwork is a business goal, a bonus system rewarding individuals who improve their productivity by themselves or at the expense of another does not make sense. Likewise, if quality is an important issue for an entrepreneur, the reward system that he or she designs should not emphasize rewarding the *quantity* of work accomplished by a business unit.

Properly measuring performance ensures the program pays off in terms of business goals. Since rewards have a real cost in terms of time or money, small business owners need to confirm that performance has actually improved before rewarding it. Often this requires meas-

uring something other than financial returns: reduced defects, happier customers, more rapid deliveries, etc.

When developing a rewards program, an entrepreneur should consider matching rewards to the end result for the company. Perfect attendance might merit a different reward than saving the company $10,000 through improved contract negotiation. It is also important to consider rewarding both individual and group accomplishments in order to promote both individual initiative and group cooperation and performance.

Lastly, in order for a rewards program to be successful, the specifics need to be clearly spelled out for every employee. Motivation depends on the individual's ability to understand what is being asked of her. Once this has been done, reinforce the original communication with regular meetings or memos promoting the program. Keep your communications simple but frequent to ensure staff members are kept abreast of changes to the system.

TYPES OF REWARD PROGRAMS

There are a number of different types of reward programs aimed at both individual and team performance.

Variable Pay Variable pay or pay-for-performance is a compensation program in which a portion of a person's pay is considered "at risk." Variable pay can be tied to the performance of the company, the results of a business unit, an individual's accomplishments, or any combination of these. It can take many forms, including bonus programs, stock options, and one-time awards for significant accomplishments. Some companies choose to pay their employees less than competitors but attempt to motivate and reward employees using a variable pay program instead. Good incentive pay packages provide an optimal challenge, one that stretches employees but remains in reach. If too much is required to reach the goal, the program will be ignored.

Bonuses Bonus programs have been used in American business for some time. They usually reward individual accomplishment and are frequently used in sales organizations to encourage salespersons to generate additional business or higher profits. They can also be used, however, to recognize group accomplishments. Indeed, increasing numbers of businesses have switched from individual bonus programs to one which reward contributions to corporate performance at group, departmental, or company-wide levels.

According to some experts, small businesses interested in long-term benefits should probably consider another type of reward. Bonuses are generally short-term motivators. By rewarding an employee's performance for the previous year, they encourage a short-term perspective rather than future-oriented accomplishments. In addition, these programs need to be carefully structured to ensure they are rewarding accomplishments above and beyond an individual or group's basic functions. Otherwise, they run the risk of being perceived of as entitlements or regular merit pay, rather than a reward for outstanding work. Proponents, however, contend that bonuses are a perfectly legitimate means of rewarding outstanding performance, and they argue that such compensation can actually be a powerful tool to encourage future top-level efforts.

Profit Sharing Profit sharing refers to the strategy of creating a pool of monies to be disbursed to employees by taking a stated percentage of a company's profits. The amount given to an employee is usually equal to a percentage of the employee's salary and is disbursed after a business closes its books for the year. The benefits can be provided either in actual cash or via contributions to employee's 401(k) plans. A benefit for a company offering this type of reward is that it can keep fixed costs low.

The idea behind profit sharing is to reward employees for their contributions to a company's achieved profit goal. It encourages employees to stay put because it is usually structured to reward employees who stay with the company; most profit sharing programs require an employee to be vested in the program over a number of years before receiving any money. Unless well managed, profit sharing may not properly motivate individuals if all receive the share anyway. A team spirit (everyone pulling together to achieve that profit) can counter this—especially if it arises from the employees and is not just management propaganda.

Stock Options Previously the territory of upper management and large companies, stock options have become an increasingly popular method in recent years of rewarding middle management and other employees in both mature companies and start-ups. Employee stock-option programs give employees the right to buy a specified number of a company's shares at a fixed price for a specified period of time (usually around ten years). They are generally authorized by a company's board of directors and approved by its shareholders. The number of options a company can award to employees is usually equal to a certain percentage of the company's shares outstanding.

Like profit sharing plans, stock options usually reward employees for sticking around, serving as a long-term motivator. Once an employee has been with a company for a certain period of time (usually around four years), he or she is fully vested in the program. If the employee leaves the company prior to being fully vested, those options are canceled. After an employee becomes fully vested in the program, he or she can purchase from the company an allotted number of shares at the strike price (or the fixed price originally agreed to). This purchase is known as "exercising" stock options. After purchasing the stock, the employee can either retain it or sell it on the open market with the difference in strike price and market price being the employee's gain in the value of the shares.

Offering additional stock in this manner presents risks for both the company and the employee. If the option's strike price is higher than the market price of the stock, the employee's option is worthless. When an employee exercises an option, the company is required to issue a new share of stock that can be publicly traded. The company's market capitalization grows by the market price of the share, rather than the strike price that the employee purchases the stock for. The possibility of reduction of company earnings (impacting both the company and shareholders) arises when the company has a greater number of shares outstanding. To keep ahead of this possibility, earnings must increase at a rate equal to the rate at which outstanding shares increase. Otherwise, the company must repurchase shares on the open market to reduce the number of outstanding shares.

One benefit to offering stock options is a company's ability to take a tax deduction for compensation expense when it issues shares to employees who are exercising their options. Another benefit to offering options is that while they could be considered a portion of compensation, current accounting methods do not require businesses to show options as an expense on their books. This tends to inflate the value of a company. Companies should think carefully about this as a benefit, however. If accounting rules were to become more conservative, corporate earnings could be impacted as a result.

GROUP-BASED REWARD SYSTEMS

As more small businesses use team structures to reach their goals, many entrepreneurs look for ways to reward cooperation between departments and individuals. Bonuses, profit sharing, and stock options can all be used to reward team and group accomplishments. An entrepreneur can choose to reward individual or group contributions or a combination of the two. Group-based reward systems are based on a measurement of team performance, with individual rewards received on the basis of this performance. While these systems encourage individual efforts toward common business goals, they also tend to reward under-performing employees along with average and above-average employees. A reward program which recognizes individual achievements in addition to team performance can provide extra incentive for employees.

RECOGNITION PROGRAMS

For small business owners and other managers, a recognition program may appear to be merely extra effort on their part with few tangible returns in terms of employee performance. While most employees certainly appreciate monetary awards for a job well done, many people merely seek recognition of their hard work. For an entrepreneur with more ingenuity than cash available, this presents an opportunity to motivate employees.

Nor will the entrepreneur be far off the mark. As Patricia Odell reported, writing for *Promo*, "Cash is no longer the ultimate motivator." Odell cited data from the Forum for People Performance Management and Measurement at Northwester University—which had discovered that non-cash awards tend to be more effective; the exception was rewarding increasing sales. "The study found," Odell wrote, "that non-cash awards programs would work better than cash in such cases as reinforcing organizational values and cultures, improving teamwork, increasing customer satisfaction and motivating specific behaviors among other programs."

In order to develop an effective recognition program, a small business owner must be sure to separate the program from the company's system of rewarding employees. This ensures a focus on recognizing the efforts of employees. To this end, although the recognition may have a monetary value (such as a luncheon, gift certificates, or plaques), money itself is not given to recognize performance.

Recognition has a timing element: it must occur so that the performance recognized is still fresh in the mind. If high performance continues, recognition should be frequent but cautiously timed so that it doesn't become automatic. Furthermore, like rewards, the method of recognition needs to be appropriate for the achievement. This also ensures that those actions which go farthest in supporting corporate goals receive the most attention. However, an entrepreneur should remain flexible in the methods of recognition, as different employees are motivated by different forms of recognition. Finally, employees need to clearly understand the behavior or action being recognized. A small business owner can ensure this by being specific in what actions will be recognized and then reinforcing this by communicating exactly what an employee did to be recognized.

Recognition can take a variety of forms. Structured programs can include regular recognition events such as banquets or breakfasts, employee of the month or year recognition, an annual report or yearbook which features the accomplishments of employees, and department or company recognition boards. Informal or spontaneous recognition can take the form of privileges such as working at home, starting late/leaving early, or long lunch breaks. A job well done can also be recognized by providing additional support or empowering the employee in ways such as greater choice of assignments, increased authority, or naming the employee as an internal consultant to other staff. Symbolic recognition such as plaques or coffee mugs with inscriptions can also be effective, provided they reflect sincere appreciation for hard work. These latter expressions of thanks, however, are far more likely to be received positively if the source is a small business owner with limited financial resources. Employees will look less kindly on owners of thriving businesses who use such inexpensive items as centerpieces of their reward programs.

Both reward and recognition programs have their place in small business. Small business owners should first determine desired employee behaviors, skills, and accomplishments that will support their business goals. By rewarding and recognizing outstanding performance, entrepreneurs will have an edge in a competitive corporate climate.

BIBLIOGRAPHY

Brandi, JoAnna. "9 Ways to Keep Employees Engaged." *Entrepreneur*. 12 April 2005.

Grimaldi, Lisa. "Study proves recognition pays off." *Meetings & Conventions*. August 2005.

Henneman, Todd. "Daniels' Scientific Method." *Workforce Management*. 10 October 2005.

Odell, Patricia. "Live from the Mo Show: Non-Cash Awards More Effective." *Promo*. 28 September 2005.

Parker, Owen, and Liz Wright. "Pay and Employee Commitment: The Missing Link." *Ivey Business Journal*. January 2001.

Rauch, Maggie. "Communications Gap: Majority of businesses give managers little guidance on recognition." *Incentive*. September 2005.

Ventrice, Cindy. "Make Their Day! Employee Recognition That Works." *Berrett-Koehler Publishers*. April 2003.

Hillstrom, Northern Lights
updated by Magee, ECDI

EMPLOYEE RIGHTS

Employee rights arise from federal and state laws that, over time, have established various rules that govern the employer-employee relationship. More broadly viewed, the phrase is often used to refer to rights not explicitly mentioned in law but inferred from legal protections. An example of this is a "right not to be bullied" derived from legislation mandating a safe work place and prohibiting hostile working environments. Many employees also assume that they have by right what they actually have at the employer's option. An example of that is paid holidays and paid vacations; these benefits are nowhere mandated by law but almost universally offered as employment benefits.

Employee rights fall under seven categories: 1) union activity, i.e., the right to organize and to bargain collectively; 2) working hours and minimum pay; 3) equal compensation for men and women doing the same or similar work for the same employer; 4) safety and health protection in the work environment and related workers' compensation; 5) unemployment benefits; 6) non-discriminatory hiring and promotion practices; 7) family and medical leave; and 8) ability to complain without retaliation (whistle-blower protection). Additional rights are guaranteed under state laws, but these vary: for instance, 15 states mandate a higher minimum wage than does the Federal Government. Sometimes considered as rights are prohibitions imposed on employers against child labor—which includes limitations on what kind of work teenagers under 18 may perform.

A partial listing of the most important federal laws that embody employee rights includes the following:

- Americans with Disabilities Act—covers rights of the disabled.

- Age Discrimination in Employment Act—covers age discrimination.

- Civil Rights Act—covers racial discrimination and sexual harassment.

- Equal Pay Act—mandates equal pay for men and women.

- Fair Labor Standards Act (FLSA)—principally relates to hourly workers and minimum pay.

- Family and Medical Leave Act—covers maternity/paternity and medical leave.

- Federal Unemployment Tax Act—covers unemployment compensation.

- Occupational Safety and Health Act—covers safety at work and workers' compensation.

- The Wagner Act—original labor union legislation followed by many other laws.

- The Whistleblower Protection Act—covers whistleblowers, but federal employees only.

One of the more important categories of rights relates to discrimination. Companies hiring people may not discriminate on the basis of seven categories: sex, age, race, national origin, religion, physical disability, or veteran status. These categories are labeled "classes"; all the categories taken together are referred to in federalese as "protected classes." Employees have the right to be considered for employment regardless of the class to which they belong—and everyone belongs minimally to three of these in having a gender, an age, and being a member of a race. Furthermore, the employer is prohibited from discussing the class-status of an employee during an employment interview even inferentially. It is prohibited, for instance, to ask: "Are you sure, Richard, that you'll do well in a caring environment, like nursing?"

Based on Title VII of the Civil Rights Act, the Equal Employment Opportunity Commission issued guidelines for defining and enforcing Title VII's requirements titled *Guidelines on Discrimination Because of Sex* (Code of Federal Regulations 29CFR1604.11). This regulation initially introduced the concept of conduct that has "the purpose or effect of unreasonably interfering with an individual's work performance or creating an *intimidating, hostile, or offensive working environment.*" [Emphasis added.] The regulation was last revised in 2002. The emphasized phrasing has gradually come to be claimed inclusive of other than just sexual conduct—such as bullying or aggressive religious or political advocacy on the job. As yet the concept has not been enlarged, but developments in the mid-2000s serve as an illustration of the manner in which employee rights established for one purpose can gradually expand to others. An earlier development along these lines was the passage of the Pregnancy Discrimination Act, amending Title VII, whereby the concept of discrimination on the basis of sex was used to expand its definition to include pregnancy.

Employee Rights that Aren't Most employees believe that they have rights they do not have under law. The most common categories have to do with paid time off. A large majority of employees (77 percent in 2005) enjoyed paid vacations and holidays—but 79 percent of those working in 1999 had such benefits and had since that time lost the privilege. Similarly, most people believe that they will be paid for time spent on jury duty—but only 69 percent actually had such benefits; and only 48 percent of people were paid for military absences. With very large numbers of people enjoying certain benefits—but at the employer's option—a sense of entitlement arises. Often, if times are good, such benefits eventually turn into perceived rights.

SEE ALSO *Employee Privacy; Drug Testing*

BIBLIOGRAPHY
"E-mail and Employee Rights: Legal decision raises bar for effective internal communications." *Employee Benefit News.* 1 April 2005.

Gallagher, Dave. "Bullying Not Just for Schoolyards Anymore: Employers need to search for warning signs." *Bellingham Business Journal.* June 2005.

Koli, Anuradha. "I Suspect My Boss Snoops Through My Desk. Is that Legal?" *Cosmopolitan.* February 2005.

Lehane, Mike. "Stand Up to Bullies: If bullying is happening in your workplace, it is up to you to take a firm stand." *Nursing Standard.* 1 June 2005.

"Questions About Employee Rights." National Federation of Independent Business. Available from http://www.nfib.com/object/1584083.html. Retrieved on 8 March 2006.

Sack, Steven Mitchell. *The Employee Rights Handbook.* Warner Business Books, 1 October 2000.

Wieber, Ryan. "It's Harassment." *Library Journal.* 1 July 2005.

Hillstrom, Northern Lights
updated by Magee, ECDI

EMPLOYEE SCREENING PROGRAMS

Every business wants trustworthy, qualified employees—especially small firms where every employee counts and interpersonal dynamics often assume heightened importance. As a result, pre-employment screening programs are a part of the business landscape in the mid-2000s. According to a 2004 survey by the American Management Association, 63 percent of companies test employees medically before employment; and earlier AMA surveys showed that 43 percent of responding members also tested prospective employees in job skills, psychological fitness, and/or basic competency in math and literacy. Screening programs generally also include some combination of reference and credit checks, verification of employment, investigations into any criminal activity (where allowed by law), and physical/drug testing. Testing before hiring is more efficient than doing so on the job: those who fail need not be engaged. Screening programs can assist in ensuring a proper fit between employer and employee. "A pre-employment test that costs less than $10 can sometimes save a company the thousands it costs to replace a bad match, or the legal fees to defend against liability lawsuits for negligence in hiring a troubled or troublesome employee," wrote Gilbert Nicholson in *Workforce.* "Tests range from evaluating cognitive skills to identifying personality traits, and can help employers avoid bad apples and match good ones to the right jobs."

Despite the potential value of screening programs, not all companies use such methods. Businesses engaged in industries with traditionally high turnover rates (e.g. restaurants) may determine through cost-benefit analysis that benefits don't warrant the upfront expenditure.

Companies that do engage in workforce screening tend to take one of two routes: they create and administer their own test or use established test and/or the services of a screening company. "Some companies are so specialized, it makes sense to tailor their own instrument to the unique features of their organization," said one testing executive in *Workforce.* "But that usually requires a company with a human-relations team skilled in test development." In addition, some small business owners choose to execute their own screening programs, but use existing tests to do so. The Buros Institute, Inc. at the University of Nebraska-Lincoln (www.unl.edu/buros) maintains a Tests in Print resource that lists more than 2,900 commercially available screening tests—and may be a good first stop. Finally, many businesses prefer to outsource the entire program. When hiring a screening company to check out prospective employees, it is important that the company itself be fully qualified. Checking it out—including checking with long-time users of the service—is good practice.

Companies using screening should be aware of local, state, and federal laws against discrimination. These may impact both the questions asked of candidates as well as reference, credit, and other checks. Aptitude tests should be job-related and uniformly implemented. Many local and state governments prohibit questions related to criminal convictions. A business should note the difference between an arrest and a conviction: merely having been arrested proves nothing.

Screening protects a business against possible lawsuits. "With the tort of negligent hiring now recognized in a majority of the states, employers have been forced to defend a growing number of suits seeking redress for crimes committed by employees, usually thefts or assaults that victimize customers or co-workers," wrote David Shaffer and Ronald Schmidt in "Personality Testing in Employment" (www.thelenreid.com). Courts may hold companies responsible for injuries their employees inflict on others while on the job. Companies found liable in a negligent hiring suit may be held responsible for punitive damages, medical bills, lost wages, etc. For a small business, such a suit could be potentially devastating. But it should be noted that if a prospective employee has a criminal record, a company's liability in a lawsuit after employment depends on the relevance of the crime to the job.

Fortunately, legal experts say that legal liability on either of these two fronts is unlikely provided that the company in question is careful in creating, maintaining, and monitoring the various aspects of its program. To ensure protection against legal trouble, business owners are well-advised to consult a specialist in employment law before establishing any of the following potential elements of a screening program:

Previous Employment and References Employers should review resumes and employment histories for gaps in employment. In regards to references, the employer should be sure to contact specific business references as opposed to merely friends and family of the prospective employee. Finally, companies may choose to contact other individuals not listed as references such as previous co-workers, who may provide additional background on the employee. This check may be subject to local or state laws or require the consent of the applicant.

Credit and Vehicle Checks These may be done through credit agencies used by banks, stores, and others. While checking an applicant's credit and vehicle records is not conclusive regarding qualifications for employment, these records may give an indication of an applicant's dependability or honesty.

Criminal Records As noted, the use of criminal record searches may be subject to local or state laws against discrimination. Small business owners and managers also must weigh whether the applicant's previous arrest or crime would have a direct bearing on the work that he or she would be doing.

IQ or Personality Tests Businesses sometimes also use personality or IQ tests to augment less formal interviews in order to round out or verify their impressions of a prospective employee. Outside agencies can run a battery of tests on applicants and provide employers with profiles on each candidate. A small business can also take advantage of current software or standardized tests to handle at least a portion of such testing. Many companies choose to outsource testing and thus cut down the number of applicants for closer view.

Physical Screening or Drug Tests These are often handled by a qualified clinic or laboratory. Prospective employees provide blood or urine samples to the contracted agency. The company is then sent results and can make a determination regarding employment.

BIBLIOGRAPHY

"Access Criminal Background Checks Online." *Arkansas Business.* 26 December 2005.

Brownlee, Ken. "Pre-Employment Screening Issues." *Claims.* July 2005.

"Employee Screening." *Security Management* . November 2005.

Graham, Cindy Schroeter. "Conduct Background Checks Right." *SportsTURF.* January 2006.

Nicholson, Gilbert. "Screen and Glean." *Workforce* October 2000.

Ross, Sativa. "Reference Checks Identify Poor Performers." *Aftermarket Business.* July 2005.

Hillstrom, Northern Lights
updated by Magee, ECDI

EMPLOYEE STOCK OWNERSHIP PLANS (ESOPs)

An Employee Stock Ownership Plan, or ESOP, is a qualified retirement program in which employees receive shares of the business rather than stock. ESOPs are said to be "qualified" because they qualify for federal income tax deferral until the stock is turned into cash at retirement. ESOPs are in most respects similar to 401(k) plans except that, instead of cash, the company providing the ESOP "pays in" its own stock. But, as in 401(k) plans, all full time employees must be eligible provided that they meet certain age and service requirements. Unlike a 401(k) plan, contributions to an ESOP by the employer do not become the property of the employee until after specified vesting periods are satisfied. Under both programs, employees receive monetary benefits on retirement or in the event of death or disability. The chief difference between ESOPs and 401(k)s is that, in the latter, the funds paid in are invested in a diversified portfolio; in the ESOP they hold only the company's own stock. The advantages and risks of ESOPs derive from this difference.

An ESOP offers employers two advantages. First, the company gets significant tax breaks. It can, for example, borrow money through the ESOP for expansion or other purposes and then deduct both the repayment and interest when it pays back the loan. In the case of ordinary loans, only interest payments are tax deductible. In addition, the business owner who sells his or her stock holdings to the ESOP can often defer or even avoid capital-gains taxes associated with the sale of the business. In this way, ESOPs have become an important tool in succession planning for business owners preparing for retirement.

A less tangible advantage many employers experience when forming an ESOP is an increase in employee loyalty and productivity. Employees become owners of the company; having a stake in it, their relationship to the company changes. An ESOP therefore provides a financial incentive—but also something that goes beyond future compensation. Small businesses are at a disadvantage over against large company because they provide less compensation and fewer benefits on average. An ESOP therefore helps small businesses recruit and retain employees by offering ownership benefits.

GROWTH OF ESOPs

The first ESOP was created in 1957, but the idea did not attract much attention until 1974 when plan details were laid out in the Employee Retirement Income Security Act (ERISA). The number of businesses sponsoring ESOPs expanded steadily during the 1980s as changes in the tax code made plans more attractive for business owners. Although the popularity of ESOPs declined during the recession of the early 1990s, the programs have expanded since. According to the National Center for Employee Ownership, the number of companies with ESOPs grew from 9,000 in 1990 to 10,000 in 1997. By 2004, there were 11,500 ESOPs with 10 million participants. The ESOPs had $500 billion in assets.

ESOP SPECIFICS

In order to establish an ESOP, a company must have been in business and shown a profit for at least three years. One of the main factors limiting the growth of ESOPs is that such plans are relatively complicated and require strict reporting; thus can be quite expensive to establish and administer. Steve Miller, writing for *Top Producer*, provided estimates of $35,000 to $50,000 for establishing ESOPs; annual fees for stock appraisals and record keeping are between $5,000 and $10,000. Appraisals are necessary in the case of closely held corporations that are not publicly traded in order to satisfy federal law. These costs are substantial—but they are tax deductible.

Employers can choose between two main types of ESOPs, loosely known as basic ESOPs and leveraged ESOPs. They differ in the ways in which the ESOP obtains the company's stock. In a basic ESOP, the employer simply contributes securities or cash to the plan every year—like an ordinary profit-sharing plan—so that the ESOP can purchase stock. Contributions are tax-deductible up to a maximum equivalent to 15 percent of payroll. In contrast, leveraged ESOPs obtain bank loans to purchase the company's stock. The employer can then use the proceeds of the stock purchase to expand the business or to fund the business owner's retirement nest egg. The business can repay the loans through contributions to the ESOP that are tax-deductible up to a maximum of 25 percent of payroll.

An ESOP can also be a useful tool in facilitating the buying and selling of small businesses. For example, a business owner nearing retirement age can sell his or her stake in the company to the ESOP in order to gain tax advantages and provide for the continuation of the business. Some experts claim that transferring ownership to the employees in this way is preferable to third-party sales. Third-party sales have negative tax implications if successful. But buyers may be difficult to find; and after the transaction, collecting installment payments may turn out to be difficult or costly. Using the ESOP, more certain results are possible. The ESOP can borrow money to buy out the owner's stake in the company. If, after the stock purchase, the ESOP holds more than 30 percent of the company's shares, the owner can defer capital-gains taxes by investing the proceeds in a Qualified Replacement Property (QRP). QRPs can include stocks, bonds, and certain retirement accounts. The income stream generated by the QRP can help provide the business owner with income during retirement.

ESOPs can also prove helpful to those interested in buying a small business. Many individuals and companies choose to raise capital to finance such a purchase by selling nonvoting stock in the business to its employees. This strategy allows the purchaser to retain the voting shares in order to maintain control of the business. At one time, banks favored this sort of purchase arrangement because they were entitled to deduct 50 percent of the interest payments as long as the ESOP loan was used to purchase a majority stake in the company. However, this tax incentive for banks was eliminated with the passage of the Small Business Jobs Protection Act of 1996.

In addition to the various advantages that ESOPs can provide to business owners, sellers, and buyers, they also offer benefits to employees. Like other types of retirement plans, the employer's contributions to an ESOP on behalf of employees are allowed to grow tax-free until the funds are distributed upon an employee's retirement. At the time an employee retires or leaves the company, he or she simply sells the stock back to the company. The proceeds of the stock sale can then be rolled over into another qualified retirement plan, e.g., an Individual Retirement Account (IRA) or a plan sponsored by another employer. Another provision of ESOPs gives participants—upon reaching the age of 55 and putting in at least ten years of service—the option of diversifying their ESOP investment away from company stock and toward more traditional investments.

The financial rewards associated with ESOPs can be particularly impressive for long-term employees who have participated in the growth of a company. Of course, employees encounter some risks with ESOPs, too: their retirement funds are invested in the stock of one small company. In fact, an ESOP may become worthless if the sponsoring company goes bankrupt. But history has shown that this scenario is unlikely to occur: only 1 percent of ESOP firms have gone under financially in last 20 years.

WHO SHOULD ESTABLISH AN ESOP

Although 1996 legislation opened the door for S corporations to establish ESOPs, the plans continue to be much more attractive for C corporations. In general, ESOPs are likely to prove too costly for very small companies, those with high employee turnover, or those that rely heavily on contract workers. ESOPs might also be problematic for businesses that have uncertain cash flow; companies are contractually obligated to repurchase stock from employees when they retire or leave the company. Finally, ESOPs are most appropriate for companies that are committed to allowing employees to participate in the management of the business. Otherwise, an ESOP might tend to create resentment among employees who become part-owners of the company and then are not treated in accordance with their status.

SEE ALSO *Retirement Planning; Succession Planning*

BIBLIOGRAPHY

Bregar, Bill. "Group Backs ESOP Awareness." *Plastic News.* 25 April 2005.

Brodzinski, Carrier. "ESOP's Fables Can Make Coverage Risky: Moral of the story is not to ignore exposures should employee stock tank." *National Underwriter Property and Casualty-Risk and Benefits Management.* 13 June 2005.

Culpepper, Robert A., John E. Gamble, and Meg G. Blubaugh. "Employee Stock Ownership Plans and Three-Component Commitment." *Journal of Occupational and Organizational Psychology.* June 2004.

Miller, Steve. "ESOP Fables." *Top Producer.* 4 December 2005.

Pratt, David A. "Focus on … ESOPs." *Journal of Pension Benefits.* Winter 2004.

Zwiebach, Elliot. "A Piece of the Pie: Companies with Employee Stock Ownership Plans Say the Structure Creates an Environment Where Workers Are more Motivated." *Supermarket News.* 23 May 2005.

Zwiebach, Elliot. "ESOPs Can Benefit Both Company and Worker." *Supermarket News.* 23 May 2005.

Hillstrom, Northern Lights
updated by Magee, ECDI

EMPLOYEE STRIKES

Strikes may affect a small business in one of two ways. First, its own employees may go on strike or carry out some collective action functionally equivalent to a strike. Second, the small business may be unable to carry on as usually because some other company or industry is experiencing labor disruptions and thus denies the business vital services or supplies.

STATUS AND TRENDS IN UNIONIZATION

Employee or labor strikes are called by labor unions usually after a strike-vote by its membership. The strike may be directed at a single organization or may be industry-wide. Two major tends in unionization suggest that small business is very unlikely to be unionized and therefore directly threatened by a strike. Based on data from the U.S. Bureau of Labor Statistics, in the 40-year period from 1964 to 2005, union members have declined from 29.3 percent to 12.5 percent of the labor force. Even as the total unionized work-force has declined, the private-sector's share of total union labor has declined and the share of the public-sector has increased. In 1983, for example, private-sector union employees were 67.2 percent of all union laborers; the public-sector share was 32.4 percent. By 2005, the private-sector share was 52.6 percent, the public-sector share 47.4 percent.

As a consequence of this general decline in the unionized workforce, labor stoppages have also declined. Major work stoppages involving 1,000 or more workers averaged 352 in the 1950s, 283 in the 1960s, 289 in the 1970s, 83 in the 1980s, 35 in the 1990s, and 28 in the five-year period 2000-2005.

In 2005, union membership was highest in the transportation and utilities industries in the private-sector (24 percent) and lowest in finance and related services (2.3 percent). In construction and manufacturing, union membership was 13 percent of the labor force; in wholesale and retail (where the highest proportion of small businesses operate) the rate was 5.2 percent. In professional and business services, another important small business sector, the rate was 2.7 percent. Furthermore, unions target for organization efforts large operations rather than small for pure cost/benefit reasons. Therefore unionized small businesses are rare. Finally, unions call strikes only when grievances are of long standing and long unresolved. Not surprisingly, a search of the business literature does not turn up any cases of small businesses struck by strikes.

TYPES OF STRIKES

The National Labor Relations Board (NLRB) provides legal protections for economic strikes and strikes based on unfair labor practices. In the first category, workers attempt to garner improvements in their wages, benefits, hours, or working conditions. An unfair labor practices strike is called when the employer allegedly violates NLRA rules that protect workers during collective bargaining. The small business owner faced with a labor organizing action is well advised, early in the process, to consult with a competent labor lawyer in order to get guidance on how to comply with NLRA regulations. Fundamental rules to observe include:

1. The business must bargain in good faith throughout the process. Workers have a fundamental right under U.S. law to organize and to bargain collectively.

2. The business must provide the union with all information to which the latter is legally entitled. Under U.S. labor law, unions can request information about management's plans regarding various operational aspects of the business during the strike. For example, the union can ask for information about where the business plans to get replacement workers and the wages that they will be paid.

3. The business has and can exercise rights of its own. It can freely communicate its own plans to employees, point out how they differ from the union's proposals, and ask employees to vote on the business's final offer. In many strike situations, the business has the option of utilizing replacement workers without penalty.

AVOIDING/MANAGING A STRIKE

In the case of a small business especially—where contact between management and the work force is closer—avoiding a strike is obviously the best strategy. If the shop was unionized during the current ownership's tenure, that fact alone should have signaled to the management that something was drastically out of order. Unionization is fundamentally an adversarial process intended to *force* the business to behave in certain ways by threatening to deny the business an indispensable resource. If the union shop was acquired, the new owner can build a new relationship with labor and, often, after some period of time—during which the labor force has learned to trust the management—even succeed in decertifying the union. If, despite best efforts, a strike appears unavoidable, early planning and effective implementation are the only ways to minimize damage. Such planning will include at minimum:

- Obtaining early legal counsel to determine if hiring replacement workers will be possible and, if yes, making early arrangements for such help.

- Effectively communicating with suppliers and customers to tailor deliveries to the new situation and to warn customers of impending problems affecting prompt shipment of products. Where possible, inventories might be built up in advance.

- Communicating effectively with non-striking employees to maintain morale.

- In the most drastic situation (more likely in a small than a large business) planning termination of operations, up to bankruptcy, if the strike will cripple the business.

MANAGING SUPPLIER'S STRIKES

Employee strikes most likely to damage a small business are likely to be strikes by *other people's* employees, not its own. In the industrial climate of the mid-2000s such disruptions were most likely to result from transportation strikes, especially if a business was highly dependent on a single delivery channel. As John Boyd pointed out in *Traffic Word,* "With a host of U.S. air cargo carriers locked in labor disputes as 2006 gets under way, shippers are bracing for what could be a turbulent year in the air but one they're hoping doesn't leave them grounded." Boyd cited a shipping manager who said: "I'm not panicking. But I am starting to think 'What if,' and planning ahead." Boyd pointed out that FedEx, UPS, and DHL were all negotiating with union pilots.

The situation described by Boyd could arise, of course, in some other sector than transportation and affect for the small business, but the generic aspects are the same. The forward-looking manager will keep up-to-speed on the issues that impact its most important suppliers of goods and services, anticipate problems, plan for a workaround, and do the necessary contingency planning and budgeting that may be necessary. For example, large customers might be notified if the business anticipates shipment delays or shortages of parts—thus giving customer's opportunities to acquire additional supplies early.

SEE ALSO *Labor Unions and Small Business*

BIBLIOGRAPHY
Boyd, John D. "Flying Into Turbulence: Shippers tighten belts and look for alternatives in case major cargo carriers face job actions, disruption." *Traffic World.* 23 January 2006.

Edelson, Sharon and David Moin. "N.Y. Stores Prepare for Transit Strike." *WWD.* 13 December 2005.

Glazer, Mark. "No More Labor Woes." *Waste Age.* 1 May 2005.

Katz, Rayna. "In The Throes of Labor: Whether to meet at a hotel suffering an employee-management discord is not a clear-cut decision." *Meeting News.* 24 October 2005.

"Organized Labor Will Lose Ground in Contract Talks This Year." *KiplingerForecasts.* 20 January 2006.

Tufel, Gary. "What to Do When Labor Strikes: Employee issues." *Tradeshow Week.* 9 January 2006.

U.S. Department of Labor. Bureau of Labor Statistics. "Major Work Stoppages (Annual)." Available from http://www. bls.gov/news.release/wkstp.toc.htm. Retrieved on 13 March 2006.

U.S. Department of Labor. Bureau of Labor Statistics. "Union Members in 2005." Press Release. 20 January 2006.

Darnay, ECDI

EMPLOYEE SUGGESTION SYSTEMS

The term "employee suggestion systems" refers to a variety of efforts businesses make to solicit and utilize input from their employees in hopes of achieving cost savings or improving product quality, workplace efficiency, customer service, or working conditions. These efforts range from simply placing suggestion boxes in common areas to implementing formal programs with committees to review ideas and rewards for those that are adopted. The ideas generated can range from simple quality of work life improvements, like putting a refrigerator in the coffee room, to larger streamlining issues that can save the company thousands of dollars per year, like switching all salespeople's cellular phones from individual contracts to a group contract with a discount vendor. "Suggestion programs create a win-win situation," Kate Walter wrote in *HR Magazine*. "More involvement and input for employees and improved efficiency and cost-savings for employers."

"Companies that set up effective suggestion systems are finding that employees have great ideas that can lower costs, increase revenues, improve efficiency, or produce greater quality," said Charles Martin, author of *Employee Suggestion Systems: Boosting Productivity and Profits*. "Employees work together better as a team and often submit ideas as a team. And they begin to think more like managers, looking beyond the scope of their own jobs."

Some companies assume that since they cultivate an open relationship between employees and management, ideas for improvements will surface informally, without explicit prompting. But experts note that formal suggestion systems encourage employees to really think about their jobs and want to participate in the operation of the company. Formal suggestion systems let employees know that their ideas are valued. Such systems may even increase motivation and foster loyalty and teamwork among employees. And these benefits come in addition to the positive impact employee suggestion systems can have on a company's bottom line. "There's no denying that the real expert is the person who does the job; therefore, that's the best place to go when improvements are sought," consultant Tomas Jensen, president of the Center for Suggestion System Development, told Susan Wells as published in *HR Magazine*. "Millions of dollars are being saved by listening to the company's greatest asset—its human resource." Wells went on to discuss a study by Employee Involvement Association (EIA) which uncovered savings of more than $624 million in 2003 in 47 companies in which 450,000 people participated in programs.

ELEMENTS OF A SUCCESSFUL SUGGESTION SYSTEM

"The goal of a successful suggestion system is to tap the reservoir of ideas and creative thinking of all employees for the improvement of the working process and products," Robert F. Bell wrote in *IIE Solutions*. "To do so requires proper understanding by everyone of the process, management support of the system, encouragement and meaningful rewards, and a structure to make sure nothing falls through the cracks." The elements of a successful employee suggestion system can be divided into four main areas: management support, program structure, program visibility and promotion, and recognition and rewards.

Management Support The first element of a successful employee suggestion system is to demonstrate buy-in from top management. Managers must show enthusiasm and commitment toward the program if it is to generate the desired results. A small business owner might begin by sharing his or her vision for the company with employees. Employees who understand the company's overall mission are more likely to submit valuable ideas that will help the company achieve its goals. The next step might be to make sure line managers support the suggestion system and do not feel threatened by it. It is also important for managers to raise the topic frequently in meetings and incorporate the positive results of employee suggestions into periodic progress reports. Managers should also be encouraged to submit suggestions themselves, although they should not generally be rewarded for ideas that fall under their normal strategic planning responsibilities.

Program Structure The next element of a successful employee suggestion system is structure. Experts recommend placing responsibility for program development and implementation with a single administrator. This person should begin by selecting a committee of employees—from all parts of the organization and representing various demographic groups—to help administer various phases. The administrator and employee committee should then develop clear rules to guide employee efforts in providing suggestions. Suggestion programs tend to be more successful when employees are encouraged to make reasonable suggestions within the parameters of their own work experience. "The real goal is to generate as many ideas as possible, and, over time, to improve the quality of the suggestions through feedback and encouragement," Bell noted. It is important to develop a clear policy statement that covers all aspects of the suggestion program and make sure that both managers and employees understand it. If employees view the process as open and above-board, it will help eliminate any suspicion about how ideas are reviewed and rewarded.

Program Visibility Another important element of successful employee suggestion programs is visibility. After all, employees cannot be expected to participate in a program if they are not made aware of it. Experts recommend launching suggestion programs in a highly public manner, with announcements, newsletters, parties, etc. Employees should come away with the idea that management intends to give full consideration to all suggestions and plans to act on the best ones in a timely manner. The suggestion system itself should also be widely publicized and promoted. Examples of possible systems include the familiar suggestion box with written forms; the old-fashioned bulletin board for posting ideas and results; a special toll-free telephone line to allow employees to phone in suggestions; or more sophisticated systems based on e-mail or postings to a dedicated Web site. Once the system has been introduced, it is important to follow up with ongoing promotional activities in order to maintain employee interest.

Recognition and Rewards Another vital element of successful employee suggestion systems is recognizing participants and providing rewards for good ideas. Employees are much more likely to participate in a suggestion program if the ideas they submit receive quick and thoughtful responses from management. Experts recommend setting a timetable in which receipt of an idea will be acknowledged (ranging from 24 hours with electronic systems to one week with more traditional systems). Then employees should be notified within 30 days whether or not their ideas will be adopted. Even in cases where an idea is not used, the employee who submitted it should be thanked for his or her participation in the program. It may be helpful to provide a small, tangible reward for employees who submit an idea to the suggestion system for the first time, such as a T-shirt, pen, or umbrella.

To ensure the success of a suggestion system, it is also important to publicize the suggestions used and their positive impact on the company. One way to do this might be to hold an annual dinner honoring the people who made suggestions over the course of the year. Many companies also establish reward systems for employee ideas that lead to cost savings or process improvements. For example, some companies distribute a fraction of all the savings provided by the employee suggestion system as part of their annual profit sharing programs. Experts acknowledge that it can be complicated to develop an appropriate reward system that recognizes valuable employee contributions without creating jealousy and resentment among fellow employees. Some suggest that this task might best be delegated to an employee advisory committee. The key is to evaluate ideas based on factors like innovation and ingenuity as well as monetary value when establishing rewards.

COMMON REASONS SUGGESTION SYSTEMS FAIL

"In some companies employees send a flood of useful ideas to upper management. In others the bottoms of suggestion boxes are coated with dust," wrote a contributor to *Executive Female*. "What's the difference? It's not the quality of the employees but the quality of leadership they receive." There are a number of reasons that suggestion systems might fail to generate a positive response among employees. In his article for *IIE Solutions*, Bell outlined several common problems companies experience in implementing and administering suggestion systems.

For example, employees may feel reluctant to offer suggestions if they believe that management is not truly interested in their ideas. If the company issues only a lukewarm invitation for suggestions or creates an atmosphere that might be perceived as intimidating, then employee suggestions are unlikely to be forthcoming. The company would probably experience similar problems in eliciting suggestions if management was unclear about who was invited to participate in the program or placed too many strict rules on participation.

Other common problems with employee suggestion systems involve management's response to suggestions. Employees are unlikely to participate in the program if they experience a slow response, or no response, to their suggestions. A suggestion system will also fail if there is no clear explanation of the acceptance or rejection of suggestions, or if employees perceive that management is making biased judgments about which suggestions to approve. Finally, suggestion systems tend to create problems for an organization when the rewards offered for good ideas are inconsistent or unpredictable.

BIBLIOGRAPHY
Bell, Robert F. "Constructing an Effective Suggestion System." *IIE Solutions.* February 1997.
Chanesky, Wayne S. "The Suggestion Box Syndrome." *Modern Machine Shop.* February 2006.

Dempsey, Mary. "Power of Suggestions." *Crain's Detroit Business.* 6 March 1995.

Martin, Charles. *Employee Suggestion Systems: Boosting Productivity and Profits.* Crisp Publications, 1997.

"Return of the Suggestion Box." *Industry Week.* 19 January 1998.

"Six Ways to Get Great Ideas from Employees." *Executive Female.* March-April 1996.

Ulfelder, Steve. "Beyond the Suggestion Box: How managers at the Best Places companies encourage the free flow of ideas, suggestions and innovations." *Computerworld.* 27 June 2005.

Walter, Kate. "Employee Ideas Make Money." *HR Magazine.* April 1996.

Wells, Susan J. "From Ideas to Results." *HR Magazine.* February 2005.

Hillstrom, Northern Lights
updated by Magee, ECDI

EMPLOYEE TERMINATION

Employee termination is the release of an employee against his or her will. Termination may be, at will, for cause, or for lack of work. The process is unavoidably painful: it imposes a certain degree of pain on the terminated employee, and the vast majority of people do not enjoy inflicting pain. Terminations, however, are a necessary part of business life and must be carried out promptly when the need for such actions becomes obvious in order to preserve the health of the enterprise.

TERMINATION-AT-WILL

An employment-at-will doctrine emerged in the United States in the mid-nineteenth century and came to be applied in both state and federal courts throughout the late 1800s and early 1900s. A concise interpretations of the doctrine was rendered by the California Supreme Court in 1910: "Precisely as may the employee cease labor at his whim or pleasure, and, whatever be his reason, good, bad, or indifferent, leave no one a legal right to complain; so, upon the other hand, may the employer discharge, and whatever be his reason, good, bad, or indifferent, no one has suffered a legal wrong."

Employees have retained their rights to be employed at will, but employers' rights to terminate workers at will have been modified over time based on the circumstances of the termination. The federal Wagner Act of 1935 made it illegal for companies to fire employees because they were engaged in union activity. Subsequent laws and court decisions during the mid-twentieth century reflected increasing concern about "wrongful discharge,"

implying that circumstances do exist in which it is legally wrong for a company to fire a worker. During the 1960s and 1970s, particularly, Congress enacted a number of new laws to protect workers from wrongful discharge in all types of cases, including those related to bias, whistle blowing, and other factors.

The practical consequences of this legal evolution have been that employment-at-will remains theoretically in force but is hemmed in—principally by many employee rights related to discrimination—to such an extent that legal advisors to business almost never unambiguously and forthrightly recommend using the right. This is understandable. Every employee belongs to several of the so-called "protected classes" in that they have an age, a gender, and are members of a race. It is always at least possible for an employee discharged at will to claim that the *real* motive behind the firing was motivated by bias. To avoid unnecessary lawsuits, many employers use workarounds although these are not exactly publicized.

Nevertheless at-will employment continues to be the rule in most businesses in the mid-2000s, the policy usually published by the company in its employment documents. The majority of employees understand this right as reciprocal to their own right to quit at any time. The small business employer's right is also indirectly maintained by the fact that those inclined to sue prefer to sue deep pockets, but the small business owner must be prepared to handle complaints, investigated by state or local agencies. The practice of at-will termination also implies significant discipline on the part of the small business manager who cannot simultaneous rely on the at-will policy and also give an explanation to the terminated employee which amounts to a list of other reasons than simply the employer's naked will.

TERMINATION FOR BEHAVIOR

Employees may be dismissed for cause, one of which is employee behavior. Common behaviors that lead to terminations include: absenteeism and tardiness; unsatisfactory performance; lack of qualifications or ability; changed job requirements; and gross misconduct; misconduct might involve drug abuse, theft, or other breaches of company or public policy. The term "behavior-related" distinguishes this type of termination from "trait-related" dismissals; traits are immutable characteristics of the employee, such as color of skin or physical disability. Trait-related terminations may be legal if the employer can prove that the trait keeps the employee from performing a job satisfactorily. However, those cases are uncommon.

Employers may terminate workers based on any type of behavior they deem unacceptable, although laws and court interpretations of these laws have protected some types of behavior when the employer's retaliatory action is deemed: 1) a violation of public policy; 2) a violation of an implied contract between the employer and the employee; or 3) an act of bad faith. An act of bad faith is vaguely defined: it is simply a recognition of an employer's duty to treat employees fairly. For example, it might be considered illegal for a company to fire a worker because he refused to engage in an activity a reasonable person would consider excessively dangerous or hazardous.

One illustration of a public policy violation would be a company that fired a worker because she refused to engage in an unlawful act, such as falsifying public financial documents or giving false testimony in court. Another example would be firing an employee who exercised a statutory right, e.g., voting in an election or worshiping at a church. A third type of infraction in this category would be dismissal of an employee for reasons stemming from his exercising a right to perform an important public obligation.

Violations of implied contracts occur when a company dismisses a worker despite the existence of an insinuated promise. For example, if an employer conveys to a worker that he will receive long-term employment in an effort to get the employee to take a job, it could be liable if it fired the worker without what the courts deem "just cause" or "due process." Implied contracts often emanate from interviews, policy manuals, or long-term patterns of behavior by the employer in a relationship with an employee.

Even when an employer acts in good faith and does not violate the public trust or an implied contract, it can be legally liable for dismissing a worker for other reasons. Specifically, a business may be found liable if it cannot prove that: 1) its decision to dismiss an employee is not founded on bias against a protected minority; or 2) the firing does not produce inequitable results. Suppose, for instance, that a company decided to fire all managers who did not have a college degree. Doing so, however, resulted in the dismissal of a disproportionate number of legally protected minorities from its work force. The company could be held liable if it could not show that having a college degree was necessary effectively to execute the duties of the position.

Steps in a Behavior-Related Termination Because of the legal risks inherent in dismissing employees, most companies terminate workers for behavior-related causes only after administering a progressive disciplinary and counseling process. Besides legal reasons, studies show that most companies try to correct behavior out of a perceived moral obligation to the employee. Furthermore, many employers benefit economically from correcting employee

behavior, rather than terminating workers, because of the high costs of employee turnover.

Correctional efforts do not always succeed, however. In instances when termination does prove necessary, business experts cite several basic steps that employers can take to ease the blow for the targeted employee, minimize damage to workplace morale and community standing, and shield themselves from legal liability. These steps include:

Develop clear, written policies for termination and follow them unswervingly. These policies should be readily accessible to employees in an employee handbook. The termination guidelines should include definitions of poor performance and gross misconduct, detailed descriptions of the review procedures that may lead to termination, and policies regarding severance, future employment references, and the return of company property.

Document reasons for termination over time, in quantifiable terms where possible.

- Conduct the termination meeting with the employee in a professional manner. The company representative conducting the meeting should be trained in dealing with the wide array of emotions—anger, denial, shock, etc.—that typically appear during such times.

- Give credit for positive contributions. Many experts contend that the shock of termination can be eased somewhat if they hear positive feedback about some aspect of their work performance. "Even in a termination based on performance, prompted by the fact that acquired skills were not adequate for a particular situation, the person's assets and liabilities can still be acknowledged," wrote Richard Bayer in *Business Horizons*. "A termination-for-performance should not be an occasion for abuse."

Prepare an information package for the terminated employee that outlines all elements of any severance package, including benefits and assistance options. Depending on laws and company policies, the company may provide severance pay, unemployment compensation, compensation for earned vacation days, career and placement counseling, ongoing health insurance, or other post-termination benefits.

- Craft considerate severance payout policies. The method of severance payout can be a major factor in easing (or increasing) an ex-employee's bitterness about termination. For example, Bayer notes that paying out severance in lump sums near the end of the calendar year will inflate the worker's W2 for the year and increase his/her tax burden. Small businesses can spare ex-employees this financial hit by absorbing the modest extra payroll expense of making regular severance payments.

Preserve an environment that enables the terminated employee to leave with dignity. "We should have no trouble arguing for compassionate termination policies that reduce stress on families, mitigate financial hardships, and decrease the chances that discharged employees will suffer debilitating emotional crises," wrote Bayer, who also cites the business advantages of dignified dismissals: "Employees who have witnessed termination with dignity will be more inclined to like the firm and support its goals and mission."

- Notify others that are impacted by the dismissal in a timely manner. This includes other employees, affected clients, and other entities with which your company has a business relationship.

REDUCTIONS IN FORCE (RIF)

Reductions in force (RIF)—also known as work force reductions, downsizing, right-sizing, restructuring, and reorganization—may include a number of methods of eliminating worker hours, including layoffs. Employee terminations in such cases are usually the result of surplus labor caused by economic factors, changing markets, poor management, or some other factor unrelated to worker behavior. Because work force reductions make a company vulnerable to many of the same legal risks inherent in behavior-related terminations, companies usually terminate workers by means of a carefully planned and documented process. The process is typically conducted in two stages: 1) selecting the workers to be dismissed and then terminating them according to the above process; and 2) providing benefits to ease the transition, including severance packages, unemployment compensation, and outplacement services.

Selecting and terminating employees is handled carefully because most profit-maximizing organizations are obviously concerned about losing talent or diluting the effectiveness of the company. But care must also be taken to ensure that the reductions do not violate state and federal laws. As with behavior-related terminations, downsizing terminations cannot be based on bias against protected minorities, or even unintentionally result in an inequitable outcome for a protected group. In fact, extensive legislation exists to protect disabled workers, racial minorities, workers over the age of forty, women, and other groups.

In addition to bias-related laws, moreover, companies must comply with a battery of laws specifically directed at corporate layoffs. For example, the federal Worker Adjustment and Retraining Notification (WARN) Act of 1988 requires companies with 100 or more employees to file at least sixty days prior notice before conducting mass layoffs or work force reductions. Among other stipulations, the notice must be in writing and addressed to employees and specified government workers.

The second stage of the downsizing process, outplacement, is also heavily influenced by legislation aimed at protecting employees. But it is also used to maintain the morale of the work force and to enhance the public image of the company conducting the work force reduction. Outplacement usually includes two activities: counseling and job search assistance. Counseling occurs on both the individual and group levels. Both are necessary to help the displaced worker 1) develop a positive attitude; 2) correctly assess career potential and direction, including background and skills, personality traits, financial requirements, geographic constraints, and aspirations; 3) develop job search skills, such as resume writing, interviewing, networking, and negotiating; and 4) adjust to life in transition or with a new employer.

Many companies assist with the job search by hiring a job-search firm to help their terminated employees find new work. In addition to providing some or all of the counseling services described above, job-search companies act as brokers, bringing together job hunters and companies looking for employees. Job-search companies can expedite the job hunting process by eliminating mismatches from the interview process and by helping both parties to negotiate employment terms. In some cases, the former employer will reimburse job hunting costs as part of the severance package of benefits.

SEE ALSO *Constructive Discharge; Layoffs and Downsizing*

BIBLIOGRAPHY
Bayer, Richard. "Termination with Dignity." *Business Horizons.* September 2000.

Craik, David. "Caught in The Act." *Commercial Motor.* 17 February 2005.

Henneman, Todd. "Ignoring Signs of Violence Can Be a Fatal, Costly Mistake." *Workforce Management.* 27 February 2006.

Jurkiewicz, John. "How Should I Fire? Four practices to have in place before terminating an employee." *Pest Control.* March 2005.

Poe, Andrea C. "Make Foresight 20/20." *HRMagazine.* February 2000.

Richard, Kerry M. "Pruning Poor Performers. *Veterinary Economics.* January 2006.

Steingold, Fred. "Firing Employees and Avoiding Trouble." *American Coin-Op.* February 2004.

Hillstrom, Northern Lights
updated by Magee, ECDI

EMPLOYEE THEFT

Employee theft is a considerable problem for many companies, but its precise extent is poorly documented. The U.S. Census Bureau does not track employee theft as a category but refers researchers to the Annual Retail Theft Survey conducted by Jack L. Hayes International. The U.S. Bureau of Justice Statistics publishes data on larceny, theft, and embezzlement but not in categories that permit inference of the extent of employee involvement. The most recent Annual Retail Theft Survey was based on data from 27 retail organizations employing 1.7 million people. In 2004, 3.7 percent of the employees were apprehended stealing from their employers to the tune of $671 per incident. By contrast, the average "take" of shoplifters in the survey was $149. Employee apprehensions were up 4 percent over 2003—the numbers breaking a multi-year trend of declining employee theft.

The Hayes International survey identifies what might be called mid-level cases of employee theft. Minor theft is the taking for at-home use of rolls of adhesive tape or boxes of paperclips, etc., for instance, a very wide-spread practice. Major theft is of the magnitude reported by Leslie Shiner writing for *The Journal of Light Construction*. Shiner analyzed the case of a high-end remodeling firm where the sole bookkeeper of the organization had embezzled $550,000 during a seven year engagement—caught in the end because the business owner could not understand how, despite very profitable contracts, his company never seemed to have any money. Shiner reported on a small business case. Major fraud by very high-ranking employees of businesses like Enron are the theft-peak of the employee crime pyramid.

FORMS OF EMPLOYEE THEFT

Employee theft may be grouped into four major categories: 1) manipulation of company records either to embezzle money outright or to hide the theft of goods; 2) direct theft of inventory, products, or cash; 3) abuse of power in order to aid and abet thievery by partners; and 4) theft of information for sale to others or for direct use (e.g., credit card theft).

Records Employees directly involved in financial administration and with access to company checks and corporate records may engage in forging company checks for personal use. Creating "ghost payroll entries" and then paying "phantom" employees is another method, sometimes quite elaborate in implementation involving phony time cards. Forged billings by non-existent vendors is another method—with the accounts payable clerk writing checks to him or herself when paying the fake billing. Employees also destroy paper records so that "lost shipments" cannot be traced—or fake orders to cover items missing from inventory through their own thefts.

Direct Theft In its simplest form employees simply take cash from cash registers to which multiple individuals have access to dip into petty cash resources generally easily accessible to several employees. Direct theft of valuable products or materials invariable relies upon trust (the employee comes and goes, often with a truck, stashes goods away, is never checked) or opportunity (the employee has access to the warehouse and the warehouse is not effectively guarded).

Abuse of Position In one form of this abuse, known as "sweethearting," an employee grants a friend a discount or rings up fewer items than are packaged for taking out—or rings up a cheaper item than the item that leaves the store actually cost. The goods acquired in this manner may later be shared. Individuals taking inventory may abuse this privileged status by counting fewer item than are present and, if this "mistake" is not detected, later personally "adjusting" the inventory by taking the uncounted items home.

STEALING INFORMATION

As reported more fully in the *Computer Crime* essay in this volume, an increasing proportion of attacks on computer systems take place from within the company. The target of this type of thievery is protected personal data, such as credit card information, which, in the wrong hands, can be turned into cash. More sophisticated forms of such theft are conducted in order to sell information to third parties.

Signs of Employee Theft Managers and small business owners need to be aware of tell-tale signs which, when they frequently repeat, may be the tracks of a thief at work inside the company. A useful checklist to keep in mind mentally includes—

- Missing records (such as shipping and/or receiving bills).

- Company checks that bounce or someone is surprised that the company is doing business with XYZ and then adds: "Who *is* XYZ anyway?"

- Customer complaints about missing, late, or short deliveries.

- Hefty payments made for "miscellaneous" purposes in employee expense claims.

- Frequent and puzzling mix-ups in inventory. And

- Managers who insist on performing clerical duties.

STOPPING EMPLOYEE THEFT

In the well-run small business employees are trusted to be honest but sensible policies and practices will be in place to detect the loss of product and closely to monitor financial and administrative transactions. Some of the tools include the following:

1. Clear Policy and Good Example. The company will have and will publish its ethical stance and its managers will be seen to adhere to it strictly in spirit and in action, inside and out, with customers, vendors, and employees alike.

2. Hiring Orientation. Newly hired employees must leave their orientation session fully aware that the company has zero-tolerance for any kind of irregularity—and the dire consequences that will follow pilfering, never mind theft.

3. Adequate Controls. Controls will be in place so that physical goods are locked up, protected at night, and closely checked on paper. In a small business particularly, where time is difficult to find, the owner will, nonetheless, show a keen interest in accounting details, probe into them occasionally, and not simply let the "number crunchers" drift unsupervised. Financial controls will include some of the following:

   • Checkbooks will be locked up, and access to cash and checks will be given only to authorized employees.

   • Few individuals will have the authority to write a check, by preference one writing and one signing the check.

   • More than one person will have insight into the total finances so that "lone wolf" strategies are forestalled.

   • Handling of cash will always be accompanied by documentation.

   • Books will be audited at intervals not necessarily known to accounting people in advance.

   • Cash will be rapidly and immediately deposited rather than accumulating in cash registers.

   • All invoices will be formally checked against deliveries before vendors are paid.

BIBLIOGRAPHY

Berta, Dina. "Toomey: Ward off employee theft with internal checks and balances." *Nation's Restaurant News.* 12 December 2005.

Brandman, Barry. "Inside Job: Many food distributors find themselves victimized by internal theft. Most are guilty of committing at least one of the Seven Sins of Distribution Center Security." *Food Logistics.* 15 September 2005.

Fishman, Neil H. "Signs of Fraud." *CPA Journal.* December 2000.

McTaggart, Jenny and Joe Tarnowski. "Employee Theft, Shoplifting Prevail at Retail." *Progressive Grocer.* 1 November 2005.

"Mojoes Coffee House." *Specialty Coffee Retailer.* December 2005.

Niehoff, Brian P., and Robert J. Paul. "Causes of Employee Theft and Strategies that HR Managers Can Use for Prevention." *Human Resource Management.* Spring 2000.

17th Annual Retail Theft Survey, 2004. Jack L. Hayes International. Available from http://www.hayesinternational.com. Retrieved on 14 March 2006.

Shiner, Leslie. "Protect Yourself from Employee Theft." *The Journal of Light Construction.* October 2005.

Hillstrom, Northern Lights
updated by Magee, ECDI

EMPLOYER IDENTIFICATION NUMBER (EIN)

A federal employer identification number (EIN), also sometimes referred to as a tax identification number, is a nine-digit code that businesses use to identify themselves for tax reporting, banking, and other purposes. Sole proprietorships without employees are allowed to use the owner's Social Security number for tax reporting purposes. But any company that has employees other than the owner—in addition to all partnerships, limited liability companies, and corporations—must instead apply for and use an EIN. The EIN is specific to a certain business, like a Social Security number is specific to a certain person. Therefore, if an individual or group owns more than one business, a separate EIN is required for each one.

There are several situations in which a business person should apply for an EIN. For example, an EIN may be needed in order to start a new business (other than a sole proprietorship with no employees) or upon the purchase of an ongoing business. An EIN is also needed when a business undergoes a change in its organization type (i.e., from a sole proprietorship to partnership or corporation) or when it hires employees for the first time. Some businesses may require an EIN in order to create a pension plan or form a trust. Still others find that they must have an EIN for banking purposes (many banks hold commercial accounts under EINs and personal accounts under Social Security numbers).

Businesses are required to file for an EIN as soon as it is needed for one of the above-mentioned reasons. In order to be assigned an EIN, the company must file Form SS-4, the Application for Employer Identification Number, with the Internal Revenue Service (IRS). The forms are available at all IRS and Social Security offices, or they can be downloaded from the IRS web site. No application fee applies, but the form can take several weeks to process. If any business tax forms are due in the meantime, the small business owner should simply write "applied for" in the space for the company's EIN. In addition to the federal EIN, states that charge their own income tax often require businesses to file for a state EIN.

The individual can apply for an EIN in various ways. Possibly the easies way to do so is by telephone. The IRS provide a toll free number (800-829-4933) which may be called anytime between 7 a.m. and 10 p.m. local time, Monday through Friday. An "assistor," as the IRS calls the person, will take information from the caller and issue the EIN over the telephone. Other methods are by FAX, mail, and over the Internet. To explore the most handy approach, the individual can look things over at IRS's website for this subject provided in the references below.

BIBLIOGRAPHY

U.S. Department of the Treasury. Internal Revenue Service. "Employer ID Numbers (EINs). Available from http://www.irs.gov/businesses/small/article/0,id=98350,00.html. Retrieved on 15 March 2006.

Hillstrom, Northern Lights
updated by Magee, ECDI

EMPLOYMENT APPLICATIONS

The employment application is an important part of the hiring process: it provides employers with clear and relevant information about applicants. An application is also a legal document and becomes a part of a person's permanent file once he or she is hired. A start-up small business without such an application can write its own or acquire forms from vendors; if the form is produced in-house, it is advisable to have it checked by a qualified attorney to avoid violating civil rights statutes at federal and state levels.

APPLICATION CONTENTS

Applications contain questions designed to help the employer make a hiring decision. In essence, they reorganize the information the employer typically finds on a resume while also furnishing additional information that can be helpful in making hiring decisions. Application contents typically include the following:

- Statement by the business that it is an equal opportunity employer and that it is the policy of the business to provide opportunities to all qualified persons without regard to race, creed, color, religious belief, sex, age, national origin, ancestry, physical or mental handicap, or veteran's status.

- Name, address, phone number, and other relevant contact information.

- Position the applicant is seeking within the company.

- Hours of availability.

- Expected salary.

- Past experience—This will make up the majority of the application form, for it is common for companies to request a listing of all positions that an applicant has held over the past three to five years. This section may include a request for supervisor names and reasons for leaving previous positions.

- Educational background—This typically includes schools attended, years attended and degrees attained.

- Other information—This might include questions about the applicant's experience with computer software programs and other office equipment, or it might ask the person to describe hobbies and other interests. This section of the application can be a tricky one for employers, as some questions may violate legal parameters. A good rule of thumb for small business owners weighing whether to include questions of this type is to always make sure that the responses could be pertinent to making a hiring decision.

- Closing statement—The statement at the end of an application usually includes legally worded information for the applicant about the application, including permissible uses of the information contained therein. The employer should mention that they are an equal opportunity employer on the document, and legal experts recommend that employment applications include a statement regarding the right of the hiring company to check references and verify information on the application. The employer should state clearly that falsifying any information on an application can be considered grounds for dismissal.

- Signature of applicant.

Again, it is advisable to have a home-made employee application checked by an attorney in order to avoid potential complications.

POTENTIAL PITFALLS

There are several possible pitfalls in designing an application form. On an application form, it is not permissible to pursue any of the following lines of questioning:

- Questions about the applicant's age, race, sex, religion, national origin, physical characteristics, or other personal information that violates Equal Employment Opportunity Commission (EEOC) guidelines.

- Questions about the applicant's health history or handicaps (if any) that violate the Americans with Disabilities Act (ADA).

- Questions that violating any state regulations (individual states may have regulations concerning employer rights to inquire about past salary history, referral sources, credit, access to transportation, or personal emergency information). It is important to check for state guidelines in employment applications before putting together a business application.

READY-MADE APPLICATIONS

In the Internet age, the start-up business can quite readily find carefully written employment applications on the Internet. A Google search on the phrase "employment forms" will produce in excess of 300,000 hits, a Yahoo search in excess of 280,000. The first couple of pages will already offer some free forms for direct downloading as well as forms for purchase. Alternatively, the business owner can purchase books with forms, some with a CD attached (examples are provided in the references below, see Fyock and Steingold) from which a form appropriate to the business can be selected.

USING THE APPLICATION

The application should be given to every person applying for a position from outside the company. It should be required regardless of level of position, so that all potential employees have a similar experience and receive similar treatment. Normally, a separate, abbreviated application form is used for people who are already employed by the company who wish to apply for positions elsewhere within the company.

Some laws require employers to retain applications—whether the person is hired or not—for up to one year after the date the application is made. The employer is not usually required to reconsider the applications on file as new positions become available, but

they must have record of the applications made to the company. Applications become a part of the permanent record of the employee once hired. Increasingly, these employee records are held in electronic files.

SEE ALSO *Employee Hiring*

BIBLIOGRAPHY
Fyock, Catherine D. *Hiring Source Book.* Society For Human Resource Management, 28 April 2004.

"Integic Lands OPM Work." *Washington Technology.* 24 January 2005.

"Made E-Z Products Inc." *Roofing Contractor.* May 2004.

"Personnel Forms." *Roofing Contractor.* October 2003.

Smith, Shawn A. and Rebecca A. Mazin. *The HR Answer Book.* AMACOM, March 2004.

Steingold, Fred. S. *Legal Forms for Starting & Running a Small Business.* Nolo, February 2006.

Hillstrom, Northern Lights
updated by Magee, ECDI

EMPLOYMENT CONTRACTS

Employment contracts replace the normal hiring arrangement between employer and employee with a legal document in which the employment relationship is spelled out in substantial detail. Important elements of employment contracts deal with compensation, bonuses, stock options, severance packages ("golden parachutes"), fringe benefits (currently and after retirement), non-compete requirements including disclosure of internal information ("post-employment confidentiality"), and non-solicitation of current employees after severance. Less obvious but nevertheless equally binding forms of an employment contract are frequently used. These usually take the form of an agreement the employee is asked to sign during the employment process. The agreement commits the employee to hold certain types of information confidential and/or to prohibits the employee to work for a competitor in any relationship for some specified period of time, e.g., three years. These lower forms of the employment contract, significantly, provide no special compensation for doing what is asked: they are conditions of employment.

BACKGROUND AND TRENDS

Employment contracts became a standard method of attracting high-powered, high-profile executives to a corporation. In the expansionary decades following World War II, personal qualities and charisma became associated (rightly or wrongly) with corporate performance; in consequence market forces worked in such a manner that such contracts became rather surprisingly rich packages—the much-courted executive able to secure, well in advance of doing anything at all, guarantees of high compensation and reward, including a golden parachute. Public resistance to this broad trend did not translate into regulatory action (including self-regulatory action) until the spectacular corporate scandals surrounding Enron and WorldCom surfaced in the early 2000s.

During the dot-com boom of the 1990s—which the retired chair of the Federal Reserve, Alan Greenspan, dubbed "irrational exuberance" in a speech to the American Enterprise Institute given on December 5, 1996—executives of many quite small corporations also got themselves employment contracts in anticipation of earning vast wealth quickly in an Internet enterprise. The dot-com bust, which came in 2000, changed the exuberant mood so that, by the mid-2000s the business press barely mentioned employment contracts except in a negative context.

The passage of legislation aimed at reforming slack or fraudulent corporate behavior (the Sarbanes-Oxley Act of 2002), followed by Securities and Exchange Commission regulations, has brought employment contracts into sharp focus. In the mid-2000s, public as well as private emphasis was on reform, including bringing executive compensation in line with total compensation of all employees. However, executive compensation—the driving force behind employment contracts—appears to be a cyclical phenomenon with periods of reform followed by periods of excess. The only certainty is change.

Employment contracts, especially of the exuberant variety, appear to be rarely used by small businesses except in certain contexts—namely to secure the owner a reasonable retirement income after the business is sold or terminated.

Crafting an Employment Contract Business owners who are considering introducing employment contracts into their operations should consider the following:

- Employment contracts imposed unilaterally by the employer—rather than by genuine mutual agreement—are at substantial risk in the courts. If the employee is found to have entered into the contract under duress, the agreement will be struck down.

- Employment contracts are an effective means of mitigating the risk of business damage at the hands of ex-employees—the motivation behind confidentiality and non-compete clauses. The

confidentiality clauses are easier to enforce. A non-compete clause written so that the employee appears unable to practice an occupation will likely be ignored—and if challenged in court, the court will side with the employee. State law may significantly curb an employer's ability to impose non-compete clauses.

- Employment contracts should, ideally, maintain the rights of the employer to terminate employment "at will"—and such clauses need to be present in the contract even if specific periods of employment are specified. If an "at will" clause is present, of course, the contract must specify how an employee with a three-year contract will be compensated if the contract is terminated after a year.

- Termination "for cause" should always be present and the triggering causes specified—legal offenses, dishonest, fraud, etc.

- Employment contracts—indeed all contracts—should be vetted by a competent attorney. Many states regulate such contracts, and the owner may be unaware of these regulations.

- Employment contracts should be used only for legitimate business relationships. Compensation for services rendered should be reasonable and should be distributed only when they are in fact completed. This element is of particular relevance to family-owned enterprises, which sometimes turn to employment contracts as part of their overall succession plan.

- Employment contracts are not "one-size-fits-all." Employers should recognize that managers and executives can and should be rewarded in different ways, depending on their contributions to the company.

- Severance arrangements should be reviewed on a regular basis to determine their suitability for inclusion in employment contracts. Most severance packages are classified as ERISA (Employment Retirement Income Security Act) welfare benefits.

- Dispute resolution mechanisms are often incorporated into employment contracts. This arbitration language is sometimes limited to certain specified issues within the contract (authority of employee, divisions of intellectual property, bonus calculations, etc.), thus leaving other aspects of the contract to the courts. Other employment agreements, however, include "blanket" arbitration clauses that provide for arbitration of all disputes between the employer and the employee under contract.

BIBLIOGRAPHY

Barlas, Stephen. "SEC Proposes Changes to Executive Pay Reporting." *Strategic Finance.* March 2006.

"Game Plan." *Network Computing.* 18 March 2004.

Lublin, Joann S. "Many Top-Level Executives Lack Employment Contracts." *The Wall Street Journal.* 12 November 2004.

"Noted and Noteworthy." *U.S. Banker.* March 2006.

Powers, Kelly A.J. "A Guide to Creating Employment Agreements That Protect Both Leaders and Their Charities." *The Chronicle of Philanthropy.* 6 March 2003.

"Reform Tenacity." *Pensions & Investments.* 20 February 2006.

Schweitzer, Carole. "Don't Ask, Don't Get: Legal expert Jed R. Mandel explains why economic conditions continue to signal caveats for executive contracts." *Association Management.* April 2004.

"10 Executive Contracts with Perks and Quirks." *Advertising Age.* 22 December 2003.

U.S. Securities and Exchange Commission. "Executive Compensation: A Guide for Investors." Available from http://www.sec.gov/investor/pubs/execomp0803.htm#employmentcontract. Retrieved on 15 March 2006.

Hillstrom, Northern Lights
updated by Magee, ECDI

EMPLOYMENT INTERVIEWS

Interviewing is an integral part of the hiring process. It provides small business owners with their primary opportunity to learn about a candidate's work experience, education, and interpersonal abilities, as well as characteristics—such as enthusiasm—that are rarely conveyed in resumes; similarly, the interview process often provides would-be employees with their best opportunity to inquire about various aspects of company operations and expectations.

BEFORE THE INTERVIEW

Before beginning the interview, the manager must define the skills needed to fill the position. This, along with careful applicant research and candidate selection, helps to ensure a smooth interview process.

Critical Skills. To secure the right person for a job, the manager must define the necessary skills for the job, often called the critical skills. These describe exactly the skills a person needs successfully to perform the tasks. Sample critical skills could be phrased as "facility with communication," "high degree of organization," or "ability to work well independently." Critical skills are expanded upon in the job description and help guide the

manager during the selection process and then provide structure for the position throughout employment.

Applicant Research. Applicants must be researched before the interview. The most common methods of receiving candidate information are the resume and cover letter, generated by the applicant, or the employment application, generated by the company. These records can be very informative. Not only do they provide basic background/historical information, but the presentation can also provide glimpses into the applicant's suitability for employment. A manager, for instance, should watch for such problems as typographical errors, spelling errors, or incomplete information about the applicant. Likewise, pay attention to the length of time an applicant has spent at a position, the responsibilities they were given in successive positions, and the chronological information on the resume. Frequent job changes, declining responsibility, or gaps in employment are all items that should be pursued for clarification. None of these call for immediate rejection of a candidate, but any could signal a potential area of exploration.

Selecting Candidates. Not all people who apply will be qualified for the position. The manager selects candidates for the position from the entire group of applicants, choosing individuals who demonstrate the best skills for the open position in their written presentation.

When putting together an interview schedule, a manager needs to balance the desire to interview all qualified people with the practical necessity of concluding the search in a timely fashion. Consider the time frame for the hiring decision, the amount of time available to interview, and select candidates carefully. A good rule of thumb is to allow from 30 to 60 minutes per interview; then add 15 minutes in between interviews, to prevent back-to-back interviews. Small business consultants caution that a day of back-to-back interviews can tire the interviewer and hinder his or her ability to make a well-reasoned decision.

THE INTERVIEW

Time well spent in the interviewing process can prevent a poor hiring decision. Preparation is the key to a successful interview. Don't scrimp on time during the interview, and be sure to let the candidate do the majority of the talking. The space for the interview should be ready, and the interviewer should have already prepared questions for the discussion.

Environment. The interviewer can make the candidate feel at ease or an interviewer can make the candidate uncomfortable. In short, the interviewer sets the tone for the meeting. To insure a successful interview, be sure that the space is free of distractions and interruptions such as telephones or other employees; allow for minimal barriers between you and the candidate (desks or tables); and always offer the candidate coffee, soda, or water. Be courteous and professional without presenting an environment that is too formal.

Behavioral Interviewing. Though there are many kinds of interviewing techniques, behavioral interviewing allows the interviewer to focus on likely future performance based on past behavior. This is one of the most popular interviewing techniques, and it is effective precisely because it focuses on specific situations and examples, not hypothetical situations. It requires that candidates draw on past experience to describe what they actually did in specific work situations, and this discourages "made up" answers or hypothetical exaggerations. It thus provides potentially valuable insights into how a candidate is likely to approach issues and problems he or she may face in your company's work environment.

Types of Questions. Interview questions are designed to explore the candidate's previous work experience, education, and other areas which will enable the interviewer to determine if the candidate has the best match of critical skills for the position. There are many types of questions.

The biggest mistake interviewers make is to ask only factual questions during an interview. Often, an interviewer asks questions that illicit a yes or no or other single response answer: "When did you join the company?" or "How long were you in the position?" Such questions limit the candidate's response; they don't require the candidate to consider or analyze any specific problem or situation.

Open ended questions allow the candidate to expand on a topic, describing experiences and actual situations. They keep the candidate talking and the interviewer listening. The focus of open ended questions is always on past performance, using wording such as "Give me an example of....", "Explain the nature of your duties at....", "Tell me about a time when you...." Such questions are the basis of behavioral interviewing and focus on specific examples of past behavior—how a candidate performed in a specific circumstance.

Probing questions are used to uncover more information than the original answer given. If a candidate answers with "yes / no" or a very general response, the interviewer can probe by encouraging the candidate to elaborate on a point within the answer. Ask very specific questions when probing. Specific questions encourage a candidate to expand on a general answer.

Avoid leading questions which direct the candidate to a specific answer and do not encourage an honest, spontaneous response. If leading, the interviewer may nod to encourage a particular response or may stack two or more questions guaranteed to produce a desired

answer. This biases the interviewer to the candidate who responds most easily with the correct answer.

Finally, increasing numbers of companies are turning to "brainteasers" or "verbal puzzles" during the interview process as tools in gauging a candidate's ability to perform under pressure. "Games and challenges can ... help interviewers overcome a tendency to make snap judgments about candidates too early in the meeting," wrote Martha Frase-Blunt in *HRMagazine.* "Tossing an unexpected question into the mix can bring a new focus for both prospect and interviewer." These types of interview questions have become particularly popular in high-tech areas such as software design and engineering. Companies are encouraged to make judicious use of these lines of questioning, however. If the quiz or puzzle has no apparent relevance to the job that needs to be filled, candidates may react negatively. "Good applicants may be turned off by what they may consider to be a frivolous or unfair process of making important selection decisions based on a five-minute exercise," one employment manager pointed out in *HRMagazine.*

Closing the Interview. When closing the interview, first offer to answer any questions the candidate may have. Have basic factual information about the company and position readily available. Make the follow-up process clear to the candidate. If there are other candidates to interview, be sure that the candidate knows this and knows when to expect your decision. Always thank the candidate for interviewing, and try to leave the candidate with the most favorable impression possible of the company, regardless of whether or not the person is offered the job.

Note Taking. There are different schools of thought on note taking. Some feel that notes during the interview distract the interviewer; others say that notes should be made both during and after the interview. If you do choose to take notes, make sure that they are specific enough to help the interviewer reconstruct the details of the interview, particularly when a number of candidates are being interviewed for the same position. Notes should never be made about the physical aspects of the candidate or any other area of potential legal liability. Note taking should be reserved to commentary about the applicant's qualifications and skills suitable to the job.

Team Interviewing. In the current atmosphere of work teams and group decision making, it may be desirable to have a group interview the candidate. "Use as many sets of ears as possible," counseled Michael Santo in *Agency Sales Magazine.* "This team interview approach helps catch the true response of the candidate. The team interview has an added benefit of keeping the interview focused on the more critical areas, as it is less likely that all the members of the interview team will be drawn into conversations that are not insightful and could cross into areas that may have legal ramifications."

When this team-based approach is deemed appropriate, be sure that every member of the team has all of the information about the candidate prior to the interview, including copies of the person's resume, cover letter, and application. Plan the interview questions that each member of the team will ask, so that the candidate is not asked the same question by more than one member of the team.

LEGAL ASPECTS OF INTERVIEWING

Interviewing is subject to both state and federal laws that define employment discrimination in all aspects of employment. It is worthwhile to check for any state hiring regulations that might apply. The main federal regulations for hiring include:

I. The Civil Rights Act of 1964 (Title VII)

II. The Age Discrimination in Employment Act of 1967 (ADEA)

III. The Americans with Disabilities Act of 1990 (ADA)

IV. The Uniformed Services Employment Reemployment Rights Act of 1994 (USERRA)

V. The Immigration Reform and Control Act

Together, these acts forbid a company to discriminate in hiring on the basis of sex, age, race, national origin, religion, physical disability or veteran status. These are called protected classes so questions about any of these topics during an interview are illegal.

The interviewer must avoid all questions that could seem legally questionable, such as those about height, weight, age, marital status, religious or political beliefs, dependents, birth control, birthplace, race, and national origin. Generally, it is a good rule to measure a question's necessity by the role it plays in the determination of a candidate's ability to perform a job.

TURNING SOMEONE DOWN

Once the job is offered and accepted by a candidate, immediately notify other candidates that they have not been selected for the position. A rejection is best done by phone—it is immediate, and it allows the manager to personally thank the candidate for taking the time to interview. When unable to phone, a letter of rejection is suitable. Although the candidate may ask, it is not necessary to be extremely specific about the types of qualities that the person lacks. An exact description of what was lacking in the candidate may open the manager to lawsuits for unfair hiring practices and discrimination.

The importance of making the right hiring decision is crucial in staffing a business. It means nothing short of selecting the right person for the right job at the right time. Since the interview is often the most decisive factor in determining who is hired for a specific position, business consultants contend that the importance of mastering the interview process should be appreciated; indeed, the interview process is ultimately an important factor in determining workforce quality and satisfaction.

SEE ALSO *Employee Hiring*

BIBLIOGRAPHY
Frase-Blunt, Martha. "Games Interviewers Play." *HRMagazine.* January 2001.

Ralston, Steven M., William G. Kirkwood and Patricia A. Burant. "Helping Interviewees Tell Their Stories." *Business Communications Quarterly.* September 2003.

Santo, Michael. "Interviewing the Chameleon." *Agency Sales Magazine.* November 2000.

"Surveys Describe Disastrous Employment Interviews." *Occupational Outlook Quarterly.* Summer 2005.

Yost, Lauren. "Playbook: The ABCs of Interviewing: How to find the right employee by conducting the perfect interview." *Parks & Recreation.* November 2005.

Hillstrom, Northern Lights
updated by Darnay, ECDI

EMPLOYMENT OF MINORS

Businesses in some industries rarely utilize minors as employees, but in many other sectors teenagers comprise a large component of the total work force; indeed, some enterprises engaged in various retail, restaurant, and other businesses rely on minors to a considerable degree. The primary advantage associated with employing minors is that compensation is far less costly than if the employer decided to hire adults as staff. But employers should be aware of the various legal restrictions that state and federal agencies have placed on the employment of minors, and they should also be cognizant of the particular challenges and rewards that accompany the decision to hire teenagers.

LEGAL CONSIDERATIONS

In addition to state laws, which have varying rules regarding child labor and compulsory school attendance laws, employers should be familiar with the federal government's Fair Labor Standards Act (FLSA). The rules in the FLSA differ from individual states in some respects; in cases where differences exist, the stricter law prevails.

Ignorance of state and federal child labor laws will not save employers from fines; fines can be quite substantial. "Many companies have discovered that there are two sides to the child labor issue," wrote Steven Slutsky in *Journal of Business Strategy.* "On the one hand, minors can be a cost-effective and flexible supplement to your core work force. But on the other hand, the penalties for violating the child labor laws can be steep." Indeed, the U.S. Department of Labor (DOL) imposes fines of up to $10,000 per minor on those businesses that violate the child labor provisions detailed in the FLSA, and in the mid-1990s the DOL upped the stakes for employers who flout or remain ignorant of American child labor law by adding fines of $10,000 per *infraction*—not per minor— and eliminating the cap on the total amount of fines that could be imposed. These latter measures were taken for the purpose of punishing employers whose violations contributed to the death or significant injury of a minor.

Slutsky admitted that the likelihood of an employer being singled out by the Department of Labor for a random compliance audit is remote unless the company is active in a high-risk industry. "But don't assume that the DOL won't find out about child labor law violations," he warned. "Word usually gets back to the agency in the form of complaints from underage employees or their parents or even unions. The publicity factor is involved here as well, since violations that result in injuries or death often are picked up by the media."

Small business owners, then, should make sure that they—and their supervisory personnel, if any—are fully aware of what minor employees are permitted to do. First, it is important to recognize that employees can basically be broken down into three age groups: workers who are 18 years old or older, and thus regarded as adults under the law; youngsters who are 16 or 17 years old; and minors who are 14 or 15 years old (employment of children under the age of 14 is severely restricted, although parents who employ their children enjoy greater leeway).

Restrictions on Minors Under Age 18 According to the Department of Labor, minors under the age of 18 are not allowed to perform jobs that the department has classified as detrimental to their physical safety, mental safety, and health. These restrictions forbid minors from operating (or setting up, repairing, adjusting, or cleaning) any power-driven machines, including woodworking machinery, metal forming machines, punching and shearing machines, paper products machines, circular and band saws, bakery machines, meat-processing equipment, or hoisting apparatus (forklifts, cranes, derricks, freight elevators). Since February 2005, under revised DOL regulations, minors under 17 are also restricted to the types of

cooking activities in which they may engage. They may not drive on the job except under certain circumstances and only if they have a valid state license, have completed state-approved driver education, and have no record of moving violations. In addition, minors are prohibited from engaging in the following activities at their place of employment:

- Operating motor vehicles or assisting as outside help on those vehicles.

- Working in any capacity on roofing, wrecking, or demolition jobs.

- Working in mining operations, unless in office, maintenance, or repair capacities away from the mine site.

- Working in areas where explosives (fireworks, dynamite, ammunition, etc.) are manufactured or stored.

- Working in logging or sawmilling operations.

- Assisting in the manufacture of brick, tile, and kindred products.

- Working at tasks that require exposure to radioactive substances.

- Undertaking excavation work (exceptions are made for manual excavation in trenches and building excavations, provided the dig does not exceed four feet in depth).

It should be noted that exceptions to some of these rules may be made for minors who are participating in recognized apprenticeship programs. On a practical basis, however, these restrictions mean that minors are of limited use in non-office settings to businesses engaged in construction, manufacturing, and the like. Still, manufacturers and construction firms do maintain staff devoted to clerical work and custodial duties, and minor employees may be suitable for these slots. The above restrictions generally have little impact on businesses looking for cashiers, salespersons, stocking personnel, and other positions that do not require handling of motor-driven equipment.

Restrictions on Minors Age 14 and 15 Additional restrictions have been put in place by both federal and state agencies concerning the employment of 14- and 15-year-old minors. "The environment in which 14-year-olds and 15-year-olds do their work also plays an important role in determining whether the duties are permissible," cautioned Slutsky. "For example, although workers in this age group may clean, wrap, seal, label, weigh, price, and stock produce, they can't perform these tasks in a freezer. And while they may assemble, pack, and shelve merchandise—as can 16-year-olds and 17-year-olds—they can't do it in a warehouse or rooms where manufacturing and processing work takes place." Moreover, owners of construction and transportation companies should be aware that minors under age 16 may not perform any kind of work (including office work) on the construction site or transportation medium. Other areas in which 14- and 15-year-olds are restricted from working include boiler/engine rooms, meat coolers, and places where products are being loaded or unloaded from conveyors or railroad cars.

In addition, 14- and 15-year-old teens are not allowed to work before 7:00 a.m. and after 7:00 p.m. during the school year. They are also not permitted to work during school hours. Finally, these minors may only work certain numbers of hours. During periods of the year when school is in session, 14- and 15-year-old minors may work no more than three hours a day on school days, no more than 18 hours total a week, no more than eight hours a day on non-school days, and no more than 40 hours total during weeks in which school is not in session (summer, vacation breaks).

The most recent revision of federal rules took place on February 14, 2005. However, rules change from time to time, therefore occasional checks are a good idea. The business owner can easily check the DOL web-site http://www.dol.gov/esa/regs/compliance/whd/childlaborcentral.htm to see what is new.

USING MINORS EFFECTIVELY

Small business owners and employment analysts agree that the key to securing skilled and motivated minors as employees lies at the very beginning, with the application and interview. Remarkably, some employers tend to lump teen employees together into one indistinguishable mass, but in reality, dramatic differences exist within this demographic group (and all other demographic groups, for that matter) in such areas as punctuality, honesty, ambition, talent, intelligence, and all-around quality. In order to find top-notch minor employees, small business owners are encouraged to pay close attention to the information provided in the job application form. Are the students high academic achievers in high school? Do they participate in extracurricular activities? Do they provide good references, such as former employers or school teachers/administrators?

In addition, employers should take the time to conduct a thorough interview with minor applicants, even if it is for a part-time entry level position. Every employee plays a part in shaping company culture, and if the new hire has a bad attitude, it has the potential to influence other employees. This is particularly true for businesses that have a significant number of minor employees. For example, an employer who hires a minor for a floor sales position only to discover that the new hire has a previously undetected predilection for emotionally distant, "cool" behavior may find other emotionally malleable—and previously customer-friendly—staffers adopting some of the same mannerisms.

Employers who hire minors also need to recognize that, as Bess Ritter May said in *Supervision,* "adolescence is a transitional period. Those who are in this age group are forming their personalities and identities." This sometimes awkward period of development will likely manifest itself in all phases of the teen's life—including work. But while employers may experience some frustration dealing with teens who are buffeted by school, societal, and peer pressures, they can take comfort in the fact "that it's easy to train these kids since they have little or no prior work experience and have consequently acquired little or no work-related bad habits," said May. "Most intelligent youngsters can also be instructed quickly concerning specific business systems and procedures, pick up and remember new things easily and have few or no preconceived ideas concerning how specific workplace tasks should be handled. Such aptitudes have surprised and astonished many supervisors." Observers also note that younger people often have considerable aptitude for office work that is done on computers, since a much greater emphasis is placed on that area in today's school environment.

Minor employees may require closer supervision than other employees. Often, they are unfamiliar with various facets of the workplace, and they may be so intimidated that they will be reluctant to ask questions about issues or tasks that they do not fully understand. Employers should anticipate this do two things, first, fully explain projects and tasks, and second, maintain a work environment that is clearly receptive to their questions. In addition, employers should adopt a firm, but positive and constructive manner in various areas of training. This includes communication that may be necessary to correct errors. Adopting a tactful, reasonable, but firm approach in such instances is important, wrote May, because "adolescents who are starting out on their first or second jobs are often more sensitive to corrections concerning their work by those who are older and (presumably) wiser. Such youngsters do not always understand that it is only their skills that are being faulted and not their innate characters and consequently are often very defensive."

Small business owners who employ minors should also consider giving their top workers opportunities to show their abilities. Young employees are fully capable of contributing to your business's success in ways other than filing paperwork or sweeping floors, and they sometimes develop into valued employees after reaching adulthood.

Finally, employers should at all times remain cognizant of the importance of adhering to state and federal laws. "Conduct periodic check-ups of your compliance with child labor law," Slutsky counseled business owners. "Be sure to keep your managers up to date on the child labor issue. Make sure they are not hiring new employees without obtaining proper age documentation, and then key them into which employers are minors and what type of job duties they may perform. After all, it won't do your company much good if you are well-versed in the laws, but the managers who directly oversee workers are unaware of the requirements." In addition, small business experts recommend that owners (or knowledgeable managers) establish a regular practice of reviewing underage employees' schedules to try and prevent violations.

BIBLIOGRAPHY

Francis-Smith, Janice. "Oklahoma Lawmaker Pushes Tighter Child Labor Laws." *Journal Record.* 30 January 2006.

May, Beth Ritter. "Youthful Problems—Adult Solutions." *Supervision.* September 1993.

Savitt, Meredith. "Businesses Need to Take Note of Child Labor Law Restrictions." *Capital District Business Review.* 20 March 2000.

Slutsky, Steven H. "No Minor Asset." *Journal of Business Strategy.* May-June 1995.

U.S. Department of Labor. Employment Standards Administration. "New and Revised Child Labor Materials." Available from http://www.dol.gov/esa/regs/compliance/whd/childlaborcentral.htm. Retrieved on 18 March 2006.

Weston, Burns. H., ed. *Child Labor and Human Rights: Making Children Matter.* Lynne Rienner Publishers, Inc., 2005.

"What Can a Child Labor Violation Cost Your Club?" *Club Management.* August 2005.

Hillstrom, Northern Lights
updated by Magee, ECDI

EMPLOYMENT PRACTICES LIABILITY INSURANCE

Employment practices liability (EPL) insurance is a type of coverage that protects businesses from the financial consequences associated with a variety of employment-related lawsuits. EPL may cover lawsuits involving a company's directors and officers, negligence lawsuits affecting a company's human resources department, and liability lawsuits over fiduciary duty. EPL can also protect against charges of racial or age discrimination, sexual harassment, wrongful termination, or noncompliance

with the Americans with Disabilities Act. Finally, EPL insurance can help protect businesses against legal conflicts that flare up between employees and third parties, such as vendors or customers, if a third-party coverage endorsement is secured as part of the EPL policy.

The market for EPL insurance coverage began to expand with large companies in 1991 and grew rapidly as employment-related lawsuits exploded in the wake of the passage of two important pieces of legislation: the Americans with Disabilities act of 1990 and the Civil Rights Act of 1991. As reported by Barbara Bowers in *Best's Review,* in the 1999-2003 period employees brought more than 403,000 charges under all laws with the Equal Employment Opportunity commission. "The median compensatory jury award for employment practices liability cases," wrote Bowers, "rose 18% in 2003 to $250,000. About 75% of employee-generated claims are proven groundless, but they are expensive to defend." The median award in 1997 was around $140,000. The usual cost of defending a groundless action is around $10,000.

In the mid-2000s EPL was still predominantly a product only large companies purchased. As reported by Steve Tuckey, writing for *National Underwriter Property and Casualty-Risk and Benefits Management,* price reductions by one insurance carrier in 2005 signaled that companies in the fewer-than-500 employee categories might soon be targeted by the insurance industry. Tuckey cited Richard Rupp, a senior vice president of Professional Indemnity Agency, to the effect that "the 500-and-under market is only about 30 percent covered." The natural inference is that those covered are likely to be closer to the 500-employee than to the 50-employee range. Employees suing an employer do so largely in order to get substantial awards. The really "small" range of small business cannot sustain a quarter-million dollar award and stay in business. Insurance costs are also high: EPL insurance pricing is usually built on a formula based on employment size, with, for example, $400 premium per employee for the first 50 and then lesser additional amounts for larger groupings. A minimum annual premium of $1,000 is likely.

Obviously the small business owner must weigh risks and costs very carefully. Standard liability insurance policies do not provide adequate coverage for employment-related risks. If such risks are high, buying EPL insurance may be a reasonable expenditure. The life savings of the small business owner are often tied up in the company and may have to be protected.

But EPL insurance policies should be studied carefully before reaching a "buy" decision. Policies vary wildly, both in terms of price and breadth of coverage. "The problem is exacerbated by the difficulty of quantifying the risk-management value of particular policy provisions," said Stephen J. Weiss in *Directors and Boards*. "For comparative valuation purposes, how do you properly account for the fact that [one policy] covers six employment practices violations, and has six exclusions and restrictive definitions, whereas [another policy] covers 15 employment practices violations but has 15 exclusions and restrictive definitions?"

In order to secure the EPL coverage that best fits the business, analysts counsel owners and executives to heed the following basic considerations:

Negotiate to build a policy that offers comprehensive coverage. Small business owners should select a reasonably priced policy, then make appropriate modifications. This is standard operating practice for insurers, and it can help ensure that the company is not left vulnerable to gaps in coverage. For instance, Weiss noted that "virtually all policies cover traditional wrongful employment practices such as harassment, discrimination, and wrongful termination of employment. However, employment practices law is rapidly evolving and the definition of 'wrongful act' in many policies has not kept pace with the creation or popularization of additional causes of action [such as] claims alleging 'negligent hiring, training, and supervision.'" Weiss also observed that many standard EPL policies expressly disclaim coverage for punitive damages. But he added that determined business owners can often negotiate shortfalls in either wrongful-act definitions or punitive damages coverage without the payment of additional premiums.

Negotiate for control of legal decisions when claims are filed. "Before you buy a policy, make sure what rights to retain counsel that it gives you," wrote Tim Bland in *Memphis Business Journal*. "Many policies give the insurance company the right to designate counsel of its own choosing.... [In such cases], more often than not it will focus more on the costs of the attorney, rather than the quality of representation the attorney provides." He also noted that some EPL policies require that the company consent to financial settlements that are approved by the insurer or forfeit their coverage. As a result, "your right to influence the selection of defense counsel and defense strategy should be clearly set forth in the policy."

Examine losses covered under the policy. The majority of employment practices business insurance policies provide coverage of back pay, lost benefits, and legal fees. However, front pay, fines, penalties, punitive damages, and cost of accommodations and travel are often not covered. "Look carefully at what types of losses are covered," counseled Bland. "A policy that looks cheap on the front end may end up costing dearly if it does not cover all losses you could face in a lawsuit."

Another possible option for small businesses in need of EPL insurance is a Business Opportunity Plan (BOP). A BOP provides basic property coverage for computers and other office equipment, plus liability protection for work-related accidents. In some cases, a BOP might also include business interruption coverage that will maintain the company's income stream for up to a year if a catastrophe disrupts business. Many BOPs also offer optional coverage against power failures and mechanical breakdowns, liability for workplace practices (including discrimination, sexual harassment, and compliance with the Americans with Disabilities Act), professional liability, and other risks.

SEE ALSO *Americans with Disabilities Act; Sexual Harassment*

BIBLIOGRAPHY

Bland, Timothy S. "Liability Insurance Needs to be Customized." *Memphis Business Journal*. 25 February 2000.

Bowers, Barbara. "Working Up a Suit: As more people sue the company they work for, employment practices liability insurance is becoming standard coverage." Best's Review. January 2005.

"EPLI." *Risk & Insurance*. November 2005.

Lynn, Jacquelyn. "You're Sued! If you have employees, you need EPL coverage." *Entrepreneur*. July 2005.

Mirza, Patrick. "Insuring a Better Process." *HRMagazine*. January 2006.

Prahl, Robert J. "Employment Practices Liability Insurance: A Review and Update." *Rough Notes*. November 2000.

Tuckey, Steve. "As EPL Coverage Comes of Age, Smaller Firms Get Insurer Attention: Despite lack of HR departments, small firms might actually be better risks." *National Underwriter Property and Casualty-Risk and Benefits Management*. 13 June 2005.

Weiss, Stephen J. "How to Eliminate EPLI Coverage Gaps." *Directors and Boards*. Fall 2000.

Hillstrom, Northern Lights
updated by Magee, ECDI

EMPOWERMENT ZONES

Empowerment zones (EZs) are economically distressed communities designated by government for aid—but this aid is intended primarily to lift the communities out of poverty by stimulating business enterprise and creating jobs. "Empowerment" is thus a somewhat euphemistic or hopeful term. The chief characteristic of targeted communities is poverty. Most of the actual dollars earmarked for empowerment zones are intended to be spent on infrastructure development. Support for business is indirect and takes the form of tax credits. To be sure, a business has to be doing well enough to *owe* taxes before credits are meaningful. Tax benefits are governed by complex rules that specifically identify classes of employees (they must be poor), types of property (they must be "qualified under the poverty rate criteria"), and types of equipment (they must be *on* qualifying property), etc. From the viewpoint of the communities themselves, a major motive for being designated an EZ was eligibility for up to $40 million in outright grants. Empowerment zones are designated as rural or urban, rural programs administered by the U.S. Department of Agriculture (USDA) and the urban programs by the U.S. Department of Housing and Urban Development (HUD). EZs were created by the Empowerment Zones and Enterprise Communities Act of 1993.

HISTORICAL BACKGROUND

Government initiatives to reduce poverty by tax incentives to business have a venerable history somewhat linked to the War on Poverty. The first such program arose in the United Kingdom. Sir Geoffrey Howe, a member of the British Parliament, announced the first "enterprise zones" in 1978 to help improve economic conditions in the dock districts of London. The system implemented in England reduced government restrictions in order to encourage the formation of new businesses in impoverished areas. It met with limited success, however, because it did not fund infrastructure upgrades in urban areas later found to be necessary for new businesses to succeed.

The first enterprise zone legislation in the United States was passed in 1987 as Title VII of the Housing and Community Development Act. The act did not offer tax incentives but was intended to relax federal regulations and to coordinate the efforts of existing programs in the designated zones. HUD received applications from 270 distressed communities for assistance under the program, but political maneuvering prevented the designation of any enterprise zones during the 1980s.

The Empowerment Zones and Enterprise Communities Act, passed by Congress in 1993, corrected for some of deficiencies of the U.K. experience and the U.S. experience under Title VII: it was designed to provide incentives to business through the tax code, provide bonding authority for infrastructure development, and offered distressed communities an attractive grant program. The act is frequently referred to as EZ/EC.

THREE ROUNDS

Developments under EZ/EC (and modifying legislation passed since 1993) are classified by the term "rounds" because three rounds of national competition have taken place in which communities vied for EZ/EC designation.

The first took place in 1994, the second in 1998, the third in 2001. Benefits offered empowerment zones changed slightly between Round I and Round II and again between Round II and III, the last changes in part due to the provisions of new legislation, the Community Renewal and New Markets Initiative of 2000. The provisions of all three rounds end on December 31, 2009—unless, of course, Congress extends that date in the intervening time.

PROGRAM SPECIFICS

For a community to be considered for designation as an empowerment zone under the act, it had to demonstrate economic distress: high levels of unemployment, a poverty rate of at least 20 percent, a declining population, and a pattern of disinvestment by businesses. In addition, an EZ community had to show the potential for economic development and the capacity to build public-private partnerships. Communities could meet this requirement by having public and private resources available to aid in the renewal process and by involving various community groups and other interested parties in developing and implementing the strategic plan.

Once a community met the economic distress and development potential criteria, it had to apply for the program with the help of its local and state governments. The application for the empowerment zone designation required communities to submit a strategic development plan—incorporating the input of all affected members of the community, from business and government to church groups and community organizations—and identify sources of private funds and support for the renewal effort. Finally, the community had to develop baseline measurements and benchmark goals to evaluate program success.

Tax Credits for Business Under Round III benefits, designated communities could offer tax benefits to business. In order to create jobs for area residents, employers received a 20 percent wage credit for the first $15,000 paid to a resident of the empowerment zone; they also received tax breaks for training such employees. Credits could be applied to full- or part-time workers. Owners themselves and relatives of owners could not qualify. Nor, surprisingly, could those employees who worked for golf courses, massage parlors, liquor stores, gambling facilities, or other ineligible business enterprises: not all businesses have the same status in EZs.

Employers who hired "targeted employees" also received a 40 percent tax credit on the first $6,000 of first-year only wages. Targeted employees are defined as high risk youth residents within the EZs, food stamp recipients, SSI recipients, vocational rehabilitation referrals, and others.

The act provided rapid depreciation on capital expenditures up to $35,000 (Round III) provided that the equipment was on land parcels meeting certain criteria.

PROGRAM RESULTS

As reported by *American City & County*, HUD conducted a study of the program's first five years (1995-2000) but focused on Round I EZs only and found that its results were mixed. In five of six EZs jobs had increased, in one they had declined. The number of resident- and minority-owned businesses increased substantially in the six EZs under HUD's oversight. But in only half of the EZs did employment growth correlate with EZ program activities. In one such area, employment increases were attributable to non-EZ activities. In looking at the businesses themselves, HUD discovered that larger companies were much more likely to make use of the tax credits available than smaller organizations. HUD also discovered that targeted population groups were very difficult to employ or keep employed. The period covered by HUD's survey, of course, also coincided with a boom period in the U.S. economy.

The auditing arm of Congress, the Government Accountability Office (newly renamed from "Government Accounting Office" but still GAO) concluded in 2004 that data for effective measurement of the EZ/EC legislation were not adequate to reach firm conclusions. GAO found that the communities, as grants recipients, were continuing to draw down on their grants and that some corporations had made use of the tax credits available to businesses in EZs. But, according to the GAO, IRS had difficulty pinning down the actual locations where these credits were being used.

BIBLIOGRAPHY

"Study Finds EZ/EC Program Results Mixed." *American City & County*. 1 April 2002.

U.S. Congress. General Accountability Office (GAO). *Federal Revitalization Programs Are Being Implemented, but Data on the Use of Tax Benefits Are Limited*. March 2004.

U.S. Department of Housing and Urban Development. "Welcome to the Community Initiative." Available from http://www.hud.gov/offices/cpd/economicdevelopment/programs/rc/index.cfm. 27 February 2006.

U.S. Department of Agriculture. Office of Community Development. "Backgrounder: Rural EZ/EC Program." Available from http://www.ezec.gov/About/backgrounder.html. 22 July 2005.

Hillstrom, Northern Lights
updated by Magee, ECDI

ENDORSEMENTS AND TESTIMONIALS

On the presumption that people are more likely to buy products other people, people they know, have already bought and liked, marketers the world over have used endorsements and testimonials to promote their products. People know celebrities and endow them with greater wisdom—how, after all, could someone become a celebrity and rich beyond the wildest dreams unless they were brighter, smarter, and more savvy? People also live vicariously live through the lives of the famous and wish to do as they do. Thus at least runs the marketing script. Therefore endorsements are associated with well-known figures. People also respect what their neighbors are saying—at least some of their neighbors. Testimonials are made by ordinary people, but advertisers chose such ordinary people because they resemble the "typical" neighbor, the "typical" sports fan, the "typical" purchaser of a riding mower, etc. A hybrid between celebrity and trusted source is the "doctor" endorsement—using actual doctors or figures in white coats. Doctors are a "generic" form of celebrity for most people. Finally, the trusted figure may be an institution widely trusted, e.g., the Centers for Disease Control and Prevention, the Food and Drug Administration, the Olympic Games, and similar entities.

Is all this true? And does it work? Very substantial sums of money have been and continue to be expended to see if advertising works in general and also on testing how it works in particular cases. Proving the effectiveness of advertising remains more art than science—and produces results similar to polling. It is certainly true that celebrities draw the attention of people watching TV, listening to the radio, and leafing through papers and magazines. It is certainly true that doctors, and experts in general, are held in high regard. It is also a matter of observation that in practice undecided buyers will tend to poll family, friends, and neighbors—which supports the effectiveness of testimonial-style advertising.

A CLOSER LOOK

Celebrity Endorsements Celebrities chosen to endorse products are almost always in some way linked to the product or service being sold. Famous male sports figures will *not* be endorsing facial creams; they'll be selling athletic shoes or clothing. People unfamiliar with a product category (e.g. snowmobiles) may have difficulty even recognizing the celebrities chosen to promote it—but insiders will know exactly who the celebrity is. For this reason, celebrity endorsement is not restricted solely to multi-million dollar ad campaigns but may be utilized by a small business in a local market—featuring, for example, a well-known local TV host or the regional winner of a beauty contest. The crucial element is that the targeted audience should recognize the celebrity and trust her or his endorsement. As *Marketing Week* pointed out advertisers benefit if the endorsement is genuine. Thus it is better to recruit a celebrity already known to use a product than simply to pay a famous face for mouthing some vaguely favorable opinion. Based on federal law, endorsements must be genuine.

Expert Endorsement The expert doing the endorsement should *be* an expert. Furthermore the expert must also have evaluated the product or service using appropriate techniques; he/she must be qualified in the relevant area. A surgeon is not by definition an expert on pharmacology. The endorsement should be backed up by tests, evaluations, and/or product comparisons. Many advertisements attempt to create an "air" of expertise in the presentation of a fictitious expert, but close examination will show that the ad does not meet the requirements of an expert presentation.

Consumer Endorsements These endorsements feature actual users of the product or service being sold. Advertising utilizing customer testimonials must reflect the typical experiences of customers and the genuine feelings and findings of the consumer being highlighted as further developed below.

Organizational Endorsements Endorsements from organizations must reflect the consensus of the organization, and must comply with that organization's standards of formal endorsement. In addition, the organization in question has to be independent (rather than one created wholly or partially for the purpose of promoting the advertising firm's products or services).

LEGAL RESTRICTIONS ON USE

Numerous federal and state laws prohibit advertising that misleads or deceives consumers. The Federal Trade Commission (FTC) is the primary law enforcement agency in the United States in this regard. Its powers range from issuing "cease and desist" orders in cases where "unfair or deceptive acts or practices in commerce" are found to arguing cases in various courts of law (these courts can hand down massive fines and other penalties to violators of endorsement restrictions).

The FTC offers several general considerations on endorsement/testimonial use. For example, it states that "endorsements must also reflect the honest opinions, findings, beliefs, or experience of the endorser. Furthermore, they may not contain any representations which would be deceptive, or could not be substantiated if made directly by the advertiser." The agency also

stipulates that while the endorsement message does not have to contain the exact phraseology used by the endorser, "the endorsement may neither be presented out of context nor reworded so as to distort in any way the endorser's opinion or experience with the product. [In addition], an advertiser may use an endorsement of an expert or celebrity only as long as it has good reason to believe that the endorser continues to subscribe to the views presented." With this in mind, the FTC urges businesses to fulfill this obligation periodically and whenever a change in the product/service's function, performance, or material composition is made.

According to the FTC, advertisers also may not state that the endorser uses the product or service being marketed unless the endorser was in fact a user at the time the endorsement was made. "Additionally," states the agency, "the advertiser may continue to run the advertisement only so long as he has good reason to believe that the endorser remains a bona fide user of the product."

The FTC provides particularly strong protections to ordinary consumers utilized in advertising campaigns. Key stipulations of this type of endorsement include: 1) the consumer endorsement should be representative "of what consumers will generally achieve with the advertised product in actual, albeit variable, conditions of use"; 2) consumer endorsements should be clearly marked as such.

Finally, the FTC requires full disclosure of "material" connections. Under these rules, advertisers must disclose all compensation being paid to endorsers, and must divulge any potentially compromising relationships between themselves and the endorser (for example, family or employee relationships). "When there exists a connection between the endorser and the seller of the advertised product which might materially affect the weight or credibility of the endorsement ... Such connection must be fully disclosed," explained the FTC. "When the endorser is neither represented in the advertisement as an expert nor is known to a significant portion of the viewing public, then the advertiser should clearly and conspicuously disclose either the payment or promise of compensation prior to and in exchange for the endorsement or the fact that the endorser knew or had reasons to know or to believe that if the endorsement favors the advertised product some benefit, such as an appearance on TV, would be extended to the endorser."

IMPLEMENTING EFFECTIVE ENDORSEMENTS AND TESTIMONIALS

In addition to adhering to existing laws and regulations governing use of endorsements and testimonials for advertising purposes, business experts cite several other considerations that should be weighed by business owners. Some of these considerations are unique to specific types of endorsements (i.e., celebrity or consumer testimonials, which are the two types most frequently utilized), while others are common to all four types.

For example, celebrity testimonials—while potentially valuable in attracting attention to a firm's products and/or services—also have a higher risk factor. For example, media attention on celebrity athletes, singers, and other personalities can turn negative quickly. In these instances, products or services with which the celebrity is associated can be stained by implication. For this reason, companies include "opt-out" clauses in most contracts so that they can end a business relationship quickly and without penalty if the celebrity's reputation is compromised.

Moreover, some analysts question the value of celebrity endorsements in increasing public allegiance to a product or service, especially if the public figure in question is of limited stature (generally, the only type of celebrity whose endorsement is within the financial grasp of smaller and mid-size companies). They instead urge companies to consider customer testimonials, which are widely regarded as more honest and believable, and less expensive and time-consuming to create. "Testimonials given by satisfied customers are far, far more effective than testimonials given by celebrities because the customer-to-be knows the celebrity is paid for their endorsement," stated businessman Murray Raphel in *Direct Marketing*. "Testimonials are easy to find. They are live, in person and visit your place of business every day in person, on the phone, or through the mail, fax, or Internet."

Another element of consumer endorsements that needs to be addressed is assurance of legality. All types of endorsements need to be specified in written form. But unlike the celebrity, expert, or association forms of endorsement, in which contracts are expected to be long and detailed, customer testimonials are usually relatively short and simple release forms. "When we originally asked our lawyer for a 'release form' he gave us (literally) a five page single spaced document!," recalled Raphel. "That will scare any potential testimonial-giver, no matter how much they like you or your business." Small business owners, then, are urged to obtain legal advice that will enable them to adopt and utilize short, easy-to-understand contracts that will not intimidate customers.

BIBLIOGRAPHY

Cates, Bill. "Get It In Writing." *On Wall Street*. April 2001.

"Insight – Celebrity Endorsements: The benefits of keeping it real." *Marketing Week*. 16 March 2006.

Raphel, Murray. "Realizing the Strength of Testimonials and How to Utilize Them in Your Business." *Direct Marketing*. June 1997.

Stark, Phyllis. "Redneck Radio: Jeff Foxworthy Style." *Billboard Radio Monitor*. 8 July 2005.

Toutant, Charles. "Federal Regulators Fault Proposed N.J. Restriction on Attorney Ads." *New Jersey Law Journal*. 13 March 2006.

"Wall-Mart Ads Tout Surprises." *Promo*. 16 February 2006.

Hillstrom, Northern Lights
updated by Magee, ECDI

ENTERPRISE RESOURCE PLANNING (ERP)

Enterprise resource planning (ERP) is a method of using computer technology to link various functions—such as accounting, inventory control, and human resources—across an entire company. ERP is intended to facilitate information sharing, business planning, and decision making on an enterprise-wide basis. ERP came into sharp visibility in the mid-1990s and was still energetically developing in the mid-2000s a decade later. ERP enjoyed a great deal of popularity among large manufacturers in the mid- to late-1990s. Most early ERP systems consisted of mainframe computers and software programs that integrated the various smaller systems used in different parts of a company. Since the early ERP systems could cost up to $2 million and take as long as four years to implement, the main market for the systems was Fortune 1,000 companies.

"Throughout the 1990s, most large industrial companies installed enterprise resource planning systems—that is, massive computer applications allowing a business to manage all of its operations (finance, requirements planning, human resources, and order fulfillment) on the basis of a single, integrated set of corporate data," Dorien James and Malcolm L. Wolf wrote in *The McKinsey Quarterly*. "ERP promised huge improvements in efficiency—for example, shorter intervals between orders and payments, lower back-office staff requirements, reduced inventory, and improved customer service. Encouraged by these possibilities, businesses around the world invested some $300 billion in ERP during the decade."

By the late 1990s sales of ERP systems began to slow. Some manufacturers had encountered implementation problems. Other factors also began to influence ERP systems both in design and deployment. Many companies developed close relationships with customers and suppliers and began conducting business over the

Internet on a massive scale. Small PC-based networks became much faster, more flexible, and cheaper than mainframes. After the slow recovery from the economic downturn that came in 2000s, ERP has become much more closely associated with web-based systems—which have also lifted it into prominence again. In 2006, for instance, *American Banker* magazine polled experts in banking who saw ERP as a new tool in business-to-business electronic commerce, with ERPs communicating with one another over the Web.

BENEFITS AND DRAWBACKS OF ERP

When the idea was first introduced, ERP was an attractive solution for many large companies because it offered so many potential uses. For example, the same system could be used to forecast demand for a product, order the necessary raw materials, establish production schedules, track inventory, allocate costs, and project key financial measures. ERP "acts as a planning backbone for a company's core business processes," Gary Forger wrote in *Modern Materials Handling.* "In addition to directing many of them, the system also ties together these varied processes using data from across the company. For instance, a typical ERP system manages functions and activities as different as the bills of materials, order entry, purchasing, accounts payable, human resources, and inventory control, to name just a few of the 60 modules available. As needed, ERP is also able to share the data from these processes with other corporate software systems." Another important benefit of ERP systems was that they allowed companies to replace a tangle of complex computer applications with a single, integrated system.

Despite these potential benefits, however, ERP systems continue to extract a cost. Implementation requires substantial time commitments from the company's information technology (IT) department or outside professionals. An article in *Computing,* for instance, citing a survey of 100 organizations, showed that only 5 percent of IT managers "were able to install ERP packages straight out of the box." On the other hand, only 9 percent reported very significant customization work. In addition, because ERP systems affected most major departments in a company, they tend to create changes in many business processes. Putting ERP in place thus requires new procedures, employee training, and both managerial and technical support. As a result, many companies find the changeover to ERP a slow and painful process. Once the implementation phase is complete, some businesses have trouble quantifying the benefits they gained from ERP.

ERP SOLUTIONS FOR SMALL BUSINESSES

As sales of ERP systems to large manufacturing companies began to slow, some vendors changed their focus to smaller companies. According to a survey by AMR research reported in *Modern Materials Handling,* the overall market for ERP systems grew 21 percent in 1998, despite the fact that sales to companies with greater than $1 billion in revenues declined 14 percent during the same period. "ERP applications are no longer just the stuff of huge corporations," Constance Loizos noted in *Industry Week.* "While billion-dollar manufacturing companies are now completing their ERP implementations, mid-size customers—witness to the improved business processes of manufacturing market leaders—are beginning to refine their own operations.... Invariably the most substantial reason for companies to implement ERP is that without it, staying competitive is a practical impossibility. The business world is moving ever closer toward a completely collaborative model, and that means companies must increasingly share with their suppliers, distributors, and customers the in-house information that they once so vigorously protected."

Of course, small and medium-sized companies—as well as those involved in service rather than manufacturing industries—have different resources, infrastructure, and needs than the large industrial corporations who provided the original market for ERP systems. Vendors had to create a new generation of ERP software that was easier to install, more manageable, required less implementation time, and entailed lower startup costs. Many of these new systems were more modular, which allowed installation to proceed in smaller increments with less support from information technology professionals. Other small businesses elected to outsource their ERP needs to vendors. For a fixed amount of money, the vendor would supply the technology and the support staff needed to implement and maintain it. This option often proved easier and cheaper than buying and implementing a whole system, particularly when the software and technology seemed likely to become outdated within a few years.

ERP AND THE INTERNET

Another trend in ERP development and use involves vendors making the software available to client companies on the Internet. Known as hosted ERP or Web-deployed ERP, this trend has also contributed to making ERP systems available to smaller businesses. When a company chooses to run its ERP systems through a Web-based host, the software is not purchased by or installed at the client company. Instead, it resides on the vendor's host computer, where clients access it through an Internet connection. "Rather than dispersing ERP to multiple corporate sites and incurring the costs of many servers needed to run the software, Web-deployed ERP centralizes the system," Forger noted. "Using the Web to access a single ERP system at a central location, companies can reduce their IT investment on two fronts—hardware and personnel."

Running ERP systems on a host computer relieves small businesses from the need to purchase a mainframe computer or hire information technology specialists to support the system. In addition, this arrangement allows client companies to save money by paying only for the ERP applications they use rather than having to buy a certain number of modules. In effect, ERP vendors act as application service providers (ASPs) for several client firms. "Systems supplied by ASPs are particularly attractive to start-up companies that can't reliably predict their future business volumes, can't afford to pay for first-tier ERP systems, and don't want to be continually replacing cheaper, less capable systems as their businesses grow," James and Wolf explained.

ERP EXPANDS ALONG THE SUPPLY CHAIN

Traditional ERP systems were concerned with automating processes and connecting disparate information systems within a business enterprise. But during the late 1990s, an increasing number of businesses turned their focus outward, toward collaboration and forging technological links to other companies in the supply chain. "Increasingly, manufacturers in developed countries are becoming part of the design and production line of their customers," Richard Adhikari wrote in *Industry Week*. "Tight scheduling requires automating the supply chain and enterprise resource planning functions and implementing electronic communications links." ERP vendors have responded to this trend by integrating ERP systems with other types of applications, such as e-commerce, and even with the computer networks of suppliers and customers. These interconnected ERP systems are known as extended enterprise solutions.

ERP systems have expanded to include several new functions. For example, application integration functions link ERP to other software systems that affect the supply chain. Visibility functions give companies an overview of inventory and its status as it moves through the supply chain. Supply chain planning software helps create optimal plans for producing and delivering goods. Similarly, customer relationship management software customizes the way that a supplier deals with each customer individually. ERP has also been adapted to support e-commerce by facilitating order fulfillment and distribution, simpli-

fying the process of electronic procurement, and tracking information about customers and their orders.

CHOOSING AN ERP VENDOR

Leading vendors in the field are SAP of Germany; Oracle; J.D. Edwards; PeopleSoft; and Baan of the Netherlands. Marketing efforts of the leaders continue to be on large business clients and concentrated on automating manufacturing, distribution, human resources, and financial systems. But numerous smaller vendors are active in the market serving smaller business clients and focused on niche applications.

Loizos outlined a series of factors for small businesses to consider in choosing an ERP vendor. For example, she emphasized that implementing an ERP system is a major information technology decision that requires time and resources, so companies should avoid choosing a vendor too quickly. Instead, she recommended that small businesses evaluate their needs carefully and come up with a list of business issues they expect the ERP system to help them address. Loizos also suggested that companies research potential ERP vendors thoroughly, looking at their reputations in the industry but also checking references and interviewing previous clients. She recommended avoiding multiple vendors if possible, and ensuring that the vendor chosen is appropriate for the small business's future growth and expansion plans. Finally, she noted that companies should ensure that project funding is in place before a contract is signed.

FACTORS IN A SUCCESSFUL ERP IMPLEMENTATION

Once a small business has decided to install an ERP system and selected a vendor, there are a number of steps the company can take to ensure a successful implementation. In his article, Forger noted that the ERP implementation is more likely to succeed if the company positions it as a strategic business issue and integrates it with a process redesign effort. Of course, the ERP system should fit the company's overall strategy and help it serve its customers. It may also be helpful to find a passionate leader for the project and select a dedicated, cross-functional project team. The small business owner should make certain that these individuals have the power to make decisions about the ERP implementation process.

Forger recommends that companies attack the implementation project in short, focused stages, working backward from targeted deadlines to create a sense of urgency. It may be helpful to begin with the most basic systems and then expand to other functional areas. Forger also suggests using change management techniques to manage the human dimension of the project, since ERP requires a great deal of support from affected areas of the company. Finally, he emphasizes that once the ERP system is in place, companies need to interpret the data collected carefully and accurately if the system is to contribute to business planning.

Although ERP systems may seem complex and costly, even small businesses are increasingly finding it necessary to invest in such technology in order to remain competitive. "ERP systems are being implemented today to provide a stable foundation for a growing number of businesses across all segments, from dot-coms to major automotive manufacturers," Dave Morrison wrote in *CMA Management*. "The number of implementations down the supply chain and into small and medium-sized companies is steadily growing as the initial costs are reduced along with the overall cost of ownership. Preconfigured and pre-tested versions are now effectively slashing the implementation costs while reducing the project complexity and risks. These new systems are providing a clean head start in development and delivering a stable and fully tested product to production. The methodology is continually evolving and the results are very positive."

SEE ALSO *Material Requirements Planning; Inventory Control Systems*

BIBLIOGRAPHY

Adhikari, Richard. "ERP Meets the Middle Market." *Industry Week.* 1 March 1999.

Brown, Alan S. "Lies Your ERP System Tells You: Enterprise resource planning has always had a hard time bridging the gap between corporate offices and the factory floor. Here's why." *Mechanical Engineering-CIME.* March 2006.

"Enterprise—ERP Requires Adjustment." *Computing.* 23 February 2006.

Forger, Gary. "ERP Goes Mid-Market." *Modern Materials Handling.* 31 January 2000.

James, Dorien, and Malcolm L. Wolf. "A Second Wind for ERP." *McKinsey Quarterly.* Spring 2000.

Loizos, Constance. "ERP: Is It the Ultimate Software Solution?" *Industry Week.* 7 September 1998.

Morrison, Dave. "Full Speed Ahead." *CMA Management.* November 2000.

"What Industry Leaders Foresee." *American Banker.* 21 February 2006.

"Wireless ERP." *Modern Plastics Worldwide.* March 2006.

Hillstrom, Northern Lights
updated by Magee, ECDI

ENTREPRENEURIAL COUPLES

If farming is considered a business, and all farms have a definite business aspect, then the reality of couples working together in a business goes back to colonial times. In colloquial speech, as well, the phrase "mom-and-pop" is commonly used to indicate a small business enterprise. In effect the couple in business is the most common form of a family business. The phrase "entrepreneurial couple" appears to have arisen initially in sociological and other academic studies but has become the standard way of referring to the "mom-and-pop" without the slightly denigrating connotations of that latter phrase.

Statistical reporting by the U.S. Census Bureau does not provide precise data on the prevalence of entrepreneurial couples, but data on business ownership—collected predominantly to track women-owned and minority owned businesses—provide a close-to-accurate estimate. Data from the 2002 economic census (the most recent available) show that in that year 2.7 million businesses were owned equally by women and men; these had $731.4 billion in receipts.

The Census data, based on ownership, may very well understate the full extent of the phenomenon—if not that of the "entrepreneurial couple" then of the "couple working together in a business." The Census Bureau reported 14 million sole-proprietorships without employees. In a very large number of these wives and husbands work together, the wife providing administrative services and handling appointments and orders, the husband, a craftsman or a professional, providing the actual "labor."

TYPES OF OPERATION

While the term "entrepreneurial couple" suggests on the one hand a couple running a little store together (hence the mom-and-pop label) and on the other a couple owning and running a substantial business together with several or many employees, the range of operations is extremely diverse with each member of the couple taking variable roles.

One useful categorization was offered by a leading expert on the subject, Kathy Marschack. distinguished three distinct and basic types of operations in her book, *Entrepreneurial Couples.* She calls the first type the solo entrepreneur with a supportive spouse. In this arrangement the supporting role may be held either by the man or the woman, and the support provided may extend from emotional backing to more practical day-to-day involvement. The distinguishing feature is that only one member of the couple carries the *entrepreneurial* load. The second type Marschack offers is the dual entrepreneurial couple. In this type of arrangement, both members of a couple run different businesses of their own and provide each other support. Here both are highly entrepreneurial but separately—yet their common interest in enterprise provides an additional bond. The third type Marschack labels coprenerial, combining the words "couple" and "entrepreneur." In this type the couple participate in the business as full partners and share all responsibilities equally.

ISSUES

Couples considering launching a business together might be well advised to read one or several books available on the subject—including Marschack's. Others include *Couples at Work* by E. W. James, *Married in Business* by Jack and Elaine Wyman, *In Business and In Love* by Chuck and April Jones, and others. Preparation is key because the combination of marriage and business while on the one hand potential very fruitful can also have unusual problems and down-sides. Some of the factors are briefly highlighted here.

1. Both partners need to bring significant value to the business—experience, talent, or skill. Spouses unable to make meaningful contributions in one or more areas of a business may take on a supportive but should avoid an operational role in that company to avoid later regret. Here the issue is finding the *right* role suitable to the different temperaments of the couple involved. An outgoing personality should not be keeping the books; the loner should not be in sales, etc. Normally the right role for each partner will be obvious to the couple based on their married life. Ideally, partners in a couple-owned business will have separate, complementary skills. When partners handle different responsibilities of the business, it tends to minimize disagreements over day-to-day matters and creates an environment in which both partners are able to exercise some autonomy and develop respect for the talents that the other brings to the enterprise.

2. Ideally partners will not be competitive with one another or avoid situations in which such competitiveness will create friction. Successful couple-owned business partners are willing to accept blame for business problems rather than simply point fingers at one another.

3. Newlyweds should exercise caution before partnering up for business—for the obvious reason that they may not know each other well enough yet to burden the marriage with a brand new set of problems.

4. Good communications are essential. Experts note that the keys to good communication in dialogue with a spouse are the same as they would be for any other business partner—listening, focusing on the issue at hand, not taking criticism personally, etc.—and that entrepreneurial couples have to recognize that business disagreements have nothing to do with their love relationship.

5. Adaptiveness to changing roles is valuable. The man may be accustomed to calling shots in business—while the woman is accustomed to running the household *her way*. In the business one or the other may have to assume an unaccustomed role. These matters need early discussion and continuing review—one reason why couples who "talk together" will fare well—see point 4 above.

6. Work life and home life must be separated. Many entrepreneurial couples warn that it is easy for husband-wife and other romantically involved business partnerships to lose sight of the personal side of the relationship in a flurry of business issues. In such cases, the romantic spark that first drew the partners together can be snuffed out by payroll concerns, worries about the landlord, proposed regulatory changes, and a plethora of other issues that are always swirling outside the doors of small business enterprises. Entrepreneurial couples can take several steps to curb this threat. Some couples agree to never discuss work at home or in bed; others actively seek out non-work activities that they can do together. Yet other couples, meanwhile, agree to have one or the other take time away from the business, so that both partners can take a step back, regain their perspective, and rekindle their personal relationship. This is particularly important in instances where children are involved.

7. Privacy set-asides. Since entrepreneurial couples spend enormous amounts of time together, successful husband-wife teams agree that one of the keys to their success is their decision to set aside solo time for each partner. Even if the solo activity (community work, a class, a sport league) is only one evening a week, this time can do a lot to recharge the partnership batteries of both people.

8. Let reason rule. Couples need objectively to assess whether they can work together well in a business. They may make a great couple precisely because they complement each other—but the business may require a different kind of match.

WHEN THE BUSINESS/MARRIAGE FAILS

A special problem of the couple-owned business is failure of the business—or of the marriage. Either one can, and often does, cause the failure or loss of the other. In a divorce settlement, for example, the business may have to be sold because one of the partners insists on a cash settlement. The loss of a business may cause such stresses that the marriage also fails. Legal precautions even for these unfortunately eventualities have been devised. As Dan Erdel reported in *Farm Journal* on the evolution of so-called antenuptial ("after marriage") agreements, contracts intended to distribute property jointly owned by a couple in the event the marriage ends in death or divorce. Erdel wrote: "The typical antenuptial agreement addresses the following issues: 1) how much of the deceased spouse's property, if any, is the surviving spouse to receive; 2) if the marriage dissolves, how is the property to be divided between the parties; and 3) how is the property that is accumulated during the marriage to be divided upon death or dissolution of the marriage?" Erdel points out that an antenuptial agreement "is not a romantic subject." True. Some entrepreneurial couples, however, may find that such an agreement may be appropriate to safeguard children—possibly from earlier marriage(s)—the business, and each of the partners.

BIBLIOGRAPHY

"A Family Business with Customers at Its Heart." *Farmers Weekly.* 24 February 2006.

Castle, Ken. "Dodge Ridge, California: A mom-and-pop mountain keeps skiers happy with a relaxed vibe and good old-fashioned home cooking." *Ski.* 2 March 2006.

Baltes, Sharon. "Brothers Open Coffeehouse." *Business Record.* 27 February 2006.

Blackburn, Vanessa. "Two Heads Really Are Better than One: Local couples make business and marriage work as paired partners selling local real estate." *Bellingham Business Journal.* March 2004.

Erdel, Dan. "Family Business." *Farm Journal.* 21 February 2006.

Jandebeur, Robert. "Change in Family: Industry Sampler: In Tulsa, reacting to the change from 'Mom & Pop' to bizav." *Airport Business.* February 2006.

Marschack, Kathy J. "Entrepreneurial Couples: Making It Work at Work and at Home." *Davies-Black Publisher.* 1998.

"Power Couples." *Florida Trend.* November 2004.

Reynolds, Gail. "The Pleasures and Pitfalls for a Homestead Business." *Countryside & Small Stock Journal.* November-December 2005.

Starr, Jennie. "What Would You Do if You Received a 'Cease and Desist' Letter?" *Searcher.* March 2006.

"Taking the Pulse of Family Business." *Business Week Online.* 13 February 2006.

U.S. Census Bureau. Press Release. "Women-Owned Businesses Grew at Twice the National Average, Census Bureau Reports." 26 January 2006.

Hillstrom, Northern Lights
updated by Magee, ECDI

ENTREPRENEURIAL NETWORKS

The definition of a "network" being a system of interconnected components, an "entrepreneurial network" is an association of entrepreneurs organized, formally or informally, with the object of increasing the effectiveness of the members' business activities. Such networks extend from very informal mutual support arrangements on up to national and international membership organizations based on formal rules, substantial membership fees, and often employing professional staffs. The phrase includes business owners meeting for breakfast once a week to trade experiences, problems, opportunities, woes, and news all the way to international industry associations that link such major activities as petroleum, steel, communications, and many other major branches of finance and of industry. Typical examples are chambers of commerce, associations of racially or ethnically similar business owners, Rotary Clubs, alumni associations focused on business development, community based business clubs, industry associations, investment clubs with thematic aims, some venture capital organizations, and SCORE (Service Corps of Retired Executives) sponsored by the Small Business Administration. In one sense OPEC (Organization of Oil Exporting Countries) may be considered an entrepreneurial network as well. What these organizational types have in common is that their members are either in business, wish to be in business, have been in business, and/or are interested in fostering a healthy business/industrial environment.

A study published by the National Commission on Entrepreneurship (NCOE), an organization populated by entrepreneurs and funded by the Kauffman Center for Entrepreneurial Leadership, posed the following question in designing the parameters of its study: "What makes a community entrepreneurial?" Why, for example, do some locales seem to generate a vibrant and exciting business environment while other places, with very similar demographic profiles, struggle to generate new businesses and to keep those that get started? What the NCOE discovered confirmed conventional wisdom on the subject: the presence of universities, access to venture capital, and good physical infrastructures are all keys to a vibrant economy. But the NCOE found one other and important ingredient that differentiated "entrepreneurial" from other areas. NCOE's study, entitled *Building Entrepreneurial Networks* summarized its findings this way: "Successful regions are not just relying on hard assets like schools, buildings, and capital. Soft, people-based assets matter, and they matter a lot. In particular, we found that entrepreneurs thrive in regions where they can effectively network with other entrepreneurs.... Regardless of their stated purpose, networks provide entrepreneurs with critical opportunities for peer learning. These learning opportunities matter as communities with more extensive peer networks in place tend to enjoy higher levels of both entrepreneurial activity and economic growth."

Business, trade, and craft associations, broadly speaking, have been around as long as business has existed.

They were not only common but government-monitored institutions during the Roman empire and, in the form of guilds, represented one of the more important organizational forms of mediaeval business activity, serving later as launching pads for the development of major sectors in the industrial age. The phrase "entrepreneurial network," however, is of recent origin and represents yet another form of association reflecting the popularity of "networking," a subject discussed in detail elsewhere in this work under that name. The emphasis in what now follows, particularly the examples cited, will be on the newly emerging form.

BENEFITS OF NETWORKING FOR THE ENTREPRENEUR

Commercial exchange is, by definition, a social activity. It involves exchange between at least two people. "No man is an island, entire of itself," as John Donne said. Nor is a business self-sufficient. A business is a social creature, "a part of the main." A company's reach, power, and effectiveness grows in proportion to is connectedness. Start-up firms often begin with a limited network. For the entrepreneur starting a business, entrepreneurial networks offer genuine benefits. Foremost among these are opportunities to build relationships. Such relations need not necessarily be with people narrowly linked to business. Any and all relationships help—but those with peers are more valuable. By cultivating membership in a peer network, a new entrepreneur can learn a great deal from others daily facing the same problems. Networking of this sort can also provide a new business owner with the chance to get a first hand look at potential service providers and/or help to combat the sense of isolation that often comes with starting a company.

As a business develops, the challenges it faces also tend to grow. The founder of a growing business is likely to be looking for different benefits from networking than he or she did during the start-up phase. The social and peer-to-peer advisory aspects of an entrepreneurial network often become secondary to more strategic networking objectives. The new objectives may be to build business alliances, to find new investors and/or partners, to get first hand reviews of potential service providers, or to search for somebody with a particular area of expertise who can be hired.

INFORMAL NETWORKS

Entrepreneurial networks start with the entrepreneur's established web of relationships—with family and with friends. Religious, avocational, and social linkages belong to this category from the outset. People in such groups can provide an unexpected source of information or contacts that may be helpful in some aspect of a business's

development. The informal aspects of such networks often mean they are taken for granted; their value *as a network* is not appreciated; in most cases, consequently, they're not exploited to the full. Although nobody much likes a person who has a one-track mind and who attempts to "do business" in inappropriate venues, it is useful to make informal networks work for a business purpose by simply being informative about one's business needs and open to the suggestions and the expertise of others.

FORMAL NETWORKS

Formal entrepreneurial networks are associations of businesses—or functions within them, like presidents' or purchasing managers' groups. Associations organized around industry groupings or types of businesses are one form of formal networking. A new business owner can gain legitimacy by joining such groups even before his or her venture has gained enough traction to become a factor on the competitive landscape. There are, of course, limits to how freely one can interact with those with whom one must compete. Nonetheless, associations of this type are a useful source of information about regulatory matter that impact a business, technical developments within the field, effective methods of communication or administration, and frequently associations also pool competitive information and share the results; thus associations hire staffs that collect but keep confidential sales data but publish overall market size information. Formal networks are often an effective means of reaching out to the public and of influencing government policy.

Chambers of commerce are a widespread and universally accepted form of "formal" entrepreneurial networking. Chambers, of course, belong to the traditional forms of business associations, but they offer modern services much valued by the same entrepreneurs who join other networks. These services include, for instance, attractively priced health insurance that a chamber negotiates with a provider under which the chamber itself is the "umbrella" organization providing a large number of "employees" to cover. Most chambers also offer training opportunities through seminars and lecture series, and virtually all offer multiple venues for contact, referral services, and technical advice for the fledgling member.

The Alternative Board® is a business established in 1990 with the objective of facilitating monthly peer advisory boards comprised of entrepreneurs and high level managers who run non-competing businesses. The Alternative Board® (TAB) is funded by membership fees based on the annual sales of each participating business. The voluntary boards TAB organizes consist of presidents, CEOs, owners, and managing partners of privately owned businesses. The boards—with up to 10 but no more than 12 members—meet monthly under the guidance of a TAB certified facilitator or coach. This cooperative venture is an example of a very formal entrepreneurial network in which business owners join together to assist one another in the development of their businesses—with an understanding that each will benefit from the cooperative endeavor.

SpeedNetworking^{TM} is a service business developed to assist entrepreneurs in the job of making connections with the "larger whole." According to the company's Web site what they offer is the following: "SpeedNewtorking.com is Web site are SpeedNetworking^{TM} events that provide a very effective and fun way of generating new business, ideas, job leads and ultimately providing participants greater professional opportunities in person."

The desire to interact and form connections is often greater than are the opportunities or time available to do so. Consequently, there is a business opportunity inherent in meeting this desire and some entrepreneurial types have taken advantage of the need and formed businesses to try and fill that need. SpeedNetworking^{TM} is only one such business. Another is LinkedIn.com, and the spread of the Internet has been an opportunity for such networking facilitation businesses.

Jodi Cohen, writing in the *Chicago Tribune,* described a SpeedNetworking^{TM} event this way: "It works like this: Following a schedule, participants sit across from each other and have five minutes to swap information about their businesses. When five minutes are up, the organizer shouts 'rotate, rotate, rotate,' and one of the guests switches seats. An hour later, each person will have made 10 contacts—and maybe plans to meet later for coffee." SpeedNetworking^{TM} events include the services of a networking "expert" who provides advice to participants. Such advice includes: 1) Ask the right questions, "What do you need?" instead of "What do you do?" 2) Develop a short, concise, and interesting description of your business, service, or product. 3) Most importantly, follow up after the event–stay in touch.

Business associations based on racial, ethnic and other similar common characteristics of its members are also types of entrepreneurial networks. Associations of this type include the U.S. Hispanic Chamber of Commerce, the National Association of Women Business Owners, the National Association of Minority Contractors, the National Black Chamber of Commerce, and the National Indian Business Association to name but a few. Like industry or business sector associations, these organizations offer members a variety of benefits as well as the opportunity to network with other business owners in a cordial and non-competitive environment.

Trade, business, and commercial organizations represent nearly 17 percent of all not-for-profit organizations in the U.S., at least as measured by Thomson Gale's *Encyclopedia of Associations (EA).* In its most recent edition, EA listed 22,270 major associations of which 3,789 were in the industrial/commercial category. Large entrepreneurial networks are a subset of this total, but the phenomenon, particularly in its more informal manifestation, is very much larger. These networks benefit small business above all, linking them into the greater fabric of American commerce.

SEE ALSO *Angle Investors; Business Incubators; Chambers of Commerce; Mentoring; Networking; Service Corps of Retired Executives*

BIBLIOGRAPHY
"About SpeedNetworking.com." SpeedNetworking^{TM}. Available from http://www.speednetworking.com/AboutUs/ 17_AboutUs.asp. Retrieved on 13 June 2006.

The Alternative Board®. "History." Available from http:// www.tabboards.com/Page-844.htm. Retrieved on 12 June 2006.

"Building Entrepreneurial Networks." National Commission on Entrepreneurship. Available from www.ncoe.org/. December 2001.

Cohen, Jodi S. "Business Networking Goes Broadband: Professionals make new connections in 5-minute intervals." *Chicago Tribune.* 30 May 2006.

Encyclopedia of Associations. Forty Third Edition. Thomson Gale, 2005.

Hitt, Michael, Duane Ireland, Michael Camp, and Donald Sexton, eds. *Strategic Entrepreneurship.* Blackwell Publishing, May 2002.

"On-line Business Networking Becomes a Profitable Alternative." *PR NewsWire.* 3 May 2006.

Rosenfeld, Stuart A. "Networks and Clusters: The Yin and Yang of Rural Development." Paper presented to Conference on Exploring Policy Options for a New Rural America, Federal Reserve Bank of Kansas City. May 2001.

Tanter, Suzanne. "Entrepreneurial Networks Feature at IT Business Conference." *The University Record (University of Michigan).* 15 November 1999.

Wee, Gillian May-Lian. "A Game of Hit or Miss: For small businesses, networking key to landing next client." *Charlotte Observer.* 24 May 2006.

"Women Leading the Way in Business Start-Ups." *Business Week Online.* 9 March 2006.

Magee, ECDI

ENTREPRENEURSHIP

Entrepreneurship comes from entrepreneur, anglicized from the original French word. It means someone who undertakes something. Merriam-Webster defines "entrepreneur" as "one who assumes the risk and management of business; enterprise; undertaker." The relevant definition of "enterprise," in turn, is "the character or disposition that leads one to attempt the difficult, the untried, etc." Starting with basic definitions is useful because entrepreneurship is valued in American culture and has therefore come to be applied to all manner of business activities, including the running of very large corporations where the managers are not genuinely at risk, did not start the business, and are simply running things; their "undertakings" might sometimes be risky—but not in relation to total assets.

Academic students of the entrepreneurial phenomenon have emphasized different aspects of behavior in business. Josef Schumpeter (1883-1950), the Austrian economist, associated entrepreneurship with **innovation.** Arthur Cole (1889-1980), Schumpeter's colleague at Harvard, associated entrepreneurship with purposeful activity and the creation of **organizations.** The management guru, Peter Drucker (1909-2005) defined entrepreneurship as a **discipline.** "Most of what you hear about entrepreneurship is all wrong," Drucker wrote in *Innovation and Entrepreneurship* (1986). "It's not magic; it's not mysterious; and it has nothing to do with genes. It's a discipline and, like any discipline, it can be learned." Drucker argued that entrepreneurship extends to all types of organizations. Two widely cited contributors to the *Encyclopedia of Entrepreneurship* (1982), A. Shapero and L. Sokol argued, from a sociological position, that all organizations and individuals have the potential to be entrepreneurial. They focused on **activities** rather than organizational make-up in examining entrepreneurship. In their view entrepreneurship is characterized by an individual or group's initiative-taking, resource gathering, autonomy, and risk taking; thus, like Drucker's their definition encompasses all types and sizes of organizations with a wide variety of functions and goals—very much in line with the observation which shows that entrepreneurship is evident in the foundation and growth of all types of organizations.

The academic approach to this subject has tended to be analytical—attempts at disassembling the entrepreneurial phenomenon in order to generate laws of business. One of Arthur Cole's intentions, for example, was to integrate the entrepreneurial phenomenon into a general theory of economics; thus he spoke of it as one of several production factors: "Entrepreneurship may be defined in simplest terms," he wrote in *Journal of Economic History*, 1953, "as the utilization of one productive factor of the other productive factors for the creation of economic goods." Much of Peter Drucker's work related to management, particularly the management of large organizations; not surprisingly he saw entrepreneurship in terms of a methodology of management—and methodologies can be learned.

Another way to look at entrepreneurship is by the study of history on the one hand—how enterprises came to be, with special emphasis on their beginnings—and looking at the reports of entrepreneurs themselves to see what they have to say. The historical approach is very instructive but in a surprising way. First, the actual entrepreneurial experience somewhat de-mystifies the concept (as Drucker did, but for other reasons): entrepreneurs very often stumble across opportunities, follow peculiar interests, or make something useful because they cannot find it. Second, history also highlights intangible aspects of the entrepreneurial personality (the very genes that Drucker dismissed): such individuals tend to be open-minded, curious, inquisitive, innovative, persistent, and energetic by temperament, thus showing many of the characteristics highlighted by the academics. But, fourth, the notion that entrepreneurs are risk-takers is not confirmed: rather, entrepreneurs are risk-averse but good at minimizing risk.

Paul Hawken, himself the founder of two successful businesses, provided a good view of entrepreneurship, from the entrepreneur's perspective, in his book *Growing A Business*. Hawken looked at many instances of start-ups (including his own companies) and highlighted the interesting mix of personal qualities, leanings, opportunities, the incremental means by which businesses get started, and the characteristics good entrepreneurs exhibit. Hawken made useful distinctions that Peter Drucker apparently overlooked. "Entrepreneurial change," Hawken wrote, "depends on static situations, and these are provided in abundance by government, large corporations, and other institutions, including educational ones. We need both entrepreneurial and institutional behavior. Each feeds on the other. The role of the former is to foment change. The role of the latter is to test that change." The distinction will ring true to anyone engaged in small business—especially those who have taken it up after working in a large organization: change is difficult inside large, bureaucratic structures; it is easier to accomplish in a small firm: no committees need to make an input, no chain of command needs climbing one link after the next... Some examples illustrating the historical view of entrepreneurship:

Sears and Kmart Sears, Roebuck (according to Sears Archives, http://www.searsarchives.com/history/history1886.htm) began because a railroad station agent in North Redwood, MN had time on his hands and, to fill it, did some minor dealings in lumber and coal. A jeweler in nearby Redwood Falls refused a shipment of watches in 1886. The young Richard Sears, the agent, bought the watches from the seller and sold them to other agents up and down the railroad line. This little venture having been successful, Sears bought more watches. Eventually he started selling the watches in a catalog of his own. The company was then called R.W. Sears Watch Company. Sears needed a watchmaker to support this business and hired another young man, Alvah Roebuck, using an ad in a Chicago paper. One thing led to another. Sears was not the first catalog seller to the then predominantly rural U.S. population. One of his innovations was to make the Sears catalog smaller than that of the dominant Montgomery Ward. Sears argued that, being smaller, the catalog would always end up on top. "Small is beautiful," you might say. Kmart also began small—as a dime-store founded by Sebastian Kresge, a category now equivalent to so-called "dollar stores." Kresge's innovation consisted in exploiting the low-price end of retail goods and concentrating on them.

McDonald's The "golden arches" had their start because Ray Kroc, McDonald's founder, sold milkshake blenders to drugstores and eateries. In 1954 he discovered that a hamburger seller owned by the MacDonald brothers was far and away the most popular in Southern California and had developed a method for serving customers in record time. Eight milkshake blenders were running at the little shop continuously. He proposed to the brothers that they open several more shops—thinking that he could sell them blenders. The brothers wondered who could open these stores for them. Kroc then said, (according to McDonald's web site, http://www.mcdonalds.com/corp/about/mcd_history_pg1.html) "Well, what about me?" The first golden arches rose a year later in Des Plains, IL. Ray Kroc himself had, by that time, already shown his entrepreneurial spirit by investing his savings and a second-mortgage on his house into the milkshake blender distributorship—which in due time led to his fortune. In this case the desire to sell more blenders resulted in the establishment of a national and now international "fast food" category.

Apple and the Macintosh Apple began when two Steves, Steve Wozniak, the technical innovator, and Steve Jobs, the entrepreneur, got together to make circuit boards for hobbyists—who, in turn, would use them to make home-grown computers. Thus Apple did not begin as a computer maker. When Jobs attempted to sell these boards to a local computer store, Paul Terrel, the owner, told him to make finished computers and promised to buy 50 of them for $500 each. Financing was a problem, but Jobs, armed with the purchase order from Terrel, managed to persuade a electronics distributor to let him have the components on credit. Thus Apple was born—financed by a sale-in-hand. This history illustrates the limited visions of the start-up enterprise and the effect of tenacious enterprise. Jobs, however, had a vision when, some eight years later, in 1979, he toured Xerox's Palo Alto

Research Corporation (PARC) and there saw, for the first time, an experimental visual interface and the computer mouse. Xerox, clearly, was miles ahead of anyone in technological innovation, but the people at Xerox PARC could not persuade their managements to commercialize the ideas already present in physical demonstration. Apple, however, independently developed the concepts and thus created the Macintosh. Visual interfaces became standard after that—and everyone now uses a mouse. This bit of history illustrates Hawken's notion that institutionalization stifles and entrepreneurship creates change.

Pepperidge Farm A classical case of entrepreneurship, mixing a challenge, a creative response, and persistent enterprise is that of Margaret Rudkin, founder of Pepperidge Farm, Inc. Margaret Rudkin moved with her family from New York to a farm in Fairfield, CT where sour gum or "Pepperidge" trees grew—hence Pepperidge Farm. Here one of her young sons developed an allergy to commercial breads laced with preservatives and artificial ingredients. This was the "challenge." The year was 1937. As the Pepperidge Farm web site reports (see http://www.pepperidgefarm.com/history.asp), Rudkin set out not only to bake wholesome bread her child could eat but "the perfect loaf of bread." She succeeded very well—her "creative response." Visitors to the home liked the bread so much they persuaded her to try to sell it. With a few loaves in hand, she approached the local grocer who, with some reluctance, agreed to try to sell them—soon he was asking for more. The business weathered the shortages created by World War II during which Rudkin sometimes suspended production rather than produce inferior product—a sign of her "persistence." On July 4, 1947 the small business suddenly grew quite a lot with the opening of a large modern bakery in Norwalk, CT. The bread was of such quality that it commanded a price of 25 cents a loaf at a time when bread sold for a dime a loaf. The product is still on the shelf everywhere—in testimony to Margaret Rudkin's persevering "enterprise."

THE ENTREPRENEURIAL PERSONALITY

Scholars, psychologists, analysts, and writers continue in efforts to define that elusive something called the "entrepreneurial" personality—but while the results usually include some of the same words (creative, innovative, committed, talented, knowledgeable, self-confident, lucky, persistent, and others), actual entrepreneurs (like actual artists, scientists, discoverers, and leaders in every walk of life) come in a bewildering variety. They may be highly trained or untrained, very knowledgeable or not.

What seems certain is that the qualities entrepreneurs exhibit are not likely to be mass producible or the consequence of a well-crafted curriculum. That such people are in many ways outstanding—and in others quite ordinary—is also clear from a study of history. Entrepreneurship, therefore, might simply be called a kind of excellence that appears sharply in organizational life—be it business or some other activity.

BIBLIOGRAPHY

Baltes, Sharon. "Brothers Open Coffeehouse." *Business Record.* 27 February 2006.

Fratt, Lisa. "The Entrepreneurial Approach: Entrepreneurship holds the power to transform education. The tough question? Is the risk of sticking with the current system greater or less than the risk of innovation?" *District Administration.* February 2006.

Gergen, David. "The New Engines of Reform." *U.S. News & World Report.* 20 February 2006.

Hawken, Paul. *Growing A Business.* Simon & Schuster, 1988.

Kent , Calvin A., Donald L. Sexton, and Karl H. Vesper, eds. *Encyclopedia of Entrepreneurship* Prentice-Hall, 1982.

Mckeough, Kevin. "Do You Believe in Angels? You Should." *Crain's Chicago Business.* 2 January 2006.

Nash, Sheryl Nance. "Freedom Through Entrepreneurship: Rohan Hall is teaching others the joy of owning a business." *Black Enterprise.* March 2006.

Velotti, Jean Paul. "West Babylon Entrepreneur, Environmentalist Developing First Privately-Owned Fuel Station." *Long Island Business News.* 24 February 2006.

"Women Leading the Way in Startups." *Business Week Online.* 9 March 2006.

Darnay, ECDI

ENVIRONMENTAL AUDIT

Environmental audits are reviews of a company's operations and processes to determine compliance with environmental regulations. Audits cover buildings and building sites; activities and procedures; industrial and commercial developments; and engineering hazard and operability studies.

Environmental audits can be costly—but, conversely, failure to carry out such audits can have much more expensive, and sometimes prohibitively expensive, consequences. They are undertaken, for these reasons, when mandated by law or prudence. Two major types of audits are conducted: 1) site inspection related to buying and selling land and 2) operational audits carried out either voluntarily in order to avoid or reduce penalties or because they are mandated under law.

SUPERFUND ESAs

Small business owners are most likely to encounter environmental audits in the context of real estate transactions. In December 1980 Congress passed the Comprehensive Environmental Response Cleanup and Liability Act (CERCLA), better known to the general public as the Superfund program. Superfund legislation is aimed at controlling and cleaning up sites contaminated with hazardous wastes—and to pin the costs of clean-up on those who contaminated or own the site. Essentially, if a site is found to be contaminated, the landowner or operator (and other parties connected to the property) are responsible for environmental cleanup costs. This liability extends to the owner/operator even if the site was contaminated by *previous* owner/operators and, in most cases, even if the current owner/operator was unaware of the contamination.

Not surprisingly, owners of land wishing to sell it, potential buyers doing "due diligence" before buying a site, and lenders standing by to finance such deals have spent—or have caused to be spent—substantial amounts of money on environmental site assessments (ESAs). These are performed by environmental auditing companies (frequently small businesses); an ESA can ensure that a property is "clean." ESAs come in a modest and expensive versions known respectively as Phase I and Phase II. Phase I audits are based on documentation about the site's history to determine if it was ever used for manufacturing or waste storage. If not, good. If yes, Phase II. Phase II is expensive because it may involve actual soil and groundwater testing. Phase I audits begin at around $1,000 but may cost more if the property is large; Phase II audits begin at around $8,000 and go up from there.

SELF-POLICING AUDITS

The U.S. Environmental Protection Agency (EPA) has been operating a program under which regulated entities (companies and other institutions) voluntarily monitor their own compliance with environmental regulations and, if they find themselves in violation, report such breaches to the EPA. The EPA calls this program *Self-Policing: Discovery, Disclosure, Correction and Prevention of Violations.* Regulations governing this program were issued by EPA in 1996 and then in revised format in April 2000.

The fundamental logic underlying self-policing is that it costs the agency much less money to ferret out offenders, to prove that violations have occurred (which may require extensive sampling and testing protocols), and to litigate cases in the courts. To achieve this cost—and potential environmental—benefit, EPA policy offers the regulated community special incentives to self-police:

self-policing entities avoid substantial penalties for violations that they report; EPA foregoes referral of such volunteers for criminal prosecution; and EPA refrains from asking for audit reports from the entity to which it has a right under law.

Penalties assessed by EPA under environmental laws include two components. The first is the economic gain the company achieves by *not* controlling its pollution; the second component is based on the gravity of the offense, e.g., the amount of spillage or air emissions and/or the toxicity of the chemicals permitted illegally to escape. Under self-policing, all penalties based on "gravity" are cancelled if the polluter complied with all of EPA's rules in carrying out its audit. Seventy-five percent of gravity-based penalties are forgiven if the polluter complied with the rules but failed to have in place a systematic method of detecting violations. Penalties based on "economic gain" continue to apply.

To avoid penalties, the entity must meet nine conditions reproduced from EPA regulations as follows:

- **Systematic discovery** of the violation through an environmental audit or the implementation of a compliance management system.

- **Voluntary discovery** of the violation was not detected as a result of a legally required monitoring, sampling or auditing procedure.

- **Prompt disclosure** in writing to EPA within 21 days of discovery or such shorter time as may be required by law. Discovery occurs when any officer, director, employee or agent of the facility has an objectively reasonable basis for believing that a violation has or may have occurred.

- **Independent discovery and disclosure** before EPA or another regulator would likely have identified the violation through its own investigation or based on information provided by a third-party.

- **Correction and remediation** within 60 calendar days, in most cases, from the date of discovery.

- **Prevent recurrence** of the violation.

- **Repeat violations** are ineligible, that is, the specific (or closely related) violations have occurred at the same facility within the past 3 years or those that have occurred as part of a pattern at multiple facilities owned or operated by the same entity within the past 5 years; if the facility has been newly acquired, the existence of a violation prior to acquisition does not trigger the repeat violations exclusion.

- **Certain types of violations** are ineligible such as those that result in serious actual harm, those that may have presented an imminent and substantial endangerment, and those that violate the specific terms of an administrative or judicial order or consent agreement.

- **Cooperation** by the disclosing entity is required.

EXISTING AUDIT AND DISCLOSURE REQUIREMENTS

Many corporate studies on environmental and safety issues, whether conducted internally (by employees) or externally (by outside consultants/experts under contract), must be disclosed to appropriate government agencies and the general public. For instance, companies are required to submit permit applications, emission reports, and other information to government agencies under the Clean Air Act, the Clean Water Act, and other environmental laws. The Federal Community Right to Know Act is another law that places specific obligations on companies. Under this law, firms are obliged to disclose the size, nature, and identity of storage and releases of toxic substances.

Companies also often engage in a wide array of other environmental and safety evaluations to assess cost and level of compliance. The practice of voluntarily checking compliance with environmental regulations through the practice of self-auditing has garnered considerable support from state lawmakers as well. As of 2000, environmental self-audits receive significant legal protections in 26 states. The body of law in these states maintains that companies can voluntarily test for violations and correct all previously undetected problems without legal penalty. Companies that report violations avoid financial penalties and receive additional time to rectify problems. Most significant of all, the results of self-audit tests and programs in these states receive significant legal protections from public disclosure.

Confidentiality privileges have been heavily criticized in some quarters. The Environmental Protection Agency (EPA), environmental groups, and other observers charge that environmental self-audit laws, when buttressed with secrecy protections, allow polluters to violate environmental statutes without suffering any adverse consequences. Detractors of secret audit privileges also contend that decreased visibility of environmental practices and decisions will produce increased "corner-cutting" in the realms of health and safety.

Supporters of increased audit secrecy privileges claim that increased confidentiality would actually encourage greater stewardship of the environment. Advocates say that if businesses do not have to publicly disclose information found in internal compliance studies—which might otherwise be used by as "roadmaps" by litigants in civil or criminal cases—the company's owners and managers will be more likely to engage in thorough studies of their true level of compliance with environmental regulations.

The EPA's own self-policing policy appears to straddle these positions—encouraging internal audits and providing incentives to conduct them but setting the rules for such studies and analyses and requiring disclosure.

BIBLIOGRAPHY

Cheney, Glenn. "Environmental Accounting: Get your 'green' eyeshades." *Accounting Today.* 10 October 2005.

"Clean-Air Inspections." *The American Prospect.* March 2005.

"Earth's Ability to Cope Taxed by Consumption." *Capper's.* 23 November 2004.

Ennis, Matthew. "Corporate Green." *Supermarket News.* 12 September 2005.

Shaw, Jane S. "Business and the Environment: Is there more to the story? Evidence of good environmental stewardship is more extensive than most economists and executives recognize." *Business Economics.* January 2005.

Toloken, Steve. "Pondering Plastics Pollution: Environmental audit just one way industry tackles issue." *Waste News.* 10 October 2005.

U.S. Environmental Protection Agency. *Incentives for Self-Policing: Discovery, Disclosure, Correction and Prevention of Violations; Notice.* Federal Register. 11 April 2000.

Hillstrom, Northern Lights
updated by Magee, ECDI

ENVIRONMENTAL LAW AND BUSINESS

Environmental laws in the United States protect air and water resources and control certain aspects of land-use as well, particularly disposal of wastes on land. Basic laws are federal but many states have laws of their own, often more stringent than that of the federal law. Laws on the books also control the environment in the workplace and noise levels caused by machinery, especially aircraft. Regulations on food purity and the safety of drugs frequently have environmental aspects. And the management of radiating substances is also within the compress of "environmental law." The chief regulatory agencies are the U.S. Environmental Protection Agency (EPA) and the Nuclear Regulatory Commission (NRC)—but some 13 other agencies are directly and yet others indirectly involved in enforcing laws. All states also have environmental agencies.

Environmental law in its current form developed in the 1960s and culminated in the passage of the National Environmental Policy Act of 1969. In the mid-2000s 18 major pieces of legislation entirely or partially administered by EPA and five laws administered by the NRC constitute the corpus of environmental law as shown below:

EPA-administered laws (in date order) are the following:

- Federal Food, Drug, and Cosmetic Act (FFDCA). 1938.

- The Freedom of Information Act (FOIA). 1966.

- National Environmental Policy Act of 1969 (NEPA). Basic environmental law.

- The Clean Air Act (CAA). 1970.

- The Occupational Safety and Health Act (OSHA). 1970.

- Federal Insecticide, Fungicide and Rodenticide Act (FIFRA). 1972.

- The Endangered Species Act (ESA). 1973.

- The Safe Drinking Water Act (SDWA). 1974.

- The Resource Conservation and Recovery Act (RCRA). 1976.

- The Toxic Substances Control Act (TSCA). 1976.

- The Clean Water Act (CWA). 1977.

- Comprehensive Environmental Response, Compensation, and Liability Act (CERCLA or Superfund). 1980. Deals with hazardous waste sites.

- The Emergency Planning & Community Right-To-Know Act (EPCRA). 1986.

- The Superfund Amendments and Reauthorization Act (SARA). 1986.

- The Pollution Prevention Act (PPA). 1990.

- The Oil Pollution Act of 1990.

- Food Quality Protection Act (FQPA). 1996.

- Chemical Safety Information, Site Security and Fuels Regulatory Relief Act. 1999. Amends the Clean Air Act.

NCR administered laws:

- Atomic Energy Act of 1954, as amended. Basic law on nuclear energy.

- Energy Reorganization Act of 1974.

- Uranium Mill Tailings Radiation Control Act of 1978.

- Nuclear Waste Policy Act of 1982.

- Low-Level Radioactive Waste Policy Amendments Act of 1985.

Other major agencies involved in the implementation of these laws include the following:

- Army Corps of Engineers—Regulates construction projects on navigable waters; coordinates administration of Superfund cleanups; engages in construction projects to protect wildlife on shorelines and in navigable waters; and other projects.

- Consumer Product Safety Commission—Charged with enforcement of various enabling acts designed to protect consumers, including responsibility for protecting consumers from toxic (hazardous) chemicals.

- Council on Environmental Quality (CEQ)—Oversees compliance with the National Environmental Policy Act (NEPA) by agencies throughout federal government.

- Bureau of Land Management—Manages federally owned lands, which total over 350 million acres, as well as the resources on those lands, including timber; oil, gas and minerals; rivers and lakes; plants, animals, and fish and their habitats.

- Federal Energy Regulatory Commission—Regulates dams and hydroelectric power.

- Federal Maritime Commission—Certifies that ships carrying oil and hazardous materials have the ability to cover the cost of any spills.

- Food and Drug Administration—Charged with enforcement of statutes designed to protect the public from harmful food or drugs. Also works with the EPA to protect the public from hazards associated with pesticide residues in food.

- Mine Safety and Health Administration—Regulates to protect the health and safety of workers in mines and to protect the public from hazards associated with mining.

- National Institute for Occupational Safety and Health (NIOSH)—Under jurisdiction of the Centers for Disease Control (CDC), conducts research on the effects of toxic substances on humans, the results of which are used by OSHA, EPA, and other agencies.

- National Park Service—Charged with managing the various parks that comprise the nation's national park system.

- Occupational Safety and Health Administration—Regulates to protect the health and safety of workers within workplaces (excluding mining).

- U.S. Fish and Wildlife Service—Manages the National Wildlife Refuge System.

- U.S. Forest Service—Manages public forest resources for lumbering, mining, farming, grazing, and recreation.

CATEGORIZING LAWS

As the old Tom Lehrer song, "Pollution," put it: "If you visit American city,/You will find it very pretty./Just two things of which you must beware:/Don't drink the water and don't breathe the air." The song appeared in 1965 and was, in a way, background music to the development of environmental legislation. The verses, however, pinpoint the chief rationale behind most environmental legislation: it is to protect human health and welfare by keeping fundamental resources, like air and water, clean and usable. Once basic legislation was in place, it came to be extended to preventing poisons reaching people indirectly through plant life and food species in toxic substances and hazardous waste legislation. Modern law goes further and also protects species endangered by human activity and regulates how industry must treat and restore land disturbed by such activities as mining.

AIR AND WATER

Air and water pollution control legislation sets strict limits on what kinds of pollutants may be emitted to the environment in what concentrations over defined periods of time—so that small amounts deemed permissible are emitted in small quantities ensuring mixing and dispersion. Emission laws result in emission standards—which may change over time. Economic pressures act at times to loosen the standards; public pressure acts to tighten them. Whatever the standard, enforcement activity may be energetic or lax, and the type of enforcement itself may be the result of policy. In addition to setting standards, the laws also specify technological means of treating effluent streams; the specifics of how to do that are elaborated in regulations. The regulations are detailed, down to specific chemicals and specific circumstances of emission. Since cities, as public bodies, are a large source of polluted water (sewage), federal law also provided financial grants to partially pay for the building of water and sewer treatment plants.

Control in these categories is based both on an administrative and a physical "process," the former requiring permits, monitoring, and periodic audits; the latter governing actual pollution control processing. Federal regulatory action in these two areas (as elsewhere) takes place through the publication of proposed regulations on which public comment is invited, followed by final regulations which incorporate some and reject other suggestions by interested parties.

Solid Wastes Federal law does not regulate land disposal of ordinary urban and commercial waste by prescribing methods, but federal guidelines describe best practice. Regulatory action may be present indirectly if groundwater contamination results from landfill leachates and, in consequence, safe drinking water standards are not met. Incineration of wastes falls under air pollution laws. State laws and regulations do control solid wasteland disposal, but requirements vary from state to state.

Toxic and Hazardous Wastes Handling of such wastes is tightly regulated relating to transport, storage, and disposal of wastes. To the extent that such wastes are liquefied before processing or are incinerated, water and air regulations apply. Many decades of haphazard toxic/hazardous waste disposal preceded the emergence of environmental regulations so that many hundreds of "legacy" sites still exist. Superfund legislation controls both the clean-up process and the assignment of responsibility for the clean-up.

DRINKING WATER

Federal law relating to drinking water is a standard-setting process under which maximum levels of contaminants are set. Federal regulators take into account water purification technology in setting or revising standards; attempts to tighten standards are usually triggered by improvements in treatment technology—and resisted because new methods have higher costs.

Other Areas The protection of endangered species takes multiple forms, including prohibitions against hunting, protection of habitats from development or restrictions on access to and exploitation of resources inside habitats. Nuclear materials handling is a world unto itself in which very tight safeguards are prescribed for every aspect of nuclear materials handling—including in such "non-atomic" environments as medical laboratories. Storage, transport, labeling, and handling of toxic and hazardous materials in the workplace are covered by Department of Transportation and OSHA regulations—again aimed at protecting people directly involved and the broader population outside the workplace in case of fires or disasters.

THE SMALL BUSINESS CONNECTION

The small business may very likely be touched in one way or another by environmental law even in businesses that do very little or very basic manufacturing. If solvents and lubricants are used—which will be likely in a machine or in a printing shop; or if chemicals are used—in a flower shop or gardening enterprise—environmental laws will be invisibly present. A careful inspection of the business, looking for chemicals, fire hazards, and inspecting the type of waste generated may be worthwhile unless the owner keeps up-to-date on the subject. A good means of doing so is through product vendors who usually provide information or track legal restrictions on chemicals closely. Trade publications also routinely report on new regulator developments in the industry they cover and thus provide early warning signals that action may be necessary to get on the right side of environmental law.

SEE ALSO *CERCLA; Clean Air Act; Clean Water Act*

BIBLIOGRAPHY

"Capital Briefs." *Waste News.* 27 February 2006.

"Enforcement Action Requires $10 Billion to Be Spent on Cleanup." *Pollution Engineering.* January 2006.

Schnitzler, Peter. "Legislators Fight Over Green Rules, Biz Lobby: Indiana standards should not exceed EPA's." *Indianapolis Business Journal.* 9 January 2006.

Sissell, Kara. "Nations Agree to Extend Kyoto Obligations." *Chemical Week.* 21 December 2005.

Sliz, Deborah and Karen Price. "NEPA: Is it time to reform the Magna Carta of environmental law?" *Bulletin (Northwest Public Power Association).* February 2006.

Tolme, Paul. "Environment: Out of the Woods?" *Newsweek.* 16 January 2006.

U.S. Environmental Protection Agency. "Major Environmental Laws." [as of 2 January 2001] Available from http://www.epa.gov/epahome/laws.htm. Retrieved on 21 March 2006.

U.S. Nuclear Regulatory Commission. "Our Governing Legislation." Available from http://www.nrc.gov/who-we-are/governing-laws.html. Retrieved on 21 March 2006.

Darnay, ECDI

ENVIRONMENTAL PROTECTION AGENCY (EPA)

The U.S. Environmental Protection Agency (EPA) was created on December 2, 1970, by executive order of President Richard Nixon to "permit coordinated and effective government action on behalf of the environment." Fifteen different environmental programs from various federal offices were combined and placed under the jurisdiction of the newly created EPA. The EPA was designed to serve as an "umbrella agency" through which most federal environmental laws, regulations, and policies would be administered.

EPA's ORGANIZATION

The administrator of the EPA is appointed by the President of the United States and approved by the Senate, along with a deputy administrator, nine assistant administrators, an inspector general, and a general counsel. The inspector general is responsible for investigating environmental crimes, and the general counsel provides legal advice. Within the EPA are four "program" offices. They are 1) Air and Radiation; 2) Water; 3) Pesticides and Toxic Substances; and 4) Solid Waste and Emergency Response. There is also an office for Research and Development which works in coordination with each of the four program offices.

The main office of the EPA, which is located in Washington, D.C., oversees implementation of national environmental laws and programs, directs the EPA's regional offices and laboratories, and submits budget requests to Congress. Research is conducted through the EPA's main office and at its regional field laboratories. There are ten regional EPA offices and field laboratories which work directly with state and local governments to coordinate pollution control efforts. The EPA uses a portion of its federal funding to provide grants and technical assistance to states and local governmental units that seek to prevent pollution.

OBJECTIVES, POWERS AND PROGRAMS

The EPA's powers and programs are established through legislation passed by Congress. (Such legislation delegating powers to an agency is known as "enabling" legislation.) Today the EPA is charged with the administration of a myriad of federal environmental laws dealing with air and water pollution, drinking water quality, radioactive wastes, pesticides, solid wastes, and noise pollution. Altogether some 18 major laws fall into EPA's "portfolio" (see *Environmental Law and Business* in this volume). In general, the EPA develops standards or regulations pursuant to environmental statutes; enforces those standards, regulations, and statutes; monitors pollutants in the environment; conducts research; and promotes public environmental education.

The EPA has five main objectives, called "core functions." These include: 1) Pollution Prevention, which is also know as "source reduction"; 2) Risk Assessment and Risk Reduction, which is the task of identifying those issues which pose the greatest risks to human health and the environment and taking action to reduce those risks; 3) Science, Research, and Technology, which involves research designed to develop innovative technologies to deal with environmental problems; 4) Regulatory Development, which involves developing standards for operations of industrial facilities—including, for exam-

ple, standards for air emissions of pollutants pursuant to Clean Air Act permits and standards for discharge of effluents under Clean Water Act permits; and 5) Environmental Education, which involves developing educational materials and providing grants to educational institutions.

COORDINATION WITH OTHER ENVIRONMENTAL PROGRAMS

The EPA works closely with state and local governments in their pollution control efforts. During the early 1980s, efforts to "downsize" federal government led the EPA to hand over more responsibility for enforcement of regulatory programs to state and local governments. States are encouraged to pass their own statutes and regulations which meet or exceed the requirements of federal statutes such as the Clean Air Act, the Clean Water Act, RCRA, and CERCLA. Upon certification by the federal EPA, such states take over day-to-day enforcement of a specific statutory program and of the regulations pertaining to that program. As a result, business people in many states find that their day-to-day contact with enforcement officials regarding environmental statutes and regulations is with a state counterpart to the EPA rather than with the federal EPA itself. However, even when a state has been certified to administer such a program, the federal EPA continues to oversee the state's enforcement activities. It provides assistance to state officials and sometimes participates directly in major enforcement actions against violators of environmental laws.

The EPA also works closely with other federal environmental control agencies, such as the National Oceanic and Atmospheric Administration and the United States Coast Guard. The National Oceanic and Atmospheric Administration engages in long-range research on pollution problems, especially problems affecting the ocean and the atmosphere. The EPA works with the Coast Guard on flood control, dredging activities, and shoreline protection. Since 1970, the EPA has worked closely with the Council on Environmental Quality (CEQ), a relatively small executive agency which was created pursuant to the National Environmental Policy Act. Its mission is to advise the president on federal policy and action in the environmental area and to ensure that other federal agencies comply with NEPA. Compliance with NEPA requires all federal agencies to pursue environmentally sound policies and prepare an Environmental Impact Statement (EIS) before undertaking any major action which might significantly affect the environment.

SEE ALSO *Environmental Law and Business*

BIBLIOGRAPHY

Atriano, Vincent. "EPA Issues New Rules Targeting 'Illegal Competitive Advantage.'" *Business First-Columbus.* 5 November 1999.

Bukro, Casey. "EPA Chief Ties Ecology to Economy." *Chicago Tribune.* 13 February 1993.

Cole, Carol. "Bush Backs Budget Cuts at EPA; Democrats Vow to Fight." *World Fuels Today.* 8 February 2006.

Collin, Robert W. The Environmental Protection Agency: Cleaning up America's act. *Greenwood Press.* 2006.

U.S. Environmental Protection Agency. "About EPA." Available from http://www.epa.gov/epahome/aboutepa.htm. 1 March 2006.

Hillstrom, Northern Lights
updated by Magee, ECDI

EQUAL EMPLOYMENT OPPORTUNITY COMMISSION

The Equal Employment Opportunity Commission (EEOC) was established to enforce provisions of Title VII of the Civil Rights Act of 1964. Title VII forbids discrimination in the workplace based on race, age, disability, religion, sex, or national origin. Title VII covers all phases and aspects of employment including but not necessarily restricted to hiring, termination of employment, layoffs, promotions, wages, on-the-job training, and disciplinary action. Businesses covered by Title VII include employers in the private sector with 15 or more employees, educational institutions, state and local governments, labor unions with 15 or more members, employment agencies, and, under certain circumstances, labor-management committees.

Originally, government-owned corporations, Indian tribes, and federal employees were not covered under the provisions of Title VII; the latter group was protected from discriminatory practices by Executive Order 11478, which was administered and enforced by the U.S. Civil Service Commission. In 1978, however, federal equal employment functions were transferred to the EEOC. Title VII—which, along with the rest of the 1964 Civil Rights Act, became operational on July 2, 1965—has since been amended several times over the years. Key amendments include the Equal Opportunity Act of 1972, the Pregnancy Discrimination Act of 1978, and the Civil Rights Act of 1991. The EEOC is also responsible for enforcing the Equal Pay Act of 1963, the Age Discrimination in Employment Act of 1967, the Rehabilitation Act of 1973 (including amendments to Section 501 prohibiting employment discrimination against federal employees with disabilities), and the

Americans with Disabilities Act of 1990. Today, the EEOC provides oversight and coordination of all federal regulations, practices, and policies affecting equal employment opportunity.

ORIGINS OF THE EEOC

Title VII and the EEOC trace their beginnings to World War II federal defense contracts. Faced with the threat of a "Negro march" on Washington to protest discrimination in hiring of defense contract workers, President Roosevelt issued Executive Order 8802 in 1941. This order called for the participation of all U.S. citizens in defense programs regardless of race, creed, color, or national origin. The order also established the Fair Employment Practices Committee (FEPC), which by 1943 was processing 8,000 employment discrimination complaints annually. The powers of the FEPC were decidedly limited. While the committee discouraged discrimination within the defense industry, it lacked the legal clout to enforce its desires. Over the next several years, both Presidents Truman and Eisenhower established committees on government contract compliance, but again enforcement power was absent. Only when President Kennedy created the President's Committee on Equal Employment Opportunity were one of these groups given enforcement powers. Even in this case, however, the committee's legal authority was limited. Moreover, Kennedy's Committee on Equal Employment Opportunity, like its predecessors, dealt only with discrimination within businesses that had government contracts, not workplace discrimination in the overall private sector. The Civil Rights Act of 1964 changed this by addressing discrimination in all areas of employment.

EEOC ENFORCEMENT ACTIVITIES

The Equal Employment Opportunity Commission's enforcement program manages between more than 80,000 charges annually. In the EEOC system, charges are prioritized into one of three categories for purposes of investigation and resource allocation: A (top priority charges to which offices devote substantial investigative and settlement efforts); B (charges deemed to have merit but needing additional investigation); and C (charges judged to be unsupported or not under the EEOC's jurisdiction, and thus are not pursued). In FY 2005 alone, the EEOC obtained nearly $173 million in benefits for charging parties through settlement and conciliation (excluding litigation awards). Litigation awards accounted for another $106 million in FY 2005.

Under EEOC rules of operation and investigation, settlements between disputing parties are encouraged at all stages of the process. With this in mind, the EEOC maintains a mediation-based alternative dispute resolution program. "The mediation program," states the EEOC, "is guided by principles of informed and voluntary participation at all stages, confidential deliberation by all parties, and neutral mediators." In FY 2005, the EEOC resolved more than 7,900 charges via its mediation program.

FILING A COMPLAINT WITH THE EEOC

Anyone who feels that he or she has suffered workplace discrimination because of his or her race, age, physical disability, religion, sex, or national origin is eligible to file a complaint with the EEOC. Complaints or charges are generally filed at an EEOC office by the aggrieved party or by his or her designated agent. All charges must be filed in writing, preferably but not necessarily on the appropriate EEOC form, within 180 days of the occurrence of the act that is the reason the complaint is being filed. Complaints may be filed at any one of 50 district, area, local, and field EEOC offices throughout the United States.

Upon receiving a discrimination charge the EEOC defers that charge to a state or local fair employment practices agency. This agency has either 60 or 120 days to act on the complaint (the allotted time depends on several factors). If no action is taken on the state or local level within that time the charge reverts back to the EEOC, which processes the charge on the 61st or 121st day. This becomes the official filing day of the complaint. Within 10 days of the filing date the EEOC notifies those parties charged with discrimination. The EEOC subsequently undertakes an investigation of the charge. If the investigation shows reasonable cause to believe that discrimination occurred, the Commission launches conciliation efforts. The reaching of an agreement between the two parties signals closure of the case. If such an agreement cannot be reached, the EEOC has the option of filing suit in court or the aggrieved party may file suit on his or her own. If no violation of Title VII is found, the EEOC removes itself from the case, though the party charging discrimination is still free to file suit in court within a specified time.

EEOC Programs The Equal Employment Opportunity Commission has established numerous programs designed to inform the public of EEOC activities and responsibilities. The Technical Assistance Program (TAPS) is a one-day educational seminar for unions and small and mid-size employers. This program highlights the rights of employers and employees under Title VII. In FY 2005, the EEOC conducted 50 TAPS that reached more than 6,000 participants. The Expanded Presence Program sends contact teams to areas that would otherwise have little immediate

accessibility to the EEOC. The EEOC also sponsors a Federal Dispute Resolution Conference, aids state and local fair practices employment agencies, and maintains liaison programs with unions, civil rights organizations, and various federal, state and local government agencies.

The EEOC's budget appropriation for FY 2004 was $325 million, while its FY 2005 budget was $327 million. Its roster of full-time employees stood at 2,640 at the end of FY 2005, a decline of about 660 employees over a two-decade period. In the meantime, however, the agency's enforcement obligations have "substantially expanded due to new statutory responsibilities," stated the EEOC. Most of these charges concern alleged violations of the Americans with Disabilities Act or sexual harassment. Overall, charge filings increased from 62,000 in FY 1990 to approximately 125,00 in FY 2005.

To contact the EEOC, write the Commission at the following address: U.S. Equal Employment Opportunity Commission, 1801 L Street, N.W., Washington, DC 20507; 202-663-4900. The EEOC also maintains a web site at www.eeoc.gov.

BIBLIOGRAPHY

Bland, Timothy S. "Heed New EEOC Discrimination Guidelines." *Memphis Business Journal.* 20 October 2000.

"Hands On." *Inc.* September 2000.

Tejeda, Carlos. "Federal Discrimination Suits Decline." *Wall Street Journal.* 18 July 2000.

U.S. Equal Employment Opportunity Commission. "EEOC Annual Reports." Available from http://www.eeoc.gov/abouteeoc/annual_reports/index.html. Retrieved on 23 March 2006.

Hillstrom, Northern Lights
updated by Magee, ECDI

EQUIPMENT LEASING

A lease is in essence an extended rental agreement under which the owner of the equipment allows the user to operate or otherwise make use of the equipment in exchange for periodic lease payments. In leasing terminology, the owner is the lessor, the user is the lessee. Equipment leasing is a popular option for companies of all sizes. The Equipment Leasing Association of America estimates that 80 percent of all companies lease at least some of their equipment, and the organization estimates that firms leased $220 billion worth of goods in 2004, projected to reach $229 billion in 2005. But equipment leasing is particularly favored by many small businesses, which often have fewer options because of limited capital.

CATEGORIZATIONS

The two primary types of leases are operating and long-term or "capital" leases. Operating leases are characterized by short-term, cancelable terms; the lessor bears the risk of obsolescence and enjoys such benefits as depreciation, including, if applicable, accelerated depreciation. These leases are generally preferable when the company needs the equipment for a short period of time. Under the usual terms of operating leases, a lessee can usually cancel the lease, assuming prior notice, without a major penalty. Long-term, "capital," non-cancelable leases, also known as full payout or financial leases, are sources of financing for assets the lessee company wants to acquire and use for longer periods of time. Most financial leases are "net" leases, meaning that the lessee is responsible for maintaining and insuring the asset and paying all property taxes, if applicable. Financial leases are often used by businesses for expensive capital equipment.

In addition to these two basic leasing models, a considerable variety of other lease arrangements are often used. These leases, each of which combine different financial and tax advantages, are actually hybrids of financial and operating leases that reflect the individual needs of lessor companies. For example, full-service leases are leases wherein the lessor is responsible for insurance and maintenance (these are commonplace with office equipment or vehicle leases). Net leases, on the other hand, are leases wherein the lessee is responsible for maintenance and insurance. Leveraged leases, meanwhile, are arrangements wherein the cost of the leased asset is financed by issuing debt and equity claims against the asset and future lease payments.

The Size of the Ticket Leases are also classified as "small ticket," "medium," and "large ticket" leases based on the value of the equipment to be leased. The small ticket lease covers items up to $100,000 in value; large ticket leases cover item costing more than $2 million. The medium, of course, is the area in between. The small ticket lease is of special interest to the small business because getting approval for such leases rarely involves much more effort than qualifying for a credit card. As the values of equipment rented increase, obtaining the lease comes more and more to resemble a major loan application.

A Bumpy Playing Field Small business owners need to keep in mind that lease rates can vary considerably from one lease company to another. Lease companies also may charge different rates for the same piece of equipment depending on various characteristics of the business that is seeking the lease. Factors that can impact the lease rate include the credit history of the lessee, the nature of

equipment wanted by the lessee, the length of the lease term, and whether the lessee or lessor is the primary beneficiary of tax credits associated with the transaction.

WHY LEASE?

Companies can finance their capital equipment by debt or equity. Capital leases are a form of debt-equity financing since such leases act like loans, must be recorded as liabilities on balance sheets, and are also treated as liabilities by the IRS. Operating leases, however, permit the company to obtain equipment with virtually no upfront capital outlay and with the lease payments treated as a deductible cost of business. For most small businesses, therefore, the principal motive for leasing is cash flow—the ability to get equipment *now* without a major expenditure of cash. Some companies able to purchase still prefer to lease because their tax situation is such that they cannot benefit from the depreciation. They may also wish to maintain a debt-equity ratio that will attract new investment more easily, and leasing rather than investment will accomplish that end. For some companies, engaged in a rapidly evolving technological market, using leased equipment under short-term leases permits them to exchange new and better equipment more rapidly than would ownership of a capital lease.

LEASING CHECKLIST

The elements of a lease agreement worth pondering in advance by the small business are on the following checklist. Each item should be viewed in light of the ultimate goal.

- Lease duration. If equipment needs are likely to change rapidly, a shorter lease period, even at a higher cost, may be desirable. When the equipment is standard, lowest price may be available for the longest duration.

- Payment due the lessor. This is one of several financial aspects the small business must consider in light of its projected cash flow.

- Financial terms (date of the month that payment is due, penalties for late payment, etc.)

- Residual values, purchase options. If the lease is just another way of purchasing equipment, the terminal point of the lease becomes important.

- Market value of equipment. The business needs to assess insurance costs (especially in capital leases).

- Tax responsibility. As outlined above, operating and capital leases have different tax implications.

- Updating or cancellation provisions—especially important when technological changes are swift.

- Lessee renewal options.
- Penalties for early cancellation without good cause.
- Miscellaneous options (security deposits, warranties).

FINDING A LEASING COMPANY

Business consultants and long-time equipment lessees agree that leasing companies vary considerably in terms of product quality, leasing terms, and customer service. Small business owners should approach a number of lease companies if possible to inquire about lease terms. They should then carefully study the terms of each outfit's lease agreements, and check into the reputation of each company (present and former customers and agencies like the Better Business Bureau can be helpful in this regard).

Finally, it is also important for entrepreneurs and business owners to take today's fast-changing technology into account when considering an equipment leasing arrangement. When dealing with computer systems or those heavily based on electronics, the owner is well advised to locate leasing companies that specifically service such needs and offer, up front, lease arrangements that facilitate rapid change.

SEE ALSO *Automobile Leasing*

BIBLIOGRAPHY
"Equipment Leasing." *Entrepreneur.* 1 December 2005.

Gallinger, Jason. "The Joys of Nonownership." *Pittsburgh Business Times.* 8 September 2000.

"Industry News." Equipment Leasing Association of America. Available from http://www.elaonline.com/. Retrieved on 23 March 2006.

Klinger, Linda. "Equipment Leasing: Money Saver or Waster?" *Washington Business Journal.* 5 May 2000.

"Long-Term Equipment Leasing Predictions: Not much new for 2006? Possibly. But recently promulgated rules for financial institutions and railroads reaching lessor leasing 'limits' may change that." *Railway Age.* October 2005.

Trebels, Ruby. "Top Reasons Why Printers Choose Leasing." *Printing News.* 29 August 2005.

Hillstrom, Northern Lights
updated by Magee, ECDI

EQUITY FINANCING

A company can finance its operation by using equity, debt, or both. *Equity* is cash paid into the business—either the owner's own cash or cash contributed by one or more investors. Equity investments are certified by issuing shares in the company. Shares are issued in direct proportional to the amount of the investment so that the person who has invested the majority of the money in effect controls the company. Investors put cash into a company in the hope of sharing in its profits and in the hope that the value of the stock will grow (appreciate). They can earn dividends of course (the share of the profit) but they can realize the value of the stock again only by selling it.

Cash obtained by incurring *debt* is the second major source of funding. It is borrowed from a lender at a fixed rate of interest and with a predetermined maturity date. The principal must be paid back in full by the fixed date, but periodic repayments of principal may be part of the loan arrangement. Debt may take the form of a loan or the sale of bonds; the form itself does not change the principle of the transaction: the lender retains a right to the money lent and may demand it back under conditions specified in the borrowing arrangement.

EQUITY DYNAMICS

The dynamics of investing cash in a business—be it the owner's cash or someone else's—revolve around risk and reward. Under the provisions of bankruptcy law, creditors are first in line when a business fails and owners (including investors) come last and are therefore at a higher risk. Not surprisingly, they expect higher returns than lenders. For these reasons the potential outside investor is very interested in the owner's personal exposure in the first place—and the exposure of other investors secondarily. The more the owner has invested personally, the more motive he or she has to make the business succeed. Similarly, if other people have invested heavily as well, the prospective new investor has greater confidence.

The liquidity of the investment is another point of pressure. If a company is privately held, selling stock in that company may be more difficult than selling the shares of a publicly traded entity: buyers have to be privately found; establishing the value of the stock requires audits of the company. When a company has grown substantially and thus its stock has appreciated, pressures tend to build to "take it public" in order to let investors cash out if they wish. But if the company pays very high dividends, such pressures may be less—the investors hesitant to "dilute" the stock by selling more of it and thus getting a smaller share of the profit.

Debt-Equity Ratio If the company also used debt as a way of financing its activities, the lender's perspective also plays a role. The company's ratio of debt to equity will influence a lender's willingness to lend. If equity is higher than debt, the lender will feel more secure. If the ratio shifts the other way, investors will be encouraged. They will see each of their dollars "leveraging" a lot more dollars from lenders. The U.S. Small Business Administration, on its web page titled "Financing Basics," draws the following conclusion for the small business: "The more money owners have invested in their business, the easier it is to attract [debt] financing. If your firm has a high ratio of equity to debt, you should probably seek debt financing. However, if your company has a high proportion of debt to equity, experts advise that you should increase your ownership capital (equity investment) for additional funds. That you way won't be over-leveraged to the point of jeopardizing your company's survival."

Control For the business owner control is an important element of equity dynamics. The ideal situation is that in which 51 percent of the equity invested is the owner's own—guaranteeing absolute control. But if substantial capital is needed, this is rarely possible. The next best thing is to have many small investors—another difficult condition for the start-up to create. The larger each investor is the less control the owner may have—especially if things get rocky down the ways.

ADVANTAGES AND DISADVANTAGES

For the small business the chief advantage of equity is that it need not be paid back. In contrast, bank loans or other forms of debt financing have an immediate impact on cash flow and carry severe penalties unless payments terms are met. Equity financing is also more likely to be available for startups with good ideas and sound plans. Equity investors primarily seek opportunities for growth; they are more willing to take a chance on a good idea. They may also be a source of good advice and contacts. Debt financiers seek security; they usually require some kind of track record before they will make a loan. Very often equity financing is the *only* source of financing.

The main disadvantage of equity financing is the above-mentioned issue of control. If investors have different ideas about the company's strategic direction or day-to-day operations, they can pose problems for the entrepreneur. These differences may not be obvious at first—but may emerge as the first bumps are hit. In addition, some sales of equity, such as limited initial public offerings, can be complex and expensive and inevitably consume time and require the help of expert lawyers and accountants.

SOURCES OF EQUITY FINANCING

Equity financing for small businesses is available from a wide variety of sources. Some possible sources of equity financing include the entrepreneur's friends and family, private investors (from the family physician to groups of local business owners to wealthy entrepreneurs known as

"angels"), employees, customers and suppliers, former employers, venture capital firms, investment banking firms, insurance companies, large corporations, and government-backed Small Business Investment Corporations (SBICs). Start-up operations, seeking so-called "first tier" financing, must almost always rely on friends and "angels," private persons, in other words, unless the business idea has real explosive, current, fad-appeal.

Venture capital firms often invest in new and young companies. Since their investments have higher risk, however, they expect a large return, which they usually realize by selling stock back to the company or on a public stock exchange at some point in the future. In general, venture capital firms are most interested in rapidly growing, new technology companies. They usually set stringent policies and standards about what types of companies they will consider for investments, based on industries, technical areas, development stages, and capital requirements. As a result, formal venture capital is not available to a large percentage of small businesses.

Closed-end investment companies are similar to venture capital firms but have smaller, fixed (or closed) amounts of money to invest. Such companies themselves sell shares to investors; they use the proceeds to invest in other companies. Closed-end companies usually concentrate on high-growth companies with good track records rather than startups. Similarly, investment clubs consist of groups of private investors that pool their resources to invest in new and existing businesses within their communities. These clubs are less formal in their investment criteria than venture capital firms, but they also are more limited in the amount of capital they can provide.

Large corporations often establish investment arms very similar to venture capital firms. However, such corporations are usually more interested in gaining access to new markets and technology through their investments than in strictly realizing financial gains. Partnering with a large corporation through an equity financing arrangement can be an attractive option for a small business. The association with a larger company can increase a small business's credibility in the marketplace, help it to obtain additional capital, and also provide it with a source of expertise that might not otherwise be available. Equity investments made by large corporations may take the form of a complete sale, a partial purchase, a joint venture, or a licensing agreement.

The most common method of using employees as a source of equity financing is an Employee Stock Ownership Plan (ESOP). Basically a type of retirement plan, an ESOP involves selling stock in the company to employees in order to share control with them rather than with outside investors. ESOPs offer small businesses a number of tax advantages, as well as the ability to borrow money through the ESOP rather than from a bank. They can also serve to improve employee performance and motivation, since employees have a greater stake in the company's success. However, ESOPs can be very expensive to establish and maintain. They are also not an option for companies in the very early stages of development. In order to establish an ESOP, a small business must have employees and must be in business for three years.

Private investors are another possible source of equity financing. A number of computer databases and venture capital networks have been developed in recent years to help link entrepreneurs to potential private investors. A number of government sources also exist to fund small businesses through equity financing and other arrangements. Small Business Investment Corporations (SBICs) are privately owned investment companies, chartered by the states in which they operate, that make equity investments in small businesses that meet certain conditions. There are also many "hybrid" forms of financing available that combine features of debt and equity financing.

METHODS OF EQUITY FINANCING

There are two primary methods that small businesses use to obtain equity financing: the private placement of stock with investors or venture capital firms; and public stock offerings. Private placement is simpler and more common for young companies or startup firms. Although the private placement of stock still involves compliance with several federal and state securities laws, it does not require formal registration with Securities and Exchange Commission. The main requirements for private placement of stock are that the company cannot advertise the offering and must make the transaction directly with the purchaser.

In contrast, public stock offerings entail a lengthy and expensive registration process. In fact, the costs associated with a public stock offering can account for more than 20 percent of the amount of capital raised. As a result, public stock offerings are generally a better option for mature companies than for startup firms. Public stock offerings may offer advantages in terms of maintaining control of a small business, however, by spreading ownership over a diverse group of investors rather than concentrating it in the hands of a venture capital firm.

Entrepreneurs interested in obtaining equity financing must prepare a formal business plan, including complete financial projections. Like other forms of financing, equity financing requires an entrepreneur to sell his or her ideas to people who have money to invest. Careful planning can help convince potential investors that the entrepreneur is a competent manager who will have an advantage over the competition. Overall, equity financ-

ing can be an attractive option for many small businesses. But experts suggest that the best strategy is to combine equity financing with other types, including the entrepreneur's own funds and debt financing, in order to spread the business's risks and ensure that enough options will be available for later financing needs. Entrepreneurs must approach equity financing cautiously in order to remain the main beneficiaries of their own hard work and long-term business growth.

SEE ALSO *Debt Financing; Capital Structure*

BIBLIOGRAPHY
Benjamin, Gerland and Joel Margulis. *Angel capital; how to raise early-stage private equity financing.* John Wile & Sons, 2005.

"The Capital Gender Gap: Despite the health and proliferation of female-owned businesses, women use less commercial credit." *Business Week Online.* 26 May 2005.

Carter, Michael. "Private Equity Capital Update." *Fairfield County Business Journal.* 27 September 2004.

Nakamura, Galen. "Choosing Debt or Equity Financing." *Hawaii Business.* December 2005.

Nugent, Eileen T. "Join the Club." *International Financial Law Review.* April 2005.

U.S. Small Business Administration. "Financing Basics." Available from http://www.sba.gov/starting_business/financing/basics.html. Retrieved on 24 March 2006.

Hillstrom, Northern Lights
updated by Magee, ECDI

ERGONOMICS

Ergonomics is the process of changing the work environment (equipment, furniture, pace of work, etc.) to fit the physical requirements and limitations of employees rather than forcing workers to adapt to jobs that can, over time, have a debilitating effect on their physical well-being. Companies of all shapes and sizes have increasingly recognized that establishing an ergonomically sensitive work environment for employees can produce bottom-line benefits in cutting absenteeism, reducing health care costs, and increasing productivity. The most progressive of these firms have—after careful analysis of the workplace environment and the tasks that their employees have to perform—taken steps to modify that environment (whether in a shop floor or an office) to better fit the physical needs and abilities of workers.

The Occupational Safety and Health Administration (OSHA), an element of the Department of Labor, defines ergonomic disorders (EDs) as a range of health ailments arising from repeated stress to the body. These disorders—which are sometimes also called repetitive strain injuries (RSIs), musculoskeletal disorders (MSDs) or cumulative trauma disorders—may affect the musculoskeletal, nervous, or neurovascular systems. They typically strike workers involved in repetitious tasks or those whose jobs require heavy lifting or awkward postures or movements. These ailments often occur in the upper body of workers, causing injuries in the back, neck, hands, wrists, shoulders, and/or elbows. Carpal tunnel syndrome is the most well-known of these maladies, but thousands of employees have also fallen victim to tendonitis and back injuries over the years. Ergonomics experts say that EDs are particularly prevalent in certain industries. Cashiers, nurses, assembly line workers, computer users, dishwashers, truck drivers, stock handlers, construction workers, meat cutters, and sewing machine operators are among those cited as being most at risk of falling victim to ergonomic disorders.

According to the Occupational Safety and Health Administration, work-related MSDs strike 1.8 million American workers each year. "These injuries are potentially disabling and can require long recovery periods," wrote Charles Jeffress in *Business Insurance*. Jeffress was OSHA's Assistant Secretary of Labor at the time of writing. "For example," Jeffress wrote, "workers need an average of 28 days to recuperate from carpal tunnel syndrome, which is more time than necessary for amputations or fractures. MSDs are also very costly injuries. Direct costs of MSDs total $15 billion to $20 billion per year. Indirect costs increase that total to $50 billion. That's an average of $135 million a day."

OSHA has cited a set of risk factors that contribute to the likelihood of repetitive strain injuries such as carpal tunnel syndrome. These include:

- Performing the same motion or pattern of motions for more than two hours at a time.

- Using tools or machines that cause vibrations for more than two hours a day.

- Handling objects that weigh more than 25 pounds more than one time in a work shift.

- Working in fixed or awkward positions for more than two hours a day.

- Performing work that is mechanically or electronically paced for more than four hours at a time.

In the mid-1990s, the issue of ergonomics became a subject of considerable debate between unions and industries. The AFL-CIO, for instance, called RSIs and job-related back injuries "the nation's biggest job safety problem," contending that more than 700,000 workers miss work each year because of these ailments. Certainly, for workers who are debilitated by carpal tunnel syndrome

or some other injury, the consequences can be dire. Long-term disability (with its attendant diminishment of financial well-being) is a real possibility for many workers who fall victim to RSIs. Some unions subsequently asked OSHA to impose minimum ergonomic standards, and OSHA responded by beginning work on basic ergonomic standards for businesses. The agency completed work on their proposal in the late 1990s; in 2000 the Clinton Administration issued regulations requiring businesses to reimburse injured workers' medical costs, inform workers about repetitive-motion injuries, and compensate them at nearly full salary (90 percent for first 90 days missed) if they miss work due to ergonomic-related injuries. Supporters contended that these new ergonomics program standards would prevent an average of 600,000 ergonomic/musculoskeletal disorders annually (and 4.6 million work-related musculoskeletal injuries over 10 years) and generate $10 billion in savings each year.

Business owners and other opponents, though, claimed that compliance with the new ergonomics standards constituted an unfair burden on small businesses. Some business interests estimated the rules would cost as much as $100 billion annually (OSHA placed the cost of the new regulations to businesses at $4.5 billion a year). Critics also contended that OSHA overstated the extent of the problem of ergonomic disorders in the workplace. In March 2001, the Bush Administration joined with the Republican-controlled Congress to reverse these new work safety rules. This move was widely applauded by small business owners and various business groups but, not surprisingly, denounced by labor unions and other workers' groups.

Whatever the prevailing regulatory atmosphere, numerous business enterprises in a wide variety of industries have shown an increased interest in factoring ergonomics in to their operational strategies, heeding business consultants who claim that an ergonomically sensitive environment can produce major economic benefits for companies. They point out that businesses boasting such environments often see a lower rate of absenteeism, lower health care expenses, lower turnover rates, and higher productivity than do other businesses in the same industry.

For small business owners, building an ergonomically sensitive work environment can depend on a number of different factors. While instituting an additional work break or two during the workday (a simple step that is sometimes cited as a deterrent to development of carpal tunnel syndrome and other repetition-related injuries) does not require the business owner to make any additional capital expenditures, instituting physical changes can be significantly more expensive, especially for established businesses that are small. Buying ergonomic furniture or making significant changes in assembly line layout can be quite expensive, and while the owner of a new business may choose to take ergonomics into account with his or her initial investment, it may be more difficult for the already-established small business owner to replace still-functional equipment and furniture. Each small business owner must determine for himself or herself whether the long-term gains that can be realized from establishing an ergonomically sound workplace (employee retention, productivity, diminished health costs, etc.) make up for the added financial investment (and possible debt) that such expenditures entail.

SEE ALSO *Workplace Safety; Workstation*

BIBLIOGRAPHY

Eckhardt, Bob. "On the Horizon." *Concrete Products.* 1 July 2005.

Ergonomics Desk Reference. J.J. Keller and Associates, 2000.

Jeffress, Charles N. "Ergonomics Standard Good for Business." *Business Insurance.* 23 October 2000.

Ryan, Sean. "President Bush's Proposed OSHA Budget Would Maintain Status Quo." *Daily Record.* 24 February 2006.

Sacks, Evelyn. "Emphasizing Ergonomics: How being proactive proves good for business." *Industrial Safety & Hygiene.* December 2004.

Warner, David. "OSHA is Moving on Ergonomics Rule." *Nation's Business.* August 1997.

Hillstrom, Northern Lights
updated by Magee, ECDI

ESTATE TAX

Estate taxes are taxes levied on the value of an estate when it is passed to heirs upon the death of its owner. Estate taxes are often informally referred to as death taxes or a death tax. The entire value of an estate is not taxed which is why most Americans never have to pay estate taxes. Calculating the taxable portion of an estate is a complicated task usually taken on by the executor of an estate, a person named in the decedent's will.

In the simplest terms, the taxable value of an estate is the gross value of all assets within the estate upon the death of its owner, plus life insurance proceeds, minus outstanding liabilities and the cost of settling the estate. From the resulting value allowable deductions can be made and a well-planned estate is able to minimize the tax owed through the proper applications of these deductions. When an estate includes the assets from a family farm and/or a family business, higher deductions are available.

Many estates, upon the death of one spouse, will transfer, tax free, all assets to the surviving spouse, so long as he or she is a U.S. citizen. The question of estate taxes is, in this way, postponed only to arise again upon the death of the surviving spouse.

Recent changes in tax law have reduced the small number of estates subject to federal estate taxes. In fact, in 2006 less than 1 percent of all U.S. estates will be liable for federal estate taxes, leaving 99 percent able, if necessary, to pass on all of their assets to heirs on a federal tax-free basis. State taxes on inherited property are another subject. Each state assesses its own estate tax.

ESTATE TAX HISTORY

Many experiments with transfer taxes were undertaken before the Federal government enacted the Revenue Act of 1916, which introduced the modern-day income tax and also contained an estate tax with many features of today's system. The act was signed into law during a period of buildup to World War I. This was a time of growing budget deficits. There was also a general concern about the risks posed to a democracy by large concentrations of wealth, the era of the robber baron being very much in the lifetime of those governing at the time.

The estate tax rose almost immediately as the U.S. entered World War I. It continued rising thereafter and reached a top rate of 77 percent for the largest estates during the depression of the 1930s. The rates and the sizes of the estates affected by those rates fluctuated throughout much of the century. During the late 1960s and early 1970s tax reformers were focused on trying to close the many tax loopholes that had evolved over time. These efforts culminated in a 1976 tax bill that rewrote estate taxation, and established the system we had for the rest of the 20th century.

CURRENT TAX RATES

In 2001 the Economic Growth and Tax Relief Reconciliation Act (EGTRRA) was enacted. This act introduced tax reductions across the board and in particular a phased reduction of the estate and gift tax. The new law increases estate tax exemption levels also called unified credits. The exemption level provides all Americans with the ability to pass on to their heirs the first X number of dollars in their estate, X being the government established exemption amount for that year. EGTRRA calls for an increase in the exemption rate every two years—from 1 million in 2003 to 3.5 million in 2009. Then, in 2010, the estate tax is completely abolished for one year. EGTRRA also gradually reduces the top marginal federal estate tax rate to a low of 45 percent in 2009. It is the "sunset" provision of the act which is most striking. In 2011, unless Congress votes to repeal the tax altogether, or establish new tax rates, estate and gift laws will revert to their pre-EGTRRA form. The very unusual single-year abolition of federal estate taxes in 2010 has led to many jokes along the lines of the one in the title of a 2006 *Money* magazine article: "Could You Please Die Sometime in 2010?"

This law has been highly controversial and there is much uncertainly surrounding what will happen with estate and gift taxes after 2010. Congress was scheduled to vote on a permanent repeal of the estate tax in 2005 but the measure was tabled in the wake of devastating hurricanes that hit along the Gulf Coast in the summer. Although no legislation has been passed as of early 2006 to address the post-2010 period, most analysts believe that EGTRRA will not be allowed to "sunset" and that some new legislation will be enacted before the end of 2010. Writing in the *Virginia Tax Review* in 2002, Karen C. Burke described the situation this way: "Virtually no one expects to see the estate tax in its current form spring back into force in 2011. Instead, the 2001 Act is best viewed as an unstable truce between two contending political camps: on one hand, the root-and-branch tax-cutters who are determined to abolish the estate tax permanently, in several strokes if the goal cannot be achieved all at once; and on the other hand, skeptics who concede the need for estate tax reform but balk at outright repeal. Both camps have introduced bills staking out their respective positions, and the outcome of the battle over the future of the estate tax remains uncertain."

ARGUMENTS FOR AND AGAINST THE ESTATE TAX

The vast majority of Americans never have to pay estate taxes. This may be hard to believe based on the vehemence with which the subject is debated. The positions taken in favor of and against an estate tax tend to rest upon deeply held beliefs. How somebody answers the following questions is a sure predictor of where that person stands on the questions of estate taxation: Do the country's richest citizens owe an extra debt to society? Do they have, in Theodore Roosevelt's words, a "peculiar obligation" to those less fortunate?

Supporters of the Estate Tax Estate tax supporters would tend to answer the questions posed in the affirmative.

Perhaps the principal argument in support of an estate tax is that it helps to make the tax burden on Americans more progressive. Proponents of an estate tax argue that such a tax serves to safeguard against the concentration of wealth and political power in the hands of a tiny minority. This in turn, they suggest, is essential for a healthy democracy. There is an underlying assumption implicit in the support of an estate tax and it

involves an understanding about what is in the common good and that, as the old French saying goes, "noblesse oblige" (or nobility obliges).

The maintenance of a vibrant economy is aided by many commonly funded goods—a national infrastructure of roads, waterways, airports, and the like; an educational system open to all; an effective system of public safety and security; a just legal and political system, among others. Those who are most fortunate benefit particularly from these systems, and institutions according to estate tax proponents. They should, consequently, be willing to pay a fair share towards their maintenance—nobility obliges.

Critics of the Estate Tax Estate tax opponents would tend to answer the questions posed in the negative.

Critics of the estate tax list three primary objectives to the taxing of accumulated wealth. First, they argue that this form of tax ends up double taxing earned income since at least a portion of any estate is made up of earned income. Second, opponents of an estate tax claim that it has a chilling effect on savings rates and on economic growth by stifling society's proven wealth builders and job creators. Third, those who wish to repeal the estate tax often state that this tax is a particular burden to family businesses and farms and makes it more difficult to pass on these assets to the next generation who can continue the businesses.

Paul J. Gessing, Director of Government Affairs for the National Taxpayers Union, explains the fundamental objection to an estate tax this way: "While the economic case against the death tax is persuasive enough, the moral case is even more powerful. Because it taxes virtue—living frugally and accumulating wealth—the tax wastes the talent of able people, both those engaged in enforcing the tax and the probably even greater number engaged in devising arrangements to escape the tax."

Complicating the debate about whether to modify the existing estate tax or repeal it all together is the stark reality of a budget deficit that has grown in every year since 2000 and is forecast by the Congressional Budget Office to continue annually for the next ten years. A repeal of the estate tax would exacerbate these annual budget deficits by reducing tax revenues by $20 billion to $60 billion a year.

ESTATE TAX PAYMENT OPTIONS

Usually, taxes on an estate are due nine months after the death of the estate holder. However, estates involving farms and closely held businesses have the option of making installment payments instead. These installment payments may be spread out over as many as 14 years and in the first five years, only interest is due. Interest charged on the taxes due from these business-related estates is set by the IRS at 4 percent. This permits a business to more easily absorb the cost of estate taxes. The deferred payment plan is jeopardized if the business is broken up or sold during the repayment period. A failure to meet the installment payment schedule too may jeopardize the deferred payment plan.

Minimizing Liability Managing a business includes taking steps to minimize the tax liability as much as possible. For family-owned closely-held businesses this planning may include planning around the estate taxes that may be due upon the death of one of its principals. Proper business and estate planning can usually prevent any unexpected or onerous tax burdens.

One step that many companies take in preparing for an expected estate tax bill is to buy life insurance on the owner or owners. The policy should be owned by the company or a life-insurance trust and the proceeds should be kept out of the deceased owner's taxable estate. Planning ahead is very important in this process since many techniques for reducing tax liability require time to implement. The use of "gifting" is one such technique. This involves the annual gift giving that is tax-free as long as it doesn't exceed $12,000 per recipient. The gifts can be in the form of stock or other assets.

Transferring ownership of a business through buy-sell agreements, partnerships, trusts, or outright gifts is a key component in many of the planning strategies available to minimize or eliminate estate tax liability. Business experts caution that taking such steps may be even more important—and also even more complicated—when a small business is owned by two or more family members, since the business can potentially be hit with estate taxes every time one of the owners passes away.

The formation of a family limited trust is another way in which to minimize potential estate tax liability. In the most basic terms, a family limited partnership allows the business to be transferred to the next generation at considerably less than its full value. This reduces the size of the estate and thus the amount of federal taxes owed. Other trusts may also be formed for use in a comprehensive plan but the use of trusts is complicated and is best handled by financial planning experts.

Because of the need for outside expertise, the job of tax planning, and in particular estate tax planning is a costly one. The expense of such planning is, in fact, one of the arguments used by those who wish to see the estate tax repealed. But, as is true with most business activities, one must deal with the realities of the environment in which one does business. Until the uncertainty surrounding the future of the estate tax is clarified by Congress, family-owned businesses are wise to make thorough and prudent plans for succession, plans that include measures to minimize the potential for estate tax liability.

SEE ALSO *Family Limited Partnerships; Retirement Planning; Succession Plans*

BIBLIOGRAPHY
Congressional Budget Office. *The Budget and Economic Outlook: Fiscal Years 2005 to 2014.* Available from http://www.cbo.gov/showdoc.cfm?index=4985&sequence=0 Retrieved on 1 March 2006.

Clifford, Denis. *Estate Planning Basics.* Nolo Press, August 2005.

Gessing, Paul J. Open Letter to Representative Cox. National Taxpayers Union. Available from http://www.ntu.org/main/letters_detail.php?letter_id=235 4 January 2005.

Harrison, Joan. "Family Business Not Fazed by Estate Tax Uncertainty." *The America's Intelligence Wire.* 10 January 2006.

"Increase in Estate Tax Exemption Highlights Changes for 2006." *Mondaq Business Briefing.* 5 January 2006.

Peterson, Carlise. "Estate Tax Seen Affecting Few." *Investment News.* 30 January 2006.

Plack, Harry J. "Form FLP to Protect Biz Assets." *Baltimore Business Journal.* 24 November 2000.

Simon, Kevin. "Estate Planning for a Closely Held Business." *Dayton Business Journal.* 17 February 2006.

Szabo, Joan. "Spreading the Wealth: Transferring Part of Your Business to Your Children Now Could Lower Their Taxes Later." *Entrepreneur.* July 1997.

Ventry, Dennis J., Jr. "Straight Talk about the 'Death' Tax: Politics, Economics, and Morality." *Tax Notes.* 27 November 2000.

Williams, Gary. "Commentary: IRS Looks More Kindly on Family Limited Partnerships That Serve Business." *Daily Record.* 22 December 2004.

Willis, Clint. "Could You Please Die Sometime in 2010? And Other Frequently Asked Questions Under Today's Crazy Estate-Tax Law." *Money.* 1 February 2006.

Magee, ECDI

EUROPEAN UNION (EU)

The European Union (EU), formerly known as the European Community (EC), was formed in the 1950s to encourage and oversee political and economic cooperation between numerous European nations. In the nearly half-century since it was formed, the EU has gradually succeeded in becoming the dominant governing economic body in Europe, and it now affects every aspect of business in its member states.

HISTORY

The EU had its origins in an upsurge of warfare which began in 1870 with the Franco-Prussian war and then continued through two world wars. World War II barely over, Winston Churchill, in a speech at Zurich University given in September 1946 called for "a kind of United States of Europe." Churchill's was a prominent voice but he expressed what many other leaders in Europe were feeling at the time. Two years later Belgium, France, Luxembourg, the Netherlands and the United Kingdom formed the West European Union aimed at mutual defense; that same year 16 other nations joined to form the Organization for European Economic Cooperation (OEEC) to oversee implementation of the U.S.-created Marshall Plan. OEEC later evolved into OECD (Organization for Economic Cooperation and Development), with the U.S. and Japan joining as well.

Communities: Coal, Atomic Energy, Economics In 1951 Belgium, West Germany, Luxembourg, France, Italy, and the Netherlands established the European Coal and Steel Community (ECSC) empowered to make decisions about these industries for the group as a whole. Jean Monnet, who had given an influential speech about this subject in 1950 was named as the ECSC president. ECSC was a great success. In 1957 the same six countries created the European Atomic Energy Community (EURATOM) and the European Economic Community (EEC) to handle atomics and economic development in the same way, principally by removing trade barriers and creating a "common market." These "communities," focused on specific areas, were a step toward a greater union.

Maastricht Milestones along the way were the merger, in 1967, of the three "communities" under a single Commission alongside a Council of Ministers and a European Parliament. In 1979 member countries' populations participated in direct elections of members of this parliament. Elections have been held at five-year intervals since. The Treaty of Maastricht, signed in 1992, created the European Union itself in 1992 by enabling member states to cooperate in defense and in the areas of justice and home affairs as well.

Common Policies and Market—and a Single Currency The collective aim of these arrangements had always been greater efficiency and the achievement of economic power on a larger and more coordinated scale. Removal of trade barriers, common policies in many fields (agriculture, culture, energy, food purity, transportation, trade, etc.), and a common point for negotiating trade and aid agreements have been aims. The EU formed an economic and monetary union in EMU in part to implement some of these goals; it created the European Central Bank and projected the use of a single currency, the euro. The euro became the official currency in 2002 of 12 of the then 15 members: Belgium, Germany, Greece, Spain, France, Ireland, Italy, Luxembourg, the Netherlands, Austria, Portugal, and Finland. Denmark, Sweden, and the U.K retained their own currencies. Since 2002 the euro has become an important global currency.

Expansion and Consolidation In 2002 the EU voted to admit ten additional countries, most of them formerly communist states. In consequence, in 2003, Cyprus, the Czech Republic, Estonia, Hungary, Latvia, Lithuania, Malta, Poland, Slovakia, and Slovenia joined the EU. The Treaty of Nice, which came into force on February 1, 2003 was intended to regulate the newly enlarged union. An EU constitution was framed and will replace Treaty of Nice regulations if all EU member nations approve it in 2006.

STRUCTURE

The EU's several governing bodies oversee different aspects of the union's operations. In addition, each country in the union takes turn acting as chairman; the position changes hands every six months. The European Commission (EC) is perhaps the most important of the governing bodies: it proposes policies and is the only body authorized to propose legislation (besides the national governments of each state). It also oversees the day-to-day operations of the union and ensures that treaties are being carried out as intended. The commission is comprised of 20 commissioners, including a president, all appointed by member states and approved by the parliament.

Once legislation is passed, it is administered by the European Council. The council is comprised of ministers who represent the national governments of the 25 members of the union. Actions of the European Council are approved on a majority vote of 13 of 25 commissioners.

Members of the European Parliament are directly elected by the people of each nation, and members serve five-year terms. While the parliament did gain some legislative power from the Maastricht Treaty, it mainly serves as the public forum of the EU, holding open debates on important issues and overseeing the activities of the council and the commission. The Court of Justice oversees EU laws and regulations and issues rulings when conflicts arise. The court sits as a "Grand Chamber" of 13 judges or in chambers of three or five judges. Decisions issued by the court are binding on member states.

Important but specialized activities of the EU are managed by nine additional bodies:

- European Economic and Social Committee (civil society, employers, and employees).

- Committee of the Regions (represents regional and local authorities).

- European Investment Bank (finances projects and helps small business by means of the European Investment Fund).

- European Central Bank (monetary policy, especially in euro-based countries).

- European Ombudsman (investigates complaints).

- European Data Protection Supervisor (concerned with data privacy).

- Office of Official Publications of the European Communities.

- European Personnel Selection office (recruitment).

- European Administrative School (staff training).

A "UNITED STATES OF EUROPE"?

Is the EU a sovereign entity comparable to the United States? The answer is no—but with the provision that the EU may in the future gradually evolve in that direction if historical forces favor that development. William Underhill wrote in *Newsweek International,* reviewing a book by Boris Johnson (*The Dream of Rome,* HarperCollins): "To Johnson, the idea of Rome is lodged in European folk memory. Deep down, he argues, the continent yearns to re-create an Augustan Age, when 80 million people from Syria to Scotland enjoyed the benefits of Pax Romana." But Johnson evidently doubts the possibility that the old Roman—or the later Holy Roman—empire could be rebuilt, basing his views on the great cultural diversity and fierce national loyalties that the patchwork of nations in Europe represents. The EU was and largely remains an economic venture aiming to present to the world a single, large market (like that of the United States). This emerges from its proposed and still pending (2006) constitution. For those in business dealing with European customers, however, the EU is a much easier entity to deal with than 25 separate states, each with specific rules—no doubt one reason why the EU is successful despite continuing and chronic disagreements among its members.

BIBLIOGRAPHY

European Union. "The History of the European Union." Available from http://europa.eu.int/abc/history/index_en.htm. Retrieved on 26 March 2006.

The European Union in the United States. Available. from http://www.eurunion.org/states/home.htm. Retrieved on 26 March 2006.

Europe's Unreformed Economies. *Global Agenda.* 24 March 2006.

Underhill, William. "The Lessons of History: In a new book, British M.P. Boris Johnson wonders: why can't the EU be more like the Roman Empire?" *Newsweek International.* 20 March 2006.

Weidenfeld, Werner. *Europe from A to Z: A Guide to European Integration.* Office for Official Publications of the European Communities, 1997.

"What is 'Your Europe – Business'?" European Commission. Available from http://europa.eu.int/business/en/advice/theeuro/index.html. Retrieved on 26 March 2006.

Darnay, ECDI

EXPENSE ACCOUNTS

Expense accounts, also called expense allowances, are plans under which companies reimburse employees for business-related expenses. These expenses include travel, entertainment, gifts, and other expenses related to the employer's business activity. Of particular interest to businesses and their employees is the tax treatment of business-related expenses, the types of expenses for which employees will be reimbursed, and the manner in which those reimbursements are made.

For tax purposes a company's expense account plan is either accountable or nonaccountable. An "accountable" plan must meet the certain requirements of the Internal Revenue Service: there must be a business connection; expenses must be substantiated (usually through a receipt); and any amount received by an employee in excess of actual expenses must be returned to the employer. Substantiation means that the employer must be able to identify the specific nature of each expense and determine that the expense was business-related. Expenses may not be aggregated into broad categories, and they may not be reported using vague terminology. If the company's plan is in fact an accountable plan, then all money received by an employee under the plan is excluded from the employee's gross income. It is not reported as wages or other compensation, and it is exempt from withholding.

Companies that fail to require employees to substantiate their expenses or allow employees to retain amounts in excess of substantiated expenses are considered by the IRS to have "nonaccountable" plans. Funds employees receive under nonaccountable plans are treated as income, subject to withholding, and such expenses are deductible by the employee only as a miscellaneous item-ized deduction. Even then, the expenses are deductible only if they exceed 2 percent of the employee's adjusted gross income.

The tax laws affecting business-related expenses change at intervals as the IRS revises its regulations based on its own experience; changes are almost yearly. In 1994, for example, deductions for meal expenses were reduced from 80 percent to 50 percent. But then, in 2000, the IRS changed restaurant rules again, requiring receipts for meals only if the meals cost $75 or more; in 2002 the IRS changed per-diem deduction rules. Changes are also triggered by the passage of new legis-lation. The corporate scandals (Enron, WorldCom) have resulted in important legislation, the Sarbanes-Oxley Act of 2002, which requires much closer tracking and record-keeping by publicly traded corporations. Sarbanes-Oxley is unlikely to affect most small businesses, but fall-out in the form of tightened record-keeping requirements or revised per-diem rates permitted by the IRS have to be watched.

For this reason, it is in the best interests of both employer and employee that all affected parties have a complete understanding of expense accounts and reim-bursable expenses. Employees who find that they are incurring business-related expenses need to determine from their employer exactly what types of expenses are reimbursable, and companies—especially small business owners—need to make sure that employees do not take advantage of expense account policies with excessive spending on lodging, food, and entertainment—never mind fraudulent reporting thereof. In an effort to control spiraling travel and other business-related expenses, some companies have developed reimbursement policies that spell out in detail the various travel expenses that qualify for reimbursement.

SPECIFIC EXPENSE ACCOUNT POLICIES FOR THE SMALL BUSINESS

Small business owners are encouraged to carefully docu-ment all business-related expenses, both for tax purposes and to minimize their exposure to expense account fraud by employees (this type of fraud cost American businesses an estimated $600 billion in 2002 according to the Association of Certified Fraud Examiners, up from $400 billion in 1996). Specific steps and policies that should be considered include:

1. Establish strong internal control systems for tracking expense accounts and activities. These systems include written policies for expense reporting and reimbursement, including what can and cannot be expensed, regular schedules for submitting expense

account reports, and original documentation requirements (receipts) for confirmation of expenses.

2. Institute report procedures to verify legitimacy of submitted expenses. Steps that can be taken in this regard include uniform standards for review of expense reports, comparisons of year-to-year costs, comparisons of submitted mileage expenses with actual mileage information for areas traveled (which can be obtained easily via various Internet travel sites).

3. Establish and maintain careful hiring practices, including comprehensive background/reference checks, before hiring new employees. Companies that take the extra effort to find quality employees for their work force are less vulnerable to fraudulent activity.

4. Be careful not to institute unreasonably stingy poli-cies. Expense accounts, if left unmonitored, can develop into a significant source of income loss for small businesses. But owners and managers should also realize that today's competitive business envi-ronment requires many companies to devote con-siderable financial resources to entertaining clients and business partners in order to ensure a stable and positive relationship.

SEE ALSO *Business Travel; Per-Diem Allowance*

BIBLIOGRAPHY

"A Welcome IRS Change." *Business Week.* 28 February 2000.

Association of Certified Fraud Examiners. Available from http://www.acfe.com/home.asp. Retrieved on 29 March 2006.

Bing, Stanley. "Expense This!" *Fortune.* 6 March 2006.

"Compliance Priority for '06." *Purchasing.* 8 December 2005.

Delahoussaye, Martin. "Teaching People to Steal." *Training.* February 2001.

Israeloff, Robert L. "Preventing Expense Report Fraud." *LI Business News.* 21 January 2000.

"SEC Opens Probe of Red Robin Ex-CEO's Expenses." *Nation's Restaurant News.* 13 February 2006.

Hillstrom, Northern Lights
updated by Magee, ECDI

EXPORT-IMPORT BANK

The United States Export-Import (Ex-Im) Bank, origi-nally established in 1945, is an independent agency cre-ated to help finance U.S. exports to industrializing and developing markets by providing loans, credit guarantees, and insurance. In its 60-year history, the agency has supported more than $400 billion in U.S. exports.

The Ex-Im Bank ranks as one of the most viable sources of financing for small- and mid-sized exporters. For instance, an estimated 1,150 small businesses used Ex-Im Bank programs for the first time from fiscal years 1997 through 1999. In FY 2004, the bank approved 2,572 small business transactions, nearly 83 percent of its total transactions; some 291 small businesses used the Ex-Im bank for the first time that fiscal year. This viability is underscored by the continued reluctance of many banks to make loans for international trade purposes, despite the growing consensus that international markets are a potentially lucrative new area for many small businesses to explore. "You've seen the statistics on the economic benefits of exporting," wrote Jan Alexander in *Working Woman.* "You've read the success stories about small companies that quadrupled their revenues through international sales. All you need is a little extra cash to get things started." But since "loan officers in the U.S. have a tendency to see nearly all foreign markets as unpredictable and all loans associated with foreign expansion as very risky," said Alexander, organizations like the Export-Import Bank and the Small Business Administration (SBA) "have a mandate to help American businesses each step of the way, offering instruction and support in everything from identifying viable foreign markets to closing and financing the deal." The Export-Import Bank confirms as much in its own words. "We want to ensure that no innovative small company loses the opportunity to make a foreign sale because it lacks working capital or competitive export financing," stated one Ex-Im executive in *Business America.*

Indeed, organizations such as the Ex-Im Bank are widely recognized as a valuable resource for small businesses that might otherwise be wholly muscled out of international markets by larger competitors. "Small business and middle market companies must be aware of the existence of export financing programs that can help them increase their export sales by providing access to competitively priced working capital financing," said William Easton in *Business Credit.* "Historically, small businesses and middle market companies have experienced a significant competitive disadvantage in obtaining working capital financing versus larger Fortune 500 companies." The programs maintained by the Ex-Im Bank are designed to address these competitive disadvantages.

PRIMARY EX-IM PROGRAMS

The primary way in which the Ex-Im Bank aids small- and medium-sized U.S. exporters is through one or more of its financing programs. These are summarized as follows:

Working Capital Guarantee Program (WCGP). The Working Capital Guarantee Program, which is operated in conjunction with the SBA's Export Working Capital Program, assists small business exporters in obtaining the capital they need to purchase inventory or raw materials, market exports, or engage in manufacturing activities. The program guarantees 90 percent of the principal and interest on working capital loans extended by commercial lenders to eligible exporters, provided the loan is fully collateralized (through inventory, accounts receivable, or other means). The loan amount may be used for a variety of business purposes, including purchase of raw materials, purchase of inventory, or manufacturing expenses (including cost of labor, engineering, and other services).

Export Credit Insurance Program. The Export-Import Bank makes available credit insurance to qualified small businesses. This insurance, which may be obtained directly or via an insurance broker, consists of a wide variety of policies designed to protect businesses against losses incurred in developing countries, where commercial and political developments can trigger defaults. In FY 2004, small businesses received $1.6 billion in credit insurance authorizations. Specifically, this program 1) protects the exporter against the failure of foreign buyers to make payment because of national political and/or economic developments; 2) encourages exporters to offer international buyers competitive terms of payment; 3) gives exporters and their lending institutions greater financial flexibility in handling overseas accounts receivable (policies are assignable from the insured exporter to financial institutions).

Small Business Insurance Policy Program. The Export-Import Bank provides short-term (no more than 180 days) policies designed to address the unique credit requirements of smaller, newer exporters. Under the policy, Ex-Im Bank assumes 95 percent of the commercial and 100 percent of the political risk involved in extending credit to the exporter's overseas customers. "This policy frees the exporter from 'first loss' commercial risk deductible provisions that are usually found in regular insurance policies," stated the Ex-Im Bank. "It is a multi-buyer type policy which requires the exporter to insure all export credit sales. It offers a special 'hold-harmless' assignment of proceeds which makes the financing of insured receivables more attractive to banks."

Short-Term Single Buyer Program. This option is available to exporters who do not wish to insure all their short-term credit sales under a multi-buyer policy when they are in fact making single or multiple sales to the same buyer. The policy offers 90 percent to 100 percent coverage for both political and commercial risks of default, depending on buyer, term of sale, and type of product. It has no deductible, and small businesses are eligible for special reduced premiums.

Other notable programs offered by the Ex-Im Bank include: 1) Umbrella Policy—allows state agencies, export trading and management companies, insurance brokers, and other agencies to act as intermediaries between the Bank and their clients. 2) Medium-Term Insurance—comprehensive (100 percent) coverage available to exporters of capital goods or services in amounts of $10 million or less and terms up to five years. 3) Guarantees to Foreign Buyers—various loans and guarantees of commercial financing that can be extended to foreign purchasers of U.S. capital goods and related services. 4) Guarantees of repayment protection for private sector loans to buyers of U.S. capital goods and related services. 5) Programs Supporting Export of Environmental Goods and Services—This Ex-Im Bank offering supports export of environmental goods and services by providing short-term environmental insurance policies that feature no deductible and comprehensive coverage in the event of default. 6) Seminars and Briefing Programs—Available to members of the small business community, these discussions and seminars cover a variety of exporting topics.

For more information on these and other Ex-Im offerings, contact the bank's central headquarters in Washington, D.C., or one of its six regional offices across the United States. For more information on these centers, or on any of the institution's other programs and services, call 1-800-565-EXIM or access their Web site at http://www.exim.gov. In addition, the United States maintains 14 U.S. Export Assistance Centers (USEACs) which serve as one-stop centers for export-related services of the Ex-Im Bank and other agencies, including the Small Business Administration and the Department of Commerce.

BIBLIOGRAPHY

Alexander, Jan. "Where the Money Is." *Working Woman.* December-January 1998.

"Ex-Im Bank Enables U.S. Companies to Increase Their International Sales." *World Trade.* January 2006.

Export-Import Bank of the United States. "Your Passport to the Global Marketplace." 2004 Annual Report. Available from http://www.exim.gov/about/reports/ar/ar2004/index.html. Retrieved on 29 March 2006.

Hoover, Kent. "Export-Import Bank of the United States." *Washington Business Journal.* 26 January 2001.

"New VP Small Business at US Ex-Im." *Trade Finance.* February 2006.

Sletten, Eric. *How to Succeed in Exporting and Doing Business Internationally.* John Wiley, 1994.

Hillstrom, Northern Lights
updated by Magee, ECDI

EXPORTING

Any enterprise doing business in the United States can also sell goods and/or services to customers located in foreign countries. A business engaged in such transactions is said to be exporting or to be an exporter. In functional terms the business is still doing what it always does—selling and delivering goods or services—but now across a border. The special phrase is used because export trade involves unusual arrangements. Exporting brings special benefits to the U.S. economy as a whole because we are a net importer of goods and commodities and have experienced a trade deficit for a very long time. The business engaged in export makes a contribution to balancing the uneven distribution of trade. For this reason government assistance is available to the business wishing to sell abroad—ranging from technical and marketing assistance to financing and guarantees of various sorts. Trade assistance is available to the small business from the Small Business Administration, the Export-Import Bank, the U.S. Department of Commerce, and frequently also from state government agencies. Trade associations also provide substantial services to the small business.

Under normal circumstances the small business will "run into" or "chance upon" export opportunities in the course of doing business—by meeting potential buyers at a trade show, for example, by attending some event sponsored by a governmental agency, or hearing of some unusual opportunity. Businesses located in states that border Canada or Mexico sometimes "grow up" exporting as a matter of course. In the Internet age businesses also sometimes get leads and inquiries because they have Web pages visible to foreigners; then, following up one or more promising leads, the business will discover the difficulties of exporting, learn the way to do it by getting help from a government agency, and, after a while, discover that it has added a substantial bit of sales to its business. Another natural route into exporting comes from the owner's personal interests in a foreign country; in the pursuit of that interest, business linkages may develop as well.

Exporting is by no means the exclusive domain of huge corporations and multinationals. In its Fiscal Year 2004 Annual Report, for instance, the U.S. Export-Import Bank reported that it approved 2,572 small business transactions—and these represented a surprising 83 percent of all of its transactions. Nor was FY 2004 unusual for the Ex-Im Bank. To be sure, these small businesses were unlikely to have been two- or three-employee shops but substantially larger (the bank did not provide a size breakdown). Nevertheless, the sheer numbers involved suggest that smallness is not a barrier to exporting. The Small Business Administration adds, by way of confirmation (in its introduction to *Breaking into the Trade Game: A Small Business Guide*) that small businesses export at the rate of $1 billion *a day*.

WHO, WHY, AND WHY NOT

Most advice to small business about exporting—what to do, what to avoid, how to go about it—comes from experts in government agencies who actively participate in brokering foreign trade. The broad consensus of such expertise may be summed up under three rules: 1) the business should be doing well in the domestic market before it attempts to sell abroad; exporting is not a cure for a faltering enterprise; 2) the business should have an innovative or unusual product or service in order to differentiate itself; and 3) the business should first do the necessary homework before incurring expenses some of which may well be wasted. SBA's guide shows the following advantages and disadvantages:

Advantages include some of the following:

- Increased sales and profits.
- Reduced dependence on local markets.
- Leveraged use of corporate technology and know-how.
- Potentially less seasonal variation in sales.
- Full use of production capacity.
- Better information about foreign competition.

These positives are balanced by some negatives:

- Need for additional staff.
- Higher travel expenses.
- Product modification for the new market.
- New promotional material.
- Higher administrative costs.
- Need for additional financing.
- Need for special export licenses.
- Slower payment of receivables.

The SBA comments on this list as follows. "The disadvantages may justify a decision to forego direct exporting at the present time, although your company may be able to pursue exporting through an intermediary. If your company's financial situation is weak, attempting to sell into foreign markets may be ill-timed. The decision to export needs to be based on careful analysis and sound planning." The list of negatives also suggests that the business owner has a fairly steep mountain of knowledge to climb: exporting is not, repeat *NOT* business as usual.

EXPORT CHANNELS

Businesses will typically choose to sell to foreign markets directly or through intermediaries, the channel likely to be chosen because the opportunity came to the business in a certain way. A business that began exporting in response to an inquiry by a foreign retailer, for instance, will likely sell directly and then, later, applying the experience gained in the process, expand by contacting other retailers. Instead of a retailer, inquiries may have come from foreign individuals by way of the Internet—and direct sales to the final customers may become the type of exporting in the business. If the impetus came by way of a solicitation from an export management or an export trading company (EMCs and ETCs respectively), the business is likely to cut its teeth in a relationship with one of these intermediaries and thus begin indirect exporting.

Direct Exporting Direct exporting may involve the business in selling abroad and, if entirely managed in-house, will require the business to master the administrative requirement of exporting in order to deliver the goods to the customer. If selling costs are high or the administrative learning-curve proves to be steep, employment of sales agents already skilled in the process may be an alternative. A commonly utilized method is to use specialized distributors. These can be found through the Department of Commerce's Agent/Distributor Service program, trade associations, and U.S. and foreign chambers of commerce located in targeted foreign markets. The legal agreement between a company and a distributor can be tricky enough so that using a legal and/or accounting professional in its review may be advisable.

If the business has no leads as yet and wishes to find foreign buyers, the Small Business Administration recommends several different approaches. Advertising in trade journals—especially the DOC's widely read *Commercial News USA*—is commonly cited as an effective way of publicizing a small business's product line to overseas markets, as are catalog and video/catalog exhibitions. Trade shows and trade missions are other potentially valuable avenues to explore, but the SBA also encourages small business owners to be proactive in their approach to finding buyers for their products. "Rather than wait for potential foreign customers to contact you," suggests the SBA, "another option is to search out foreign companies looking for the particular product you produce" by investigating information held on the DOC's Economic Bulletin Board, the World Trade Centers Network, and other government and business sources.

Indirect Exporting Export management companies represent the interests of a range of companies; acting as agents for their client companies, EMCs solicit and transact business with prospective foreign buyers. Unlike distributors, however, they do not handle financial matters. The business is responsible for its own debt collection. EMCs typically handle market research, assess the viability of various distribution channels, arrange financing, handle export logistics (prepare invoices, arrange insurance, etc.), and provide legal advice on trade matters. Some EMCs also provide help in negotiating export contracts and after-sales support.

Export trading companies are similar to EMCs in many functional respects, but their standing is more neutral. ETCs act as agents between buyers and sellers, directly paying manufacturers for goods that they subsequently sell to purchasers. Since a small business does not have to rely on the end purchaser to receive compensation under this arrangement, an ETC is seen as a fairly risk-free indirect exporting option. ETC cooperatives, meanwhile, are described by the SBA as U.S. government-sanctioned cooperatives of companies with similar product lines who are interested in securing increased foreign market share. Agricultural interests and trade associations have enjoyed notable success with such cooperatives over the years.

Finally, small companies that choose not to enter into any of the above agreements may still explore foreign markets through agreements with export merchants or via a practice commonly known as "piggyback exporting." Export merchants or agents are businessmen and women who will purchase and repackage products for export. They assume all risks associated with selling the goods, but analysts caution that such arrangements can also compromise a business's control over the pricing and marketing of its product in key markets. Piggyback exporting, meanwhile, is a practice wherein another company armed with an already-established export distribution system sells both its own products and those of other, often smaller enterprises who are not similarly equipped.

WHERE TO GET HELP

A wide range of sources are available to help the small business owner research these issues. Trade associations, exporters' associations, state and federal government agencies, and foreign governments are all potential sources of valuable information.

Relevant trade associations include the Small Business Exporter's Association, the American Association of Exporters and Importers, the National Association of Export Companies (NEXCO), the National Federation of Export Associations (NFEA), and the National Federation of International Trade Associations (NFITA). In addition, the United States

houses more than 5,000 trade and professional organizations with a wide range of industry specializations, many of which actively promote exporting among their members. The federal government, meanwhile, maintains a number of agencies that can be tremendously helpful to the small business owner who is pondering expansion into international markets. These include the United States and Foreign Commercial Service (US&FCS), the Small Business Administration (SBA) and its various programs (Service Corps of Retired Executives-SCORE, Small Business Development Centers-SBDCs, Small Business Institute-SBI), and the International Trade Administration (ITA), which is an arm of the U.S. Department of Commerce (DOC). Resources available through the ITA include international trade specialists and District Export Councils (DECs). The latter groups, which are scattered around the country, are comprised of thousands of executives with experience in international trade who have volunteered their time to help small businesses.

Finally, the U.S. government maintains several databases that can provide small business owners with important data on various exporting factors. These are the SBA's Automated Trade Locator Assistance System (SBAtlas), the National Trade Data Bank (NTDB), and Foreign Trade Report FT925. SBAtlas provides current market information to SBA clients on world markets suitable for their products and services. Foreign Trade Report FT925, meanwhile, provides users with a monthly breakdown of imports and exports by Standard Industrial Trade Classification (SITC) number for each country. The National Trade Data Bank, which is maintained by the Department of Commerce, includes thousands of government documents on various aspects of export promotion and international economics.

SEE ALSO *Export-Import Bank; Exporting—Financing and Pricing; Tariffs*

BIBLIOGRAPHY

"Get Exports Moving." *Entrepreneur.* September 2000.

Powers, Marsha. "Going Global? Take Advantage of Ohio's Export Financing Options." *Crain's Cleveland Business.* 12 September 2005.

"Small Business, Global Reach." *KiplingerForecasts.* 10 June 2005.

Thomson, Amy. "New Guarantee Program Has More Lenders Going Global." *American Banker.* 14 July 2005.

U.S. Commercial Service. Export.gov. "Let Us Help You Export." Available from http://www.export.gov/comm_svc/. Retrieved on 27 March 2006.

U.S. Department of State. *Entrepreneurship and Small Business.* Available from http://usinfo.state.gov/journals/ites/0106/ijee/ijee0106.htm. Retrieved on 28 March 2006.

U.S. Small Business Administration. *Breaking into the Trade Game: A Small Business Guide.* 2005.

U.S. Small Business Administration. "Network of U.S. Export Assistance Centers." Available from http://www.sba.gov/oit/export/useac.html. Retrieved on 28 March 2006.

Hillstrom, Northern Lights
updated by Magee, ECDI

EXPORTING— FINANCING AND PRICING

The financing of export sales concerns arrangements to get payment for the goods shipped or the services provided—exactly the same issue domestically as well, but in the foreign setting the seller's power and leverage, ability to assess credit-worthiness, and his or her ability to collect are constrained by distance and differences in the legal system. For this reason export financing is a specialty and is handled as a distinct transaction of all export deals. Export pricing, similarly, is the same issue as domestic pricing but it must be based on the conditions prevailing in a foreign economy.

MODES OF PAYMENT

In the overwhelming majority of business-to-business transactions domestically, the payment mechanism used is "open account," meaning that goods are shipped by the seller and then billed, with payment expected within 30 days. Occasionally the seller will require "payment in advance" from customers who have a poor credit rating or credit history. Occasionally as well, by prior arrangement, goods are shipped "on consignment" to a buyer, meaning that payment is received only after the buyer in turn has sold the goods and not before.

All three of these modes of payment are used in foreign trade, but because of the special situation prevailing between distant sellers and buyers in different countries, what best suits the seller very rarely pleases the buyers, and vice versa. The respected foreign buyer, for example, does not want to pay in advance—risking that some little business far away fails to deliver. The relatively weak seller does not wish to sell on open account—risking very costly collection efforts if the buyer, far away, fails to pay. Shipping on consignment has the same risks for the seller—with the additional problem of waiting for a sale hundreds or thousands of miles away. For these reasons two other major forms of payment are commonly used in foreign trade: letters of credit and documentary collection.

Letters of Credit Letters of credit (LCs) are issued by banks and, in effect, guarantee that the importer's credit is good. Under this arrangement, the bank makes payment to the importer. Financial experts note that if a letter of credit comes from a U.S. bank, it virtually eliminates the commercial credit risk of an export sale. In other words, the exporter is assured of receiving his or her due compensation for the sale. The terms of an irrevocable letter of credit cannot be changed without the express permission of the exporter once it has been opened. The letter of credit also extends some protection to importers: it includes steps that ensure that the exporter has fully complied with the terms of sale discussed in the LC. But some importers balk at the added costs that LC arrangements bring on them.

Documentary Collection Documentary Collection, also known as a draft, is roughly equivalent to cash on delivery. Under this system of payment, a draft is drawn that requires the buyer to make payment either on sight (sight draft) or by a specified date (time draft). Legal possession of the products does not pass from the exporter to the importer until the draft has been paid or accepted. Analysts note that this arrangement serves to protect both parties, although an exporter may still have to pursue legal options to secure payment if the buyer defaults.

Trade Financing Trade financing is borrowing specifically for an export venture, with the loan backed by the export inventory and the accounts payable due to the seller after completion of the sale. Trade finance loans are self-liquidating, meaning that proceeds of the sale are first used to pay off the loan; the remainder, thereafter, is credited to the borrower. These are project-oriented loans and quite unlike ordinary working capital loans. If the business does not need up-front money for raw materials and labor, it may still wish to engage in more limited trade financing, especially if payments of receivables are likely to be slow. This type of financing involves sales of the receivables to a third party or borrowing on the receivables themselves.

Sources of trade financing are 1) banks, 2) factoring houses, 3) export trading companies, 4) export management companies, 5) private trade finance companies, and 6) U.S. government agencies.

The small business's local bank may be a very good source of financing if it is experienced in international trade, has a department specializing in such business, or is affiliated with another bank with which it routinely deals on such transactions. For trade financing particularly, the U.S. Small Business Administration (SBA) recommends the business owner to work with an experienced international banker. As always when obtaining any kind of credit, but especially in dealing with a bank on international ventures, the owner should anticipate having to provide financial statements, business plans, and other documentation all depending on the size and nature of the transaction.

Factoring houses purchase export receivables—but at a discount. They may also act as middlemen (the word "factor" means "agent," derived from "doer"). They will purchase exports but at a certain percentage below invoice value; the percentage rate will be dependent on, among other things, the intended market and the type of buyer. Under this arrangement, the exporter does not receive full value for its goods but gets paid immediately and does not have to worry about future collection hassles with foreign customers who are tardy with their payments. Export trading companies (ETCs) and export management companies (EMCs) provide assistance in arranging financing for exporters. In addition they may offer a wide range of potentially helpful other services, including international market research, legal assistance, insurance, administration, warehousing and distribution, and product design. Private trade finance companies provide a range of financing options to small businesses in exchange for fees, commissions, or outright involvement in the transactions under consideration.

Finally, small business owners may choose to seek assistance from the government. Several federal agencies—and some state agencies—maintain programs that offer financial aid to small enterprises seeking to sell to foreign markets. Loan programs offered by the Small Business Administration, for example, include the International Trade Loan Program, a long-term financing option; the ERLC (Export Revolving Line of Credit) Program, which lasts for up to 36 months, and regular SBA business loans. Businesses may also seek loans through the Small Business Investment Company (SBIC), the Department of Agriculture's Commodity Credit Corporation (CCC), or the Export-Import Bank of the United States (Ex-Im Bank). The latter is an independent federal agency charged with assisting U.S. exporters of goods and services through a wide range of programs. Some of these export assistance programs are maintained in cooperation with various state governments. Lastly, some small business owners choose to secure financing for deals in moderate- to high-risk emerging markets through the Overseas Private Investment Corporation (OPIC), an organization that guarantees and/or provides project loans to American companies in developing nations around the world, or the U.S. Agency for International Development (USAID). USAID makes loans and grants to foreign countries some of which require the country to purchase U.S. supplies. The agency, therefore, is a source of leads

for the small business prospecting for business overseas with safe payment arrangements.

PRICING FOR THE FOREIGN MARKET

Pricing for the foreign market—as for the domestic—is a circular process which involves market research to determine current pricing structures in the targeted market, estimating the cost of production to see if prevailing prices can support the production, projecting a tentative price, testing it in the market if possible, and then making changes in production, packaging, distribution, and marketing until the "right" price emerges. The difference lies in such factors as currency conversion, difficulties in getting information, additional costs associated with foreign trade which may impose higher costs (fees, licenses, etc.), translation costs, special packaging requirements, and higher costs of money (if payments are slow or must be discounted to factoring companies). It is obvious from this brief sketch above that the business with good market contacts and well-developed sources of information will be more successful in setting the right price yielding the maximum profit than a business largely groping in the dark or pricing entirely by analogy to the domestic market.

SBA's principal Guide (*Breaking into the Trade Game: A Small Business Guide*) recommends that the business develop its cost picture based on the marginal-cost method, assuming that export sales are "additional" sales. Under this method, all costs are classified as fixed or variable. If the business is profitable now and the owner does not need to add buildings or machinery to produce for export, these "fixed" costs are excluded from the costing and only "variable" costs of raw materials, purchased parts, energy, and labor are measured. To these costs are added export costs unique to that business along with prorated overhead costs. Thus if the export sale represents 8 percent of total sales, 8 percent of overhead costs would be added. The anticipated profit would then be added to determine a tentative initial price from the business's own point of view.

With price initially set, the business needs some data about pricing in the target market. According to the SBA, "pricing information can be obtained in several ways: a) from overseas distributors and agents of similar products of equivalent quality; b) whenever feasible, traveling to the country where your products will be sold to gather information; and c) through the U.S. Commercial Service which can assist in determining appropriate prices through its *Customized Sales Survey.* For more information, go to www.export.gov/tic."

Prices obtained must be translated to U.S. dollars before comparisons to the business's own "tentative price" can be made. If the business has a genuinely innovative product, comparisons will not be exact because products now sold may not offer the company's superior features. But the "market prices" will be an indicator both of the venture's feasibility and likely degree of success. If pricing in the market is generally lower but the company's product has desirable features, a green light may flash immediately if those features are obvious. If not, marketing expenses may have to be raised—and the process of pricing iterated. Sometimes the "feature" of the company's product may be precisely that it is inexpensive yet in all other ways equivalent. In that case, too, additional costs may be indicated to get the message of quality and durability across or, if the price differential is high in favor of the seller, perhaps the price needs to be hiked.

Currency values fluctuate, in some markets more than others. For this reason the SBA recommends that small businesses new to exporting arrange transactions in U.S. dollars; that is, they should both price their goods and request payment for them in U.S. dollars. If a buyer balks at conducting the transaction in U.S. dollars, an exporter can still protect him or herself through factoring or hedging. Hedging guarantees a set exchange rate through the use of option and forward contracts, but these types of transactions involve the small business in activities likely to be far removed from its core business.

The small business pursuing export business with some care and tenacity will, needless to say, develop a fairly extensive circle of advisors and participants so that neither its financing nor its pricing activities will be taking place in a vacuum. Aside from having something of real value to sell, the most important factor for success will be information—about the market, about methods of financing, channels of distribution, and (not least) about the customer. The more extensive the business's contacts and the more intensive its relationships, the better will be its information and the more refined will be its pricing.

SEE ALSO *Exporting*

BIBLIOGRAPHY

Burpitt, William J., and Dennis A. Rondinelli. "Small Firms' Motivations for Exporting: To Earn and Learn?" *Journal of Small Business Management.* October 2000.

"Consistent Performance for the Client." *Trade Finance.* February 2006.

Powers, Marsha. "Going Global? Take advantage of Ohio's export financing options." *Crain's Cleveland Business.* 12 September 2005.

"Support for SMEs from US Ex-Im Continues Apace." *Trade Finance.* March 2003.

Thomson, Amy. "New Guarantee Program Has More Lenders Going Global." *American Banker.* 14 July 2005.

U.S. Small Business Administration. *Breaking into the Trade Game: A Small Business Guide.* 2005.

Hillstrom, Northern Lights
updated by Magee, ECDI

F

FACILITY LAYOUT AND DESIGN

Facility layout and design is an important component of a business's overall operations, both in terms of maximizing the effectiveness of the production process and meeting the needs of employees. The basic objective of layout is to ensure a smooth flow of work, material, and information through a system. The basic meaning of facility is the space in which a business's activities take place. The layout and design of that space impact greatly how the work is done—the flow of work, materials, and information through the system. The key to good facility layout and design is the integration of the needs of people (personnel and customers), materials (raw, finishes, and in process), and machinery in such a way that they create a single, well-functioning system.

FACTORS IN DETERMINING LAYOUT AND DESIGN

Small business owners need to consider many operational factors when building or renovating a facility for maximum layout effectiveness. These criteria include the following:

1. Ease of future expansion or change—Facilities should be designed so that they can be easily expanded or adjusted to meet changing production needs. "Although redesigning a facility is a major, expensive undertaking not to be done lightly, there is always the possibility that a redesign will be necessary," said Weiss and Gershon in their book *Production and Operations Management*. "Therefore,

any design should be flexible . . . . Flexible manufacturing systems most often are highly automated facilities having intermediate-volume production of a variety of products. Their goal is to minimize changeover or setup times for producing the different products while still achieving close to assembly line (single-product) production rates."

2. Flow of movement—The facility design should reflect a recognition of the importance of smooth process flow. In the case of factory facilities, the editors of *How to Run a Small Business* state that "ideally, the plan will show the raw materials entering your plant at one end and the finished product emerging at the other. The flow need not be a straight line. Parallel flows, U-shaped patterns, or even a zig-zag that ends up with the finished product back at the shipping and receiving bays can be functional. However, backtracking is to be avoided in whatever pattern is chosen. When parts and materials move against or across the overall flow, personnel and paperwork become confused, parts become lost, and the attainment of coordination becomes complicated."

3. Materials handling—Small business owners should make certain that the facility layout makes it possible to handle materials (products, equipment, containers, etc.) in an orderly, efficient—and preferably simple—manner.

4. Output needs—The facility should be laid out in a way that is conducive to helping the business meet its production needs.

5. Space utilization—This aspect of facility design includes everything from making sure that traffic lanes are wide enough to making certain that inventory storage warehouses or rooms utilize as much vertical space as possible.

6. Shipping and receiving—The J. K. Lasser Institute counseled small business owners to leave ample room for this aspect of operations. "While space does tend to fill itself up, receiving and shipping rarely get enough space for the work to be done effectively," it said in *How to Run a Small Business.*

7. Ease of communication and support—Facilities should be laid out so that communication within various areas of the business and interactions with vendors and customers can be done in an easy and effective manner. Similarly, support areas should be stationed in areas that help them to serve operating areas.

8. Impact on employee morale and job satisfaction—Since countless studies have indicated that employee morale has a major impact on productivity, Weiss and Gershon counsel owners and managers to heed this factor when pondering facility design alternatives: "Some ways layout design can increase morale are obvious, such as providing for light-colored walls, windows, space. Other ways are less obvious and not directly related to the production process. Some examples are including a cafeteria or even a gymnasium in the facility design. Again, though, there are costs to be traded off. That is, does the increase in morale due to a cafeteria increase productivity to the extent that the increased productivity covers the cost of building and staffing the cafeteria."

9. Promotional value—If the business commonly receives visitors in the form of customers, vendors, investors, etc., the small business owner may want to make sure that the facility layout is an attractive one that further burnishes the company's reputation. Design factors that can influence the degree of attractiveness of a facility include not only the design of the production area itself, but the impact that it has on, for instance, ease of fulfilling maintenance/cleaning tasks.

10. Safety—The facility layout should enable the business to effectively operate in accordance with Occupational Safety and Health Administration guidelines and other legal restrictions.

"Facility layout must be considered very carefully because we do not want to constantly redesign the facility," summarized Weiss and Gershon. "Some of the goals in designing the facility are to ensure a minimum amount of materials handling, to avoid bottlenecks, to minimize machine interference, to ensure high employee morale and safety, and to ensure flexibility. Essentially, there are two distinct types of layout. *Product layout* is synonymous with assembly line and is oriented toward the products that are being made. *Process layout* is oriented around the processes that are used to make the products. Generally, product layout is applicable for high-volume repetitive operations, while process layout is applicable for low-volume custom-made goods."

DIFFERENCES BETWEEN OFFICE AND FACTORY LAYOUTS

Offices and manufacturing facilities are typically designed in much different ways—a reflection of the disparate products that the two entities make. "A factory produces things," wrote Stephen Konz in *Facility Design.* "These things are moved with conveyors and lift trucks; factory utilities include gas, water, compressed air, waste disposal, and large amounts of power as well as telephones and computer networks. A layout criterion is minimization of transportation cost." Konz pointed out, however, that the mandate of business offices is to produce information, whether disseminated in physical (reports, memos, and other documents), electronic (computer files), or oral (telephone, face-to-face encounters) form. "Office layout criteria, although hard to quantify, are minimization of communication cost and maximization of employee productivity," wrote Konz.

Layout requirements can also differ dramatically by industry. The needs of service-oriented businesses, for instance, are often predicated on whether customers receive their services at the physical location of the business (such as at a bank or pet grooming shop, for instance) or whether the business goes to the customer's home or place of business to provide the service (as with exterminators, home repair businesses, plumbing services, etc.) In the latter instances, these businesses will likely have facility layouts that emphasize storage space for equipment, chemicals, and paperwork rather than spacious customer waiting areas. Manufacturers may also have significantly different facility layouts, depending on the unique needs that they have. After all, the production challenges associated with producing jars of varnish or mountaineering equipment are apt to be considerably different than those of making truck chassis or foam beach toys. Retail outlets comprise yet another business sector that has unique facility layout needs. Such establishments typically emphasize sales floor space, inventory logistics, foot-traffic issues, and overall store attractiveness when studying facility layout issues.

Konz also observed that differences in factory and office layouts can often be traced to user expectations. "Historically, office workers have been much more concerned with status and aesthetics than factory workers," he noted. "A key consideration in many office layouts is 'Who will get the best window location?' To show their status, executives expect, in addition to preferred locations, to have larger amounts of space. Rank expects more privacy and more plush physical surroundings." In addition, he stated, "Offices are designed to be 'tasteful' and to 'reflect the organization's approach to business dealings.'" Conversely, in the factory setting, aesthetic elements take a back seat to utility.

Given these emphases, it is not surprising that, as a general rule, office workers will enjoy advantages over their material production brethren in such areas as ventilation, lighting, acoustics, and climate control.

BIBLIOGRAPHY

Baykasoglu, Adil, Turkay Dereli, and Ibrahim Sabuncu. "An Ant Colony Algorithm for Solving Budget Constrained and Unconstrained Dynamic Facility Layout Problems." *Omega.* August 2006.

Cornacchia, Anthony J. "Facility Management: Life in the Fast Lane." *The Office.* June 1994.

Groover, M. P. *Automation, Production Systems, and Computer-Integrated Manufacturing.* Prentice-Hall, 1987.

J. K. Lasser Institute. *How to Run a Small Business.* Seventh Edition. McGraw-Hill, 1994.

Konz, Stephen. *Facility Design.* John Wiley & Sons, 1985.

Myers, John. "Fundamentals of Production that Influence Industrial Facility Designs." *Appraisal Journal.* April 1994.

Sherali, Hanif D., Barbara M.P. Fraticelli, and Russell D. Melle. "Enhanced Model Formulations for Optimal Facility Layout." *Operations Research.* July-August 2003.

Weiss, Howard J., and Mark E. Gershon. *Production and Operations Management.* Allyn and Bacon, 1989.

Hillstrom, Northern Lights
updated by Magee, ECDI

FACILITY MANAGEMENT

Facility management is the coordination of the physical workplace with the people and work of an organization. It is the integration of business administration, architecture, and the behavioral and engineering sciences. In the most basic terms, facility management encompasses all activities related to keeping a complex operating. Facilities include grocery stores, auto shops, sports complexes, jails, office buildings, hospitals, hotels, retail establishments, and all other revenue-generating or government institutions.

Responsibilities associated with facility management typically include a wide range of function and support services, including janitorial services; security; property or building management; engineering services; space planning and accounting; mail and messenger services; records management; computing, telecommunications and information systems; safety; and other support duties. It is the job of the facility manager to create an environment that encourages productivity, is safe, is pleasing to clients and customers, meets government mandates, and is efficient.

DIFFERENT BUSINESSES AND THEIR DIFFERENT FACILITY NEEDS

The term "facility" is used to refer to a broad spectrum of buildings, complexes, and other physical entities. "The only thread common among these entities is the fact that they are all *places*," wrote Alan M. Levitt in *Disaster Planning and Recovery: A Guide for Facility Professionals.* "A 'facility' may be a space or an office or suite of offices; a floor or group of floors within a building; a single building or a group of buildings or structures. These structures may be in an urban setting or freestanding in a suburban or rural setting. The structures or buildings may be a part of a complex or office park or campus."

The key is to define the facility as a physical place where business activities are done, and to make facility management plans in accordance with the needs and demands of those business activities. After all, the facility needs of a movie theatre, a museum, a delicatessen, a plastics manufacturer, and a bank are apt to be considerably different, even though there will likely be certain basic needs that all will share (furniture, office space, air conditioning systems, light fixtures, etc.). Good facility management is concerned with addressing those needs in the best and most cost-effective ways possible. Indeed, facility management encompasses a wide range of responsibilities, including the following:

- Monitoring organization efficiency. The coordination of personnel, machines, supplies, work in progress, finished products, and deliveries must all be done if your plant is to be successful.

- Ensuring that the business receives the most it can for its facility-related expenditures (this is often done through standardization of company-wide needs so that high-volume purchases of necessary products can be made).

  Real estate procurement, leasing, and disposal (or facility construction, renovation, and relocation).

- Ensuring that the divergent processes, procedures, and standards present in a business complement rather than interfere with one another.

- Monitoring all aspects of facility maintenance and upkeep so that the business can operate at highest capacity.

- Tracking and responding to environmental, health, safety, and security issues.

- Ensuring facility compliance with relevant regulatory codes and regulations

- Anticipating future facility needs in areas as diverse as fluorescent light procurement, new space for expanded assembly lines, automation, and wiring for new computer networks.

- Educating the work force about all manner of standards and procedures, from ordering office supplies to acting in the event of a disaster.

THE EVOLVING CHARACTER OF FACILITY MANAGEMENT

Facility management has traditionally been associated with janitorial services, mailrooms, and security. Since the middle of the twentieth century, facility management has evolved into a demanding discipline. Factors driving the complexity of the facility manager's job are numerous. For example, facilities have become much larger and more complicated, often relying on computerized and electronic support systems that require expertise to operate and repair. Personal computer networks, sophisticated telecommunications systems and other technological tools have significantly increased the requirements of facility management in the past 20 years.

Of course, many other factors have impacted on the challenges of facility management in recent years. For example, the newfound corporate cost-consciousness that emerged during the 1980s has generated an emphasis on operational efficiency. Writing in *IIE Solutions*, Steven M. Price summarized the facility manager's situation thusly: "Facilities professionals are being asked to contain costs while achieving maximum beneficial use—that is, to achieve more with less." In addition, philosophical changes such as increased reliance on teamwork, cross-functional teams, and telecommuting have created new spacing and infrastructure demands. Finally, the responsibilities of facility managers have continued to broaden into all areas of facility upkeep, including insuring that the business adheres to regulatory requirements in such areas as handicapped access, hazardous material handling and disposal, and other "safe workplace" issues.

The end result of new technology, efficiency pressures, and government regulations has been an expansion of the facility management role. By the 1990s, facility managers were often highly trained and educated and prepared to wear several hats. Depending on the size of the complex, the manager will likely be responsible for

directing a facility management and maintenance staff. In addition to overseeing the important duties related to standard maintenance, mailroom, and security activities, he or she may also be responsible for providing engineering and architectural services, hiring subcontractors, maintaining computer and telecommunications systems, and even buying, selling, or leasing real estate or office space.

For example, suppose that a company has decided to consolidate five branch offices into a central computerized facility. It may be the facility manager's job to plan, coordinate, and manage the move. He or she may have to find the new space and negotiate a purchase. And he or she will likely have to determine which furniture and equipment can be moved to the new office, and when and how to do so with a minimal disruption of the operation. This may include negotiating prices for new furniture and equipment or balancing needs with a limited budget. The facility management department may also furnish engineering and architectural design services for the new space, and even provide input for the selection of new computer and information systems. Of import will be the design and implementation of various security measures and systems that reduce the risk of theft and ensure worker safety. The manager will also be responsible for considering federal, state, and local regulations. He or she will need to ensure that the complex conforms to mandates associated with the Americans with Disabilities Act (ADA), clean air and other environmental protection regulations, and other rules. The ADA dictates a list of requirements related to disabled employee and patron access with which most facilities must comply, while clean air laws impose standards for indoor air quality and hazardous emissions. Similarly, other laws regulate energy consumption, safety, smoking, and other factors that fall under the facility manager's umbrella of responsibility.

FACILITY MANAGEMENT IN THE FUTURE

Analysts have suggested that evolving business realities in the realms of process improvement, cost containment, speed-to-market accelerations, quality control, and workplace arrangements and concepts will all have a big impact on future notions of facility management. The challenge for facility managers will be to integrate knowledge workers into a dynamic business environment of global competition, technological developments, security threats and changing values. Writing in *IIE Solutions*, Steven M. Price, in the *IIE Solutions* article entitled "Facilities Planning: A Perspective for the Information Age" laid out four primary precepts that will likely form the underpinnings of future financial management planning:

1. Understanding the evolving nature of knowledge-based business—"The new workforce and the content of its work is migrating from a bureaucratic control of resources and the movement of materials through a process toward a highly flexible and networked organization whose added value is exploiting specialized knowledge and information to solve complex problems," wrote Price.

2. Understanding workspace trends—Price and other business analysts believe that computing and communications technologies are fundamentally transforming the workplace landscape. As shared jobs, telecommuting, home-based businesses, flexible work hours and other trends make further inroads in the business world, facility management philosophies will have to keep pace.

3. Understanding how new technologies have removed old restrictions on conducting business—This, said Price, basically entails recognizing that "the removal of physical limitations caused by transportation and communications technology has changed the scope, strategy, and structure of the business world."

4. Understanding "Job Factor" basics—Price noted that IBM and other companies have developed facility management philosophies that study the interaction of all job factors, including those of physical environment and job content.

CONTRACT FACILITY MANAGEMENT

Increasing numbers of large businesses are choosing to outsource their facility management tasks to specialized facility management companies that operate the complex for the owner on a contract basis. This arrangement has become more common in part because of the increasing scope and complexity of facility management. Companies that hire contract managers prefer to focus on other goals, such as producing a product or providing a service. Many of these firms find that outsourcing facility management duties to a specialist reduces costs and improves operations.

Contract facility managers may be hired to manage an entire complex or just one part of a large operation. For example, some companies hire contract managers that specialize in operating mailrooms or providing janitorial services. In any case, the company expects to benefit from the expertise of the manager/management firm it hires. A contractor that manages data processing systems, for example, may bring technical know-how that its employer would have great difficulty cultivating in-house. Likewise, a recreation facility owner that employs a facility manager specializing in the operation of sport complexes may benefit from the contractor's mix of knowledge related to grounds keeping, accounting and reporting, and sports marketing, among other functions.

Besides expertise and efficiency, several other benefits are provided by contract facility managers. One such benefit is the reduced liability to owner's or occupant's for personnel. By contracting a firm to manage one of its factories, an organization can substantially reduce its involvement in staffing, training, worker's compensation expenses and litigation, employee benefits, and worker grievances. It also eliminates general management and payroll responsibilities—rather than tracking hours and writing checks for an entire staff, it simply pays the facility management company. In addition, a company that hires a facility management firm can quickly reduce or increase its staff as it chooses without worrying about hiring or severance legalities.

Whether a small business chooses to outsource or maintain internal control of its facility management processes the ultimate goals are the same. As Raymond O'Brien commented in *Managing Office Technology*, "both the in-house facility management department and outsourced services must recognize that the facility management business is changing. While, traditionally, interior planning has been driven by preconceived notions of what is appropriate, business today increasingly is not being conducted in a traditional manner or in traditional locations.... Changing roles, combined with changing technology, drives the environment of the future."

Although he concurred that the field of facility management is in a state of flux at the moment, O'Brien argued that quality facility management could became an even greater advantage for attentive businesses in the future: "[Facility management] offers those with entrepreneurial spirit enormous opportunity. Whether working within a corporation or as an outsourced service provider, imaginative facility managers can find myriad ways to improve service to the company or the client while creating an interesting, challenging position for themselves."

BIBLIOGRAPHY
Alder, Steve. "Disaster and Recovery Planning: A Guide for Facility Managers." *Security Management*. June 2005.

Brown, Malcolm. "Rulers of the New Frontier." *Management Today*. March 1996.

Friday, Stormy. *Organization Development for Facility Managers*. AMACOM, a Division of the American Management Association, 2003.

Huston, John. "Mastering the Facility." *Buildings*. December 1999.

Kruk, Leonard B. "Facilities Planning Supports Changing Office Technologies." *Managing Office Technology.* December 1996.

Levitt, Alan M. *Disaster Planning and Recovery: A Guide for Facility Professionals.* John Wiley & Sons, 1997.

Lewis, Bernard T. and Richard P. Payant. *The Facility Manager's Emergency Preparedness Handbook.* AMACOM, a Division of the American Management Association, 2003.

O'Brien, Raymond. "Facility Managers Provide Invaluable Services." *Managing Office Technology.* September 1995.

Price, Steven M. "Facilities Planning: A Perspective for the Information Age." *IIE Solutions.* August 1997.

Sopko, Sandy. "Smaller Staffs and Budgets Boost FM Outsourcing." *The Office.* August 1993.

Tuveson, Kit. "Facility Management in the 21st Century." *Managing Office Technology.* May 1998.

Hillstrom, Northern Lights
updated by Magee, ECDI

FACTORING

Factoring is a form of financing in which a business sells its receivables to a third party or "factor company" at a discounted price. Under this arrangement, a factor company agrees to provide financing and other services to the selling business in return for interest and fees on the money that they advanced against the seller's accounts receivables. Businesses in need of cash can thus secure about 80 percent of their accounts receivables' face value. In rare cases, a higher percentage can be secured, but in most instances 20 percent of the value of the accounts receivable is held in reserve until the accounts are collected.

Factoring is a tool used by many established firms to avoid the sorts of cash flow problems that arise because of a customer's slow payment patterns. Economic downturns are often accompanied by an elongating of the average invoice payment time. Cash is the lifeblood of a business. Managing it efficiently is essential for success. It is often a lack of cash flow rather than a lack of sales that prevents companies from developing beyond their initial stages. Factoring agreements are one way that businesses with established sales can, for a price, guarantee smooth cash flow. Since factoring is a practice based on lending against accounts receivable, it is not a realistic source of capital for start-ups.

There are two primary financing agreements entered into by factor companies, recourse and nonrecourse financing. Recourse financing is an agreement under which the borrower maintains the responsibility for any bad debt or uncollectible invoices that it has issued. Nonrecourse financing is the term used when the factor company bears the risk of collecting from its client's clients. It takes on the responsibility for collecting and covers uncollectible invoices.

HOW FACTORING WORKS

The factoring process varies from agreement to agreement but the basics are similar in most situations. A business that is working with a factoring company, upon invoicing its clients, will send a copy of each invoice issued to the factoring company. On receipt of the invoices, the factoring company immediately provides its client with 80 to 85 percent of the value of the invoices received.

Once the outstanding invoices are paid by the business's customers to the factoring company it pays the business the remaining 20 percent of the value of those invoices less prearranged charges. Factoring charges include a fee and interest on the 80 to 85 percent paid in advance of collections.

In some respects, the factoring process is roughly comparable to credit card arrangements. Just as MasterCard buys a retailer's receivables and pays the store as soon as a sale is made, factoring companies do much the same thing on the wholesale level. For example, assume a toaster manufacturer ships a $150,000 order to one of its customers. Rather than waiting for the customer to pay, the manufacturer can sell the receivables to a factor, receiving up to 85 percent of the $150,000 total as soon as the goods leave the shipping dock and an invoice is sent. This speeds the collection process. The balance is paid, less factoring charges, when the factor collects from the toaster manufacturer's customer.

Small business owners should be aware that factoring is different in several fundamental respects from bank financing. For one thing, it is much more expensive. Factoring charges can cost between 2 percent and 10 percent of sales. Arrangements for fees vary widely, depending on the credit quality of the borrower's customer account balances and the range of services that are purchased from the factor. In addition, small business owners should recognize that utilizing a factor company is an all-or-nothing proposition. Factors generally demand 100 percent of a client's receivables. They will not limit their efforts to those receivables considered marginal or high risk.

GROWTH OF FACTORING

Factor companies are an increasingly mainstream choice for small business owners seeking capital. According to the World Bank, in its report entitled *Financing Small- and Medium-Size Enterprises with Factoring*, the volume of business handled by factors in the United States increased 15.2 percent between 1998 and 2003. Indeed, even though factoring carries some risks for small enterprises, it is regarded as a viable short-term cash management tool.

Factoring companies usually include a range of accounts receivable services as a part of their overall service. These services include such things as bookkeeping, collections, and credit verification. By reducing the in-house cost of managing these tasks it is more likely that a business will be able to justify the cost of working with a factoring company.

Although the cost of working with a factoring company is high, it may still be more cost effective than offering customers a 6 percent early payment discount in order to encourage the early payment of invoices. A factor will provide a business with cash almost immediately upon shipping a product whereas early payment discounts will usually only bring in payments marginally sooner than would be the case without the discount. Working with a factor is far more likely to offer substantial cash flow benefits than simply speeding up the collection period. The growth of factoring suggests that many companies are finding it a profitable way in which to help manage cash flow.

SELECTING A FACTOR

Selecting a factor is much like selecting any other service provider. The objective is to find the best price for the services provided. Several considerations that should be weighed by the small business owner in making fee arrangements with a factor include:

- Recourse—Small business enterprises that elect to go with a recourse factor (in which they bear final responsibility for collecting monies owed) over nonrecourse factors (where the factor company bears that responsibility) will find that they may gain lower fees and more money from the factor in return for increasing their risk.

- Customer Base—The larger the number of customers a business has, the more cost advantages the factor can offer the business. Automation provides factors with significant economies of scale when a large number of customers are involved.

- Creditworthiness of Customers—Factor companies will assess the credit worthiness of a business's clients and use this as an important element in pricing the factoring services for that business. Factors will not purchase substandard customer balances.

- Size and Age of the Average Invoice—Smaller receivables that have been on the books for a while will result in less advantageous factoring arrangements for small business owners than will large, current receivables.

- Factor Preferences—Some factors tend to work with larger businesses, while others concentrate their efforts on smaller enterprises. Large factor companies tend to focus their attentions on companies that have at least $10 million in annual sales, while smaller factor companies—sometimes known as ''re-factors''—may provide services to companies with annual sales as low as $300,000.

- Industry Knowledge—Most factors that reach agreements with small businesses will have a fairly solid understanding of the industry and competitive environment in which those businesses operate. Such factor companies can provide help to small businesses in determining who they should (and should not) extend credit to. In addition, factor companies can be helpful in settling upon credit limits for both new and existing customers.

- System Compatibility—Most businesses in today's environment have implemented automated processes to calculate and monitor accounts receivable and cash applications of cash received. Small business owners should make sure that their systems are compatible with those of the factor before agreeing to a factoring arrangement.

- Collections—As indicated above, this can be a tricky area for the small business owner. Handing over collection duties to a factor company is expensive, and over-aggressive collection efforts on their part can damage a small business's relations with legitimate clients. However, factor companies often have better luck in collecting money owed than do small business enterprises, which have more limited resources to dedicate to the collections process. Business owners should recognize, however, that the factor is only interested in business transactions in which their client is owed money. Factors will not be responsible for non-payment that is attributed to other issues, such as vendor disputes or defective merchandise.

A variety of institutions, including bank subsidiaries and finance companies, provide factoring services. These companies can be found via several different methodologies. The Commercial Finance Association offers a list of its members and their service offerings online at www.cfa.com. Many factoring businesses also advertise in local yellow pages under such headings as ''factors,'' ''financing commercial,'' ''accounts receivable financing,'' or ''billing service.''

SEE ALSO *Accounts Receivable; Cash Flow; Discounted Cash Flow*

BIBLIOGRAPHY

Andresky Fraser, Jill. "Show Me the Money: You Can Look for Money in All the Wrong Places." *Inc.* March 1997.

Baker, Marie H. R., Leora Klapper, and Gregory F. Udell. *Financing Small- and Mdedium-Size Enterprises with Factoring: Global Growth in Factoring—and Its Potential in Eastern Europe.* The World Bank, 2004.

Banchero, Paola. "Financing Fight: Nonbank Lenders Want Nothing More Than to Take Business Away from Traditional Banks." *Kansas City Business Journal.* 10 October 1997.

Dresser, Guy. "Factoring: The Way to Cash." *Director.* January 1997.

Fiordelisi, Franco, and Philip Molyneux. "Efficiency in the Factoring Industry." *Applied Economics.* 20 May 2004.

"How to Make Them Give You the Money." *Money.* June 1995.

Reynes, Roberta. "A Big Factor in Expansion." *Nation's Business.* January 1999.

Sherman, Andrew J. *The Complete Guide to Running and Growing Your Business.* Times Books, 1997.

Story, Mary. "When Money Flows: Smoothing the business cycle makes sense." *New Zealand Managment.* March 2005.

Tucker, Ross, and Arthur Zackiewicz. "Selling to Fewer Stores? Call a Factor." *Daily News Record.* 6 June 2005.

Warren, Carl S., Philip E. Fess, and James M. Reeve. *Accounting.* Thomson South-Western, 2004.

Whittemore, Meg. "Creative Financing that Succeeds." *Nation's Business.* April 1995.

Hillstrom, Northern Lights
updated by Magee, ECDI

FAMILY LIMITED PARTNERSHIP

Family limited partnerships (sometimes known as FLPs and pronounced "flip" by tax experts) are an increasingly popular tool utilized by owners of family businesses who wish to pass on their companies to their children while minimizing the federal tax burden that sometimes accompanies such a transfer. The family limited partnership is a legal agreement that allows business owners and their children to address tax issues, business-succession, and estate-planning needs all at once. In simple terms, a parent may transfer assets, such as a family business, into a family limited partnership formed with the children. The parents, as general partners, maintain control of the assets. The children are limited partners. The assets that are transferred to the FLP are restricted—less liquid, harder to sell—and consequently, their value is discounted for tax purposes. The result is that a typical business may have a discounted tax value of 20 to 50 percent under its pre-FLP value. After the older family member dies, the FLP is taxed as part of his or her estate

but the amount due is reduced since the value within the FLP has been reduced. Thus, a tax saving is realized. The resulting reduction in tax burden has propelled family limited partnerships to the forefront of estate-planning techniques.

ESTATE PLANNING IN THE FAMILY-OWNED BUSINESS

When considered in the context of family-owned businesses, estate planning is basically the practice of transferring ownership of the family business to the next generation. Families must plan to minimize their tax burden at the time of the owner's death so that the resources can stay within the company and the family. The complexity of American tax law, however, makes it necessary for most estate planning to be undertaken with the assistance of professionals in the realms of accounting and law.

Since estate planning is such a vital element of long-term family business strategies, consultants encourage business owners to establish an estate plan as soon as their enterprise becomes successful, and to make sure that they update it as necessary as business or family circumstances change. A variety of options are available that can help a business owner defer or otherwise minimize the transfer taxes associated with handing down a family business. A marital deduction trust, for example, passes property along to a surviving spouse in the event of the owner's death, and no taxes are owed until the spouse dies. It is also possible to pay the estate taxes associated with the transfer of a family business on an installment basis, so that no taxes are owed for five years and the balance is paid in annual installments over a ten-year period.

CURRENT ESTATE TAX RATES

Recent changes in estate tax law have resulted in a great reduction in the number of estates that are subject to **any** federal estate taxes. In fact, in 2006 only 0.27 percent of all U.S. estates will be affected by federal estate tax, leaving 99.23 percent able, if necessary, to pass on all of their assets to heirs on a federal tax-free basis. State taxes on inherited property are another subject. Each state assesses its own estate tax.

In 2001, the Economic Growth and Tax Relief Reconciliation Act (EGTRRA) was passed. This act substantially changed federal estate and gift tax laws. The new law increases estate exemption levels every two years—from 1 million in 2003 to 3.5 million in 2009—and abolished the estate tax completely in 2010. EGTRRA also gradually reduces the top marginal federal estate tax rate to a low of 45 percent in 2009. In 2011, unless Congress votes to repeal the tax altogether, estate and gift laws will revert to their pre-EGTRRA form. The very unusual single-year abolition of federal estate taxes in 2010 has led to many jokes along the lines of the one in the title of a 2006*Money* magazine article: "Could You Please Die Sometime in 2010?"

This law has been highly controversial and there is much uncertainty surrounding what will happen with estate taxes after 2010. Congress was scheduled to vote on a permanent repeal of the estate tax in 2005 but the measure was tabled in the wake of devastating hurricanes that hit along the Gulf Coast in the summer. According to editors of *Mondaq Business Briefing,* "The consensus among observers appears to be that permanent repeal is not likely to occur in the immediate future, if at all. While a total permanent repeal would obviously remove a major obstacle in estate planning, we will probably have to settle for legislation that would set the exemption at a definite amount (e.g., $3- $5 million) with an inflation index." In the absence of legislation clarifying what will occur after 2010, the prudent action is to plan well and as flexibly as possible. Family limited partnerships are one useful tool for preparing to minimize estate taxes now and in the uncertain tax environment future.

ADVANTAGES OF FAMILY LIMITED PARTNERSHIPS

The primary purpose of family limited partnerships is to blunt the impact of estate taxes. Estate taxes can hit family businesses hard because the full value of a parent's business may be included in the parent's estate when he or she dies. The estate tax is one of the highest taxes levied. It is only born by individuals with very large estates. The first $2 million of an individual's estate is exempt from federal estate tax, but amounts above the exempt portion are subject to a tax rate of 46 percent (in 2006). One way to dampen the impact of this tax is to make use of an Internal Revenue Service (IRS) rule that allows individuals to make annual gifts of up to $12,000 ($22,000 if joined by your spouse) to other individuals without incurring gift taxes. The other way to elude the full brunt of this tax is via an FLP.

A basic family limited partnership operates as follows. The parents (or a single parent) retain a general partnership interest in the property—as little as 1 percent—and give limited-partnership interests to their children, usually over a number of years. The general partner, or partners, retain complete control over the assets in the partnership, and no management authority is given to the limited partner(s).

In the most basic terms, a family limited partnership allows the business to be transferred to the next generation at considerably less than its full value. This reduces the size of the estate and thus the amount of federal taxes

owed. Indeed, observers indicate that these discounts can amount to as much as 50 percent of a business's value. The discounted valuation occurs because the shares cannot be easily sold or otherwise transferred and because such partnership interests do not carry any voting rights or control in the business in question. Since the gifted shares are discounted, the partnership pays lower gift taxes on those shares. For example, if a $15,000 limited partnership share is appraised at $8,000, the parents can transfer that share to a child plus $4,000 worth of something else in a single year and stay within the $12,000 annual tax exclusion on gifts. Second, this reevaluation also applies to the shares in the FLP that the parents continue to hold. Third, because the parents are transferring shares out of their estate, they're reducing the value of the estate for annual tax purposes as well.

OTHER CONSIDERATIONS

Many estate planners and business consultants encourage their clients to look into FLPs, but they do note that family business owners should weigh some other non-tax factors as well. These include:

Lawsuit Protection A family limited partnership may serve as asset protection in the case of a lawsuit. Because the assets within an FLP are not the personal property of its partners, any legal judgement against one of the partners does not include the assets held by the FLP. The portion of the plaintiff's assets that are located within the FLP are thus protected from a legal judgment until disbursements are made from the FLP to the partner.

Timing of the Formation of the Limited Partnership Estate planners and business consultants warn that the Internal Revenue Service will not necessarily approve a family limited partnership if it is transparently obvious that the FLP was formed simply to skirt paying taxes. Family business owners who attempt to institute an FLP a few weeks before their death from some foreseeable illness will likely find their efforts blocked.

Divorce In most instances, a child's ownership of limited partnership shares will not be impacted by a divorce action by his or her parents, but business owners seeking to ensure protection for their child can take a couple of steps to provide additional insurance. Since limited partners (children) receive their shares as a gift and are not permitted to vote or otherwise exercise any authority in the partnership, the child's shares will not be considered part of the marital assets. Instead, they will remain the sole and separate property of the child. The key, say legal experts, is to make sure that the shares were never formally made part of the marital property.

Expense of Setting Up an FLP Establishing a family limited partnership can be somewhat expensive, although the price tag depends in large part on the size of the company, the value of its assets, the number of intended minority owners, and other factors. As of 2006, a family-owned company would need to have a value in excess of $2 million (or $4 million if a husband and wife team were partners in the business) before it would have any estate tax liability upon the death of its principal. If the value of the firm exceeds this threshold than the cost of setting up an FLP will likely be justified by the savings it will be able to generate by reducing the tax obligations due upon the transfer of the company.

Compatibility with Business FLPs are better suited to some businesses than others. The effectiveness of FLPs is greatest when used in family companies related to real estate or companies whose business relies greatly on capital assets. For service-oriented companies—firms that do consulting, computer networking, software development, landscaping, childcare, and/or small retailers, for example—the vehicle is not as beneficial since firms of this kind tend not to have large asset balances that they wish to protect from taxation.

Increased Risk of IRS Audits Although family limited partnerships can be very valuable, and their use is increasing, accountants and estate planning attorneys do caution family business owners that the use of an FLP will almost certainly lead to an IRS audit. This is not a reason to avoid forming an FLP but it does emphasize the need to do so with care and to keep thorough and complete documentation on its formation and activities.

A string of recent court cases in which the IRS successfully challenged the legitimacy of particular FLPs can provide guidelines to follow in forming FLPs that will withstand an IRS challenge. Gary Williams explains why FLPs based on true family-owned businesses are more likely to survive an IRS challenge in his *Daily Record* article entitled "Commentary: IRS Looks More Kindly on Family Limited Partnerships That Serve Business." He states that "commentators think you'll be on safest ground if the FLP includes an active family business or investment that requires active management by the FLP's

partners, such as rental property."

Another measure that can be taken to improve one's likelihood of a successful audit outcome is to have the business appraised by an experienced, respected professional who can provide a solid valuation. For information

on securing the services of an established appraiser, contact the American Society of Appraisers at (800) 272-8258.

Dissatisfaction Among Minority Owners Ironically, some family businesses find that FLPs actually spark difficulties between parents and their children, despite the formidable savings that such a plan can provide and the ultimate aim—reduced estate taxes upon succession—of the partnership. This is certainly not always the case; many families put together family limited partnerships that garner tax savings without a ripple of internal dissension or dissatisfaction. But it is a factor that can crop up, depending on the personalities and financial situations of the persons involved. When conflict arises it is usually caused by the minority owners who may feel constrained, unable to sell their shares and convert them into a liquid asset as desired. This feeling of not having control often manifests in the form of harassing the management, criticizing business decisions, lobbying for dividends, and generally causing unrest.

Need for Professional Guidance Establishing a family limited partnership is a complex estate-planning strategy, made even more complicated by the uncertainty of the regulatory environment. Subsequently, business owners are strongly encouraged to secure qualified legal and/or accounting help in setting up such plans.

SEE ALSO *Estate Planning; Tax Planning; Succession Planning*

BIBLIOGRAPHY
Cleary, Jay, and Dave Hunter. "The Family Limited Partnership." *Denver Business Journal.* 19 November 1999.

Clifford, Denis. *Estate Planning Basics.* Nolo Press, August 2005.

Harrison, Joan. "Family Business Not Fazed by Estate Tax Uncertainty." *The America's Intelligence Wire.* 10 January 2006.

"Increase in Estate Tax Exemption Highlights Changes for 2006." *Mondaq Business Briefing.* 5 January 2006.

Peterson, Carlise. "Estate Tax Seen Affecting Few." *Investment News.* 30 January 2006.

Plack, Harry J. "Form FLP to Protect Biz Assets." *Baltimore Business Journal.* 24 November 2000.

"Planning With Family Limited Partnership." *Mondaq Business Briefing.* 24 May 2004.

Szabo, Joan. "Spreading the Wealth: Transferring Part of Your Business to Your Children Now Could Lower Their Taxes Later." *Entrepreneur.* July 1997.

Williams, Gary. "Commentary: IRS Looks More Kindly on Family Limited Partnerships That Serve Business." *Daily Record.* 22 December 2004.

Willis, Clint. "Could You Please Die Sometime in 2010? And Other Frequently Asked Questions Under Today's Crazy Estate-Tax Law." *Money.* 1 February 2006.

Hillstrom, Northern Lights
updated by Magee, ECDI

FAMILY AND MEDICAL LEAVE ACT

The Family and Medical Leave Act (FMLA) provides employees who qualify with up to 12 work weeks of unpaid, job-protected leave in a 12-month period for specified family and medical reasons. It also requires group health benefits to be maintained during the leave as if employees continued to work instead of taking leave. The employer can elect to use the calendar year, a fixed 12-month fiscal year, or a 12-month period prior to or after the commencement of leave as the 12-month period. The Act became effective on August 5, 1993 and applies to **all** companies who employ 50 or more people. It is primarily administered and enforced by the U.S. Department of Labor's Employment Standards Division, Wage and Hour Division.

ELIGIBILITY FOR FMLA

To qualify for FMLA benefits, an employee must; 1) work for an employer who employees 50 or more people; 2) have worked for that employer for a total of 12 months; 3) have worked at least 1,250 hours over the previous 12 months; 4) work at a location in the United States or in any territory or possession of the United States where at least 50 employees are employed by the employer within 75 miles. This latter stipulation exempts many small business owners from FMLA rules and guidelines.

But while FMLA does not apply to small businesses that employ fewer than 50 people, it does apply to small and mid-size companies that employed 50 or more employees in 20 or more work weeks in the current or preceding calendar year. FMLA also applies to all public agencies, including local, state, and federal employers; large companies; and school administrations.

Leave Entitlement There are several different situations under which employers subject to FMLA must grant eligible employees unpaid leave from work without penalty. Reasons include:

- Situations in which the employee is unable to work because of illness or other health difficulties.

- Placement with the employee of a child for adoption or foster care.

- Birth and care of the newborn child of the employee.

- Caring for an immediate family member with serious health difficulties (immediate family members are defined as spouse, child, or parent).

In addition, spouses employed by the same company or agency are jointly entitled to a combined total of 12 work weeks of family leave for the birth and care of a newborn child, for placement of a child for adoption or foster care, or to care for a parent suffering from a serious health condition.

Finally, depending on the circumstances, some employees may be able to take leave in blocks of time or by scaling back their normal work schedule. In addition, employers or employees may sometimes choose to use accrued paid leave to cover some or all of the FMLA leave.

Illnesses and Other Conditions Covered Under FMLA The FMLA was written so that employees who have family members in "serious health condition"—or who themselves are in such condition—can use the law to protect their job during the time that they are on leave. The Department of Labor defines "serious health condition" as an illness, injury, impairment, or physical or mental condition that involves any of the following:

- Any period of incapacity or treatment connected with overnight stays in a hospital or other residential medical care facility, and any period of incapacity or subsequent treatment in connection with such inpatient care.

- Continuing treatment by a health care provider that includes any period of incapacity due to: 1) a health condition (including treatment of, or recovery from) lasting more than three consecutive days, and any subsequent treatment or period of incapacity relating to the same condition; 2) pregnancy or prenatal care; 3) a chronic serious health condition which continues over an extended period of time, requires periodic visits to a doctor or other health care professional, and may involve occasional episodes of incapacity (diabetes, asthma); 4) permanent or long-term conditions for which treatment may not work (cancer, stroke); 5) absences to receive treatments for restorative surgery or for a condition which would likely result in incapacitation for more than three days if not treated (radiation or chemotherapy treatments for cancer).

EMPLOYER REQUIREMENTS UNDER FMLA

Employers who are subject to FMLA regulations must maintain group health insurance coverage for any employee taking FMLA leave whenever that employee already had that insurance. The employer is not allowed to make any changes in the terms of that insurance coverage, either. There are some situations, however, where an employer may be able to recover any insurance premiums that it paid out to maintain health coverage for an employee if that worker fails to return to work from FMLA leave.

In instances where the employee does return from FMLA leave, that employee is entitled to be restored to his or her original job, or to an equivalent job, complete with equivalent pay, benefits, and other terms of employment. Moreover, FMLA stipulates that an employee cannot lose any employment benefit that he or she earned prior to using FMLA leave once the employee returns to work. There are exceptions to the above rules, but they come into play only in extreme circumstances wherein returning an employee to his or her previous station will cause "substantial and grievous economic injury" to the business. Obviously, such circumstances arise only when the company is in deep financial jeopardy.

Employers who are subject to FMLA law are required to post notices that explain the Family and Medical Leave Act in the workplace. These notices are approved by the Secretary of Labor. Companies that willfully violate this requirement are subject to fines. This requirement is part of a general mandate that directs employers to inform employees of all pertinent aspects of FMLA, including employee responsibilities.

THE FIRST SEVEN YEARS OF FMLA

The Bureau of Labor Statistics oversaw two surveys of employers and employees in the year 2000, surveys designed to gather information about the implementation of the FMLA during its first seven years. As of early 2006 no new national-level surveys on the subject have been published.

According to the BLS report, "Family Medical Leave: Evidence from the 2000 survey," 46.9 percent of private-sector employees were covered and eligible for FMLA leave in the year 2000 (eligibility having to do with the employee's tenure with their employer). "One-sixth of all employees (16.5 percent) took leave for family or medical reasons in the 18 months prior to the 2000 survey, about the same percentage as did in the 1995 survey (16.0 percent)" stated the BLS report. In both the 1995 and the 2000 surveys the employee's own health was the most commonly cited

reason for taking leave (61.4 percent and 47.2 percent, respectively). The second most commonly cited reason for taking leave in both 1995 and 2000 was for the care of a newborn, newly adopted child, or newly placed foster child (14.3 percent and 17.9 percent, respectively).

STEPS TO SECURING FMLA LEAVE

Employees who wish to take advantage of the Family and Medical Leave Act must adhere to certain steps so as to soften the impact on the businesses where they are employed. Workers using FMLA must first provide 30-day advance notice of their intention to take leave in all instances where advanced notice is possible. In addition, some employers require employees using FMLA to do some or all of the following:

- Provide medical certification supporting the need for leave.

- Provide second or third medical opinions (at the employer's expense)

- Give periodic re-certification of health status.

- Provide periodic reports on employee status and intentions regarding returning to work.

- Adhere to limitations on intermittent leave.

In their article for *Entrepreneur,* Steven C. Bahls and Jane Easter Bahls admitted that adhering to the FMLA can be difficult for employers, but they also claimed that businesses benefit by retaining good employees. "Keeping a job open for months, tracking the employee's illness, determining if medical certification is adequate, keeping records on which absences are covered and which are not—clearly, it's not easy to administer an FMLA leave and avoid legal trouble," they wrote. "And there remains the possibility of abuse of the system. Still, try to keep in mind what your employees gain from knowing there's a good job waiting on the other side of their problems, and what your company gains by retaining a valued employee."

SEE ALSO *Employee Benefits; Pregnancy in the Workplace*

BIBLIOGRAPHY
Bahls, Steven C., and Jane Easter Bahls. "Statute of Liberty." *Entrepreneur.* January 2001.

The HR Focus Guide to the Family and Medical Leave Act. American Management Association, n.d.

U.S. Department of Labor. *Compliance Guide to the Family and Medical Leave Act.* 1996.

U.S. Department of Labor. Waldfogel, Jane. "Family and Medical Leave: Evidence from the 2000 surveys." *Monthly Labor Review.* September 2001.

Hillstrom, Northern Lights
updated by Magee, ECDI

FAMILY-OWNED BUSINESSES

A family-owned business may be defined as any business in which two or more family members are involved and the majority of ownership or control lies within a family. Family-owned businesses may be the oldest form of business organization. Farms were an early form of family business in which what we think of today as the private life and work life were intertwined. In urban settings it was once normal for a shopkeeper or doctor to live in the same building in which he or she worked and family members often helped with the business as needed.

Since the early 1980s the academic study of family business as a distinct and important category of commerce has developed. Today family owned businesses are recognized as important and dynamic participants in the world economy. According to the U.S. Bureau of the Census, about 90 percent of American businesses are family-owned or controlled. Ranging in size from two-person partnerships to *Fortune 500* firms, these businesses account for half of the nation's employment and half of her Gross National Product. Family businesses may have some advantages over other business entities in their focus on the long term, their commitment to quality (which is often associated with the family name), and their care and concern for employees. But family businesses also face a unique set of management challenges stemming from the overlap of family and business issues.

ISSUES IN FAMILY BUSINESSES

A family business can be described as an interaction between two separate but connected systems—the business and the family—with uncertain boundaries and different rules. Graphically, this concept can be presented as two intersecting circles. Family businesses may include numerous combinations of family members in various business roles, including husbands and wives, parents and children, extended families, and multiple generations playing the roles of stockholders, board members, working partners, advisors, and employees. Conflicts often arise due to the overlap of these roles. The ways in which individuals typically communicate within a family, for example, may be inappropriate in business situations.

Likewise, personal concerns or rivalries may carry over into the work place to the detriment of the firm. In order to succeed, a family business must keep lines of communication open, make use of strategic planning tools, and engage the assistance of outside advisors as needed.

Family versus Non-family Employees There are a number of common issues that most family businesses face at one time or another. Attracting and retaining non-family employees can be problematic because such employees may find it difficult to deal with family conflicts on the job, limited opportunities for advancement, and the special treatment sometimes accorded family members. In addition, some family members may resent outsiders being brought into the firm and purposely make things unpleasant for non-family employees. But outsiders can provide a stabilizing force in a family business by offering a fair and impartial perspective on business issues. Family business leaders can conduct exit interviews with departing non-family employees to determine the cause of turnover and develop a course of action to prevent it.

Employment Qualifications Many family businesses also have trouble determining guidelines and qualifications for family members hoping to participate in the business. Some companies try to limit the participation of people with certain relationships to the family, such as in-laws, in order to minimize the potential for conflicts. Family businesses often face pressure to hire relatives or close friends who may lack the talent or skill to make a useful contribution to the business. Once hired, such people can be difficult to fire, even if they cost the company money or reduce the motivation of other employees by exhibiting a poor attitude. A strict policy of only hiring people with legitimate qualifications to fill existing openings can help a company avoid such problems, but only if the policy is applied without exception. If a company is forced to hire a less-than-desirable employee, analysts suggest providing special training to develop a useful talent, enlisting the help of a non-family employee in training and supervising, and assigning special projects that minimize negative contact with other employees.

Salaries and Compensation Another challenge frequently encountered by family businesses involves paying salaries to and dividing the profits among the family members who participate in the firm. In order to grow, a small business must be able to use a relatively large percentage of profits for expansion. But some family members, especially those who are owners but not employees of the company, may not see the value of expenditures that reduce the amount of current dividends they receive. This is a source of conflict for many family firms and an added level of difficulty in making the necessary investments into the business for continued success. To ensure that salaries are distributed fairly among family and non-family employees, business leaders should match them to industry guidelines for each job description. When additional compensation is needed to reward certain employees for their contributions to the company, fringe benefits or equity distributions can be used.

Succession Another important issue relating to family businesses is succession—determining who will take over leadership and/or ownership of the company when the current generation retires or dies. The key to avoiding conflicts about who will take over a business is having a well-defined plan in place. A family retreat, or a meeting on neutral ground without distractions or interruptions, can be an ideal setting to open discussions on family goals and future plans, the timing of expected transitions, and the preparation of the current generation for stepping down and the future generation for taking over. When succession is postponed, older relatives who remain involved in the family firm may develop a preference for maintaining the status quo. These people may resist change and refuse to take risks, even though such an attitude can inhibit business growth. The business leaders should take steps to gradually remove these relatives from the daily operations of the firm, including encouraging them to become involved in outside activities, arranging for them to sell some of their stock or convert it to preferred shares, or possibly restructuring the company to dilute their influence.

Family business leaders can take a number of steps in order to avoid becoming caught up in these common pitfalls. Having a clear statement of goals, an organized plan to accomplish the goals, a defined hierarchy for decision-making, an established plan for succession, and strong lines of communication will help to prevent many possible problems from arising. All family members involved in the business must understand that their rights and responsibilities are different at home and at work. While family relationships and goals take precedence at home, the success of the business comes first at work.

When emotion intrudes upon work relationships, something that happens in all businesses from time to time, and the inevitable conflicts between family members arise, the manager must intervene and make the objective decisions necessary to protect the interests of the firm. Rather than taking sides in a dispute, the manager must make it clear to all employees that personal disagreements will not be allowed to interfere with work. This approach should discourage employees from jockeying for position or playing politics. The business leader may also find it useful to have regular meetings

with family members, and to put all business agreements and policy guidelines in writing.

THE PLANNING PROCESS

Strategic planning—centering around both business and family goals—is vital to successful family businesses. In fact, planning may be more crucial to family businesses than to other types of business entities, because in many cases families have a majority of their assets tied up in the business. Since much conflict arises due to a disparity between family and business goals, planning is required to align these goals and formulate a strategy for reaching them. The ideal plan will allow the company to balance family and business needs to everyone's advantage.

Family Planning In family planning, all interested members of the family get together to develop a mission statement that describes why they are committed to the business. In allowing family members to share their goals, needs, priorities, strengths, weaknesses, and ability to contribute, family planning helps create a unified vision of the company that will guide future dealings.

A special meeting called a family retreat or family council can guide the communication process and encourage involvement by providing family members with a venue to voice their opinions and plan for the future in a structured way. By participating in the family retreat, children can gain a better understanding of the opportunities in the business, learn about managing resources, and inherit values and traditions. It also provides an opportunity for conflicts to be discussed and settled. Topics brought to family councils can include: rules for joining the business, treatment of family members working and not working in the business, role of in-laws, evaluations and pay scales, stock ownership, ways to provide financial security for the senior generation, training and development of the junior generation, the company's image in the community, philanthropy, opportunities for new businesses, and diverse interests among family members. Leadership of the family council can be on a rotating basis, or an outside family business consultant may be hired as a facilitator.

Business Planning Business planning begins with the long-term goals and objectives the family holds for themselves and for the business. The business leaders then integrate these goals into the business strategy. In business planning, management analyzes the strengths and weaknesses of the company in relation to its environment, including its organizational structure, culture, and resources. The next stage involves identifying opportunities for the company to pursue, given its strengths, and threats for the company to manage, given its weaknesses. Finally, the planning process concludes with the creation of a mission statement, a set of objectives, and a set of general strategies and specific action steps to meet the objectives and support the mission. This process is often overseen by a board of directors, an advisory board, or professional advisors.

Succession Planning Succession planning involves deciding who will lead the company in the next generation. Unfortunately, less than one-third of family-owned businesses survive the transition from the first generation of ownership to the second, and only 13 percent of family businesses remain in the family over 60 years. Problems making the transition can occur for any number of reasons: 1) the business was no longer viable; 2) the next generation did not wish to continue the business, or 3) the new leadership was not prepared for the burden of full operational control. Lack of planning, however, is by far the most common underlying reason for a company to fail in the generational transition. At any given time, a full 40 percent of American firms are facing the succession issue, yet relatively few make succession plans. Business owners may be reluctant to face the issue because they do not want to relinquish control, feel their successor is not ready, have few interests outside the business, or wish to maintain the sense of identity they have for so long gotten from their work.

But it is vital that the succession process be carefully planned before it becomes necessary due to the owner's illness or death. Family businesses are advised to follow a five-stage process in planning for succession: initiation, selection, education, finance preparation, and transition.

- In the initiation phase, possible successors are introduced to the business and guided through a variety of work experiences of increasing responsibility.

- In the selection phase, a successor is chosen and a schedule is developed for the transition. Analysts almost unanimously recommend that the successor be a single individual and not a group of siblings or cousins. To some degree, by selecting a group, the existing leadership is merely postponing the decision or leaving it to the next generation to sort out.

- During the education phase, the business owner gradually hands over the reigns to the successor, one task at a time, so that he or she may learn the requirements of the position.

- Finance preparation involves making arrangements so that the departing management team can withdraw funds enough to retire. The more time is used in preparing for the financial implications of

this transition the more likely a business will be able to avoid being burdened in the process.

- In the transition phase, the business changes hands—the business owner removes himself or herself from the daily operations of the firm. This final stage can be the most difficult, as many entrepreneurs experience great difficulty in letting go of the family business. It helps when the business owner establishes outside interests, creates a sound financial base for retirement, and gains confidence in the abilities of the successor.

Estate Planning Estate planning involves the financial and tax aspects of transferring ownership of the family business to the next generation. Families must plan to minimize their tax burden at the time of the owner's death so that the resources can stay within the company and the family. Unfortunately, tax laws today provide disincentives for families wishing to continue the business. Heirs are taxed upon the value of the business at a high rate when ownership is transferred. Due to its complexity, estate planning is normally handled by a team of professional advisors who include a lawyer, accountant, financial planner, insurance agent, and perhaps a family business consultant. An estate plan should be established as soon as the business becomes successful and then updated as business or family circumstances change.

One technique available to family business owners in planning their estate is known as "estate freeze." This technique enables the business owner to "freeze" the value of the business at a particular point in time by creating preferred stock, which does not appreciate in value, and then transferring the common stock to his or her heirs. Since the majority of shares in the firm are preferred and do not appreciate, estate taxes are reduced. The heirs are required to pay gift taxes, however, when the preferred stock is transferred to them.

A variety of tools are available that can help a business owner defer the transfer taxes associated with handing down a family business. A basic will outlines the owner's wishes regarding the distribution of property upon his or her death. A living trust creates a trustee to manage the owner's property not covered by the will, for example during a long illness. A marital deduction trust passes property along to a surviving spouse in the event of the owner's death, and no taxes are owed until the spouse dies. It is also possible to pay the estate taxes associated with the transfer of a family business on an installment basis, so that no taxes are owed for five years and the remainder are paid in annual installments over a ten-year period. Other techniques exist that allow business owners to exclude some or all of their assets from estate taxes, including a unified credit/exemption trust, a dynamic trust, and an annual exclusion gift. Since laws change frequently, retaining legal assistance is highly advisable.

ASSISTANCE IN PLANNING

A professional family business consultant can be a tremendous asset when confronting planning issues. The consultant is a neutral party who can stabilize the emotional forces within the family and bring the expertise of working with numerous families across many industries. Most families believe theirs is the only company facing these difficult issues, and a family business consultant brings a refreshing perspective. In addition, the family business consultant can establish a family council and advisory board and serve as a facilitator to those two groups.

Advisory boards can be established to advise the company's president or board of directors. These boards consist of five to nine non-family members who meet regularly to provide advice and direction to the company. They too can take the emotions out of the planning process and provide objective input. Advisory board members should have business experience and be capable of helping the business to get to the next level of growth. In most cases, the advisory board is compensated in some manner.

As the family business grows, the family business consultant may suggest different options for the family. Often professional non-family managers or an outside CEO are recruited to play a role in the future growth of the business. Some families simply retain ownership of the business and allow it to operate with few or no family members involved.

THE FUTURE OF FAMILY BUSINESSES

As Tracy Perman explains in her *Business Week* article entitled "Taking the Pulse of Family Business," two broad trends are visible in the realm of family business as we get comfortable in the 21st Century. First, the aging of the baby boom generation signals a coming ownership change for many family businesses within the next ten years. Second, more and more of these businesses will be taken over by women, continuing a trend that has been visible since the turn of the century. Perman goes on to highlight some statistics about women owned family businesses that makes this trend towards female ownership seem quite positive. Recent studies have shown, Perman explains, that "women-owned businesses were more likely to focus on succession planning, have a 40 percent lower rate of family-member attrition, tend to be more fiscally conservative, and carry less debt than male-owned businesses."

Some family-owned businesses are finding that it is no longer assumed that children will wish to take over a family business. If the founders of a firm wish to keep it in the family's hands, they should be sure to take proactive measures to attract future generations to the business.

- Expose family members to all aspects of the business, including employees, customers, products, and services.

- Define the business's attractive qualities in terms that will appeal to the listener.

- Recognize those factors that have the potential to dissuade family members from staying involved in the business. These factors can range from personal interests that lie in other areas to conflicts with other family members.

- Reward family members who decide to join or stay with the family business. The 'price' successors pay to join and operate a family business may include giving up career options that they find financially and personally attractive. It may seem to a new family member coming into a family business that he or she is suffering a loss of privacy. Conflicts may arise between parent and child when their management styles conflict. A business may make compromises—such as making it possible for the successor to spend more time with his or her family or hiring an interim senior manager to buffer conflicts between parent and child. But the company's 'cost' and the successor's 'price' must be affordable to both.

- Give family members outlets to explore their ideas, interests, and concerns.

The rewards of a family-owned business are many as are the challenges. Those family members who manage the family business should enjoy the business itself if they are to be successful and pass along a sense of enthusiasm for the business when the time comes for them to hand over the reins.

SEE ALSO *Family Limited Partnerships; Closely Held Corporations; Succession Plans*

BIBLIOGRAPHY

Astrachan, Joseph H. "Commentary on the Special Issue: The Emergence of a Field." *Journal of Business Venturing.* 2003.

Caselli, Stefano, and Stefano Gatti. *Banking for Family Business.* Springer, March 2005.

Dammon Loyalka, Michelle. "Family-Biz Circle: The Boomer Handoff." *Business Week.* 14 February 2006.

Gangemi, Jeff, and Francesca Di Meglio. "Making an Educated Decision." *Business Week Online.* Available from http://www.businessweek.com/smallbiz/content/feb2006/sb20060213_733893.htm?campaign_id=search 15 February 2006.

Karofsky, Paul. "Can Business Bring a Family Together?" *Business Week.* 22 February 2006.

Lea, James. "The Best Way to Teach Responsibility is to Delegate It." *South Florida Business Journal.* 25 July 1997.

McMenamin, Brigid. "Close-Knit: Keeping Family Businesses Private and in the Family." *Forbes.* 25 December 2000.

Nelton, Sharon. "Family Business: Major Shifts in Leadership Lie Ahead." *Nation's Business.* June 1997.

O'Hare, William T. *Centuries of Success.* Adams Media, September 2004.

Perman, Stacy. "Taking the Pulse of Family Business." *Business Week.* 13 February 2006.

Hillstrom, Northern Lights
updated by Magee, ECDI

FEASIBILITY STUDY

A feasibility study is done by an organization in order to determine if a particular action makes sense from an economic and operational standpoint. Such a study is usually designed to provide an overview of the essential issues related to a course of action being considered. The goal is to test the feasibility of a proposed course of action and to identify any "make or break" issues that would argue against the action being taken or suggest that a successful outcome were unlikely.

Businesses find it helpful to conduct a feasibility study whenever they anticipate making an important strategic decision. For example, a company might perform a feasibility study to evaluate a proposed change in location, the acquisition of another company, a purchase of major equipment or a new computer system, the introduction of a new product or service, or the hiring of additional employees. A feasibility study is advisable as a means of fully studying an action in advance of taking the action. This allows managers a chance to fully assess the impact that any major changes they are consider may have before implementing the change.

As David E. Gumpert, wrote in his book *How to Really Create a Successful Business Plan,* "Although [an unsuccessful feasibility study] may appear to be a failure, it's not. The failure would have been if you had invested your own and others' money and then lost it due to barriers you failed to research in advance."

STEPS IN CONDUCTING A FEASIBILITY STUDY

The main objective of a feasibility study is to determine whether or not a certain plan of action is likely to produce the anticipated result—that is, whether or not it will work, and whether or not it is worth doing economically. Although the primary objective of the study is dedicated to showing the outcomes of specific actions, it should begin with an evaluation of the entire operation.

A good feasibility study would review a company's strengths and weaknesses, its position in the marketplace, and its financial situation. It would also include information on a company's major competitors, primary customers, and any relevant industry trends. This sort of overview provides small business owners and managers with an objective view of the company's current situation and opportunities. By providing information on consumer needs and how best to meet them, a feasibility study can also lead to new ideas for strategic changes.

The second part of a good feasibility study should focus on the proposed plan of action and provide a detailed estimate of its costs and benefits. In some cases, a feasibility study may lead management to determine that the company could achieve the same benefits through easier or cheaper means. For example, it may be possible to improve a manual filing system rather than purchase an expensive new computerized database. If the proposed project is determined to be both feasible and desirable, the information provided in the feasibility study can prove valuable in implementation. It can be used to develop a strategic plan for the project, translating general ideas into measurable goals. The goals can then be broken down further to create a series of concrete steps and outline how the steps can be implemented. Throughout the process, the feasibility study will show the various consequences and impacts associated with the plan of action.

In some cases, a company may wish to hire a qualified consultant to perform a feasibility study. To be able to provide a meaningful analysis of the data, the consultant chosen should have expertise in the industry. It is also important for small businesses to assign an internal person to help gather information for the feasibility study. The small business owner must be sure that those conducting the study have full access to the company and the specific information they need.

BIBLIOGRAPHY

Capko, Judy, and Rebecca Anwar. "Feasibility Studies Can Help You Control Your Destiny." *American Medical News.* 23 September 1996.

Gumpert, David E. *How to Really Create a Successful Business Plan.* Fourth Edition. Lauson Publishing Company, 2003.

Phillips, Joseph. *PMP Project Management Professional Study Guide.* McGraw-Hill Professional, 22 December 2003.

"Weigh the Benefits, Consider the Costs." *Dallas Business Journal.* 23 June 2000.

Hillstrom, Northern Lights
updated by Magee, ECDI

FEDERAL TRADE COMMISSION (FTC)

The Federal Trade Commission (FTC) was established as an independent administrative agency pursuant to the Federal Trade Commission Act of 1914. The purpose of the FTC is to enforce the provisions of the Federal Trade Commission Act, which prohibits "unfair or deceptive acts or practices in commerce." The Clayton Antitrust Act (1914) also granted the FTC the authority to act against specific and unfair monopolistic practices. The FTC is considered to be a law enforcement agency, and like other such agencies it lacks punitive authority. Although the FTC cannot punish violators—that is the responsibility of the judicial system—it can issue cease and desist orders and argue cases in federal and administrative courts.

Today, the Federal Trade Commission serves an important function as a protector of both consumer and business rights. While the restrictions that it imposes on business practices often receive the most attention, other laws enforced by the FTC—such as the 1979 Franchise Rule, which directed franchisors to provide full disclosure of franchise information to prospective franchisees—have been of great benefit to entrepreneurs and small business owners. Basically, all business owners should educate themselves about the guidelines set forth by the FTC on various business practices. Some of its rules can be helpful to small businesses and entrepreneurs. Conversely, businesses that flout or remain ignorant of the FTC's operating guidelines are apt to regret it.

CREATION OF THE FTC

The FTC was created in response to a public outcry against the abuses of monopolistic trusts during the late 19th and early 20th centuries. The Sherman Antitrust Act of 1890 had proven inadequate in limiting trusts, and the widespread misuse of economic power by companies became so problematic that it became a significant factor in the election of Woodrow Wilson to the White House in 1912. Once Wilson assumed the office of the Presidency, he followed through on his campaign promises to address the excesses of America's trusts. Wilson's

State of the Union Message of 1913 included a call for extensive antitrust legislation. Wilson's push, combined with public displeasure with the situation, resulted in the passage of two acts. The first was the Federal Trade Commission Act, which created and empowered the FTC to define and halt "unfair practice" in trade and commerce. It was followed by the Clayton Antitrust Act, which covered specific activities of corporations that were deemed to be not in the public interest. Activities covered by this act included those mergers which inhibited trade by creating monopolies. The FTC began operating in 1915; the Bureau of Operations, which had previously monitored corporate activity for the federal government, was folded into the FTC.

The FTC is empowered to enforce provisions of both acts following specific guidelines. The offense must fall under the jurisdiction of the various acts and must affect interstate commerce. The violations must also affect the public good; the FTC does not intervene in disputes between private parties. As noted, the FTC lacks authority to punish or fine violators, but if an FTC ruling—such as a cease and desist order—is ignored, the FTC can seek civil penalties in federal court and seek compensation for those harmed by the unfair or deceptive practices.

Since 1914 both the Federal Trade Commission Act and the Clayton Act have been amended numerous times, thus expanding the legal responsibilities of the FTC. Some of the more notable amendments are:

- Webb-Pomerene Export Trade Act of 1918—This act promoted exports by encouraging cooperative activities

- Robinson-Patman Act of 1936—This act strengthened the Clayton Act and addressed pricing practices of suppliers and wholesalers

- Wool Products Labeling Act of 1939—This act ensured the purity of wool products

- Lanham Trademark Act of 1946—This act required the registration and protection of trademarks used in commerce

- Fair Packaging and Labeling Act of 1966—This act legislated against unfair or deceptive labeling and packaging

- Truth in Lending Act of 1969—This legislation offered increased protection to consumers by requiring that companies provide full disclosure of credit terms and limit consumer liability concerning stolen credit cards; it also established regulations for advertising for credit services

- Fair Credit Reporting Act of 1970—This act established regulations and fair operating practices for credit reporting agencies

- Magnuson-Moss Warranty-Federal Trade Commission Improvement Act of 1975—This legislation expanded the authority of the FTC by allowing it to seek redress for consumers and civil penalties for repeat offenders. It also increased the FTC's authorization to pursue violations "affecting commerce" rather than violations "in commerce." This was an important distinction. Under the terms of the act, manufacturers are not required to warrant their products but if they do they must specify whether their warranties are "full" or "limited." The law also introduced rules requiring businesses to explain any limitations on warranties in writing

- FTC Franchise Rule of 1979—This rule requires franchisors to provide prospective franchisees with a full disclosure of relevant information about the franchise

- Telemarketing and Consumer Fraud and Abuse Prevention Act of 1994—This law, commonly referred to as the "Telemarketing Sales Rule," was put together in response to widespread consumer complaints about fraudulent and/or bothersome telemarketing practices. The act imposed meaningful curbs on such activities. Among the restrictions imposed by the legislation were specific identity disclosure requirements, prohibitions on misrepresentations, limitations on time during which telemarketers can make their calls, prohibitions on making calls to consumers who specifically ask not to be called, restrictions on sales of certain goods and services, and new recordkeeping requirements. The FTC and many consumer and business advocates, however, contend that FTC penalties for deceptive telemarketing practices are insufficient to meaningful curtail such activities. They are currently engaged in efforts to increase the size of FTC fines and support stiffer penalties (including jail time) for offending parties.

- The Children's Online Privacy Protection Act of 1998—This act protects children's privacy by giving parents the tools to control what information is collected from their children online. Under the act, operators of commercial Web sites and online services that include children as their intended audience, are obliged to carry out a list of actions meant to protect children and in some cases to assure parental knowledge of a child's online activity.

- Do-Not-Call Registry Act of 2003—This act authorizes the FTC, under sections of the Telemarketing and Consumer Fraud and Abuse Prevention Act, to implement and enforce a do-not-call registry to be established and run by the commission. The registry is nationwide in scope, applies to all telemarketers (with the exception of certain non-profit organizations), and covers both interstate and intrastate telemarketing calls. Commercial telemarketers are not allowed to call a number that is on the registry, subject to certain exceptions.

- Fair and Accurate Credit Transactions Act of 2003—This act's provisions are designed to improve the accuracy of consumers' credit-related records. It gives consumers the right to one free copy of their credit report a year from the credit reporting agencies, and consumers may also purchase for a reasonable fee a credit score along with information about how the credit score is calculated. The act also includes provisions to prevent and mitigate identity theft, to enable consumers to place fraud alerts in their credit files, and to grant consumers additional rights with respect to how their information is used.

In recent years, the Federal Trade Commission has been very attentive to developments related to e-commerce and online activities generally. With the growth of globalization and the information economy, the FTC is likely to continue exploring the ways in which these movements converge and impact consumer protection. This is the area most likely to see expanded FTC regulations in the future.

FTC BUREAUS

The FTC is administered by a five-member commission. Each commissioner is appointed by the President for a seven-year term with the advice and consent of the Senate. The commission must represent at least three political parties and the President chooses from its ranks one commissioner to be chairperson. The chairperson appoints an executive director with the consent of the full commission; the executive director is responsible for general staff operations.

Three bureaus of the FTC interpret and enforce jurisdictional legislation: the Bureau of Consumer Protection, the Bureau of Competition, and the Bureau of Economics.

Bureau of Consumer Protection The Bureau of Consumer Protection is charged with protecting the consumer from unfair, deceptive, and fraudulent practices. It enforces congressional consumer protection laws and regulations issued by the Commission. In order to meet its various responsibilities, the Bureau often becomes involved in federal litigation, consumer, and business education, and conducts various investigations under its jurisdiction. The Bureau has divisions of advertising, marketing practices, credit, and enforcement.

Bureau of Competition The FTC's Bureau of Competition is responsible for antitrust activity and investigations involving restraint of trade. The Bureau of Competition works with the Antitrust Division of the U.S. Department of Justice, but while the Justice Department concentrates on criminal violations, the Bureau of Competition deals with the technical and civil aspects of competition in the marketplace.

Bureau of Economics The Bureau of Economics predicts and analyzes the economic impact of FTC activities, especially as these activities relate to competition, interstate commerce, and consumer welfare. The Bureau provides Congress and the Executive Branch with the results of its investigations and undertakes special studies on their behalf when requested.

APPLICATIONS FOR COMPLAINTS

The FTC becomes aware of alleged unfair or deceptive trade practices as a result of its own investigations or complaints from consumers, business people, trade associations, other federal agencies, or local and state governmental agencies. These complaints become known as "applications for complaints" and are reviewed to determine whether or not they fall under FTC jurisdiction. If the application does fall under FTC jurisdiction, the case can be settled if the violator agrees to a consent order. This is a document issued by the FTC after a formal—and in some cases—public hearing to hear the complaint. Consent orders are handed down in situations where the offending company or person agrees to discontinue or correct the challenged practices. If an agreement is not reached via a consent order, the case is litigated before an FTC Administrative Law Judge. After the judge has handed down his or her decision, either the FTC counsel or the respondent can appeal the decision to the Commission. The Commission may either dismiss the case or issue a cease and desist order. If a cease and desist order is issued, the respondent has sixty days to take all necessary steps to obey the order or launch an appeal process through the federal court system.

For further information on the FTC, its various responsibilities, and its impact on small business owners, contact the agency at one of the following addresses: Federal Trade Commission, CRC-240, Washington, D.C. 20580, or online at http://www.ftc.gov/.

BIBLIOGRAPHY

Holt, William Stull. *The Federal Trade Commission: Its History, Activities, and Organization.* AMS Press, 1974.

Hoover, Kent. "FTC Faces Tough Task Stemming Tide of Fraudulent Sales." *Tampa Bay Business Journal.* April 14, 2000.

Labaree, Robert V. *The Federal Trade Commission: A Guide to Sources.* Garland, 2000.

"Online Enforcement Efforts Outlined." *New York Times.* November 1, 2000.

U. S. Federal Trade Commission. *National Do Not Call Registry.* Available from http://www.ftc.gov/donotcall/. Retrieved on 23 February 2006.

Hillstrom, Northern Lights
updated by Magee, ECDI

FICA TAXES

FICA taxes are those arising from the 1937 law—the Federal Insurance Contribution Act (FICA). These taxes include contributions to both the federal Social Security and Medicare programs, and must be paid by all American workers, whether they are employed by a company or are self-employed. The way in which the payment is made varies but anyone employed for pay owes FICA taxes.

Small businesses that employ persons other than the owner or partners are required to withhold FICA taxes—along with regular income taxes—from the wages paid to employees. These taxes are remitted on a monthly or semi-weekly basis, depending on the quantity owed. Businesses are also required to make regularly scheduled reports to the IRS about the amount of taxes owed and paid. Businesses are not required to withhold FICA taxes on wages paid to independent contractors. Self employed persons are responsible for paying their own FICA taxes directly to the IRS on a quarterly basis.

FICA taxes are assigned to two programs and the tax rate for each program is different. In 2006, the employer is required to withhold 6.2 percent of the first $94,200 of an employee's income for the Social Security portion of the employee's FICA taxes (also known as Old Age Survivors and Disability Insurance or OASDI). The Medicare portion is 1.45 percent of the employee's entire income. As a result, the full employee's portion of the FICA tax is 7.65 percent on the first $94,200 of income and 1.45 percent on all income over $94,200. The FICA tax percentages have remained constant since 1990 but the top income rate taxable for Social Security is adjusted annually.

In addition to the portion withheld from employees, employers are required to match the 7.65 percent employee contribution, so that the total FICA contribution is 15.3 percent. Self-employed persons are required to pay both the employer and employee portions of the FICA tax.

The timeliness of FICA tax payments to the IRS is very important. The IRS penalizes late payers with significant penalties and interest. The regular income taxes and the portion of the FICA taxes that are withheld from employees' wages each pay period must be remitted to the IRS monthly (or semi-weekly in the case of an employer whose payroll taxes owed exceed $50,000 in the period), along with a Federal Tax Deposit Coupon (Form 8109-B). If the total tax due is less than $500, however, the business is allowed to make the payments quarterly. FICA tax payments also must be reported on Form W-2, the Annual Statement of Taxes Withheld, which must be sent to all employees and to the Social Security Administration before January 31 of the following year.

Small businesses are also required to maintain specific employment records regarding FICA tax withholding and remittance in order to meet federal requirements. These records, which must be kept for every employee, include the amount of each payment subject to FICA taxes, the amount of FICA tax collected from each payment, along with the date, and an explanation for any difference between the amount subject to FICA taxes and the amount of tax collected.

Many small businesses fall behind in paying their FICA taxes or filing the associated reports at some time during their existence. A company struggling with cash flow may opt to pay suppliers and worker salaries in order to stay in business, rather than remitting its FICA tax withholdings on time. This is a very bad practice, however, because significant interest and penalties apply for late payment or nonpayment of FICA taxes. In fact, the Trust Fund Recovery Penalty allows the IRS to hold a small business owner or accountant personally liable for 100 percent of the amount owed, even in cases where the business has gone bankrupt. "Therefore, it is critical that owners and officers be aware of their liability if they are directly or indirectly responsible for withholding tax deposits," Carl Grassi wrote in *Crain's Cleveland Business.* "Those owners and officers taking a passive role within a business should remove themselves from the financial affairs to help ensure that they will not be made responsible for unremitted withholding taxes."

There are certain situations in which small businesses can avoid owing FICA taxes. For example, special rules apply to sole proprietorships and husband-and-wife partnerships that pay their minor (under 18) children for work performed in the business. These small businesses receive an exemption from withholding FICA taxes from their children's paychecks, and are also not required to pay the employer portion of the FICA taxes. In this way, the parent and child each save 7.65 percent, for a total of 15.3 percent. In addition, the child's wages can still be deducted from the parents' income taxes as a business expense.

There is no limit on how much children can earn and still receive the FICA tax exemption. However, it is important that the wages paid to the child are reasonable for the job performed, and that the hours worked by the child are carefully documented, so it will be clear to the IRS that the child has not been paid for nothing. In addition, parents should note that their child's financial aid for college may be reduced if they earn more than $1,750 per year.

SEE ALSO *Payroll Taxes; Tax Withholding*

BIBLIOGRAPHY

Dailey, Frederick W. *Tax Savvy for Small Business.* Second Edition. Nolo Press, 1997.

DeJong, David S., and Ann Gray Jakabcin. *J.K. Lasser's Year-Round Tax Strategies.* Macmillan, 1997.

Glen, Heidi. "Young Americans Face Higher FICA Taxes or Lower Benefits." *Tax Notes.* 18 March 1996.

Grassi, Carl. "Federal Withholding Rules Enforced with an Iron Fist." *Crain's Cleveland Business.* 12 June 2000.

Marullo, Gloria Gibbs. "Hiring Your Child: Tax Breaks and Trade-Offs." *Nation's Business.* June 1997.

Hillstrom, Northern Lights
updated by Magee, ECDI

FIDUCIARY DUTY

Fiduciary duty is a legal requirement of loyalty and care that applies to any person or organization that has a fiduciary relationship with another person or organization. A fiduciary is a person, committee, or organization that has agreed to accept legal ownership or control and management of an asset or group of assets belonging to someone else. Some examples of fiduciary relationships might include an investment manager to participants in a pension plan, a majority stockholder in a corporation to minority investors, the members of a partnership to one another, a banker to customers, an attorney to a client, or even a parent to a child.

A fiduciary duty is one of complete trust and utmost good faith. While fiduciaries take legal title to assets, the assets do not belong to them. Rather, legal title allows fiduciaries to administer and manage the assets for a temporary period and for a specific purpose. In taking control of another's assets, fiduciaries also agree to manage those assets in accordance with the wishes of the individual who established the fiduciary relationship. The powers and duties of fiduciaries are often established in a document that formally establishes the fiduciary relationship. The conduct of fiduciaries is governed by common law as well as by specific federal and state laws. The Uniform Fiduciary Act and the Uniform Trustees' Powers Act serve as models for state legislation.

Fiduciaries owe two main duties to their clients: a duty of loyalty and a duty of care. The duty of loyalty requires that fiduciaries act solely in the interest of their clients, rather than in their own interest. Thus fiduciaries must not derive any direct or indirect profit from their position, and must avoid potential conflicts of interest. The duty of care requires that fiduciaries perform their functions with a high level of competence and thoroughness, in accordance with industry standards.

Corporate directors have a special fiduciary duty to their shareholders. They are accountable not only for the safekeeping of assets but also for their efficient and effective use. Directors may not profit personally at the expense of, or contrary to, the corporation's shareholders. In other words, corporate directors must place the interests of shareholders above their own interests. The concept of fiduciary duty has a wide variety of other applications in the business world. But a particular area of concern for small businesses is the expanded definition of fiduciary duty that applies to employers that offer certain types of benefit plans to their employees.

EMPLOYEE BENEFIT PLANS

Employers that offer employee benefit plans—such as 401(k) plans or other types of pension plans—are bound by the definition of fiduciary duty set forth in the Employee Retirement Income Security Act of 1974 (ERISA). ERISA, in regulating employee benefit plans, established higher standards of fiduciary duty for individuals who have control over a plan's assets than had existed for other types of fiduciaries under common law.

Under ERISA, each pension plan must have a named fiduciary. In many cases, the named fiduciary is the CEO or CFO. It is common for the CEO or CFO to designate someone else to act as the administrator, fiduciary, and manager of the pension or retirement plan itself. It is important, however, to note that designating another person or entity to manage a plan does not relieve the CEO—or other named fiduciary—of ultimate responsibility. The named fiduciary has a responsibility to monitor the performance of all others responsible for the plan.

In spelling out fiduciary duties with regard to employee benefit plans, ERISA covers the duty of loyalty, the duty to use prudence, and the duty to comply with the plan. The duty of loyalty means that fiduciaries must act in the best interests of the plan and its participants. If fiduciaries are also plan participants, they must subordinate their own interests to those of the plan. In cases where plan participants form a diverse group with different interests, it may be difficult to balance the interests of all concerned.

ERISA expands the concept of care beyond that found in common law. Section 404(a)(1) of ERISA states that a fiduciary shall discharge his duties with respect to a plan "with the care, skill, prudence, and diligence under the circumstances then prevailing that a prudent man acting in a like capacity and familiar with such matters would use in the conduct of an enterprise of a like character and with like aims." Thus, fiduciaries of employee benefit plans must discharge their duties with adequate expertise. The courts have found that fiduciary duties were breached when nonexpert laypersons failed to seek independent qualified counsel when making decisions affecting plan assets. Plan fiduciaries are under an obligation not only to use their special skills and expertise, but also to engage qualified advisers and managers if they lack the expertise themselves.

The prudent person standard, as expressed in ERISA, also requires that fiduciaries "diversify the investments of the plan so as to minimize the risk of large losses, unless under the circumstances it is clearly prudent not to do so." ERISA also makes note of prohibited transactions. Additional specific duties of plan fiduciaries may be set forth in the plan document, and fiduciaries have a duty to administer the plan "in accordance with the documents and instruments governing the plan." Fiduciary duties outlined in the plan document must be consistent with ERISA.

Retirement plan fiduciaries are advised, in an *HR Focus* article from 2006, to address the following points in order to assure that they are covering all of their fiduciary responsibilities under ERISA.

- Ensure that the plan fiduciaries have adopted a statement of investment policies to be followed by the trustee and investment manager. This must include compliance with ERISA requirements of prudence, diversification, and avoidance of prohibited transactions. The statement of investment policy should be reviewed periodically and updated as necessary.

- Ensure that the named fiduciary submits a report at least annually to the company's board on plan administration and compliance with ERISA and the Internal Revenue Code.

- The named fiduciary must regularly review the performance of all other fiduciaries involved in administering and servicing the plan. Documentation of these reviews should also be maintained.

- Obtain an unqualified opinion on the plan's financial statement.

- Have a policy or procedure for the selection, retention, and monitoring of the plan's service providers.

- Ensure that the policy or procedure for selection of service providers is thorough, includes a check of credentials, educational preparation, and professional associations.

- Consider the service providers' general financial condition—credit or other ratings.

- Verify that the service providers are not performing multiple services for the company that could create a possible conflict of interest.

- Check to make sure that "free" services from the service provider are actually "free."

- Make sure that the service provider's fees are clearly defined and that they are reasonable and within industry standards.

Under ERISA, retirement plans are not extensions of the companies who establish them. They are entirely separate entities and should be seen as holding assets in trust. These assets must be managed solely in the interest of the plan, its participants and beneficiaries.

SEE ALSO *Pension Plans; 401(k) Plans; Retirement Planning*

BIBLIOGRAPHY
"Fifteen Ways to Help Your Company Avoid Fiduciary Trouble." *HR Focus.* January 2006.

Foster, Douglas, and Wayne Miller. "Who's the Fiduciary?" *CFO, The Magazine for Senior Financial Executives.* February 2006.

Karol, Bernard. "Fiduciaries Must Beware of Potential Conflicts." *American Banker.* 26 June 1997.

MacDonald, John. "'Traditional' Pension Assets Lost Dominance a Decade Ago, IRA's and 401(k)s Have Long Been Dominant." *Fast Facts from EBRI.* Employee Benefit Research Institute, 3 February 2006.

Rutherford, Elizabeth A. "Fiduciary Liability 101: Do You Pass?" *Employee Benefits Journal.* March 2000.

Welbourn, Thomas. "Fiduciary Liability Insurance: A Necessary Means of Protection." *Leaders' Edge.* May 1998.

Hillstrom, Northern Lights
updated by Magee, ECDI

FINANCE COMPANIES

Commercial finance companies have in recent years become a favorite option for entrepreneurs seeking small business loans. Commercial financing institutions generally charge higher interest rates than banks and credit unions, but they are also more likely to approve a loan request. Most loans obtained through finance companies are secured and the assets used as collateral can be seized if the entrepreneur defaults on the loan.

Consumer finance companies make small loans against personal assets and provide an option for individuals with poor credit ratings. Commercial finance companies provide small businesses with loans for inventory and equipment purchases and are a good resource of capital for manufacturing enterprises. Insurance companies often make commercial loans as a way of reinvesting their income. They usually provide payment terms and interest rates comparable to a commercial bank, but require a business to have more assets available as collateral.

"In general, finance companies want to see strong assets to back up a loan and will monitor those assets much more carefully," one expert told *Entrepreneur.* "For that reason, they can loan more against the assets. So chances are a smaller business might get a larger loan from a finance company" than from a bank. Paola Banchero of *Kansas City Business Journal* noted that commercial finance companies have also grown because they are more flexible in arranging loan repayment schedules than are banks. Whereas banks typically require a seven-year repayment schedule on term loans and 15-year schedules for loans on commercial property, finance companies may extend payment schedules up to 10 years for term loans and up to 25 years for loans on commercial real estate.

Finance companies have experienced sustained growth throughout the 1990s. By the end of the decade, finance companies had become America's second largest source of business credit, behind banking institutions. Larger commercial finance companies often offer small business owners a variety of lending options from which to choose. These include factoring, working capital loans, equipment financing and leasing, working capital loans, specialized equity investments, collateral-based financing, and cash-flow financing. Some also offer additional services in connection with those loans, such as assistance with collections.

Commercial finance companies come in all shapes and sizes. The size of the firm usually has some bearing on the exact services it offers. The nation's largest finance firms (The Money Store, AT&T Small Business Lending Corp.) have established networks of offices across the country, and they sometimes offer lending services that even banks do not. For example, The Money Store—which made more than 1,700 loans worth $635 million in fiscal year 1996—offers loans to entrepreneurs looking to take ownership of a franchise, an option that is not available at all banks. But as *Entrepreneur's* Cynthia Griffin noted, "in addition to the mega players, the commercial finance industry is populated by hundreds of smaller firms." These firms generally make asset-based loans, providing services to small business owners who are unable to secure loans from their banks.

BIBLIOGRAPHY
Andresky Fraser, Jill. "Show Me the Money: You Can Look for Money in All the Wrong Places." *Inc.* March 1997.

Banchero, Paola. "Financing Fight: Nonbank Lenders Want Nothing More Than to Take Business Away from Traditional Banks." *Kansas City Business Journal.* 10 October 1997.

Griffin, Cynthia E. "Breaking the Bank." *Entrepreneur.* March 1998.

Kuehner-Herbert, Katie. "Asset-Based Lending: Whole Different Ball Game." *American Banker.* 3 January 2006.

Prins, Ruth. "From the Frying Pan to the Fire?" *U.S. Banker.* December 1997.

Sherman, Andrew J. *The Complete Guide to Running and Growing Your Business.* Times Books, 1997.

Smith, Sharon. "Techno Mecca: The Use of Factoring and Commercial Finance Companies." *Accountancy.* September 2000.

Hillstrom, Northern Lights
updated by Magee, ECDI

FINANCE AND FINANCIAL MANAGEMENT

Finance and financial management encompass numerous business and governmental activities. In the most basic sense, the term *finance* can be used to describe the activities of a firm attempting to raise capital through the sale of stocks, bonds, or other promissory notes. Similarly, *public finance* is a term used to describe government capital-raising activities through the issuance of bonds or the imposition of taxes. Financial management can be defined as those business activities undertaken with the goal of maximizing shareholder wealth, utilizing the principles of the time value of money, leverage, diversification, and an investment's expected rate of return versus its risk.

Within the discipline of finance, there are three basic components. First, there are financial instruments. These instruments—stocks and bonds—are recorded evidence of obligations on which exchanges of resources are founded. Effective investment management of these financial instruments is a vital part of any organization's financing activities. Second, there are financial markets, which are the mechanisms used to trade the financial instruments. Finally, there are banking and financial institutions, which facilitate the transfer of resources among those buying and selling the financial instruments.

In today's business environment, corporate finance addresses issues relating to individual firms. Specifically, the field of corporate finance seeks to determine the optimal investments that firms should make, the best methods of paying for those investments, and the best ways of managing daily financial activities to ensure that firms have adequate cash flow. Financial management influences all segments of corporate activity, for both profit-oriented firms and non-profit firms. Through the acquisition of funds, the allocation of resources, and the tracking of financial performance, financial management provides a vital function for any organization's activities. Furthermore, finance provides stockholders and other interested parties a tool with which to assess management activities.

Large corporations usually employ managers who specialize in finance as treasurers, controllers, and/or a chief financial officer (CFO). In a small business, many of the functions that would be performed by these specialists fall upon the small business owner or manager. He or she is usually responsible for obtaining financing, maintaining the company's relationship with banks and other financial institutions, ensuring that the company meets its obligations to investors and creditors, analyzing and deciding upon capital investment projects, and conducting overall financial policymaking and planning. For this reason, a basic understanding of financial management can be very helpful for a small business owner.

BIBLIOGRAPHY
Beyond Irrelevance: Economic Focus." *The Economist.* 11 February 2006.

Crawford, Richard D., Henry A. Davis, and William W. Sihler. *Smart Financial Management: The Essential Reference for the Successful Small Business.* AMACOM, 2004.

Culp, Christopher L., and William A. Niskanen. *Corporate Aftershock.* John Wiley & Sons, 2003.

Higgins, Robert C. *Analysis for Financial Management.* McGraw-Hill, 2000.

Noe, Thomas H. "Corporate Finance, Incentives, and Strategy." *Financial Review.* November 2000.

"Small Business Finance: Certified Bookkeepers Replacing MBAs." *PR Newswire.* 1 March 2006.

Tirole, Jean. *The Theory of Corporate Finance.* Princeton University Press, 2005.

Hillstrom, Northern Lights
updated by Magee, ECDI

FINANCIAL ANALYSIS

Financial analysis is an aspect of the overall business finance function that involves examining historical data to gain information about the current and future financial health of a company. Financial analysis can be applied in a wide variety of situations to give business managers the information they need to make critical decisions. The ability to understand financial data is essential for any business manager. Finance **is** the language of business. Business goals and objectives are set in financial terms and their outcomes are measured in financial terms. Among the skills required to understand and manage a business is fluency in the language of finance—the ability to read and understand financial data as well as present information in the form of financial reports.

The finance function in business involves evaluating economic trends, setting financial policy, and creating long-range plans for business activities. It also involves applying a system of internal controls for the handling of cash, the recognition of sales, the disbursement of expenses, the valuation of inventory, and the approval of capital expenditures. In addition, the finance function reports on these internal control systems through the preparation of financial statements, such as income statements, balance sheets, and cash flow statements.

Finally, finance involves analyzing the data contained in financial statements in order to provide valuable information for management decisions. In this way, financial analysis is only one part of the overall function of finance, but it is a very important one. A company's accounts and statements contain a great deal of information. Discovering the full meaning contained in the statements is at the heart of financial analysis. Understanding how accounts relate to one another is part of financial analysis. Another part of financial analysis involves using the numerical data contained in company statements to uncover patterns of activity that may not be apparent on the surface.

DOCUMENTS USED IN FINANCIAL ANALYSIS

The three main sources of data for financial analysis are a company's balance sheet, income statement, and cash flow statement.

Balance Sheet The balance sheet outlines the financial and physical resources that a company has available for business activities in the future. It is important to note, however, that the balance sheet only lists these resources, and makes no judgment about how well they will be used by management. For this reason, the balance sheet is

more useful in analyzing a company's current financial position than its expected performance.

The main elements of the balance sheet are assets and liabilities. Assets generally include both current assets (cash or equivalents that will be converted to cash within one year, such as accounts receivable, inventory, and prepaid expenses) and noncurrent assets (assets that are held for more than one year and are used in running the business, including fixed assets like property, plant, and equipment; long-term investments; and intangible assets like patents, copyrights, and goodwill). Both the total amount of assets and the makeup of asset accounts are of interest to financial analysts.

The balance sheet also includes two categories of liabilities, current liabilities (debts that will come due within one year, such as accounts payable, short-term loans, and taxes) and long-term debts (debts that are due more than one year from the date of the statement). Liabilities are important to financial analysts because businesses have same obligation to pay their bills regularly as individuals, while business income tends to be less certain. Long-term liabilities are less important to analysts, since they lack the urgency of short-term debts, though their presence does indicate that a company is strong enough to be allowed to borrow money.

Income Statement In contrast to the balance sheet, the income statement provides information about a company's performance over a certain period of time. Although it does not reveal much about the company's current financial condition, it does provide indications of its future viability. The main elements of the income statement are revenues earned, expenses incurred, and net profit or loss. Revenues consist mainly of sales, though financial analysts may also note the inclusion of royalties, interest, and extraordinary items. Likewise, operating expenses usually consists primarily of the cost of goods sold, but can also include some unusual items. Net income is the "bottom line" of the income statement. This figure is the main indicator of a company's accomplishments over the statement period.

Cash Flow Statement The cash flow statement is similar to the income statement in that it records a company's performance over a specified period of time. The difference between the two is that the income statement also takes into account some non-cash accounting items such as depreciation. The cash flow statement strips away all of this and shows exactly how much actual money the company has generated. Cash flow statements show how companies have performed in managing inflows and outflows of cash. It provides a sharper picture of a company's ability to pay bills, creditors, and finance growth better than any other one financial statement.

ELEMENTS OF FINANCIAL HEALTH

A company's overall financial health can be assessed by examining three major factors: its liquidity, leverage, and profitability. All three of these factors are internal measures that are largely within the control of a company's management. It is important to note, however, that they may also be affected by other conditions—such as overall trends in the economy—that are beyond management's control.

Liquidity Liquidity refers to a company's ability to pay its current bills and expenses. In other words, liquidity relates to the availability of cash and other assets to cover accounts payable, short-term debt, and other liabilities. All small businesses require a certain degree of liquidity in order to pay their bills on time, though start-up and very young companies are often not very liquid. In mature companies, low levels of liquidity can indicate poor management or a need for additional capital. Of course, any company's liquidity may vary due to seasonal variations, the timing of sales, and the state of the economy.

Companies tend to run into problems with liquidity because cash outflows are not flexible, while income is often uncertain. Creditors expect their money when promised, and employees expect regular paychecks. However, the cash coming in to a business does not often follow a set schedule. Sales volumes fluctuate as do collections from customers. Because of this difference between cash generation and cash payments, businesses should maintain a certain ratio of current assets to current liabilities in order to ensure adequate liquidity.

Leverage Leverage refers to the proportion of a company's capital that has been contributed by investors as compared to creditors. In other words, leverage is the extent to which a company has depended upon borrowing to finance its operations A company that has a high proportion of debt in relation to its equity would be considered highly leveraged. Leverage is an important aspect of financial analysis because it is reviewed closely by both bankers and investors. A high leverage ratio may increase a company's exposure to risk and business downturns, but along with this higher risk also comes the potential for higher returns.

Profitability Profitability refers to management's performance in using the resources of a business. Many measures of profitability involve calculating the financial return that the company earns on the money that has been invested. Most entrepreneurs decide to start their own businesses in order to earn a better return on their money than would be available through a bank or other low-risk investments. If profitability measures demonstrate that this is not occurring—particularly once a small business has moved beyond the start-up phase—then the entrepreneur should consider selling the business and reinvesting his or her money elsewhere. However, it is important to note that many factors can influence profitability measures, including changes in price, volume, or expenses, as well the purchase of assets or the borrowing of money.

PERFORMING ANALYSES WITH FINANCIAL RATIOS

Measuring the liquidity, leverage, and profitability of a company is not a matter of how many dollars the company has in the form of assets, liabilities, and equity. The key is the proportions in which such items occur in relation to one another. A company is analyzed by looking at ratios rather than just dollar amounts. Financial ratios are determined by dividing one number by another, and are usually expressed as a percentage. They enable business owners to examine the relationships between seemingly unrelated items and thus gain useful information for decision-making. Financial ratios are simple to calculate, easy to use, and provide a wealth of information that cannot be gotten anywhere else. Ratios are tools that aid judgment and cannot take the place of experience. They do not replace good management, but they can make a good manager better.

Virtually any financial statistics can be compared using a ratio. Small business owners and managers only need to be concerned with a small set of ratios in order to identify where improvements are needed. Determining which ratios to compute depends on the type of business, the age of the business, the point in the business cycle, and any specific information sought. For example, if a small business depends on a large number of fixed assets, ratios that measure how efficiently these assets are being used may be the most significant.

There are a few general ratios that can be very useful in an overall financial analysis. To assess a company's liquidity, analysts recommend using the current, quick, and liquidity ratios. The current ratio can be defined as Current Assets/Current Liabilities. It measures the ability of an entity to pay its near-term obligations. Though the ideal current ratio depends to some extent on the type of business, a general rule of thumb is that it should be at least 2:1. A lower current ratio means that the company may not be able to pay its bills on time, while a higher ratio means that the company has money in cash or safe investments that could be put to better use in the business.

The quick ratio, also known as the "acid test," can be defined as Quick Assets (cash, marketable securities, and receivables) / Current Liabilities. This ratio provides a stricter definition of the company's ability to make payments on current obligations. Ideally, this ratio should be 1:1. If it is higher, the company may keep too much cash on hand or have a poor collection program for accounts receivable. If it is lower, it may indicate that the company relies too heavily on inventory to meet its obligations. The liquidity ratio, also known as the cash ratio, can be defined as Cash/Current Liabilities. This measure eliminates all current assets except cash from the calculation of liquidity.

To measure a company's leverage, the debt/equity ratio is the appropriate tool. Defined as Debt / Owners' Equity, this ratio indicates the relative mix of the company's investor-supplied capital. A company is generally considered safer if it has a low debt to equity ratio—that is, a higher proportion of owner-supplied capital—though a very low ratio can indicate excessive caution. In general, debt should be between 50 and 80 percent of equity.

Finally, to measure a company's level of profitability, analysts recommend using the return on equity (ROE) ratio, which can be defined as Net Income/Owners' Equity. This ratio indicates how well the company is utilizing its equity investment. ROE is considered to be one of the best indicators of profitability. It is also a good figure to compare against competitors or an industry average. Experts suggest that companies usually need at least 10-14 percent ROE in order to fund future growth. If this ratio is too low, it can indicate poor management performance or a highly conservative business approach. On the other hand, a high ROE can mean that management is doing a good job, or that the firm is undercapitalized.

In conclusion, financial analysis can be an important tool for small business owners and managers to measure their progress toward reaching company goals, as well as toward competing with larger companies within an industry. When performed regularly over time, financial analysis can also help small businesses recognize and adapt to trends affecting their operations. It is also important for small business owners to understand and use financial analysis because it provides one of the main measures of a company's success from the perspective of bankers, investors, and outside analysts.

SEE ALSO *Balance Sheets; Cash Flow Statements; Income Statements; Return on Assets*

BIBLIOGRAPHY

Casteuble, Tracy. "Using Financial Ratios to Assess Performance." *Association Management.* July 1997.

"Financial Analysis: 17 Areas to Review." *Business Owner.* January-February 1999.

Gil-Lafuente, Anna Maria. *Fuzzy Logic In Financial Analysis.* Springer, 2005.

Helfert, Erich A. *Techniques of Financial Analysis.* Irwin, 1997.

Hey-Cunningham, David. *Financial Statements Demystified.* Allen & Unwin, 2002.

Higgins, Robert C. *Analysis for Financial Management.* McGraw-Hill, 2000.

Jones, Allen N. "Financial Statements: When Properly Read, They Share a Wealth of Information." *Memphis Business Journal.* 5 February 1996.

Larkin, Howard. "How to Read a Financial Statement." *American Medical News.* 11 March 1996.

Hillstrom, Northern Lights
updated by Magee, ECDI

FINANCIAL PLANNERS

Financial planners are individuals who advise both people and companies about how to invest their assets. Most financial planners are professionals who help their clients with a variety of financial tasks and aids in making investment decisions to plan for the future.

A financial planner, unlike a Certified Financial Planner or Chartered Financial Consultant, is a title that is self-bestowed, it may be used by anyone. As a result, small business owners wishing to hire a financial planner must be diligent in obtaining referrals, checking qualifications and licenses, and inquiring about fees. "The real pros can help you map out a route to goals like retirement and estate planning, asset allocation, and tax and cash-flow planning," Laura Koss-Feder wrote in an article for *Money.*

A good financial planner will conduct an in-depth interview to gather information about the client's income, expenses, assets, liabilities, future goals, and risk tolerance. Then the planner will use this information to develop a detailed, written financial plan specifically for the client. Financial planners may steer their clients into a wide range of investment products, including stocks, bonds, mutual funds, money market accounts, independent retirement accounts (IRAs), and insurance. In most cases, clients receive monthly or quarterly reports detailing the progress of their investment portfolios.

FINDING A GOOD FINANCIAL PLANNER

"There is no shortage of good financial planners, but the challenge is to identify them among as many as 450,000 stockbrokers, insurance salespeople, and outright cranks who claim to be effective planners. Unlike, say, a plumber, hairdresser, or neurosurgeon, a financial planner does not necessarily have to open a book, take an exam, or otherwise demonstrate any competence before hanging out a shingle," Koss-Feder explained.

The first step in finding a good financial planner is obtaining referrals from friends and business associates, preferably those who are in similar financial situations and have similar financial needs. If personal recommendations are not available, trade groups such as the National Association of Personal Financial Advisors, the International Association for Financial Planning, and the Institute of Certified Financial Planners provide referrals for their members.

After obtaining referrals, experts recommend that small business owners interview at least three potential planners before making a decision. It may be helpful to examine financial plans that each planner has prepared for clients with similar circumstances, and to gather information about the problems the planners have solved for other clients. Though it may not be necessary if the referral came from a trusted friend, the small business owner may wish to contact some of these clients directly and ask about the planners' strengths and weaknesses, responsiveness to phone calls, and willingness to explain things. Since financial planners often work with other professionals—such as attorneys and accountants—the small business owner may wish to ask for professional references as well.

The next step in hiring a financial planner is to conduct a thorough examination of their qualifications and experience. Experts recommend that financial planners have a strong background in finance, accounting, banking, stock brokerage, or a related field, as well as five years experience. Potential financial planners should also be able to show proof that they are licensed with regulatory bodies. In order to obtain a credential such as Certified Financial Planner (CFP) or Chartered Financial Consultant (ChFC), a planner must pass a series of tests, take continuing education courses, and comply with a code of ethics. In addition, financial planners who provide advice about securities must file a disclosure document known as an ADV with the Securities and Exchange Commission (SEC). They are required to show potential clients part II of this document upon request, which gives information on their educational background, qualifications, fees charged for services, and any business affiliations that could cause a conflict of interest. Although financial planners are not obliged to show clients part I of their ADVs, small business owners may want to avoid any planner who is unwilling to do so, as part I outlines any disciplinary problems the planner has experienced.

FEE-BASED OR COMMISSION-BASED PLANNERS

The final step in hiring a financial planner is to find out how the planner will be compensated—through client fees or brokerage commissions. Fee-based planners charge their clients various fees depending on the type of work they perform. In contrast, commission-based planners do not charge their clients up-front fees, but instead take a commission on the investments they recommend. Commission-based planners generally work with their clients to create an investment plan for free, then charge commissions ranging from 1 percent on money-market accounts to 90 percent of first-year insurance premiums. In some ways, choosing a fee-based planner may seem preferable because it promotes objectivity and eliminates the potential for conflict of interest. But the fees charged can be expensive; according to Koss-Feder, the average fee to create a basic financial plan was over $1,100. "As long as you have confidence in the planner, it really doesn't matter which type you choose—as long as you know how he is making his money," Koss-Feder concluded. The fee structure should always be spelled out in a written agreement.

Until an atmosphere of trust develops between the small business owner and the financial planner, it may be best to start slowly, by investing around 25 percent of assets. The amount can then increase over time if the client is satisfied with the planner's performance. In order to establish a strong relationship with a financial planner, Lorayne Fiorillo of *Entrepreneur* recommended that small business owners "treat your financial advisor and his or her staff with respect. Don't call your advisor with paperwork questions; that's a job for his or her assistant. If you have a complex question, call when the stock market is closed—your advisor will have more time to talk. Most of all, keep the lines of communication open."

BIBLIOGRAPHY

Chatzky, Jean Sherman. "How to Pick a Pro: Financial Planning Works, but All Financial Planners Are Not Equal." *Money.* 1 December 2000.

Fairley, Juliette. "The Right Choice: Choosing a Financial Planner You Can Trust." *Black Enterprise.* March 1996.

Fiorillo, Lorayne. "Rope One In: How to Spot the Good, the Bad, and the Ugly When Looking for a Financial Advisor." *Entrepreneur.* December 1997.

Glover, Hannah. "Comprehensive Financial Plans Falling Short." *Money Management Executive.* 20 February 2006.

Kahn, Virginia Munger. "Defining, and Finding, a Fee-Only Planner." *New York Times.* 12 January 1997.

Koss-Feder, Laura. "Smart Ways to Find a Financial Planner." *Money.* March 1997.

Nissenbaum, Martin and Barbara J. Raasch, Charles L. Ratner. *Ernst & Young's Personal Financial Planning Guide.* John Wiley & Sons, 17 September 2004.

Stovall, Robert H. "Selecting a Financial Planner." *Sales and Marketing Management.* February 1998.

Hillstrom, Northern Lights
updated by Magee, ECDI

FINANCIAL RATIOS

Financial ratios are relationships determined from a company's financial information and used for comparison purposes. Examples include such often referred to measures as return on investment (ROI), return on assets (ROA), and debt-to-equity, to name just three. These ratios are the result of dividing one account balance or financial measurement with another. Usually these measurements or account balances are found on one of the company's financial statements—balance sheet, income statement, cashflow statement, and/or statement of changes in owner's equity. Financial ratios can provide small business owners and managers with a valuable tool with which to measure their progress against predetermined internal goals, a certain competitor, or the overall industry. In addition, tracking various ratios over time is a powerful means of identifying trends in their early stages. Ratios are also used by bankers, investors, and business analysts to assess a company's financial status.

Ratios are calculated by dividing one number by another, total sales divided by number of employees, for example. Ratios enable business owners to examine the relationships between items and measure that relationship. They are simple to calculate, easy to use, and provide business owners with insight into what is happening within their business, insights that are not always apparent upon review of the financial statements alone. Ratios are aids to judgment and cannot take the place of experience. But experience with reading ratios and tracking them over time will make any manager a better manager. Ratios can help to pinpoint areas that need attention before the looming problem within the area is easily visible.

Virtually any financial statistics can be compared using a ratio. In reality, however, small business owners and managers only need to be concerned with a small set of ratios in order to identify where improvements are needed.

It is important to keep in mind that financial ratios are time sensitive; they can only present a picture of the business at the time that the underlying figures were prepared. For example, a retailer calculating ratios before and after the Christmas season would get very different results. In addition, ratios can be misleading when taken singly, though they can be quite valuable when a small

business tracks them over time or uses them as a basis for comparison against company goals or industry standards.

Perhaps the best way for small business owners to use financial ratios is to conduct a formal ratio analysis on a regular basis. The raw data used to compute the ratios should be recorded on a special form monthly. Then the relevant ratios should be computed, reviewed, and saved for future comparisons. Determining which ratios to compute depends on the type of business, the age of the business, the point in the business cycle, and any specific information sought. For example, if a small business depends on a large number of fixed assets, ratios that measure how efficiently these assets are being used may be the most significant. In general, financial ratios can be broken down into four main categories—1) profitability or return on investment; 2) liquidity; 3) leverage, and 4) operating or efficiency—with several specific ratio calculations prescribed within each.

PROFITABILITY OR RETURN ON INVESTMENT RATIOS

Profitability ratios provide information about management's performance in using the resources of the small business. Many entrepreneurs decide to start their own businesses in order to earn a better return on their money than would be available through a bank or other low-risk investments. If profitability ratios demonstrate that this is not occurring—particularly once a small business has moved beyond the start-up phase—then entrepreneurs for whom a return on their money is the foremost concern may wish to sell the business and reinvest their money elsewhere. However, it is important to note that many factors can influence profitability ratios, including changes in price, volume, or expenses, as well as the purchase of assets or the borrowing of money. Some specific profitability ratios follow, along with the means of calculating them and their meaning to a small business owner or manager.

Gross profitability: Gross Profits/Net Sales—measures the margin on sales the company is achieving. It can be an indication of manufacturing efficiency, or marketing effectiveness.

Net profitability: Net Income/Net Sales—measures the overall profitability of the company, or how much is being brought to the bottom line. Strong gross profitability combined with weak net profitability may indicate a problem with indirect operating expenses or non-operating items, such as interest expense. In general terms, net profitability shows the effectiveness of management. Though the optimal level depends on the type of business, the ratios can be compared for firms in the same industry.

Return on assets: Net Income/Total Assets—indicates how effectively the company is deploying its assets. A very low return on asset, or ROA, usually indicates inefficient management, whereas a high ROA means efficient management. However, this ratio can be distorted by depreciation or any unusual expenses.

Return on investment 1: Net Income/Owners' Equity—indicates how well the company is utilizing its equity investment. Due to leverage, this measure will generally be higher than return on assets. ROI is considered to be one of the best indicators of profitability. It is also a good figure to compare against competitors or an industry average. Experts suggest that companies usually need at least 10-14 percent ROI in order to fund future growth. If this ratio is too low, it can indicate poor management performance or a highly conservative business approach. On the other hand, a high ROI can mean that management is doing a good job, or that the firm is undercapitalized.

Return on investment 2: Dividends +/- Stock Price Change/Stock Price Paid—from the investor's point of view, this calculation of ROI measures the gain (or loss) achieved by placing an investment over a period of time.

Earnings per share: Net Income/Number of Shares Outstanding—states a corporation's profits on a per-share basis. It can be helpful in further comparison to the market price of the stock.

Investment turnover: Net Sales/Total Assets—measures a company's ability to use assets to generate sales. Although the ideal level for this ratio varies greatly, a very low figure may mean that the company maintains too many assets or has not deployed its assets well, whereas a high figure means that the assets have been used to produce good sales numbers.

Sales per employee: Total Sales/Number of Employees—can provide a measure of productivity. This ratio will vary widely from one industry to another. A high figure relative to one's industry average can indicate either good personnel management or good equipment.

LIQUIDITY RATIOS

Liquidity ratios demonstrate a company's ability to pay its current obligations. In other words, they relate to the availability of cash and other assets to cover accounts payable, short-term debt, and other liabilities. All small businesses require a certain degree of liquidity in order to pay their bills on time, though start-up and very young companies are often not very liquid. In mature companies, low levels of liquidity can indicate poor management or a need for additional capital. Any company's liquidity may vary due to seasonality, the timing of sales, and the state of the economy. But liquidity ratios can provide small business owners with useful limits to help

them regulate borrowing and spending. Some of the best-known measures of a company's liquidity include:

Current ratio: Current Assets/Current Liabilities—measures the ability of an entity to pay its near-term obligations. "Current" usually is defined as within one year. Though the ideal current ratio depends to some extent on the type of business, a general rule of thumb is that it should be at least 2:1. A lower current ratio means that the company may not be able to pay its bills on time, while a higher ratio means that the company has money in cash or safe investments that could be put to better use in the business.

Quick ratio (or "acid test"): Quick Assets (cash, marketable securities, and receivables)/Current Liabilities—provides a stricter definition of the company's ability to make payments on current obligations. Ideally, this ratio should be 1:1. If it is higher, the company may keep too much cash on hand or have a poor collection program for accounts receivable. If it is lower, it may indicate that the company relies too heavily on inventory to meet its obligations.

Cash to total assets: Cash/Total Assets—measures the portion of a company's assets held in cash or marketable securities. Although a high ratio may indicate some degree of safety from a creditor's viewpoint, excess amounts of cash may be viewed as inefficient.

Sales to receivables (or turnover ratio): Net Sales/Accounts Receivable—measures the annual turnover of accounts receivable. A high number reflects a short lapse of time between sales and the collection of cash, while a low number means collections take longer. Because of seasonal changes this ratio is likely to vary. As a result, an annual floating average sales to receivables ratio is most useful in identifying meaningful shifts and trends.

Days' receivables ratio: 365/Sales to receivables ratio—measures the average number of days that accounts receivable are outstanding. This number should be the same or lower than the company's expressed credit terms. Other ratios can also be converted to days, such as the cost of sales to payables ratio.

Cost of sales to payables: Cost of Sales/Trade Payables—measures the annual turnover of accounts payable. Lower numbers tend to indicate good performance, though the ratio should be close to the industry standard.

Cash turnover: Net Sales/Net Working Capital (current assets less current liabilities)—reflects the company's ability to finance current operations, the efficiency of its working capital employment, and the margin of protection for its creditors. A high cash turnover ratio may leave the company vulnerable to creditors, while a low ratio may indicate an inefficient use of working capital. In general, sales five to six times greater than working capital are needed to maintain a positive cash flow and finance sales.

LEVERAGE RATIOS

Leverage ratios look at the extent to which a company has depended upon borrowing to finance its operations. As a result, these ratios are reviewed closely by bankers and investors. Most leverage ratios compare assets or net worth with liabilities. A high leverage ratio may increase a company's exposure to risk and business downturns, but along with this higher risk also comes the potential for higher returns. Some of the major measurements of leverage include:

Debt to equity ratio: Debt/Owners' Equity—indicates the relative mix of the company's investor-supplied capital. A company is generally considered safer if it has a low debt to equity ratio—that is, a higher proportion of owner-supplied capital—though a very low ratio can indicate excessive caution. In general, debt should be between 50 and 80 percent of equity.

Debt ratio: Debt/Total Assets—measures the portion of a company's capital that is provided by borrowing. A debt ratio greater than 1.0 means the company has negative net worth, and is technically bankrupt. This ratio is similar, and can easily be converted to, the debt to equity ratio.

Fixed to worth ratio: Net Fixed Assets/Tangible Net Worth—indicates how much of the owner's equity has been invested in fixed assets, i.e., plant and equipment. It is important to note that only tangible assets (physical assets like cash, inventory, property, plant, and equipment) are included in the calculation, and that they are valued less depreciation. Creditors usually like to see this ratio very low, but the large-scale leasing of assets can artificially lower it.

Interest coverage: Earnings before Interest and Taxes/Interest Expense—indicates how comfortably the company can handle its interest payments. In general, a higher interest coverage ratio means that the small business is able to take on additional debt. This ratio is closely examined by bankers and other creditors.

EFFICIENCY RATIOS

By assessing a company's use of credit, inventory, and assets, efficiency ratios can help small business owners and managers conduct business better. These ratios can show how quickly the company is collecting money for its credit sales or how many times inventory turns over in a given time period. This information can help management decide whether the company's credit terms are appropriate and whether its purchasing efforts are handled in an efficient manner. The following are some of the main indicators of efficiency:

Annual inventory turnover: Cost of Goods Sold for the Year/Average Inventory—shows how efficiently the company is managing its production, warehousing, and distribution of product, considering its volume of sales. Higher ratios—over six or seven times per year—are generally thought to be better, although extremely high inventory turnover may indicate a narrow selection and possibly lost sales. A low inventory turnover rate, on the other hand, means that the company is paying to keep a large inventory, and may be overstocking or carrying obsolete items.

Inventory holding period: 365/Annual Inventory Turnover—calculates the number of days, on average, that elapse between finished goods production and sale of product.

Inventory to assets ratio: Inventory/Total Assets—shows the portion of assets tied up in inventory. Generally, a lower ratio is considered better.

Accounts receivable turnover: Net (credit) Sales/Average Accounts Receivable—gives a measure of how quickly credit sales are turned into cash. Alternatively, the reciprocal of this ratio indicates the portion of a year's credit sales that are outstanding at a particular point in time.

Collection period: 365/Accounts Receivable Turnover—measures the average number of days the company's receivables are outstanding, between the date of credit sale and collection of cash.

SUMMARY

Although they may seem intimidating at first glance, all of the aforementioned financial ratios can be derived by simply comparing numbers that appear on a small business's income statement and balance sheet. Small business owners would be well-served by familiarizing themselves with ratios and their uses as a tracking device for anticipating changes in operations.

Financial ratios can be an important tool for small business owners and managers to measure their progress toward reaching company goals, as well as toward competing with larger companies. Ratio analysis, when performed regularly over time, can also help small businesses recognize and adapt to trends affecting their operations. Yet another reason small business owners need to understand financial ratios is that they provide one of the main measures of a company's success from the perspective of bankers, investors, and business analysts. Often, a small business's ability to obtain debt or equity financing will depend on the company's financial ratios.

Despite all the positive uses of financial ratios, however, small business managers are still encouraged to know the limitations of ratios and approach ratio analysis with a degree of caution. Ratios alone do not make give one all the information necessary for decision making. But decisions made without a look at financial ratios, the decision is being made without all the available data.

SEE ALSO *Balance Sheets; Cash Flow Statements; Income Statements; Return on Assets*

BIBLIOGRAPHY

Casteuble, Tracy. "Using Financial Ratios to Assess Performance." *Association Management.* July 1997.

Clark, Scott. "Financial Ratios Hold the Key to Smart Business." *Birmingham Business Journal.* 11 February 2000.

Clark, Scott. "You Can Read the Tea Leaves of Financial Ratios." *Birmingham Business Journal.* 25 February 2000.

Gil-Lafuente, Anna Maria. *Fuzzy Logic In Financial Analysis.* Springer, 2005.

Hey-Cunningham, David. *Financial Statements Demystified.* Allen & Unwin, 2002.

Taulli, Tom. *The Edgar Online Guide to Decoding Financial Statements.* J. Ross Publishing, 2004.

Hillstrom, Northern Lights
updated by Magee, ECDI

FINANCIAL STATEMENTS

Financial statements are written records of a business's financial situation. They include standard reports like the balance sheet, income or profit and loss statements, and cash flow statement. They stand as one of the more essential components of business information, and as the principal method of communicating financial information about an entity to outside parties. In a technical sense, financial statements are a summation of the financial position of an entity at a given point in time. Generally, financial statements are designed to meet the needs of many diverse users, particularly present and potential owners and creditors. Financial statements result from simplifying, condensing, and aggregating masses of data obtained primarily from a company's (or an individual's) accounting system.

FINANCIAL REPORTING

According to the Financial Accounting Standards Board, financial reporting includes not only financial statements but also other means of communicating financial information about an enterprise to its external users. Financial statements provide information useful in investment and credit decisions and in assessing cash flow prospects. They provide information about an enterprise's resources, claims to those resources, and changes in the resources.

Financial reporting is a broad concept encompassing financial statements, notes to financial statements and parenthetical disclosures, supplementary information (such as changing prices), and other means of financial reporting (such as management discussions and analysis, and letters to stockholders). Financial reporting is but one source of information needed by those who make economic decisions about business enterprises.

The primary focus of financial reporting is information about earnings and its components. Information about earnings based on accrual accounting usually provides a better indication of an enterprise's present and continuing ability to generate positive cash flows than that provided by cash receipts and payments.

MAJOR FINANCIAL STATEMENTS

The basic financial statements of an enterprise include the 1) balance sheet (or statement of financial position), 2) income statement, 3) cash flow statement, and 4) statement of changes in owners' equity or stockholders' equity. The balance sheet provides a snapshot of an entity as of a particular date. It list the entity's assets, liabilities, and in the case of a corporation, the stockholders' equity on a specific date. The income statement presents a summary of the revenues, gains, expenses, losses, and net income or net loss of an entity for a specific period. This statement is similar to a moving picture of the entity's operations during this period of time. The cash flow statement summarizes an entity's cash receipts and cash payments relating to its operating, investing, and financing activities during a particular period. A statement of changes in owners' equity or stockholders' equity reconciles the beginning of the period equity of an enterprise with its ending balance.

Items currently reported in financial statements are measured by different attributes (for example, historical cost, current cost, current market value, net reliable value, and present value of future cash flows). Historical cost is the traditional means of presenting assets and liabilities.

Notes to financial statements are informative disclosures appended to the end of financial statements. They provide important information concerning such matters as depreciation and inventory methods used, details of long-term debt, pensions, leases, income taxes, contingent liabilities, methods of consolidation, and other matters. Notes are considered an integral part of the financial statements. Schedules and parenthetical disclosures are also used to present information not provided elsewhere in the financial statements.

Each financial statement has a heading, which gives the name of the entity, the name of the statement, and the date or time covered by the statement. The information provided in financial statements is primarily financial in nature and expressed in units of money. The information relates to an individual business enterprise. The information often is the product of approximations and estimates, rather than exact measurements. The financial statements typically reflect the financial effects of transactions and events that have already happened (i.e., historical).

Financial statements presenting financial data for two or more periods are called comparative statements. Comparative financial statements usually give similar reports for the current period and for one or more preceding periods. They provide analysts with significant information about trends and relationships over two or more years. Comparative statements are considerably more significant than are single-year statements. Comparative statements emphasize the fact that financial statements for a single accounting period are only one part of the continuous history of the company.

Interim financial statements are reports for periods of less than a year. The purpose of interim financial statements is to improve the timeliness of accounting information. Some companies issue comprehensive financial statements while others issue summary statements. Each interim period should be viewed primarily as an integral part of an annual period and should generally continue to use the generally accepted accounting principles (GAAP) that were used in the preparation of the company's latest annual report. Financial statements are often audited by independent accountants for the purpose of increasing user confidence in their reliability.

Every financial statement is prepared on the basis of several accounting assumptions: that all transactions can be expressed or measured in dollars; that the enterprise will continue in business indefinitely; and that statements will be prepared at regular intervals. These assumptions provide the foundation for the structure of financial accounting theory and practice, and explain why financial information is presented in a given manner.

Financial statements also must be prepared in accordance with generally accepted accounting principles, and must include an explanation of the company's accounting procedures and policies. Standard accounting principles call for the recording of assets and liabilities at cost; the recognition of revenue when it is realized and when a transaction has taken place (generally at the point of sale), and the recognition of expenses according to the matching principle (costs to revenues). Standard accounting principles further require that uncertainties and risks related to a company be reflected in its accounting reports and that, generally, anything that would be of interest to an informed investor should be fully disclosed in the financial statements.

ELEMENTS OF FINANCIAL STATEMENTS

The Financial Accounting Standards Board (FASB) has defined the following elements of financial statements of business enterprises: assets, liabilities, equity, revenues, expenses, gains, losses, investment by owners, distribution to owners, and comprehensive income. According to FASB, the elements of financial statements are the building blocks with which financial statements are constructed. These FASB definitions, articulated in its "Elements of Financial Statements of Business Enterprises," are as follows:

- **Assets** are probable future economic benefits obtained or controlled by a particular entity as a result of past transactions or events.

- **Comprehensive income** is the change in equity (net assets) of an entity during a period from transactions and other events and circumstances from nonowner sources. It includes all changes in equity during a period except those resulting from investments by owners and distributions to owners.

- **Distributions to owners** are decreases in net assets of a particular enterprise resulting from transferring assets, rendering services, or incurring liabilities to owners. Distributions to owners decrease ownership interest or equity in an enterprise.

- **Equity** is the residual interest in the assets of an entity that remains after deducting its liabilities. In a business entity, equity is the ownership interest.

- **Expenses** are outflows or other uses of assets or incurring of liabilities during a period from delivering or producing goods or rendering services, or carrying out other activities that constitute the entity's ongoing major or central operation.

- **Gains** are increases in equity (net assets) from peripheral or incidental transactions of an entity and from all other transactions and other events and circumstances affecting the entity during a period except those that result from revenues or investments by owner.

- **Investments by owners** are increases in net assets of a particular enterprise resulting from transfers to it from other entities of something of value to obtain or increase ownership interest (or equity) in it.

- **Liabilities** are probable future sacrifices of economic benefits arising from present obligations of a particular entity to transfer assets or provide services to other entities in the future as a result of past transactions or events.

- **Losses** are decreases in equity (net assets) from peripheral or incidental transactions of an entity and from all other transactions and other events and circumstances affecting the entity during a period except those that result from expenses or distributions to owners.

- **Revenues** are inflows or other enhancements of assets of an entity or settlement of its liabilities (or a combination of both) during a period from delivering or producing goods, rendering services, or other activities that constitute the entity's ongoing major or central operations.

SUBSEQUENT EVENTS

In accounting terminology, a subsequent event is an important event that occurs between the balance sheet date and the date of issuance of the annual report. Subsequent events must have a material effect on the financial statements. A "subsequent event" note must be issued with financial statements if the event (or events) is considered to be important enough that without such information the financial statement would be misleading if the event were not disclosed. The recognition and recording of these events often requires the professional judgment of an accountant or external auditor.

Events that effect the financial statements at the date of the balance sheet might reveal an unknown condition or provide additional information regarding estimates or judgments. These events must be reported by adjusting the financial statements to recognize the new evidence. Events that relate to conditions that did not exist on the balance sheet date but arose subsequent to that date do not require an adjustment to the financial statements. The effect of the event on the future period, however, may be of such importance that it should be disclosed in a footnote or elsewhere.

PERSONAL FINANCIAL STATEMENTS

The reporting entity of personal financial statements is an individual, a husband and wife, or a group of related individuals. Personal financial statements are often prepared to deal with obtaining bank loans, income tax planning, retirement planning, gift and estate planning, and the public disclosure of financial affairs.

For each reporting entity, a statement of financial position is required. The statement presents assets at estimated current values, liabilities at the lesser of the discounted amount of cash to be paid or the current cash settlement amount, and net worth. A provision should also be made for estimated income taxes on the differences between the estimated current value of assets. Comparative statements for one or more periods should be presented. A statement of changes in net worth is optional.

DEVELOPMENT STAGE COMPANIES

A company is considered to be a development stage company if substantially all of its efforts are devoted to establishing a new business and either of the following is present: 1) principal operations have not begun, or 2) principal operations have begun but revenue is insignificant. Activities of a development stage enterprise frequently include financial planning, raising capital, research and development, personnel recruiting and training, and market development.

A development stage company must follow generally accepted accounting principles applicable to operating enterprises in the preparation of financial statements. In its balance sheet, the company must report cumulative net losses separately in the equity section. In its income statement it must report cumulative revenues and expenses from the inception of the enterprise. Likewise, in its cash flow statement, it must report cumulative cash flows from the inception of the enterprise. Its statement of stockholders' equity should include the number of shares issued and the date of their issuance as well as the dollar amounts received. The statement should identify the entity as a development stage enterprise and describe the nature of development stage activities. During the first period of normal operations, the enterprise must disclose its former developmental stage status in the notes section of its financial statements.

FRAUDULENT FINANCIAL REPORTING

Fraudulent financial reporting is defined as intentional or reckless reporting, whether by act or by omission, that results in materially misleading financial statements. Fraudulent financial reporting can usually be traced to the existence of conditions in either the internal environment of the firm (e.g., inadequate internal control), or in the external environment (e.g., poor industry or overall business conditions). Excessive pressure on management, such as unrealistic profit or other performance goals, can also lead to fraudulent financial reporting.

The legal requirements for a publicly traded company when it comes to financial reporting are, not surprisingly, much more rigorous than for privately held firms. And they became even more rigorous in 2002 with the passage of the Sarbanes-Oxley Act. This legislation was passed in the wake of the stunning bankruptcy filing in 2001 by Enron, and subsequent revelations about fraudulent accounting practices within the company. Enron was only the first in a string of high-profile bankruptcies. Serious allegations of accounting fraud followed and extended beyond the bankrupt firms to their accounting firms. The legislature acted quickly to fortify financial reporting requirements and stem the decline in confidence that resulted from the wave of bankruptcies. Without confidence in the financial reports of publicly traded firms, no stock exchange can exist for long.

The Sarbanes-Oxley Act is a complex law that imposes heavy reporting requirements on all publicly traded companies. Meeting the requirements of this law has increased the workload of auditing firms. In particular, Section 404 of the Sarbanes-Oxley Act requires that a company's financial statements and annual report include an official write-up by management about the effectiveness of the company's internal controls. This section also requires that outside auditors attest to management's report on internal controls. An external audit is required in order to attest to the management report.

Private companies are not covered by the Sarbanes-Oxley Act. However, analysts suggest that even private firms should be aware of the law as it has influenced accounting practices and business expectations generally.

AUDITING

The preparation and presentation of a company's financial statements are the responsibility of the management of the company. Published financial statements may be audited by an independent certified public accountant. In the case of publicly traded firms, an audit is required by law. For private firms it is not, although banks and other lenders often require such an independent check as a part of lending agreements.

During an audit, the auditor conducts an examination of the accounting system, records, internal controls, and financial statements in accordance with generally accepted auditing standards. The auditor then expresses an opinion concerning the fairness of the financial statements in conformity with generally accepted accounting principles. Four standard opinions are possible:

1. Unqualified opinion—This opinion means that all materials were made available, found to be in order, and met all auditing requirements. This is the most favorable opinion that can be rendered by an external auditor about a company's operations and records. In some cases, a company may receive an unqualified opinion with explanatory language added. Circumstances may require that the auditor add an explanatory paragraph to his or her report. When this is done the opinion is prefaced with the term, "explanatory language added."

2. Qualified opinion—This type of opinion is used for instances in which most of the company's financial materials were in order, with the exception of a certain account or transaction.

3. Adverse opinion—An adverse opinion states that the financial statements do not accurately or completely represent the company's financial position, results of operations, or cash flows in conformity with generally accepted accounting principles. Such an opinion is obviously not good news for the business being audited.

4. Disclaimer of opinion—A disclaimer of opinion states that the auditor does not express an opinion on the financial statements, generally because he or she feels that the company did not present sufficient information. Again, this opinion casts an unfavorable light on the business being audited.

The auditor's standard opinion typically includes the following statements, among others:

The financial statements are the responsibility of the company's management; the audit was conducted according to generally accepted auditing standards; the audit was planned and performed to obtain reasonable assurance that the statements are free of material misstatements, and the audit provided a reasonable basis for an expression of an opinion concerning the fair presentation of the audit. The audit report is then signed by the auditor and a principal of the firm and dated.

SEE ALSO *Annual Report; Audits, External; Balance Sheets; Cash Flow Statements; Income Statements*

BIBLIOGRAPHY

"Adjust Financial Statements to Better Present Your Company." *Business Owner.* May-June 1999.

Atrill, Peter. *Accounting and Finance for Nonspecialists.* Prentice Hall, 1997.

Hey-Cunningham, David. *Financial Statements Demystified.* Allen & Unwin, 2002.

Kwok, Benny K.B. *Accounting Irregularities in Financial Statements.* Gower Publishing, Ltd., 2005.

Stittle, John *Annual Reports.* Gower Publishing Ltd., 2004.

Taulli, Tom. *The Edgar Online Guide to Decoding Financial Statements.* J. Ross Publishing, 2004.

Taylor, Peter. *Book-Keeping & Accounting for Small Business.* Business & Economics, 2003.

Hillstrom, Northern Lights
updated by Magee, ECDI

FIREWALLS

A firewall is a computer security device that is situated between a small business's internal network and the Internet. It can work at either the software or the hardware level to prevent unwanted outside access to the company's computer system. Matthew Sarrel, writing for *PC Magazine,* provided the following definition: "A firewall must contain a stateful packet inspection (SPI) engine, which examines the content of packets and grants access to your network only if the traffic appears legitimate. Firewalls can also block inappropriate inbound and outbound traffic based on rules or filters. Internet Protocol (IP) filtering, for example, can block employees behind the firewall from accessing or receiving mail from specific IP addresses. Also, traffic can be blocked based on your network card's unique identifier, called a MAC (media access control) address. Many firewalls can control traffic using keyword and domain filters, letting you block traffic to specific sites. More sophisticated firewalls let you create complex rules." The firewall thus basically acts as a guard, identifying each packet of information before it is allowed to pass through. It is one of the most effective forms of protection yet developed against hackers operating on the Internet. A "stateful" engine, by the way, is electronics parlance for software able to remember its earlier states, usually by saving values in memory.

Ideally, a firewall will detect intruders, block them from entering the company's computer network, notify the system administrator, record information about the source of the attempted break-in, and produce reports to help authorities track down the culprits. Since firewalls can be set to monitor both incoming and outgoing Internet traffic, they can also be used to prevent employees from accessing games, newsgroups, or adult sites on the Internet.

Despite the potential advantages of firewalls, however, some small businesses remain unprotected. Owners sometimes believe that firewalls are too expensive or demand too much technical expertise. Others believe that no hacker would be interested in the information contained on their computers. Wrong! Intruders often seek unprotected computers to serve as unknowing transmitters for spam mail. Later the company may discover this when many sites that *have* protected themselves refuse the company's own mail. Many hackers also seek to disrupt companies' operations just for the hell of it. A small business may lose valuable information or cause itself no end of hassle by failing to erect a firewall.

EVALUATING THE NEED FOR A FIREWALL

Any computer connected to the Internet is vulnerable to hackers. Networked computers require more robust protection than free-standing machines. The free-standing machine connected to the Internet may be sufficiently protected by software arrangements—and the protection provided to its e-mail by the Internet portal operator.

Although firewalls have a number of potential advantages, they do not provide foolproof protection and also have some potential disadvantages. As Steffano Korper and Juanita Ellis wrote in *The E-Commerce Book,* firewalls cannot protect against computer viruses or against data theft by authorized users of a company's computer network. In addition, firewalls have some expense. Ideally they will be installed by a service organization.

Some small businesses avoid the need for a firewall by using a simple security measure known as "air gapping." This means that the company's computer network is kept completely separate from the Internet. One method of air gapping involves accessing the Internet only from a standalone computer not connected to the internal network; that machine, of course, will not hold any valuable or confidential information. This approach may be cheap but will not serve an organization that actively uses the Internet in its business operations. Another method involves only running Web servers that outsiders can reach on a secure system belonging to an Internet Service Provider (ISP).

TYPES OF FIREWALL PROTECTION

The hardware security systems that act as firewalls vary in configuration and sophistication. One relatively simple device involves using a router—which controls the sending and receiving of messages—equipped with packet filters to examine the messages. This system can be configured to block traffic to or from certain Internet destinations or all unknown destinations. This type of security system is relatively inexpensive and easy to set up, but it also offers only minimal protection from hackers. A slightly more sophisticated and secure system is a proxy server. A proxy server works by stopping all incoming and outgoing traffic for inspection before forwarding it. One advantage of this type of system is that it can create a log of all messages sent and received. Proxy servers can be difficult to install, however, and can also make Internet use less convenient for employees.

Both routers and proxy servers have one major disadvantage in terms of the security they provide. These systems base their evaluation and approval of messages on the header, which lists the sender, recipient, source, and destination. But hackers can easily create false headers to fool the filtering systems. One way to overcome this problem is through type enforcement, which also scans the content of messages. Another system, already mentioned, is the stateful inspection firewall; it uses an even more sophisticated method of verifying the sources of messages. Finally, it is possible to use any combination of routers, filters, proxy servers, and firewalls to create a layered security system. A large company like Motorola, for example, might place a firewall at the outside of the system, and connect it to a gateway computer, and then connect that machine to a router with packet filters, and finally connect the router to the internal computer network.

TIPS ON BUYING A FIREWALL

Before purchasing a firewall, a small business owner should consider what type of information must be protected, and how severe the consequences of an attack might be. These factors will help determine how much money and time the company should spend on the firewall purchase. It is important to remember that the true costs of a firewall include installation and setup, training, maintenance, and regular updates. In addition, understanding the distinctions between different products—and installing the product properly—requires technical expertise and may involve hiring an outside computer expert.

Firewall protection comes in a wide variety of forms. Some basic firewall software is available for free on the World Wide Web. These simple packages can be downloaded and installed fairly easily, but they provide fewer options for users and do not offer technical support in case of problems. Many other software solutions are available at retail computer stores or via mail order. These firewalls are also easy to install and often feature technical support. The most sophisticated firewalls are complete hardware systems that can cost thousands of dollars. These systems usually include a number of additional features. For example, they often can be used as routers for directing traffic among computers in a network. Some of the top firewall vendors include Ascend, Cisco, Sterling Commerce, CyberGuard, LanOptics, and Microsoft.

Besides meeting the small business's basic computer security needs, a firewall should work with your hardware and software, as well as that used by your ISP. It also should not slow down your Internet connection too noticeably. The most versatile products conform to the Open Platform for Secure Enterprise Connectivity (OPSEC), a standard that is supported by many top vendors and that makes it easier to combine security products from different sources.

When evaluating possible firewalls, it may be helpful to look for product reviews in computer magazines or on the World Wide Web. Once the purchase decision has been made and the firewall is up and running, it is important to test the product. Many firewalls are breached by hackers due to faulty installation or configuration. In fact, Emery recommends having a team of technically minded employees try to break into the system from outside. This exercise may help the internal

experts understand the strengths and limitations of the firewall, as well as how it fits into the context of the small business's overall computer security policy.

SEE ALSO *Internet Security*

BIBLIOGRAPHY

Cert Coordination Center. Carnegie Mellon Software Engineering Institute. Available from http://www.cert.org. Retrieved on 29 April 2006.

Korper, Steffano, and Juanita Ellis. *The E-Commerce Book: Building the E-Empire.* Academic Press, 2000.

Passmore, David. "Inside-Out Security. *Business Communications Review.* March 2006.

Rae-Dupree, Janet. "Risky Business Online." *U.S. News & World Report.* 4 September 2000.

Sarrel, Matthew D. "Business Body Armor: All sorts of enemy combatants want to penetrate your network, but you can turn attacks aside with the right combo of hardware and tactics." *PC Magazine.* 7 March 2006.

Smith, Tim. "Firewalls Explained." *Computer Act!ve.* 2 February 2006.

Hillstrom, Northern Lights
updated by Magee, ECDI

FISCAL YEAR

A fiscal year is any 52-week period used consistently by an organization for the purposes of financial reporting and policy setting. It may or may not correspond with the typical calendar year of January to December. A company may choose to designate a different time period as its fiscal year as a way of recognizing seasonal variations in its business, as a method of minimizing its tax burden, or for any number of other reasons.

Fiscal years are used by companies as the basis on which to report financial information. To be useful, information must reach decision makers frequently and promptly. To provide this timely information, accounting systems are designed to produce periodic reports at regular intervals. As a result, the accounting process is based on the time period principle.

According to this principle, an organization's activities are identified with specific time periods, such as a month, a three-month quarter, or a year. Then, financial statements are prepared for each reporting period. The time periods covered by the reports are called accounting periods. Most organizations use one year as their primary accounting period and prepare annual financial statements. However, nearly all organizations also prepare interim financial reports that cover one or three months of activity.

HOW FISCAL YEAR PERIODS ARE DETERMINED

The annual reporting period or company's fiscal year is not always the same as the calendar year ending December 31. In fact, an organization can adopt a fiscal year consisting of any 12 consecutive months. An acceptable variation of this rule is to adopt an annual reporting period of 52 weeks.

Companies that do not experience much seasonal variation in sales volume within the year often choose the calendar year as their fiscal year. On the other hand, companies that experience major seasonal variations in sales often choose a fiscal year that corresponds to their natural business year. The natural business year ends when sales activities are at their lowest point during the year. For example, the natural business year for retail merchants ends around January 31, after the Christmas holidays and the January pre-inventory selling seasons. As a result, retailers often start their fiscal year on February 1st each year.

The federal budget of the U.S. Government extends from October 1, 2000, to September 30, 2001. This period encompasses the government's fiscal year. In another example, the State of Texas has designated a fiscal year that extends from September 1, 2000, through August 31, 2001. Texas uses this fiscal year for financial reporting and for establishing basic policies, such as those setting the base fares for travel on state business.

BIBLIOGRAPHY

Larson, Kermit D. *Fundamental Accounting Principles.* McGraw-Hill, 1997.

Pinson, Linda. *Keeping the Books: Basic Record Keeping and Accounting for Successful Small Business.* Business & Economics, 2004.

Hillstrom, Northern Lights
updated by Magee, ECDI

FIXED AND VARIABLE EXPENSES

Business expenses are categorized in two ways: fixed expenses and variable expenses. Fixed expenses or costs are those that do not fluctuate with changes in production level or sales volume. They include such expenses as rent, insurance, dues and subscriptions, equipment leases, payments on loans, depreciation, management salaries, and advertising. Variable costs are those that respond directly and proportionately to changes in activity level or volume, such as raw materials, hourly production wages, sales commissions, inventory, packaging supplies, and shipping costs.

Bookkeeping and accounting systems track activities by assigning each transaction to a particular account—phones, travel expense, materials purchase, etc... The accounts are all given a number of defining attributes and among those is a designation of fixed expense or variable expense. This is important because most business planning activities require that expenses be easily segregated into these two categories. Those managing businesses soon learn how crucial it is to track expenses in a way that helps to make planning, forecasting and bidding as easy as possible.

Although fixed costs do not vary with changes in production or sales volume, they may change over time. As a result, fixed costs are sometimes called period costs. Some fixed costs are incurred at the discretion of a company's management, such as advertising and promotional expense, while others are not. It is important to remember that all non-discretionary fixed costs will be incurred even if production or sales volume falls to zero. Although production and sales volume are the main factors determining the level of variable costs incurred by a company, these costs also may fluctuate in relation to other factors, such as changes in suppliers' prices or seasonal promotional efforts. Some expenses may have both fixed and variable elements. For example, a company may pay a sales person a monthly salary (a fixed cost) plus a percentage commission for every unit sold above a certain level (a variable cost).

It is important to understand the behavior of the different types of expenses as production or sales volume increases. Total fixed costs remain unchanged as volume increases, while fixed costs per unit decline. For example, if a bicycle business had total fixed costs of $1,000 and only produced one bike, then the full $1,000 in fixed costs must be applied to that bike. On the other hand, if the same business produced 10 bikes, then the fixed costs per unit decline to $100. Variable costs behave differently. Total variable costs increase proportionately as volume increases, while variable costs per unit remain unchanged. For example, if the bicycle company incurred variable costs of $200 per unit, total variable costs would be $200 if only one bike was produced and $2,000 if 10 bikes were produced. However, variable costs applied per unit would be $200 for both the first and the tenth bike. The company's total costs are a combination of the fixed and variable costs. If the bicycle company produced 10 bikes, its total costs would be $1,000 fixed plus $2,000 variable equals $3,000, or $300 per unit.

It is very important for small business owners to understand how their various costs respond to changes in the volume of goods or services produced. The breakdown of a company's underlying expenses determines the profitable price level for its products or services, as well as many aspects of its overall business strategy. A small business owner can use a knowledge of fixed and variable expenses to determine the company's break-even point (the number of units or dollars at which total revenues equal total costs, so the company breaks even), and in making decisions related to pricing goods and services.

Economies of scale are another area of business that can only be understood within the framework of fixed and variable expenses. Economies of scale are possible because in most production operations the fixed costs are not related to production volume; variable costs are. Large production runs therefore "absorb" more of the fixed costs. An example is a printing run. Setting up the run requires burning a plate after a photographic process, mounting the plate on the printing press, adjusting ink flow, and running five or six pages to make sure everything is correctly set up. The cost of setting up will be the same whether the printer produces one copy or 10,000. If the set-up cost is $55 and the printer produces 500 copies, each copy will carry 11 cents worth of the set-up cost—the fixed costs. But if 10,000 pages are printed, each page carries only 0.55 cents of set-up cost. The reduction in cost per unit is an economy due to scale.

Determining the fixed and variable expenses is the first step in performing a break-even analysis. The number of units needed to break even = fixed costs / (price - variable costs per unit). This equation provides a small business owner with a great deal of valuable information by itself, and it can also be changed to answer a number of important questions, like whether a planned expansion will be profitable. Knowing how to work with information about fixed and variable expenses can be particularly helpful for individuals who are considering buying a small business. Many businesses, particularly franchises, are reluctant to give out information about projected profits, but will provide information about costs and unit prices. The potential purchaser can then use this information to calculate the number of units and the dollar volume that would be needed to make a profit, and determine whether these numbers seem realistic.

SEE ALSO *Accounting; Bookkeeping; Cost-Benefit Analysis; Economies of Scale*

BIBLIOGRAPHY
Bannester, Anthony. *Bookkeeping and Accounting for Small Business.* Straighforward Co. Ltd., April 2004.

Pinson, Linda. *Keeping the Books.* Dearborn Trade Publishing, 2004.

Ragan, Robert C. *Step-By-Step Bookkeeping.* Sterling Publishing Company, Inc., 2001.

Rohr, Ellen. "The Best Bookkeeper." *Reefing Contractor.* March 2005.

Taylor, Peter. *Book-Keeping and Accounting for the Small Business.* How To Books, Ltd., 2003.

Hillstrom, Northern Lights
updated by Magee, ECDI

FLEXIBLE BENEFIT PLANS

Flexible benefit plans allow employees to choose the benefits they want or need from a package of programs offered by an employer. Flexible benefit plans may include health insurance, retirement benefits such as 401(k) plans, and reimbursement accounts that employees can use to pay for out-of-pocket health or dependent care expenses. In a flexible benefit plan, employees contribute to the cost of these benefits through a payroll deduction of their before-tax income, reducing the employer's contribution. In addition, the ability to pay for benefits with pre-tax income lowers an employee's taxable income while raising the amount of their take-home pay — an added "benefit." In the short term, companies obviously benefit from sharing costs with employees. But a business may also choose to cap its future contributions to benefits by passing along increased costs to employees through these plans.

Flexible benefit plans have become increasingly popular with employers. Health and child-care costs have risen tremendously over the past several decades. This has had a major effect on a business' ability to offer benefits, yet most employees still expect to receive benefits as a result of employment. Small businesses in particular are often unable to take advantage of the economies of scale that larger companies can use to their advantage in securing benefits programs. These companies, as well as larger ones, have subsequently sought palatable means by which their employees can contribute to the cost of benefits. One option is a flexible benefit plan. Indeed, many businesses have begun to offer flexible benefits in order to retain a competitive benefits package for employees. There are several types of flexible benefit plans, including cafeteria plans and flexible spending accounts.

CAFETERIA PLANS

A type of flexible benefit plan known as a cafeteria plan enables employees to choose between receiving some or all of an employer's nontaxable benefits, or receiving cash or other taxable benefits such as stock. These plans were established by the Revenue Act of 1978 and are regulated by Section 125 of the Internal Revenue Code. Only certain benefits can be offered under a cafeteria plan, though employers may offer any or all of these benefits. These include: health and group life insurance as well as medical reimbursement plans for non-insured expenses; disability, dental, and vision coverage; day care or elder care; 401(k) plans; and vacation days. Tuition assistance and other fringe benefits are exempt from the plans, even if they are not taxable. Funding for cafeteria plans may come from the employer, employee or both. Often, the employee receives a spending credit, with which he or she may choose to "buy" benefits from a list of options such as health insurance, life insurance, etc. The benefits themselves may be provided in cash or via actual coverage.

In order to ensure these plans are fair to all employees and to limit the number of changes employees can make to their plan, the IRS has set up a number of restrictions. For example, employees are unable to carry over unused credits or benefits to the next plan year. In addition, employers need to be sure that no more than 25 percent of the tax-favored benefits go to "highly compensated" employees. These employees could be officers earning above a certain salary range or those who have a percentage of ownership in the company greater than 1 percent (if they earn over $150,000) or greater than 5 percent (for others).

FLEXIBLE SPENDING ACCOUNTS

A flexible spending account (FSA) is a tax-deferred savings account established by an employer to help employees meet certain medical and dependent-care expenses that are not covered under the employer's insurance plan. FSAs allow employees to contribute pre-tax dollars to an account set up by their employer. They can later withdraw these funds tax-free to pay for qualified health insurance premiums, out-of-pocket medical costs, day care provider fees, or private pre-school and kindergarten expenses.

There are three main types of FSAs. First, premium-only plans, which allow employees to set aside funds to pay medical and life insurance premiums. Second, unreimbursed medical expense plans, which allow employees to set aside money for projected health care expenses not covered by insurance. Third, dependent care reimbursement plans, which allow employees to set aside money for day care of dependent children. Employees must prove they have a legitimate expense in order to be reimbursed from these accounts. Invoices from health care professionals or day care facilities would serve this purpose. However, employees must also prove that the claim has not been reimbursed by other coverage, such as a spouse's insurance. Funds placed in reimbursement accounts generally must be used during the calendar year in which they were contributed; otherwise, the employee forfeits the funds. For this reason, participating in a flexible spending account requires careful planning on the part of both employees and employers.

SET-UP AND TAX IMPLICATIONS

A small business can manage its own flexible benefit plan with the proper software. Since these plans are under the watchful eye of the IRS, it is important that record keeping and benefit payments be accurate and timely. Many companies hire an outside firm to manage their plan, which reduces internal headaches but at a higher cost to the company. Some insurance companies also provide administrative services for flexible plans.

Employer contributions to cafeteria plans are tax deductible for the employer and are not subject to income tax for the employee. The contributions are taken before taxes, and therefore are not subject to Social Security (FICA) or federal unemployment (FUTA) taxes unless the monies are contributed to 401(k) plans. Many states follow the same guidelines regarding state taxes but companies should check with their accountant or the state's tax department to be sure.

Obviously, flexible benefit plans are not without their drawbacks. But for small businesses looking to attract and retain key personnel with competitive benefit packages while keeping their own costs low, they can be an attractive alternative to standard benefit plans. Further information about setting up and administering flexible benefit plans is available from the Employee Benefits Institute of America at www.ebia.com/cafeteria.html.

SEE ALSO *Employee Benefits*

BIBLIOGRAPHY
"Flex Plan Enrollment Rules Eased." *Employee Benefit News.* 1 February 2001.

Henricks, Mark. "Take Your Pick: Want to keep health-care costs low and employees happy in today's economy?" *Entrepreneur.* May 2003.

Gould, Jay. "Flexible Spending Accounts Benefit Both Employees, Employers." *San Antonio Business Journal.* 24 November 2000.

"How to Set Up a Cafeteria Plan." *Capital District Business Review.* 11 December 2000.

Hunt, Kelly A. "Survey Finds Flexible Benefits on the Rise, Particularly Among Public Employers." *Government Finance Review.* August 1997.

"Let's Be Flexible." *Journal of Accountancy.* March 1998.

Rosen, Lori. *HR Networking.* CCH Incorporated, 2004.

Hillstrom, Northern Lights
updated by Magee, ECDI

FLEXIBLE SPENDING ACCOUNT (FSA)

A flexible spending account (FSA) is a tax-deferred savings account established by an employer to help employees meet certain medical and dependent-care expenses that are not covered under the employer's insurance plan. Established under Section 125 of the Internal Revenue Code, FSAs were once known as medical Individual Retirement Accounts (IRAs). FSAs allow employees to contribute pre-tax dollars to an account set up by their employer. They can later withdraw these funds tax-free to pay for qualified health insurance premiums, out-of-pocket medical costs, day care provider fees, or private pre-school and kindergarten expenses.

FSAs provide an attractive benefit for many employees, and they also offer tax savings for both employees and employers. As the cost of providing health insurance to employees has risen rapidly over the last decade, many companies have greatly increased the employee portion of the insurance premium. Co-pays and deductibles have increased as well in an attempt to manage the overall premium cost. The use of a health care FSA is one way in which employers may help their employees to self-fund with tax-free dollars the growing costs that they are asked to bear for their partial company-funded health insurance.

TAX BENEFITS OF FSAs

Internal Revenue Service guidelines allow employees to make contributions to employer-sponsored FSAs out of pre-tax income. Thus employees save federal and state income taxes, as well as the employee portion of Social Security taxes, on the amount they authorize their employer to withdraw from their paychecks and place in the FSA each year. By reducing their taxable income, employees can increase their take-home pay. For example, say that an employee of ABC Company whose annual salary was $50,000 contributed $5,000 to an FSA in 2000. This action would reduce the employee's taxable income to $45,000. If the employee typically paid taxes amounting to 30 percent of her income, she would save $1,500 in taxes for 2000. Furthermore, the money contributed to an FSA is not taxable for the employee when it is withdrawn, provided it is used to pay for qualified medical or dependent-care expenses.

Employers also receive a tax benefit by establishing flexible spending accounts. Employers are not required to pay the employer portion of the Social Security tax—which amounts to 7.65 percent of each employee's taxable income—on employee contributions to FSAs. In effect, payroll taxes are reduced by 7.65 percent of the total employee contributions to the FSA.

In the earlier example, say that ABC Company is a small business with 10 employees and an annual payroll of $500,000. Without the tax advantage of an FSA, the company would owe Social Security taxes of 7.65 percent on its total payroll of $500,000, or $38,250, in 2000. But if, in a most optimistic scenario, all 10 employees each contributed the maximum allowable contribution of $5,000, the company's taxable payroll would be reduced by $50,000, and the company would save $3,825 in taxes for the year. Combined with the tax savings of $1,500 per employee, the total tax reduction for the company and its workers resulting from the FSA would be $18,825 for the year.

In reality, a company can expect a participation rate closer to 20 percent. In a 2005 *Business Insurance* article entitled "Grace Period Complicates FSAs," author Jerry Geisel states that "Currently, about 15 percent of eligible employees contribute to health care FSAs, with employees contributing on average between $1,100 and $1,200 a year."

One potential reason for low participation rates has to do with the "use it or loss it" rule limiting the ability to cumulate funds in an FSA account. Money deposited into an FSA account is forfeit if not used in the benefit year—forfeit by the employee and received back by the company. Until 2005, when the IRS issued an FSA grace period amendment, all funds contributed to an FSA had to be used within one year. The dates for that year were defined as the company's benefit plan year, a period which may or may not correspond with the calendar year. As of 2005, a company may amend its FSA Plan document to incorporate a two and one half-month grace period. This allows an employee to use the first two and half months of the next year to use up his or her FSA balance from the prior year. Anything not used within this period would be forfeit. Proponents of this new grace period hope that it will reduce concerns about losing money and encourage participation in FSA plans.

LEGAL REQUIREMENTS FOR FSAs

Employers are required to follow the guidelines established in Section 125 of the Internal Revenue Code when setting up an FSA. The first step involves preparing a plan document that states the conditions for eligibility, the benefits provided, and the rules that apply to implementation of the FSA. The employer must distribute these rules to eligible employees and follow them consistently. Employers are also required to file Form 5500 with the U.S. Department of Labor each year, as well as complete a series of nondiscrimination tests outlined by the IRS.

Each part of the process of implementing and administering an FSA plan for employees involves legal requirements. These requirements apply to the plan document, summary plan description, nondiscrimination testing, government filings, claims administration, and plan updates. Since compliance with these requirements tends to be complex, and since the IRS imposes serious penalties for noncompliance, most companies outsource FSA administration to a third party. The costs of outsourcing these administrative tasks are high. Many experts say that such costs may be off-set by the tax saving that FSA plans generate along with the savings associated with any funds forfeit by participants.

Any employer considering an FSA for her firm must be careful to plan for the potential cash flow needs that may be generated by early disbursements. If an employee agrees to have $2,500 withheld from his paychecks for deposit into his FSA account during the year, those funds must be available to him as needed, which may be within the first month of the year. Since the money going into his account will be collected over a twelve-month period, the company must have cash reserves set aside to address cash disbursements that occur prior to collections.

USING FSAs FOR DEPENDENT CARE EXPENSES

Employers can set up FSAs in a number of ways, depending on what options their employees would find most valuable. For example, FSAs can cover only health insurance premiums, or they can only be used to reimburse medical expenses not otherwise covered by the employer's health insurance plan. FSAs can also cover only dependent care expenses, or they can offer a full plate of benefits including both health care and dependent care.

Dependent care reimbursement FSAs have become increasingly common in recent years. Employees with children can use these accounts to cover day care and educational expenses up to and including private kindergarten.

With a dependent care FSA, employees can begin making pre-tax contributions when a child is born and continue until the child completes kindergarten. The maximum contribution is $5,000 annually per child. The employee decides how much to contribute based on his or her anticipated child-care expenses for each year. The employer deducts that amount in installments from the employee's gross pay each pay period, and sets the money aside in an FSA. The employee's income taxes are calculated based on his or her remaining pay, which reduces taxable income. The employee can withdraw money from the FSA tax-free to make tuition payments. In most cases, employees are required to submit proof that their deductions are put toward qualifying dependent care expenses.

SEE ALSO *Child-Care; Employee Benefits; Health Insurance Options*

BIBLIOGRAPHY

Geisel, Jerry. "Grace Period Complicates FSAs." *Business Insurance.* 22 August 2005.

Gould, Jay. "Flexible Spending Accounts Benefit Both Employees, Employers." *San Antonio Business Journal.* 24 November 2000.

"How Tax Savings Play Out." *Inc.* March 2000.

"Letting Easy Money Slip Away." *Work & Family Newsbrief.* November 2005.

"One-Third of Employers to Extend FSA Deadlines." *Managing Benefits Plans.* October 2005.

Seiden, Richard. "IRS Offers 'Use It or Lose It' Grace Period for Flexible Spending Accounts." *San Fernando Valley Business Journal.* 29 August 2005.

"Some Good News About Health Care Flexible-Spending Accounts." *Managing Benefits Plans.* February 2006.

Hillstrom, Northern Lights
updated by Magee, ECDI

FLEXIBLE WORK ARRANGEMENTS

Flexible work programs are work arrangements wherein employees are given greater scheduling freedom in how they fulfill the obligations of their positions. The most commonplace of these programs is flextime, which gives workers far greater leeway in terms of the time when they begin and end work, provided they put in the total number of hours required by the employer. Other common flexible working arrangements involve telecommuting, job-sharing, and compressed work weeks.

Supporters of flexible work programs hail them as important recognition of the difficulties that many employees have in balancing their family obligations and their work duties, and they note that such programs can make a company more attractive to prospective employees. Critics contend, however, that while flexible employment initiatives do attempt to redress some long-time inequities in the work life-family life balance, ill-considered plans can have a deleterious impact on a company.

PRIMARY FLEXIBLE WORK PROGRAMS

Flexible work arrangements can take any number of forms, from basic flextime programs to innovative child- and elder-care programs.

- Flextime—This is a system wherein employees choose their starting and quitting times from a range of available hours. These periods are usually at either end of a "core" time during which most company business takes place. Formerly regarded as a rare, cutting-edge workplace arrangement, flextime is now commonly practiced in a wide variety of industries.

- Compressed Work Week—Under this arrangement, the standard work week is compressed into fewer than five days. The most common incarnation of the compressed work week is one of four 10-hour days. Other options include three 12-hour days or arrangements in which employees work 9- or 10-hour days over two weeks and are compensated with an extra day or two of time off during that time.

- Flexplace—This term encompasses various arrangements in which an employee works from home or some other non-office location. Telecommuting is the most commonly practiced example of this type of flexible employment.

- Job Sharing—Under these arrangements, two people voluntarily share the duties and responsibilities of one full-time position, with both salary and benefits of that position prorated between the two individuals.

- Work Sharing—These programs are increasingly used by companies that wish to avoid layoffs. It allows businesses to temporarily reduce hours and salary for a portion of their workforce while maintaining the number of employees.

- Expanded Leave—This option gives employees greater flexibility in terms of requesting extended periods of time away from work without losing their rights as employees. Expanded leave, which can be granted on either a paid or unpaid basis, is used for a variety of reasons, including sabbaticals, education, community service, family problems, and medical care (the latter two reasons are now largely covered by the terms of the Family and Medical Leave Act).

- Phased Retirement—Under these arrangements, the employee and employer agree to a schedule wherein the employee's full-time work commitments are gradually reduced over a period of months or years.

- Partial Retirement—These programs allow older employees to continue working on a part time basis, with no established end date.

- Work and Family Programs—These programs are still relatively rare, although some larger companies have reported good results with pilot initiatives in this area. These programs are ones in which employers provide some degree of assistance to their employees in the realms of child-care and elder-care. The best-known of these programs are in-house facilities providing care for the children of employees, but even basic flex-time programs can ease child-care logistics for employees.

ADVANTAGES OF FLEXIBLE WORK PROGRAMS

Defenders of flexible work initiatives point to the competitive advantages that such programs bring to companies that offer these sorts of programs. Perhaps the single most cited reason for introducing a flexible work environment is employee retention. Indeed, many businesses contend that the recent trend toward flextime and other programs has made it necessary for them to introduce their own programs or risk losing valued employees. "Another business argument for flexible work arrangements is that they allow companies to match the peaks and valleys of activity," wrote Elizabeth Sheley in *HRMagazine*. "More organizations have shifted their focus to how potential changes in schedule will affect the product. Reduced absenteeism, though often overlooked, is also a legitimate business rationale; flexible options not only strengthen commitment, but also give employees more time to handle the very situations that sometimes lead to absenteeism."

Proponents also note that, in many respects, flexible work programs provide a way for businesses to increase employee loyalty without resorting to making fundamental changes in their operations. Indeed, Sheley observed that "the most popular flexible work options are those that involve the least change. Flex-time and compressed work weeks, for example, call for the same number of hours, at the same workplace, as in traditional work arrangements."

In addition, some supporters of flexible work arrangements argue that such programs can actually have a positive impact on the productivity of employees. They contend that employees who are better able to attend to family needs through flex-time are more likely to be contented and productive, while good employees who telecommute may get even more work done if they are freed up from office interruptions.

Business can also use flexible programs to address institutional problems. For instance, a small- or mid-sized business that is crammed into a small facility or office may want to explore telecommuting programs in order to relieve the situation without resorting to an expensive relocation or expansion. Finally, proponents say the flexible work programs can be beneficial to companies by enhancing their public image and expanding the number of hours during which customers can be serviced.

DISADVANTAGES OF FLEXIBLE WORK PROGRAMS

Flexible work programs have many apparent advantages, but critics point out that ill-conceived programs can have a negative impact on businesses, and they add that even good programs often present challenges that a business has to address.

First of all, business owners and managers need to recognize that flexible work arrangements are not always appropriate for all people, jobs, or industries. Telecommuting and other "flexplace" arrangements, for example, can be disastrous (or at the very least a productivity drain) if used by employees who are unwilling or unable to put in a full day of work amid the non-work temptations (television, pleasure reading, housecleaning, etc.) of a home setting. Other companies, meanwhile, find that employees "flex" in and out of the business at such different hours that overhead costs increase, customer service suffers (i.e., no one comes in until 9:30 a.m., a state of affairs that forces customers and vendors to cool their heels until then), and manufacturing output suffers. This latter factor makes flex-time a difficult fit for many manufacturing facilities. In a manufacturing setting, many of the factory operations depend on a single set of operational hours across operations. When one is dealing with a firm the uses a work-cell team manufacturing concept, flex-time is not an option.

Critics also contend that flex programs often leave managers in exceedingly difficult situations. "Far too often, flex is embraced ... for its 'family-friendly' aspects long before the corporate support needed to manage it takes root," wrote Martha H. Peak in *Management Review.* "In these companies, flex policies are outlined in the employee manual but implementation is left up to individual managers. Then, when managers try to implement these programs, they discover that to be fair, flex requires them to treat different employees differently."

Finally, many observers argue that businesses launch flexible work plans without adequate preparation. "I know that flex is a basic element of family-friendly and that family-friendly is a requisite for competitive companies," stated Peak. "But it takes more than a statement in the policy manual to institutionalize flex. It takes new methodologies to measure job success and investment in technologies to keep employees in constant communication."

INSTITUTING A FLEXIBLE WORK ENVIRONMENT

Business experts and companies that have instituted flexible work programs offer a variety of recommendations to businesses that are pondering a move to a flexible work environment.

Research Research the pros and cons of instituting a flexible work program in your company. Every company's needs and operating environment are different; just because a flex program worked for a neighboring

business, that does not necessarily mean that it will work for your company. Conversely, a program that fails in another firm may work in yours. Detailed research into the needs and pressures of both the operations and the employees of each business, then, is a necessary component of any decision. So is an honest assessment of the qualities of the business's work force.

A company that is blessed with a work force of dedicated and conscientious employees is far more likely to be productive in a flex environment than is one that is saddled with a heavy sprinkling of unmotivated employees. A thorough and honest assessment of a company's existing workforce as well as future labor needs is important in determining whether a flexible work program is likely to succeed for that company.

Guidelines Create guidelines and systems of flex program administration that: 1) address all business needs, and 2) stand up to tests of fairness and comprehensiveness. The process used to create guidelines for a flexible work program should include steps to ensure that new policies are compatible with existing company objectives. Issues like eligibility, application processes, reversibility, and changes to employee status should be plainly addressed. Finally, companies should formalize guidelines to head off complaints about favoritism or unfair treatment. Because a balanced and equitable treatment of all employees is important, the terminology used in the formal guidelines should be as general as possible—family obligations may be used instead of child-care obligations, for example.

Training Employees should be educated about policies and feel comfortable using them. This can only happen if the company actively promotes the program. Employees need to know that participation in such initiatives will not hurt their career. Indeed, *HRMagazine* noted that a mid-1990s report by the Catalyst research organization indicated that this can be a significant deterrent: "Many of the options for flexible scheduling are perceived as being bad for one's career by management and by co-workers who have more traditional working arrangements. A job-share partner or part-time employee cannot be as committed, the thinking goes. A positive experience with less than full-time work depends on the cultural values of the employee's organization. In some organizations, people who have taken less traditional schedules have been perceived as committing career suicide."

Employees are not the only workers who need to be reassured. Companies instituting flex work plans must also develop resource materials and training programs for managers. In fact, in many respects, managers of personnel and projects are the people who must make the biggest adjustment to a flexible work environment. "Workplace flexibility requires managers to develop a new set of skills," wrote Sheley. "Managers used to manage by sight, and defined work by hours on site. If a worker was in the office for eight hours, the boss assumed that person did eight hours of work." With flex-time and other developments, however, managers need to develop new skills that emphasize work flow and productivity. Managers and employees will need to be flexible themselves in order to make these arrangement successful.

Control Ultimately, a flexible work program is only worth keeping if it benefits your company's financial, strategic, and production goals. A key to making sure that those needs are met is to maintain control of the program. Employees and work teams can be very helpful in shaping flexible work guidelines, but business owners and managers should be wary of handing over too much control. Indeed, they need to make sure that business considerations remain paramount in any discussion of flex-time and other options, and that ultimate control over flexible work programs rests with them. Dysfunctional work teams, for example, will reduce flex-time to a shambles if they are left to institute and supervise it themselves.

Evaluation Businesses should evaluate their flex work programs on a regular basis. Too many businesses introduce workplace flexibility programs that are flawed, but rather than review the program and make the necessary corrections, they throw up their arms and ask their personnel (managers and eligible employees alike) to reshape their responsibilities, priorities, and planning to match the flawed program. Other companies launch good programs that lose their effectiveness over time because of neglect. Instead, business managers and owners need to practice continuous improvement in their workplace flexibility programs, just as they do in other aspects of their operations. "Fine-tune the program," wrote Sheley. "The evaluation process will provide at least some of the information necessary to make the adjustments that will make a workplace flexibility program of optimum benefit to both the company and its employees."

CONTINUED CHANGE IN FLEXIBLE WORK PROGRAMS

In today's business world, flexible employment staples such as flextime and telecommuting continue to grow, in large measure because businesses that introduce them continue to prosper while simultaneously improving the quality of life of their employees. Looking ahead, it seems clear that flexible work programs will continue to be used and be used more frequently. With the rise of the Internet and rapid spread of high-speed connections to the Internet in homes and offices alike, the tools necessary to make flexible work programs successful are multiplying. Creating a flexible work program suitable for a particular business and company will continue to be an individual endeavor but one that is made ever easier with new technologies and communication tools.

SEE ALSO *Comp Time; Job Sharing; Telecommuting*

BIBLIOGRAPHY

Dreike Almer, Elizabeth, and Louis E. Single. "Career Consequences of Flexible Work Arrangements: The Daddy Track." *The CPA Journal.* September 2004.

"Flexible Working Practices Boost Business Success." *Leadership & Organization Development Journal.* February-March 1997.

Graham, Baxter W. "The Business Argument for Flexibility." *HRMagazine.* May 1996.

Leveen-Sher, Margery. "Flexibility Is the Key to Small Business Benefits." *Washington Business Journal.* 16 February 1996.

Peak, Martha H. "Why I Hate Flextime." *Management Review.* February 1994.

Sheley, Elizabeth. "Flexible Work Options." *HRMagazine.* February 1996.

Skyrme, David J. "Flexible Working: Building a Lean and Responsive Organization." *Long Range Planning.* October 1994.

Whittard, Mark. "Flexible Work Arrangements: Friend or Foe?" *Keeping Good Companies.* December 2005.

"A Workstyle Revolution? A Survey of Flexible Employment Practices." *Leadership and Organization Development Journal.* November 1999.

Hillstrom, Northern Lights
updated by Magee, ECDI

FLOW CHARTS

A flow chart, or flow diagram, is a graphical representation of a process or system that details the sequencing of steps required to create output. A typical flow chart uses a set of basic symbols to represent various functions, and shows the sequence and interconnection of functions with lines and arrows. Flow charts can be used to document virtually any type of business system, from the movement of materials through machinery in a manufacturing operation to the flow of applicant information through the hiring process in a human resources department.

Each flow chart is concerned with one particular process or system. It begins with the input of data or materials into the system and traces all the procedures needed to convert the input into its final output form. Specialized flow chart symbols show the processes that take place, the actions that are performed in each step, and the relationship between various steps. Flow charts may include different levels of detail as needed, from a high-level overview of an entire system to a detailed diagram of one component process within a larger system. In any case, the flow chart shows the overall structure of the process or system, traces the flow of information and work through it, and highlights key processing and decision points.

Flow charts are an important tool for the improvement of processes. By providing a graphical representation, they help project teams to identify the different elements of a process and understand the interrelationships among the various steps. Flow charts may also be used to gather information and data about a process as an aid to decision making or performance evaluation. For example, the owner of a small advertising agency who hopes to reduce the time involved in creating a print ad might be able to use a flow chart of the process to identify and eliminate unnecessary steps. Though flow charts are relatively old design tools, they remain popular among computer programmers working on systems analysis and design. In recent years, many software programs have been developed to assist business people in creating flow charts.

CONSTRUCTING FLOW CHARTS

Flow charts typically utilize specialized symbols. Some of the main symbols that are used to construct flow charts include:

- A round-edged rectangle to represent starting and ending activities, which are sometimes referred to as terminal activities.

- A rectangle to represent an activity or step. Each step or activity within a process is indicated by a single rectangle, which is known as an activity or process symbol.

- A diamond to signify a decision point. The question to be answered or decision to be made is written inside the diamond, which is known as a decision symbol. The answer determines the path that will be taken as a next step.

- Flow lines show the progression or transition from one step to another.

Constructing a flow chart involves the following main steps: 1) Define the process and identify the scope of the flow diagram; 2) Identify project team members that are to be involved in the construction of the process flow diagram; 3) Define the different steps involved in the process and the interrelationships between the different steps (all team members should help develop and agree upon the different steps for the process); 4) Finalize the diagram, involving other concerned individuals as needed and making any modifications necessary; and 5) Use the flow diagram and continuously update it as needed.

BIBLIOGRAPHY
Harris, Robert L. *Information Graphics.* Oxford University Press, 2000.

Laudon, Kenneth C., and Jane Price Laudon. *Management Information Systems: A Contemporary Perspective.* Macmillan, 1991.

Lehman, Mark W. "Flowcharting Made Simple." *Journal of Accountancy.* October 2000.

Hillstrom, Northern Lights
updated by Magee, ECDI

FOCUS GROUPS

A focus group is a marketing research tool in which a small group of people (typically eight to ten individuals) engages in a roundtable discussion of selected topics of interest in an informal setting. The focus group discussion is typically directed by a moderator who guides the discussion in order to obtain the group's opinions about or reactions to specific products or marketing-oriented issues, known as test concepts. While focus groups can provide marketing managers, product managers, and market researchers with a great deal of helpful information, their use as a research tool is limited in that it is difficult to measure the results objectively. In addition, the cost and logistical complexity of focus group research is frequently cited as a deterrent, especially for small companies. Nonetheless, many small businesses find focus groups to be useful a means of staying close to consumers and their ever-changing attitudes and feelings. By providing qualitative information from well-defined target audiences, focus groups can aid businesses in decision making and in the development of marketing strategies and promotional campaigns.

APPLICATIONS

Traditionally, focus groups have been used by makers of consumer products to gather qualitative data from target groups of consumers. They are often used in the new product development process, for example, to test consumer reaction to new product concepts and prototypes. Focus groups are also used to test marketing programs, as they can provide an indication of how consumers will react to specific advertising messages and other types of marketing communications. In this way, focus groups can help advertising and promotion managers position a particular product, service, or institution with respect to their target audience. Reactions to new types of product packaging can also be tested with focus groups. In addition, many companies have used focus groups as a tool to learn more about consumer habits, product usage, and service expectations.

As focus groups increased in popularity during the 1980s and 1990s, they were increasingly used to explore relatively narrow information niches. For example, pharmaceutical companies have convened focus groups consisting of medical professionals to test concepts related to new drug products. The legal profession has used focus groups to improve the quality of their cases. Nonprofit organizations have used focus groups to test fundraising campaigns. Focus groups have been used in industrial settings by business-to-business marketers. Some companies have even set up employee focus groups to learn more about employee motivation.

CHARACTERISTICS

A key factor in determining the success of focus groups is the composition of the group in terms of the participants' age, gender, and product usage. Focus group participants are generally selected on the basis of their use of, knowledge, attitudes, or feelings about the products, services, or other test concepts that are the subject of the focus group. In selecting participants, the objective is to find individuals who can knowledgeably discuss the topics at hand and provide quality output that meets the specified research objectives.

The most common method of selecting participants for focus groups is from some type of database that contains demographic, psychographic, and lifestyle information about a large number of consumers. Such databases are available from a variety of commercial vendors. A list of desired characteristics is drawn up and matched with the database to select participants for focus groups. These characteristics may include purchase behavior, attitudes, and demographic data such as age and gender. The goal is to select participants who would likely be in the target audience for the products, services, or concepts being tested.

There is no absolute ideal in terms of the number of participants, although eight to ten participants is the norm. Different moderators are comfortable with different sizes of focus groups, but most consultants encourage companies to utilize groups in the eight-ten person range. Those who prefer this size focus group contend that these groups are large enough to provide a nice range of perspectives and make it difficult for one or two individuals to dominate the discussion (moderators should guard against such developments). Groups that include more than ten participants are usually more difficult for moderators to control. Group interaction in larger groups is also more difficult, and moderators have a harder time stimulating discussion. In addition, it is often more difficult for a moderator to spend time following up on the insights voiced by one individual when there are a dozen or more participants.

Focus groups that are relatively homogeneous in terms of age, gender, and product usage generally work better than mixed groups. When it is desirable to obtain data from different age and gender groups, most experts recommend scheduling a series of focus groups using homogeneous participants. They claim that group dynamics tend to become inhibited in mixed-gender or age-focus groups. In addition, specific topics can be explored in greater depth when there is homogeneity among the participants with regard to usage of or attitudes toward the products being tested.

MODERATORS

Moderators play an important role in determining the success of focus groups. Well-trained moderators can provide a great deal of added value in terms of their past experience, skills, and techniques. On the other hand, poorly trained moderators are likely to fail to generate quality output from their focus groups. In addition to professional, full-time focus group moderators, other types of individuals who often serve as moderators include professional researchers, academicians, marketing consultants, psychologists or psychiatrists, and company representatives.

Focus group moderators serve as discussion leaders. They try to stimulate discussion while saying as little as possible. They are not interviewers. They usually work from a guide that provides them with an outlined plan of how the discussion should flow. The guide includes topics to be covered together with probing questions that can be used to stimulate further discussion. Moderators try to include everyone in the discussion. They allocate available time to make sure the required topics are covered. When the discussion digresses, it is up to the moderator to refocus the group on the topic at hand.

SESSIONS

When setting up a focus group session, it is important to give careful consideration to the physical setting where it will take place. The location should be one that encourages relaxed participation and informal, spontaneous comments. The focus group facility must be of adequate size and have comfortable seating for all of the participants. Living room and conference room settings both provide good locations for focus groups, but public places—such as restaurants and auditoriums—are generally regarded as too distracting for gaining optimal results. In selecting a focus group site it is also important to make it geographically convenient for the participants. Locations that are hard to find or located in out of the way places may cause delays and scheduling problems. Finally, sites should be determined with an eye toward the schedules and locations of managers and executives who should be in attendance.

The facility should also be relatively soundproof, to minimize outside noises and distractions. While focus group sessions are almost always audiotaped and many are videotaped, client company representatives usually like to observe their focus groups firsthand. With this in mind, many focus group discussion areas are equipped with one-way mirrors that allow company representatives to observe without intruding. An alternative viewing arrangement would be to use a remote video hookup that would allow company representatives to view the proceedings on a video screen. Having company representatives in the same room as the focus group is the least desirable arrangement.

Once the facility, moderator, and participants have been selected, typical focus group sessions begin with an introduction. During the introductory part of the session the moderator welcomes the participants, informs them of what will take place during the session, and generally sets the stage for the discussion to follow. Prior to the main discussion there is usually a warm-up phase. The warm-up is designed to make the participants feel at ease. During the warm-up participants generally introduce themselves to the group. General topic discussions, usually related to the specific topics that will be covered later, also form part of the warm-up stage. These general discussions help participants focus their attention. They also provide the moderator with some insight into the different participants.

Gradually the moderator moves the level of discussion from general topics to more specific ones. The moderator may present different concepts for discussion. These include the test concepts for which the group was convened. The moderator may choose to use props to focus the group's attention. Typical props include product samples, actual or concept ads, concept statements that participants read together, photographs, and television commercials.

Once all of the test concepts have been discussed and evaluated by the group, the moderator moves the discussion into a wrap-up phase. During this phase the best concepts are identified and their strengths and weaknesses discussed. Participants may be asked to write down their reactions to what they have seen and discussed.

During this final phase, any outstanding issues that were omitted are covered. When all of the substantive discussions have been completed, the moderator closes the session by thanking the participants and giving them any final instructions. Participants should leave with a positive feeling about the experience and the company, if the company that arranged the focus group has been identified. After the participants have left, it is standard practice for the moderator and the client company observers to have a post-group discussion.

Following the conclusion of the focus group or series of focus group sessions, the moderator may prepare a report for the client company. The report generally provides a written summary of the results of the session or sessions as interpreted by the moderator. Focus group reports may be very detailed or may be a simple summary of the discussion. In some cases the client company may not require a written report.

ONLINE FOCUS GROUPS

One recent innovation in focus group research has been the emergence of online focus group sessions, which permit business owners and managers to directly observe group discussions without going to the time and expense of traveling to the locale in which the exercise is taking place. Using the Internet as a medium to conduct focus groups is a logical—and vastly superior—successor to videoconferencing. Videoconferencing enabled companies to conduct focus group research without incurring major business travel expenses. But equipment glitches, the logistical challenge of gathering observers at a central location, and the expense of purchasing and implementing this high-tech option made it a decidedly imperfect vehicle. Nonetheless, as business writer Alf Nucifora observed, "the advent of video streaming technology now means that focus groups can be observed 'live' from the comfort of one's desk.... A camera captures all the action close-up... and broadcasts the action via video streaming to an unlimited number of viewers who can watch real-time from the comfort of their desktop computers at any time, in any place." The completed focus group session can then be saved in computer-readable form for future use.

Analysts cite online focus groups as a particularly exciting development for small business owners with limited resources. *Business Week* noted that traditional focus group research can take several months and a great deal of expense (as much as $100,000) to complete. But growing numbers of market research firms offer online focus group research services for less than $5,000 a session, the results of which can be studied and tabulated within a matter of weeks. Still, not all business ventures are equally suited to pursue this electronic alternative.

"If your customers aren't tech-savvy, or if your product relies heavily on touch and taste, you may be wiser to foot the bill for a traditional group," counseled *Business Week*. "But if all you require is a quick glimpse into your customers' minds, an online group could be the way to go."

SEE ALSO *Market Research*

BIBLIOGRAPHY

Greenbaum, Thomas L. *The Handbook for Focus Group Research.* Lexington Books, 1993.

"I've Asked You Here Because . . . " *Business Week.* 14 August 2000.

James, William, James Langford, and Joseph D. McDouglad. *Focus Groups.* Taylor & Foster, 2002.

Krueger, Richard A. *Focus Groups: A Practical Guide for Applied Research.* Sage Publications, 1988.

Nucifora, Alf. "Internet is Revolutionizing the Use of Focus Groups." *Memphis Business Journal.* 9 September 2000.

"Trend Spotting Beyond Focus Groups." *Financial Express.* 15 January 2006.

Hillstrom, Northern Lights
updated by Magee, ECDI

FORECASTING

Forecasting can be broadly considered as a method or a technique for estimating many future aspects of a business or other operation. Planning for the future is a critical aspect of managing any organization, and small business enterprises are no exception. Indeed, their typically modest capital resources make such planning particularly important. In fact, the long-term success of both small and large organizations is closely tied to how well the management of the organization is able to foresee its future and to develop appropriate strategies to deal with likely future scenarios. Intuition, good judgment, and an awareness of how well the industry and national economy are doing may give the manager of a business firm a sense of future market and economic trends. Nevertheless, it is not easy to convert a feeling about the future into a precise and useful number, such as next year's sales volume or the raw material cost per unit of output. Forecasting methods can help estimate many such future aspects of a business operation.

The goal of forecasting is to come as close to possible to an accurate picture of the future. But, as with other forms of fortune telling, it can never be fully accurate. There are simply too many interactive variables. A change in any one of these may cause the forecasted scenario to change. For example, unexpected shocks to the economy, as occurred after the terrorist attacks of 9/11, are extremely difficult to anticipate and plan around. Such extreme situations are, happily, very rare. But there are far more subtle events that may also cause major changes in the assumptions upon which a forecast is based, things like: sharply increased material costs resulting from storms or wars, the unexpected demise or buyout of a large competitor, and/or an increase in demand due to an unexpected fashion trend shift. Despite the fact that forecasting is an imprecise art, a company must do the best it can to plan for the future and an important part of this planning is forecasting.

The task of forecasting can be approached in a number of ways and the best forecasting outcomes are usually the result of applying several forecasting methods. To supplement their judgment, forecasters rely on a variety of data sources and forecasting methods. For example, forecasting may involve the use of econometric models that can take into account the interactions between economic variables. In other cases the forecaster may employ statistical techniques for analyzing sets of historical data referred to simply as time series. Other frequently used data sources are recent consumer surveys and forecasts produced by other institutions—industry associations, investment banks, and economists generally.

FORECASTING AND ITS PRACTICAL APPLICATIONS

In an era where forecasts drive entire supply chain networks forecasting is an increasingly critical organizational capability. Forecasting the future may sound like a lofty and theoretical activity when in reality it is a practical business tool like many others. Here is an example. How should a business go about preparing the quarterly sales volume forecasts for their primary product, say, window-glass? The company will certainly want to review the actual sales data for window glass over the last few years. Suppose that the forecaster has access to actual sales data for each quarter over the 15-year period the firm has been in business. Using these historical data, the forecaster can see the general level of sales but more importantly, he or she can also determine what pattern the sales history produces, what trends are visible. A thorough review of the data may reveal some type of seasonal pattern, such as peak sales occurring in the spring as people do spring-cleaning and others prepare to sell their homes during the summer school break. In addition, if the forecaster is able to identify other factors that influence sales, like weather patterns or housing starts, historical data on these factors can also be used in generating forecasts of future sales volumes.

FORECASTING METHODS

Academics divide forecasting methods into two broad categories: qualitative and quantitative. The division of forecasting methods into qualitative forecasting and quantitative forecasting is based on the availability of historical time series data. If historical data and time series are available, than quantitative methods may be used. If not, qualitative methods are the only option.

Qualitative Forecasting Methods Qualitative forecasting techniques generally employ the judgment of experts to generate forecasts. A key advantage of these procedures is that they can be applied in situations where historical data are simply not available. Even in situations where such data are available, quantitative forecasting methods are a useful addition to successful forecasting. Three important qualitative forecasting methods are: the Delphi method, scenario writing, and the subject approach.

Delphi Method In the Delphi method, an attempt is made to develop forecasts through "group consensus."

A group of experts in a particular field participate. Usually, a panel of these experienced people is asked to respond to a series of questionnaires. The panel members, who should ideally come from a variety of backgrounds (marketing, production, management, finance, purchasing, etc.) are asked to respond to an initial questionnaire. A second questionnaire is then created which incorporates information and opinions gathered in the responses to the first questionnaire. The second questionnaire is then distributed. Each panelist is asked to reconsider and revise his or her initial response to the questions based on the new information. This process is continued until some degree of consensus among the panelists is reached. It should be noted that the objective of the Delphi method is not to produce a single answer at the end. Instead, it attempts to produce a relatively narrow range of opinions—a range into which most of the panelists' opinions fall.

Scenario Writing Method Under the scenario writing approach, the forecaster starts with different sets of assumptions. For each set of assumptions, a likely scenario of the business outcome is charted. Thus, the forecaster generates several different future scenarios (corresponding to different sets of assumptions). The decision maker or business person is presented with the different scenarios, and has to decide which scenario is most likely to prevail.

A Subjective Approach Method The subjective approach allows individuals participating in the forecasting decision to arrive at a forecast based on their feelings, ideas, and personal experiences. Many corporations in the United States have started to increasingly use the subjective approach. Internally, these subjective approaches

sometimes take the form of "brainstorming sessions," in which managers, executives, and employees work together to develop new ideas or to solve complex problems. At other times, the subjective approach may take the form of a survey of the company's sales people. This approach, which is known as the sales force composite or grass roots method, is relied on because salespeople interact directly with purchasers and it is assumed therefore that they have a good feel for which products will or will not sell and in what quantities.

The advantage of using the salespeople's forecasts is that salespeople are highly qualified to explain the demand for products, especially in their own territories. The disadvantage is that salespeople may tend to be optimistic in their estimates since optimism is a characteristic often found in good salespeople. Also, those working in sales may fear that a low sales forecast will lead to layoffs in the sales area. The opinions of salespeople should not be relied on to the exclusion of all else for one additional reason. Salespeople may not be aware of impending changes in other related areas, such as availability of raw materials, national economic developments, or the arrival of a formidable new competitor.

Quantitative Forecasting Methods Quantitative forecasting methods are used when historical data on variables of interest are available—these methods are based on an analysis of historical data concerning the time series of the specific variable of interest. There are two quantitative forecasting methods. The first uses the past trend of a particular variable in order to make a future forecast of the variable. In recognition of this method's reliance on time series, it is commonly called the "time series method." The second quantitative forecasting method also uses historical data. This method is often referred to as the causal method because it relies on the use of several variables and their "cause-and-effect" relationships. Examples of variables that may have this cause-and-effect relationship are: 1) interest rate levels and levels of disposable income; 2) winter weather patterns and demand for heating oil; 3) increasing gas prices and a decline in demand for sports utility vehicles (SUVs). By studying the time series data on two or more variables that have a cause-and-effect relationship with the item for which a forecast is needed, effort is made to incorporate as many relevant factors as possible into the forecast.

In practice, most business people use some combination of these methods and techniques in trying to plan for the future and put together accurate forecasts. With each cycle of forecasting, more is learned about what factor to consider and how to weight their importance in projecting future events.

SEE ALSO *Business Planning; Sales Forecasts*

BIBLIOGRAPHY

Aston, Adam, and Joseph Weber. "The Worst Isn't Over: Smarter science is helping companies and insurers plan for hurricanes. The Bad News: This year could be another doozy." *Business Week*. 16 January 2006.

Chase, Charles W. Jr. "Composite Forecasting: Combining Forecasts for Improved Accuracy." *Journal of Business Forecasting*. Summer 2000.

Engerman, Stanley. "On the Accuracy of Some Past and Present Forecasts." *International Monetary Fund Staff Papers*. Annual 2005.

Evans, Michael. *Practical Business Forecasting*. Blackwell Publishing, 2002.

Gaber, Tal, Jacob Goldenberg, Barak Libai, and Eitan Mullerray. "From Density to Destiny: Using spatial dimension of sales data for early prediction of new product success." *Marketing Science*. Summer 2004.

Gray, Andi. "How Forecasting Can Help the Bottom Line." *Fairfield County Business Journal*. 27 June 2005.

Jones, Vernon Dale, Stuart Bretschneider, and Wilpen L. Gorr. "Organization Pressures on Forecast Evaluation: Managerial, Political, and Procedural Influences." *Journal of Forecasting*. July 1997.

Mentzer, John T., and Mark A. Moon. *Sales Forecasting Management*. Sage Publications, Inc., 2004.

O'Connor, Marcus, William Remus, and Ken Griggs. "Going Up—Going Down: How Good are People at Forecasting Trends and Changes in Trends?" *Journal of Forecasting*. May 1997.

Sanders, Nada R., and Karl B. Manrodt. "The Efficacy of Using Judgmental versus Quantitative Forecasting Methods in Practice." *Omega*. December 2003.

Rasmussen, Rasmus. "On Time Series Data and Optimal Parameters." *Omega*. April 2004.

Hillstrom, Northern Lights
updated by Magee, ECDI

FORTUNE 500

The term Fortune 500 refers to an annual listing by *Fortune* magazine of the top 500 public companies in the U.S., as ranked by sales, assets, earnings, and capitalization. This list ranks only public companies, or those which have issued securities through an offering and which are traded on the stock market. This list is important to a number of financial groups, but particularly to investors, who study the performance of these select companies. In addition, academic and business researchers look to these companies to learn about best practices in various industries and to discover the secrets to their business and financial success. The requirements and typical characteristics of Fortune 500 companies can be found at: http://money.cnn.com/magazines/fortune/.

RANKING FACTORS USED IN DETERMINING THE FORTUNE 500

Sales Growth Ranking Tracking the increase in sales of a company is a way to determine if the company is indeed growing. This is very important to investors. Sales growth is also indicative of the state of the economy. One would expect a company's sales to grow during a healthy period of economic activity. When a company's sales grow faster than the general economy in the markets in which the firm operates, the firm is obviously outperforming the market due to some process within the company. It could be due to a superior quality product, low-cost production or service delivery methods, excellent customer service and support, or innovations in production and/or processing. Companies on the Fortune 500 list typically exhibit more than one success measure that may be important for competitors to emulate.

Assets Ranking Companies listed on the Fortune 500 usually have large and growing asset balances. An asset is any item of economic value owned by the corporation, including cash, securities, accounts receivable, inventory, office equipment, and property.

Earnings Ranking A firm's earnings are calculated by subtracting the cost of sales, operating expenses, and taxes from its revenues. Earnings are often the single most important determinant of a corporation's stock price.

Capitalization Ranking Capitalization is the sum of a corporation's long-term debt, stock, and retained earnings. It may also be called invested capital. By multiplying the number of shares outstanding by the price per share, it is possible to determine the market price of an entire company or its market capitalization.

MOST ADMIRED COMPANIES

Another popular feature of the Fortune 500 list is the top 10 rankings of the most admired companies. The most recent list can be found at:

http://money.cnn.com/magazines/fortune/mostadmired/index.html. The top 10 most admired list for 2005 includes the following companies: General Electric; FedEx; Southwestern Airlines; Procter & Gamble; Starbucks; Johnson & Johnson; Berkshire Hathaway, Dell, Toyota Motor, and Microsoft. The top ten "most admired" ranking is based on all the votes a company received from all respondents across all industries to the *Fortune* survey.

According to the Fortune 500 study, the annual list of 500 companies represents the bedrock of American business and remains an important tool for both researchers and investors. The Fortune 500 list is well established and has been a standard of performance for over 50 years. In recent years, the companies of the Fortune 500—whether ranked by growth, return, or market capitalization—were led by computer firms and telecommunications companies. *Fortune* also compiles the Global 500 list, a list of the most admired international companies, and a list of top employers on an annual basis.

SEE ALSO *Blue Chip*

BIBLIOGRAPHY

Filbeck, Greg, Raymond Gorman, and Diana Preece. "Fortune's Most Admired Firms: An Investor's Perspective." *Studies in Economics and Finance.* Fall 1997.

Huey, John. "The Real 500." *Fortune.* 27 April 1998.

Hillstrom, Northern Lights
updated by Magee, ECDI

401(K) PLANS

A 401(k) plan is a tax-deferred, defined-contribution retirement plan. The name comes from a section of the Internal Revenue Code that permits an employer to create a retirement plan to which employees may voluntarily contribute a portion of their compensation on a pre-tax basis. This section also allows the employer to match employee contributions with tax-deductible company contributions, or to contribute additional funds to employee accounts at the company's discretion as a form of profit-sharing. Earnings on all contributions are allowed to accumulate tax-deferred until the employee withdraws them upon retirement. In many cases, employees are able to borrow from their 401(k) accounts prior to retirement at below-market interest rates. In addition, employees may decide to roll over funds in their 401(k) accounts to another qualified retirement plan without penalty if they change jobs.

Popularity of 401(k) plans during the 1990s and 2000s has been great. For the first time ever, in 1997, 401(k) type defined-contribution plans surpassed the more traditional defined-benefit pension plans in terms of the total retirement assets held by each. And the growth of defined-contribution plans continued thereafter. According to the Employee Benefit Research Institute, as of the close of 2005, defined-contribution plans held 61 percent of private-sector retirement assets, compared with 39 percent in defined-benefit pensions. The 401(k) plan has a reasonably short history yet it has already changed the face of retirement planning in America.

HISTORY

The 401(k) provision was created in 1978 as part of that year's Tax Revenue Act, but went largely unnoticed for two years until Ted Benna, a Pennsylvania benefits consultant, devised a creative and rewarding application of the law. Section 401(k) stipulated that cash or deferred-bonus plans qualified for tax deferral. Most observers of tax law had assumed that contributions to such plans could be made only after income tax was withheld, but Benna noticed that the clause did not preclude pre-tax salary reduction programs.

Benna came up with his innovative interpretation of the 401(k) provision in 1980 in response to a client's proposal to transfer a cash-bonus plan to a tax-deferred profit-sharing plan. The now-familiar features he sought were an audit-inducing combination then—pre-tax salary reduction, company matches, and employee contributions. Benna called his interpretation of the 401(k) rule "Cash-Op," and even tried to patent it, but most clients were wary of the plan, fearing that once the government realized its tax revenue-reducing implications, legislators would pull the plug on it.

Luckily for Benna and the millions of participants who have since utilized his idea, the concept of employee savings was gaining political ascendancy at that time. Ronald Reagan had made personal saving through tax-deferred individual retirement accounts, or IRAs, a component of his campaign and presidency. Payroll deductions for IRAs were allowed in 1981 and Benna hoped to extend that feature to his new plan. He established a salary-reducing 401(k) plan even before the Internal Revenue Service had finished writing the regulations that would govern it. The government agency surprised many observers when it provisionally approved the plan in spring 1981 and specifically sanctioned Benna's interpretation of the law that fall.

401(k) plans quickly became a leading factor in the evolving retirement benefits business. From 1984 to 1991, the number of plans increased more than 150 percent, and the rate of participation grew from 62 percent to 72 percent. The number of employees able to participate in 401(k) plans rose to more than 48 million by 1991 from only 7 million in 1983, and Benna's breakthrough earned him the appellation "the grandfather of 401(k)s." As expected, the government soon realized the volume of salary reductions it was unable to tax and tried to quash the revolution—the Reagan administration made two attempts to invalidate 401(k)s in 1986—but public outrage prevented the repeal.

The advent of 401(k) plans helped effect a philosophical shift among employers, from the provision of defined-benefit pension plans for employees to the administration of defined-contribution retirement plans. In the past, companies had offered true pension plans that guaranteed all individuals a predetermined retirement benefit. But after 1981, rather than providing an employer-funded pension, many companies began to give employees the opportunity to save for their own retirement through a cash or deferred arrangement such as a 401(k). This change helped level the playing field for small businesses, which were now able to offer the same type of retirement benefits as many larger employers. Small businesses thus found themselves better able to attract and retained qualified employees who may previously have opted for the security of a large company and its pension plan.

THE BASICS OF 401(K) PLANS

In benefits parlance, employers offering 401(k)s are sometimes called "plan sponsors" and employees are often known as "plan participants." Most 401(k)s are qualified plans, meaning that they conform to criteria established in the Economic Recovery Tax Act of 1981 (ERTA). ERTA expanded upon and refined the Employee Retirement Income Security Act of 1974 (ERISA), which had been enacted to protect participants and beneficiaries from abusive employer practices and created guidelines that were intended to ensure adequate funding of retirement benefits and minimum standards for pension plans.

Basic eligibility standards were set up with this legislation, though they have changed frequently since and may vary slightly from plan to plan. As of 1996, an employee had to be at least 21 years of age and have put in at least one year of service with the company to participate in the 401(k) program. Some union employees, nonresident aliens, and part-time employees were excluded from participation.

401(k) plans incorporate many attractive features for long-term savers, including tax deferral, flexibility, and control. Taxes on both income and interest are delayed until participants begin receiving distributions from the plan. Rollovers (the direct transfer of 401(k) funds into another qualified plan, such as a new employer's 401(k), an IRA, or a self-employed pension plan)—as well as emergency or hardship loans for medical expenses, higher-education tuition, and home purchases—allayed participants' fears about tying up large sums for the long term. While there are restrictions on these loans' availability, terms, and amounts, the net cost of borrowing may be quite reasonable because the interest cost is partly offset by the investment return.

Employees may also receive lump sum distributions of their accounts upon termination. If an employee elects to take his or her distribution in cash before retirement age, however, the employer is required by law to withhold 20 percent of the distribution. If the account is rolled over into another qualified plan, nothing is withheld. Employees' self-determination of investments has allowed tailoring of accounts according to individual needs. For example, younger participants may wish to emphasize higher-risk (and potentially higher-return) investments, while employees who are closer to retirement age can focus on more secure holdings. These features have been refined over the years through legislation, especially after the government realized the tax revenue losses engendered by the popular plans.

Passage of the Economic Growth and Tax Relief Reconciliation Act of 2001 (EGTRRA) changed the taxation landscape in the Untied States. With respect to 401(k) plans, several changes were made. For the most part these changes helped to increase the amount that individuals and companies are able to contribute to 401(k) plans on a tax-deferred basis.

As of 2006, the amount an employee could defer annually under such programs was set at $15,000. In addition, the sum of employer and employee contributions to one individual's account was set at either 100 percent of annual compensation or $40,000, whichever was higher. The employer was further limited to an annual contribution of 15 percent of total payroll, including both employee deferrals and employer matching and profit-sharing contributions. Finally, the amount of compensation that could be considered in determining an employee's deferral was limited to $200,000 per year. The contribution limits and percentage rates used to calculate plan-wide limits change from year to year and make the administering of these plans a very complex task.

These limits tend to restrict senior executives and other highly paid employees more than the majority of employees. Mandatory "top heavy" tests prevent 401(k) programs from favoring highly compensated employees by restricting the amount that a company's top earners can contribute to 401(k) plans. Known as "nondiscrimination tests" in the benefits industry, top heavy rules separate employers and employees into two groups: those who are highly compensated and all the rest. The amount that the highly paid employees may defer is based upon what the lower-paid employees deferred during the year. If the average lower-paid employee only contributed 2 percent of his or her compensation to the corporate 401(k), for example, highly paid employees may only divert 4 percent of their pay. Benefits and tax specialists have, of course, devised strategies to circumvent these restrictions, such as 401(k) wrap-arounds, "rabbi trust arrangements," and other "non-qualified" plans that consciously and legally operate outside the bounds of "qualified" 401(k)s. Such plans are costly to administer and run and are not often seen in small company settings.

ADVANTAGES AND DISADVANTAGES OF 401(K) PLANS

The shift from defined-benefit plans to defined-contribution plans such as 401(k)s has had both positive and negative ramifications. On the downside for employees is their need to shoulder more of the financial burden for their retirement. Compared to defined-benefit plans, defined-contribution plans are risky. Instead of a federally guaranteed pension pay-out upon retirement, 401(k) plan holders make their own investments which offer the hope of great gains but also contain the potential for great losses. The story of Enron and the stock market declines of the early 2000s both showed what could happen to investments in a 401(k) plan. Nonetheless, most observers have applauded the movement towards greater reliance on 401(k) plans. Employees have gained greater control over their retirement assets. The plans provide immediate tax advantages as the contributions are not subject to federal income taxes nor to most state and local taxes. They also provide long-term tax advantages, as earnings accumulate tax-free until withdrawal at retirement, when withdrawals can presumably receive favorable tax treatment. In addition, 401(k)s offer loan provisions that many other pension plans lack.

For employers, 401(k) plans offer many advantages. For example, employers have been able to share or entirely eliminate their pension contributions. And if employers do choose to contribute, the employer too gets a tax deduction. 401(k)s have evolved into a valuable perk to attract and retain qualified employees. Employers can even link contributions to a profit-sharing arrangement to increase employee incentive toward higher productivity and commitment to the company. By enabling employees to become active participants in saving and investing for their retirement, 401(k) plans can raise the level of perceived benefits provided by the employer.

Small business owners can set up a 401(k) plan by filling out the necessary forms at any financial institution (a bank, mutual fund, insurance company, brokerage firm, etc.). There are several types of 401(k) plans that may be used, one of which is the SIMPLE 401(k) plan. The IRS Web site explains that this sort of plan was especially created so that small businesses could have an effective cost-efficient way to offer retirement benefits to their employees. A SIMPLE 401(k) plan is not subject to the annual nondiscrimination tests that apply to the traditional plans. The employer is required to make employer contributions that are fully vested. This type of 401(k) plan is available to employers with 100 or fewer employees who received at least $5,000 in

compensation from the employer for the preceding calendar year. In addition, employees that are covered by a SIMPLE 401(k) plan may not receive any contributions or benefit accruals under any other plans of the employer.

The fees involved in establishing and administering a 401(k) plan can be relatively high, since sponsors of this type of plan are required to file Form 5500 annually to disclose plan activities to the IRS. The preparation and filing of this complicated document can increase the administrative costs associated with a plan, as the business owner may require help from a tax advisor or plan administration professional. Fortunately, for companies with fewer than 100 employees, a SIMPLE 401(k) plan is an option and one that entails fewer fees and administrative costs.

SEE ALSO *Employee Benefits; Retirement Planning*

BIBLIOGRAPHY
Blakely, Stephen. "Pension Power." *Nation's Business.* July 1997.

"401k Plan Costs." *The Controller's Report.* June 2005.

MacDonald, John. "'Traditional' Pension Assets Lost Dominance a Decade Ago, IRAs and 401(k)s Have Long Been Dominant." *Fast Facts from EBRI.* Employee Benefit Research Institute, 3 February 2006.

"Retirement Planning: Squeeze on Retirement Savings." *The Practical Accountant.* February 2006.

Sifleet, Jean D. *Beyond 401(k)s for Small Business Owners.* John Wiley & Sons, 2003.

U.S. Internal Revenue Service. "401(k) Resource Guide – Plan Participants – Limitations on Elective Deferrals." Available from http://www.irs.gov/retirement/participant/article/0, id=151786,00.html Retrieved on 9 March 2006.

Weller, Christian E., and Ross Eisenbrey "No More Enrons: Protection 401(k) Plans for a Safe Retirement." *EPI Issue Brief.* Economic Policy Institute, 7 February 2002.

Hillstrom, Northern Lights
updated by Magee, ECDI

FRANCHISING

Franchising is a kind of licensing arrangement wherein a business owner, known as the "franchisor," distributes or markets a trademarked product or service through affiliated dealers, who are known as "franchisees." While these franchisees own their establishments, terms of franchising agreements typically require them to share operational responsibilities with the franchisor.

Over the past few decades, franchising has emerged as an integral part of America's commercial landscape. Indeed, companies as diverse as McDonald's, The Gap, and Jiffy Lube owe their ubiquitous presence in the marketplace to the practice. Department of Commerce figures indicate that franchises exceeded $1 trillion in annual sales in the year 2000. The International Franchising Association (IFA) estimates that 40 percent of all U.S. retail sales took place in franchise outlets in the early 2000s. Although the U.S. Census Bureau has not counted franchises in previous Economic Censuses, International Franchise Association President Matthew Shay announced in a late 2005 press release that plans were being finalized by the Bureau to include questions about franchising in the 2007 Census of Business.

Franchising has been embraced by many entrepreneurs eager to run their own company. But the characteristics of a franchising business are dissimilar in some crucial respects from those of other start-up businesses. Some businesspeople have even gone so far as to characterize franchisees as glorified employees of the franchisor, the company that owns the trademark and business concept that the franchisees use. Other observers find this description of the relationship to be misleading and simplistic, but they also acknowledge that there are many aspects of franchising that a prospective small business owner should learn about before entering into such an agreement.

Three different kinds of franchising arrangements are commonly found in the United States today. Business format franchises are the most popular of the franchise types. Under this arrangement, the franchisee pays an initial fee and an ongoing royalty to the franchisor in exchange for a proven business operation and identity. Benefits of this package include the franchisor's name and its product line, marketing techniques, production and administration systems, and operating procedures. A second option is to pursue a product or trade name franchise in which the franchisee becomes part of a franchisor's distribution network. Some small business owners choose to combine their resources under the banner of a single operating network. These affiliate franchises are thus able to pool their assets together for purchasing, advertising, and marketing visibility purposes.

BENEFITS OF FRANCHISE OWNERSHIP

There are many significant advantages to franchise ownership. In most instances, an entrepreneur who decides to buy a franchise is purchasing a business concept with a proven track record of success. In addition, a franchise agreement provides instant name recognition for the business, which can be a huge advantage if the name enjoys a solid reputation in the marketplace. But franchising provides benefits in many other areas of business operation as well. These include:

Advertising and Promotion Franchisees benefit from any national advertising campaigns launched by the corporation with which they have gone into business. In addition, many franchisors provide their franchisees with a wide range of point-of-sale advertising materials, ranging from posters to mobiles to brochures. Since such materials are often expensive to produce, they would otherwise be beyond the reach of some individual franchisees.

Operations Franchisors provide franchisees with a wide range of help in the areas of administration and general operations. The entrepreneur who becomes a franchise owner is instantly armed with proven products and production systems; inventory systems; financial and accounting systems; and human resources guidelines. Many franchisors also provide management training to new franchisees, and ongoing seminar workshops for established owners.

Buying Power Franchisees are often able to fill inventory needs at discount prices because of their alliance with the franchisor, which typically has made arrangements to buy supplies at large-volume prices. This is an increasingly great advantage because today one has to compete with national chains, conglomerates, buying consortiums, and other large franchises. The small-business person who purchases in small quantities can not easily compete in terms of buying power. By becoming a franchisee, a business has the collective buying power of the entire franchise system.

Research and Development Most small business owners are able to devote little time or money to research and development efforts. Franchising, then, can provide a huge lift in this regard, for many franchisors maintain ongoing research and development systems to develop new products and forecast market trends.

Consulting Services It is in the franchisor's best interests to do all it can to ensure the success of all of its franchisees. As a result, the entrepreneur who decides to become a franchisee can generally count on a wide range of training and consulting services from the larger company. Such services can be particularly helpful during the start-up phase of operations.

DRAWBACKS OF FRANCHISE OWNERSHIP

While the benefits of franchising are many and varied, there are well-documented drawbacks that should be considered as well. These include:

Cost The initial franchise fee, which in some cases is not refundable, can be quite expensive. Some fees are only a few thousand dollars, but others can require an up-front investment of several hundred thousand dollars. In addition, some franchisors require their franchisees to pay them regular royalty fees—a percentage of their weekly or monthly gross income—in exchange for permission to use their name. Some franchisors also require their franchise owners to help pay for their national advertising expenditures. Other costs include insurance, initial inventory purchases, and other expenses associated with equipping a new business.

Limited Control Franchisees are subject to many franchisor regulations concerning various aspects of business operation and conduct. As the Federal Trade Commission (FTC) acknowledged to prospective franchisees in its *Consumer Guide to Buying a Franchise,* "these controls may significantly restrict your ability to exercise your own business judgment." Areas in which franchisors generally wield significant control include the following:

Site Approval—Many franchise agreements include stipulations that give the franchisor final say in site selection. Some franchisors also limit franchise territories, and while such restrictions generally prevent other company franchisees from impinging on your territory, they can also act to restrict your ability to relocate once you have become established.

Operating Restrictions—Franchise agreements include many instructions on the ways in which a franchisee must conduct business. These encompass all aspects of a business's operation, from operating hours to accounting procedures to the goods or services that are offered. "These restrictions may impede you from operating your outlet as you deem best," admitted the FTC. "The franchisor also may require you to purchase supplies only from an approved supplier, even if you can buy similar goods elsewhere at a lower cost."

Appearance Many franchisors cultivate a certain readily recognizable look to their outlets, for they know that such standards, when applied consistently, contribute to national recognition of the company name and its products and services. Franchisees generally accept these regulations willingly, for these standards of appearance in the areas of decor, design, and uniforms have proven to be part of a winning formula elsewhere. This is just as well, for the franchise owner who does wish to make changes in his business's appearance often has little freedom to do so.

Association with the Franchisor For the small business owner whose franchise is attached to a highly regarded,

financially robust franchisor, the association can be a powerful positive in his or her business. Business experts note, however, that a franchise outlet can suffer severe damage if its franchisor is beset with financial difficulties or public relations problems. "If the franchisor hits hard times, you'll most likely feel them as well," noted the editors of the *Small Business Advisor.* "You are inevitably tied to the franchisor, not only by contract, but by concept, name, product, and services sold."

Prospective franchisees, then, need to weigh many factors in their decision making about entering the burgeoning world of franchising. But most small business consultants acknowledge that these factors usually boil down to a couple of fundamental concerns. The choice of becoming a franchisee or starting a stand-alone business hinges on the answers one gives to two important questions: Is risk sufficiently mitigated by the trademark value, operating system, economies of scale, and support process of the franchise to justify a sharing of equity with the franchisor? Is my personality and management style compatible with sharing decision-making responsibilities with the franchisor and other franchisees?"

SELECTING A FRANCHISE

It is imperative for prospective franchise owners to make an intelligent, informed decision regarding franchise selection, for once a contract has been signed, the franchisee has committed himself to the enterprise. But the selection process can be a bewildering one for the unprepared entrepreneur. Franchise opportunities are available in a wide array of industries, each of which offers its own potential benefits and drawbacks. Moreover, every franchisor has its own strengths and weaknesses. Several business areas, then, need to be investigated as part of any effective franchise selection process.

Analysis of Self Experts counsel prospective franchise owners to evaluate their own personal strengths and weaknesses before signing any franchise contract. Prospective franchisees should also have an understanding of their ultimate business and personal objectives before beginning the search for an appropriate franchise. The entrepreneur who is most interested in achieving financial security may want to look in an entirely different industry than the entrepreneur who hopes to land a franchise that will enable him or her to devote more time to family life.

Analysis of Industry and Market Prospective franchise owners need to evaluate which industries interest them. They also need to determine whether the franchisor's principal goods or services are in demand in the community in which he or she hopes to operate. Other industry-wide factors, such as the cost of raw materials used and the amount of industry competition, need to be weighed as well. The latter issue is a particularly important one, for it can be a fundamental factor in a franchisee's success or failure. The presence of some competition, for instance, often indicates a healthy demand for goods or services in that industry area. A dearth of competitors, though, might indicate that demand is low (or nonexistent). Similarly, the presence of several competitors might necessitate an examination of whether the market can support another provider in that area, or whether you might have to take meaningful market share from already existing businesses in order to survive.

Analysis of Franchisor Entrepreneurs interested in franchising should be knowledgeable about the strengths and weaknesses of companies that offer such arrangements. Factors that should be considered include the franchisor's profitability, organizational structure, growth patterns, public reputation, litigation history, financial management capabilities, fee requirements, and relationship with other franchisees.

Perhaps the best source of information on these and many other issues is the franchisor's disclosure document. This important document, which must be given to prospective franchise owners at least ten business days before any contract is signed or any deposits are owed, usually takes the form of the Uniform Franchise Offering Circular (UFOC). The UFOC contains important information on key aspects of the franchisor's business and the nature of its dealings with franchisees. Information contained in the UFOC includes a franchise history; audited financial statements and other financial history documents; franchise fee and royalty structures; background on the franchise's leading executives; terms of franchise agreements; estimated start-up costs for franchisees (including equipment, inventory, operating capital, and insurance); circumstances under which the franchisor can terminate its relationship with a franchisee; franchisor training and assistance programs; franchisee advertising costs (if any); data on the success (or lack thereof) of current and former franchisee operations; and litigation history.

Some prospective franchise owners pay less attention to a company's litigation history than other information included in the UFOC, but a company's past litigation experiences can, in some cases, provide important insights into the franchisor's business ethics and/or operating style. "The disclosure document tells you if the franchisor, or any of its executive officers, has been convicted of felonies involving, for example, fraud, any violation of franchise law or unfair or deceptive practices law, or are subject to any state or federal injunctions

involving similar misconduct," noted the Federal Trade Commission. "It also will tell you if the franchisor, or any of its executives, has been held liable or settled a civil action involving the franchise relationship. A number of claims against the franchisor may indicate that it has not performed according to its agreements, or, at the very least, that franchisees have been dissatisfied with the franchisor's performance. Be aware that some franchisors may try to conceal an executive's litigation history by removing the individual's name from their disclosure documents."

The inclusion of other information on a franchisor's business dealings with franchisees is up to the discretion of the franchisor. For example, while franchisors are required by law to provide prospective franchisees with documentation of expected start-up costs, they are not required to provide long-term earnings projections. Those who do provide such information are obligated by the FTC's Franchise Rule to have a reasonable basis for the claims they make and provide prospective franchisees with written information substantiating their projections.

It is important, then, to utilize other sources of information in addition to the disclosure document when pondering a move into the world of franchising. For example, small business consultants often urge prospective franchisees to conduct interviews with franchisor representatives about various business issues. Other sources of information often cited include financial institutions (for financial evaluations of the franchisor), state agencies (for information on franchisee rights in the state in which the franchisee is operating), the Better Business Bureau (for news of possible complaints against the franchisor), industry surveys, and associations (such as the Franchise Consultants International Association and the International Franchise Association).

Many experts also encourage prospective small business owners to interview current and former franchisees associated with the franchisor. Would-be franchisees can thus gain first-hand information on a great many business subjects, including: likely size of total investment, hidden or unexpected costs, satisfaction with franchisor performance (in training, advertising, operating, etc.), franchisee backgrounds, and business trends in the industry. Franchisee lists can be a valuable resource, but consultants caution their clients to make certain that they receive a complete list, rather than a list of selected franchisees who are compensated by the franchisor for giving positive appraisals of the company.

FRANCHISING LAWS

The United States has developed an extensive regulatory system designed to govern franchising practices throughout the business world. Chief among the federal guidelines are the FTC's Franchising and Business Opportunity Ventures Trade Regulation Rules and Subsequent Guidelines. In addition, many state governments have fashioned pieces of legislation that directly impact on franchising operations. A good many of the laws governing franchising—both at the state and federal level—are expressly designed to protect prospective small business owners from unscrupulous franchisors who misrepresent themselves.

Franchising experts commonly urge prospective franchisees to enlist the help of an attorney during the franchise selection process. Indeed, since franchising is such a complicated business, many entrepreneurs secure an attorney's services throughout the process. Legal assistance is especially helpful when the time comes to sign the franchise or license agreement, the document that lays out the terms of the partnership between a franchisee and a franchisor. "The franchise agreement is the foundation on which your franchise is built," stated the *Entrepreneur Magazine Small Business Advisor*. "The agreement gives both parties a clear understanding of the basis on which they are going to continue to operate."

The franchise contract covers all aspects of the franchisee-franchisor agreement, from record keeping to site selection to quality control provisions. The contract is designed to cover both relatively minor issues—such as sign display requirements—to matters of major importance—such as the franchisee's schedule of royalty payments and required insurance provisions. Franchise agreements also include a section devoted to detailing the length of the contract, and any possibilities for extending the terms of the contract beyond the termination date. Long term agreements (15 years or more) give franchisees more security, though this can be problematic if their relations with the franchisor take a bad turn. Since shorter terms do make it easier for franchisors to rid themselves of under performing or troublesome franchisees, some prefer to go this route. Others, however, place a higher value on securing the franchisee royalties that often pour in under the longer agreements.

Information included in the franchise contract includes the following:

- Accounting and recordkeeping provisions
- Existence (and terms) of any performance quotas
- Fairness of the franchise fee
- Fairness of the royalty arrangement
- Franchisor's continuing services to franchisee
- Insurance protection (if any) under franchisor's patent or liability insurance coverage

- Operating provisions (including quality control, human resource management, and other areas)
- Restrictions (if any) on business activities outside the franchise
- Restrictions (if any) on selling the franchise
- Start-up investment required
- Termination or default terms (as well as arbitration clauses)
- Terms of contributions, if any, to parent company's national advertising campaigns
- Terms of inventory and ordering practices
- Terms of renewing the franchise agreement
- Territorial protections

Given the scope of its coverage—and its importance as the binding legal document between franchisee and franchisor—the franchise contract is, in its final form, an imposing and complicated document. Again, the importance of the agreement makes it imperative that prospective franchise owners consult with an attorney before signing the contract.

SEE ALSO *Buying an Existing Business*

BIBLIOGRAPHY

Blair, Roger D., and Francine LaFontaine. *The Economics of Franchising*. Cambridge University Press, June 2005.

Caffey, Andrew A. "Now You're Cooking." *Entrepreneur*. January 1999.

Federal Trade Commission. *Consumer Guide to Buying a Franchise*. Available from http://www.ftc.gov/bcp/conline/pubs/invest/buyfran.htm Retrieved on 9 March 2006.

Goldstein, Joel. "Successful Franchisees Investigate before They Invest: Why franchise shows are invaluable to the decision-making process." *Franchising World*. November 2005.

"Great Business—Why Not Franchise it?" *Inc.* 29 May 2001.

Harris, Pat Lopes. "Fickle Franchising: Buying a Franchise May Seem Like a Low-Risk Way to Becoming a Successful Entrepreneur, But It's Not Necessarily a Sure Thing." *Washington Business Journal*. 6 November 1998.

Hill, Terry, and Amy Bannon. "Economic Census will Count Franchise Business." Press Release. International Franchising Association. Available from http://www.franchise.org/article.asp?article=1290&paper=93&cat=303 22 November 2005.

"Many Franchises are Services, Fitness." *UPI NewTrack*. 5 March 2006.

Hillstrom, Northern Lights
updated by Magee, ECDI

FREE-LANCE EMPLOYMENT/ INDEPENDENT CONTRACTORS

Free-lance employees, also known as independent contractors, are individuals who work on their own, without a long-term contractual commitment to any one employer. A free-lance employee usually performs services or completes work assignments under short-term contracts with several employers, or clients, who have the right to control only the final result of the individual's work, rather than the specific means used to get the work done. Examples of positions held by independent contractors range from doctors and computer programmers to maids and farm workers. Free-lance employment can offer a number of advantages to individuals, including flexible work arrangements, independence, variety, and some tax deductions. It can also hold some pitfalls, however, such as assuming risk in business dealings, paying self-employment taxes, and taking personal responsibility for health insurance, disability, and retirement coverage.

Specifically, individuals who are classified as independent contractors can deduct work-related expenses for tax purposes. In contrast, the first 2 percent of expenses are not deductible for those classified as employees. In addition, independent contractors often qualify for tax deductions for using part of their home as an office and for salaries paid to other people, while employees usually do not. Independent contractors also have the benefit of sheltering 15 percent of their annual income, or up to $30,000, for retirement, while employees are limited to $15,000 annually. Finally, independent contractors must pay the full amount of Social Security and Medicare taxes and make quarterly estimated tax payments to the federal government. Employers must withhold taxes for their employees and pay half of their Social Security and Medicare taxes.

Free-lance employment boomed in the United States during the 1980s, as many companies sought to reduce their payroll costs in order to remain competitive. Instead of hiring new employees and paying an additional 30 percent or more in payroll taxes and benefits, many companies chose to make "work-for-hire" arrangements with independent contractors (ICs). Businesses, and especially small businesses, can gain several advantages from such arrangements. For example, employers are not responsible for paying taxes for free-lance employees, and they avoid the high costs of providing health insurance, paid vacation and sick leave, and other benefits often granted to regular, full-time employees. In addition, employers that use independent contractors relieve themselves of the risk of costly litigation over hiring, promotion, firing, and other employment practices. These employers simply file Form 1099 with the government to report the total compensation paid to each independent contractor for the year.

There are disadvantages to using independent contractors instead of hiring a staff as well. The loyalty of a free-lance worker is not likely to be as great as that of an employee who is a part of the organization. The knowledge that an independent contractor gains about how a company likes things done is also in greater jeopardy than would be the case with an employee. Thus the investment in working with somebody is more easily lost with an independent contractor. However, small businesses often lack the financial security to make the longer-term commitment that taking on an employee requires. Hiring free-lancers is, consequently, an attractive option when help is needed.

FREE-LANCE TREND CAUSES CONTROVERSY

The boom in free-lance employment led to increased scrutiny by the U.S. Internal Revenue Service (IRS) in the early 1990s. Section 1706 of the Internal Revenue Code provides a 20-part test to determine whether workers are employees or independent contractors. The IRS began using this test to reclassify many independent contractors—particularly those engaged in high-paying professions—as employees in order to eliminate tax deductions and increase tax revenues.

The IRS has made reclassification of independent contractors a priority, since fraudulent IC arrangements are estimated to cost the government between $6 and $20 billion per year in tax revenue. The IRS would also argue that they are attempting to protect individuals from unfair treatment by employers—such as being fired and then rehired as an independent contractor without benefits—but few of the reclassifications have involved exploited low-wage laborers, because they generate minimal tax revenues.

Although the controversy surrounding free-lance employment has received increased attention in recent years, it is not new. As early as the 1960s, the IRS started looking more closely at household employees—such as maids, nannies, and gardeners—who often received income "under the table" and thus did not pay taxes. The main cause of dissension over current application of the law is that it often tends to penalize individuals who wish to be classified as independent contractors and take advantage of tax breaks (as well as the small businesses that depend on them), while it often fails to protect individuals who should be classified as employees and be eligible for benefits. For example, the IRS would be likely to review the case of a highly paid engineer who markets her services to several companies as an independent contractor and deducts various expenses of doing business. However, the IRS would be unlikely to review the case of a migrant farm worker who is employed by a large producer but, as an independent contractor, makes less than minimum wage and receives no disability or old-age benefits.

ELEMENTS OF THE IRS TEST

The IRS applies a 20-part test in order to determine whether a certain worker should be classified as an employee or an independent contractor. The main issue underpinning the test is who sets the work rules: employees must follow rules set by their bosses, while independent contractors set their own rules. The hours during which a job is performed is one determination of work rules. For example, if the employer dictates an individual's work hours or pays an individual by the hour rather than by the job, that individual is likely to be considered an employee rather than an independent contractor. Likewise, if the employer requires that an individual work full-time or not be employed by another company simultaneously, that individual would appear to be an employee. On the other hand, an individual who sets her own hours, receives payment by the job, and divides her time between work for several different employers would probably be classified as an independent contractor.

Other criteria involve who provides the tools and materials needed to complete the work. For example, an individual who works at an employer's facility and uses the employer's equipment would be considered an employee, while one who works at a separate location and provides his own equipment would be classified as an independent contractor. Another element of the IRS test involves termination of the work relationship. Employees can usually quit their jobs at will, and can also be fired by their employers. However, a free-lance employee would have a contractual obligation to complete a specific amount of work for an employer, and neither party could break the agreement without cause. Finally, an independent contractor usually pays his own expenses of doing business and takes the risk of not receiving payment when work is not completed in accordance with a contract, while an employee is usually reimbursed for business-related expenses by the employer and receives a paycheck whether his work is completed or not.

FREE-LANCE EMPLOYMENT AND SMALL BUSINESSES

The rules governing independent contractors affect small businesses in two significant ways. First, many entrepreneurs are themselves free-lance employees, and they must understand and adhere to the IRS guidelines in offering services to clients. Otherwise, they risk being reclassified as an employee of their client in an IRS audit of the same. An entrepreneur who is reclassified as an employee of a major client loses a variety of tax breaks and other advantages of self-employment.

In order to be considered independent contractors, entrepreneurs must establish that they are in business for themselves for the purpose of making a profit. They might demonstrate that their enterprise is a business—rather than a hobby or the work of an employee—by registering a business name, obtaining an occupational permit or license, establishing an office, soliciting clients, and printing stationery and business cards. Even if the majority of work will be performed for one client, entrepreneurs should make clear their intention of soliciting work from other clients.

Next, the entrepreneur should subject his or her business activities to the IRS 20-step test in order to avoid the appearance of being an employee. For example, the entrepreneur should be certain that the client does not set his or her hours, determine the location where work is performed, pay withholding taxes on his or her income, or provide needed equipment, tools, supplies, or transportation. Instead, the entrepreneur should sign a contract specifying an amount of work that will be completed by a certain deadline. The contract should include a specific disclaimer stating that this work will be performed as an independent contractor. The entrepreneur should also be certain to obtain a 1099 form (a statement of miscellaneous income) from the client for tax purposes, rather than a W-2 form (a statement of income from employment).

The rules governing independent contractors affect small businesses in another significant way. Many small businesses lack the resources to hire permanent employees to provide support for short-term projects or to provide expertise in highly technical fields, so instead they enlist the services of independent contractors. In these cases, it is to the benefit of the small business owner as well as the independent contractor to spell out the details of the work arrangement in a contract. The small business owner should also choose free-lance employees carefully to be sure that they present themselves as being in business to make a profit.

BIBLIOGRAPHY

Fishman, Stephen. *Working for Yourself.* Nolo Press, 2004.

Fishman, Stephen. *Working With Independent Contractors.* Fifth Edition. Nolo Press, July 2005.

Lankford, Kimberly. "Freelancers, Meet Schedule C." *Kiplinger's Starting Out Web Column.* 27 January 2005.

Mullings, Monique. "Freelancers Can be Enhancers." *European Intelligence Wire.* 19 September 2005.

Russman, Joel, and Cindy Gomerdinger. "Pros and Cons of Contractors vs. Employees." *Denver Business Journal.* 17 March 2000.

U. S. Internal Revenue Service. "Independent Contractor vs. Employee." Available from http://www.irs.gov/businesses/small/article/0,id=99921,00.html Retrieved on 10 March 2006.

Hillstrom, Northern Lights
updated by Magee, ECDI

G

---•---

GENDER DISCRIMINATION

Gender discrimination, also known as sexual discrimination, is any action that specifically denies opportunities, privileges, or rewards to a person (or a group) because of gender. The practice of letting a person's gender become a factor when deciding who receives a job or a promotion, is gender discrimination. When gender is a factor in other decisions about employment opportunities or benefits, that too is gender discrimination. While most discrimination charges claim that a woman (or women) was discriminated against in favor of a man (or men), there have also been cases where males have claimed that they have been discriminated against on the basis of gender. These cases are usually referred to as "reverse discrimination."

Court rulings handed down through the years have determined that a company's responsibility not to discriminate based on sex begins even before an individual is hired. Companies can be held liable if pre-employment screening or testing is determined to be discriminatory, if applications ask unacceptable questions designed to screen for sex, or if the overall selection process is deemed to be unfair. One of the main indicators that gender discrimination has occurred in the hiring process involves the qualifications of the job applicants. While a slight difference in qualifications between a female and a male candidate does not automatically indicate gender bias (if a lesser qualified male candidate is hired instead of a female candidate, that is), a drastic difference in qualifications has almost always been upheld by the courts as a sure sign of gender discrimination. For example, if a male who dropped out of high school without receiving a diploma is hired in an administrative position over a female who had obtained her master's degree, then it is likely bias was a factor.

In addition to gender discrimination in hiring and other circumstances, there is a particular form of sexual discrimination called sexual harassment. This form of discrimination involves inappropriate words or actions of a sexual nature directed at one employee by another. To meet the criteria for harassment, the behavior in question must be both unwanted and sexual in nature. The U.S. legal system has determined that there are two main types of sexual harassment, the first being "quid pro quo," or "this for that," which occurs when one employee offers another employee a job or benefit in exchange for sexual favors, or threatens to deny that job or benefit unless sexual favors are granted. The second type of sexual harassment is referred to as "hostile work environment." In these types of cases, an employee, or a group of employees, repeatedly make lewd comments or suggestive noises, make unwanted sexual advances, or otherwise use sex to create a work environment that is intimidating or threatening to others.

FEDERAL LAWS STRONGLY PROHIBIT GENDER DISCRIMINATION

Since the social unrest of the 1960s, the federal government has been actively involved in preventing gender discrimination in the workplace. One of the most important laws covering gender discrimination on the job is the Civil Rights Act of 1964—specifically, Title VII of that act, which strictly prohibits all forms of discrimination on the basis of race, color, religion, sex, or national origin in all aspects of employment. Written during a tumultuous period in American history when many people expected the federal government to right social wrongs, the law was a monumental piece of legislation that changed the American employment landscape.

The law was passed after heated debate in both the Senate and the House of Representatives. It stated that it was unlawful for an employer to "fail or refuse to hire or to discharge any individual, or otherwise discriminate against any individual with respect to his compensation, terms, conditions, or privileges or employment, because of such individual's race, color, religion, sex, or national origin." The law covers hiring, dismissals, compensation, and all other aspects of employment, while also covering actual employment opportunities that are available. Examples of gender discrimination or sexual harassment that would fall under the scope of the act include:

I. An employee who alleges that his or her manager only promotes male employees and keeps females in entry-level positions.

II. An employee who alleges that a manager or other person in power tells jokes or makes statements that are demeaning, insulting, or offensive to women.

III. A manager who makes it clear, either through his actions or words, that he wants to have sexual relations with a female employee.

IV. A manager who asks inappropriate and unnecessary questions about a female employee's sex life.

V. A manager who touches his female employees in inappropriate ways without consent.

The law covers business with 15 or more employees, and applies to all private, federal, state, and local employers. In many states, businesses with fewer than 15 employees face the same rules thanks to local or state statutes. In addition to the hiring provisions, the law dictates that employers cannot limit or segregate employees based on sex in any way that would adversely affect their chances at promotions. It does allow for two narrow exceptions to the law—businesses may use a "bona fide" seniority or merit system to measure performance and earnings based on a quantity or quality measuring system, and employers may use ability tests to determine the most qualified candidates for a job as long as the test does not discriminate by gender in any way.

The Civil Rights Act was originally intended to address only racial discrimination. Just as the law was about to be passed, however, Representative Howard Smith of Virginia added the word "sex" to one of the opening sentences, meaning the law would also prevent sexual discrimination. This was a controversial action, as many people actually saw it as an attempt to kill the bill. The argument made by critics was that Smith added the word sex to the law knowing that many people would oppose the addition and the bill would be defeated, thus preventing racial protection from occurring as well. Smith denied this accusation and swore he had added the provision after working with the National Women's Party. Whatever his motivation, thanks to the efforts of Representative Martha Griffiths and others, the revised bill was passed into law.

One year before the landmark civil rights legislation act was passed, one specific problem regarding gender discrimination had also been addressed by the U.S. Congress. Until 1963, it was legal for employers to pay women lower wages for the same job performed by men. During World War II, when many women worked at jobs traditionally held by men while the men fought in the war, there had been an attempt by the National War Labor Board to get companies to pay women the same rate as men, but that attempt failed miserably. In fact, most of the women lost their jobs when the men came home from the war.

Before 1963, newspapers routinely ran separate Help Wanted sections in the classifieds—one for men, and one for women. It was not uncommon for the same job to be posted in both sections, but with different—and much lower—pay scales for women. In 1963, women earned 59 percent of what men earned for the same job, or for every dollar a man earned, a woman earned 59 cents.

The Equal Pay Act of 1963 was intended to end that discrepancy. The law stated that "no employer... shall discriminate, within any establishment in which such employees are employed, between employees on the basis of sex by paying wages to employees in such establishment at a rate less than the rate at which he pays wages to employees of the opposite sex in such establishment for equal work on jobs the performance of which requires equal skill, effort, and responsibility, and which are performed under similar working conditions." The only exemptions to the law were for seniority, established merit systems that paid all employees based on job performance, systems that paid wages based on the quantity or quality of the work produced, and wage differences that were based on some factor other than sex.

While the law did not put an end to unequal pay, it did improve things in many cases. Between 1964, when the law went into effect, and 1971, more than $26 million in back pay was issued to women as a result of court cases filed after the law was passed. Two cases that made their way through the U.S. court system—*Schultz v. Wheaton Glass Co.* (1970) and *Corning Glass Works v. Brennan* (1974)— modified the 1963 law by eliminating common loopholes. The ruling in the Schultz case said that jobs only had to be "substantially equal" rather than identical to earn protection under the law. In the Corning Glass case, the U.S. Supreme Court decided that companies could not pay women a lower wage than men simply because there was a "lower going rate" for female employees in the local marketplace. The court ruled that the only reason such a lower rate existed was because male employees would refuse to work for the lower rate that was offered to women.

The Equal Pay Act officially gives women protection under the law in regards to equal pay for equal work, but inequities still exist in almost every employment sector. According to the U.S. Census Bureau, women working full-time in 2004 still earned only 77 cents for every dollar earned by a man. Some employers still resist the need to pay men and women equally for equal work. Some even go so far as to change job titles or employment requirements just to find a way to make jobs seem different enough to justify paying women less than men. Consequently, courts are starting to use a "comparable worth" test to determine if two jobs merit the same amount of pay instead of relying on the description of the exact tasks performed on a job. There is hope that the situation will continue to improve, as it has slowly for the last 40 years.

Above and beyond standard sexual discrimination, sexual harassment has been the centerpiece of numerous court cases and legal decisions that have established government standards regarding harassment. In 1998, the U.S. Supreme Court made two important rulings that have had a significant effect on harassment claims. In *Burlington Industries, Inc. v. Ellerth,* the court ruled that, even if an employee did not report incidents of alleged harassment when they occurred, the company was still liable for the behavior of the employee who committed the sexual acts. In *Faragher v. City of Boca Raton,* the court held that an employer could be held liable for harassment if a supervisor made threats regarding punishment if an employee did not have sex with him, even if those threats were never carried out. Together, the two decisions made it clear that the court holds companies strictly liable for actions carried out by supervisors who have direct authority over the person they are harassing, if the supervisor can alter the victim's employment status through hiring, firing, refusal to promote, etc.

THE EQUAL EMPLOYMENT OPPORTUNITY COMMISSION

To oversee the federal civil rights legislation, including the Equal Pay Act, a separate administrative body was created as part of the Civil Rights Act of 1964. The Equal Employment Opportunity Commission, or EEOC, was created to enforce laws that prevent discrimination based on race, sex, color, religion, national origin, disability, or age when hiring, firing, or promoting employees. Four groups—race, color, sex, and creed—were given "protected status" under the law, which was to be upheld by the EEOC. The commission is an independent regulatory body that has the power to launch investigations, file lawsuits, and create programs to eliminate discrimination.

The EEOC has been a controversial organization throughout its nearly 40-year history. Liberal politicians believe that the agency was long overdue and that it is absolutely imperative that it be proactive in identifying and fighting discrimination in the courts, while conservatives believe that the organization is a perfect example of "big government" that intrudes far too deeply into citizens' lives. The agency's strong enforcement of affirmative action policies (which actively seek to promote minorities over equally qualified nonminorities in order to address past discrimination) has been its most controversial action, as many Americans oppose affirmative action.

STEPS TAKEN BY EMPLOYERS TO END GENDER DISCRIMINATION

To prevent gender discrimination or sexual harassment from occurring in the workplace, more and more employers are adopting a zero tolerance policy towards all acts of discrimination. This usually includes the creation of an official written policy against discrimination that is circulated to all employees, as well as education and training courses for all managers (and often for all employees). In addition, the companies have to show that they are serious about implementing and enforcing the new policy by creating disciplinary standards for violations of the policy.

Another step employers can take is to conduct a thorough investigation every time a claim of discrimination or harassment is lodged. If a company identifies a situation where it believes discrimination has occurred and the company is going to be held liable, it can ease the amount of punishment handed down if it conducts a thorough in-house investigation that culminates in appropriate action taken against the person who committed the discrimination, up to and including dismissal of that employee.

When managers are trained to recognize instances of sexual discrimination or harassment, they should be told one thing above all others—not to try to handle the complaint by themselves. Instead, they should always immediately notify the human resources department that an incidence of discrimination or harassment has been reported and needs to be investigated. If the training is also provided to all employees, primary efforts should be spent on teaching employees what is and is not considered to be appropriate behavior and on helping employees understand each other better so that they can work together more effectively.

THE CURRENT STATE OF GENDER DISCRIMINATION

While many cases of sexual discrimination or harassment involve men victimizing women, there is a new backlash that has seen allegations of reverse sexual discrimination. A male cosmetics counter employee at a Dillard's department store in Florida became angry when his suit was stained by the make-up he was selling. When he asked the store for a uniform of some sort, which the female employees who worked at the make-up counter at another store in the same mall wore, he was ignored by store management. The man also alleged that he was passed over for promotions and was ineligible to win store sales contests because all of the prizes were for women. The employee filed a sexual discrimination claim with the EEOC and later filed a lawsuit against the store.

In another case, a male employee of Vision Quest National in Philadelphia filed a lawsuit alleging sexual discrimination when he was fired after complaining that he had to work nights for the company while women did not. The company had instituted a policy saying women did not have to work the night shift because the company was in a high-crime area; several female employees had threatened to quit if forced to work nights. The company claimed the policy was a bona fide occupational qualification (which is one of the EEOC's exemptions in discrimination cases), but the courts ruled that this was not the case and sided with the male employee.

In addition to reverse discrimination cases, there have also been recent instances of same-sex discrimination cases. While the EEOC holds that Title VII of the Civil Rights Act *does* protect against same-sex discrimination, the courts have been reluctant to rule on the matter. In 1998, however, the U.S. Supreme Court reversed the ruling of a lower court and in so doing held that same-sex discrimination was in fact covered by Title VII because the law referred to sex in every context.

Discrimination against employees on the basis of gender (as well as race, national origin, age, and/or disability) is wrong. It may also be very costly. Charges of employment discrimination that are successfully brought before the EEOC are usually resolved, in part, by issuing the plaintiff a monetary award. The trend towards larger awards has been steady and although it is unclear whether that trend will continue, some people clearly believe that it will. As a result, a new form of commercial liability insurance emerged in the late 1990s in answer to the

rising costs associated with employment discrimination actions. It is called Employment Practices Liability Insurance (EPLI) and it may one day be a standard policy within commercial insurance packages.

Avoiding the need for such an insurance policy is, of course, preferable. Establishing serious policies to prevent discrimination is essential. Making these efforts visible and apparent to all will help to create a work environment free of discrimination, or at least one in which discriminatory acts are brought to the attention of management right away.

SEE ALSO *Equal Employment Opportunity Commission; Sexual Harassment*

BIBLIOGRAPHY

Bible, Jon B. "Disorder in the Courts: Proving same-sex sex discrimination in Title VII cases via 'gender stereotyping'." *Employee Relations Law Journal.* Spring 2006.

"Discriminatory Protective Rules Illegal." *Workforce.* December 2000.

Equal Employment Opportunity Commission. "EEOC Litigation Statistics, FY 1992 through FY 2005." Available from http://www.eeoc.gov/stats/litigation.html Retrieved on 10 March 2006

McDonald, James J. Jr. "Be Nice, or Be Sued." *Employee Relations Law Journal.* Spring 2006.

"Sexual Harassment Interpretations Give Cause for New Concerns." *Workforce.* May 1999.

"Title VII Sex Discrimination in the Public Sector in the 1990s: The Courts' View." *Public Personnel Management.* Summer 1998.

U.S. Census Bureau. "Historical Income Tables – People." Available on http://www.census.gov/hhes/www/income/histinc/p03.html. Retrieved on 5 March 2006.

U.S. National Archives and Records Administration. "The Civil Rights Act of 1964 and the Equal Opportunity Employment Commission." Available from http://www.archives.gov/index.html Retrieved on 10 March 2006

Hillstrom, Northern Lights
updated by Magee, ECDI

GLOBAL BUSINESS

Global business refers to international trade whereas *a* global business is a company doing business across the world. The exchange of goods over great distances goes back a very long time. Anthropologists have already established long-distance trading in Europe in the Stone Age. Sea-borne trading was commonplace in many regions of the world in times predating Greek civilization. Such trade, of course, was not by definition "global" but had the same characteristics. In the 16th century all of the continents came to be routinely linked by ocean-based communications. Trading activity in the modern sense rapidly followed at the beginning of the 17th century; it might be more accurate to say that it "returned" again because trading of such character had taken place in Roman times as well.

It is not intended here to discuss another and related subject covered separately in this volume: globalization. Globalization is a long-standing program advocated by the economically advanced nations to free up international trade across the globe through treaties. It has also come to mean the relocation of production or service activities to places that have much lower labor costs. Global business in the past—or currently—does not require what advocates of globalization seek, namely a so-called level playing field. International trade has always had a mixed character in which national organizations and private enterprises have both participated, in which monopolies have been imposed, frequently defended by armed forces, in which all manner of restraints and tariffs have been common and participants have made all sorts of efforts to counter such interference or to profit from it.

GLOBAL ENTERPRISES

Fernand Braudel, a prominent historian of commerce, describes early trading with distant points around the globe—from Europe to the Americas and from Europe to India and Asia—in what then was still called Christendom, as speculative ventures funded by high-interest loans from patrons: traders had to pay back double the money they borrowed; failure to pay the money back—unless they had been shipwrecked—meant a period of slavery until the debt was satisfied. Very high profits could be achieved trading in spices and silk with the "Indies"; such profits justified the risks. In parallel with such private trading, government-sponsored ventures also took to the oceans; they became the dominant form of international trade shortly before and all through the period of colonialism. Thus Spain exploited its discoveries in South America by shipping gold and silver from America to Europe—thus setting off a great inflationary period. Global enterprise, thus, in the modern sense, began to develop during the Age of Discovery. It was instrumental in stimulating colonialism. Single merchants or groups of explorers went forth and came back with treasures. Government-sponsored consortia, the early global businesses, followed in the adventurers' wake.

The two earliest global companies, both government chartered, were the British East India Company begun in 1600 and the Dutch East India Company, established in 1602. Both have now passed into history. The British company dissolved in 1874, but in its nearly 300-year

history it had launched and for a long period had practically run the British Empire. The Dutch company was dissolved in 1798 after nearly 200 years of operations in Asia, India, Sri Lanka, and Africa. But the Hudson Bay Company, another British-founded monopoly to exploit the North American fur trade, was established in 1670 and is still going—so much so that Canadians explain that the company's initials stand for "Here Before Christ." HBC has long since ceased to be a global monopoly and is known today in Canada as a department store.

Early global companies were usually state-chartered *trading* companies. The Danes, the French, and the Swedes all had East India companies. Japan established companies known as the *sogo shosha* (for "general trading company") in the 19th century. Japan had tried and failed to preserve its isolation. When it opened itself to the world, it channeled trade through these ventures. Great trading companies were and continue to be important in transportation as well; operating shipping supports their activities. A contemporary American example is the privately held Cargill Corporation which trades internationally in agricultural, food, pharmaceutical, and financial products.

Commodity-based international corporations emerged in the 19th century with oil. The first global oil company was Standard Oil, founded by John D. Rockefeller. That honor was held by others since, including Exxon Corporation and Royal Dutch/Shell Group until, in the mid-2000s, Saudi Arabia's Aramco became Number 1. Major companies in turn emerged in chemicals and in artificial fibers, in automobiles, in aircraft manufacturing, and then in virtually every industry in the second part of the 20th century.

Multinationals The term "multinationals" came into currency during the same time to designate corporations that operated in at least two different countries—but the actual use of the label applies to corporations that have a global presence. The term is used in a neutral sense simply to indicate very large size and participation in global markets. A more negative connotation of the term is that such corporations are effectively beyond the full reach of national laws because they have a presence in many locations, can move money and resources around at will, can sometimes escape taxation, and thus represent a power beyond public control.

Business Week has compiled what it labeled the "Top 100 Global Brands Scoreboard." It gives some indication of the characteristics and distribution of multinationals. The "scoreboard" is based on unique products (thus the "brand" label applied here) and by definition excludes some very important multinationals that operate in unbranded commodities like crude oil, grains, food products, minerals and similar categories; Phillips, British Petroleum, and Shell, for instance, make the top 100 but Aramco does not. Based on this scorecard, the U.S. dominates the category with 53 of the 100 top brands; the U.S. also holds 8 of the first 10 spots. Others in rank order are Germany (9), France (8), Japan (7), Switzerland (5), Britain and Italy both with 4, the Netherlands and South Korea with 3 each, and Finland, Spain, and Sweden with 1 each. Additionally, one company. Royal Dutch Petroleum, is listed as both British and Dutch. The top 10, in order of brand value, are Coca-Cola, Microsoft, IBM, General Electric, Intel, Nokia (Finland), Disney, McDonald's, Toyota (Japan), and Marlboro's producer, Altria Group. The two largest industrial categories are electronics and software with 17 brands and autos and related with 11. As Coca-Cola with its sweet soda leads the list so Heineken with its beer closes the list in the 100th spot.

GLOBAL MARKETS

From the point of view of a seller, a global market is an export market; from the buyer's vantage point, the global market represents imports from abroad. World statistics on international trade are collected by the World Trade Organization (WTO) located in Geneva. The most current data available in early 2006 were for the year 2004; all economic data lag the current time, but international data more so than national. In 2004, the global market for exports was $11.28 trillion, with merchandise exports representing 81.2 and commercial services 18.8 percent of that total. Merchandise exports, using WTO's definition, include commodities as well as manufactured and semi-manufactured goods. Services are divided into transportation, travel, and the "other services" categories.

Merchandise Trade The largest category of foreign trade is in machinery and transportation equipment, representing 16.8 percent of the total—but the category pointedly excludes both automobiles and related equipment as well as office and telecommunications equipment. Fuels and Mining Products is second with 14.4 percent of share. The other major categories are Office and Telecom Equipment (12.7 percent), Chemicals (11.0), Automobiles and Related (9.5), Agricultural Products (8.8), Other Manufactured Products not already mentioned (8.6), Semi-Manufactures (like parts and components, 7.1 percent), Iron and Steel (3.0), Clothing (2.9), and Textiles other than clothing (2.2 percent).

Just ten countries around the world represent 54.8 percent of all merchandise exports. Germany led the world in 2004 with a 10 percent share of all exports, followed by the U.S. with an 8.9 percent share. Other leading exporters in order of share were China (6.5), Japan (6.2), France (4.9), the Netherlands (3.9), Italy (3.8), United Kingdom (3.8), Canada (3.5), and Belgium (10 percent of total).

At the top of world trading, anyway, the same countries were also the top importers, but not in the same order. The U.S. was top importer: 16.1 percent of all world imports were bought by U.S. consumers; Germany was second with 7.6 percent of imports. The others were China (5.9 percent), France and the United Kingdom (both 4.9), Japan (4.8), Italy (3.7), the Netherlands (3.4), Belgium (3.0), and Canada (2.9).

More interestingly, six of 10 countries achieved a trade surplus and the others had a trade deficit. The U.S. had the largest negative, a deficit of $706.7 billion, followed by the United Kingdom ($116.6 billion), France ($16.7 billion), and Italy ($1.9 billion).

Commercial Services In the export and import of commercial services, the U.S. ranked first on both sides of this ledger, representing 15 percent of exports and 12 percent of services imports—and achieved a $58.3 billion trade surplus—not enough, however, to erase its very large merchandise trade deficit. The other leading exporters of services were United Kingdom (8.1 percent of services exports resulting in a $35.7 billion services trade surplus), Germany (6.3 percent, a $59.1 billion *deficit*— which reduced its healthy merchandise surplus), France (5.1 percent of exports, achieving $13.1 billion in surplus, which almost wiped out its merchandise trade deficit), and Japan (4.5 percent, experiencing a $39.1 billion *deficit* in this category of trade).

TOP U.S. TRADING PARTNERS

Trade is by its very nature a reciprocal activity. Not surprisingly, the United States' top nine trading partners, established by adding both exports to them to imports received from them, are also in the top 15 of export and of import viewed separately. These countries are (arranged by total trade volume) Canada, Mexico, China, Japan, Germany, United Kingdom, South Korea, France, and Taiwan. Countries that are part of the top 15 to which the U.S. exports, in addition to those just named, are the Netherlands, Belgium, Australia, Brazil, and Hong Kong. On the import side, in addition to the largest trade partners, the top 15 import partners include Venezuela, Malaysia, Italy, Ireland, Saudi Arabia, and Nigeria. These listings are for trade results achieved in March 2006, but looking back at intervals over several years, much the same results obtain. It is also notable that the world's top foreign traders, discussed above, are on the U.S. list—strongly suggesting that foreign trade in noticeable volume, is between major developed industrial countries in the first instance, between neighbors in the second, and then come important suppliers of oil.

Related Parties When a company imports from or exports to a foreign-based element of its own company—to a branch, a subsidiary, or a partner—the goods or services nevertheless cross country borders and are handled as foreign trade. In 2005, 47 percent of all U.S. imports were from "related parties" and 31 percent of exports went to such entities. These ratios have been fairly steady over time; the import ratio in 2001 was the same and the export ratio just one percentage point higher. Related party trading is, of course, an indirect measure of globalization—especially the rather high import percentage: it shows that companies are importing goods made by themselves, most likely in lower labor-cost markets, for sale domestically.

BALANCING THE TRADE

In the grand scheme of international trading, a balance in trade has always been the rational goal of sovereign states. Balanced trade means that exports will be the same as imports, one balancing the other. Exports generate the currency with which imports must be bought. A country that persistently experiences trade deficits slides into debt or dependency on foreign investment—the current situation of the U.S. The United States has experienced trade deficits continuously since 1971; it has been able to sustain its way of life only because of foreign investment here.

Current trends point to continued and ever-growing trade deficits. The only bright spot in the picture is a trade surplus in the commercial services export category. Such surpluses, however, would have to increase 12-fold (based on 2004 data) before they erased the merchandise trade deficit. The other alternatives open are as yet invisible innovations that lead to the creation of new, proprietary exports no one else can match—or a drastic diet of consumption so that imports take a dive and exports can catch up. The future will tell which way the problem will be resolved.

SEE ALSO *Globalization*

BIBLIOGRAPHY
"Aramco No. 1 Oil Company." *The New York Times.* 20 May 2006.

Braudel, Fernand. *The Wheels of Commerce.* Harper & Row, 1979.

"International Trade Statistics." World Trade Organization. Available from http://www.wto.org/english/res_e/statis_e/statis_e.htm. Retrieved on 19 May 2006.

Jones, Geoffrey. *Merchants to Multinationals: British Trading Companies in the Nineteenth and Twentieth Centuries.* Oxford University Press, 2000.

"Top 100 Global Brands Scoreboard." *Business Week Online.* Available from http://bwnt.businessweek.com/brand/2005/. Retrieved on January 10, 2006.

U.S. Census Bureau. Bernard, Andrew B., J. Bradford Jensen, and Peter K. Schott. "Importers, Exporters and Multinationals: A Portrait of Firms in the U.S. That Trade Goods." Center for Economic Studies. October 2005.

U.S. Census Bureau. News Release. "U.S. Goods Trade: Imports & Exports by Related Parties; 2005." 12 May 2006.

U.S. Census Bureau. "Top Trading Partners – Total Trade, Exports, Imports." March 2006. Available from http://www.census.gov/foreign-trade/statistics/highlights/top/top0603.html. Retrieved on 19 May 2006.

Darnay, ECDI

GLOBALIZATION

Viewed narrowly, globalization is a governmental policy favoring free trade, open borders, the free movement of capital and goods (but not always of people), elimination of tariffs and price controls (including artificial control of currency values), and the privatization of publicly-owned or controlled enterprises. Globalization is also a word used to describe all manner of phenomena associated with such a policy—both positive and negative. In the U.S., the positive consequences of globalization so far have been inexpensive imports and the ability of companies to more easily invest abroad; the negative consequences have been the loss of jobs to off-shored operations and outsourced functions, large trade deficits, and foreign ownership of domestic assets. Globalization is a polarizing issue generally favored by the right in the name of free markets and opposed by the left as a policy that favors "Big Capital" and hence a small corporate elite.

HISTORICAL CONTEXT

The International Monetary Fund, an organization of 184 countries, suggests in its definition that globalization is something of a natural process. Globalization, according to the IMF, is "a historical process, the result of human innovation and technological progress. It refers to the increasing integration of economies around the world, particularly through trade and financial flows. The term sometimes also refers to the movement of people (labor) and knowledge (technology) across international borders. There are also broader cultural, political and environmental dimensions of globalization. . . ."

Trade, of course, is as old as humanity. Anthropologists have traced enormous trade routes that Cro-Magnon man used all across Europe before the dawn of history. Trade over land and by ship became common, the principal trade goods being agricultural products like olives and grains. In pre-industrial times high dependence either on exports or imports tended to lead to war as countries tried either to secure their supplies or their markets. Rome became seriously dependent on grain imports from Egypt and eventually conquered its supplier. The British Empire evolved as a series of steps attempting to protect its far flung trading centers. In modern times oil and gas are the "must have" commodities and are producing wars and tensions. The relevant phrase in the IMF's definition therefore is "increasing integration." Integration implies mutual dependency and therefore the danger of being cut off in times of trouble.

Underlying trade is the uneven distribution of the world's resources. Some people have grain, others have timber. Some can raise animals on plains others can mine metal in mountains. We encounter a formulation of this argument in Adam Smith's *The Wealth of Nations* (18th century): "If a foreign country can supply us with a commodity cheaper than we ourselves can make it, better buy it of them with some part of the produce of our own industry, employed in a way in which we have some advantage." In the 19th century David Ricardo refined this concept and called it "comparative advantage." Ricardo factored in opportunity costs as well as direct costs. In any event, the value underlying free trade is that both sides benefit because of differential advantages.

Trade is the expression of economic power, but a more basic power underlies it: political power expressed as force. Trade-based policies in the past have been balanced by policies of autarky, a word Merriam-Webster defines to mean "national economic self-sufficiency; a policy of establishing independence of imports from other countries." No country is genuinely self-sufficient, but attempts to gain the optimum advantage by a mixture of trade and force tends to be practiced at all times. Thus the U.S. government, for instance, despite a broadly favorable view on globalization, still imposed a tariff on Brazilian ethanol imports in the mid-2000s. The relative power of a country, the relative importance of a commodity, and the relative influence of vital constituencies within that country combine to determine how much a country will rely on trade, how much on force, and in which categories particularly.

A fundamental reason for opposition to globalization arises from its chief feature, integration and therefore mutual dependence. In democratically organized countries political blocks can only hope to influence their own government—not that of scores of others. But unreachable foreign governments will influence the local economy. And narrow constituencies that benefit disproportionately from free trade may be able to control the government. The free trade philosophy, based on the vitality of competition, is also opposed by a socialist philosophy, based on the virtue of cooperation.

INSTITUTIONAL EXPRESSION

Globalization is taking place under international treaties to which a majorities of countries are signatories. Traditionally these treaties have been negotiated in so-called "rounds" and have resulted in "agreements." The last "round" was the Uruguay Round in which agreements were signed on April 24, 1994; they went into effect on January 1, 1995, and established the World Trade Organization (WTO). Several other agreements were annexed to the "WTO Agreement;" these include the General Agreement on Tariffs and Trade (GATT), the General Agreement on Trade and Services (GATS), and the Agreement on Trade-Related Aspects of Intellectual Property Rights (TRIPS). The first GATT was negotiated and signed in 1947. WTO is now the successor to all of these agreements.

The WTO is headquartered in Geneva, Switzerland, and had a membership (as of December 2005) of 145 countries. The organization describes itself as "the only global international organization dealing with the rules of trade between nations. At its heart are the WTO agreements, negotiated and signed by the bulk of the world's trading nations and ratified in their parliaments. The goal is to help producers of goods and services, exporters, and importers conduct their business."

In the mid-2000s the WTO was engaged in the Doha Round of negotiations (based in Doha, Qatar and begun in 2001). The chief aims of the round, strongly backed by the U.S. government, were further liberalization of trade in agricultural goods and services. The future of this round, and thus indirectly of the WTO, was murky at the time of writing (2006) because ratification of the new agreements was widely opposed and not certain to be ratified even by the U.S. Congress.

U.S. TREATIES AND INITIATIVES

Within the U.S. government, the institutional body managing trade activities is the Office of the United States Trade Representative (USTR), a 200-person organization that takes the lead in negotiating trade agreements. The legal basis of this governmental element was the Trade Expansion Act of 1962, modified by subsequent trade acts, most recently by the Trade and Development Act of 2000.

Official U.S. participation in the globalization movement takes the form of participation in the global agreements that formed the WTO. In addition, the U.S. is a party to three regional agreements and is a promoter of three regional initiatives.

The agreements include APEC (for Asia-Pacific Economic Cooperation, signed in 1989), NAFTA (North American Free Trade Agreement, which became effective in 1994), and CAFTA (Central American Free Trade Agreement, which became effective in 2005). CAFTA includes the Dominican Republic and all Central American States except Costa Rica which has thus far not ratified the treaty. The USTR lists CAFTA as a bilateral agreement although it includes a group of nations.

The U.S. is also active in pursuing several free trade initiatives. These include the FTAA Initiative (for Free Trade Area of the Americas, begun 1994), the ASEAN Initiative (for Association of Southeast Asian Nations, begun 2002), and the MEFTA Initiative (for Middle East Free Trade Area, begun 2003). The treatment of CAFTA as a bilateral agreement may be the consequence of difficulties in bringing the FTAA Initiative to an agreement in more than a decade of ministerial meetings.

With CAFTA removed, the U.S. also has 13 bilateral agreements with Australia, Bahrain, Chile, Columbia, Israel, Jordan, Malaysia, Morocco, Oman, Panama, Peru, Singapore, and the South African Customs Union.

Most Favored Nations Just to keep things straight, special trade agreements *are not the same* as the often-mentioned "most-favored-nation" designations. The Library of Congress Research Service provides the following definition for the phrase: "Under the provisions of the General Agreement on Tariffs and Trade (GATT), when one country accords another most-favored-nation status, it agrees to extend to that country the same trade concessions, such as lower tariffs or reduced nontariff barriers, that it grants to any other recipient having most-favored-nation status." Each country, therefore, has its own definition of "most favored nation." All those so designated are treated alike. But some countries may be treated more favorably still. In that case they will not bear the "most favored" label. NAFTA members are an example. The phrasing is unfortunate because one is reminded of George Orvell's *Animal Farm*. Many nations may be "most favored," but some are more favored than others.

COSTS AND BENEFITS

The costs and benefits of globalization depend on who you are, where you are, and even on what you are doing at any one point in time. Are you shopping? Working? Looking for work? Do you work for a multinational? For a small business? From the U.S. perspective, globalization has resulted in massive imports of goods available at very attractive prices in major outlets like Wal-Mart. This has helped consumers but has brought hardship on many small-business retailers unable to purchase goods in high quantity in foreign markets at rock-bottom prices. Globalization has not only made it possible to import low-priced goods but also to export well-paid jobs to low-wage regions of the world, thus causing job-losses domestically. Lost jobs may be replaced, but the general

consequences of intense competition with lower-paid labor elsewhere is to depress income domestically.

The benefits of lower prices have sent U.S. consumers on a shopping spree. Robert Samuelson reported in *Newsweek* on this phenomenon, citing Sara Johnson of Global Insight: "From 1996 to 2005," Samuelson wrote, "the United States generated almost 45 percent of global growth in consumer spending… That dwarfs the U.S. share of the world economy, [which is] about 20 percent." A consequence of this has been an increase in the U.S. trade deficit from $191 billion in 1996 to $784 billion in 2005. But trade deficits extend unbroken many decades back (to 1971—when it was only $4.9 billion), indicating that the U.S. consistently sells less abroad than it buys from others. This, in effect, represents a net loss of U.S. assets to foreign owners. In the case of the U.S., "increased integration" has produced rapidly growing "dependence"—which, unless righted by energetic corrective measures, can only be paid for, ultimately, by a decline in the standard of living.

The near term beneficiaries of globalization are consumers. And they need help because their incomes are stagnant or declining. The clearest beneficiaries are the stockholders of big multinational corporations that reap the rewards of greatly increased flexibilities in sourcing labor and raw materials while still retaining the large U.S. market. The somewhat conflicting outcomes of globalization are typically justified by appeals to technological progress: The U.S. can afford to shed jobs and enjoy the benefits of lower prices because the country's prowess in technology and innovation will generate whole new waves of much better employment. Thus goes the argument. But the argument is, to some extent, a "bird-in-the-bush" rather than a "bird-in-the-hand" argument. For this reason energetic public opposition to globalization has emerged. If it finds political resonance, globalization may in time be slowed or curbed.

SEE ALSO *Global Business; Tariffs*

BIBLIOGRAPHY

"Globalization: Threat or Opportunity?" International Monetary Fund. January 2002. Available from http://www.imf.org/external/np/exr/ib/2000/041200.htm#chart1a. Retrieved on 6 May 2006.

Levine, Robert A. "Globalization's Grave Challenges for the West." *International Herald Tribune*. 9 May 2006.

Mathema, Cain. "Globalization as Defined in the West." Chronicle (Bulawayo, Zimbabwe). 16 May 2006.

Office of the United States Trade Representative. Official Web Site. Available from http://www.ustr.gov/. Retrieved on 16 May 2006.

Samuelson, Robert. "Will America Pass the Baton? The world is addicted to America's shopping spree. But some experts see emerging markets increasingly driving the world economy." *Newsweek*. 6 March 2006.

Suranovic, Steven M. "International Trade Theory and Policy Lecture Notes." 20 August 2003. Available from http://internationalecon.com/v1.0/ch40/40c000.html. Retrieved on 7 May 2006.

U.S. Library of Congress/Federal Research Division/Country Studies. "Glossary." Available from http://lcweb2.loc.gov/frd/cs/belarus/by_glos.html. Retrieved on 16 May 2006.

"US Not Ready to Scale Back WTO Hopes: USTR Nominee." *Reuters.* 16 May 2006.

World Trade Organization. Official Web Site. Available from http://www.wto.org/. Retrieved on 16 May 2006.

Darnay, ECDI

GOODWILL

Goodwill is a type of intangible business asset. It is defined as the difference between the fair market value of a company's assets (less its liabilities) and the market price or asking price for the overall company. In other words, goodwill is the amount in excess of the company's book value that a purchaser would be willing to pay to acquire it. A combination of advertising, research, management talent, and timing may give a particular company a dominant market position for which another company is willing to pay a high price. This ability to command a premium price for a business is the result of goodwill. If a sale is realized, the new owner of the company lists the difference between book value and the price paid as goodwill in financial statements.

The sale of a business may involve a number of intangible assets. Some of these may be specifically identifiable intangibles—such as trademarks, patents, copyrights, licensing agreements—that can be assigned a value. The remaining intangibles—which may include the business's reputation, brand names, customer lists, unique market position, knowledge of new technology, good location, and special skills or operating methods—are usually lumped into the category of goodwill. Although these factors that contribute to goodwill do not necessarily have an assignable value, they nonetheless add to the overall value of the business by convincing the purchaser that the company will be able to generate abnormally high future earnings.

Although goodwill undoubtedly has value, it is still an intangible asset and as such is not recorded on a company's books. In fact, many companies use a value of one dollar for goodwill in their everyday accounting procedures. Many companies could be sold for a premium price based on the good reputation they have established. But such goodwill is never recorded on the books until an actual acquisition occurs. The acquisition price determines the amount of goodwill that is recorded following the purchase of a company. For example, if a small business with assets of $40,000 is purchased for $50,000, then the purchaser records $10,000 of goodwill.

In general, determining the sales price of a business begins with an assessment of its equity, which includes tangible assets such as real estate, equipment, inventory, and supplies. Then an additional amount is added on for intangible assets (sometimes called a "blue sky" amount), which may include things like patent rights, a trade name, a non-compete clause, and goodwill. Experts note that in small business sales, the combined total of "blue sky" additions should rarely be more than a year's net income, because few purchasers are willing to work longer than that for free. For public companies, the amount of goodwill is often dependent on the vagaries of the stock market. Since the share price determines the purchase price, the value attributed to goodwill may fluctuate wildly during the course of an acquisition.

Standard accounting procedures state that, following an acquisition, the purchaser should amortize goodwill over a period of 15 years using the straight-line method. In other words, one-fifteenth of the original amount attributed to goodwill is deducted each year. Since this writeoff period is longer than that required for most tangible assets, it is usually a good idea to allocate as much of the purchase price as possible to business equipment. The shorter depreciation period would enable the purchaser to accelerate deductions and thus achieve earlier tax savings.

On occasion, the goodwill booked after the sale of a business may be written down or reduced. Such occasions usually occur because of some larger shift within the market in which the business is active, a shift that causes a reevaluation of the business. An example of such is the mobile phone market. During the 2000s the market grew quickly, as many new companies entered the market, and many mergers and acquisitions occurred. In late 2005 and early 2006 T-Mobile and Vodafone announced large write-downs of the goodwill on their books in order to more accurately reflect the competitive marketplace in which they operate.

Over the years, there has been some dissatisfaction expressed with the way that goodwill is handled for accounting purposes. First, since goodwill is sometimes a huge component of a company's acquisition price (particularly in the case of large public companies), the amortization of goodwill can have a significant negative effect on the purchaser's net income. Second, the treatment of goodwill under U.S. law differs from many other countries, which sometimes puts American companies at a disadvantage in international mergers and acquisitions.

SEE ALSO *Business Appraisers*

BIBLIOGRAPHY

Anthony, Robert N., and Leslie K. Pearlman. *Essentials of Accounting.* Prentice Hall, 1999.

Best, Jo. "T-Mobile Goodwill Cut by 1.5 Billion Euros." *Mobile and Wireless.* Silicon.com Available from http://networks.silicon.com/mobile/0,39024665,39156963,00.htm 3 March 2006.

Bragg, Steven M. *Accounting Best Practices.* John Wiley, 1999.

Weatherholt, Nancy D., and David W. Cornell. "Accounting for Goodwill Revisited." *Ohio CPA Journal.* October-December 1998.

Hillstrom, Northern Lights
updated by Magee, ECDI

GOVERNMENT PROCUREMENT

Many small businesses maintain and increase their operations through doing work for local, state, and federal government entities. While these businesses may also secure business through the offering of competitive bids on jobs offered by the private sector, small business owners should be aware of the differences in procuring work from the public and private sectors. The most fundamental difference between the procurement process in the public and private sectors concerns the process itself; whereas some private companies may have fairly streamlined processes for awarding contracts to outside bidders—or may not even bother with competitive bidding at all, if they are comfortable with a certain contractor—governments at the local, state, and federal level are all obligated to adhere to a significant body of law designed to ensure that 1) taxpayer money is spent wisely, 2) contracts are not awarded for less-than-legitimate reasons, and 3) all businesses are provided with a fair opportunity to make their case for the contract in question. Because government buyers are expected to spend taxpayer money wisely, their purchases are usually subject to significant oversight. Formal procurement rules are established to prevent both the reality and appearance of favoritism.

Submitting bids for public contracts can be a frustrating experience for businesses. The process of awarding contracts—at the local, state, or national levels—is a sometimes cumbersome one that is still heavy on bureaucracy, despite recent streamlining. In addition, government contracts are far more exposed to public scrutiny than are private ones. But business analysts and government procurement officers agree that the potential benefits of securing public contracts far outweigh the disadvantages. After all, local, state, and federal government offices and agencies comprise the single biggest customer block in the nation. For many small businesses, then, government procurement is a potentially lucrative avenue to long-term organizational growth and success.

Government agencies and legislators recognize this reality as well. In recognition of the importance of federal contracts to many small business establishments, U.S. legislation requires that a certain percentage of its contracts go to companies that qualify as small businesses. These goals, which are arrived at through the combined input of the Small Business Administration (SBA) and individual agencies, classify bidding companies not only by their size, but also by other classifications (minority-owned businesses, women-owned businesses, businesses located in high unemployment areas, etc.), and government purchasing agents work to fill these slots as well. In fact, some contracts are specifically set-aside for the "exclusive participation" of small businesses, small disadvantaged businesses (minority- and women-owned enterprises), and businesses in high unemployment areas.

CHANGES IN GOVERNMENT PROCUREMENT RULES

The foundation of modern-day government contracting at the federal level is based on two laws—the Armed Services Procurement Act of 1947 and the Federal Property and Administrative Services Act of 1949. These laws sought to codify all the various contract laws that had sprouted up over the years and provide overarching guidelines on government procurement. The laws also resulted in the creation of two sets of regulations designed to oversee affairs in the realm of government contracts—Armed Services Procurement Regulation (ASPR) for military agencies and Federal Procurement Regulation (FPR) for civilian agencies. These voluminous guidelines, though, were rife with exceptions, alternate procurement procedures, etc., and in 1979, Congress passed the Office of Federal Procurement Policy Act Amendments. These pieces of legislation called on the federal government to develop a single set of simplified procurement regulations for all government agencies.

The result of that directive was the Federal Acquisition Regulation (FAR), which covered all federal agencies. The FAR changed no laws, rather it was written in simpler language, arranged subject matter in a more logical sequence, and eliminated many of the contradictions and ambiguities that bedeviled everyone. The FAR is the 'bible' for those who wish to conduct business with the federal government. Government business is conducted in accordance with FAR rules, and contractors must comply with its procedures or risk being eliminated from consideration. That same year, Congress also passed the Competition in Contracting Act of 1984 (CICA), which opened up the doors to competitive bidding in numerous areas that had previously only allowed limited bidding practices.

Today, bidding for government contracts at all levels, but especially the state and federal levels, is intense. Many small businesses are in the thick of the battle, fighting for contracts that look to be within their financial and operational grasp. But making a bid for a government project is a time-consuming process, and consultants often counsel small business enterprises to be selective in their bid choices.

Federal procurement offices have recognized that the process takes a toll on small businesses as well. In 1995, Congress passed the Federal Acquisitions Reform Act, which arranged for a two-phase process of contract awarding in which the agency office selects a limited group of bidders based on their qualifications and general approach to the project, then examines detailed proposals from those "short listed" bidders, choosing the ultimate winner on a "best value" basis. The "best value" method calls for ranking proposals based on the scores each receives for a list of different items that are laid out in the solicitation document. The purchasing agency may award the contract after this evaluation, or it may discuss proposals with those considered competitive and then permit the short listed bidders to submit their best and final offers.

Small business owners currently engaged in soliciting government contracts—or weighing the possibility of doing so—should make sure that they obtain a copy of the Federal Acquisition Regulation. FAR is available through the Government Printing Office (GPO). In addition, business owners should be aware that the FAR is updated in two different ways. 1) Federal Acquisition Circulars (FACs) contain changes to the FAR as a result of federal legislation; these are easy to use, because they are distributed as replacement pages that can be instituted in place of outdated FAR regulations. 2) Each federal department also has its own materials that supplement— not supplant—FAR guidelines. These supplementary materials, which can be quite extensive, are also available through the GPO. Obviously, it is not necessary for potential suppliers to obtain every agency's supplemental FAR guidelines. Acquire the guidelines from those agencies or departments for whom you have particular bidding interests.

As of 2002, the Federal Business Opportunities Web site is the primary information source for businesses seeking federal contracts, replacing the *Commerce Business Daily.* It is through the new Internet site that all government agencies notify the public sector of upcoming solicitations and decisions on contracts over $25,000 in value. Through this single portal—FedBizOpps.gov—commercial vendors seeking federal markets for their products and services can search, monitor and retrieve opportunities solicited by any entity within the federal contracting community.

METHODS OF SOLICITATION

Small businesses hoping to secure a federal contract will turn to one of three methods of solicitation: Request For Proposals (RFP), Invitation For Bid (IFB), or oral solicitation. RFPs are the most commonly utilized of these solicitation methods.

For smaller contracts, government purchasing agents typically use a simplified system of awarding in order to minimize administrative costs. In such instances, a purchasing agent may simply call a few potential contractors from their bidders list and ask for a quote, awarding the contract to whoever comes in with the lowest responsible quote. The vast majority of all federal contractual actions are made through simplified procedures. This may seem surprising but one must remember that these smaller purchases are the government's equivalent of buying a cup of coffee or a newspaper, the sort of purchasing that is done routinely to meet recurring needs.

Not surprisingly, awards for larger contracts—which can, after all, run into millions of dollars—are bestowed only after a more comprehensive process. When a government agency has a project for which it wishes to receive bids it may: 1) Ask for sealed bids through the use of an IFB, or 2) Negotiate with a bidder on specific terms of the agreement. This latter methodology is more frequently used.

8(A) PROGRAM

The 8(a) Program is a Small Business Administration (SBA) program intended to provide assistance to economically and/or socially disadvantaged business owners. The initiative, which originated out of Section 8(a) of the Small Business Act provides participants with access to a variety of business development services, including the opportunity to receive federal contracts on a sole-source or limited competition basis.

Becoming a participant in the 8(a) Program is a laborious process but one that may be beneficial for eligible companies who wish to become involved in bidding on federal government projects. For more details on this program, please refer to the essay on 8(a) Programs earlier in this publication.

KEYS TO SUCCESSFUL BIDS FOR GOVERNMENT CONTRACTS

Business consultants, executives, managers, and purchasing officers alike note that there are several keys to successfully pursuing government contracts, no matter what their size or other characteristics. For the most part, these are recommendations that hold true when bidding for any large job/project.

Learn about the process and the impact of successful bids on business operations. In addition to conducting basic research on the agencies and project areas in which they are interested, small business owners need to educate themselves on the nuances of bidding, the repercussions of a successful bid on company operations (workforce allocation, needed facility upgrades, etc.), and a host of other considerations.

Review RFPs on a regular basis. Small business owners should faithfully check FedBizOpps.gov to make sure that possible projects do not pass by unnoticed.

Make bids judiciously. Small business owners should consider many factors when weighing whether to put in a bid on a project, such as current workload, delivery schedule, expectations of the agency, etc.

Submit a strong proposal in accordance with agency guidelines and time table. Businesses do not always allow for sufficient time to put together an adequately researched and detailed bid. Company leadership should make sure that adequate resources—both in terms of time and effort—are allocated for this purpose. Agencies who receive tardy, incomplete, or shoddy proposals will quickly discard them.

Prepare for the awarding of the project. Businesses are sometimes subjected to pre-award surveys to determine their ability to fulfill all contract obligations; this is especially true if the government office has never worked with the bidder before.

Key competency areas typically examined by government purchasing agents include:

- Adequacy of financial resources, organizational talent, technical knowledge, and operational controls to perform the duties detailed in the contract

- Ability to comply with the required delivery or performance schedule

- Good prior performance record and business reputation

- Access to all production, construction, and technical equipment and facilities necessary for completion of project

- Eligibility to receive the contract under all relevant laws and regulations

Contractors are often asked for extensive information by government purchasing agents, and they should be prepared to hand it over and accommodate surveys and other information-gathering activities by the government office in question. Information that may be requested from the contractor includes financial data, personnel information, and reports on all aspects of production (from technical capability to quality assurance capability), but the agent may also contact suppliers, trade and business associations, customers, financial institutions, and contract administrators of previous government jobs that your company has completed.

INCREASED POPULARITY OF ALTERNATIVES TO LOW BID CONTRACTS

In recent years, various government offices at all levels have followed the federal government's lead and pursued "low bid" alternatives when awarding contracts to the private sector. In previous eras, cities, counties, states, and federal offices all generally awarded contracts to the lowest responsible bidder, reasoning that such decisions minimized exposure to charges of favoritism, corruption, and backroom dealing. Both contractors and purchasing agents have observed, however, that this dynamic has undergone considerable change, especially in such high-cost areas as public works projects (building and road construction, etc.).

The use of "best value" and "performance-based" evaluations as a means of deciding on a winning bidder has begun to supplant the exclusive use of the lowest bidder as the deciding factor. Agencies at local levels have increasingly followed the lead of federal offices in this shift. As mentioned above, "best value" calls for ranking various proposals on a whole range of criteria and selecting the winner based on all those factors, not just price. "Performance-based" contracting, on the other hand, is an arrangement wherein the contract defines the required performance standards for the project but leaves it up to the contractor to devise the means of accomplishing the task in accordance with relevant laws. Several procurement policymaking agencies in the federal government, including the Office of Federal Procurement Policy, have touted performance-based contracting as superior to traditional low-bid contracting in every way, including cost, service, and delivery time.

SEE ALSO *8(a) Program*

BIBLIOGRAPHY

Cloutier, George A. "How to Do Business with Uncle Sam: For many entrepreneurs, an impenetrable bureaucracy and time-consuming paperwork rule out any thought of bidding for government contracts. That need not be the case." *Business Week Online.* 26 August 2004.

Day, Jennifer. "Before It's Too Late: It's never too early to identify construction project opportunities. Here's how your firm can get a leg up on the government bidding process." *Construction Today.* March-April 2005.

Kress, Stacie. "How to Do Business with Uncle Sam: The government's bidding process can seem overwhelming. Know how to prepare." *Florida Trend.* May 2003.

"Selling to the Government." *Corporate Counsel.* April 2000.

"SBA Annoucnes 8(a) Online Applications." *St. Charles County Business Record.* 16 September 2004.

U.S. General Services Administration. *Federal Business Opportunities.* Available from http://www.fedbizopps.gov/ Retrieved on 10 March 2006.

U.S. Small Business Association. *8(a) Business Development.* Available from http://www.sba.gov/med April 27, 2001.

Hillstrom, Northern Lights
updated by Magee, ECDI

GRAPHICAL USER INTERFACE

A graphical user interface (GUI, pronounced "gooey") is a computer environment that simplifies the user's inter-action with the computer by representing programs, commands, files, and other options as visual elements, such as icons, pull-down menus, buttons, scroll bars, windows, and dialog boxes. By selecting one of these graphical elements, through either use of a mouse or a selection from a menu, the user can initiate different activities, such as starting a program or printing a docu-ment. Prior to the introduction of GUI environments, most interactive user interface programs were text ori-ented and required the user to learn a set of often com-plex commands that are unique to a given program. The first GUI was developed in the 1970s by Xerox Corporation, although GUIs did not become popular until the 1980s with the emergence of the Apple Macintosh computer. Today, the most familiar GUI interfaces are Apple Computer's Macintosh and Microsoft Corporation's Windows operating systems.

Computer software applications, such as word proc-essing and spreadsheet packages, typically use the set of GUI elements built into the operating system and then add other elements of their own. The advantage of the GUI element of any software program is that it provides a standard method for performing a given task (i.e., copying a file, formatting text, printing a document) each time the user requests that option, rather than creating a set of commands unique to each potential request. Many GUI elements are standard across all packages built on the same operating system, so once a user is familiar with the GUI elements of one package, it is easier to then work in other packages.

GUI interfaces typically offer more than one method for initiating a particular action. For example, to print a document from a program within the Windows environ-ment, a user can select the "Print" option from the "File" menu, click the printer icon, or, as an alternative, use the keyboard shortcut of holding down the Ctrl key and pressing the letter "P." A user can then employ the option that feels most comfortable to him or her across all Windows programs.

The GUI interface has also been instrumental in making the World Wide Web easily accessible to indi-viduals through the use of GUI-based "browser" pro-grams. Netscape Navigator, Internet Explorer, and similar programs enable a user to access and search the Web using the familiar GUI format.

BIBLIOGRAPHY
Compact American Dictionary of Computer Words. Houghton Mifflin Company, 1998.

Hillstrom, Northern Lights
updated by Magee, ECDI

GREEN MARKETING

Environmentally-responsible or "green" marketing is a business practice that takes into account consumer concerns about promoting preservation and conservation of the nat-ural environment. Green marketing campaigns highlight the superior environmental protection characteristics of a company's products and services. The sorts of characteristics usually highlighted include such things as reduced waste in packaging, increased energy efficiency of the product in use, reduced use of chemicals in farming, or decreased release of toxic emissions and other pollutants in production.

Marketers have responded to growing consumer demand for environment-friendly products in several ways, each of which is a component of green marketing. These include: 1) promoting the environmental attrib-utes of products; 2) introducing new products specifically for those concerned with energy efficiency, waste reduc-tion, sustainability, and climate control, and 3) redesign-ing existing products with an eye towards these same consumers. Marketing campaigns touting the environ-mental ethics of companies and the environmental advantages of their products are on the rise.

Most observers agree that some businesses engage in green marketing solely because such an emphasis will enable them to make a profit. Other businesses, however, conduct their operations in an environmentally-sensitive fashion because their owners and managers feel a respon-sibility to preserve the integrity of the natural environ-ment even as they satisfy consumer needs and desires. Indeed, true green marketing emphasizes environmental stewardship. Green or environmental marketing may be defined as any marketing activity that recognizes environmental stewardship as a fundamental business development responsibility and business growth responsibility. This expands, to some extent, the traditional understanding of a business's responsibilities and goals.

REACTIONS TO "GREEN CONSUMERISM"

A number of factors have caused business firms in some industries to incorporate an environmental ethic into their operations. The principal factor, of course, is the growing public awareness of the environmental degradation that has resulted as a consequence of the growth in population and natural resource consumption throughout the world during the last 50 years. The issue is particularly relevant in America, which accounts for fully one quarter of world consumption despite having only a small fraction of the world's population. This growing public awareness of environmental issues has brought with it a corresponding change in the buying decisions of a significant segment of American consumers. Many consumers, and not just the most environmentally conscious, have begun in recent years to incorporate environmental concerns in their personal buying decisions through the purchase and use of products and services perceived to be more environmentally friendly. In some cases, changes in commodity availability have been the motivation behind such shifts in purchasing patterns. For example, the gas price increases seen in 2004 and 2005 caused a sharp decline in sales of sport utility vehicles (SUVs) in favor of hybrid and other flexible-fuel vehicles.

Businesses took heed of this growth in "green consumerism," and new marketing campaigns were devised to reflect this new strain of thought among consumers. Companies with product lines that were created in an environmentally friendly fashion (i.e., with recycled products, comparatively low pollutant emissions, and so on) quickly learned to shape their marketing message to highlight such efforts and to reach those customers most likely to appreciate those efforts (an advertisement highlighting a company's recycling efforts, for instance, is more likely to appear in an outdoor/nature magazine than a general interest periodical).

Ironically, the most environmentally aware consumers are also the ones most likely to view green claims of companies with skepticism. The attempt to portray oneself as "green" may fall flat if they are perceived to be false advertising, particularly among those most educated about environmental issues. Corporate reputation, then, has emerged as a tremendously important factor in reaching and keeping these consumers. A company that touts its sponsorship of an outdoor-oriented event or utilizes nature scenery in its advertising, but also engages in practices harmful to the environment, is unlikely to gain a significant portion of the green consumer market. Of course, such tactics are sometimes effective in reaching less informed sectors of the marketplace.

GREEN PRODUCTS

In their book *The Green Consumer,* John Elkington, Julia Hailes, and John Makower discussed several characteristics that a product must have to be regarded as a "green" product. They contended that a green product should not:

- Endanger the health of people or animals
- Damage the environment at any stage of its life, including manufacture, use, and disposal
- Consume a disproportionate amount of energy and other resources during manufacture, use, or disposal
- Cause unnecessary waste, either as a result of excessive packaging or a short useful life
- Involve the unnecessary use of or cruelty to animals
- Use materials derived from threatened species or environments

J. Stephen Shi and Jane M. Kane, meanwhile, noted in *Business Horizons* that the consulting firm FIND/SVP also judged a product's friendliness to the environment by ultimately simple measurements: "FIND/SVP considers a product to be 'green' if it runs cleaner, works better, or saves money and energy through an efficiency. Businesses practice being green when they voluntarily recycle and attempt to reduce waste in their daily operations. Practicing green is inherently proactive; it means finding ways to reduce waste and otherwise be more environmentally responsible, before being forced to do so through government regulations. Green promotion, however, requires businesses to be honest with consumers and not mislead them by over promising."

Life Cycle Analysis Most analysts agree that the "life" of the product and its parts is one of the most important components in determining whether a product is "green" or not. Most people think only of the process of creating a product when gauging whether a product is green, but in reality, products impact on the environment at several additional stages of their useful lives. Life cycle analysis (LCA) and/or product line analysis (PLA) studies measure the cumulative environmental impact of products over their entire life cycle—from extraction of the resources used to create the product to all aspects of production (refining, manufacturing, and transportation) to its use and ultimate disposal. These studies are sometimes referred to as "cradle to grave" studies. Since such studies track resource use, energy requirements, and waste generation in order to provide comparative benchmarks, both manufacturers and consumers can select products that have the least impact upon the natural environment. Some detractors of LCA studies, though—while granting that they do provide useful information—contend that they are subjective in setting analysis boundaries and claim that it is difficult to compare the environmental impact of disparate products.

GREEN PROMOTION

Perhaps no area of green marketing has received as much attention as promotion. In fact, green advertising claims grew so rapidly during the late 1980s that the Federal Trade Commission (FTC) issued guidelines to help reduce consumer confusion and prevent the false or misleading use of terms such as "recyclable," "degradable," and "environmentally friendly" in environmental advertising. Since that time, the FTC has continued to offer general guidelines for companies wishing to make environmental claims as part of their promotional efforts:

- Qualifications and disclosures should be sufficiently clear and prominent to prevent deception.

- Environmental claims should make clear whether they apply to the product, the package, or a component of either. Claims need to be qualified with regard to minor, incidental components of the product or package.

- Environmental claims should not overstate the environmental attribute or benefit. Marketers should avoid implying a significant environmental benefit where the benefit is, in fact, negligible.

- A claim comparing the environmental attributes of one product with those of another product should make the basis for the comparison sufficiently clear and should be substantiated.

The FTC regulations apply to all aspects and forms of marketing, including labeling, advertising, and promotional materials. "When a business makes any environmental claim, it must be able to support that claim with reliable scientific evidence," summarized Shi and Kane. "A corporation trumpeting an environmental benefit that it is unable to substantiate is treading on thin ice and leaving itself open to substantial penalties if a legal suit is brought against the company."

In addition to delineating marketing claims that might be regarded as false or misleading, the FTC also provides guidance to businesses on how to make specific claims about environmentally-friendly aspects of their operation, in part by clarifying the definitions of such commonly used terms as "recyclable," "biodegradable," and "compostable."

"Organic" is another term commonly used in marketing. Its popularity has grown with the growing demand for organic agricultural products. For a company to promote and label a product as organic, that product must meet the strict guidelines established by the Department of Agriculture (USDA). The guidelines for both production and labeling of organic agricultural goods are laid out in the USDA's National Organic Program Web site located at http://www.ams.usda.gov/nop/indexIE.htm.

The popularity of green products created a need to regulate and standardize claims about the environmental characteristics of products. Many regulatory guidelines were issued (and remain in force) to accomplish this job. They are designed not only to curb businesses engaged in misleading advertising practices, but also to clarify the regulatory environment for companies and make it easier for the consumer to differentiate between products that are truly "green" and those that are not.

ECO-SPONSORING

One avenue commonly used by companies to promote their specific ecological concerns (or polish their overall reputations as good corporate citizens) is to affiliate themselves with groups or projects engaged in environmental improvements. In the simplest form, firms engaged in eco-sponsoring activities contribute funds directly to an environmental organization to further the organization's objectives. Another approach is to "adopt" a particular environmental cause (community recycling programs are popular), thus demonstrating the company's interest in supporting environmental protection efforts. Sponsorships of educational programs, wildlife refuges, and park or nature area clean-up efforts also communicate concern for environmental issues. Environmental organizations charge, however, that some businesses use eco-sponsorships to hide fundamentally rapacious attitudes toward the environment.

ECO-LABELING

Another vehicle that has been used with increasing frequency in recent years to convey environmental information to consumers is "eco-labeling." Eco-labeling programs are typically voluntary, third-party expert assessments of the environmental impacts of products. Two firms that are involved in such third party label verification work are Green Seal and Energy Star.

Eco-labeling programs increase awareness of environmental issues, set high standards for firms to work towards, and help reduce consumer uncertainty regarding a product's environmental benefits. Thus far, however, the U.S. government has resisted instituting an officially-sanctioned eco-labeling program.

BIBLIOGRAPHY

Baker, Michael. *The Marketing Book.* Fifth Edition. Elsevier, 2002.

Federal Trade Commission. Frequently Asked Advertising Questions: A Guide for Small Business. Available from http://www.ftc.gov/bcp/conline/pubs/buspubs/ad-faqs.htm Retrieved on 13 March 2006.

Meiklejohn, Gregg. "The Marketing Value of Environmental Stewardship." *Direct Marketing.* October 2000.

Meyer, Harvey. "The Greening Corporate America." *Journal of Business Strategy.* January 2000.

"Nearly Two-Thirds of Americans Have Tried Organic Foods and Beverages." Press Release. Whole Foods Market. Available from http://www.wholefoodsmarket.com/company/pr_11-18-05.html 18 November 2005.

Ottman, Jacquelyn A. *Green Marketing.* Second Edition. BookSurge Publishing, May 2004.

Smith, Allison E. "Green Markets: Survey shows consumers' desire for environmentally-sensitive products." *Incentive.* August 2005.

U.S. Department of Agriculture. The National Organic Program Available from http://www.ams.usda.gov/nop/indexNet.htm Retrieved on 13 March 2006.

Wagner, Marcus, and S. Schaltegger. *How Does it Pay to Be Green?* Tectum Verlag DE, 2003.

Webb, Tom. "Organic Farms See Soaring Demand: Supporters say more are needed in Minnesota, Wisconsin." *Saint Paul Pioneer Press.* 11 March 2006.

Hillstrom, Northern Lights
updated by Magee, ECDI

GREEN PRODUCTION

The color green is closely associated with environmentalism—and therefore "green production," "green enterprise," "green business," and similar tags signal activities related to environmental goals in a positive way.

Environmentalism arose in the 1960s as the younger, more politically active post-war embodiment of an earlier conservation movement that is still active today. The latter is associated with President Theodore Roosevelt (1858-1919). Environmental interest reached its peak in the 1970s. The first major environmental law, the National Environmental Policy Act of 1969, came just before the first Earth Day was celebrated on April 22, 1970 (coinciding then and every year since with the older Arbor Day on which, once, people planted trees). The eight years between 1969 and 1976 saw passage of nine of the 18 fundamental environmental laws.

Since those days environmentalism is an undeniable public movement, ranging from political activism to a general sort of mild piety. Since 9/11, two analysts (Michael Shellenberger and Ted Nordhaus) have produced much discussion with an influential paper titled *The Death of Environmentalism*, but environmental polls, tracked by PollingReport.com (http://www.pollingreport.com/enviro.htm), show that public support for environmental causes was very high in the mid-2000s whether measured by Gallup, Harris, or one of the major media polls. Regarding this topic, no real differences in public opinion are discernible between the 1980s and the 2000s. A great majority (around three quarters) are favorably inclined toward the environment; more than half participate in some form of environmental activity (like recycling); and around 30 percent are actively involved in the cause.

This is the general "environment" in which green enterprise operates. Green products and services have a substantial market and command a premium price. The movement now embraces much more than simply pollution-free manufacturing and also encompasses healthy foods (organically produced, if possible), opposition to all manners of artificial ingredients, alternative fuels and modes of transportation (e.g., solar power, bicycles), alternative methods of construction to save energy (e.g., earth-sheltered homes), holistic and alternative forms of medicine, "green investment" in the securities of environmentally sensitive corporations, and many other forms of day-to-day or recreational behaviors, some of which can be supplied by business.

CORPORATE RESPONSE

The corporate response to environmentalism has taken many forms. These range from simple exploitation of the phenomenon to a deeply committed entrepreneurship by those who share the values of the environmentalists and attempt to incorporate those values into the production process itself in every possible way.

Exploitation typically takes the form of offering a few higher-priced versions of a product line which will appeal to environmentalists or positioning traditional products in marketing to highlight and emphasize the environmental aspects of the product.

The middle-ground is occupied by companies that deliberately make and sell only products that are environmentally superior, have been produced by a non-polluting process, or are made of natural ingredients only. A Google search on the phrase "environmental products," for example, will produce more than 2 million hits; a Yahoo search around 900,000. The products offered cover a bewildering variety of literally anything and everything—including even surprisingly technical items such as automotive catalysts.

Finally there are corporations in which environmental values are central to corporate values and all operations are deliberately and consciously managed with those principles guiding all choices. Often these are major publicly-traded corporations. And investment funds sold to environmentally-aware investors will feature such stocks. Sellers of such portfolios like the term "sustainable" industry as an alternative to "environmentally friendly" or "green" industry.

ENVIRONMENTAL PRODUCTION

All manufacturing processes, of course, are regulated under federal and state laws that deal with air and water pollution; the transportation and final management of toxic, hazardous, radioactive, and infectious wastes; land management and restoration in the mining of resources or the extraction of timber; the raising of animals and the management of their wastes; etc. "Green production," however, represents an effort to go the extra mile, not merely to meet all relevant environmental laws. This type of production involves, principally, four strategies: 1) methods of growing, harvesting, or extracting new raw materials in such a manner that energy is conserved and few or no artificial chemicals are introduced into the process; 2) methods of reusing materials to minimize waste and, indirectly, to save energy; 3) techniques for avoiding where possible high-energy or chemicals-intensive processes; and 4) schemes for processing production wastes back into the process or into secondary uses.

Extraction The first strategy typically involves growing agricultural commodities with minimal or no artificial fertilizers, utilizing natural method of pest and weed control, and labor-intensive rather than machine-intensive methods of harvesting—including selective timber cutting rather than clear cutting. People engaged in green production understand that substantial amounts of energy are consumed in making fertilizers and pest/weed-control chemicals—and both the extraction and use of energy harms the environment. Chemical methods of control disturb the natural ecosystem and have far-reaching down-stream consequences as run-off carries residues into waterways and the tissues of aquatic life absorb and cumulate poisons. Modern agriculture and forestry, of course, has been optimized using energy and chemicals. Therefore "green production" tends to be more costly on average.

Reuse/Recycling Where at all possible, green production will make use of waste materials and residues as raw material although, typically, such substances require more processing. Here again the motivation is to reduce production waste and to capture for continued use energy already embedded in the waste. Economic forces have, of course, long favored such reuse where the wastes are

relatively uniform or abundant. Secondary paper mills and electric furnaces to remelt scrap steel predate the environmental movement. Green production is an extension of this market-driven recycling achieved by redesign of processes.

Minimizing Energy Use Modern processing has evolved around the use of machines driven by energy and the use of chemical solvents and catalyst in preparing raw materials. The two environmentally superior means of getting the same job done are to use labor instead of machines—and time. High-powered paint-spraying, for example, requires more energy, produces more pollution (unless very carefully shielded) and, especially if combined with high-heat drying systems, is much more rapid than hand painting followed by just letting time pass as the painted objects dry. Many variants of this general approach are used.

Waste Handling In green production wastes are intensively managed to keep them useful for immediate recovery or reuse as energy in on-site furnaces. In many such production facilities, organic wastes are further treated—by composting, for instance. The waste-handling aspects of production may therefore, in turn, produce additional products for sale.

ECONOMIC AND OTHER AMBIGUITIES

Green production specifically, but green commerce as a whole, has ambiguous aspects arising from higher costs generally and the form of the dominant production culture, particularly, the nature of the U.S. consumer market. U.S. industry has evolved from a dominantly agricultural past in which the small farmer was the "typical" American to a high-geared energy/chemical culture where the typical American works in or out of an office. Automation is the norm of production—which depends, ultimately, on oil fueling machines. Green business looks back and, —once oil resources are depleted—perhaps also forward to a simpler and much more labor-intensive time. But that time is not yet. For that reason, green goods generally cost more. But they are consumed by a public wealthy from the exploitation of oil and technology.

Using 2003 data released by the Central Intelligence Agency (*The CIA World Factbook*), the U.S. had 4.6 percent of the world's population but consumed 25.9 percent of global oil—the highest consumption rate in the world. Oil consumption may be viewed as a proxy of all other consumption. Consumption of goods and energy is the cause of virtually all environmental pressures—and the U.S. consumption "footprint" is the largest. The American (and for that matter European) embrace of environmentalism can thus be seen in a cynical light as perhaps a well-meaning but naïive and sentimental activity: the recycling bin, after all, is sitting right there, next to the SUV. Another view of this situation—the reason why it is ambiguous—is that the broad public reflects a dim but clear realization that the current culture is not "sustainable" and needs to change. And many members of it are willing to pay for that by paying higher prices for green goods.

THE SMALL GREEN BUSINESS

Small business is not only well-represented in the green market but, judging by the products on offer out there, also the largest supplier, in terms of enterprises, of this sector. Small business typically leads in innovation—because it is less weighed down by institutional inertia. As the 21st century advances, small business owners are perhaps, like the public at large, hearing the beat of a different drummer.

BIBLIOGRAPHY

"Arizona—It Pays to Go Green." *Pollution Engineering.* September 2005.

"Channel Urged to Consider Green Business Approach." *MicroScope.* 4 July 2005.

"Citigroup Donates $1.5M to Support Green Enterprise." *Real Estate Weekly.* 30 November 2005.

Clarke, Philip. "Long Tradition of Green Production in Germany." *Farmers Weekly.* 4 October 2002.

"Firms Finding it Easier to Go Green." *KiplingerForecasts.* 7 October 2005.

Gunningham, Neil, Robert Kagan, and Dorothy Thornton. *Shades of Green: Business, Regulation, and Environment.* Stanford University Press, 2003.

Shellenberger, Michael and Ted Nordhaus. "The Death of Environmentalism." Paper presented to Environmental Grantmakers Association. *Grist Magazine.* Available from http://www.grist.org/news/maindish/2005/01/13/doe-reprint/. October 2004.

Sloan, Julie. "The Green CEO: A plastics maker breaks the mold." *FSB.* 1 February 2005.

Snyder, Paul. "Green Business Park Gets Approval from Madison City Council." *The Daily Reporter.* 14 March 2006.

Stern, Alissa J., and Tim Hicks. *The Process of Business/ Environmental Collaborations: Partnering for Sustainability.* Quorum Books, 2000.

Darnay, ECDI

GRIEVANCE PROCEDURES

Grievance procedures are a means of dispute resolution that can be used by a company to address complaints by employees, suppliers, customers, and/or competitors. A grievance procedure provides a hierarchical structure for presenting and settling workplace disputes. The procedure typically defines the type of grievance it covers, the stages through which the parties proceed in attempting to resolve matters, individuals responsible at each stage, the documentation required, and the time limits by which the grievance must be presented and dealt with at each stage. The best-known application of grievance procedures is as a formal process outlined in labor union contracts.

Grievance procedures do not necessarily have to be so formal and elaborate, and in fact, overly formal grievance procedures often discourage the airing of disputes in a timely manner. In small businesses, the procedures may consist of a few lines in an employee manual or the designation of a single ombudsman to deal with problems as they develop. Peer review of employee concerns is another popular way to address grievances. On the other hand, some larger companies may create an entire department dedicated to fielding complaints from employees or customers.

Whatever form they may take, grievance procedures are intended to allow companies to hear and resolve complaints in a timely and cost-effective manner, before they result in litigation. Knowing that formal procedures are available often encourages employees to raise concerns or question company policies before major problems develop. It also makes managers less likely to ignore problems, because they know that upper management may become involved through the grievance process. In union settings, grievance procedures help protect employees against arbitrary decisions of management regarding discipline, discharge, promotions, or benefits. They also provide labor unions and employers with a formal process for enforcing the provisions of their contracts.

Although having grievance procedures in place is important in both unionized and non-unionized settings, companies must support their written policies with consistent actions if they hope to maintain good employee relations. To make a grievance procedure work, all parties must approach it with the attitude that it serves their mutual interests. Ideally, an effective grievance procedure helps management discover and correct problems within an operation before they cause serious trouble. It can provide a vehicle through which employees can communicate their concerns to upper management.

For grievance procedures to be effective, both parties should view them as a positive force that facilitates the open discussion of issues. In some cases, the settling of grievances becomes a sort of scorecard that reinforces an "us versus them" mentality between labor and management. In other cases, employees are hesitant to use the grievance process out of fear of recrimination. Some studies have shown that employees who raise grievances tend to have lower performance evaluations, promotion rates, and work attendance afterwards. This suggests that some employers may retaliate against employees who raise complaints. It is vital that a company's grievance procedures include steps to prevent a backlash against those who choose to use them.

A TYPICAL GRIEVANCE PROCESS

In a union environment, a typical grievance procedure begins with an employee presenting a problem to his or her immediate supervisor within a certain time period after the offending event has occurred. The supervisor then has a set amount of time to either respond or send the grievance on to be addressed by the head of the department. At this point, a union representative enters the negotiations on behalf of the employee. If the situation is still not resolved, the grievance continues up the chain of command to the plant manager and the president of the local union. If the labor union fails to follow the procedures at any point, the contract usually specifies that it must drop the grievance. Conversely, the company is usually obligated to resolve the grievance in the employee's favor if management fails to follow the procedures outlined in the collective bargaining agreement.

If the situation still cannot be resolved, the final step in the grievance process is for both parties to present their side to a pre-designated arbitrator. The arbitrator's role is to determine the rights of both parties under the labor agreement, and his or her decision is usually final. The labor contract generally specifies the type of arbitrator used, the method of selecting the arbitrator, the scope of the arbitrator's authority, and the arrangements for the arbitrator's payment. A potential intermediate step involves presenting the grievance to a mediator, whose job is to help the parties solve their own differences before they reach the formal arbitration phase. Mediation is usually less time consuming and expensive than arbitration. In addition, the mediator may be able to teach the two parties dispute resolution skills that may be helpful in solving future problems.

SEE ALSO *Alternative Dispute Resolution; Labor Unions and Small Business*

BIBLIOGRAPHY

Dreyfack, Raymond. "Fight Grievances But Don't Retaliate." *Plant Engineering.* September 2003.

"Legal Q&A Statutory Grievance Procedures." *Personnel Today.* 10 January 2006.

Lewin, David, and Richard B. Peterson. "Behavioral Outcomes of Grievance Activity." *Industrial Relations.* October 1999.

Mathis, Robert L., and John H. Jackson. *Human Resource Management.* Thomson South-Western, 2005.

Rollinson, Derek J. "Supervisor and Manager Approaches to Handling Discipline and Grievance." *Personnel Review.* December 2000.

"When is a Grievance Not a Grievance?" *Mondaq Business Briefing.* 25 January 2006.

Hillstrom, Northern Lights
updated by Magee, ECDI

GROUPTHINK

Groupthink occurs when the pressure to conform within a group interferes with that group's analysis of a problem and causes poor group decision making. Individual creativity, uniqueness, and independent thinking are lost in the pursuit of group cohesiveness, as are the advantages that can sometimes be obtained by making a decision as a group—bringing different sources of ideas, knowledge, and experience together to solve a problem. Psychologist Irving Janis coined the phrase groupthink in the 1970s. He defines groupthink as: "a mode of thinking people engage in when they are deeply involved in a cohesive in-group, when the members' striving for unanimity override their motivation to realistically appraise alternative courses of action. Groupthink refers to a deterioration of mental efficiency, reality testing, and moral judgment that results from in-group pressures." It can also refer to the tendency of groups to agree with powerful, intimidating bosses.

The concept of groupthink provides a summary explanation of reasons groups sometimes make poor decisions. Indeed, groups are supposed to be better than individuals at making complex decisions, because, through the membership, a variety of differing perspectives are brought to bear. Group members not only serve to bring new ideas into the discussion but also act as error-correcting mechanisms. Groups also provide social support, which is especially critical for new ideas. But when new perspectives are rejected (as in the "not invented here" syndrome), it is hard to correct errors. And if the social support is geared toward supporting the group's "accepted wisdom," the elements that can make groups better decision makers than individuals become inverted, and instead make them worse. Just as groups can work to promote effective thinking/decision making, the same processes which enhance the group's operation can backfire and lead to disastrous results.

HOW GROUPTHINK WORKS

Janis identified seven points on how groupthink works. First, the group's discussions are limited to a few alternative courses of action (often only two), without a survey of the full range of alternatives. Second, the group does not survey the objectives to be fulfilled and the values implicated by the choice. Third, the group fails to reexamine the course of action initially preferred by the majority of members from the standpoint of the non-obvious risks and drawbacks that had not been considered when it was originally evaluated. Fourth, the members neglect courses of action initially evaluated as unsatisfactory—they spend little or no time discussing whether they have overlooked non-obvious gain. Fifth, the members make little or no attempt to obtain information from experts who can supply sound estimates of gains and losses to be expected from alternative courses of action. Sixth, selective bias is shown in the way the group reacts to factual information and relevant judgments from experts. Seventh, the members spend little time deliberating how the chosen policy might be hindered by bureaucratic inertia or sabotaged by political opponents; consequently, they fail to work out contingency plans.

Three general problems seem to be at work: overestimation of group power and morality, closed-mindedness, and pressures toward uniformity. Groupthink occurs when a group feels too good about itself. The group feels both invulnerable and optimistic. The group feels morally right. Linked to this attitude of perfection is a correlative closed-mindedness. Warnings are ignored. Messengers of difference are dismissed. Negative, stereotypical views of opponents are created and used. Finally, there is pressure for uniformity. A certain amount of self-censorship occurs. If individuals have questions, they keep them to themselves. This lack of dissent results in what Janis calls an "illusion of unanimity." If any difference does occur, group pressure is applied to bring the dissident into line. Janis also mentions "the emergence of self-appointed mindguards—members who protect the group from adverse information that might shatter their shared complacency."

If these precipitating problems support tendencies to groupthink, there are predisposing conditions as well. Janis suggests four conditions that predispose a group to groupthink: cohesiveness, group isolation/insulation, leader intimidation, and an absence of decision-making procedures. As a group "hangs together" and members grow to like each other, there will be greater pressure not to introduce disturbing information and opinion that might tear at that cohesiveness. Maintaining the good feelings that come from such cohesion become part of the group's "hidden agenda."

The insulation of the policy-making group is another factor. Frequently groupthinking groups are removed from interaction with others, perhaps because of their position within the organization. Lack of impartial leadership is a third contributing cause. When powerful leaders want to "get their way" they can overtly and covertly pressure the group into agreement. Finally, the lack of a template or protocol for decision making, or what Janis calls "norms requiring methodological procedures for dealing with decision making tasks," can also contribute to groupthink.

HOW TO AVOID GROUPTHINK

There are several things businesspeople can do to avoid groupthink: follow good meeting procedures, including the development of an agenda; aim for proper and balanced staff work; present competing views; and attend to correlative meeting problems, like exhaustion. A template for discussion might also be useful. One suggestion is to use an "options memo technique" in which information is presented as a problem statement, a list of options, and a preliminary recommendation. The group then looks at the preliminary recommendation with at least four questions in mind: 1) is the logic correct? (in selecting the preliminary recommendation from among the options); 2) is the judgment correct? (the logic may be fine, but the judgment may be poor); 3) are there any problems or errors remaining in the preliminary recommendation?; and 4) can the preliminary recommendation be improved? In order to prevent group isolation, it may be helpful to bring in new participants on a regular basis, use outside experts, and invite the group to meet off-site so that changes in settings and surroundings are stimulants.

To avoid groupthink, it is vital for the group leader to become a statesperson or conductor instead of a partisan virtuoso. Leadership almost always involves getting work done through others. High-quality decisions are not made through intimidation, whether intentional or unintentional. Some bosses have no idea why people do not speak up, while the reason they do not is they are likely to be attacked. Bosses encourage the best performance from groups when they can alert them to the kind of review that is expected. If the leader can be clear, and temperate, there is a greater likelihood that norms of disagreement will develop.

Finally, there is the cohesion process itself. Decision making tears at the fabric of group cohesion, and it is the desire to preserve cohesion that is an underlying dynamic of groupthink. But if decisions lower group cohesion it is not necessary to avoid decisions; an alternative is to rebuild cohesion each time. One way to accomplish this rebuilding is to complete decision making by about 65 percent of the way through the meeting, then move on to brainstorming for the next 20-30 percent of the meeting. People who have differed before have a chance to continue to interact, now around less threatening, future-oriented items. This meeting technique allows for decompression, and for rebonding of the group.

Because of the flaws of individual decision making—selective perception, excessive self-interest, limited knowledge, limited time—most important decisions today are made in groups. And groups can do a spectacular job; but they often do not. Meetings, the place where groups do their decision-making work, have a bad reputation these days, largely because of processes such as groupthink. Groupthink is the result of flawed procedures, poor leadership, insulation, and an unmanaged desire for the maintenance of group cohesion and its good feelings. These factors can be addressed positively, and group decision making improved, while groupthink is kept to a minimum.

BIBLIOGRAPHY

"Creating a Team of Individuals." *Journal of Management Development.* September 1995.

Esser, James K. "Alive and Well after 25 Years: A Review of Groupthink Research." *Organizational Behavior and Human Decision Processes.* February-March 1998.

Janis, I. *Crucial Decisions.* Free Press, 1989.

Janis, I. *Groupthink: Psychological Studies of Policy Decisions and Fiascoes.* Houghton Mifflin, 1983.

Moorhead, Gregory, Christopher P. Neck, and Mindy S. West. "The Tendency Toward Defective Decision Making within Self-Managing Teams: The Relevance of Groupthink for the 21st Century." *Organizational Behavior and Human Decision Processes.* February-March 1998.

Neck, Christopher P., and Charles C. Manz. "From Groupthink to Teamthink: Toward the Creation of Effective Thought Patterns in Self-Managing Work Teams." *Human Relations.* August 1994.

Scharff, M.M. Understanding WorldCom's Acounting Fraud: Did groupthink play a role?" *Journal of Leadership and Organizational Studies.* Spring 2005.

Tropman, John E. *Effective Meetings.* Sage Publications, 1995.

Hillstrom, Northern Lights
updated by Magee, ECDI

GROUPWARE

Groupware is a category of software designed to help groups work together by facilitating the exchange of information among group members who may or may not be located in the same office. Often, groupware users are collaborating on the same project, although groupware can be used to share a variety of information throughout an entire organization and can also be extended to clients, suppliers, and other users outside the organization. Groupware is an ideal mechanism for sharing less-structured information (for example, text or diagrams, as opposed to fielded or structured data) that might not otherwise be accessible to others. It is also used to define workflow, so that as one user completes a step in a project or process, the person responsible for the next step is notified automatically.

Groupware packages offered by different software vendors will include different features and functions, but most typically include the following components:

1. Calendaring and Scheduling—Each user maintains an online calendar to track appointments, days out of the office, and other times when he or she is unavailable. Other users can view their colleagues' calendars to look for "free" time for scheduling a new meeting. The user arranging a meeting may then send an announcement to meeting invitees and track their responses. Some packages also incorporate the ability to reserve a meeting room and any needed equipment, such as a video projector.

2. Discussion Databases—These are topic-specific databases where a user can post an idea, question, or suggestion on a given subject, and other users can post their responses. A discussion board may be set up for a short period of time to gather comments, for example, on an upcoming event, or left up indefinitely, say to solicit new product ideas on an ongoing basis. Usually, the name of each person who posted an item is recorded, but anonymous postings are an option.

3. Reference Libraries—These are collections of reference materials, such as employee handbooks, policy and procedure manuals, and similar documents. Typically, only certain users are able to post materials to a reference database, while other users have "read only" access—that is, they can view the materials but are not authorized to make any changes to them.

4. E-mail—This is probably the most heavily used groupware feature and is used to send messages to other groupware users. A message may be addressed to one or more individuals or sent to a group, such as "Sales," that includes the names of all people within a given department. Generally, users are also able to send messages to individuals located outside the organization.

Although e-mail is an essential component of groupware, e-mail and groupware employ different methods for disseminating information. Every e-mail message that is sent must have one or more recipients listed in the "To:" field. This is called the "push" model because it pushes the message out to the recipients whether or not a given recipient is interested in receiving it. Groupware uses the "pull" model, in that each user accesses and pulls from the various groupware applications that information which is of relevance to him or her.

In addition to these typical features, some groupware packages provide the functionality for users to design their own custom database applications. By using this capability, a department could create and use a database that is tailored to its specific needs. However, for more complex applications, an organization may want to consider hiring an outside developer to design the application.

Groupware functionality may also include the ability to control who sees a given piece of information. Access can be limited to specifically named individuals or to members of a group, such as all managers, members of the accounting department, or those employees working on a sensitive or confidential project. For example, job descriptions may be accessible to all users, but access to related salary information may be limited to managers and members of the human resources department.

HOW GROUPWARE WORKS

Groupware software can be divided into two categories: *server* and *client*. Depending on the size of an organization and the number of users, the software is installed on one or more computers (called "servers") in a network. Server software can also be installed on computers located in other locations, from a nearby city to another state or country. The server houses the actual applications and the associated information entered into it by the various users. If more than one server is used, the servers will "speak" to one another in a process called "replication." In this way, information held in the same database, but in different locations or on a different server, is exchanged between the servers. Once this is accomplished, the servers are said to be "synchronized."

Each person using the groupware has the client software installed on his or her computer. The client software enables the user to access and interact with the applications stored on the servers. Some users may be "remote;" that is, they are not in the office on a full-time basis but rather use a network interface card (NIC) for connecting at high speed with the groupware server. A high-speed connection allows a person to work remotely with almost if not equal speed as could be done from within the same office.

GROUPWARE IN ACTION

When faced with a lawsuit from a former partner, Bill Wright of the New Jersey law firm Farr, Buke, Bambacorta & Wright turned to groupware to help organize his firm's response. "We had to find a way to help us handle the flood of information," says Wright. Using groupware, the firm created a repository of memos and other documents related to the case, and this repository was available to Wright and others to post their own documents as well as read materials posted by others. With just one place to look, Wright was able to more quickly prepare required materials. Although the suit has long since been settled, the firm continues to use groupware to discuss key issues, share case notes, and maintain other information.

Groupware enabled employees of an accounting firm in Atlanta, Georgia, to stay out of the office and still keep in touch and functioning for several weeks when access to the center of the city was limited during the 1996 Summer Olympics. Most of the 40 employees of Porter, Keadle, Moore LLP used laptops to work from home for the duration of the games. As partner Bill Keadle noted, "I hardly saw anyone for a month, but we managed to stay in touch." The firm relied not just on the groupware's e-mail capabilities, but also on various applications, including discussion and reference databases.

For David Johnson, extending groupware beyond his own firm was key to speeding the completion of construction projects. Johnson, co-owner of an architectural firm based in Nashville, Tennessee, was looking to simplify the process of routing blueprints and other documents to as many as 50 subcontractors who may be involved in a given project. Sending materials via "snail mail" to one subcontractor, who would review them and send them along to the next subcontractor for review, was a time-consuming process. It was also, as Johnson notes, frustrating dealing with "the problems and confusion caused when 15 people in 15 far-flung locations each has a copy of important materials then somehow can't find the document when you finally get hold of them." By using groupware, Johnson was able to create a knowledge base for each project that everyone involved could access. "I wanted it to seem like we were all in the same office," he said. When Johnson tested his new system on a project designing a 60,000-square-foot medical office building, the results were exactly what he wanted—the project took about four fewer months to complete than it would have using the old system.

BIBLIOGRAPHY

Caggiano, Christopher. "Who Needs an Office, Anyway?" *Inc.* Mary 1998.

Field, Anne. "Group Think." *Inc.* 17 September 1996.

Freedman, Alan. *Computer Desktop Encyclopedia.* The Computer Language Company Inc., 1996.

Glyn-Jones, Glyn. "The Groupware Grapevine." *Management Today.* April 1995.

"IT News: New software to cut groupware costs." *Software World.* November 2005.

Hillstrom, Northern Lights
updated by Magee, ECDI

H

HEALTH INSURANCE OPTIONS

Health insurance is a contractual agreement between an individual or group and an insurance provider through which the insurance provider agrees to pay for some or all of the health care costs incurred by the person or group in exchange for their regular payment of a sum known as a premium. In this way, the insurance company assumes the financial risk of reimbursing health care costs, but it is able to offset that risk by collecting premiums from a large number of people, many of whom will have very low medical expenses. Traditionally, health insurance has been provided as an employee benefit by large companies, so many people have come to think of health insurance as part of an employment compensation package. Self-employed people and small business owners, lacking such coverage, must wade through the many available options to find plans that meet their own health insurance needs.

The seemingly ever-rising cost of health care has become a serious problem for the nation as a whole. In 2006, *Business Week Online* reported on statistics gathered by the Kaiser Family Foundation. They report that 45 million Americans are uninsured. Slightly more than half of these uninsured Americans (51 percent) work for small companies, defined as having fewer than 100 employees. Complicating this already dramatic situation is the fact that health insurance premiums have risen by 60 percent since 2001 and, according to the Kaiser Family Foundation, are expected to nearly double between 2005 and 2013.

"Premium increases are hitting the smallest of businesses the hardest, most of whom already have a difficult time affording health insurance," said Kaiser Family Foundation President Drew Altman in the *Indianapolis Business Journal.* "These increases will make it even harder for small businesses to provide health insurance for their employees in the future." Many small business owners found it necessary to consider modifying their health insurance plans for greater affordability, requiring employees to pay more of the monthly premium costs, or dropping their group health care coverage altogether. This last option could pose a problem for small businesses hoping to remain competitive in the job market, however, since 88 percent of employees consider health care benefits to be more of an incentive than any other type of benefit.

A small business' options for health care insurance have increased in recent years and this trend may expand further in coming years. A new bill is working its way through Congress. In early March of 2006, the Senate Committee on Health Education Labor and Pensions passed the Health Insurance Marketplace Modernization and Affordability Act. The act, which has passed the House and awaits full Senate passage, allows for the creation of Small Business Health Plans (SBHPs). These plans are designed to help small businesses realize economies of scale by banding together into ever larger entities that span state lines and industry categories. If this bill becomes law, small businesses may be one step closer to more affordable health care.

Assessing a Company's Needs The type of coverage a business needs depends upon its work force. For example, a company with a work force consisting primarily of married people with dependent children will need more comprehensive coverage than a company with a mostly unmarried, childless work force. Many plans can be specifically tailored to the needs of a company's work force. For example, firms whose employees work at computers may wish to provide eye care as part of their health insurance plans, while other firms may find that employees would value a fitness program.

Many insurance companies offer computer models that enable small businesses to determine the most economical insurance plan given the previous year's health care expenses. Another option that can reduce premiums is pooling insurance with other small businesses through trade associations or other organizations. Experts note that business owners may find it helpful in comparing different plans to ask the providers for references to other small business clients. Even though health insurance coverage can be expensive for small businesses, plan costs are tax deductible. In addition, providing such benefits can help smaller companies compete with larger ones to attract talented employees and can act to reduce employee turnover. It is important to note that, under the terms of the Consolidated Omnibus Budget Reconciliation Act (COBRA), all businesses that employ more than twenty people and offer a group health insurance plan must give employees the option of continuing coverage at their own expense for a limited period of time when they lose eligibility for company-provided benefits.

There are a variety of health insurance plans available from commercial insurance companies, hospital and medical service plan providers, and health maintenance organizations (HMOs). Coverage can generally be purchased on an individual or group basis. Group plans may be handled through an employer or through various organizations, including professional associations, colleges, labor unions, and health cooperatives. These plans usually have lower premiums than individual plans, cannot be canceled, and do not depend on the physical condition of individuals within the group. Most types of policies cover part of the costs of hospitalization, diseases and illnesses, surgery, and injuries from accidents, but the extent of coverage depends on the particular policy. Most policies do not cover cosmetic surgery, self-inflicted injuries, or preexisting conditions. Supplemental coverage is usually required to pay for eye and dental care, special hazards (such as football, skiing, hunting), rehabilitation services, and travel accidents. Some policies have a deductible that requires the insured to pay a certain amount out-of-pocket before benefits kick in, while others have a co-payment that requires the insured to pay a percentage of the costs after satisfying the deductible.

The most popular types of health insurance plans in the United States are: prepaid plans, which include popular managed care options such as HMOs; and fee-for-service plans, which encompass traditional indemnity insurance. Other possibilities include self-insurance, which basically involves a company or individual covering their own health care costs, and medical savings accounts (MSAs), which allow people to set aside money before taxes to be used for medical expenses. In addition, government-backed health care plans are available to federal employees, members of the military, veterans, the elderly, low-income families, Native Americans, and other societal groups.

As a result of the proliferation of health insurance options, deciding upon a plan can be a complicated process for a self-employed person or small business owner. Experts recommend that individuals and companies choose a plan that protects them against experiencing financial harm from an unexpected injury or illness, but is not prohibitively costly to maintain. In deciding on an appropriate amount of coverage, it is important to consider the amount of money available for emergencies, the unusual hazards that may exist, the family or work force health history, the extent of protection already available, and the level of health care costs in the community.

TYPES OF PLANS

The most common types of health insurance plans are prepaid (also known as managed care) and fee-for-service. Under traditional fee-for-service plans, the insurer pays the insured directly for any covered hospital or physician costs. Under a prepaid plan, insurance companies arrange to pay health care providers for any service for which an enrollee has coverage. The insurer effectively agrees to provide the insured with health care services, rather than reimbursement dollars. Prepaid plans offer the advantage of lower costs, which result from reduced administrative expenses and a greater emphasis on cost control. However, such plans also restrict enrollees' choices as to the doctors and hospitals from which they receive service.

Fee-for-Service Fee-for-service health insurance plans waned in popularity during the late 1980s and 1990s. In fact, the percentage of insured Americans covered by such plans declined from 96 to 28 percent between 1984 and 1991, and was expected to reach 20 percent by 2000. The primary reason for this decline was that fee-for-service arrangements do not emphasize preventative care or containment of costs. Fee-for-service health insurance plans are available to both individuals and groups. By spreading the costs among a pool of enrollees, group health insurance offers benefits derived from economies of scale. Group insurance generally features lower premiums and deductibles, more comprehensive coverage, and fewer restrictions than individual policies.

Most fee-for-service plans cover basic costs related to: hospitalization, including room and board, drugs, and emergency room care; professional care, such as physician visits; and surgery, including any procedures performed by surgeons, radiologists, or other specialists. Insured persons generally have their choice of hospitals and doctors. More inclusive health insurance plans are referred to as major medical insurance. Two types of major medical plans are: 1) supplemental, which provides higher dollar limits for coverage or covers miscellaneous services not encompassed in some basic plans, such as medical appliances and psychiatric care; and 2) comprehensive, which usually covers all costs included in basic and supplemental plans, and may also eliminate deductible and coinsurance requirements. Basic, supplemental, and comprehensive plans usually do not insure dental, vision, or hearing care.

Most health care options related to fee-for-service plans relate to different degrees of coverage. For instance, insureds may select a high deductible as a way of lowering the cost of the plan. Likewise, different levels of coinsurance are usually available. For example, the plan participant may agree to pay for 20 percent of all costs incurred after the deductible amount, up to a total of, say, $50,000 (for a total disbursement by the insured of $10,000). A more expensive plan may reduce the participant's share of those costs to 5 or 10 percent. The total limit on insurer payments can also be adjusted; an individual lifetime maximum of $1 million is not uncommon.

Prepaid Plans The second major category of health insurance is prepaid, or managed care, plans. Managed care plans typically arrange to provide medical services for members in exchange for subscription fees paid to the plan sponsor. Members receive services from physicians or hospitals that also have a contract with the sponsor. Thus, managed care plan administrators act as middlemen by contracting with both health care providers and enrollees to deliver medical services. Subscribers benefit from reduced health care costs, and the health care providers profit from a guaranteed client base.

Although they serve the same basic function as traditional health insurance, managed care plans differ because the plan sponsors play a greater role in administering and managing the services that the health care providers furnish. For this reason, advocates of managed care believe that it provides a less expensive alternative to traditional insurance plans. For instance, plan sponsors can work with health care providers to increase outpa-

tient care, reduce administrative costs, eliminate complicated claim forms and procedures, and minimize unnecessary tests.

Managed care sponsors accomplish these tasks by: reviewing each patient's needs before treatment, sometimes requiring a second opinion before allowing doctors to administer care; providing authorization before hospitalization; and administering prior approval of services performed by specialists. Critics of managed care claim that some techniques the sponsors use, such as giving bonuses to doctors for reducing hospitalization time, lead to undertreatment. Some plans also offer controversial bonuses to doctors for avoiding expensive tests and costly services performed by specialists.

Managed care plan sponsors also have more of an incentive to emphasize preventive maintenance procedures that help patients avoid serious future health problems and expenses. For instance, they typically provide physicals and checkups at little or no charge to their members, which helps them detect and prevent many long-term complications. Many plans offer cancer screenings, stress reduction classes, programs to help members stop smoking, and other services that save the sponsor money in the long run. Some plans also offer financial compensation to members who lose weight or achieve fitness goals. For example, one plan offers $175 to overweight members who lose 10 pounds and gives $100 to members who participate in a fitness program.

Another difference between traditional insurance and managed care is that members typically have less freedom to choose their health care providers and have less control over the quality and delivery of care in a managed system. Members of managed care plans usually must select a "primary care physician" from a list of doctors provided by the plan sponsor.

Managed care plans can take many forms. The most popular plans are health maintenance organizations (HMOs) and preferred provider organizations (PPOs). Other services that mimic these two plans include point-of-service plans (POSs) and competitive medical organizations. In addition to these established plans, many employers and organizations offer hybrid plans that combine various elements of fee-for-service and managed care options.

The most popular plan, the basic HMO, is the purest form of the managed care concept. HMOs are differentiated by four organizational models that define the relationship between plan sponsors, physicians, and subscribers. Under the first model, called individual practice associations (IPAs), HMO sponsors contract with independent physicians who agree to deliver services to enrollees for a fee. Under this plan, the sponsor pays the provider on a per-capita, or fee-for-service, basis each time it treats a plan member. Under the second model, the group plan, HMOs contract with groups of physicians to deliver client services. The sponsor then compensates the medical group on a negotiated per-capita rate. The physicians determine how they will compensate each member of their group.

A third model, the network model, is similar to the group model but the HMO contracts with various groups of physicians based on the specialty that a particular group of doctors practices. Enrollees then obtain their service from a network of providers based on their specialized needs. Under the fourth model, the staff arrangement, doctors are actually employed by the managed care plan sponsor. The HMO owns the facility and pays salaries to the doctors on its staff. This type of arrangement allows the greatest control over costs but also entails the highest start-up costs.

A PPO is a variation of the basic HMO. It combines features of both indemnity insurance and HMO plans. A PPO is typically organized by a large insurer or a group of doctors or hospitals. Under this arrangement, networks of health care providers contract with large organizations to offer their services at reduced rates. The major difference from the HMO is that PPO enrollees retain the option of seeking care outside of the network with a doctor or hospital of their choice. They are usually charged a penalty for doing so, however. Doctors and hospitals are drawn to PPOs because they provide prompt payment for services as well as access to a large client base.

Other Options Various other health insurance options exist for small businesses and self-employed individuals. One possibility is self-insurance, which requires a company to absorb most of the financial risk of its own health care coverage. An outside administrator may handle the paperwork, but the company pays its own claims. Self-insurance can provide a company with greater control over its health care costs and improved cash flow, but it can also be prohibitively expensive in cases of severe illness or injury. As a result, some companies choose to limit their liability by purchasing stop-loss insurance, which covers expenses after they reach a certain limit.

Finally, a company may chose to make health savings accounts (HSAs) available for employees to use in paying for their own health insurance. HSAs were established under federal law with the signing of the Medicare Prescription Drug Improvement and Modernization Act of 2003. HSAs are the successors to the Medical Savings Accounts of the 1990s. In essence, HSAs are personal accounts into which employees may set aside pre-tax dollars that can be used later to pay for health care

expenditures. Disbursements from these accounts are tax-free as long as they are used for approved medical expenses. HSAs may be used as the sole form of health insurance vehicle provided by a company or they may be offered as a means of supplementing a more employer-funded type of insurance policy. In most cases, the HSA option is coupled with a high-deductible insurance policy and HSA funds are used to pay for the deductible and other out-of-pocket expenditures that an employee may have.

The patchwork pattern that is health care in the United States makes it a challenge for small businesses and sole proprietorships to acquire and maintain health insurance. Large firms too struggle with the high costs of healthcare, and with what are often referred to as legacy costs associated with providing health care insurance to retirees. For small businesses, there is the promise of new legislation that may help in the struggle to provide health care benefits to their employees. However, barring the implementation of a national health care system, which appears very unlikely for now, businesses will have to continue to weigh their options and search for the best possible coverage with what resources they have available.

SEE ALSO *Employee Benefits*

BIBLIOGRAPHY

DiFiore, Bernard. "Small Companies Don't Have to Settle for Less." *Dallas Business Journal.* 22 September 2000.

"Fighting Off Health-Care Headaches: Rising premiums have made it difficult for small businesses to provide health insurance." *Business Week Online.* 16 March 2006.

Lehman, Raymond J. "Survey: Voters Overwhelmingly Favor Small-Business Health Plans." *A.M. Best Newswire.* 31 March 2006.

May, Troy. "Health Insurance Costs Put Small Firms in a Money Crunch." *Business Journal.* 27 October 2000.

"Premium Pain Relief: Association Health Plans." *Business Week.* 12 June 2000.

Rettig, Ellen. "Small Biz Feels Brunt of Premium Increases." *Indianapolis Business Journal.* 16 October 2000.

"Smaller Firms Can and Do Find Health Insurance." *Crain's Chicago Business.* 18 October 2004.

U.S. Small Business Administration. Anastasio, Susan. *Small Business Insurance and Risk Management Guide.* n.d.

Webb, Marion. "How to Beat the High Cost of Business: For some small-business owners, it means paying little or none of workers' health care insurance." *San Diego Business Journal.* 19 September 2005.

Hillstrom, Northern Lights
updated by Magee, ECDI

HEALTH MAINTENANCE ORGANIZATIONS AND PREFERRED PROVIDER ORGANIZATIONS

Health Maintenance Organizations (HMOs) and Preferred Provider Organizations (PPOs) administer the most common types of managed care health insurance plans. Managed care plans typically arrange to provide medical services for members in exchange for subscription fees paid to the plan sponsor—usually an HMO or PPO. Members receive services from a network of approved physicians or hospitals that also have a contract with the sponsor. Thus, managed care plan administrators act as middlemen by contracting with both health care providers and enrollees to deliver medical services. Subscribers benefit from reduced health care costs, and the health care providers profit from a guaranteed client base.

Managed care plans emerged during the 1990s as the main alternative to traditional, fee-for-service health insurance arrangements. In a fee-for-service arrangement, employees can go to the hospital or doctor of their choice. The plan reimburses costs at a set rate—for example, the insurance company might pay 80 percent and the company or individual enrollee might pay 20 percent—for all medically necessary services. Although they serve the same basic function as traditional health insurance plans, managed care plans differ because the plan sponsors play a greater role in administering and managing the services that the health care providers furnish. For this reason, advocates of managed care believe that it provides a less expensive alternative to traditional insurance plans. For instance, plan sponsors can work with health care providers to increase outpatient care, reduce administrative costs, eliminate complicated claims forms and procedures, and minimize unnecessary tests.

Managed care sponsors accomplish these tasks by reviewing each patient's needs before treatment, requiring a second opinion before allowing doctors to administer care, providing authorization before hospitalization, and administering prior approval of services performed by specialists. Critics of managed care claim that some techniques the sponsors use—such as giving bonuses to doctors for reducing hospitalization time—lead to under treatment. Some plans also offer controversial bonuses to doctors for avoiding expensive tests and costly services performed by specialists.

On the plus side, managed care plan sponsors also have more of an incentive to emphasize preventive maintenance procedures that can help patients avoid serious future health problems and expenses. For instance, they typically provide physicals and checkups at little or no charge to their members, which helps them detect and prevent many long-term complications. Many plans offer cancer screenings, pre-natal care, stress reduction classes, programs to help members stop smoking, and other services that save the sponsor money in the long run. Some plans also offer financial compensation to members who lose weight or achieve fitness goals.

Another difference between traditional health insurance and managed care plans is that members typically have less freedom to choose their health care providers and have less control over the quality and delivery of care in a managed system. Participants in managed care plans usually must select a "primary care physician" from a list of doctors provided by the plan sponsor. The sponsor pays the health care provider a predetermined price for each covered service. The individual participant may have to meet a deductible and make a small co-payment.

The trend away from traditional fee-for-service health care plans has been steady over the last 25 years. According to statistics from the U.S. Department of Labor, fee-for-service plans accounted for 96 percent of health care plans offered by medium and large public employers in 1984 and 20 years later they account for less than 15 percent of employer provided health insurance. Managed health care policies have effectively displaced traditional fee-for-service health insurance plans. These new plans come in three flavors: health management organizations (HMOs), preferred provider organizations (PPOs), and point of service plans (POSs).

HMOs HMOs provide a wide range of comprehensive health care services to their members in exchange for a fixed periodic payment. In most cases, participants must select a "primary care physician" from a list of approved providers which usually includes internists, pediatricians, and general practitioners. These doctors act as "gatekeepers" to coordinate all the basic health care needs for their patients. A patient with a knee injury, for example, would be required to see his or her primary care physician, who would then decide whether referral to a specialist for surgery or rehabilitation was warranted. In this way, the primary care physician helps eliminate unnecessary care that would cause an increase in plan costs. Another way in which HMOs seek to reduce costs is by providing care only within a restricted geographical area. Most HMOs provide local service and do not cover visits to doctors or hospitals outside the network except when the patient is traveling or has an emergency.

HMOs can be classified into four organizational models that define the relationship between plan sponsors, physicians, and subscribers. Under the first model, called individual practice associations (IPA), HMO sponsors contract with independent physicians who agree to deliver services to enrollees for a fee. Under this plan, the sponsor pays the provider on a per capita, or fee-for-service, basis each time it treats a plan member. Under the second model, the group plan, HMOs contract with groups of physicians to deliver client services. The sponsor then compensates the medical group on a negotiated per capita rate. The physicians determine how they will compensate each member of their group.

A third model, the network model, is similar to the group model but the HMO contracts with various groups of physicians based on the specialty that a particular group of doctors practices. Enrollees then obtain their service from a network of providers based on their specialized needs. Under the fourth model, the staff arrangement, doctors are actually employed by the managed care plan sponsor. The HMO owns the facility and pays salaries to the doctors on its staff. This type of arrangement allows the greatest control over costs but also entails the highest start-up costs.

For small businesses in the market for a health care plan, HMOs offer relatively low costs, broad coverage, and little administrative work. Many HMOs began establishing plans for smaller companies by the mid-1990s, although some of the larger HMOs still did not provide coverage for individuals. Experts recommend that small business owners check the financial security of an HMO before signing a contract, since many managed care providers went bankrupt in the early 1990s. Although employees have a reduced ability to choose their own doctors and limited out-of-area coverage with an HMO, they benefit from low out-of-pocket costs, comprehensive services, preventative care, and no claim forms. In addition, there is no waiting period for coverage of preexisting conditions, and no maximum lifetime limits on benefits. Many HMOs also provide other services, like dental care and eye exams.

PPOs A PPO is a variation of the basic HMO that combines features of traditional insurance with those of managed care. With a PPO, the plan sponsor negotiates discounts with participating doctors and hospitals, then pays them on a fee-for-service basis rather than prepaying. Patients are usually permitted to choose from a fairly extensive list of doctors and hospitals. The patient is required to pay a set amount per visit, and the insurer pays the rest. The amount of the co-payment depends on the type of plan—those with higher premiums usually feature lower out-of-pocket costs.

The major difference between PPOs and HMOs is that PPO enrollees retain the option of seeking care outside of the network with a doctor or hospital of their choice. They are usually charged a penalty for doing so,

however, as the percentage of costs paid by the PPO is reduced. Doctors and hospitals are drawn to PPOs because they provide prompt payment for services as well as access to a large client base. There are still restrictions on patients that are intended to control the frequency and cost of health care services, but not as many as with a typical HMO. PPOs are a popular choice for sole proprietors or owners of very small companies, since they require employees to pay a larger percentage of their own health care costs. Most insurance agents and brokers can provide information on the various PPO plans available to small businesses.

POSs A point of service plan (POS) is a sort of hybrid health insurance model that combines features of HMOs and PPOs. Like an HMO or PPO, the patient only pays a co-payment or low co-insurance for contracted services within a network of preferred providers for what is termed in-network care. However, like traditional fee-for-service insurance, enrollees have the flexibility to seek out-of-network care under the terms of traditional indemnity plans with a deductible and a percentage co-insurance charge.

THE DEBATE OVER MANAGED CARE

Health care reform was a major topic of debate during the 2000 elections. Political candidates were reacting to growing public outrage over cost increases and increasing restrictions imposed by managed care health insurance plans, especially HMOs. As HMOs increased in popularity during the 1990s, many people came to believe that, as for-profit companies, they placed a greater emphasis on making money than on providing needed care. The media was full of stories about HMOs denying medically necessary services to patients, ostensibly in order to control costs.

In response, the U.S. Congress began considering several major pieces of legislation that would regulate managed care providers and affect the way health insurance companies operate. As of 2006 they are still considering and debating the subject. Meanwhile, many states have passed rules and regulations that provide protections of the sort envisioned in Patients' Bill of Rights. The laws vary by state but include such mandates as: a ban on gag clauses, which prevent physicians from telling patients about all possible treatment options; a ban on pre-authorization requirements for emergency room care; and the creation of independent grievance panels to settle disputes between patients and HMOs.

SEE ALSO *Employee Benefits; Health Insurance Options*

BIBLIOGRAPHY

Benko, Laura B. "New Call for Patients' Bill of Rights: Docs worry ruling limiting HMO suits will boost medical malpractice filings." *Modern Healthcare.* 28 June 2004.

Blakely, Stephen. "The Backlash against Managed Care." *Nation's Business.* July 1998.

Lynn, Jacquelyn. "A Quick Guide to Insurance." *Entrepreneur.* June 1997.

Newman, Carlise. "HMOs Hammer Small Business with Rate Hikes." *Milwaukee Business Journal.* 11 December 1998.

U.S. Department of Labor. "A Look at Employers' Costs of Providing Health Benefits." Prepared by the Office of the Chief Economist. Available from http://www.dol.gov/asp/ programs/history/reich/reports/costs.htm Retrieved on 27 March 2006.

Weizman, Steve. "FTCR: Assault on State HMO 'Patients' Bill of Rights' Movement Unveiled in Senate Today Would Deregulate Health Insurance Nationally." *The America's Intelligence Wire.* 8 March 2006.

Wolfson, Bernard J. "Choice Between HMOs, PPOs One of Cost Versus Flexibility." *The Orange County Register.* 10 October 2004.

Hillstrom, Northern Lights
updated by Magee, ECDI

HEALTH PROMOTION PROGRAMS

A health promotion program—sometimes known as a wellness program—is a type of employee benefit that encompasses the various efforts companies make to promote and maintain their employees' health. Examples of health promotion programs might include company-sponsored smoking cessation training, visits with a nutritionist to receive information about healthy cooking, discounted fitness center memberships, or free cholesterol testing.

Offering health promotion programs to employees provides small businesses with a number of potential benefits. For example, they may decrease their health care costs, increase worker productivity, reduce absenteeism, and encourage employee loyalty. In addition to improving their general health, work-based health promotion programs also make employees feel that the company is concerned about their welfare, which tends to increase their job satisfaction. "Keeping your workers healthy year-round is a great way to decrease absenteeism and improve morale," Ellen Paris wrote in an article for *Entrepreneur.* "Free cancer screenings, educational seminars, and flu shots may not sound like fun perks, but employees appreciate them."

Health promotion programs have increased in popularity in recent years. A study by the consulting firm Hewitt Associates reported in *HR Focus* found that 93 percent of American large companies—those with 200 or more employees—offered some sort of health promotion program, an increase of 7 percent since 1995. Among the most popular wellness programs or elements within programs were educational workshops and seminars, a smoke-free workplace, counseling on lifestyle habits that contribute to chronic conditions, screenings for high cholesterol and high blood pressure, and flu shots. The Hewitt study revealed that 72 percent of U.S. companies offer education and training as part of their wellness programs, while 27 percent offer health risk appraisals to promote early detection of treatable conditions. About 40 percent of employers offer some sort of incentive for employees who participate in company-sponsored health programs.

The cost of health promotion programs is relatively low, given the potential savings small businesses might realize in reduced health care costs. Flu shots cost about $20 per employee, according to Paris, while cholesterol screening costs about $5 per employee. Many basic wellness services are available through the employer outreach programs of local hospitals and visiting nurse associations. Another option for companies is to provide employees with access to health information on the Internet. "We are also finding that employers are increasingly using online technology to deliver health education incentives," health care consultant Camille Haltom told Bill Leonard in *HR Magazine.* "Online technology provides convenient access for participants, can potentially increase participation in health management, and is cost-effective for employers when compared with traditional approaches."

Introducing a health promotion program can be an extremely daunting undertaking because its success usually requires meaningful changes in attitudes and behaviors. Changing behaviors and attitudes can be extremely difficult, as anyone knows who has undertaken to break a bad habit. Behaviors related to health risk factors are often among the most challenging to modify, because they are very basic lifestyle activities like eating, sleeping, exercising, and smoking. Since people do not easily change their habits without good reason, a successful health promotion program should include some sort of incentive. Incentives may take the form of desirable rewards or undesirable consequences. For the most part, employers implementing health promotion programs find the use of desirable incentives more conducive to establishing a program that projects a positive image.

Inspiring others to change their behavior takes persistence, patience, and time. The benefits to be gained by a company from a health promotion program may not manifest themselves quickly. So, assessments of the success of such a program should be measured only after sufficient time has elapsed. A healthier workforce is a goal that most business owners will agree is desirable, even if it takes time to achieve.

BIBLIOGRAPHY

Hall, Barry. "Good Health Pays Off! Fundamentals of Health Promotion Incentives." *Journal of Deferred Compensation.* Winter 2006.

"How Midsize Employers Can Use Health Promotion Programs to Cut Costs." *Managing Benefits Plans.* December 2003.

Johnson, David. "What's Wrong With Wellness? Healthcare Costs are Soaring. But Not Health Promotion Programs." *Industrial Safety & Hygiene News.* October 2004.

Leonard, Bill. "Health Promotion Programs Grow in Popularity." *HR Magazine.* May 2000.

"More Employers Now Use Health Promotion Programs to Cut Costs." *HR Focus.* October 2003.

Paris, Ellen. "Fit for Work: Everyone Wins with Health Promotion Programs." *Entrepreneur.* April 2001.

Powell, Don R. "Characteristics of Successful Wellness Programs." *Employee Benefits Journal.* September 1999.

Hillstrom, Northern Lights
updated by Magee, ECDI

HIGH-TECH BUSINESS

High-technology businesses are those engaged in securing growth and revenue from industry sectors characterized by new and rapidly changing technology. In fact, advanced technology has come to be utilized in so many different industries that members of the business community now often regard it as its own unique industry subset, with applications across the spectrum of the world of commerce. Today, high-tech businesses are involved in industries as diverse as food exporting, retail product design, oil extraction, and a host of others.

Businesses immersed in the world of high technology range from huge corporations (Microsoft, Intel, Amazon. com, etc.) to small start-ups hoping to be the next huge corporations. The differences between these organizations are many, but it is perhaps more consequential that their leaders—whether the president of a multinational computer chip manufacturer or the owner of a ten-employee CAD/CAM outfit—share one thing. They understand and recognize the changes that technological advances are bringing to the global marketplace and the opportunities that such changes are creating. Early and successful adopters of new technologies are often able to gain advantages that enable them to establish new

ground in a market before the technology becomes more widely used, a more standard feature within the market.

Successful high-tech firms are adept at recognizing the possibilities associated with technological advancements, and nurture corporate cultures that enable them to seize on those opportunities.

CHANGE AND UNCERTAINTY IN THE GLOBAL MARKETPLACE

Observers agree that today's high-tech companies operate in a business world that is changing at an alternately exciting and unnerving pace. Economists, business executives, consultants, and entrepreneurs alike have debated fiercely about the ultimate character of these changes. As *The Economist* observed, "the belief that technology and globalization promise unbounded prosperity and render old economic rules redundant has infected American managers, investors, and politicians with remarkable speed.... Why has the belief in the New Economy spread so quickly? One reason is that some of its elements really do exist. Imports and exports **do** play a bigger role than they did a generation ago. Information technology **is** altering the nature of America's economic output, as well as the ways that companies operate." Indeed, it is this latter factor that is often touted as the most dependable and significant engine of economic growth. After all, exciting new technologies have revolutionized huge areas of the business landscape, from manufacturing to communications and marketing. Neil Gross and John Carey, writing in *Business Week,* pointed out two other important reasons why observers expect many high-tech businesses to continue to soar: 1) There is a relatively low cost associated with purchasing and implementing the necessary equipment and other infrastructure for high-tech ventures, at least when compared with many other industries; and 2) breakthrough technologies in such areas as computers and communication equipment can be rapidly designed into commodity products.

Moreover, researchers point out that unlike other growth sectors, high technology ventures are not limited to larger corporations. Indeed, small business enterprises have carved out an impressive niche in the industry, and they are expected to remain firmly entrenched in the world of high-tech for years to come. "Despite a long list of hurdles," wrote *Entrepreneur'* Heather Page, "high-tech entrepreneurs can still look to the future with well-founded optimism. Thanks to a recent convergence of opportunities—namely changing market needs and the evolution of technologies to address them, ready access to capital, and a larger pool of talented technical personnel to hire or partner with—the odds have swung in favor of high-tech businesses in recent years."

KEYS TO LAUNCHING AND MAINTAINING A SUCCESSFUL HIGH-TECH BUSINESS

In addition to adhering to common-sense entrepreneurial guidelines—don't spread your finances too thin, devise a sound marketing strategy, hire good employees, weigh the impact of your actions on your family, etc.—people hoping to start or add to a high-technology business should take into account the following keys, many of which concern taking advantage of available opportunities in such areas as education, training, and financing:

Keep up with industry changes. This can be a daunting task, but the entrepreneur who stays up to date on new technologies and innovations, new applications, and changing markets will be far better equipped to spot the gaps in products and services that still dot the high-tech landscape and fill that spot with their own company's offerings.

Make full use of technology transfer opportunities. In recent years, laboratories and research institutions operated by universities, government agencies, and corporations have all shown a much greater inclination to share their knowledge and technology with entrepreneurs and other business enterprises in commercial industries. "These types of programs are effectively placing technology in the hands of those most capable of turning it into viable ventures: entrepreneurs," claimed Page. "Moreover, not only is it now easier to identify which technologies can make the shift into the commercial sector, but more systems are being created to facilitate their transfer."

Use the Internet and other Information Technology (IT) markets to full advantage.

Reward and challenge employees. Workforce stability and reliability is an important factor in small business success for just about any entrepreneur, but its importance may be particularly pronounced in one of the fast-paced high-tech industries. Indeed, it is a far more serious matter to replace a software programmer three months before a new product launch than it is to replace a cashier or stock-person. For many small high-tech companies, workers are among their most valuable assets; the smart entrepreneur will compensate them accordingly, via salary, benefits, promotion, responsibility, or some combination thereof, to best ensure a high degree of employee retention.

Admit mistakes. Given the rapid pace at which high-tech industries are changing, companies need to be aggressive in their prosecution of new strategies and initiatives. Yet almost inevitably, a high-tech business will find itself pursuing a product or market that, for whatever reason, comes to look decidedly less appetizing

than it appeared when it was first targeted. The key to weathering such disappointments, say many analysts, lies not only in diligent research and detailed planning, but also in pulling the plug on plans that have gone sour rather than pouring additional money and resources into it while your competitors pursue more promising avenues.

Explore various funding options. High-technology companies in such areas as communications, networking, the Internet, and various other software applications were major recipients of funding from venture capital companies in the 1990s. This trend declined noticeably in 1999 and 2000 due to convulsions in the stock value of numerous high-tech firms and the subsequent economic slowdown in the early 2000s. Another option for high-tech start-ups and small businesses is one of large number of programs sponsored by federal, state, and regional agencies to help them secure risk capital and research and development funding.

Utilize education and training opportunities. Entrepreneurial programs have proliferated across the country in recent years, and many of these feature a heavy emphasis on technology.

BIBLIOGRAPHY

Allen, Mike. "Software Firms Look to Go Small for Right Deal: Infommersion, Web Technologies are Snatched Up as Bigger Firms See Opportunities." *San Diego Business Journal.* 10 October 2005.

Arthur, Brian. "The New Rules of the Game." *U.S. News & World Report.* 8 July 1996.

"Assembling the New Economy: A New Economic Paradigm is Sweeping America; It Could Have Dangerous Consequences." *The Economist.* 13 September 1997.

Baum, Geoff. "Bouncing Back: In High Tech, Failure is Rarely a Dead End, It's Just Another Opportunity." *Forbes.* 2 June 1997.

"Forecast: Long-Term Growth." *PC Magazine.* August 1997.

Kirkpatrick, David. "Riding the Real Trends in Technology." *Fortune.* 19 February 1996.

Page, Heather. "Power Play." *Entrepreneur.* June 1997.

Sager, Ira. "Cloning the Best of the Valley." *Business Week.* 18 August 1997.

Viardot, Eric. *Successful Marketing Strategy for High-Tech Firms.* Artech House, 2004.

Wyman, J. "Technological Myopia: The Need to Think Strategically about Technology." *Sloan Management Review.* Summer 1985.

Hillstrom, Northern Lights
updated by Magee, ECDI

HOME OFFICES

A home office is a space within an individual's personal residence that is used for business purposes. It may be a corner of a spare bedroom equipped with nothing more than a desk. Or, it could be one whole floor of a house filled with the latest in computer and communications devices. Whatever its size and composition, however, the home office is increasingly common in American business today. A majority of the estimated 40 million Americans who work from their homes are self-employed small business owners. In addition, many professionals maintain two offices, and a growing number are equipping their home computers with modems that allow them access to their office computer files. Many large corporations are also expanding experiments in "telecommuting," which enables employees to work from home, using modem-equipped computers, just as they would in the office.

Establishing a home office involves a number of important considerations. For example, individuals interested in working out of their homes must gather information on local zoning restrictions, find and set aside an appropriate work area, and gain the support of family and neighbors for the home office. Other considerations include whether the home office will offer sufficient privacy, will be convenient for customers and vendors, and will provide room for future expansion and growth. The expense involved in furnishing a home office and purchasing necessary computers, office supplies, and other equipment is another factor to consider.

The use of part of a home as a business office may enable an individual to qualify for tax deductions. The "home office deduction" allows individuals who meet certain criteria to deduct a portion of mortgage interest or rent, depreciation of the space used as an office, utility bills, home insurance costs, and cleaning, repairs, and security costs from their federal income taxes. Although the Internal Revenue Service (IRS) has set strict regulations about who qualifies for the deduction, about 1.6 million people claim the deduction each year. According to Gloria Gibbs Marullo in an article for *Nation's Business,* the savings can be considerable: a sole proprietor living in a $150,000 home stands to save about $2,500 in actual taxes annually.

HOME OFFICE TAX DEDUCTION

The most important aspects of setting up a home office are the potential tax and legal implications. Home office operators may claim a deduction for those offices on IRS Form 8829 (Expenses for Business Use of Your Home), which is filed along with Schedule C (Profit or Loss From Your Business). There are restrictions, however, which are covered in IRS Publication 587 (*Business Use*

of Your Home). Failing to abide by these restrictions may put a red flag on a home office user's federal income tax return, which could result in an audit.

In general, a home office deduction is allowed if the home office meets at least one of three criteria: 1) the home office is the principal place of business; 2) the home office is the place where the business owner meets with clients and customers as part of the normal business day; or 3) the place of business is a separate structure on the property, but is not attached to the house or residence. The deduction is figured on the size of the home office as a percentage of the total house or residence. For example, if the total house size is 2,400 square feet and the home office is 240 square feet, 10 percent of the total house is considered used for business. That would allow the business owner to deduct 10 percent of the household's costs for electricity, real estate taxes, mortgage interest, insurance, repairs, etc. as business expenses.

Be warned, however, that the home office deduction cannot be used by everyone who has a home office. A 1993 United States Supreme Court decision made the home office deduction more difficult to apply outside of these very carefully worded circumstances. In the case in question, a doctor worked in three different hospitals, but did not maintain an office in any of them. Therefore, he established a home office, which he claimed was necessary to keep up with his billing and patient records, and claimed a home office deduction. But the Supreme Court ruled that since the doctor spent most of his working hours visiting patients, the hospitals were his principal place of work, and his home office deduction was denied.

This ruling, which more narrowly defined the concept of "principal place of business" affected a large number of people, particularly professionals such as sales agents who see customers at the customers' places of business. Since the demonstration and sale of the merchandise occurs away from the home office, the IRS ruling says that those offices are not critical to conducting that business. As a general rule, if the income-producing activity takes place away from the office, a deduction is not allowed. On the other hand, a second job conducted exclusively from the home office may qualify for the deduction. The key is that the income must be generated from the home office.

A home office deduction is still possible, however, if the space is set aside exclusively to meet with clients or customers, even if it is not always the principal place of business. The IRS uses an example of a lawyer who works three days in an office and two days at home in an office set up so that clients can come to his home. The last test for an unchallenged home office deduction is that it can be a separate structure—such as a studio or garage apartment—that is essential for running the business. For example, a floral shop owner who runs a greenhouse on her property would qualify under this rule.

In July 1997, responding to the concerns of small business advocates, the U.S. Congress passed a tax bill that effectively overturned the 1993 Supreme Court ruling. The legislation redefined an individual's "principal place of business" to include a home office that meets the following two criteria: 1) it is used to conduct the management or administrative activities of a business; and 2) it is the only place in which the small business owner conducts those management or administrative activities. When this change became effective on January 1, 1999, it was expected to enable many business owners who perform services outside of their homes to claim the home office deduction.

Even after meeting the criteria to qualify for the home office deduction, a myriad of different IRS rules apply to exactly what expenses can be deducted. These rules cover depreciation of the home, depreciation of equipment, how to recover that depreciation if the home is sold, etc. One important thing to note is that the monthly residential telephone charge cannot be deducted, even if most of the calls pertain to the business. However, long distance business-related calls can be deducted. Individuals are advised to consult an accountant to stay within the law on home office deductions.

Simplification of the home office deduction may be coming. Colleen DeBaise wrote, in an early 2006 article entitled "Locking In The Home-Office Deduction," about efforts being made to simplify this tax deduction. She wrote, "The National Association for the Self-Employed, a small-business group in Washington, D.C., supports a simplified, standard deduction to ease the burden on home-based businesses. And perhaps someday, sweet relief will be granted: Two bills introduced in 2005 contain language for a standard home-office deduction, although neither has passed. One of the bills, the Small Employer Tax Relief Act of 2005, specifically calls for a standard home-office deduction of $2,500.... In the meantime, small-business owners have little choice other than to muddle through the form — or hire a tax adviser for help."

OTHER CONSIDERATIONS

Besides the IRS regulations, some municipal governments have zoning laws that restrict or license home offices. Originally designed to protect residential neighborhoods from becoming commercial zones, the zoning laws have sometimes been strictly interpreted to keep residents from conducting any sort of business from their home, even if it does not have a commercial impact on the rest of the neighborhood. Zoning laws and ordinan-

ces may affect such varied issues as parking for customers, access for deliveries, the number and types of employees permitted, and the use of signs or other forms of advertising. As a result, people wishing to set up home offices should check with their city's zoning office and licensing board for restrictions that may apply to the city, or even to their particular neighborhood.

If a home-based business is allowed at the site, the next step is to determine whether a home office is a workable option in the residence. For example, individuals interested in working from their homes must consider where the office should be located, how much it will cost to equip the area for business use, and what adjustments will need to be made in living arrangements. While a home office offers an entrepreneur a number of tax and lifestyle benefits, it can also pose problems relating to limited space, isolation, household distractions, and security concerns.

Providing that a home office is feasible, the next step is to choose a location for the office. This location may be a spare bedroom, a den or study, a basement, an attic, a garage, a kitchen table, or a corner of a living room. When choosing a location for the home office, entrepreneurs should take into consideration their own working needs, the needs of clients who may visit, and the lifestyle needs of other members of their family. Though it is important for the home office to be located out of the mainstream of household activities, it also should be located in a desirable spot that will offer a pleasant working environment. The location of a home office is very significant; "in fact, almost every problem people have in working from home... is either aggravated or alleviated by where they put their offices," Paul and Sarah Edwards noted in their book *Working from Home*. At a minimum, the location chosen must be large enough to contain a desk and chair, computer and phone equipment, storage and shelf space, and contemplation or meeting space.

After a location has been determined, the work space must be clearly defined in order to eliminate potential distractions and create a good working atmosphere. "A peaceful marriage of home and office depends on establishing effective boundaries," according to Paul and Sarah Edwards. If no extra room is available in the home, it is possible to use room dividers or office partitions to creatively define the office space. It is vital that the space be well-lit, as lighting is a key contributor to productivity. In addition, if clients are expected to visit the home office, then ideally the office should be the only part of the home they see. Thus if clients will visit regularly, it might be helpful to have an outside entrance to the office space. Besides defining the work space, it is important for an individual working out of his or her home to establish specific working hours and stick to them. Home-based business owners should let family, friends, and neighbors know when they are available for socializing and when they will be working. Otherwise, family members may interrupt business activities, or friends and neighbors may impinge upon work time with visits or requests for favors or baby-sitting services.

After a home office space has been defined, that space needs to be outfitted with the necessary equipment to conduct business activities. In her book *Organizing Your Home Office for Success,* Lisa Kanarek recommended plotting the available office space on a grid in order to help select and organize appropriate furniture and equipment. It may also be helpful to think in terms of vertical space as well as horizontal. For example, it may be possible to install storage shelves above a desk, or to use office walls for bulletin boards, dry-erase boards, or planning calendars. The most important consideration in selecting office furniture, besides fit with the available space, is ergonomics. After all, an average person spends 75 percent of his or her day sitting at a desk. If that desk is the wrong height, or the chair is uncomfortable, the entrepreneur may experience back pain, fatigue, carpal tunnel syndrome, or a variety of other productivity-reducing problems. In addition, Kanarek noted that individuals shopping for home office furniture should avoid the temptation simply to seek out bargains. Poorly designed or constructed furniture will only need to be replaced, which may make it more expensive than selecting high-quality materials in the first place.

Some of the most costly equipment commonly purchased for home offices includes computers, printers, and other technological devices. According to Mike Brennan in an article for the *Detroit Free Press,* the first step in buying computer equipment for a home office is to evaluate what tasks it will need to accomplish. For example, a business that depends upon professional presentations may require a computer system capable of handling complex desktop publishing programs. The next step is to decide whether to buy the best computer model available to meet these needs, or to spend less money for an older, yet serviceable model. In general, experts recommend that entrepreneurs buy the best computer that they can afford. Renting or leasing computer equipment may be an attractive option for small business owners who anticipate that they will not be able to afford top-of-the-line equipment, or who want to keep up with the rapid changes in technology prevalent in today's market.

In addition to the computer itself, home office workers today usually need to invest in a computer equipped with a network interface card (NIC) necessary for most high-speed connections to the Internet. This is essential in order to communicate with customers and to facilitate e-mail and fax capabilities. The majority of home offices also purchase one or more peripheral devices—such as a printer, scanner, copier, or fax machine—depending on their needs. Brennan noted that a multiple function machine encompassing several of these peripherals may be a good way for home offices to save space, although such machines generally entail a tradeoff in the quality of any one function. Finally, a home office must also invest in software to perform work on the computer. Many new computers come with a variety of useful software already installed. One good general option for small businesses is Microsoft Office, which includes word processing, spreadsheet, and database programs, as well as a variety of other business applications.

When establishing the physical layout of the home office space, it is also important to provide for storage of office supplies and business records. Most home-based businesses require at least one filing cabinet, shelves for books or manuals, and space to store paper and other office supplies. Office superstores, mail-order office supply companies, and computer shopping are all convenient options for home business owners in restocking their office supplies. Home-based businesses also need to provide the means for customer contact. Experts recommend establishing a separate phone line for business contacts, and equipping it with a reliable answering machine or voice mail system to handle calls during non-business hours. A separate phone line, which can be answered in a professional manner, gives more credibility and control to the small business owner, and also acts to solidify boundaries between an individual's business and personal life. Some entrepreneurs choose not to use their home address in business dealings, either because of the image it projects or to protect their privacy and security. Home-based business owners may want to consider obtaining a post office box, renting an address from an office suite service, or using a mail receiving service as alternatives to using a home address for business correspondence.

Finally, individuals investing in a home office often need to make significant changes in their insurance coverage to ensure that their business is protected. For example, fire and theft coverage must be expanded to include business equipment, and liability coverage needs to include customers, vendors, and delivery persons visiting the premises. Depending on the type of home-based business, additional coverage may be needed to protect against business interruption, product or workmanship liability, and business use of a vehicle.

BIBLIOGRAPHY
Brennan, Mike. "Do Your Homework: Setting Up an Office in Your House Can Be a Disaster if You're Not Computer Literate." *Detroit Free Press.* 24 November 1997.

DeBaise, Colleen. "Locking In That Home-Office Deduction." *SmartMoney.com.* Available from http://www.smartmoney.com/smallbiz/askedandanswered/index.cfm?story=20060110 10 January 2006.

Edwards, Paul, and Sarah Edwards. *Working from Home: Everything You Need to Know about Living and Working under the Same Roof.* Tarcher, 1990.

Kanarek, Lisa. *Organizing Your Home Office for Success: Expert Strategies That Can Work for You.* Penguin, 1993.

Kelsey, Dick. "IDC: New Technology Makes Home-Office Life Easier." *Newsbytes.* 5 September 2000.

Marullo, Gloria Gibbs. "Redefining the Home-Office Deduction." *Nation's Business.* September 1997.

Hillstrom, Northern Lights
updated by Magee, ECDI

HOME-BASED BUSINESS

A home-based business is any enterprise for which the principal administrative and managerial activities take place within an individual's personal residence. People start home-based business ventures for a wide variety of reasons. For example, some people are forced to leave the corporate world as a result of downsizing or early retirement, while others leave voluntarily out of a desire to be their own boss, to avoid the hassles associated with commuting, or to facilitate caring for children or elderly relatives. Whatever the reason, home-based businesses have become a significant trend in recent years. Once viewed as a way for an unemployed person to make some money until a "real" job came along, home-based businesses are now taken much more seriously. Today, home-based businesses run the gamut from consulting firms and advertising agencies to photography studios and free-lance writing services.

The main driving force behind the growth of home-based businesses is the increasing capability and availability of computer and communications technology. Powerful yet affordable home computer systems equipped with modems allow people to send and receive messages, transfer data, and conduct research from their homes, largely eliminating the need for those employed in such endeavors from having to commute to a place of employment. Similarly, sophisticated software programs offering applications in desktop publishing, database management, financial management, and word processing enable one individual to do the work formerly handled by an entire support staff. In addition, the widespread use of cellular phones, pagers, voice-mail systems, and toll-free telephone numbers has enhanced the ability of home-based business owners to remain connected to the outside business world. Rapid improvements in technology have enabled large numbers of home-based business people to earn the same income they could at a regular jobs while also gaining a number of lifestyle benefits. Another important factor in the growth of home-based businesses is the transformation of the American economy from a product orientation to a service orientation. Since service businesses generally have no need to store inventory or run production machinery, they are less disruptive and more adaptable to a neighborhood environment.

As a result of these and other factors, an estimated 40 million Americans now work from their homes. This number includes employees working from home for a larger employer as well as self-employed. Not surprisingly, two-thirds of home-based business owners are women, who choose this option either because of childcare concerns or because of a perceived glass ceiling limiting their earnings potential in the corporate world. Running a business out of the home offers a number of advantages, including time savings, control over working hours and conditions, independence, and flexibility. Starting a home-based business is also considerably cheaper than starting a business in rented facilities. In addition to saving money on overhead expenses, commuting costs, and wardrobe expenditures, many home-based business owners can deduct a portion of their rent or mortgage interest from their personal income taxes.

There are also several disadvantages to home-based businesses, however, including uncertain income, reduced benefits, isolation, and distractions. In addition, home-based business owners, like other self-employed individuals, must be able to handle all sorts of business-related tasks, like bookkeeping, billing, marketing and sales, and tax compliance. Still, home-based businesses do tend to be more successful than other types of small business ventures. According to the editors of *Income Opportunities* magazine in their *Home Business Handbook*, only 20 to 25 percent of home-based businesses fail within five years, compared to a failure rate of over 50 percent for all small business ventures. Several organizations are available to assist people in forming home-based businesses, including the National Association of Home-Based Businesses (www.ameribiz.com), Home Office Association of America (www.hoaa.com), and National Association for the Self-Employed (www.nase.org).

REQUIREMENTS FOR A SUCCESSFUL HOME-BASED BUSINESS

As Paul and Sarah Edwards noted in their book *Working from Home,* successful home-based business owners are usually good at what they do and enjoy doing it. It is also helpful to be independent, self-sufficient, and flexible. Other keys to success include being able to sell oneself and the business, and staying on top of personal and business finances. Since it is often difficult to associate being at home with working, home-based business people must be able to maintain boundaries between their personal and professional lives. In addition, they require a great deal of self-discipline to overcome the sense of isolation, frequent distractions, and lack of motivation and concentration that commonly affect those working from home.

Formal planning can help ease the transition for a person starting a home-based business. By being aware of the potential pitfalls and creating a plan to overcome them, a home-based business owner can significantly increase his or her chances for success. The main planning tool recommended by experts is a business plan. A formal business plan, which is generally created in anticipation of starting a new business venture, includes a description of the business; a statement of purpose; information about the business's structure, organization, and management; a marketing plan; and a financial plan.

The process of gathering information and writing a business plan helps the entrepreneur take an objective, critical look at the business idea and its chances for success. A home-based business may be related to an individual's previous occupation, but may also be based upon a hobby or the discovery of a unique business opportunity. In any case, the idea should be evaluated with an eye toward market potential and competition. Once the business is up and running, the business plan sets forth goals and standards for management and serves as an operational tool to measure progress. Although there are many ways to start a home-based business—including "moonlighting" while employed full-time, working part-time for an employer and part-time at home, and just taking the plunge—planning is important to all of them.

After creating a plan for the home-based business, the entrepreneur is ready to put the plan in action. One of the earliest steps involves preparing family members and enlisting their support. The loss of a reliable source of income may cause some anxiety or resentment among other members of the household. In addition, the creation of a home office will probably necessitate changes in family members' schedules or lifestyle. Dealing with such issues in advance can help avoid problems later. Another important step is to establish an area of the home as a business office. The most important consideration when choosing a location for a home office is that it allow the entrepreneur room to work comfortably and efficiently without too many distractions. The office should be as physically separate from the living area of the home as possible, and should project an air of professionalism to potential visitors as well as to its occupant.

Other steps in the process of forming a home-based business include selecting a legal structure, filing a fictitious name or "doing business as" statement, and obtaining any needed permits or licenses. The entrepreneur should also evaluate the risks associated with the business venture and make any necessary arrangements for health, life, liability, property, or business interruption insurance. Since it is sometimes difficult for a home-based business to be taken seriously by customers or creditors, it may be helpful to communicate a professional image through stationery and business cards, a separate phone line answered with a formal greeting, and distinct working hours.

OVERCOMING COMMON PROBLEMS

Many people start home-based businesses in the hopes of setting their own work schedules and increasing their free time, but few people realize the careful planning that is required to achieve these goals. In fact, time management is one of the more important challenges a home-based business owner may face. Experts recommend that home-based business owners set up a workable schedule immediately upon starting their ventures in order to establish good habits. In many cases, the limited amount of work available in the early stages of a home-based business's existence may cause the entrepreneur to establish a pattern of running personal errands or watching television during work time. In this way, lethargy and unproductive use of time become ingrained and perpetuate themselves. Instead, downtime that has been reserved for working should be used to market and promote the business.

Once the home-based business gets off the ground, many entrepreneurs tend to go to the opposite extreme and overcommit themselves. In their need to attract clients, they become uncomfortable turning down work. But unlike people who work for a large employer in an outside office, home-based business owners cannot leave their work behind and go home, because home is where their work is. As a result, some entrepreneurs work too many hours and abandon their personal lives, resulting in stress and burnout. Instead, experts recommend that home-based business owners set up realistic work schedules in order to reinforce the boundaries between their personal and business lives. It may be helpful to establish the following day's schedule the previous afternoon and prioritize the activities. The schedule should be realistic and allow for inevitable interruptions. Some experts claim that an important factor in successful time management for home-based business owners is arising early in the morning to get a jump start on work. Others stress the importance of dressing comfortably yet professionally in order to establish a positive psychological state for working. Although these methods do not apply to everyone, it is important for home-based business people to find a pattern that maximizes their productivity and stick with it.

Another common problem faced by those who work from home is isolation. In a standard business environment, people are dealing with co-workers constantly, as well as the noise of ringing phones and running machines. There are also meetings, breaks, and lunch hours that serve to break up the day and provide opportunities for socializing. This contact with other people provides a built-in system of motivation to at least appear busy at work. In contrast, many people who start a home-based business are faced with nothing but a quiet, empty house. Some find it difficult to motivate themselves and succumb to boredom and loneliness. But such isolation does have a positive side: working at home increases productivity by an average of 20 percent, so home-based business owners can often get more work done in less time. Planning is necessary to overcome the negative effects of isolation, however. Experts recommend that home-based business owners schedule interaction with other people on a regular basis, using such means as business meals, outside meetings and appointments, clubs and associations, and networking.

Yet another common problem encountered by home-based business people is frequent distractions that reduce productivity. In fact, distractions are everywhere for people who work from home. When faced with a difficult work task, it sometimes seems far preferable to run the vacuum, clean out a closet, walk the dog, have a snack, take a nap, raid the refrigerator, pull some weeds in the garden, or do any of the myriad other things that need doing around a normal household. In addition, people who work from home lack the motivation that peer pressure can provide in a regular office. They also face spouses and children who demand time and attention, as well as friends and neighbors who call to chat or stop by to ask favors.

To be successful, home-based business owners need to be aware that time-stealing temptations exist and take steps to counteract digressions before they turn into habits. If distractions seem overwhelming, the first step is to analyze the situation. If the problem lies with household chores, eating, or the television, the solution may be to get the distractions out of sight. If the problem involves family members or friends and neighbors, it may be necessary to have a frank discussion or family meeting concerning work time and free time. Options for resolving people conflicts include moving the office to another part of the house, hiring a baby-sitter or arranging for day care, or not taking personal calls during business hours. Ideally, an entrepreneur should set up a

daily work schedule, try to work diligently for several hours at a time, and then take a break as a reward.

FINANCIAL AND TAX ASPECTS

Like other forms of self-employment, home-based businesses face a number of challenges relating to financial management and tax compliance. Part of the business plan that is prepared prior to forming a home-based business is a financial plan detailing how much it will cost to begin the new venture and keep it running. After the business has been established, it is vital that the entrepreneur set up a good bookkeeping system to manage cash flow and ensure compliance with tax laws. Bookkeeping systems can be manual or computer based. Experts also recommend that entrepreneurs set up a separate checking account for their home-based businesses in order to better document business expenses. Canceled checks, paid bills, invoices, sales slips, receipts, and other financial documentation should be kept on file in case of an audit. Another important aspect of financial planning for a home-based business is tracking working capital—the difference between current assets (cash, accounts receivable, and inventory) and current liabilities (operating expenses, debts, and taxes)—in order to maintain a realistic picture of where the business stands financially.

Taxes become significantly more complicated with a home-based business. Self-employed persons are allowed to deduct business-related expenses—such as wages paid to others, the cost of professional services, shipping and postage charges, advertising costs, the cost of office supplies and equipment, professional dues and publications, insurance premiums, automobile expenses, and some entertainment and travel costs—from their income taxes, but are also required to pay self-employment taxes. People who work from their homes may be eligible for another tax deduction known as a home office deduction. The home office deduction allows individuals who meet certain criteria to deduct a portion of mortgage interest or rent, depreciation of the space used as an office, utility bills, home insurance costs, and cleaning, repairs, and security costs from their federal income taxes. Although the Internal Revenue Service (IRS) has set strict regulations about who qualifies for the deduction, about 1.6 million people claim the deduction each year. According to Gloria Gibbs Marullo in an article for *Nation's Business,* the savings can be considerable: a sole proprietor living in a $150,000 home stands to save about $2,500 in actual taxes annually.

In general, a home office deduction is allowed if the home office meets at least one of three criteria: 1) the home office is the principal place of business; 2) the home office is the place where the business owner meets with clients and customers as part of the normal business day; or 3) the place of business is a separate structure on the property, but is not attached to the house or residence. The deduction is figured on the size of the home office as a percentage of the total house or residence. For example, if the total house size is 2,400 square feet and the home office is 240 square feet, 10 percent of the total house is considered used for business. That would allow the business owner to deduct 10 percent of the household's costs for electricity, real estate taxes, mortgage interest, insurance, repairs, etc. as business expenses.

For many years, the IRS has followed a very strict interpretation of "principal place of business," which prevented some self-employed persons—such as an accountant who maintained a home office but also spent a great deal of time visiting clients—from claiming the deduction. But in July 1997, responding to the concerns of small business advocates, the U.S. Congress passed a tax bill that redefined an individual's "principal place of business" to include a home office that meets the following two criteria: 1) it is used to conduct the management or administrative activities of a business; and 2) it is the only place in which the small business owner conducts those management or administrative activities. When this change became effective on January 1, 1999, it was expected to enable many home-based business owners who also perform services outside of their homes to claim the home office deduction.

The home office deduction may become even easier to use in the near future. Colleen DeBaise wrote, in an early 2006 article entitled "Locking In The Home-Office Deduction," about efforts being made to simplify this tax deduction. She wrote, "The National Association for the Self-Employed, a small-business group in Washington, D.C., supports a simplified, standard deduction to ease the burden on home-based businesses. And perhaps someday, sweet relief will be granted: Two bills introduced in 2005 contain language for a standard home-office deduction, although neither has passed. One of the bills, the Small Employer Tax Relief Act of 2005, specifically calls for a standard home-office deduction of $2,500.... In the meantime, small-business owners have little choice other than to muddle through the form — or hire a tax adviser for help."

As home-based businesses continue to play an important role in our economy, institutions and regulations will adapt to working well with these businesses and their unique support requirements.

BIBLIOGRAPHY

Bates, Steve. "Following Their Homing Instinct: A Special Breed, Home-Based Business People Seek Lucrative Niches." *Nation's Business.* June 1998.

Beech, Wendy M. "Home Alone? Fighting Isolation in Home-Based Businesses." *Black Enterprise.* January 2000.

"Bring it Home: Get moving with our ranking of the top 101 home-based franchises." *Entrepreneur.* March 2006.

Clark, Scott. "The Home-Based Business Boom Brings Problems and Opportunities." *Houston Business Journal.* 7 January 2000.

DeBaise, Colleen. "Locking In That Home-Office Deduction." *SmartMoney.com.* Available from http://www.smartmoney.com/smallbiz/askedandanswered/index.cfm?story=20060110 10 January 2006.

Edwards, Paul, and Sarah Edwards. *Working from Home: Everything You Need to Know about Living and Working under the Same Roof.* Tarcher, 1990.

Hausman, Carl. *The Complete Small Business Sourcebook: Information, Services, and Experts Every Small and Home-Based Business Needs.* Times Business, 1999.

Home Business Handbook: Expert Advice for Running a Successful Business Out of Your Home. Perigee Books, 1990.

Marullo, Gloria Gibbs. "Redefining the Home-Office Deduction." *Nation's Business.* September 1997.

Hillstrom, Northern Lights
updated by Magee, ECDI

HOTELING

Hoteling is a term used to describe the practice of providing office space to employees on an as-needed basis instead of by means of a permanent workspace—cubicle or office. Hoteling, often referred to as office hoteling, is possible because of new office and communication technologies. Computer networks, laptops and other mobile devices, as well as sophisticated wireless communications systems all make moving a person and his or her productive tools from one place to another relatively easy. This, in turn, allows the employer to make more efficient use of office space and thus reduce costs. Hoteling systems tend to work particularly well for organizations whose employees travel frequently.

Hoteling was adopted by many consulting and accounting firms in the late 1990s. It had also found proponents among companies with traveling sales forces or large numbers of telecommuters. Basically, hoteling allows employees who spend a great deal of time off-site to return to the home office and plug a laptop computer into a cubicle for a few hours. Hoteling is similar to "free addressing" or "hot desking," in which employees occupy whatever desks or offices are available. All of these strategies make innovative use of office space in order to accommodate the flexible schedules and work habits of employees. "Today's worker spends less and less time in the office, using it chiefly to touch base or to interact for short periods with team members," Sandra M. Paret explained in the *Dallas Business Journal.* "In a traditional office, up to 50 percent of desks, offices, and workstations are unused at any given point on a typical workday."

THE ALTERNATIVE OFFICING TREND

Hoteling is part of a larger trend known as alternative officing (AO), which encompasses a variety of methods of redesigning office space to reduce costs, improve productivity, adapt to new technology, and accommodate the increased mobility of employees. More and more companies are changing to open office environments with informal meeting rooms, snack areas, project rooms, and focus rooms for individual work. These innovative office designs are intended to foster teamwork and interaction among employees.

The most common complaints about alternative officing setups involve a lack of privacy and problems with technological support. "AO strategies also place greater demands on systems and building infrastructures," Paret noted. "Work stations must be flexible enough to accommodate different workers at different times. Scheduling software must evolve so companies can plan for their workspace usage on a daily basis. Telecommunications systems must take into account that employees and their equipment will not be fixed in one location."

Small business owners who consider redesigning their office space to take advantage of hoteling or other alternative officing setups should first identify their goals. Some companies undertake office redesigns in order to improve teamwork and collaboration, while others need to create private areas to improve employee concentration. It may be helpful to conduct a formal workflow analysis or usage pattern study to determine the best use of space.

It is also important to consider the culture of the organization before undertaking an office redesign. Employees at some companies may like the hierarchy provided by a traditional office setting, in which people's status is tied to their office space. Alternative officing, on the other hand, requires people to operate in nonterritorial ways and respect shared space. Small business owners should investigate a variety of possible arrangements and make sure employees support the plan before making radical changes. "An office redesign can do a lot more than provide a facelift," Katherine C. Berg wrote in the *Dallas Business Journal.* "It can spark productivity, improve employee morale, and ultimately boost the bottom line."

SEE ALSO *Flexible Work Arrangements; Workstation*

BIBLIOGRAPHY

Berg, Katherine C. "Office Updates Bring Efficiency to the Workplace." *Dallas Business Journal.* 26 January 2001.

Brouillard, Sarah. "Hoteling Adapts to Mobile Workers." *Minneapolis-St. Paul City Business.* 16 February 2001.

Gilligan, Eugene. "Flex Time: Corporations bring back hoteling to improve efficiency." *Commercial Property News.* 1 February 2006.

Paret, Sandra M. "Alternative Officing Demands New Approach." *Dallas Business Journal.* 26 January 2001.

Wise, David T. "Identify Goals before Setting Up Open-Floor Office." *Los Angeles Business Journal.* 19 February 2001.

Hillstrom, Northern Lights
updated by Magee, ECDI

HTML

Hypertext Markup Language (HTML) is an authoring tool that is used in creating Internet Web pages. When using HTML a block of text is surrounded with tags that indicate to an Internet browser how the text is to appear (for example, in bold face or italics). HTML is a collection of platform-independent styles (indicated by markup tags) that define the various components of a Web document. It is the preferred tool for creating Web pages because it is understood by all Internet browsers. Many Web designers who use HTML find it simple to learn and easy to use, because it offers a stripped-down approach to Web design that does not rely a lot on extraneous features. Another aspect of its popularity is its ability to deal quickly with bandwidth-friendly text documents.

Internet lingo is full of acronyms and buzzwords. When you consider what each letter in HTML stands for, it may be easier to understand exactly what it does and how it works.

As Joe Burns stated on www.htmlgoodies.com:

"**H**yper is the opposite of linear. It used to be that computer programs had to move in a linear fashion. This before this, this before this, and so on. HTML does not hold to that pattern and allows the person viewing the World Wide Web page to go anywhere, any time they want.

"**T**ext is what you will use. Real, honest to goodness English letters.

"**M**ark up is what you will do. You will write in plain English and then mark up what you wrote. More to come on that in the next Primer.

"**L**anguage because they needed something that started with "L" to finish HTML and Hypertext

Markup Louie didn't flow correctly. Because it's a language, really -- but the language is plain English.

THE HISTORY OF HTML

HTML, along with Hypertext Transport Protocol (HTTP) and uniform resource locator (URL), were created by Tim Berners-Lee in the latter part of the 1980s. Berners-Lee was collaborating in Switzerland at the CERN physics laboratory with another scientist by the name of Robert Calliau. When Berners-Lee was faced with the problem of organizing his notes, he created HTML to make the information accessible and easy to link.

At first, Berners-Lee was faced with the problem of only being able to use his creations on his own personal computer. In an article on Berners-Lee for *Time* magazine, Joshua Quittner asked the question: "But what if he wanted to add stuff that resided on someone else's computer? First he would need that person's permission, and then he would have to do the dreary work of adding the new material to a central database. An even better solution would be to open up his document—and his computer—to everyone and allow them to link their stuff to his. He could limit access to his colleagues at CERN, but why stop there? Open it up to scientists everywhere! Let it span the networks! In Berners-Lee's scheme there would be no central manager, no central database and no scaling problems. The thing could grow like the Internet itself, open-ended and infinite.... So he cobbled together a relatively easy-to-learn coding system—HTML—that has come to be the lingua franca of the Web. It's the way Web-content creators put those little colored, under-lined links in text, add images, and so on."

Because of his accomplishments, Berners-Lee is considered the father of the World Wide Web and he has received many awards and accolades for his contributions to the world of computers and technology. Awards and accolades may be the only thing he received for his creations. As Quittner put it: "You'd think he would have at least got rich; he had plenty of opportunities. But at every juncture, Berners-Lee chose the non-profit road, both for himself and for his creation."

HOW HTML WORKS

HTML helps to define the structure of a Web page. It is useful to help set up paragraphs, headers, and default fonts so that a user can always read the text regardless of whether or not they have the font installed on their own personal computer. The acceptance of HTML by Web page designers has allowed them to think of a document as a way of accessing information, rather than a collection of static pages that can only be read when downloaded.

When someone types in a URL or clicks on a Web page link, the browser requests a document from a Web server via the Hypertext Transport Protocol, or HTTP. The server then sends the document back to the user, which is displayed on the browser. The things that the are contained in the document (text, photos, audio and video files, etc.) were all put there using HTML structure.

THE DRAWBACKS OF HTML

HTML is not a perfect tool for designing graphic-intensive sites or those that contain a large overall amount of information. The fact that the documents contained in a HTML structure are static pages does not make it the tool of choice for sites that contain animation, either. It is getting better in that department thanks to the development of different HTML extensions and other upgrades.

HTML also lacks the ability to create custom window sizes, compress files, and other standard navigational controls. Distribution size is also a crucial issue because the standard HTML file format is not suited for delivering a large amount of content over a network. In addition, an HTML programmer may have difficulty dealing with a large number of HTML and graphics files at once. Certain software does exist to help deal with all of these problems.

DYNAMIC HTML AND OTHER COMPETING TOOLS

Because of HTML's weaknesses in the area of graphics, dynamic HTML was created to enhance the capabilities in Web page design. As William R. Stanek stated in *PC Magazine:* "With dynamic HTML, you can create Web pages with eye-popping special effects, animation, and much more without relying on server-side scripts, database engines and hundreds of lines of complicated markup code. One of the key design goals in creating dynamic HTML was easing the complexities involved in interactive multimedia presentations on the Web. An important part of that goal was building the necessary support framework into the browser. The result is that you don't have to rely on controls, plug-ins, or other helper applications to achieve special effects, animation, or anything else that dynamic HTML enables."

Dynamic HTML allows Web page designers to create impressive graphics and animation with minimal coding. These features are visible to viewers almost instantaneously. As Stanek explained, "The key to dynamic HTML in both Internet Explorer and Navigator is a live update mechanism that allows a browser to modify sections of a Web page in the background. Once the page has been modified, the browser reformats it as necessary and displays the changes. Anyone viewing the page sees the updates instantly and doesn't have to wait for the browser to reload the page or access another page. The browser makes the changes without ever having to go back to the Web server for additional content."

In addition to dynamic HTML and other advancements in that area, there are several other tools that were designed to directly compete with HTML. One such tool is Java, which is hailed as a complete programming language, with many features that are compatible with other applications. Another innovation is eXtensible Markup Language (XML) that allows for the standardized exchange of information between computers. XML is being touted as the next big Internet standard, the heir apparent to the HTML throne. It is still an evolving tool that has a maximum potential which remains to be seen. Another tool known as XHTML is also being developed. It is a version of HTML that is based on XML.

HTML AND SMALL BUSINESS

If a small business owner intends to set up his own Web site, there are several steps to consider. First, the site should be carefully planned out, and its content should be determined. The Web site should be designed by a person with a strong sense of graphic design in order to make it visually appealing for the users. When the site enters the programming phase, a basic knowledge of HTML will come into play. If someone within the company is familiar with HTML, then he or she could easily do it. If not, a professional programmer should be called upon to lend his or her expertise. This person will then write the code around a text that the company provides and build the graphics and aspects of the Web site's structure.

The person doing the implementation of the HTML code should take into consideration the range of browsers and browser versions that exist. Since the Web site is a potentially important part of any company with an online presence, a knowledgeable programmer should be hired to do the design work. After the programming is done, a Web host should be chosen and efforts should be made to promote the site once it is posted on the Internet. Only through proper promotion will traffic to the site be generated.

SEE ALSO *Web Site Design*

BIBLIOGRAPHY
Klein, Leo Robert. "The Joys of Interactivity." *Library Journal.* January 2000.

Quittner, Joshua. "Network Designer: Tim Berners-Lee. From Thousands of Interconnected Threads of the Internet, He Wove the World Wide Web and Created a Mass Medium for the 21st Century." *Time.* 29 March 1999.

Slocombe, Mike. "Construct a Foolproof Navigation System: Notch up more hits by helping visitors find their way around your site." *Internet Magazine.* October 2003.

Stanek, William R. "Creativity and Control." *PC Magazine.* 20 January 1998.

Hillstrom, Northern Lights
updated by Magee, ECDI

HUBZONE EMPOWERMENT CONTRACTING PROGRAM

The HUBZone Empowerment Contracting Program is an initiative of the U.S. Small Business Administration (SBA) that gives preference in securing federal contracts to small businesses located in "historically underutilized business zones," or HUBZones. There are three types of HUBZones: urban areas as defined by U.S. census figures; "non-metropolitan counties" or rural areas that meet certain median household income parameters; and Native American lands (lands on federally recognized Indian reservations). As of 2005 there were nearly 8,500 HUBZones in the United States.

The HUBZone program—which was established under the Small Business Reauthorization Act of 1997—provides access to federal contracting opportunities for small businesses that maintain a principal office in one of these areas and employ people who live there. It is intended to improve the economic status of distressed communities by encouraging the growth and long-term viability of small businesses, thus helping to create jobs and attract private investment.

As of October 1, 2000, all U.S. government agencies were required to give preference to HUBZone businesses when awarding federal contracts. The goal of the program was to award 2 percent of federal contracts to HUBZone businesses in 2001, 2.5 percent in 2002, and 3 percent in each year thereafter. In 2000, Federal agencies reported that they had awarded only $663 million in contracts to HUBZone companies, a number that represented 0.33 percent of all primer contracts. This was far short of the goal set for that year. In 2001, the budget for the program was cut sharply and the Small Business Administration (SBA) was forced to maintain the program with limited funds. The program has been maintained and as of 2005, $8 million of the SBA's budget was earmarked for the HUBZone Program.

The SBA is responsible for determining which businesses are eligible for HUBZone contracts, maintaining a list of qualified small businesses, and reporting to Congress on the results of the program. As of May 31, 2005, 12,983 firms were HUBZone-certified. To qualify as a HUBZone contractor, a small business must meet the following criteria: it must be a small business according to SBA size standards; it must have a principal office located in a HUBZone; it must be owned or controlled by U.S. citizens; and at least 35 percent of its employees must be HUBZone residents. If any of a firm's locations meet these standards, then the entire company is eligible for HUBZone status.

HUBZone contracts are awarded in three principal ways. When more than one qualified HUBZone business is expected to submit a bid, then the contract is awarded competitively at a fair market price. If only one qualified HUBZone business submits a bid, that business can receive a sole source contract at a fair price. In some situations, contracts are awarded via a full and open competition in which qualified HUBZone businesses receive a preference if their bid is less than 10 percent higher than those of other bidders.

In addition to preferences in securing federal contracts, HUBZone businesses also can qualify for higher SBA guaranteed surety bonds on contract bids. In cases where the HUBZone is also designated as a federal Empowerment Zone/Enterprise Community, small businesses may also qualify for other tax credits and deductions. To find out more about the HUBZone program, see the Small Business Administration Web site at http://www.sba.gov/hubzone.

SEE ALSO *8(a) Programs; Empowerment Zones*

BIBLIOGRAPHY
Hoover, Kent. "Funds for HUBZones Sliced by Congress." *Philadelphia Business Journal.* 7 December 2001.

U.S. Small Business Administration. *SBA Profile: Who We Are and What We Do.* 2000.

U.S. White House. ExpectMore.gov *Detailed Information on the Historically Underutilized Business Zone - HUBZone Assessment.* Available from http://www.whitehouse.gov/omb/expectmore/detail.10004421.2005.html Retrieved on 14 March 2006.

Hillstrom, Northern Lights
updated by Magee, ECDI

HUMAN RESOURCE MANAGEMENT

Human Resource Management (HRM) is the term used to describe formal systems devised for the management of people within an organization. The responsibilities of a

human resource manager fall into three major areas: staffing, employee compensation and benefits, and defining/designing work. Essentially, the purpose of HRM is to maximize the productivity of an organization by optimizing the effectiveness of its employees. This mandate is unlikely to change in any fundamental way, despite the ever-increasing pace of change in the business world. As Edward L. Gubman observed in the *Journal of Business Strategy,* "the basic mission of human resources will always be to acquire, develop, and retain talent; align the workforce with the business; and be an excellent contributor to the business. Those three challenges will never change."

Until fairly recently, an organization's human resources department was often consigned to lower rungs of the corporate hierarchy, despite the fact that its mandate is to replenish and nourish what is often cited—legitimately—as an organization's greatest resource, it's work force. But in recent years recognition of the importance of human resources management to a company's overall health has grown dramatically. This recognition of the importance of HRM extends to small businesses, for while they do not generally have the same volume of human resources requirements as do larger organizations, they too face personnel management issues that can have a decisive impact on business health. As Irving Burstiner commented in *The Small Business Handbook,* "Hiring the right people—and training them well—can often mean the difference between scratching out the barest of livelihoods and steady business growth.... Personnel problems do not discriminate between small and big business. You find them in all businesses, regardless of size."

PRINCIPLES OF HUMAN RESOURCE MANAGEMENT

Business consultants note that modern human resource management is guided by several overriding principles. Perhaps the paramount principle is a simple recognition that human resources are the most important assets of an organization; a business cannot be successful without effectively managing this resource. Another important principle, articulated by Michael Armstrong in his book *A Handbook of Human Resource Management,* is that business success "is most likely to be achieved if the personnel policies and procedures of the enterprise are closely linked with, and make a major contribution to, the achievement of corporate objectives and strategic plans." A third guiding principle, similar in scope, holds that it is the HR's responsibility to find, secure, guide, and develop employees whose talents and desires are compatible with the operating needs and future goals of the company. Other HRM factors that shape corporate culture—whether by encouraging integration and cooperation across the company, instituting quantitative performance measurements, or taking some other action—are also commonly cited as key components in business success. HRM, summarized Armstrong, "is a strategic approach to the acquisition, motivation, development and management of the organization's human resources. It is devoted to shaping an appropriate corporate culture, and introducing programs which reflect and support the core values of the enterprise and ensure its success."

POSITION AND STRUCTURE OF HUMAN RESOURCE MANAGEMENT

Human resource department responsibilities can be subdivided into three areas: individual, organizational, and career. Individual management entails helping employees identify their strengths and weaknesses; correct their shortcomings; and make their best contribution to the enterprise. These duties are carried out through a variety of activities such as performance reviews, training, and testing. Organizational development, meanwhile, focuses on fostering a successful system that maximizes human (and other) resources as part of larger business strategies. This important duty also includes the creation and maintenance of a change program, which allows the organization to respond to evolving outside and internal influences. Finally, there is the responsibility of managing career development. This entails matching individuals with the most suitable jobs and career paths within the organization.

Human resource management functions are ideally positioned near the theoretic center of the organization, with access to all areas of the business. Since the HRM department or manager is charged with managing the productivity and development of workers at all levels, human resource personnel should have access to—and the support of—key decision makers. In addition, the HRM department should be situated in such a way that it is able to communicate effectively with all areas of the company.

HRM structures vary widely from business to business, shaped by the type, size, and governing philosophies of the organization that they serve. But most organizations organize HRM functions around the clusters of people to be helped—they conduct recruiting, administrative, and other duties in a central location. Different employee development groups for each department are necessary to train and develop employees in specialized areas, such as sales, engineering, marketing, or executive education. In contrast, some HRM departments are completely independent and are organized purely by function. The same training department, for example, serves all divisions of the organization.

In recent years, however, observers have cited a decided trend toward fundamental reassessments of human resources structures and positions. "A cascade of changing business conditions, changing organizational structures, and changing leadership has been forcing human resource departments to alter their perspectives on their role and function almost overnight," wrote John Johnston in *Business Quarterly*. "Previously, companies structured themselves on a centralized and compartmentalized basis—head office, marketing, manufacturing, shipping, etc. They now seek to decentralize and to integrate their operations, developing cross-functional teams.... Today, senior management expects HR to move beyond its traditional, compartmentalized 'bunker' approach to a more integrated, decentralized support function." Given this change in expectations, Johnston noted that "an increasingly common trend in human resources is to decentralize the HR function and make it accountable to specific line management. This increases the likelihood that HR is viewed and included as an integral part of the business process, similar to its marketing, finance, and operations counterparts. However, HR will retain a centralized functional relationship in areas where specialized expertise is truly required," such as compensation and recruitment responsibilities.

HUMAN RESOURCE MANAGEMENT— KEY RESPONSIBILITIES

Human resource management is concerned with the development of both individuals and the organization in which they operate. HRM, then, is engaged not only in securing and developing the talents of individual workers, but also in implementing programs that enhance communication and cooperation between those individual workers in order to nurture organizational development.

The primary responsibilities associated with human resource management include: job analysis and staffing, organization and utilization of work force, measurement and appraisal of work force performance, implementation of reward systems for employees, professional development of workers, and maintenance of work force.

Job analysis consists of determining—often with the help of other company areas—the nature and responsibilities of various employment positions. This can encompass determination of the skills and experiences necessary to adequately perform in a position, identification of job and industry trends, and anticipation of future employment levels and skill requirements. "Job analysis is the cornerstone of HRM practice because it provides valid information about jobs that is used to hire and promote people, establish wages, determine training needs, and make other important HRM decisions," stated Thomas S. Bateman and Carl P. Zeithaml in *Management: Function and Strategy.* Staffing, meanwhile, is the actual process of managing the flow of personnel into, within (through transfers and promotions), and out of an organization. Once the recruiting part of the staffing process has been completed, selection is accomplished through job postings, interviews, reference checks, testing, and other tools.

Organization, utilization, and maintenance of a company's work force is another key function of HRM. This involves designing an organizational framework that makes maximum use of an enterprise's human resources and establishing systems of communication that help the organization operate in a unified manner. Other responsibilities in this area include safety and health and worker-management relations. Human resource maintenance activities related to safety and health usually entail compliance with federal laws that protect employees from hazards in the workplace. These regulations are handed down from several federal agencies, including the Occupational Safety and Health Administration (OSHA) and the Environmental Protection Agency (EPA), and various state agencies, which implement laws in the realms of worker's compensation, employee protection, and other areas. Maintenance tasks related to worker-management relations primarily entail: working with labor unions; handling grievances related to misconduct, such as theft or sexual harassment; and devising communication systems to foster cooperation and a shared sense of mission among employees.

Performance appraisal is the practice of assessing employee job performance and providing feedback to those employees about both positive and negative aspects of their performance. Performance measurements are very important both for the organization and the individual, for they are the primary data used in determining salary increases, promotions, and, in the case of workers who perform unsatisfactorily, dismissal.

Reward systems are typically managed by HR areas as well. This aspect of human resource management is very important, for it is the mechanism by which organizations provide their workers with rewards for past achievements and incentives for high performance in the future. It is also the mechanism by which organizations address problems within their work force, through institution of disciplinary measures. Aligning the work force with company goals, stated Gubman, "requires offering workers an employment relationship that motivates them to take ownership of the business plan."

Employee development and training is another vital responsibility of HR personnel. HR is responsible for researching an organization's training needs, and for initiating and evaluating employee development pro-

grams designed to address those needs. These training programs can range from orientation programs, which are designed to acclimate new hires to the company, to ambitious education programs intended to familiarize workers with a new software system.

"After getting the right talent into the organization," wrote Gubman, "the second traditional challenge to human resources is to align the workforce with the business—to constantly build the capacity of the workforce to execute the business plan." This is done through performance appraisals, training, and other activities. In the realm of performance appraisal, HRM professionals must devise uniform appraisal standards, develop review techniques, train managers to administer the appraisals, and then evaluate and follow up on the effectiveness of performance reviews. They must also tie the appraisal process into compensation and incentive strategies, and work to ensure that federal regulations are observed.

Responsibilities associated with training and development activities, meanwhile, include the determination, design, execution, and analysis of educational programs. The HRM professional should be aware of the fundamentals of learning and motivation, and must carefully design and monitor training and development programs that benefit the overall organization as well as the individual. The importance of this aspect of a business's operation can hardly be overstated. As Roberts, Seldon, and Roberts indicated in *Human Resources Management,* "the quality of employees and their development through training and education are major factors in determining long-term profitability of a small business.... Research has shown specific benefits that a small business receives from training and developing its workers, including: increased productivity; reduced employee turnover; increased efficiency resulting in financial gains; [and] decreased need for supervision."

Meaningful contributions to business processes are increasingly recognized as within the purview of active human resource management practices. Of course, human resource managers have always contributed to overall business processes in certain respects—by disseminating guidelines for and monitoring employee behavior, for instance, or ensuring that the organization is obeying worker-related regulatory guidelines. Now, increasing numbers of businesses are incorporating human resource managers into other business processes as well. In the past, human resource managers were cast in a support role in which their thoughts on cost/benefit justifications and other operational aspects of the business were rarely solicited. But as Johnston noted, the changing character of business structures and the marketplace are making it increasingly necessary for business owners and executives to pay greater attention to the human resource aspects of operation: "Tasks that were once neatly slotted into well-defined and narrow job descriptions have given way to broad job descriptions or role definitions. In some cases, completely new work relationships have developed; telecommuting, permanent part-time roles and outsourcing major non-strategic functions are becoming more frequent." All of these changes, which human resource managers are heavily involved in, are important factors in shaping business performance.

THE CHANGING FIELD OF HUMAN RESOURCE MANAGEMENT

In recent years, several business trends have had a significant impact on the broad field of HRM. Chief among them was new technologies. These new technologies, particularly in the areas of electronic communication and information dissemination and retrieval, have dramatically altered the business landscape. Satellite communications, computers and networking systems, fax machines, and other devices have all facilitated change in the ways in which businesses interact with each other and their workers. Telecommuting, for instance, has become a very popular option for many workers, and HRM professionals have had to develop new guidelines for this emerging subset of employees.

Changes in organizational structure have also influenced the changing face of human resource management. Continued erosion in manufacturing industries in the United States and other nations, coupled with the rise in service industries in those countries, have changed the workplace, as has the decline in union representation in many industries (these two trends, in fact, are commonly viewed as interrelated). In addition, organizational philosophies have undergone change. Many companies have scrapped or adjusted their traditional, hierarchical organizational structures in favor of flatter management structures. HRM experts note that this shift in responsibility brought with it a need to reassess job descriptions, appraisal systems, and other elements of personnel management.

A third change factor has been accelerating market globalization. This phenomenon has served to increase competition for both customers and jobs. The latter development enabled some businesses to demand higher performances from their employees while holding the line on compensation. Other factors that have changed the nature of HRM in recent years include new management and operational theories like Total Quality Management (TQM), rapidly changing demographics, and changes in health insurance and federal and state employment legislation.

SMALL BUSINESS AND HUMAN RESOURCE MANAGEMENT

A small business's human resource management needs are not of the same size or complexity of those of a large firm. Nonetheless, even a business that carries only two or three employees faces important personnel management issues. Indeed, the stakes are very high in the world of small business when it comes to employee recruitment and management. No business wants an employee who is lazy or incompetent or dishonest. But a small business with a work force of half a dozen people will be hurt far more by such an employee than will a company with a work force that numbers in the hundreds (or thousands). Nonetheless, "most small business employers have no formal training in how to make hiring decisions," noted Jill A. Rossiter in *Human Resources: Mastering Your Small Business.* "Most have no real sense of the time it takes nor the costs involved. All they know is that they need help in the form of a 'good' sales manager, a 'good' secretary, a 'good' welder, and so on. And they know they need someone they can work with, who is willing to put in the time to learn the business and do the job. It sounds simple, but it isn't."

Before hiring a new employee, the small business owner should weigh several considerations. The first step the small business owner should take when pondering an expansion of employee payroll is to honestly assess the status of the organization itself. Are current employees being utilized appropriately? Are current production methods effective? Can the needs of the business be met through an arrangement with an outside contractor or some other means? Are you, as the owner, spending your time appropriately? As Rossiter noted, "any personnel change should be considered an opportunity for rethinking your organizational structure."

Small businesses also need to match the talents of prospective employees with the company's needs. Efforts to manage this can be accomplished in a much more effective fashion if the small business owner devotes energy to defining the job and actively taking part in the recruitment process. But the human resource management task does not end with the creation of a detailed job description and the selection of a suitable employee. Indeed, the hiring process marks the beginning of HRM for the small business owner.

Small business consultants strongly urge even the most modest of business enterprises to implement and document policies regarding human resource issues. "Few small enterprises can afford even a fledgling personnel department during the first few years of business operation," acknowledged Burstiner. "Nevertheless, a large mass of personnel forms and data generally accumulates rather rapidly from the very beginning. To hold problems to a minimum, specific personnel policies should be established as early as possible. These become useful guides in all areas: recruitment and selection, compensation plan and employee benefits, training, promotions and terminations, and the like." Depending on the nature of the business enterprise (and the owner's own comfort zone), the owner can even involve his employees in this endeavor. In any case, a carefully considered employee handbook or personnel manual can be an invaluable tool in ensuring that the small business owner and his or her employees are on the same page. Moreover, a written record can lend a small business some protection in the event that its management or operating procedures are questioned in the legal arena.

Some small business owners also need to consider training and other development needs in managing their enterprise's employees. The need for such educational supplements can range dramatically. A bakery owner, for instance, may not need to devote much of his resources to employee training, but a firm that provides electrical wiring services to commercial clients may need to implement a system of continuing education for its workers in order to remain viable.

Finally, the small business owner needs to establish and maintain a productive working atmosphere for his or her work force. Employees are far more likely to be productive assets to your company if they feel that they are treated fairly. The small business owner who clearly communicates personal expectations and company goals, provides adequate compensation, offers meaningful opportunities for career advancement, anticipates work force training and developmental needs, and provides meaningful feedback to his or her employees is far more likely to be successful than the owner who is neglectful in any of these areas.

SEE ALSO *Employee Benefits; Employee Compensation; Employee Manual*

BIBLIOGRAPHY

Armstrong, Michael. *A Handbook of Human Resource Management Practice.* Kogan Page Limited, 1999.

Burstiner, Irving. *The Small Business Handbook.* Prentice Hall, 1988.

Green, Paul C. *Building Robust Competencies: Linking Human Resource Systems to Organizational Strategies.* Jossey-Bass, 1999.

Gubman, Edward L. "The Gauntlet is Down." *Journal of Business Strategy.* November-December 1996.

Phillip, Harris. *Managing the Knowledge Culture.* Human Resource Development Press, March 2005.

Johnston, John. "Time to Rebuild Human Resources." *Business Quarterly.* Winter 1996.

Mathis, Robert L., and John H. Jackson. *Human Resource Management.* Thomson South-Western, 2005.

Rossiter, Jill A. *Human Resources: Mastering Your Small Business.* Upstart Publishing, 1996.

Solomon, Charlene Marmer. "Working Smarter: How HR Can Help." *Personnel Journal.* June 1993.

Ulrich, Dave. *Delivering Results: A New Mandate for HR Professionals.* Harvard Business School Press, 1998.

U.S. Small Business Administration. Roberts, Gary, Gary Seldon, and Carlotta Roberts. "Human Resources Management." n.d.

Hillstrom, Northern Lights
updated by Magee, ECDI

HUMAN RESOURCE POLICIES

Human resource policies are the formal rules and guidelines that businesses put in place to hire, train, assess, and reward the members of their workforce. These policies, when organized and disseminated in an easily used form, can serve to preempt many misunderstandings between employees and employers about their rights and obligations in the business place. It is tempting, as a new small business owner, to focus on the concerns of the business at hand, and put off the task of writing up a human resource policy. All business analysts and employment lawyers will advise a new business owner to get a policy down on paper, even if it is a simple one drafted from a boilerplate model. Having policies written is important so that it is clear to all what the policies are and that they are applied consistently and fairly across the organization. Moreover, when issues concerning employee rights and company policies come before federal and state courts, it is standard practice to assume that the company's human resource policies, whether written or verbal, are a part of an employment contract between the employee and the company. Without clearly written policies, the company is at a disadvantage.

Small businesses—and especially business start-ups—can not afford to fritter away valuable time and resources on drawn-out policy disputes or potentially expensive lawsuits. Having a human resource policy in place from the start can help to avoid this situation. The business owner who takes the time to establish sound, comprehensive human resource policies will be far better equipped to succeed over the long run than the business owner who deals with each policy decision as it erupts. The latter ad hoc style is much more likely to produce inconsistent, uninformed, and legally questionable decisions that may cripple an otherwise prosperous business. For as many small business consultants state, human resource policies that are inconsistently applied or based on faulty or incomplete data will almost inevitably result in declines in worker morale, deterioration in employee loyalty, and increased vulnerability to legal penalties. To help ensure that personnel management policies are applied fairly, business owners and consultants alike recommend that small business enterprises produce and maintain a written record of its HR policies and of instances in which those policies came into play.

SUBJECTS COVERED BY COMPANY HR POLICIES

Small business owners should make sure that they address the following basic human resource issues when putting together their personnel policies:

- Equal Employment Opportunity policies
- Employee classifications
- Workdays, paydays, and pay advances
- Overtime compensation
- Meal periods and break periods
- Payroll deductions
- Vacation policies
- Holidays
- Sick days and personal leave (for bereavement, jury duty, voting, etc.)
- Performance evaluations and salary increases
- Performance improvement
- Termination policies

Templates that may be used to create a first human resource policy document are available from many sources. Two such sources that are reputable and offer information of a full range of employment issues are the National Human Resource Association and the Society for Human Resource Managers. Each maintains a Web site with information on the services it provides and pointers to other reputable service providers. Those Web sites are, respectively, http://www.humanresources.org and http://www.shrm.org/.

A broad spectrum of issues can be addressed in human resource policies, depending on the nature of the business in question. Examples of such issues include promotion policies; medical/dental benefits provided to employees; use of company equipment/resources (access to Internet, personal use of fax machines and telephones, etc.); continuity of policies; sexual harassment; substance abuse and/or drug testing; smoking; flextime and telecommuting policies; pension, profit-sharing, and retirement plans; reimbursement of employee expenses (for traveling expenses and other expenses associated with conducting company business); child or elder care; edu-

cational assistance; grievance procedures; employee privacy; dress codes; parking; mail and shipping; and sponsorship of recreational activities.

ADVANTAGES OF FORMAL HUMAN RESOURCE POLICIES

Small business owners who have prepared and updated good personnel management policies have cited several important ways in which they contribute to the success of business enterprises. Many observers have pointed out that even the best policies will falter if the business owners or managers who are charged with administering those policies are careless or incompetent in doing so. But for those businesses that are able to administer their HR policies in an intelligent and consistent manner, benefits can accrue in several areas:

Communication with employees. A well written and thoughtfully presented human resource policy manual can establish the tone that a new business person wishes to maintain within his or her business. Such a policy also serves to disseminating information about what employees may expect from the company as well as what the employer expects from the employees regarding work performance and behavior while on the job.

Communication with managers and supervisors. Formal policies can be helpful to managers and other supervisory personnel faced with hiring, promotion, and reward decisions concerning people who work under them.

Time Savings. Prudent and comprehensive human resource management policies can save companies significant amounts of management time that can then be spent on other business activities, such as new product development, competitive analysis, marketing campaigns, etc.

Curbing litigation. Members of the legal and business communities agree that organizations can do a lot to cut off legal threats from disgruntled current or ex-employees simply by creating—and applying—a fair and comprehensive set of personnel policies.

MAKING CHANGES TO EXISTING HR POLICIES

Companies typically have to make revisions to established HR policies on a regular basis, as the company grows and as the regulatory and business environments in which it operates evolve. When confronted with the challenge of updating HR policies, however, it is important for small businesses to proceed cautiously. For example, if an employee asks the owner of a small business if he might telecommute from his home one day a week, the owner may view the request as a reasonable, relatively innocuous one. But even minor variations in personnel policy can have repercussions that extend far beyond the initially visible parameters of the request. If the employee is granted permission to work from home one day a week, will other employees ask for the same benefit? Does the employee expect the business to foot the bill for any aspect of the telecommuting endeavor—purchase of computer, modem, etc.? Do customers or vendors rely on the employee (or employees) to be in the office five days a week? Do other employees need that worker to be in the office to answer questions? Is the nature of the employee's workload such that he can take meaningful work home? Can you implement the telecommuting variation on a probationary basis?

Small business owners need to recognize that changes in HR policy have the potential to impact, in one way or another, every person in the company, *including* the owner. Proposed changes should be examined carefully and in consultation with others in the organization who may recognize potential pitfalls that other managers, or the business owner herself, may have failed to detect. Once a change in policy is made, it should be disseminated widely and effectively so that everyone within the business is working from the same human resource policy at all times.

BIBLIOGRAPHY

Armstrong, Michael. *Handbook of Human Resource Management Practice*. Kogan Page, 1999.

"How to Develop Essential HR Policies and Procedures." *HRMagazine*. February 2005.

Green, Paul C. *Building Robust Competencies: Linking Human Resource Systems to Organizational Strategies*. Jossey-Bass, 1999.

Johnston, John. "Time to Rebuild Human Resources." *Business Quarterly*. Winter 1996.

Koch, Marianne J., and Rita Gunther McGrath. "Improving Labor Productivity: Human Resource Management Policies Do Matter." *Strategic Management Journal*. May 1996.

Mathis, Robert L., and John H. Jackson. *Human Resource Management*. Thomson South-Western, 2005.

Rossiter, Jill A. *Human Resources: Mastering Your Small Business*. Upstart Publishing, 1996.

Ulrich, Dave. *Delivering Results: A New Mandate for Human Resource Professionals*. Harvard Business School Press, 1998.

U.S. Small Business Administration. Roberts, Gary, Gary Seldon, and Carlotta Roberts. "Human Resources Management." n.d..

Hillstrom, Northern Lights
updated by Magee ECDI

HUMAN RESOURCES MANAGEMENT AND THE LAW

The field of human resources management is greatly influenced and shaped by the state and federal laws governing employment issues. Indeed, regulations and laws govern all aspects of human resource management—recruitment, placement, development, and compensation.

One of the most important pieces of HRM legislation, which affects all of the functional areas, is Title VII of the Civil Rights Act of 1964 and subsequent amendments, including the Civil Rights Act of 1991. These acts made illegal the discrimination against employees or potential recruits for reasons of race, color, religion, sex, and national origin. It forces employers to follow—and often document—fairness practices related to hiring, training, pay, benefits, and virtually all other activities and responsibilities related to HRM. The 1964 act established the Equal Employment Opportunity Commission to enforce the act, and provides for civil penalties in the event of discrimination. The net result of the all-encompassing civil rights acts is that businesses must carefully design and document numerous procedures to ensure compliance, or face potentially significant penalties. Another important piece of legislation that complements the civil rights laws discussed above is the Equal Pay Act of 1963. This act forbids wage or salary discrimination based on sex, and mandates equal pay for equal work with few exceptions. Subsequent court rulings augmented the act by promoting the concept of comparable worth, or equal pay for unequal jobs of equal value or worth.

Other important laws that govern significant aspects of labor relations and human resource management include the following:

- Davis-Bacon Act of 1931—This law requires the payment of minimum wages to nonfederal employees.

- The Norris-Laguardia Act of 1932—This law protects the rights of unions to organize, and prohibits employers from forcing job applicants to promise not to join a union in exchange for employment.

- The Wagner Act of 1935—This law, also known as the National Labor Relations Act, is the main piece of legislation governing union/management relations, and is a chief source of regulation for HRM departments.

- Social Security Act of 1935— This law was enacted in order to protect the general welfare by establishing a variety of systems to assist the aging, the disabled, and children.

- The Walsh-Healy Public Contracts Act of 1936— This law was designed to ensure that employees working as contractors for the federal government would be compensated fairly.

- Fair Labor Standards Act of 1938—this important law mandated employer compliance with restrictions related to minimum wages, overtime provisions, child labor, and workplace safety.

- Taft-Hartley Act of 1947—This law created provisions that severely restrict the activities and power of labor unions in the United States.

- Landrum-Griffin Act of 1959— Also known as the Labor-Management Reporting and Disclosure Act (LMRDA), the Landrum-Griffin Act deals primarily with the relationship between a union and its members. This law grants certain rights to union members and protects their interests by promoting democratic procedures within labor organizations.

- Age Discrimination in Employment Act of 1967— This legislation, which was strengthened by amendments in the early 1990s, essentially protects workers 40 years of age and older from discrimination.

- Occupational Safety and Health Act of 1970—This act, which established the Occupational Safety and Health Administration, was designed to force employers to provide safe and healthy work environments and to make organizations liable for workers' safety. Today, thousands of regulations, backed by civil and criminal penalties, have been implemented in various industries to help ensure that employees are not subjected to unnecessarily hazardous working conditions.

- Family and Medical Leave Act of 1993—This law was passed to provide employees who qualify with up to 12 work weeks of unpaid, job-protected leave in a 12-month period for specified family and medical reasons. It also requires group health benefits to be maintained during the leave as if employees continued to work instead of taking leave. The Act became effective on August 5, 1993 and applies to companies who employ 50 or more people.

The network of state and federal laws that exist to regulate employment and labor relations is extensive. In many cases, rules only apply to firms with a specified minimum number of employees and thus do not regulate small companies. But, other regulations apply to all employee/employer relationships, regardless of enterprise size. So, companies of all sizes must make an effort to stay abreast of legislative and regulatory developments in this area. Trade associations are a good source of news on new regulations as is the Society of Human Resource Managers (SHRM). The SHRM tracks developments at the state and federal level regarding human resource matters and makes much of this available on its Web site, located at http://www.shrm.org/.

SEE ALSO *Employee Manual ; Employment Contracts; Employment Practices Liability Insurance*

BIBLIOGRAPHY

Armstrong, Michael. *Handbook of Human Resource Management Practice.* Kogan Page, 1999.

Mathis, Robert L., and John H. Jackson. *Human Resource Management.* Thomson South-Western, 2005.

Rossiter, Jill A. *Human Resources: Mastering Your Small Business.* Upstart Publishing, 1996.

Society of Human Resource Managers. "Federal Government Information." Available from http://www.shrm.org/issues/ps/federal.asp Retrieved on 22 March 2006.

U.S. Small Business Administration. Roberts, Gary, Gary Seldon, and Carlotta Roberts. "Human Resources Management." n.d..

U.S. Social Security Administration. "Legislative History." Available from http://www.ssa.gov/history/35actinx.html Retrieved on 15 March 2006.

Hillstrom, Northern Lights
updated by Magee, ECDI

I

INCOME STATEMENTS

An income statement presents the results of a company's operations for a given period—a quarter, a year, etc. The income statement presents a summary of the revenues, gains, expenses, losses, and net income or net loss of an entity for the period. This statement is similar to a moving picture of the entity's operations during the time period specified. Along with the balance sheet, the statement of cash flows, and the statement of changes in owners' equity, the income statement is one of the primary means of financial reporting. The key item listed on the income statement is the net income or loss. A company's net income for an accounting period is measured as follows: Net income = Revenues − Expenses + Gains - Losses.

Within the income statement there is a wealth of information. A person knowledgeable about reading financial statements can find, in a company's income statement, information about its return on investment, risk, financial flexibility, and operating capabilities. Return on investment is a measure of a firm's overall performance. Risk is the uncertainty associated with the future of the enterprise. Financial flexibility is the firm's ability to adapt to problems and opportunities. Operating capability relates to the firm's ability to maintain a given level of operations.

The current view of the income statement is that income should reflect all items of profit and loss recognized during the accounting period, except for a few items that would be entered directly under retained earnings on the balance sheet, notably prior period adjustments (i.e., correction of errors). The main area

of transaction that is not included in the income statement involves changes in the equity of owners. The following summary income statement illustrates the format under generally accepted accounting principles:

Revenues	$1,000,000
Expenses	(400,000)
Gains (losses) that are not extraordinary	(100,000)
Other gains (losses)	20,000
Income from continuing operations	520,000
Gains (losses) from discontinued operations	75,000
Extraordinary gains (losses)	20,000
Cum. effect of changes in accounting principles	10,000
Net income	$625,000
Pre-tax earnings per share (2,000 shares)	$3.13

TERMS ON THE INCOME STATEMENT

The Financial Accounting Standards Board provides broad definitions of revenues, expenses, gains, losses, and other terms that appear on the income statement in its Statement of Concepts No. 6. Revenues are inflows or other enhancements of assets of an entity or settlement of its liabilities (or both) during a period, based on production and delivery of goods, provisions of services, and other activities that constitute the entity's major operations. Examples of revenues are sales revenue, interest revenue, and rent revenue.

Expenses are outflows or other uses of assets during a period as a result of delivering or producing goods, rendering services, or carrying out other activities that constitute the entity's ongoing major or central operations. Examples are cost of goods sold, salaries expense, and interest expense.

Gains are increases in owners' equity (net assets) from peripheral or incidental transactions of an entity and from all other transactions and events affecting the entity during the accounting period, except those that result from revenues or investments by owners. Examples are a gain on the sale of a building and a gain on the early retirement of long-term debt.

Losses are decreases in owners' equity (net assets) from peripheral or incidental transactions of an entity and from all other transactions and events affecting the entity during the accounting period except those that result from expenses or distributions to owners. Examples are losses on the sale of investments and losses from litigation.

Discontinued operations are those operations of an enterprise that have been sold, abandoned, or otherwise disposed. The results of continuing operations must be reported separately in the income statement from discontinued operations, and any gain or loss from the disposal of a segment must be reported along with the operating results of the discontinued separate major line of business or class of customer. Results from discontinued operations are reported net of income taxes.

Extraordinary gains or losses are material events and transactions that are both unusual in nature and infrequent in occurrence. Both of these criteria must be met for an item to be classified as an extraordinary gain or loss. To be considered unusual in nature, the underlying event or transaction should possess a high degree of abnormality and be clearly unrelated to, or only incidentally related to, the ordinary and typical activities of the entity, taking into account the environment in which the entity operates. To be considered infrequent in occurrence, the underlying event or transaction should be a type that would not reasonably be expected to recur in the foreseeable future, taking into account the environment in which the entity operates.

Extraordinary items could result if gains or losses were the direct result of any of the following events or circumstances: 1) a major casualty, such as an earthquake, 2) an expropriation of property by a foreign government, or 3) a prohibition under a new act or regulation. Extraordinary items are reported net of income taxes.

Gains and losses that are not extraordinary refer to material items that are unusual or infrequent, but not both. Such items must be disclosed separately and would be not be reported net of tax.

An **accounting change** refers to a change in accounting principle, accounting estimate, or reporting entity. Changes in accounting principles result when an accounting principle is adopted that is different from the one previously used. Changes in estimate involve revisions of estimates, such as the useful lives or residual value of depreciable assets, the loss for bad debts, and warranty costs. A change in reporting entity occurs when a company changes its composition from the prior period, as occurs when a new subsidiary is acquired.

Net income is the excess of all revenues and gains for a period over all expenses and losses of the period. Net loss is the excess of expenses and losses over revenues and gains for a period.

Generally accepted accounting principles require disclosing earnings per share amounts on the income statement of all public reporting entities. Earnings per share data provide a measure of the enterprise's management and past performance and enables users of financial statements to evaluate future prospects of the enterprise and assess dividend distributions to shareholders. Disclosure of earnings per share for effects of discontinued operations and extraordinary items is optional, but it is required for income from continuing operations, income before extraordinary items, cumulative effects of a change in accounting principles, and net income.

Primary earnings per share and fully diluted earnings per share may also be required. Primary earnings per share is a presentation based on the outstanding common shares and those securities that are in substance equivalent to common shares and have a diluting effect on earnings per share. Convertible bonds, convertible preferred stock, stock options, and warrants are examples of common stock equivalents. The fully diluted earnings per share presentation is a pro forma presentation that shows the dilution of earnings per share that would have occurred if all contingent issuances of common stock that would individually reduce earnings per share had taken place at the beginning of the period.

RECOGNIZING REVENUES AND EXPENSES

There are two methods of accounting for revenues and expenses. The key difference between them has to do with how each records transactions—cash coming into and going out of the company.

Cash Basis Accounting records and statements prepared using the cash basis recognize income and expenses according to real-time cash flow. Income is recorded upon receipt of funds, rather than based upon when it is actually earned; expenses are recorded as they are paid, rather than as they are actually incurred. Under this accounting method, therefore, it is possible to defer taxable income by delaying billing so that payment is not received in the current year. Likewise, it is possible to accelerate expenses by paying them as soon as the bills are received, in advance of the due date.

Accrual Basis A company using an accrual basis for accounting recognizes both income and expenses at the time they are earned or incurred, regardless of when cash associated with those transactions changes hands. Under this system, revenue is recorded when it is earned rather than when payment is received; expenses are recorded when they are incurred rather than when payment is made. At any one point in time, a company's statements will look very different depending on which accounting method was used in their preparation. Over time, however, these differences diminish since all expenses and revenues are eventually recorded.

Companies using the generally preferred accrual method of accounting use what is called the revenue recognition principle. This Financial Accounting Standards Board principle generally requires that revenue be recognized in the financial statements when: 1) realized or realizable, and 2) earned. Revenues are realized when products or other assets are exchanged for cash or claims to cash or when services are rendered. Revenues are realizable when assets received or held are readily convertible into cash or claims to cash. Revenues are considered earned when the entity has substantially accomplished what it must do to be entitled to the benefits represented by the revenues. Recognition through sales or the providing (performance) of services provides a uniform and reasonable test of realization. Limited exceptions to the basic revenue principle include recognizing revenue during production (on long-term construction contracts), at the completion of production (for many commodities), and subsequent to the sale at the time of cash collection (on installment sales).

In recognizing expenses, an effort must be made to match the costs with any revenues for which they are related. This is called the matching principle because expense and revenues are "matched." For example, matching, or associating, the cost of goods sold with the revenues that resulted directly and jointly from the same transaction is reasonable and practical. To recognize costs for which it is difficult to adopt some association with revenues, accountants use a rational and systematic allocation policy that assigns expenses to the periods during which the related assets are expected to provide benefits, such as depreciation, amortization, and insurance. Some costs are charged to the current period as expenses (or losses) merely because no future benefit is anticipated, no connection with revenue is apparent, or no allocation is rational and systematic under the circumstances, i.e., an immediate recognition principle.

The current operating concept of income would include only those value changes and events that are controllable by management and that are incurred in the current period from ordinary, normal, and recurring operations. Any unusual and nonrecurring items of income or loss would be recognized directly in the statement of retained earnings. Under this concept, investors are primarily interested in continuing income from operations.

The all-inclusive concept of income includes the total changes in equity recognized during a specific period, except for dividend distributions and capital transactions. Under this concept, unusual and nonrecurring income or loss items are part of the earning history of a company and should not be overlooked. Currently, the all-inclusive concept is generally recognized; however, certain material prior period adjustments should be reflected adjustments of the opening retained earnings balance.

FORMATS OF THE INCOME STATEMENT

The income statement can be prepared using either the single-step or the multiple-step format. The single-step format lists and totals all revenue and gain items at the beginning of the statement. All expense and loss items are then fixed and the total is deducted from the total revenue to give the net income. The multiple-step income statement presents operating revenue at the beginning of the statement and non-operating gains, expenses, and losses near the end of the statement. However, various items of expenses are deducted throughout the statement at intermediate levels. The statement is arranged to show explicitly several important amounts, such as gross margin on sales, operating income, income before taxes, and net income. Extraordinary items, gains and losses, accounting changes, and discontinued operations are always shown separately at the bottom of the income statement ahead of net income, regardless of which format is used.

Each format of the income statement has its advantages. The advantage of the multiple-step income statement is that it explicitly displays important financial and managerial information that the user would have to calculate from a single-step income statement. The single-step format has the advantage of being relatively simple to prepare and to understand.

SEE ALSO *Annual Reports; Balance Sheet; Cash Flow Statement; Financial Statements*

BIBLIOGRAPHY
Orr, Jayson. "Making Your Numbers Talk: The Income Statement." *CMA Management.* November 2000.

Pinson, Linda. *Keeping the Books: Basic Record Keeping and Accounting for Successful Small Business.* Business & Economics, 2004.

Rappaport, Alfred. "Show Me the Cash Flow! The income statement badly needs an overhaul." *Fortune.* 16 September 2002.

Taylor, Peter. *Book-Keeping & Accounting for Small Business.* Business & Economics, 2003.

Hillstrom, Northern Lights
updated by Magee, ECDI

INCORPORATION

Corporate ownership is one of three broad categories defining the legal ownership structure of a business. The other two broad categories are sole proprietorship and partnership. In a sole proprietorship, the owner is personally liable for his or her business's debts and losses, there is little distinction made between personal and business income, and the business terminates upon the death of the owner or the owner's decision to change the legal character of the firm (by relinquishing part or all of his or her ownership in the enterprise). A partnership is merely joint ownership, and in terms of personal liability, is similar to a sole proprietorship. Sole proprietorships and partnerships are categories of business ownership that may be entered into and dissolved fairly easily. Incorporation, on the other hand, is a more complex process. Incorporating involves the creation of a legal entity that serves as a sort of "person" who can enter into and dissolve contracts; incur debts; initiate or be the recipient of legal action; and own, acquire, and sell goods and property. A corporation, which must be chartered by a state or the federal government, is recognized as having rights, privileges, assets, and liabilities distinct from those of its owners.

In the 1990s, a new form of business structure became available to those operating businesses in many states. By the year 2002 this form, the limited liability company (LLC) or limited liability partnership (LLP), was available in all 50 states of the union and has become the business form of choice for newly formed businesses. These limited liability entities are the only forms of business structure other than the corporation in which the personal liability of the owners is limited. This feature accounts for their popularity. For the majority of small businesses, the relative simplicity and flexibility of the LLC makes it the better choice of business structure. However, there are situations in which incorporation may still be preferable. If a company wishes to do any of the following three things, incorporation is preferable to forming a limited liability company: 1) The company expects to have multiple investors or offer stock to the public; 2) The company wishes to offer extensive fringe benefits to owner-employees, and/or 3) The company hopes to use stock options or stock bonuses as part of an incentive program. In each of these three instances, IRS rules regulating corporations makes the desired activity either possible or more easily done than would be the case for limited liability companies.

Prospective entrepreneurs and established business-people operating sole proprietorships and partnerships are encouraged to weigh several factors when considering incorporating. Indeed, incorporation can have a fundamental impact on many aspects of business operation, from taxes and document keeping requirements to raising capital and owner liability.

ADVANTAGES OF INCORPORATION

- Raising Capital—Incorporation is generally regarded as an indication that the owners are serious about their business enterprise, and intend to devote time and resources to the venture for a significant period of time. This factor, as well as the reporting requirements of incorporation and—in some cases—the owners' more formidable financial resources—make corporations more attractive to some lending institutions. In addition, corporations have the option of raising capital by selling shares in their business to investors. Stockholders know that if the business they are investing in is a corporation, their personal assets are safe if the company gets into litigation or debt trouble.

- Ease of Ownership Transfer—Ownership of the company can be transferred fairly easily by simply selling stock (though some corporations attach restrictions in this regard).

- Tax Advantages—Some businesses enjoy lower tax rates under the incorporated designation than they would if they operated as a partnership or sole proprietorship. For instance, business owners can adjust the salaries they pay themselves in ways that impact the corporation's profits and, subsequently, its tax obligations. It can also be easier for a business to invest in pension plans and other fringe benefits as a corporation because the cost of these benefits can be counted as tax-deductible business expenses.

- Liability—This factor is often cited as far and away the most important advantage to incorporation. When a company incorporates, the shareholders or owners of the corporation are liable only up to the amount of money they contribute to the firm. Moreover, while a corporation can be targeted in legal actions such as lawsuits, the personal assets of the company's owners cannot be touched if a judgement is rendered against their establishment since it is recognized as a legal entity separate from the owners/shareholders.

Still, while incorporation provides business owners with far greater liability protection than they would enjoy if they operated as a standard partnership or sole proprietorship, business experts note that certain instances remain wherein the personal assets of business owners may be vulnerable:

- Many small business owners who approach banks to secure financing for a new corporation are asked to sign a personal guarantee that assures the lending institution that they will pay back the loan if the corporation is unable to do so. Banks sometimes require similar guarantees from entrepreneurs and small business owners seeking financial assistance to lease equipment or facilities. Owners are also held personally responsible for ensuring that the corporation makes its required tax payments.

- Protection from liability can also be compromised in situations in which legal action is brought against a director or officer who is alleged to have committed some transgression outside the parameters of his or her job description. In other words, a business owner or shareholder can still be sued for personal actions.

- In some cases, key personnel of a corporation—such as board members or officers—can be held personally liable if the establishment that they operate has been found criminally negligent or guilty of willful criminal acts.

- The personal assets of business owners operating a corporation can also be threatened if it is determined that the business has not been properly established and adequately maintained. In such instances, a plaintiff may claim that the corporation and the owner are one and the same, and therefore the owner's personal assets can be used to satisfy the judgement. This is called 'piercing the corporate veil.' There are several steps that business owners can take, however, to ensure that their corporation protection is maintained. These include: 1) Keeping up with taxes and regulatory requirements; 2) Staying in full compliance with guidelines regarding corporate minutes and various organizational bylaws; 3) Keeping personal and corporate accounts completely separated from one another; and 4) Showing proper capitalization by maintaining a satisfactory debt-to-equity ratio.

DISADVANTAGES OF INCORPORATION

- Regulatory and Record keeping Requirements— Corporate operations are governed by local, state, and federal regulations to a greater degree than are other businesses.

- Added Cost of Doing Business—Regulatory and record keeping guidelines and requirements often make it necessary for corporations to make additional investments (in accounting staffing, etc.) devoted to seeing that those legal requirements are met. In addition, there are fees associated with incorporating to which business partnerships and sole proprietorships are not subject.

- "Double" Taxation—People who are owners of a corporation, and who also work as an employee of the business, can receive financial compensation in two different ways. In addition to receiving a salary or wages for work performed, the owner may also receive a dividend or distribution on the stock that he or she owns. Any distribution of income to stockholders via dividends is taxable, however, if the corporation is organized as a "C corporation." This is sometimes called "double taxation" in recognition of the fact that such income has in reality been taxed twice, first when the corporation paid taxes on its profits, and secondly when the dividends were distributed. Companies that register as an "S corporation," however, are able to avoid this added tax.

- Separation of Finances—While incorporation provides significant protection of owners' personal assets from repercussions of business downturns, it also means that a business owner is not allowed to tap into the corporation's account for assistance in meeting personal debts.

S CORPORATIONS AND C CORPORATIONS

Small business owners can choose to incorporate as one of two basic types of corporations. The C corporation is the more traditional of the arrangements, and is more frequently employed by large companies. With a regular corporation, the business's profits or losses are absorbed directly into the company. With the alternative corporate arrangement—the S corporation (also sometimes known as the Subchapter S corporation)—profits and losses pass through to the company's shareholders.

The S corporation option was actually put together by the federal government in recognition of the fact that the operating challenges faced by small businesses and large businesses can often be quite different. Indeed, the

S corporation was shaped specifically to accommodate small business owners. S corporations give their owners the limited liability protections provided by corporate status, while also providing them with a more advantageous tax environment. In fact, S corporation status puts companies in the same basic tax situation as partnerships and sole proprietorships. Whereas C corporations are subject to the above-mentioned double taxation, profits registered by an S corporation are taxed only once, when they reach the company's shareholders.

To qualify as an S corporation, a business must meet the following requirements: 1) It must be a U.S. corporation; 2) It can have only a limited number of shareholders (75 in 2006); 3) It may not offer more than one class of outstanding stock. In terms of the maximum number of shareholders, starting with taxable years beginning after December 31, 2004, a family may elect to have all the members of the family that hold stock directly or indirectly in an S corporation treated as one shareholder for purposes of the number-of-shareholders limitation. This election may be made by any family member and a "members of the family" is defined as individuals with a common ancestor, lineal descendants of the common ancestor, and the spouses (or former spouses) of such lineal descendants or common ancestor. These are the primary requirements for seekers of S corporation status, although the government has additional stipulations regarding the citizenship of owners/shareholders and affiliations with other business entities. Prospective S corporations must be in accordance with all these restrictions.

THE PROCESS OF INCORPORATION

The actual fees required to incorporate generally amount to several hundred dollars, although the total cost differs from state to state (corporations usually pay both an initial filing fee and an annual fee to the states in which they operate). Hiring an attorney to assist in the process can raise the cost, but several services are available on the Internet to assist businesses with the incorporation process. The Small Business Administration has noted that the owners of a business that is going to be incorporated must agree on several important issues, including the nature of the business; the total number of shares of stock the corporation will make available; the stock that the owners will be able to purchase; the amount of financial investment that each of the owners will make; the bylaws by which the corporation will operate; the management structure of the corporation; and the name under which the business will operate.

Indeed, it is a good idea to reserve the proposed name of the corporation with the state before filing articles of incorporation. The owners of the business must make sure that they have a clear right to that name, since only one corporation may possess any given name in each state. If a business owner files articles of incorporation using a name that already belongs to another corporation, the application will be rejected. The name of the business must also include either *corporation, company, limited,* or *incorporated* as part of its legal name; such terms serve notice to people and businesses outside the company that it is a legal entity unto itself and thus subject to different laws than other business types.

Since the corporation will be a legal entity separate from its owners, separate financial accounts and record keeping practices also need to be established. Once the shareholders have reached agreement on these issues, they must prepare and file articles of incorporation or a certificate of incorporation with the corporate office of the state in which they have decided to incorporate. Any corporation—with the exception of banks and insurance companies—can incorporate under Section 3 of the Model Business Corporation Act.

Business experts also counsel organizers of a corporation to put together a pre-incorporation agreement that specifies the various roles and responsibilities that each owner will take on in the corporation once it has come into being. Pre-incorporation agreements typically cover many of the above-mentioned issues, and can be supplemented with other legal documents governing various business operations, such as inventory purchases and lease agreements. Pre-incorporation agreements are also sometimes drawn up with third parties. Such contracts generally address: 1) Scope of potential liability; 2) Rights and obligations for both the corporation and its organizers once it has been formed; 3) Provisions to address business issues if incorporation never occurs for some reason; and 4) Provisions for declining the contract once the corporation has been formed.

Once a company has incorporated, stock can be distributed and the shareholders can elect a board of directors to take formal control of the business. Small corporations often institute buy-sell agreements for their shareholders. Under this agreement, stock that is given up by a shareholder—either because of death or a desire to sell—must first be made available to the business's other established shareholders. Stock issues and shareholder responsibilities are usually fairly straightforward in smaller companies, but larger corporations with large numbers of shareholders generally have to register with state regulatory agencies or the federal Securities and Exchange Commission (SEC).

In addition, incorporation requires the adoption of corporate bylaws. The bylaws, which are not public record, include more specific information about how the corporation will be run. These are the rules and regulations that govern the internal affairs of the corporation, although they may not conflict with the Articles of Incorporation or the corporate laws of your state. The bylaws are adopted by the board or the corporation's shareholders and may be amended or repealed at a later date. When preparing bylaws, it is sometimes easiest to start with the model bylaws that typically arrive with corporate kits or incorporation guides, although these may be altered. The bylaws should specify such information as:

- The location of corporate offices
- The names and powers of shareholders and directors
- The date and time for regular shareholders' and board of directors' meetings
- The content of such meetings
- The period of notice required before such meetings
- Voting eligibility
- Voting procedures
- Election procedures for seating directors and officers
- The names and duties of officers
- How financial transactions will be conducted
- The procedures for amending or repealing bylaws
- Stipulations as to whether powers or duties of board of directors may be relegated to ad hoc committees
- Procedures to be followed in the event of a merger with another company or the dissolution of the corporation itself

CORPORATE OWNERSHIP AND CONTROL

The owners of a corporation remain the ultimate controllers of that business's operations, but exercising that control is a more complicated process than it is for owners of partnerships or sole proprietorships. Control depends in part on whether the owners decide to make the corporation a public company—in which shares in the company are available to the general public—or a private or closely held corporation, where shares are concentrated in the hands of a few owners.

In most cases, small businesses have a modest number of shareholders or owners. When it comes to the day-to-day operations of the corporation, shareholders generally have very few powers. They are responsible for electing the board of directors and removing them from office. In smaller corporations, the shareholders can give themselves more operational powers by including provisions in the articles and bylaws of the corporation. In most cases, however, it is the shareholder-appointed board of directors that runs the company. Directors are responsible for all aspects of the company's operation, and it is the board that appoints the key personnel responsible for overseeing the business's daily operations. The officers (president, vice-president, treasurer, etc.), though appointed by the board of directors, often wield the greatest power in a corporation; indeed, in some corporations, officers are also members of the board of directors. Of course, in situations where only one person owns the incorporated company, he or she will bear many of the above responsibilities.

INCORPORATING IN DELAWARE AND NEVADA

Over the years, many companies have chosen to incorporate in Delaware or Nevada because of those states' business-friendly environment regarding taxation and liability issues. But some business experts caution small businesses from automatically casting their lots with these states. Small businesses with a small number of shareholder-employees should probably incorporate within their own state of operation. Although Delaware may offer some tax breaks and potentially more statutory protection from liability for corporate directors than most other states, for a small corporation the advantages are usually outweighed by the disadvantages. For instance, a company incorporated in Delaware but operating elsewhere must appoint someone in Delaware to be an agent for the corporation (there are companies in Delaware that do this). In addition, such a firm will have to pay an annual franchise (corporate) tax to the state of Delaware as well as file an application in its home state to do business as a foreign corporation. This designation will require them to pay a franchise fee in addition to their usual state income taxes.

SEE ALSO *Articles of Incorporation; C Corporation; Limited Liability Company; S Corporation*

BIBLIOGRAPHY

Colville, John. "Incorporation: Pros and Cons." *Accountancy*. July 2000.

Fink, Philip R. "Limited Liability Companies: Tax and Business Law." *The Tax Adviser*. June 2005.

"How–and Why–to Incorporate Your Business." *Entrepreneur.com*. Available from http://www.entrepreneur.com/article/ 0,4621,321322,00.html. 11 May 2005.

Krebsbach, Karen. "Community Banks Press IRS Change: De novo and startup banks are eager to consider LLC status. But to be truly worthwhile, an IRS rule change is needed to make the switch more tax advantageous. So what's the holdup?" *US Banker*. October 2005.

Lee, Min-Yun. "Incorporating Could Become Your Company's Profitable First Step." *Houston Business Journal*. 22 September 2000.

Mancuso, Anthony. *LLC or Corporation? How to Choose the Right Form for Your Business.* Nolo Press, 2004.

Oster, Rick. "S Corporation Vs. LLCs, The Pros and Cons of Each Business Form." *Entrepreneur.* 23 April 2001.

Schnee, Edward J. "Debt Allocation and LLCs." *Journal of Accountancy.* September 2004.

Thompson, Margaret Gallagher. "Where We Were and Where We Are in Family Limited Partnerships." *The Legal Intelligencer.* 1 August 2005.

U.S. Department of the Treasury. Internal Revenue Service. "S Corporations." Available from http://www.irs.gov/businesses/small/article/0,,id=98263,00.html Retrieved on 10 April 2006.

U.S. Small Business Administration Brittin, Jocelyn West. *Selecting the Legal Structure for Your Business.* n.d.

Hillstrom, Northern Lights
updated by Magee, ECDI

INDIVIDUAL RETIREMENT ACCOUNTS (IRAs)

An individual retirement account (IRA) is a tax-deferred retirement program in which any employed person can participate, including self-employed persons and small business owners. In most cases, the money placed in an IRA is deducted from the worker's income before taxes and is allowed to grow tax-deferred until the worker retires. IRA funds can be invested in a variety of ways, including stocks and bonds, money market accounts, treasury bills, mutual funds, and certificates of deposit. Intended to make it easier for individuals to save money for their own retirement, IRAs are nonetheless subject to a number of complex government regulations and restrictions. The amount of annual contributions permitted, and the tax deductibility thereof, is dependent on the individual worker's situation.

The main difference between IRAs and employer-sponsored retirement plans is that IRA funds—although held by a trust or annuity—are under the complete discretion of the account holder as far as withdrawals and choice of investments. For this reason, IRAs are known as self-sponsored and self-directed retirement accounts. Even combination plans that allow employers to make contributions, like Simplified Employee Pension (SEP) IRAs, are considered self-sponsored since they require the employee to set up his or her own IRA account. A special provision of IRAs allows individuals to roll over funds from an employer-sponsored retirement plan to an IRA without penalty.

IRAs were authorized by Congress in 1974 as part of a broader effort to reform laws governing pensions. Recognizing that employers facing intense competition might decide to cut costs by reducing the retirement benefits provided to employees—and that government programs such as Social Security would not be enough to fill in the gaps—Congress sought to encourage individual taxpayers to undertake long-term savings programs for their own retirement. The Internal Revenue Service responded by making provisions for individual retirement accounts in section 408 of the tax code. IRAs quickly became recognized as one of the most opportunistic and flexible retirement options available, enabling workers to control their own preparations for the conclusion of their working lives.

IRA PROVISIONS

In the original provisions, elective pre-tax contributions to IRAs were limited to $1,500 per year. The maximum annual contribution increased to $2,000 in 1982, but new restrictions were imposed upon workers who were covered under an employer's retirement plan. For example, such workers were not eligible to deduct their total IRA contributions unless their adjusted gross income was less than $25,000 if unmarried, or less than $40,000 if married. A partial deduction was available for single workers who earned up to $35,000 and married workers who earned up to $50,000, but no deductions were allowed for people with higher income levels. These restrictions did not apply to self-employed individuals and others who did not participate in an employer's plan. For tax year 2006, if you are covered by a retirement plan at work, your deduction for contributions to a traditional IRA will be phased out if your modified adjusted gross income is: 1) more than $75,000 but less than $85,000 for a married couple filing a joint return or a qualifying widow(er), or 2) more than $50,000 but less than $60,000 for a single individual or head of household, or 3) less than $10,000 for a married individual filing a separate return.

The way the tax code was written, individuals were intended to begin making regular withdrawals from their IRAs upon retirement. These withdrawals would be considered income and subjected to income tax, but the individual was presumed to be in a lower tax bracket by this time than they had been during their working years. "Ordinary" distributions from an IRA are those taken when a worker is between the ages of 59 ½ and 70 ½. Though workers are not required to begin receiving distributions until they reach age 70 ½, most establish a regular schedule of distributions to supplement their income during this time.

The total annual distributions from an IRA cannot exceed $150,000 per year, or they are subject to a

15 percent penalty in addition to the regular income tax. "Early" withdrawals, or those taken before a worker reaches age 59 ½, are subject to a 10 percent penalty on top of the regular income tax, except in cases of death or disability of the account holder. In addition, there are ten other reasons that the government will let you access the money, such as higher education expenses and first-time homeownership. The rules on such distributions are very rigid and one must carefully document any reasons for early withdrawal or face IRS penalties. The early distribution penalty is intended to discourage younger people from viewing an IRA as a tax-deferred savings account.

Legislation passed over the years since the IRA's initial authorization has refined the scope, provisions, and requirements of IRAs so that other forms are available besides the basic, individual "contributory" IRA. As outlined by W. Kent Moore in *The Guide to Tax-Saving Investing,* the different IRA variations include:

1. Spousal IRAs, which enable a working spouse to contribute to an IRA opened for a nonworking partner

2. Third-party-sponsored IRAs, which are used by employee organizations, labor unions, and others wishing to contribute on workers' behalf

3. Simplified Employee Pensions (SEPs), which enable employers to provide retirement benefits by contributing to workers' IRAs

4. Savings Incentive Match Plan for Employees (SIMPLE) IRAs, which require employers to match up to 3 percent of an employee's salary, or $6,000 annually, plus allow employees to contribute another $6,000 per year to their own accounts

5. Rollover contribution accounts, which allow distributions from an IRA or an employer's qualified retirement plan to be reinvested in another IRA without penalty

6. Roth IRAs, which enable single people with an annual income of less than $95,000 and married couples with an annual income of less than $150,000 to make a nondeductible contribution of $2,000 per year, whether they are covered by an employer's plan or not.

It is also possible for those earning less than $100,000 per year to convert a regular IRA to a Roth IRA by paying any deferred income tax. Though money placed in Roth IRAs is subject to taxes when invested, the earnings grow tax-deferred and the withdrawals are tax-free after five years.

FACTORS TO CONSIDER

Those interested in opening an IRA should familiarize themselves with the current regulations governing the amounts that may be contributed, the timing of contributions, the criteria for tax deductibility, and the penalties for making early withdrawals. They should also shop around when investigating financial institutions that offer IRAs—such as banks, credit unions, mutual funds, brokerage firms, and insurance companies—inasmuch as fees vary from institution to institution, ranging from no charge to a one-time fee for opening the account to an annual fee for maintaining the IRA. Financial institutions also differ in the amount of minimum investment, how often interest is compounded, and the type and frequency of account statement provided. There is no limit to the number of IRAs an individual can open, as long as he or she does not exceed the maximum allowable annual contribution.

Another important factor to consider, in addition to the trustee of the account, is where the IRA funds should be invested. Individuals have a wide range of investment options available to choose from—including bank accounts, certificates of deposit, stocks, bonds, annuities, mutual funds, or a combination thereof—each offering different levels of risk and rates of growth. According to many investment advisors, the ideal IRA investment is one that is reasonably stable, can be held for the long term, and provides a level of comfort for the individual investor. Most financial advisors advise against playing the stock market or investing in a single security with funds that have been earmarked for retirement, due to the risk involved. Instead, they recommend that individuals take a more diversified approach with their IRAs, such as investing in a growth-income mutual fund, in order to protect themselves against inflation and the inevitable swings of the stock market.

The decision about where IRA funds should be invested can be changed at any time, as often as the individual deems necessary. Switching to a different type of investment or to a mutual fund with a different objective usually only requires filling out a transfer form from the sponsoring financial institution. Since the IRA simply changes custodians in this type of transaction, and never passes through the hands of the individual investor, it is not subject to any sort of penalty or tax, and it is not considered a rollover.

Despite the number of decisions involved, IRAs nonetheless provide an important means for people to save for their retirement. "The advantages of IRAs far outweigh the disadvantages," as Moore noted. "Earnings for either deductible or nondeductible IRAs grow faster than ordinary savings accounts, because IRA earnings are tax deferred, allowing all earnings to be reinvested. Even when withdrawals are made, the remaining funds continue to grow as tax-deferred assets."

SEE ALSO *401(k) Plans; Retirement Planning*

BIBLIOGRAPHY
Blakely, Stephen. "Pension Power." *Nation's Business*. July 1997.

Crouch, Holmes F. *Decisions When Retiring*. Allyear Tax Guides, 1995.

"Deduction Phaseout for Regular IRAs Begins at Higher Levels in 2006." *The Kiplinger Tax Letter* 30 December 2005.

Internal Revenue Service. "What's New in 2006." Available from http://www.irs.gov/publications/p590/ar01.html. Retrieved on 14 March 2006.

Korn, Donald Jay. "Tax-Deferred Vehicles That Will Last a Lifetime." *Black Enterprise*. October 2000.

Moore, W. Kent. "Deferring Taxes with Retirement Accounts." *The Guide to Tax-Saving Investing* Globe Pequot Press, 1995.

Wiener, Leonard. "How to Keep One Step Ahead: Hot Tips for Turning an Annual Chore into Many Happy Returns." *U.S. News and World Report*. 9 March 1998.

Wiener, Leonard. "How to Unscramble a Nest Egg." *U.S. News & World Report*. 5 July 1999.

Hillstrom, Northern Lights
updated by Magee, ECDI

INDUSTRIAL SAFETY

The issue of industrial safety evolved concurrently with industrial development in the United States. Of central importance was the establishment of protective legislation, most significantly the worker's compensation laws, enacted at the start of the twentieth century, and the Occupational Safety and Health Act, enacted in 1970. The discussion of industrial safety began to shift in the 1970s from one concerned primarily with compensation issues to one concerned with prevention and with the study of long-term effects of occupational hazards. This shift in emphasis was encouraged by insurance companies who, in order to protect themselves from workers' compensation expenses, found that it made good business sense for them to promote industrial safety programs and research industrial safety issues. Today, industrial safety is widely regarded as one of the most important factors that any business, large or small, must consider in its operations.

Worker's compensation laws vary widely from state to state but have key objectives in common. Employers are required to compensate employees for work-related injuries or sickness by paying medical expenses, disability benefits, and compensation for lost work time. In return, workers are barred in many instances from suing their employers, a provision that protects employers from large liability settlements (of course, employers may still be found liable in instances where they are found guilty of neglect or other legal violations). In his *Industrial Safety: Management and Technology*, David Colling contended that "workmen's compensation laws have done more to promote safety than all other measures collectively, because employers found it more cost-effective to concentrate on safety than to compensate employees for injury or loss of life."

THE CREATION OF OSHA

One of the key developments in industrial safety legislation was the Occupational Safety and Health Act of 1970. The Act, which was the first comprehensive industrial safety legislation passed at the federal level, passed nearly unanimously through both houses of Congress. One of the factors contributing to strong support for the act was the rise in the number of work-related fatalities in the 1960s, and particularly the Farmington, West Virginia, mine disaster of 1968, in which 78 miners were killed. The Occupational Safety and Health Act was distinguished by its emphasis on the prevention of—rather than compensation for—industrial accidents and illnesses. The legislation provided for the establishment of the Occupational Safety and Health Administration (OSHA) and the National Institute of Occupational Safety and Health (NIOSH). Among the key provisions of the act were the development of mandatory safety and health standards, the enforcement of these standards, and standardized record-keeping and reporting procedures for businesses.

OSHA regulations cover all private-sector employers with one or more workers and are therefore an area of regulatory law about which small businesses must be away. OSHA regulations do not, however, cover employers in the public sector (municipal, county, state, or federal government agencies); self-employed individuals; family members operating a farm; or domestic household workers.

OSHA issues regulations governing a wide range of worker safety areas, all intended to meet OSHA's overriding principle that "each employer shall furnish to each of his employees employment and a place of employment which are free from recognized hazards that are causing or are likely to cause death or serious physical harm to his [or her] employees." OSHA regulations include both safety standards, designed to prevent accidents, and health standards, designed to protect against exposure to toxins and to address the more long-term effects of occupational hazards. So-called "horizontal" standards apply to all industries whereas "vertical" standards apply to specific industries or occupations. Some of OSHA's standards were adopted from private national organizations, such as the American National Standards Institute, the National Fire Protection Association, and the American Society of Mechanical Engineers. Other standards are developed by OSHA itself, often based on recommendations from NIOSH.

When OSHA drafts a proposal for a permanent standard, it first consults with industry and labor representatives and collects whatever scientific, medical, and engineering data is necessary to ensure that the standard adequately reflects workplace realities. Proposed standards are published in the *Federal Register*. A comment period is then held, during which input is received from interested parties including, but not limited to, representatives of industry and labor. At the close of the comment period, the proposal may be withdrawn and set aside, withdrawn and re-proposed with modifications, or approved as a final standard that is legally enforceable. All standards that become legally binding are first published in the *Federal Register* and then compiled and published in the *Code of Federal Regulations*. The cause of industrial safety has also been reinforced by the passage of significant "right-to-know" laws. Right-to-Know laws require that dangerous materials in the workplace be identified and that workers be informed of these dangers as well as trained in their safe use.

In addition to federal worker health and safety laws, individual states are permitted to develop and operate their own job safety and health programs. If the state can show that its job safety and health standards are "at least as effective as" comparable federal standards, the state can be certified to assume OSH Act administration and enforcement in that state. OSHA approves and monitors state plans, and provides up to 50 percent of operating costs for approved plans.

INDUSTRIAL HAZARDS

One of the important aspects of industrial safety programs is the identification of hazards. Managers typically determine hazards by the examination of accident records, interviews with engineers and equipment operators, and the advice of safety specialists, such as OSHA or insurance companies. Industrial health hazards are typically categorized into three classes: chemical hazards, in which the body absorbs toxins; ergonomic hazards, such as those resulting from improper lifting or repetitive stress; and physical hazards, in which the worker is exposed to temperature extremes, atmospheric pressure, dangerous conditions, or excessive noise.

About one-tenth of industrial accidents result from operating machinery, and these accidents often result in severe injury. Among the most dangerous types of machinery are power presses and woodworking tools, which most commonly cause injury to the hands. A number of mechanisms have been developed to safeguard against such injuries. The simplest of these are barrier guards, in which the moving parts of machinery are enclosed in a protective housing. These safeguards are typically used in conjunction with sensors so that the machine cannot be operated without them. Other types of safeguards include those which prevent a machine from operating unless a worker has both hands properly in place, automated material feeding devices, warning labels, and color coding.

Toxins are most commonly ingested through inhalation, and the most commonly inhaled substances are dust, fumes, and smoke. Toxins are also commonly absorbed through the skin, and this is a bigger problem than many business owners and managers realize. Indeed, some studies indicate that skin disorders result in approximately 200,000 lost working days each year. The most common of these disorders is dermatitis, which is particularly problematic in the food preparation and chemical industries.

Among the most commonly-used toxins are industrial solvents. The toxicity of solvents varies widely by type, but the most toxic of these are carcinogens and can cause permanent damage to the nervous system through prolonged occupational overexposure. In addition, organic solvents, such as those made from petroleum, are often highly flammable. Tightly-fitted respirators with activated charcoal filters are used to protect against inhalation of organic solvents, particularly in spraying applications in which solvents are atomized. Ventilation systems comprised of fans and ducts are also used to control airborne toxins of all types. Rubber gloves are commonly used to prevent skin absorption of organic solvents.

One of the most rapidly-growing types of reported occupational injury is what the U.S. Bureau of Labor Statistics refers to as "disorders associated with repeated trauma." These conditions result from repeatedly performing the same tasks over a prolonged period of time.

SMALL BUSINESSES AND INDUSTRIAL SAFETY

All companies, including small businesses, are required to keep records on various aspects of their operations that are relevant to employee safety and health. All employers covered by the OSH Act are required to keep records regarding enforcement of OSHA standards; research records; job-related injury, illness, and death records; and job hazard records.

But while small businesses must adhere to many of the same regulations that govern the operations or larger companies, there also are several federal industrial safety programs available exclusively to smaller business enterprises, and OSHA and state regulatory agencies both enjoy some discretion in adjusting penalties for industrial safety violations for small companies. For example, OSHA has discretion to grant monetary penalty reductions of up to 60 percent for businesses that qualify as small firms. It also gives smaller firms greater flexibility in certain safety areas (i.e., lead in construction, emergency evacuation plans, process safety management) in recognition of their limited resources, and provides grants to nonprofit groups with explicit mandates of addressing safety and health issues in small business settings.

SEE ALSO *Occupational Safety and Health Administration; Workers Compensation; Workplace Safety*

BIBLIOGRAPHY

Colling, David A. *Industrial Safety: Management and Technology.* Prentice Hall, 1990.

Genn, Adina. "Three Bills Would Expand OSHA Standards." *Daily Record (Kansas City, MO).* 13 February 2006.

Karr, Al. "Behavior-Based Safety: Is It the Holy Grail of the Workplace?" *Safety and Health.* March 2000.

Marsh, Barbara. "Workers at Risk: Chance of Getting Hurt is Generally Far Higher at Small Companies." *Wall Street Journal.* 3 February 1994.

U.S. Department of Labor. Occupational Safety and Health Administration. *OSHA's Small Business Outreach Training Program.* Available from http://www.osha.gov/SLTC/smallbusiness/index.html Retrieved on 14 March 2006.

Willen, Janet. "Safety Incentive Programs: Problem Solver or Troublemaker?" *Safety and Health.* September 2000.

Yohay, Stephen C. "Recent Court Decisions on Important OSHA Enforcement Issues." *Employee Relations Law Journal.* Spring 1997.

Hillstrom, Northern Lights
updated by Magee, ECDI

INDUSTRY ANALYSIS

Industry analysis is a tool that facilitates a company's understanding of its position relative to other companies that produce similar products or services. Understanding the forces at work in the overall industry is an important component of effective strategic planning. Industry analysis enables small business owners to identify the threats and opportunities facing their businesses, and to focus their resources on developing unique capabilities that could lead to a competitive advantage.

"Many small business owners and executives consider themselves at worst victims, and at best observers of what goes on in their industry. They sometimes fail to perceive that understanding your industry directly impacts your ability to succeed. Understanding your industry and anticipating its future trends and directions gives you the knowledge you need to react and control your portion of that industry," Kenneth J. Cook wrote in his book *The AMA Complete Guide to Strategic Planning for Small Business.* "However, your analysis of this is significant only in a relative sense. Since both you and your competitors are in the same industry, the key is in finding the differing abilities between you and the competition in dealing with the industry forces that impact you. If you can identify abilities you have that are superior to competitors, you can use that ability to establish a competitive advantage."

An industry analysis consists of three major elements: the underlying forces at work in the industry; the overall attractiveness of the industry; and the critical factors that determine a company's success within the industry.

One way in which to compare a particular business with the average of all participants in the industry is through the use of ratio analysis and comparisons. Ratios are calculated by dividing one measurable business factor by another, total sales divided by number of employees, for example. Many of these ratios may be calculated for an entire industry with data available from many reports and papers published by the U.S. Departments of Commerce and Labor.

By comparing a particular ratio for one company with that of the industry as a whole, a business owner can learn much about where her business stands in comparison with the industry average. For example, a small nursing home business can compare its "payroll per employee" ratio with the average for all residential care operators in the U.S. in order to determine if it is within a competitive range. If her business's "payroll per employee" figure is higher than the industry average, she may wish to investigate further. Checking the "employees per establishment" ratio would be a logical place to look next. If this ratio is lower than the industry average it may justifying the higher per-employee payroll figure. This sort of comparative analysis is one important way in which to assess how one's business compares with all others involved in the same line of work. There are various sources for the industry average ratios, among them is the industry analysis series published by Thomson Gale as the *USA series.*

Another premier model for analyzing the structure of industries was developed by Michael E. Porter in his classic 1980 book *Competitive Strategy: Techniques for Analyzing Industries and Competitors.* Porter's model shows that rivalry among firms in industry depends upon five forces: 1) the potential for new competitors to enter the market; 2) the bargaining power of buyers; 3) the bargaining power of suppliers; 4) the availability of substitute goods; and 5) the competitors and nature of competition. These factors are outlined below.

INDUSTRY FORCES

The first step in performing an industry analysis is to assess the impact of Porter's five forces. "The collective strength of these forces determines the ultimate profit potential in the industry, where profit potential is measured in terms of long term return on invested capital," Porter stated. "The goal of competitive strategy for a business unit in an industry is to find a position in the industry where the company can best defend itself against these competitive forces or can influence them in its favor." Understanding the underlying forces determining the structure of the industry can highlight the strengths and weaknesses of a small business, show where strategic changes can make the greatest difference, and illuminate areas where industry trends may turn into opportunities or threats.

Ease of Entry Ease of entry refers to how easy or difficult it is for a new firm to begin competing in the industry. The ease of entry into an industry is important because it determines the likelihood that a company will face new competitors. In industries that are easy to enter, sources of competitive advantage tend to wane quickly. On the other hand, in industries that are difficult to enter, sources of competitive advantage last longer, and firms also tend to benefit from having a constant set of competitors.

The ease of entry into an industry depends upon two factors: the reaction of existing competitors to new entrants; and the barriers to market entry that prevail in the industry. Existing competitors are most likely to react strongly against new entrants when there is a history of such behavior, when the competitors have invested substantial resources in the industry, and when the industry is characterized by slow growth. Some of the major barriers to market entry include economies of scale, high capital requirements, switching costs for the customer, limited access to the channels of distribution, a high degree of product differentiation, and restrictive government policies.

Power of Suppliers Suppliers can gain bargaining power within an industry through a number of different situations. For example, suppliers gain power when an industry relies on just a few suppliers, when there are no substitutes available for the suppliers' product, when there are switching costs associated with changing suppliers, when each purchaser accounts for just a small portion of the suppliers' business, and when suppliers have the resources to move forward in the chain of distribution and take on the role of their customers. Supplier power can affect the relationship between a small business and its customers by influencing the quality and price of the final product. "All of these factors combined will affect your ability to compete," Cook noted. "They will impact your ability to use your supplier relationship to establish competitive advantages with your customers."

Power of Buyers The reverse situation occurs when bargaining power rests in the hands of buyers. Powerful buyers can exert pressure on small businesses by demanding lower prices, higher quality, or additional services, or by playing competitors off one another. The power of buyers tends to increase when single customers account for large volumes of the business's product, when a substitutes are available for the product, when the costs associated with switching suppliers are low, and when buyers possess the resources to move backward in the chain of distribution.

Availability of Substitutes "All firms in an industry are competing, in a broad sense, with industries producing substitute products. Substitutes limit the potential returns of an industry by placing a ceiling on the prices firms in the industry can profitably charge," Porter explained. Product substitution occurs when a small business's customer comes to believe that a similar product can perform the same function at a better price. Substitution can be subtle—for example, insurance agents have gradually moved into the investment field formerly controlled by financial planners—or sudden—for example, compact disc technology has taken the place of vinyl record albums. The main defense available against substitution is product differentiation. By forming a deep understanding of the customer, some companies are able to create demand specifically for their products.

Competitors "The battle you wage against competitors is one of the strongest industry forces with which you contend," according to Cook. Competitive battles can take the form of price wars, advertising campaigns, new product introductions, or expanded service offerings—all of which can reduce the profitability of firms within an industry. The intensity of competition tends to increase when an industry is characterized by a number of well-balanced competitors, a slow rate of industry growth, high fixed costs, or a lack of differentiation between products. Another factor increasing the intensity of competition is high exit barriers—including specialized assets, emotional ties, government or social restrictions, strategic interrelationships with other business units, labor agreements, or other fixed costs—which make competitors stay and fight even when they find the industry unprofitable.

INDUSTRY ATTRACTIVENESS AND INDUSTRY SUCCESS FACTORS

"Industry attractiveness is the presence or absence of threats exhibited by each of the industry forces," Cook explained. "The greater the threat posed by an industry force, the less attractive the industry becomes." Small businesses, in particular, should attempt to seek out markets in which the threats are low and the attractiveness is high. Understanding what industry forces are at work enables small business owners to develop strategies to deal with them. These strategies, in turn, can help small businesses to find unique ways to satisfy their customers in order to develop a competitive advantage over industry rivals.

Success factors are those elements that determine whether a company succeeds or fails in a given industry. They vary greatly by industry. Some examples of possible success factors include quick response to market changes, a complete product line, fair prices, excellent product quality or performance, knowledgeable sales support, a good record for deliveries, solid financial standing, or a strong management team. "The reason for identifying success factors is that it will help lead you to areas where you can establish competitive advantages," Cook noted. The first step is to determine whether or not the company possesses each success factor identified. Then the small business owner can decide whether the company can and should develop additional success factors.

THE IMPORTANCE OF INDUSTRY ANALYSIS

A comprehensive industry analysis requires a small business owner to take an objective view of the underlying forces, attractiveness, and success factors that determine the structure of the industry. Understanding the company's operating environment in this way can help the small business owner to formulate an effective strategy, position the company for success, and make the most efficient use of the limited resources of the small business. "Once the forces affecting competition in an industry and their underlying causes have been diagnosed, the firm is in a position to identify its strengths and weaknesses relative to the industry," Porter wrote. "An effective competitive strategy takes offensive or defensive action in order to create a *defendable* position against the five competitive forces." Some of the possible strategies include positioning the firm to use its unique capabilities as defense, influencing the balance of outside forces in the firm's favor, or anticipating shifts in the underlying industry factors and adapting before competitors do in order to gain a competitive advantage.

SEE ALSO *Financial Ratios; Small Business Dominated Industries*

BIBLIOGRAPHY
Anker, David. *Developing Business Strategies.* Wiley, 1998.

Clark, Scott. "Financial Ratios Hold the Key to Smart Business." *Birmingham Business Journal.* 11 February 2000.

Cook, Kenneth J. *The AMA Complete Guide to Strategic Planning for Small Business.* American Marketing Association, 1995.

Darnay, Arsen J., ed. *Service Industries USA..* Fourth Edition. Thomson Gale, 1999.

Gil-Lafuente, Anna Maria. *Fuzzy Logic In Financial Analysis.* Springer, 2005.

Gitman, Lawrence, J., and Carl McDaniel. *The Future of Business.* Thomson South-Western, March 2005.

Goodstein, Leonard. *Applied Strategic Planning: How to Develop a Plan That Really Works.* McGraw-Hill, 1992.

Porter, Michael E. *Competitive Strategy: Techniques for Analyzing Industries and Competitors.* Free Press, 1980.

Hillstrom, Northern Lights
updated by Magee, ECDI

INDUSTRY LIFE CYCLE

Life cycle models are not just a phenomenon of the life sciences. Industries experience a similar cycle of life. Just as a person is born, grows, matures, and eventually experiences decline and ultimately death, so too do industries and product lines. The stages are the same for all industries, yet every industry will experience these stages differently, they will last longer for some and pass quickly for others. Even within the same industry, various firms may be at different life cycle stages. A firms strategic plan is likely to be greatly influenced by the stage in the life cycle at which the firm finds itself. Some companies or even industries find new uses for declining products, thus extending their life cycle.

The growth of an industry's sales over time is used to chart the life cycle. The distinct stages of an industry life cycle are: introduction, growth, maturity, and decline. Sales typically begin slowly at the introduction phase, then take off rapidly during the growth phase. After leveling out at maturity, sales then begin a gradual decline. In contrast, profits generally continue to increase throughout the life cycle, as companies in an industry take advantage of expertise and economies of scale and scope to reduce unit costs over time.

STAGES OF THE LIFE CYCLE

Introduction In the introduction stage of the life cycle, an industry is in its infancy. Perhaps a new, unique product offering has been developed and patented, thus beginning a new industry. Some analysts even add an embryonic stage before introduction. At the introduction stage, the firm may be alone in the industry. It may be a small entrepreneurial company or a proven company which used research and development funds and expertise to develop something new. Marketing refers to new product offerings in a new industry as "question marks" because the success of the product and the life of the industry is unproven and unknown.

A firm will use a focused strategy at this stage to stress the uniqueness of the new product or service to a small group of customers. These customers are typically referred to in the marketing literature as the "innovators" and "early adopters." Marketing tactics during this stage are intended to explain the product and its uses to consumers and thus create awareness for the product and the industry. According to research by Hitt, Ireland, and Hoskisson, firms establish a niche for dominance within an industry during this phase. For example, they often attempt to establish early perceptions of product quality, technological superiority, or advantageous relationships with vendors within the supply chain to develop a competitive advantage.

Because it costs money to create a new product offering, develop and test prototypes, and market the product, the firm's and the industry's profits are usually negative at this stage. Any profits generated are typically reinvested into the company to solidify its position and help fund continued growth. Introduction requires a significant cash outlay to continue to promote and differentiate the offering and expand the production flow from a job shop to possibly a batch flow. Market demand will grow from the introduction, and as the life cycle curve experiences growth at an increasing rate, the industry is said to be entering the growth stage. Firms may also cluster together in close proximity during the early stages of the industry life cycle to have access to key materials or technological expertise, as in the case of the U.S. Silicon Valley computer chip manufacturers.

Growth Like the introduction stage, the growth stage also requires a significant amount of capital. The goal of marketing efforts at this stage is to differentiate a firm's offerings from other competitors within the industry. Thus the growth stage requires funds to launch a newly focused marketing campaign as well as funds for continued investment in property, plant, and equipment to facilitate the growth required by the market demands. However, the industry is experiencing more product

standardization at this stage, which may encourage economies of scale and facilitate development of a line-flow layout for production efficiency.

Research and development funds will be needed to make changes to the product or services to better reflect customers' needs and suggestions. In this stage, if the firm is successful in the market, growing demand will create sales growth. Earnings and accompanying assets will also grow and profits will be positive for the firms. Marketing often refers to products at the growth stage as "stars." These products have high growth and market share. The key issue in this stage is market rivalry. Because there is industry-wide acceptance of the product, more new entrants join the industry and more intense competition results.

The duration of the growth stage, as all the other stages, depends on the particular industry or product line under study. Some items—like fad clothing, for example—may experience a very short growth stage and move almost immediately into the next stages of maturity and decline. A hot toy this holiday season may be nonexistent or relegated to the back shelves of a deep-discounter the following year. Because many new product introductions fail, the growth stage may be short or nonexistent for some products. However, for other products the growth stage may be longer due to frequent product upgrades and enhancements that forestall movement into maturity. The computer industry today is an example of an industry with a long growth stage due to upgrades in hardware, services, and add-on products and features.

During the growth stage, the life cycle curve is very steep, indicating fast growth. Firms tend to spread out geographically during this stage of the life cycle and continue to disperse during the maturity and decline stages. As an example, the automobile industry in the United States was initially concentrated in the Detroit area and surrounding cities. Today, as the industry has matured, automobile manufacturers are spread throughout the country and internationally.

Maturity As the industry approaches maturity, the industry life cycle curve becomes noticeably flatter, indicating slowing growth. Some experts have labeled an additional stage, called expansion, between growth and maturity. While sales are expanding and earnings are growing from these "cash cow" products, the rate has slowed from the growth stage. In fact, the rate of sales expansion is typically equal to the growth rate of the economy.

Some competition from late entrants will be apparent, and these new entrants will try to steal market share from existing products. Thus, the marketing effort must remain strong and must stress the unique features of the product or the firm to continue to differentiate a firm's offerings from industry competitors. Firms may compete on quality to separate their product from other lower-cost offerings, or conversely the firm may try a low-cost/low-price strategy to increase the volume of sales and make profits from inventory turnover. A firm at this stage may have excess cash to pay dividends to shareholders. But in mature industries, there are usually fewer firms, and those that survive will be larger and more dominant. While innovations continue they are not as radical as before and may be only a change in color or formulation to stress "new" or "improved" to consumers. Laundry detergents are examples of mature products.

Decline Declines are almost inevitable in an industry. If product innovation has not kept pace with other competing products and/or service, or if new innovations or technological changes have caused the industry to become obsolete, sales suffer and the life cycle experiences a decline. In this phase, sales are decreasing at an accelerating rate. This is often accompanied by another, larger shake-out in the industry as competitors who did not leave during the maturity stage now exit the industry. Yet some firms will remain to compete in the smaller market. Mergers and consolidations will also be the norm as firms try other strategies to continue to be competitive or grow through acquisition and/or diversification.

PROLONGING THE LIFE CYCLE

Management efficiency can help to prolong the maturity stage of the life cycle. Production improvements, like just-in-time methods and lean manufacturing, can result in extra profits. Technology, automation, and linking suppliers and customers in a tight supply chain are also methods to improve efficiency.

New uses of a product can also revitalize an old brand. A prime example is Arm & Hammer baking soda. In 1969, sales were dropping due to the introduction of packaged foods with baking soda as an added ingredient and an overall decline in home baking. New uses for the product as a deodorizer for refrigerators and later as a laundry additive, toothpaste additive, and carpet freshener extended the life cycle of the baking soda industry. Promoting new uses for old brands can increase sales by increasing usage frequency. In some cases, this strategy is cheaper than trying to convert new users in a mature market.

To extend the growth phase as well as industry profits, firms approaching maturity can pursue expansion into other countries and new markets. Expansion into another geographic region is an effective response to declining demand. Because organizations have control over internal factors and can often influence external factors, the life cycle does not have to end.

An example is feminine hygiene products. Sales in the United States have reached maturity due to a number of external reasons, like the stable to declining population growth rate and the aging of the baby boomers, who may no longer be consumers for these products. But when makers of these products concentrated on foreign markets, sales grew and the maturity of the product was prolonged. Often so-called "dog" products can find new life in other parts of the world. However, once world saturation is reached, the eventual maturity and decline of the industry or product line will result.

LIFE CYCLES ARE EVERYWHERE

Just as industries experience life cycles, studies have documented life cycles in many other areas. Countries have life cycles, for example, and we traditionally classify them as ranging from the First World countries to Third World or developing countries, depending on their levels of capital, technological change, infrastructure, or stability. Products also experience life cycles. Even within an industry, various individual companies may be at different life cycle stages depending upon when they entered the industry. The life cycle phenomenon is an important and universally accepted concept to help managers better understand sales growth and change over time.

BIBLIOGRAPHY

Hitt, Michael A., R. Duane Ireland, and Robert E. Hoskisson. *Strategic Management: Competitiveness and Globalization.* Fourth Edition. South-Western College Publishing, 2001.

Porter, M. *Competitive Strategy.* Free Press, 1980.

Porter, M. E. "Towards a Dynamic Theory of Strategy." *Strategic Management Journal.* 1991.

Wang, Zhu. "Learning, Diffusion, and Industry Life Cycle." Federal Reserve Bank of Kansas City, Working Paper 04-01 Available from www.kansascityfed.org/PUBLICAT/PSR/ RWP/NBER-WangPaper.pdf 15 January 2006.

Wansink, Brian, and Jennifer Marie Gilmore. "New Uses that Revitalize Old Brands." *Journal of Advertising Research.* March 1999.

Hillstrom, Northern Lights
updated by Magee, ECDI

INFORMATION BROKERS

Information brokers provide, for a fee, information retrieval from publicly accessible data sources, most often online databases. Information brokering first emerged as a business opportunity for individuals in the mid-1950s. Also known as independent information specialists, brokers often do much more than gather the information. In this day and age, when almost anyone can access huge amounts of data over the Internet, brokers provide a number of special services, including: writing reports that analyze the data they obtain, creating internal databases for clients to manage their in-house information, maintaining current awareness services that update a client whenever new information on a given topic becomes available, and more.

A good broker can save a client time and money. While it may be tempting to try to jump on the Internet and do the research yourself (especially for a small businessperson with limited financial resources), searching for data can be an arduous and time-consuming process, especially if you are not an expert in the realm of online searching. In addition, most brokers subscribe to online databases that are not available to the public, even on the Internet. Subscriptions to these databases, which often contain high-level professional, business, and/or scientific information, can cost up to several thousand dollars a year. Clearly, that cost is prohibitive for many small businesses, especially when a one-time information search is all that is needed.

Finding a good broker is important. A good broker will tell you when you actually can find the information yourself for free, but will also make it clear when his or her services are needed. Check to see what online services the broker subscribes to, and how long the broker has been in business. The growth of the Internet and commercial services such as America Online have led to an explosion in the number of people who call themselves information brokers or specialists, but not all of these businesses are legitimate. Relatively new information broker businesses may be perfectly legitimate, but business consultants still urge small business owners to be careful about selecting a specialist without first conducting adequate research into the company's history and other clients. Analysts indicate that the best information brokers in the field often have a background in library science (many brokers have been employed at public or corporate libraries) or have started out actually working for one of the large database provider companies. Other factors to consider include education, rates, specialty areas, subcontracting capability, and business practices.

Be aware that information brokers can do more than collect online data. They can search public records, conduct competition checks when you are starting a new business, or visit a local library to comb through materials there. Perhaps most importantly, they can, if needed, conduct phone research by interviewing people and then preparing a report based on those interviews. As one broker said in *Searcher* magazine, "The most desired information is, and will continue to be, in people's heads."

Housebrokers If a one-time search is needed, one should also keep in mind that many of the online services maintain their own in-house information brokering services. Sometimes known as "housebrokers," these in-house retrieval specialists work for one of the data providers. For example, LEXIS/NEXIS, which specializes in legal information, maintains a staff of information retrieval specialists for customers. A businessperson can call LEXIS/NEXIS, explain that he or she needs a one-time search (as opposed to a full-time subscription to their databases, which again can cost thousands of dollars), and the company will hand the job off to one of their housebrokers. This person will conduct the search and provide the clients with the results for a reasonable fee. Using a housebroker can be advantageous if the information you need is limited to one topic and will not require extensive searches of numerous databases from several vendors. In the latter instance, however, it may be preferable to secure the services of a private broker who can take advantage of many sources.

BIBLIOGRAPHY

Ardito, Stephanie C. "Information Brokers and Cyberstalking." *Information Today.* May 2003.

Bond, Patti. "Proposed Identity Theft Law Applies Only to Information Brokers, Critics Say." *The Atlantic Journal-Constitution.* 24 May 2005.

"Government Information Brokers Fail To Protect Privacy: Information resellers often fail to follow privacy protection guidelines when dealing with the federal government, a government report says." *InternetWeek.* 5 April 2006.

Noorlander, Willem. "Information Management: Who's Controlling Who?" *Online.* January 2001.

Hillstrom, Northern Lights
updated by Magee, ECDI

INITIAL PUBLIC OFFERINGS

An initial public offering (IPO) is the process through which a privately held company issues shares of stock to the public for the first time. Also known as "going public," an IPO transforms a business from a privately owned and operated entity into one that is owned by public stockholders. An IPO is a significant stage in the growth of many businesses, as it provides them with access to the public capital market and also increases their credibility and exposure. Becoming a public entity, however, also involves significant changes for a business including a loss of flexibility and control for management. In some cases an IPO may be the only means left of financing rapid growth and expansion. The decision to go public is sometimes influenced by venture capitalists or founders who wish to cash in on their early investment.

Staging an IPO is a very time-consuming and expensive process. A business interested in going public must apply to the Securities and Exchange Commission (SEC) for permission to sell stock to the public. The SEC registration process is quite complex and requires the company to disclose a great deal of detailed information to potential investors. The IPO process can take as little as six months or as long as two years, during which time management's attention is distracted away from day-to-day operations. It can also cost a company between $50,000 and $250,000 in underwriting fees, legal and accounting expenses, and printing costs.

Overall, going public is an enormous undertaking and the decision to go public requires careful consideration and planning. Experts recommend that business owners consider all the alternatives first (such as securing venture capital, forming a limited partnership or joint venture, or selling shares through private placement), examine their current and future capital needs, and be aware of how an IPO will affect the availability of future financing.

According to Jennifer Lindsey in her book *The Entrepreneur's Guide to Capital,* the ideal candidate for an IPO is a small- to medium-sized company in an emerging industry, with annual revenues of at least $10 million and a profit margin of over 10 percent of revenues. It is also important that the company have a stable management group, growth of at least 10 percent annually, and capitalization featuring no more than 25 percent debt. Companies that meet these basic criteria still need to time their IPO carefully in order to gain the maximum benefits. Lindsey suggested going public when the stock markets are receptive to new offerings, the industry is growing rapidly, and the company needs access to more capital and public recognition to support its strategies for expansion and growth.

ADVANTAGES OF GOING PUBLIC

The primary advantage a business stands to gain through an initial public stock offering is access to capital. In addition, the capital does not have to be repaid and does not involve an interest charge. The only reward that IPO investors seek is an appreciation of their investment and possibly dividends. Besides the immediate infusion of capital provided by an IPO, a business that goes public may also find it easier to obtain capital for future needs through new stock offerings or public debt offerings. A related advantage of an IPO is that it provides the business's founders and venture capitalists with an opportunity to cash out on their early investment. Those shares

of equity can be sold as part of the IPO, in a special offering, or on the open market some time after the IPO. However, it is important to avoid the perception that the owners are seeking to bail out of a sinking ship, or the IPO is unlikely to be a success.

Another advantage of an IPO is increased public awareness of the company. This sort of attention and publicity may lead to new opportunities and new customers. As part of the IPO process, information about the company is printed in newspapers across the country. The excitement surrounding an IPO may also generate increased attention in the business press. There are a number of laws covering the disclosure of information during the IPO process, however, so business owners must be careful not to get carried away with the publicity. A related advantage is that the public company may have enhanced credibility with its suppliers, customers, and lenders, which may lead to improved credit terms.

Yet another advantage of going public involves the ability to use stock in creative incentive packages for management and employees. Offering shares of stock and stock options as part of compensation may enable a business to attract better management talent, and to provide them with an incentive to perform well. Employees who become part-owners through a stock plan may be motivated by sharing in the company's success. Finally, an initial public offering provides a public valuation of a business. This means that it will be easier for the company to enter into mergers and acquisitions, because it can offer stock rather than cash.

DISADVANTAGES OF GOING PUBLIC

The biggest disadvantages involved in going public are the costs and time involved. Experts note that a company's management is likely to be occupied with little else during the entire IPO process, which may last as long as two years. The business owner and other top managers must prepare registration statements for the SEC, consult with investment bankers, attorneys, and accountants, and take part in the personal marketing of the stock. Many people find this to be an exhaustive process and would prefer to simply run their company.

An IPO is extremely expensive. In fact, it is not unusual for a business to pay between $50,000 and $250,000 to prepare and publicize an offering. In his article for *The Portable MBA in Finance and Accounting,* Paul G. Joubert noted that a business owner should not be surprised if the cost of an IPO claims between 15 and 20 percent of the proceeds of the sale of stock. Some of the major costs include the lead underwriter's commission; out-of-pocket expenses for legal services, accounting services, printing costs, and the personal marketing "road show" by managers; .02 percent filing costs with the SEC; fees for public relations to bolster the company's image; plus ongoing legal, accounting, filing, and mailing expenses. Despite such expense, it is always possible that an unforeseen problem will derail the IPO before the sale of stock takes place. Even when the sale does take place, most underwriters offer IPO shares at a discounted price in order to ensure an upward movement in the stock during the period immediately following the offering. The effect of this discount is to transfer wealth from the initial investors to new shareholders.

Other disadvantages involve the public company's loss of confidentiality, flexibility, and control. SEC regulations require public companies to release all operating details to the public, including sensitive information about their markets, profit margins, and future plans. An untold number of problems and conflicts may arise when everyone from competitors to employees know all about the inner workings of the company. By diluting the holdings of the company's original owners, going public also gives management less control over day-to-day operations. Large shareholders may seek representation on the board and a say in how the company is run. If enough shareholders become disgruntled with the company's stock value or future plans, they can stage a takeover and oust management. The dilution of ownership also reduces management's flexibility. It is not possible to make decisions as quickly and efficiently when the board must approve all decisions. In addition, SEC regulations restrict the ability of a public company's management to trade their stock and to discuss company business with outsiders.

Public entities also face added pressure to show strong short-term performance. Earnings are reported quarterly, and shareholders and financial markets always want to see good results. Unfortunately, long-term strategic investment decisions may tend to have a lower priority than making current numbers look good. The additional reporting requirements for public companies also add expense, as the business will likely need to improve accounting systems and add staff. Public entities also encounter added costs associated with handling shareholder relations.

THE PROCESS OF GOING PUBLIC

Once a business has decided to go public, the first step in the IPO process is to select an underwriter to act as an intermediary between the company and the capital markets. Joubert recommended that business owners solicit proposals from a number of investment banks, then evaluate the bidders on the basis of their reputation, experience with similar offerings, experience in the industry, distribution network, record of post-offering support, and type of underwriting arrangement. Other considerations include the bidders' valuation of the company and recommended share price.

There are three basic types of underwriting arrangements: best efforts, which means that the investment bank does not commit to buying any shares but agrees to put forth its best effort to sell as many as possible; all or none, which is similar to best efforts except that the offering is canceled if all the shares are not sold; and firm commitment, which means that the investment bank purchases all the shares itself. The firm commitment arrangement is probably best for the small business, since the underwriter holds the risk of not selling the shares. Once a lead underwriter has been selected, that firm will form a team of other underwriters and brokers to assist it in achieving a broad distribution of the stock.

The next step in the IPO process is to assemble an underwriting team consisting of attorneys, independent accountants, and a financial printer. The attorneys for the underwriter draft all the agreements, while the attorneys for the company advise management about meeting all SEC regulations. The accountants issue opinions about the company's financial statements in order to reassure potential investors. The financial printer handles preparation of the prospectus and other written tools involved in marketing the offering.

After putting together a team to handle the IPO, the business must then prepare an initial registration statement according to SEC regulations. The main body of the registration statement is a prospectus containing detailed information about the company, including its financial statements and a management analysis. The management analysis is perhaps the most important and time-consuming part of the IPO process. In it, the business owners must simultaneously disclose all of the potential risks faced by the business and convince investors that it is a good investment. This section is typically worded very carefully and reviewed by the company's attorneys to ensure compliance with SEC rules about truthful disclosure.

The SEC rules regarding public stock offerings are contained in two main acts: the Securities Act of 1933 and the Securities Act of 1934. The former concerns the registration of IPOs with the SEC in order to protect the public against fraud, while the latter regulates companies after they have gone public, outlines registration and reporting procedures, and sets forth insider trading laws. Upon completion of the initial registration statement, it is sent to the SEC for review. During the review process, which can take up to two months, the company's attorneys remain in contact with the SEC in order to learn of any necessary changes. Also during this time, the company's financial statements must be audited by independent accountants in accordance with SEC rules. This audit is more formal than the usual accounting review and provides investors with a much higher degree of assurance about the company's financial position.

Throughout the SEC review period—which is sometimes called the "cooling off" or "quiet" period—the company also begins making controlled efforts to market the offering. The company distributes a preliminary prospectus to potential investors, and the business owners and top managers travel around to make personal presentations of the material in what are known as "road shows." It is important to note, however, that management cannot disclose any further information beyond that contained in the prospectus during the SEC review period. Other activities taking place during this time include filing various forms with different states in which the stock will be sold (the differing state requirements are known as "blue sky laws") and holding a due diligence meeting to review financial statements one last time.

At the end of the cooling off period, the SEC provides comments on the initial registration statement. The company then must address the comments, agree to a final offering price for the shares, and file a final amendment to the registration statement. Technically, the actual sale of stock is supposed to become effective 20 days after the final amendment is filed, but the SEC usually grants companies an acceleration so that it becomes effective immediately. This acceleration grows out of the SEC's recognition that the stock market can change dramatically over a 20-day period. The actual selling of shares then takes place, beginning on the official offering date and continuing for seven days. The lead investment banker supervises the public sale of the security. During the offering period, the investment bankers are permitted to "stabilize" the price of the security by purchasing shares in the secondary market. This process is called pegging, and it is permitted to continue for up to ten days after the official offering date. The investment bankers may also support the offering through over allotment, or selling up to 15 percent more stock when demand is high.

After a successful offering, the underwriter meets with all parties to distribute the funds and settle all expenses. At that time the transfer agent is given authorization to forward the securities to the new owners. An IPO closes with the transfer of the stock, but the terms of the offering are not yet completed. The SEC requires the filing of a number of reports pertaining to the appropriate use of the funds as described in the prospectus. If the offering is terminated for any reason, the underwriter returns the funds to the investors.

IMPROVING THE PROSPECTS FOR A SUCCESSFUL IPO

For most businesses, the decision to go public is made gradually over time as changes in the company's performance

and capital needs make an IPO seem more desirable and necessary. But many companies still fail to bring their plans to sell stock to completion due to a lack of planning. In an article for *Entrepreneur,* David R. Evanson outlined a number of steps business owners can take to improve the prospects of an IPO long before their company formally considers going public. One step involves assessing and taking action to improve the company's image, which will be scrutinized by investors when the time comes for an IPO. It is also necessary to reorganize as a corporation and begin keeping detailed financial records.

Another step business owners can take in advance to prepare their companies to go public is to supplement management with experienced professionals. Investors like to see a management team that generates confidence and respect within the industry, and that can be a source of innovative ideas for future growth. Forming this sort of management team may require a business owner to hire outside of his or her own local network of business associates. It may also involve setting up lucrative benefit plans to help attract and retain top talent. Similarly, the business owner should set about building a solid board of directors that will be able to help the company maximize shareholder value once it has become a public entity. It is also helpful for the business owner to begin making contacts with investment banks, attorneys, and accountants in advance of planning an IPO. In 1997, Evanson recommended using one of the "Big Six" accounting firms based on their trustworthy reputations nationally. Unfortunately, the reputations of these firms took a hit in 2001 and 2002 with a string of high-profile bankruptcy filing. Serious allegations of accounting fraud followed and extended beyond the bankrupt firms to their "Big Six" accounting firms. In 2005, the ranks of the "Big Six" accounting firms had been reduced. The remaining "Big Four" accounting firms are: Deloitte & Touche, Ernst & Young, KPMG Peat Marwick, and PricewaterhouseCoopers.

Businesses interested in eventually going public are advised to begin acting like a large corporation well in advance of an IPO. Although many deals involving small businesses are sealed with an informal handshake, investors like to see a pattern of formal, professional contracts with customers, suppliers, and independent contractors. They also favor formal human resource programs, including hiring procedures, performance reviews, and benefit plans. It is also important for businesses to protect their unique products and ideas by applying for patents and trademarks as needed. All of these steps, when taken in advance, can help to smooth a business's passage to becoming a public entity.

The pace of IPOs reached a peak in 1999, when a record 509 companies went public, raising an unprecedented $66 billion. IPO fever was fueled by "dotcoms," or new Internet-based companies, which accounted for 290 of the initial public stock offerings that year. These fledgling companies went public to take advantage of a unique climate in the stock market, as giddy investors trying to catch the next Internet fad did not demand much in terms of profitability. New Internet-based companies with limited track records were able to use the public markets as a form of venture capital. In fact, new issues of stock in dotcoms jumped an average of 70 percent on their first day of trading in 1999. By the middle of 2000, however, drops in the tech-heavy National Association of Securities Dealers Automated Quotation (NASDAQ) made investors more cautious and dramatically changed the situation for Internet IPOs. Studies showed that 40 percent of high-tech IPOs were trading below their original offering price by that time. As a result, 52 companies decided to cancel or postpone their IPOs in the first six months of 2000. During the first 10 months of 2005, 147 IPOs took place, fewer than took place in 2004 (331) but almost twice as many as there had been in 2003 (75). Business owners must keep a close eye on market conditions and make sure their companies are well positioned and show a strong chance of long-term viability before engaging in an IPO.

SEE ALSO *Direct Public Offering; Private Placement*

BIBLIOGRAPHY

"2005 Annual IPO Review" IPOHome, Renaissance Capital. Available from http://www.ipohome.com/marketwatch/review/2005main.asp Retrieved on 15 March 2006.

Draho, Jason. *IPO Decision, Why and How Companies Go Public.* Edward Elgar Publishing, 2004.

Evanson, David R. "Public School: Learning How to Prepare for an IPO." *Entrepreneur.* October 1997.

Joubert, Paul G. "Going Public." *The Portable MBA in Finance and Accounting.* Wiley, 1992.

Lardner, James, and Paul Sloan. "The Anatomy of Sickly IPOs." *U.S. News & World Report.* 29 May 2000.

Lindsey, Jennifer. *The Entrepreneur's Guide to Capital: The Techniques for Capitalizing and Refinancing New and Growing Businesses.* Probus, 1986.

MacAdam, Donald H. *Startup to IPO.* Xlibris Corporation, 2004.

O'Brien, Sarah. "Red Tape Said to Strangle Small-Business IPOs." *Investment News.* 9 July 2001.

Tucker, Andy. "IPO Ahead? Try These Steps to Avoid Hitting Roadblocks." *Business First-Columbus.* 17 March 2000.

Hillstrom, Northern Lights
updated by Magee, ECDI

INNOVATION

Innovation is the basic driving force behind entrepreneurship and the creation of small businesses. When an individual comes up with an idea that has not previously been explored, or a niche that larger businesses have not been able to exploit, he or she may be able to turn that idea into a successful business venture. "Ideas are the fuel that keep entrepreneurial fires blazing," I. Satya Sreenivas wrote in *The Business Journal.* "Savvy entrepreneurs realize the fact that ideas can originate from anywhere at anytime, and a random idea could be more worthwhile than a well-researched project."

Of course, not every new idea has the potential to become a successful business. And in many cases, individuals with good, marketable ideas fail to come up with the capital needed to turn their ideas into reality. But innovation is still a necessary first step for small business success in many instances. Moreover, entrepreneurs cannot afford to stop innovating once they have established a successful business. Innovation applies not only to new business and product ideas, but also to the internal workings of a company. Successful business owners continually innovate with regards to internal systems and processes in order to create and sustain a source of competitive advantage. "The global economy requires that companies generate an unending stream of new products, systems, technologies, and services," Claus Weyrich wrote in *Electronic News.* "And innovation has to be applied to things other than products."

According to Weyrich, sustaining innovation in a business organization requires an understanding of the company's core competencies, an innovative corporate culture, and a systematic approach. He described three phases in the innovation process: 1) the invention phase, in which ideas are generated; 2) the implementation phase, in which the best ideas are selected and developed further; and 3) the market penetration phase, in which ideas are exploited for commercial gain. This process is an ongoing one, with feedback used to close the loop.

Analysts agree that companies of all sizes need to place innovation into a broader context than just traditional research and development. The process of innovation needs to be managed in a structured way. "Companies need to establish a seamless innovation process—an enterprise-wide exchange of ideas that will ensure that the information and expertise required to create, market, and service breakthrough products is available and accessible to those who need it," *Chemical Week* contributor Ken Cottrill explained. "If all the people able to extract value from a new product or technology are in the information loop, there is a smaller chance that opportunities will be squandered." Making use of the information resources available within a company allows employees to benefit from "corporate memory." They are better able to focus on innovation because they know where others have been before them.

Innovation is something that takes time, quite literally. To be innovative, people need time to clear their minds, to read about interesting and unrelated fields, and to ponder these things in a non-urgent environment. According to a *Harvard Business Review* study entitled "Creativity Under the Gun," people are rarely creative when they are under deadline. "When creativity is under the gun, it usually ends up getting killed. Our study indicates that the more time pressure people feel on a given day, the less likely they will be to think creatively." What is needed to jumpstart the process of innovation is time away from the day-to-day pressures of multitasking. Managers should avoid extreme time pressure when possible and should try to structure work for others so that they too may avoid working under deadline at least part of the time. Part of any program designed to stimulate innovation must be a measure of free time. After all, complex cognitive processing takes time.

It is important to include the whole company in the innovation process, because the germ of an idea can come from anywhere, and the best ideas often grow out of a combination of functional areas. Establishment of a network structure can provide a framework for this desired innovation. A network structure includes cross-functional groups within the company, cross-links between the various groups, and can even include linkages with external parties such as customers and suppliers. "Companies of all sizes can adopt this approach to innovation," said Cottrill. "There is no standard blueprint for these networks, because they are shaped by a company's business goals and organizational structure. However, the individuals who make up these groups are unified by a common mission and are in regular communication."

Small businesses face a number of obstacles on the road to effective innovation, the most obvious being limited financial, knowledge, and manpower resources. They also have some advantages over larger firms when it comes to the flexibility, a characteristic that is important for the successful implementation of an innovation fostering process. In fact, one of the most important factors in promoting company-wide innovation is the support of owners, managers, and those in positions of authority. "A corporation's synapses may be buzzing with creative ideas and initiatives, but without support from the top echelons, this effort can lose momentum, and innovation becomes stifled," Cottrill stated.

SEE ALSO *Managing Organizational Change*

BIBLIOGRAPHY
Amabile, Teresa A., Constance N. Hadley, Steven J. Kramer. "Creativity Under the Gun." *Harvard Business Review.* 1 August 2002.

Cottrill, Ken. "Networking for Innovation." *Chemical Week.* 25 February 1998.

Pisa, Regina M. "Formally Foster Innovation and Inevitable Change." *Boston Herald.* 1 February 2006.

Sreenivas, I. Satya. "First Idea May Not Be the Best." *The Business Journal.* 3 November 1997.

Weyrich, Claus. "The Meaning of Innovation." *Electronic News.* 16 February 1998.

Hillstrom, Northern Lights
updated by Magee, ECDI

INSURANCE POOLING

Insurance pooling is a practice wherein a group of small firms join together to secure better insurance rates and coverage plans by virtue of their increased buying power as a block. This practice is primarily used for securing health and disability insurance coverage. Those doing insurance pooling are often referred to as insurance purchasing cooperatives.

Small business enterprises have long complained that insurers hand out discounts to big clients, who have substantial purchasing power and large numbers of employees, and that those insurers too often try to make up those discount losses by hiking rates for their smaller clients. Unable to buy good coverage on their own, smaller companies were forced to rely on pooling plans created and managed by trade associations or other affiliated business groups, or pass on providing coverage altogether. In recent years, however, another alternative, in which private businesses band together and organize their own pools, has emerged. Distinct entities have been created to address both health and disability coverage needs.

Health Insurance Pools Health insurance coverage has long been a difficult benefit for many small businesses to incorporate into their compensation packages. Premiums for even modest health packages constitute a significant outlay for small businesses, and increases in premiums and deductibles attributable to employee illness forced many owners with the unpleasant choice of placing their business at financial risk or ending health insurance for their employees. "Insurers had come to evaluate small firms separately by such factors as claims experience, worker's health status, and even type of business," explained *Nation's Business*. "As a result, many small companies couldn't buy health insurance at any price. Those that did have coverage lived in fear of a single serious illness because it could trigger skyrocketing rates or cancellation of coverage."

Health insurance pools, which are also sometimes called insurance purchasing alliances or health insurance purchasing co-ops, were originally created to address this problem. They provide group health policies exclusively to small businesses. Rules governing these alliances vary from state to state, with some states offering eligibility to sole proprietorships and others providing coverage to businesses with up to 100 employees. On average, however, these health insurance pools target employers of three to 50 people.

Small businesses that join one of these pools can typically count on the following benefits:

1. A community premium rate that is significantly lower than any individual rate it could demand, because the membership gains collective leverage that forces insurance carriers to modify premium and deductible demands

2. In many cases, premium increases are capped for the first several years of the policy

3. Centralized administration of the policy among all of companies covered under it, which results in savings in work hours and paperwork

4. Standard rates and benefits that do not fluctuate according to company size or work force health history

5. Selection of plans from multiple insurers (some plans allocate plan selection power exclusively with employers, while others allow workers to select from a menu of plans)

First tried in California in the early 1990s, these types of pools could be found in 15 states by the early 2000s. In addition, several more states are slated to open their doors to such pooling strategies over the next few years. Analysts warn, however, that the rules and regulations governing health insurance pools vary considerably from state to state, and note that the laws of a number of states make it unlikely that these alliances will make an appearance within their borders any time soon. "Because they are usually locally based and privately operated, health co-ops or alliances have evolved quite differently in the 15 states where they are functioning," explained Stephen Blakely in *Nation's Business*. "For instance, California's co-op plan is run by an independent state agency that defines the benefits and negotiates with insurers. Florida and Texas have less state control and permit more autonomy among alliances. In New York and some other states, local business-sponsored health alliances operate on their own.... Some states have long-standing laws expressly prohibiting businesses from coming together to obtain insurance. Other states have not enacted laws that would enable small firms to buy health insurance regardless of their workers' health status, that would limit insurance-rate variability between companies of similar size and labor characteristics, and that would prohibit insurers from canceling small groups' coverage without cause."

Disability Insurance Pools Disability insurance pools, also called risk-purchasing groups, operate under the same guiding principles as health insurance alliances—by joining together into one single negotiating group, small businesses can increase their bargaining power when dealing with insurers. These groups are usually composed of companies that hail from the same industry sector, and thus face many of the same disability risks.

These disability insurance pools arose in the aftermath of the 1986 Risk Retention Act, which was passed by Congress in an effort to address the growing inability of small business owners to obtain liability insurance because of its rapidly growing cost. "Risk-retention groups enable companies in the same industry, such as plastics or chemicals, to cut insurance costs by forming what are, in effect, mini insurance companies to self-insure against liability claims," explained Lynn Woods in *Nation's Business*. "Risk-purchasing groups, on the other hand, permit group purchasing of liability coverage."

Interestingly, insurance companies have been among the biggest boosters of this new type of disability coverage arrangement. Woods pointed out that "insurance companies find risk-purchasing groups attractive prospects because the companies can save costs in two ways—by using a single agent or broker for multiple states and by tailoring a policy for a group based on a similar level of risk."

SEE ALSO *Employee Benefits; Health Insurance Options*

BIBLIOGRAPHY

Blakely, Stephen. "An Update on Health-Care Pools." *Nation's Business*. May 1997.

Kaufman, Steve. "Insurance Pooling System Makes Health Care Affordable for Small Firms." *Knight-Ridder Tribune News*. April 7, 1997.

Maynard, Roberta, and Roger Thompson. "The Power of Pooling." *Nation's Business*. March 1995.

U.S. Small Business Administration. Anastasio, Susan. *Small Business Insurance and Risk Management Guide*. n.d.

Wicks, Elliot K. "Health Insurance Purchasing Cooperatives." *Taskforce on the Issue of Health Insurance – Issue Brief*. The Commonwealth Fund, November 2002.

Woods, Lynn. "Gaining an Edge on Liability." *Nation's Business*. June 1996.

Hillstrom, Northern Lights
updated by Magee, ECDI

INTELLECTUAL PROPERTY

Intellectual property (IP) is an intangible creation of the human mind, usually expressed or translated into a tangible form, that is assigned certain rights of property. Examples of intellectual property include an author's copyright on a book or article, a distinctive logo design representing a soft drink company and its products, unique design elements of a web site, or a patent on a particular process to, for example, manufacture chewing gum. Intellectual property law covers the protection of copyrights, patents, trademarks, and trade secrets, as well as other legal areas, such as unfair competition. In effect, intellectual property laws give the creator of a new and unique product or idea a temporary monopoly on its use. The value of intellectual property to an individual or company is not based on physical properties, such as size and structure. Instead, intellectual property is valuable because it represents ownership and an exclusive right to use, manufacture, reproduce, or promote a unique creation or idea. In this way, it has the potential to be one of the most valuable assets a person or small business can own.

In an era of globalization, IP rights must be protected and regulated at an international level. The U.S. Department of State explains why countries protect inventions; literary and artistic works; and symbols, images, names, and designs used in commerce on a Web site it dedicates to this subject. Countries protect IP "because they know safeguarding these property rights fosters economic growth, provides incentives for technological innovation, and attracts investment that will create new jobs and opportunities for all their citizens.... In the United States alone, for example, studies in the past decade have estimated that over 50 percent of U.S. exports now depend on some form of intellectual property protection, compared to less then 10 percent 50 years ago."

DEVELOPMENT OF INTELLECTUAL PROPERTY LAWS

The laws protecting intellectual property in the United States exist at both the state and federal levels. State laws cover a broad spectrum of intellectual property fields, from trade secrets to the right of publicity. The laws differ somewhat from state to state. At the federal level, the Constitution and legislation authorized under the Constitution deal exclusively with patents and copyrights, and partially with trademarks and related areas of unfair competition.

Intellectual property protection first became an important issue at an international level during trade and tariff negotiations in the nineteenth century, and has remained so ever since. One of the first international treaties relating to intellectual property in the broadest sense was the International Convention for the Protection of Industrial Property, or the Paris Convention. Written in 1883, the treaty created under the Paris Convention provided protection for such properties as patents, industrial models and designs, trademarks, and trade names. Over 100 countries have signed the Paris Convention treaty, and it has been modified several times. Two of the most important provisions of the treaty relate to the rights of national treatment and priority.

The right of national treatment ensures that those individuals seeking a patent or trademark in a foreign country will not be discriminated against and will receive the same rights as a citizen of that country. The right of priority provides an inventor one year from the date of filing a patent application in his or her home country (six months for a trademark or design application) to file an application in a foreign country. The legal, effective date of application in the foreign country is then retroactively the legal, effective filing date in the home country, provided the application is made within the protection period. If the invention is made public prior to filing the home country application, however, the right of priority in a foreign country is no longer applicable.

Enforcement and protection of IP at the international level has historically been extremely complex. Laws have varied significantly from country to country, and the political climate within each country has influenced the extent of protection available. Separate legislation and treaties specifically addressed relevant procedures, conventions, and standards for each area within the scope of intellectual property, such as copyright or trade secrets.

Many U.S. and international laws relating to intellectual property were significantly altered with the 1994 passage of the General Agreement on Tariffs and Trade (GATT). In fact, the member nations that signed the GATT committed themselves to a higher degree of intellectual property protection than had been provided under any earlier multinational treaties. Under the guidance of the World Trade Organization (WTO), all member nations were required to adopt specific provisions for the enforcement of rights and settlement of disputes relating to intellectual property. Under these provisions, trademark counterfeiting and commercial copyright piracy are subject to criminal penalties.

Today, the strong protections of intellectual property are recognized as one of the cornerstones of the formation and growth of small businesses in the United States, especially since the advent of the Internet and other new technologies have placed a premium on new ideas and innovations. Intellectual property allows individuals who come up with a new idea to enjoy the exclusive use of that idea for a certain period of time, which can be a significant monetary incentive for entrepreneurs. But intellectual property law is extraordinarily complex, so small business owners interested in IP issues should consult a legal expert in order to protect themselves to the full extent of the law. "The law on intellectual property... is everywhere both comparatively new and in flux," observed *The Economist (US)*. The rapid and worldwide spread of access to the Internet as well as the ease with which electronic data may be copied and manipulated pose new challenges to the existing network of IP regulations. Laws surrounding IP rights will likely see many changes in the coming years as we adjust them to the new demands created by the information age.

SEE ALSO *Inventions and Patents; Work for Hire*

BIBLIOGRAPHY

Epstein, Eve. "What Is Intellectual Property?" *InfoWorld*. 19 June 2000.

Foster, Frank H., and Robert L. Shook. *Patents, Copyrights & Trademarks*. Wiley, 1993.

Gartman, John, and Kevin McNeely. "A Summary Checklist for Dealing with Intellectual Property." *Providence Business News*. 26 June 2000.

Lickson, Charles P. *A Legal Guide for Small Business*. Crisp Publications, 1994.

"Markets for Ideas: Rights in Intellectual Property." *The Economist (US)*. 14 April 2001.

Prencipe, Loretta W. "Intellectual Property Due Diligence." *InfoWorld*. 30 October 2000.

"Protecting Intellectual Property: An Introductory Guide for U.S. Businesses on Protecting Intellectual Property Abroad." *Business America*. July 1991.

Spinello, Richar A., and Herman T. Tavani. *Intellectual Property Rights in a Networked World*. Idea Group, Inc. (IGI), 2004.

Tabalujan, Benny. "Keeping the Fruits of Your Intellectual Pursuit to Yourself." *Business Times*. July 1993.

U.S. Department of State. International Information Programs. Field, Thomas G. Jr. "What is Intellectual Property." Available from http://usinfo.state.gov/products/pubs/intelprp/ January 2006.

World Trade Commission. "Intellectual Property: Protection and Enforcement." Available from http://www.wto.org/english/thewto_e/whatis_e/tif_e/agrm7_e.htm Retrieved on 16 March 2006.

Hillstrom, Northern Lights
updated by Magee, ECDI

INTERCULTURAL COMMUNICATION

The term "intercultural communication" is often used to refer to the wide range of communication issues that inevitably arise within an organization composed of individuals from a variety of religious, social, ethnic, and educational backgrounds. Each of these individuals brings a unique set of experiences and values to the workplace, many of which can be traced to the culture in which they grew up and now operate. Businesses that are able to facilitate effective communication—both written and verbal—between the members of these various cultural groups will be far better equipped to succeed than will those organizations that allow conflicts that arise from internal cultural differences to fester and harden. The failure to address and resolve culturally based conflicts and tensions will inevitably show up in the form of diminished performance and decreased productivity.

The importance of effective intercultural communication can hardly be overstated. Indeed, as Trudy Milburn pointed out in *Management Review*, communication serves not only as an expression of cultural background, but as a *shaper* of cultural identity. "Cultural identities, like meaning, are socially negotiated," she wrote. "Ethnic identities, class identities, and professional identities are formed and enacted through the process of communication. What it means to be white, Jewish, or gay is based on a communication process that constructs those identities. It is more than just how one labels oneself, but how one acts in the presence of like and different others, that constructs a sense of identity and membership."

LANGUAGE—THE CORNERSTONE OF INTERCULTURAL COMMUNICATION

Differences in culture reflect themselves in a variety of ways. For instance, one cultural norm may have a significantly different conception of time than another, or a different idea of what constitutes appropriate body language and personal space when engaged in conversation. But most researchers, employees, and business owners agree that the most important element in effective intercultural communication concerns language. "A great deal of ethnocentrism is centered around language," said John P. Fernandez in *Managing a Diverse Work Force: Regaining the Competitive Edge*. "Language issues are becoming a considerable source of conflict and inefficiency in the increasingly diverse work force throughout the world.... No corporation can be competitive if co-workers avoid, don't listen to, perceive as incompetent, or are intolerant of employees who have problems with the language. In addition, these attitudes could be carried over into their interactions with customers who speak English as a second language, resulting in disastrous effects on customer relations and, thus, the corporate bottom line."

Small business owners should try and avoid making assumptions about the abilities of another person—either a vendor, employee, or partner—based on ethnocentric assumptions of their own culture's superiority in the realm of communication. "Withhold evaluative statements on foreign communication styles until you recognize that different cultures use different communication methods," counseled Herta A. Murphy and Herbert W. Hildebrandt in *Effective Business Communications.*

Often overlooked in discussion of intercultural communication are the sometimes significant cultural differences that exist concerning the practice of listening. Tips about establishing culturally sensitive verbal and written communication practices within an organization are plentiful, but in many cases, relatively short shrift is given to cultural differences in listening, the flip side of the communication coin. "Codes of conduct that specify how listening should be demonstrated are based upon certain cultural assumptions about what counts as listening," said Milburn. But while the prevailing norms of communication in American business may call for the listener to be quiet and offer body language (steady eye contact, for instance) intended to assure the speaker that his or her words are being heeded, many cultures have different standards that may strike the uninitiated as rude or disorienting. "A person who communicates by leaning forward and getting close may be very threatening to someone who values personal space," pointed out *Oregon Business's* Megan Monson. "And that person could be perceived as hostile and unfriendly, simply because of poor eye contact." The key, say analysts, is to make certain that your organization recognizes that cultural differences abound in listening as well as speaking practices, and to establish intercultural communication practices accordingly.

DIVERSITY/INTERCULTURAL COMMUNICATION POLICIES

In recent years, companies of various shapes, sizes, and in many different fields of endeavor have embraced programs designed to celebrate diversity and encourage communication between individuals and groups from different cultural backgrounds. But according to Milburn, "diversity is one of those concepts that is very context-bound. It does not have a singular meaning for everyone. Companies that try to institute diversity programs without understanding the cultural assumptions upon which these programs are based may find it difficult to enact meaningful diversity policies.... Many companies believe that through sharing they can promote diverse cultural values. Yet, how a company defines sharing may actually hinder its diversity initiatives since some cultures have specific rules about sharing. These rules are enacted in everyday communication practices."

Most business owners recognize that their companies are far more likely to be successful if they are able to establish effective systems of intercultural communication between employees of different religious, social, and ethnic backgrounds. But profound differences in communication styles can also be found within functional areas of a company as well, and these too need to be addressed to ensure that the organization is able to operate at its highest level of efficiency. For example, employees engaged in technical fields (computers, mechanical engineering, etc.) often have educational and work backgrounds that are considerably different from workers who are engaged in "creative" areas of the company (marketing, public relations, etc.). These differences often manifest themselves in the modes of communication that the respective parties favor. "Engineers tend to be introverted and analytical with very logical ways of solving problems," observed one software industry veteran in an interview with Monson. "Those in marketing tend to be extroverted and intuitive. It's a perennial source of possible contention, and really, it's just a matter of style."

Consultants and researchers agree, though, that many differences between these distinct functional cultures can be addressed through proactive policies that recognize that such differences exist and work to educate everyone about the legitimacy of each culture. "Today's dynamic marketplace demands that high-tech companies be able to move quickly, which in turn needs accurate communication, both with customers and among employees. Poor communication can mean loss of morale, production plunges, and perhaps even a failed start-up," said Monson.

SEE ALSO *Communication Systems; Globalization; International Markets*

BIBLIOGRAPHY

Beeth, Gunnar. "Multicultural Managers Wanted." *Management Review.* May 1997.

Cox, Taylor, Jr. *Cultural Diversity in Organizations.* Berrett-Koehler Publishers, 1993.

Faird, Elashmawia, and Philip Harris. *Multicultural Management.* Gulf Publishing Company, 1993.

Fernandez, John P. *Managing a Diverse Work Force: Regaining the Competitive Edge.* Lexington Books, 1991.

Gancel, Charles, and Chilina Hills. "Managing the Pitfalls and Challenges of Intercultural Communication." *Communication World.* December 1997.

Gardenswartz, Lee, and Anita Rowe. "Cross-Cultural Awareness." *HRMagazine.* March 2001.

Jandt, Fred E. *Intercultural Communications.* Sage Publications, Inc., 2003.

Lieberman, Simma, Kate Berardo, Simons George, Berardo Kate, and George F. Simons. *Putting Diversity to Work.* Thomson Crisp Learning, 2003.

Milburn, Trudy. "Bridging Cultural Gaps." *Management Review.* January 1997.

Monson, Megan. "Talking to Techweenies." *Oregon Business.* February 1997.

Murphy, Herta A., and Herbert W. Hildebrandt. *Effective Business Communications.* McGraw-Hill, 1991.

Hillstrom, Northern Lights
updated by Magee, ECDI

INTEREST RATES

Lenders of money profit from such transactions by arranging for the borrower to pay back an additional amount of money over and above the sum that they borrow. This difference between what is lent and what is returned is known as interest. The interest on a loan is determined through the establishment of an interest rate, which is expressed as a percentage of the amount of the loan.

Borrowing is a staple in many arenas of the U.S. economy. This has resulted in a dizzying array of borrowing arrangements, many of which feature unique wrinkles in the realm of interest rates. Common borrowing and lending arrangements include business and personal loans (from government agencies, banks, and commercial finance companies), credit cards (from corporations), mortgages, various federal and municipal government obligations, and corporate bonds. In addition, interest is used to reward investors and others who place money in savings accounts, individual retirement accounts (IRAs), Certificates of Deposit (CDs), and many other financial vehicles.

TYPES OF INTEREST RATES

The "prime rate" is probably the best-known interest rate. It is the rate at which commercial banks lend money to their best—most creditworthy—customers. However, in order to track interest rates logically, one should start with the Federal Reserve's "discount rate." The discount rate is the interest rate that banks are charged when they borrow money overnight from one of the Federal Reserve Banks. There are twelve Federal Reserve Banks, each of which is a part of the nation's central bank and plays a part in setting the monetary policy of the United States.

Commercial banks pass along the cost of borrowing money when they establish the rates at which they lend money. One factor in establishing those rates is the discount rate established by the Federal Reserve Bank, although other factors play into the calculation. The prime rate is the lowest rate at which commercial banks lend. Although often thought of as a set interest rate, the prime lending rate is not actually a uniform rate.

National City Bank may, for example, have one rate while CitiBank has another slightly different rate. As a result, the most widely quoted prime rate figure in the United States is the one published in the *Wall Street Journal.* What they publish is an average rate that results from polling the nation's thirty largest banks; when twenty-three of those institutions have changed their prime rates, the *Wall Street Journal* responds by updating the published rate. The reason that the prime rate is so well known is that it is used as a basis off of which most other interest rates are calculated.

Other important interest rates that are used in making capital investment decisions include:

- Commercial Paper Rate—These are short-term discount bonds issued by established corporate borrowers. These bonds mature in six months or less.

- Treasury Bill Rate—A Treasury bill is a short-term (one year or less) risk-free bond issued by the U.S. government. Treasury bills are made available to buyers at a price that is less than its redemption value upon maturity.

- Treasury Bond Rate—Unlike the short-term Treasury bills, Treasury bonds are bonds that do not mature for at least one year, and most of them have a duration of 10 to 30 years. The interest rates on these bonds vary depending on their maturity.

- Corporate Bond Rate—The interest rate on long-term corporate bonds can vary depending on a number of factors, including the time to maturity (20 years is the norm for corporate bonds) and risk classification.

How interest rates are established, why they fluctuate, and why they vary from lender to lender and borrower to borrower are complicated matters. Two terms used in banking whose definitions it will be helpful to know in reading further about interest rates are "real" and "nominal." The "real" interest rate on a loan is the current interest rate minus inflation. It is, in essence, the effective rate for the duration of the loan. The "nominal" interest rate is the rate that appears on the loan agreements, the stated rate that does not account in any way for inflation.

FACTORS THAT INFLUENCE INTEREST RATES

Interest rate levels are determined by the laws of supply and demand and fluctuate as supply and demand change. In an economic environment in which demand for loans is high, lending institutions are able to command more lucrative lending arrangements. Conversely, when banks and other institutions find that the market for loans is a tepid one (or worse), interest rates are typically lowered accordingly to encourage businesses and individuals to take out loans.

Interest rates are a key instrument of American fiscal policy. The Federal Reserve determines the interest rate at which the federal government will bestow loans, and banks and other financial institutions, which establish their own interest rates to parallel those of the "Fed," typically follow suit. This ripple effect can have a dramatic impact on the U.S. economy. In a recessionary climate, for instance, the Federal Reserve might lower interest rates in order to create an environment that encourages spending. Conversely, the Federal Reserve often implements interest rate hikes when its board members become concerned that the economy is "overheating" and prone to inflation.

By raising or lowering its discount interest rate on loans to banks, the Federal Reserve can make it attractive or unattractive for banks to borrow funds. By influencing the commercial bank's cost of money, changes in the discount rate tend to influence the whole structure of interest rates, either tightening or loosening money. When interest rates are high, we have what we call tight money. This means not only that borrowers have to pay higher rates, but that banks are more selective in judging the creditworthiness of businesses applying for loans. Conversely, when interest rates decline, money is called easy, meaning that it is both cheaper and easier to borrow. The monetary tools of the Federal Reserve work most directly on short-term interest rates. Interest rates charged for loans of longer duration are indirectly affected through the market's perception of government policy and its impact on the economy.

Another key factor in determining interest rates is the lending agency's confidence that the money—and the interest on that money—will be paid in full and in a timely fashion. Default risk encompasses a wide range of circumstances, from borrowers who completely fail to fulfill their obligations to those that are merely late with a scheduled payment. If lenders are uncertain about the borrower's ability to adhere to the specifications of the loan arrangement, they will often demand a higher rate of return or risk premium. Borrowers with an established credit history, on the other hand, qualify for what is known as the prime interest rate, which is a low interest rate.

TERM STRUCTURE OF INTEREST RATES

The actual interest on a loan is not fully known until the duration of the borrowing arrangement has been specified. Interest rates on loans are typically figured on an annual basis, though other periods are sometimes specified. This does not mean that the loan is supposed to be paid back in a year; indeed, many loans—especially in the realm of small business—do not mature for five or ten years, or even longer. Rather, it refers to the frequency with which the interest and "principal owed"—the original amount borrowed—are recalculated according to the terms of the loan.

Interest is usually charged in such a way that both the principal lent and the accrued interest is used to calculate future interest owed. This is called compounding. For small business owners and other borrowers, this means that the unpaid interest due on the principal is added to that base figure in determining interest for future payments. Most loans are arranged so that interest is compounded on an annual basis, but in some instances, shorter periods are used. These latter arrangements are more beneficial to the loaner than to the borrower, for they require the borrower to pay more money in the long run.

While annual compound interest is the accepted measure of interest rates, other equations are sometimes used. The yield or interest rate on bonds, for instance, is normally computed on a semiannual basis, and then converted to an annual rate by multiplying by two. This is called simple interest. Another form of interest arrangement is one in which the interest is "discounted in advance." In such instances, the interest is deducted from the principal, and the borrower receives the net amount. The borrower thus ends up paying off the interest on the loan at the very beginning of the transaction. A third interest payment method is known as a floating- or variable-rate agreement. Under this common type of business loan, the interest rate is not fixed. Instead, it moves with the bank's prime rate in accordance with the terms of the loan agreement. A small business owner might, for instance, agree to a loan in which the interest on the loan would be the prime rate plus 3 percent. Since the prime rate is subject to change over the life of the loan, interest would be calculated and adjusted on a daily basis.

THE INTEREST RATE AND SMALL BUSINESSES

Entrepreneurs and small business owners often turn to loans in order to establish or expand their business ventures. Business enterprises that choose this method of securing funding, which is commonly called debt financing, need to be aware of all components of those loan agreements, including the interest.

Business consultants point out that interest paid on debt financing is tax deductible. This can save entrepreneurs and small business owners thousands of dollars at tax time, and analysts urge business owners to factor those savings in when weighing their company's capacity to accrue debt. But other interest rate elements can cut into those tax savings if borrowers are not careful. Because interest paid on a loan is tax deductible, while other loan charges and fees are not, it may be in the best interest of a small business owner to accept a loan with a slightly higher interest rate if it offers fewer handling charges than a similar loan with a slightly lower interest rate but higher handling fees. The full impact of loan charges and interest rates over time should be made before deciding upon a lender.

Commercial banks remain the primary source of loans for small business firms in America, especially for short-term loans. Small business enterprises who are able to secure loans from these lenders must also be prepared to negotiate several important aspects of the loan agreement which directly impact interest rate payments. Both the interest rate itself and the schedule under which the loan will be repaid are, of course, integral factors in determining the ultimate cost of the loan to the borrower, but a third important subject of negotiation between the borrowing firm and the bank concerns the *manner* in which the interest on a loan is actually paid. There are three primary methods by which the borrowing company can pay back interest on a loan to a bank: a simple- or ordinary-interest plan, a discounted-interest plan, or a floating interest rate plan.

Securing long-term financing is more problematic for many entrepreneurs and small business owners, and this is reflected in the interest rate arrangements that they must accept in order to secure such financing. Small businesses are often viewed by creditors as having an uncertain future, and making an extended-term loan to such a business means being locked into a high-risk agreement for a prolonged period. To make this type of loan, a lender will want to feel comfortable with the business, the quality of its management, and will want to be compensated for what it sees as higher-than-usual risk exposure. This compensation usually includes the imposition of interest rates that are considerably higher than those charged for short-term financing. As with short-term financing arrangements, interest on long-term agreements can range from floating interest plans to those tied to a fixed rate. The actual cost of the interest rate method that is ultimately chosen appears in interest rate disclosures (which are required by law) as a figure known as the annual percentage rate (APR).

SEE ALSO *Banks and Banking; Credit; Loans*

BIBLIOGRAPHY
Cooper, James C. "U.S.: From Here On Out, The Fed Is Winging It; More uncertainty over future rate decisions will mean bumpier markets." *Business Week.* 10 April 2006.

Federal Reserve Board of the United States. *Discount Rate.* Available from http://www.federalreserve.gov/monetarypolicy/discountrate.htm 16 March 2006.

Walter, Robert. *Financing Your Small Business.* Barron's Educational Series, March 2004.

Hillstrom, Northern Lights
updated by Magee, ECDI

INTERNAL REVENUE SERVICE (IRS)

The Internal Revenue Service (IRS) is the agency of the U.S. Department of the Treasury responsible for collecting federal taxes of all kinds. In addition to income taxes from individuals, companies and organizations, the IRS collects several other kinds of taxes, including Social Security, estate, excise, and gift taxes (they are not responsible for collecting taxes based on the revenue derived from the sale of alcohol, tobacco, or firearms). For the tax year 2005 the IRS reported processing 227 million tax returns in it's publication *2005 Data Book.* The net tax collected on these 2005 returns totaled $1.999 billion; 44 percent was from individual income taxes; 38.3 percent from employment taxes; 13.7 from corporate income taxes; and 4 percent from estate, gift, and excise taxes.

In addition to processing hundreds of thousands of tax returns each year the Internal Revenue Service's responsibilities include enforcement of U.S. tax laws, distribution of forms and instructions necessary for the filing of tax returns, and provision of counseling for businesses and individuals subject to its regulations.

HISTORY OF THE IRS

The IRS, which is a part of the U.S. Department of the Treasury, was first created by Congress in 1862. In the first years of the IRS, its money-gathering activities were very modest. Until the Civil War, the United States gathered approximately as much money from customs duties as it did from taxation, and the federal government's financial needs were slight because it offered few programs for its citizens. In 1913 IRS responsibilities increased with the introduction of the federal income tax system. Since that time, the government has imposed steadily higher taxes on its citizenry to pay for national defense, social programs, transportation and other infrastructure, and other aspects of modern American society. As internal revenue gathering increased in scope during the past century, the Internal Revenue Service saw similar growth. The IRS, which employed approximately 86,000 workers in the mid-1990s, was reorganized in 2000 into four operating divisions: wage and investment; small business and self-employed; large and mid-size business (those with assets greater than $5 million); and tax exempt and governmental entities. Further information on these divisions can be found on the official IRS web site (www.irs.gov).

The Internal Revenue Service processes more than 180 million tax returns on an annual basis. On a small percentage of these returns, the IRS performs a more detailed tax return examination called an "audit." If an individual or business is audited, the IRS representative conducting the examination typically asks for proof of the various deductions and exemptions claimed on the tax return. Depending on how the audit unfolds, the IRS agent may ultimately decide that additional taxes are owed (or, less frequently, that the taxpayer actually paid too much). Taxpayers who object to these audit findings have the option of appealing to an independent division within the IRS specifically created to deal with such cases. If negotiations still do not satisfy the taxpayer, appeals can be filed in U.S. Tax Court or other federal courts, depending on the nature of the case.

SMALL BUSINESS AND THE IRS

The Internal Revenue Service sponsors several different programs designed to help entrepreneurs and small business owners fulfill their revenue reporting and taxpaying obligations. These include the Small Business Tax Education Program (STEP), which is designed to help small business owners maneuver through the plethora of business tax issues that they face.

Other recent IRS initiatives have met with opposition from small business groups, however. For example, IRS regulations requiring businesses that paid more than $50,000 in employment taxes in 1995 to file federal payments electronically—and implementing heavy penalties for those not in compliance—deeply angered many small business owners. The IRS's new Market Segment Specialization Program (MSSP) has also been a subject of some controversy within the small business community. The MSSP is described as a research initiative intended to provide the IRS with a greater understanding of the typical structure and operation of several dozen kinds of small businesses. The initiative, which arose as a result of studies that indicated that independent business owners had a relatively high rate of noncompliance with tax laws, is designed to ultimately provide auditors with greater understanding of how each business is conducted and the compliance problems that they sometimes have. While supporters argue that the MSSP will give the IRS greater insights into the tax difficulties that small businesses face,

critics contend that the program could ultimately result in tougher audits for small businesses.

THE CHANGING IRS

The rapidly changing face of technology and communications has presented small businesses and multinational corporations alike with a wide array of challenges. The Internal Revenue Service has not been immune to these changes. Indeed, the agency has struggled to modernize its operations, especially in the realm of computers. The IRS recently announced that it is considering outsourcing of its tax-return data entry after replacing some aging computers. According to *Computerworld*, IRS priorities now include finding an interim solution to the data input situation and solving remittance processing problems.

With the spread of technologies that facilitate the electronic transfer of data, the data input portion of the IRS's processing task shrinks. The IRS has seen a steady increase in the numbers of tax returns that are filed electronically every year. In 2005, according to the IRS's publication *2005 Data Book,* more than half of all individual tax returns were filed electronically. The trend towards electronic filing of tax returns is expected to continue. As technologies create new way in which to pay our bills and exchange data so too will the tools used by the IRS to collect our taxes.

SEE ALSO *Tax Returns*

BIBLIOGRAPHY
Faulkner, Crystal. "IRS Expanding 'Customer Service' to Businesses." *Business Courier-Cincinnati/Northern Kentucky.* 18 August 2000.

Gearan, Anne. "IRS e-file and Direct Deposit Outpace Last Year's Results." *The America's Intelligence Wire.* 15 March 2006.

Griffin, Cynthia E. "Audit Alert: The Key to Surviving an IRS Audit, Know the Rules." *Entrepreneur.* July 1997.

Guttman, George. "IRS Finishing Up New Strategic Plan." *Tax Notes.* 27 November 2000.

Hodges, Susan. "Getting Wired for the IRS." *Nation's Business.* October 1996.

Machlis, Sharon. "Newly Candid IRS Has Year 2000 Fix, Mulls Outsourcing." *Computerworld.* 10 February 1997.

Stern, Linda. "The IRS's New Focus on Small Business." *Home Office Computing.* April 1994.

U.S. Department of Treasury Internal Revenue Service. *2005 Data Book.* 2006

U.S. Department of Treasury Internal Revenue Service. *Tax Guide for Small Business.* n.d.

Hillstrom, Northern Lights
updated by Magee, ECDI

INTERNATIONAL EXCHANGE RATE

An international exchange rate, also known as a foreign exchange (FX) rate, is the price of one country's currency in terms of another country's currency. Foreign exchange rates are relative and are expressed as the value of one currency compared to another. When selling products internationally, the exchange rate for the two trading countries' currencies is an important factor. Foreign exchange rates, in fact, are one of the most important determinants of a countries relative level of economic health, ranking just after interest rates and inflation. Exchange rates play a vital role in a country's level of trade, which is critical to most every free market economy in the world. Consequently, exchange rates are among the most watched, analyzed, and manipulated economic measures.

Recent History Prior to 1971, foreign exchange rates were fixed by an agreement among the world's central banks called the Bretton Woods Accord. This agreement was entered into after World War II. The world was in a shambles and the Bretton Woods Accord was established to help stabilize the volatile situation by pegging the U.S. dollar to gold and all other currencies of the world to the U.S. dollar. In 1971 a new agreement was formulated to replace the Bretton Woods Accord but it was short lived. In 1973 the world's currencies began to be valued and exchanged based on a free-float system, a system still in place in 2006. The free-float system is a default system of currency trading. It works strictly on supply and demand of currencies. There are no limits on how much currencies can appreciate or depreciate in value measured against other currencies. Because this can cause volatility, central banks and governments have tried to regulate the values of their currencies, but it has become an increasingly costly proposition. Although no longer an official standard, the U.S. dollar remains the benchmark currency, with the Japanese yen (¥) and European euro (€) close behind.

Currency Value Factors A number of factors influence exchange rates. These include all of the following:

- Relative rates of inflation
- Comparative interest rates
- Growth of domestic money supply
- Size and trend of a country's balance of payments
- Economic growth (as measured by the gross national product)
- Dependency on outside energy sources
- Central bank intervention

In addition to these measures of economic activity, the consensus perception of a majority of countries about the overall strength of one country's currency can have a strong impact on how that one country's currency is valued.

THE FOREIGN EXCHANGE MARKET

As nations and their economies have become increasingly interdependent, the FX market has emerged as a global focal point. With an estimated daily FX turnover exceeding $1 trillion, this is by far the world's largest market. In order to remain competitive in the world economy, it is vital to manage the risk of adverse currency fluctuations. In recent times, the worldwide trend has been toward the consolidation of markets and currencies, as in the case of the European Economic Union.

The largest users of the FX market are commercial banks, which serve as intermediaries between currency buyers and sellers. Corporations and financial institutions also trade currencies, primarily to safeguard their foreign currency-denominated assets and liabilities against adverse FX rate movement. Banks and fund managers trade currencies to profit from FX rate movements. Individuals also are subject to fluctuating FX rates, most commonly when a traveler exchanges his/her native currency for a foreign one before embarking on a business trip or vacation.

When the Chicago Mercantile Exchange introduced trading in foreign currency futures in 1972, it enabled all currency market participants, including individual investors, to capitalize on FX rate fluctuations without having to make or take delivery of the actual currencies. Foreign currency futures offer risk management and profit opportunities to individual investors, as well as to small firms and large companies.

There are two types of potential users of foreign currency futures: the hedger and the speculator. The hedger seeks to reduce and manage the risk of financial losses that can arise from transacting business in currencies other than one's native currency. Speculators provide risk capital and assume the risk the hedger is seeking to transfer in the hope of making a profit by correctly forecasting future price movement.

THE EFFECT OF EXCHANGE RATE CHANGES ON BUSINESS

The results of companies that operate in more than one nation often must be "translated" from foreign currencies into U.S. dollars. Exchange rate fluctuations make financial forecasting more difficult for these companies, and also have a marked effect on unit sales, prices, and costs. For example, assume that current market conditions dictate that one U.S. dollar can be exchanged for

125 Japanese yen. In this business environment, an American auto dealer plans to import a Japanese car with a price of 2.5 million yen, which translates to a price in dollars of $20,000. If that dealer also incurred $2,000 in transportation costs and decided to mark up the price of the car by another $3,000, then the vehicle would sell for $25,000 and provide the dealer with a profit margin of 12 percent.

But if the exchange rate changed before the deal was made so that one dollar was worth 100 yen—in other words, if the dollar weakened or depreciated compared to the yen—it would have a dramatic effect on the business transaction. The dealer would then have to pay the Japanese manufacturer $25,000 for the car. Adding in the same costs and mark up, the dealer would have to sell the car for $30,000, yet would only receive a 10 percent profit margin. The dealer would either have to negotiate a lower price from the Japanese manufacturer or cut his profit margin further to be able to sell the vehicle.

Under this FX scenario, the price of American goods would compare favorably to that of Japanese goods in both domestic and foreign markets. The opposite would be true if the dollar strengthened or appreciated against the yen, so that it would take more yen to buy one dollar. This type of exchange rate change would lower the price of foreign goods in the U.S. market and hurt the sales of U.S. goods both domestically and overseas.

SEE ALSO *Exporting*

BIBLIOGRAPHY

"Factors Affecting Exchange Rates." *Consensus Economics.* Available from http://consensuseconomics.com/special_data.htm Retrieved on 21 March 2006.

Faff, Raboert W., and Andrew Marshall. "International Evidence on the Determinants of Foreign Exchange Rate Exposure of Multinational Corporations." *Journal of International Business Studies.* September 2005.

Federal Reserve Bank of San Francisco. "Long-run Determinants of East Asian Real Exchange Rates." Available from http://www.frbsf.org/econrsrch/wklyltr/wklyltr98/el98-11.html Retrieved on 20 March 2006.

"It All Depends." *The Economist.* 30 January 1999.

"Might the Dollar Eventually Follow the Precedent of the Pound and Cede Its Status as Leading International Reserve Currency?" *NBER Reporter.* Summer 2005.

Miller, Kent D., and Jeffrey J. Reuer. "Firm Strategy and Economic Exposure to Foreign Exchange Rate Movements." *Journal of International Business Studies.* Fall 1998.

Hillstrom, Northern Lights
updated by Magee, ECDI

INTERNET DOMAIN NAMES

An Internet domain name is a string of typographic characters used to describe the location of a specific location online. Formally known as the Uniform Resource Locator or URL, it is often considered to be the address of a certain Web site. Obtaining an Internet domain name is a vital step for small businesses hoping to establish a presence on the Internet. "To be a major league team in the Internet game, your business will want a domain name of its own," Vince Emery wrote in *How to Grow Your Business on the Internet.* "These valuable intellectual assets. . . make the difference in your image between Internet pro and fumbling amateur. Your domain name is more than your address. It tells the world who you are and what you do."

A typical domain name consists of several parts. As an example, consider an auto parts business with the domain www.spareparts.com. The letters "www." before the domain name mean that what follows describes the location of a site on the World Wide Web. The last two or three letters of a domain name or URL are known as its top-level domain. The top-level domain for the sample used earlier, www.spareparts.com is .com. Some of the most common top-level domains include .com, which usually indicates a business or commercial site; .org, which generally describes a nonprofit, charity, or cultural organization site; .gov, which indicates a governmental site; and .net, which is most often used by network-related businesses. Other common top-level domains are country codes, like .us for United States and .au for Australia, etc. Small businesses can put as many subdomains as needed in front of their domain names. For example, the customer service department of the aforementioned auto parts business might be designated as www.service.spareparts.com.

Internet domain names are fairly easy and inexpensive to obtain. The process of registering a domain name involves searching to see if the desired name is already taken, filling out a form online, and paying a fee of around $35 for the first year. Maintaining the domain name will require a small annual fee. But small businesses may find it exceedingly difficult to secure the exact domain name they want. As Jacqueline Emigh noted in *Computerworld,* the supply of available domain names is dwindling rapidly, particularly in the popular .com top-level domain. In some cases, the best domain names are already being used by other individuals or firms. Some larger businesses will register several different domain names in case they might be needed in the future, or in order to protect themselves against competing sites. But in other cases, the best domain names are held by cybersquatters or cyberpirates. These individuals register a number of domain names that are likely to be coveted by businesses in hopes of selling them in the future for a significant profit. This practice has developed into a sort of low level marketplace in which there are Web sites dedicated to trading—purchasing and selling—of registered domain names. One such Wed based trading business is located online at www.sedo.com.

CHOOSING AND REGISTERING A DOMAIN NAME

For small businesses hoping to establish a presence on the World Wide Web, choosing an Internet domain name is nearly as important as choosing a company name. The name must fit the firm's overall marketing strategy and convey a positive message to potential customers. In addition to registering a domain name for the company's Web site, small business owners might also consider registering the names of major products, important markets, or well-known slogans. As Bill Roberts explained in *Electronic Business,* small business owners must make sure that the domain names they choose are not overly long and avoid unconventional spellings that may be difficult for people to remember. Since doing business on the Internet immediately exposes companies to international markets, it is also important to be careful of trademark infringement issues and cultural problems in other languages.

There are a number of ways to handle the registration of an Internet domain name. In most cases, an Internet Service Provider (ISP) can register a small business's domain name and maintain the company's Web site on its server. The ISP can conduct an online search to make sure that the domain name does not duplicate any existing name or infringe on the trademark of any other business. Although registering through an ISP can simplify the process for small businesses, it is important for the business to secure ownership of the domain name. Otherwise, it may be difficult to keep the domain name if the company decides to change ISPs.

Small business owners can also register a domain name through Network Solutions Inc. (NSI), a private company which began registering names in 1993 through a cooperative agreement with the U.S. government. The process involves conducting a free online search, filling out a form on the NSI Web site (networksolutions.com), and paying a fee of approximately $35 for a single year of domain name ownership. Finally, small businesses can register domain names through the Internet Corporation for Assigned Names and Numbers (ICANN), a non-profit organization that has been taking over increased responsibility for the registration process (details are available online at www.icann.org).

With authority from the U.S. government, ICANN has begun addressing the problems of Internet site regis-

tration, including the diminishing supply of domain names and the resolution of disputes over names. As Walter Eidson outlined in the *Washington Business Journal,* ICANN implemented a new dispute resolution policy on January 1, 2000, to settle questions over ownership and use of popular domain names. In order to dispute another party's use of a domain name, a small business must prove that the name is identical or confusingly similar to a previously registered trademark and that the other party has no legitimate business interest in it. Businesses are unlikely to prevail in such disputes if the other party had registered the name in good faith and was using it for legitimate purposes. But businesses do have recourse in cases where the other party is using the name in bad faith—for example, holding it for the purpose of selling it, blocking the legitimate owner from using it, or attracting customers through deception.

SEE ALSO *Search Engine; Web Page Design*

BIBLIOGRAPHY
Dowling, Paul J., Jr., et al. *Web Advertising and Marketing.* Prima, 1996.

Eidson, Walter. "How to Protect, Defend an Internet Domain Name." *Washington Business Journal.* 14 January 2000.

Emery, Vince. *How to Grow Your Business on the Internet.* Third Edition. Coriolis Group, 1997.

Emigh, Jacqueline. "Domain Naming." *Computerworld.* 27 September 1999.

Porter, Monica. "Addressing an Investment Issue—Money Maverick Domain Names." *The Financial Times.* 11 March 2006.

Roberts, Bill. "The Name Game." *Electronic Business.* November 1999.

"The Value of a Domain Name." *Web Marketing Today Free Weekly.* 15 March 2006.

Hillstrom, Northern Lights
updated by Magee, ECDI

INTERNET PAYMENT SYSTEMS

In 2003, the most recent year for which statistics on electronic commerce were available at the time of writing, e-commerce had reached a record volume of $1,679 billion. The bulk of the volume, $1,573 billion, took the form of business-to-business transactions which, in the mid-2000s, still continued to be settled in the traditional manner—by sellers sending out invoices and receiving checks in the mail. But a small—if by any measure still significant—part of this e-commerce volume, $106 billion, represented online consumer purchases. Consumers used

Internet payment systems to pay for most of the goods or services bought. Payments were dominated by credit card transactions in which credit card information (owner's name, card number, type of card, expiration date) moved over secure communications lines in encrypted form to the vendor. According to Visa, more than 90 percent of all online sales are by way of credit cards. Payment also took other forms such as e-cash transactions involving prepaid credit cards and direct transactions between the vendor and the customer's bank. Some of this commerce, of course, took traditional off-line forms: orders were placed over the Internet but payments were arranged over the telephone or sent in before shipments took place; or shipments were made COD (cash on delivery).

SECURITY: THE DOMINANT ISSUE

The most important aspect of Internet payment systems is the security of the transactions—because human contact in online interactions is wholly replaced by images on screens and messages that come and go. The identity of the seller is often difficult for the buyer to confirm. Neither the seller's physical address nor telephone number may be listed on the Web page; the Web page may be a mirage created by images and photographs hiding a scam. The buyer therefore is at least initially wary in online purchasing situations. Can he or she trust this site to 1) safeguard credit card data, 2) actually ship something in exchange for a payment, and 3) guard its records from Internet bandits after the transaction closes?

In the same manner, the seller cannot see the buyer. When the buyer sends credit card information and the card checks out, the seller still doesn't know with any certainty that the party on the other end, hidden by the fog of cyberspace, is *real*: the buyer may have stolen the card or may maliciously intend later to deny that he or she actually made a purchase.

Linda Punch, writing for *Credit Card Management*, assembled some numbers from current research to show the extent of the security problem. Citing GartnerG2, a technology research service, Punch noted that 16 percent of consumers surveyed had been victimized by credit card fraud and 8 percent had been victims of identity theft. A 2005 Visa survey found that more than half of consumers responding (56 percent) avoided online shopping because they did not wish to give out their credit card numbers. Consumers are thus aware of problems and the majority may still be avoiding this type of purchasing.

Punch also noted that merchants are also victimized. In credit card parlance the word "chargeback" is used to indicate reversals of credit purchases when the buyer disputes having used the card or refuses payment claiming product defects. Merchants' chargeback experience

with Internet sales is significantly higher, at 1.14 percent of charges, than the same experience rate in physical stores (0.08 percent) and in mail-order/telephone-order situations (0.36 percent).

TECHNOLOGICAL DEVELOPMENTS

All communications over the Internet, indeed over any electronic system whatsoever, take place by means of protocols. The sender's and the receiver's systems are both designed to understand the protocol. Using the protocols' pre-set sequences of codes, the parties are able to establish a common set of rules for the dialogue to follow, not least such details as speed of transmission. This process is also known as handshaking. Once a communications channel is thus established, packets of information may be exchanged, each packet having a header, body, and trailer. Error checking is performed. Both sender and receiver calculate mathematical abbreviation of the message, a single number called its CRC (for cyclic redundancy check). The receiver checks its CRC against the one transmitted by the sender. If the two numbers match, all is well. If the CRCs don't match, the receiver requests retransmission. Packet follows packet until the transmission is terminated using the orderly etiquette prescribed by the protocol.

Heightened levels of security are introduced by using encryption of all or some of the data. The most widely used secure method of communication is known as SSL (for secure socket layer), a "layer" of security. SSL was first introduced by Netscape. SSL is an extension of standard protocols under which the level of security to be used is first established between a pair of communicators. Under SSL, the method of encryption to be used can be set or negotiated and encryption keys are exchanged. Use of encryption in either one or in both directions may be agreed upon. All this, of course, takes place automatically, machines murmuring to each other; users do not have to know the deep details. The cryptographic element, thus, becomes central to the security of the channel.

Modern Internet cryptography is known as public-key cryptography introduced by cryptologists Whitfield Diffie and Martin Hellman in 1976. Before the invention of this method, cryptology required that two parties exchanging encrypted information both had to possess the same key, one in order to encrypt the data and the other to use the same key to decode the message. Public-key cryptography requires two keys: a public key, known to both parties, and a private key, known only to the receiver of the data. Data can only be *en*coded by the public key, therefore the sender must have this key; but the data can only be *de*coded by the private key that the receiver controls. A mathematical relationship between the two keys, known only to the receiver, provides the security. A criminal or hacker who has the public key and the encoded message is virtually unable to derive the private key from these two elements of information. Thus this method is very safe. In a typical transaction the parties exchange public keys. Each encodes its message to the other by using the other's public key; each decodes the message received by its private key. Very sophisticated implementations of these systems are available. RSA Security Inc. is the leading provider of such encryption systems.

This level of security, while it protects credit card numbers very well, does not guarantee that the credit card holder isn't using a stolen card. For this reason the same public-key cryptography is used to encrypt additional information: authentication certificates and digital signatures. The certificates carry information about the parties and the digital signatures, which can be combined with digital date stamps, add yet another layer of authentication to a transaction.

The highest form of security, developed by Visa and MasterCard—with the contributions of Microsoft, IBM, GTE, Netscape, and others—is known as Secure Electronic Transport (SET). Under this protocol, the identities and rights of three parties are simultaneously established during a transaction: the card holder, the merchant, and the card issuing institution, each using certificates, signatures, and date stamps under the protective cloak of cryptography.

SET has not yet established itself widely in the mid-2000s because of its complexity. SSL transactions are still the dominant method of passing credit card information. Visa and MasterCard have introduced another less sophisticated authentication method—primarily to offer credit card holders added security. Card holders can register with the issuer of the card and provide additional authentication data (mother's maiden name, pet's name, and so on) maintained by the issuer. Once the card is thus registered, merchants are notified of this registration and can query card holders for additional authentication data before closing a sale.

GETTING PAID ONLINE

A small business intending to sell its products online must establish a merchant account at a bank and engage the services of a payment processing firm. The business may wish to begin by looking at processing firms which frequently represent banks. Conversely, many banks work with processing firms and will recommend those that they prefer. If the company already accepts credit cards in a store, its natural route is by way of the service bureau it uses for off-line sales. A set-up fee (around $50), monthly services fees (ranging from $40 to $300

based on volume), and transaction fees levied on the volume itself (ranging from 1.5 to 0.75 percent, depending on volume) should be anticipated. The numbers cited come from Yahoo's Small Business Merchants Solutions and, while representative, will vary from vendor to vendor. Three basic types of transactions are available: credit card, online check payment, and small-transaction payment systems (where transactions are a few dollars each), A merchant can sign up for one or two or three of these—each having a different cost. A very wide array of such services has developed—and thus a fair amount of homework is implied. Entering the phrase "payment processing firms" into a search engine like Google or Yahoo will produce an extensive listing of links and ads that will get the business started. Another way of testing the waters, of course, is to ask other merchants about the services they use.

Qualifying for a merchant account may require administrative efforts similar to getting a loan—because the bank will wish to satisfy itself about the business's qualifications. Working with the processing firm will involve the business in installation and testing of card authorization software that will communicate with the processing firm. The processing firm normally handles checking the validity of the credit card number, expiration date, and purchase amount, then provides the merchant with an authorization number. The preferred method for handling online sales is to pass the transaction information along to the payment processing firm for authorization while the customer is still online. An e-mail confirmation completes the transaction.

Internet payment systems, while already highly developed, are still evolving—becoming more secure, more straightforward, and, from the small business point of vantage, more competitive in price. In the mid-2000s many services are available. As electronic retailing continues its rapid growth, it is likely that a handful of major services will begin to emerge and dominate the market until, for the small business, getting online and getting paid online, will become ever more simple.

SEE ALSO *Online Auction*

BIBLIOGRAPHY

Beaudoin, Maria. "Web Checks." *Newsweek*. 11 August 2003.

Beaumier, Carol M. "Multifactor Authentication: A blow to identity theft?" *Bank Accounting & Finance*. February-March 2006.

Bick, Jonathan. "Authenticating and Enforcing E-signatures." *New Jersey Law Journal*. 7 June 2004.

Paret, Dominique. *RFID and Contactless Smart Card Applications*. John Wiley & Sons, 2005.

Lim, Chae Hoom, and Moti Yung, eds. *Information Security Applications*. Springer, 2005.

Loshin, Peter, John Vacca, and Paul Murphy. *Electronic Commerce.* Charles River Media, 2004.

O'Mahony, Donal, Michael A. Pierce, and Hitesh Tewari. *Electronic Payment Systems for E-Commerce.* Artech House, 2001.

Punch Linda. "Authentication's Tentative Gins: Visa and MasterCard have developed authentication systems that will make Internet transactions less vulnerable to fraud." *Credit Card Management.* May 2002.

"What is Public-Key Cryptography?" RSA Laboratories. Available from http://www.rsasecurity.com/rsalabs/node.asp?id=2165. Retrieved on 4 June 2006.

"With PayPal Backing, Will Micropayments Work This Time?" *CioInsight.* 12 September 2005.

Wolf, Daniel. "When Dial-Up Link Blocks the Extra Verification Call." *American Banker.* 9 May 2006.

Darnay, ECDI

INTERNET SECURITY

Internet security is a subset of actions aimed at securing information based on computers and in transit between them. In the modern environment the two subjects are closely linked. Neither computers nor the networks that connect them are inherently secure. Computers were subject to attack before the Internet became a public utility—because illegitimate software hidden on commercial diskettes could be fashioned to load itself on a computer and play havoc with data in memory or placed on a fixed drive. The Internet, by its very nature—initially conceived of as an open network to facilitate free exchange of ideas and information—is vulnerable. According to the Internet Systems Consortium (ISC), which conducts four surveys each year, in January 2006 there were some 395 million Internet *hosts* in operation—and billions of computers consulting billions of pages carried by those hosts. Despite best efforts, a system of this size and complexity will inevitably have points of entry that can be abused—and software programs frequently have unknown weaknesses that hackers (for fun) or criminals (for gain) discover and turn to their advantage until the flaws are fixed.

Computer networks hold valuable and often protected, private information, not least data on identities; credit cards; financial data; technical, trade, and government secrets; mailing lists; medical records; and the list could be continued. These data are vulnerable *on* the computer and *in transit.* The Internet, as a connector between computer systems, is also a highway of access to valuable data stores. The vulnerabilities are loss of data through malicious erasure, the acquisition of proprietary information, the manipulation of the data such as illegal withdrawals and transfers of funds, the capture and criminal use of credit cards or identities, and any and all unauthorized uses to which information may be put. Internet security breaches can also potentially have direct physical consequences if the wrong people hijack systems that control transportation or power systems. Computers have become so pervasive, and their networking so universal, that Internet security and security in general are closely linked objectives of society.

FORMS OF ATTACK

Internet security deals narrowly with one means by which computer crime (covered in more detail elsewhere in this volume) is committed. In the mid-2000s Internet-based criminal activity appears to be less of a threat than localized computer crime. This point was emphasized by Andrew Harbinson, a computer crime fighter working for Ernst & Young in Ireland. Harbinson wrote in *Accountancy Ireland* that the ratio between "insider" and Internet crime is roughly 3 or 4 to 1—and this despite a different trend in some reports. Since the corporate scandals of the early 2000s, many companies have been reluctant to report internal frauds fearing an adverse response from the stock market. Significant crime, according to Harbinson, reflects motive and opportunity—and insiders know systems much better and can exploit them more effectively than hackers fishing around from the outside.

Systems disruptions arising from the immaturity of teenaged hackers, the malicious intent of grownups, and the organized activities of pressure groups are the most common forms of Internet attack. These take the form of destructive or simply irritating software programs (viruses) that minimally "send a message," more seriously disrupt operation or cause shut downs, and in extreme forms cause serious loss of data. Other names associated with viruses are worms, Trojan horses, logic bombs, and sniffers—described further under *Computer Crimes* in this volume. Deliberate, organized, and sometimes automated programs to overload selected sites so that they are forced out of action are sometimes mounted by dissident groups. This type of action is known as "distributed denial of service." A common Internet-based crime is the theft of valuable lists—either for use or resale by the thief or as a means of blackmailing the target. Finally, spam, in the sense of undesired e-mail, is a nuisance and a bother but does not rise to the level of a vulnerability.

The National Institute of Standards and Technology (NIST), a government agency, defines seven categories of "incidents" (but numbered in good computer fashion from 0) used to sort out unusual network events in the federal government. These are Cat 0, Scheduled and

Planned Tests (and therefore not actual breaches, even if they appear as such); Cat 1, Unauthorized Access (actual penetration without authority); Cat 2, Denial of Service (by exhausting resources); Cat 3, Malicious Code (viruses, etc.); Cat 4, Improper Usage (a user violating established policies); Cat 5, Scans/Probes/Attempted Access (unsuccessful but potentially preparatory to an attack later); and Cat 6, Investigation (unconfirmed attempts not yet fully reviewed).

Notably, perhaps—and perhaps an indication of the general health of the Internet and its chief managers (the hosts, portals, the communications companies, and the government)—no major blackout of the Internet has taken place to date literally shutting down the World Wide Web as a whole or in some region of the world.

VULNERABILITIES

Internet vulnerability arises from human factors, failures of "defensive" technologies, and from weaknesses in software products or their interactions.

Access to systems is usually protected by passwords. Careless assignment, use, and storage of passwords is in part a human factor leading to vulnerabilities. The MITRE Corporation, with funding from the U.S. Department of Homeland Security (DHS), maintains Common Vulnerabilities and Exposures (CVE), a dictionary and reference system to databases that hold CVE data by many other organizations. MITRE's CVE Website identifies, from among 7,000 CVE entries, 1,117 which relate to password vulnerabilities. These vulnerabilities have frequently arisen because passwords, particularly Systems Manager passwords, have been stored in forms easily recognized by outsiders.

Perhaps the best known protection technology is the firewall, a software system that monitors a network's or a single computer's interactions with the Internet. Firewalls are designed to capture, store, and analyze "on the fly" a series of recent commands received from the Internet. The firewall accepts these commands and temporarily puts them in a buffer to look at them before letting them execute. It has its own database of patterns of commands which signal trouble. When it finds such a pattern in its buffer, it ignores that set of commands and thus protects the system.

Virus detection and monitoring programs work by incorporating logic and data which enable them to scan and thus to recognize viruses in their many forms before these are able to do any damage. Virus detection software, of course, is constantly updated as malicious ingenuity creates ever newer attempts at slipping into computers disguised in innocent forms like e-mail attachments. When intruders discover ways to penetrate firewalls or slip viruses past virus detectors, the system becomes vulnerable.

By far the largest number of vulnerabilities are created by undiagnosed weaknesses in operating systems and in ordinary software. Attackers probing systems either know about these weaknesses, or chance across and then learn to exploit them. Software development takes many people. Programs of real use tend to be complex. To test or debug programs developers use so-called "back doors" to enable them to interact with a running program; such back doors are sometimes "left open" but become known in the hacker community. The same aims are usually achieved in the same way in programming as in other fields; thus skilled developers will know where to look for exploitable features of a software system.

Hi-Tech Obscurity The diagnosis and cure of security breaches is a hi-tech specialization where even the highly computer-literate—indeed skilled programmers—will be entirely at sea without help. Three examples of CVE definitions from MITRE, plucked more or less at random, will make the point. CVE 2000-1936, for example, states: "UTStarcom BAS 1000 3.1.10 creates several default or back door accounts and passwords, which allows remote attackers to gain access via (1) field account with a password of '*field', (2) guru account with a password of '*3noguru', (3) snmp account with a password of 'snmp', or (4) dbase account with a password of 'dbase'." Come again? CVE 2006-1136 states: "Buffer overflow in the PostScript file interpreter code for Xerox CopyCentre and Xerox WorkCentre Pro, running software 1.001.02.073 or earlier, or 1.001.02.074 before 1.001.02.715, allows attackers to cause a denial of service via unknown vectors." CVE 2005-4660 states: "IPCop (aka IPCop Firewall) before 1.4.10 has world-readable permissions for the backup.key file, which might allow local users to overwrite system configuration files and gain privileges by creating a malicious encrypted backup archive owned by 'nobody', then executing ipcoprscfg to restore from this backup."

With some 7,000 such problem definitions on file, growing at the rate of around 100 per month, it is clear that the vulnerabilities of the highly sophisticated technical universe of the Internet are themselves hi-tech phenomena and therefore the preserve of specialists.

WHAT TO DO

Systems of defense against Internet attacks have evolved side-by-side with the aggression in a kind of serious version of the "Spy vs. Spy" cartoon series made famous by *Mad Magazine*. The three important actions available to individuals and businesses, however small, are 1) disciplined use of computer systems including careful password and e-mail control, 2) installation and upgrading of firewalls between internal networks and the Internet, 3) alertness to news stories about new viruses and breaches and promptly carrying out public recommendations, and 4) prompt reporting of breaches to the authorities as soon as they are detected.

The business owner has the chief responsibility to deny access to his or her systems to individuals who should not be using them. This is normally accomplished by using password control. In the modern environment we are required to use far too many passwords. Not surprisingly, we pick one we like and tend to stick with it. We use the same password for a number of different online accounts, at home, at the office. The capture of one somewhere can lead to its use elsewhere. In cases where good discipline is enforced, new passwords are issued at intervals—but people tend to forget them, with the consequence that they are often scribbled on the computer monitor lightly in pencil. Such careless practices, needless to say, are in part responsible for major breaches and much damage. Most viruses are transmitted as attachments to e-mails. Opening attachments from unknown e-mail transmitters is generally a bad idea—even when the message sounds plausible. A good rule to follow in such cases is that if the sender *really* wants me to open that mail, he or she will call. Idle curiosity causes many viruses to spread.

Most small businesses with networks will either engage a service firm to maintain and periodically check its system or will have in-house staff managing the function. Firewalls and virus-detection software require periodic maintenance and upgrading. Failure to do so can turn open the company's system to spammers who will use it as a transmission point—using up valuable processor power and eventually causing the company's own mail to be rejected by others—or worse. Old virus monitoring packages will be unaware of new worms, Trojan horses, and logic bombs. When news breaks indicating that some software program has a major flaw, producers of the software soon have "patches" ready to repair the vulnerability. It is a nuisance to download and install such patches, but failure to do so may be more costly. Pay me now or pay me later! Several Web sites provide free virus warnings and downloadable antivirus patches for Web browsers. Examples include www.symantec.com/ avcenter and www.ciac.org. The Computer Security Institute provides annual surveys on security breaches at www.gocsi.com. Another useful resource is the National Computer Security Association (www.ncsa.com), which provides tips on Internet security for business owners and supplies definitions of high-tech terms.

Systems breaches should be reported promptly. The business can do so by contacting US-CERT (United States Computer Emergency Readiness Team). This federal organization, formed in 2003, works with the Internet community to raise awareness of security issues and organize the response to security threats. The CERT Web site posts the latest security alerts and also provides security-related documents, tools, and training seminars. Finally, CERT offers 24-hour technical assistance in the event of Internet security breaches. Small business owners who contact CERT about a security problem will be asked to provide their company's Internet address, the computer models affected, the types of operating systems and software used, and the security measures that were in place.

For most small businesses, the Internet is a valuable resource. The effort required to play by the rules is relatively low. The costs, minimally in time, often in dollars, can be quite high even for minor problems like having one's server hijacked for spamming. When viruses destroy disks holding valuable data, costs can skyrocket. Caution, alertness, and discipline can prevent the worst of such problems. A good security policy therefore should be high on the agenda of the business owner.

SEE ALSO *Biometrics; Computer Crime; Data Encryption; Downloading Issues; Firewall; Spam; Virus*

BIBLIOGRAPHY
"Common Vulnerabilities and Exposures (CVE). The MITRE Corporation. 27 February 2006. Available from http:// cve.mitre.org/cve/index.html. Retrieved on 1 June 2006.

Federal Bureau of Investigation. *2005 FBI Computer Crime Survey.* Available from www.fbi.gov/publications/ ccc2005.pdf. Retrieved on 28 May 2006.

Gordon, Lawrence A., Martin P. Loeb, William Lucyshyn, and Robert Richardson. *2005 CSI/FBI Computer Crime and Security Survey.* Computer Security Institute. Available from http://www.gocsi.com. Retrieved on 29 May 2006.

Harbinson, Andrew. "Understanding Computer Crime: A beginner's guide." *Accountancy Ireland.* August 2005.

National Vulnerability Database. National Institute of Standards and Technology. Available from http://nvd.nist.gov/. Retrieved on 1 June 2006.

United States Department of Homeland Security. US-CERT. Available from http://www.us-cert.gov/. Retrieved on 1 June 2006.

Wallace, Ryan P., Adam M. Lusthaus, and Jong Hwan Kim. "Computer Crimes." *American Criminal Law Review.* Spring 2005.

Darnay, ECDI

INTERNET SERVICE PROVIDERS (ISPs)

An Internet Service Provider (ISP) is a company that provides third parties access to the Internet. Many ISP also offer other related services such as Web site design and virtual hosting. An ISP has the equipment and the telecommunication line access required to have a point-of-presence on the Internet for the geographic area served. An ISP acts as an intermediary between its client's computer system and the Internet. ISPs take several forms and offer a wide variety of services. They generally charge their customers for Internet access depending on their usage needs and the level of service provided.

TYPES OF ISPs

Internet access is available from a wide range of companies, including telephone and cable companies, online services, large national ISPs, and small independent ISPs. There are no reliable data on the number of ISPs in the market. An article in the *Philadelphia Business Journal* estimated that there were more than 7,000 firms providing Internet access in the United States by the middle of 2000. Other industry observers and participants dispute this figure suggesting that the number of ISPs is much lower. Whatever the actual number of ISPs may be, what is certainly clear is that those interested in setting up an Internet access account have many choices available. Choosing one that best suits one's needs takes a little study.

Online Services The first Internet service providers to become widely known weren't even full ISPs but rather what were known as online services because of their members-only offerings and somewhat limited full Internet access. These were America Online (AOL) and CompuServe. It is usually very easy to set up an account with one of the major online services. A computer user equipped with a modem can establish an account of this sort and begin surfing the Internet with just a few clicks of a mouse.

Although easy to establish and set up, an account with one of these large online services may not be the most appropriate way for a small business to access the Internet. Online services have some disadvantages. For example, access to a small business's web site and promotional information may be limited to members of the online service. In addition, many online services charge high advertising fees—or collect a percentage of sales—when they are used to conduct Internet commerce. Finally, some online services monitor and restrict the content of information sent via e-mail or posted to newsgroups.

National ISPs Another type of ISP is the national ISP. These include such companies as Earthlink and MindSpring who offer Internet access in a broad geographical area. Compared to local ISPs, these companies tend to offer higher-speed connections and greater long-term stability. Many national providers also offer a broad range of services, including long-distance telephone service, web site hosting, and secure electronic transactions. They are generally a good choice for small businesses that want employees to be able to access the Internet while traveling. They may also be convenient for businesses that operate in several locations and wish to use the ISP for all locations. The main disadvantages of the larger ISPs are that they rarely offer the level of personalized service available from smaller providers, and they may have so many customers that a small business's employees could have trouble gaining access during prime business hours.

Small ISPs Small, independent ISPs operate in many local or regional markets. These companies vary widely in size, stability, and quality of service. On the plus side, their access lines may be less busy than national ISPs. In addition, many smaller providers specialize in offering services to small businesses. Some of these ISPs may visit a small business customer's work site, evaluate the company's Internet access needs, and present different service packages. They may even assign a personal account representative to handle the small business's growing electronic needs.

FINDING AN ISP

The first step in selecting an Internet Service Provider for your small business is to compile a list of potential vendors. According to Vince Emery in *How to Grow Your Business on the Internet,* looking in the local telephone directory is not the best place to start. ISPs are typically classified under a variety of confusing headings in the yellow pages. In addition, making a random selection based on a advertisement is no way to guarantee good service.

Instead, Emery recommends beginning your search for an ISP on the Internet. There are several sites that list ISPs by geographic region and also include pricing and contact information. The oldest and best-known of these sites is The List (www.thelist.com), a searchable site with information on 8,300 providers worldwide. Another possible source of information is an organization named "The Directory" (www.thedirectory.org), which lists 13,000 ISPs. Yahoo! and other search engines also yield a great deal of information about service providers. Those without access to the Internet can obtain a printed guide to ISPs from Light Reading (www.lightreading.com).

Small business owners might also benefit from calling business associates, professional organizations, chambers of commerce, and local computer users groups to obtain suggestions and references for potential ISPs.

Another option is to hire a consultant to help you evaluate your business's Internet access needs, sort through the various options, deal with the telephone company and ISP candidates, and avoid unnecessary costs or services. In any case, Emery recommends obtaining at least three quotes, encompassing both price and services provided, before selecting an ISP for your small business.

CONSIDERATIONS IN CHOOSING AN ISP

In choosing among the various ISP options, the most important thing to consider is the needs of the business. How much work will be done online and how dependent will the business's communications be on e-mail and other online services? The answer to these questions will determine the range of bandwidth needed—a simple dial-up connection or a broad band connection capable of providing a number of people with high-speed connections simultaneously. By determining the bandwidth or speed requirements for the Internet connection one may help to limit the number of ISPs to consider.

The next step in choosing an ISP is eliminating those providers that 1) cost too much, 2) do not offer the services you need, or 3) cannot provide the right type of connection. One important factor for small businesses to consider is the availability of technical support. According to William Kilmer in *Getting Your Business Wired,* ISPs vary widely in the level of support they offer to customers. Online services make it easy to set up an Internet account, for example, but may not be able to provide the personal assistance a small business owner needs. It may be helpful to check the hours that customer support is offered by telephone, and also to inquire about the average time it takes the ISP to respond to requests for assistance.

A Web site for the company is something that many firms hope to establish while they get themselves connected to the Internet. Most ISPs are able to provide assistance to users in setting up a web site, and many ISPs provide space on their servers to host client Web sites. But Kilmer noted that small businesses may need to work with national providers or local providers that specialize in business services in order to establish a professional site with its own domain name. Otherwise, the business may be limited as to the size or usage of its site. Ideally, an ISP should be able to register a domain name, offer web designers to help create the site, and provide statistics on the number of people who access the site.

Another important factor to consider in choosing an ISP is the provider's tier rating. ISPs are rated according to their proximity to the backbone of the Internet, known as their point of presence (POP). Tier 1 providers—usually big companies like AT&T and Sprint—are linked directly to the Internet. Tier 2 providers lease their connections from Tier 1 companies, and so on down the line. The lower an ISP's tier rating, the further its connections lie from the Internet and the slower its access is likely to be. Kilmer recommends that small businesses work with ISPs rated Tier 3 or better.

Other technical considerations in choosing an ISP include the speed and redundancy of its connections. Ideally, an ISP should maintain several different connections to balance traffic and make sure that one is always available in case another fails. Finally, small business owners may wish to seek out an ISP that offers special packages for small businesses. For example, some providers offer several dial-up accounts or mailboxes for a reduced price. Others may offer special deals on registering a domain name and hosting a company web site.

ASPECTS OF THE INTERNET SERVICE AGREEMENT

When you have evaluated your business's needs as well as the various services available, it is time to sign a contract with an ISP. Kilmer emphasizes that small business owners should negotiate the terms of the contract rather than accepting a stock agreement. He also mentions a number of potential pitfalls avoid when making the final arrangements for Internet access through an ISP.

First, small business owners should look out for hidden charges. Sometimes the rate quoted by an ISP is a low monthly fee, but the contract specifies additional charges for such services as installing lines, providing training and technical support, or registering a domain name. Some ISPs even charge fees by volume of incoming or outgoing e-mail messages, or by the hour for access above a certain time limit. Second, Kilmer says to be sure that any contract specifies the length of time an ISP has to forward Internet traffic to and from your business. Otherwise, your small business may encounter delays ranging from minutes to days.

Third, you should make sure that your small business—rather than the ISP—owns the domain name of your web site. Registering a domain name online is a fairly simple and inexpensive process, and most ISPs will agree to host your site for a reasonable fee. If you decide to change ISPs in the future, owning the domain name allows you to take it with you to a new provider. Fourth, Kilmer warns small business owners never to allow an ISP to claim rights to any information or intellectual property from their companies. You may even wish to include language in the contract that prohibits the ISP from using your property (such as software stored on its server) or disclosing any information about your company.

Finally, once a small business signs up with an ISP and begins using the Internet, it is important to maintain a relationship with the provider. Most ISPs add new equipment on a regular basis, but they may not always notify customers of advances and updates. It may be a good policy to call technical support or your account representative several times per year in order to review your current settings and take advantage of potential performance improvements.

BIBLIOGRAPHY

Alwang, Greg. "At Your Internet Service." *PC Magazine.* 20 April 1999.

"Choosing An ISP." *National Underwriter Property & Casualty-Risk & Benefits Management.* 8 March 2004.

Dysart, Joe. "How to Choose an ISP to Meet Your Needs." *Selling.* April 2000.

Emery, Vince. *How to Grow Your Business on the Internet.* Third Edition. Coriolis Group, 1997.

Freeman, Paul. "How to... Select an Internet Service Provider." *Philadelphia Business Journal.* 14 July 2000.

Hise, Phaedra. *Growing Your Business Online: Small Business Strategies for Working the World Wide Web.* Holt, 1996.

Kilmer, William. *Getting Your Business Wired: Using Computer Networking and the Internet to Grow Your Business.* AMACOM, 1999.

Lake, Matt. "Unlimited Access." *Home Office Computing.* August 1998.

Hillstrom, Northern Lights
updated by Magee, ECDI

INTERNSHIPS

Internships are arrangements in which college students and career changers lend their talents to companies in return for an opportunity to develop business skills, learn about a new industry, and gain exposure to the work environment. Internship programs are set up as either non-compensated or compensated internships. Whether paid or unpaid, an internship position is often quite beneficial to the student who participates, for he or she receives "real world" business experience and an early opportunity to impress potential employers. Employers too benefit from internship programs by obtaining the services of skilled personnel for modest cost and by being exposed to new ideas and perspectives.

BENEFITS OF INTERNSHIP PROGRAMS

Internships are seen by college students as potentially valuable tools to explore general career avenues as well as specific companies. Such arrangements can provide them with valuable work experience (both practical and for résumé enhancement) and an opportunity to line up a job before graduation. In addition to securing good work experience, students also may be able to gain academic credit and financial compensation (albeit modest in size) for internships. As Steven Bahls and Jane Easter Bahls observed in *Entrepreneur,* "when an internship is set up through a local college or university, students can often obtain academic credit for their effort. The fact that they're receiving credit, though, doesn't mean they're not also entitled to minimum wage if your business derives immediate benefit from their labor."

Internship programs are also potentially valuable to employers. Unfortunately, some companies continue to regard interns as little more than a free source of labor to catch up on filing and other tedious office tasks. But many business owners and managers realize that internship programs can provide them with an early opportunity to gauge the talents of a new generation of workers and, in many cases, sell themselves as a quality place for students to begin their careers after they graduate.

Internship programs are understandably most prevalent in larger companies. But small companies can realize significant benefits as well. In many respects, interns can be ideal workers for small- and mid-sized companies. They are typically hungry to gain experience, eager to perform well, and willing to perform less-desirable tasks (although a steady diet of such tasks is apt to wilt their enthusiasm). Moreover, their fresh perspectives often challenge entrenched processes and attitudes that have outlived their usefulness. In addition, internship programs enable businesses to sort through a pool of potential employees. As the weeks pass, intern performances can be evaluated, and the pool can be culled down to good workers who are already familiar with the company. "The organization has the opportunity to observe the student at work and review work habits, technical ability, interpersonal skills, and adaptability before making a full-time commitment," wrote Larry Crumbley and Glenn Sumners in *Internal Auditor.* "Internships substantially reduce the risks in cases where offers of permanent employment might be made. Not only can the organization pre-screen the intern; the student also can learn about the company. The possibility of dissatisfied employees seems far less likely when both employers and employees have clear expectations of each other."

Interns also often prove to be invaluable recruiting tools when they return to campus. "A student returning from an internship with a favorable impression becomes an on-campus advertisement," observed Crumbley and Sumners. "Students listen to their peers and often trust their opinions more than those of campus representatives or professors. The cost of recruiting permanent employees is reduced as students become familiar with the opportunities the organization has to offer and top students are attracted to permanent positions."

SETTING UP INTERNSHIPS

Small businesses can benefit enormously when they establish an internship program, but such initiatives should not be launched in haphazard fashion. "Before you bombard colleges with leaflets announcing the availability of internships, decide what it is you want to achieve," counseled Deborah Brightman in *Public Relations Journal.* "These goals will help you determine the length of your program (two months should be a minimum) and the number of interns you should hire. The latter will also depend on your experience in managing an internship program, the available budget and space, and the number of people on staff who are available to supervise and train interns." In addition, companies should have a full understanding of the specific tasks to which interns will be assigned, and make plans to ensure that interns will have an opportunity to receive meaningful feedback on their performance.

A written plan providing details of the plan should then be prepared. This plan serves to educate potential interns and internship directors at colleges and universities, and can serve as a blueprint and guide for the company after the program is launched. "The plan," wrote Brightman, "should cover the program's purpose, recruitment, activities and responsibilities, evaluation, and follow-up steps. Be sure to make those employees who will be involved in the program aware of their parts before the interns arrive." Once these materials have been created, companies can go about the process of contacting appropriate colleges and universities, many of whom have established internship centers in recent years.

The Internet offers resources for publicizing an internship program as well. Bulletin boards exist that offer to match up students and others interested in participating in an internship program with employers offering such programs. One such service is offered by Wetfeet.com and can be located online at http://www.internshipprograms.com/.

The interviewing process for internships is not unlike the regular interview process in many respects. Factors such as attitude, academic achievement, and suitability for the job are paramount. Small business consultants also counsel their clients to set up summer internship programs when possible, since the pool of both full- and part-time students available for internships is deepest at that time of the year.

Internship programs need oversight and the choice of the supervisor is often essential in determining whether the program will be successful, mediocre, or an outright failure. Business experts recommend that interns be monitored by enthusiastic people who have time to tackle

the responsibilities associated with the job. "The internship director should have regular contact with both the interns and their . . . supervisors, monitoring the quality of work that's being performed, the experience the interns are gaining, and how happy they and their supervisors are with the program," wrote Brightman. "The supervisor must also be available to mediate any problems, oversee the recruitment process, and handle administrative details such as salary, office space, and evaluations." Finally, the supervisor should be able to handle necessary communications with the intern's university.

DISTINGUISHING INTERNS FROM EMPLOYEES

Internship programs can be tremendously helpful to small businesses, but there are legal hazards associated with such programs of which employers should be aware. "Unless your internship program is essentially educational," caution *Entrepreneur* contributors Steven Bahls and Jane Easter Bahls, "your interns may look suspiciously like employees, who are entitled to the federal minimum wage." Companies that operate internship programs that are found to be *not* primarily educational may run the risk of being found in violation of the Fair Labor Standards Act (FLSA), which applies to all companies with two or more employees and annual sales of at least $500,000.

Bahls and Bahls note that the U.S. Labor Department's *Wage and Hour Field Operations Manual* establishes six criteria for distinguishing interns from employees:

1. Interns may be trained using equipment and procedures specific to the employer, but internship experiences must be akin to experiences that they would be able to gain in a vocational school.

2. Regular employees cannot be displaced by interns, who should be closely supervised. "Farming work out to unpaid interns after a regular employee quits would raise a red flag," said Bahls and Bahls.

3. Interns are not guaranteed jobs at the completion of their internship. "If they are," wrote Bahls and Bahls, "the experience looks more like the training period at the start of a new job, for which they'd be entitled to fair wages."

4. Both employer and intern need to understand that training time does not entitle interns to wages.

5. Training should be primarily for the benefit of the intern.

6. Companies providing training to interns, noted Bahls and Bahls, "must derive no immediate advantage from the activities of the intern. . . .

Although an internship program will benefit your business over the long term by providing a pool of trained applicants with familiar work habits, it's not meant to be a source of free labor."

Most business consultants offer soothing advice to small companies that might be scared off by such criteria. They point out that the overwhelming majority of firms that establish internship programs are pleased with them, and as Bahls and Bahls wrote, "while the Labor Department closely adheres to its six criteria, courts tend to look at the spirit of the internship program as a whole."

Business owners and managers also need to be aware that, generally speaking, even unpaid interns have the same legal rights as employees when it comes to protection against discrimination or harassment. "It's best to cover them for workers' compensation, too," said Bahls and Bahls, "because if they're injured on the job and not covered, they can sue your business for medical expenses and possibly for negligence, which can subject your business to unlimited damages." However, interns do not have the same rights as employees in the realms of unemployment compensation or termination procedures.

BIBLIOGRAPHY

Atkinson, William. "Hiring Older Interns: With career-switching on the rise, your internship applicants might be more experienced than you'd expect." *HRMagazine* June 2005.

Bahls, Steven C., and Jane Easter Bahls. "Internal Affairs." *Entrepreneur*. November 1997.

Bell, Justine. "Marketing Academic Internships in the Public Sector." *Public Personnel Management*. Fall 1994.

"The Best 109 Internships." *The Princeton Review*. 28 January 2003.

Brightman, Deborah E. "How to Build an Internship Program." *Public Relations Journal*. January 1989.

Crumbley, Larry, and Glenn E. Sumners. "How Businesses Profit from Internships." *Internal Auditor*. October 1998.

Gornstein, Leslie. "Heard at Downsized Firms: 'Hey! Let the Intern Do It!'" *Crain's Chicago Business*. 5 September 1994.

Kaplan, Rochelle. "Hiring Student Interns." *Small Business Reports*. May 1994.

Ray Roberts. "Hiring Interns Can Lead to Real Insight into Your Company." *Conference & Incentive Travel*. October 2005.

Hillstrom, Northern Lights
updated by Magee, ECDI

INTERPERSONAL COMMUNICATION

Although interpersonal communication encompasses all forms of communicating, oral, written, and nonverbal, the term is usually applied to spoken communication that takes place between two or more individuals on a personal, face-to-face level. Some of the types of interpersonal communication that are commonly used within a business organization include staff meetings, formal project discussions, employee performance reviews, and informal chats. Interpersonal communication with those outside of the business organization can take a variety of forms as well, including client meetings, employment interviews, or sales visits. In order to understand the principles of effective interpersonal communication, it is helpful to look at the basic process of communication.

The basic process of communication begins when a fact is observed or an idea formulated by one person. That person (the sender) decides to translate the observation into a message, and then transmits the message through some communication medium to another person (the receiver). The receiver then must interpret the message and provide feedback to the sender indicating that the message has been understood and appropriate action taken.

Unfortunately, errors can be introduced during any phase of the communication process. For example, misunderstandings can occur when the sender does not possess a clear idea of the message he or she is trying to communicate, or has a clear idea but is not able to express it well. Errors in the process can also occur when the receiver does not listen carefully, infers a different meaning than what was intended by the sender, or fails to provide feedback. Ultimately, unclear, inaccurate, or inconsiderate business communication can waste valuable time, alienate employees or customers, and destroy goodwill toward management or the overall business.

INTERPERSONAL COMMUNICATION STYLES

In general terms, interpersonal communication can be classified as either one-way or two-way. One-way communication occurs when the sender transmits information in the form of direction, without any expectation of discussion or feedback. For example, a manager may stop by an employee's desk to inform him that a certain project will be due the following day. One-way communication is faster and easier for the sender—because he or she does not have to deal with potential questions or disagreement from the receiver—but tends to be overused in business situations.

In contrast, two-way communication involves the sharing of information between two or more parties in a constructive exchange. For example, a manager may hold a staff meeting in order to establish the due dates for a number of projects. Engaging in two-way communication indicates that the sender is receptive to feedback and willing to provide a response. Although it is more difficult and time-consuming for the sender than one-way communication, it tends to enable a clearer communications exchange by involving both parties.

In addition to being classified as one-way or two-way, interpersonal communication can also be broken down into a variety of styles, or specialized sets of behaviors. Bateman and Zeithaml identified six main styles of interpersonal communication that are used in business settings: controlling, egalitarian, structuring, dynamic, relinquishing, and withdrawal. "Different individuals use different communication styles," the authors noted. "A communicator should realize that some styles are more effective than others in certain situations."

Controlling The controlling style is a form of one-way communication that is used to direct others and gain their compliance. Managers using this style usually do not want feedback, and they tend to employ power and even manipulation to reinforce their message. Although the controlling style can be effective when it is used on occasion by respected individuals, particularly in times of crisis, it can also alienate workers.

Egalitarian In contrast, the egalitarian style is a form two-way communication that involves sharing information rather than directing behavior. It is used to stimulate others to express their ideas and opinions in order to reach a mutual understanding. In most situations—particularly when cooperation is needed—it is more effective than the controlling style.

Structuring The structuring style of interpersonal communication is used to establish schedules or impose organization. Managers using this style would be likely to cite company standards or rules. Though the structuring style may be necessary to inform others of goals or procedures when complex tasks must be performed by a group, it should usually be counterbalanced with the egalitarian style.

Dynamic The dynamic style is a high-energy approach that uses inspirational pleas to motivate another person to take action. This style can be effective in crisis situations, but it is generally ineffective when the receivers do not have enough knowledge or experience to take the required action.

Relinquishing The relinquishing style of interpersonal communication is deferential rather than directive. It is highly receptive to the ideas of others, to the point of shifting responsibility for communication to the receiver. For example, a manger employing this style might allow her staff to discuss and develop the final solution to a problem while making little comment. This style is particularly effective when the receivers have the knowledge, experience, and willingness to assume responsibility.

Withdrawal The withdrawal style is more like a lack of communication. Managers using this style try to avoid using their influence and may indicate a disinterest or unwillingness to participate in the discussion.

Finally, an often overlooked element of interpersonal communication is being a good receiver, which involves developing listening skills. Good listening skills can be vital in finding a solution to grievances or making successful sales calls. Listening involves showing an interest in the speaker, concentrating on the message, and asking questions to ensure understanding. One useful listening technique is reflection, or attempting to repeat and clarify the other person's message rather than immediately responding to it with a message of your own. Used correctly, reflection can allow managers to view issues from their employees' point of view. Some other keys to effective listening include: keeping an open mind rather than allowing emotions to intervene; finding a part of the subject that may have application to your own experience; and resisting distractions such as the speaker's mannerisms or clothing. It also helps to be prepared for the discussion, to take notes as needed, and to summarize the speaker's statements.

Strong interpersonal communication skills, utilizing a variety of styles and techniques, are particularly important for small business owners who must supervise the work of others. Bateman and Zeithaml described some of the characteristics of supervisors who receive high marks from their employees. First, these managers tend to communicate more than other managers, explaining the reasons behind decisions and providing advance warning of changes. Second, they tend to employ an egalitarian rather than controlling style when communicating with subordinates, asking for instead of demanding their compliance. Third, they tend to take others' needs and feelings into account when communicating. Finally, most effective managers are good listeners, giving careful consideration to employee concerns and taking the time to respond to questions and complaints.

SEE ALSO *Communication Systems; Intercultural Communications*

BIBLIOGRAPHY

Bateman, Thomas S., and Carl P. Zeithaml. *Management: Function and Strategy.* Irwin, 1990.

Clampitt, Phillip G. *Communicating for Managerial Effectiveness.* Sage Publications, Inc., 2004.

Koonce, Richard. "Language, Sex, and Power: Women and Men in the Workplace." *Training and Development.* September 1997.

Roper, Greg. "Managing Employee Relations: Develop interpersonal communications and conflict-management skills to better manage employee relations." *HRMagazine.* May 2005.

Smart, Karl L, and Carol Barnum. "Communication in Cross-Functional Teams." *Technical Communication.* February 2000.

Hillstrom, Northern Lights
updated by Magee, ECDI

INTRANET

An intranet often gets confused with the Internet. While there are a lot of similarities between them, they really are two different things. Simply put, the Internet is the global World Wide Web, while an intranet is a private computer network operating within a company. Both the Internet and an intranet use similar communication protocols (like TCP/IP) and offer many of the same functional features like e-mail and bulletin boards. One main difference is that an intranet is an internal and private network. Access to a company network (an intranet) is controlled whereas access to the Internet is open to anyone with physical access. Most company intranets are set up to include Internet access as one of the functions provided but the inter company network, or intranet is a separate entity and not part of the Internet.

When they were first introduced, intranets were dismissed by critics as the latest in a seemingly endless parade of technological fads and buzzwords. That soon changed as businesses with intranets began to reap benefits that were apparent to others.

A company may wish to set up an intranet for many reasons. Among them is the speed of communication that can be gained by the broad bandwidths that are used in intranets. These speeds allow for fast e-mail systems and the rapid exchange of documents. The private internal networks offer security and protection in the form of the aforementioned firewalls as well as password-protected access and secure servers. The use of an intranet allows companies to share information internally easily and in so doing to manage the efforts of many employees quickly. Less paperwork, increased productivity, added flexibility, and versatility are other benefits that may be gained through the use of a well-designed intranet. All of this adds up to a bottom line that is attractive in any business decision: the ability to save money and increase profits.

An **ex**tranet is a part of a company's **in**tranet that can be accessed by users outside of the company. Clients, vendors, suppliers, and business partners are just a few examples of the types of people who would benefit from this type of private network. They can exchange large volumes of data using Electronic Data Interchange (EDI), share exclusive information, collaborate on joint business ventures, participate in training programs, and share services between the companies. An extranet is a way to telecommunicate and share business information securely without having to worry about it being intercepted over the Internet. This is achieved for an extranet in much the same way that it is done for an intranet, namely through the use of extra security and privacy measures which include firewalls, password restrictions, and data encryption.

INTRANET APPLICATIONS

Intranets may be set up to provide a company with any of a number of functions. Most of these are related to communications in one form or another and use the same basic computer software applications as are used on the Internet. Often these applications are referred to as Web applications but in the context of an intranet it is important to distinguish between the "web" like functionality and the fact that it is being applied within an intranet and not on the Internet.

E-mail The most popular intranet application is interoffice e-mail. This capability allows the employees of a company to communicate with each other swiftly and easily. If the intranet has access to the Internet, e-mail can be accessed through the Internet connection. If the intranet is running without the Internet, special e-mail software packages can be bought and installed so that employees can take advantage of its many benefits.

Electronic Publishing An intranet has many other different applications that can be utilized by a company. These include the electronic publishing of corporate documents, electronic or Web forms, and interactive database links that allow users to access information. Newsletters, information on benefits and 401(k) enrollment, job listings and classifieds, libraries, stock quotes, maps, historical data, catalogs, price lists, information on competitors' products, and customer service data are just a few examples of these types of applications. In addition, there are several other main applications that are very popular in the intranet format.

E-forms Every type of company has to deal with forms of some sort. This is another area where paperwork can become a problem for a business. Intranet servers can be equipped with programs that allow for forms to be filled out electronically. They could also be downloaded and printed out by the users themselves, which would cut down on the time it would take to distribute these forms manually.

Organizational policy and procedure manuals are also handy to have on an intranet. Unlike printed hard copies, online manuals can be easily accessed by all employees at any time. They are also easier to organize online, and can be indexed by subject and attached to a search engine to provide for easier navigation through the manual. In addition, changes can be made more quickly and easily when they are in this format. Converting printed materials to Web browser readable formats is fairly simple and requires either an appropriate html translator or a way for the original word processor documents to be launched with a specific application.

Inter-company Directories Phone directories are another useful intranet applications. Again, this type of application cuts down on paperwork and the time and money it takes to produce hard copies of these directories. Instead, employee names, titles, duties, departments, phone and fax numbers, e-mail addresses, and even photographs can be stored in an online directory. They then can be easily searched and updated at any time with minimal effort. It is suggested that a few paper copies of the employee directory and other important records be kept on hand in the event that the intranet is experiencing technical difficulties.

Organizational Charts Online organizational charts are a useful way for employees to see the hierarchy of their company. These charts can describe who reports to whom, the specific duties of a person or department, and the structure of the organization. They can be set up in either graphic or text formats on an intranet and updated every time there is employee turnover or a change in job title or responsibilities.

Chat Rooms While somewhat complicated, intranets can be equipped with software to allow for live chat rooms or instant messages so that employees can communicate with each other online about work-related subjects. If a company is considering this form of communication, they should first form a policy about what can be discussed in an intranet chat. Chat room moderators and software to log the chats for future reference should also be considered. Despite these options, it is still difficult to see live online chats replacing traditional company meetings anytime soon.

DESIGNING AN INTRANET

There are many tools at managers' disposal to successfully implement an intranet. These include html editors, data-base and forms interfaces, java applets, and java script. An intranet must use these tools to be designed well enough to fully maximize its potential. When designing an intranet, careful attention must be paid to the details that will allow employees to find the information that they are looking for in an easy manner. Just because an intranet is only seen by employees and not by clients or the general public, this is no excuse for a company to take the easy way out and cut corners with design. Well-organized intranets with a pleasing graphic design sense are usually more efficient and much appreciated by the employees who use them.

According to intranet experts Anthony Schneider and Christopher Davis, "Successful process-oriented intranets look and work as differently as the processes they enable, but they share several common characteristics. First, they are built on smart information design. Second, they focus on tasks, not documents, and aim to integrate those tasks into distinct processes. Finally, the best intranets encourage collaboration by creating shared and familiar spaces that reflect the personality of the company and create a common ground for all employees."

Since individual tasks are generally a small portion of a bigger task, intranets should be organized in such a way that the related individual tasks are grouped together. These tasks can be simple or complex, but as long as they all contribute to the same overall process, employees will benefit from the easy access to information that this sort of design provides.

Intranets are useful in bringing employees from different departments together. They can even help employees of the same company who work in different locations to communicate more successfully. Through an effective design, these departments can collaborate and solve problems by using the intranet as a tool rather than relying on more traditional business ideas like meetings and conference calls.

The bottom line is that an intranet, like any corporate communications tool, is a reflection of the business that runs it. A company that is well organized will be able to design an intranet in such a way to best suit their needs. As Schneider and Davis state, "As the intranet creates new forms of collaboration, it will challenge traditional ways of doing work and obtaining information. For the intranet to be successful, it must provide ways of empowering all employees, offering concrete incentives for employees to use, and encourage the use, of the intranet. The process-oriented intranet, then, is 'in sync' with the company it works for. And this is where graphic design, tone and standards emerge as vital to the intranet's success. Like it or not, intranets have personalities, which are amalgams of visual style, tone and content. An intranet that reflects the culture of its company will make employees feel more at home, will help dispersed employees feel that they share the same space, and will encourage collaboration and communication around the processes they support."

THE COST OF SETTING UP AND RUNNING AN INTRANET

Initially, a business that wishes to set up an intranet has to consider the following costs: 1) hardware (including the server and network adapter); 2) software and utilities, and 3) installation and maintenance. A simple intranet may be set-up rather quickly if the company involved already has computers that are networked using the common TCP/IP communications protocol. To this network of computers one need only add an extra machine to act as a server. This extra machine will have to have the proper Web server software and network card installed. After everything is up and running, upgrades to the hardware will have to made from time to time to handle increasing traffic. New software like multimedia applications and interactive forums as well as upgrades to existing applications are all essential. The labor of employees who maintain the intranet is an ongoing cost, as are the costs to publish and archive data.

On the other hand, since intranets were designed to save time, they can usually be counted on to save money over time. By cutting down on routine communication, employees can refocus their efforts to better performing their duties. Employees who use the intranet to its fullest potential will discover that the benefits of e-mail, reduced paperwork, and easy access to information will increase their productivity. Both the employee and the employer benefit in this situation. As mentioned previously, company literature that is stored and distributed online rather than through traditional hard paper copies also cuts down printing and distribution costs. Large companies sometimes notice a savings of tens of thousands of dollars when they post their documents online.

In an article that appeared in *Intranet Communicator*, however, Schneider and McGrath warned managers not to expect too much too soon: "Review the existing return on investment studies or question company executives on their claims of multimillion dollar savings, and one finds that calculating intranet ROI is more art than science and more 'guesstimate' than calculation. Like the sweeping claims made for corporate Web sites a few years ago, many of the projections of ROI measured in thousands of percent may fade as organizations begin to experience the cost of ramping up, maintaining and administering intranets across thousands of users. Not to mention incorporating the inevitable upgrades and conducting enterprise-wide training."

MANAGING AN INTRANET

As the cost to maintain an intranet grows over time, so does the time and effort to maintain it. Managers often spend considerable energy trying to keep up with increased traffic and other forms of growth. Proper planning (including having the best Web and network tools available) is one way to cut down on the manpower required to run an intranet. Employees who maintain the intranet must be experts in the area of Web publishing. Managing the server, developing applications, and converting documents and databases to html format are just some of the duties found in this area.

Many companies decide to hire an outside firm to run their intranet rather than do so themselves. This cuts down on the number of internal problems and potential disasters and gives management peace of mind to know that trained professionals are handling this task. If this route is taken, it is important for management to keep some employees dedicated to intranet issues in case the relationship with the outside supplier does not end up working out.

Once the intranet is set up, it is important to keep its content current in order to keep employees using it in the manner for which it was intended. Regular updates regarding company news and the promotion of the intranet from upper management are just two ways to keep it from growing obsolete before its time.

Large corporations like IBM, Ford Motor Company, and the Turner Entertainment Group have all had success implementing intranets into their corporate structure. But these giant companies are not the only ones who have been able to exploit the benefits of intranets to their fullest advantage. Small businesses have taken notice as to how intranets help cut down on costs and increase productivity. Since small businesses often also have less red tape to deal with than larger corporations, a full-fledged intranet or even a test version can often be set up quickly and easily. Once management and employees become familiar with how the intranet works, the possibilities for successful utilization are great.

BIBLIOGRAPHY

Denton, Keith D. *Empowering Intranets to Implement Strategy, Build Teamwork, and Manage Change* Praeger/Greenwood, 30 December 2002.

Hopkins, Bryan, and James Markham. *Using Intranets to Improve the Effectiveness of Your People.* Gower Publishing Limited, August 2004.

Schneider, Anthony, and Christopher Davis. "Intranet Architecture: Integrating Information Design with Business Planning." *The Complete Intranet Resource* Available from http://www.intrack.com/intranet/.

McGrath, George, and Anthony Schneider. "Measuring Intranet Return On Investment." *Intranet Communicator.* June/July 1997.

Hillstrom, Northern Lights
updated by Magee, ECDI

INTRAPRENEURSHIP

Intrapreneurs are employees who work within a business in an entrepreneurial capacity, creating innovative new products and processes for the organization. Intrapreneurship is often associated with larger companies that have taken notice of the rise in entrepreneurial activity in recent years; these firms endeavor to create an environment wherein creative employees can pursue new ways of doing things and new product ideas within the context of the corporation. But smaller firms can instill a commitment to intrapreneurship within their workforces as well. In fact, small businesses, which often originate as entrepreneurial ventures, are ideally suited to foster an intrapreneurial environment, since their owners have first-hand knowledge of the opportunities and perils that accompany new business initiatives. For larger companies, nurturing an environment of intrapreneurship is a way to recapture a dynamic spirit while for smaller companies, it can be a way of maintaining the entrepreneurial drive from which they began.

Intrapreneurship practices have developed in response to the modern world's rapidly changing marketplace. Businesses of all sizes have long had internal units dedicated to research and development and new product development. Nonetheless, the task of maintaining a creative environment in which innovative ideas may be nurtured is not an easy one and the larger the organization the more difficult that may be. As an organization grows it naturally becomes more bureaucratic and for people of a creative bent a bureaucratic environment can be stifling. Frequently, organizations loose creative people as they grow. Intrapreneuring in its current form represents the determination of employers to solve the resulting brain drain. They are doing so by creating the environment and incentives for entrepreneurship within their existing business operations.

Small businesses have a natural advantage in terms of establishing such an environment, although it may not come naturally even for a smaller business. Internal "incubators" are one innovative example of the trend towards intrapreneurship. In these programs, employees can use the company's resources (including their already established name and reputation, as well as management experience, financial assistance, and infrastructure) to build and promote their own new business ideas. These and similar arrangements enable companies to stem the loss of ambitious and talented employees to entrepreneurial ventures. Entrepreneurial-minded employees, meanwhile, "get the challenge—and the profits—of creating their own 'companies' with little of the risk they would face on their own," observed David Cuthill in *Los Angeles Business Journal.*

ORGANIZATIONAL CHARACTERISTICS THAT ENCOURAGE INTRAPRENEURSHIP

The single most important factor in establishing an "intrapreneur-friendly" organization is making sure that your employees are placed in an innovative working environment. Rigid and conservative organizational structures often have a stifling effect on intrapreneurial efforts. Conservative firms are capable of operating at a high level of efficiency and profitability, but they generally do not provide an environment that is conducive to intrapreneurial activity. Some keys to instilling an intrapreneurial environment in a business include the following:

1. Support from ownership and top management. This support should not simply consist of passive approval of innovative ways of thinking. Ideally, it should also take the form of active support, such as can be seen in mentoring relationships. Indeed, the small business owner's own entrepreneurial experiences can be valuable to his firm's intrapreneurial employees if he makes himself available to them.

2. Recognition that the style of intrapreneurialism that is encouraged needs to be compatible with business operations and the organization's overall culture.

3. Make sure that communication systems within the company are strong so that intrapreneurs who have new ideas for products or processes can be heard.

4. Intelligent allocation of resources to pursue intrapreneurial ideas.

5. Reward intrapreneurs. All in all, intrapreneurs tend to be creative, dedicated, and talented in a variety of areas. They are thus of significant value even to companies that do not feature particularly innovative environments. Their importance is heightened, then, to firms that do rely on intrapreneurial initiatives for growth. Since they are such important resources, they should be rewarded accordingly (both in financial and emotional terms). For while intrapreneurs may not want to go into business for themselves, they still have a hunger to make use of their talents and a wish to be compensated for their contributions. If your small business is unable or

unwilling to provide sufficient rewards, then it should be prepared to lose that intrapreneur to another organization that can meet his/her desires for professional fulfillment.

6. Allow intrapreneurs to follow through. Intrapreneurs who think of a new approach or process deserve to be allowed to maintain their involvement on the project, rather than have it be handed off to some other person or task force. Ensuring that the individual stays involved with the initiative makes sense for several important reasons. The intrapreneur's creativity and emotional investment in the project can be tremendously helpful in further developing the process or product for future use. Moreover, they usually possess the most knowledge and understanding of the various issues under consideration. Most importantly, however, the small business enterprise should make sure that its talented and creative employees have continued input because not allowing them to do so can have a profoundly morale-bruising impact.

SEE ALSO *Entrepreneurship; Innovation*

BIBLIOGRAPHY

Carrier, Camille. "Intrapreneurship in Large Firms and SMEs: A Comparative Study." *International Small Business Journal.* April-June 1994.

Carrier, Camille. "Intrapreneurship in Small Businesses: An Exploratory Study." *Entrepreneurship: Theory and Practice.* Fall 1996.

Cutbill, David. "Incubators: The Blueprint for New Economy Companies." *Los Angeles Business Journal.* 27 March 2000.

Fattal, Tony. "Intrapreneurship at Work: Championing projects to push innovation in your company." *CMA Management.* November 2003.

Huggins, Sheryl E. "Internal Moonlighting: Use Your Day Job to Branch Out on Your Own." *Black Enterprise.* October 1997

Millner, Marlon. "Intrapreneurship: Techie Turns System He Built for Former Employer into a Small Business." *Washington Business Journal.* 1 May 1998.

Oden, Howard W. *Managing Corporate Culture, Innovation, and Intrapreneurship.* Greenwood Press, 1998.

Pinchot, Gifford, and Ron Pellman. *Intrapreneuring in Action: A Handbook for Business Innovation.* Berrett-Koehler, 1999.

Pryor, Austin K., and E. Michael Shays. "Growing the Business with Intrapreneurs." *Business Quarterly.* Spring 1993.

Sathe, Vijay. *Corporate Entrepreneurship: Top Managers and New Business Creation.* Cambridge University Press, 26 June 2003.

Hillstrom, Northern Lights
updated by Magee, ECDI

INVENTIONS AND PATENTS

A patent is a document that secures to an inventor the exclusive right to sell, make, or otherwise use his or her invention for a specified number of years. The document details the terms under which the government has granted the inventor full possession of the invention. These terms of possession or "intellectual property right" include specifications designed to exclude all others from making, using, or selling the invention in the United States for the life of the patent. The patent also provides rightful patent holders with specific legal steps that can be taken to stop (or be compensated for) instances in which others have infringed on the patent.

Patented inventions have spawned thousands of small businesses over the years. Not all of these businesses have succeeded, of course; some were predicated on new products or designs that were fundamentally flawed, while others faded because of operational problems, economic trends, or personal frailties. But countless successful entrepreneurs have launched their businesses on the strength of a single invention, and patents continue to stand as among the most valuable assets of thousands of small business owners across the nation.

TYPES OF PATENTS

Inventors may apply for patents on inventions in three major categories: utility patents, design patents, and plant patents.

Utility Patents Utility Patents are the most common kind of patents. They are granted to inventors who, according to the U.S. Patent and Trademark Office (PTO), invent or discover any new and useful process, machine, manufacture, or compositions of matter (mixtures of ingredients, chemical compounds), or any new and useful variations of existing products, processes, or compositions. The legal definition of "process" in this instance includes new industrial or technical methods. Utility patents are the most complex of the three kinds of patents, for they require the patent applicant to provide a full description of the invention's functional and/or structural features (often including detailed drawings) as well as the inventor's explanation of what he or she feels is "patentable." Inventors filing utility patents subsequently are more likely to secure legal help in making certain that all details of the patent are adequately addressed. In recent years, the greatest increase in this kind of patent application has been seen in Internet-related business methodologies and innovations. In 2005, 381,797 Utility Patent applications were filed with the PTO and 151,079 were issued.

Design Patents Inventors can also obtain patents on the appearance of a product, provided that it is a new and original design. As Richard C. Levy noted in his *Inventor's Desktop Companion,* "if you've invented any new, original, and ornamental designs for an article of manufacture, a design patent may be appropriate. A design patent protects only the appearance of an article and not its structure or utilitarian features." Thomas Field, author of the Small Business Administration's *Avoiding Patent, Trademark and Copyright Problems,* pointed out that both design patents and utility patents "do more than prevent copying; they forbid the making, using or selling of an invention similar to or the same as the protected invention," even in situations where the second invention was independently created. In 2005, 25,304 Design Patent applications were filed with the PTO and 13,395 were issued.

Plant Patents This kind of patent is granted to anyone who invents or discovers and asexually reproduces any distinct and new variety of plant, including cultivated sports, mutants, hybrids, and newly found seedlings. The PTO does not grant plant patents, however, for tuber-propagated plants or plants found in an uncultivated state. Asexually propagated plants, noted Levy, are those that are reproduced by means other than from seeds, such as rooting of cuttings, layering, budding, grafting, and inarching. Plant patents comprise only a small minority of the total number of patents that have been bestowed by the PTO. In 2005, 1,288 Plant Patent applications were filed with the PTO and 816 were issued.

Although millions of patents have been granted in the United States and other countries over the years, there are many things that are not eligible to receive patent protection. These include general business ideas and strategies, printed material, scientific theories, mathematical formulas, and obvious changes to existing items, although some of the above can be legally protected in other ways. Printed material, for instance, can be protected through copyrights.

FILING A PATENT

Patents are arranged according to a massive classification system encompassing more than 400 subject classes and 115,000 subject subclasses. The *Index to the U.S. Patent Classification System,* an alphabetical subject listing of these various classes and subclasses, is produced by the PTO to aid searchers of the system. "The Classifications," wrote Levy, "are to searching a patent what the card catalog is to looking for a library book. It is the only way to discover what exists in the field of prior art [prior patents]. The Classifications are a star to steer by, without which no meaningful patent search can be completed."

The *Index,* coupled with the *Official Gazette of the United States Patent and Trademark Office,* the *Manual of Classification,* are among the most important tools available to patent searchers.

Another important cog in the PTO's efforts to disseminate information about patents to the public is the Patent and Trademark Depository Library (PTDL), a national network of academic, research, and public libraries. Many inventors are frequent users of often-extensive PTDL resources.

Conducting a Patent Search Inventors, lawyers, and patent experts all advise inventors armed with a possible new product or design to undertake a comprehensive patent search before taking any other steps. "You cannot avoid doing a search," Levy flatly stated. "The [Patent and Trademark Office] examiner will do one anyway and if your application is rejected based upon prior art (patents that have previously issued), you'll have lost the application cost not to mention the significant time and energy you invested."

Patent searches can be mounted in one of three ways. Some inventors choose to undertake the task themselves, often with the aid of patent software programs. But the majority chooses to secure the services of a patent attorney or a professional patent search firm. Patent attorneys typically hire professional researchers to do the actual patent search; the turnaround time with lawyers who specialize in handling such searches is usually fast, but they are also expensive because of the mark-up charge that attorneys impose. Other options include inventor associations, university intellectual property departments, or patent search firms. Patent search companies can be found in local yellow pages, but inventors need to be careful in making agreements with such firms. Some are perfectly legitimate, but others prey on unsuspecting inventors, saddling them with service contracts or other bad business arrangements. Given this reality, inventors should ask for references, evidence that the search firm has prior experience in the field in which their inventions are classified, and a signed letter of non-disclosure before agreeing to any arrangement with a search firm.

The cost of a search can vary substantially, depending on the nature of the search. As Levy remarked, "there are different charges for different assignments (for example, searching utility patents versus design patents). Electronic, chemical, biological, botanical, and medical searches are often more expensive. And, in most cases, there will be incidental charges for copies, phone and fax, online fees, and shipping and handling of your materials. This is all standard." Another fact that can influence the final cost is turnaround time. Some patent search services now offer same-day service, but at higher prices than their usual searches.

Once a patent search has been completed, the inventor can proceed accordingly. In instances where the invention is in the public domain (a patent on the invention has expired), the inventor is, according to Field, "free to manufacture and market it without concern for the patent laws. Also, even if the inventor didn't find exactly what he or she originally had in mind, a host of good and freely used ideas that are even better might have been discovered. These alone could be worth several times the price of the search in saving research and development time."

If the inventor finds that any part of his or her proposed product or design is covered by a current patent, then the inventor can either drop the idea or approach the patent holder about securing a license to use it. "Infringing on a current patent exposes one to a suit for damages as well as an injunction against future use," warned Field. "Even an injunction might mean substantial costs, including the loss of current inventory, and a patent covering even a small feature of the new [product] might give rise to the need to retool. Although deliberate infringement is more serious, ignorance of others' patents is no defense."

If one or more elements of the proposed product or design appear to be new, with notable advantages over prior patents, then the inventor can submit a patent application. Inventors should be sure that they do not let their enthusiasm get the better of them in such instances. If he or she begins selling the product or design without first filing an application for patent, then he or she forfeits any possibility of securing patent rights in the United States after one year. In addition, the inventor loses all possible protection in most other countries.

APPLYING FOR A PATENT

Most experts counsel inventors to retain patent counsel to handle utility patents (although they are permitted to make utility patent applications themselves if they so desire). Utility patent applications are complex documents with myriad requirements, and as Levy indicated, "smart inventors use experienced patent counsel to assure that they obtain the strongest patent protection available on their inventions. There is too much at stake. Smart inventors do not rely on patent-it-yourself books." Design patent applications, however, are far less complicated, so many inventors take care of those documents themselves.

Patent Attorneys Before making an arrangement with a patent attorney, savvy inventors take steps to ensure that they have found competent, responsible legal counsel. The first step is to make sure that the lawyer is registered

with the Patent and Trademark Office. Attorneys listed with the PTO are required to have minimum academic and professional qualifications, and must pass a PTO examination.

Inventors should also make certain that their legal counsel is familiar with the field or industry in which the invention would be used. In addition, they should do their best to insure that their attorney has all relevant information needed to make the best possible patent application. Finally, experts counsel inventors to shop around to find the best combination of price and value, and they encourage them to secure written agreements on attorney fees.

Patent Drawings Patent experts advise inventors to secure the services of an experienced patent draftsman when the time comes to make patent drawings. "The requirements for drawings are strictly enforced," warned Levy. "Professional draftsmen will stand behind their work and guarantee revisions if requested by the PTO due to inconsistencies in the drawings.... Because the design patent is granted for the appearance of the article, the drawing in the design patent is more critical than the drawing in a utility patent. The design drawing is the disclosure of the claimed design, whereas the utility drawing is intended to provide only an exemplary illustration of some aspects of the mechanism described in the specification and claims."

Patents and the PTO It generally takes the Patent and Trademark Office a little over 18 months to process patent applications and issue approved patents. Examinations of patent applications, which are undertaken in the order in which they are received, are arduous exercises, encompassing inspection of legal compliance and comprehensive searches to ensure the invention's legitimacy.

If an application is approved, then the inventor can proceed with his business plan, whether that involved launching a small business or seeking buyers for the invention. Many applications, however, are rejected when they are first submitted. Even applications for genuinely new products or designs sometimes need changes to meet PTO requirements. In instances in which the application is rejected, the inventor has limited options. The inventor can prepare a response to the examiner's stated grounds for rejection, explaining why he or she believes that the examiner erred; this is a viable step, and one which sometimes convinces examiners to reconsider. The inventor can also offer amendments to the application designed to assuage the examiner's objections.

On many occasions, however, the examiner will remain unpersuaded and will reject the inventor's claims.

If this happens, the inventor can lodge appeals with the PTO commissioner and, after that, the Board of Patent Appeals and Interferences. If the application is still deemed unacceptable, and the inventor remains determined to pursue the issue, he or she can then turn to the U.S. court system. The Court of Appeals for the Federal Circuit and the U.S. District Court for the District of Columbia have both heard such cases.

Fees Receivers of patents must pay fees to the PTO for services rendered when a patent is reviewed. In 1982 a law was passed that cut some of these fees (patent application, extension of time, revival, appeal, patent issues, statutory disclaimer, maintenance on patents) for "small entities." Small entities were held to include independent inventors, small businesses, and nonprofit organizations. In addition, all utility patents are subject to the payment of maintenance fees that must be paid to keep the patent going. These payments are made at several different points of the patent's life. Inventors need to heed this payment schedule closely, for nonpayment may result in the premature expiration of the patent (a six-month grace period is typically provided during which the fee can be paid, albeit with a surcharge). Inventors who secure the services of a patent attorney generally do not have to worry about this scenario as much, since a competent attorney will notify them of impending maintenance fee payments.

In recent years, the government's decision to retool the PTO so that it could operate without federal funding has triggered significant increases in PTO fees. In 1991 Congress dramatically raised patent application fees to cover the Office's operating costs, but by the mid-1990s this income was being redistributed to pay for other government programs or address the federal budget deficit. The PTO was subsequently forced to mull additional fee increases, which angered many members of the small business community who felt that such increases disproportionately impact individual inventors and entrepreneurs. However, one of the provisions of the American Inventors Protection Act of 1999 reduced certain patent fees.

In December 2004 a new Patent and Trademark Office fee schedule went into effect for the years 2005 and 2006 as part of the Consolidated Appropriations Act. Fees vary widely for different application forms and services. The range for initial patent application fees is between $50 and $300 and for each it is half the full fee for applicants that qualify as small entities. A full list of fees is posted on the PTO Web site located at http://www.uspto.gov/.

U.S. Patents and GATT The 1994 General Agreement on Tariffs and Trade (GATT) also brought significant changes to U.S. patent law. The biggest one changed the duration of patent protection. Prior to GATT, patents lasted for 17 years (14 years for design patents) from the date that the patent was granted. After GATT, patent terms were extended to 20 years *from the date at which the patent application was first filed.* This is a significant change, for as Levy noted, under the new arrangement, a competitor could conceivably file a long stream of fraudulent interference objections (claims that it had developed a similar product or design at the same time) in order to delay the issuance of a patent, "thereby reducing the patent's life when it does issue." Many observers fear that entrepreneurs and small businesses could be hurt by this arrangement.

GATT does provide some patent rules of potential advantage to small inventors. For example, it provides for the issuance of "provisional patent applications," which in effect allows inventors to file a preliminary application that establishes the date of invention. The provisional application does not replace the regular PTO application, but it gives inventors additional time to prepare for that step. Other GATT rules changed import/export rules regarding intellectual property and expanded the number of scenarios under which interference proceedings could be launched.

American Inventors Protection Act The most recent domestic legislation that has impacted the patent and invention process is the American Inventors Protection Act of 1999. This law contained many provisions of interest to inventors, including the following:

- Establishes the Patent and Trademark Office as an agency within the Department of Commerce.

- Reduced the risk of patent infringement lawsuits against various industries, most notably financial services companies, whose "methods of doing business" had been claimed as proprietary by patent holders.

- Requires invention promotion companies to provide complete disclosure of various aspects of their operational history, including their customers success in receiving net financial profit and license agreements as a direct result of the invention promotion services.

- Reduces fees for international patent applications and initial maintenance fees, and authorizes the PTO director to adjust trademark fees without regard to fluctuations in the Consumer Price Index.

- Extends the terms of patents to compensate for processing delays and delays in the prosecution of applications pending for more than three years.

Provides a minimum of 17-year patent term for
diligent applicants.

- Provides for publication of patent applications 18
months after filing unless the applicant requests
otherwise and certifies that the invention has not and
will not be patented in another country.

FILING PATENTS IN THE U.S. AND ABROAD

Most experienced inventors and patent experts counsel
inventors to file for a patent as soon as possible. In the
United States you have to apply for a patent within one
year of the time you first disclose the device or start
selling it. At the conclusion of that year, a valid patent
may not be obtained. Inventors should also note that a
U.S. patent will not provide him or her with protection
in other countries; patent applications need to be made
in every country in which protection is desired.
Moreover, in other countries, inventors have to apply
for the patent before it is publicly disclosed.

Finally, the PTO notes that in most instances,
American inventors seeking to secure a patent in another
country must first get a license from the Commissioner
of Patents and Trademarks. This requirement is waived,
however, if the filing in the foreign country takes place
more than six months after the U.S. filing took place.

There are two major international patent treaties
that should be studied by inventors hoping to market
their products abroad. The Paris Convention for the
Protection of Industrial Property, which was signed by
the United States and nearly 100 other nations, stipulates
that each signing nation provide the same rights in patents and trademarks to citizens of other participating
nations that it does to its own. The Patent Cooperation
Treaty, meanwhile, is a patent agreement that includes
more than 50 nations.

SEE ALSO *Copyright; Intellectual Property; Licensing*

BIBLIOGRAPHY

Campanelli, Melissa. "Patent Fever." *Entrepreneur.* December
2000.

Chun, Janean. "Patent Lather." *Entrepreneur.* June 1997.

GATT Implementing Legislation. Intellectual Property Owners
Association, 1994.

Levy, Richard C. *The Inventor's Desktop Companion.* Visible Ink
Press, 1995.

Signore, Philippe. "The New Provisional Rights Provision."
Journal of the Patent and Trademark Office Society. October
2000.

U.S. Patent and Trademark Office. Dzenitis, Talis. "American
Inventors Protection Act of 1999 Summary." 1999.

U.S. Patent and Trademark Office. *Performance and
Accountability Report Fiscal Year 2005.* Available from

http://www.uspto.gov/web/offices/com/annual/2005/
index.html Retrieved on 22 March 2006.

U.S. Small Business Administration. Field, Thomas. *Avoiding
Patent, Trademark and Copyright Problems.* 1992.

Hillstrom, Northern Lights
updated by Magee, ECDI

INVENTORY

An inventory is the entirety of those things owned by a
company and intended for resale or the raw materials and
parts to be used in producing salable goods and products.
Inventories are time-sensitive storage systems that can be
divided into three categories. First are cycle stocks: the
order quantity or lot size received from the plant or
vendor. Second are in-transit stocks: inventory in shipment from the plant or vendor or between distribution
centers. Third are safety stocks: the items in inventory
that serve as a buffer against forecast error and lead time
variability.

Historically, there have been two basic inventory
systems: the continuous review system and the periodic
review system. With continuous review systems, the level
of a company's inventory is monitored at all times.
Under these arrangements, businesses typically track
inventory until it reaches a predetermined point of
"low" holdings, whereupon the company makes an order
(also of a generally predetermined level) to push its
holdings back up to a desirable level. Since the same
amount is ordered on each occasion, continuous review
systems are sometimes also referred to as event-triggered
systems, fixed order size systems (FOSS), or economic
order quantity systems (EOQ). Periodic review systems,
on the other hand, check inventory levels at fixed intervals rather than through continuous monitoring. These
periodic reviews (weekly, biweekly, or monthly checks are
common) are also known as time-triggered systems, fixed
order interval systems (FOIS), or economic order interval
systems (EOI).

INVENTORY AND THE GROWING COMPANY

Most successful small companies find that as their economic fortunes rise, so too do the complexities of their
inventory system logistics. The resulting need for
increased inventory management procedures is due primarily to two factors: 1) greater volume and variety of
products, and 2) increased allocation of company resources (such as physical space and financial capital) to
accommodate the growth in inventory. For a small company used to ordering parts and materials in an as-needed

and informal basis, the transition to a formal and documented system of purchasing and inventory management can be a significant step. It requires the creation of new job functions to identify the costs (holding, shortage) associated with inventory and to implement and manage a formal inventory system. Formal inventory systems require extensive record keeping and on a periodic basis, they must be audited by someone. In addition, this transition to a formal inventory system requires substantial coordination between different functional areas of the company. Such a transition often leads into computerization of inventory management. This can be a challenging project, particularly for companies lacking employees with appropriate backgrounds in data management.

Just-In-Time Inventory Control Just-in-time production is a straightforward idea that may be somewhat difficult to implement. The basic concept is that finished goods should be produced just in time for delivery, and raw materials should be delivered just in time for production. When this occurs, materials or goods never sit idle. This, in turn, means that a minimum amount of money is tied up in raw materials, semi-finished goods, and finished goods. The result of a well-managed inventory system capable of supporting a just-in-time production system is sustained productivity and quality improvement with greater flexibility and delivery responsiveness. This production concept, which originated in Japan and became immensely popular in American industries in the early and mid-1990s, continues to be hailed by proponents as a viable alternative for businesses looking for a competitive edge.

SETTING AN INVENTORY STRATEGY

No single inventory strategy is effective for all businesses. When a company is faced with a need to establish or reevaluate its inventory control systems, a practice commonly known as "inventory segmenting" or "inventory partitioning" is a helpful tool. This practice is, in essence, a way of breaking down and reviewing total inventory so that a thorough assessment of each category may be made. The inventory may be broken down by product classifications, inventory stages (raw materials, intermediate inventories, finished products), sales and operations groupings, and excess inventories. Proponents of this method of study say that such categorical segmentations break the company's total inventory into much more manageable parts for analysis.

Key Considerations Inventory management is a key factor in the successful operation of any business for which inventories are an integral part. For both large and small companies, determining whether their inventory systems are successful can be done by answering one question: Does the inventory strategy insure that the company has adequate stock for production and goods shipments while at the same time minimizing inventory costs? If the answer is yes, then the company in question is far more likely to be successful. If, however, the answer is no, then the business is operating under twin burdens that can be of considerable consequence to its ability to survive, let alone flourish.

No factor is more important in ensuring successful inventory management than regular analysis of policies, practices, and results. A useful checklist of actions for those wishing to establish and maintain an effective inventory system includes:

- Regularly reviewing product offerings, including the breadth of the product line and the impact that peripheral products have on inventory.

- Ensuring that inventory strategies are in place for each product and that they are reviewed on a regular basis.

- Reviewing transportation alternatives and their impact on inventory/warehouse capacities.

- Undertaking periodic reviews to ensure that inventory is held at the level that best meets customer needs; this applies to all levels of business, including raw materials, intermediate assembly, and finished products.

- Regularly canvassing key employees for ideas and information that may inform future inventory control plans.

- Determining what level of service (lead time, etc.) is necessary to meet the demands of customers.

- Establishing a system for effectively identifying and managing excess or obsolete inventory, and determining why these goods reached such status.

- Devising a workable system wherein "safety" inventory stocks can be reached and distributed on a timely basis when the company sees an unexpected rise in product demand.

- Calculating the impact of seasonal inventory fluctuations and incorporating them into inventory management strategies.

- Reviewing the company's forecasting mechanisms and the volatility of the marketplace, both of which can (and do) have a big impact on inventory decisions.

- Instituting a "continuous improvement" philosophy in inventory management.

• Making inventory management decisions that reflect a recognition that inventory is deeply interrelated with other areas of business operation.

To summarize, inventory management systems should be regularly reviewed from top to bottom as an essential part of the annual strategic and business planning processes.

Indeed, even cursory examinations of inventory statistics can provide business owners with valuable insights into how things are going generally. Business consultants and managers alike note that if an individual business has an inventory turnover ratio that is low in relation to the average for the industry in which it operates, this may be a sign that the business is carrying a surplus of obsolete or otherwise unsalable inventory. Conversely, if a business is experiencing unusually high inventory turnover when compared with industry or business averages, then the company may be losing out on sales because of a lack of adequate stock on hand. Determining and tracking the turnover rate of all items in inventory helps in building up an inventory assessment.

INVENTORY ACCOUNTING

The way in which a company accounts for its inventory can have a visible effect on its financial statements. Inventory is a current asset on the balance sheet. One may think that inventory valuation is relatively simple. For a retailer, inventory should be valued for what it cost to acquire that inventory. When an inventory item is sold, the inventory account should be reduced (credited) and cost of goods sold should be increased (debited) for the amount paid for each inventory item. This works if a company is operating under the Specific Identification Method. That is, a company knows the cost of every individual item that is sold. This method works well when the amount of inventory a company has is limited and each inventory item is unique. Examples would include car dealerships, jewelers, and art galleries.

The Specific Identification Method, however, is cumbersome in situations where a company owns a great deal of inventory and the items within that inventory are not easily distinguished one from another. As a result, other inventory valuation methods have been developed. The best known of these are the FIFO (first-in, first out) and LIFO (last-in, first-out) methods.

FIFO First-in, first-out is a method of inventory accounting in which the oldest stock items in a company's inventory are assumed to have been the first items sold. Therefore, the inventory that remains is from the most recent purchases. In a period of rising prices, this accounting method yields a higher ending inventory, a lower cost of goods sold, a higher gross profit, and a higher taxable income.

The FIFO method may come the closest to matching the actual physical flow of inventory. Since FIFO assumes that the oldest inventory is always sold first, the valuation of inventory still on hand is at the most recent price. Assuming inflation, this will mean that cost of goods sold will be at its lowest possible amount. Therefore, a major advantage of FIFO is that it has the effect of maximizing net income within an inflationary environment.

LIFO Last-in, first-out, on the other hand, is an accounting approach that assumes that the most recently acquired items are the first ones sold. Therefore, the inventory that remains is always the oldest inventory. During economic periods in which prices are rising, this inventory accounting method yields a lower ending inventory, a higher cost of goods sold, a lower gross profit, and a lower taxable income. The LIFO method is preferred by many companies because it has the effect of reducing a company's taxes, thus increasing cash flow. However, these attributes of LIFO are only present in an inflationary environment.

The other major advantage of LIFO is that it can have an income smoothing effect. Again, assuming inflation and a company that is doing well, one would expect inventory levels to expand. Therefore, a company is purchasing inventory, but under LIFO, the majority of the cost of these purchases will be on the income statement as part of cost of goods sold. Thus, the most recent and, assuming an inflationary period, most expensive purchases will be the first items sold. As they are sold, the cost of goods sold will rise and net income will be reduced. Net income is still high, but it does not reach the levels that it would if the company used the FIFO method.

Given the important differences that exist between the various inventory accounting methods, it is important that the inventory footnote be read carefully in financial statements, for this part of the document will inform the reader of the method of inventory valuation chosen by a company. Assuming inflation, FIFO will result in higher net income during growth periods and a higher, and more realistic inventory balance. In periods of growth, LIFO will result in lower net income and lower income tax payments, thus enhancing a company's cash flow. During periods of contraction, LIFO will result in higher income levels, but it will also undervalue inventory over time.

Small business owners weighing a switch to a LIFO inventory valuation method should note that while making the change is a relatively simple process (the company files IRS Form 970 with its tax return), switching away from LIFO is not so easy. Once a company adopts the LIFO method, it can not switch to FIFO without securing IRS approval.

DONATING EXCESS INVENTORY

In recent years, many small (and large) businesses have gained valuable tax deductions by donating obsolete or excess inventory to charitable organizations, churches, and disaster relief efforts. The type of deduction that can be claimed depends on the business structure of the donating company. "If you're organized as an S corporation, a partnership, or a sole proprietorship and you donate inventory to a charity that uses the goods to assist the sick, the poor, or children, you're generally able to take a tax deduction for the cost of producing the inventory," stated Joan Szabo in *Entrepreneur*. C Corporations, meanwhile, can deduct the cost of the inventory *plus* half the difference between the production cost and the inventory's fair market value, provided the deduction does not exceed twice the cost of the donated goods.

A number of organizations have been established for the express purpose of distributing donated inventory. Gifts in Kind International (based in Alexandria, Virginia) distributes used computers, high-tech equipment, and other donated inventory to approximately 50,000 domestic and international charities. The Galesburg, Illinois-based National Association for the Exchange of Industrial Resources (NAEIR), meanwhile, distributes excess inventory to more than 5,000 schools, churches, homeless shelters, and other charitable organizations. Office supplies comprise much of the NAEIR goods, but clothing, janitorial supplies, and computer equipment are also distributed. The NAEIR estimates that it has distributed more than $1 billion in corporate inventory donations to American schools and nonprofit organizations since 1977.

SEE ALSO *Automated Storage and Retrieval Systems; Enterprise Resource Planning; Inventory Control Systems; Material Requirements Planning*

BIBLIOGRAPHY

Allen, Kelley L. "Lose that Inventory Baggage." *Across the Board.* January 2000.

Haaz, Mort. "How to Establish Inventory Levels." *Gift and Decorative Accessories.* April 1999.

Muller, Max. *Essentials of Inventory Management.* AMACOM Division of American Management Association, November 2002.

Szabo, Joan. "Spring Cleaning." *Entrepreneur.* April 1999.

Toomey, John W. *Inventory Management.* Springer, June 2000.

Hillstrom, Northern Lights
updated by Magee, ECDI

INVENTORY CONTROL SYSTEMS

An inventory control system is a system the encompasses all aspects of managing a company's inventories; purchasing, shipping, receiving, tracking, warehousing and storage, turnover, and reordering. In different firms the activities associated with each of these areas may not be strictly contained within separate subsystems, but these functions must be performed in sequence in order to have a well-run inventory control system. Computerized inventory control systems make it possible to integrate the various functional subsystems that are a part of the inventory management into a single cohesive system.

In today's business environment, even small and mid-sized businesses have come to rely on computerized inventory management systems. Certainly, there are plenty of small retail outlets, manufacturers, and other businesses that continue to rely on manual means of inventory tracking. Indeed, for some small businesses, like convenience stores, shoe stores, or nurseries, purchase of an electronic inventory tracking system might constitute a wasteful use of financial resources. But for other firms operating in industries that feature high volume turnover of raw materials and/or finished products, computerized tracking systems have emerged as a key component of business strategies aimed at increasing productivity and maintaining competitiveness. Moreover, the recent development of powerful computer programs capable of addressing a wide variety of record keeping needs—including inventory management—in one integrated system have also contributed to the growing popularity of electronic inventory control options.

Given such developments, it is little wonder that business experts commonly cite inventory management as a vital element that can spell the difference between success and failure in today's keenly competitive business world. Writing in *Production and Inventory Management Journal*, Godwin Udo described telecommunications technology as a critical organizational asset that can help a company realize important competitive gains in the area of inventory management. He noted that companies that make good use of this technology are far better equipped to succeed than those who rely on outdated or unwieldy methods of inventory control.

COMPUTERS AND INVENTORY

Automation can dramatically impact all phases of inventory management, including counting and monitoring of inventory items; recording and retrieval of item storage location; recording changes to inventory; and anticipating inventory needs, including inventory handling requirements. This is true even of stand-alone systems that are not integrated with other areas of the business, but many analysts indicate that productivity—and hence profitability—gains that are garnered through use of automated systems can be further increased when a business integrates its inventory control systems with other systems such as accounting and sales to better control inventory levels. As Dennis Eskow noted in *PC Week,* business executives are "increasingly integrating financial data, such as accounts receivable, with sales information that includes customer histories. The goal: to control inventory quarter to quarter, so it doesn't come back to bite the bottom line. Key components of an integrated system . . . are general ledger, electronic data interchange, database connectivity, and connections to a range of vertical business applications."

The Future of Inventory Control Systems New technologies have greatly improved the tools used to manage inventories. Powerful computer systems that are linked into networks are now able to receive information from handheld devises. The wireless handheld devices scan bar codes on inventory items and send data to a tracking database in real time. The increased efficiency of inventory systems over the past 25 years made some things possible that would have been impossible in earlier times, like the popular just-in-time manufacturing system.

The newest trend in the area of inventory control and management are vendor-managed inventory (VMI) systems and agreements. In a VMI system distributors and/or manufacturers agree to take over the inventory management for their customers. Based on daily reports sent automatically from the customer to the distributor, the distributor replenishes the customers stocks as needed. The distributor or manufacturer sees what is selling and makes all necessary arrangements to send the customer new products or parts automatically. No phone calls or paperwork are necessary allowing the supply chain process to remain uninterrupted.

The benefits that can accrue to both parties in a VMI arrangement are noteworthy. Both parties should experience a savings of time and labor. The customer is able to maintain fewer items in stock and can rely upon a steady flow of products or parts. The vendor or distributor benefits in two ways. First, a supplier is able to better anticipate production requirements. Second, the supplier benefits from a strong relationship with the customer, one that is more difficult to alter than would be a vendor-customer relationship in which such automated systems did not exist.

As with all outsourcing arrangements, there are potential negatives to a VMI system. The first is the partial loss of control experienced by the customer in managing his or her own inventories. Second is the problem this type of system poses on a vendor in the case of volatile sales periods. It is very difficult for a distributor or manufacturer to hold large inventories for one customer on a VMI system who is experiencing a slowdown in sales while having to ramp up for another customer who is experiencing rising demand. Both parties to a VMI agreement must weight the pros and cons of such a system thoroughly and be sure to include in any VMI agreement prearranged methods for dealing with periods of volatile sales patterns. The popularity of VMI suggests that there are many applications in which these systems produce net benefits for both parties.

WAREHOUSE LAYOUT AND OPERATION

The trend toward automation in inventory management naturally has moved into the warehouse as well. Citing various warehousing experts, Sarah Bergin contended in *Transportation and Distribution* magazine that "the key to getting productivity gains from inventory management . . . is placing real-time intelligent information processing in the warehouse. This empowers employees to take actions that achieve immediate results. Real-time processing in the warehouse uses combinations of hardware including material handling and data collection technologies. But according to these executives, the intelligent part of the system is sophisticated software which automates and controls all aspects of warehouse operations."

Another important component of good inventory management is creation and maintenance of a sensible, effective warehousing design. A well-organized, user-friendly warehouse layout can be of enormous benefit to small business owners, especially if they are involved in processing large volumes of goods and materials. Conversely, an inefficient warehouse system can cost businesses dearly in terms of efficiency, customer service, and, ultimately, profitability.

Transportation and Distribution magazine cited several steps that businesses utilizing warehouse storage systems can take to help ensure that they get the most out of their facilities. It recommended that companies utilize the following tools:

Stock locator database—"The stock locator database required for proactive decision making will be an adjunct of the inventory file in a state-of-the-art space management system. A running record will be maintained of the stock number, lot number, and number of pallet loads in each storage location. Grid coordinates of the reserve area, including individual rack tier positions, must therefore be established, and the pallet load capacity of all storage locations must be incorporated into the database."

Grid coordinate numbering system—Warehouse numbering system should be developed in conjunction with the storage layout, and should be user-friendly so that workers can quickly locate currently stocked items and open storage spaces alike.

Communication systems—Again, this can be a valuable investment if the business's warehouse requirements are significant. Such facilities often utilize fork lift machinery that can be used more effectively if their operators are not required to periodically return to a central assignment area. Current technology, makes it possible for the warehouse computer system to interact with terminal displays or other communications devices on the fork lifts themselves. "Task assignment can then be made by visual display or printout, and task completion can be confirmed by scanning, keyboard entry, or voice recognition," observed *Transportation and Distribution.*

Maximization of storage capacity—Warehouses that adhere to rigid "storage by incoming lot size" storage arrangements do not always make the best use of their space. Instead, businesses should settle on a strategy that eases traffic congestion and best eases problems associated with ongoing turnover in inventory.

Some companies choose to outsource their warehouse functions. "This allows a company that isn't as confident in running their own warehousing operations to concentrate on their core business and let the experts worry about keeping track of their inventory," wrote Bergin. Third-party inventory control operations can provide companies with an array of valuable information, including analysis of products and spare parts, evaluations of their time sensitivity, and information on vendors. Of course, businesses weighing whether to outsource such a key component of their operation need to consider the expense of such a course of action, as well as their feelings about relinquishing that level of control.

SEE ALSO *Automated Storage and Retrieval Systems; Enterprise Resource Planning; Material Requirements Planning*

BIBLIOGRAPHY

Andel, Tom, and Daniel A. Kind. "Flow It, Don't Stow It." *Transportation and Distribution.* May 1996.

Baljko, Jennifer. "As VMI Programs Proliferate, Some Questions Come to Fore." *EBN.* 25 November 2002.

Bergin, Sarah. "Make Your Warehouse Deliver: New Developments in Warehouse Management Systems Inspire New Productivity in Needy Operations." *Transportation and Distribution.* February 1997.

Eskow, Dennis. "Rising Stock: Integrated Inventory Systems Help Companies Shoot Economic Rapids." *PC Week.* 5 June 1995.

Haaz, Mort. "How to Establish Inventory Levels." *Gift and Decorative Accessories.* April 1999.

Harris, Angela D. "Vendor-Managed Inventory Growing." *Air Conditioning, Heating & Refrigeration News.* 24 October 2005.

Safizadeh, M. Hossein, and Larry P. Rizman. "Linking Peformance Drivers in Production Planning and Inventory Control to Process Choice." *Journal of Operations Management.* November 1997.

Udo, Godwin J. "The Impact of Telecommunications on Inventory Management." *Production and Inventory Management Journal.* Spring 1993.

Weisfeld, Barry. "Automated Ordering Puts Profits in Sight." *Transportation and Distribution.* February 1997.

Hillstrom, Northern Lights
updated by Magee, ECDI

INVESTOR PRESENTATIONS

Investor presentations are an important but often overlooked aspect of entrepreneurial efforts to secure financing for their businesses. Presentations are particularly important to small business owners hoping to raise money from private investors. Whereas institutional investors such as banks rely primarily on financial statements, business plans, etc., in making their lending decisions, private investors are more likely to be swayed by other factors, such as the owner's vision of a new product's appeal, knowledge of the marketplace, or ability to present a compelling picture of future profits for both the owner and the investor.

Poor investor presentation may close the door on potential avenues of financing, even if the entrepreneur's idea for a new business or product is a good one. "Putting together a winning presentation isn't as easy as it might seem," said David R. Evanson in *Nation's Business.* "Whatever the forum—a formal dog-and-pony show before a roomful or institutional investors, a clubby luncheon with 10 to 15 wealthy individuals, or a one-on-one meeting with a venture capitalist—founders . . . have often shown they can shoot themselves in the foot with deadly accuracy." Entrepreneurs and small business owners seeking expansion capital need to make certain that their presentations grab the attention of investors and inspire them.

KEYS TO SUCCESSFUL INVESTOR PRESENTATIONS

Several considerations should be kept in mind when planning a presentation to potential investors. These considerations range from tips on public speaking to recommendations on presentation content.

Tailor Presentation to Audience Some business owners make investor presentations that are only negligibly different from presentations that they make to internal salespeople or to customers. This choice—which is often a byproduct of laziness more than anything else—can have a negative impact on the owner's chances of landing an investor. "Topics such as product features, new technology and customer service—the things that matter to customers—are of interest to investors only as part of an overall menu of competitive advantages that will help drive sales," said Evanson. Moreover, no two investors are alike; one individual may have a reputation for daring business initiatives; another may be predisposed toward (or away from) involvement in a specific industry; still another may be most interested in receiving assurances about the competence of the enterprise's management team. Entrepreneurs preparing to make a pitch toward private investors should find out as much as possible about their audience's interests and investment philosophies beforehand.

Judicious Use of Visual Aids Visual aids should augment the presentation, not dominate it. Slides and overheads can be valuable tools in a presentation, but their use contains a number of potential pitfalls for entrepreneurs. Some people place so much importance on the visual component of their presentation that they flounder in situations where they have to deviate from their script. Others cram their visual aids so full of information that viewers are unable to digest it all, which merely triggers resentment or annoyance from potential investors. However, visual support—when intelligently utilized—can be most helpful in providing context and illustrating key points.

Presentation software programs, like Microsoft's Power Point, for example, are utilized frequently today for public speaking events. Such programs have several advantages. They can compose impressive displays and their content can be altered quickly to reflect needed changes. Moreover, their portability is a big improvement over big slide carousels, overhead projectors, and display boards. But many of the advantages associated with computer displays hinge on a certain level of program mastery and design skill. Always remember: a visually interesting presentation is a very good idea, but substance should **always** trump style.

Live Demonstrations It may be tempting for an entrepreneur to make a live demonstration or his or her product as part of the total presentation package, but demonstrations have a pretty hefty downside. This is especially true of technology products, which can end up looking hopeless because of some minor glitch. "As people with sales experience will tell you, the customer

has a picture in mind of what the product is and what it's supposed to do," wrote Evanson. "Any uncontrolled situation that distorts that image is ultimately counterproductive to closing the sale." Of course, there may be situations wherein the presenter is pointedly asked for a live demonstration by a potential investor. Not granting such a request may throw prospects for financial assistance in jeopardy as well, so entrepreneurs should be prepared to make such a demonstration if it seems necessary. Finally, there are certain categories of products (generally involving simpler, non-technological designs) that can be demonstrated with less worry for a negative outcome because of a technical glitch. Each presenter has to judge the potential risks of a live demonstration for him or herself.

Relevance Presentations that spend excessive amounts of time on relatively unimportant points are unlikely to attract investors. Instead, presentations should remain focused on the basic information that investors are likely to want to hear, such as company background, ownership/management background, key employees, product development, market opportunities, existing competition, present and future marketing plans, and financial analysis.

Communication Abilities This element of presentation encompasses several different areas. First of all, the presenter should ideally be able to speak in an authoritative, confident, and smooth manner. Fairly or not, public speaking ability can make a profound difference in an entrepreneur's success in securing investors for his or her business or product. "There are a number of golden rules in making a presentation and plenty of speakers break them all," observed Sue Bryant in *Marketing*. "No eye contact. No pauses. Patronizing the audience by putting text on screen and reading it out loud. Writing a speech, failing to rehearse and reading it woodenly. Fumbling with equipment and muttering: 'Now, how do I work this thing...'" Indeed, Bryant pointed out that excessive use of visual aids can often be traced to a presenter's discomfort with public speaking. Given the importance of a good delivery, an entrepreneur who is uncomfortable with speaking in public should consider investing in a course designed to help people with public speaking and presentation skills.

Presenters also need to make sure that the presentation itself is appropriately focused and understandable. Karen Kalish, author of *How to Give a Terrific Presentation*, stated that effective presentations have seven key organizational elements:

- Audience-grabbing opening

- Well-organized information (including examples, analogies, and anecdotes where appropriate)

- Logical transitions
- Short sentences
- Understandable language
- Good closing
- Appropriate responses to questions

Entrepreneurs are often very intimately involved in the details of their products or services. This may lead to a tendency to drift off into a lengthy discussion of technical matters. The last thing that one wants is to bore prospective investors. Avoid lengthy explanations of relatively esoteric subjects. "Yes, the technical aspects of your company's product or service are important," wrote Evanson and Art Beroff in *Entrepreneur,* "inasmuch as they deliver competitive advantages, open new markets or change the balance of power in an existing market—but to investors, technology is not important in and of itself."

Honest Presentation Presenting projected financial performance for a company or product is an important and delicate part of the investor presentation process. Entrepreneurs naturally want to put their prospects in a good light, but consultants warn that private investors are wary of overly optimistic numbers, and view misleading data in this area as a clear sign that they should withhold assistance. "With so many exciting opportunities in the marketplace, you've got to walk a very fine line between numbers that are exciting enough to attract investors and those that will turn them off because they're simply unrealistic," one successful business founder told *Entrepreneur.*

Length of Presentation Most experts advise entrepreneurs to limit their presentation to between 20 and 30 minutes. It may be tempting to devote more time than that—and in some cases it may be warranted (the potential investor has already indicated that he or she wants a full accounting, the entrepreneur's idea is a complex one)—but for the most part, entrepreneurs should limit themselves as indicated above. Whereas excessively long presentations can bore investors and unduly short ones can leave investors wondering if they are being told everything, presentations of 20-30 minutes can usually provide an adequate overview and leave sufficient time to answer investor questions.

Question-and-Answer Sessions Questions from investors are an inevitable part of investor presentations. Entrepreneurs who avoid answering certain questions, answer with rambling sermons in "tech-speak," or respond in an arrogant, "know it all" fashion are unlikely to favorably impress their audience.

Follow-Up Entrepreneurs should follow up with investors within a few days of the presentation, but they should be careful not to badger him or her with multiple queries. "When raising capital, particularly from individual investors, the old rule is that *yes* comes fast, and *no* takes forever," commented Evanson and Beroff [emphasis added]. "Still, many investors test the mettle of the business owner by seeing how long it takes him or her to follow up. If it's not forthcoming, even for reasons of perceived courtesy, many investors get turned off. On the other side of the coin, calling every day doesn't work, either."

Finally, rehearse both the presentation and various responses to anticipated questions. Entrepreneurs seeking funding from private investors are competing with many others. Take full advantage of the limited time afforded during an investor presentation to convince the audience that your business strategy makes sense and that your management team is capable of successfully executing the plan.

SEE ALSO *Business Plan*

BIBLIOGRAPHY

Arthur, Audrey. "Keeping Up Public Appearances: Master the Fine Art of Public Speaking and Give a Great Presentation Every Time." *Black Enterprise.* July 1997.

Bryant, Sue. "Speak for Yourself." *Marketing.* 31 October 1996.

Casteel, Lynn E. "Tips from the Pros: Effective Investor Presentations." *Community Banker.* April 2004.

"Elements of a Great Speech." *Industry Week.* 17 February 1997.

Evanson, David R. "Capital Pitches that Succeed." *Nation's Business.* May 1997.

Evanson, David R., and Art Beroff. "Perfect Pitch." *Entrepreneur.* March 1998.

Greer, John, and Francie Murphy. "Be Prepared When Making Multimedia Presentations." *Los Angeles Business Journal.* 22 September 1997.

Kalish, Karen. *How to Give a Terrific Presentation.* AMACOM, 1997.

Weissman, Jerry. *Presenting to Win: The Art of Telling Your Story.* Financial Times Prentice Hall, 2003.

Hillstrom, Northern Lights
updated by Magee, ECDI

INVESTOR RELATIONS AND REPORTING

Once a privately held company issues shares of stock to the public—through an initial public offering (IPO), for example—it incurs a number of new responsibilities related to investor relations and reporting requirements.

Also known as "going public," an IPO transforms a business from a privately owned and operated entity into one that is owned by public stockholders. An IPO is a significant stage in the growth of many businesses, as it provides them with access to the public capital market and also increases their credibility and exposure. Becoming a public entity also involves significant changes for a business, changes that include a substantial increase in both the number and complexity of the reports the company is legally required to file.

LEGAL REPORTING REQUIREMENTS

In 1934, the Securities Act was passed. This act provided for the establishment of the Security and Exchange Commission (SEC) as the agency authorized to oversee the act's provisions. The SEC regulates all publicly traded companies. SEC reporting requirements are extensive. In addition to the periodic reports known as 8A, 10K, and 10Q, public companies must issue annual reports, quarterly reports, proxy statements, and press releases in order to keep shareholders, financial analysts, and regulatory agencies informed of their actions.

Form 8A This is the main form for registering a stock issue with the SEC. It must be filed if the shares will be traded on a major stock exchange (NYSE, AMEX, or NASDAQ), if the firm will have more than 500 shareholders, or if it has more than $3 million in assets. Companies that register their stock offerings using Form 8A must also file periodic reports until they no longer meet the aforementioned requirements. These updates are an important means of communication with shareholders, who use the information in making investment decisions.

Form 10K All public companies are required to file Form 10K annually within 90 days of end of their fiscal year. This form requires disclosure of the company's audited financial statements, a summary of operations, a description of the overall business and its physical property, identification of any subsidiaries or affiliates, disclosure of the revenues contributed by major products or departments, and information on the number of shareholders, the management team and their salaries, and the interests of management and shareholders in certain transactions. The idea of Form 10K is to update on an annual basis the information that the company provided for its initial filing.

Form 10Q Another SEC required form is Form 10Q. This form must be filed within 45 days of the end of each of the first three quarters in a company's fiscal year, includes audited financial statements with management discussion, as well as details of any corporate events that had a significant impact on the company.

Form 8K Another important reporting requirement is Form 8K, which discloses major changes in corporate control or assets due to such events as mergers, acquisitions, or bankruptcy. Several other types of filings are required for specific events, such as a significant increase or decrease in the amount of outstanding stock, or distributions to shareholders in the form of stock splits or dividends. In addition, public companies are required to inform stockholders of impending meetings or votes and send out proxy statements. Finally, insider trading laws require that public companies disclose any changes in the holdings of managers or directors who own more than 10 percent of the company's stock.

The Fair Disclosure Regulation, enacted in 2000, stipulates that publicly traded companies broadly and publicly disseminate information instead of distributing it selectively to certain analysts or investors only. Companies are encouraged to use several means of information dissemination including news releases, Web sites or Web casts, and press releases.

In 2002 Congress passed the Sarbanes-Oxley Act and it was signed into law. This act came about in the wake of serious allegations of accounting fraud and a string of bankruptcies of very high-profile, publicly traded companies. The act established stricter reporting requirements and increased the personal responsibility that both CEOs and CFOs must take on when signing corporate reports. Meeting the requirements of this law has increased the workload for publicly traded firms and the firms that do their auditing work. In particular, Section 404 of the Sarbanes-Oxley Act requires that a company's annual report include an official write-up by management about the effectiveness of the company's internal controls. The section also requires that outside auditors attest to management's report on internal controls. An external audit is required in order to attest to the management report.

BEYOND SEC REQUIREMENTS

In addition to SEC reporting requirements, public companies also face the responsibility of maintaining good investor relations. Although it is not legally required, it is nonetheless important for all companies to establish systems to deal with stockholders, financial analysts, the media, and the overall community. One of management's key responsibilities in addition to managing the business and overseeing all regulatory reporting requirements is to keep the investor's informed about company activities.

It is therefore vital that interested outsiders are presented with a complete and accurate picture of what is happening within the company. In some cases, this may entail obtaining the services of a public relations firm that specializes in investor relations. Such firms can guide newly public companies through the maze of information that they must disseminate. In addition, many smaller companies with limited resources will utilize the services of outside consultants who can help them meet their goal of providing full, accurate, and accessible information for disclosure to investors. Companies who decide to pursue this route should consider the following when selecting a consultant:

Reputation. References, qualifications, and experience of prospective investor relations firms should be closely examined.

Methodology. Consultants have different methodologies, strategies, and philosophies, and it is the small business owner's obligation to research these variables and determine which firm is the best fit for his or her own company.

Compensation structure. Investor relations consultants maintain a wide array of compensation and billing structures. "Understand how the billing is done, how expenses are allocated, and what services the company will receive," counseled Michael Noonan in *Houston Business Journal.* "Clearly identify the terms and responsibility for each party and put the deal in writing." At the same time, companies seeking assistance in this area need to undertake a frank appraisal of their own budgetary constraints.

SEE ALSO *Financial Statements; SEC Disclosure Laws and Regulations*

BIBLIOGRAPHY
Cole, Benjamin Mark. *The New Investor Relations: Expert Perspectives on the State of the Art.* Bloomberg Press, October 2003.

"Fresh Strategies are Needed for the New SEC Reporting Requirements." *Corporate Board.* March-April 2003.

MacAdam, Donald H. *Startup to IPO.* Xlibris Corporation, 2004.

Mirza, Patrick. "Some Companies Struggle to Meet SEC Reporting Requirements." *HRMagazine.* May 2004.

Noonan, Michael D. "Proper Investor Relations Plans May Require Outside Consultants." *Houston Business Journal.* 15 September 2000.

Roberts, Holme, and Harold A. S. Bloomenthal. *Going Public Handbook.* Clark Boardman, 1991.

Hillstrom, Northern Lights
updated by Magee, ECDI

IRS AUDITS

Each year, the Internal Revenue Service (IRS) conducts audits on individuals and businesses to ensure that they are in compliance with U.S. tax law. The percentage of people and businesses subject to these audits is relatively small—for tax year 2004, for instance, the IRS audited only 1 percent of tax returns filed by individuals and 2 percent of returns filed by all corporations. Of small businesses, one in 127 is likely to face an audit, based on audits performed in 2004. Nonetheless, the prospect of being targeted does provoke dread among a certain portion of the American public.

Indeed, many business analysts believe that smaller businesses in certain industries are at greater risk of being subjected to an audit because of historically higher levels of noncompliance in those industries, many of which are primarily composed of small firms. Home-based businesses that are characterized by cash-based transactions are particularly likely to undergo formal IRS review. Many business and tax experts, however, contend that small businesses that conduct their operations honestly and maintain good record keeping practices should be able to weather an IRS audit without too much difficulty. Indeed, some small business owners have been known to actually request an audit in instances where they have a dispute with the IRS over tax obligations.

When providing advice on IRS audits, tax advisors counsel small business owners to adhere to the following guidelines:

- Be honest in business operations and in claiming deductions.

- If you prepare your own returns, be familiar with IRS rules regarding deductions and other tax matters; if not, make certain that you hire an accountant or tax advisor who is knowledgeable in these areas.

- Keep all receipts and maintain sound and thorough record keeping practices.

- Keep expenses in line with industry norms.

- Make sure that the auditing agent is knowledgeable about the industry in which you operate.

- Be cooperative; promptly answer all communications from the IRS and make every effort to provide the auditing agent with all requested information.

- If you are unhappy with the results of an IRS audit, consider making a written appeal; the Internal Revenue service maintains an independent division specifically designed to hear such appeals.

TAX FRAUD AND THE IRS

As the Internal Revenue Service goes about the annual routine of gathering and processing tax statements from businesses and individuals, one of the agency's principal responsibilities is to be on the lookout for cases of potential tax evasion or fraud. Business experts cite several primary scenarios that are likely to prompt further investigation:

- Accounting irregularities, such as discrepancies between amounts reported on various financial statements.

- Inadequate record keeping, such as missing or incomplete financial records.

- Failure to report all income.

- Improper claims for deductions (such as inflated claims of business costs).

- Allocation of income to related taxpayers, especially if the recipient pays lower taxes.

Financial Status Audit. One of the primary means by which the IRS conducts audits is the financial status audit. Under this form of audit, the investigating agent compares the amount of income reported against the assets and lifestyle of the taxpayer. The visibility of this type of audit has fluctuated in recent years, however. In fact, the financial status audit became a lightning rod for criticism of the IRS in the mid-1990s, when the agency announced that it intended to provide increased training in this area in order to increase its use of this type of audit. Resistance to this focus was strong and immediate. Many accountants and the AICPA [Association of Independent Certified Public Accountants] were concerned about the intrusive nature of these audits and the intention of the IRS to perform them in large numbers. The adverse reaction to the IRS decision reached a culmination in 1998, when legislators took action to curb the use of this sort of audit. The legislation written, in part, to address financial status audits is the IRS Restructuring and Reform Act of 1998. This legislation placed limits on the use of the financial status audit, although it did not put an end to them.

MARKET SEGMENT SPECIALIZATION PROGRAM (MSSP)

The Market Segment Specialization Program, established in 1992, is an IRS initiative designed to conduct and analyze in-depth studies and actual audits of industries with unique business practices. MSSP Audit Technique Guides aim to improve the auditing process by creating and distributing auditor training guides on these specific industries. These guides, which were originally developed for reference use by auditors and IRS revenue agents, can also be useful to businesses preparing for IRS audits or researching their tax liability. Each of the available guides—which cover industries ranging from air charter services and architectural firms to mortuaries and gas retailers—include an overview of industry issues, outlines of the books and records that may be maintained for tax purposes, examination techniques, industry terminology, and highlights of the prevailing business practices in that industry. All MSSP Audit Technique Guides are available on the Internal Revenue Service Web site, located at http://www.irs.gov/index.html.

SEE ALSO *Record Retention; Tax Returns*

BIBLIOGRAPHY
"Burden of Proof: Your Rights in IRS Audits and Examinations." *The Business Owner.* May-June 2000.

Daily, Frederick W. *Stand Up to the IRS.* Eighth Edition. Nolo, 2005.

David, Theodore M. *Dealing with the New IRS: Laws, Forms, and Practices.* American Law Institute, 2001.

"IRS is Turning Up the Heat, Doing More Audits." *Kiplinger Forecasts.* 23 November 2005.

KattZeff, Paul. "IRS Steps Up Audits Of Small Business; S Corps. In Cross Hairs; Uncle Sam is Worried That Popular Structures are Used as Tax Dodges." *Investor's Business Daily.* 15 August 2005.

U.S. Department of Treasury. Internal Revenue Service. "2005 Data Book Details Rise in Audits." Available from http://www.irs.gov/newsroom/article/0,,id=155371,00.html. 17 March 2006.

Hillstrom, Northern Lights
updated by Magee, ECDI

ISO 9000

ISO 9000 is a set of international standards of quality management that have become increasingly popular for large and small companies alike. Adherence is accomplished through an application process for ISO 9000 certification in company standards for inspecting production processes, updating records, maintaining equipment, training employees and handling customer relations. "ISO is grounded on the 'conformance to specification' definition of quality," wrote Francis Buttle in the *International Journal of Quality and Reliability Management.* "The standards specify how management operations shall be conducted. ISO 9000's purpose is to ensure that suppliers design, create, and deliver products and services which meet predetermined standards; in other words, its goal is to prevent non-conformity." Used by both manufacturing and service firms, ISO 9000 had been adopted by more than 100 nations as their national quality management/quality assurance standard by the end of 2005.

This quality standard was first introduced in 1987 by the International Organization for Standards (ISO) in hopes of establishing an international definition of the essential characteristics and language of a quality system for all businesses, irrespective of industry or geographic location. Initially, it was used almost exclusively by large companies, but by the mid-1990s, increasing numbers of small- and mid-sized companies had embraced ISO 9000 as well. In fact, small and moderate-sized companies account for much of the growth in ISO 9000 registration over the past several years. As of December 15, 2003 a revised standard replaced the 1994 edition of the ISO 9000. The new standard is referred to as ISO 9001:2000 but is often still referred to simply as ISO 9000. Revisions of the ISO standards occur periodically.

The increased involvement of small and mid-sized firms in seeking ISO 9000 registration is generally attributed to several factors. Many small businesses have decided to seek ISO 9000 certification because of their corporate customers, who began to insist on it as a method of ensuring that their suppliers were paying adequate attention to quality. Other small business owners, meanwhile, have pursued ISO 9000 certification in order to increase their chances of securing new business or simply as a means of improving the quality of their processes. "The pressure for companies to become ISO 9000-certified is absolutely increasing and will continue to increase," predicted one management consultant in an interview with *Nation's Business*. "The question many smaller companies have to ask is when, not if, they [will] get ISO 9000-registered."

ELEMENTS OF ISO 9000 QUALITY MANAGEMENT SYSTEMS

The standards of ISO 9000 detail 20 requirements for an organization's quality management system in the following areas:

- Management Responsibility
- Quality System
- Order Entry
- Design Control
- Document and Data Control
- Purchasing
- Control of Customer Supplied Products
- Product Identification and Tractability
- Process Control
- Inspection and Testing

- Control of Inspection, Measuring, and Test Equipment
- Inspection and Test Status
- Control of Nonconforming Products
- Corrective and Preventive Action
- Handling, Storage, Packaging, and Delivery
- Control of Quality Records
- Internal Quality Audits
- Training
- Servicing
- Statistical Techniques

MODELS OF ISO 9000

The ISO 9000 quality standards were broken into three model sets—ISO 9001, ISO 9002, and ISO 9003. Each of these models, noted *Industrial Management* contributors Stanislav Karapetrovic, Divakar Rajamani, and Walter Willborn, "stipulate a number of requirements on which an organization's quality system can be assessed by an external party (registrar)" in accordance with the ISO's quality system audits standard. "A quality system," they added, "involves organizational structure, processes, and documented procedures constituted towards achieving quality objectives."

In the late 2003 revision of the ISO 9000 these three standards were combined into a single ISO 9001:2000. The new standard was published in 2000 and companies migrated to the new standards during the first three years of the new century. Organizations and companies that were certified under the older ISO 9000, ISO 9001, ISO 9002, and ISO 9003 systems were required to take steps to transfer or upgrade their certification to the new standard. An organization was required to demonstrate to an accredited registration body that its quality management system met the requirements of the new ISO 9001:2000.

ADVANTAGES OF ISO 9000 SYSTEM

The advantages associated with the ISO 9000 certification system are numerous, as both business analysts and business owners will attest. These benefits, which can impact nearly all corners of a company, range from increased stature to bottom-line operational savings. They include:

- Increased marketability—Nearly all observers agree that ISO 9000 registration provides businesses with markedly heightened credibility with current and prospective clients alike. Basically, it proves that the company is dedicated to providing quality to its customers, which is no small advantage whether the company is negotiating with a long-time customer or endeavoring to pry a potentially lucrative customer away from a competitor. This benefit manifests itself not only in increased customer retention, but also in increased customer acquisition and heightened ability to enter into new markets; indeed, ISO 9000 registration has been cited as being of particular value for small and mid-sized businesses hoping to establish a presence in international markets.

- Reduced operational expenses—Sometimes lost in the many discussions of ISO 9000's public relations cache is the fact that the rigorous registration process often exposes significant shortcomings in various operational areas. When these problems are brought to light, the company can take the appropriate steps to improve its processes. These improved efficiencies can help companies garner savings in both time and money. "The cost of scrap, rework, returns, and the employee time spent analyzing and troubleshooting various products are all considerably reduced by initiating the discipline of ISO 9000," confirmed Richard B. Wright in *Industrial Distribution*.

- Better management control—The ISO 9000 registration process requires so much documentation and self-assessment that many businesses that undergo its rigors cite increased understanding of the company's overall direction and processes as a significant benefit.

- Increased customer satisfaction—Since the ISO 9000 certification process almost inevitably uncovers areas in which final product quality can be improved, such efforts often bring about higher levels of customer satisfaction. In addition, by seeking and securing ISO 9000 certification, companies can provide their clients with the opportunity to tout their suppliers' dedication to quality in their own business dealings.

- Improved internal communication—The ISO 9000 certification process's emphasis on self-analysis and operations management issues encourages various internal areas or departments of companies to interact with one another in hopes of gaining a more complete understanding of the needs and desires of their internal customers.

- Improved customer service—The process of securing ISO 9000 registration often serves to refocus company priorities on pleasing their customers in all respects, including customer service areas. It also helps heighten awareness of quality issues among employees.

- Reduction of product-liability risks—Many business experts contend that companies that achieve ISO 9000 certification are less likely to be hit with product liability lawsuits, etc., because of the quality of their processes.

- Attractiveness to investors—Business consultants and small business owners alike agree that ISO-9000 certification can be a potent tool in securing funding from venture capital firms.

DISADVANTAGES OF ISO 9000 SYSTEM

Despite the many advantages associated with ISO 9000, however, business owners and consultants caution companies to research the rigorous certification process before committing resources to it. Following is a list of potential hurdles for entrepreneurs to study before committing to an initiative to gain ISO 9000 certification:

- Owners and managers do not have an adequate understanding of the ISO 9000 certification process or of the quality standards themselves—Some business owners have been known to direct their company's resources toward ISO 9000 registration, only to find that their incomplete understanding of the process and its requirements results in wasted time and effort.

- Funding for establishing the quality system is inadequate—Critics of ISO 9000 contend that achieving certification can be a very costly process, especially for smaller firms. Indeed, according to a 1996 *Quality Systems Update* survey, the average cost of ISO certification for small firms (those registering less than $11 million in annual sales) was $71,000.

- Heavy emphasis on documentation—The ISO 9000 certification process relies heavily on documentation of internal operating procedures in many areas, and as Meyer stated, "many say ISO's exacting documentation requirements gobble up time. Indeed, there are horror stories about companies losing substantial business because a documentation obsession redirected their priorities." According to *Nation's Business*, small business owners need to find an appropriate balance between ISO documentation requirements, which are admittedly "one is ISO 9000's hallmarks," and attending to the fundamental business of running a company: "Strike a balance among obsessively writing down every employee's task, offering training for the work, and letting common sense dictate how a task is to be performed."

- Length of the process—Business executives and owners familiar with the ISO 9000 registration process warn that it is a process that takes many months to complete. The 1996 *Quality Systems*

Update survey indicated that it took businesses an average of 15 months to move from the early stages of the process to passage of the final audit, and that processes of 18-20 months or even longer were not that uncommon.

SELECTING A LEADER FOR THE ISO 9000 REGISTRATION PROCESS

ISO 9000 experts and businesses that have gone through the rigorous process of certification agree that businesses that appoint someone to guide the process are much more likely to be able to undergo the process in a healthy, productive manner than are firms that have murky reporting relationships. Hiring an outside consultant is one option for businesses. "An ISO 9000 advisor could give you a rough sketch of the registration process and help you get started," stated *Nation's Business.* "Or the consultant could counsel you through the entire process, writing the company's quality policy statement and even specific operating procedures." In addition, firms should hire an ISO-9000 registrar with a background in their industry, legitimacy with international customers, and knowledge of small business issues.

Some small firms choose to appoint an employee as their ISO 9000 representative rather than hire an outside consultant. Many companies have done this successfully, but small business owners should take great care in making this decision. "The ISO 9000 representative [should be] a person who encompasses a genuine and passionate commitment to quality and success, knowledge of processes and systems within the company, and power to influence employees at all levels," wrote Karapetrovic, Rajamani, and Willborn. "He should be familiar with the standards. If this is not the case, there are ample training opportunities available to acquire sufficient expertise."

For more information on ISO 9000 registration, small business owners can contact several different organizations. One organization that offers help with ISO 9000 registrations is the American Society for Quality, located at 600 North Plankinton Avenue, Milwaukee, WI 53203. They can be reached by telephone at 800-248-1946, and online at http://www.asq.org/. Another such organization is the American National Standards Institute, located at 1819 L Street, NW, Washington DC, 20036. They can be reached by phone at 202-293-8020, and online at http://www.ansi.org/.

SEE ALSO *Quality Control; Total Quality Management*

BIBLIOGRAPHY
Buttle, Francis. "ISO 9000: Marketing Motivations and Benefits." *International Journal of Quality and Reliability Management.* July 1997.

"ISO 9000 Certifications Expire." *Business and the Environment.* February 2004.

Kanji, G.K. "An Innovative Approach to Make ISO 9000 Standards More Effective." *Total Quality Management.* February 1998.

Karapetrovic, Stanislav, Divakar Rajamani, and Walter Willborn. "ISO 9000 for Small Business: Do It Yourself." *Industrial Management.* May-June 1997.

Meyer, Harvey R. "Small Firms Flock to Quality System." *Nation's Business.* March 1998.

Peach, Robert. *The ISO 9000 Handbook.* QSU Publishing Company, 2002.

Simmons, Bret L., and Margaret A. White. "The Relationship between ISO 9000 and Business Performance: Does Registration Really Matter?" *Journal of Managerial Issues.* Fall 1999.

Van der Wiele, Tom, et al. "ISO 9000 Series and Excellence Models: Fad to Fashion to Fit." *Journal of General Management.* Spring 2000.

Wilson, L. A. "Eight-Step Process to Successful ISO 9000 Implementation: A Quality Management System Approach." *Quality Progress.* January 1996.

Wright, Richard B. "Why We Need ISO 9000." *Industrial Distribution.* January 1997.

Hillstrom, Northern Lights
updated by Magee, ECDI